The Sporting News

HOCKEY GUIDE

1999-2000 EDITION

Editor/Hockey Guide

CRAIG CARTER

The Sporting News

A Times Mirror Company

CONTENTS

ON THE COVER:Mike Modano (Cover designed by Michael Behrens. Large photo by Albert Dickson/THE SPORTING NEWS; small photo by THE SPORTING NEWS.).

Spine photo: Patrick Roy (File photo).

ISBN: 0-89204-617-1

10 9 8 7 6 5 4 3 2 1

1999-2000 NHL SEASON

NHL directory

Team information

Schedule

NATIONAL HOCKEY LEAGUE
DIRECTORY

LEAGUE OFFICES

OFFICERS

Commissioner
Gary Bettman
Executive vice president
Stephen Solomon
Exec. vice president & chief legal officer
William Daly
Exec. v.p. and dir. of hockey operations
Colin Campbell
V.p. of corporate communications
Bernadette Mansur
Vice president of media relations
Frank Brown
Exec. vice president and general counsel
David Zimmerman
Vice president of corporate marketing
Ed Horn
Vice president of broadcasting
Glenn Adamo
Director of club marketing
Scott Carmichael
Vice president, security
Dennis Cunningham
Sr. v.p. hockey operations (Toronto)
Jim Gregory
Vice president and CFO
Craig Harnett
Vice president event marketing
Frank Supovitz
Dir. of admin. and exec. assistant to the commissioner
Debbie Jordan

BROADCASTING/NHL PRODUCTIONS

Vice president
Glenn Adamo
Executive producer
Ken Rosen
Producer
Darryl Lepik
Director, broadcasting/TV
Adam Acone
Director, broadcast operations/NHLP
Patti Fallick
Director, scheduling and operations
Steve HatzePetros
Managers, broadcasting
Todd Goodman
Anthony Triano

CORPORATE COMMUNICATIONS

Manager
Tracey Warshaw
Manager, community relations
Adrienne Brautigan
Manager, corporate communications
Sandra Carreon
Publicist
Joy Kalfus

PUBLIC RELATIONS

V.p., public relations and media services
Gary Meagher
Chief statistician (Toronto)
Benny Ercolani
Director, public relations
Andrew McGowan
Manager, media services
Susan Aglietti
Manager, news services
Greg Inglis
Manager, media relations
Amy Early
Public relations coordinator (Toronto)
David Keon
News service assistant
Adam Schwartz
Public relations assistant (Toronto)
Chris Tredree

NEW YORK OFFICE (NHL AND NHLE)

Address
1251 Avenue of the Americas
47th Floor
New York, NY 10020
Phone
212-789-2000
FAX
212-789-2020

TORONTO OFFICE

Address
50 Bay Street, 11th Floor
Toronto, Ont. M5J 2X8
Phone
416-981-2777
FAX
416-981-2779

MONTREAL OFFICE

Address
1800 McGill College Avenue
Suite 2600
Montreal, Que., Canada H3A 3J6
Phone
514-841-9220
FAX
514-284-0300

DIVISIONAL ALIGNMENT

EASTERN CONFERENCE

ATLANTIC DIVISION
New Jersey Devils
New York Islanders
New York Rangers
Philadelphia Flyers
Pittsburgh Penguins

NORTHEAST DIVISION
Boston Bruins
Buffalo Sabres
Montreal Canadiens
Ottawa Senators
Toronto Maple Leafs

SOUTHEAST DIVISION
Atlanta Thrashers
Carolina Hurricanes
Florida Panthers
Tampa Bay Lightning
Washington Capitals

WESTERN CONFERENCE

CENTRAL DIVISION
Chicago Blackhawks
Detroit Red Wings
Nashville Predators
St. Louis Blues

NORTHWEST DIVISION
Calgary Flames
Colorado Avalanche
Edmonton Oilers
Vancouver Canucks

PACIFIC DIVISION
Mighty Ducks of Anaheim
Dallas Stars
Los Angeles Kings
Phoenix Coyotes
San Jose Sharks

MIGHTY DUCKS OF ANAHEIM
WESTERN CONFERENCE/PACIFIC DIVISION

Mighty Ducks Schedule

Home games shaded; D—Day game; *—All-Star Game at Toronto.

October

SUN	MON	TUE	WED	THU	FRI	SAT
					1	2 DAL
3	4	5 PHO	6	7	8 DAL	9
10	11 D SJ	12	13 NJ	14	15 TB	16 FLA
17	18	19 WAS	20	21 CHI	22 DET	23
24 BOS	25	26	27 PIT	28	29 WAS	30
31 PHO						

November

SUN	MON	TUE	WED	THU	FRI	SAT
	1	2	3 PHI	4	5	6
7 EDM	8	9 TOR	10	11 MON	12	13 OTT
14	15	16	17 CAL	18	19 CHI	20
21	22 MON	23	24 NJ	25	26 D DAL	27 NSH
28	29	30				

December

SUN	MON	TUE	WED	THU	FRI	SAT
			1 TB	2	3 LA	4 PHO
5	6	7	8 VAN	9	10 COL	11
12 ATL	13	14	15 COL	16	17 CHI	18
19 DET	20	21	22 PHO	23	24	25
26 D SJ	27 EDM	28	29 CAL	30	31 DAL	

January

SUN	MON	TUE	WED	THU	FRI	SAT
						1
2	3	4	5 FLA	6	7 CAR	8 DET
9	10	11	12 OTT	13	14 STL	15 PHO
16	17 BUF	18	19 DAL	20	21 COL	22 SJ
23	24	25	26 NYI	27	28	29 PIT
30	31 BOS					

February

SUN	MON	TUE	WED	THU	FRI	SAT
		1 BUF	2	3 PHI	4	5
6 *	7	8 LA	9 DAL	10	11	12 STL
13	14 CHI	15	16 CAL	17	18 SJ	19
20	21 STL	22	23 VAN	24	25	26
27 EDM	28	29 SJ				

March

SUN	MON	TUE	WED	THU	FRI	SAT
			1	2 VAN	3 CAL	4
5 NSH	6	7	8 NYR	9	10	11 D STL
12	13	14 COL	15 LA	16	17 SJ	18
19 DET	20	21 LA	22 EDM	23	24 VAN	25
26 PHO	27	28	29	30	31	

April

SUN	MON	TUE	WED	THU	FRI	SAT
						1 D LA
2	3 NSH	4	5 CHI	6	7 NSH	8
9 D LA	10	11	12	13	14	15

1999-2000 SEASON
CLUB DIRECTORY

Chairman and governor
Tony Tavares
President and general manager
Pierre Gauthier
Vice president of hockey operations
Jack Ferreira
Assistant general manager
David McNab
Chief amateur scout
Alain Chainey
Pro scout
Lucien DeBlois
Head coach
Craig Hartsburg
Assistant coaches
Newell Brown
George Burnett
Dir. of communications/team services
Rob Scichili
Media relations coordinator
Alex Gilchrist
Media relations assistant
Mark Janko
Head athletic trainer
Chris Phillips
Equipment manager
Mark O'Neill
Assistant equipment manager
John Allaway

DRAFT CHOICES

Rd.— Player	Ht./Wt.	Overall	Pos.	Last team
2— Jordan Leopold	6-0/193	44	D	Minnesota (WCHA)
3— Niklas Havelid	5-11/200	83	D	Malmo, Sweden
4— Alexandr Chagodayev	6-1/185	105	C	CSKA Moskow, Russia
5— Maxim Rybin	5-9/167	141	RW	Spartak Moscow, Rus.
6— Jan Sandstrom	6-0/191	173	D	AIK, Sweden
8— Petr Tenkrat	5-11/176	230	W	Kladno, Czech Rep.
9— Brian Gornick	6-4/200	258	C	Air Force Academy

MISCELLANEOUS DATA

Home ice (capacity)
The Arrowhead Pond of Anaheim (17,174)
Address
2695 E. Katella Avenue
P.O. Box 61077
Anaheim, CA 92803-6177
Business phone
714-940-2900
Club colors
Purple, jade, silver and white
Radio affiliation
XTRA Sports (690 AM)
TV affiliation
KCAL (Channel 9), FOX Sports Midwest (Cable)

TRAINING CAMP ROSTER

No.	FORWARDS	Ht./Wt.	BORN Place	BORN Date	NHL exp.	1998-99 clubs
14	Antti Aalto (C)	6-2/195	Lappeenrana, Finland	3-4-75	2	Anaheim
	Maxim Balmochnykh (LW)	6-0/185	Lipetsk, U.S.S.R.	3-7-79	0	Lada Togliatti (Russian)
29	Frank Banham (RW)	6-0/204	Calahoo, Alta.	4-14-75	2	Cincinnati (AHL)
	Alexander Chagodayev (C)	6-1/180	Moscow, U.S.S.R.	1-15-81	0	HC CSKA Moscow (Russian Div. II)
	Marc Chouinard (C)	6-5/203	Charlesbourg, Ont.	5-5-77	0	Cincinnati (AHL)
11	Matt Cullen (C)	6-1/195	Virginia, Minn.	11-2-76	2	Anaheim, Cincinnati (AHL)
22	Johan Davidsson (C/RW)	6-1/187	Jonkoping, Sweden	1-6-76	1	Anaheim, Cincinnati (AHL)
21	Ted Donato (LW)	5-10/183	Boston	4-28-68	8	Boston, New York Islanders, Ottawa
18	Ted Drury (C/LW)	6-0/206	Boston	9-13-71	6	Anaheim
32	Stu Grimson (LW)	6-5/239	Kamloops, B.C.	5-20-65	11	Anaheim
9	Paul Kariya (LW)	5-10/180	Vancouver	10-16-74	5	Anaheim
	Peter LeBoutillier (RW)	6-2/200	Minnedosa, Man.	1-11-75	2	Cincinnati (AHL)
12	Mike LeClerc (LW)	6-1/206	Winnipeg	11-10-76	3	Anaheim, Cincinnati (AHL)
16	Marty McInnis (C/LW)	5-11/190	Weymouth, Mass.	6-2-70	8	Calgary, Anaheim
33	Jim McKenzie (LW)	6-4/229	Gull Lake, Sask.	11-3-69	10	Anaheim
	Tony Mohagen (LW)	6-4/225	Regina, Saskatchewan	7-13-78	0	Cincinnati (AHL)
19	Jeff Nielsen (RW)	6-0/195	Grand Rapids, Minn.	9-20-71	3	Anaheim
20	Steve Rucchin (C)	6-2/212	Thunder Bay, Ont.	7-4-71	5	Anaheim
	Maxim Rybin (RW)	5-9/176	Moscow, U.S.S.R.	6-15-81	0	Spartak Moscow (Russian)
8	Teemu Selanne (RW)	6-0/201	Helsinki, Finland	7-3-70	7	Anaheim
40	Jeremy Stevenson (LW)	6-1/215	San Bernardino, Calif.	7-28-74	3	Cincinnati (AHL)
	Bob Wren (LW)	5-10/180	Preston, Ont.	9-16-74	1	Cincinnati (AHL)
	DEFENSEMEN					
25	Mike Crowley	5-11/190	Bloomington, Minn.	7-4-75	2	Cincinnati (AHL), Anaheim
21	Scott Ferguson	6-1/191	Camrose, Alta.	1-6-73	2	Cincinnati (AHL), Anaheim
5	Kevin Haller	6-2/195	Trochu, Alta.	12-5-70	10	Anaheim
	Niklas Havelid	5-11/200	Enkoping, Sweden	4-12-73	0	Malmo (Sweden)
	Joel Kwiatkowski	6-2/206	Kendersley, Saskatchewan	3-22-77	0	Cincinnati (AHL)
	Jordan Leopold	6-0/193	Golden Valley, Minn.	8-3-80	0	Univ. of Minnesota (WCHA)
23	Jason Marshall	6-2/200	Cranbrook, B.C.	2-22-71	6	Anaheim
	Antti-Jussi Niemi	6-1/183	Vantaa, Finland	9-22-77	0	Jokerit Helsinki (Finland)
2	Fredrik Olausson	6-0/198	Dadesjo, Sweden	10-5-66	13	Anaheim
24	Ruslan Salei	6-1/206	Minsk, U.S.S.R.	11-2-74	3	Anaheim
	Jan Sandstrom	6-0/191	Pitea, Sweden	1-24-78	0	AIK Solna (Sweden)
	Lloyd Shaw	6-3/206	Regina, Sask.	9-26-76	0	Cincinnati (AHL), Huntington (ECHL)
34	Dan Trebil	6-3/210	Bloomington, Minn.	4-10-74	3	Cincinnati (AHL), Anaheim
27	Pascal Trepanier	6-0/205	Gaspe, Que.	4-9-73	2	Anaheim
7	Pavel Trnka	6-3/200	Plzen, Czechoslovakia	7-27-76	2	Anaheim
10	Oleg Tverdovsky	6-0/200	Donetsk, U.S.S.R.	5-18-76	5	Phoenix
	Vitali Vishnevsky	6-2/190	Kharkov, U.S.S.R.	3-18-80	0	Torpedo Yaroslavl (Russian)
	GOALTENDERS					
67	Tom Askey	6-2/194	Kenmore, N.Y.	10-4-74	2	Cincinnati (AHL), Anaheim
31	Guy Hebert	5-11/186	Troy, N.Y.	1-7-67	8	Anaheim
30	Dominic Roussel	6-1/191	Hull, Que.	2-22-70	6	Anaheim

1998-99 REVIEW

INDIVIDUAL STATISTICS

SCORING

	Games	G	A	Pts.	PIM	+/-	PPG	SHG	Shots	Shooting Pct.
Teemu Selanne	75	47	60	107	30	18	25	0	281	16.7
Paul Kariya	82	39	62	101	40	17	11	2	429	9.1
Steve Rucchin	69	23	39	62	22	11	5	1	145	15.9
Fredrik Olausson	74	16	40	56	30	17	10	0	121	13.2
Marty McInnis*	75	18	34	52	36	-14	11	1	139	12.9
Tomas Sandstrom	58	15	17	32	42	-5	7	0	107	14.0
Travis Green	79	13	17	30	81	-7	3	1	165	7.9
Matt Cullen	75	11	14	25	47	-12	5	1	112	9.8
Ruslan Salei	74	2	14	16	65	1	1	0	123	1.6
Ted Drury	75	5	6	11	83	2	0	0	79	6.3
Jim McKenzie	73	5	4	9	99	-18	1	0	59	8.5
Jeff Nielsen	80	5	4	9	34	-12	0	0	94	5.3
Johan Davidsson	64	3	5	8	14	-9	1	0	48	6.3
Antti Aalto	73	3	5	8	24	-12	2	0	61	4.9
Jason Marshall	72	1	7	8	142	-5	0	0	63	1.6
Kevin Haller	82	1	6	7	122	-1	0	0	64	1.6
Pascal Trepanier	45	2	4	6	48	0	0	0	49	4.1
Mike Crowley	20	2	3	5	16	-10	1	0	41	4.9

	Games	G	A	Pts.	PIM	+/-	PPG	SHG	Shots	Shooting Pct.
Pavel Trnka	63	0	4	4	60	-6	0	0	50	0.0
Stu Grimson	73	3	0	3	158	0	0	0	10	30.0
Jamie Pushor	70	1	2	3	112	-20	0	0	75	1.3
Scott Ferguson	2	0	1	1	0	0	0	0	1	0.0
Josef Marha*	10	0	1	1	0	-4	0	0	13	0.0
Guy Hebert (goalie)	69	0	1	1	0	0	0	0	0	0.0
Daniel Trebil	6	0	0	0	0	-2	0	0	1	0.0
Mike Leclerc	7	0	0	0	4	-2	0	0	1	0.0
Dominic Roussel (goalie)	18	0	0	0	0	0	0	0	0	0.0

GOALTENDING

	Games	Min.	Goals	SO	Avg.	W	L	T	Shots	Sv. Pct.
Guy Hebert	69	4083	165	6	2.42	31	29	9	2114	.922
Dominic Roussel	18	884	37	1	2.51	4	5	4	478	.923

Empty-net goals (do not count against a goaltender's average): Hebert 3, Roussel 1.
*Played with two or more NHL teams.

RESULTS

OCTOBER

10— At Washington ....L 0-1
11— At Philadelphia..................L 1-4
13— At Montreal.......................L 0-1
15— At Chicago.......................W 5-3
21— Boston.............................W 3-0
25— Phoenix ....T *2-2
28— Tampa Bay ....W 5-3
30— At Dallas...........................T *3-3
31— At St. Louis.......................T *2-2

NOVEMBER

4— St. Louis ....L 1-3
6— San Jose............................T *2-2
8— Detroit ....L 2-3
11— Carolina............................W *5-4
13— At Vancouver ....L 2-5
14— At Calgary ....W 1-0
16— Los Angeles ....W 3-1
18— N.Y. Rangers ....W 3-1
20— Edmonton..........................L *2-3
22— Chicago ....W 4-1
25— At Detroit..........................L 2-5
27— At Nashville ....L 1-3
29— At Carolina........................L 1-3

DECEMBER

1— At Pittsburgh ....T *4-4
3— At Chicago...........................L 1-4
6— At San Jose........................W 2-1
9— Vancouver ....T *4-4
11— Washington ....W 1-0
13— Los Angeles ....W 3-0
16— Nashville...........................W 6-1
18— N.Y. Islanders ....T *2-2
21— Colorado ....L 2-4
22— At Colorado ....W 1-0
28— At Ottawa...........................T *2-2
30— At Toronto ....L 1-4

JANUARY

1— At Buffalo ....W 7-2
2— At Boston.............................L 1-2
4— At Nashville ....L 1-2
6— Buffalo ....L *2-3
8— Phoenix ....W 4-1
10— Edmonton.........................W 6-4
13— Calgary ....L 1-2
15— Dallas.................................L 1-3
18— Pittsburgh ....W 5-3
20— New Jersey.........................L 3-4
21— At Phoenix..........................T *3-3
27— Colorado ....L 3-4
28— At Colorado ....L 2-6
30— At Edmonton ....L 0-1

FEBRUARY

3— Chicago ....W 3-0
5— At Tampa Bay ....W 5-3
6— At St. Louis ....W 4-3
10— Philadelphia.....................W 5-4
12— Dallas.................................L 2-3
14— At Phoenix........................W 5-1
15— At Los Angeles ....W 3-1
17— Edmonton...........................L 2-6
19— At Calgary ....L 3-6
20— At Vancouver....................W 5-1
24— At Edmonton ....W 2-1
26— San Jose ....W 3-1
27— At San Jose ....W 4-1

MARCH

3— Los Angeles ....W 2-1
5— Nashville...........................W 3-2
7— Detroit ....W 3-1
10— Vancouver ....T *4-4
12— At Dallas ....L 0-4
13— At Phoenix..........................L 0-1
17— Ottawa ....T *2-2
18— At Los Angeles ....W 4-2
21— Florida ....L 2-5
26— Dallas ....W 5-1
28— Calgary ....W 5-1
31— At New Jersey ....L 1-7

APRIL

2— At N.Y. Rangers ....W 4-1
3— At N.Y. Islanders ....T *2-2
5— At Detroit.............................L 2-3
7— At Dallas ....L 1-5
9— San Jose.............................L 1-4
11— Phoenix ....W 3-0
14— St. Louis.............................L 1-3
15— At Los Angeles ....L *3-4
17— At San Jose ....T *3-3

*Denotes overtime game.

ATLANTA THRASHERS

EASTERN CONFERENCE/SOUTHEAST DIVISION

Thrashers Schedule

Home games shaded; D—Day game; *—All-Star Game at Toronto.

October

SUN	MON	TUE	WED	THU	FRI	SAT
					1	2 NJ
3	4	5	6	7 DET	8	9 BUF
10	11	12	13	14 NYI	15	16 TB
17 NYR	18	19	20	21	22	23 COL
24	25	26 CAL	27 TOR	28	29	30
31 OTT						

November

SUN	MON	TUE	WED	THU	FRI	SAT
	1	2	3 TB	4	5	6 BOS
7	8	9	10 FLA	11	12 NJ	13 MON
14	15	16	17 TB	18	19 BUF	20 BUF
21	22 VAN	23	24	25 OTT	26	27 FLA
28 DAL	29	30				

December

SUN	MON	TUE	WED	THU	FRI	SAT
			1	2	3 FLA	4 NYI
5	6 NSH	7	8 LA	9	10 SJ	11
12 ANA	13	14	15 WAS	16	17 BOS	18 CAR
19	20	21	22 FLA	23 PHI	24	25
26 TB	27 DET	28	29	30 NSH	31	

January

SUN	MON	TUE	WED	THU	FRI	SAT
						1 CAR
2	3	4 BUF	5	6 WAS	7	8 WAS
9	10	11	12 WAS	13	14 PHI	15
16 D NYR	17 D BOS	18	19 BOS	20	21 FLA	22
23	24 NYR	25	26 PHO	27 PIT	28	29 TB
30	31 PIT					

February

SUN	MON	TUE	WED	THU	FRI	SAT
		1	2 DAL	3 NYR	4	5
6 *	7	8	9 PIT	10 11	SJ 12	CHI 13
14	15	STL 16	MON 17	18	19	20
PHO 21	22	COL 23	24	25	EDM 26	CAL 27
28	29	TOR 1				

March

SUN	MON	TUE	WED	THU	FRI	SAT
			2	STL 3	4	OTT 5
6	MON 7	8	9	10	NJ 11	12 D
CAR 13	EDM 14	15	16	NYI 17	18	TOR 19
20	21	OTT 22	MON 23	24	PIT 25	26
LA 27	28	WAS 29	30	31	NJ 1	

April

SUN	MON	TUE	WED	THU	FRI	SAT
						2 D
NYI 3	4	PHI 5	6	PHI 7	8 D	CAR 9 D
CAR 10	11	12	13	14	15	

1999-2000 SEASON

CLUB DIRECTORY

President and governor
Dr. Harvey W. Schiller
Executive vice president
Dave Maggard
Vice president and general manager
Dave Waddell
Vice president of sales and marketing
Derek Schiller
Vice president of public relations
Greg Hughes
Assistant general manager
Les Jackson
Dir. of player evaluation and dev.
Bob Owen
Director of marketing
Jim Pfeifer
Director of media relations
Tom Hughes
Director of team services
Michele Zarzaca
Director of ticket sales
Dan Froehlich
Manager of hockey operations
Jordy Bowman
Manager of hockey administration
Larry Simmons
Manager of community relations
Terry Hickman
Manager of fan development
David Cole
Manager of marketing
Rob Preiditsch
Manager of media relations
Rob Koch
Manager of ticket sales
Keith Brennan
Manager of ticket operations
Wendell Byrne
Manager of ticket promotions
Elaine Keller
Head coach
Curt Fraser
Assistant coaches
Jay Leach
George Kingston
Head trainer
Scott Green
Equipment manager
Bobby Stewart
Strength & conditioning coach
Chris Reichert
Massage therapist
Inar Treiguts

DRAFT CHOICES

Rd.— Player	Ht./Wt.	Overall	Pos.	Last team
1— Patrik Stefan	6-2/205	1	C	Long Beach (IHL)
2— Luke Sellars	6-1/195	30	D	Ottawa (OHL)
3— Zdenek Blatny	6-1/187	68	C/LW	Seattle (WHL)
4— David Kaczowka	6-2/208	98	LW	Seattle (WHL)
4— Rob Zepp	6-1/160	99	G	Plymouth (OHL)
5— Derek MacKenzie	5-11/169	128	C	Sudbury (OHL)
6— Yuri Dobryshkin	6-0/189	159	W	Krylja Sovetov, Russia
7— Stephan Baby	6-5/226	188	RW	Green Bay (USHL)
8— Garnet Exelby	6-1/194	217	D	Saskatoon (WHL)
9— Tommy Santala	6-2/198	245	C/RW	Jokerit Helsinki, Fin.
9— Ray DiLauro	6-2/215	246	D	St. Lawrence (ECAC)

MISCELLANEOUS DATA

Home ice (capacity)
Philips Arena (18,517)
Address
1 CNN Center, Box 105583
Atlanta, GA 30348-5583
Business phone
404-827-5300
Club colors
Navy, blue, copper, bronze and gold
Radio affiliation
To be announced
TV affiliation
Turner South, WUPA/WPN (Channel 69)

TRAINING CAMP ROSTER

No.	FORWARDS	Ht./Wt.	BORN Place	BORN Date	NHL exp.	1998-99 clubs
	Bryan Adams (LW)	6-0/185		3-20-77	0	Michigan State (CCHA)
	Zdenek Blatny (C/LW)	6-1/187	Brno, Czechoslovakia	1-14-81	0	Seattle (WHL)
	Jason Botterill (LW)	6-3/205	Edmonton	5-19-76	2	Dallas, Michigan (IHL)
18	Andrew Brunette (LW)	6-2/212	Sudbury, Ont.	8-24-73	4	Nashville
16	Kelly Buchberger (RW)	6-2/210	Langenburg, Sask.	12-2-66	13	Edmonton
14	Sylvain Cloutier (C)	6-0/195	Mont-Laurier, Que.	2-13-74	1	Indianapolis (IHL), Chicago
	Yuri Dobryshkin (RW)	6-0/189	Penza, U.S.S.R.	7-19-79	0	Kryla Sov. Moscow (Russian)
	Nelson Emerson (RW)	5-11/175	Hamilton, Ont.	8-17-67	9	Carolina, Chicago, Ottawa
	Ray Ferraro (C)	5-10/192	Trail, B.C.	8-23-64	15	Los Angeles
29	Johan Garpenlov (LW)	5-11/185	Stockholm, Sweden	3-21-68	9	Florida
21	Jody Hull (RW)	6-2/195	Cambridge, Ont.	2-2-69	11	Philadelphia
17	Matt Johnson (LW)	6-5/232	Welland, Ont.	11-23-75	5	Los Angeles
	David Kaczowka (LW)	6-2/208	Regina, Sask.	7-5-81	0	Seattle (WHL)
	Tomi Kallio (LW)	6-1/180	Turku, Finland	1-27-77	0	TPS Turku (Finland)
	Andreas Karlsson (C)	6-2/180	Leksand, Sweden	8-19-75	0	Leksand (Sweden)
	Bob Lachance (RW)	6-0/194	Northampton, Mass.	2-1-74	0	Indianapolis (IHL)
	Derek MacKenzie (C)	5-11/169	Sudbury, Ont.	6-11-81	0	Sudbury (OHL)
	Martin Prochazka (LW)	5-11/180	Slany, Czechoslovakia	3-3-72	1	Vsetin (Czech Rep.)
16	Randy Robitaille (C)	5-11/190	Ottawa	10-12-75	3	Providence (AHL), Boston
14	Mike Stapleton (C)	5-10/185	Sarnia, Ont.	5-5-66	12	Phoenix
	Patrik Stefan (C)	6-2/205	Pribram, Czechoslovakia	9-16-80	0	Long Beach (IHL)
	Per Svartvadet (C)	6-1/180	Solleftea, Sweden	5-17-75	0	MoDo Ornskoldvik (Sweden)
46	Dean Sylvester (RW)	6-2/185	Hanson, Mass.	12-30-72	1	Rochester (AHL), Buffalo
37	Herbert Vasiljevs (C)	5-11/170	Rigo, U.S.S.R.	5-27-76	1	Kentucky (AHL), Florida
42	Ed Ward (RW)	6-3/215	Edmonton	11-10-69	6	Calgary
27	Terry Yake (C)	5-11/190	New Westminster, B.C.	10-22-68	9	Worcester (AHL), St. Louis
	Alexei Yegorov (LW)	5-11/185	St. Petersburg, U.S.S.R.	5-21-75	2	Torpedo Yaroslavl (Russian), SKA St. Petersburg (Russian)
	DEFENSEMEN					
34	Petr Buzek	6-0/205	Jihlava, Czechoslovakia	4-26-77	2	Michigan (IHL), Dallas
29	Brett Clark	6-0/182	Wapella, Sask.	12-23-76	2	Montreal, Fredericton (AHL)
28	Kevin Dean	6-3/205	Madison, Wis.	4-1-69	5	New Jersey
4	Maxim Galanov	6-1/195	Krasnoyarsk, U.S.S.R.	3-13-74	2	Pittsburgh
6	David Harlock	6-2/205	Toronto	3-16-71	5	New York Islanders
5	Gord Murphy	6-2/195	Willowdale, Ont.	3-23-67	11	Florida
	Luke Sellars	6-1/195	Toronto	5-21-81	0	Ottawa (OHL)
8	Darryl Shannon	6-2/208	Barrie, Ont.	6-21-68	11	Buffalo
25	Steve Staios	6-0/200	Hamilton, Ont.	7-28-73	4	Vancouver
2	Chris Tamer	6-1/207	Dearborn, Mich.	11-17-70	6	Pittsburgh, New York Rangers
	Daniel Tjarnqvist	6-2/180	Umea, Sweden	10-14-76	0	Djur. Stockholm (Sweden)
38	Yannick Tremblay	6-2/185	Pointe-aux-Trembles, Que.	11-15-75	3	Toronto
	Sergei Vyshedkevich	6-0/195	Moscow, U.S.S.R.	1-3-75	0	Albany (AHL)
	GOALTENDERS					
31	Scott Langkow	5-11/190	Sherwood Park, Alta.	4-21-75	3	Las Vegas (IHL), Utah (IHL), Phoenix
40	Norm Maracle	5-9/175	Belleville, Ont.	10-2-74	2	Adirondack (AHL), Detroit
1	Damian Rhodes	6-0/180	St. Paul, Minn.	5-28-69	7	Ottawa
32	Corey Schwab	6-0/180	North Battleford, Sask.	11-4-70	4	Cleveland (IHL), Tampa Bay
	Rob Zepp	6-1/160	Scarborough, Ont.	9-7-81	0	Plymouth (OHL)

BOSTON BRUINS
EASTERN CONFERENCE/NORTHEAST DIVISION

Bruins Schedule

Home games shaded; D—Day game; *—All-Star Game at Toronto.

October

SUN	MON	TUE	WED	THU	FRI	SAT
					1	2 CAR
3	4 TOR	5	6	7 OTT	8	9 PHI
10	11 D COL	12	13 COL	14	15 DAL	16 PHO
17	18	19	20 LA	21	22	23 SJ
24 ANA	25	26	27	28 TB	29	30 BUF
31						

November

SUN	MON	TUE	WED	THU	FRI	SAT
	1	2	3	4 NJ	5	6 ATL
7	8	9	10 BUF	11 TOR	12	13 NYR
14	15	16	17 NJ	18 NYR	19	20 WAS
21	22 CAR	23	24 NSH	25	26 D VAN	27
28 NYI	29	30				

December

SUN	MON	TUE	WED	THU	FRI	SAT
			1	2 WAS	3	4 CHI
5	6	7	8	9 EDM	10	11 DET
12	13 PHO	14 PIT	15	16	17 ATL	18 STL
19	20	21 NSH	22	23 MON	24	25
26	27 NYI	28	29 NJ	30 OTT	31	

January

SUN	MON	TUE	WED	THU	FRI	SAT
						1 NJ
2	3	4 NYI	5	6 CAR	7	8 NYI
9	10	11 TOR	12	13 BUF	14	15 MON
16	17 D ATL	18	19 ATL	20 TB	21	22 FLA
23	24 CAL	25	26	27 MON	28	29 BUF
30	31 ANA					

February

SUN	MON	TUE	WED	THU	FRI	SAT
		1 OTT	2	3 TOR	4	5
6 *	7	8 WAS	9	10	11 NYR	12 FLA
13	14	15	16 TOR	17	18	19
20	21 VAN	22	23 EDM	24	25 WAS	26 PIT
27	28	29 OTT				

March

SUN	MON	TUE	WED	THU	FRI	SAT
			1	2	3	4 D PHI
5	6 OTT	7	8 BUF	9	10 CAR	11 MON
12	13	14	15	16 CHI	17	18 D PIT
19 D PHI	20	21 TB	22	23 FLA	24	25 D LA
26	27	28	29 MON	30 STL	31	

April

SUN	MON	TUE	WED	THU	FRI	SAT
						1 D NYR
2	3	4 TB	5 FLA	6	7	8 D PHI
9 PIT	10	11	12	13	14	15

1999-2000 SEASON

CLUB DIRECTORY

Owner and governor
Jeremy M. Jacobs
Alternative governor
Louis Jacobs
President, g.m. and alternate governor
Harry Sinden
V.p. of hockey operations and asst. g.m.
Mike O'Connell
Senior assistant to the president
Nate Greenberg
Asst. to the v.p. of hockey operations
Jeff Gorton
General counsel
Michael Wall
Director of administration
Dale Hamilton
Assistant to the president
Joe Curnane
Team travel coordinator/admin. asst.
Carol Gould
Coach
Pat Burns
Assistant coach
Jacques Laperriere
Director of scouting
Scott Bradley
Director of development
Bob Tindall
Scouting staff
Nickolai Bobrov, Gerry Cheevers, Daniel Dore, Ernie Gare, Yuri Karmanov, Don Matheson, Scott McLellan, Tom McVie, Jim Morrison, Tim O'Connell, Jean Ratelle, Don Saatzer, Sven-Ake Svensson
Director of media relations
Heidi Holland
Media relations assistant
Mark Awdycki
Dir. of marketing and community rel.
Sue Byrne
Athletic trainer
Don Del Negro
Physical therapist
Scott Waugh
Equipment manager
Peter Henderson
Assistant equipment manager
Chris "Muggsy" Aldrich

DRAFT CHOICES

Rd.— Player	Ht./Wt.	Overall	Pos.	Last team
1— Nicholas Boynton	6-2/210	21	D	Ottawa (OHL)
2— Matt Zultek	6-4/222	56	LW	Ottawa (OHL)
3— Kyle Wanvig	6-2/197	89	RW	Kootenay (WHL)
4— Jaakko Harikkala	6-1/200	118	D	Lukko, Finland
5— Seamus Kotyk	5-11/185	147	G	Ottawa (OHL)
6— Donald Choukalos	6-2/186	179	G	Regina (WHL)
7— Greg Barber	6-0/185	207	RW	Victoria (BCJHL)
8— John Cronin	6-2/200	236	D	Nobles Prep H.S.
9— Mikko Eloranta	6-0/185	247	W	Jokerit Helsinki, Fin.
9— Georgijs Pujacs	6-1/185	264	D	Dynamo Riga, Latvia

MISCELLANEOUS DATA

Home ice (capacity)
FleetCenter (17,565)
Address
One FleetCenter, Suite 250
Boston, MA 02114-1303
Business phone
617-624-1900
Club colors
Gold, black and white
Radio affiliation
WBZ (1030 AM) & Bruins Radio Network
TV affiliation
WSBK (Channel 38) & NESN (New England Sports Network)

TRAINING CAMP ROSTER

No.	FORWARDS	Ht./Wt.	BORN Place	BORN Date	NHL exp.	1998-99 clubs
41	Jason Allison (C)	6-3/205	North York, Ont.	5-29-75	6	Boston
	Dave Andreychuk (LW)	6-4/220	Hamilton, Ont.	9-29-63	17	New Jersey
11	P.J. Axelsson (RW)	6-1/174	Kungalv, Sweden	2-26-75	2	Boston
17	Shawn Bates (C)	5-11/205	Melrose, Mass.	4-3-75	2	Providence (AHL), Boston
22	Ken Baumgartner (LW)	6-1/205	Flin Flon, Man.	3-11-66	12	Boston
16	Ken Belanger (LW)	6-4/225	Sault Ste. Marie, Ont.	5-14-74	5	New York Islanders, Boston
33	Anson Carter (LW)	6-1/185	Toronto	6-6-74	3	Utah (IHL), Boston
19	Rob DiMaio (LW)	5-10/190	Calgary	2-19-68	11	Boston
45	Aaron Downey (RW)	6-0/210	Shelburne, Ontario	9-27-74	0	Providence (AHL)
	Peter Ferraro (RW)	5-10/180	Port Jefferson, N.Y.	1-24-73	4	Boston, Providence (AHL)
	Lee Goren (RW)	6-3/190	Winnipeg	12-26-77	0	Univ. of North Dakota (WCHA)
23	Steve Heinze (RW)	5-11/202	Lawrence, Mass.	1-30-70	8	Boston
	Jay Henderson (LW)	5-11/188	Edmonton	9-17-78	1	Providence (AHL), Boston
	Joe Hulbig (LW)	6-3/215	Norwood, Mass.	9-29-73	3	Hamilton (AHL), Edmonton
	Mattias Karlin (C)	5-11/183	Ornskoldsvik, Sweden	7-4-79	0	MoDo Ornskoldvik (Sweden)
12	Dimitri Khristich (RW)	6-2/195	Kiev, U.S.S.R.	7-23-69	9	Boston
	Antti Laaksonen (LW)	6-0/180	Tammela, Finland	10-3-73	1	Boston, Providence (AHL)
10	Cameron Mann (RW)	6-0/194	Thompson, Man.	4-20-77	2	Providence (AHL), Boston
	Marquis Mathieu (C)	5-11/190	Hartford, Conn.	5-31-73	1	Providence (AHL), Boston
72	Eric Nickulas (C)	5-11/190	Cape Cod, Mass.	3-25-75	1	Providence (AHL), Boston
	Peter Nordstrom (RW)	6-1/200	Munkfors, Sweden	7-26-74	1	Boston, Providence (AHL), Farjestad Karlstad (Sweden)
39	Joel Prpic (C)	6-7/225	Sudbury, Ont.	9-25-74	1	Providence (AHL)
14	Sergei Samsonov (LW)	5-8/184	Moscow, U.S.S.R.	10-27-78	2	Boston
	Andre Savage (C)	6-0/195	Ottawa	5-27-75	1	Providence (AHL), Boston
6	Joe Thornton (C)	6-4/225	London, Ont.	7-2-79	2	Boston
	Kyle Wanvig (RW)	6-2/197	Calgary	1-29-81	0	Kootenay (WHL)
27	Landon Wilson (RW)	6-2/216	St. Louis	3-15-75	4	Providence (AHL), Boston
	Matt Zultek (LW)	6-3/218	Windsor, Ont.	3-12-79	0	Ottawa (OHL)
	DEFENSEMEN					
	Elias Abrahamsson	6-3/240	Uppsala, Sweden	6-15-77	0	Providence (AHL)
	Johnathan Aitken	6-4/215	Edmonton, Alta.	5-24-78	0	Providence (AHL)
	Bobby Allen	6-1/198	Braintree, Mass.	11-14-78	0	Boston College (Hockey East)
77	Ray Bourque	5-11/219	Montreal	12-28-60	20	Boston
	Nicholas Boynton	6-2/215	Etobicoke, Ont.	1-14-79	0	Ottawa (OHL)
	Ben Clymer	6-1/195	Edina, Minn.	4-11-78	0	Seattle (WHL)
44	Dave Ellett	6-2/205	Cleveland	3-30-64	15	Boston
25	Hal Gill	6-7/240	Concord, Mass.	4-6-75	2	Boston
	Jonathan Girard	5-11/192	Joliette, Que.	5-27-80	1	Acadie-Bathurst (QMJHL), Boston
	Jaakko Harikkala	6-2/215	Kalanti, Finland	3-30-81	0	Lukko Rauma (Finland), UJK (Finland Div. 2), Lukko Rauma (Finland Jr.)
18	Kyle McLaren	6-4/219	Humboldt, Sask.	6-18-77	4	Boston
	Brandon Smith	6-1/196	Hazelton, B.C.	2-25-73	1	Providence (AHL), Boston
32	Don Sweeney	5-10/184	St. Stephen, N.B.	8-17-66	11	Boston
37	Mattias Timander	6-3/210	Solleftea, Sweden	4-16-74	3	Providence (AHL), Boston
20	Darren Van Impe	6-1/205	Saskatoon, Sask.	5-18-73	5	Boston
	GOALTENDERS					
	Donald Choukalos	6-2/186	Calgary	4-11-81	0	Calgary (WHL), Regina (WHL)
34	Byron Dafoe	5-11/190	Sussex, England	2-25-71	7	Boston
47	John Grahame	6-2/210	Denver	8-31-75	0	Providence (AHL)
	Seamus Kotyk	5-11/185	London, Ont.	10-7-80	0	Ottawa (OHL)
	Andrew Raycroft	6-0/150	Belleville, Ont.	5-4-80	0	Sudbury (OHL)
35	Rob Tallas	6-0/170	Edmonton	3-20-73	4	Boston

1998-99 REVIEW

INDIVIDUAL STATISTICS

SCORING

	Games	G	A	Pts.	PIM	+/-	PPG	SHG	Shots	Shooting Pct.
Jason Allison	82	23	53	76	68	5	5	1	158	14.6
Dmitri Khristich	79	29	42	71	48	11	13	1	144	20.1
Ray Bourque	81	10	47	57	34	-7	8	0	262	3.8
Sergei Samsonov	79	25	26	51	18	-6	6	0	160	15.6
Joe Thornton	81	16	25	41	69	3	7	0	128	12.5
Anson Carter	55	24	16	40	22	7	6	0	123	19.5
Steve Heinze	73	22	18	40	30	7	9	0	146	15.1
Kyle McLaren	52	6	18	24	48	1	3	0	97	6.2
Rob DiMaio	71	7	14	21	95	-14	1	0	121	5.8

	Games	G	A	Pts.	PIM	+/-	PPG	SHG	Shots	Shooting Pct.
Darren Van Impe	60	5	15	20	66	-5	4	0	92	5.4
P.J. Axelsson	77	7	10	17	18	-14	0	0	146	4.8
Peter Ferraro	46	6	8	14	44	10	1	0	61	9.8
Grant Ledyard	47	4	8	12	33	-8	1	0	47	8.5
Don Sweeney	81	2	10	12	64	14	0	0	79	2.5
Tim Taylor	49	4	7	11	55	-10	0	0	76	5.3
Hal Gill	80	3	7	10	63	-10	0	0	102	2.9
Shawn Bates	33	5	4	9	2	3	0	0	30	16.7
Chris Taylor	37	3	5	8	12	-3	0	1	60	5.0
Cameron Mann	33	5	2	7	17	0	1	0	42	11.9
Landon Wilson	22	3	3	6	17	0	0	0	32	9.4
Mattias Timander	22	0	6	6	10	4	0	0	22	0.0
Dave Ellett	54	0	6	6	25	11	0	0	45	0.0
Ken Belanger*	45	1	4	5	152	-2	0	0	16	6.3
Ted Donato*	14	1	3	4	4	0	0	0	22	4.5
Ken Baumgartner	69	1	3	4	119	-6	0	0	15	6.7
Antti Laaksonen	11	1	2	3	2	-1	0	0	8	12.5
Randy Robitaille	4	0	2	2	0	-1	0	0	5	0.0
Byron Dafoe (goalie)	68	0	2	2	25	0	0	0	0	0.0
Andre Savage	6	1	0	1	0	2	0	0	8	12.5
Eric Nickulas	2	0	0	0	0	0	0	0	0	0.0
Peter Nordstrom	2	0	0	0	0	-1	0	0	0	0.0
Jonathan Girard	3	0	0	0	0	1	0	0	3	0.0
Dennis Vaske	3	0	0	0	6	-3	0	0	0	0.0
Jay Henderson	4	0	0	0	2	-1	0	0	4	0.0
Terry Virtue	4	0	0	0	0	2	0	0	2	0.0
Brandon Smith	5	0	0	0	0	2	0	0	2	0.0
Marquis Mathieu	9	0	0	0	8	-1	0	0	4	0.0
Robbie Tallas (goalie)	17	0	0	0	0	0	0	0	0	0.0

GOALTENDING

	Games	Min.	Goals	SO	Avg.	W	L	T	Shots	Sv. Pct.
Byron Dafoe	68	4001	133	10	1.99	32	23	11	1800	.926
Robbie Tallas	17	987	43	1	2.61	7	7	2	421	.898

Empty-net goals (do not count against a goaltender's average): Dafoe 3, Tallas 2.

*Played with two or more NHL teams.

RESULTS

OCTOBER

10—St. Louis ....T *3-3
12—N.Y. Islanders ....W 3-0
14—At Colorado ....W 3-0
16—At Los Angeles ....L *1-2
18—At San Jose ....W 3-0
19—At Phoenix ....L 1-3
21—At Anaheim ....L 0-3
24—At New Jersey ....L 1-3
28—At Montreal ....W 9-2
29—Montreal ....T *1-1
31—Carolina ....L 0-2

NOVEMBER

3—At Buffalo ....L 2-4
5—Toronto ....W 4-1
7—At Pittsburgh ....T *0-0
8—At Carolina ....W 5-2
13—At N.Y. Rangers ....T *3-3
14—Dallas ....L 1-3
19—Florida ....T *5-5
21—Washington ....W *5-4
24—At Tampa Bay ....W 4-1
25—At Florida ....W 1-0
27—Montreal ....W 5-1

DECEMBER

1—Vancouver ....T *1-1
5—Pittsburgh ....W 2-1
10—At Carolina ....W 3-2
12—Buffalo ....L 1-4
16—At Detroit ....L 3-5
17—Ottawa ....W 5-2
19—Detroit ....W 4-1
21—Tampa Bay ....W 3-2
23—Philadelphia ....L 1-2
26—At N.Y. Islanders ....L 2-4
28—At Washington ....L 1-5
30—At Nashville ....W 5-2
31—At Dallas ....L 1-6

JANUARY

2—Anaheim ....W 2-1
4—Calgary ....W 5-1
7—Toronto ....W 2-1
9—At Toronto ....L 3-6
15—At Buffalo ....L 1-2
16—Tampa Bay ....T *2-2
18—Nashville ....W 8-1
21—Ottawa ....L 1-3
26—At N.Y. Islanders ....L 1-4
28—New Jersey ....L 0-2
30—At Pittsburgh ....L 2-5
31—Carolina ....T *0-0

FEBRUARY

2—Colorado ....L 2-3
4—N.Y. Islanders ....L 4-5
6—At Philadelphia ....T *2-2
7—N.Y. Rangers ....W 3-2
9—At Edmonton ....W 2-0
12—At Calgary ....L 3-4
13—At Vancouver ....L 1-3
18—At Ottawa ....L 0-2
21—At Chicago ....W 6-3
23—Ottawa ....W 5-2
25—New Jersey ....T *3-3
27—Washington ....W 4-3

MARCH

2—Phoenix ....W 3-2
3—At Carolina ....L 1-2
5—At New Jersey ....W 4-1
7—N.Y. Rangers ....L 1-3
9—Florida ....W 2-0
12—At N.Y. Rangers ....W 5-4
13—At Buffalo ....L 1-3
17—At Toronto ....W 4-1
20—San Jose ....T *2-2
21—At Washington ....W 4-1
24—At Ottawa ....W 3-0
25—Chicago ....T *3-3
27—At Toronto ....T *2-2
30—Los Angeles ....L *1-2

APRIL

1—At Montreal ....W 3-2
3—Philadelphia ....W 3-0
5—Montreal ....W 3-0
7—At Florida ....W 5-2
8—At Tampa Bay ....L 0-3
10—Tampa Bay ....W 3-2
15—Pittsburgh ....W 4-2
17—Buffalo ....W *2-1
18—At Philadelphia ....L 1-3

*Denotes overtime game.

BUFFALO SABRES

EASTERN CONFERENCE/NORTHEAST DIVISION

Sabres Schedule

Home games shaded; D—Day game; *—All-Star Game at Toronto.

October

SUN	MON	TUE	WED	THU	FRI	SAT
					1	2 DET
3	4	5	6	7	8 WAS	9 ATL
10	11 PHO	12	13	14	15	16 MON
17 PHI	18	19	20 NSH	21	22 CAR	23 OTT
24	25	26	27 TB	28	29 FLA	30 BOS
31						

November

SUN	MON	TUE	WED	THU	FRI	SAT
	1	2	3 DAL	4 CHI	5	6 NYI
7	8	9	10 BOS	11	12 TB	13 FLA
14	15	16 PIT	17	18	19 ATL	20 ATL
21	22	23	24 WAS	25	26 STL	27
28 TB	29	30 PIT				

December

SUN	MON	TUE	WED	THU	FRI	SAT
			1	2 PHI	3	4 NYR
5	6 TOR	7	8 OTT	9	10 CHI	11
12	13	14 PHI	15	16	17 FLA	18 NYI
19	20	21 NYR	22	23 COL	24	25
26	27 NJ	28 DET	29	30	31	

January

SUN	MON	TUE	WED	THU	FRI	SAT
						1 TOR
2	3 TOR	4 ATL	5	6 NJ	7	8 OTT
9	10	11	12	13 BOS	14 MON	15
16	17 ANA	18 LA	19	20 PHO	21	22 D CAR
23	24	25 TB	26	27	28 OTT	29 BOS
30	31					

February

SUN	MON	TUE	WED	THU	FRI	SAT
		1 ANA	2	3 OTT	4	5
6 *	7	8 COL	9	10 NSH	11	12 D PHI
13 D EDM	14	15	16 PIT	17 VAN	18	19 LA
20	21 NJ	22	23	24	25 NYR	26 TOR
27	28 FLA	29				

March

SUN	MON	TUE	WED	THU	FRI	SAT
			1 NYR	2	3	4 D NYI
5 D WAS	6	7	8 BOS	9	10 MON	11
12 D NYI	13	14	15 SJ	16 VAN	17	18 CAL
19	20 MON	21	22	23 CAL	24	25
26	27 CAR	28	29	30	31 CAR	

April

SUN	MON	TUE	WED	THU	FRI	SAT
						1 MON
2	3 TOR	4	5	6 NJ	7 PIT	8
9 D WAS	10	11	12	13	14	15

1999-2000 SEASON

CLUB DIRECTORY

Chairman of the board
John J. Rigas
Vice chairman of the board and counsel
Robert O. Swados
Vice chairman of the board
Robert E. Rich Jr.
Chief executive officer
Timothy J. Rigas
Executive vice president/administration
Ron Bertovich
Exec. v.p./finance & bus. development
Ed Hartman
Exec. v.p./integrated marketing
John Cimperman
Senior v.p./corporate sales
Kerry Atkinson
Senior v.p./legal and business affairs
Kevin Billet
Senior vice president/marketing
Christye Peterson
Vice president/communications
Michael Gilbert
Vice president/corporate relations
Seymour H. Knox IV
V.p./ticket sales and operations
John Sinclair
General manager
Darcy Regier
Assistant general manager
Larry Carriere
Director of media relations
Gil Chorbajian
Graduate assistant communications
Gregg Huller
Director of player personnel
Don Luce
Professional scouts
Kevin Devine, Frank Effinger, Terry Martin
Scouting staff
Don Barrie, Jim Benning, Bo Berglund, Paul Merritt, Darryl Plandowski, Mike Racicot, Rudy Migay, David Volek
Head coach
Lindy Ruff
Associate coach
Don Lever
Assistant coach
Mike Ramsey
Strength and conditioning coach
Doug McKenney
Assistant strength coach
Dennis Cole
Goaltender coach
Jim Corsi
Administrative assistant coach
Jeff Holbrook
Head trainer/massage therapist
Jim Pizzutelli
Head equipment manager
Rip Simonick
Assistant equipment manager
George Babcock
On-site travel coordinator
Kim Christiano
Club doctor
Dr. John Marzo

DRAFT CHOICES

Rd.— Player	Ht./Wt.	Overall	Pos.	Last team
1— Barrett Heisten	6-1/189	20	LW	Maine (H. East)
2— Milan Bartovic	5-11/183	35	RW	Trencin, Slovakia
2— Doug Janik	6-2/198	55	D	Maine (H. East)
2— Michael Zigomanis	6-0/183	64	C	Kingston (OHL)
3— Tim Preston	6-0/193	73	LW	Seattle (WHL)
4— Karel Mosovsky	6-2/198	117	LW	Regina (WHL)
5— Ryan Miller	6-1/150	138	G	Soo (NAHL)
5— Matthew Kinch	5-11/189	146	D	Calgary (WHL)
6— Seneque Hyacinthe	6-0/180	178	LW	Val d'Or (QMJHL)
7— Bret DeCecco	5-10/189	206	RW	Seattle (WHL)
8— Brad Self	5-11/165	235	C	Peterborough (OHL)
9— Craig Brunel	6-0/198	263	RW	Prince Albert (WHL)

MISCELLANEOUS DATA

Home ice (capacity)
Marine Midland Arena (18,595)
Address
Marine Midland Arena
One Seymour H. Knox III Plaza
Buffalo, NY 14203
Business phone
716-855-4100
Club colors
Black, white, red, gray and silver
Radio affiliation
WHTT (104.1 FM)
TV affiliation
Empire Sports Network

TRAINING CAMP ROSTER

No.	FORWARDS	Ht./Wt.	BORN Place	BORN Date	NHL exp.	1998-99 clubs
	Maxim Afinogenov (RW)	5-11/176	Moscow, U.S.S.R.	9-4-79	0	Dynamo Moscow (Russian)
41	Stu Barnes (C)	5-11/186	Spruce Grove, Alta.	12-25-70	8	Pittsburgh, Buffalo
	Milan Bartovic (LW)	5-11/183	Trencin, Czechoslovakia	4-20-81	0	Dukla Trencin Jrs. (Slovakia Jrs.)
37	Curtis Brown (C/LW)	6-0/190	Unity, Sask.	2-12-76	5	Buffalo
17	Randy Cunneyworth (LW)	6-0/198	Etobicoke, Ont.	5-10-61	16	Rochester (AHL), Buffalo
18	Michal Grosek (LW)	6-2/216	Vyskov, Czechoslovakia	6-1-75	6	Buffalo
55	Denis Hamel (LW)	6-2/200	Lachute, Que.	5-10-77	0	Rochester (AHL)
	Barrett Heisten (LW)	6-1/189	Anchorage, Alaska	3-19-80	0	Univ. of Maine (Hockey East)
19	Brian Holzinger (C/RW)	5-11/190	Parma, Ohio	10-10-72	5	Buffalo
	Seneque Hyacinthe (LW)	6-0/180	Montreal	2-22-81	0	Acadie-Bathurst (QMJHL), Val-d'Or (QMJHL)
	Jaroslov Kristek (RW)	6-0/183	Zlin, Czechoslovakia	3-16-80	0	Tri-City (WHL)
24	Paul Kruse (LW)	6-0/214	Merritt, B.C.	3-15-70	9	Buffalo
	Jeff Martin (C)	6-1/177	Stratford, Ont.	4-26-79	0	Windsor (OHL)
	Norman Milley (RW)	5-11/185	Toronto	2-14-80	0	Sudbury (OHL)
	Karel Mosovsky (LW)	6-2/198	Pisek, Czechoslovakia	8-22-81	0	Regina (WHL)
27	Michael Peca (C)	5-11/181	Toronto	3-26-74	6	Buffalo
83	Domenic Pittis (C)	5-11/180	Calgary	10-1-74	2	Rochester (AHL), Buffalo
	Tim Preston (LW)	6-0/193	Vancouver	6-30-81	0	Seattle (WHL)
22	Wayne Primeau (C)	6-3/225	Scarborough, Ont.	6-4-76	5	Buffalo
9	Erik Rasmussen (LW/C)	6-2/205	Minneapolis	3-28-77	2	Rochester (AHL), Buffalo
32	Rob Ray (RW)	6-0/215	Stirling, Ont.	6-8-68	10	Buffalo
80	Geoff Sanderson (LW)	6-0/190	Hay River, NW Territories	2-1-72	9	Buffalo
81	Miroslav Satan (LW/RW)	6-1/195	Topolcany, Czechoslovakia	10-22-74	4	Buffalo
	Darren Van Oene (LW)	6-3/207	Edmonton	1-18-78	0	
25	Vaclav Varada (RW)	6-0/215	Vsetin, Czechoslovakia	4-26-76	4	Buffalo
15	Dixon Ward (RW/LW)	6-0/200	Leduc, Alta.	9-23-68	7	Buffalo
	Mike Zigomanis (C)	6-0/183	North York, Ont.	1-17-81	0	Kingston (OHL)
	DEFENSEMEN					
	Brian Campbell	5-11/185	Strathroy, Ont.	5-23-79	0	Ottawa (OHL)
34	Jean-Luc Grand-Pierre	6-3/207	Montreal	2-2-77	1	Rochester (AHL), Buffalo
29	Jason Holland	6-2/193	Morinville, Alta.	4-30-76	3	Buffalo, Rochester (AHL)
6	Doug Houda	6-1/208	Blairmore, Alta.	6-3-66	13	Adirondack (AHL), Detroit
21	Mike Hurlbut	6-2/200	Massena, N.Y.	7-10-66	4	Rochester (AHL), Buffalo
	Doug Janik	6-2/198	Agawam, Mass.	3-26-80	0	Univ. of Maine (Hockey East)
	Dmitri Kalinin	6-2/198	Chelyabinsk, U.S.S.R.	7-22-80	0	Moncton (QMJHL), Rochester (AHL)
	Matt Kinch	5-11/189	Red Deer, Alta.	2-17-80	0	Calgary (WHL)
74	Jay McKee	6-3/205	Kingston, Ont.	9-8-77	4	Buffalo
	James Patrick	6-2/200	Winnipeg	6-14-63	16	Buffalo
6	Cory Sarich	6-3/175	Saskatoon, Sask.	8-16-78	1	Rochester (AHL), Buffalo
42	Richard Smehlik	6-3/222	Ostrava, Czechoslovakia	1-23-70	7	Buffalo
	Henrik Tallinder	6-3/194	Stockholm, Sweden	1-10-79	0	AIK Solna (Sweden)
	Luc Theoret	6-2/197	Winnipeg	7-30-79	0	Lethbridge (WHL), Portland (WHL)
4	Rhett Warrener	6-1/210	Shaunavon, Sask.	1-27-76	4	Florida, Buffalo
5	Jason Woolley	6-1/207	Toronto	7-27-69	8	Buffalo
44	Alexei Zhitnik	5-11/215	Kiev, U.S.S.R.	10-10-72	7	Buffalo
	GOALTENDERS					
43	Martin Biron	6-1/154	Lac St. Charles, Que.	8-15-77	2	Rochester (AHL), Buffalo
39	Dominik Hasek	5-11/168	Pardubice, Czechoslovakia	1-29-65	9	Buffalo
	Ryan Miller	6-1/150	East Lansing, Mich.	7-17-80	0	Soo (NAHL)
30	Dwayne Roloson	6-1/190	Simcoe, Ont.	10-12-69	3	Buffalo, Rochester (AHL)

1998-99 REVIEW

INDIVIDUAL STATISTICS

SCORING

	Games	G	A	Pts.	PIM	+/-	PPG	SHG	Shots	Shooting Pct.
Miroslav Satan	81	40	26	66	44	24	13	3	208	19.2
Michael Peca	82	27	29	56	81	7	10	0	199	13.6
Michal Grosek	76	20	30	50	102	21	4	0	140	14.3
Curtis Brown	78	16	31	47	56	23	5	1	128	12.5
Dixon Ward	78	20	24	44	44	10	2	1	101	19.8
Jason Woolley	80	10	33	43	62	16	4	0	154	6.5
Brian Holzinger	81	17	17	34	45	2	5	0	143	11.9
Alexei Zhitnik	81	7	26	33	96	-6	3	1	185	3.8
Vaclav Varada	72	7	24	31	61	11	1	0	123	5.7
Geoff Sanderson	75	12	18	30	22	8	1	0	155	7.7
Matthew Barnaby*	44	4	14	18	143	-2	0	0	52	7.7

	Games	G	A	Pts.	PIM	+/-	PPG	SHG	Shots	Shooting Pct.
Derek Plante*	41	4	11	15	12	3	0	0	66	6.1
Darryl Shannon	71	3	12	15	52	28	1	0	80	3.8
Richard Smehlik	72	3	11	14	44	-9	0	0	61	4.9
Wayne Primeau	67	5	8	13	38	-6	0	0	55	9.1
Erik Rasmussen	42	3	7	10	37	6	0	0	40	7.5
James Patrick	45	1	7	8	16	12	0	0	31	3.2
Jay McKee	72	0	6	6	75	20	0	0	57	0.0
Randy Cunneyworth	14	2	2	4	0	1	0	0	12	16.7
Stu Barnes*	17	0	4	4	10	1	0	0	25	0.0
Rob Ray	76	0	4	4	261	-2	0	0	23	0.0
Paul Kruse	43	3	0	3	114	0	0	0	33	9.1
Mike Wilson*	30	1	2	3	47	10	0	0	40	2.5
Joe Juneau*	9	1	1	2	2	-1	0	0	8	12.5
Rhett Warrener*	13	1	0	1	20	3	0	0	11	9.1
Jean-Luc Grand-Pierre	16	0	1	1	17	0	0	0	11	0.0
Mike Hurlbut	1	0	0	0	0	2	0	0	2	0.0
Dean Sylvester	1	0	0	0	0	-1	0	0	1	0.0
Jason Holland	3	0	0	0	8	-1	0	0	2	0.0
Domenic Pittis	3	0	0	0	2	0	0	0	1	0.0
Cory Sarich	4	0	0	0	0	3	0	0	2	0.0
Martin Biron (goalie)	6	0	0	0	0	0	0	0	0	0.0
Rumun Ndur*	8	0	0	0	16	1	0	0	1	0.0
Dwayne Roloson (goalie)	18	0	0	0	4	0	0	0	0	0.0
Dominik Hasek (goalie)	64	0	0	0	14	0	0	0	0	0.0

GOALTENDING

	Games	Min.	Goals	SO	Avg.	W	L	T	Shots	Sv. Pct.
Dominik Hasek	64	3817	119	9	1.87	30	18	14	1877	.937
Martin Biron	6	281	10	0	2.14	1	2	1	120	.917
Dwayne Roloson	18	911	42	1	2.77	6	8	2	460	.909

Empty-net goals (do not count against a goaltender's average): Hasek 2, Biron 1, Roloson 1.
*Played with two or more NHL teams.

RESULTS

OCTOBER
10—At Dallas ....L......1-4
12—At Colorado ....W......3-0
16—Florida ....T....*2-2
17—At Montreal ....W......4-3
23—Washington ....L......0-1
24—At N.Y. Islanders ....L......4-5
27—At N.Y. Rangers ....T....*0-0
30—Toronto ....W......4-1
31—At Toronto ....W......6-3

NOVEMBER
3—Boston ....W......4-2
7—At Philadelphia ....T....*2-2
10—Ottawa ....T....*2-2
12—At Washington ....W......2-0
14—Chicago ....W......6-1
20—Toronto ....W......4-1
21—At Toronto ....L......1-2
25—N.Y. Rangers ....W......4-2
28—At Florida ....L......2-6
29—At Tampa Bay ....W......6-3

DECEMBER
2—Florida ....W......2-1
4—Philadelphia ....W......3-0
5—At Nashville ....W......3-1
8—At St. Louis ....T....*2-2
11—N.Y. Rangers ....W......2-0
12—At Boston ....W......4-1
18—Montreal ....W......4-2
19—Carolina ....L......2-3
21—At Carolina ....W......4-1
23—Tampa Bay ....W......2-0
26—At New Jersey ....W......2-0
28—New Jersey ....L......4-7
30—Ottawa ....L....*2-3

JANUARY
1—Anaheim ....L......2-7
2—Calgary ....W......7-1
6—At Anaheim ....W....*3-2
7—At Los Angeles ....L......2-4
9—At San Jose ....T....*2-2
11—At Phoenix ....L......0-1
13—St. Louis ....L......2-4
15—Boston ....W......2-1
16—At Ottawa ....T....*1-1
18—At Florida ....W......4-0
19—At Tampa Bay ....L......1-2
26—Phoenix ....T....*1-1
28—Nashville ....L......2-4
30—Los Angeles ....W......4-1

FEBRUARY
2—At Pittsburgh ....L......3-5
3—Colorado ....L......3-5
6—At Montreal ....L......2-3
7—At Washington ....L......1-3
9—At Ottawa ....T....*1-1
11—Montreal ....W......5-2
13—N.Y. Islanders ....T....*2-2
15—Carolina ....W......3-2
17—Toronto ....L....*2-3
19—San Jose ....W......4-2
21—Detroit ....T....*4-4
24—At Calgary ....T....*2-2
26—At Edmonton ....L......3-6
28—At Vancouver ....W......2-0

MARCH
3—Edmonton ....L......3-5
5—Dallas ....W......2-1
7—Philadelphia ....T....*1-1
8—At Carolina ....L......1-4
11—Tampa Bay ....L......2-5
13—Boston ....W......3-1
15—N.Y. Islanders ....W......2-1
19—At N.Y. Rangers ....W....*3-2
23—At New Jersey ....T....*1-1
24—At Detroit ....L......1-2
27—At Pittsburgh ....T....*1-1
28—Pittsburgh ....W....*4-3
31—At Chicago ....L......1-2

APRIL
3—At Montreal ....L......1-2
5—Pittsburgh ....W......3-1
6—At N.Y. Islanders ....W......4-3
9—Florida ....W......3-1
10—At Ottawa ....T....*1-1
13—At Philadelphia ....T....*2-2
14—New Jersey ....L......1-2
17—At Boston ....L....*1-2
18—Washington ....W......3-0

*Denotes overtime game.

CALGARY FLAMES
WESTERN CONFERENCE/NORTHWEST DIVISION

Flames Schedule

Home games shaded; D—Day game; *—All-Star Game at Toronto.

October

SUN	MON	TUE	WED	THU	FRI	SAT
					1	2 SJ
3	4	5	6 STL	7	8 MON	9
10	11 D CAR	12	13 VAN	14	15 LA	16 VAN
17	18	19 STL	20	21	22 FLA	23 TB
24	25	26 ATL	27	28 OTT	29	30 TOR
31						

November

SUN	MON	TUE	WED	THU	FRI	SAT
	1	2	3 NSH	4	5	6 FLA
7	8	9	10 SJ	11	12	13 COL
14	15	16 PHO	17 ANA	18	19 DET	20
21	22	23 NYI	24	25 CHI	26	27 COL
28	29	30 CAR				

December

SUN	MON	TUE	WED	THU	FRI	SAT
			1	2 NYI	3	4 NJ
5	6 NYR	7 MON	8	9	10 VAN	11
12 CHI	13	14 STL	15 DAL	16	17	18 OTT
19	20	21 DAL	22	23 EDM	24	25
26 VAN	27 PHI	28	29 ANA	30	31	

January

SUN	MON	TUE	WED	THU	FRI	SAT
						1
2 D VAN	3	4	5 COL	6 CHI	7	8 TB
9	10	11	12 DAL	13	14	15 TOR
16	17	18 DET	19 EDM	20	21 NSH	22
23	24 BOS	25	26 WAS	27	28 DET	29 NSH
30	31					

February

SUN	MON	TUE	WED	THU	FRI	SAT
		1 STL	2	3 CHI	4	5
6 *	7	8	9 VAN	10 COL	11	12 PHO
13	14 LA	15	16 ANA	17	18 EDM	19 EDM
20	21	22	23 LA	24	25 PHO	26 ATL
27	28	29				

March

SUN	MON	TUE	WED	THU	FRI	SAT
			1 PIT	2	3 ANA	4
5 NJ	6	7 COL	8	9 TOR	10	11 LA
12	13 SJ	14	15 OTT	16	17	18 BUF
19 EDM	20	21	22 DET	23 BUF	24	25 NSH
26	27	28	29	30	31 PHO	

April

SUN	MON	TUE	WED	THU	FRI	SAT
						1 SJ
2	3 DAL	4	5 STL	6	7 COL	8 EDM
9	10	11	12	13	14	15

1999-2000 SEASON

CLUB DIRECTORY

Co-owners
Grant A. Bartlett
N. Murray Edwards
Harley N. Hotchkiss
Ronald V. Joyce
Alvin G. Libin
Allan P. Markin
J.R. (Bud) McCaig
Byron J. Seaman
Daryl K. Seaman

President/chief executive officer
Ron Bremner

Executive v.p./general manager
Al Coates

V.p., finance and administration
Michael Holditch

Vice president, marketing
Garry McKenzie

V.p., corporate development
Lanny McDonald

Director, player personnel
Nick Polano

Director, hockey operations
Al MacNeil

Head coach
Brian Sutter

Assistant coaches
Rich Preston
Jamie Hislop

Director, hockey administration
Mike Burke

Director, communications
Peter Hanlon

Assistant director, communications
Kathy Gieck

Pro scout
Tod Button

Scouts
Guy Lapointe
Ian McKenzie

Scouting staff
Glen Giovanucci
Jiri Hrdina
Larry Johnston
Lars Norrman
Dave Polano
Mike Polano

Controller
Jackie Manwaring

Equipment manager
Gus Thorson

Physcal therapist
Terry Kane

Athletic therapist
Morris Boyer

Strength & conditioning coordinator
Rich Hesketh

DRAFT CHOICES

Rd.— Player	Ht./Wt.	Overall	Pos.	Last team
1— Oleg Saprykin	6-0/173	11	C/LW	Seattle (WHL)
2— Dan Cavanaugh	6-1/190	38	C/RW	Boston U. (H. East)
3— Craig Andersson	6-2/170	77	G	Guelph (OHL)
4— Roman Rozakov	6-1/198	106	D	Togliatti, Russia
5— Matt Doman	6-1/218	135	RW	Wisconsin (WCHA)
5— Jesse Cook	6-6/210	153	D	Denver (WCHA)
6— Cory Pecker	6-0/190	166	C	Sault Ste. Marie (OHL)
6— Matt Underhill	6-2/195	170	G	Cornell (ECAC)
7— Blair Stayzer	6-3/207	190	LW	Windsor (OHL)
9— Dimitri Kirilenko	5-11/183	252	C	CSKA Moskow, Russia

MISCELLANEOUS DATA

Home ice (capacity)
Canadian Airlines Saddledome
(17,104)

Address
P.O. Box 1540
Station M
Calgary, Alta. T2P 3B9

Business phone
403-777-2177

Club colors
Red, white, gold and black

Radio affiliation
66 CFR (660 AM)

TV affiliation
Calgary 7, CBC-TV, CTV, RDTV

TRAINING CAMP ROSTER

No.	FORWARDS	Ht./Wt.	BORN Place	BORN Date	NHL exp.	1998-99 clubs
57	Steve Begin (C)	5-11/185	Trois-Rivieres, Que.	8-14-78	1	Saint John (AHL)
43	Travis Brigley (LW)	6-1/195	Coronation, Alta.	6-16-77	1	Saint John (AHL)
8	Valeri Bure (RW)	5-10/180	Moscow, U.S.S.R.	6-13-74	5	Calgary
	Dan Cavanaugh (C/RW)	6-1/190	Springfield, Mass.	3-3-80	0	Boston University (Hockey East)
	Chris Clark (RW)	6-0/190	South Windsor, Conn.	3-8-76	0	Saint John (AHL)
20	Rene Corbet (LW)	6-0/187	St. Hyacinte, Que.	6-25-73	6	Colorado, Calgary
	Matt Doman (RW)	6-1/218	St. Cloud, Minn.	2-10-80	0	Univ. of Wisconsin (WCHA)
17	Hnat Domenichelli (C)	6-0/190	Edmonton	2-17-76	3	Saint John (AHL), Calgary
18	Steve Dubinsky (C/LW)	6-0/190	Montreal	7-9-70	6	Chicago, Calgary
44	Rico Fata (RW)	5-11/202	Sault Ste. Marie, Ont.	2-12-80	1	London (OHL), Calgary
12	Jarome Iginla (C/RW)	6-1/205	Edmonton	7-1-77	4	Calgary
62	Andrei Nazarov (LW)	6-5/230	Chelyabinsk, U.S.S.R.	4-22-74	6	Tampa Bay, Calgary
	Cory Pecker (C)	6-0/190	Montreal	3-20-81	0	Sault Ste. Marie (OHL)
	Ronald Petrovicky (RW)	5-11/172	Zilina, Czechoslovakia	2-15-77	0	Saint John (AHL)
25	Dave Roche (C)	6-4/230	Lindsay, Ont.	6-13-75	3	Calgary, Saint John (AHL)
	Oleg Saprykin (C/LW)	6-0/187	Moscow, U.S.S.R.	2-12-81	0	Seattle (WHL)
10	Marc Savard (C)	5-11/185	Ottawa	7-17-77	2	Hartford (AHL), New York Rangers
11	Jeff Shantz (C)	6-0/184	Edmonton	10-10-73	6	Chicago, Calgary
15	Martin St. Louis (C)	5-9/180	Laval, Que.	9-8-71	1	Calgary, Saint John (AHL)
16	Cory Stillman (C)	6-0/195	Peterborough, Ont.	12-20-73	5	Calgary
22	Rocky Thompson (RW)	6-2/205	Calgary	8-8-77	2	Saint John (AHL), Calgary
	Daniel Tkaczuk (C)	6-0/195	Toronto	6-10-79	0	Barrie (OHL)
58	Sergei Varlamov (RW)	5-11/190	Kiev, U.S.S.R.	7-21-78	1	Saint John (AHL)
24	Jason Wiemer (C)	6-1/225	Kimberley, B.C.	4-14-76	5	Calgary
23	Clarke Wilm (C)	6-0/195	Central Butte, Sask.	10-24-76	1	Calgary
	DEFENSEMEN					
5	Tommy Albelin	6-1/195	Stockholm, Sweden	5-21-64	12	Calgary
29	Wade Belak	6-4/213	Saskatoon, Sask.	7-3-76	3	Colorado, Hershey (AHL), Saint John (AHL), Calgary
38	Eric Charron	6-3/192	Verdun, Que.	1-14-70	7	Calgary, Saint John (AHL)
	Jesse Cook	6-6/210	Denver	10-11-79	0	Univ. of Denver (WCHA)
3	Denis Gauthier	6-2/205	Montreal	10-1-76	2	Saint John (AHL), Calgary
6	Phil Housley	5-10/185	St. Paul, Minn.	3-9-64	17	Calgary
32	Cale Hulse	6-3/215	Edmonton	11-10-73	4	Calgary
53	Derek Morris	6-0/200	Edmonton	8-24-78	2	Calgary
	Robyn Regehr	6-2/210	Recife, Brazil	4-19-80	0	Kamloops (WHL)
	Rail Rozakov	6-1/198	Murmansk, U.S.S.R.	3-29-81	0	Lada-2 Togliatti (Russian Div. III)
27	Todd Simpson	6-3/215	Edmonton	5-28-73	4	Calgary
55	Steve Smith	6-4/215	Glasgow, Scotland	4-30-63	15	Calgary
33	Lee Sorochan	6-1/210	Edmonton	9-9-75	1	Fort Wayne (IHL), Hartford (AHL), Saint John (AHL), Calgary
	GOALTENDERS					
	Craig Andersson	6-2/170	Park Ridge, Ill.	5-21-81	0	Chicago (NAHL), Guelph (OHL)
40	Fred Brathwaite	5-7/170	Ottawa	11-24-72	4	Canadian nat'l team (Int'l), Calgary
1	Tyrone Garner	6-1/170	Stoney Creek, Ont.	7-27-78	1	Oshawa (OHL), Calgary
47	Jean-Sebastien Giguere	6-0/175	Montreal	6-16-77	2	Saint John (AHL), Calgary
30	Tyler Moss	6-0/195	Ottawa	6-29-75	2	Calgary, Saint John (AHL), Orlando (IHL)
35	Andrei Trefilov	6-0/190	Moscow, U.S.S.R.	8-31-69	7	Chicago, Indianapolis (IHL), Calgary, Detroit (IHL), Ak Bars Kazan (Russia)
	Matt Underhill	6-2/195	Campbell River, B.C.	9-16-79	0	Cornell University (ECAC)

1998-99 REVIEW

INDIVIDUAL STATISTICS

SCORING

	Games	G	A	Pts.	PIM	+/-	PPG	SHG	Shots	Shooting Pct.
Theoren Fleury*	60	30	39	69	68	18	7	3	250	12.0
Cory Stillman	76	27	30	57	38	7	9	3	175	15.4
Phil Housley	79	11	43	54	52	14	4	0	193	5.7
Valeri Bure	80	26	27	53	22	0	7	0	260	10.0
Jarome Iginla	82	28	23	51	58	1	7	0	211	13.3
Andrew Cassels	70	12	25	37	18	-12	4	1	97	12.4
Derek Morris	71	7	27	34	73	4	3	0	150	4.7
Jeff Shantz*	69	12	17	29	40	15	1	1	77	15.6
Jason Wiemer	78	8	13	21	177	-12	1	0	128	6.3
Clarke Wilm	78	10	8	18	53	11	2	2	94	10.6
Steve Smith	69	1	14	15	80	3	0	0	42	2.4
Andrei Nazarov*	36	5	9	14	30	1	0	0	53	9.4
Steve Dubinsky*	61	4	10	14	14	-7	0	2	69	5.8
Cale Hulse	73	3	9	12	117	-8	0	0	83	3.6
Hnat Domenichelli	23	5	5	10	11	-4	3	0	45	11.1

	Games	G	A	Pts.	PIM	+/-	PPG	SHG	Shots	Shooting Pct.
Todd Simpson	73	2	8	10	151	18	0	0	52	3.8
Rene Corbet*	20	5	4	9	10	-2	1	0	45	11.1
Ed Ward	68	3	5	8	67	-4	0	0	56	5.4
Denis Gauthier	55	3	4	7	68	3	0	0	40	7.5
Dave Roche	36	3	3	6	44	-1	1	0	30	10.0
Tommy Albelin	60	1	5	6	8	-11	0	0	54	1.9
Michael Nylander*	9	2	3	5	2	1	1	0	7	28.6
Bob Bassen	41	1	2	3	35	-13	0	0	47	2.1
Greg Pankewicz	18	0	3	3	20	0	0	0	10	0.0
Marty McInnis*	6	1	1	2	6	-1	0	0	7	14.3
Martin St. Louis	13	1	1	2	10	-2	0	0	14	7.1
Fred Brathwaite (goalie)	28	0	2	2	2	0	0	0	0	0.0
Eric Landry	3	0	1	1	0	1	0	0	1	0.0
Wade Belak*	9	0	1	1	23	3	0	0	2	0.0
Chris O'Sullivan	10	0	1	1	2	-1	0	0	10	0.0
Tyler Moss (goalie)	11	0	1	1	0	0	0	0	0	0.0
Eric Charron	12	0	1	1	14	-6	0	0	9	0.0
Jean-Sebastien Giguere (goalie)	15	0	1	1	4	0	0	0	0	0.0
Rico Fata	20	0	1	1	4	0	0	0	13	0.0
Ken Wregget (goalie)	27	0	1	1	8	0	0	0	0	0.0
Chris Dingman*	2	0	0	0	17	-2	0	0	1	0.0
Lee Sorochan	2	0	0	0	0	-3	0	0	5	0.0
Tyrone Garner (goalie)	3	0	0	0	0	0	0	0	0	0.0
Rocky Thompson	3	0	0	0	25	0	0	0	0	0.0
Sami Helenius*	4	0	0	0	8	-2	0	0	1	0.0
Andrei Trefilov* (goalie)	4	0	0	0	0	0	0	0	0	0.0
Tom Chorske*	7	0	0	0	2	-5	0	0	13	0.0

GOALTENDING

	Games	Min.	Goals	SO	Avg.	W	L	T	Shots	Sv. Pct.
Fred Brathwaite	28	1663	68	1	2.45	11	9	7	796	.915
Tyler Moss	11	550	23	0	2.51	3	7	0	295	.922
Ken Wregget	27	1590	67	1	2.53	10	12	4	712	.906
Jean-Sebastien Giguere	15	860	46	0	3.21	6	7	1	447	.897
Andrei Trefilov*	4	162	11	0	4.07	0	3	0	84	.869
Tyrone Garner	3	139	12	0	5.18	0	2	0	74	.838

Empty-net goals (do not count against a goaltender's average): Brathwaite 3, Giguere 2, Wregget 2.

*Played with two or more NHL teams.

RESULTS

OCTOBER

9— San Jose† ......T *3-3
10—At San Jose† ......W 5-3
16—Toronto ......L 3-7
18—At Detroit ......L 0-2
20—At Dallas ......L 1-3
23—At Nashville ......W 4-3
24—At St. Louis ......L 3-4
28—Pittsburgh ......L 2-5
30—Washington ......T *0-0

NOVEMBER

1— At Chicago ......W 4-1
3— At Detroit ......W 5-2
6— Nashville ......L 1-2
8— Colorado ......W 3-1
10—Los Angeles ......W *5-4
12—Vancouver ......L 3-4
14—Anaheim ......L 0-1
16—Detroit ......W 5-3
19—At Montreal ......L 3-4
21—At Ottawa ......L 1-4
23—At Toronto ......L 2-3
25—At Nashville ......L 3-4
27—Edmonton ......L 2-3
28—Chicago ......W 5-4

DECEMBER

3— Tampa Bay ......W 4-1
5— Phoenix ......L 2-3
7— Dallas ......L 2-3
11—At Tampa Bay ......W 2-1
12—At Florida ......W 4-2
14—At N.Y. Rangers ......L 2-5
17—At Philadelphia ......T *3-3
18—At New Jersey ......W 5-2
22—Vancouver ......L 3-5
23—At Vancouver ......L 2-5
27—Colorado ......L 1-2
29—Philadelphia ......L *3-4
31—Montreal ......L 1-2

JANUARY

2— At Buffalo ......L 1-7
4— At Boston ......L 1-5
5— At Pittsburgh ......L 1-5
8— Dallas ......W 1-0
10—Florida ......L 1-2
13—At Anaheim ......W 2-1
14—At Los Angeles ......L 0-3
16—At San Jose ......T *3-3
19—Detroit ......W 3-1
21—At Colorado ......L 2-4
28—Chicago ......T *6-6
30—St. Louis ......W *4-3

FEBRUARY

1— At Dallas ......T *2-2
2— At Phoenix ......T *2-2
4— Nashville ......T *2-2
6— Ottawa ......L 1-2
8— Edmonton ......W 2-1
9— At Colorado ......W 2-1
12—Boston ......W 4-3
19—Anaheim ......W 6-3
20—Los Angeles ......T *2-2
22—N.Y. Rangers ......W 6-2
24—Buffalo ......T *2-2
26—St. Louis ......L 2-4

MARCH

1— San Jose ......L 1-2
5— At Vancouver ......W 5-1
6— At Los Angeles ......W 4-1
9— At St. Louis ......W 7-4
12—At Carolina ......L 1-2
13—At Washington ......W *5-4
16—At Nashville ......W 4-2
17—At Chicago ......L 1-3
21—N.Y. Islanders ......W 2-1
22—At Edmonton ......T *2-2
25—Montreal ......W 2-1
27—At Phoenix ......L 1-2
28—At Anaheim ......L 1-5
30—At Colorado ......T *3-3

APRIL

1— Phoenix ......L 1-4
3— Toronto ......L 1-5
7— At Edmonton ......L 2-4
9— Edmonton ......L 1-4
12—Vancouver ......L 0-2
14—At Vancouver ......W 5-4
15—Colorado ......W 5-1
17—At Edmonton ......L 2-3

*Denotes overtime game.
†Game played in Tokyo, Japan.

CAROLINA HURRICANES
EASTERN CONFERENCE/SOUTHEAST DIVISION

Hurricanes Schedule

Home games shaded; D—Day game; *—All-Star Game at Toronto.

October

SUN	MON	TUE	WED	THU	FRI	SAT
					1	2 BOS
3	4	5	6	7 PHI	8 NYR	9
10	11 D CAL	12	13 EDM	14	15 VAN	16
17	18	19	20 TOR	21	22 BUF	23 PIT
24	25	26	27	28	29 NJ	30 NYI
31						

November

SUN	MON	TUE	WED	THU	FRI	SAT
	1	2	3 TOR	4	5 DET	6
7 WAS	8	9	10 NYI	11 PHI	12	13 TB
14	15	16	17 OTT	18	19 WAS	20 DAL
21	22 BOS	23	24 VAN	25	26 TB	27 PIT
28	29	30 CAL				

December

SUN	MON	TUE	WED	THU	FRI	SAT
			1	2 TOR	3	4 COL
5	6	7 STL	8 DAL	9	10 TB	11
12	13	14	15 PIT	16	17	18 ATL
19	20 COL	21	22 DET	23 OTT	24	25
26 FLA	27	28 NSH	29	30	31	

January

SUN	MON	TUE	WED	THU	FRI	SAT
						1 ATL
2	3	4 OTT	5	6 BOS	7 ANA	8
9 NYR	10	11 PHI	12	13	14 FLA	15
16	17 NJ	18 NYR	19	20 NYR	21	22 D BUF
23	24 MON	25 PHO	26	27	28 NJ	29
30 D MON	31					

February

SUN	MON	TUE	WED	THU	FRI	SAT
		1 FLA	2	3 WAS	4	5
6 *	7	8 NYI	9	10	11	12 TB
13	14 TOR	15 OTT	16	17 MON	18	19 TB
20	21 D WAS	22	23	24 FLA	25	26 FLA
27	28	29				

March

SUN	MON	TUE	WED	THU	FRI	SAT
			1 PHO	2 LA	3	4 SJ
5	6	7	8 CHI	9	10 BOS	11
12 D ATL	13	14	15 EDM	16	17 WAS	18 MON
19	20	21 NJ	22 STL	23	24	25
26 D NYI	27 BUF	28	29 NSH	30	31 BUF	

April

SUN	MON	TUE	WED	THU	FRI	SAT
						1
2 D PHI	3 PIT	4	5	6	7	8 D ATL
9 D ATL	10	11	12	13	14	15

1999-2000 SEASON

CLUB DIRECTORY

Chief executive officer/governor
Peter Karmanos Jr.
General partner
Thomas Thewes
President and general manager
Jim Rutherford
President and COO, Gale Force Holdings, LLP
Dean Jordan
Assistant general manager
Jason Karmanos
Vice president of hockey operations
Terry McDonnell
Head coach
Paul Maurice
Assistant coaches
Randy Ladouceur
Kevin McCarthy
Director of amateur scouting
Sheldon Ferguson
Amateur scouts
Laurence Ferguson
Willy Langer
Willy Lindstrom
Tony MacDonald
Bert Marshall
Terry E. McDonnell
Pro scout
Claude Larose
Goaltender coach/pro scout
Steve Weeks
Head athletic therapist/strength and conditioning coach
Peter Friesen
Assistant athletic therapist
Stu Lemke
Equipment managers
Skip Cunningham
Wally Tatomir
Assistant equipment managers
Bob Gorman
Rick Szuber
Director of media and public relations
Chris Brown
Media relations manager
Jerry Peters

DRAFT CHOICES

Rd.— Player	Ht./Wt.	Overall	Pos.	Last team
1— David Tanabe	6-1/190	16	D	Wisconsin (WCHA)
2— Brett Lysak	6-0/190	49	C	Regina (WHL)
3— Brad Fast	6-0/185	84	D	Prince George (WHL)
4— Ryan Murphy	6-1/192	113	LW	Bowling Green (CCHA)
6— Damian Surma	5-9/202	174	LW	Plymouth (OHL)
7— Jim Baxter	6-3/204	202	D	Oshawa (OHL)
8— David Evans	6-3/185	231	RW	Clarkson (ECAC)
8— Antti Jokela	5-11/165	237	G	Lukko, Finland
9— Yauhenni Kurlin	6-0/183	259	C	

MISCELLANEOUS DATA

Home ice (capacity)
Raleigh Entertainment & Sports Arena (18,715)
Address
5000 Aerial Center
Suite 100
Morrisville, NC 27560
Business phone
919-467-7825
Club colors
Red, black and silver
Radio affiliation
WRBZ (850 AM)
TV affiliation
FOX Sports South, HTS (Cable)

TRAINING CAMP ROSTER

No.	FORWARDS	Ht./Wt.	BORN Place	BORN Date	NHL exp.	1998-99 clubs
13	Bates Battaglia (LW)	6-2/185	Chicago	12-13-75	2	Carolina
21	Ron Francis (C)	6-3/200	Sault Ste. Marie, Ont.	3-1-63	18	Carolina
23	Martin Gelinas (LW)	5-11/195	Shawinigan, Que.	6-5-70	11	Carolina
	Jeff Heerema (RW)	6-1/171	Thunder Bay, Ont.	1-17-80	0	Sarnia (OHL)
24	Sami Kapanen (RW)	5-10/173	Helsinki, Finland	6-14-73	4	Carolina
36	Greg Koehler (C)	6-2/195	Scarbourough, Ont.	2-27-75	0	New Haven (AHL), Florida (ECHL)
51	Andrei Kovalenko (RW)	5-10/215	Gorky, U.S.S.R.	7-7-70	7	Edmonton, Philadelphia, Carolina
18	Robert Kron (RW)	5-11/182	Brno, Czechoslovakia	2-27-67	9	Carolina
56	Andrew Luciuk (LW)	6-1/195	Barrhead, Alta.	2-17-77	0	Florida (ECHL), Asheville Smoke (UHL)
	Brett Lysak (C)	6-0/190	Edmonton	12-30-80	0	Regina (WHL)
31	Craig MacDonald (LW)	6-2/185	Antigonish, Nova Scotia	4-7-77	1	New Haven (AHL), Carolina
	Ian MacNeil (C)	6-2/178	Halifax, Nova Scotia	4-27-77	0	New Haven (AHL)
44	Kent Manderville (C)	6-3/200	Edmonton	4-12-71	8	Carolina
61	Brent McDonald (C)	5-11/170	Olds, Alta.	10-7-79	0	Red Deer (WHL), Prince George (WHL)
	Ryan Murphy (LW)	6-1/185	Van Nuys, Calif.	8-14-80	0	Bowling Green (CCHA)
92	Jeff O'Neill (C)	6-1/195	King City, Ont.	2-23-76	4	Carolina
	Andrei Petrunin (RW)	5-9/167	Moscow, U.S.S.R.	2-2-78	0	Muskegon (UHL)
55	Keith Primeau (C)	6-5/220	Toronto	11-24-71	9	Carolina
57	Askhat Rakhmatullin (LW)	5-11/165	Ufa, U.S.S.R.	5-31-78	0	Florida (ECHL), Fayetteville (CHL), Asheville (UHL)
28	Paul Ranheim (LW)	6-1/210	St. Louis	1-25-66	11	Carolina
15	Byron Ritchie (C)	5-10/185	Burnaby, B.C.	4-24-77	1	New Haven (AHL), Carolina
10	Gary Roberts (LW)	6-1/190	North York, Ont.	5-23-66	13	Carolina
	Damian Surma (LW)	5-9/202	Lincoln Park, Mich.	1-22-81	0	Plymouth (OHL)
	Josef Vasicek (C)	6-4/196	Havlickuv Brod, Czech.	9-12-80	0	Sault Ste. Marie (OHL)
	Tommy Westlund (RW)	6-0/202	Fors, Sweden	12-29-74	0	New Haven (AHL)
45	Shane Willis (RW)	6-0/176	Edmonton	6-13-77	1	New Haven (AHL), Carolina
	DEFENSEMEN					
77	Paul Coffey	6-0/200	Weston, Ont.	6-1-61	19	Chicago, Carolina
	Brad Fast	6-0/185	Fort St. John, Sask.	2-21-80	0	Prince George (BCJHL)
	Sergei Fedotov	6-2/180	Moscow, U.S.S.R.	1-24-77	0	Salavat Yulayev Ufa (Russian), New Haven (AHL), Florida (ECHL)
14	Steve Halko	6-1/200	Etobicoke, Ont.	3-8-74	2	New Haven (AHL), Carolina
22	Sean Hill	6-1/203	Duluth, Minn.	2-14-70	9	Carolina
33	Dave Karpa	6-1/210	Regina, Sask.	5-7-71	8	Carolina
7	Curtis Leschyshyn	6-1/205	Thompson, Man.	9-21-69	11	Carolina
5	Marek Malik	6-5/210	Ostrava, Czechoslovakia	6-24-75	4	HC Vitkovice (Czech Republic), New Haven (AHL), Carolina
4	Nolan Pratt	6-2/208	Fort McMurray, Alta.	8-14-75	3	Carolina
46	Mike Rucinski	5-11/188	Trenton, Mich.	3-30-75	2	Carolina, New Haven (AHL)
	David Tanabe	6-1/195	Minneapolis, Minn.	7-19-80	0	Univ. of Wisconsin (WCHA)
	Nikos Tselios	6-5/200	Oak Park, Ill.	1-20-79	0	Plymouth (OHL)
2	Glen Wesley	6-1/201	Red Deer, Alta.	10-2-68	12	Carolina
	GOALTENDERS					
	Eric Fichaud	5-11/171	Montreal	11-4-75	4	Milwaukee (IHL), Nashville
	Mark Fitzpatrick	6-2/198	Toronto	11-13-68	11	Chicago
1	Arturs Irbe	5-8/175	Riga, U.S.S.R.	2-2-67	8	Carolina
	Randy Petruk	5-9/178	Cranbrook, B.C.	4-23-78	0	New Haven (AHL), Florida (ECHL)

1998-99 REVIEW

INDIVIDUAL STATISTICS

SCORING

	Games	G	A	Pts.	PIM	+/-	PPG	SHG	Shots	Shooting Pct.
Keith Primeau	78	30	32	62	75	8	9	1	178	16.9
Sami Kapanen	81	24	35	59	10	-1	5	0	254	9.4
Ray Sheppard	74	25	33	58	16	4	5	0	188	13.3
Ron Francis	82	21	31	52	34	-2	8	0	133	15.8
Gary Roberts	77	14	28	42	178	2	1	1	138	10.1
Jeff O'Neill	75	16	15	31	66	3	4	0	121	13.2
Martin Gelinas	76	13	15	28	67	3	0	0	111	11.7
Robert Kron	75	9	16	25	10	-13	3	1	134	6.7
Glen Wesley	74	7	17	24	44	14	0	0	112	6.3
Nelson Emerson*	35	8	13	21	36	1	3	0	84	9.5
Paul Ranheim	78	9	10	19	39	4	0	2	67	13.4
Kevin Dineen	67	8	10	18	97	5	0	0	86	9.3
Jon Battaglia	60	7	11	18	22	7	0	0	52	13.5
Kent Manderville	81	5	11	16	38	9	0	0	71	7.0
Nolan Pratt	61	1	14	15	95	15	0	0	46	2.2

	Games	G	A	Pts.	PIM	+/-	PPG	SHG	Shots	Shooting Pct.
Andrei Kovalenko*	18	6	6	12	0	3	1	0	21	28.6
Marek Malik	52	2	9	11	36	-6	1	0	36	5.6
Paul Coffey*	44	2	8	10	28	-1	1	0	79	2.5
Sean Hill	54	0	10	10	48	9	0	0	44	0.0
Curtis Leschyshyn	65	2	7	9	50	-1	0	0	35	5.7
Steve Chiasson	28	1	8	9	16	7	1	0	74	1.4
Steven Halko	20	0	3	3	24	5	0	0	6	0.0
Adam Burt*	51	0	3	3	46	3	0	0	37	0.0
Dave Karpa	33	0	2	2	55	1	0	0	21	0.0
Mike Rucinski	15	0	1	1	8	1	0	0	8	0.0
Byron Ritchie	3	0	0	0	0	0	0	0	0	0.0
Shane Willis	7	0	0	0	0	-2	0	0	1	0.0
Craig MacDonald	11	0	0	0	0	0	0	0	5	0.0
Trevor Kidd (goalie)	25	0	0	0	0	0	0	0	0	0.0
Arturs Irbe (goalie)	62	0	0	0	10	0	0	0	0	0.0

GOALTENDING

	Games	Min.	Goals	SO	Avg.	W	L	T	Shots	Sv. Pct.
Arturs Irbe	62	3643	135	6	2.22	27	20	12	1753	.923
Trevor Kidd	25	1358	61	2	2.70	7	10	6	640	.905

Empty-net goals (do not count against a goaltender's average): Irbe 3, Kidd 3.
*Played with two or more NHL teams.

RESULTS

OCTOBER

10—Tampa Bay....T....*4-4
13—At Nashville....L......2-3
15—Dallas....T....*2-2
17—Philadelphia....T....*1-1
20—Vancouver....W......3-1
24—At Ottawa....W......3-1
25—Los Angeles....L......2-3
28—Chicago....W......2-0
30—At N.Y. Rangers....L......0-1
31—At Boston....W......2-0

NOVEMBER

2—Colorado....L......2-3
5—At N.Y. Islanders....W......6-3
6—At Washington....W......3-2
8—Boston....L......2-5
11—At Anaheim....L....*4-5
12—At San Jose....L......0-3
14—At Los Angeles....W......5-3
17—Montreal....W......5-4
19—At New Jersey....L....*2-3
20—Philadelphia....L......1-3
22—New Jersey....L......2-5
25—San Jose....W......3-0
28—At N.Y. Islanders....W......3-1
29—Anaheim....W......3-1

DECEMBER

2—Montreal....W......4-1
4—Pittsburgh....T....*3-3
5—At Florida....T....*3-3
10—Boston....L......2-3
12—Detroit....W......3-0
15—Edmonton....W......3-0
18—At Ottawa....L......1-5
19—At Buffalo....W......3-2
21—Buffalo....L......1-4
23—At N.Y. Rangers....W......1-0
26—N.Y. Rangers....L......3-6
30—Tampa Bay....W......4-3

JANUARY

1—At Florida....T....*3-3
2—Nashville....W......4-1
4—Ottawa....T....*4-4
7—At Pittsburgh....L......2-4
9—At Philadelphia....L......0-2
14—Florida....W......3-2
16—Washington....L....*2-3
18—Toronto....W......4-2
21—At Detroit....L......1-4
26—At Pittsburgh....W......5-3
28—N.Y. Rangers....W....*3-2
30—At Montreal....W......3-1
31—At Boston....T....*0-0

FEBRUARY

3—New Jersey....L......1-4
5—At Washington....L......1-4
6—Florida....T....*3-3
10—At Toronto....W......6-5
12—At N.Y. Rangers....W......3-1
13—At New Jersey....L......4-6
15—At Buffalo....L......2-3
18—Washington....T....*2-2
20—At Tampa Bay....W......3-2
21—N.Y. Islanders....W......4-1
24—At Toronto....T....*2-2
26—At Vancouver....L......0-1
27—At Edmonton....T....*2-2

MARCH

3—Boston....W......2-1
6—At Florida....T....*2-2
8—Buffalo....W......4-1
10—Pittsburgh....L....*2-3
12—Calgary....W......2-1
15—At Phoenix....T....*5-5
18—At Colorado....L......2-3
21—At Dallas....L....*2-3
22—At St. Louis....L......2-5
24—N.Y. Islanders....W......2-1
26—Toronto....L......2-7
28—Tampa Bay....T....*3-3
30—At Philadelphia....T....*3-3

APRIL

3—At Chicago....L......1-2
6—New Jersey....W......4-2
7—At Montreal....L......0-2
10—At N.Y. Islanders....W......6-1
14—Washington....W......3-0
16—At Tampa Bay....T....*2-2
17—Ottawa....T....*1-1

*Denotes overtime game.

CHICAGO BLACKHAWKS

WESTERN CONFERENCE/CENTRAL DIVISION

Blackhawks Schedule

Home games shaded; D—Day game; *—All-Star Game at Toronto.

October

SUN	MON	TUE	WED	THU	FRI	SAT
					1	2
3	4 SJ	5	6 VAN	7	8 PHO	9
10 NSH	11	12	13	14	15 TOR	16 PIT
17	18	19	20	21 ANA	22	23 DET
24	25	26	27 MON	28	29 DET	30 LA
31						

November

SUN	MON	TUE	WED	THU	FRI	SAT
	1	2	3	4 BUF	5 NSH	6
7 NYR	8	9	10 NSH	11	12 NYI	13
14 EDM	15	16 LA	17	18	19 ANA	20 PHO
21	22	23	24 EDM	25 CAL	26	27 STL
28	29	30 OTT				

December

SUN	MON	TUE	WED	THU	FRI	SAT
			1	2	3 DET	4 BOS
5	6 EDM	7	8	9 NJ	10 BUF	11
12 CAL	13	14 SJ	15	16	17 ANA	18 LA
19	20	21	22	23 DAL	24	25
26 PIT	27 WAS	28	29	30 FLA	31 DET	

January

SUN	MON	TUE	WED	THU	FRI	SAT
						1
2 SJ	3	4	5	6 CAL	7	8 NSH
9 COL	10	11	12 VAN	13 DET	14	15 COL
16	17 D SJ	18	19 NJ	20	21 STL	22
23 DAL	24	25	26	27 COL	28	29
30 VAN	31					

February

SUN	MON	TUE	WED	THU	FRI	SAT
		1	2 EDM	3 CAL	4	5
6 *	7	8	9	10	11	12 ATL
13	14 ANA	15	16 LA	17	18 WAS	19
20 D DET	21	22 PHI	23 NSH	24	25 DAL	26
27 D STL	28	29				

March

SUN	MON	TUE	WED	THU	FRI	SAT
			1 MON	2	3 TB	4
5 D PHO	6	7 NSH	8 CAR	9	10	11 FLA
12 TB	13	14	15 TOR	16 BOS	17	18 D DAL
19	20	21 PHO	22	23	24 DAL	25
26 D STL	27 COL	28	29	30 TOR	31	

April

SUN	MON	TUE	WED	THU	FRI	SAT
						1 D NYI
2 D VAN	3	4	5 ANA	6	7 STL	8
9 D STL	10	11	12	13	14	15

1999-2000 SEASON

CLUB DIRECTORY

President
William W. Wirtz
Senior vice president
Robert J. Pulford
Vice president
Jack Davison
General manager
Bob Murray
Director of player personnel
Dale Tallon
Head coach
Lorne Molleken
Assistant coaches
Denis Savard
Trent Yawney
Goaltending consultant
Vladislav Tretiak
Pro scout
Phil Russell
Scouts
Ron Anderson, Jan Blomgren, Michel Dumas, Bruce Franklin, Tim Higgins, Steve Richmond
Assistant to the general manager
Steve Williams
Manager of team services
David Stensby
Head trainers
Michael Gapski
Equipment manager
Troy Parchman
Assistant equipment manager
Lou Varga
Massage therapist
Pawel Prylinski
Vice president of marketing
Peter R. Wirtz
Exec. director of public relations
Jim De Maria
Dir. of community relations/p.r. asst.
Barbara Davidson
Director of publications/p.r. assistant
Brad Freeman
Exec. dir. of marketing/merchandising
Jim Sofranko
Manager, special events
Matt Colleran
Manager, game operations
Kellett McConville
Director of ticket operations
James K. Bare
Sales manager
Doug Ryan

DRAFT CHOICES

Rd.— Player	Ht./Wt.	Overall	Pos.	Last team
1— Steve McCarthy	6-0/197	23	D	Kootenay (WHL)
2— Dimitri Levinski	6-1/183	46	RW	Cherepovec, Russia
2— Stepan Mokhov	6-1/183	63	D	Cherepovec, Russia
5— Michael Jacobsen	6-1/207	134	D	Belleville (OHL)
6— Michael Leighton	6-2/175	165	G	Windsor (OHL)
7— Mattias Wennerberg	5-11/176	194	C	Modo Ornsk., Sweden
7— Yorick Treille	6-3/185	195	RW	Mass.-Lowell (H. East)
8— Andrew Carver	6-2/205	223	D	Hull (QMJHL)

MISCELLANEOUS DATA

Home ice (capacity)
United Center (20,500)
Address
1901 W. Madison Street
Chicago, IL 60612
Business phone
312-455-7000
Club colors
Red, black and white
Radio affiliation
WMAQ (670 AM)
TV affiliation
FOX Sports Chicago

TRAINING CAMP ROSTER

CHICAGO BLACKHAWKS

No.	FORWARDS	Ht./Wt.	BORN Place	BORN Date	NHL exp.	1998-99 clubs
10	Tony Amonte (LW/RW)	6-0/195	Hingham, Mass.	8-2-70	9	Chicago
	Mark Bell (C/LW)	6-3/185	St. Paul's, Ont.	8-5-80	0	Ottawa (OHL)
	Kyle Calder (C)	5-11/180	Mannville, Alta.	1-5-79	0	Regina (WHL), Kamloops (WHL)
	Wendel Clark (LW)	5-10/194	Kelvington, Sask.	10-25-66	14	Tampa Bay, Detroit
55	Eric Daze (LW)	6-6/222	Montreal	7-2-75	5	Chicago
17	Jean-Pierre Dumont (RW)	6-1/187	Montreal	5-1-78	1	Portland (AHL), Chicago
	Pete Gardiner (RW)	6-5/220	Toronto	9-29-77	0	Rensselaer Poly. Inst. (ECAC)
93	Doug Gilmour (C)	5-11/175	Kingston, Ont.	6-25-63	16	Chicago
	Casey Hankinson (LW)	6-1/187	Edina, Minn.	5-8-76	0	Portland (AHL)
20	Mark Janssens (C)	6-3/216	Surrey, B.C.	5-19-68	12	Chicago
27	Ty Jones (RW)	6-3/218	Richland, Wash.	2-22-79	1	Spokane (WHL), Kam. (WHL), Chicago
23	Jean-Yves Leroux (LW)	6-2/211	Montreal	6-24-76	3	Chicago
	Dmitri Levinsky (LW)	6-1/183	Ust-Kamenogorsk, U.S.S.R.	6-23-81	0	Severstal-2 Cherepovets (Russia)
44	Josef Marha (C)	6-1/205	Havlickov Brod, Czech.	6-2-76	4	Ana., Cin. (AHL), Chi., Portland (AHL)
34	Dean McAmmond (C)	5-11/200	Grand Cache, Alta.	6-15-73	7	Edmonton, Chicago
39	Craig Mills (RW)	6-0/195	Toronto	8-27-76	3	Chicago, Chicago (IHL), Indianapolis (IHL)
15	Chris Murray (RW)	6-2/209	Port Hardy, B.C.	10-25-74	5	Ottawa, Chicago
	Jeff Paul (RW)	6-3/196	London, Ont.	3-1-78	0	Portland (AHL), Indianapolis (IHL)
	Colin Pepperall (LW)	5-10/180	Niagara Falls, Ont.	4-28-78	0	Portland (AHL), Greenville (ECHL), Indianapolis (IHL)
	Geoff Peters (C)	6-0/174	Hamilton, Ont.	4-30-78	0	Canadian nat'l team (Int'l), Portland (AHL)
24	Bob Probert (LW)	6-3/225	Windsor, Ont.	6-5-65	14	Chicago
	Ben Simon (C)	5-11/178	Shaker Heights, Ohio	6-14-78	0	Univ. of Notre Dame (CCHA)
33	Reid Simpson (LW)	6-2/220	Flin Flon, Man.	5-21-69	7	Chicago
19	Ryan VandenBussche	6-0/200	Simcoe, Ontario	2-28-73	3	Ind. (IHL), Portland (AHL), Chicago
26	Todd White (C)	5-10/181	Kanata, Ont.	5-21-75	2	Chicago (IHL), Chicago
36	Alexei Zhamnov (C)	6-1/195	Moscow, U.S.S.R.	10-1-70	7	Chicago
	DEFENSEMEN					
38	Jamie Allison	6-1/190	Lindsay, Ont.	5-13-75	4	Saint John (AHL), Chicago, Ind. (IHL)
32	Radim Bicanek	6-1/195	Uherske Hradiste, Czech.	1-18-75	4	Ottawa, Grand Rapids (IHL), Chicago
2	Brad Brown	6-3/206	Baie Verte, Ont.	12-27-75	2	Montreal, Chicago
8	Anders Eriksson	6-3/220	Bollnas, Sweden	1-9-75	4	Detroit, Chicago
	Jason Hamilton	6-2/218	Montreal	1-25-77	0	Greenville (ECHL), Portland (AHL)
	Michael Jacobsen	6-1/207	Thunder Bay, Ont.	7-24-81	0	Belleville (OHL)
22	Dave Manson	6-3/220	Prince Albert, Sask.	1-27-67	13	Montreal, Chicago
4	Bryan McCabe	6-1/210	Toronto	6-8-75	4	Vancouver
	Steve McCarthy	6-0/197	Trail, B.C.	2-3-81	0	Kootenay (WHL)
3	Boris Mironov	6-3/223	Moscow, U.S.S.R.	3-21-72	6	Edmonton, Chicago
	Stepan Mokhov	6-1/183	Ust-Kamenogorsk, U.S.S.R.	1-22-81	0	Severstal-2 Cherepovets (Russia)
37	Bryan Muir	6-4/220	Winnipeg	6-8-73	4	N.J., Alb. (AHL), Chi., Portland (AHL)
6	Remi Royer	6-2/200	Donnacona, Que.	2-12-78	1	Chicago, Portland (AHL), Ind. (IHL)
5	Trent Yawney	6-3/195	Hudson Bay, Sask.	9-29-65	12	Chicago
4	Doug Zmolek	6-2/220	Rochester, Minn.	11-3-70	7	Chicago
	GOALTENDERS					
	Michael Leighton	6-2/175	Petrolia, Ont.	5-19-81	0	Windsor (OHL)
29	Steve Passmore	5-9/165	Thunder Bay, Ont.	1-29-73	1	Hamilton (AHL), Edmonton
	Jonathan Pelletier	5-11/165	Riviere-du-Loup, Que.	4-14-80	0	Drummondville (QMJHL)
41	Jocelyn Thibault	5-11/185	Montreal	1-12-75	6	Montreal, Chicago

1998-99 REVIEW

INDIVIDUAL STATISTICS

SCORING

	Games	G	A	Pts.	PIM	+/-	PPG	SHG	Shots	Shooting Pct.
Tony Amonte	82	44	31	75	60	0	14	3	256	17.2
Alexei Zhamnov	76	20	41	61	50	-10	8	1	200	10.0
Doug Gilmour	72	16	40	56	56	-16	7	1	110	14.5
Eric Daze	72	22	20	42	22	-13	8	0	189	11.6
Chris Chelios*	65	8	26	34	89	-4	2	1	172	4.7
Chad Kilger*	64	14	11	25	30	-1	2	1	68	20.6
Ed Olczyk	61	10	15	25	29	-3	2	1	88	11.4
Bob Probert	78	7	14	21	206	-11	0	0	87	8.0
Dave Manson*	64	6	15	21	107	4	2	0	134	4.5
Jean-Pierre Dumont	25	9	6	15	10	7	0	0	42	21.4
Ethan Moreau*	66	9	6	15	84	-5	0	0	80	11.3
Nelson Emerson*	27	4	10	14	13	8	0	0	94	4.3
Doug Zmolek	62	0	14	14	102	1	0	0	33	0.0
Todd White	35	5	8	13	20	-1	2	0	43	11.6
Christian Laflamme*	62	2	11	13	70	0	0	0	53	3.8
Reid Simpson	53	5	4	9	145	2	1	0	23	21.7
Daniel Cleary	35	4	5	9	24	-1	0	0	49	8.2
Boris Mironov*	12	0	9	9	27	7	0	0	35	0.0
Jean-Yves Leroux	40	3	5	8	21	-7	0	0	47	6.4

	Games	G	A	Pts.	PIM	+/-	PPG	SHG	Shots	Shooting Pct.
Brad Brown*	61	1	7	8	184	-4	0	0	26	3.8
Anders Eriksson*	11	0	8	8	0	6	0	0	12	0.0
Mike Maneluk*	28	4	3	7	8	2	1	0	29	13.8
Josef Marha*	22	2	5	7	4	5	1	0	32	6.3
Dean McAmmond*	12	1	4	5	2	3	0	0	16	6.3
Bryan Muir*	53	1	4	5	50	1	0	0	78	1.3
Jamie Allison	39	2	2	4	62	0	0	0	24	8.3
Eric Weinrich*	14	1	3	4	12	-13	0	0	24	4.2
Paul Coffey*	10	0	4	4	0	-6	0	0	8	0.0
Jeff Shantz*	7	1	0	1	4	-1	0	0	5	20.0
Mark Janssens	60	1	0	1	65	-11	0	0	27	3.7
Mark Fitzpatrick (goalie)	27	0	1	1	8	0	0	0	0	0.0
Jocelyn Thibault* (goalie)	52	0	1	1	2	0	0	0	0	0.0
Steve Dubinsky*	1	0	0	0	0	0	0	0	1	0.0
Andrei Trefilov* (goalie)	1	0	0	0	0	0	0	0	0	0.0
Roman Vopat*	3	0	0	0	4	-4	0	0	0	0.0
Chris Murray*	4	0	0	0	14	0	0	0	4	0.0
Ryan Vandenbussche	6	0	0	0	17	0	0	0	3	0.0
Radim Bicanek*	7	0	0	0	6	-3	0	0	7	0.0
Sylvain Cloutier	7	0	0	0	0	-1	0	0	3	0.0
Craig Mills	7	0	0	0	2	-2	0	0	1	0.0
Alain Nasreddine*	7	0	0	0	19	-2	0	0	2	0.0
Cam Russell*	7	0	0	0	10	1	0	0	1	0.0
Ty Jones	8	0	0	0	12	-1	0	0	3	0.0
Jeff Hackett* (goalie)	10	0	0	0	6	0	0	0	0	0.0
Dennis Bonvie	11	0	0	0	44	-4	0	0	1	0.0
Remi Royer	18	0	0	0	67	-10	0	0	24	0.0
Trent Yawney	20	0	0	0	32	-6	0	0	11	0.0

GOALTENDING

	Games	Min.	Goals	SO	Avg.	W	L	T	Shots	Sv. Pct.
Jocelyn Thibault*	52	3014	136	4	2.71	21	26	5	1435	.905
Mark Fitzpatrick	27	1403	64	0	2.74	6	8	6	682	.906
Jeff Hackett*	10	524	33	0	3.78	2	6	1	256	.871
Andrei Trefilov*	1	25	4	0	9.60	0	1	0	20	.800

Empty-net goals (do not count against a goaltender's average): Thibault 6, Hackett 3, Fitzpatrick 2.

*Played with two or more NHL teams.

RESULTS

OCTOBER

10—New Jersey......W......2-1
13—At Dallas......L......1-3
15—Anaheim......L......3-5
17—Dallas......W......4-3
19—At Montreal......W......2-1
22—San Jose......T....*2-2
24—Nashville......W......5-4
28—At Carolina......L......0-2
30—Florida......L......3-7

NOVEMBER

1—Calgary......L......1-4
4—At Florida......L......1-2
6—At Tampa Bay......T....*2-2
8—Edmonton......L....*2-3
10—At St. Louis......L......2-5
12—Toronto......L....3-10
14—At Buffalo......L......1-6
15—Ottawa......T....*2-2
17—At Nashville......W......2-1
21—At Los Angeles......L......0-5
22—At Anaheim......L......1-4
24—At Phoenix......L......2-3
28—At Calgary......L......4-5
29—At Edmonton......W......3-2

DECEMBER

3—Anaheim......W......4-1
6—Tampa Bay......W......7-5
8—At Detroit......L......2-3
9—Edmonton......W......3-1
11—Toronto......L......2-3
13—Dallas......T....*2-2
17—Washington......L......1-3
19—At Philadelphia......L......1-3
20—Los Angeles......L......1-4
23—Phoenix......W......4-3
26—Philadelphia......L......2-3
31—N.Y. Islanders......W......1-0

JANUARY

2—At Detroit......L......2-5
3—Detroit......L......1-3
5—At N.Y. Islanders......T....*1-1
7—At St. Louis......L......2-4
9—At Nashville......T....*3-3
10—Colorado......L....*2-3
12—At Colorado......L......1-4
15—At N.Y. Rangers......W......3-1
17—Phoenix......T....*1-1
21—Montreal......W......3-0
27—At Edmonton......W....*4-3
28—At Calgary......T....*6-6
30—At Vancouver......L......2-3

FEBRUARY

1—At San Jose......L......1-5
3—At Anaheim......L......0-3
4—At Los Angeles......L......2-3
6—At Phoenix......L......0-3
10—San Jose......L......2-5
12—Detroit......L......1-2
13—At Toronto......W......6-2
15—At Ottawa......L......2-6
17—Vancouver......W......4-0
19—At Dallas......L......1-5
21—Boston......L......3-6
24—At St. Louis......W......3-1
26—Los Angeles......L......1-2
28—St. Louis......L......1-3

MARCH

6—At San Jose......W......4-0
7—At Vancouver......T....*2-2
10—Nashville......W......5-2
12—At Nashville......L......3-5
14—St. Louis......L......2-5
17—Calgary......W......3-1
20—At Colorado......T....*5-5
21—Colorado......W......4-3
23—At Pittsburgh......L......2-5
25—At Boston......T....*3-3
27—At New Jersey......T....*4-4
28—St. Louis......W......3-1
31—Buffalo......W......2-1

APRIL

2—At Detroit......L......3-5
3—Carolina......W......2-1
5—Vancouver......W......2-1
8—N.Y. Rangers......W......6-2
12—At Washington......W......4-2
15—Nashville......W......4-2
17—Detroit......W......3-2

*Denotes overtime game.

COLORADO AVALANCHE
WESTERN CONFERENCE/NORTHWEST DIVISION

COLORADO AVALANCHE

Avalanche Schedule

Home games shaded; D—Day game; *—All-Star Game at Toronto.

October

SUN	MON	TUE	WED	THU	FRI	SAT
					1	2
3	4	5 NSH	6 TOR	7	8 PIT	9
10 D NYI	11 D BOS	12	13 BOS	14	15	16 OTT
17	18	19	20 MON	21 OTT	22	23 ATL
24	25	26	27 DET	28 PHI	29	30 D PHO
31						

November

SUN	MON	TUE	WED	THU	FRI	SAT
	1	2	3 STL	4	5 NYR	6
7	8	9	10	11 LA	12	13 CAL
14	15 VAN	16	17 FLA	18	19 NYI	20
21	22 DAL	23 LA	24	25	26 PHO	27 CAL
28	29	30 VAN				

December

SUN	MON	TUE	WED	THU	FRI	SAT
			1 EDM	2	3	4 CAR
5	6 VAN	7	8 SJ	9	10 ANA	11
12 VAN	13	14	15 ANA	16	17 DET	18 NSH
19	20 CAR	21	22	23 BUF	24	25
26	27 STL	28	29 LA	30	31	

January

SUN	MON	TUE	WED	THU	FRI	SAT
						1
2	3 EDM	4	5 CAL	6	7 MON	8
9 CHI	10	11 NSH	12	13 PIT	14	15 CHI
16	17 PHO	18	19 SJ	20	21 ANA	22
23 D LA	24	25 SJ	26	27 CHI	28	29 STL
30	31					

February

SUN	MON	TUE	WED	THU	FRI	SAT
		1 VAN	2	3 SJ	4	5
6 *	7	8 BUF	9	10 CAL	11	12
13 DET	14	15 WAS	16	17 NJ	18 NYR	19
20 D DAL	21	22 ATL	23	24	25 STL	26
27 DAL	28	29 EDM				

March

SUN	MON	TUE	WED	THU	FRI	SAT
			1	2 NJ	3	4 TB
5	6	7 CAL	8	9	10 EDM	11
12 PHI	13	14 ANA	15	16 NSH	17	18 D DET
19	20 VAN	21	22	23 PHO	24	25
26 D DAL	27 CHI	28	29 EDM	30	31	

April

SUN	MON	TUE	WED	THU	FRI	SAT
						1
2 D DAL	3	4	5 EDM	6	7 CAL	8
9 D DET	10	11	12	13	14	15

1999-2000 SEASON
CLUB DIRECTORY

Owner
Donald Sturm
President and general manager
Pierre Lacroix
Assistant general manager
Francois Giguere
Head coach
Bob Hartley
Assistant coaches
Jacques Cloutier
Bryan Trottier
Video coach
Paul Fixter
Director of player personnel
Michel Goulet
Director of hockey administration
Charlotte Grahame
Team services assistant
Heide Roberson
Consultant to the president
Dave Draper
Chief scout
Brian MacDonald
Pro scout
Brad Smith
Scouts
Yvon Gendron, Jim Hammett, Garth Joy, Steve Lyons, Don Paarup, Orval Tessier
Computer research consultant
John Donohue
Strength & conditioning coach
Paul Goldberg
Head athletic trainer
Pat Karns
Kinesiologist
Matt Sokolowski
Massage Therapist
Leo Vyssokov
Equipment managers
Wayne Flemming
Mark Miller
Assistant equipment manager
Eric Swartz
Visiting team attendant
Chris Moody
Dir. of media relations & team services
Jean Martineau
Dir. of special projects & new media
Hayne Ellis
Assistant director of media relations
Damen Zier

DRAFT CHOICES

Rd.— Player	Ht./Wt.	Overall	Pos.	Last team
1— Mihail Kuleshov	6-2/200	25	LW	Cherepovec, Russia
2— Martin Grenier	6-5/231	45	D	Quebec (QMJHL)
3— Branko Radivojevic	6-1/183	93	RW	Belleville (OHL)
4— Sanny Lindstrom	6-2/194	112	D	Huddinge, Sweden
4— Kristian Kovac	6-3/213	122	RW	Kosice, Slovakia
5— William Magnuson	6-5/232	142	D	Lake Superior (CCHA)
5— Jordan Krestanovich	6-0/168	152	LW	Calgary (WHL)
6— Anders Lovdahl	6-3/189	158	C	HV-71 Jonkoping, Swe.
6— Riku Hahl	6-0/187	183	C	Hameenlinna, Finland
7— Radim Vrbata	6-0/175	212	RW	Hull (QMJHL)
8— Jeff Finger	6-1/194	240	D	Green Bay (USHL)

MISCELLANEOUS DATA

Home ice (capacity)
Pepsi Center (18,139)
Address
1635 Clay St.
Denver, CO 80204
Business phone
303-893-6700
Club colors
Burgundy, steel blue, black, white and silver
Radio affiliation
KKFN (95.5 AM)
TV affiliation
FOX Sports Rocky Mountain (Cable)

TRAINING CAMP ROSTER

No.	FORWARDS	Ht./Wt.	BORN Place	BORN Date	NHL exp.	1998-99 clubs
	Ramzi Abid (LW)	6-2/195	Montreal	3-24-80	0	Chicoutimi (QMJHL), Acadie-Bathurst (QMJHL)
44	Serge Aubin (C)	6-0/180	Val d'Or, Que.	2-15-75	1	Hershey (AHL), Colorado
	Vincent Auger (C)	5-10/175	Quebec City	3-7-75	0	
	Yuri Babenko (C)	6-0/185	Penza, U.S.S.R.	1-2-78	0	Hershey (AHL)
18	Adam Deadmarsh (RW)	6-0/195	Trail, B.C.	5-10-75	5	Colorado
	Chris Dingman (LW)	6-4/245	Edmonton	7-6-76	2	Saint John (AHL), Calgary, Hershey (AHL), Colorado
12	Shean Donovan (RW)	6-3/210	Timmins, Ont.	1-22-75	5	Colorado
37	Chris Drury (C)	5-10/180	Trumbull, Conn.	8-20-76	1	Colorado
21	Peter Forsberg (C)	6-0/190	Ornskoldsvik, Sweden	7-20-73	5	Colorado
	Riku Hahl (C)	6-0/187	Hameenlinna, Finland	11-1-80	0	HPK Hameenlinna (Finland)
23	Milan Hejduk (RW)	5-11/165	Sstnad-Laberm, Czech.	2-14-76	1	Colorado
	Kristian Kovac (RW)	6-3/213	Kosice, Czechoslovakia	1-1-81	0	VSZ Kosice (Slovakia)
	Jordan Krestanovich	6-0/168	Langley, B.C.	6-14-81	0	Calgary (WHL)
	Mikhail Kuleshov (LW)	6-2/200	Perm, U.S.S.R.	1-7-81	0	Severstal Cherepovets (Russian)
	Yevgeny Lazarev (LW)	6-2/215	Kharkov, U.S.S.R.	4-25-80	0	Hershey (AHL)
22	Claude Lemieux (RW)	6-1/215	Buckingham, Que.	7-16-65	16	Colorado
	Anders Lovdahl (C)	6-3/189	Borlange, Sweden	2-4-81	0	HV 71 Jonkoping (Sweden Jr.)
	Christian Matte (RW)	5-11/170	Hull, Que.	1-20-75	3	Hershey (AHL), Colorado
	Steve Moore (C)	6-2/190	Windsor, Ont.	9-22-78	0	Harvard University (ECAC)
	Ville Nieminen (RW)	5-11/205	Tampere, Finland	4-6-77	0	Hershey (AHL)
36	Jeff Odgers (RW)	6-0/200	Spy Hill, Sask.	5-31-69	8	Colorado
	Samual Pahlsson (C)	5-11/190	Ornskoldsvik, Sweden	12-17-77	0	MoDo Ornskoldvik (Sweden)
25	Shjon Podein (LW)	6-2/200	Eden Prarie, Minn.	3-5-68	7	Philadelphia, Colorado
19	Joe Sakic (C)	5-11/185	Burnaby, B.C.	7-7-69	11	Colorado
	Alex Tanguay (C)	6-0/180	Ste.-Justine, Que.	11-21-79	0	Halifax (QMJHL), Hershey (AHL)
26	Stephane Yelle (C)	6-1/190	Ottawa	5-9-74	4	Colorado
	DEFENSEMEN					
7	Greg de Vries	6-3/218	Sundridge, Ont.	1-4-73	4	Nashville, Colorado
52	Adam Foote	6-1/205	Toronto	7-10-71	8	Colorado
	Mike Gaul	6-1/197	Lachine, Que.	4-22-73	1	Lowell (AHL), Hershey (AHL), Colorado
	Martin Grenier	6-5/231	Laval, Que.	11-2-80	0	Quebec (QMJHL)
	Alexei Gusarov	6-3/185	Leningrad, U.S.S.R.	7-8-64	9	Colorado
24	Jon Klemm	6-3/200	Cranbrook, B.C.	1-8-70	7	Colorado
	Sanny Lindstrom	6-2/194	Huddinge, Sweden	12-24-79	0	Huddinge (Sweden Dv. 2)
	Will Magnuson	6-5/232	Anchorage, Alaska	2-19-80	0	Lake Superior State (CCHA)
29	Eric Messier	6-2/200	Drummondville, Que.	10-29-73	4	Colorado, Hershey (AHL)
3	Aaron Miller	6-3/200	Buffalo	8-11-71	6	Colorado
8	Sandis Ozolinsh	6-3/205	Riga, U.S.S.R.	8-3-72	7	Colorado
27	Scott Parker	6-4/220	Hanford, Calif.	1-29-78	1	Hershey (AHL), Colorado
	Martin Skoula	6-2/195	Litvinov, Czechoslovakia	10-28-79	0	Barrie (OHL)
43	Dan Smith	6-2/195	Fernie, B.C.	10-19-76	1	Hershey (AHL), Colorado
59	Brian White	6-1/180	Winchester, Mass.	2-7-76	1	Hershey (AHL), Colorado
	GOALTENDERS					
30	Marc Denis	6-0/190	Montreal	8-1-77	2	Hershey (AHL), Colorado
33	Patrick Roy	6-0/192	Quebec City	10-5-65	15	Colorado

1998-99 REVIEW

INDIVIDUAL STATISTICS

SCORING

	Games	G	A	Pts.	PIM	+/-	PPG	SHG	Shots	Shooting Pct.
Peter Forsberg	78	30	67	97	108	27	9	2	217	13.8
Joe Sakic	73	41	55	96	29	23	12	5	255	16.1
Claude Lemieux	82	27	24	51	102	0	11	0	292	9.2
Adam Deadmarsh	66	22	27	49	99	-2	10	0	152	14.5
Milan Hejduk	82	14	34	48	26	8	4	0	178	7.9
Chris Drury	79	20	24	44	62	9	6	0	138	14.5
Valeri Kamensky	65	14	30	44	28	1	2	0	123	11.4
Sandis Ozolinsh	39	7	25	32	22	10	4	0	81	8.6
Theoren Fleury*	15	10	14	24	18	8	1	0	51	19.6
Rene Corbet*	53	8	14	22	58	3	2	0	82	9.8
Adam Foote	64	5	16	21	92	20	3	0	83	6.0
Sylvain Lefebvre	76	2	18	20	48	18	0	0	64	3.1
Shean Donovan	68	7	12	19	37	4	1	0	81	8.6
Aaron Miller	76	5	13	18	42	3	1	0	87	5.7
Stephane Yelle	72	8	7	15	40	-8	1	0	99	8.1

	Games	G	A	Pts.	PIM	+/-	PPG	SHG	Shots	Shooting Pct.
Alexei Gusarov	54	3	10	13	24	12	1	0	28	10.7
Shjon Podein*	41	2	6	8	24	-3	0	0	49	4.1
Eric Messier	31	4	2	6	14	0	1	0	30	13.3
Dale Hunter*	12	2	4	6	17	0	0	0	6	33.3
Jeff Odgers	75	2	3	5	259	-3	1	0	39	5.1
Keith Jones*	12	2	2	4	20	-6	1	0	11	18.2
Greg De Vries*	67	1	3	4	60	-3	0	0	56	1.8
Cam Russell*	35	1	2	3	84	-5	0	0	14	7.1
Jon Klemm	39	1	2	3	31	4	0	0	28	3.6
Christian Matte	7	1	1	2	0	-2	0	0	9	11.1
Warren Rychel	28	0	2	2	63	3	0	0	15	0.0
Patrick Roy (goalie)	61	0	2	2	28	0	0	0	0	0.0
Ted Crowley*	7	0	1	1	2	-1	0	0	10	0.0
Serge Aubin	1	0	0	0	0	0	0	0	1	0.0
Chris Dingman*	1	0	0	0	7	0	0	0	0	0.0
Michael Gaul	1	0	0	0	0	0	0	0	1	0.0
Brian White	2	0	0	0	0	0	0	0	0	0.0
Marc Denis (goalie)	4	0	0	0	0	0	0	0	0	0.0
Jeff Buchanan	6	0	0	0	6	1	0	0	1	0.0
Eric Lacroix*	7	0	0	0	2	-2	0	0	4	0.0
Dan Smith	12	0	0	0	9	5	0	0	6	0.0
Craig Billington (goalie)	21	0	0	0	2	0	0	0	0	0.0
Wade Belak*	22	0	0	0	71	-2	0	0	5	0.0
Scott Parker	27	0	0	0	71	-3	0	0	3	0.0

GOALTENDING

	Games	Min.	Goals	SO	Avg.	W	L	T	Shots	Sv. Pct.
Patrick Roy	61	3648	139	5	2.29	32	19	8	1673	.917
Marc Denis	4	217	9	0	2.49	1	1	1	110	.918
Craig Billington	21	1086	52	0	2.87	11	8	1	492	.894

Empty-net goals (do not count against a goaltender's average): Roy 4, Billington 1.
*Played with two or more NHL teams.

RESULTS

OCTOBER

10—Ottawa ....L 3-4
12—Buffalo ....L 0-3
14—Boston ....L 0-3
15—At Phoenix ....L 2-5
18—At Los Angeles ....T *5-5
24—Edmonton ....W 6-4
26—Phoenix ....L 1-5
29—San Jose ....W 4-2
31—At Nashville ....L 2-3

NOVEMBER

2—At Carolina ....W 3-2
4—At Toronto ....L 0-3
6—At Edmonton ....W 5-2
8—At Calgary ....L 1-3
10—At Phoenix ....T *1-1
13—Tampa Bay ....W 8-1
15—At Vancouver ....W 2-1
17—N.Y. Islanders ....W 5-2
19—Vancouver ....L 0-5
21—At Montreal ....W 3-2
25—At Edmonton ....L 0-3
28—New Jersey ....L 2-3

DECEMBER

2—Detroit ....W 4-2
4—St. Louis ....W 2-0
5—At St. Louis ....W 3-1
8—At N.Y. Islanders ....W 2-1
9—At N.Y. Rangers ....W 2-1
12—At New Jersey ....L 3-5
14—St. Louis ....T *0-0
17—At Vancouver ....L 1-2
19—At San Jose ....L 1-2
21—At Anaheim ....W 4-2
22—Anaheim ....L 0-1
26—Dallas ....L 2-4
27—At Calgary ....W 2-1
29—At Vancouver ....W 4-2
31—N.Y. Rangers ....L 3-6

JANUARY

2—At Los Angeles ....L 2-4
4—Montreal ....W 4-3
6—Florida ....T *2-2
9—At Detroit ....L 2-3
10—At Chicago ....W *3-2
12—Chicago ....W 4-1
16—St. Louis ....W 2-0
19—At Los Angeles ....W 5-4
21—Calgary ....W 4-2
27—At Anaheim ....W 4-3
28—Anaheim ....W 6-2
30—San Jose ....W 5-0

FEBRUARY

2—At Boston ....W 3-2
3—At Buffalo ....W 5-3
5—At Detroit ....W 3-1
7—At Dallas ....W 3-0
9—Calgary ....L 1-2
13—Phoenix ....L 1-4
14—Philadelphia ....T *4-4
19—At Nashville ....T *4-4
21—At Dallas ....T *1-1
23—Vancouver ....T *4-4
25—Pittsburgh ....L 2-3
27—Nashville ....W 3-1

MARCH

1—Edmonton ....L 3-4
3—At Florida ....W 7-5
4—At Tampa Bay ....L 1-2
7—At Pittsburgh ....W 3-1
9—At Washington ....W *3-2
11—At Philadelphia ....W 5-3
14—Detroit ....L 1-3
18—Carolina ....W 3-2
20—Chicago ....T *5-5
21—At Chicago ....L 3-4
24—Vancouver ....W 5-2
26—Washington ....W 3-1
28—Los Angeles ....W 7-2
30—Calgary ....T *3-3
31—At San Jose ....W 3-2

APRIL

3—Edmonton ....W 5-2
5—Los Angeles ....W 4-1
7—Nashville ....W 4-1
11—At St. Louis ....W 4-2
15—At Calgary ....L 1-5
16—At Edmonton ....L 1-5
18—Dallas ....W 2-1

*Denotes overtime game.

DALLAS STARS
WESTERN CONFERENCE/PACIFIC DIVISION

Stars Schedule

Home games shaded; D—Day game; *—All-Star Game at Toronto.

October

SUN	MON	TUE	WED	THU	FRI	SAT
					1 PIT	2 ANA
3	4	5 DET	6	7	8 ANA	9 SJ
10	11	12	13 SJ	14	15 BOS	16 NSH
17	18	19	20 EDM	21	22 NJ	23
24	25 TOR	26	27	28	29	30 TB
31						

November

SUN	MON	TUE	WED	THU	FRI	SAT
	1	2	3 BUF	4	5 PHO	6 SJ
7	8	9 STL	10 DET	11	12	13
14	15	16	17 WAS	18 PHI	19	20 CAR
21	22 COL	23	24 LA	25	26 D ANA	27
28 ATL	29	30 NYI				

December

SUN	MON	TUE	WED	THU	FRI	SAT
			1 MON	2	3	4 OTT
5	6 PHO	7	8 CAR	9	10 FLA	11 STL
12	13	14	15 CAL	16	17 EDM	18 VAN
19	20	21 CAL	22	23 CHI	24	25
26	27 SJ	28	29 NYR	30	31 ANA	

January

SUN	MON	TUE	WED	THU	FRI	SAT
						1
2	3 LA	4	5 NSH	6	7 VAN	8
9	10	11 EDM	12 CAL	13	14	15 VAN
16	17	18	19 ANA	20 LA	21	22
23 CHI	24	25	26 LA	27	28 STL	29
30	31 EDM					

February

SUN	MON	TUE	WED	THU	FRI	SAT
		1	2 ATL	3 PHO	4	5
6 *	7	8	9 ANA	10	11 LA	12
13 WAS	14	15	16 NSH	17	18 PHO	19
20 D COL	21 NSH	22	23 DET	24	25 CHI	26
27 COL	28	29				

March

SUN	MON	TUE	WED	THU	FRI	SAT
			1 PHI	2	3 PHO	4
5 DET	6	7	8 VAN	9	10 NYI	11
12 D STL	13 NYR	14	15 NJ	16	17	18 D CHI
19 D SJ	20	21	22	23	24 CHI	25
26 D COL	27	28 TB	29 FLA	30	31	

April

SUN	MON	TUE	WED	THU	FRI	SAT
						1
2 D COL	3 CAL	4	5 SJ	6	7 LA	8
9 D PHO	10	11	12	13	14	15

1999-2000 SEASON
CLUB DIRECTORY

Owner and governor
Thomas O. Hicks
President and alternate governor
James R. Lites
General manager
Bob Gainey
Assistant general manager
Doug Armstrong
Director of player personnel
Craig Button
Chief amateur scout
Tim Bernhardt
Head coach
Ken Hitchcock
Assistant coaches
Doug Jarvis
Rick Wilson
Strength and conditioning coach
J.J. McQueen
Coaching assistant/video coordinator
Leon Friedrich
Head athletic trainer
Dave Surprenant
Head equipment manager
Dave Smith
Equipment manager
Rich Matthews
Equipment assistant
Dave Wanner
Director of public relations
Larry Kelly
Public relations manager
Kurt Daniels

DRAFT CHOICES

Rd.— Player	Ht./Wt.	Overall	Pos.	Last team
2— Michael Ryan	6-1/170	32	C	Boston College H.S.
2— Dan Jancevski	6-3/208	66	D	London (OHL)
3— Mathias Tjarnqvist	6-1/183	96	C	Rogle, Sweden
4— Jeff Bateman	5-11/165	126	C	Brampton (OHL)
5— Gregor Baumgartner	6-2/185	156	C	A.-Bathurst (QMJHL)
6— Justin Cox	6-0/160	184	RW	Prince George (WHL)
6— Brett Draney	6-1/179	186	LW	Kamloops (WHL)
7— Jeff MacMillan	6-3/198	215	D	Oshawa (OHL)
8— Brian Sullivan	6-3/185	243	D	Thayer Academy
9— Jamie Chamberlain	6-0/178	265	RW	Peterborough (OHL)
9— Mikhail Donika	6-0/185	272	D	Torp. Yaroslavl, Russia

MISCELLANEOUS DATA

Home ice (capacity)
Reunion Arena (17,001)
Office address
211 Cowboys Parkway
Irving, TX 75063
Business phone
972-868-2890
Club colors
Black, gold, green and white
Radio affiliation
WBAP (820 AM)
TV affiliation
FOX Sports Southwest (Cable), KXTX (Channel 39)

TRAINING CAMP ROSTER

No.	FORWARDS	Ht./Wt.	BORN — Place	BORN — Date	NHL exp.	1998-99 clubs
	Jeff Bateman (C)	5-11/165	Belleville, Ont.	8-29-81	0	Brampton (OHL)
	Gregor Baumgartner (C)	6-2/185	Leoben, Austria	7-13-79	0	Acadie-Bathurst (QMJHL)
	Tyler Bouck (RW)	6-0/185	Camrose, Alta.	1-13-80	0	Prince George (WHL)
	Ryan Christie (LW)	6-2/175	Beamsville, Ont.	7-3-78	0	Michigan (IHL)
	Justin Cox (RW)	6-0/160	Merritt, B.C.	3-13-81	0	Prince George (WHL)
	Brett Draney (LW)	6-1/179	Merritt, B.C.	3-12-81	0	Kamloops (WHL)
39	Kelly Fairchild (C)	5-11/188	Hibbing, Minn.	4-9-73	3	Michigan (IHL), Dallas
	Steve Gainey (C)	6-0/180	Montreal	1-26-79	0	Kamloops (WHL)
23	Aaron Gavey (C)	6-1/175	Sudbury, Ont.	2-22-74	4	Dallas, Michigan (IHL)
22	Brett Hull (RW)	5-10/204	Belleville, Ont.	8-9-64	14	Dallas
	Niko Kapanen (C)	5-9/180	Hameenlinna, Finland	4-29-78	0	HPK Hameenlinna (Finland)
12	Mike Keane (RW)	5-10/185	Winnipeg	5-29-67	11	Dallas
15	Jamie Langenbrunner (C)	5-11/185	Duluth, Minn.	7-24-75	5	Dallas
	Greg Leeb (C)	5-9/160	Red Deer, Alta.	5-31-77	0	Michigan (IHL)
26	Jere Lehtinen (RW)	6-0/185	Espoo, Finland	6-24-73	4	Dallas
11	Juha Lind (LW)	5-11/180	Helsinki, Finland	1-2-74	1	Jokerit (Finland)
	Roman Lyashenko (C)	6-0/174	Murmansk, U.S.S.R.	5-2-79	0	Torpedo Yaroslavl (Russian)
29	Grant Marshall (RW)	6-1/185	Mississauga, Ont.	6-9-73	5	Dallas
9	Mike Modano (C)	6-3/200	Livonia, Mich.	6-7-70	11	Dallas
	Brenden Morrow (LW)	5-11/195	Carlyle, Sask.	1-16-79	0	Portland (WHL)
25	Joe Nieuwendyk (C)	6-1/195	Oshawa, Ont.	9-10-66	13	Dallas
	Pavel Patera (C)	6-1/172	Kladno, Czechoslovakia	9-6-71	0	Vsetin (Czech Republic)
18	Derek Plante (C)	5-11/181	Cloquet, Minn.	1-17-71	6	Buffalo, Dallas
	Michael Ryan (C)	6-1/170	Milton, Mass.	5-16-80	0	Boston College H.S. (USHS (East))
49	Jon Sim (C)	5-9/175	New Glasgow, Nova Scotia	9-29-77	1	Michigan (IHL), Dallas
10	Brian Skrudland (C)	6-0/200	Peace River, Alta.	7-31-63	14	Dallas
11	Blake Sloan (RW)	5-10/193	Park Ridge, Ill.	7-27-75	1	Houston (IHL), Dallas
	Mathias Tjarnqvist (C)	6-1/183	Umea, Sweden	4-15-79	0	Rogle (Sweden Dv. 2)
46	Jamie Wright (LW)	6-0/170	Kitchener, Ont.	5-13-76	2	Dallas, Michigan (IHL)
	DEFENSEMEN					
27	Shawn Chambers	6-2/200	Sterling Heights, Mich.	10-11-66	12	Dallas
	John Erskine	6-4/197	Kingston, Ont.	6-26-80	0	London (OHL)
2	Derian Hatcher	6-5/225	Sterling Heights, Mich.	6-4-72	8	Dallas
	Richard Jackman	6-2/180	Toronto	6-28-78	0	Michigan (IHL)
	Dan Jancevski	6-3/208	Windsor, Ont.	6-15-81	0	London (OHL)
37	Brad Lukowich	6-1/170	Cranbrook, B.C.	8-12-76	2	Michigan (IHL), Dallas
24	Richard Matvichuk	6-2/190	Edmonton	2-5-73	7	Dallas
	Jamie Pushor	6-3/225	Lethbridge, Alta.	2-11-73	4	Anaheim
5	Darryl Sydor	6-0/195	Edmonton	5-13-72	8	Dallas
4	Mark Wotton	6-0/190	Foxwarren, Man.	11-16-73	3	Syracuse (AHL)
56	Sergei Zubov	6-1/200	Moscow, U.S.S.R.	7-22-70	7	Dallas
	GOALTENDERS					
20	Ed Belfour	5-11/182	Carman, Man.	4-21-65	11	Dallas
30	Manny Fernandez	6-0/185	Etobicoke, Ont.	8-27-74	4	Houston (IHL), Dallas
	Marty Turco	5-11/175	Sault Ste. Marie, Ont.	8-13-75	0	Michigan (IHL)

1998-99 REVIEW

INDIVIDUAL STATISTICS

SCORING

	Games	G	A	Pts.	PIM	+/-	PPG	SHG	Shots	Shooting Pct.
Mike Modano	77	34	47	81	44	29	6	4	224	15.2
Brett Hull	60	32	26	58	30	19	15	0	192	16.7
Joe Nieuwendyk	67	28	27	55	34	11	8	0	157	17.8
Jere Lehtinen	74	20	32	52	18	29	7	1	173	11.6
Sergei Zubov	81	10	41	51	20	9	5	0	155	6.5
Darryl Sydor	74	14	34	48	50	-1	9	0	163	8.6
Jamie Langenbrunner	75	12	33	45	62	10	4	0	145	8.3
Pat Verbeek	78	17	17	34	133	11	8	0	134	12.7
Grant Marshall	82	13	18	31	85	1	2	0	112	11.6
Derian Hatcher	80	9	21	30	102	21	3	0	125	7.2
Mike Keane	81	6	23	29	62	-2	1	1	106	5.7
Tony Hrkac	69	13	14	27	26	2	2	0	67	19.4
Dave Reid	73	6	11	17	16	0	1	0	81	7.4
Guy Carbonneau	74	4	12	16	31	-3	0	0	60	6.7
Richard Matvichuk	64	3	9	12	51	23	1	0	54	5.6
Shawn Chambers	61	2	9	11	18	6	1	0	82	2.4
Craig Ludwig	80	2	6	8	87	5	0	0	39	5.1

	Games	G	A	Pts.	PIM	+/-	PPG	SHG	Shots	Shooting Pct.
Brian Skrudland	40	4	1	5	33	2	0	0	33	12.1
Derek Plante*	10	2	3	5	4	1	1	0	24	8.3
Sergey Gusev*	22	1	4	5	6	5	0	0	30	3.3
Benoit Hogue*	12	1	3	4	4	2	0	0	20	5.0
Brad Lukowich	14	1	2	3	19	3	0	0	8	12.5
Brent Severyn	30	1	2	3	50	-2	0	0	22	4.5
Jonathan Sim	7	1	0	1	12	1	0	0	8	12.5
Dan Keczmer*	22	0	1	1	22	-2	0	0	12	0.0
Kelly Fairchild	1	0	0	0	0	0	0	0	4	0.0
Emmanuel Fernandez (goalie)	1	0	0	0	0	0	0	0	0	0.0
Petr Buzek	2	0	0	0	2	0	0	0	0	0.0
Aaron Gavey	7	0	0	0	10	-1	0	0	4	0.0
Jamie Wright	11	0	0	0	0	-3	0	0	10	0.0
Blake Sloan	14	0	0	0	10	-1	0	0	7	0.0
Jason Botterill	17	0	0	0	23	-2	0	0	8	0.0
Doug Lidster	17	0	0	0	10	0	0	0	7	0.0
Roman Turek (goalie)	26	0	0	0	0	0	0	0	0	0.0
Ed Belfour (goalie)	61	0	0	0	26	0	0	0	0	0.0

GOALTENDING

	Games	Min.	Goals	SO	Avg.	W	L	T	Shots	Sv. Pct.
Ed Belfour	61	3536	117	5	1.99	35	15	9	1373	.915
Emmanuel Fernandez	1	60	2	0	2.00	0	1	0	29	.931
Roman Turek	26	1382	48	1	2.08	16	3	3	562	.915

Empty-net goals (do not count against a goaltender's average): Turek 1.

*Played with two or more NHL teams.

RESULTS

OCTOBER

10—Buffalo ... W ... 4-1
13—Chicago ... W ... 3-1
15—At Carolina ... T ... *2-2
17—At Chicago ... L ... 3-4
20—Calgary ... W ... 3-1
22—Phoenix ... W ... 2-1
24—San Jose ... W ... 2-1
30—Anaheim ... T ... *3-3
31—Detroit ... W ... 3-2

NOVEMBER

4—At San Jose ... L ... 0-4
7—At Los Angeles ... W ... 4-3
11—Phoenix ... L ... 0-2
13—At Detroit ... W ... 5-1
14—At Boston ... W ... 3-1
20—N.Y. Islanders ... W ... 4-2
21—At St. Louis ... T ... *3-3
23—San Jose ... W ... 3-2
25—New Jersey ... L ... 2-5
27—Washington ... W ... 4-0

DECEMBER

2—At San Jose ... W ... 3-0
4—At Vancouver ... L ... 1-4
6—At Edmonton ... W ... 6-2
7—At Calgary ... W ... 3-2
9—San Jose ... T ... *3-3
11—Montreal ... W ... 3-2
13—At Chicago ... T ... *2-2
15—St. Louis ... W ... 7-3
18—At Detroit ... W ... 3-1
20—At Ottawa ... W ... 3-2
21—At Montreal ... T ... *2-2
23—At Toronto ... W ... 5-1
26—At Colorado ... W ... 4-2
28—Nashville ... W ... 1-0
31—Boston ... W ... 6-1

JANUARY

1—At Phoenix ... W ... *2-1
6—Vancouver ... W ... 6-4
8—At Calgary ... L ... 0-1
10—At Vancouver ... L ... 0-2
12—At Edmonton ... T ... *2-2
13—At San Jose ... W ... 2-1
15—At Anaheim ... W ... 3-1
18—Vancouver ... L ... 3-5
20—Toronto ... L ... 4-6
27—Los Angeles ... W ... 3-2
29—At Tampa Bay ... W ... 4-1
30—At Florida ... W ... 5-2

FEBRUARY

1—Calgary ... T ... *2-2
7—Colorado ... L ... 0-3
12—At Anaheim ... W ... 3-2
13—At Los Angeles ... W ... 3-2
15—Edmonton ... W ... 4-1
17—Florida ... W ... 2-1
19—Chicago ... W ... 5-1
21—Colorado ... T ... *1-1
23—At Nashville ... W ... 4-3
24—Nashville ... L ... 1-2
26—Pittsburgh ... W ... 6-4
28—Los Angeles ... W ... 1-0

MARCH

2—At N.Y. Rangers ... T ... *2-2
4—At N.Y. Islanders ... W ... *3-2
5—At Buffalo ... L ... 1-2
7—St. Louis ... W ... 4-3
10—Edmonton ... W ... 7-4
12—Anaheim ... W ... 4-0
14—At Philadelphia ... T ... *1-1
16—At Pittsburgh ... T ... *2-2
17—At Washington ... L ... *1-2
19—Ottawa ... L ... 1-2
21—Carolina ... W ... *3-2
23—At Phoenix ... W ... 3-2
25—At Los Angeles ... W ... 2-1
26—At Anaheim ... L ... 1-5
28—At Nashville ... W ... 3-0
31—Tampa Bay ... W ... 6-4

APRIL

3—At St. Louis ... L ... 2-5
4—Detroit ... L ... 0-3
7—Anaheim ... W ... 5-1
9—N.Y. Rangers ... W ... 3-1
11—Los Angeles ... W ... 6-2
14—Phoenix ... W ... 4-2
17—At Phoenix ... L ... 0-2
18—At Colorado ... L ... 1-2

*Denotes overtime game.

DETROIT RED WINGS
WESTERN CONFERENCE/CENTRAL DIVISION

Red Wings Schedule

Home games shaded; D—Day game; *—All-Star Game at Toronto.

October

SUN	MON	TUE	WED	THU	FRI	SAT
					1	2 BUF
3	4	5 DAL	6	7 ATL	8	9 FLA
10	11	12	13 STL	14	15	16 PHI
17	18	19	20 SJ	21	22 ANA	23 CHI
24	25	26	27 COL	28	29 CHI	30 STL
31						

November

SUN	MON	TUE	WED	THU	FRI	SAT
	1	2	3 LA	4	5 CAR	6
7 TB	8	9	10 DAL	11	12 PIT	13 TOR
14	15	16	17 VAN	18	19 CAL	20 EDM
21	22	23	24 STL	25	26 EDM	27
28 D PHO	29	30				

December

SUN	MON	TUE	WED	THU	FRI	SAT
			1 SJ	2	3 CHI	4 NSH
5	6	7	8 NSH	9	10 LA	11 BOS
12	13	14	15 EDM	16	17 COL	18
19 ANA	20 SJ	21	22 CAR	23	24	25
26	27 ATL	28 BUF	29	30	31 CHI	

January

SUN	MON	TUE	WED	THU	FRI	SAT
						1
2 PIT	3	4 PHO	5	6 NSH	7	8 ANA
9	10	11 MON	12	13 CHI	14	15
16 EDM	17	18 CAL	19 VAN	20	21	22 OTT
23	24	25	26 TOR	27	28 CAL	29 NJ
30	31 PHO					

February

SUN	MON	TUE	WED	THU	FRI	SAT
		1	2	3 LA	4	5
6 *	7	8 STL	9	10 STL	11	12
13 COL	14 PHO	15	16 VAN	17	18 LA	19
20 D CHI	21 D NYI	22	23 DAL	24	25 NYI	26
27 TB	28	29				

March

SUN	MON	TUE	WED	THU	FRI	SAT
			1	2	3 WAS	4
5 DAL	6	7 LA	8 SJ	9	10 NSH	11
12	13	14 NSH	15	16 TOR	17	18 D COL
19 ANA	20	21	22 CAL	23 NSH	24	25
26 D NYR	27 NYR	28	29 VAN	30	31	

April

SUN	MON	TUE	WED	THU	FRI	SAT
						1 D STL
2 MON	3	4	5	6	7 WAS	8
9 D COL	10	11	12	13	14	15

1999-2000 SEASON

CLUB DIRECTORY

Owner
Michael Ilitch
Owner and secretary/treasurer
Marian Ilitch
Vice presidents
Atanas Ilitch
Christopher Ilitch
Senior vice president
Jim Devellano
General manager
Ken Holland
Assistant general manager
Jim Nill
Head coach
Scotty Bowman
Associate coaches
Dave Lewis
Barry Smith
Goaltending consultant
Jim Bedard
NHL scout
Dan Belisle
Scouts
Hakan Andersson, Paul Crowley, Bruce Haralson, Vladimir Havluj, Mark Howe, Mark Leach, Joe McDonnell, Ruslan Shabanov, Marty Stein
Athletic trainer
John Wharton
Equipment manager
Paul Boyer
Assistant equipment manager
Tim Abbott
Masseur
Bob Huddleston
Team physicians
Dr. John Finley
Dr. David Collon
Team dentist
C.J. Regula

DRAFT CHOICES

Rd.— Player	Ht./Wt.	Overall	Pos.	Last team
4— Jari Toulsa	6-0/172	120	C	Frolunda, Sweden
5— Andrei Maximenko	5-11/172	149	LW	Krylja Sovetov, Russia
6— Kent McDonnell	6-2/195	181	RW	Guelph (OHL)
7— Henrik Zetterberg	5-11/176	210	LW	Timra, Sweden
8— Anton Borodkin	5-11/177	238	LW	Kamloops (WHL)
9— Ken Davis	6-4/210	266	RW	Portland (WHL)

MISCELLANEOUS DATA

Home ice (capacity)
Joe Louis Arena (19,983)
Address
600 Civic Center Drive
Detroit, MI 48226
Business phone
313-396-7544
Club colors
Red and white
Radio affiliation
WJR (760 AM)
TV affiliation
WKBD (Channel 50), FOX Sports Detroit (Cable)

TRAINING CAMP ROSTER

No.	FORWARDS	Ht./Wt.	BORN Place	BORN Date	NHL exp.	1998-99 clubs
	Philippe Audet (LW)	6-2/175	Ottawa	6-4-77	1	Adirondack (AHL), Detroit
	Ryan Barnes (LW)	6-1/201	Dunnville, Ont.	1-30-80	0	Sudbury (OHL), Toronto (OHL), Barrie (OHL)
17	Doug Brown (RW)	5-11/185	New Haven, Conn.	6-12-64	13	Detroit
	Yuri Butsayev (C)	6-1/183	Togliatti, U.S.S.R.	10-11-78	0	Lada Togliatti (Russia), Dynamo Moscow (Russia)
33	Kris Draper (C)	5-10/190	Toronto	5-24-71	9	Detroit
91	Sergei Fedorov (C)	6-2/200	Pskov, U.S.S.R.	12-13-69	9	Detroit
	Johan Forsander (LW)	6-1/174	Jonkoping, Sweden	4-28-78	0	HV 71 Jonkoping (Sweden)
41	Brent Gilchrist (LW)	5-11/180	Moose Jaw, Sask.	4-3-67	11	Detroit
96	Tomas Holmstrom (LW)	6-0/198	Pieta, Sweden	1-23-73	3	Detroit
26	Joey Kocur (RW)	6-0/222	Calgary	12-21-64	15	Detroit
13	Slava Kozlov (LW)	5-10/195	Voskresensk, U.S.S.R.	5-3-72	8	Detroit
	Darryl Laplante (C)	6-0/193	Calgary	3-28-77	2	Adirondack (AHL), Detroit
20	Martin Lapointe (RW)	5-11/215	Lachine, Que.	9-12-73	8	Detroit
8	Igor Larionov (C)	5-10/170	Voskresensk, U.S.S.R.	12-3-60	9	Detroit
18	Kirk Maltby (RW)	6-0/190	Guelph, Ont.	12-22-72	6	Detroit
	Andrei Maximenko (LW)	5-11/172	Moscow, U.S.S.R.	10-1-81	0	Kryla Sov. Moscow (Russian)
25	Darren McCarty (RW)	6-1/215	Burnaby, B.C.	4-1-72	6	Detroit
	Kent McDonell (RW)	6-2/198	Cornwall, Ont.	3-1-79	0	Guelph (OHL)
23	Stacy Roest (C)	5-9/185	Lethbridge, Alta.	3-15-74	1	Detroit, Adirondack (AHL)
14	Brendan Shanahan (LW)	6-3/215	Mimico, Ont.	1-23-69	12	Detroit
	Jari Tolsa (C)	6-0/172	Goteborg, Sweden	4-20-81	0	V. Frolunda Goteborg (Sweden Jr.)
	Tomek Valtonen (LW)	6-1/198	Piotrkow Trybunalski, Poland	1-8-80	0	Plymouth (OHL)
	B.J. Young (RW)	5-11/177	Anchorage, Alaska	7-23-77	0	Adirondack (AHL)
19	Steve Yzerman (C)	5-10/185	Cranbrook, B.C.	5-9-65	16	Detroit
	DEFENSEMEN					
24	Chris Chelios	6-1/190	Chicago	1-25-62	16	Chicago, Detroit
11	Mathieu Dandenault	6-1/196	Magog, Que.	2-3-76	4	Detroit
	Jiri Fischer	6-5/210	Horovice, Czechoslovakia	7-31-80	0	Hull (QMJHL)
28	Yan Golubovsky	6-3/205	Novosibirsk, U.S.S.R.	3-9-76	2	Detroit, Adirondack (AHL)
4	Uwe Krupp	6-6/233	Cologne, West Germany	6-24-65	13	Detroit
	Maxim Kuznetsov	6-5/235	Pavlodar, U.S.S.R.	3-24-77	0	Adirondack (AHL)
5	Nicklas Lidstrom	6-2/190	Vasteras, Sweden	4-28-70	8	Detroit
55	Larry Murphy	6-1/215	Scarborough, Ont.	3-8-61	19	Detroit
	Jesse Wallin	6-2/190	Saskatoon, Sask.	3-10-78	0	Adirondack (AHL)
27	Aaron Ward	6-2/225	Windsor, Ont.	1-17-73	5	Detroit
	John Wikstrom	6-3/200	Lulea, Sweden	1-30-79	0	
	GOALTENDERS					
	Jason Elliott	6-2/183	Chapman, Australia	10-11-75	0	Adirondack (AHL)
	Manny Legace	5-9/162	Toronto	2-4-73	1	Long Beach (IHL), Los Angeles
	Aren Miller	6-2/208	Oxbow, Sask.	1-13-78	0	Toledo (ECHL), Adirondack (AHL)
30	Chris Osgood	5-11/181	Peace River, Alta.	11-26-72	6	Detroit
31	Ken Wregget	6-1/200	Brandon, Man.	3-25-64	16	Calgary

1998-99 REVIEW

INDIVIDUAL STATISTICS

SCORING

	Games	G	A	Pts.	PIM	+/-	PPG	SHG	Shots	Shooting Pct.
Steve Yzerman	80	29	45	74	42	8	13	2	231	12.6
Sergei Fedorov	77	26	37	63	66	9	6	2	224	11.6
Igor Larionov	75	14	49	63	48	13	4	2	83	16.9
Brendan Shanahan	81	31	27	58	123	2	5	0	288	10.8
Vyacheslav Kozlov	79	29	29	58	45	10	6	1	209	13.9
Nicklas Lidstrom	81	14	43	57	14	14	6	2	205	6.8
Larry Murphy	80	10	42	52	42	21	5	1	168	6.0
Darren McCarty	69	14	26	40	108	10	6	0	140	10.0
Tomas Holmstrom	82	13	21	34	69	-11	5	0	100	13.0
Martin Lapointe	77	16	13	29	141	7	7	1	153	10.5
Doug Brown	80	9	19	28	42	5	3	1	180	5.0
Kris Draper	80	4	14	18	79	2	0	1	78	5.1
Kirk Maltby	53	8	6	14	34	-6	0	1	76	10.5
Mathieu Dandenault	75	4	10	14	59	17	0	0	94	4.3
Stacy Roest	59	4	8	12	14	-7	0	0	50	8.0
Anders Eriksson*	61	2	10	12	34	5	0	0	67	3.0
Aaron Ward	60	3	8	11	52	-5	0	0	46	6.5
Jamie Macoun	69	1	10	11	36	-1	0	0	62	1.6

	Games	G	A	Pts.	PIM	+/-	PPG	SHG	Shots	Shooting Pct.
Joey Kocur	39	2	5	7	87	0	0	0	20	10.0
Wendel Clark*	12	4	2	6	2	1	0	0	44	9.1
Uwe Krupp	22	3	2	5	6	0	0	0	32	9.4
Todd Gill*	23	2	2	4	11	-4	0	0	25	8.0
Chris Osgood (goalie)	63	0	3	3	8	0	0	0	0	0.0
Chris Chelios*	10	1	1	2	4	5	1	0	15	6.7
Brent Gilchrist	5	1	0	1	0	-1	0	0	4	25.0
Petr Klima	13	1	0	1	4	-3	0	0	12	8.3
Doug Houda	3	0	1	1	0	-2	0	0	1	0.0
Yan Golubovsky	17	0	1	1	16	4	0	0	10	0.0
Darryl Laplante	3	0	0	0	0	0	0	0	0	0.0
Philippe Audet	4	0	0	0	0	-2	0	0	3	0.0
Kevin Hodson* (goalie)	4	0	0	0	0	0	0	0	0	0.0
Bill Ranford* (goalie)	4	0	0	0	0	0	0	0	0	0.0
Ulf Samuelsson*	4	0	0	0	6	-1	0	0	2	0.0
Norm Maracle (goalie)	16	0	0	0	0	0	0	0	0	0.0

GOALTENDING

	Games	Min.	Goals	SO	Avg.	W	L	T	Shots	Sv. Pct.
Bill Ranford*	4	244	8	0	1.97	3	0	1	98	.918
Norm Maracle	16	821	31	0	2.27	6	5	2	379	.918
Chris Osgood	63	3691	149	3	2.42	34	25	4	1654	.910
Kevin Hodson*	4	175	9	0	3.09	0	2	0	79	.886

Empty-net goals (do not count against a goaltender's average): Osgood 4, Maracle 1.
*Played with two or more NHL teams.

RESULTS

OCTOBER

10—At Toronto L 1-2
13—At Washington W 3-2
16—St. Louis W 4-1
18—Calgary W 2-0
21—Nashville W 5-2
23—Toronto L 3-5
24—At Montreal W 3-0
28—At Florida W 7-2
29—At St. Louis L 1-3
31—At Dallas L 2-3

NOVEMBER

3—Calgary L 2-5
6—At Phoenix L 1-3
8—At Anaheim W 3-2
11—St. Louis W 6-2
13—Dallas L 1-5
16—At Calgary L 3-5
18—At Edmonton W 6-2
21—At Vancouver W 4-2
25—Anaheim W 5-2
27—Vancouver W 7-1
29—San Jose W 4-1

DECEMBER

2—At Colorado L 2-4
4—At San Jose T *2-2
5—At Los Angeles W 4-3
8—Chicago W 3-2
11—Edmonton W 3-2
12—At Carolina L 0-3
16—Boston W 5-3
18—Dallas L 1-3
19—At Boston L 1-4
22—Phoenix L 2-6
23—At Nashville L 3-5
26—At St. Louis L 3-4
28—St. Louis T *4-4
31—Toronto L 2-4

JANUARY

2—Chicago W 5-2
3—At Chicago W 3-1
6—Ottawa L 0-2
9—Colorado W 3-2
10—At Ottawa L 1-4
12—Montreal W 5-1
14—Nashville W *2-1
16—At Vancouver T *2-2
17—At Edmonton L 1-4
19—At Calgary L 1-3
21—Carolina W 4-1
26—At Nashville W 4-1
30—N.Y. Rangers L 2-3

FEBRUARY

1—At New Jersey T *2-2
3—N.Y. Islanders W 5-1
5—Colorado L 1-3
7—At Pittsburgh L 1-2
9—At Nashville W 5-2
11—Edmonton W 4-2
12—At Chicago W 2-1
14—At N.Y. Rangers W 4-2
17—San Jose W 3-1
19—New Jersey W 3-1
21—At Buffalo T *4-4
24—Los Angeles L *2-3
26—Florida T *5-5
27—At N.Y. Islanders L 1-3

MARCH

5—At Phoenix W 7-2
7—At Anaheim L 1-3
9—At Los Angeles L 2-4
12—At San Jose L 0-2
14—At Colorado W 3-1
17—Phoenix L 3-4
19—At Tampa Bay W 5-3
21—At Philadelphia L 4-5
24—Buffalo W 2-1
26—Tampa Bay W 6-1
28—Philadelphia W *3-2
31—Los Angeles W 2-1

APRIL

2—Chicago W 5-3
4—At Dallas W 3-0
5—Anaheim W 3-2
7—Vancouver W 6-1
9—At St. Louis T *1-1
11—Pittsburgh L 0-3
14—Nashville W 4-2
17—At Chicago L 2-3

*Denotes overtime game.

EDMONTON OILERS
WESTERN CONFERENCE/NORTHWEST DIVISION

Oilers Schedule

Home games shaded; D—Day game; *—All-Star Game at Toronto.

October

SUN	MON	TUE	WED	THU	FRI	SAT
					1 NYR	2
3	4	5	6 MON	7 SJ	8	9 STL
10	11	12	13 CAR	14	15	16 LA
17	18	19	20 DAL	21 STL	22	23 NSH
24	25	26 PHO	27	28	29	30
31 NSH						

November

SUN	MON	TUE	WED	THU	FRI	SAT
	1	2	3 FLA	4	5 STL	6
7 ANA	8	9 LA	10 PHO	11	12 STL	13
14 CHI	15	16	17	18	19	20 DET
21 NYI	22	23	24 CHI	25	26 DET	27 TOR
28	29	30				

December

SUN	MON	TUE	WED	THU	FRI	SAT
			1 COL	2 VAN	3	4 VAN
5	6 CHI	7	8 NYR	9 BOS	10	11 D NJ
12	13	14 NYI	15 DET	16	17 DAL	18
19 OTT	20	21 WAS	22	23 CAL	24	25
26	27 ANA	28	29	30 LA	31	

January

SUN	MON	TUE	WED	THU	FRI	SAT
						1 PHO
2	3 COL	4	5 SJ	6	7 TB	8
9	10	11 DAL	12	13	14 TOR	15
16 DET	17	18	19 CAL	20	21	22 VAN
23	24 NSH	25 VAN	26	27	28 TB	29 FLA
30	31 DAL					

February

SUN	MON	TUE	WED	THU	FRI	SAT
		1	2 CHI	3	4	5
6 *	7	8 MON	9	10 PHI	11 PIT	12
13 D BUF	14	15 NSH	16	17	18 CAL	19 CAL
20	21 LA	22	23 BOS	24	25 ATL	26
27 ANA	28	29 COL				

March

SUN	MON	TUE	WED	THU	FRI	SAT
			1	2	3	4 PIT
5	6	7 TOR	8	9	10 COL	11
12 D NSH	13 ATL	14	15 CAR	16	17 OTT	18
19 CAL	20	21	22 ANA	23	24	25 VAN
26	27 SJ	28	29 COL	30	31	

April

SUN	MON	TUE	WED	THU	FRI	SAT
						1 PHO
2	3 SJ	4	5 COL	6	7 VAN	8 CAL
9	10	11	12	13	14	15

1999-2000 SEASON

CLUB DIRECTORY

Owner
Edmonton Investors Group, Ltd.
Governor
Jim Hole
President/general manager
Glen Sather
Exec. v.p./assistant general manager
Bruce MacGregor
Vice president, hockey operations
Doug Risebrough
Coach
Kevin Lowe
Assistant coach
Craig MacTavish
Chief scout
Barry Fraser
Dir. of hockey personnel/hockey ops.
Kevin Prendergast
Director of hockey administration
Peter Stephan
Video coordinator
Brian Ross
Scouting staff
Ed Chadwick, Brad Davis, Lorne Davis, Harry Howell, Gilles Leger, Chris McCarthy, Kent Nilsson, Dave Semenko, Tom Thompson
Athletic trainer/therapist
Ken Lowe
Equipment manager
Barrie Stafford
Assistant equipment manager
Lyle Kulchisky
Massage therapist
Stewart Poirier
Team physicians
Dr. David C. Reid
Dr. Boris Boyko
Vice president, public relations
Bill Tuele
Information coordinator
Steve Knowles
Public relations manager
Bryn Griffiths
Public & community relations coord.
Fiona Liew
Executive v.p., business operations
Doug Piper
Executive v.p., finance
Doug Thomson
V.p., corporate communications
Trish Kerr
V.p., sponsorships, sales & services
Allan Watt
Director of ticketing
John Yeomans
Director of properties
Darrell Holowaychuk
Director of broadcast
Don Metz

DRAFT CHOICES

Rd.— Player	Ht./Wt.	Overall	Pos.	Last team
1— Jani Rita	6-1/206	13	RW	Jokerit Helsinki, Fin.
2— Alexei Semenov	6-6/210	36	D	Sudbury (OHL)
2— Tony Salmelainen	5-9/176	41	LW	IFK Helsinki, Finland
3— Adam Hauser	6-2/192	81	G	Minnesota (WCHA)
3— Mike Comrie	5-9/172	91	C	Michigan (CCHA)
5— Jonathan Fauteux	6-2/232	139	D	Val d'Or (QMJHL)
6— Chris Legg	5-11/177	171	C	London Jr. B (OHA)
7— Christian Chartier	6-0/219	199	D	Saskatoon (WHL)
9— Tomas Groschl	6-2/183	256	W	Hungary

MISCELLANEOUS DATA

Home ice (capacity)
Skyreach Centre (17,100)
Address
11230 110 Street
Edmonton, Alta. T5G 3H7
Business phone
780-414-4000
Club colors
White, midnight blue, metallic copper and red
Radio affiliation
CHED (630 AM)
TV affiliation
The A Channel, CBXT TV & CTV SportsNet

EDMONTON OILERS

TRAINING CAMP ROSTER

No.	FORWARDS	Ht./Wt.	BORN Place	BORN Date	NHL exp.	1998-99 clubs
20	Josef Beranek (C)	6-2/195	Litvinov, Czechoslovakia	10-25-69	7	Edmonton
	Dan Cleary (LW)	6-0/200	Carbonear, Nfld.	12-18-78	2	Chicago, Portland (AHL), Hamilton (AHL)
	Mike Comrie (C)	5-9/172	Edmonton	9-11-80	0	Univ. of Michigan (CCHA)
	Paul Comrie (C)	5-11/188	Edmonton	2-7-77	0	Univ. of Denver (WCHA), Hamilton (AHL)
19	Boyd Devereaux (C)	6-2/195	Seaforth, Ont.	4-16-78	2	Edmonton, Hamilton (AHL)
34	Jim Dowd (C)	6-1/190	Brick, N.J.	12-25-68	8	Hamilton (AHL), Edmonton
10	Pat Falloon (RW)	5-11/200	Foxwarren, Man.	9-22-72	8	Edmonton
25	Mike Grier (RW)	6-1/227	Detroit	1-5-75	3	Edmonton
9	Bill Guerin (RW)	6-2/210	Wilbraham, Mass.	11-9-70	8	Edmonton
	Michael Henrich (RW)	6-2/206	Thornhill, Ont.	3-3-80	0	Barrie (OHL)
	Mike Houde (C)	5-11/186	Montreal	12-9-76	3	Fredericton (AHL), Montreal
15	Chad Kilger (C)	6-4/215	Cornwall, Ont.	11-27-76	4	Chicago, Edmonton
	Dan LaCouture (LW)	6-2/201	Hyannis, Mass.	4-13-77	1	Hamilton (AHL), Edmonton
27	Georges Laraque (RW)	6-3/240	Montreal	12-7-76	2	Hamilton (AHL), Edmonton
	Chris Legg (C)	5-11/177		2-19-80	0	London Jr. B (OHA)
	Fredrik Lindquist (C/RW)	6-0/190	Sodertalje, Sweden	6-21-73	1	Edmonton, Hamilton (AHL)
26	Todd Marchant (LW)	5-10/178	Buffalo, N.Y.	8-12-73	6	Edmonton
18	Ethan Moreau (LW)	6-2/205	Orillia, Ont.	9-22-75	4	Chicago, Edmonton
17	Rem Murray (LW)	6-2/195	Stratford, Ont.	10-9-72	3	Edmonton
	Michel Riesen (LW)	6-2/183	Oberbalm, Switzerland	4-11-79	0	Hamilton (AHL)
	Jani Rita (LW/RW)	6-1/206	Helsinki, Finland	7-25-81	0	Jokerit Helsinki (Finland)
	Tony Salmelainen (LW)	5-9/176	Espoo, Finland	8-8-81	0	HIFK Helsinki (Finland Jr.)
	Peter Sarno (C)	5-11/185	Toronto	7-26-79	0	Sarnia (OHL)
28	Alexander Selivanov	6-0/206	Moscow, U.S.S.R.	3-23-71	5	Cleveland (IHL), Tampa Bay, Edmonton
94	Ryan Smyth (LW)	6-1/195	Banff, Alta.	2-21-76	5	Edmonton
39	Doug Weight (C)	5-11/200	Warren, Mich.	1-21-71	9	Edmonton
	DEFENSEMEN					
23	Sean Brown	6-3/205	Oshawa, Ont.	11-5-76	3	Edmonton
	Mathieu Descoteaux	6-3/200	Pierreville, Que.	9-23-77	0	Hamilton (AHL)
	Jonathan Fauteaux	6-2/232	Terrebonne, Que.	12-3-80	0	Val-d'Or (QMJHL)
	Chris Hajt	6-3/210	Amherst, N.Y.	7-5-78	0	Hamilton (AHL)
22	Roman Hamrlik	6-2/215	Gottwaldov, Czechoslovakia	4-12-74	7	Edmonton
	Alex Henry	6-5/216	Elliot Lake, Ont.	10-18-79	0	London (OHL)
24	Christian LaFlamme	6-1/202	St. Charles, Que.	11-24-76	3	Chicago, Portland (AHL), Edmonton
8	Frank Musil	6-3/215	Pardubice, Czechoslovakia	12-17-64	13	Edmonton
44	Janne Niinimaa	6-2/220	Raahe, Finland	5-22-75	3	Edmonton
5	Tom Poti	6-3/215	Worcester, Mass.	3-22-77	1	Edmonton
46	Todd Reirden	6-5/220	Deerfield, Ill.	6-25-71	1	Hamilton (AHL), Edmonton
	Alexei Semenov	6-6/210	Murmansk, U.S.S.R.	4-10-81	0	Sudbury (OHL)
21	Jason Smith	6-3/208	Calgary	11-2-73	6	Toronto, Edmonton
	GOALTENDERS					
	Alex Fomitchev	5-10/180	Moscow, U.S.S.R.	2-19-79	0	Calgary (WHL)
	Adam Hauser	6-2/192	Bovey, Minn.	5-27-80	0	Univ. of Minnesota (WCHA)
	Bill Ranford	5-11/185	Brandon, Man.	12-14-66	14	Tampa Bay, Detroit
35	Tommy Salo	5-11/173	Surahammar, Sweden	2-1-71	5	New York Islanders, Edmonton

1998-99 REVIEW

INDIVIDUAL STATISTICS

SCORING

	Games	G	A	Pts.	PIM	+/-	PPG	SHG	Shots	Shooting Pct.
Bill Guerin	80	30	34	64	133	7	13	0	261	11.5
Josef Beranek	66	19	30	49	23	6	7	0	160	11.9
Mike Grier	82	20	24	44	54	5	3	2	143	14.0
Pat Falloon	82	17	23	40	20	-4	8	0	152	11.2
Boris Mironov*	63	11	29	40	104	6	5	0	138	8.0
Rem Murray	78	21	18	39	20	4	4	1	116	18.1
Doug Weight	43	6	31	37	12	-8	1	0	79	7.6
Todd Marchant	82	14	22	36	65	3	3	1	183	7.7
Roman Hamrlik	75	8	24	32	70	9	3	0	172	4.7
Ryan Smyth	71	13	18	31	62	0	6	0	161	8.1
Janne Niinimaa	81	4	24	28	88	7	2	0	142	2.8
Andrei Kovalenko*	43	13	14	27	30	-4	2	0	75	17.3
Dean McAmmond*	65	9	16	25	36	5	1	0	122	7.4
Tom Poti	73	5	16	21	42	10	2	0	94	5.3
Mats Lindgren*	48	5	12	17	22	4	0	1	53	9.4
Alexander Selivanov*	29	8	6	14	24	0	1	0	57	14.0
Boyd Devereaux	61	6	8	14	23	2	0	1	39	15.4
Kelly Buchberger	52	4	4	8	68	-6	0	2	29	13.8

	Games	G	A	Pts.	PIM	+/-	PPG	SHG	Shots	Shooting Pct.
Sean Brown	51	0	7	7	188	1	0	0	27	0.0
Kevin Brown	12	4	2	6	0	-2	2	0	13	30.8
Ethan Moreau*	14	1	5	6	8	2	0	0	16	6.3
Georges Laraque	39	3	2	5	57	-1	0	0	17	17.6
Todd Reirden	17	2	3	5	20	-1	0	0	26	7.7
Marty McSorley	46	2	3	5	101	-5	0	0	29	6.9
Frank Musil	39	0	3	3	34	0	0	0	9	0.0
Vladimir Vorobiev	2	2	0	2	2	1	0	0	5	40.0
Jason Smith*	12	1	1	2	11	0	0	0	15	6.7
Chad Kilger*	13	1	1	2	4	-3	0	0	13	7.7
Craig Millar	24	0	2	2	19	-6	0	0	18	0.0
Chris Ferraro	2	1	0	1	0	1	0	0	1	100.0
Steve Passmore (goalie)	6	0	1	1	2	0	0	0	0	0.0
Christian Laflamme*	11	0	1	1	0	-3	0	0	15	0.0
Bob Essensa (goalie)	39	0	1	1	0	0	0	0	0	0.0
Jim Dowd	1	0	0	0	0	0	0	0	1	0.0
Joe Hulbig	1	0	0	0	2	1	0	0	2	0.0
Bill Huard	3	0	0	0	0	0	0	0	2	0.0
Dan Lacouture	3	0	0	0	0	1	0	0	0	0.0
Daniel Lacroix	4	0	0	0	13	0	0	0	5	0.0
Fredrik Lindquist	8	0	0	0	2	-2	0	0	6	0.0
Tommy Salo* (goalie)	13	0	0	0	0	0	0	0	0	0.0
Mikhail Shtalenkov* (goalie)	34	0	0	0	2	0	0	0	0	0.0

GOALTENDING

	Games	Min.	Goals	SO	Avg.	W	L	T	Shots	Sv. Pct.
Tommy Salo*	13	700	27	0	2.31	8	2	2	279	.903
Mikhail Shtalenkov*	34	1819	81	3	2.67	12	17	3	782	.896
Bob Essensa	39	2091	96	0	2.75	12	14	6	974	.901
Steve Passmore	6	362	17	0	2.82	1	4	1	183	.907

Empty-net goals (do not count against a goaltender's average): Essensa 2, Shtalenkov 2, Passmore 1.

*Played with two or more NHL teams.

RESULTS

OCTOBER

10—Los Angeles .... L 1-2
13—Toronto .... L 2-3
14—At Vancouver .... W 4-1
17—At New Jersey .... W 4-2
20—At N.Y. Rangers .... L 2-3
21—At N.Y. Islanders .... W 4-2
24—At Colorado .... L 4-6
28—Washington .... W 8-2
31—Pittsburgh .... W 4-1

NOVEMBER

2—Vancouver .... W 5-3
4—Nashville .... W 3-2
6—Colorado .... L 2-5
8—At Chicago .... W *3-2
11—At Toronto .... L 2-3
12—At Ottawa .... T *1-1
14—At Montreal .... W 4-1
18—Detroit .... L 2-6
20—At Anaheim .... W *3-2
21—At Phoenix .... L *2-3
25—Colorado .... W 3-0
27—At Calgary .... W 3-2
29—Chicago .... L 2-3

DECEMBER

2—Phoenix .... W 4-3
4—Tampa Bay .... L 1-2
6—Dallas .... L 2-6
8—At Nashville .... T *3-3
9—At Chicago .... L 1-3
11—At Detroit .... L 2-3
13—At Philadelphia .... T *2-2
15—At Carolina .... L 0-3
18—At Tampa Bay .... W 4-1
19—At Florida .... L 1-3
23—San Jose .... L 3-5
27—Vancouver .... W 3-0
29—Montreal .... L 2-5

JANUARY

3—Philadelphia .... T *3-3
5—Los Angeles .... L *3-4
7—At Phoenix .... W 7-1
9—At Los Angeles .... T *1-1
10—At Anaheim .... L 4-6
12—Dallas .... T *2-2
14—At Vancouver .... W 3-1
17—Detroit .... W 4-1
21—At San Jose .... T *3-3
27—Chicago .... L *3-4
30—Anaheim .... W 1-0

FEBRUARY

1—St. Louis .... L *3-4
3—Ottawa .... T *2-2
5—Nashville .... W 4-2
8—At Calgary .... L 1-2
9—Boston .... L 0-2
11—At Detroit .... L 2-4
13—At St. Louis .... W 3-2
15—At Dallas .... L 1-4
17—At Anaheim .... W 6-2
18—At Los Angeles .... L 2-3
21—N.Y. Rangers .... L *1-2
24—Anaheim .... L 1-2
26—Buffalo .... W 6-3
27—Carolina .... T *2-2

MARCH

1—At Colorado .... W 4-3
3—At Buffalo .... W 5-3
5—At Pittsburgh .... T *2-2
6—At Washington .... L 3-4
10—At Dallas .... L 4-7
13—At St. Louis .... L 4-6
14—At Nashville .... L 1-3
17—New Jersey .... L 1-4
20—Vancouver .... W 4-3
22—Calgary .... T *2-2
24—Montreal .... L 0-2
26—St. Louis .... W 2-1
28—San Jose .... W 5-2
30—Phoenix .... L 4-7

APRIL

1—Toronto .... L 1-5
3—At Colorado .... L 2-5
7—Calgary .... W 4-2
9—At Calgary .... W 4-1
10—At Vancouver .... T *1-1
12—At San Jose .... W *5-4
16—Colorado .... W 5-1
17—Calgary .... W 3-2

*Denotes overtime game.

FLORIDA PANTHERS
EASTERN CONFERENCE/SOUTHEAST DIVISION

Panthers Schedule

Home games shaded; D—Day game; *—All-Star Game at Toronto.

October

SUN	MON	TUE	WED	THU	FRI	SAT
					1	2 WAS
3	4	5	6 LA	7	8	9 DET
10	11	12 MON	13 TOR	14	15	16 ANA
17	18	19	20 VAN	21	22 CAL	23
24 PHI	25	26	27 NYI	28	29 BUF	30 OTT
31						

November

SUN	MON	TUE	WED	THU	FRI	SAT
	1	2	3 EDM	4	5 VAN	6 CAL
7	8	9	10 ATL	11	12	13 BUF
14	15	16	17 COL	18 STL	19	20 PIT
21	22	23	24 PHI	25	26 NYR	27 ATL
28	29	30				

December

SUN	MON	TUE	WED	THU	FRI	SAT
			1	2	3 ATL	4 WAS
5	6	7	8 PHO	9	10 DAL	11 NSH
12	13	14	15 NSH	16	17 BUF	18 PIT
19	20 TOR	21	22 ATL	23	24	25
26 CAR	27 TB	28	29	30 CHI	31	

January

SUN	MON	TUE	WED	THU	FRI	SAT
						1 D TB
2	3	4	5 ANA	6 LA	7	8 SJ
9	10	11	12 NYI	13	14 CAR	15 TB
16	17 D PHI	18	19 WAS	20	21 ATL	22 BOS
23	24	25	26 NJ	27 PHI	28	29 EDM
30	31					

February

SUN	MON	TUE	WED	THU	FRI	SAT
		1 CAR	2 MON	3	4	5
6 *	7	8	9 SJ	10	11 OTT	12 BOS
13	14 MON	15	16 NYR	17	18	19 PIT
20	21 D OTT	22	23 WAS	24 CAR	25	26 CAR
27	28 BUF	29				

March

SUN	MON	TUE	WED	THU	FRI	SAT
			1 TOR	2	3 NYR	4 STL
5	6	7 WAS	8	9	10 TB	11 CHI
12	13	14	15	16 PIT	17	18 NYI
19 NJ	20	21 NYR	22	23 BOS	24	25 MON
26	27	28	29 DAL	30	31 OTT	

April

SUN	MON	TUE	WED	THU	FRI	SAT
						1 TB
2	3 NJ	4	5 BOS	6	7	8 D NJ
9 D NYI	10	11	12	13	14	15

1999-2000 SEASON

CLUB DIRECTORY

Chairman & chief executive officer
H. Wayne Huizenga

President & governor
William A. Torrey

V.p. and general manager
Bryan Murray

Assistant general manager
Chuck Fletcher

Head coach
Terry Murray

Assistant coaches
Slavomir Lener
Bill Smith

Pro scouts
Michael Abbamont
Duane Sutter

Director of amateur scouting
Tim Murray

Director of player development
Paul Henry

Amateur scouts
Ron Harris, Matti Vaisanen, Wayne Meier, Billy Dea

Head medical trainer
David Smith

Strength & conditioning coach
Ian Pyka

Equipment manager
Mark Brennan

Vice president of marketing
Declan J. Bolger

V.p., corporate sales and sponsorship
Kimberly Terranova

Vice president of operations
Steve Dangerfield

Director of communications
Mike Hanson

Communications/media relations coord.
Chris Kelleher

Director of finance/controller
Evelyn Lopez

DRAFT CHOICES

Rd.— Player	Ht./Wt.	Overall	Pos.	Last team
1— Denis Shvidki	6-0/195	12	RW	Barrie (OHL)
2— Alexander Auld	6-4/196	40	G	North Bay (OHL)
3— Niklas Hagman	5-11/183	70	LW	IFK Helsinki, Finland
3— Jean-Francois Laniel	6-2/170	80	G	Shawinigan (QMJHL)
4— Morgan McCormick	6-4/199	103	RW	Kingston (OHL)
4— Rod Sarich	6-3/178	109	D	Calgary (WHL)
6— Brad Woods	6-3/165	169	D	Brampton (OHL)
7— Travis Eagles	6-4/195	198	RW	Prince George (WHL)
8— Jonathan Charron	6-2/180	227	G	Val d'Or (QMJHL)

MISCELLANEOUS DATA

Home ice (capacity)
National Car Rental Center (19,250)

Address
One Panther Parkway
Sunrise, FL 33323

Business phone
954-835-7000

Club colors
Red, navy blue, yellow and gold

Radio affiliation
WQAM (560 AM)

TV affiliation
SportsChannel

TRAINING CAMP ROSTER

No.	FORWARDS	Ht./Wt.	BORN Place	BORN Date	NHL exp.	1998-99 clubs
10	Pavel Bure (RW)	5-10/189	Moscow, U.S.S.R.	3-31-71	8	Florida
	Jiri Dopita (C)	6-3/209	Sumperk, Czechoslovakia	12-2-68	0	Vsetin (Czech Republic)
19	Radek Dvorak (RW)	6-1/194	Tabor, Czechoslovakia	3-9-77	4	Florida
	Niklas Hagman (LW)	5-11/183	Espoo, Finland	12-5-79	0	HIFK Helsinki (Finland), HIFK Helsinki (Finland Jr.), Blues Espoo (Finland)
12	Dwayne Hay (LW)	6-0/219	London, Ont.	2-11-77	2	Florida, New Haven (AHL)
18	Alex Hicks (LW)	6-0/190	Calgary	9-4-69	4	San Jose, Florida
15	John Jakopin (LW)	6-5/239	Toronto	5-16-75	2	New Haven (AHL), Florida
17	Ryan Johnson (C)	6-1/180	Thunder Bay, Ont.	6-14-76	2	New Haven (AHL), Florida
25	Viktor Kozlov (C)	6-5/232	Togliatti, U.S.S.R.	2-14-75	5	Florida
16	Oleg Kvasha (LW)	6-5/216	Moscow, U.S.S.R.	7-26-78	1	Florida
11	Bill Lindsay (LW)	6-0/195	Big Fork, Mont.	5-17-71	8	Florida
	Morgan McCormick (RW)	6-4/199	Guelph, Ont.	2-21-81	0	Kingston (OHL)
27	Scott Mellanby (RW)	6-1/205	Montreal	6-11-66	14	Florida
44	Rob Niedermayer (C)	6-2/204	Cassiar, B.C.	12-28-74	6	Florida
12	Marcus Nilson (C)	6-2/193	Balsta, Sweden	3-1-78	1	New Haven (AHL), Florida
	Ivan Novoseltsev (RW)	6-1/200	Golitsino, U.S.S.R.	1-23-79	0	Sarnia (OHL)
21	Mark Parrish (RW)	5-11/191	Edina, Minn.	2-2-77	1	Florida, New Haven (AHL)
	Denis Shvidky (RW)	6-0/195	Kharkov, U.S.S.R.	11-21-80	0	Barrie (OHL)
23	Chris Wells (C/LW)	6-6/223	Calgary	11-12-75	4	Florida, New Haven (AHL)
14	Ray Whitney (LW)	5-10/175	Fort Saskatchewan, Alta.	5-8-72	8	Florida
28	Peter Worrell (RW)	6-6/235	Pierrefonds, Que.	8-18-77	2	Florida, New Haven (AHL)
	DEFENSEMEN					
12	Chris Allen	6-2/197	Chatham, Ont.	5-8-78	2	New Haven (AHL), Florida
26	Dan Boyle	5-11/190	Ottawa	7-12-76	1	Kentucky (AHL), Florida
	Brad Ference	6-3/196	Calgary	4-2-79	0	Spokane (WHL), Tri-City (WHL)
4	Bret Hedican	6-2/205	St. Paul, Minn.	8-10-70	8	Vancouver, Florida
33	Filip Kuba	6-3/202	Ostrava, Czechoslovakia	12-29-76	1	Kentucky (AHL), Florida
3	Paul Laus	6-1/212	Beamsville, Ont.	9-26-70	6	Florida
2	Lance Pitlick	5-11/211	Fridley, Minn.	11-5-67	5	Ottawa
6	Peter Ratchuk	6-1/185	Buffalo	9-10-77	1	New Haven (AHL), Florida
	Rod Sarich	6-3/178	Saskatoon, Sask.	3-23-81	0	Calgary (WHL)
8	Jaroslav Spacek	5-11/198	Rokycany, Czechoslovakia	2-11-74	1	Florida, New Haven (AHL)
24	Robert Svehla	6-1/210	Martin, Czechoslovakia	1-2-69	5	Florida
15	Jeff Ware	6-4/215	Toronto	5-19-77	3	St. John's (AHL), New Haven (AHL), Florida
7	Mike Wilson	6-6/212	Brampton, Ont.	2-26-75	4	Las Vegas (IHL), Buffalo, Florida
	Brad Woods	6-3/165	Cambridge, Ont.	3-4-81	0	Brampton (OHL)
	GOALTENDERS					
	Alexander Auld	6-4/196	Cold Lake, Alta.	1-7-81	0	North Bay (OHL)
	Ryan Bach	6-1/195	Sherwood Park, Alta.	10-21-73	1	Utah (IHL), Los Angeles, Long Beach (IHL)
31	Sean Burke	6-4/210	Windsor, Ont.	1-29-67	11	Florida
37	Trevor Kidd	6-2/190	Dugald, Man.	3-29-72	7	Carolina
	Jean-Francois Laniel	6-2/170	Montreal	6-16-81	0	Shawinigan (QMJHL)

1998-99 REVIEW

INDIVIDUAL STATISTICS

SCORING

	Games	G	A	Pts.	PIM	+/-	PPG	SHG	Shots	Shooting Pct.
Ray Whitney	81	26	38	64	18	-3	7	0	193	13.5
Rob Niedermayer	82	18	33	51	50	-13	6	1	142	12.7
Viktor Kozlov	65	16	35	51	24	13	5	1	209	7.7
Scott Mellanby	67	18	27	45	85	5	4	0	136	13.2
Radek Dvorak	82	19	24	43	29	7	0	4	182	10.4
Mark Parrish	73	24	13	37	25	-6	5	0	129	18.6
Robert Svehla	80	8	29	37	83	-13	4	0	157	5.1
Bill Lindsay	75	12	15	27	92	-1	0	1	135	8.9
Oleg Kvasha	68	12	13	25	45	5	4	0	138	8.7
Johan Garpenlov	64	8	9	17	42	-9	0	1	71	11.3
Pavel Bure	11	13	3	16	4	3	5	1	44	29.5
Ed Jovanovski*	41	3	13	16	82	-4	1	0	68	4.4
Kirk Muller	82	4	11	15	49	-11	0	0	107	3.7
Jaroslav Spacek	63	3	12	15	28	15	2	1	92	3.3
Dave Gagner*	36	4	10	14	39	-7	2	0	50	8.0
Terry Carkner	62	2	9	11	54	0	0	0	25	8.0
Bret Hedican*	25	3	7	10	17	-2	0	0	38	7.9

	Games	G	A	Pts.	PIM	+/-	PPG	SHG	Shots	Shooting Pct.
Paul Laus	75	1	9	10	218	-1	0	0	54	1.9
Peter Worrell	62	4	5	9	258	0	0	0	50	8.0
Dan Boyle	22	3	5	8	6	0	1	0	31	9.7
Dino Ciccarelli	14	6	1	7	27	-1	5	0	23	26.1
Rhett Warrener*	48	0	7	7	64	-1	0	0	33	0.0
Gord Murphy	51	0	7	7	16	4	0	0	56	0.0
Alex Hicks*	51	0	6	6	58	-4	0	0	47	0.0
Sean Burke (goalie)	59	0	4	4	27	0	0	0	0	0.0
Marcus Nilson	8	1	1	2	5	2	0	0	7	14.3
Peter Ratchuk	24	1	1	2	10	-1	0	0	34	2.9
Chris Wells	20	0	2	2	31	-4	0	0	28	0.0
Ryan Johnson	1	1	0	1	0	0	0	0	1	100.0
David Nemirovsky	2	0	1	1	0	1	0	0	2	0.0
Filip Kuba	5	0	1	1	0	2	0	0	5	0.0
Jeff Ware	6	0	1	1	6	-6	0	0	1	0.0
Chris Allen	1	0	0	0	0	1	0	0	0	0.0
Viacheslav Butsayev*	1	0	0	0	2	-1	0	0	0	0.0
John Jakopin	3	0	0	0	0	-1	0	0	0	0.0
Jeff Norton*	3	0	0	0	2	0	0	0	2	0.0
Steve Washburn*	4	0	0	0	4	-1	0	0	0	0.0
Mike Wilson*	4	0	0	0	0	2	0	0	8	0.0
Herbert Vasiljevs	5	0	0	0	2	-1	0	0	6	0.0
Dwayne Hay	9	0	0	0	0	-1	0	0	3	0.0
Kirk McLean (goalie)	30	0	0	0	2	0	0	0	0	0.0

GOALTENDING

	Games	Min.	Goals	SO	Avg.	W	L	T	Shots	Sv. Pct.
Sean Burke	59	3402	151	3	2.66	21	24	14	1624	.907
Kirk McLean	30	1597	73	2	2.74	9	10	4	727	.900

Empty-net goals (do not count against a goaltender's average): Burke 3, McLean 1.
*Played with two or more NHL teams.

RESULTS

OCTOBER

9— Tampa Bay ....W......4-1
10—At Nashville ....W......1-0
16—At Buffalo....................T....*2-2
21—Los Angeles....................T....*1-1
23—Vancouver ....L......0-5
24—At Washington....................T....*2-2
28—Detroit ....L......2-7
30—At Chicago....................W......7-3
31—At New Jersey ....L......1-3

NOVEMBER

2— At N.Y. Islanders....................L......2-6
4— Chicago ....W......2-1
7— New Jersey....................L......3-4
11—N.Y. Rangers ....W......4-1
12—At Philadelphia ....W......2-1
14—At Pittsburgh ....L......0-4
19—At Boston....................T....*5-5
21—At New Jersey ....T....*3-3
22—Philadelphia....................L....*1-2
25—Boston ....L......0-1
27—At Tampa Bay ....W......2-1
28—Buffalo....................W......6-2

DECEMBER

1— At N.Y. Rangers ....L....*4-5
2— At Buffalo....................L......1-2
5— Carolina ....T....*3-3
9— Ottawa....................W......6-5
12—Calgary ....L......2-4
16—Pittsburgh ....W......4-1
19—Edmonton....................W......3-1
23—Washington ....L......0-4
26—At Tampa Bay ....W......3-1
28—N.Y. Islanders ....W......5-1
30—At Pittsburgh ....L......4-7

JANUARY

1— Carolina ....T....*3-3
2— Pittsburgh....................L......2-4
5— At Phoenix....................T....*2-2
6— At Colorado ....T....*2-2
8— At Vancouver ....T....*1-1
10—At Calgary ....W......2-1
13—Toronto....................T....*3-3
14—At Carolina....................L......2-3
16—N.Y. Islanders ....W......1-0
18—Buffalo ....L......0-4
20—At N.Y. Islanders....................W......5-2
21—At N.Y. Rangers....................W......2-1
26—At Philadelphia....................T....*3-3
27—Montreal....................W......2-1
30—Dallas....................L......2-5

FEBRUARY

3— Toronto....................W......5-2
5— At Pittsburgh ....L......0-3
6— At Carolina....................T....*3-3
8— St. Louis ....L......4-5
11—At Ottawa ....W......3-1
13—At Montreal....................L......0-4
15—San Jose....................T....*2-2
17—At Dallas ....L......1-2
18—At St. Louis....................T....*0-0
20—Phoenix ....W......7-1
24—Philadelphia....................W......5-3
26—At Detroit ....T....*5-5
27—At Toronto ....L......1-4

MARCH

3— Colorado ....L......5-7
6— Carolina ....T....*2-2
8— At Montreal ....W......5-2
9— At Boston....................L......0-2
11—At Washington ....W......2-1
13—Tampa Bay ....W......1-0
17—At San Jose ....L......2-4
20—At Los Angeles ....L......3-4
21—At Anaheim....................W......5-2
24—N.Y. Rangers....................L......1-2
26—Nashville....................W......4-1
28—New Jersey ....T....*2-2
31—N.Y. Islanders ....L......3-5

APRIL

1— At Washington....................L......3-5
3— Ottawa ....L......4-6
5— Washington ....L......0-3
7— Boston ....L......2-5
9— At Buffalo....................L......1-3
10—At Toronto ....L......1-9
12—At Ottawa ....W......2-0
14—Montreal....................W....*3-2
17—Tampa Bay ....W......6-2

*Denotes overtime game.

LOS ANGELES KINGS
WESTERN CONFERENCE/PACIFIC DIVISION

Kings Schedule

Home games shaded; D—Day game; *—All-Star Game at Toronto.

October

SUN	MON	TUE	WED	THU	FRI	SAT
					1	2 NSH
3	4 STL	5	6 FLA	7 TB	8	9 WAS
10	11	12	13	14	15 CAL	16 EDM
17	18	19	20 BOS	21	22 PHO	23
24 SJ	25	26 WAS	27	28 PIT	29	30 CHI
31						

November

SUN	MON	TUE	WED	THU	FRI	SAT
	1	2 PIT	3 DET	4	5	6 PHI
7	8	9 EDM	10	11 COL	12	13
14 PHO	15	16 CHI	17	18 PHO	19	20 MON
21	22	23 COL	24 DAL	25	26	27 D SJ
28	29	30				

December

SUN	MON	TUE	WED	THU	FRI	SAT
			1	2	3 ANA	4 TB
5	6	7	8 ATL	9	10 DET	11 MON
12	13	14 NJ	15 NYR	16	17	18 CHI
19	20	21	22 SJ	23	24	25
26 PHO	27	28	29 COL	30 EDM	31	

January

SUN	MON	TUE	WED	THU	FRI	SAT
						1
2	3 DAL	4 STL	5	6 FLA	7	8
9	10	11 OTT	12	13 STL	14	15 SJ
16	17	18 BUF	19	20 DAL	21	22
23 D COL	24	25	26 DAL	27 NSH	28	29 TOR
30	31 NYI					

February

SUN	MON	TUE	WED	THU	FRI	SAT
		1	2	3 DET	4	5
6 *	7	8 ANA	9 PHO	10	11 DAL	12
13	14 CAL	15	16 CHI	17	18 DET	19 BUF
20	21 EDM	22	23 CAL	24	25 VAN	26 SJ
27	28	29 VAN				

March

SUN	MON	TUE	WED	THU	FRI	SAT
			1	2 CAR	3	4 NSH
5	6	7 DET	8	9 NYR	10	11 CAL
12	13 VAN	14	15 ANA	16	17 STL	18
19 NSH	20	21 ANA	22	23 PHI	24	25 D BOS
26 ATL	27	28	29 SJ	30	31	

April

SUN	MON	TUE	WED	THU	FRI	SAT
						1 D ANA
2	3 PHO	4	5 VAN	6	7 DAL	8
9 D ANA	10	11	12	13	14	15

1999-2000 SEASON
CLUB DIRECTORY

Owners
Philip F. Anschutz
Edward P. Roski, Jr.
Governor
Robert Sanderman
President
Tim Leiweke
Sr. vice president, general manager
Dave Taylor
Coach
Andy Murray
Assistant coaches
Ray Bennett
Mark Hardy
Dave Tippett
Assistant general manager
Kevin Gilmore
Assistant to general manager
John Wolf
Director of amateur scouting
Al Murray
Director of pro scouting
Ace Bailey
Scouting staff
Serge Aubry
Greg Drechsel
Rob Laird
Vaclav Nedomansky
John Stanton
Ari Vuori
Vice president of marketing
John Rizzardini
Dir., media relations and team services
Mike Altieri
Mgr., media relations and team services
Jeff Moeller
Media relations assistant
Jason Pommier
Trainers
Pete Demers
Peter Millar
Rick Garcia
Robert Zole
Assistant trainer
Rick Burrill

DRAFT CHOICES

Rd.— Player	Ht./Wt.	Overall	Pos.	Last team
2— Andrei Shefer	6-1/194	43	LW	Cherepovec, Russia
3— Jason Crain	6-3/190	74	D	Ohio State (CCHA)
3— Frantisek Kaberle	6-0/185	76	D	Modo Ornsk., Sweden
3— Cory Campbell	6-0/192	92	G	Belleville (OHL)
4— Brian McGrattan	6-3/210	104	RW	Sudbury (OHL)
4— Daniel Johansson	5-11/176	125	C	Modo Ornsk., Sweden
5— Jean-Francois Nogues	6-2/154	133	G	Victoriaville (QMJHL)
7— Kevin Baker	6-0/192	193	RW	Belleville (OHL)
8— George Parros	6-4/210	222	RW	Chicago (NAHL)
9— Noah Clarke	5-9/175	250	LW	Des Moines (USHL)

MISCELLANEOUS DATA

Home ice (capacity)
Staples Center (18,500)
Address
555 N. Nash Street
El Segundo, CA 90245
Business phone
310-419-3160
Club colors
Purple, silver, black and white
Radio affiliation
KRLA (1110 AM)
TV affiliation
FOX Sports West

TRAINING CAMP ROSTER

No.	FORWARDS	Ht./Wt.	BORN Place	BORN Date	NHL exp.	1998-99 clubs
10	Donald Audette (RW)	5-8/184	Laval, Que.	9-23-69	10	Los Angeles
	Scott Barney (C)	6-4/198	Oshawa, Ont.	3-27-79	0	Peterborough (OHL), Springfield (AHL)
	Eric Belanger (LW)	6-0/177	Sherbrooke, Que.	12-16-77	0	Springfield (AHL), Long Beach (IHL)
11	Jason Blake (C)	5-10/180	Moorhead, Minn.	9-2-73	1	Univ. of North Dakota (WCHA), Orlando (IHL), Los Angeles
42	Dan Bylsma (RW)	6-2/205	Grand Haven, Mich.	9-19-70	4	L. Beach (IHL), L.A., Springfield (AHL)
	Bill Huard (LW)	6-1/215	Welland, Ont.	6-24-67	7	Edmonton, Houston (IHL)
	Daniel Johansson (C)	5-11/176	Ornskoldsvik, Sweden	7-5-81	0	MoDo Ornskoldsvik Jrs. (Sweden Jr.)
23	Craig Johnson (LW)	6-2/197	St. Paul, Minn.	3-8-72	5	Los Angeles, Houston (IHL)
24	Nathan LaFayette (RW)	6-1/200	New Westminster, B.C.	2-17-73	6	Los Angeles, Long Beach (IHL)
22	Ian Laperriere (C)	6-1/197	Montreal	1-19-74	6	Los Angeles
	Donald MacLean (C)	6-2/199	Sydney, Nova Scotia	1-14-77	1	Springfield (AHL), Grand Rapids (IHL)
	Brian McGrattan (RW)	6-3/210	Hamilton, Ont.	9-2-81	0	Guelph (OHL), Sudbury (OHL)
7	Steve McKenna (LW)	6-8/247	Toronto	8-21-73	3	Los Angeles
52	Jason Morgan (C)	6-1/200	Kitchener, Ont.	10-9-76	2	Long Beach (IHL), Springfield (AHL)
27	Glen Murray (RW)	6-3/222	Halifax, Nova Scotia	11-1-72	8	Los Angeles
16	Zigmund Palffy (RW)	5-10/183	Skalica, Czechoslovakia	5-5-72	6	HK 36 Skalica (Slovakia), N.Y. Islanders
	Justin Papineau (C)	5-10/160	Ottawa	1-15-80	0	Belleville (OHL)
	Greg Phillips (RW)	6-2/205	Winnipeg	3-27-78	0	Springfield (AHL)
28	Jason Podollan (RW/C)	6-1/181	Vernon, B.C.	2-18-76	2	St. John's (AHL), Toronto, Long Beach (IHL), Los Angeles
20	Luc Robitaille (LW)	6-1/205	Montreal	2-17-66	13	Los Angeles
55	Pavel Rosa (RW)	5-11/180	Most, Czechoslovakia	6-7-77	1	Long Beach (IHL), Los Angeles
	Andrei Shefer (LW)	6-1/180	Sverdlovsk, U.S.S.R.	7-26-81	0	Severstal Cherepovets (Russian)
20	Bryan Smolinski (C)	6-1/205	Toledo, Ohio	12-27-71	7	New York Islanders
15	Jozef Stumpel (C)	6-3/216	Nitra, Czechoslovakia	7-20-72	8	Los Angeles
9	Vladimir Tsyplakov (LW)	6-1/197	Moscow, U.S.S.R.	4-18-69	4	Los Angeles
	Marko Tuomainen (RW)	6-3/203	Kuopio, Finland	4-25-72	1	HIFK Helsinki (Finland)
	DEFENSEMEN					
5	Aki Berg	6-3/203	Turku, Finland	7-28-77	3	TPS Turku (Finland)
4	Rob Blake	6-4/220	Simcoe, Ont.	12-10-69	10	Los Angeles
	Sean Blanchard	5-11/198	Sudbury, Ont.	3-29-78	0	Springfield (AHL), Mississippi (ECHL)
43	Philippe Boucher	6-2/214	St. Apollnaire, Que.	3-24-73	7	Los Angeles
	Kip Brennan	6-4/196	Kingston, Ont.	8-27-80	0	Sudbury (OHL)
	Jason Crain	6-3/190	Pittsburgh	1-3-80	0	Ohio State (CCHA)
3	Garry Galley	6-0/207	Ottawa	4-16-63	15	Los Angeles
	Peter Hogan	6-3/183	Scarborough, Ont.	1-10-78	0	Springfield (AHL)
	Frantisek Kaberle	6-0/185	Kladno, Czechoslovakia	11-8-73	0	MoDo Ornskoldvik (Sweden)
	Jere Karalahti	6-2/185	Helsinki, Finland	3-25-75	0	HIFK Helsinki (Finland)
33	Jaroslav Modry	6-2/219	Ceske-Budejovice, Czech.	2-27-71	5	Long Beach (IHL), Los Angeles
54	Jan Nemecek	6-1/215	Pisek, Czechoslovakia	2-14-76	1	Long Beach (IHL), Los Angeles
14	Mattias Norstrom	6-2/201	Stockholm, Sweden	1-2-72	6	Los Angeles
6	Sean O'Donnell	6-3/230	Ottawa	9-13-71	5	Los Angeles
	Richard Seeley	6-2/199	Powell River, B.C.	4-30-79	0	Prince Albert (WHL)
	Tomas Zizka	6-1/198	Sternberk, Czechoslovakia	10-10-79	0	ZPS Zlin (Czech Republic)
	GOALTENDERS					
	Cory Campbell	6-0/192	Stratford, Ont.	7-27-81	0	Belleville (OHL)
1	Marcel Cousineau	5-9/180	Delson, Que.	4-30-73	3	Lowell (AHL), New York Islanders
35	Stephane Fiset	6-1/198	Montreal	6-17-70	10	Los Angeles
	Jean-Francois Nogues	6-2/154	Acton Vale, Que.	5-10-81	0	Victoriaville (QMJHL)
1	Jamie Storr	6-2/198	Brampton, Ont.	12-28-75	5	Los Angeles
	Alexei Volkov	6-1/185	Yekaterinburg, U.S.S.R.	3-15-80	0	Halifax (QMJHL)

1998-99 REVIEW

INDIVIDUAL STATISTICS

SCORING

	Games	G	A	Pts.	PIM	+/-	PPG	SHG	Shots	Shooting Pct.
Luc Robitaille	82	39	35	74	54	-1	11	0	292	13.4
Donald Audette	49	18	18	36	51	7	6	0	152	11.8
Rob Blake	62	12	23	35	128	-7	5	1	216	5.6
Jozef Stumpel	64	13	21	34	10	-18	1	0	131	9.9
Glen Murray	61	16	15	31	36	-14	3	3	173	9.2
Ray Ferraro	65	13	18	31	59	0	4	0	84	15.5
Yanic Perreault*	64	10	17	27	30	-3	2	2	113	8.8
Vladimir Tsyplakov	69	11	12	23	32	-7	0	2	111	9.9
Steve Duchesne*	60	4	19	23	22	-6	1	0	99	4.0
Olli Jokinen	66	9	12	21	44	-10	3	1	87	10.3
Craig Johnson	69	7	12	19	32	-12	2	0	94	7.4
Russ Courtnall	57	6	13	19	19	-9	0	1	77	7.8

	Games	G	A	Pts.	PIM	+/-	PPG	SHG	Shots	Shooting Pct.
Pavel Rosa	29	4	12	16	6	0	0	0	61	6.6
Garry Galley	60	4	12	16	30	-9	3	0	77	5.2
Doug Bodger	65	3	11	14	34	1	0	0	67	4.5
Sean O'Donnell	80	1	13	14	186	1	0	0	64	1.6
Ian Laperriere	72	3	10	13	138	-5	0	0	62	4.8
Philippe Boucher	45	2	6	8	32	-12	1	0	87	2.3
Mattias Norstrom	78	2	5	7	36	-10	0	1	61	3.3
Sandy Moger	42	3	2	5	26	-9	0	0	28	10.7
Nathan LaFayette	33	2	2	4	35	0	0	1	42	4.8
Josh Green	27	1	3	4	8	-5	1	0	35	2.9
Mark Visheau	28	1	3	4	107	-7	0	0	10	10.0
Matt Johnson	49	2	1	3	131	-5	0	0	14	14.3
Dave Babych*	8	0	2	2	2	-2	0	0	5	0.0
Jason Blake	1	1	0	1	0	1	0	0	5	20.0
Jan Nemecek	6	1	0	1	4	-1	0	0	8	12.5
Steve McKenna	20	1	0	1	36	-3	0	0	12	8.3
Jaroslav Modry	5	0	1	1	0	1	0	0	11	0.0
Sean Pronger*	13	0	1	1	4	2	0	0	8	0.0
Manny Legace (goalie)	17	0	1	1	0	0	0	0	0	0.0
Eric Lacroix*	27	0	1	1	12	-5	0	0	17	0.0
Jamie Storr (goalie)	28	0	1	1	6	0	0	0	0	0.0
Ryan Bach (goalie)	3	0	0	0	0	0	0	0	0	0.0
Brandon Convery*	3	0	0	0	4	-1	0	0	2	0.0
Roman Vopat*	3	0	0	0	6	0	0	0	2	0.0
Jason Podollan*	6	0	0	0	5	-3	0	0	7	0.0
Dan Bylsma	8	0	0	0	2	-1	0	0	3	0.0
Stephane Fiset (goalie)	42	0	0	0	2	0	0	0	0	0.0

GOALTENDING

	Games	Min.	Goals	SO	Avg.	W	L	T	Shots	Sv. Pct.
Jamie Storr	28	1525	61	4	2.40	12	12	2	724	.916
Manny Legace	17	899	39	0	2.60	2	9	2	439	.911
Stephane Fiset	42	2403	104	3	2.60	18	21	1	1217	.915
Ryan Bach	3	108	8	0	4.44	0	3	0	66	.879

Combination shutout: Fiset and Legace.
Empty-net goals (do not count against a goaltender's average): Legace 5, Storr 3, Fiset 2.
*Played with two or more NHL teams.

RESULTS

OCTOBER

10—At Edmonton .... W 2-1
12—At Vancouver .... L 2-4
16—Boston .... W *2-1
18—Colorado .... T *5-5
21—At Florida .... T *1-1
23—At Tampa Bay .... L 2-3
25—At Carolina .... W 3-2
27—At N.Y. Islanders .... L 0-1
28—At New Jersey .... W 4-0
30—Tampa Bay .... L 0-3

NOVEMBER

1—Phoenix .... L 0-3
5—St. Louis .... T *2-2
7—Dallas .... L 3-4
9—At Vancouver .... W 4-3
10—At Calgary .... L *4-5
12—Nashville .... L 1-3
14—Carolina .... L 3-5
16—At Anaheim .... L 1-3
18—At San Jose .... L 4-5
19—N.Y. Rangers .... L 1-5
21—Chicago .... W 5-0
28—Phoenix .... L 0-4
30—At Montreal .... L 1-3

DECEMBER

2—At Toronto .... L 1-3
3—At Ottawa .... L 1-3
5—Detroit .... L 3-4
9—Washington .... W 2-1
12—Vancouver .... W 3-0
13—At Anaheim .... L 0-3
17—N.Y. Islanders .... L *4-5
19—At St. Louis .... L 2-5
20—At Chicago .... W 4-1
22—At Pittsburgh .... W 3-0
26—Phoenix .... L 1-2
28—At Phoenix .... W 4-2
30—San Jose .... W 5-1

JANUARY

2—Colorado .... W 4-2
5—At Edmonton .... W *4-3
7—Buffalo .... W 4-2
9—Edmonton .... T *1-1
11—At San Jose .... L 0-4
14—Calgary .... W 3-0
16—Pittsburgh .... L 1-5
19—Colorado .... L 4-5
21—New Jersey .... L 2-3
27—At Dallas .... L 2-3
29—At Washington .... W 6-3
30—At Buffalo .... L 1-4

FEBRUARY

1—At Philadelphia .... L 2-4
4—Chicago .... W 3-2
6—San Jose .... W 2-0
10—At Phoenix .... L 0-3
11—Philadelphia .... W 4-3
13—Dallas .... L 2-3
15—Anaheim .... L 1-3
18—Edmonton .... W 3-2
20—At Calgary .... T *2-2
22—At St. Louis .... L 1-5
24—At Detroit .... W *3-2
26—At Chicago .... W 2-1
28—At Dallas .... L 0-1

MARCH

3—At Anaheim .... L 1-2
4—Nashville .... L 3-4
6—Calgary .... L 1-4
9—Detroit .... W 4-2
13—Vancouver .... W 3-1
15—Ottawa .... W 4-0
18—Anaheim .... L 2-4
20—Florida .... W 4-3
21—At Phoenix .... L 1-4
25—Dallas .... L 1-2
28—At Colorado .... L 2-7
30—At Boston .... W *2-1
31—At Detroit .... L 1-2

APRIL

3—At Nashville .... L 2-3
5—At Colorado .... L 1-4
8—San Jose .... W 3-2
11—At Dallas .... L 2-6
12—At Nashville .... W 4-3
15—Anaheim .... W *4-3
16—At San Jose .... W 2-0
18—St. Louis .... L 2-3

*Denotes overtime game.

MONTREAL CANADIENS

EASTERN CONFERENCE/NORTHEAST DIVISION

Canadiens Schedule

Home games shaded; D—Day game; *—All-Star Game at Toronto.

October

SUN	MON	TUE	WED	THU	FRI	SAT
					1	2 TOR
3	4	5	6 EDM	7	8 CAL	9 VAN
10	11	12 FLA	13	14 PHI	15	16 BUF
17	18 NYI	19	20 COL	21	22	23 TOR
24	25	26	27 CHI	28	29	30 NYR
31						

November

SUN	MON	TUE	WED	THU	FRI	SAT
	1	2	3 NJ	4 NYI	5	6 OTT
7	8	9	10 PIT	11 ANA	12	13 ATL
14	15	16 SJ	17	18 NSH	19	20 LA
21	22 ANA	23 SJ	24	25	26	27 VAN
28	29	30				

December

SUN	MON	TUE	WED	THU	FRI	SAT
			1 DAL	2	3 NYR	4 PHI
5	6	7 CAL	8	9 NYI	10	11 LA
12	13 WAS	14	15	16 NJ	17	18 TOR
19	20 PIT	21	22	23 BOS	24	25
26	27 OTT	28	29 OTT	30	31	

January

SUN	MON	TUE	WED	THU	FRI	SAT
						1
2 NYR	3	4 WAS	5	6 STL	7 COL	8
9	10	11 DET	12	13	14 BUF	15 BOS
16	17	18	19 NYI	20	21	22 PIT
23	24 CAR	25	26	27 BOS	28	29 D PHI
30 D CAR	31					

February

SUN	MON	TUE	WED	THU	FRI	SAT
		1	2 FLA	3 TB	4	5
6 *	7	8 EDM	9	10 WAS	11	12 OTT
13	14 FLA	15	16 ATL	17 CAR	18	19 TOR
20	21	22 PHO	23	24 NJ	25	26 WAS
27 NJ	28	29				

March

SUN	MON	TUE	WED	THU	FRI	SAT
			1 CHI	2	3	4 TOR
5	6 ATL	7	8 PIT	9	10 BUF	11 BOS
12	13	14 TB	15	16 PHI	17	18 CAR
19	20 BUF	21	22 ATL	23	24	25 FLA
26 TB	27	28	29 BOS	30	31	

April

SUN	MON	TUE	WED	THU	FRI	SAT
						1 BUF
2 DET	3	4	5 NYR	6 TB	7	8 OTT
9	10	11	12	13	14	15

1999-2000 SEASON

CLUB DIRECTORY

Vice president and general manager
Rejean Houle
V.p., com. and marketing services
Bernard Brisset
Vice president, building operations
Aldo Giampaolo
Vice president, finance and admin.
Fred Steer
Administrative assistant to the g.m.
Phil Sheuer
Consultant to the general manager
Jacques Lemaire
Coach
Alain Vigneault
Assistant coaches
Clement Jodoin
Dave King
Roland Melanson
Dir. of player development and scout
Claude Ruel
Pro scouts
Pierre Mondou
Mario Tremblay
Chief scout
Pierre Dorion
Scouts
Neil Armstrong, Bred Bandel, Elmer Benning, Mats Naslund, Gerry O'Flaherty, Doug Robinson, Antonio Routa, Richard Scammell
Director of team services
Michele Lapointe
Club physician
Dr. D.G. Kinnear
Athletic trainer
Gaetan Lefebvre
Assistant to the athletic trainer
Graham Rynbend
Strength and conditioning coach
Stephane Dube
Equipment manager
Pierre Gervais
Assistants to the equipment manager
Robert Boulanger
Pierre Ouellette

DRAFT CHOICES

Rd.— Player	Ht./Wt.	Overall	Pos.	Last team
2— Alexander Buturlin	5-11/183	39	LW	CSKA Moskow, Russia
2— Matt Carkner	6-4/222	58	D	Peterborough (OHL)
4— Chris Dyment	6-3/201	97	D	Boston U. (H. East)
4— Evan Lindsay	6-2/192	107	G	Prince Albert (WHL)
5— Dustin Jamieson	6-2/180	136	LW	Sarnia (OHL)
5— Marc-Andre Thinel	5-11/158	145	RW	Victoriaville (QMJHL)
5— Matt Shasby	6-3/188	150	D	Des Moines (USHL)
6— Sean Dixon	6-3/186	167	D	Erie (OHL)
7— Vadim Tarasov	5-11/158	196	G	Novokuznetsk, Russia
8— Mikko Hyytia	6-0/180	225	C	Jyvaskyla, Finland
9— Jerome Marois	6-1/181	253	LW	Quebec (QMJHL)

MISCELLANEOUS DATA

Home ice (capacity)
Molson Centre (21,273)
Address
1260 rue de La Gauchetiere Ouest
Montreal, Que. H3B 5E8
Business phone
514-932-2582
Club colors
Red, white and blue
Radio affiliation
CJAD (800 AM), CBF (690 AM)
TV affiliation
CFJP-TV (TQS Cable 5)

TRAINING CAMP ROSTER

No.	FORWARDS	Ht./Wt.	BORN Place	BORN Date	NHL exp.	1998-99 clubs
	Aaron Asham (C)	5-11/194	Portage-La-Prairie, Man.	4-13-78	1	Fredericton (AHL), Montreal
35	Andrei Bashkirov (LW)	6-0/198	Shelekhov, U.S.S.R.	6-22-70	1	Fred. (AHL), Montreal, F. Wayne (IHL)
	Marc Beaucage (C)	5-11/179	Trois-Rivieres, Que.	2-14-73	0	Fredericton (AHL)
17	Benoit Brunet (LW)	5-11/198	Montreal	8-24-68	10	Montreal
	Alexander Buturlin (LW)	5-11/183	Moscow, U.S.S.R.	9-3-81	0	CSKA Moscow (Russian)
27	Shayne Corson (LW)	6-1/199	Barrie, Ont.	8-13-66	14	Montreal
15	Jim Cummins (RW)	6-2/216	Dearborn, Mich.	5-17-70	8	Phoenix
	Jonathan Delisle (RW)	5-10/180	Montreal	6-30-77	1	Fredericton (AHL), Montreal
46	Matt Higgins (C)	6-2/188	Vernon, B.C.	10-29-77	2	Montreal, Fredericton (AHL)
	Dusty Jamieson (LW)	6-2/180	Sarnia, Ont.	5-26-81	0	Guelph (OHL), Sarnia (OHL)
	Scott King (C)	5-11/191	Saskatoon, Sask.	1-21-77	0	Fredericton (AHL)
11	Saku Koivu (C)	5-10/183	Turku, Finland	11-23-74	4	Montreal
32	Trevor Linden (C/RW)	6-4/210	Medicine Hat, Alta.	4-11-70	11	New York Islanders
6	Trent McCleary (C)	6-0/180	Swift Current, Sask.	9-8-72	3	Montreal
	Dave Morissette (LW)	6-1/224	Baie Comeau, Que.	12-24-71	1	Montreal
37	Patrick Poulin (C)	6-0/218	Vanier, Que.	4-23-73	8	Montreal
	Mike Ribeiro (C)	5-11/150	Montreal	2-10-80	0	Rouyn-Noranda (QMJHL)
26	Martin Rucinsky (LW)	6-1/205	Most, Czechoslovakia	3-11-71	8	Montreal
14	Terry Ryan (LW)	6-1/202	St. John's, Nfld.	1-14-77	3	Fredericton (AHL), Montreal
49	Brian Savage (RW)	6-2/192	Sudbury, Ont.	2-24-71	6	Montreal
23	Turner Stevenson (RW)	6-3/226	Port Alberni, B.C.	5-18-72	7	Montreal
	Marc-Andre Thinel (RW)	5-11/158	St. Jerome, Que.	3-24-81	0	Victoriaville (QMJHL)
24	Scott Thornton (C)	6-3/216	London, Ont.	1-9-71	9	Montreal
	Jason Ward (RW/C)	6-2/192	Chapleau, Ont.	1-16-79	0	Windsor (OHL), Plymouth (OHL)
34	Sergei Zholtok (C)	6-1/190	Riga, U.S.S.R.	12-2-72	5	Montreal, Fredericton (AHL)
28	Dainius Zubrus (RW)	6-3/220	Elektrenai, U.S.S.R.	6-16-78	3	Philadelphia, Montreal
	DEFENSEMEN					
	Francis Bouillon	5-8/186	New York	10-17-75	0	Fredericton (AHL)
43	Patrice Brisebois	6-2/204	Montreal	1-27-71	9	Montreal
	Matt Carkner	6-4/222	Winchester, Ont.	11-3-80	0	Peterborough (OHL)
	Sean Dixon	6-2/180	Kitchener, Ont.	2-22-81	0	Erie (OHL)
	Chris Dyment	6-3/201	Stoneham, Mass.	10-24-79	0	Boston University (Hockey East)
	Miroslav Guren	6-2/209	Uherske Hradiste, Czech.	9-24-76	1	Montreal, Fredericton (AHL)
20	Scott Lachance	6-1/209	Charlottesville, Va.	10-22-72	8	New York Islanders, Montreal
38	Vladimir Malakhov	6-4/227	Sverdlovsk, U.S.S.R.	8-30-68	7	Montreal
	Ilkka Mikkola	6-0/189	Oulu, Finland	1-18-79	0	TPS Turku (Finland)
	Alain Nasreddine	6-1/201	Montreal	7-10-75	1	Chicago, Portland (AHL), Fredericton (AHL), Montreal
	Barry Richter	6-2/200	Madison, Wis.	9-11-70	3	New York Islanders
52	Craig Rivet	6-2/197	North Bay, Ont.	9-13-74	5	Montreal
	Stephane Robidas	5-11/180	Sherbrooke, Que.	3-3-73	0	Fredericton (AHL)
	Matt Shasby	6-3/188	Sioux Falls, S.D.	7-2-80	0	Des Moines (USHL)
55	Igor Ulanov	6-3/211	Kraskokamsk, U.S.S.R.	10-1-69	8	Montreal
22	Eric Weinrich	6-1/215	Roanoke, Va.	12-19-66	11	Chicago, Montreal
	GOALTENDERS					
39	Frederic Chabot	5-11/187	Hebertville, Que.	2-12-68	5	Houston (IHL), Montreal
	Mathieu Garon	6-2/187	Chandler, Que.	1-9-78	0	Fredericton (AHL)
31	Jeff Hackett	6-1/195	London, Ont.	6-1-68	10	Chicago, Montreal
	Evan Lindsay	6-2/192	Calgary	5-15-79	0	Prince Albert (WHL)
60	Jose Theodore	5-11/182	Laval, Que.	9-13-76	4	Montreal, Fredericton (AHL)

1998-99 REVIEW

INDIVIDUAL STATISTICS

SCORING

	Games	G	A	Pts.	PIM	+/-	PPG	SHG	Shots	Shooting Pct.
Mark Recchi*	61	12	35	47	28	-4	3	0	152	7.9
Saku Koivu	65	14	30	44	38	-7	4	2	145	9.7
Vincent Damphousse*	65	12	24	36	46	-7	3	2	147	8.2
Martin Rucinsky	73	17	17	34	50	-25	5	0	180	9.4
Vladimir Malakhov	62	13	21	34	77	-7	8	0	143	9.1
Shayne Corson	63	12	20	32	147	-10	7	0	142	8.5
Benoit Brunet	60	14	17	31	31	-1	4	2	115	12.2
Turner Stevenson	69	10	17	27	88	6	0	0	102	9.8
Stephane Quintal	82	8	19	27	84	-23	1	1	159	5.0
Brian Savage	54	16	10	26	20	-14	5	0	124	12.9
Patrick Poulin	81	8	17	25	21	6	0	1	87	9.2
Sergei Zholtok	70	7	15	22	6	-12	2	0	102	6.9
Jonas Hoglund	74	8	10	18	16	-5	1	0	122	6.6

	Games	G	A	Pts.	PIM	+/-	PPG	SHG	Shots	Shooting Pct.
Eric Weinrich*	66	6	12	18	77	-12	4	0	95	6.3
Patrice Brisebois	54	3	9	12	28	-8	1	0	90	3.3
Igor Ulanov	76	3	9	12	109	-3	0	0	55	5.5
Scott Thornton	47	7	4	11	87	-2	1	0	56	12.5
Craig Rivet	66	2	8	10	66	-3	0	0	39	5.1
Jason Dawe*	37	4	5	9	14	0	1	0	52	7.7
Dainius Zubrus*	17	3	5	8	4	-3	0	0	31	9.7
Brett Clark	61	2	2	4	16	-3	0	0	36	5.6
Eric Houde	8	1	1	2	2	-2	0	0	4	25.0
Scott Lachance*	17	1	1	2	11	-2	0	0	22	4.5
Dave Manson*	11	0	2	2	48	-3	0	0	11	0.0
Matt Higgins	25	1	0	1	0	-2	0	0	12	8.3
Miloslav Guren	12	0	1	1	4	-1	0	0	11	0.0
Jeff Hackett* (goalie)	53	0	1	1	6	0	0	0	0	0.0
Jonathan Delisle	1	0	0	0	0	0	0	0	0	0.0
Terry Ryan	1	0	0	0	5	0	0	0	0	0.0
Sylvain Blouin	5	0	0	0	19	0	0	0	1	0.0
Brad Brown*	5	0	0	0	21	0	0	0	0	0.0
Jean-Francois Jomphe*	6	0	0	0	0	0	0	0	4	0.0
Arron Asham	7	0	0	0	0	-4	0	0	5	0.0
Alain Nasreddine*	8	0	0	0	33	1	0	0	1	0.0
Andrei Bashkirov	10	0	0	0	0	-3	0	0	4	0.0
Dave Morissette	10	0	0	0	52	1	0	0	2	0.0
Jocelyn Thibault* (goalie)	10	0	0	0	0	0	0	0	0	0.0
Frederic Chabot (goalie)	11	0	0	0	2	0	0	0	0	0.0
Jose Theodore (goalie)	18	0	0	0	0	0	0	0	0	0.0
Trent McCleary	46	0	0	0	29	-1	0	0	18	0.0

GOALTENDING

	Games	Min.	Goals	SO	Avg.	W	L	T	Shots	Sv. Pct.
Frederic Chabot	11	430	16	0	2.23	1	3	0	188	.915
Jeff Hackett*	53	3091	117	5	2.27	24	20	9	1360	.914
Jocelyn Thibault*	10	529	23	1	2.61	3	4	2	250	.908
Jose Theodore	18	913	50	1	3.29	4	12	0	406	.877

Empty-net goals (do not count against a goaltender's average): Hackett 2, Theodore 1.
*Played with two or more NHL teams.

RESULTS

OCTOBER

10—N.Y. Rangers ..... W 7-1
13—Anaheim ..... W 1-0
16—At Washington ..... T *2-2
17—Buffalo ..... L 3-4
19—Chicago ..... L 1-2
21—Ottawa ..... W 3-2
24—Detroit ..... L 0-3
28—Boston ..... L 2-9
29—At Boston ..... T *1-1
31—At Ottawa ..... L 1-5

NOVEMBER

4—At N.Y. Rangers ..... W 4-1
7—N.Y. Islanders ..... W 4-2
9—Philadelphia ..... W 5-1
11—At New Jersey ..... L 0-3
12—At N.Y. Islanders ..... L 0-4
14—Edmonton ..... L 1-4
17—At Carolina ..... L 4-5
19—Calgary ..... W 4-3
21—Colorado ..... L 2-3
27—At Boston ..... L 1-5
28—Pittsburgh ..... L 3-4
30—Los Angeles ..... W 3-1

DECEMBER

2—At Carolina ..... L 1-4
4—At New Jersey ..... T *1-1
5—Toronto ..... L *3-4
9—At Phoenix ..... L 2-4
11—At Dallas ..... L 2-3
12—At Nashville ..... T *2-2
14—Phoenix ..... T *2-2
18—At Buffalo ..... L 2-4
19—New Jersey ..... T *1-1
21—Dallas ..... T *2-2
23—At Ottawa ..... L 1-3
26—At Toronto ..... W 2-1
29—At Edmonton ..... W 5-2
31—At Calgary ..... W 2-1

JANUARY

2—At Vancouver ..... W 2-1
4—At Colorado ..... L 3-4
7—Tampa Bay ..... W 4-1
9—N.Y. Islanders ..... W 3-2
11—St. Louis ..... W 3-1
12—At Detroit ..... L 1-5
15—At Washington ..... W 3-0
16—N.Y. Rangers ..... W 3-0
18—Washington ..... T *4-4
21—At Chicago ..... L 0-3
26—At Tampa Bay ..... W 2-1
27—At Florida ..... L 1-2
30—Carolina ..... L 1-3
31—Pittsburgh ..... L 3-5

FEBRUARY

3—Vancouver ..... W 2-1
4—At Philadelphia ..... L 2-5
6—Buffalo ..... W 3-2
9—At Pittsburgh ..... L *2-3
11—At Buffalo ..... L 2-5
13—Florida ..... W 4-0
17—At N.Y. Rangers ..... W 6-3
18—At Philadelphia ..... W 3-1
20—At Toronto ..... L *2-3
25—At Ottawa ..... L 1-3
27—Ottawa ..... W 4-1

MARCH

2—Philadelphia ..... W 4-1
3—At Pittsburgh ..... T *4-4
6—Tampa Bay ..... L 1-6
8—Florida ..... L 2-5
11—At St. Louis ..... W 3-0
13—Toronto ..... W 2-1
18—Nashville ..... W 3-2
20—Washington ..... L 0-1
22—San Jose ..... T *1-1
24—At Edmonton ..... W 2-0
25—At Calgary ..... L 1-2
27—At Vancouver ..... L 1-5

APRIL

1—Boston ..... L 2-3
3—Buffalo ..... W 2-1
5—At Boston ..... L 0-3
7—Carolina ..... W 2-0
8—At N.Y. Islanders ..... L 1-3
10—New Jersey ..... L 2-6
13—At Tampa Bay ..... T *2-2
14—At Florida ..... L *2-3
17—Toronto ..... W 3-2

*Denotes overtime game.

NASHVILLE PREDATORS

WESTERN CONFERENCE/CENTRAL DIVISION

Predators Schedule

Home games shaded; D—Day game; *—All-Star Game at Toronto.

October

SUN	MON	TUE	WED	THU	FRI	SAT
					1	2 LA
3	4	5 COL	6	7	8	9
10 CHI	11 TOR	12	13	14 SJ	15	16 DAL
17	18	19	20 BUF	21	22	23 EDM
24	25	26	27	28 SJ	29	30 VAN
31 EDM						

November

SUN	MON	TUE	WED	THU	FRI	SAT
	1	2	3 CAL	4	5 CHI	6
7	8	9	10 CHI	11 OTT	12	13 PIT
14	15	16	17	18 MON	19	20 VAN
21	22 STL	23	24 BOS	25	26 WAS	27 ANA
28	29	30 PHO				

December

SUN	MON	TUE	WED	THU	FRI	SAT
			1	2 STL	3	4 DET
5	6 ATL	7	8 DET	9	10 STL	11 FLA
12	13	14 TB	15 FLA	16	17	18 COL
19 PHI	20	21 BOS	22	23 STL	24	25
26 STL	27	28 CAR	29	30 ATL	31	

January

SUN	MON	TUE	WED	THU	FRI	SAT
						1 D SJ
2	3	4	5 DAL	6 DET	7	8 CHI
9	10	11 COL	12	13 VAN	14	15 PIT
16	17	18 PHO	19	20	21 CAL	22
23 VAN	24 EDM	25	26	27 LA	28	29 CAL
30	31 NYR					

February

SUN	MON	TUE	WED	THU	FRI	SAT
		1	2 NYI	3 NJ	4	5
6 *	7	8	9	10 BUF	11	12 WAS
13	14	15 EDM	16 DAL	17	18 STL	19
20	21 DAL	22	23 CHI	24	25	26 TB
27	28	29 NJ				

March

SUN	MON	TUE	WED	THU	FRI	SAT
			1	2 SJ	3	4 LA
5 ANA	6	7 CHI	8	9	10 DET	11
12 D EDM	13	14 DET	15	16 COL	17 PHO	18
19 LA	20	21 PHI	22	23 DET	24	25 CAL
26	27	28 NYI	29 CAR	30	31 VAN	

April

SUN	MON	TUE	WED	THU	FRI	SAT
						1
2	3 ANA	4	5 PHO	6	7 ANA	8
9	10	11	12	13	14	15

1999-2000 SEASON

CLUB DIRECTORY

Owner, chairman and governor
Craig Leipold
Alternate governor
Terry London
President, COO and alternate governor
Jack Diller
Exec. v.p./g.m. and alternate governor
David Poile
Assistant general manager
Ray Shero
Mgr. of media relations/team services
Frank Buonomo
Communications coordinator
Judd Hancock
Communications assistant
Greg Harvey
Head coach
Barry Trotz
Assistant coaches
Paul Gardner
Brent Peterson
Chief amateur scout
Craig Channell
Director of player personnel
Paul Fenton
Strength and conditioning coach
Mark Nemish
Goaltending consultant
Mitch Korn
Head athletic trainer
Dan Redmond
Equipment manager
Pete Rogers
Assistant equipment manager
Chris Scoppetto
Massage therapist
Anthony Garrett
Video coordinator
Robert Bouchard

DRAFT CHOICES

Rd.— Player	Ht./Wt.	Overall	Pos.	Last team
1— Brian Finley	6-2/180	6	G	Barrie (OHL)
2— Jonas Andersson	6-2/189	33	RW	AIK, Sweden
2— Adam Hall	6-3/200	52	RW	Michigan State (CCHA)
2— Andrew Hutchinson	6-2/186	54	D	Michigan State (CCHA)
2— Ed Hill	6-3/215	61	D	Barrie (OHL)
2— Jan Lasak	6-0/189	65	G	Zvolen, Slovakia
3— Brett Angel	6-5/221	72	D	North Bay (OHL)
4— Yevgeny Pavlov	6-1/191	121	C/RW	Togliatti, Russia
4— Alexandr Krevsun	5-11/174	124	RW	Samara, Russia
5— Konstantin Panov	6-0/186	131	RW	Kamloops (WHL)
6— Timo Helbling	6-2/183	162	D	Davos, Switzerland
7— Martin Erat	5-11/176	191	LW	ZPS-Barum-Zlin, Czech
7— Kyle Kettles	6-1/170	205	G	Neepawa, Manitoba Jr.
8— Miroslav Durak	6-3/183	220	D	Bratislava, Slovakia
9— Darren Haydar	5-9/160	248	RW	New Hamp. (H. East)

MISCELLANEOUS DATA

Home ice (capacity)
Nashville Arena (17,298)
Address
501 Broadway
Nashville, TN 37203
Business phone
615-770-2300
Club colors
Blue, gold, silver, steel and orange
Radio affiliation
WTN (99.7 FM)
TV affiliation
FOX Sports South (Cable), WNAB (Channel 58)

TRAINING CAMP ROSTER

No.	FORWARDS	Ht./Wt.	BORN Place	Date	NHL exp.	1998-99 clubs
	Jonas Andersson (RW)	6-2/189	Lidingo, Sweden	2-24-81	0	AIK Solna Jrs. (Sweden Jr.)
	Denis Arkhipov (RW)	6-3/195	Kazan, U.S.S.R.	5-19-79	0	Ak Bars Kazan (Russian)
	Martin Bartek (LW)	6-0/192	Kindgssed Jill, Czech.	7-17-80	0	Zvolen (Slovakia)
71	Sebastien Bordeleau (C)	5-11/188	Vancouver	2-15-75	4	Nashville
	Marian Cisar (RW)	6-0/196	Bratislava, Czechoslovakia	2-25-78	0	Milwaukee (IHL)
17	Patrick Cote (LW)	6-3/199	Lasalle, Que.	1-24-75	4	Nashville
	Phil Crowe (LW)	6-2/230	Nanton, Alta.	4-14-70	5	Ottawa, Detroit (IHL), Cincinnati (IHL), Las Vegas (IHL)
21	Tom Fitzgerald (RW/C)	6-0/191	Billerica, Mass.	8-28-68	11	Nashville
	Adam Hall (RW)	6-3/200	Kalamazoo, Mich.	8-14-80	0	Michigan State (CCHA)
47	Matt Henderson (RW)	6-1/205	White Bear Lake, Minn.	3-1-74	1	Milwaukee (IHL), Nashville
22	Greg Johnson (C)	5-10/194	Thunder Bay, Ont.	3-16-71	6	Nashville
10	Patric Kjellberg (LW)	6-2/196	Trelleborg, Sweden	6-17-69	2	Nashville
	Alexander Krevsun (RW)	5-11/174	Togliatti, U.S.S.R.	2-6-80	0	CSK VVS Samara (Russian)
25	Sergei Krivokrasov (RW)	5-10/185	Angarsk, U.S.S.R.	4-15-74	7	Nashville
28	Denny Lambert (LW)	5-11/200	Wawa, Ont.	1-7-70	5	Nashville
11	David Legwand (C)	6-2/180	Detroit	8-17-80	1	Plymouth (OHL), Nashville
	Mark Mowers (C)	5-11/188	Whitesboro, N.Y.	2-16-74	1	Milwaukee (IHL), Nashville
	Konstantin Panov (RW)	6-0/186	Chelyabinsk, U.S.S.R.	6-29-80	0	Kamloops (WHL)
	Yevgeny Pavlov (C/RW)	6-1/191	Togliatti, U.S.S.R.	1-10-81	0	Lada Togliatti (Russian)
16	Ville Peltonen (LW)	5-11/180	Vantaa, Finland	5-24-73	3	Nashville
	Brent Peterson (LW)	6-3/206	Calgary	7-20-72	3	Cleveland (IHL), Tampa Bay, Grand Rapids (IHL)
	Branko Radivojevic (RW)	6-1/183	Piestany, Czechoslovakia	11-24-80	0	Belleville (OHL)
7	Cliff Ronning (C)	5-8/170	Vancouver	10-1-65	13	Phoenix, Nashville
50	Petr Sykora (C)	6-2/180	Pardubice, Czechoslovakia	12-21-78	1	Milwaukee (IHL), Nashville
9	Darren Turcotte (C)	6-0/190	Boston	3-2-68	11	Nashville
12	Rob Valicevic (C)	6-2/200	Detroit	1-6-71	1	Houston (IHL), Nashville
24	Scott Walker (C)	5-9/185	Cambridge, Ont.	7-19-73	5	Nashville
	Steve Washburn (C)	6-2/198	Ottawa	4-10-75	4	Florida, New Haven (AHL), Vancouver, Syracuse (AHL)
43	Vitali Yachmenev (RW)	5-9/180	Chelyabinsk, U.S.S.R.	1-8-75	4	Milwaukee (IHL), Nashville
	DEFENSEMEN					
	Brett Angel	6-5/221	Kingston, Ont.	4-29-81	0	North Bay (OHL)
15	Drake Berehowsky	6-2/211	Toronto	1-3-72	8	Nashville
	Bubba Berenzweig	6-2/195	Arlington Heights, Ill.	8-8-77	0	Univ. of Michigan (CCHA)
42	Joel Bouchard	6-0/200	Montreal	1-23-74	5	Nashville
6	Bob Boughner	6-0/206	Windsor, Ont.	3-8-71	4	Nashville
	Jayme Filipowicz	6-2/212			0	New Hampshire (Hockey East)
	Timo Helbling	6-2/183	Basel, Switzerland	7-21-81	0	Davos (Switzerland)
	Ed Hill	6-3/215	Newburyport, Mass.	10-24-80	0	Barrie (OHL)
	Andrew Hutchinson	6-2/186	Evanston, Ill.	3-24-80	0	Michigan State (CCHA)
2	Dan Keczmer	6-1/190	Mt. Clemens, Mich.	5-25-68	9	Dallas, Michigan (IHL), Nashville
	Richard Lintner	6-3/194	Trencin, Czechoslovakia	11-15-77	0	Springfield (AHL), Milwaukee (IHL)
	Craig Millar	6-2/205	Winnipeg, Man.	7-12-76	3	Edmonton, Hamilton (AHL)
4	Jay More	6-2/210	Souris, Man.	1-12-69	10	Nashville
40	Karlis Skrastins	6-1/196	Riga, U.S.S.R.	7-9-74	1	Nashville
44	Kimmo Timonen	5-9/180	Kuopio, Finland	3-18-75	1	Milwaukee (IHL), Nashville
5	Jan Vopat	6-0/207	Most, Czechoslovakia	3-22-73	4	Nashville
	GOALTENDERS					
1	Mike Dunham	6-3/195	Johnson City, N.Y.	6-1-72	3	Nashville
	Brian Finley	6-2/180	Sault Ste. Marie, Ont.	7-3-81	0	Barrie (OHL)
	Corey Hirsch	5-10/175	Medicine Hat, Alta.	7-1-72	5	Vancouver, Syracuse (AHL)
	Jan Lasak	6-0/202	Zvolen, Czechoslovakia	4-10-79	0	HKM Zvolen (Slovakia Jrs.)
30	Chris Mason	6-0/204	Red Deer, Alta.	4-20-76	1	Milwaukee (IHL), Nashville
29	Tomas Vokoun	5-11/180	Karlovy Vary, Czechoslovakia	7-2-76	2	Milwaukee (IHL), Nashville

1998-99 REVIEW

INDIVIDUAL STATISTICS

SCORING

	Games	G	A	Pts.	PIM	+/-	PPG	SHG	Shots	Shooting Pct.
Cliff Ronning*	72	18	35	53	40	-6	8	0	239	7.5
Greg Johnson	68	16	34	50	24	-8	2	3	120	13.3
Sergei Krivokrasov	70	25	23	48	42	-5	10	0	208	12.0
Sebastien Bordeleau	72	16	24	40	26	-14	1	2	168	9.5
Scott Walker	71	15	25	40	103	0	0	1	96	15.6
Tom Fitzgerald	80	13	19	32	48	-18	0	0	180	7.2
Patric Kjellberg	71	11	20	31	24	-13	2	0	103	10.7
Andrew Brunette	77	11	20	31	26	-10	7	0	65	16.9
Jamie Heward	63	6	12	18	44	-24	4	0	124	4.8
Vitali Yachmenev	55	7	10	17	10	-10	0	1	83	8.4
Drake Berehowsky	74	2	15	17	140	-9	0	0	79	2.5
Denny Lambert	76	5	11	16	218	-3	1	0	66	7.6

	Games	G	A	Pts.	PIM	+/-	PPG	SHG	Shots	Shooting Pct.
Joel Bouchard	64	4	11	15	60	-10	0	0	78	5.1
Blair Atcheynum*	53	8	6	14	16	-10	2	0	70	11.4
John Slaney	46	2	12	14	14	-12	0	0	84	2.4
Bob Boughner	79	3	10	13	137	-6	0	0	59	5.1
Kimmo Timonen	50	4	8	12	30	-4	1	0	75	5.3
Jan Vopat	55	5	6	11	28	0	0	0	46	10.9
Ville Peltonen	14	5	5	10	2	1	1	0	31	16.1
Darren Turcotte	40	4	5	9	16	-11	0	0	73	5.5
Robert Valicevic	19	4	2	6	2	4	0	0	23	17.4
Mark Mowers	30	0	6	6	4	-4	0	0	24	0.0
J.J. Daigneault*	35	2	2	4	38	-4	1	0	38	5.3
Jeff Daniels	9	1	3	4	2	-1	0	0	8	12.5
Jeff Nelson	9	2	1	3	2	-1	0	0	8	25.0
Patrick Cote	70	1	2	3	242	-7	0	0	21	4.8
Jay More	18	0	2	2	18	2	0	0	24	0.0
Doug Friedman	2	0	1	1	14	0	0	0	3	0.0
Karlis Skrastins	2	0	1	1	0	0	0	0	0	0.0
Tomas Vokoun (goalie)	37	0	1	1	6	0	0	0	1	0.0
David Legwand	1	0	0	0	0	0	0	0	2	0.0
Matt Henderson	2	0	0	0	2	-1	0	0	0	0.0
Petr Sykora	2	0	0	0	0	-1	0	0	2	0.0
Rob Zettler	2	0	0	0	2	-2	0	0	0	0.0
Chris Mason (goalie)	3	0	0	0	0	0	0	0	0	0.0
Brad Smyth	3	0	0	0	6	-1	0	0	5	0.0
Greg De Vries*	6	0	0	0	4	-4	0	0	1	0.0
Eric Fichaud (goalie)	9	0	0	0	0	0	0	0	0	0.0
Dan Keczmer*	16	0	0	0	12	-3	0	0	12	0.0
Mike Dunham (goalie)	44	0	0	0	4	0	0	0	0	0.0

GOALTENDING

	Games	Min.	Goals	SO	Avg.	W	L	T	Shots	Sv. Pct.
Tomas Vokoun	37	1954	96	1	2.95	12	18	4	1041	.908
Mike Dunham	44	2472	127	1	3.08	16	23	3	1387	.908
Eric Fichaud	9	447	24	0	3.22	0	6	0	229	.895
Chris Mason	3	69	6	0	5.22	0	0	0	44	.864

Empty-net goals (do not count against a goaltender's average): Vokoun 4, Dunham 3, Fichaud 1.
*Played with two or more NHL teams.

RESULTS

OCTOBER

10—Florida ....L 0-1
13—Carolina ....W 3-2
17—At Ottawa ....L 1-3
19—At Toronto ....T *2-2
21—At Detroit ....L 2-5
23—Calgary ....L 3-4
24—At Chicago ....L 4-5
27—Vancouver ....W 5-4
31—Colorado ....W 3-2

NOVEMBER

4—At Edmonton ....L 2-3
6—At Calgary ....W 2-1
7—At Vancouver ....L 3-5
10—At San Jose ....W 4-2
12—At Los Angeles ....W 3-1
14—At St. Louis ....L 1-5
17—Chicago ....L 1-2
19—St. Louis ....W 3-2
21—N.Y. Islanders ....L 3-6
24—At St. Louis ....L 0-4
25—Calgary ....W 4-3
27—Anaheim ....W 3-1
29—At N.Y. Rangers ....L 1-5

DECEMBER

1—Ottawa ....L 1-3
5—Buffalo ....L 1-3
8—Edmonton ....T *3-3
10—San Jose ....W 2-1
12—Montreal ....T *2-2
16—At Anaheim ....L 1-6
17—At San Jose ....L 1-3
19—At Vancouver ....W 6-4
23—Detroit ....W 5-3
26—Washington ....W 3-1
28—At Dallas ....L 0-1
30—Boston ....L 2-5

JANUARY

1—St. Louis ....L 5-6
2—At Carolina ....L 1-4
4—Anaheim ....W 2-1
7—San Jose ....L 3-4
9—Chicago ....T *3-3
11—At Philadelphia ....L 0-8
14—At Detroit ....L *1-2
15—Phoenix ....W 2-0
18—At Boston ....L 1-8
19—Vancouver ....W 4-1
21—Tampa Bay ....L 2-3
26—Detroit ....L 1-4
28—At Buffalo ....W 4-2
30—At New Jersey ....W *3-2
31—Phoenix ....L 1-5

FEBRUARY

4—At Calgary ....T *2-2
5—At Edmonton ....L 2-4
9—Detroit ....L 2-5
12—At N.Y. Islanders ....W 2-1
13—Pittsburgh ....L *2-3
15—N.Y. Rangers ....L 4-7
19—Colorado ....T *4-4
20—At St. Louis ....W 4-3
23—Dallas ....L 3-4
24—At Dallas ....W 2-1
27—At Colorado ....L 1-3

MARCH

2—St. Louis ....L 1-5
4—At Los Angeles ....W 4-3
5—At Anaheim ....L 2-3
7—At Phoenix ....L 3-4
10—At Chicago ....L 2-5
12—Chicago ....W 5-3
14—Edmonton ....W 3-1
16—Calgary ....L 2-4
18—At Montreal ....L 2-3
20—At Pittsburgh ....T *1-1
24—At Tampa Bay ....W 3-0
26—At Florida ....L 1-4
28—Dallas ....L 0-3
30—At Washington ....W 3-2

APRIL

1—Philadelphia ....L 1-2
3—Los Angeles ....W 3-2
7—At Colorado ....L 1-4
9—At Phoenix ....W 4-3
12—Los Angeles ....L 3-4
14—At Detroit ....L 2-4
15—At Chicago ....L 2-4
17—New Jersey ....L 1-4

*Denotes overtime game.

NEW JERSEY DEVILS
EASTERN CONFERENCE/ATLANTIC DIVISION

Devils Schedule

Home games shaded; D—Day game; *—All-Star Game at Toronto.

October

SUN	MON	TUE	WED	THU	FRI	SAT
					1	2 ATL
3	4	5	6	7 PIT	8	9 TB
10	11 D OTT	12	13 ANA	14	15	16 NYI
17	18	19	20	21	22 DAL	23 STL
24	25	26	27 STL	28	29 CAR	30 PHI
31						

November

SUN	MON	TUE	WED	THU	FRI	SAT
	1	2	3 MON	4 BOS	5	6 TOR
7	8	9 PHI	10	11	12 ATL	13 WAS
14	15	16	17 BOS	18	19	20 D OTT
21	22	23	24 ANA	25 PHO	26	27
28 SJ	29	30				

December

SUN	MON	TUE	WED	THU	FRI	SAT
			1 NYR	2	3 OTT	4 CAL
5	6	7 PIT	8	9 CHI	10	11 D EDM
12	13	14 LA	15	16 MON	17	18 WAS
19 NYI	20	21	22 PHI	23 TOR	24	25
26 D NYR	27 BUF	28	29 BOS	30	31	

January

SUN	MON	TUE	WED	THU	FRI	SAT
						1 BOS
2	3 D OTT	4	5 PIT	6 BUF	7	8 PHO
9	10	11 TB	12	13	14 WAS	15 PHI
16	17 CAR	18	19 CHI	20	21 NYI	22
23	24	25	26 FLA	27	28 CAR	29 DET
30	31					

February

SUN	MON	TUE	WED	THU	FRI	SAT
		1	2 NYR	3 NSH	4	5
6 *	7	8 NYR	9 NYR	10	11	12
13 D SJ	14	15 PHI	16	17 COL	18	19 D NYI
20	21 BUF	22	23	24 MON	25 TOR	26
27 MON	28	29 NSH				

March

SUN	MON	TUE	WED	THU	FRI	SAT
			1	2 COL	3	4 VAN
5 CAL	6	7	8	9	10 ATL	11 WAS
12	13 PIT	14	15 DAL	16	17 TB	18
19 FLA	20	21 CAR	22	23	24 NYI	25 TOR
26	27	28 PIT	29	30	31 ATL	

April

SUN	MON	TUE	WED	THU	FRI	SAT
						1
2 TB	3 FLA	4	5	6 BUF	7	8 D FLA
9	10	11	12	13	14	15

1999-2000 SEASON

CLUB DIRECTORY

Chairman
John J. McMullen
President and general manager
Louis A. Lamoriello
Head coach
Robbie Ftorek
Assistant coaches
Vyacheslav Fetisov
Larry Robinson
Goaltending coach
Jacques Caron
Medical trainer
Bill Murray
Strength & conditioning coordinator
Michael Vasalani
Equipment manager
Dana McGuane
Assistant equipment manager
Lou Centanni
V.p., communications and broadcasting
Rick Minch
Director, public relations
Kevin Dessart
Director, information & publications
Mike Levine

DRAFT CHOICES

Rd.— Player	Ht./Wt.	Overall	Pos.	Last team
1— Ari Ahonen	6-2/172	27	G	Jyvaskyla, Finland
2— Mike Commodore	6-4/225	42	D	North Dakota (WCHA)
2— Brett Clouthier	6-4/215	50	LW	Kingston (OHL)
3— Andre Lakos	6-6/210	95	D	Barrie (OHL)
4— Teemu Kesa	6-0/183	100	D	Ilves Tampere, Finland
6— Scott Cameron	6-0/182	185	C	Barrie (OHL)
7— Chris Hartsburg	6-0/190	214	C/RW	Colorado Col. (WCHA)
8— Justin Dziama	6-2/215	242	RW	Nobles Prep H.S.

MISCELLANEOUS DATA

Home ice (capacity)
Continental Airlines Arena (19,040)
Address
P.O. Box 504
50 Route 120 North
East Rutherford, N.J. 07073
Business phone
201-935-6050
Club colors
Red, black and white
Radio affiliation
WABC (770 AM)
TV affiliation
FOX Sports Net New York

TRAINING CAMP ROSTER

No.	FORWARDS	Ht./Wt.	BORN Place	BORN Date	NHL exp.	1998-99 clubs
25	Jason Arnott (C)	6-3/220	Collingworth, Ont.	10-11-74	6	New Jersey
	Christian Berglund (RW)	5-11/183	Orebro, Sweden	3-12-80	0	Farjestad Karlstad (Sweden)
	Eric Bertrand (LW)	6-0/205	St. Ephrem, Que.	4-16-75	0	Albany (AHL)
	Jiri Bicek (LW)	5-11/185	Kosice, Czechoslovakia	12-3-78	0	Albany (AHL)
	Steve Brule (RW)	6-0/195	Montreal	1-15-75	0	Albany (AHL)
18	Sergei Brylin (C)	5-10/190	Moscow, U.S.S.R.	1-13-74	5	New Jersey
	Scott Cameron (C)	6-0/182	Sudbury, Ont.	4-11-81	0	Barrie (OHL)
	Brett Clouthier (LW)	6-4/215	Ottawa	6-9-81	0	Kingston (OHL)
	Pierre Dagenais (LW)	6-4/200	Blainville, Que.	3-4-78	0	Albany (AHL)
26	Patrik Elias (LW)	6-0/195	Trebic, Czechoslovakia	4-13-76	4	New Jersey
	Scott Gomez (C)	5-11/180	Anchorage, Alaska	12-23-79	0	Tri-City (WHL)
	Stanislav Gron (C)	6-1/190	Bratislava, Czechoslovakia	10-28-78	0	Kootenay (WHL), Utah (IHL)
16	Bobby Holik (C)	6-3/225	Jihlava, Czechoslovakia	1-1-71	9	New Jersey
32	Sasha Lakovic (LW)	6-0/205	Vancouver	9-7-71	3	New Jersey, Albany (AHL)
11	John Madden (C)	5-11/185	Barrie, Ont.	5-4-73	1	Albany (AHL), New Jersey
21	Randy McKay (RW)	6-2/210	Montreal	1-25-67	11	New Jersey
9	Brendan Morrison (C)	5-11/180	Pitt Meadows, B.C.	8-12-75	2	New Jersey
12	Sergei Nemchinov (C)	6-0/210	Moscow, U.S.S.R.	1-14-64	8	New York Islanders, New Jersey
29	Krzysztof Oliwa (RW)	6-5/235	Tychy, Poland	4-12-73	3	New Jersey
20	Jay Pandolfo (LW)	6-1/200	Winchester, Mass.	12-27-74	3	New Jersey
10	Denis Pederson (C)	6-2/205	Prince Albert, Sask.	9-10-75	4	New Jersey
	Richard Rochefort (C)	5-10/185	North Bay, Ont.	1-7-77	0	Albany (AHL)
14	Brian Rolston (LW)	6-2/200	Flint, Mich.	2-21-73	5	New Jersey
8	Vadim Sharifijanov (RW)	6-0/205	Ufa, U.S.S.R.	12-23-75	2	New Jersey, Albany (AHL)
17	Petr Sykora (C)	5-11/185	Plzen, Czechoslovakia	11-19-76	4	New Jersey
	Jeff Williams (LW)	6-0/195	Pointe-Claire, Que.	2-11-76	0	Albany (AHL)
	DEFENSEMEN					
6	Brad Bombardir	6-1/205	Powell River, B.C.	5-5-72	2	New Jersey
	Mike Commodore	6-4/225	Fort Saskatchewan, Alta.	11-7-79	0	Univ. of North Dakota (WCHA)
3	Ken Daneyko	6-0/215	Windsor, Ont.	4-17-64	16	New Jersey
	Joshua DeWolf	6-2/190	Bloomington, Minn.	7-25-77	0	Albany (AHL)
	Sascha Goc	6-2/195	Schwenningen, West Germany	4-14-79	0	Albany (AHL)
	Teemu Kesa	6-1/189	Nurmijarvi, Finland	6-7-81	0	Ilves Tampere (Finland Jr.)
	Geordie Kinnear	6-1/195	Simcoe, Ont.	7-9-73	0	Albany (AHL)
	Andre Lakos	6-6/210	Vienna, Austria	7-29-79	0	Barrie (OHL)
	Josh MacNevin	6-2/185	Calgary	7-14-77	0	Providence College (Hockey East)
27	Scott Niedermayer	6-0/205	Edmonton	8-31-73	8	Utah (IHL), New Jersey
24	Lyle Odelein	5-11/210	Quill Lake, Sask.	7-21-68	10	New Jersey
2	Sheldon Souray	6-4/235	Elk Point, Alta.	7-13-76	2	New Jersey
4	Scott Stevens	6-1/215	Kitchener, Ont.	4-1-64	17	New Jersey
7	Ken Sutton	6-2/205	Edmonton	11-5-69	8	Albany (AHL), New Jersey
	Mike Van Ryn	6-1/190	London, Ont.	5-14-79	0	University of Michigan (WCHA)
	Colin White	6-3/215	New Glasgow, Nova Scotia	12-12-77	0	Albany (AHL)
	GOALTENDERS					
	Ari Ahonen	6-2/172	Jyvaskyla, Finland	2-6-81	0	JyP HT Jyvaskyla Jrs. (Finland Jr.)
30	Martin Brodeur	6-1/205	Montreal	5-6-72	7	New Jersey
	J.F. Damphousse	6-0/175	St. Alexis des Monts, Que.	7-21-79	0	Moncton (QMJHL), Albany (AHL)
	Frederic Henry	5-11/170	Cap Rouge, Que.	8-9-77	0	Albany (AHL)
31	Chris Terreri	5-9/160	Providence, R.I.	11-15-64	12	New Jersey

1998-99 REVIEW

INDIVIDUAL STATISTICS

SCORING

	Games	G	A	Pts.	PIM	+/-	PPG	SHG	Shots	Shooting Pct.
Petr Sykora	80	29	43	72	22	16	15	0	222	13.1
Bobby Holik	78	27	37	64	119	16	5	0	253	10.7
Brian Rolston	82	24	33	57	14	11	5	5	210	11.4
Jason Arnott	74	27	27	54	79	10	8	0	200	13.5
Patrik Elias	74	17	33	50	34	19	3	0	157	10.8
Brendan Morrison	76	13	33	46	18	-4	5	0	111	11.7
Scott Niedermayer	72	11	35	46	26	16	1	1	161	6.8
Randy McKay	70	17	20	37	143	10	3	0	136	12.5
Lyle Odelein	70	5	26	31	114	6	1	0	101	5.0
Dave Andreychuk	52	15	13	28	20	1	4	0	110	13.6
Jay Pandolfo	70	14	13	27	10	3	1	1	100	14.0
Vadim Sharifijanov	53	11	16	27	28	11	1	0	71	15.5
Scott Stevens	75	5	22	27	64	29	0	0	111	4.5
Denis Pederson	76	11	12	23	66	-10	3	0	145	7.6

	Games	G	A	Pts.	PIM	+/-	PPG	SHG	Shots	Shooting Pct.
Sergei Brylin	47	5	10	15	28	8	3	0	51	9.8
Krzysztof Oliwa	64	5	7	12	240	4	0	0	59	8.5
Ken Daneyko	82	2	9	11	63	27	0	0	63	3.2
Kevin Dean	62	1	10	11	22	4	1	0	51	2.0
Bob Carpenter	56	2	8	10	36	-3	0	0	69	2.9
Brad Bombardir	56	1	7	8	16	-4	0	0	47	2.1
Sheldon Souray	70	1	7	8	110	5	0	0	101	1.0
Sergei Nemchinov*	10	4	0	4	6	4	1	0	13	30.8
Martin Brodeur (goalie)	70	0	4	4	4	0	0	0	0	0.0
Sasha Lakovic	16	0	3	3	59	0	0	0	10	0.0
Ken Sutton	5	1	0	1	0	1	0	0	5	20.0
John Madden	4	0	1	1	0	-2	0	0	4	0.0
Chris Terreri (goalie)	12	0	1	1	0	0	0	0	0	0.0
Scott Daniels	1	0	0	0	0	0	0	0	0	0.0
Bryan Muir*	1	0	0	0	0	0	0	0	4	0.0

GOALTENDING

	Games	Min.	Goals	SO	Avg.	W	L	T	Shots	Sv. Pct.
Martin Brodeur	70	4239	162	4	2.29	39	21	10	1728	.906
Chris Terreri	12	726	30	1	2.48	8	3	1	294	.898

Empty-net goals (do not count against a goaltender's average): Brodeur 4.
*Played with two or more NHL teams.

RESULTS

OCTOBER

10—At Chicago ....L.....1-2
14—Pittsburgh ....L.....1-3
16—At N.Y. Rangers ....W.....2-1
17—Edmonton ....L.....2-4
22—At Philadelphia ....W.....3-2
24—Boston ....W.....3-1
28—Los Angeles ....L.....0-4
29—At N.Y. Islanders ....W.....2-1
31—Florida ....W.....3-1

NOVEMBER

3—N.Y. Rangers ....W.....3-1
7—At Florida ....W.....4-3
8—At Tampa Bay ....L.....1-3
11—Montreal ....W.....3-0
13—Pittsburgh ....W.....4-3
14—At Philadelphia ....L.....1-6
19—Carolina ....W....*3-2
21—Florida ....T....*3-3
22—At Carolina ....W.....5-2
25—At Dallas ....W.....5-2
26—At Phoenix ....L.....2-3
28—At Colorado ....W.....3-2

DECEMBER

1—At Washington ....W.....4-0
4—Montreal ....T....*1-1
5—At N.Y. Islanders ....W.....7-5
8—Philadelphia ....T....*5-5
10—At Philadelphia ....W....*5-4
12—Colorado ....W.....5-3
16—N.Y. Rangers ....W.....6-3
18—Calgary ....L.....2-5
19—At Montreal ....T....*1-1
23—St. Louis ....W.....4-2
26—Buffalo ....L.....0-2
28—At Buffalo ....W.....7-4
30—At Washington ....W.....3-2

JANUARY

2—At Ottawa ....L.....0-6
5—San Jose ....T....*3-3
6—At N.Y. Rangers ....W.....5-2
9—Washington ....L.....2-3
11—Ottawa ....L.....2-4
14—At Ottawa ....L.....2-3
15—Tampa Bay ....W.....3-1
18—At San Jose ....L.....1-3
20—At Anaheim ....W.....4-3
21—At Los Angeles ....W.....3-2
26—Ottawa ....W.....4-1
28—At Boston ....W.....2-0
30—Nashville ....L....*2-3

FEBRUARY

1—Detroit ....T....*2-2
3—At Carolina ....W.....4-1
4—At St. Louis ....W.....2-0
6—Toronto ....L.....2-3
9—Vancouver ....L.....3-4
12—Washington ....L.....2-3
13—Carolina ....W.....6-4
15—Toronto ....T....*3-3
17—Tampa Bay ....W.....7-1
19—At Detroit ....L.....1-3
20—N.Y. Islanders ....L.....2-3
22—At Tampa Bay ....W.....3-2
25—At Boston ....T....*3-3
28—Phoenix ....W.....4-1

MARCH

3—At Toronto ....W.....5-2
5—Boston ....L.....1-4
7—At N.Y. Islanders ....W.....4-2
9—At Pittsburgh ....W.....3-2
15—At Vancouver ....W.....2-1
17—At Edmonton ....W.....4-1
20—At Toronto ....L.....1-3
23—Buffalo ....T....*1-1
25—Pittsburgh ....W.....5-3
27—Chicago ....T....*4-4
28—At Florida ....T....*2-2
31—Anaheim ....W.....7-1

APRIL

3—At Pittsburgh ....W.....4-2
4—N.Y. Rangers ....W.....4-1
6—At Carolina ....L.....2-4
8—Washington ....W.....1-0
10—At Montreal ....W.....6-2
12—N.Y. Islanders ....L.....2-4
14—At Buffalo ....W.....2-1
16—Philadelphia ....W....*3-2
17—At Nashville ....W.....4-1

*Denotes overtime game.

NEW YORK ISLANDERS

EASTERN CONFERENCE/ATLANTIC DIVISION

Islanders Schedule

Home games shaded; D—Day game; *—All-Star Game at Toronto.

October

SUN	MON	TUE	WED	THU	FRI	SAT
					1	2 TB
3	4	5	6	7	8	9
10 D COL	11 NYR	12	13	14 ATL	15	16 NJ
17	18 MON	19	20	21	22	23 VAN
24	25	26	27 FLA	28	29	30 CAR
31						

November

SUN	MON	TUE	WED	THU	FRI	SAT
	1	2	3 NYR	4 MON	5	6 BUF
7	8	9	10 CAR	11	12 CHI	13 STL
14	15	16	17	18	19 COL	20
21 EDM	22	23 CAL	24	25	26	27 WAS
28 BOS	29	30 DAL				

December

SUN	MON	TUE	WED	THU	FRI	SAT
			1	2 CAL	3	4 ATL
5	6	7 WAS	8	9 MON	10	11 D OTT
12	13	14 EDM	15 TOR	16	17	18 BUF
19 NJ	20	21 PIT	22	23 NYR	24	25
26	27 BOS	28	29 TOR	30 PIT	31	

January

SUN	MON	TUE	WED	THU	FRI	SAT
						1
2 D PHI	3	4 BOS	5	6 PHI	7	8 BOS
9	10 PHO	11	12 FLA	13 TB	14	15 D NYR
16	17 D OTT	18	19 MON	20	21 NJ	22 TB
23	24	25	26 ANA	27	28	29 SJ
30	31 LA					

February

SUN	MON	TUE	WED	THU	FRI	SAT
		1	2 NSH	3 PIT	4	5
6 *	7	8 CAR	9	10 TB	11	12 PIT
13 NYR	14	15 SJ	16	17 PHI	18	19 D NJ
20	21 D DET	22	23	24	25 DET	26 PHI
27	28 WAS	29				

March

SUN	MON	TUE	WED'	THU	FRI	SAT
			1	2 OTT	3	4 D BUF
5 PHI	6	7	8	9 PHO	10 DAL	11
12 D BUF	13	14	15 WAS	16 ATL	17	18 FLA
19	20	21 PIT	22 TOR	23	24 NJ	25
26 D CAR	27	28 NSH	29	30	31	

April

SUN	MON	TUE	WED	THU	FRI	SAT
						1 D CHI
2 D ATL	3	4	5	6 OTT	7 TOR	8
9 D FLA	10	11	12	13	14	15

1999-2000 SEASON

CLUB DIRECTORY

Owners
Steven Gluckstern
Howard Milstein
Ed Milstein

President
John Sanders

General manager
Mike Milbury

Head coach
Butch Goring

Associate coach
Lorne Henning

Assistant coach
Greg Cronin

Head certified athletic trainer
Rich Campbell

Head equipment manager
Joe McMahon

Assistant certified athletic trainer
Sean Donellan

Assistant equipment managers
Rick Harper
Eric Miklich

Director of media and public relations
Chris Botta

Media relations assistant
Jason Lagnese

Publications assistant
Kerry Gwydir

DRAFT CHOICES

Rd.— Player	Ht./Wt.	Overall	Pos.	Last team
1— Tim Connolly	6-0/186	5	C	Erie (OHL)
1— Taylor Pyatt	6-4/220	8	LW	Sudbury (OHL)
1— Branislav Mezei	6-5/221	10	D	Belleville (OHL)
1— Kristian Kudroc	6-6/229	28	D	Michalovce, Slovakia
3— Mattias Weinhandl	6-0/183	78	RW	Modo Ornsk., Sweden
3— Brian Collins	6-1/190	87	C	St. John's H.S.
4— Juraj Kolnik	5-10/182	101	RW	Rimouski (QMJHL)
4— Johan Halvardsson	6-3/198	102	D	HV-71 Jonkoping, Swe.
5— Justin Mapletoft	6-1/180	130	C	Red Deer (WHL)
5— Adam Johnson	6-6/220	140	D	Greenway H.S., Minn.
6— Bjorn Melin	6-1/178	163	RW	HV-71 Jonkoping, Swe.
8— Radek Martinek		228	W	C.-Budejovice, Czech
9— Brett Henning	6-1/203	255	C	Notre Dame (CCHA)
9— Tyler Scott	6-1/215	268	D	Upper Canada College

MISCELLANEOUS DATA

Home ice (capacity)
Nassau Veterans Memorial Coliseum (16,297)

Address
Uniondale, NY 11553

Business phone
516-794-4100

Club colors
Blue and orange

Radio affiliation
WJWR (620 AM), WLUX (530 AM)

TV affiliation
FOX Sports New York

TRAINING CAMP ROSTER

No.	FORWARDS	Ht./Wt.	BORN Place	BORN Date	NHL exp.	1998-99 clubs
	Brian Collins (C)	6-1/190	Worcester, Mass.	9-13-80	0	St. John's Prep (Mass. H.S.)
	Tim Connolly (C)	6-0/186	Baldwinsville, N.Y.	5-7-81	0	Erie (OHL)
25	Mariusz Czerkawski (RW)	6-0/195	Radomski, Poland	4-13-72	6	New York Islanders
38	Chris Ferraro (C)	5-10/185	Port Jefferson, N.Y.	1-24-73	4	Hamilton (AHL), Edmonton
	Josh Green (LW)	6-4/212	Camrose, Alta.	11-16-77	1	Los Angeles, Springfield (AHL)
	Sean Haggerty (LW)	6-1/186	Rye, N.Y.	2-11-76	2	Lowell (AHL)
	Tony Hrkac (C)	5-11/180	Thunder Bay, Ont.	7-7-66	9	Dallas
15	Brad Isbister (LW)	6-4/227	Edmonton	5-7-77	2	Las Vegas (IHL), Springfield (AHL), Phoenix
	Olli Jokinen (C)	6-3/208	Kuopio, Finland	12-5-78	2	Springfield (AHL), Los Angeles
	Jorgen Jonsson (LW)	6-0/195	Angelholm, Sweden	9-29-72	0	Farjestad Karlstad (Sweden)
	Juraj Kolnik (RW)	5-10/182	Nitra, Czechoslovakia	11-13-80	0	Quebec (QMJHL), Rimouski (QMJHL)
	Jason Krog (C)	5-11/191	Fernie, B.C.	10-9-75	0	Univ. of New Hampshire (ECAC)
13	Claude Lapointe (C)	5-9/181	Lachine, Que.	10-11-68	9	New York Islanders
44	Mark Lawrence (RW)	6-4/215	Burlington, Ont.	1-27-72	4	Lowell (AHL), New York Islanders
10	Mats Lindgren (LW/C)	6-2/202	Skelleftea, Sweden	10-1-74	3	Edmonton, New York Islanders
48	Warren Luhning (RW)	6-2/185	Edmonton	7-3-75	2	Lowell (AHL), New York Islanders
	Justin Mapletoft (C)	6-1/180	Lloydminster, Sask.	6-11-81	0	Red Deer (WHL)
	Bjorn Melin (RW)	6-1/178	Jonkoping, Sweden	7-4-81	0	HV 71 Jonkoping (Sweden Jr.)
	Petr Mika (C)	6-4/195	Prague, Czechoslovakia	2-12-79	0	Slavia Praha (Czech Republic)
37	Dimitri Nabokov (C/LW)	6-2/209	Novosibirsk, U.S.S.R.	1-4-77	2	Lowell (AHL), New York Islanders
	Chris Nielsen (C)	6-2/185	Moshi, Tanzania	2-16-80	0	Calgary (WHL)
24	Gino Odjick (LW)	6-3/210	Maniwaki, Que.	9-7-70	9	New York Islanders
49	Vladimir Orszagh (RW)	5-11/173	Banska Bystrica, Czech.	5-24-77	2	Lowell (AHL), New York Islanders
	Taylor Pyatt (LW)	6-4/220	Thunder Bay, Ont.	8-19-81	0	Sudbury (OHL)
	Michael Rupp (LW)	6-5/218	Cleveland	1-13-80	0	Erie (OHL)
12	Mike Watt (LW/C)	6-2/212	Seaforth, Ont.	3-31-76	2	New York Islanders
8	Steve Webb (RW)	6-0/195	Peterborough, Ont.	4-30-75	3	Lowell (AHL), New York Islanders
	Mattias Weinhandl (RW)	6-0/183	Ljungby, Sweden	6-1-80	0	Troja-Ljungby (Sweden Dv. 2)
	DEFENSEMEN					
	Mathieu Biron	6-6/212	Lac St. Charles, Que.	4-29-80	0	Shawinigan (QMJHL)
4	Eric Brewer	6-3/195	Verona, B.C.	4-17-79	1	New York Islanders
33	Eric Cairns	6-6/230	Oakville, Ont.	6-27-74	3	Hartford (AHL), Lowell (AHL), New York Islanders
3	Zdeno Chara	6-9/255	Trencin, Czechoslovakia	3-18-77	2	Lowell (AHL), New York Islanders
55	Vladimir Chebaturkin	6-2/212	Tyumen, U.S.S.R.	4-23-75	2	Lowell (AHL), New York Islanders
	Ray Giroux	5-11/185	North Bay, Ont.	7-20-76	0	Lowell (AHL)
	Johan Halvardsson	6-3/198	Jonkoping, Sweden	12-26-79	0	HV 71 Jonkoping (Sweden)
	Jamie Heward	6-2/207	Regina, Sask.	3-30-71	3	Nashville
	Adam Johnson	6-6/220	Minneapolis, Minn.	8-2-80	0	Greenway H.S. (USHS (West))
29	Kenny Jonsson	6-3/195	Angelholm, Sweden	10-6-74	5	New York Islanders
	Evgeny Korolev	6-1/186	Moscow, U.S.S.R.	7-24-78	0	Lowell (AHL), Roanoke (ECHL)
	Kristian Kudroc	6-6/229	Michalovce, Czechoslovakia	5-21-81	0	Michalovce (Slovakia)
39	Dean Malkoc	6-3/200	Vancouver	1-26-70	4	Lowell (AHL), New York Islanders
	Branislav Mezei	6-5/221	Nitra, Czechoslovakia	10-8-80	0	Belleville (OHL)
2	Rich Pilon	6-0/205	Saskatoon, Sask.	4-30-68	11	New York Islanders
36	Ray Schultz	6-2/200	Red Deer, Alta.	11-14-76	2	Lowell (AHL), New York Islanders
	GOALTENDERS					
	Roberto Luongo	6-3/175	St. Leonard, Que.	4-4-79	0	Val-d'Or (QMJHL), Acadie-Bathurst (QMJHL)
28	Felix Potvin	6-1/195	Anjou, Que.	6-23-71	8	Toronto, New York Islanders

1998-99 REVIEW

INDIVIDUAL STATISTICS

SCORING

	Games	G	A	Pts.	PIM	+/-	PPG	SHG	Shots	Shooting Pct.
Robert Reichel*	70	19	37	56	50	-15	5	1	186	10.2
Zigmund Palffy	50	22	28	50	34	-6	5	2	168	13.1
Trevor Linden	82	18	29	47	32	-14	8	1	167	10.8
Bryan Smolinski	82	16	24	40	49	-7	7	0	223	7.2
Mariusz Czerkawski	78	21	17	38	14	-10	4	0	205	10.2
Claude Lapointe	82	14	23	37	62	-19	2	2	134	10.4
Mark Lawrence	60	14	16	30	38	-8	4	0	88	15.9
Kenny Jonsson	63	8	18	26	34	-18	6	0	91	8.8
Mike Watt	75	8	17	25	12	-2	0	0	75	10.7
Barry Richter	72	6	18	24	34	-4	0	0	111	5.4
Ted Donato*	55	7	11	18	27	-10	2	0	68	10.3
Sergei Nemchinov*	67	8	8	16	22	-17	1	0	61	13.1
Bryan Berard*	31	4	11	15	26	-6	2	0	72	5.6
Eric Brewer	63	5	6	11	32	-14	2	0	63	7.9
Scott Lachance*	59	1	8	9	30	-19	1	0	37	2.7

	Games	G	A	Pts.	PIM	+/-	PPG	SHG	Shots	Shooting Pct.
Mats Lindgren*	12	5	3	8	2	2	3	0	30	16.7
Zdeno Chara	59	2	6	8	83	-8	0	1	56	3.6
David Harlock	70	2	6	8	68	-16	0	0	35	5.7
Gino Odjick	23	4	3	7	133	-2	1	0	28	14.3
Kevin Miller	33	1	5	6	13	-5	0	0	37	2.7
Jason Dawe*	22	2	3	5	8	0	0	0	29	6.9
Craig Janney*	18	1	4	5	4	-2	0	0	9	11.1
Richard Pilon	52	0	4	4	88	-8	0	0	27	0.0
Joe Sacco	73	3	0	3	45	-24	0	1	84	3.6
Eric Cairns	9	0	3	3	23	1	0	0	2	0.0
Ted Crowley*	6	1	1	2	0	0	1	0	10	10.0
Ken Belanger*	9	1	1	2	30	1	0	0	3	33.3
Dmitri Nabokov	4	0	2	2	2	4	0	0	4	0.0
Vladimir Orsagh	12	1	0	1	6	2	0	0	5	20.0
Tom Chorske*	2	0	1	1	2	1	0	0	9	0.0
Dean Malkoc	2	0	1	1	7	3	0	0	1	0.0
Mike Kennedy	1	0	0	0	2	0	0	0	0	0.0
Ray Schultz	4	0	0	0	7	-2	0	0	2	0.0
Marcel Cousineau (goalie)	6	0	0	0	0	0	0	0	0	0.0
Vlad Chebaturkin	8	0	0	0	12	6	0	0	4	0.0
Mike Hough	11	0	0	0	2	-2	0	0	4	0.0
Warren Luhning	11	0	0	0	8	-4	0	0	11	0.0
Felix Potvin* (goalie)	11	0	0	0	0	0	0	0	0	0.0
Wade Flaherty (goalie)	20	0	0	0	4	0	0	0	0	0.0
Steve Webb	45	0	0	0	32	-10	0	0	18	0.0
Tommy Salo* (goalie)	51	0	0	0	12	0	0	0	0	0.0

GOALTENDING

	Games	Min.	Goals	SO	Avg.	W	L	T	Shots	Sv. Pct.
Tommy Salo*	51	3018	132	5	2.62	17	26	7	1368	.904
Marcel Cousineau	6	293	14	0	2.87	0	4	0	119	.882
Wade Flaherty	20	1048	53	0	3.03	5	11	2	491	.892
Felix Potvin*	11	606	37	0	3.66	2	7	1	345	.893

Empty-net goals (do not count against a goaltender's average): Salo 5, Flaherty 3.

*Played with two or more NHL teams.

RESULTS

OCTOBER

10— Pittsburgh ....L....3-4
12— At Boston ....L....0-3
14— At Tampa Bay ....W....2-0
17— At St. Louis ....W....1-0
21— Edmonton ....L....2-4
22— At N.Y. Rangers ....L....2-3
24— Buffalo ....W....5-4
27— Los Angeles ....W....1-0
29— New Jersey ....L....1-2
31— Philadelphia ....W....3-2

NOVEMBER

2— Florida ....W....6-2
5— Carolina ....L....3-6
7— At Montreal ....L....2-4
9— At Toronto ....W....3-1
10— At Pittsburgh ....L....2-3
12— Montreal ....W....4-0
14— Washington ....L....3-5
17— At Colorado ....L....2-5
20— At Dallas ....L....2-4
21— At Nashville ....W....6-3
25— Philadelphia ....W....4-2
26— At Ottawa ....L....1-4
28— Carolina ....L....1-3

DECEMBER

2— N.Y. Rangers ....L....2-3
4— At Washington ....L....1-5
5— New Jersey ....L....5-7
8— Colorado ....L....1-2
12— Tampa Bay ....L....*1-2
15— At San Jose ....W....1-0
17— At Los Angeles ....W....*5-4
18— At Anaheim ....T....*2-2
20— At Phoenix ....L....2-4
22— St. Louis ....T....*3-3
26— Boston ....W....4-2
28— At Florida ....L....1-5
29— At Tampa Bay ....L....0-3
31— At Chicago ....L....0-1

JANUARY

2— San Jose ....L....*3-4
5— Chicago ....T....*1-1
7— At Philadelphia ....L....0-5
9— At Montreal ....L....2-3
11— At Washington ....L....3-4
13— At N.Y. Rangers ....L....*3-4
16— At Florida ....L....0-1
20— Florida ....L....2-5
21— At Pittsburgh ....W....5-2
26— Boston ....W....4-1
29— Phoenix ....T....*4-4
30— At Ottawa ....L....2-9

FEBRUARY

3— At Detroit ....L....1-5
4— At Boston ....W....5-4
7— Vancouver ....T....*3-3
9— Washington ....L....1-2
12— Nashville ....L....1-2
13— At Buffalo ....T....*2-2
15— Tampa Bay ....T....*3-3
17— Pittsburgh ....W....3-1
20— At New Jersey ....W....3-2
21— At Carolina ....L....1-4
25— Toronto ....L....1-4
27— Detroit ....W....3-1

MARCH

2— Ottawa ....L....2-4
4— Dallas ....L....*2-3
6— At Philadelphia ....T....*3-3
7— New Jersey ....L....2-4
9— Philadelphia ....T....*2-2
11— Toronto ....L....1-2
14— N.Y. Rangers ....L....*2-3
15— At Buffalo ....L....1-2
19— At Vancouver ....W....3-1
21— At Calgary ....L....1-2
24— At Carolina ....L....1-2
27— Ottawa ....L....3-7
29— At N.Y. Rangers ....L....1-3
31— At Florida ....W....5-3

APRIL

3— Anaheim ....T....*2-2
6— Buffalo ....L....3-4
8— Montreal ....W....3-1
10— Carolina ....L....1-6
12— At New Jersey ....W....4-2
14— At Toronto ....L....*2-3
17— At Pittsburgh ....W....7-2

*Denotes overtime game.

NEW YORK RANGERS

EASTERN CONFERENCE/ATLANTIC DIVISION

Rangers Schedule

Home games shaded; D—Day game; *—All-Star Game at Toronto.

October

SUN	MON	TUE	WED	THU	FRI	SAT
					1 EDM	2 VAN
3	4	5 OTT	6	7	8 CAR	9
10 D PHO	11 NYI	12	13	14 PIT	15	16
17 ATL	18	19 SJ	20 PHI	21	22 PHI	23
24 VAN	25	26	27	28	29	30 MON
31						

November

SUN	MON	TUE	WED	THU	FRI	SAT
	1	2	3 NYI	4	5 COL	6
7 CHI	8	9	10 OTT	11 WAS	12	13 BOS
14	15	16	17	18 BOS	19	20 TOR
21	22	23	24 TB	25	26 FLA	27
28	29	30				

December

SUN	MON	TUE	WED	THU	FRI	SAT
			1 NJ	2	3 MON	4 BUF
5	6 CAL	7	8 EDM	9	10	11
12	13	14	15 LA	16	17 WAS	18
19 TB	20	21 BUF	22	23 NYI	24	25
26 D NJ	27	28 PHO	29 DAL	30	31	

January

SUN	MON	TUE	WED	THU	FRI	SAT
						1
2 MON	3 STL	4	5 TOR	6	7	8 TOR
9 CAR	10	11	12	13	14	15 D NYI
16 D ATL	17	18 CAR	19	20 CAR	21	22 STL
23	24 ATL	25 PIT	26	27 TOR	28	29 OTT
30	31 NSH					

February

SUN	MON	TUE	WED	THU	FRI	SAT
		1	2 NJ	3 ATL	4	5
6 *	7	8 NJ	9 NJ	10	11 BOS	12
13 NYI	14	15 TB	16 FLA	17	18 COL	19
20 PHI	21	22 PIT	23	24	25 BUF	26 OTT
27	28	29				

March

SUN	MON	TUE	WED	THU	FRI	SAT
			1 BUF	2	3 FLA	4
5	6 SJ	7	8 ANA	9 LA	10	11 PIT
12	13 DAL	14	15 TB	16	17	18 D PHI
19 PIT	20	21 FLA	22	23 WAS	24	25
26 D DET	27 DET	28	29	30	31	

April

SUN	MON	TUE	WED	THU	FRI	SAT
						1 D BOS
2	3 WAS	4	5 MON	6	7	8
9 D PHI	10	11	12	13	14	15

1999-2000 SEASON

CLUB DIRECTORY

Chief executive officer/governor
David W. Checketts

President and g.m./alternate governor
Neil Smith

Executive v.p. and general counsel
Kenneth W. Munoz

Vice president and business manager
Francis P. Murphy

V.p., legal and business affairs
Marc Schoenfeld

Vice president, controller
John Cudmore

Alternate governors
Marc Lustgarten
Kenneth W. Munoz

Assistant general manager
Don Maloney

Head coach
John Muckler

Assistant coaches
Keith Acton
Charlie Huddy
John Tortorella

Development coach
John Paddock

Assistant development coach
Mike Busniuk

Goaltending analyst
Sam St. Laurent

Director of scouting
Martin Madden

Amateur scouting staff
Darwin Bennett, Ray Clearwater, Herb Hammond, Martin Madden Jr., Christer Rockstom, Dick Todd

Scouting manager
Bill Short

Video assistant
Jerry Dineen

Vice president of business operations
Mark Piazza

Vice president of marketing
Jeanie Baumgartner

Director of public relations
John Rosasco

Manager of public relations
Jason Vogel

Public relations assistant
Jeff Schwartzenberg

Community relations assistant
Jennifer Schoenfeld

Team physician and orthopedic surgeon
Dr. Barton Nisonson

Assistant team physician
Dr. Anthony Maddalo

Medical trainer
Jim Ramsay

Equipment trainer
Mike Folga

DRAFT CHOICES

Rd.— Player	Ht./Wt.	Overall	Pos.	Last team
1— Pavel Brendl	6-0/204	4	RW	Calgary (WHL)
1— Jamie Lundmark	6-0/174	9	C	Moose Jaw (WHL)
2— David Inman	6-1/180	59	C	Notre Dame (CCHA)
3— Johan Asplund	6-1/180	79	G	Brynas Gavle, Sweden
3— Patrick Aufiero	6-2/186	90	D	Boston U. (H. East)
5— Garett Bembridge	6-0/164	137	RW	Saskatoon (WHL)
6— Jay Dardis	6-3/190	177	C	Proctor H.S., Minn.
7— Arto Laatikainen	6-0/187	197	D	Espoo, Finland
8— Evgeny Gusakov	6-6/235	226	LW	Togliatti, Russia
9— Petter Henning	6-0/200	251	W	Modo Ornsk., Sweden
9— Alexei Bulatov	5-11/178	254	LW	Yekateringburg, Russia

MISCELLANEOUS DATA

Home ice (capacity)
Madison Square Garden (18,200)

Address
2 Pennsylvania Plaza
New York, NY 10121

Business phone
212-465-6486

Club colors
Blue, red and white

Radio affiliation
WFAN (660 AM)

TV affiliation
MSG Network

TRAINING CAMP ROSTER

No.	FORWARDS	Ht./Wt.	BORN Place	Date	NHL exp.	1998-99 clubs
38	Derek Armstrong (C)	6-1/193	Ottawa	4-23-73	4	Hartford (AHL), New York Rangers
	Garrett Bembridge (RW)	6-0/164	Melfort, Sask.	7-6-81	0	Saskatoon (WHL)
	Pavel Brendl (RW)	6-0/204	Opocno, Czechoslovakia	3-23-81	0	Calgary (WHL)
	Stefan Cherneski (RW)	6-0/195	Winnipeg	9-19-78	0	Hartford (AHL)
	Jay Dardis (C)	6-3/190	Duluth, Minn.	7-4-80	0	Proctor (USHS (West))
14	Theo Fleury (RW)	5-6/180	Oxbow, Sask.	6-29-68	11	Calgary, Colorado
	Scott Fraser (C)	6-1/178	Moncton, N. B.	5-3-72	3	New York Rangers, Hartford (AHL)
9	Adam Graves (LW)	6-0/205	Tecumseh, Ont.	4-12-68	12	New York Rangers
20	Todd Harvey (RW)	6-0/200	Hamilton, Ont.	2-17-75	5	New York Rangers
	Jan Hlavac (LW)	6-0/183	Prague, Czechoslovakia	9-20-76	0	Sparta Praha (Czech Republic)
	David Inman (C)	6-1/180	New York	6-13-80	0	Notre Dame (CCHA)
13	Valeri Kamensky (LW)	6-2/200	Voskresensk, U.S.S.R.	4-18-66	8	Colorado
22	Mike Knuble (RW)	6-3/225	Toronto	7-4-72	3	New York Rangers
28	Eric Lacroix (LW)	6-2/210	Montreal	7-15-71	6	Colorado, Los Angeles, N.Y. Rangers
19	Darren Langdon (LW)	6-1/205	Deer Lake, Nfld.	1-8-71	5	New York Rangers
	Patrick Leahy (RW)	6-3/190	Brighton, Mass.	6-9-79	0	Miami of Ohio (CCHA)
	Jamie Lundmark (C)	6-0/174	Edmonton	1-16-81	0	Moose Jaw (WHL)
15	John MacLean (RW)	6-0/200	Oshawa, Ont.	11-20-64	16	New York Rangers
6	Manny Malhotra (C)	6-2/210	Mississauga, Ont.	5-18-80	1	New York Rangers
93	Petr Nedved (C)	6-3/195	Liberec, Czechoslovakia	12-9-71	8	Las Vegas (IHL), New York Rangers
	Brad Smyth (RW)	6-0/200	Ottawa	3-13-73	4	Mil. (IHL), Nashville, Hartford (AHL)
17	Kevin Stevens (LW)	6-3/230	Brockton, Mass.	4-15-65	12	New York Rangers
28	P.J. Stock (C)	5-10/190	Victoriaville, Que.	5-26-75	2	New York Rangers, Hartford (AHL)
	Dmitri Subbotin (RW)	6-1/183	Tomsk, U.S.S.R.	10-20-77	0	Lada Togliatti (Russian), Dynamo Moscow (Russian)
	Brian Swanson (C)	5-10/180	Eagle River, Alaska	3-24-76	0	Colorado Col. (WCHA), Hartford (AHL)
26	Tim Taylor (C)	6-1/185	Stratford, Ont.	2-6-69	6	Boston
14	Johan Witehall (RW)	6-1/198	Goteborg, Sweden	1-7-72	1	Hartford (AHL), New York Rangers
	Michael York (C)	5-10/185	Pontiac, Mich.	1-3-78	0	Michigan State (CCHA), Hartford (AHL)
	DEFENSEMEN					
	Pat Aufiero	6-2/186	Winchester, Mass.	7-1-80	0	Boston University (Hockey East)
	Jeff Brown	6-1/190	Toronto	4-24-78	0	Canadian nat'l team (Int'l), Hartford (AHL), Charlotte (ECHL)
55	Jason Doig	6-2/220	Montreal	1-29-77	3	Phoenix, Springfield (AHL), Hart. (AHL)
	Burke Henry	6-2/190	Ste. Rose, Manitoba	1-21-79	0	
	Wes Jarvis	6-4/203	Toronto	4-16-79	0	Can. nat'l team (Int'l), Kitchener (OHL)
	Kim Johnsson	6-1/175	Malmo, Sweden	3-16-76	0	Malmo (Sweden)
	Tomi Kallarsson	6-3/194	Lempaala, Finland	3-15-79	0	HPK Hameenlinna (Finland)
	Tomas Kloucek	6-2/205	Prague, Czechoslovakia	3-7-80	0	Cape Breton (QMJHL)
	Alexander Korobolin	6-2/189	Chelyabinsk, U.S.S.R.	3-12-76	0	Mechel Chelyabinsk (Russian)
2	Brian Leetch	6-1/190	Corpus Christi, Tex.	3-3-68	12	New York Rangers
	Sylvain Lefebvre	6-2/205	Richmond, Que.	10-14-67	10	Colorado
	Jan Mertzig	6-4/215	Stockholm, Sweden	7-18-70	1	N.Y. Rangers, Hartford (AHL), Utah (IHL)
36	Rumun Ndur	6-2/222	Zaria, Nigeria	7-7-75	3	Buffalo, N.Y. Rangers, Hartford (AHL)
34	Peter Popovic	6-6/239	Koping, Sweden	2-10-68	6	New York Rangers
5	Stephane Quintal	6-3/228	Boucherville, Que.	10-22-68	11	Montreal
25	Mathieu Schneider	5-10/192	New York	6-12-69	11	New York Rangers
	Alexei Vasiliev	6-1/190	Yaroslavl, U.S.S.R.	9-1-77	1	Hartford (AHL)
	Terry Virtue	6-0/197	Scarborough, Ont.	8-8-70	1	Providence (AHL), Boston
	GOALTENDERS					
	Johan Asplund	6-1/180	Slutskar, Sweden	12-15-80	0	Brynas Gavle (Sweden)
	Johan Holmqvist	6-1/200	Tierp, Sweden	5-24-78	0	Brynas Gavle (Sweden)
	Jason Labarbera	6-2/205	Burnaby, B.C.	1-18-80	0	Portland (WHL)
	Jean-Francois Labbe	5-9/170	Sherbrooke, Que.	6-15-72	0	Hartford (AHL)
1	Kirk McLean	6-0/180	Willowdale, Ont.	6-26-66	14	Florida
35	Mike Richter	5-11/185	Philadelphia	9-22-66	11	New York Rangers

1998-99 REVIEW

INDIVIDUAL STATISTICS

SCORING

	Games	G	A	Pts.	PIM	+/-	PPG	SHG	Shots	Shooting Pct.
Wayne Gretzky	70	9	53	62	14	-23	3	0	132	6.8
John MacLean	82	28	27	55	46	5	11	1	231	12.1
Brian Leetch	82	13	42	55	42	-7	4	0	184	7.1
Adam Graves	82	38	15	53	47	-12	14	2	239	15.9
Petr Nedved	56	20	27	47	50	-6	9	1	153	13.1
Marc Savard	70	9	36	45	38	-7	4	0	116	7.8
Kevin Stevens	81	23	20	43	64	-10	8	0	136	16.9
Niklas Sundstrom	81	13	30	43	20	-2	1	2	89	14.6
Mike Knuble	82	15	20	35	26	-7	3	0	113	13.3
Mathieu Schneider	75	10	24	34	71	-19	5	0	159	6.3

	Games	G	A	Pts.	PIM	+/-	PPG	SHG	Shots	Shooting Pct.
Todd Harvey	37	11	17	28	72	-1	6	0	58	19.0
Manny Malhotra	73	8	8	16	13	-2	1	0	61	13.1
Ulf Samuelsson*	67	4	8	12	93	6	0	0	37	10.8
Brent Fedyk	67	4	6	10	30	-11	0	1	47	8.5
Jeff Beukeboom	45	0	9	9	60	-2	0	0	8	0.0
Alexei Kovalev*	14	3	4	7	12	-6	1	0	35	8.6
Scott Fraser	28	2	4	6	14	-12	1	0	35	5.7
Chris Tamer*	52	1	5	6	92	-12	0	0	46	2.2
Peter Popovic	68	1	4	5	40	-12	0	0	64	1.6
Richard Brennan	24	1	3	4	23	-4	0	0	36	2.8
Rumun Ndur*	31	1	3	4	46	-2	0	0	21	4.8
Eric Lacroix*	30	2	1	3	4	-5	0	0	17	11.8
Sean Pronger*	14	0	3	3	4	-3	0	0	3	0.0
Esa Tikkanen	32	0	3	3	38	-5	0	0	25	0.0
Jan Mertzig	23	0	2	2	8	-5	0	0	10	0.0
Alexander Karpovtsev*	2	1	0	1	0	1	0	0	4	25.0
Jeff Finley*	2	0	0	0	0	-1	0	0	0	0.0
Derek Armstrong	3	0	0	0	0	0	0	0	1	0.0
Mike Maneluk*	4	0	0	0	4	-1	0	0	3	0.0
Geoff Smith	4	0	0	0	2	-5	0	0	0	0.0
Johan Witehall	4	0	0	0	0	0	0	0	1	0.0
P.J. Stock	5	0	0	0	6	-1	0	0	0	0.0
Harry York*	5	0	0	0	4	-1	0	0	5	0.0
Christian Dube	6	0	0	0	0	0	0	0	0	0.0
Stan Neckar*	18	0	0	0	8	-1	0	0	8	0.0
Dan Cloutier (goalie)	22	0	0	0	2	0	0	0	0	0.0
Darren Langdon	44	0	0	0	80	-3	0	0	8	0.0
Mike Richter (goalie)	68	0	0	0	0	0	0	0	0	0.0

GOALTENDING

	Games	Min.	Goals	SO	Avg.	W	L	T	Shots	Sv. Pct.
Mike Richter	68	3878	170	4	2.63	27	30	8	1898	.910
Dan Cloutier	22	1097	49	0	2.68	6	8	3	570	.914

Empty-net goals (do not count against a goaltender's average): Richter 6, Cloutier 2.
*Played with two or more NHL teams.

RESULTS

OCTOBER

9— Philadelphia .... L 0-1
10—At Montreal .... L 1-7
12—St. Louis .... L 2-4
16—New Jersey .... L 1-2
17—At Pittsburgh .... T *3-3
20—Edmonton .... W 3-2
22—N.Y. Islanders .... W 3-2
24—At Philadelphia .... T *2-2
27—Buffalo .... T *0-0
30—Carolina .... W 1-0

NOVEMBER

3— At New Jersey .... L 1-3
4— Montreal .... L 1-4
7— At Toronto .... T *6-6
10—At Tampa Bay .... W 10-2
11—At Florida .... L 1-4
13—Boston .... T *3-3
18—At Anaheim .... L 1-3
19—At Los Angeles .... W 5-1
21—At San Jose .... T *2-2
25—At Buffalo .... L 2-4
27—At Pittsburgh .... T *2-2
29—Nashville .... W 5-1

DECEMBER

1— Florida .... W *5-4
2— At N.Y. Islanders .... W 3-2
5— At Ottawa .... W 2-1
7— Toronto .... W 6-2
9— Colorado .... L 1-2
11—At Buffalo .... L 0-2
14—Calgary .... W 5-2
16—At New Jersey .... L 3-6
19—At Toronto .... L 4-7
23—Carolina .... L 0-1
26—At Carolina .... W 6-3
30—At Phoenix .... L 1-3
31—At Colorado .... W 6-3

JANUARY

2— At St. Louis .... W 1-0
4— San Jose .... W 4-3
6— New Jersey .... L 2-5
7— At Washington .... L 1-5
10—Tampa Bay .... W 5-2
13—N.Y. Islanders .... W *4-3
15—Chicago .... L 1-3
16—At Montreal .... L 0-3
19—Ottawa .... L 1-2
21—Florida .... L 1-2
26—At Washington .... W 4-1
28—At Carolina .... L *2-3
30—At Detroit .... W 3-2

FEBRUARY

1— Washington .... L 1-3
4— Vancouver .... W 8-4
7— At Boston .... L 2-3
12—Carolina .... L 1-3
14—Detroit .... L 2-4
15—At Nashville .... W 7-4
17—Montreal .... L 3-6
19—Pittsburgh .... W 6-1
21—At Edmonton .... W *2-1
22—At Calgary .... L 2-6
26—Phoenix .... W 3-0
28—Philadelphia .... W 6-5

MARCH

2— Dallas .... T *2-2
4— At Washington .... W 4-2
7— At Boston .... W 3-1
8— Toronto .... W *3-2
10—Ottawa .... L 0-3
12—Boston .... L 4-5
14—At N.Y. Islanders .... W *3-2
15—Washington .... T *1-1
19—Buffalo .... L *2-3
21—Pittsburgh .... T *2-2
22—At Tampa Bay .... L 3-6
24—At Florida .... W 2-1
27—At Philadelphia .... L 1-3
29—N.Y. Islanders .... W 3-1

APRIL

2— Anaheim .... L 1-4
4— At New Jersey .... L 1-4
5— At Philadelphia .... W 5-1
8— At Chicago .... L 2-6
9— At Dallas .... L 1-3
12—Tampa Bay .... W 2-1
15—At Ottawa .... T *2-2
18—Pittsburgh .... L *1-2

*Denotes overtime game.

OTTAWA SENATORS

EASTERN CONFERENCE/NORTHEAST DIVISION

Senators Schedule

Home games shaded; D—Day game; *—All-Star Game at Toronto.

October

SUN	MON	TUE	WED	THU	FRI	SAT
					1	2 PHI
3	4	5 NYR	6	7 BOS	8	9 TOR
10	11 D NJ	12	13	14 PHO	15	16 COL
17	18	19	20	21 COL	22	23 BUF
24	25	26	27	28 CAL	29	30 FLA
31 ATL						

November

SUN	MON	TUE	WED	THU	FRI	SAT
	1	2	3 WAS	4 PIT	5	6 MON
7	8	9	10 NYR	11 NSH	12	13 ANA
14	15	16	17 CAR	18 SJ	19	20 D NJ
21	22	23	24	25 ATL	26 PIT	27
28 D PHI	29	30 CHI				

December

SUN	MON	TUE	WED	THU	FRI	SAT
			1	2	3 NJ	4 DAL
5	6	7	8 BUF	9	10	11 D NYI
12	13 TOR	14	15	16 VAN	17	18 CAL
19 EDM	20	21	22	23 CAR	24	25
26	27 MON	28	29 MON	30 BOS	31	

January

SUN	MON	TUE	WED	THU	FRI	SAT
						1
2	3 D NJ	4 CAR	5	6 PHO	7	8 BUF
9	10	11 LA	12 ANA	13	14	15
16 D WAS	17 D NYI	18	19	20 PHI	21	22 DET
23	24 TOR	25	26 STL	27	28 BUF	29 NYR
30	31					

February

SUN	MON	TUE	WED	THU	FRI	SAT
		1 BOS	2	3 BUF	4	5
6 *	7	8	9	10	11 FLA	12 MON
13	14	15 CAR	16	17 TB	18	19 D VAN
20	21 D FLA	22	23	24 TB	25	26 NYR
27	28 PIT	29 BOS				

March

SUN	MON	TUE	WED	THU	FRI	SAT
			1	2 NYI	3	4 ATL
5	6 BOS	7	8	9 PIT	10	11 TOR
12	13	14	15 CAL	16	17 EDM	18 VAN
19	20	21 ATL	22	23 TOR	24	25 WAS
26	27	28 PHI	29	30 TB	31 FLA	

April

SUN	MON	TUE	WED	THU	FRI	SAT
						1
2 D STL	3	4 WAS	5	6 NYI	7	8 MON
9 TB	10	11	12	13	14	15

1999-2000 SEASON

CLUB DIRECTORY

Chairman, governor
Rod Bryden
President and CEO & alt. governor
Roy Mlakar
General manager
Marshall Johnston
Executive vice president
Steve Violetta
COO & alternate governor
Cyril Leeder
Head coach
Jacques Martin
Assistant coaches
Perry Pearn
Mike Murphy
Director of hockey operations
Trevor Timmins
Vice president, broadcast
Jim Steel
Vice president, communications
Phil Legault
Director, media relations
Morgan Quarry
Manager, media relations
Steve Keogh
Media relations assistant
Jen Eves
Video coordinator & conditioning coach
Randy Lee
Head equipment manager
Ed Georgica
Assistant equipment manager
John Gervais
Head athletic trainer
Kevin Wagner
Massage therapist
Brad Joyal
Team doctor
Jamie Kissick, M.D.
Scouts
Paul Castron, Dale Engel, George Fargher, Gary Harker, Jarmo Kekalainen, Phil Myre, John Phelan, Andre Savard, Boris Shagus

DRAFT CHOICES

Rd.— Player	Ht./Wt.	Overall	Pos.	Last team
1— Martin Havlat	6-1/178	26	C/LW	Trinec, Czech Republic
2— Simon Lajeunesse	6-0/175	48	G	Moncton (QMJHL)
2— Teemu Sainomaa	6-3/202	62	LW	Jokerit Helsinki, Fin.
3— Chris Kelly	6-0/179	94	C/LW	London (OHL)
5— Andrew Ianiero	6-0/188	154	LW	Kingston (OHL)
6— Martin Prusek	6-1/158	164	G	HC Vitkovice, Czech
7— Mikko Ruutu	6-4/183	201	W	IFK Helsinki, Finland
7— Layne Ulmer	6-0/193	209	C	Swift Current (WHL)
7— Alexandre Giroux	6-2/165	213	C/LW	Hull (QMJHL)
9— Konstantin Gorovikov	5-11/172	269	F	St. Petersburg, Russia

MISCELLANEOUS DATA

Home ice (capacity)
Corel Centre (18,500)
Address
1000 Palladium Drive
Kanata, Ont. K2VIA5
Business phone
613-599-0250
Club colors
Black, red and gold
Radio affiliation
OSR (1200 AM), STAR (96 FM)
TV affiliation
CHRO TV, CTV Sportsnet

TRAINING CAMP ROSTER

No.	FORWARDS	Ht./Wt.	BORN Place	BORN Date	NHL exp.	1998-99 clubs
11	Daniel Alfredsson (RW)	5-11/194	Partille, Sweden	12-11-72	4	Ottawa
20	Magnus Arvedson (LW)	6-2/198	Karlstad, Sweden	11-25-71	2	Ottawa
	Chris Bala (LW)	6-1/180	Alexandria, Va.	9-24-78	0	Harvard University (ECAC)
14	Radek Bonk (C)	6-3/210	Koprivnice, Czechoslovakia	1-9-76	5	Ottawa
22	Slava Butsayev (C)	6-2/200	Togliatti, U.S.S.R.	6-13-70	5	Fort Wayne (IHL), Florida, Ottawa
	Ivan Ciernik (RW)	6-1/198	Levice, Czechoslovakia	10-30-77	1	Adirondack (AHL), Cincinnati (AHL)
10	Andreas Dackell (RW)	5-11/191	Gavle, Sweden	12-29-72	3	Ottawa
	Mike Fisher (C)	6-0/183	Peterborough, Ont.	6-5-80	0	Sudbury (OHL)
25	Bruce Gardiner (C)	6-1/193	North York, Ont.	2-11-72	3	Ottawa
	Martin Havlat (C/LW)	6-1/178	Brno, Czechoslovakia	4-19-81	0	Zelezarny Trinec (Czech Republic)
18	Marian Hossa (LW)	6-1/194	Stara Lubovna, Czechoslovakia	1-12-79	2	Ottawa
	Andrew Ianiero (LW)	6-0/188	St. Catherines, Ont.	1-10-81	0	Kingston (OHL)
	Chris Kelly (C/LW)	6-0/179	Toronto	11-11-80	0	London (OHL)
16	Steve Martins (C)	5-9/180	Gatineau, Que.	4-13-72	4	Detroit (IHL), Ottawa
15	Shawn McEachern (LW)	5-11/196	Waltham, Mass.	2-28-69	8	Ottawa
	Chris Neil (RW)	6-0/210	Markdale, Ont.	6-18-79	0	North Bay (OHL)
	Rastislav Pavlikovsky	5-10/195	Dubnica, Czechoslovakia	3-2-77	0	Cincinnati (IHL), Cincinnati (AHL)
13	Vaclav Prospal (C)	6-2/190	Ceske-Budejovice, Czech.	2-17-75	3	Ottawa
	Teemu Sainomaa (LW)	6-3/202	Helsinki, Finland	5-15-81	0	Jokerit Helsinki (Finland Jr.)
	Yves Sarault (LW)	6-0/200	Valleyfield, Que.	12-23-72	5	Detroit (IHL), Ottawa
	Petr Schastlivy (LW)	6-0/198	Angarsk, U.S.S.R.	4-18-79	0	Torpedo Yaroslavl (Russian)
22	Shaun Van Allen (C)	6-1/200	Calgary	8-29-67	8	Ottawa
	Sergei Verenikin (RW)	5-11/187	Yaroslavl, U.S.S.R.	9-8-79	0	Torpedo Yaroslavl (Russian)
19	Alexei Yashin (C)	6-3/225	Sverdlovsk, U.S.S.R.	11-5-73	6	Ottawa
7	Rob Zamuner (LW)	6-2/206	Oakville, Ont.	9-17-69	8	Tampa Bay
	DEFENSEMEN					
	Erich Goldmann	6-3/208	Dingolfing, West Germany	4-7-76	0	Cincinnati (IHL), Hershey (AHL), Cincinnati (AHL)
	John Gruden	6-0/208	Virginia, Minn.	4-6-70	4	Detroit (IHL), Ottawa
29	Igor Kravchuk	6-0/200	Ufa, U.S.S.R.	9-13-66	8	Ottawa
27	Janne Laukkanen	6-0/180	Lahti, Finland	3-19-70	5	Ottawa
4	Chris Phillips	6-2/213	Fort McMurray, Alta.	3-9-78	2	Ottawa
6	Wade Redden	6-2/205	Lloydminster, Sask.	6-12-77	3	Ottawa
5	Sami Salo	6-3/210	Turku, Finland	9-2-74	1	Ottawa, Detroit (IHL)
3	Patrick Traverse	6-3/190	Montreal	3-14-74	2	Ottawa
	Julien Vauclair	6-0/200	Delemont, Switzerland	10-2-79	0	Lugano (Switzerland)
33	Jason York	6-2/198	Nepean, Ont.	5-20-70	7	Ottawa
	GOALTENDERS					
	Mathieu Chouinard	6-1/209	Laval, Que.	4-11-80	0	Shawinigan (QMJHL)
	Jani Hurme	6-0/185	Turku, Finland	1-18-75	0	Detroit (IHL), Cincinnati (IHL)
	Simon Lajeunesse	6-0/170	Quebec City, Que.	1-22-81	0	Moncton (QMJHL)
	Martin Prusek	6-0/176	Vitkovice, Czechoslovakia	12-11-75	0	HC Vitkovice (Czech Republic)
31	Ron Tugnutt	5-11/165	Scarborough, Ont.	10-22-67	11	Ottawa

1998-99 REVIEW

INDIVIDUAL STATISTICS

SCORING

	Games	G	A	Pts.	PIM	+/-	PPG	SHG	Shots	Shooting Pct.
Alexei Yashin	82	44	50	94	54	16	19	0	337	13.1
Shawn McEachern	77	31	25	56	46	8	7	0	223	13.9
Andreas Dackell	77	15	35	50	30	9	6	0	107	14.0
Magnus Arvedson	80	21	26	47	50	33	0	4	136	15.4
Andreas Johansson	69	21	16	37	34	1	7	0	144	14.6
Vaclav Prospal	79	10	26	36	58	8	2	0	114	8.8
Jason York	79	4	31	35	48	17	2	0	177	2.3
Daniel Alfredsson	58	11	22	33	14	8	3	0	163	6.7
Radek Bonk	81	16	16	32	48	15	0	1	110	14.5
Marian Hossa	60	15	15	30	37	18	1	0	124	12.1
Wade Redden	72	8	21	29	54	7	3	0	127	6.3
Igor Kravchuk	79	4	21	25	32	14	3	0	171	2.3
Sami Salo	61	7	12	19	24	20	2	0	106	6.6
Shaun Van Allen	79	6	11	17	30	3	0	1	47	12.8
Bruce Gardiner	59	4	8	12	43	6	0	0	70	5.7
Janne Laukkanen	50	1	11	12	40	18	0	0	46	2.2
Patrick Traverse	46	1	9	10	22	12	0	0	35	2.9
Lance Pitlick	50	3	6	9	33	7	0	0	34	8.8
Steve Martins	36	4	3	7	10	4	1	0	27	14.8

	Games	G	A	Pts.	PIM	+/-	PPG	SHG	Shots	Shooting Pct.
David Oliver	17	2	5	7	4	1	0	0	18	11.1
Chris Murray*	38	1	6	7	65	-2	0	0	33	3.0
Chris Phillips	34	3	3	6	32	-5	2	0	51	5.9
Ted Donato*	13	3	2	5	10	2	1	0	16	18.8
Bill Berg	44	2	2	4	28	4	0	0	40	5.0
Nelson Emerson*	3	1	1	2	2	-1	0	0	10	10.0
Damian Rhodes (goalie)	45	1	1	2	4	0	0	0	1	100.0
Stan Neckar*	3	0	2	2	0	-1	0	0	2	0.0
Stephen Leach*	9	0	2	2	6	-1	0	0	4	0.0
Viacheslav Butsayev*	2	0	1	1	2	0	0	0	5	0.0
Philip Crowe	8	0	1	1	4	1	0	0	2	0.0
Yves Sarault	11	0	1	1	4	1	0	0	7	0.0
John Gruden	13	0	1	1	8	0	0	0	10	0.0
Radim Bicanek*	7	0	0	0	4	-1	0	0	6	0.0
Ron Tugnutt (goalie)	43	0	0	0	0	0	0	0	0	0.0

GOALTENDING

	Games	Min.	Goals	SO	Avg.	W	L	T	Shots	Sv. Pct.
Ron Tugnutt	43	2508	75	3	1.79	22	10	8	1005	.925
Damian Rhodes	45	2480	101	3	2.44	22	13	7	1060	.905

Empty-net goals (do not count against a goaltender's average): Tugnutt 2, Rhodes 1.
*Played with two or more NHL teams.

RESULTS

OCTOBER
10—At Colorado W 4-3
11—At Phoenix W 4-1
17—Nashville W 3-1
21—At Montreal L 2-3
22—St. Louis L 3-5
24—Carolina L 1-3
29—Philadelphia W 3-1
31—Montreal W 5-1

NOVEMBER
1—At Philadelphia W 5-4
5—Pittsburgh L 2-4
7—Washington L 5-8
10—At Buffalo T *2-2
12—Edmonton T *1-1
14—At Toronto L 1-2
15—At Chicago T *2-2
20—At Washington W 4-1
21—Calgary W 4-1
23—Vancouver W 4-3
26—N.Y. Islanders W 4-1
28—At Toronto L *2-3

DECEMBER
1—At Nashville W 3-1
3—Los Angeles W 3-1
5—N.Y. Rangers L 1-2
8—At Tampa Bay W 4-2
9—At Florida L 5-6
12—Phoenix L 0-2
17—At Boston L 2-5
18—Carolina W 5-1
20—Dallas L 2-3
23—Montreal W 3-1
26—At Pittsburgh L *1-2
28—Anaheim T *2-2
30—At Buffalo W *3-2

JANUARY
1—At Washington W 4-3
2—New Jersey W 6-0
4—At Carolina T *4-4
6—At Detroit W 2-0
8—Tampa Bay W 5-1
10—Detroit W 4-1
11—At New Jersey W 4-2
14—New Jersey W 3-2
16—Buffalo T *1-1
18—Philadelphia L 0-5
19—At N.Y. Rangers W 2-1
21—At Boston W 3-1
26—At New Jersey L 1-4
30—N.Y. Islanders W 9-2

FEBRUARY
1—At Vancouver W 1-0
3—At Edmonton T *2-2
6—At Calgary W 2-1
9—Buffalo T *1-1
11—Florida L 1-3
13—Washington W 2-1
15—Chicago W 6-2
18—Boston W 2-0
20—Philadelphia W 4-1
23—At Boston L 2-5
25—Montreal W 3-1
27—At Montreal L 1-4

MARCH
2—At N.Y. Islanders W 4-2
4—At Philadelphia W 5-0
6—Toronto W 3-1
8—Tampa Bay W 9-3
10—At N.Y. Rangers W 3-0
13—At San Jose L 2-3
15—At Los Angeles L 0-4
17—At Anaheim T *2-2
19—At Dallas W 2-1
20—At St. Louis W 3-2
24—Boston L 0-3
26—San Jose T *1-1
27—At N.Y. Islanders W 7-3
30—At Pittsburgh W 6-4

APRIL
1—Pittsburgh T *3-3
3—At Florida W 6-4
5—At Tampa Bay T *4-4
7—At Toronto L 2-4
8—Toronto W 3-1
10—Buffalo T *1-1
12—Florida L 0-2
15—N.Y. Rangers T *2-2
17—At Carolina T *1-1

*Denotes overtime game.

PHILADELPHIA FLYERS

EASTERN CONFERENCE/ATLANTIC DIVISION

Flyers Schedule

Home games shaded; D—Day game; *—All-Star Game at Toronto.

October

SUN	MON	TUE	WED	THU	FRI	SAT
					1	2 OTT
3	4	5	6	7 CAR	8	9 BOS
10	11	12 WAS	13	14 MON	15	16 DET
17 BUF	18	19	20 NYR	21	22 NYR	23
24 FLA	25	26 VAN	27	28 COL	29	30 NJ
31						

November

SUN	MON	TUE	WED	THU	FRI	SAT
	1	2	3 ANA	4	5 SJ	6 LA
7	8	9 NJ	10	11 CAR	12	13 D SJ
14	15	16	17	18 DAL	19	20 TB
21	22 TB	23	24 FLA	25	26 D TOR	27
28 D OTT	29	30				

December

SUN	MON	TUE	WED	THU	FRI	SAT
			1	2 BUF	3	4 MON
5 STL	6	7	8	9 TOR	10	11 TOR
12	13	14 BUF	15	16 PHO	17	18 TB
19 NSH	20	21	22 NJ	23 ATL	24	25
26	27 CAL	28	29 VAN	30	31	

January

SUN	MON	TUE	WED	THU	FRI	SAT
						1
2 D NYI	3	4	5	6 NYI	7	8 PIT
9	10	11 CAR	12	13	14 ATL	15 NJ
16	17 D FLA	18	19	20 OTT	21	22
23 PIT	24	25	26	27 FLA	28	29 D MON
30 D WAS	31					

February

SUN	MON	TUE	WED	THU	FRI	SAT
		1	2	3 ANA	4	5
6 *	7	8	9 TOR	10 EDM	11	12 D BUF
13	14	15 NJ	16	17 NYI	18	19 WAS
20 NYR	21	22 CHI	23	24 PIT	25	26 NYI
27	28	29 STL				

March

SUN	MON	TUE	WED	THU	FRI	SAT
			1 DAL	2	3	4 D BOS
5 NYI	6	7	8 TB	9 WAS	10	11
12 COL	13 PHO	14	15	16 MON	17	18 D NYR
19 D BOS	20	21 NSH	22	23 LA	24	25
26 D PIT	27	28 OTT	29	30	31	

April

SUN	MON	TUE	WED	THU	FRI	SAT
						1 D PIT
2 D CAR	3	4 ATL	5	6 ATL	7	8 D BOS
9 D NYR	10	11	12	13	14	15

1999-2000 SEASON

CLUB DIRECTORY

Chairman
Edward M. Snider
President and general manager
Bob Clarke
Chairman of the board emeritus
Joseph C. Scott
Executive vice president
Keith Allen
Chief operating officer
Ron Ryan
Assistant general manager
Paul Holmgren
Coach
Roger Neilson
Assistant coaches
Wayne Cashman
Craig Ramsay
Goaltending coach
Rejean Lemelin
Pro scout
Al Hill
Chief scout
Dennis Patterson
Scouts
Inge Hammarstrom
Vaclav Slansky
Simon Nolet
Evgeny Zimin
John Chapman
Blair Reid
Ticket manager
Ceil Baker
Vice president, sales
Jack Betson
Director of public relations
Zack Hill
Director of publications
Joe Klueg
Medical trainer
John Worley
Head equipment manager
Jim Evers
Equipment managers
Rusty Pearl
Anthony Oratorio
Orthopedic surgeon
Arthur Bartolozzi

DRAFT CHOICES

Rd.— Player	Ht./Wt.	Overall	Pos.	Last team
1— Maxime Ouellet	6-0/180	22	G	Quebec (QMJHL)
4— Jeff Feniak	6-5/210	119	D	Calgary (WHL)
6— Konstantin Rudenko		160		Cherepovec, Russia
7— Pavel Kasparik	6-2/198	200	C	Czech Republic
7— Vaclav Pletka	5-10/172	208	LW	Trinec, Czech Republic
8— David Nystrom	6-0/174	224	W	Frolunda, Sweden

MISCELLANEOUS DATA

Home ice (capacity)
First Union Center (19,519)
Address
First Union Center
3601 South Broad Street
Philadelphia, PA 19148
Business phone
215-465-4500
Club colors
Orange, white and black
Radio affiliation
WIP (610 AM)
TV affiliation
Comcast SportsNet (cable);
UPN 57 WPSG-TV

TRAINING CAMP ROSTER

No.	FORWARDS	Ht./Wt.	BORN Place	BORN Date	NHL exp.	1998-99 clubs
14	Mikael Andersson (LW)	5-11/184	Malmo, Sweden	5-10-66	14	Tampa Bay, Philadelphia
	Francis Belanger (LW)	6-2/216	Bellefuille, Que.	1-15-78	0	Chicoutimi (QMJHL), Philadelphia (AHL)
17	Rod Brind'Amour (LW/C)	6-1/200	Ottawa	8-9-70	11	Philadelphia
28	Marc Bureau (C/RW)	6-1/200	Trois-Rivieres, Que.	5-19-66	10	Philadelphia
	Simon Gagne (C)	6-0/165	Ste. Foy, Que.	2-29-80	0	Quebec (QMJHL)
	Mark Greig (RW)	5-11/190	High River, Alta.	1-25-70	6	Philadelphia (AHL), Philadelphia
	Paul Healey (RW)	6-2/185	Edmonton	3-20-75	2	Philadelphia (AHL)
20	Keith Jones (RW)	6-2/200	Brantford, Ont.	11-8-68	7	Colorado, Philadelphia
18	Daymond Langkow (C)	5-11/175	Edmonton	9-27-76	4	Cleveland (IHL), Tampa Bay, Philadelphia
10	John LeClair (LW)	6-3/226	St. Albans, Vt.	7-5-69	9	Philadelphia
88	Eric Lindros (C)	6-4/236	London, Ont.	2-28-73	7	Philadelphia
	Mike Maneluk (RW)	5-11/190	Winnipeg	10-1-73	1	Philadelphia, Chicago, N.Y. Rangers
21	Sandy McCarthy (RW)	6-3/225	Toronto	6-15-72	6	Tampa Bay, Philadelphia
	Richard Park (C)	5-11/190	Seoul, South Korea	5-27-76	5	Philadelphia (AHL), Philadelphia
11	Mark Recchi (RW)	5-10/185	Kamloops, B.C.	2-1-68	11	Montreal, Philadelphia
19	Mikael Renberg (RW)	6-2/215	Pitea, Sweden	5-5-72	6	Tampa Bay, Philadelphia
29	Roman Vopat (LW)	6-3/223	Litvinov, Czechoslovakia	4-21-76	4	Chicago, Los Angeles, Philadelphia
	Brian Wesenberg (RW)	6-3/173	Peterborough, Ont.	5-9-77	1	Philadelphia (AHL), Philadelphia
	Peter White (C)	5-11/200	Montreal	3-15-69	4	Philadelphia (AHL), Philadelphia
26	Valeri Zelepukin (LW)	6-1/195	Voskresensk, U.S.S.R.	9-17-68	8	Philadelphia
	Jason Zent (LW)	5-11/216	Buffalo	4-15-71	3	Philadelphia (AHL), Philadelphia
	DEFENSEMEN					
	Ryan Bast	6-2/190	Spruce Grove, Alta.	8-27-75	1	Saint John (AHL), Philadelphia (AHL), Philadelphia
	Jesse Boulerice	6-1/200	Plattsburgh, N.Y.	8-10-78	0	Philadelphia (AHL), New Orleans (ECHL)
2	Adam Burt	6-2/205	Detroit	1-15-69	11	Carolina, Philadelphia
	Mikhail Chernov	6-2/196	Prokopjevsk, U.S.S.R.	11-11-78	0	Philadelphia (AHL)
	Andy Delmore	6-0/180	Windsor, Ont.	12-26-76	1	Philadelphia (AHL), Philadelphia
37	Eric Desjardins	6-1/205	Rouyn, Que.	6-14-69	11	Philadelphia
24	Karl Dykhuis	6-3/214	Sept-Iles, Que.	7-8-72	7	Tampa Bay, Philadelphia
	Mark Eaton	6-2/205	Washington, Del.	5-6-77	0	Philadelphia (AHL)
	Jeff Feniak	6-5/210	Edmonton	1-31-81	0	Calgary (WHL)
	Jeff Lank	6-3/185	Indianhead, Sask.	3-1-75	0	Philadelphia (AHL)
3	Dan McGillis	6-2/225	Hawkesbury, Ont.	7-1-72	3	Philadelphia
	Dean Melanson	5-11/211	Antigonish, Nova Scotia	11-19-73	1	Rochester (AHL)
22	Luke Richardson	6-3/210	Kanata, Ont.	3-26-69	12	Philadelphia
6	Chris Therien	6-5/235	Ottawa	12-14-71	5	Philadelphia
	GOALTENDERS					
	Brian Boucher	6-1/180	Woonsocket, R.I.	8-1-77	0	Philadelphia (AHL)
	Maxime Ouellet	6-0/180	Beauport, Que.	6-17-81	0	Quebec (QMJHL)
	Jean-Marc Pelletier	6-3/195	Atlanta	3-4-78	1	Philadelphia (AHL), Philadelphia
34	John Vanbiesbrouck	5-8/176	Detroit	9-4-63	17	Philadelphia

1998-99 REVIEW

INDIVIDUAL STATISTICS

SCORING

	Games	G	A	Pts.	PIM	+/-	PPG	SHG	Shots	Shooting Pct.
Eric Lindros	71	40	53	93	120	35	10	1	242	16.5
John LeClair	76	43	47	90	30	36	16	0	246	17.5
Rod Brind'Amour	82	24	50	74	47	3	10	0	191	12.6
Eric Desjardins	68	15	36	51	38	18	6	0	190	7.9
Keith Jones*	66	18	31	49	78	29	2	0	124	14.5
Daniel McGillis	78	8	37	45	61	16	6	0	164	4.9
Mikael Renberg*	46	11	15	26	14	7	4	0	112	9.8
Valeri Zelepukin	74	16	9	25	48	0	0	0	129	12.4
Daymond Langkow*	56	10	13	23	24	-8	3	1	109	9.2
Chris Therien	74	3	15	18	48	16	1	0	115	2.6
Colin Forbes*	66	9	7	16	51	0	0	0	92	9.8
Jody Hull	72	3	11	14	12	-2	0	0	73	4.1
Marc Bureau	71	4	6	10	10	-2	0	0	52	7.7
Dmitri Tertyshny	62	2	8	10	30	-1	1	0	68	2.9
Dainius Zubrus*	63	3	5	8	25	-5	0	1	49	6.1
Mike Maneluk*	13	2	6	8	8	4	0	0	23	8.7
Chris Gratton*	26	1	7	8	41	-8	0	0	54	1.9
Steve Duchesne*	11	2	5	7	2	0	1	0	19	10.5
Mark Recchi*	10	4	2	6	6	-3	0	0	19	21.1
Petr Svoboda*	25	4	2	6	28	5	1	1	37	10.8
Dave Babych*	33	2	4	6	20	0	2	0	44	4.5

	Games	G	A	Pts.	PIM	+/-	PPG	SHG	Shots	Shooting Pct.
Karl Dykhuis*	45	2	4	6	32	-2	1	0	61	3.3
Luke Richardson	78	0	6	6	106	-3	0	0	49	0.0
Alexandre Daigle*	31	3	2	5	2	-1	1	0	26	11.5
Mark Greig	7	1	3	4	2	1	0	0	9	11.1
Mike Sillinger*	25	0	3	3	8	-9	0	0	23	0.0
Roman Vopat*	48	0	3	3	80	-3	0	0	25	0.0
Ron Hextall (goalie)	23	0	2	2	2	0	0	0	0	0.0
Shjon Podein*	14	1	0	1	0	-2	0	0	26	3.8
Ryan Bast	2	0	1	1	0	0	0	0	1	0.0
Andy Delmore	2	0	1	1	0	-1	0	0	2	0.0
Mikael Andersson*	7	0	1	1	0	1	0	0	11	0.0
Andrei Kovalenko*	13	0	1	1	2	-5	0	0	8	0.0
Sandy McCarthy*	13	0	1	1	25	-2	0	0	18	0.0
Adam Burt*	17	0	1	1	14	1	0	0	24	0.0
John Vanbiesbrouck (goalie)	62	0	1	1	12	0	0	0	0	0.0
Jean-Marc Pelletier (goalie)	1	0	0	0	0	0	0	0	0	0.0
Brian Wesenberg	1	0	0	0	5	1	0	0	0	0.0
Chris Joseph	2	0	0	0	2	0	0	0	1	0.0
Trent Klatt*	2	0	0	0	0	0	0	0	2	0.0
Dan Kordic	2	0	0	0	2	-1	0	0	0	0.0
Jason Zent	2	0	0	0	0	0	0	0	1	0.0
Peter White	3	0	0	0	0	0	0	0	0	0.0
Richard Park	7	0	0	0	0	-1	0	0	5	0.0
Craig Berube*	11	0	0	0	28	-3	0	0	7	0.0

GOALTENDING

	Games	Min.	Goals	SO	Avg.	W	L	T	Shots	Sv. Pct.
John Vanbiesbrouck	62	3712	135	6	2.18	27	18	15	1380	.902
Ron Hextall	23	1235	52	0	2.53	10	7	4	464	.888
Jean-Marc Pelletier	1	60	5	0	5.00	0	1	0	29	.828

Combination shutout: Hextall and Vanbiesbrouck.
Empty-net goals (do not count against a goaltender's average): Vanbiesbrouck 4.
*Played with two or more NHL teams.

RESULTS

OCTOBER

9— At N.Y. Rangers ....W......1-0
11—Anaheim ....W......4-1
16—At Tampa Bay ....W......5-2
17—At Carolina........................T....*1-1
20—San Jose ....W......3-1
22—New Jersey ....L......2-3
24—N.Y. Rangers......................T....*2-2
27—St. Louis...........................W......2-1
29—At Ottawa..........................L......1-3
31—At N.Y. Islanders...............L......2-3

NOVEMBER

1— Ottawa ....L......4-5
3— At Pittsburgh ....T....*4-4
7— Buffalo...............................T....*2-2
9— At Montreal.........................L......1-5
12—Florida ....L......1-2
14—New Jersey........................W......6-1
17—At Pittsburgh......................W......4-1
20—At Carolina ....W......3-1
22—At Florida..........................W....*2-1
25—At N.Y. Islanders...............L......2-4
27—Toronto.............................W......4-3
29—Vancouver ....W......6-2

DECEMBER

4— At Buffalo..........................L......0-3
5— Washington ....W......2-1
8— At New Jersey ....T....*5-5
10—New Jersey........................L....*4-5
12—At Toronto ....W......3-0
13—Edmonton...........................T....*2-2
17—Calgary ....T....*3-3
19—Chicago ....W......3-1
20—Tampa Bay.........................T....*2-2
23—At Boston ....W......2-1
26—At Chicago.......................W......3-2
28—At San Jose ....T....*1-1
29—At Calgary ....W....*4-3
31—At Vancouver....................W......6-2

JANUARY

3— At Edmonton ....T....*3-3
7— N.Y. Islanders ....W......5-0
9— Carolina...........................W......2-0
11—Nashville...........................W......8-0
13—At Washington ....W......3-0
16—Toronto ....L......3-4
18—At Ottawa ....W......5-0
21—Washington.......................W......4-1
26—Florida ....T....*3-3
28—Phoenix............................W......4-2
30—Tampa Bay ....W......6-2

FEBRUARY

1— Los Angeles ....W......4-2
4— Montreal...........................W......5-2
6— Boston ....T....*2-2
10—At Anaheim.........................L......4-5
11—At Los Angeles ....L......3-4
14—At Colorado ....T....*4-4
16—At Phoenix........................W......4-1
18—Montreal ....L......1-3
20—At Ottawa...........................L......1-4
21—Pittsburgh ....W......2-1
24—At Florida...........................L......3-5
26—At Tampa Bay ....L......1-4
28—At N.Y. Rangers ....L......5-6

MARCH

2— At Montreal..........................L......1-4
4— Ottawa ....L......0-5
6— N.Y. Islanders ....T....*3-3
7— At Buffalo............................T....*1-1
9— At N.Y. Islanders.................T....*2-2
11—Colorado..............................L......3-5
13—At Pittsburgh ....L......0-4
14—Dallas...................................T....*1-1
16—At St. Louis..........................L......2-5
21—Detroit ....W......5-4
22—At Toronto ....W......3-1
27—N.Y. Rangers ....W......3-1
28—At Detroit............................L....*2-3
30—Carolina ....T....*3-3

APRIL

1— At Nashville........................W......2-1
3— At Boston.............................L......0-3
5— N.Y. Rangers.......................L......1-5
8— Pittsburgh ....W......3-1
10—At Washington ....W......2-1
13—Buffalo ....T....*2-2
16—At New Jersey ....L....*2-3
18—Boston..............................W......3-1

*Denotes overtime game.

PHILADELPHIA FLYERS

PHOENIX COYOTES
WESTERN CONFERENCE/PACIFIC DIVISION

Coyotes Schedule

Home games shaded; D—Day game; *—All-Star Game at Toronto.

October

SUN	MON	TUE	WED	THU	FRI	SAT
					1	2 STL
3	4	5 ANA	6	7	8 CHI	9
10 D NYR	11 BUF	12	13	14 OTT	15	16 BOS
17	18	19	20	21	22 LA	23 WAS
24	25	26 EDM	27	28 VAN	29	30 D COL
31 ANA						

November

SUN	MON	TUE	WED	THU	FRI	SAT
	1	2	3 SJ	4	5 DAL	6
7	8	9	10 EDM	11	12 VAN	13
14 LA	15	16 CAL	17	18 LA	19	20 CHI
21	22	23	24	25 NJ	26 COL	27
28 D DET	29	30 NSH				

December

SUN	MON	TUE	WED	THU	FRI	SAT
			1	2 TB	3	4 ANA
5	6 DAL	7	8 FLA	9	10	11 PIT
12	13 BOS	14	15	16 PHI	17	18
19 D SJ	20	21 STL	22 ANA	23	24	25
26 LA	27	28 NYR	29	30	31	

January

SUN	MON	TUE	WED	THU	FRI	SAT
						1 EDM
2	3	4 DET	5	6 OTT	7	8 NJ
9	10 NYI	11	12 PIT	13	14	15 ANA
16	17 COL	18 NSH	19	20 BUF	21	22
23 SJ	24	25 CAR	26 ATL	27	28 WAS	29
30	31 DET					

February

SUN	MON	TUE	WED	THU	FRI	SAT
		1 SJ	2	3 DAL	4	5
6 *	7	8	9 LA	10	11	12 CAL
13	14 DET	15	16	17	18 DAL	19
20 ATL	21	22 MON	23 TOR	24	25 CAL	26
27 VAN	28	29				

March

SUN	MON	TUE	WED	THU	FRI	SAT
			1 CAR	2	3 DAL	4
5 D CHI	6	7 STL	8	9 NYI	10	11 VAN
12	13 PHI	14	15 STL	16	17 NSH	18
19	20	21 CHI	22	23 COL	24 SJ	25
26 ANA	27	28	29	30	31 CAL	

April

SUN	MON	TUE	WED	THU	FRI	SAT
						1 EDM
2	3 LA	4	5 NSH	6	7 SJ	8
9 D DAL	10	11	12	13	14	15

1999-2000 SEASON

CLUB DIRECTORY

Owner & governor
Richard Burke
General manager
Bobby Smith
Assistant general manager
Taylor Burke
Director of hockey operations
Laurence Gilman
Head coach
Bob Francis
Assistant coaches
Rick Bowness
Wayne Fleming
Goaltending coach
Benoit Allaire
Strength & conditioning coach
Stieg Theander
Athletic therapist
Gord Hart
Massage therapist
Jukka Nieminen
Equipment managers
Stan Wilson
Tony DaCosta
Assistant equipment manager
Tony Silva
V.p. of media and player relations
Richard Nairn
Manager of media relations
Rick Braunstein
Publications manager
Merit Tully

DRAFT CHOICES

Rd.— Player	Ht./Wt.	Overall	Pos.	Last team
1— Scott Kelman	6-2/185	15	C	Seattle (WHL)
1— Kirill Safronov	6-2/196	19	D	St. Petersburg, Russia
2— Brad Ralph	6-2/198	53	LW	Oshawa (OHL)
3— Jason Jaspers	6-0/185	71	C/LW	Sudbury (OHL)
4— Ryan Lauzon	5-10/185	116	C	Hull (QMJHL)
4— Preston Mizzi	5-11/193	123	C	Peterborough (OHL)
6— Erik Leverstrom	6-2/198	168	D	Grums, Sweden
8— Goran Bezina	6-3/203	234	D	Fribourg Jr., Switz.
9— Alexei Litvinenko		262		

MISCELLANEOUS DATA

Home ice (capacity)
America West Arena (16,210)
Address
Cellular One Ice Den
9375 E. Bell Road
Scottsdale, AZ 85260
Business phone
602-473-5600
Club colors
Red, green, sand, sienna and purple
Radio affiliation
KDUS (1060 AM) and KDKB (93.3 FM)
TV affiliation
FOX Sports Net Arizona, WB 61, KTVK (Channel 3)

TRAINING CAMP ROSTER

No.	FORWARDS	Ht./Wt.	BORN Place	BORN Date	NHL exp.	1998-99 clubs
17	Greg Adams (LW)	6-3/195	Nelson, B.C.	8-15-63	15	Phoenix
8	Daniel Briere (C)	5-9/160	Gatineau, Que.	10-6-77	2	Las Vegas (IHL), Phoe., Springfield (AHL)
29	Louie DeBrusk (LW)	6-2/215	Cambridge, Ont.	3-19-71	8	Las Vegas (IHL), Phoenix, Springfield (AHL), Long Beach (IHL)
19	Shane Doan (RW)	6-2/217	Halkirk, Alta.	10-10-76	4	Phoenix
11	Dallas Drake (RW)	6-0/185	Trail, B.C.	2-4-69	7	Phoenix
	Robert Francz (LW)	6-1/194	Bad Muskau, East Germany	3-30-78	0	Peterborough (OHL), Springfield (AHL)
39	Travis Green (C)	6-2/196	Castlegar, B.C.	12-20-70	7	Anaheim
47	Tavis Hansen (C/RW)	6-1/180	Prince Albert, Sask.	6-17-75	3	Springfield (AHL), Phoenix
	Jason Jaspers (C/LW)	6-0/185	Thunder Bay, Ont.	4-8-81	0	Sudbury (OHL)
	Scott Kelman (C)	6-2/185	Winnipeg	5-7-81	0	Seattle (WHL)
	Ryan Lauzon (C)	5-10/185	Halifax, Nova Scotia	10-8-80	0	Hull (QMJHL)
50	Trevor Letowski (C)	5-10/170	Thunder Bay, Ont.	4-5-77	1	Springfield (AHL), Phoenix
	Preston Mizzi (C)	5-11/193	Sault Ste. Marie, Ont.	12-22-80	0	Peterborough (OHL)
12	Rob Murray (C)	6-1/185	Toronto	4-4-67	8	Springfield (AHL), Phoenix
	David Oliver (RW)	5-11/190	Sechelt, B.C.	4-17-71	4	Ottawa, Houston (IHL)
	Brad Ralph (LW)	6-2/198	Ottawa	10-17-80	0	Oshawa (OHL)
16	Robert Reichel (C)	5-10/186	Litvinov, Czechoslovakia	6-25-71	8	New York Islanders, Phoenix
97	Jeremy Roenick (C)	6-0/192	Boston	1-17-70	11	Phoenix
	Mike Sullivan (LW)	6-2/196	Marshfield, Mass.	2-28-68	8	Phoenix
7	Keith Tkachuk (LW)	6-2/220	Melrose, Mass.	3-28-72	8	Phoenix
22	Rick Tocchet (RW)	6-0/214	Scarborough, Ont.	4-9-64	15	Phoenix
36	Juha Ylonen (C)	6-1/180	Helsinki, Finland	2-13-72	3	Phoenix
	DEFENSEMEN					
3	Keith Carney	6-2/205	Providence, R.I.	2-3-70	8	Phoenix
	David Cullen	6-1/195	St. Catherine's, Ont.	12-30-76	0	Univ. of Maine (Hockey East)
33	J.J. Daigneault	5-10/186	Montreal	10-12-65	14	Nashville, Phoenix
	Dan Focht	6-6/226	Reginan, Sask.	12-31-77	0	Springfield (AHL), Mississippi (ECHL)
48	Sean Gagnon	6-2/210	Sault Ste. Marie, Ont.	9-11-73	2	Springfield (AHL), Phoenix
5	Todd Gill	6-0/185	Brockville, Ont.	11-9-65	15	St. Louis, Detroit
	Juha Gustafsson	6-3/200	Espoo, Finland	4-26-79	0	
	Jay Leach	6-3/202	Syracuse, N.Y.	9-2-79	0	Providence College (Hockey East)
	Erik Lewerstrom	6-2/198	Grums, Sweden	5-28-80	0	Grums (Sweden Dv. 2)
20	Jyrki Lumme	6-1/210	Tampere, Finland	7-16-66	11	Phoenix
	Per-Anton Lundstrom	6-2/185	Umea, Sweden	9-29-77	0	Bjorkloven (Sweden)
	Mike Martone	6-2/200	Sault Ste. Marie, Ont.	9-26-77	0	Springfield (AHL), Mississippi (ECHL)
24	Stan Neckar	6-1/212	Ceske-Budejovice, Czech.	12-22-75	5	New York Rangers, Ottawa, Phoenix
27	Teppo Numminen	6-1/195	Tampere, Finland	7-3-68	11	Phoenix
5	Deron Quint	6-2/201	Durham, N.H.	3-12-76	4	Phoenix
	Kirill Safronov	6-2/196	Leningrad, U.S.S.R.	2-26-81	0	SKA St. Petersburg (Russian)
57	Robert Schnabel	6-6/216	Prague, Czechoslovakia	11-10-78	0	Springfield (AHL)
63	Radoslav Suchy	6-1/185	Poprad, Czechoslovakia	4-7-76	0	Springfield (AHL)
39	Brad Tiley	6-1/185	Markdale, Ont.	7-5-71	2	Springfield (AHL), Phoenix
	Ossi Vaananen	6-3/200	Vantaa, Finland	8-18-80	0	Jokerit Helsinki (Finland Jr.)
	GOALTENDERS					
	Patrick DesRochers	6-3/195	Penetang, Ont.	10-27-79	0	Sarnia (OHL), Kingston (OHL), Canadian nat'l team (Int'l)
42	Robert Esche	6-0/188	Utica, N.Y.	1-22-78	1	Springfield (AHL), Phoenix
35	Nikolai Khabibulin	6-1/196	Sverdlovsk, U.S.S.R.	1-13-73	5	Phoenix
30	Mikhail Shtalenkov	6-2/185	Moscow, U.S.S.R.	10-20-65	6	Edmonton, Phoenix

1998-99 REVIEW

INDIVIDUAL STATISTICS

SCORING

	Games	G	A	Pts.	PIM	+/-	PPG	SHG	Shots	Shooting Pct.
Jeremy Roenick	78	24	48	72	130	7	4	0	203	11.8
Keith Tkachuk	68	36	32	68	151	22	11	2	258	14.0
Rick Tocchet	81	26	30	56	147	5	6	1	178	14.6
Greg Adams	75	19	24	43	26	-1	5	0	176	10.8
Teppo Numminen	82	10	30	40	30	3	1	0	156	6.4
Dallas Drake	53	9	22	31	65	17	0	0	105	8.6
Jyrki Lumme	60	7	21	28	34	5	1	0	121	5.8
Oleg Tverdovsky	82	7	18	25	32	11	2	0	117	6.0
Juha Ylonen	59	6	17	23	20	18	2	0	66	9.1
Daniel Briere	64	8	14	22	30	-3	2	0	90	8.9
Shane Doan	79	6	16	22	54	-5	0	0	156	3.8
Bob Corkum	77	9	10	19	17	-9	0	0	146	6.2
Mike Stapleton	76	9	9	18	34	-6	0	2	106	8.5
Keith Carney	82	2	14	16	62	15	0	2	62	3.2
Robert Reichel*	13	7	6	13	4	2	3	0	50	14.0

	Games	G	A	Pts.	PIM	+/-	PPG	SHG	Shots	Shooting Pct.
Deron Quint	60	5	8	13	20	-10	2	0	94	5.3
Brad Isbister	32	4	4	8	46	1	0	0	48	8.3
Jim Cummins	55	1	7	8	190	3	0	0	26	3.8
Cliff Ronning*	7	2	5	7	2	3	2	0	18	11.1
J.J. Daigneault*	35	0	7	7	32	-8	0	0	27	0.0
Mike Sullivan	63	2	4	6	24	-11	0	1	66	3.0
Trevor Letowski	14	2	2	4	2	1	0	0	8	25.0
Tavis Hansen	20	2	1	3	12	-4	0	0	14	14.3
Rob Murray	13	1	2	3	4	2	0	0	11	9.1
Stephen Leach*	22	1	1	2	37	-6	0	0	23	4.3
Gerald Diduck	44	0	2	2	72	9	0	0	39	0.0
Jason Doig	9	0	1	1	10	2	0	0	0	0.0
Jamie Huscroft*	11	0	1	1	27	-1	0	0	7	0.0
Stan Neckar*	11	0	1	1	10	3	0	0	6	0.0
Jean-Francois Jomphe*	1	0	0	0	2	0	0	0	0	0.0
Scott Langkow (goalie)	1	0	0	0	0	0	0	0	0	0.0
Andrei Vasilyev	1	0	0	0	0	-2	0	0	0	0.0
Joe Dziedzic	2	0	0	0	0	-2	0	0	1	0.0
Sean Gagnon	2	0	0	0	7	-2	0	0	1	0.0
Robert Esche (goalie)	3	0	0	0	0	0	0	0	0	0.0
Mikhail Shtalenkov* (goalie)	4	0	0	0	0	0	0	0	0	0.0
Brian Noonan	7	0	0	0	0	-3	0	0	1	0.0
Brad Tiley	8	0	0	0	0	-1	0	0	1	0.0
Bryan Helmer*	11	0	0	0	23	2	0	0	11	0.0
Louie Debrusk	15	0	0	0	34	-2	0	0	6	0.0
Jim Waite (goalie)	16	0	0	0	2	0	0	0	0	0.0
Nikolai Khabibulin (goalie)	63	0	0	0	8	0	0	0	0	0.0

GOALTENDING

	Games	Min.	Goals	SO	Avg.	W	L	T	Shots	Sv. Pct.
Nikolai Khabibulin	63	3657	130	8	2.13	32	23	7	1681	.923
Mikhail Shtalenkov*	4	243	9	0	2.22	1	2	1	104	.913
Jim Waite	16	898	41	1	2.74	6	5	4	390	.895
Robert Esche	3	130	7	0	3.23	0	1	0	50	.860
Scott Langkow	1	35	3	0	5.14	0	0	0	17	.824

Empty-net goals (do not count against a goaltender's average): Khabibulin 6, Shtalenkov 1.
*Played with two or more NHL teams.

RESULTS

OCTOBER

11—Ottawa ....L 1-4
15—Colorado ....W 5-2
19—Boston ....W 3-1
22—At Dallas ....L 1-2
25—At Anaheim ....T *2-2
26—At Colorado ....W 5-1
28—At San Jose ....W 4-2

NOVEMBER

1—At Los Angeles ....W 3-0
6—Detroit ....W 3-1
10—Colorado ....T *1-1
11—At Dallas ....W 2-0
14—Tampa Bay ....W 4-1
18—Vancouver ....W 4-2
20—At San Jose ....W *2-1
21—Edmonton ....W *3-2
24—Chicago ....W 3-2
26—New Jersey ....W 3-2
28—At Los Angeles ....W 4-0

DECEMBER

2—At Edmonton ....L 3-4
5—At Calgary ....W 3-2
6—At Vancouver ....T *3-3
9—Montreal ....W 4-2
12—At Ottawa ....W 2-0
14—At Montreal ....T *2-2
16—At Toronto ....L 2-5
17—At St. Louis ....L 2-3
20—N.Y. Islanders ....W 4-2
22—At Detroit ....W 6-2
23—At Chicago ....L 3-4
26—At Los Angeles ....W 2-1
28—Los Angeles ....L 2-4
30—N.Y. Rangers ....W 3-1

JANUARY

1—Dallas ....L *1-2
5—Florida ....T *2-2
7—Edmonton ....L 1-7
8—At Anaheim ....L 1-4
11—Buffalo ....W 1-0
13—Pittsburgh ....W 5-3
15—At Nashville ....L 0-2
17—At Chicago ....T *1-1
19—St. Louis ....W 4-2
21—Anaheim ....T *3-3
26—At Buffalo ....T *1-1
28—At Philadelphia ....L 2-4
29—At N.Y. Islanders ....T *4-4
31—At Nashville ....W 5-1

FEBRUARY

2—Calgary ....T *2-2
4—San Jose ....W 3-1
6—Chicago ....W 3-0
8—San Jose ....L 0-3
10—Los Angeles ....W 3-0
13—At Colorado ....W 4-1
14—Anaheim ....L 1-5
16—Philadelphia ....L 1-4
19—At Tampa Bay ....L 2-4
20—At Florida ....L 1-7
22—At Pittsburgh ....L 1-4
24—At Washington ....W 2-1
26—At N.Y. Rangers ....L 0-3
28—At New Jersey ....L 1-4

MARCH

2—At Boston ....L 2-3
5—Detroit ....L 2-7
7—Nashville ....W 4-3
9—At San Jose ....L 2-4
11—Vancouver ....L 0-3
13—Anaheim ....W 1-0
15—Carolina ....T *5-5
17—At Detroit ....W 4-3
18—At St. Louis ....T *2-2
21—Los Angeles ....W 4-1
23—Dallas ....L 2-3
25—Washington ....W 4-2
27—Calgary ....W 2-1
29—At Vancouver ....L 0-1
30—At Edmonton ....W 7-4

APRIL

1—At Calgary ....W 4-1
6—San Jose ....L 0-1
9—Nashville ....L 3-4
11—At Anaheim ....L 0-3
14—At Dallas ....L 2-4
15—St. Louis ....L 4-6
17—Dallas ....W 2-0

*Denotes overtime game.

PITTSBURGH PENGUINS
EASTERN CONFERENCE/ATLANTIC DIVISION

Penguins Schedule

Home games shaded; D—Day game; *—All-Star Game at Toronto.

October

SUN	MON	TUE	WED	THU	FRI	SAT
					1 DAL	2
3	4	5	6	7 NJ	8 COL	9
10	11	12	13	14 NYR	15	16 CHI
17	18	19	20	21	22	23 CAR
24	25	26	27 ANA	28 LA	29	30 SJ
31						

November

SUN	MON	TUE	WED	THU	FRI	SAT
	1	2 LA	3	4 OTT	5	6 TB
7	8	9	10 MON	11	12 DET	13 NSH
14	15	16 BUF	17	18 TB	19	20 FLA
21	22	23 TOR	24	25	26 OTT	27 CAR
28	29	30 BUF				

December

SUN	MON	TUE	WED	THU	FRI	SAT
			1	2 SJ	3	4 TOR
5	6	7 NJ	8	9 WAS	10	11 PHO
12	13	14 BOS	15 CAR	16	17	18 FLA
19	20 MON	21 NYI	22	23 TB	24	25
26 CHI	27	28	29 WAS	30 NYI	31	

January

SUN	MON	TUE	WED	THU	FRI	SAT
						1
2 DET	3	4	5 NJ	6	7 TOR	8 PHI
9	10	11	12 PHO	13 COL	14	15 NSH
16	17	18	19 STL	20	21	22 MON
23 PHI	24	25 NYR	26	27 ATL	28	29 ANA
30	31 ATL					

February

SUN	MON	TUE	WED	THU	FRI	SAT
		1 WAS	2	3 NYI	4	5
6	*7	8	9 ATL	10	11 EDM	12 NYI
13	14 VAN	15	16 BUF	17	18	19 FLA
20	21 TB	22 NYR	23	24 PHI	25	26 BOS
27	28 OTT	29				

March

SUN	MON	TUE	WED	THU	FRI	SAT
			1 CAL	2	3	4 EDM
5	6	7	8 MON	9 OTT	10	11 NYR
12	13 NJ	14	15	16 FLA	17	18 D BOS
19 NYR	20	21 NYI	22	23	24 ATL	25
26 D PHI	27	28 NJ	29	30 WAS	31	

April

SUN	MON	TUE	WED	THU	FRI	SAT
						1 D PHI
2	3 CAR	4	5 TOR	6	7 BUF	8
9 BOS	10	11	12	13	14	15

1999-2000 SEASON
CLUB DIRECTORY

Owners/co-managing directors
Howard Baldwin
Roger Marino
Executive v.p. and general manager
Craig Patrick
Assistant general manager
Ed Johnston
Head coach
Kevin Constantine
Assistant coaches
Mike Eaves
Don Jackson
Troy Ward
Scouts
Les Binkley
Herb Brooks
Ralph Cox
Charlie Hodge
Mark Kelley
Greg Malone
Gilles Meloche
Vice president, general counsel
Greg Cribbs
Vice president, advertising
David Soltesz
V.p., finance and administration
Bob Vogel
V.p., communications
Tom McMillan
Controller
Kevin Hart
Director of media relations
Steve Bovino
Assistant director of media relations
Brian Coe
Vice president, ticket sales
Mark Anderson
Strength and conditioning coach
John Welday
Equipment manager
Steve Latin
Team physician
Dr. Charles Burke

DRAFT CHOICES

Rd.— Player	Ht./Wt.	Overall	Pos.	Last team
1— Konstantin Koltsov	6-0/187	18	LW	Cherepovec, Russia
2— Matt Murley	6-1/192	51	LW	Rensselaer (ECAC)
2— Jeremy Van Hoof	6-3/200	57	D	Ottawa (OHL)
3— Sebastien Caron	6-1/150	86	G	Rimouski (QMJHL)
4— Ryan Malone	6-3/190	115	LW	Omaha (USHL)
5— Tomas Skvaridlo	6-1/180	144	C/LW	Zvolen, Slovakia
5— Vladimir Malenkykh	6-1/187	157	D	Lada Togliatti, Russia
6— Doug Meyer	6-2/197	176	LW	Minnesota (WCHA)
7— Tom Kostopoulos	6-0/204	204	RW	London (OHL)
8— Darcy Robinson	6-4/220	233	D	Saskatoon (WHL)
9— Andrew McPherson	6-2/175	261	LW	Rensselaer (ECAC)

MISCELLANEOUS DATA

Home ice (capacity)
Civic Arena (16,958)
Address
Civic Arena
66 Mario Lemieux Place
Pittsburgh, PA 15219
Business phone
412-642-1300
Club colors
Black, gold and white
Radio affiliation
WDVE (102.5 FM)
TV affiliation
FOX Sports Pittsburgh

TRAINING CAMP ROSTER

No.	FORWARDS	Ht./Wt.	BORN Place	BORN Date	NHL exp.	1998-99 clubs
36	Matthew Barnaby (RW)	6-0/188	Ottawa	5-4-73	7	Buffalo, Pittsburgh
44	Rob Brown (RW)	5-11/185	Kingston, Ont.	4-10-68	10	Pittsburgh
	Robert Dome (C/LW)	6-0/215	Skalica, Czechoslovakia	1-29-79	1	Syracuse (AHL), Houston (IHL)
38	Jan Hrdina (C)	5-11/180	Hradec Kralove, Czech.	2-5-76	1	Pittsburgh
68	Jaromir Jagr (RW)	6-2/228	Kladno, Czechoslovakia	2-15-72	9	Pittsburgh
	Alexei Kolkunov (C)	6-0/201	Belgorod, U.S.S.R.	2-3-77	0	Syracuse (AHL)
	Konstantin Koltsov (LW)	6-0/187	Minsk, U.S.S.R.	4-17-81	0	Cherepovets (Russian)
27	Alexei Kovalev (RW)	6-2/210	Moscow, U.S.S.R.	2-24-73	7	New York Rangers, Pittsburgh
	Milan Kraft (C)	6-3/191	Plzen, Czechoslovakia	1-17-80	0	Prince Albert (WHL)
20	Robert Lang (C)	6-2/200	Teplice, Czechoslovakia	12-19-70	6	Pittsburgh
	Ryan Malone (LW)	6-3/190	Pittsburgh	12-1-79	0	Omaha (USHL)
	Eric Meloche (RW)	5-11/195	Montreal	5-1-76	0	Ohio State (CCHA)
	Doug Meyer (LW)	6-2/197	Bloomington, Minn.	2-21-81	0	Univ. of Minnesota (WCHA)
37	Kip Miller (C)	5-10/185	Lansing, Mich.	6-11-69	7	Pittsburgh
24	Ian Moran (RW)	6-0/206	Cleveland	8-24-72	5	Pittsburgh
95	Alexei Morozov (RW)	6-1/195	Moscow, U.S.S.R.	2-16-77	2	Pittsburgh
	Valentin Morozov (C)	5-11/196	Moscow, U.S.S.R.	6-1-75	0	Syracuse (AHL)
	Matt Murley (LW)	6-1/192	Troy, N.Y.	12-17-79	0	Rensselaer Poly. Inst. (ECAC)
32	Boris Protsenko (RW)	6-0/185	Kiev, U.S.S.R.	8-21-78	0	Syracuse (AHL)
	Tomas Skvaridlo (C/LW)	6-1/180	Zvolen, Czechoslovakia	6-19-81	0	HKM Zvolen (Slovakia Jrs.), Zvolen (Slovakia)
12	Martin Sonnenberg (LW)	6-1/185	Wetaskiwin, Alta.	1-23-78	1	Syracuse (AHL), Pittsburgh
82	Martin Straka (C)	5-10/175	Plzen, Czechoslovakia	9-3-72	7	Pittsburgh
9	German Titov (C)	6-1/201	Moscow, U.S.S.R.	10-16-65	6	Pittsburgh
	Alexander Zevakhin (C)	6-0/187	Perm, U.S.S.R.	6-4-80	0	CSKA Moscow (Russian)
	DEFENSEMEN					
22	Sven Butenschon	6-5/215	Itzehoe, West Germany	3-22-76	2	Houston (IHL), Pittsburgh
	Andrew Ference	5-10/190	Edmonton	3-17-79	0	Portland (WHL), Kansas City (IHL)
4	Kevin Hatcher	6-3/232	Detroit	9-9-66	15	Pittsburgh
11	Darius Kasparaitis	5-11/209	Elektrenai, U.S.S.R.	10-16-72	7	Pittsburgh
3	Chris Kelleher	6-2/220	Cambridge, Mass.	3-23-75	0	Syracuse (AHL)
	Vladimir Malenkikh	6-1/187	Togliatti, U.S.S.R.	10-1-80	0	Lada Togliatti (Russian)
	Josef Melichar	6-3/204	Ceske Budejovice, Czech.	1-20-79	0	Tri-City (WHL)
	Michal Rozsival	6-1/200	Vlasim, Czechoslovakia	9-3-78	0	Syracuse (AHL)
46	Pavel Skrbek	6-3/200	Kladno, Czechoslovakia	8-9-78	1	Syracuse (AHL), Pittsburgh
71	Jiri Slegr	6-0/217	Jihlava, Czechoslovakia	5-30-71	6	Pittsburgh
	Jeremy Van Hoof	6-3/200	Lindsay, Ont.	8-12-81	0	Ottawa (OHL)
5	Brad Werenka	6-1/221	Two Hills, Alta.	2-12-69	5	Pittsburgh
	GOALTENDERS					
30	Jean-Sebastien Aubin	5-11/179	Montreal	7-19-77	1	Kansas City (IHL), Pittsburgh
35	Tom Barrasso	6-3/210	Boston	3-31-65	16	Pittsburgh
	Sebastien Caron	6-1/150	Amqui, Que.	6-25-80	0	Rimouski (QMJHL)
40	Craig Hillier	6-1/174	Cole Harbour, Nova Scotia	2-28-78	0	Syracuse (AHL)
1	Peter Skudra	6-1/177	Riga, U.S.S.R.	4-24-73	2	Pittsburgh

1998-99 REVIEW

INDIVIDUAL STATISTICS

SCORING

	Games	G	A	Pts.	PIM	+/-	PPG	SHG	Shots	Shooting Pct.
Jaromir Jagr	81	44	83	127	66	17	10	1	343	12.8
Martin Straka	80	35	48	83	26	12	5	4	177	19.8
German Titov	72	11	45	56	34	18	3	1	113	9.7
Alexei Kovalev*	63	20	26	46	37	8	5	1	156	12.8
Robert Lang	72	21	23	44	24	-10	7	0	137	15.3
Kip Miller	77	19	23	42	22	1	1	0	125	15.2
Jan Hrdina	82	13	29	42	40	-2	3	0	94	13.8
Kevin Hatcher	66	11	27	38	24	11	4	2	131	8.4
Stu Barnes*	64	20	12	32	20	-12	13	0	155	12.9
Rob Brown	58	13	11	24	16	-15	9	0	78	16.7
Brad Werenka	81	6	18	24	93	17	1	0	77	7.8
Jiri Slegr	63	3	20	23	86	13	1	0	91	3.3
Alexei Morozov	67	9	10	19	14	5	0	0	75	12.0
Dan Kesa	67	2	8	10	27	-9	0	0	33	6.1
Bobby Dollas	70	2	8	10	60	-3	0	0	34	5.9
Ian Moran	62	4	5	9	37	1	0	1	65	6.2
Maxim Galanov	51	4	3	7	14	-8	2	0	44	9.1
Jeff Serowik	26	0	6	6	16	-4	0	0	26	0.0
Darius Kasparaitis	48	1	4	5	70	12	0	0	32	3.1

	Games	G	A	Pts.	PIM	+/-	PPG	SHG	Shots	Shooting Pct.
Matthew Barnaby*	18	2	2	4	34	-10	1	0	27	7.4
Tom Barrasso (goalie)	43	0	3	3	20	0	0	0	0	0.0
Martin Sonnenberg	44	1	1	2	19	-2	0	0	12	8.3
Patrick Lebeau	8	1	0	1	2	-2	0	0	4	25.0
Greg Andrusak	7	0	1	1	4	4	0	0	2	0.0
Victor Ignatjev	11	0	1	1	6	-3	0	0	15	0.0
Sean Pronger*	2	0	0	0	0	0	0	0	3	0.0
Harry York*	2	0	0	0	0	0	0	0	0	0.0
Ryan Savoia	3	0	0	0	0	-1	0	0	0	0.0
Pavel Skrbek	4	0	0	0	2	2	0	0	1	0.0
Brian Bonin	5	0	0	0	0	-2	0	0	2	0.0
Chris Tamer*	11	0	0	0	32	-2	0	0	2	0.0
J-Sebastien Aubin (goalie)	17	0	0	0	0	0	0	0	0	0.0
Sven Butenschon	17	0	0	0	6	-7	0	0	8	0.0
Neil Wilkinson	24	0	0	0	22	-2	0	0	11	0.0
Peter Skudra (goalie)	37	0	0	0	2	0	0	0	0	0.0
Tyler Wright	61	0	0	0	90	-2	0	0	16	0.0

GOALTENDING

	Games	Min.	Goals	SO	Avg.	W	L	T	Shots	Sv. Pct.
Jean-Sebastien Aubin	17	756	28	2	2.22	4	3	6	304	.908
Tom Barrasso	43	2306	98	4	2.55	19	16	3	993	.901
Peter Skudra	37	1914	89	3	2.79	15	11	5	822	.892

Empty-net goals (do not count against a goaltender's average): Skudra 6, Barrasso 4.
*Played with two or more NHL teams.

RESULTS

OCTOBER

10—At N.Y. Islanders .... W 4-3
14—At New Jersey .... W 3-1
17—N.Y. Rangers .... T *3-3
21—At Tampa Bay .... L 0-5
24—Toronto .... L 4-6
26—At Toronto .... W 2-0
28—At Calgary .... W 5-2
30—At Vancouver .... T *2-2
31—At Edmonton .... L 1-4

NOVEMBER

3—Philadelphia .... T *4-4
5—At Ottawa .... W 4-2
7—Boston .... T *0-0
10—N.Y. Islanders .... W 3-2
13—At New Jersey .... L 3-4
14—Florida .... W 4-0
17—Philadelphia .... L 1-4
19—At Tampa Bay .... W 5-1
21—Tampa Bay .... W 5-2
25—At Washington .... L 4-5
27—N.Y. Rangers .... T *2-2
28—At Montreal .... W 4-3

DECEMBER

1—Anaheim .... T *4-4
4—At Carolina .... T *3-3
5—At Boston .... L 1-2
12—At St. Louis .... W 4-3
15—Tampa Bay .... W *3-2
16—At Florida .... L 1-4
19—Washington .... W 3-0
21—At Toronto .... L 1-7
22—Los Angeles .... L 0-3
26—Ottawa .... W *2-1
30—Florida .... W 7-4

JANUARY

2—At Florida .... W 4-2
5—Calgary .... W 5-1
7—Carolina .... W 4-2
9—St. Louis .... W 2-1
13—At Phoenix .... L 3-5
15—At San Jose .... L 2-3
16—At Los Angeles .... W 5-1
18—At Anaheim .... L 3-5
21—N.Y. Islanders .... L 2-5
26—Carolina .... L 3-5
28—Toronto .... W 6-0
30—Boston .... W 5-2
31—At Montreal .... W 5-3

FEBRUARY

2—Buffalo .... W 5-3
5—Florida .... W 3-0
7—Detroit .... W 2-1
9—Montreal .... W *3-2
11—Vancouver .... W *6-5
13—At Nashville .... W *3-2
15—Washington .... W 7-3
17—At N.Y. Islanders .... L 1-3
19—At N.Y. Rangers .... L 1-6
21—At Philadelphia .... L 1-2
22—Phoenix .... W 4-1
25—At Colorado .... W 3-2
26—At Dallas .... L 4-6
28—At Washington .... L 3-4

MARCH

3—Montreal .... T *4-4
5—Edmonton .... T *2-2
7—Colorado .... L 1-3
9—New Jersey .... L 2-3
10—At Carolina .... W *3-2
13—Philadelphia .... W 4-0
16—Dallas .... T *2-2
17—At Tampa Bay .... W 2-0
20—Nashville .... T *1-1
21—At N.Y. Rangers .... T *2-2
23—Chicago .... W 5-2
25—At New Jersey .... L 3-5
27—Buffalo .... T *1-1
28—At Buffalo .... L *3-4
30—Ottawa .... L 4-6

APRIL

1—At Ottawa .... T *3-3
3—New Jersey .... L 2-4
5—At Buffalo .... L 1-3
8—At Philadelphia .... L 1-3
11—At Detroit .... W 3-0
15—At Boston .... L 2-4
17—N.Y. Islanders .... L 2-7
18—At N.Y. Rangers .... W *2-1

*Denotes overtime game.

ST. LOUIS BLUES
WESTERN CONFERENCE/CENTRAL DIVISION

Blues Schedule

Home games shaded; D—Day game; *—All-Star Game at Toronto.

October

SUN	MON	TUE	WED	THU	FRI	SAT
					1	2 PHO
3	4 LA	5	6 CAL	7	8	9 EDM
10	11	12	13 DET	14	15	16 TOR
17	18	19 CAL	20	21 EDM	22	23 NJ
24	25	26	27 NJ	28	29	30 DET
31						

November

SUN	MON	TUE	WED	THU	FRI	SAT
	1	2	3 COL	4	5 EDM	6
7 VAN	8	9 DAL	10	11	12 EDM	13 NYI
14	15	16	17 TOR	18 FLA	19	20 SJ
21	22 NSH	23	24 DET	25	26 BUF	27 CHI
28	29	30				

December

SUN	MON	TUE	WED	THU	FRI	SAT
			1	2 NSH	3	4 SJ
5 PHI	6	7 CAR	8	9	10 NSH	11 DAL
12	13	14 CAL	15	16	17	18 BOS
19	20	21 PHO	22	23 NSH	24	25
26 NSH	27 COL	28	29	30 SJ	31	

January

SUN	MON	TUE	WED	THU	FRI	SAT
						1 WAS
2	3 NYR	4 LA	5	6 MON	7	8 VAN
9	10	11 SJ	12	13 LA	14 ANA	15
16	17	18	19 PIT	20	21 CHI	22 NYR
23	24	25	26 OTT	27	28 DAL	29 COL
30	31					

February

SUN	MON	TUE	WED	THU	FRI	SAT
		1 CAL	2	3 VAN	4	5
6 *	7	8 DET	9	10 DET	11	12 ANA
13	14	15 ATL	16	17	18 NSH	19
20	21 ANA	22	23 SJ	24	25 COL	26
27 D CHI	28	29 PHI				

March

SUN	MON	TUE	WED	THU	FRI	SAT
			1	2 ATL	3	4 FLA
5	6	7 PHO	8	9 VAN	10	11 D ANA
12 D DAL	13	14	15 PHO	16	17 LA	18
19	20 WAS	21	22 CAR	23	24 TB	25
26 D CHI	27	28	29 TOR	30 BOS	31	

April

SUN	MON	TUE	WED	THU	FRI	SAT
						1 D DET
2 D OTT	3	4	5 CAL	6	7 CHI	8
9 D CHI	10	11	12	13	14	15

1999-2000 SEASON

CLUB DIRECTORY

Chairman of the board
Jerry Ritter

President & chief executive officer
Mark Sauer

Sr. vice president and general manager
Larry Pleau

Assistant general manager
John Ferguson Jr.

Head coach
Joel Quenneville

Assistant coaches
Jim Roberts
Mike Kitchen

Goaltending coordinator
Keith Allain

Athletic trainer
Ray Barile

Strength and conditioning coordinator
Robb Rogers

Video coordinator
Jamie Kompon

Equipment manager
Bert Godin

Assistant equipment manager
Eric Bechtol

Director of communications
Jeff Trammel

Assistant director of communications
Tony Ommen

Communications manager
Joe Campbell

DRAFT CHOICES

Rd.— Player	Ht./Wt.	Overall	Pos.	Last team
1— Barret Jackman	6-1/200	17	D	Regina (WHL)
3— Peter Smrek	6-1/194	85	D	Des Moines (USHL)
4— Chad Starling	6-6/207	114	D	Kamloops (WHL)
5— Trevor Byrne	6-3/200	143	D	Deerfield H.S., Mass.
6— Tore Vikingstad	6-4/202	180	W	Farjestad, Sweden
7— Phil Osaer	6-1/189	203	G	Ferris State (CCHA)
8— Colin Hemingway	5-11/167	221	W	Surrey (BCJHL)
8— Alexander Khavanov	6-1/192	232	D	Dynamo, Russia
9— Brian McMeekin	6-2/195	260	D	Cornell (ECAC)
9— James Desmarais	5-10/170	270	C	R.-Noranda (QMJHL)

MISCELLANEOUS DATA

Home ice (capacity)
Kiel Center (19,260)

Address
1401 Clark
St. Louis, MO 63103

Business phone
314-622-2500

Club colors
Blue, gold, navy and white

Radio affiliation
KMOX (1120 AM)

TV affiliation
KPLR (Channel 11) & FOX Sports Midwest

TRAINING CAMP ROSTER

No.	FORWARDS	Ht./Wt.	BORN Place	BORN Date	NHL exp.	1998-99 clubs
56	Lubos Bartecko (LW)	6-1/200	Kezmarok, Czechoslovakia	7-14-76	1	Worcester (AHL), St. Louis, Poprad (Slovakia)
	Derek Bekar (LW/C)	6-2/195	Burnaby, B.C.	9-15-75	0	Worcester (AHL)
10	Jim Campbell (RW)	6-3/204	Worcester, Mass.	2-3-73	4	St. Louis
39	Kelly Chase (RW)	6-0/200	Porcupine Plain, Sask.	10-25-67	10	St. Louis
22	Craig Conroy (C)	6-2/200	Potsdam, N.Y.	9-4-71	5	St. Louis
	Daniel Corso (C)	5-10/184	St. Hubert, Que.	4-3-78	0	Worcester (AHL)
14	Geoff Courtnall (LW)	6-1/204	Victoria, B.C.	8-18-62	16	St. Louis
38	Pavol Demitra (LW/C)	6-0/196	Dubnica, Czechoslovakia	11-29-74	6	St. Louis
32	Mike Eastwood (C)	6-3/209	Cornwall, Ont.	7-1-67	8	St. Louis
26	Michal Handzus (C)	6-5/210	Banska Bystrica, Czech.	3-11-77	1	St. Louis
55	Jochen Hecht (C)	6-1/191	Mannheim, West Germany	6-21-77	1	Worcester (AHL), St. Louis
	Reed Low (RW)	6-5/228	Moose Jaw, Sask.	6-26-76	0	Worcester (AHL)
21	Jamal Mayers (C)	6-1/205	Toronto	10-24-74	2	Worcester (AHL), St. Louis
	Ladislav Nagy (C)	5-11/183	Presov, Yugoslavia	6-1-79	0	Halifax (QMJHL)
9	Tyson Nash (LW)	6-0/180	Edmonton	3-11-75	1	Worcester (AHL), St. Louis
33	Scott Pellerin (LW)	5-10/189	Shediac, N.B.	1-9-70	6	St. Louis
	Andrei Podkonicky (C)	6-2/195	Zvolen, Czechoslovakia	5-9-78	0	Worcester (AHL)
15	Marty Reasoner (C)	6-1/185	Rochester, N.Y.	2-26-77	1	St. Louis, Worcester (AHL)
	Tyler Rennette (C)	6-2/180	North Bay, Ont.	4-16-79	0	Erie (OHL)
25	Pascal Rheaume (C)	6-1/209	Quebec City	6-21-73	3	St. Louis
77	Pierre Turgeon (C)	6-1/199	Rouyn, Que.	8-28-69	12	St. Louis
	Tore Vikingstad (C)	6-4/202	Oslo, Norway	10-8-75	0	Farjestad Karlstad (Sweden)
48	Scott Young (RW)	6-0/200	Clinton, Mass.	10-1-67	11	St. Louis
	DEFENSEMEN					
	Christian Backman	6-2/187	Alingsas, Sweden	4-28-80	0	Vastra Frolunda HC Goteborg (Sweden)
4	Marc Bergevin	6-1/214	Montreal	8-11-65	15	St. Louis
	Trevor Byrne	6-3/200	Hingham, Mass.	5-7-80	0	Deerfield Academy (USHS (East))
37	Jeff Finley	6-2/205	Edmonton	4-14-67	10	Hartford (AHL), N.Y. Rangers, St. Louis
42	Rory Fitzpatrick	6-2/205	Rochester, N.Y.	1-11-75	3	Worcester (AHL), St. Louis
	Tyler Harlton	6-3/210	Regina, Sask.	1-11-76	0	Worcester (AHL), Peoria (ECHL)
36	Bryan Helmer	6-1/190	Sault Ste. Marie, Ont.	7-15-72	1	Phoenix, Las Vegas (IHL), St. Louis, Worcester (AHL)
	Jan Horacek	6-4/206	Benesov, Czechoslovakia	5-22-79	0	Worcester (AHL), Slavia Praha (Czech Republic)
	Barret Jackman	6-1/200	Trail, B.C.	3-5-81	0	Regina (WHL)
2	Al MacInnis	6-2/209	Inverness, Nova Scotia	7-11-63	18	St. Louis
19	Chris McAlpine	6-0/208	Roseville, Minn.	12-1-71	4	St. Louis
	Jaroslav Obsut	6-1/185	Presov, Czechoslovakia	9-3-76	0	Manitoba (IHL), Augusta (ECHL), Worcester (AHL)
7	Ricard Persson	6-2/210	Ostersund, Sweden	8-24-69	4	Worcester (AHL), St. Louis
20	Rudy Poeschek	6-2/220	Terrace, B.C.	9-29-66	11	St. Louis
	Jame Pollock	6-1/190	Quebec City	6-16-79	0	Seattle (WHL)
	Libor Prochazka	6-1/190	Slany, Czechoslovakia	4-25-74	0	HC Zelezarny Trinec (Czech Republic)
44	Chris Pronger	6-6/210	Dryden, Ont.	10-10-74	6	St. Louis
6	Jamie Rivers	6-0/197	Ottawa	3-16-75	4	St. Louis
	Bryce Salvador	6-1/194	Brandon, Man.	2-11-94	0	Worcester (AHL)
	Matt Smith	6-5/229	Kent, England	12-23-76	0	Worcester (AHL), Peoria (ECHL)
	Peter Smrek	6-1/194	Martin, Czechoslovakia	2-16-79	0	Des Moines (USHL)
	Chad Starling	6-6/207	Saskatoon, Sask.	9-16-80	0	Kamloops (WHL)
	Didier Tremblay	6-1/198	Laval, Que.	5-4-79	0	Val-d'Or (QMJHL)
	GOALTENDERS					
31	Grant Fuhr	5-10/201	Spruce Grove, Alta.	9-28-62	18	St. Louis
	Brent Johnson	6-2/185	Farmington, Mich.	3-12-77	1	Worcester (AHL), St. Louis
29	Jamie McLennan	6-0/190	Edmonton, Alta.	6-30-71	5	St. Louis
30	Rich Parent	6-3/215	Montreal	1-12-73	2	Worcester (AHL), St. Louis
	Cody Rudkowsky	6-1/200	Willingdon, Alta.	7-21-78	0	Seattle (WHL)
1	Roman Turek	6-3/190	Pisek, Czechoslovakia	5-21-70	3	Dallas

1998-99 REVIEW

INDIVIDUAL STATISTICS

SCORING

	Games	G	A	Pts.	PIM	+/-	PPG	SHG	Shots	Shooting Pct.
Pavol Demitra	82	37	52	89	16	13	14	0	259	14.3
Pierre Turgeon	67	31	34	65	36	4	10	0	193	16.1
Al MacInnis	82	20	42	62	70	33	11	1	314	6.4
Scott Young	75	24	28	52	27	8	8	0	205	11.7
Chris Pronger	67	13	33	46	113	3	8	0	172	7.6
Scott Pellerin	80	20	21	41	42	1	0	5	138	14.5
Craig Conroy	69	14	25	39	38	14	0	1	134	10.4
Mike Eastwood	82	9	21	30	36	6	0	0	76	11.8
Pascal Rheaume	60	9	18	27	24	10	2	0	85	10.6

	Games	G	A	Pts.	PIM	+/-	PPG	SHG	Shots	Shooting Pct.
Terry Yake	60	9	18	27	34	-9	3	0	59	15.3
Jim Campbell	55	4	21	25	41	-8	1	0	99	4.0
Michel Picard	45	11	11	22	16	5	0	0	69	15.9
Lubos Bartecko	32	5	11	16	6	4	0	0	37	13.5
Michal Handzus	66	4	12	16	30	-9	0	0	78	5.1
Ricard Persson	54	1	12	13	94	4	0	0	52	1.9
Geoff Courtnall	24	5	7	12	28	2	1	0	60	8.3
Marty Reasoner	22	3	7	10	8	2	1	0	33	9.1
Kelly Chase	45	3	7	10	143	2	0	0	25	12.0
Jamal Mayers	34	4	5	9	40	-3	0	0	48	8.3
Tony Twist	63	2	6	8	149	0	0	0	23	8.7
Jamie Rivers	76	2	5	7	47	-3	1	0	78	2.6
Todd Gill*	28	2	3	5	16	-6	1	0	36	5.6
Blair Atcheynum*	12	2	2	4	2	2	0	0	23	8.7
Bryan Helmer*	29	0	4	4	19	3	0	0	38	0.0
Jeff Finley*	30	1	2	3	20	12	0	0	16	6.3
Chris McAlpine	51	1	1	2	50	-10	0	0	56	1.8
Marc Bergevin	52	1	1	2	99	-14	0	0	40	2.5
Rory Fitzpatrick	1	0	0	0	2	-3	0	0	0	0.0
Tyson Nash	2	0	0	0	5	-1	0	0	1	0.0
Jochen Hecht	3	0	0	0	0	-2	0	0	4	0.0
Jim Carey (goalie)	4	0	0	0	0	0	0	0	0	0.0
Brent Johnson (goalie)	6	0	0	0	0	0	0	0	0	0.0
Rich Parent (goalie)	10	0	0	0	2	0	0	0	0	0.0
Brad Shaw*	12	0	0	0	4	0	0	0	10	0.0
Rudy Poeschek	16	0	0	0	33	0	0	0	8	0.0
Jamie McLennan (goalie)	33	0	0	0	0	0	0	0	0	0.0
Grant Fuhr (goalie)	39	0	0	0	12	0	0	0	0	0.0

GOALTENDING

	Games	Min.	Goals	SO	Avg.	W	L	T	Shots	Sv. Pct.
Brent Johnson	6	286	10	0	2.10	3	2	0	127	.921
Jamie McLennan	33	1763	70	3	2.38	13	14	4	640	.891
Grant Fuhr	39	2193	89	2	2.44	16	11	8	827	.892
Rich Parent	10	519	22	1	2.54	4	3	1	193	.886
Jim Carey	4	202	13	0	3.86	1	2	0	76	.829

Empty-net goals (do not count against a goaltender's average): McLennan 3, Fuhr 1, Parent 1.
*Played with two or more NHL teams.

RESULTS

OCTOBER

10—At Boston....T....*3-3
12—At N.Y. Rangers....W......4-2
16—At Detroit....L......1-4
17—N.Y. Islanders....L......0-1
22—At Ottawa....W......5-3
24—Calgary....W......4-3
27—At Philadelphia....L......1-2
29—Detroit....W......3-1
31—Anaheim....T....*2-2

NOVEMBER

4—At Anaheim....W......3-1
5—At Los Angeles....T....*2-2
7—At San Jose....T....*2-2
10—Chicago....W......5-2
11—At Detroit....L......2-6
14—Nashville....W......5-1
19—At Nashville....L......2-3
21—Dallas....T....*3-3
24—Nashville....W......4-0
27—San Jose....L......2-4
28—Washington....W......4-2

DECEMBER

4—At Colorado....L......0-2
5—Colorado....L......1-3
8—Buffalo....T....*2-2
12—Pittsburgh....L......3-4
14—At Colorado....T....*0-0
15—At Dallas....L......3-7
17—Phoenix....W......3-2
19—Los Angeles....W......5-2
22—At N.Y. Islanders....T....*3-3
23—At New Jersey....L......2-4
26—Detroit....W......4-3
28—At Detroit....T....*4-4

JANUARY

1—At Nashville....W......6-5
2—N.Y. Rangers....L......0-1
4—Vancouver....W......4-0
7—Chicago....W......4-2
9—At Pittsburgh....L......1-2
11—At Montreal....L......1-3
13—At Buffalo....W......4-2
16—At Colorado....L......0-2
19—At Phoenix....L......2-4
21—Toronto....L......2-4
26—At San Jose....W......3-0
28—At Vancouver....W......4-2
30—At Calgary....L....*3-4

FEBRUARY

1—At Edmonton....W....*4-3
4—New Jersey....L......0-2
6—Anaheim....L......3-4
8—At Florida....W......5-4
10—At Tampa Bay....W......5-4
11—San Jose....L......1-5
13—Edmonton....L......2-3
15—Vancouver....W......8-1
18—Florida....T....*0-0
20—Nashville....L......3-4
22—Los Angeles....W......5-1
24—Chicago....L......1-3
26—At Calgary....W......4-2
28—At Chicago....W......3-1

MARCH

2—At Nashville....W......5-1
4—Toronto....L......0-4
7—At Dallas....L......3-4
9—Calgary....L......4-7
11—Montreal....L......0-3
13—Edmonton....W......6-4
14—At Chicago....W......5-2
16—Philadelphia....W......5-2
18—Phoenix....T....*2-2
20—Ottawa....L......2-3
22—Carolina....W......5-2
25—At Vancouver....W......4-1
26—At Edmonton....L......1-2
28—At Chicago....L......1-3

APRIL

1—Tampa Bay....W......3-0
3—Dallas....W......5-2
5—At Toronto....T....*2-2
7—At Washington....W......4-2
9—Detroit....T....*1-1
11—Colorado....L......2-4
14—At Anaheim....W......3-1
15—At Phoenix....W......6-4
18—At Los Angeles....W......3-2

*Denotes overtime game.

SAN JOSE SHARKS
WESTERN CONFERENCE/PACIFIC DIVISION

Sharks Schedule

Home games shaded; D—Day game; *—All-Star Game at Toronto.

October

SUN	MON	TUE	WED	THU	FRI	SAT
					1	2 CAL
3	4 CHI	5	6	7 EDM	8	9 DAL
10	11 D ANA	12	13 DAL	14 NSH	15	16 WAS
17	18	19 NYR	20 DET	21	22	23 BOS
24 LA	25	26	27	28 NSH	29	30 PIT
31 WAS						

November

SUN	MON	TUE	WED	THU	FRI	SAT
	1	2	3 PHO	4	5 PHI	6 DAL
7	8	9 VAN	10 CAL	11	12	13 D PHI
14	15 TOR	16 MON	17	18 OTT	19	20 STL
21	22	23 MON	24	25	26	27 D LA
28 NJ	29	30				

December

SUN	MON	TUE	WED	THU	FRI	SAT
			1 DET	2 PIT	3	4 STL
5	6 TB	7	8 COL	9	10 ATL	11
12	13	14 CHI	15	16	17	18
19 D PHO	20 DET	21	22 LA	23	24	25
26 D ANA	27 DAL	28	29	30 STL	31	

January

SUN	MON	TUE	WED	THU	FRI	SAT
						1 D NSH
2 CHI	3	4	5 EDM	6	7	8 FLA
9	10	11 STL	12	13	14	15 LA
16	17 D CHI	18	19 COL	20	21	22 ANA
23 PHO	24	25 COL	26	27	28 VAN	29 NYI
30	31					

February

SUN	MON	TUE	WED	THU	FRI	SAT
		1 PHO	2	3 COL	4	5
6 *	7	8 TB	9 FLA	10	11 ATL	12
13 D NJ	14	15 NYI	16	17	18 ANA	19
20	21	22	23 STL	24	25	26 LA
27	28	29 ANA				

March

SUN	MON	TUE	WED	THU	FRI	SAT
			1	2 NSH	3	4 CAR
5	6 NYR	7	8 DET	9	10	11
12	13 CAL	14	15 BUF	16	17 ANA	18
19 D DAL	20	21	22 VAN	23	24 PHO	25
26	27 EDM	28	29 LA	30	31	

April

SUN	MON	TUE	WED	THU	FRI	SAT
						1 CAL
2	3 EDM	4	5 DAL	6	7 PHO	8
9 D VAN	10	11	12	13	14	15

1999-2000 SEASON

CLUB DIRECTORY

Owner & chairman
George Gund III
Co-owner
Gordon Gund
President & chief executive officer
Greg Jamison
Sr. v.p. & chief operating officer
Frank Jirik
Exec. v.p., development
Matt Levine
Exec. v.p. and general manager
Dean Lombardi
Vice president, chief financial officer
Gregg Olson
Vice chairman
Tom McEnery
Assistant general manager
Wayne Thomas
Head coach
Darryl Sutter
Assistant coaches
Paul Baxter
Bob Berry
Bernie Nicholls
Strength & conditioning coach
Mac Read
Assistant to the general manager
Joe Will
Executive assistant
Brenda Will
Director of media relations
Ken Arnold
Media relations manager
Roger Ross
Media relations assistant
Chris Kelleher
Director of pro development
Doug Wilson
Head trainer
Tom Woodcock
Equipment manager
Mike Aldrich
Assistant equipment manager
Kurt Harvey
Team physician
Dr. Arthur J. Ting
Director of marketing and publicity
Beth Brigino

DRAFT CHOICES

Rd.— Player	Ht./Wt.	Overall	Pos.	Last team
1— Jeff Jillson	6-3/219	14	D	Michigan (CCHA)
3— Mark Concannon	6-0/200	82	LW	Winchendon H.S.
4— Willie Levesque	6-0/195	111	RW	Northeastern (H. East)
5— Nicholas Dimitrakos	5-11/190	155	RW	Maine (H. East)
8— Eric Betournay	6-1/176	229	C	A.-Bathurst (QMJHL)
8— Doug Murray	6-3/220	241	D	Apple Core (EJHL)
9— Hannes Hyvonen	6-2/196	257	D	TPS Turko, Finland

MISCELLANEOUS DATA

Home ice (capacity)
San Jose Arena (17,483)
Address
525 West Santa Clara Street
San Jose, CA 95113
Business phone
408-287-7070
Club colors
Deep pacific teal, shimmering gray, burnt orange and black
Radio affiliation
KARA (105.7 FM)
TV affiliation
FOX Sports Bay Area

TRAINING CAMP ROSTER

No.	FORWARDS	Ht./Wt.	BORN Place	BORN Date	NHL exp.	1998-99 clubs
13	Jamie Baker (C)	6-0/195	Nepean, Ont.	8-31-66	10	San Jose
	Matt Bradley (RW)	6-2/195	Stittsville, Ont.	6-13-78	0	Kentucky (AHL)
	Michal Bros (C)	6-1/195	Olomouc, Czechoslovakia	1-25-76	0	Petra Vsetin (Czech Republic)
	Jonathan Cheechoo (RW)	6-0/205	Moose Factory, Ont.	7-15-80	0	Belleville (OHL)
	Adam Colagiacomo (RW)	6-2/205	Toronto	3-17-79	0	Plymouth (OHL)
	Mark Concannon (LW)	6-0/200	Boston	6-12-80	0	Winchendon (USHS (East))
25	Mike Craig (RW)	6-1/188	London, Ont.	6-6-71	8	Kentucky (AHL), San Jose
32	Murray Craven (LW)	6-3/190	Medicine Hat, Alta.	7-20-64	17	San Jose
25	Vincent Damphousse (C)	6-1/190	Montreal	12-17-67	13	Montreal, San Jose
	Nicholas Dimitrakos	5-11/190	Boston	5-21-79	0	Univ. of Maine (Hockey East)
39	Jeff Friesen (LW)	6-0/200	Meadow Lake, Sask.	8-5-76	5	San Jose
21	Tony Granato (RW)	5-10/180	Downers Grove, Ill.	6-25-64	11	San Jose
15	Alexander Korolyuk (RW)	5-9/190	Moscow, U.S.S.R.	1-15-76	2	Kentucky (AHL), San Jose
	Eric Landry (C)	5-11/185	Gatineau, Que.	1-20-75	2	Saint John (AHL), Calgary
	Willie Levesque (RW)	6-0/195	Oak Bluffs, Mass.	1-22-80	0	Northeastern Univ. (Hockey East)
14	Patrick Marleau (C)	6-2/205	Swift Current, Sask.	9-15-79	2	San Jose
37	Stephane Matteau (LW)	6-4/220	Rouyn-Noranda, Que.	9-2-69	9	San Jose
33	Brantt Myhres (RW)	6-3/220	Edmonton	3-18-74	4	San Jose, Kentucky (AHL)
11	Owen Nolan (RW)	6-1/205	Belfast, Northern Ireland	2-12-72	9	San Jose
18	Mike Ricci (C)	6-0/190	Scarborough, Ont.	10-27-71	9	San Jose
	Teemu Riihijarvi (RW)	6-6/220	Espoo, Finland	3-1-77	0	Blues Espoo (Finland)
8	Jarrod Skalde (C)	6-0/170	Niagara Falls, Ont.	2-26-71	7	San Jose, Kentucky (AHL)
	Mark Smith (C)	5-10/190	Eyebrow, Sask.	10-24-77	0	Kentucky (AHL)
22	Ronnie Stern (RW)	6-0/200	Ste. Agatha Des Mont, Que.	1-11-67	12	San Jose
19	Marco Sturm (C)	6-0/195	Dingolfing, West Germany	9-8-78	2	San Jose
	Niklas Sundstrom (LW)	6-0/195	Ornskoldsvik, Sweden	6-6-75	4	New York Rangers
12	Ron Sutter (C)	6-0/180	Viking, Alta.	12-2-63	17	San Jose
	DEFENSEMEN					
	Christian Gosselin	6-5/235	Laval, Que.	8-21-76	0	Kentucky (AHL)
6	Scott Hannan	6-1/210	Richmond, B.C.	1-23-79	1	San Jose, Kelowna (WHL), Kentucky (AHL)
23	Shawn Heins	6-4/215	Eganville, Ont.	12-24-73	1	Canadian nat'l team (Int'l), San Jose, Kentucky (AHL)
	Jeff Jillson	6-3/219	North Smithfield, R.I.	7-24-80	0	Univ. of Michigan (CCHA)
27	Bryan Marchment	6-1/205	Scarborough, Ont.	5-1-69	11	San Jose
	Jeff Norton	6-2/200	Acton, Mass.	11-25-65	12	Florida, San Jose
10	Marcus Ragnarsson	6-1/215	Ostervala, Sweden	8-13-71	4	San Jose
40	Mike Rathje	6-5/230	Mannville, Alta.	5-11-74	6	San Jose
3	Bob Rouse	6-2/220	Surrey, B.C.	6-18-64	16	San Jose
	Brad Stuart	6-2/210	Rocky Mountain House, Alta.	11-6-79	0	Regina (WHL), Calgary (WHL)
20	Gary Suter	6-0/205	Madison, Wis.	6-24-64	14	San Jose
42	Andy Sutton	6-6/240	Kingston, Ont.	3-10-75	1	San Jose, Kentucky (AHL)
	GOALTENDERS					
	Johan Hedberg	5-11/180	Leksand, Sweden	5-5-73	0	Leksand (Sweden)
	Miikka Kiprusoff	6-0/180	Turku, Finland	10-26-76	0	TPS Turku (Finland)
	Michel Larocque	5-11/200	Lahr, West Germany	10-3-76	0	Boston University (Hockey East)
	John Nabokov	6-0/180	Ust-Kamenogorsk, U.S.S.R.	7-25-75	0	Kentucky (AHL)
31	Steve Shields	6-3/215	Toronto	7-19-72	4	San Jose
	Vesa Toskala	5-9/172	Tampere, Finland	5-20-77	0	Ilves Tampere (Finland)
29	Mike Vernon	5-9/180	Calgary	2-24-63	16	San Jose

1998-99 REVIEW

INDIVIDUAL STATISTICS

SCORING

	Games	G	A	Pts.	PIM	+/-	PPG	SHG	Shots	Shooting Pct.
Jeff Friesen	78	22	35	57	42	3	10	1	215	10.2
Joe Murphy	76	25	23	48	73	10	7	0	176	14.2
Patrick Marleau	81	21	24	45	24	10	4	0	134	15.7
Owen Nolan	78	19	26	45	129	16	6	2	207	9.2
Mike Ricci	82	13	26	39	68	1	2	1	98	13.3
Marco Sturm	78	16	22	38	52	7	3	2	140	11.4
Bill Houlder	76	9	23	32	40	8	7	0	115	7.8
Alexander Korolyuk	55	12	18	30	26	3	2	0	96	12.5
Stephane Matteau	68	8	15	23	73	2	0	0	72	11.1
Jeff Norton*	69	4	18	22	42	2	2	0	68	5.9
Ronnie Stern	78	7	9	16	158	-3	1	0	94	7.4

	Games	G	A	Pts.	PIM	+/-	PPG	SHG	Shots	Shooting Pct.
Dave Lowry	61	6	9	15	24	-5	2	0	58	10.3
Mike Rathje	82	5	9	14	36	15	2	0	67	7.5
Murray Craven	43	4	10	14	18	-3	0	1	55	7.3
Vincent Damphousse*	12	7	6	13	4	3	3	0	43	16.3
Marcus Ragnarsson	74	0	13	13	66	7	0	0	87	0.0
Tony Granato	35	6	6	12	54	4	0	1	65	9.2
Bob Rouse	70	0	11	11	44	0	0	0	75	0.0
Ron Sutter	59	3	6	9	40	-8	0	0	67	4.5
Bryan Marchment	59	2	6	8	101	-7	0	0	49	4.1
Andrei Zyuzin	25	3	1	4	38	5	2	0	44	6.8
Stephen Guolla	14	2	2	4	6	3	0	0	22	9.1
Andy Sutton	31	0	3	3	65	-4	0	0	24	0.0
Jarrod Skalde	17	1	1	2	4	-6	0	0	17	5.9
Scott Hannan	5	0	2	2	6	0	0	0	4	0.0
Bernie Nicholls	10	0	2	2	4	-4	0	0	11	0.0
Brantt Myhres	30	1	0	1	116	-2	0	0	7	14.3
Jamie Baker	1	0	1	1	0	1	0	0	1	0.0
Alex Hicks*	4	0	1	1	4	-1	0	0	4	0.0
Shawn Burr	18	0	1	1	29	-3	0	0	22	0.0
Steve Shields (goalie)	37	0	1	1	6	0	0	0	0	0.0
Mike Craig	1	0	0	0	0	-1	0	0	1	0.0
Sean Gauthier (goalie)	1	0	0	0	0	0	0	0	0	0.0
Gary Suter	1	0	0	0	0	0	0	0	1	0.0
Shawn Heins	5	0	0	0	13	0	0	0	4	0.0
Mike Vernon (goalie)	49	0	0	0	8	0	0	0	0	0.0

GOALTENDING

	Games	Min.	Goals	SO	Avg.	W	L	T	Shots	Sv. Pct.
Sean Gauthier	1	3	0	0	0.00	0	0	0	2	1.000
Steve Shields	37	2162	80	4	2.22	15	11	8	1011	.921
Mike Vernon	49	2831	107	4	2.27	16	22	10	1200	.911

Empty-net goals (do not count against a goaltender's average): Vernon 3, Shields 1.

*Played with two or more NHL teams.

RESULTS

OCTOBER

9— At Calgary† ....T....*3-3
10— Calgary† ....L......3-5
18— Boston ....L......0-3
20— At Philadelphia ....L......1-3
22— At Chicago ....T....*2-2
24— At Dallas ....L......1-2
28— Phoenix ....L......2-4
29— At Colorado ....L......2-4
31— Tampa Bay ....W......6-1

NOVEMBER

4— Dallas ....W......4-0
6— At Anaheim ....T....*2-2
7— St. Louis ....T....*2-2
10— Nashville ....L......2-4
12— Carolina ....W......3-0
18— Los Angeles ....W......5-4
20— Phoenix ....L....*1-2
21— N.Y. Rangers ....T....*2-2
23— At Dallas ....L......2-3
25— At Carolina ....L......0-3
27— At St. Louis ....W......4-2
29— At Detroit ....L......1-4

DECEMBER

2— Dallas ....L......0-3
4— Detroit ....T....*2-2
6— Anaheim ....L......1-2
9— At Dallas ....T....*3-3
10— At Nashville ....L......1-2
12— Washington ....W......2-1
15— N.Y. Islanders ....L......0-1
17— Nashville ....W......3-1
19— Colorado ....W......2-1
23— At Edmonton ....W......5-3
26— Vancouver ....W......2-0
28— Philadelphia ....T....*1-1
30— At Los Angeles ....L......1-5

JANUARY

2— At N.Y. Islanders ....W....*4-3
4— At N.Y. Rangers ....L......3-4
5— At New Jersey ....T....*3-3
7— At Nashville ....W......4-3
9— Buffalo ....T....*2-2
11— Los Angeles ....W......4-0
13— Dallas ....L......1-2
15— Pittsburgh ....W......3-2
16— Calgary ....T....*3-3
18— New Jersey ....W......3-1
21— Edmonton ....T....*3-3
26— St. Louis ....L......0-3
30— At Colorado ....L......0-5

FEBRUARY

1— Chicago ....W......5-1
4— At Phoenix ....L......1-3
6— At Los Angeles ....L......0-2
8— At Phoenix ....W......3-0
10— At Chicago ....W......5-2
11— At St. Louis ....W......5-1
13— At Tampa Bay ....W......3-1
15— At Florida ....T....*2-2
17— At Detroit ....L......1-3
19— At Buffalo ....L......2-4
20— At Washington ....L......1-3
24— Vancouver ....T....*1-1
26— At Anaheim ....L......1-3
27— Anaheim ....L......1-4

MARCH

1— At Calgary ....W......2-1
3— At Vancouver ....W......4-3
6— Chicago ....L......0-4
9— Phoenix ....W......4-2
12— Detroit ....W......2-0
13— Ottawa ....W......3-2
17— Florida ....W......4-2
20— At Boston ....T....*2-2
22— At Montreal ....T....*1-1
24— At Toronto ....W......8-5
26— At Ottawa ....T....*1-1
28— At Edmonton ....L......2-5
31— Colorado ....L......2-3

APRIL

2— At Vancouver ....W......7-0
3— Vancouver ....W......5-2
6— At Phoenix ....W......1-0
8— At Los Angeles ....L......2-3
9— At Anaheim ....W......4-1
12— Edmonton ....L....*4-5
16— Los Angeles ....L......0-2
17— Anaheim ....T....*3-3

*Denotes overtime game.

†Game played in Tokyo, Japan.

TAMPA BAY LIGHTNING
EASTERN CONFERENCE/SOUTHEAST DIVISION

Lightning Schedule

Home games shaded; D—Day game; *—All-Star Game at Toronto.

October

SUN	MON	TUE	WED	THU	FRI	SAT
					1	2 NYI
3	4	5	6	7 LA	8	9 NJ
10	11	12	13	14	15 ANA	16 ATL
17	18	19 VAN	20	21	22	23 CAL
24	25	26	27 BUF	28 BOS	29	30 DAL
31						

November

SUN	MON	TUE	WED	THU	FRI	SAT
	1	2	3 ATL	4	5	6 PIT
7 DET	8	9 WAS	10	11	12 BUF	13 CAR
14	15	16	17 ATL	18 PIT	19	20 PHI
21	22 PHI	23	24 NYR	25	26 CAR	27
28 BUF	29	30				

December

SUN	MON	TUE	WED	THU	FRI	SAT
			1 ANA	2 PHO	3	4 LA
5	6 SJ	7	8	9	10 CAR	11
12	13	14 NSH	15	16	17	18 PHI
19 NYR	20	21 TOR	22	23 PIT	24	25
26 ATL	27 FLA	28	29	30	31	

January

SUN	MON	TUE	WED	THU	FRI	SAT
						1 D FLA
2	3	4	5 VAN	6	7 EDM	8 CAL
9	10	11 NJ	12	13 NYI	14	15 FLA
16	17 D WAS	18	19	20 BOS	21	22 NYI
23	24 WAS	25 BUF	26	27	28 EDM	29 ATL
30	31					

February

SUN	MON	TUE	WED	THU	FRI	SAT
		1 TOR	2	3 MON	4	5
6 *	7	8 SJ	9	10 NYI	11	12 CAR
13	14	15 NYR	16	17 OTT	18	19 CAR
20	21 PIT	22	23	24 OTT	25	26 NSH
27 DET	28	29				

March

SUN	MON	TUE	WED	THU	FRI	SAT
			1 WAS	2	3 CHI	4 COL
5	6	7	8 PHI	9	10 FLA	11
12 CHI	13	14 MON	15 NYR	16	17 NJ	18
19 D WAS	20	21 BOS	22	23	24 STL	25
26 MON	27	28 DAL	29	30 OTT	31	

April

SUN	MON	TUE	WED	THU	FRI	SAT
						1 FLA
2 NJ	3	4 BOS	5	6 MON	7	8 TOR
9 OTT	10	11	12	13	14	15

1999-2000 SEASON
CLUB DIRECTORY

Chief executive officer & governor
Thomas Wilson
President
Ron Campbell
Vice president & general manager
Rick Dudley
Assistant general manager
Jay Feaster
Senior advisor to the general manager
Cliff Fletcher
Head coach
Steve Ludzik
Assistant coach
John Cullen
Goaltending consultant
Jeff Reese
Vice president of public relations
Bill Wickett
Director of public relations
Jay Preble
Media relations manager
Brian Potter

DRAFT CHOICES

Rd.— Player	Ht./Wt.	Overall	Pos.	Last team
2— Sheldon Keefe	5-10/176	47	RW	Barrie (OHL)
3— Evegeny Konstantinov	6-0/167	67	G	Ak-Bars Kazan, Russia
3— Brett Scheffelmaier	6-5/200	75	D	Medicine Hat (WHL)
3— Jimmie Olvestad	6-1/194	88	LW	Djurgarden, Sweden
5— Kaspars Astashenko	6-2/183	127	D	Riga HC, Latvia
5— Michal Lanicek	6-1/172	148	G	Slavia Praha, Czech
6— Fedor Fedorov	6-3/187	182	C	Port Huron (UHL)
7— Ivan Rachunek	5-10/172	187	LW	ZPS-Barum-Zlin, Czech
8— Erkki Rajamaki	6-1/189	216	W	IFK Helsinki, Finland
9— Mikko Kuparinen	6-3/211	244	D	Grand Rapids (IHL)

MISCELLANEOUS DATA

Home ice (capacity)
Ice Palace (19,758)
Address
401 Channelside Drive
Tampa, Fla. 33602
Business phone
813-229-2658
Club colors
Black, blue, silver and white
Radio affiliation
WDAE (1250 AM)
TV affiliation
Sunshine Network (Cable)

TAMPA BAY LIGHTNING

TRAINING CAMP ROSTER

No.	FORWARDS	Ht./Wt.	BORN Place	BORN Date	NHL exp.	1998-99 clubs
	Eric Beaudoin (LW)	6-3/188	Ottawa	5-3-80	0	Guelph (OHL)
	Shawn Burr (LW/C)	6-1/205	Sarnia, Ont.	7-1-66	15	San Jose, Kentucky (AHL)
21	Alexandre Daigle (C/RW)	6-0/202	Montreal	2-7-75	6	Philadelphia, Tampa Bay
43	Xavier Delisle (RW)	5-11/193	Quebec City	5-24-77	1	Cleveland (IHL), Tampa Bay
	Matt Elich (RW)	6-3/196	Detroit	9-22-79	0	Kingston (OHL)
	Fedor Fedorov (C)	6-3/187	Moscow, U.S.S.R.	6-11-81	0	Port Huron (UHL)
27	Colin Forbes (LW)	6-3/205	New Westminister, B.C.	2-16-76	3	Philadelphia, Tampa Bay
77	Chris Gratton (C)	6-3/219	Brantford, Ont.	7-5-75	6	Philadelphia, Tampa Bay
	Steve Guolla (C)	6-0/180	Scarborough, Ont.	3-15-73	3	Kentucky (AHL), San Jose
38	Andreas Johansson	6-2/209	Hofors, Sweden	5-19-73	4	Ottawa
	Sheldon Keefe (RW)	5-11/176	Brampton, Ont.	9-17-80	0	Toronto (OHL), Barrie (OHL)
11	Steve Kelly (C)	6-1/200	Vancouver	10-26-76	3	Tampa Bay, Cleveland (IHL)
8	Vincent Lecavalier (C)	6-4/190	Ile-Bizard, Que.	4-21-80	1	Tampa Bay
9	Michael Nylander (C)	5-11/195	Stockholm, Sweden	10-3-72	6	Calgary, Tampa Bay
	Jimmie Olvestad (LW)	6-1/194	Stockholm, Sweden	2-16-80	0	Djur. Stockholm (Sweden)
14	Robert Petrovicky (C)	5-11/180	Kosice, Czechoslovakia	10-26-73	6	Grand Rapids (IHL), Tampa Bay
	Brad Richards (LW)	6-0/175	Montague, P.E.I.	5-2-80	0	Rimouski (QMJHL)
44	Stephane Richer (RW)	6-3/226	Buckingham, Que.	6-7-66	15	Tampa Bay
26	Mike Sillinger (C/RW)	5-11/191	Regina, Sask.	6-29-71	9	Philadelphia, Tampa Bay
	Eero Somervuori (RW)	5-10/167	Jarvenpaa, Finland	2-7-79	0	Jokerit Helsinki (Finland)
20	Corey Spring (C)	6-4/214	Cranbrook, B.C.	5-31-71	2	Cleveland (IHL), Tampa Bay
	Jan Sulc (C)	6-3/180	Litvinov, Czechoslovakia	2-17-79	0	Kingston (OHL), Owen Sound (OHL)
16	Darcy Tucker (C)	5-11/185	Castor, Alta.	3-15-75	4	Tampa Bay
	DEFENSEMEN					
	Kaspars Astashenko	6-2/183	Riga, U.S.S.R.	2-7-75	0	Cincinnati (IHL)
55	Drew Bannister	6-2/200	Belleville, Ont.	9-4-74	4	Las Vegas (IHL), Tampa Bay
6	Karel Betik	6-2/210	Karvina, Czechoslovakia	10-28-78	1	Cleveland (IHL), Tampa Bay
4	Cory Cross	6-5/219	Lloydminster, Alta.	7-31-75	6	Tampa Bay
5	Jassen Cullimore	6-5/220	Simcoe, Ont.	12-4-72	5	Tampa Bay
3	Sergey Gusev	6-1/195	Nizhny Tagil, U.S.S.R.	7-31-75	2	Dallas, Michigan (IHL), Tampa Bay
	Bill Houlder	6-2/215	Thunder Bay, Ont.	3-11-67	12	San Jose
	Kyle Kos	6-3/197	Hope, B.C.	5-25-79	0	Red Deer (WHL), Kamloops (WHL)
13	Pavel Kubina	6-3/213	Caledna, Czechoslovakia	4-15-77	2	Tampa Bay, Cleveland (IHL)
71	Mario Larocque	6-2/195	Montreal	4-24-78	1	Cleveland (IHL), Tampa Bay
22	Paul Mara	6-3/185	Ridgewood, N.J.	9-7-79	1	Plymouth (OHL), Tampa Bay
2	Mike McBain	6-2/203	Kimberley, B.C.	1-12-77	2	Cleveland (IHL), Tampa Bay
	Jason Robinson	6-2/197	Goderich, Ont.	8-22-78	0	Cleveland (IHL), Chesapeake (ECHL)
	Brett Scheffelmaier	6-4/200	Coronation, Alta.	3-31-81	0	Medicine Hat (WHL)
46	Andrei Skopintsev	6-0/185	Moscow, U.S.S.R.	9-28-71	1	Cleveland (IHL), Tampa Bay
23	Petr Svoboda	6-1/183	Most, Czechoslovakia	2-14-66	15	Philadelphia, Tampa Bay
	Mark Thompson	6-6/219	St. Albert, Alta.	4-26-79	0	Kootenay (WHL)
	Andrei Zyuzin	6-1/200	Ufa, U.S.S.R.	1-21-78	2	San Jose, Kentucky (AHL)
	GOALTENDERS					
1	Zac Bierk	6-4/205	Peterborough, Ont.	9-17-76	2	Cleveland (IHL), Tampa Bay
34	Dan Cloutier	6-1/192	Mont-Laurier, Que.	4-22-76	2	New York Rangers
31	Kevin Hodson	6-0/182	Winnipeg	3-27-72	4	Detroit, Adirondack (AHL), Tampa Bay
	Yevgeny Konstantinov	6-0/167	Kazan, U.S.S.R.	3-29-81	0	Ak Bars-2 Kazan (Russian Div. III)
	Michal Lanicek	6-1/172	Benesov, Czechoslovakia	7-6-81	0	Slavia Praha Jrs. (Czech Republic)
93	Daren Puppa	6-4/205	Kirkland Lake, Ont.	3-23-65	14	Tampa Bay

1998-99 REVIEW

INDIVIDUAL STATISTICS

SCORING

	Games	G	A	Pts.	PIM	+/-	PPG	SHG	Shots	Shooting Pct.
Darcy Tucker	82	21	22	43	176	-34	8	2	178	11.8
Wendel Clark*	65	28	14	42	35	-25	11	0	171	16.4
Stephane Richer	64	12	21	33	22	-10	3	2	139	8.6
Vincent Lecavalier	82	13	15	28	23	-19	2	0	125	10.4
Chris Gratton*	52	7	19	26	102	-20	1	0	127	5.5
Benoit Hogue*	62	11	14	25	50	-12	2	0	101	10.9
Craig Janney*	38	4	18	22	10	-13	2	0	36	11.1
Pavel Kubina	68	9	12	21	80	-33	3	1	119	7.6
Rob Zamuner	58	8	11	19	24	-15	1	1	89	9.0
Alexander Selivanov*	43	6	13	19	18	-8	1	0	120	5.0
Cory Cross	67	2	16	18	92	-25	0	0	96	2.1
Jassen Cullimore	78	5	12	17	81	-22	1	1	73	6.8
Petr Svoboda*	34	1	16	17	53	-4	0	0	46	2.2
Alexandre Daigle*	32	6	6	12	2	-12	3	0	56	10.7
Sandy McCarthy*	67	5	7	12	135	-22	1	0	89	5.6
Mikael Renberg*	20	4	8	12	4	-2	2	0	42	9.5
Mike Sillinger*	54	8	2	10	28	-20	0	2	69	11.6
Daymond Langkow*	22	4	6	10	15	0	1	0	40	10.0
Michael Nylander*	24	2	7	9	6	-10	0	0	26	7.7
David Wilkie	46	1	7	8	69	-19	0	0	35	2.9

	Games	G	A	Pts.	PIM	+/-	PPG	SHG	Shots	Shooting Pct.
Robert Petrovicky	28	3	4	7	6	-8	0	0	32	9.4
Mike McBain	37	0	6	6	14	-11	0	0	22	0.0
Mikael Andersson*	40	2	3	5	4	-8	0	0	40	5.0
Kjell Samuelsson	46	1	4	5	38	-6	0	0	22	4.5
Colin Forbes*	14	3	1	4	10	-5	0	1	25	12.0
Steve Kelly	34	1	3	4	27	-15	0	0	15	6.7
Corey Schwab (goalie)	40	0	4	4	4	0	0	0	0	0.0
Brent Peterson	20	2	1	3	0	-2	0	0	16	12.5
Karl Dykhuis*	33	2	1	3	18	-21	0	0	27	7.4
Michal Sykora	10	1	2	3	0	-7	0	0	24	4.2
Drew Bannister	21	1	2	3	24	-4	0	0	29	3.4
Sergey Gusev*	14	0	3	3	10	-8	0	0	16	0.0
Jason Bonsignore	23	0	3	3	8	-4	0	0	12	0.0
Andrei Nazarov*	26	2	0	2	43	-5	0	0	18	11.1
Paul Mara	1	1	1	2	0	-3	1	0	1	100.0
Enrico Ciccone*	16	1	1	2	24	-1	0	0	9	11.1
Andrei Skopintsev	19	1	1	2	10	1	0	0	17	5.9
Karel Betik	3	0	2	2	2	-3	0	0	2	0.0
Sami Helenius*	4	1	0	1	15	-3	0	1	3	33.3
Corey Spring	8	0	1	1	2	0	0	0	6	0.0
Paul Ysebaert	10	0	1	1	2	-5	0	0	10	0.0
Daren Puppa (goalie)	13	0	1	1	0	0	0	0	0	0.0
Zac Bierk (goalie)	1	0	0	0	0	0	0	0	0	0.0
Xavier Delisle	2	0	0	0	0	0	0	0	1	0.0
John Cullen	4	0	0	0	2	-2	0	0	3	0.0
Kevin Hodson* (goalie)	5	0	0	0	0	0	0	0	0	0.0
Mario Larocque	5	0	0	0	16	-4	0	0	3	0.0
Derek Wilkinson (goalie)	5	0	0	0	0	0	0	0	0	0.0
Bill Ranford* (goalie)	32	0	0	0	2	0	0	0	0	0.0

GOALTENDING

	Games	Min.	Goals	SO	Avg.	W	L	T	Shots	Sv. Pct.
Zac Bierk	1	59	2	0	2.03	0	1	0	21	.905
Kevin Hodson*	5	238	11	0	2.77	2	1	1	118	.907
Daren Puppa	13	691	33	2	2.87	5	6	1	350	.906
Derek Wilkinson	5	253	13	0	3.08	1	3	1	128	.898
Corey Schwab	40	2146	126	0	3.52	8	25	3	1153	.891
Bill Ranford*	32	1568	102	1	3.90	3	18	3	858	.881

Combination shutout: Schwab and Hodson.
Empty-net goals (do not count against a goaltender's average): Ranford 2, Schwab 2, Puppa 1.
*Played with two or more NHL teams.

RESULTS

OCTOBER

9— At Florida ..... L 1-4
10— At Carolina ..... T *4-4
14— N.Y. Islanders ..... L 0-2
16— Philadelphia ..... L 2-5
18— Washington ..... L 1-4
21— Pittsburgh ..... W 5-0
23— Los Angeles ..... W 3-2
25— Vancouver ..... W 3-2
28— At Anaheim ..... L 3-5
30— At Los Angeles ..... W 3-0
31— At San Jose ..... L 1-6

NOVEMBER

4— At Washington ..... W 5-2
6— Chicago ..... T *2-2
8— New Jersey ..... W 3-1
10— N.Y. Rangers ..... L 2-10
13— At Colorado ..... L 1-8
14— At Phoenix ..... L 1-4
19— Pittsburgh ..... L 1-5
21— At Pittsburgh ..... L 2-5
24— Boston ..... L 1-4
27— Florida ..... L 1-2
29— Buffalo ..... L 3-6

DECEMBER

3— At Calgary ..... L 1-4
4— At Edmonton ..... W 2-1
6— At Chicago ..... L 5-7
8— Ottawa ..... L 2-4
11— Calgary ..... L 1-2
12— At N.Y. Islanders ..... W *2-1
15— At Pittsburgh ..... L *2-3
18— Edmonton ..... L 1-4
20— At Philadelphia ..... T *2-2
21— At Boston ..... L 2-3
23— At Buffalo ..... L 0-2
26— Florida ..... L 1-3
29— N.Y. Islanders ..... W 3-0
30— At Carolina ..... L 3-4

JANUARY

4— At Toronto ..... L *4-5
7— At Montreal ..... L 1-4
8— At Ottawa ..... L 1-5
10— At N.Y. Rangers ..... L 2-5
12— Toronto ..... L 3-4
15— At New Jersey ..... L 1-3
16— At Boston ..... T *2-2
19— Buffalo ..... W 2-1
21— At Nashville ..... W 3-2
26— Montreal ..... L 1-2
29— Dallas ..... L 1-4
30— At Philadelphia ..... L 2-6

FEBRUARY

2— Toronto ..... L 0-3
3— At Washington ..... L 1-10
5— Anaheim ..... L 3-5
10— St. Louis ..... L 4-5
13— San Jose ..... L 1-3
15— At N.Y. Islanders ..... T *3-3
17— At New Jersey ..... L 1-7
19— Phoenix ..... W 4-2
20— Carolina ..... L 2-3
22— New Jersey ..... L 2-3
26— Philadelphia ..... W 4-1

MARCH

2— Washington ..... L 2-8
4— Colorado ..... W 2-1
6— At Montreal ..... W 6-1
8— At Ottawa ..... L 3-9
9— At Toronto ..... L 1-6
11— At Buffalo ..... W 5-2
13— At Florida ..... L 0-1
17— Pittsburgh ..... L 0-2
19— Detroit ..... L 3-5
22— N.Y. Rangers ..... W 6-3
24— Nashville ..... L 0-3
26— At Detroit ..... L 1-6
28— At Carolina ..... T *3-3
31— At Dallas ..... L 4-6

APRIL

1— At St. Louis ..... L 0-3
3— Washington ..... W 4-3
5— Ottawa ..... T *4-4
8— Boston ..... W 3-0
10— At Boston ..... L 2-3
12— At N.Y. Rangers ..... L 1-2
13— Montreal ..... T *2-2
16— Carolina ..... T *2-2
17— At Florida ..... L 2-6

*Denotes overtime game.

TORONTO MAPLE LEAFS

EASTERN CONFERENCE/NORTHEAST DIVISION

Maple Leafs Schedule

Home games shaded; D—Day game; *—All-Star Game at Toronto.

October

SUN	MON	TUE	WED	THU	FRI	SAT
					1	2 MON
3	4 BOS	5	6 COL	7	8	9 OTT
10	11 NSH	12	13 FLA	14	15 CHI	16 STL
17	18	19	20 CAR	21	22	23 MON
24	25 DAL	26	27 ATL	28	29	30 CAL
31						

November

SUN	MON	TUE	WED	THU	FRI	SAT
	1	2	3 CAR	4	5 WAS	6 NJ
7	8	9 ANA	10	11 BOS	12	13 DET
14	15 SJ	16	17 STL	18	19	20 NYR
21	22	23 PIT	24	25	26 D PHI	27 EDM
28	29 WAS	30				

December

SUN	MON	TUE	WED	THU	FRI	SAT
			1	2 CAR	3	4 PIT
5	6 BUF	7	8	9 PHI	10	11 PHI
12	13 OTT	14	15 NYI	16	17	18 MON
19	20 FLA	21 TB	22	23 NJ	24	25
26	27	28	29 NYI	30	31	

January

SUN	MON	TUE	WED	THU	FRI	SAT
						1 BUF
2	3 BUF	4	5 NYR	6	7 PIT	8 NYR
9	10	11 BOS	12	13	14 EDM	15 CAL
16	17 VAN	18	19	20	21	22 WAS
23	24 OTT	25	26 DET	27 NYR	28	29 LA
30	31					

February

SUN	MON	TUE	WED	THU	FRI	SAT
		1 TB	2	3 BOS	4	5
6 *	7	8	9 PHI	10	11	12 VAN
13	14 CAR	15	16 BOS	17	18	19 MON
20	21	22	23 PHO	24	25 NJ	26 BUF
27	28	29 ATL				

March

SUN	MON	TUE	WED	THU	FRI	SAT
			1 FLA	2	3	4 MON
5	6 VAN	7 EDM	8	9 CAL	10	11 OTT
12	13	14	15 CHI	16 DET	17	18 ATL
19	20	21	22 NYI	23 OTT	24	25 NJ
26	27	28	29 STL	30 CHI	31	

April

SUN	MON	TUE	WED	THU	FRI	SAT
						1 WAS
2	3 BUF	4	5 PIT	6	7 NYI	8 TB
9	10	11	12	13	14	15

1999-2000 SEASON

CLUB DIRECTORY

Chairman of the board and governor
Steve A. Stavro
Alternate governor
Brian P. Bellmore
President and alternate governor
Ken Dryden
General manager and head coach
Pat Quinn
Assistant to the president
Bill Watters
Asst. g.m. & dir. of player development
Anders Hedberg
Marketing/community representative
Darryl Sittler
Dir. of pro scouting and player personnel
Nick Beverley
Director of player evaluation
Joe Yannetti
Assistant coaches
Rick Ley
Alpo Suhonen
Manager, hockey operations
Casey Vanden Heuvel
Vice president, sports communications & community development
John Lashway
Media relations manager
Pat Park
Senior manager of ticket operations
Donna Henderson
Scouts
George Armstrong, Thommie Bergman, Jack Gardiner, Mark Hillier, Larry Horning, Bob Johnson, Peter Johnson, Floyd Smith, Leonid Vaysfeld
Prospect developer
Chris MacDonald
Strength & conditioning coach
Phil Walker
Video coach & applied psychologist
Paul Dennis
Head athletic therapist
Chris Broadhurst
Athletic therapist
Brent Smith
Equipment manager
Brian Papineau
Assistant equipment manager
Dave Aleo
Trainer
Scott McKay

DRAFT CHOICES

Rd.— Player	Ht./Wt.	Overall	Pos.	Last team
1— Luca Cereda	6-2/200	24	C	Ambri, Switzerland
2— Peter Reynolds	6-3/195	60	D	London (OHL)
4— Mirko Murovic	6-3/190	108	LW	Moncton (QMJHL)
4— Jonathan Zion	6-0/187	110	D	Ottawa (OHL)
5— Vaclav Zavoral	6-3/198	151	D	Litvinov, Czech Rep.
6— Jan Sochor	6-0/198	161	RW	Slavia Praha, Czech
7— Vladimir Kulkov		211		CSKA Moskow, Russia
8— Pierre Hedin	6-1/198	239	D	Modo Ornsk., Sweden
9— Peter Metcalf	6-0/190	267	D	Maine (H. East)

MISCELLANEOUS DATA

Home ice (capacity)
Air Canada Centre (18,800)
Address
Air Canada Centre
40 Bay Street
Toronto, Ont. MSJ 2X2
Business phone
416-815-5700
Club colors
Blue and white
Radio affiliation
TALK 640 (AM)
TV affiliation
CBC, ON TV, Global TV, TSN

TRAINING CAMP ROSTER

No.	FORWARDS	Ht./Wt.	BORN Place	BORN Date	NHL exp.	1998-99 clubs
42	Kevyn Adams (C)	6-1/195	Washington, D.C.	10-8-74	2	St. John's (AHL), Toronto
34	Niklas Andersson (LW)	5-9/175	Kunglav, Sweden	5-20-71	4	Chicago (IHL)
	Vladimir Antipov (RW)	5-11/180	Appatity, U.S.S.R.	1-17-78	0	Torpedo Yaroslavl (Russian)
	Nikolai Antropov (C)	6-5/191	Vost, Kazakhstan	2-18-80	0	Dynamo Moscow (Russian)
94	Sergei Berezin (RW)	5-10/197	Voskresensk, U.S.S.R.	11-5-71	3	Toronto
16	Lonny Bohonos (RW)	5-11/192	Winnipeg	5-20-73	4	St. John's (AHL), Toronto
64	Jason Bonsignore (C)	6-4/220	Rochester, N.Y.	4-15-76	4	Cleveland (IHL), Tampa Bay
	Luca Cereda (C)	6-2/200	Lugano, Switzerland	9-7-81	0	Ambri-Piotta (Switzerland)
28	Tie Domi (RW)	5-10/205	Windsor, Ont.	11-1-69	10	Toronto
	Mikael Hakansson (C)	6-1/196	Stockholm, Sweden	3-31-74	0	Djur. Stockholm (Sweden)
44	Jonas Hoglund (LW)	6-3/218	Karlstad, Sweden	8-29-72	3	Montreal
20	Mike Johnson (RW)	6-2/197	Scarborough, Ont.	10-3-74	3	Toronto
	Konstantin Kalmikov (C)	6-4/215	Kharkov, U.S.S.R.	6-14-78	0	St. John's (AHL)
7	Derek King (LW)	5-11/212	Hamilton, Ont.	2-11-67	13	Toronto
12	Kris King (LW)	5-11/208	Bracebridge, Ont.	2-18-66	12	Toronto
26	Ladislav Kohn (RW)	5-11/184	Uherske Hrada, Czech.	3-4-75	3	St. John's (AHL), Toronto
22	Igor Korolev (C/LW)	6-1/187	Moscow, U.S.S.R.	9-6-70	7	Toronto
	Adam Mair (C)	6-2/194	Hamilton, Ont.	2-15-79	1	Owen Sound (OHL), Toronto
18	Alyn McCauley (C)	5-11/191	Brockville, Ont.	5-29-77	2	Toronto
19	Fredrik Modin (RW)	6-4/220	Sundsvall, Sweden	10-8-74	3	Toronto
	Frantisek Mrazek (LW)	6-5/220	Ceske Budejovice, Czech.	5-16-79	0	Red Deer (WHL)
	Mirko Murovic (LW)	6-3/190	Montreal	2-2-81	0	Moncton (QMJHL)
26	David Nemirovsky (RW)	6-2/205	Toronto	8-1-76	4	Fort Wayne (IHL), Florida, St. John's (AHL)
	Doug Nolan (LW)	6-2/198	Quincy, Mass.	1-5-76	0	Mass.-Lowell (Hockey East)
44	Yanic Perreault (C)	5-11/189	Sherbrooke, Que.	4-4-71	6	Los Angeles, Toronto
	Jan Sochor (RW)	6-0/198	Usti Nad Labem, Czech.	1-17-80	0	Slavia Praha (Czech Republic)
11	Steve Sullivan (C)	5-9/155	Timmins, Ont.	7-6-74	4	Toronto
13	Mats Sundin (C)	6-4/230	Bromma, Sweden	2-13-71	9	Toronto
32	Steve Thomas (LW)	5-11/185	Stockport, England	7-15-63	15	Toronto
18	Garry Valk (LW)	6-1/221	Edmonton	11-27-67	9	Toronto
8	Todd Warriner (LW)	6-1/200	Blenheim, Ont.	1-3-74	5	Toronto
	DEFENSEMEN					
	Greg Andrusak	6-1/185	Cranbrook, B.C.	11-14-69	4	Eisbaren Berlin (Germany), Houston (IHL), Pittsburgh
34	Bryan Berard	6-1/190	Woonsocket, R.I.	3-5-77	3	New York Islanders, Toronto
3	Sylvain Cote	6-0/190	Quebec City	1-19-66	15	Toronto
	Tomas Kaberle	6-2/200	Rakovnik, Czechoslovakia	3-2-78	1	Toronto
25	Alexander Karpovtsev	6-3/215	Moscow, U.S.S.R.	4-7-70	6	New York Rangers, Toronto
55	Daniil Markov	6-1/190	Moscow, U.S.S.R.	7-11-76	2	Toronto
	Chris McAllister	6-6/235	Saskatoon, Sask.	6-16-75	2	Vancouver, Syracuse (AHL), Toronto
	Marek Posmyk	6-5/224	Jihlava, Czechoslovakia	9-15-78	0	St. John's (AHL)
	Peter Reynolds	6-3/195	Waterloo, Ont.	4-27-81	0	London (OHL)
	D.J. Smith	6-1/205	Windsor, Ont.	5-13-77	1	St. John's (AHL)
	Dmitri Yakushin	6-2/215	Kharkiv, Ukraine	1-21-78	0	St. John's (AHL)
36	Dimitri Yushkevich	6-0/208	Yaroslavl, U.S.S.R.	11-19-71	7	Toronto
	Vaclav Zavoral	6-3/198	Teplice, Czechoslovakia	5-22-81	0	Chemopetrol Litvinov Jrs. (Czech. Jrs.)
	Jon Zion	6-0/187	Nepean, Ont.	5-21-81	0	Ottawa (OHL)
	GOALTENDERS					
30	Glenn Healy	5-9/192	Pickering, Ont.	8-23-62	13	Chicago (IHL), Toronto
31	Curtis Joseph	5-11/190	Keswick, Ont.	4-29-67	10	Toronto
	Francis Larivee	6-2/195	Verdun, Que.	11-8-77	0	St. John's (AHL), Chicago (IHL), Huntington (ECHL)
	Marc Robitaille	5-10/185	Gloucester, Ont.	6-7-76	0	St. John's (AHL)

1998-99 REVIEW

INDIVIDUAL STATISTICS

SCORING

	Games	G	A	Pts.	PIM	+/-	PPG	SHG	Shots	Shooting Pct.
Mats Sundin	82	31	52	83	58	22	4	0	209	14.8
Steve Thomas	78	28	45	73	33	26	11	0	209	13.4
Sergei Berezin	76	37	22	59	12	16	9	1	263	14.1
Derek King	81	24	28	52	20	15	8	0	150	16.0
Igor Korolev	66	13	34	47	46	11	1	0	99	13.1
Mike Johnson	79	20	24	44	35	13	5	3	149	13.4
Steve Sullivan	63	20	20	40	28	12	4	0	110	18.2
Fredrik Modin	67	16	15	31	35	14	1	0	108	14.8
Garry Valk	77	8	21	29	53	8	1	0	93	8.6

	Games	G	A	Pts.	PIM	+/-	PPG	SHG	Shots	Shooting Pct.
Sylvain Cote	79	5	24	29	28	22	0	0	119	4.2
Dimitri Yushkevich	78	6	22	28	88	25	2	1	95	6.3
Alexander Karpovtsev*	56	2	25	27	52	38	1	0	61	3.3
Alyn McCauley	39	9	15	24	2	7	1	0	76	11.8
Tie Domi	72	8	14	22	198	5	0	0	65	12.3
Tomas Kaberle	57	4	18	22	12	3	0	0	71	5.6
Todd Warriner	53	9	10	19	28	-6	1	0	96	9.4
Bryan Berard*	38	5	14	19	22	7	2	0	63	7.9
Yanic Perreault*	12	7	8	15	12	10	2	1	28	25.0
Jason Smith*	60	2	11	13	40	-9	0	0	53	3.8
Daniil Markov	57	4	8	12	47	5	0	0	34	11.8
Yannick Tremblay	35	2	7	9	16	0	0	0	37	5.4
Darby Hendrickson*	35	2	3	5	30	-4	0	0	34	5.9
Curtis Joseph (goalie)	67	0	5	5	6	0	0	0	0	0.0
Kris King	67	2	2	4	105	-16	0	1	34	5.9
Ladislav Kohn	16	1	3	4	4	1	0	0	23	4.3
Lonny Bohonos	7	3	0	3	4	3	0	0	13	23.1
Dallas Eakins	18	0	2	2	24	3	0	0	11	0.0
Chris McAllister*	20	0	2	2	39	4	0	0	12	0.0
Kevyn Adams	1	0	0	0	0	0	0	0	1	0.0
Jeff Reese (goalie)	2	0	0	0	0	0	0	0	0	0.0
Kevin Dahl	3	0	0	0	2	0	0	0	0	0.0
Jason Podollan*	4	0	0	0	0	0	0	0	2	0.0
Felix Potvin* (goalie)	5	0	0	0	0	0	0	0	0	0.0
Glenn Healy (goalie)	9	0	0	0	0	0	0	0	0	0.0

GOALTENDING

	Games	Min.	Goals	SO	Avg.	W	L	T	Shots	Sv. Pct.
Curtis Joseph	67	4001	171	3	2.56	35	24	7	1903	.910
Glenn Healy	9	546	27	0	2.97	6	3	0	257	.895
Felix Potvin*	5	299	19	0	3.81	3	2	0	142	.866
Jeff Reese	2	106	8	0	4.53	1	1	0	51	.843

Empty-net goals (do not count against a goaltender's average): Joseph 4, Healy 1, Potvin 1.

*Played with two or more NHL teams.

RESULTS

OCTOBER

10—Detroit W 2-1
13—At Edmonton W 3-2
16—At Calgary W 7-3
17—At Vancouver L 1-4
19—Nashville T *2-2
23—At Detroit W 5-3
24—At Pittsburgh W 6-4
26—Pittsburgh L 0-2
30—At Buffalo L 1-4
31—Buffalo L 3-6

NOVEMBER

4— Colorado W 3-0
5— At Boston L 1-4
7— N.Y. Rangers T *6-6
9— N.Y. Islanders L 1-3
11—Edmonton W 3-2
12—At Chicago W 10-3
14—Ottawa W 2-1
18—At Washington L 1-4
20—At Buffalo L 1-4
21—Buffalo W 2-1
23—Calgary W 3-2
25—Vancouver W 5-1
27—At Philadelphia L 3-4
28—Ottawa W *3-2

DECEMBER

2— Los Angeles W 3-1
5— At Montreal W *4-3
7— At N.Y. Rangers L 2-6
11—At Chicago W 3-2
12—Philadelphia L 0-3
16—Phoenix W 5-2
19—N.Y. Rangers W 7-4
21—Pittsburgh W 7-1
23—Dallas L 1-5
26—Montreal L 1-2
30—Anaheim W 4-1
31—At Detroit W 4-2

JANUARY

2— Washington L 2-5
4— Tampa Bay W *5-4
7— At Boston L 1-2
9— Boston W 6-3
12—At Tampa Bay W 4-3
13—At Florida T *3-3
16—At Philadelphia W 4-3
18—At Carolina L 2-4
20—At Dallas W 6-4
21—At St. Louis W 4-2
28—At Pittsburgh L 0-6
30—Washington W 5-3

FEBRUARY

2— At Tampa Bay W 3-0
3— At Florida L 2-5
6— At New Jersey W 3-2
10—Carolina L 5-6
13—Chicago L 2-6
15—At New Jersey T *3-3
17—At Buffalo W *3-2
20—Montreal W *3-2
22—At Washington L 3-4
24—Carolina T *2-2
25—At N.Y. Islanders W 4-1
27—Florida W 4-1

MARCH

3— New Jersey L 2-5
4— At St. Louis W 4-0
6— At Ottawa L 1-3
8— At N.Y. Rangers L *2-3
9— Tampa Bay W 6-1
11—At N.Y. Islanders W 2-1
13—At Montreal L 1-2
17—Boston L 1-4
20—New Jersey W 3-1
22—Philadelphia L 1-3
24—San Jose L 5-8
26—At Carolina W 7-2
27—Boston T *2-2
31—At Vancouver W 6-5

APRIL

1— At Edmonton W 5-1
3— At Calgary W 5-1
5— St. Louis T *2-2
7— Ottawa W 4-2
8— At Ottawa L 1-3
10—Florida W 9-1
14—N.Y. Islanders W *3-2
17—At Montreal L 2-3

*Denotes overtime game.

VANCOUVER CANUCKS

WESTERN CONFERENCE/NORTHWEST DIVISION

Canucks Schedule

Home games shaded; D—Day game; *—All-Star Game at Toronto.

October

SUN	MON	TUE	WED	THU	FRI	SAT
					1	2 NYR
3	4	5	6 CHI	7	8	9 MON
10	11	12	13 CAL	14	15 CAR	16 CAL
17	18	19 TB	20 FLA	21	22	23 NYI
24 NYR	25	26 PHI	27	28 PHO	29	30 NSH
31						

November

SUN	MON	TUE	WED	THU	FRI	SAT
	1	2	3	4	5 FLA	6
7 STL	8	9 SJ	10	11	12 PHO	13
14	15 COL	16	17 DET	18	19	20 NSH
21	22 ATL	23	24 CAR	25	26 D BOS	27 MON
28	29	30 COL				

December

SUN	MON	TUE	WED	THU	FRI	SAT
			1	2 EDM	3	4 EDM
5	6 COL	7	8 ANA	9	10 CAL	11
12 COL	13	14	15	16 OTT	17	18 DAL
19	20	21	22 WAS	23	24	25
26 CAL	27	28	29 PHI	30	31	

January

SUN	MON	TUE	WED	THU	FRI	SAT
						1
2 D CAL	3	4	5 TB	6	7 DAL	8 STL
9	10	11	12 CHI	13 NSH	14	15 DAL
16	17 TOR	18	19 DET	20	21	22 EDM
23 NSH	24	25 EDM	26	27	28 SJ	29
30 CHI	31					

February

SUN	MON	TUE	WED	THU	FRI	SAT
		1 COL	2	3 STL	4	5
6 *	7	8	9 CAL	10	11	12 TOR
13	14 PIT	15	16 DET	17 BUF	18	19 D OTT
20	21 BOS	22	23 ANA	24	25 LA	26
27 PHO	28	29 LA				

March

SUN	MON	TUE	WED	THU	FRI	SAT
			1	2 ANA	3	4 NJ
5	6 TOR	7	8 DAL	9 STL	10	11 PHO
12	13 LA	14	15	16 BUF	17	18 OTT
19	20 COL	21	22 SJ	23	24 ANA	25 EDM
26	27	28	29 DET	30	31 NSH	

April

SUN	MON	TUE	WED	THU	FRI	SAT
						1
2 D CHI	3	4	5 LA	6	7 EDM	8
9 D SJ	10	11	12	13	14	15

1999-2000 SEASON

CLUB DIRECTORY

Chairman and governor
John E. McCaw Jr.
Alternate governor
Stanley B. McCammon
President and CEO, alternate governor
Stephen T. Bellringer
President and g.m., alternate governor
Brian P. Burke
Executive v.p., business
David Cobb
Vice president, finance and CFO
Victor de Bonis
Vice president, communications and community investment
Kevin Gass
V.p. and general manager, operations
Harvey Jones
Sr. v.p., director of hockey operations
David M. Nonis
Vice president, player personnel
Steve Tambellini
Vice president, amateur scouting
Mike Penny
Executive assistant
Patti Timms
Head coach
Marc Crawford
Assistant coaches
Jack McIlhargey
Mike Johnston
Strength & conditioning coach
Peter Twist
Scouting information coordinator
Jonathan Wall
Manager, media relations
Chris Brumwell
Assistant, media relations
Reid Mitchell
Manager, community relations
Veronica Varhaug
Coordinator, education programs & community relations
Lisa Ryan
Asst., comm. rel. & hockey development
Cheryl Reardon
Medical trainer
Mike Bernstein
Massage therapist
Dave Schima
Equipment manager
Pat O'Neill
Assistant equipment manager
Darren Granger

DRAFT CHOICES

Rd.— Player	Ht./Wt.	Overall	Pos.	Last team
1— Daniel Sedin	6-1/194	2	LW	Modo Ornsk., Sweden
1— Henrik Sedin	6-2/196	3	C	Modo Ornsk., Sweden
3— Rene Vydareny	6-1/198	69	D	Bratislava, Slovakia
5— Ryan Thorpe	6-4/202	129	LW	Spokane (WHL)
6— Josh Reed	6-2/204	172	D	Cowichan (BCJHL)
7— Kevin Swanson	5-10/170	189	G	Kelowna (WHL)
8— Markus Kankaanpera	6-1/191	218	D	Jyvaskyla, Finland
9— Darrell Hay	6-0/190	271	D	Tri-City (WHL)

MISCELLANEOUS DATA

Home ice (capacity)
General Motors Place (18,422)
Address
800 Griffiths Way
Vancouver, B.C. V6B 6G1
Business phone
604-899-4600
Club colors
Deep blue, sky blue, deep red, white and silver
Radio affiliation
CKNW (980 AM)
TV affiliation
VTV (Channel 9), CTV Sportsnet (Cable)

TRAINING CAMP ROSTER

No.	FORWARDS	Ht./Wt.	BORN Place	BORN Date	NHL exp.	1998-99 clubs
44	Todd Bertuzzi (LW)	6-3/230	Sudbury, Ont.	2-2-75	4	Vancouver
8	Donald Brashear (LW)	6-2/230	Bedford, Ind.	1-7-72	6	Vancouver
	Mike Brown (C)	6-4/209	Surrey, B.C.	4-27-79	0	Kamloops (WHL)
21	Andrew Cassels (C)	6-1/185	Mississauga, Ont.	7-23-69	10	Calgary
	Artem Chubarov (C)	6-1/189	Gorky, U.S.S.R.	12-13-79	0	Dynamo Moscow (Russian)
	Matt Cooke (LW)	5-11/205	Belleville, Ont.	9-7-78	1	Vancouver, Syracuse (AHL)
	Harold Druken (LW)	6-0/200	St. John's, Nfld.	1-26-79	0	Plymouth (OHL)
14	Darby Hendrickson (C)	6-1/195	Richfield, Minn.	8-28-72	6	Toronto, Vancouver
21	Josh Holden (C)	6-2/200	Calgary	1-18-78	1	Syracuse (AHL), Vancouver
	Steve Kariya (LW)	5-7/170	Vancouver	12-22-77	0	Univ. of Maine (Hockey East)
26	Trent Klatt (RW)	6-1/210	Minneapolis, Minn.	1-30-71	8	Philadelphia, Vancouver
9	Brad May (LW)	6-1/210	Toronto	11-29-71	8	Vancouver
11	Mark Messier (C)	6-1/205	Edmonton	1-18-61	20	Vancouver
89	Alexander Mogilny (RW)	5-11/205	Khabarovsk, U.S.S.R.	2-18-69	10	Vancouver
	Justin Morrison (RW)	6-3/205	Los Angeles	9-10-79	0	Colorado College (WCHA)
17	Bill Muckalt (RW)	6-0/200	Surrey, B.C.	7-15-74	1	Vancouver
19	Markus Naslund (LW)	6-0/186	Ornskoldsvik, Sweden	7-30-73	6	Vancouver
	Ryan Ready (LW)	6-2/190	Peterborough, Ont.	11-7-78	0	Belleville (OHL)
	Jarkko Ruutu (LW)	6-2/194	Vantaa, Finland	8-23-75	0	HIFK Helsinki (Finland)
20	Dave Scatchard (C)	6-2/215	Hinton, Alta.	2-20-76	2	Vancouver
29	Peter Schaefer (LW)	5-11/195	Regina, Sask.	7-12-77	1	Syracuse (AHL), Vancouver
	Daniel Sedin (LW)	6-1/194	Ornskoldsvik, Sweden	9-26-80	0	MoDo Ornskoldvik (Sweden)
	Henrik Sedin (C)	6-2/196	Ornskoldsvik, Sweden	9-26-80	0	MoDo Ornskoldvik (Sweden)
	Ryan Thorpe (LW)	6-4/202	Vancouver	2-6-81	0	Kamloops (WHL), Spokane (WHL)
27	Harry York (C)	6-2/220	Panoka, Alta.	4-16-74	3	N.Y. Rangers, Pittsburgh, Vancouver
	DEFENSEMEN					
	Chad Allan	6-1/210	Davidson, Sask.	7-12-76	0	Syracuse (AHL)
7	Bryan Allen	6-4/210	Kingston, Ont.	8-21-80	0	Oshawa (OHL)
6	Adrian Aucoin	6-2/210	Ottawa	7-3-73	5	Vancouver
23	Murray Baron	6-3/225	Prince George, B.C.	6-1-67	10	Vancouver
	Doug Bodger	6-2/210	Chemainus, B.C.	6-18-66	15	Los Angeles
	Ryan Bonni	6-4/190	Winnipeg	2-18-79	0	Saskatoon (WHL), Red Deer (WHL)
55	Ed Jovanovski	6-2/210	Windsor, Ont.	6-26-76	4	Florida, Vancouver
2	Mattias Ohlund	6-3/210	Pitea, Sweden	9-9-76	2	Vancouver
	Josh Reed	6-2/204	Vernon, B.C.	5-21-79	0	Cowichan (BCJHL)
3	Brent Sopel	6-1/205	Saskatoon, Sask.	1-7-77	1	Syracuse (AHL), Vancouver
34	Jason Strudwick	6-3/220	Edmonton	7-17-75	3	Vancouver
	Rene Vydareny	6-1/198	Bratislava, Czechoslovakia	5-6-81	0	Bratislava (Slov. Jr.)
	GOALTENDERS					
	Alfie Michaud	5-10/184	Selkirk, Man.	11-6-76	0	Univ. of Maine (Hockey East)
30	Garth Snow	6-3/210	Wrentham, Mass.	7-28-69	6	Vancouver
35	Kevin Weekes	6-0/195	Toronto	4-4-75	2	Detroit (IHL), Vancouver

1998-99 REVIEW

INDIVIDUAL STATISTICS

SCORING

	Games	G	A	Pts.	PIM	+/-	PPG	SHG	Shots	Shooting Pct.
Markus Naslund	80	36	30	66	74	-13	15	2	205	17.6
Mark Messier	59	13	35	48	33	-12	4	2	97	13.4
Alexander Mogilny	59	14	31	45	58	0	3	2	110	12.7
Bill Muckalt	73	16	20	36	98	-9	4	2	119	13.4
Mattias Ohlund	74	9	26	35	83	-19	2	1	129	7.0
Adrian Aucoin	82	23	11	34	77	-14	18	2	174	13.2
Dave Scatchard	82	13	13	26	140	-12	0	2	130	10.0
Bryan McCabe	69	7	14	21	120	-11	1	2	98	7.1
Donald Brashear	82	8	10	18	209	-25	2	0	112	7.1
Brad May	66	6	11	17	102	-14	1	0	91	6.6
Todd Bertuzzi	32	8	8	16	44	-6	1	0	72	11.1
Harry York*	49	7	9	16	20	-2	1	0	55	12.7
Peter Zezel	41	6	8	14	16	5	1	0	45	13.3
Trent Klatt*	73	4	10	14	12	-3	0	0	58	6.9
Dave Gagner*	33	2	12	14	24	-9	0	0	50	4.0
Bret Hedican*	42	2	11	13	34	7	0	2	52	3.8
Ed Jovanovski*	31	2	9	11	44	-5	0	0	41	4.9
Brandon Convery*	12	2	7	9	8	5	0	0	12	16.7
Peter Schaefer	25	4	4	8	8	-1	1	0	24	16.7
Murray Baron	81	2	6	8	115	-23	0	0	53	3.8

	Games	G	A	Pts.	PIM	+/-	PPG	SHG	Shots	Shooting Pct.
Josh Holden	30	2	4	6	10	-10	1	0	44	4.5
Darby Hendrickson*	27	2	2	4	22	-15	1	0	36	5.6
Bert Robertsson	39	2	2	4	13	-7	0	0	13	15.4
Jason Strudwick	65	0	3	3	114	-19	0	0	25	0.0
Chris McAllister*	28	1	1	2	63	-7	0	0	6	16.7
Dana Murzyn	12	0	2	2	21	1	0	0	7	0.0
Matt Cooke	30	0	2	2	27	-12	0	0	22	0.0
Steve Staios	57	0	2	2	54	-12	0	0	33	0.0
Brent Sopel	5	1	0	1	4	-1	1	0	5	20.0
Jamie Huscroft*	26	0	1	1	63	-3	0	0	20	0.0
Garth Snow (goalie)	65	0	1	1	34	0	0	0	0	0.0
Robb Gordon	4	0	0	0	2	0	0	0	1	0.0
Steve Washburn*	8	0	0	0	2	0	0	0	6	0.0
Kevin Weekes (goalie)	11	0	0	0	0	0	0	0	0	0.0
Corey Hirsch (goalie)	20	0	0	0	0	0	0	0	0	0.0

GOALTENDING

	Games	Min.	Goals	SO	Avg.	W	L	T	Shots	Sv. Pct.
Garth Snow	65	3501	171	6	2.93	20	31	8	1715	.900
Corey Hirsch	20	919	48	1	3.13	3	8	3	435	.890
Kevin Weekes	11	532	34	0	3.83	0	8	1	257	.868

Empty-net goals (do not count against a goaltender's average): Snow 5.

*Played with two or more NHL teams.

RESULTS

OCTOBER

12—Los Angeles W 4-2
14—Edmonton L 1-4
17—Toronto W 4-1
20—At Carolina L 1-3
21—At Washington W 2-1
23—At Florida W 5-0
25—At Tampa Bay L 2-3
27—At Nashville L 4-5
30—Pittsburgh T *2-2

NOVEMBER

1—Washington W 4-1
2—At Edmonton L 3-5
7—Nashville W 5-3
9—Los Angeles L 3-4
12—At Calgary W 4-3
13—Anaheim W 5-2
15—Colorado L 1-2
18—At Phoenix L 2-4
19—At Colorado W 5-0
21—Detroit L 2-4
23—At Ottawa L 3-4
25—At Toronto L 1-5
27—At Detroit L 1-7
29—At Philadelphia L 2-6

DECEMBER

1—At Boston T *1-1
4—Dallas W 4-1
6—Phoenix T *3-3
9—At Anaheim T *4-4
12—At Los Angeles L 0-3
17—Colorado W 2-1
19—Nashville L 4-6
22—At Calgary W 5-3
23—Calgary W 5-2
26—At San Jose L 0-2
27—At Edmonton L 0-3
29—Colorado L 2-4
31—Philadelphia L 2-6

JANUARY

2—Montreal L 1-2
4—At St. Louis L 0-4
6—At Dallas L 4-6
8—Florida T *1-1
10—Dallas W 2-0
14—Edmonton L 1-3
16—Detroit T *2-2
18—At Dallas W 5-3
19—At Nashville L 1-4
28—St. Louis L 2-4
30—Chicago W 3-2

FEBRUARY

1—Ottawa L 0-1
3—At Montreal L 1-2
4—At N.Y. Rangers L 4-8
7—At N.Y. Islanders T *3-3
9—At New Jersey W 4-3
11—At Pittsburgh L *5-6
13—Boston W 3-1
15—At St. Louis L 1-8
17—At Chicago L 0-4
20—Anaheim L 1-5
23—At Colorado T *4-4
24—At San Jose T *1-1
26—Carolina W 1-0
28—Buffalo L 0-2

MARCH

3—San Jose L 3-4
5—Calgary L 1-5
7—Chicago T *2-2
10—At Anaheim T *4-4
11—At Phoenix W 3-0
13—At Los Angeles L 1-3
15—New Jersey L 1-2
19—N.Y. Islanders L 1-3
20—At Edmonton L 3-4
24—At Colorado L 2-5
25—St. Louis L 1-4
27—Montreal W 5-1
29—Phoenix W 1-0
31—Toronto L 5-6

APRIL

2—San Jose L 0-7
3—At San Jose L 2-5
5—At Chicago L 1-2
7—At Detroit L 1-6
10—Edmonton T *1-1
12—At Calgary W 2-0
14—Calgary L 4-5

*Denotes overtime game.

WASHINGTON CAPITALS
EASTERN CONFERENCE/SOUTHEAST DIVISION

Capitals Schedule

Home games shaded; D—Day game; *—All-Star Game at Toronto.

October

SUN	MON	TUE	WED	THU	FRI	SAT
					1	2 FLA
3	4	5	6	7	8 BUF	9 LA
10	11	12 PHI	13	14	15	16 SJ
17	18	19 ANA	20	21	22	23 PHO
24	25	26 LA	27	28	29 ANA	30
31 SJ						

November

SUN	MON	TUE	WED	THU	FRI	SAT
	1	2	3 OTT	4	5 TOR	6
7 CAR	8	9 TB	10	11 NYR	12	13 NJ
14	15	16	17 DAL	18	19 CAR	20 BOS
21	22	23	24 BUF	25	26 NSH	27 NYI
28	29 TOR	30				

December

SUN	MON	TUE	WED	THU	FRI	SAT
			1	2 BOS	3	4 FLA
5	6	7 NYI	8	9 PIT	10	11
12	13 MON	14	15 ATL	16	17 NYR	18 NJ
19	20	21 EDM	22 VAN	23	24	25
26	27 CHI	28	29 PIT	30	31	

January

SUN	MON	TUE	WED	THU	FRI	SAT
						1 STL
2	3	4 MON	5	6 ATL	7	8 ATL
9	10	11	12 ATL	13	14 NJ	15
16 D OTT	17 D TB	18	19 FLA	20	21	22 TOR
23	24 TB	25	26 CAL	27	28 PHO	29
30 D PHI	31					

February

SUN	MON	TUE	WED	THU	FRI	SAT
		1 PIT	2	3 CAR	4	5
6 *	7	8 BOS	9	10 MON	11	12 NSH
13 DAL	14	15 COL	16	17	18 CHI	19 PHI
20	21 D CAR	22	23 FLA	24	25 BOS	26 MON
27	28 NYI	29				

March

SUN	MON	TUE	WED	THU	FRI	SAT
			1 TB	2	3 DET	4
5 D BUF	6	7 FLA	8	9 PHI	10	11 NJ
12	13	14	15 NYI	16	17 CAR	18
19 D TB	20 STL	21	22	23 NYR	24	25 OTT
26	27	28 ATL	29	30 PIT	31	

April

SUN	MON	TUE	WED	THU	FRI	SAT
						1 TOR
2	3 NYR	4 OTT	5	6	7 DET	8
9 D BUF	10	11	12	13	14	15

1999-2000 SEASON

CLUB DIRECTORY

Owners
Ted Leonsis
Jonathan Ledecky
President and governor
Dick Patrick
Senior v.p. of business operations
Declan J. Bolger
Vice president/general manager
George McPhee
Director of hockey operations
Shawn Simpson
Assistant to the general manager
Frank Provenzano
Director of amateur scouting
Ross Mahoney
Head coach
Ron Wilson
Assistant coaches
Tim Army
Tim Hunter
Goaltender consultant
Dave Prior
Team physician
Dr. Ben Shaffer
Trainer
Greg Smith
Equipment manager
Doug Shearer
Assistant equipment manager
Craig Leydig
Equipment assistant
Brian Metzger
Strength and conditioning coach
Frank Costello
Massage therapist
Curt Millar
Director, public relations
Doug Hicks
Assistant director, public relations
Jesse Price

DRAFT CHOICES

Rd.— Player	Ht./Wt.	Overall	Pos.	Last team
1— Kris Breech	6-2/178	7	C	Calgary (WHL)
2— Michal Sivec	6-3/209	29	C	Kladno, Czech Rep.
2— Charlie Stephens	6-4/225	31	C/RW	Guelph (OHL)
2— Ross Lupaschuk	6-1/211	34	D	Prince Albert (WHL)
2— Nolan Yonkman	6-5/218	37	D	Kelowna (WHL)
5— Roman Tyrdon	6-1/189	132	C/LW	Trencin, Slovakia
6— Kyle Clark	6-7/210	175	RW	Harvard (ECAC)
7— David Johansson	6-0/176	192	D	AIK, Sweden
8— Maxim Orlov	6-0/176	219	C	CSKA Moskow, Russia
9— Igor Shadilov	6-2/189	249	D	Dynamo, Russia

MISCELLANEOUS DATA

Home ice (capacity)
MCI Center (19,740)
Address
601 F St., NW
Washington, DC 20004
Business phone
202-661-5000
Club colors
Bronze and blue
Radio affiliation
WTEM (980 AM)
TV affiliation
HTS, WBDC (Channel 50)

TRAINING CAMP ROSTER

No.	FORWARDS	Ht./Wt.	BORN Place	BORN Date	NHL exp.	1998-99 clubs
	Kris Beech (C)	6-2/178	Salmon Arm, B.C.	2-5-81	0	Calgary (WHL)
28	James Black (LW)	6-0/202	Regina, Sask.	8-15-69	9	Chicago (IHL), Washington
12	Peter Bondra (RW)	6-1/200	Luck, Ukraine	2-7-68	9	Washington
8	Jan Bulis (C)	6-0/208	Pardubice, Czechoslovakia	3-18-78	2	Washington, Cincinnati (IHL)
	Kyle Clark (RW)	6-7/210	Essex, Vt.	2-14-80	0	Harvard University (ECAC)
36	Mike Eagles (C)	5-10/192	Sussex, N.B.	3-7-63	15	Washington
48	Benoit Gratton (C)	5-10/182	Montreal	12-28-76	2	Portland (AHL), Washington
18	Trevor Halverson (LW)	6-2/203	White River, Ont.	4-6-71	1	Washington, Portland (AHL)
26	Matt Herr (LW)	6-2/204	Hackensack, N.J.	5-26-76	1	Washington, Portland (AHL)
2	Ken Klee (RW)	6-1/212	Indianapolis	4-24-71	5	Washington
22	Steve Konowalchuk (LW).	6-2/207	Salt Lake City	11-11-72	8	Washington
	Jeff Nelson (C)	6-0/190	Prince Albert, Sask.	12-18-72	3	Nashville, Milwaukee (IHL)
13	Andrei Nikolishin (C)	5-11/202	Vorkuta, U.S.S.R.	3-25-73	5	Dynamo Moscow (Russian), Washington
77	Adam Oates (C)	5-11/185	Weston, Ont.	8-27-62	14	Washington
20	Michal Pivonka (C)	6-2/200	Kladno, Czechoslovakia	1-28-66	13	Washington
	Joe Sacco (RW)	6-1/195	Medford, Mass.	2-4-69	9	N.Y. Islanders
17	Chris Simon (LW)	6-4/235	Wawa, Ont.	1-30-72	7	Washington
	Michal Sivek (C)	6-3/209	Nachod, Czechoslovakia	1-21-81	0	Sparta Praha (Czech Republic), Velvana Kladno (Czech Republic)
	Charlie Stephens (C/RW).	6-3/229	Nilestown, Ont.	4-5-81	0	Toronto (OHL), Guelph (OHL)
34	Jaroslav Svejkovsky (RW)	6-1/194	Plzen, Czechoslovakia	10-1-76	3	Washington
21	Jeff Toms (LW)	6-5/210	Swift Current, Sask.	6-4-74	4	Portland (AHL), Washington
	Roman Tvrdon (C/LW)	6-1/189	Trencin, Czecholslovakia	1-29-81	0	Dukla Trencin Jrs. (Slovakia Jrs.)
	Trent Whitfield (C)	5-10/175	Alameda, Sask.	6-17-77	0	Portland (AHL), Hampton Roads (ECHL)
44	Richard Zednik (RW)	6-0/199	Bystrica, Czechoslovakia	1-6-76	4	Washington
	DEFENSEMEN					
38	Nolan Baumgartner	6-1/195	Calgary	3-23-76	3	Portland (AHL), Washington
41	Patrick Boileau	6-0/194	Montreal	2-22-75	2	Portland (AHL), Indianapolis (IHL), Washington
39	Enrico Ciccone	6-5/220	Montreal	4-10-70	8	Tampa Bay, Cleveland (IHL), Washington
58	Jean-Francois Fortin	6-2/200	Laval, Que.	3-15-79	0	Sherbrooke (QMJHL)
55	Sergei Gonchar	6-2/212	Chelyabinsk, U.S.S.R.	4-13-74	5	Washington
	Jamie Huscroft	6-2/210	Creston, B.C.	1-9-67	9	Vancouver, Phoenix
6	Calle Johansson	5-11/203	Goteborg, Sweden	2-14-67	12	Washington
	Ross Lupaschuk	6-1/211	Edmonton	1-19-81	0	Prince Albert (WHL)
3	Stewart Malgunas	6-0/211	Prince George, B.C.	4-21-70	6	Portland (AHL), Washington, Detroit (IHL)
15	Dmitri Mironov	6-3/224	Moscow, U.S.S.R.	12-25-65	8	Washington
33	Steve Poapst	6-0/200	Cornwall, Ont.	1-3-69	2	Portland (AHL), Washington
29	Joe Reekie	6-3/220	Victoria, B.C.	2-22-65	14	Washington
4	Alexei Tezikov	6-1/198	Togliatti, U.S.S.R.	6-22-78	1	Moncton Alpines (QMJHL), Rochester (AHL), Cincinnati (IHL), Washington
19	Brendan Witt	6-2/226	Humboldt, Sask.	2-20-75	5	Washington
	Nolan Yonkman	6-5/218	Punnichy, Sask.	4-1-81	0	Kelowna (WHL)
	GOALTENDERS					
	Craig Billington	5-10/170	London, Ont.	9-11-66	11	Colorado
	Curtis Cruickshank	6-3/206	Ottawa	3-21-79	0	Kingston (OHL), Sarnia (OHL)
37	Olaf Kolzig	6-3/232	Johannesburg, South Africa	4-9-70	8	Washington

1998-99 REVIEW

INDIVIDUAL STATISTICS

SCORING

	Games	G	A	Pts.	PIM	+/-	PPG	SHG	Shots	Shooting Pct.
Peter Bondra	66	31	24	55	56	-1	6	3	284	10.9
Adam Oates	59	12	42	54	22	-1	3	0	79	15.2
Joe Juneau*	63	14	27	41	20	-3	2	1	142	9.9
Brian Bellows	76	17	19	36	26	-12	8	0	166	10.2
Andrei Nikolishin	73	8	27	35	28	0	0	1	121	6.6
Sergei Gonchar	53	21	10	31	57	1	13	1	180	11.7
James Black	75	16	14	30	14	5	1	1	135	11.9
Calle Johansson	67	8	21	29	22	10	2	0	145	5.5
Steve Konowalchuk	45	12	12	24	26	0	4	1	98	12.2
Jan Bulis	38	7	16	23	6	3	3	0	57	12.3
Ken Klee	78	7	13	20	80	-9	0	0	132	5.3
Richard Zednik	49	9	8	17	50	-6	1	0	115	7.8
Dmitri Mironov	46	2	14	16	80	-5	2	0	86	2.3
Jaroslav Svejkovsky	25	6	8	14	12	-2	4	0	50	12.0
Michal Pivonka	36	5	6	11	12	-6	2	0	30	16.7
Chris Simon	23	3	7	10	48	-4	0	0	29	10.3
Joe Reekie	73	0	10	10	68	11	0	0	81	0.0

	Games	G	A	Pts.	PIM	+/-	PPG	SHG	Shots	Shooting Pct.
Craig Berube*	66	5	4	9	166	-7	0	0	45	11.1
Benoit Gratton	16	4	3	7	16	-1	0	0	24	16.7
Brendan Witt	54	2	5	7	87	-6	0	0	51	3.9
Kelly Miller	62	2	5	7	29	-5	0	0	49	4.1
Mike Eagles	52	4	2	6	50	-5	0	0	41	9.8
Jeff Toms	21	1	5	6	2	0	0	0	30	3.3
Mark Tinordi	48	0	6	6	108	-6	0	0	32	0.0
Dale Hunter*	50	0	5	5	102	-7	0	0	18	0.0
Matthew Herr	30	2	2	4	8	-7	1	0	40	5.0
Trevor Halverson	17	0	4	4	28	-5	0	0	16	0.0
Enrico Ciccone*	43	2	0	2	103	-6	0	0	43	4.7
Tom Chorske*	17	0	2	2	4	-4	0	0	22	0.0
Olaf Kolzig (goalie)	64	0	2	2	19	0	0	0	0	0.0
Patrick Boileau	4	0	1	1	2	-4	0	0	7	0.0
Mike Rosati (goalie)	1	0	0	0	0	0	0	0	0	0.0
Patrick Augusta	2	0	0	0	0	0	0	0	4	0.0
Martin Brochu (goalie)	2	0	0	0	2	0	0	0	0	0.0
Patrice Lefebvre	3	0	0	0	2	-2	0	0	2	0.0
Brad Shaw*	4	0	0	0	4	0	0	0	5	0.0
Nolan Baumgartner	5	0	0	0	0	-3	0	0	1	0.0
Alexei Tezikov	5	0	0	0	0	-1	0	0	4	0.0
Stewart Malgunas	10	0	0	0	6	-5	0	0	2	0.0
Steve Poapst	22	0	0	0	8	-8	0	0	11	0.0
Rick Tabaracci (goalie)	23	0	0	0	2	0	0	0	0	0.0

GOALTENDING

	Games	Min.	Goals	SO	Avg.	W	L	T	Shots	Sv. Pct.
Mike Rosati	1	28	0	0	0.00	1	0	0	12	1.000
Rick Tabaracci	23	1193	50	2	2.51	4	12	3	530	.906
Olaf Kolzig	64	3586	154	4	2.58	26	31	3	1538	.900
Martin Brochu	2	120	6	0	3.00	0	2	0	55	.891

Empty-net goals (do not count against a goaltender's average): Kolzig 5, Tabaracci 3.
*Played with two or more NHL teams.

RESULTS

OCTOBER

10—Anaheim W 1-0
13—Detroit L 2-3
16—Montreal T *2-2
18—At Tampa Bay W 4-1
21—Vancouver L 1-2
23—At Buffalo W 1-0
24—Florida T *2-2
28—At Edmonton L 2-8
30—At Calgary T *0-0

NOVEMBER

1—At Vancouver L 1-4
4—Tampa Bay L 2-5
6—Carolina L 2-3
7—At Ottawa W 8-5
12—Buffalo L 0-2
14—At N.Y. Islanders W 5-3
18—Toronto W 4-1
20—Ottawa L 1-4
21—At Boston L *4-5
25—Pittsburgh W 5-4
27—At Dallas L 0-4
28—At St. Louis L 2-4

DECEMBER

1—New Jersey L 0-4
4—N.Y. Islanders W 5-1
5—At Philadelphia L 1-2
9—At Los Angeles L 1-2
11—At Anaheim L 0-1
12—At San Jose L 1-2
17—At Chicago W 3-1
19—At Pittsburgh L 0-3
23—At Florida W 4-0
26—At Nashville L 1-3
28—Boston W 5-1
30—New Jersey L 2-3

JANUARY

1—Ottawa L 3-4
2—At Toronto W 5-2
7—N.Y. Rangers W 5-1
9—At New Jersey W 3-2
11—N.Y. Islanders W 4-3
13—Philadelphia L 0-3
15—Montreal L 0-3
16—At Carolina W *3-2
18—At Montreal T *4-4
21—At Philadelphia L 1-4
26—N.Y. Rangers L 1-4
29—Los Angeles L 3-6
30—At Toronto L 3-5

FEBRUARY

1—At N.Y. Rangers W 3-1
3—Tampa Bay W 10-1
5—Carolina W 4-1
7—Buffalo W 3-1
9—At N.Y. Islanders W 2-1
12—At New Jersey W 3-2
13—At Ottawa L 1-2
15—At Pittsburgh L 3-7
18—At Carolina T *2-2
20—San Jose W 3-1
22—Toronto W 4-3
24—Phoenix L 1-2
27—At Boston L 3-4
28—Pittsburgh W 4-3

MARCH

2—At Tampa Bay W 8-2
4—N.Y. Rangers L 2-4
6—Edmonton W 4-3
9—Colorado L *2-3
11—Florida L 1-2
13—Calgary L *4-5
15—At N.Y. Rangers T *1-1
17—Dallas W *2-1
20—At Montreal W 1-0
21—Boston L 1-4
25—At Phoenix L 2-4
26—At Colorado L 1-3
30—Nashville L 2-3

APRIL

1—Florida W 5-3
3—At Tampa Bay L 3-4
5—At Florida W 3-0
7—St. Louis L 2-4
8—At New Jersey L 0-1
10—Philadelphia L 1-2
12—Chicago L 2-4
14—At Carolina L 0-3
18—At Buffalo L 0-3

*Denotes overtime game.

SCHEDULE

DAY BY DAY

*Denotes afternoon game.

FRIDAY, OCTOBER 1
Pittsburgh at Dallas
N.Y. Rangers at Edmonton

SATURDAY, OCTOBER 2
Carolina at Boston
Toronto at Montreal
Ottawa at Philadelphia
New Jersey at Atlanta
N.Y. Islanders at Tampa Bay
Washington at Florida
Buffalo at Detroit
Phoenix at St. Louis
Los Angeles at Nashville
Anaheim at Dallas
N.Y. Rangers at Vancouver
Calgary at San Jose

MONDAY, OCTOBER 4
Boston at Toronto
Los Angeles at St. Louis
Chicago at San Jose

TUESDAY, OCTOBER 5
Ottawa at N.Y. Rangers
Dallas at Detroit
Colorado at Nashville
Anaheim at Phoenix

WEDNESDAY, OCTOBER 6
Colorado at Toronto
Los Angeles at Florida
St. Louis at Calgary
Montreal at Edmonton
Chicago at Vancouver

THURSDAY, OCTOBER 7
Boston at Ottawa
Pittsburgh at New Jersey
Carolina at Philadelphia
Detroit at Atlanta
Los Angeles at Tampa Bay
Edmonton at San Jose

FRIDAY, OCTOBER 8
Washington at Buffalo
Carolina at N.Y. Rangers
Colorado at Pittsburgh
Phoenix at Chicago
Montreal at Calgary
Dallas at Anaheim

SATURDAY, OCTOBER 9
Philadelphia at Boston
Toronto at Ottawa
Tampa Bay at New Jersey
Los Angeles at Washington
Buffalo at Atlanta
Detroit at Florida
St. Louis at Edmonton
Montreal at Vancouver
Dallas at San Jose

SUNDAY, OCTOBER 10
Colorado at N.Y. Islanders*
Phoenix at N.Y. Rangers*
Nashville at Chicago

MONDAY, OCTOBER 11
Colorado at Boston*
Phoenix at Buffalo
Nashville at Toronto
New Jersey at Ottawa*
N.Y. Rangers at N.Y. Islanders
Carolina at Calgary*
San Jose at Anaheim*

TUESDAY, OCTOBER 12
Florida at Montreal
Philadelphia at Washington

WEDNESDAY, OCTOBER 13
Florida at Toronto
Anaheim at New Jersey
St. Louis at Detroit
San Jose at Dallas
Boston at Colorado
Carolina at Edmonton
Calgary at Vancouver

THURSDAY, OCTOBER 14
Atlanta at N.Y. Islanders
Pittsburgh at N.Y. Rangers
Montreal at Philadelphia
San Jose at Nashville
Ottawa at Phoenix

FRIDAY, OCTOBER 15
Anaheim at Tampa Bay
Toronto at Chicago
Boston at Dallas
Los Angeles at Calgary
Carolina at Vancouver

SATURDAY, OCTOBER 16
Buffalo at Montreal
N.Y. Islanders at New Jersey
Chicago at Pittsburgh
San Jose at Washington
Atlanta at Tampa Bay
Anaheim at Florida
Philadelphia at Detroit
Toronto at St. Louis
Dallas at Nashville
Ottawa at Colorado
Vancouver at Calgary
Los Angeles at Edmonton
Boston at Phoenix

SUNDAY, OCTOBER 17
Atlanta at N.Y. Rangers
Buffalo at Philadelphia

MONDAY, OCTOBER 18
N.Y. Islanders at Montreal

TUESDAY, OCTOBER 19
San Jose at N.Y. Rangers
Anaheim at Washington
Vancouver at Tampa Bay
Calgary at St. Louis

WEDNESDAY, OCTOBER 20
Nashville at Buffalo
Carolina at Toronto
Colorado at Montreal
N.Y. Rangers at Philadelphia
Vancouver at Florida
San Jose at Detroit
Edmonton at Dallas
Boston at Los Angeles

THURSDAY, OCTOBER 21
Colorado at Ottawa
Anaheim at Chicago
Edmonton at St. Louis

FRIDAY, OCTOBER 22
Carolina at Buffalo
Philadelphia at N.Y. Rangers
Calgary at Florida
Anaheim at Detroit
New Jersey at Dallas
Phoenix at Los Angeles

SATURDAY, OCTOBER 23
Montreal at Toronto
Buffalo at Ottawa
Vancouver at N.Y. Islanders
Carolina at Pittsburgh
Colorado at Atlanta
Calgary at Tampa Bay
Detroit at Chicago
New Jersey at St. Louis
Edmonton at Nashville
Washington at Phoenix
Boston at San Jose

SUNDAY, OCTOBER 24
Vancouver at N.Y. Rangers
Florida at Philadelphia
Boston at Anaheim
San Jose at Los Angeles

MONDAY, OCTOBER 25
Dallas at Toronto

TUESDAY, OCTOBER 26
Vancouver at Philadelphia
Calgary at Atlanta
Phoenix at Edmonton
Washington at Los Angeles

WEDNESDAY, OCTOBER 27
Tampa Bay at Buffalo
Atlanta at Toronto
Chicago at Montreal
St. Louis at New Jersey
N.Y. Islanders at Florida
Colorado at Detroit
Pittsburgh at Anaheim

THURSDAY, OCTOBER 28
Tampa Bay at Boston
Calgary at Ottawa
Colorado at Philadelphia
Phoenix at Vancouver
Pittsburgh at Los Angeles
Nashville at San Jose

FRIDAY, OCTOBER 29
Florida at Buffalo
New Jersey at Carolina
Chicago at Detroit
Washington at Anaheim

SATURDAY, OCTOBER 30
Buffalo at Boston
Calgary at Toronto
N.Y. Rangers at Montreal
Florida at Ottawa
Carolina at N.Y. Islanders
New Jersey at Philadelphia
Los Angeles at Chicago
Detroit at St. Louis
Tampa Bay at Dallas

Phoenix at Colorado*
Nashville at Vancouver
Pittsburgh at San Jose

SUNDAY, OCTOBER 31

Ottawa at Atlanta
Nashville at Edmonton
Phoenix at Anaheim
Washington at San Jose

TUESDAY, NOVEMBER 2

Los Angeles at Pittsburgh

WEDNESDAY, NOVEMBER 3

Montreal at New Jersey
N.Y. Islanders at N.Y. Rangers
Ottawa at Washington
Toronto at Carolina
Tampa Bay at Atlanta
Los Angeles at Detroit
Buffalo at Dallas
St. Louis at Colorado
Nashville at Calgary
Florida at Edmonton
Philadelphia at Anaheim
Phoenix at San Jose

THURSDAY, NOVEMBER 4

New Jersey at Boston
Pittsburgh at Ottawa
Montreal at N.Y. Islanders
Buffalo at Chicago

FRIDAY, NOVEMBER 5

Toronto at Washington
Carolina at Detroit
Chicago at Nashville
N.Y. Rangers at Colorado
St. Louis at Edmonton
Florida at Vancouver
Dallas at Phoenix
Philadelphia at San Jose

SATURDAY, NOVEMBER 6

Atlanta at Boston
N.Y. Islanders at Buffalo
Montreal at Ottawa
Toronto at New Jersey
Tampa Bay at Pittsburgh
Florida at Calgary
Philadelphia at Los Angeles
Dallas at San Jose

SUNDAY, NOVEMBER 7

Washington at Carolina
Detroit at Tampa Bay
N.Y. Rangers at Chicago
St. Louis at Vancouver
Edmonton at Anaheim

TUESDAY, NOVEMBER 9

Anaheim at Toronto
Philadelphia at New Jersey
Tampa Bay at Washington
Dallas at St. Louis
San Jose at Vancouver
Edmonton at Los Angeles

WEDNESDAY, NOVEMBER 10

Boston at Buffalo
Ottawa at N.Y. Rangers
Montreal at Pittsburgh
N.Y. Islanders at Carolina
Atlanta at Florida
Nashville at Chicago
Detroit at Dallas
San Jose at Calgary
Edmonton at Phoenix

THURSDAY, NOVEMBER 11

Toronto at Boston
Anaheim at Montreal
Nashville at Ottawa
Carolina at Philadelphia
N.Y. Rangers at Washington
Colorado at Los Angeles

FRIDAY, NOVEMBER 12

Atlanta at New Jersey
Buffalo at Tampa Bay
Pittsburgh at Detroit
N.Y. Islanders at Chicago
Edmonton at St. Louis
Vancouver at Phoenix

SATURDAY, NOVEMBER 13

Detroit at Toronto
Atlanta at Montreal
Anaheim at Ottawa
St. Louis at N.Y. Islanders
Boston at N.Y. Rangers
San Jose at Philadelphia*
Nashville at Pittsburgh
New Jersey at Washington
Tampa Bay at Carolina
Buffalo at Florida
Colorado at Calgary

SUNDAY, NOVEMBER 14

Edmonton at Chicago
Los Angeles at Phoenix

MONDAY, NOVEMBER 15

San Jose at Toronto
Colorado at Vancouver

TUESDAY, NOVEMBER 16

San Jose at Montreal
Buffalo at Pittsburgh
Calgary at Phoenix
Chicago at Los Angeles

WEDNESDAY, NOVEMBER 17

St. Louis at Toronto
Boston at New Jersey
Dallas at Washington
Ottawa at Carolina
Tampa Bay at Atlanta
Florida at Colorado
Detroit at Vancouver
Calgary at Anaheim

THURSDAY, NOVEMBER 18

N.Y. Rangers at Boston
San Jose at Ottawa
Dallas at Philadelphia
Pittsburgh at Tampa Bay
Florida at St. Louis
Montreal at Nashville
Phoenix at Los Angeles

FRIDAY, NOVEMBER 19

Carolina at Washington
Buffalo at Atlanta
N.Y. Islanders at Colorado
Detroit at Calgary
Chicago at Anaheim

SATURDAY, NOVEMBER 20

Washington at Boston
Atlanta at Buffalo
N.Y. Rangers at Toronto
Ottawa at New Jersey*
Tampa Bay at Philadelphia
Dallas at Carolina
Pittsburgh at Florida
San Jose at St. Louis
Vancouver at Nashville
Detroit at Edmonton
Chicago at Phoenix
Montreal at Los Angeles

SUNDAY, NOVEMBER 21

N.Y. Islanders at Edmonton

MONDAY, NOVEMBER 22

Boston at Carolina
Vancouver at Atlanta
Philadelphia at Tampa Bay
Nashville at St. Louis
Colorado at Dallas
Montreal at Anaheim

TUESDAY, NOVEMBER 23

Toronto at Pittsburgh
Los Angeles at Colorado
N.Y. Islanders at Calgary
Montreal at San Jose

WEDNESDAY, NOVEMBER 24

Washington at Buffalo
Vancouver at Carolina
N.Y. Rangers at Tampa Bay
Philadelphia at Florida
St. Louis at Detroit
Boston at Nashville
Los Angeles at Dallas
Chicago at Edmonton
New Jersey at Anaheim

THURSDAY, NOVEMBER 25

Ottawa at Atlanta
Chicago at Calgary
New Jersey at Phoenix

FRIDAY, NOVEMBER 26

Vancouver at Boston*
St. Louis at Buffalo
Toronto at Philadelphia*
Ottawa at Pittsburgh
Nashville at Washington
Carolina at Tampa Bay
N.Y. Rangers at Florida
Edmonton at Detroit
Anaheim at Dallas*
Colorado at Phoenix

SATURDAY, NOVEMBER 27

Edmonton at Toronto
Vancouver at Montreal
Washington at N.Y. Islanders
Pittsburgh at Carolina
Atlanta at Florida
Chicago at St. Louis
Anaheim at Nashville
Calgary at Colorado
San Jose at Los Angeles*

SUNDAY, NOVEMBER 28

N.Y. Islanders at Boston
Philadelphia at Ottawa*
Dallas at Atlanta
Buffalo at Tampa Bay
Phoenix at Detroit*
New Jersey at San Jose

MONDAY, NOVEMBER 29

Washington at Toronto

TUESDAY, NOVEMBER 30

Pittsburgh at Buffalo
Chicago at Ottawa
Dallas at N.Y. Islanders
Calgary at Carolina
Phoenix at Nashville
Colorado at Vancouver

WEDNESDAY, DECEMBER 1
Dallas at Montreal
N.Y. Rangers at New Jersey
San Jose at Detroit
Colorado at Edmonton
Tampa Bay at Anaheim

THURSDAY, DECEMBER 2
Philadelphia at Buffalo
Calgary at N.Y. Islanders
San Jose at Pittsburgh
Boston at Washington
Toronto at Carolina
Nashville at St. Louis
Edmonton at Vancouver
Tampa Bay at Phoenix

FRIDAY, DECEMBER 3
Ottawa at New Jersey
Montreal at N.Y. Rangers
Florida at Atlanta
Detroit at Chicago
Los Angeles at Anaheim

SATURDAY, DECEMBER 4
Chicago at Boston
N.Y. Rangers at Buffalo
Pittsburgh at Toronto
Philadelphia at Montreal
Dallas at Ottawa
Calgary at New Jersey
Atlanta at N.Y. Islanders
Washington at Florida
San Jose at St. Louis
Detroit at Nashville
Carolina at Colorado
Vancouver at Edmonton
Anaheim at Phoenix
Tampa Bay at Los Angeles

SUNDAY, DECEMBER 5
St. Louis at Philadelphia

MONDAY, DECEMBER 6
Buffalo at Toronto
Calgary at N.Y. Rangers
Nashville at Atlanta
Edmonton at Chicago
Phoenix at Dallas
Vancouver at Colorado
Tampa Bay at San Jose

TUESDAY, DECEMBER 7
Calgary at Montreal
Pittsburgh at New Jersey
N.Y. Islanders at Washington
Carolina at St. Louis

WEDNESDAY, DECEMBER 8
Ottawa at Buffalo
Edmonton at N.Y. Rangers
Nashville at Detroit
Carolina at Dallas
Florida at Phoenix
Vancouver at Anaheim
Atlanta at Los Angeles
Colorado at San Jose

THURSDAY, DECEMBER 9
Edmonton at Boston
Montreal at N.Y. Islanders
Toronto at Philadelphia
Washington at Pittsburgh
New Jersey at Chicago

FRIDAY, DECEMBER 10
Chicago at Buffalo
Carolina at Tampa Bay
Los Angeles at Detroit
St. Louis at Nashville
Florida at Dallas
Vancouver at Calgary
Colorado at Anaheim
Atlanta at San Jose

SATURDAY, DECEMBER 11
Detroit at Boston
Philadelphia at Toronto
Los Angeles at Montreal
N.Y. Islanders at Ottawa*
Edmonton at New Jersey*
Phoenix at Pittsburgh
Dallas at St. Louis
Florida at Nashville

SUNDAY, DECEMBER 12
Calgary at Chicago
Colorado at Vancouver
Atlanta at Anaheim

MONDAY, DECEMBER 13
Phoenix at Boston
Ottawa at Toronto
Montreal at Washington

TUESDAY, DECEMBER 14
Philadelphia at Buffalo
Los Angeles at New Jersey
Edmonton at N.Y. Islanders
Boston at Pittsburgh
Nashville at Tampa Bay
Calgary at St. Louis
Chicago at San Jose

WEDNESDAY, DECEMBER 15
N.Y. Islanders at Toronto
Los Angeles at N.Y. Rangers
Pittsburgh at Carolina
Washington at Atlanta
Nashville at Florida
Edmonton at Detroit
Calgary at Dallas
Anaheim at Colorado

THURSDAY, DECEMBER 16
New Jersey at Montreal
Phoenix at Philadelphia
Ottawa at Vancouver

FRIDAY, DECEMBER 17
Florida at Buffalo
Washington at N.Y. Rangers
Boston at Atlanta
Colorado at Detroit
Dallas at Edmonton
Chicago at Anaheim

SATURDAY, DECEMBER 18
Montreal at Toronto
Washington at New Jersey
Buffalo at N.Y. Islanders
Tampa Bay at Philadelphia
Florida at Pittsburgh
Atlanta at Carolina
Boston at St. Louis
Colorado at Nashville
Ottawa at Calgary
Dallas at Vancouver
Chicago at Los Angeles

SUNDAY, DECEMBER 19
New Jersey at N.Y. Islanders
Tampa Bay at N.Y. Rangers
Nashville at Philadelphia
Ottawa at Edmonton
San Jose at Phoenix*
Detroit at Anaheim

MONDAY, DECEMBER 20
Pittsburgh at Montreal
Colorado at Carolina
Toronto at Florida
Detroit at San Jose

TUESDAY, DECEMBER 21
Nashville at Boston
Pittsburgh at N.Y. Islanders
Buffalo at N.Y. Rangers
Toronto at Tampa Bay
Dallas at Calgary
Washington at Edmonton
St. Louis at Phoenix

WEDNESDAY, DECEMBER 22
Philadelphia at New Jersey
Detroit at Carolina
Atlanta at Florida
Washington at Vancouver
Phoenix at Anaheim
Los Angeles at San Jose

THURSDAY, DECEMBER 23
Montreal at Boston
Colorado at Buffalo
New Jersey at Toronto
Carolina at Ottawa
N.Y. Rangers at N.Y. Islanders
Atlanta at Philadelphia
Tampa Bay at Pittsburgh
Dallas at Chicago
St. Louis at Nashville
Edmonton at Calgary

SUNDAY, DECEMBER 26
New Jersey at N.Y. Rangers*
Florida at Carolina
Tampa Bay at Atlanta
Pittsburgh at Chicago
Nashville at St. Louis
Calgary at Vancouver
Phoenix at Los Angeles
Anaheim at San Jose*

MONDAY, DECEMBER 27
Montreal at Ottawa
Buffalo at New Jersey
Boston at N.Y. Islanders
Chicago at Washington
Florida at Tampa Bay
Atlanta at Detroit
San Jose at Dallas
St. Louis at Colorado
Philadelphia at Calgary
Anaheim at Edmonton

TUESDAY, DECEMBER 28
Detroit at Buffalo
Carolina at Nashville
N.Y. Rangers at Phoenix

WEDNESDAY, DECEMBER 29
Ottawa at Montreal
Boston at New Jersey
Toronto at N.Y. Islanders
Pittsburgh at Washington
N.Y. Rangers at Dallas
Los Angeles at Colorado
Anaheim at Calgary
Philadelphia at Vancouver

THURSDAY, DECEMBER 30
Boston at Ottawa
N.Y. Islanders at Pittsburgh
Florida at Chicago
San Jose at St. Louis
Atlanta at Nashville
Edmonton at Los Angeles

FRIDAY, DECEMBER 31
Chicago at Detroit
Anaheim at Dallas

SATURDAY, JANUARY 1
New Jersey at Boston
Toronto at Buffalo
St. Louis at Washington
Carolina at Atlanta
Tampa Bay at Florida*
San Jose at Nashville*
Edmonton at Phoenix

SUNDAY, JANUARY 2
N.Y. Rangers at Montreal
Philadelphia at N.Y. Islanders*
Detroit at Pittsburgh
San Jose at Chicago
Vancouver at Calgary*

MONDAY, JANUARY 3
Buffalo at Toronto
New Jersey at Ottawa*
St. Louis at N.Y. Rangers
Los Angeles at Dallas
Edmonton at Colorado

TUESDAY, JANUARY 4
Atlanta at Buffalo
Boston at N.Y. Islanders
Montreal at Washington
Ottawa at Carolina
Phoenix at Detroit
Los Angeles at St. Louis

WEDNESDAY, JANUARY 5
Toronto at N.Y. Rangers
New Jersey at Pittsburgh
Nashville at Dallas
Calgary at Colorado
San Jose at Edmonton
Tampa Bay at Vancouver
Florida at Anaheim

THURSDAY, JANUARY 6
Carolina at Boston
New Jersey at Buffalo
Phoenix at Ottawa
N.Y. Islanders at Philadelphia
Washington at Atlanta
Nashville at Detroit
Calgary at Chicago
Montreal at St. Louis
Florida at Los Angeles

FRIDAY, JANUARY 7
Toronto at Pittsburgh
Anaheim at Carolina
Vancouver at Dallas
Montreal at Colorado
Tampa Bay at Edmonton

SATURDAY, JANUARY 8
N.Y. Islanders at Boston
N.Y. Rangers at Toronto
Buffalo at Ottawa
Phoenix at New Jersey
Pittsburgh at Philadelphia
Atlanta at Washington
Anaheim at Detroit
Vancouver at St. Louis
Chicago at Nashville
Tampa Bay at Calgary
Florida at San Jose

SUNDAY, JANUARY 9
N.Y. Rangers at Carolina
Colorado at Chicago

MONDAY, JANUARY 10
Phoenix at N.Y. Islanders

TUESDAY, JANUARY 11
Toronto at Boston
Detroit at Montreal
Philadelphia at Carolina
New Jersey at Tampa Bay
Nashville at Colorado
Dallas at Edmonton
Ottawa at Los Angeles
St. Louis at San Jose

WEDNESDAY, JANUARY 12
Washington at Atlanta
N.Y. Islanders at Florida
Vancouver at Chicago
Dallas at Calgary
Pittsburgh at Phoenix
Ottawa at Anaheim

THURSDAY, JANUARY 13
Buffalo at Boston
N.Y. Islanders at Tampa Bay
Chicago at Detroit
Vancouver at Nashville
Pittsburgh at Colorado
St. Louis at Los Angeles

FRIDAY, JANUARY 14
Montreal at Buffalo
Washington at New Jersey
Philadelphia at Atlanta
Carolina at Florida
Toronto at Edmonton
St. Louis at Anaheim

SATURDAY, JANUARY 15
Boston at Montreal
N.Y. Rangers at N.Y. Islanders*
New Jersey at Philadelphia
Florida at Tampa Bay
Pittsburgh at Nashville
Chicago at Colorado
Toronto at Calgary
Dallas at Vancouver
Anaheim at Phoenix
Los Angeles at San Jose

SUNDAY, JANUARY 16
Atlanta at N.Y. Rangers*
Ottawa at Washington*
Detroit at Edmonton

MONDAY, JANUARY 17
Atlanta at Boston*
Carolina at New Jersey
Ottawa at N.Y. Islanders*
Washington at Tampa Bay*
Philadelphia at Florida*
San Jose at Chicago*
Phoenix at Colorado
Toronto at Vancouver
Buffalo at Anaheim

TUESDAY, JANUARY 18
Carolina at N.Y. Rangers
Phoenix at Nashville
Detroit at Calgary
Buffalo at Los Angeles

WEDNESDAY, JANUARY 19
N.Y. Islanders at Montreal
Chicago at New Jersey
St. Louis at Pittsburgh
Boston at Atlanta
Washington at Florida
San Jose at Colorado
Calgary at Edmonton
Detroit at Vancouver
Dallas at Anaheim

THURSDAY, JANUARY 20
Ottawa at Philadelphia
N.Y. Rangers at Carolina
Boston at Tampa Bay
Buffalo at Phoenix
Dallas at Los Angeles

FRIDAY, JANUARY 21
N.Y. Islanders at New Jersey
Florida at Atlanta
St. Louis at Chicago
Nashville at Calgary
Colorado at Anaheim

SATURDAY, JANUARY 22
Washington at Toronto
Pittsburgh at Montreal
Detroit at Ottawa
Tampa Bay at N.Y. Islanders
Buffalo at Carolina*
Boston at Florida
N.Y. Rangers at St. Louis
Vancouver at Edmonton
Anaheim at San Jose

SUNDAY, JANUARY 23
Philadelphia at Pittsburgh
Dallas at Chicago
Nashville at Vancouver
San Jose at Phoenix
Colorado at Los Angeles*

MONDAY, JANUARY 24
Calgary at Boston
Ottawa at Toronto
Tampa Bay at Washington
Montreal at Carolina
N.Y. Rangers at Atlanta
Nashville at Edmonton

TUESDAY, JANUARY 25
Tampa Bay at Buffalo
N.Y. Rangers at Pittsburgh
Phoenix at Carolina
Edmonton at Vancouver
Colorado at San Jose

WEDNESDAY, JANUARY 26
St. Louis at Ottawa
Calgary at Washington
Phoenix at Atlanta
New Jersey at Florida
Toronto at Detroit
Los Angeles at Dallas
N.Y. Islanders at Anaheim

THURSDAY, JANUARY 27
Montreal at Boston
Toronto at N.Y. Rangers
Florida at Philadelphia
Atlanta at Pittsburgh
Colorado at Chicago
Los Angeles at Nashville

FRIDAY, JANUARY 28
Ottawa at Buffalo
Phoenix at Washington
New Jersey at Carolina
Edmonton at Tampa Bay
Calgary at Detroit
St. Louis at Dallas
San Jose at Vancouver

SATURDAY, JANUARY 29
Buffalo at Boston
Los Angeles at Toronto
Philadelphia at Montreal*
N.Y. Rangers at Ottawa
Anaheim at Pittsburgh
Atlanta at Tampa Bay
Edmonton at Florida
New Jersey at Detroit
Colorado at St. Louis
Calgary at Nashville
N.Y. Islanders at San Jose

SUNDAY, JANUARY 30
Carolina at Montreal*
Philadelphia at Washington*
Chicago at Vancouver

MONDAY, JANUARY 31
Anaheim at Boston
Nashville at N.Y. Rangers
Pittsburgh at Atlanta
Edmonton at Dallas
Detroit at Phoenix
N.Y. Islanders at Los Angeles

TUESDAY, FEBRUARY 1
Anaheim at Buffalo
Boston at Ottawa
Washington at Pittsburgh
Florida at Carolina
Toronto at Tampa Bay
Vancouver at Colorado
St. Louis at Calgary
Phoenix at San Jose

WEDNESDAY, FEBRUARY 2
Nashville at N.Y. Islanders
New Jersey at N.Y. Rangers
Montreal at Florida
Atlanta at Dallas
Chicago at Edmonton

THURSDAY, FEBRUARY 3
Toronto at Boston
Ottawa at Buffalo
Nashville at New Jersey
Anaheim at Philadelphia
N.Y. Islanders at Pittsburgh
Carolina at Washington
N.Y. Rangers at Atlanta
Montreal at Tampa Bay
San Jose at Colorado
Chicago at Calgary
St. Louis at Vancouver
Dallas at Phoenix
Detroit at Los Angeles

SUNDAY, FEBRUARY 6
All-Star Game at Toronto*

TUESDAY, FEBRUARY 8
Washington at Boston
Edmonton at Montreal
Carolina at N.Y. Islanders
New Jersey at N.Y. Rangers
San Jose at Tampa Bay
St. Louis at Detroit
Buffalo at Colorado
Anaheim at Los Angeles

WEDNESDAY, FEBRUARY 9
Philadelphia at Toronto
N.Y. Rangers at New Jersey
Atlanta at Pittsburgh
San Jose at Florida
Calgary at Vancouver
Los Angeles at Phoenix
Dallas at Anaheim

THURSDAY, FEBRUARY 10
Washington at Montreal
Tampa Bay at N.Y. Islanders
Edmonton at Philadelphia
Detroit at St. Louis
Buffalo at Nashville
Calgary at Colorado

FRIDAY, FEBRUARY 11
Florida at Ottawa
Boston at N.Y. Rangers
Edmonton at Pittsburgh
San Jose at Atlanta
Dallas at Los Angeles

SATURDAY, FEBRUARY 12
Florida at Boston
Vancouver at Toronto
Ottawa at Montreal
Pittsburgh at N.Y. Islanders
Buffalo at Philadelphia*
Chicago at Atlanta
Carolina at Tampa Bay
Anaheim at St. Louis
Washington at Nashville
Calgary at Phoenix

SUNDAY, FEBRUARY 13
Edmonton at Buffalo*
San Jose at New Jersey*
N.Y. Islanders at N.Y. Rangers
Washington at Dallas
Detroit at Colorado

MONDAY, FEBRUARY 14
Carolina at Toronto
Florida at Montreal
Vancouver at Pittsburgh
Anaheim at Chicago
Detroit at Phoenix
Calgary at Los Angeles

TUESDAY, FEBRUARY 15
Carolina at Ottawa
Philadelphia at New Jersey
San Jose at N.Y. Islanders
Colorado at Washington
N.Y. Rangers at Tampa Bay
Atlanta at St. Louis
Edmonton at Nashville

WEDNESDAY, FEBRUARY 16
Boston at Toronto
Buffalo at Pittsburgh
Montreal at Atlanta
N.Y. Rangers at Florida
Vancouver at Detroit
Los Angeles at Chicago
Nashville at Dallas
Calgary at Anaheim

THURSDAY, FEBRUARY 17
Vancouver at Buffalo
Tampa Bay at Ottawa
Colorado at New Jersey
N.Y. Islanders at Philadelphia
Montreal at Carolina

FRIDAY, FEBRUARY 18
Colorado at N.Y. Rangers
Los Angeles at Detroit
Washington at Chicago
St. Louis at Nashville
Phoenix at Dallas
Edmonton at Calgary
San Jose at Anaheim

SATURDAY, FEBRUARY 19
Los Angeles at Buffalo
Toronto at Montreal
Vancouver at Ottawa*
N.Y. Islanders at New Jersey*
Washington at Philadelphia
Tampa Bay at Carolina
Pittsburgh at Florida
Calgary at Edmonton

SUNDAY, FEBRUARY 20
Philadelphia at N.Y. Rangers
Detroit at Chicago*
Dallas at Colorado*
Atlanta at Phoenix

MONDAY, FEBRUARY 21
New Jersey at Buffalo
Detroit at N.Y. Islanders*
Washington at Carolina*
Pittsburgh at Tampa Bay
Ottawa at Florida*
Dallas at Nashville
Los Angeles at Edmonton
Boston at Vancouver
St. Louis at Anaheim

TUESDAY, FEBRUARY 22
Phoenix at Montreal
Pittsburgh at N.Y. Rangers
Chicago at Philadelphia
Atlanta at Colorado

WEDNESDAY, FEBRUARY 23
Phoenix at Toronto
Florida at Washington
Dallas at Detroit
Nashville at Chicago
Los Angeles at Calgary
Boston at Edmonton
Vancouver at Anaheim
St. Louis at San Jose

THURSDAY, FEBRUARY 24
New Jersey at Montreal
Pittsburgh at Philadelphia
Florida at Carolina
Ottawa at Tampa Bay

FRIDAY, FEBRUARY 25
N.Y. Rangers at Buffalo
Toronto at New Jersey
Boston at Washington
N.Y. Islanders at Detroit
Colorado at St. Louis
Chicago at Dallas
Phoenix at Calgary
Atlanta at Edmonton
Los Angeles at Vancouver

SATURDAY, FEBRUARY 26
Buffalo at Toronto
Washington at Montreal
N.Y. Rangers at Ottawa
Philadelphia at N.Y. Islanders
Boston at Pittsburgh
Carolina at Florida
Tampa Bay at Nashville
Atlanta at Calgary
Los Angeles at San Jose

SUNDAY, FEBRUARY 27
Montreal at New Jersey
Tampa Bay at Detroit
Chicago at St. Louis*
Colorado at Dallas
Phoenix at Vancouver
Edmonton at Anaheim

MONDAY, FEBRUARY 28
Washington at N.Y. Islanders
Ottawa at Pittsburgh
Buffalo at Florida

TUESDAY, FEBRUARY 29
Ottawa at Boston
Toronto at Atlanta
Philadelphia at St. Louis
New Jersey at Nashville
Edmonton at Colorado
Vancouver at Los Angeles
Anaheim at San Jose

WEDNESDAY, MARCH 1
Buffalo at N.Y. Rangers
Washington at Tampa Bay
Toronto at Florida
Montreal at Chicago
Philadelphia at Dallas
Pittsburgh at Calgary
Carolina at Phoenix

THURSDAY, MARCH 2
Ottawa at N.Y. Islanders
St. Louis at Atlanta
New Jersey at Colorado
Anaheim at Vancouver
Carolina at Los Angeles
Nashville at San Jose

FRIDAY, MARCH 3
Florida at N.Y. Rangers
Detroit at Washington
Tampa Bay at Chicago
Anaheim at Calgary
Dallas at Phoenix

SATURDAY, MARCH 4
Philadelphia at Boston*
Montreal at Toronto
Atlanta at Ottawa
Buffalo at N.Y. Islanders*
St. Louis at Florida
Tampa Bay at Colorado
Pittsburgh at Edmonton
New Jersey at Vancouver
Nashville at Los Angeles
Carolina at San Jose

SUNDAY, MARCH 5
N.Y. Islanders at Philadelphia
Buffalo at Washington*
Phoenix at Chicago*
Detroit at Dallas
New Jersey at Calgary
Nashville at Anaheim

MONDAY, MARCH 6
Ottawa at Boston
Atlanta at Montreal
Toronto at Vancouver
N.Y. Rangers at San Jose

TUESDAY, MARCH 7
Florida at Washington
Phoenix at St. Louis
Chicago at Nashville
Colorado at Calgary
Toronto at Edmonton
Detroit at Los Angeles

WEDNESDAY, MARCH 8
Boston at Buffalo
Montreal at Pittsburgh
Chicago at Carolina
Philadelphia at Tampa Bay
Vancouver at Dallas
N.Y. Rangers at Anaheim
Detroit at San Jose

THURSDAY, MARCH 9
Pittsburgh at Ottawa
Washington at Philadelphia
Vancouver at St. Louis
Toronto at Calgary
N.Y. Islanders at Phoenix
N.Y. Rangers at Los Angeles

FRIDAY, MARCH 10
Montreal at Buffalo
Boston at Carolina
New Jersey at Atlanta
Florida at Tampa Bay
Detroit at Nashville
N.Y. Islanders at Dallas
Colorado at Edmonton

SATURDAY, MARCH 11
Boston at Montreal
Toronto at Ottawa
N.Y. Rangers at Pittsburgh
New Jersey at Washington
Chicago at Florida
Anaheim at St. Louis*
Vancouver at Phoenix
Calgary at Los Angeles

SUNDAY, MARCH 12
N.Y. Islanders at Buffalo*
Atlanta at Carolina*
Chicago at Tampa Bay
Edmonton at Nashville*
St. Louis at Dallas*
Philadelphia at Colorado

MONDAY, MARCH 13
Dallas at N.Y. Rangers
New Jersey at Pittsburgh
Edmonton at Atlanta
Philadelphia at Phoenix
Vancouver at Los Angeles
Calgary at San Jose

TUESDAY, MARCH 14
Tampa Bay at Montreal
Nashville at Detroit
Anaheim at Colorado

WEDNESDAY, MARCH 15
Chicago at Toronto
Dallas at New Jersey
Tampa Bay at N.Y. Rangers
N.Y. Islanders at Washington
Edmonton at Carolina
Ottawa at Calgary
St. Louis at Phoenix
Los Angeles at Anaheim
Buffalo at San Jose

THURSDAY, MARCH 16
Montreal at Philadelphia
Florida at Pittsburgh
N.Y. Islanders at Atlanta
Toronto at Detroit
Boston at Chicago
Nashville at Colorado
Buffalo at Vancouver

FRIDAY, MARCH 17
Tampa Bay at New Jersey
Carolina at Washington
Ottawa at Edmonton
Nashville at Phoenix
San Jose at Anaheim
St. Louis at Los Angeles

SATURDAY, MARCH 18
Pittsburgh at Boston*
Atlanta at Toronto
Carolina at Montreal
Florida at N.Y. Islanders
N.Y. Rangers at Philadelphia*
Dallas at Chicago*
Detroit at Colorado*
Buffalo at Calgary
Ottawa at Vancouver

SUNDAY, MARCH 19
Florida at New Jersey
Boston at Philadelphia*
N.Y. Rangers at Pittsburgh
Tampa Bay at Washington*
San Jose at Dallas*
Calgary at Edmonton
Detroit at Anaheim
Nashville at Los Angeles

MONDAY, MARCH 20
Montreal at Buffalo
Washington at St. Louis
Vancouver at Colorado

TUESDAY, MARCH 21
Tampa Bay at Boston
Atlanta at Ottawa
Carolina at New Jersey
Pittsburgh at N.Y. Islanders
Florida at N.Y. Rangers
Philadelphia at Nashville
Chicago at Phoenix
Anaheim at Los Angeles

WEDNESDAY, MARCH 22
N.Y. Islanders at Toronto
St. Louis at Carolina
Montreal at Atlanta
Calgary at Detroit
Anaheim at Edmonton
Vancouver at San Jose

THURSDAY, MARCH 23
Florida at Boston
Calgary at Buffalo
Toronto at Ottawa
Washington at N.Y. Rangers
Los Angeles at Philadelphia
Detroit at Nashville
Colorado at Phoenix

FRIDAY, MARCH 24
New Jersey at N.Y. Islanders
Pittsburgh at Atlanta
St. Louis at Tampa Bay
Chicago at Dallas
Anaheim at Vancouver
Phoenix at San Jose

SATURDAY, MARCH 25
Los Angeles at Boston*
New Jersey at Toronto
Washington at Ottawa
Montreal at Florida
Calgary at Nashville
Vancouver at Edmonton

SUNDAY, MARCH 26
Pittsburgh at Philadelphia*
N.Y. Islanders at Carolina*
Los Angeles at Atlanta
Montreal at Tampa Bay
N.Y. Rangers at Detroit*
St. Louis at Chicago*
Colorado at Dallas*
Phoenix at Anaheim

MONDAY, MARCH 27
Detroit at N.Y. Rangers
Buffalo at Carolina
Chicago at Colorado
Edmonton at San Jose

TUESDAY, MARCH 28
Philadelphia at Ottawa
New Jersey at Pittsburgh
Atlanta at Washington
Dallas at Tampa Bay
N.Y. Islanders at Nashville

WEDNESDAY, MARCH 29
Boston at Montreal
Nashville at Carolina
Dallas at Florida
Vancouver at Detroit
Toronto at St. Louis
Edmonton at Colorado
San Jose at Los Angeles

THURSDAY, MARCH 30
St. Louis at Boston
Pittsburgh at Washington
Ottawa at Tampa Bay
Toronto at Chicago

FRIDAY, MARCH 31
Carolina at Buffalo
Atlanta at New Jersey
Ottawa at Florida
Vancouver at Nashville
Phoenix at Calgary

SATURDAY, APRIL 1
N.Y. Rangers at Boston*
Buffalo at Montreal
Chicago at N.Y. Islanders*
Philadelphia at Pittsburgh*
Toronto at Washington
Tampa Bay at Florida
Detroit at St. Louis*
San Jose at Calgary
Phoenix at Edmonton
Anaheim at Los Angeles*

SUNDAY, APRIL 2
Philadelphia at Carolina*
N.Y. Islanders at Atlanta*
New Jersey at Tampa Bay
Montreal at Detroit
Vancouver at Chicago*
Ottawa at St. Louis*
Dallas at Colorado*

MONDAY, APRIL 3
Toronto at Buffalo
Carolina at Pittsburgh
N.Y. Rangers at Washington
New Jersey at Florida
Calgary at Dallas
San Jose at Edmonton
Los Angeles at Phoenix
Nashville at Anaheim

TUESDAY, APRIL 4
Washington at Ottawa
Philadelphia at Atlanta
Boston at Tampa Bay

WEDNESDAY, APRIL 5
Pittsburgh at Toronto
Montreal at N.Y. Rangers
Boston at Florida
Anaheim at Chicago
Calgary at St. Louis
Colorado at Edmonton
Los Angeles at Vancouver
Nashville at Phoenix
Dallas at San Jose

THURSDAY, APRIL 6
Tampa Bay at Montreal
N.Y. Islanders at Ottawa
Buffalo at New Jersey
Atlanta at Philadelphia

FRIDAY, APRIL 7
Pittsburgh at Buffalo
Toronto at N.Y. Islanders
Washington at Detroit
Chicago at St. Louis
Anaheim at Nashville
Colorado at Calgary
Edmonton at Vancouver
San Jose at Phoenix
Dallas at Los Angeles

SATURDAY, APRIL 8
Tampa Bay at Toronto
Ottawa at Montreal
Florida at New Jersey*
Boston at Philadelphia*
Carolina at Atlanta*
Edmonton at Calgary

SUNDAY, APRIL 9
Pittsburgh at Boston
Tampa Bay at Ottawa
Florida at N.Y. Islanders*
Philadelphia at N.Y. Rangers*
Buffalo at Washington*
Atlanta at Carolina*
St. Louis at Chicago*
Phoenix at Dallas*
Detroit at Colorado*
Los Angeles at Anaheim*
Vancouver at San Jose*

1998-99 NHL REVIEW

Regular season

Stanley Cup playoffs

All-Star Game

Awards

Player draft

REGULAR SEASON

FINAL STANDINGS

EASTERN CONFERENCE

NORTHEAST DIVISION

	G	W	L	T	Pts.	GF	GA	Home	Away	Div. Rec.
Ottawa Senators	82	44	23	15	103	239	179	22-11-8	22-12-7	8-8-4
Toronto Maple Leafs	82	45	30	7	97	268	231	23-13-5	22-17-2	8-11-1
Boston Bruins	82	39	30	13	91	214	181	22-10-9	17-20-4	11-7-2
Buffalo Sabres	82	37	28	17	91	207	175	23-12-6	14-16-11	10-6-4
Montreal Canadiens	82	32	39	11	75	184	209	21-15-5	11-24-6	7-12-1

ATLANTIC DIVISION

	G	W	L	T	Pts.	GF	GA	Home	Away	Div. Rec.
New Jersey Devils	82	47	24	11	105	248	196	19-14-8	28-10-3	15-4-1
Philadelphia Flyers	82	37	26	19	93	231	196	21-9-11	16-17-8	7-8-5
Pittsburgh Penguins	82	38	30	14	90	242	225	21-10-10	17-20-4	5-11-4
New York Rangers	82	33	38	11	77	217	227	17-19-5	16-19-6	8-8-4
New York Islanders	82	24	48	10	58	194	244	11-23-7	13-25-3	7-11-2

SOUTHEAST DIVISION

	G	W	L	T	Pts.	GF	GA	Home	Away	Div. Rec.
Carolina Hurricanes	82	34	30	18	86	210	202	20-12-9	14-18-9	5-2-8
Florida Panthers	82	30	34	18	78	210	228	17-17-7	13-17-11	6-4-5
Washington Capitals	82	31	45	6	68	200	218	16-23-2	15-22-4	8-5-2
Tampa Bay Lightning	82	19	54	9	47	179	292	12-25-4	7-29-5	2-10-3

WESTERN CONFERENCE

CENTRAL DIVISION

	G	W	L	T	Pts.	GF	GA	Home	Away	Div. Rec.
Detroit Red Wings	82	43	32	7	93	245	202	27-12-2	16-20-5	12-4-2
St. Louis Blues	82	37	32	13	87	237	209	18-17-6	19-15-7	10-6-2
Chicago Blackhawks	82	29	41	12	70	202	248	20-17-4	9-24-8	7-10-1
Nashville Predators	82	28	47	7	63	190	261	15-22-4	13-25-3	4-13-1

PACIFIC DIVISION

	G	W	L	T	Pts.	GF	GA	Home	Away	Div. Rec.
Dallas Stars	82	51	19	12	114	236	168	29-8-4	22-11-8	18-4-2
Phoenix Coyotes	82	39	31	12	90	205	197	23-13-5	16-18-7	11-11-2
Anaheim Mighty Ducks	82	35	34	13	83	215	206	21-14-6	14-20-7	12-7-5
San Jose Sharks	82	31	33	18	80	196	191	17-15-9	14-18-9	7-14-3
Los Angeles Kings	82	32	45	5	69	189	222	18-20-3	14-25-2	6-18-0

NORTHWEST DIVISION

	G	W	L	T	Pts.	GF	GA	Home	Away	Div. Rec.
Colorado Avalanche	82	44	28	10	98	239	205	21-14-6	23-14-4	8-8-2
Edmonton Oilers	82	33	37	12	78	230	226	17-19-5	16-18-7	12-4-2
Calgary Flames	82	30	40	12	72	211	234	15-20-6	15-20-6	6-10-2
Vancouver Canucks	82	23	47	12	58	192	258	14-21-6	9-26-6	6-10-2

INDIVIDUAL LEADERS

SCORING

TOP SCORERS

	Games	G	A	Pts.	PIM	+/-	PPG	SHG	Shots	Shooting Pct.
Jaromir Jagr, Pittsburgh	81	44	*83	*127	66	17	10	1	343	12.8
Teemu Selanne, Anaheim	75	*47	60	107	30	18	*25	0	281	16.7
Paul Kariya, Anaheim	82	39	62	101	40	17	11	2	*429	9.1
Peter Forsberg, Colorado	78	30	67	97	108	27	9	2	217	13.8
Joe Sakic, Colorado	73	41	55	96	29	23	12	†5	255	16.1
Alexei Yashin, Ottawa	82	44	50	94	54	16	19	0	337	13.1
Eric Lindros, Philadelphia	71	40	53	93	120	35	10	1	242	16.5
Theoren Fleury, Calgary-Colorado	75	40	53	93	86	26	8	3	301	13.3

	Games	G	A	Pts.	PIM	+/-	PPG	SHG	Shots	Shooting Pct.
John LeClair, Philadelphia	76	43	47	90	30	36	16	0	246	17.5
Pavol Demitra, St. Louis	82	37	52	89	16	13	14	0	259	14.3
Martin Straka, Pittsburgh	80	35	48	83	26	12	5	4	177	19.8
Mats Sundin, Toronto	82	31	52	83	58	22	4	0	209	14.8
Mike Modano, Dallas	77	34	47	81	44	29	6	4	224	15.2
Jason Allison, Boston	82	23	53	76	68	5	5	1	158	14.6
Tony Amonte, Chicago	82	44	31	75	60	0	14	3	256	17.2
Luc Robitaille, Los Angeles	82	39	35	74	54	-1	11	0	292	13.4
Steve Yzerman, Detroit	80	29	45	74	42	8	13	2	231	12.6
Rod Brind'Amour, Philadelphia	82	24	50	74	47	3	10	0	191	12.6
Steve Thomas, Toronto	78	28	45	73	33	26	11	0	209	13.4
Petr Sykora, New Jersey	80	29	43	72	22	16	15	0	222	13.1
Jeremy Roenick, Phoenix	78	24	48	72	130	7	4	0	203	11.8

The scoring leader is awarded the Art Ross Memorial Trophy.
*Led league.
†Tied for league lead.

Games
Robert Reichel, NYI-Pho. 83
Many players with 82

Points
Jaromir Jagr, Pittsburgh 127
Teemu Selanne, Anaheim 107
Paul Kariya, Anaheim 101
Peter Forsberg, Colorado 97
Joe Sakic, Colorado 96
Alexei Yashin, Ottawa 94
Eric Lindros, Philadelphia 93
Theoren Fleury, Cal.-Col. 93
John LeClair, Philadelphia 90
Pavol Demitra, St. Louis 89

Points by a defenseman
Al MacInnis, St. Louis 62
Nicklas Lidstrom, Detroit 57
Ray Bourque, Boston 57
Fredrik Olausson, Anaheim 56
Brian Leetch, N.Y. Rangers 55

Goals
Teemu Selanne, Anaheim 47
Tony Amonte, Chicago 44
Jaromir Jagr, Pittsburgh 44
Alexei Yashin, Ottawa 44
John LeClair, Philadelphia 43
Joe Sakic, Colorado 41
Theoren Fleury, Cal.-Col. 40
Eric Lindros, Philadelphia 40
Miroslav Satan, Buffalo 40
Paul Kariya, Anaheim 39
Luc Robitaille, Los Angeles 39

Assists
Jaromir Jagr, Pittsburgh 83
Peter Forsberg, Colorado 67
Paul Kariya, Anaheim 62
Teemu Selanne, Anaheim 60
Joe Sakic, Colorado 55
Jason Allison, Boston 53
Theoren Fleury, Cal.-Col. 53
Wayne Gretzky, N.Y. Rangers 53
Eric Lindros, Philadelphia 53
Pavol Demitra, St. Louis 52
Mats Sundin, Toronto 52

Power-play goals
Teemu Selanne, Anaheim 25
Alexei Yashin, Ottawa 19
Adrian Aucoin, Vancouver 18
John LeClair, Philadelphia 16
Brett Hull, Dallas 15
Markus Naslund, Vancouver 15
Petr Sykora, New Jersey 15

Shorthanded goals
Scott Pellerin, St. Louis 5
Brian Rolston, New Jersey 5
Joe Sakic, Colorado 5
Magnus Arvedson, Ottawa 4
Radek Dvorak, Florida 4
Mike Modano, Dallas 4
Martin Straka, Pittsburgh 4

Game-winning goals
Brett Hull, Dallas 11
Pavol Demitra, St. Louis 10
Tony Amonte, Chicago 8
Bobby Holik, New Jersey 8
Claude Lemieux, Colorado 8
Joe Nieuwendyk, Dallas 8
Michael Peca, Buffalo 8
Sergei Samsonov, Boston 8

Game-tying goals
Curtis Brown, Buffalo 3
Eric Daze, Chicago 3
Robert Lang, Pittsburgh 3
John LeClair, Philadelphia 3
Eric Lindros, Philadelphia 3
Scott Mellanby, Florida 3

Shots
Paul Kariya, Anaheim 429
Jaromir Jagr, Pittsburgh 343
Alexei Yashin, Ottawa 337
Al MacInnis, St. Louis 314
Theoren Fleury, Cal.-Col. 301

Shooting percentage (82 shots minimum)
Dmitri Khristich, Boston 20.1
Martin Straka, Pittsburgh 19.8
Dixon Ward, Buffalo 19.8
Anson Carter, Boston 19.5
Miroslav Satan, Buffalo 19.2

Plus/minus
Alexander Karpovtsev, NYR-Tor. 39
John LeClair, Philadelphia 36
Eric Lindros, Philadelphia 35
Magnus Arvedson, Ottawa 33
Al MacInnis, St. Louis 33

Penalty minutes
Rob Ray, Buffalo 261
Jeff Odgers, Colorado 259
Peter Worrell, Florida 258
Patrick Cote, Nashville 242
Krzysztof Oliwa, New Jersey 240
Denny Lambert, Nashville 218
Paul Laus, Florida 218
Donald Brashear, Vancouver 209
Bob Probert, Chicago 206
Brad Brown, Mon.-Chi. 205

Consecutive-game point streaks
Eric Lindros, Philadelphia 18
Teemu Selanne, Anaheim 17
Jaromir Jagr, Pittsburgh 13
Sergei Fedorov, Detroit 11
Paul Kariya, Anaheim 11
Alexei Yashin, Ottawa 11

Consecutive-game goal streaks
Miroslav Satan, Buffalo 8
Teemu Selanne, Anaheim 8
Eric Lindros, Philadelphia 7
Tony Amonte, Chicago 6
Rob Brown, Pittsburgh 6
Bobby Holik, New Jersey 6
Kip Miller, Pittsburgh 6
Miroslav Satan, Buffalo 6
Ray Sheppard, Carolina 6

Consecutive-game assist streaks
John LeClair, Philadelphia 9
Jaromir Jagr, Pittsburgh 8
Rod Brind'Amour, Philadelphia 7
Peter Forsberg, Colorado (twice) 7
Paul Kariya, Anaheim 7
Andrei Kovalenko, Edmonton 7
Eric Lindros, Philadelphia 7
Teemu Selanne, Anaheim 7
Alexei Yashin, Ottawa 7

Most games scoring three or more goals
Peter Bondra, Washington 3
Wendel Clark, Tampa Bay 3
Theoren Fleury, Cal.-Col. 3
Mike Modano, Dallas 3
Many tied with 2

Points by a rookie
Milan Hejduk, Colorado 48
Brendan Morrison, New Jersey 46
Chris Drury, Colorado 44
Jan Hrdina, Pittsburgh 42
Mark Parrish, Florida 37

Goals by a rookie
Mike Parrish, Florida 24
Chris Drury, Colorado 20
Bill Muckalt, Vancouver 16
Marian Hossa, Ottawa 15
Milan Hejduk, Colorado 14

Assists by a rookie
Milan Hejduk, Colorado 34
Brendan Morrison, New Jersey 33
Jan Hrdina, Pittsburgh 29
Chris Drury, Colorado 24
Bill Muckalt, Vancouver 20

GOALTENDING

Games

Martin Brodeur, New Jersey.....70
Guy Hebert, Anaheim.....69
Byron Dafoe, Boston.....68
Mike Richter, N.Y. Rangers.....68
Curtis Joseph, Toronto.....67

Minutes

Martin Brodeur, New Jersey.....4239
Guy Hebert, Anaheim.....4083
Byron Dafoe, Boston.....4001
Curtis Joseph, Toronto.....4001
Mike Richter, N.Y. Rangers.....3878

Goals allowed

Curtis Joseph, Toronto.....171
Garth Snow, Vancouver.....171
Mike Richter, N.Y. Rangers.....170
Guy Hebert, Anaheim.....165
Martin Brodeur, New Jersey.....162

Shutouts

Byron Dafoe, Boston.....10
Dominik Hasek, Buffalo.....9
Nikolai Khabibulin, Phoenix.....8
Guy Hebert, Anaheim.....6
Arturs Irbe, Carolina.....6
Garth Snow, Vancouver.....6
John Vanbiesbrouck, Philadelphia.....6

Lowest goals-against average (25 games played minimum)

Ron Tugnutt, Ottawa.....1.79
Dominik Hasek, Buffalo.....1.87
Byron Dafoe, Boston.....1.9845
Ed Belfour, Dallas.....1.9953
Roman Turek, Dallas.....2.08

Highest goals-against average (25 games played minimum)

Bill Ranford, T.B.-Det......3.64
Corey Schwab, Tampa Bay.....3.52
Mike Dunham, Nashville.....3.08
Tomas Vokoun, Nashville.....2.95
Garth Snow, Vancouver.....2.93

Games won

Martin Brodeur, New Jersey.....39
Ed Belfour, Dallas.....35
Curtis Joseph, Toronto.....35
Chris Osgood, Detroit.....34
Byron Dafoe, Boston.....32
Nikolai Khabibulin, Phoenix.....32
Patrick Roy, Colorado.....32

Best winning percentage (25 games played minimum)

Roman Turek, Dallas (16-3-3)..... .795
Ed Belfour, Dallas (35-15-9)..... .669
Ron Tugnutt, Ottawa (22-10-8)..... .650
Martin Brodeur, N.J. (39-21-10)..... .629
Patrick Roy, Colorado (32-19-8)..... .610

Worst winning percentage (25 games played minimum)

Corey Schwab, T.B. (8-25-3)..... .264
Bill Ranford, T.B.-Det. (6-18-4)..... .286
Garth Snow, Vancouver (20-31-8)..... .407
Tomas Vokoun, Nash. (12-18-4)..... .412
Mike Dunham, Nash. (16-23-3)..... .417

Games lost

Olaf Kolzig, Washington.....31
Garth Snow, Vancouver.....31
Mike Richter, N.Y. Rangers.....30
Jocelyn Thibault, Mon.-Chi......30
Guy Hebert, Anaheim.....29

Tie games

John Vanbiesbrouck, Philadelphia.....15
Sean Burke, Florida.....14
Dominik Hasek, Buffalo.....14
Arturs Irbe, Carolina.....12
Byron Dafoe, Boston.....11

Shots against

Guy Hebert, Anaheim.....2114
Curtis Joseph, Toronto.....1903
Mike Richter, N.Y. Rangers.....1898
Dominik Hasek, Buffalo.....1877
Byron Dafoe, Boston.....1800

Saves

Guy Hebert, Anaheim.....1949
Dominik Hasek, Buffalo.....1758
Curtis Joseph, Toronto.....1732
Mike Richter, N.Y. Rangers.....1728
Byron Dafoe, Boston.....1667

Highest save percentage (25 games played minimum)

Dominik Hasek, Buffalo..... .937
Byron Dafoe, Boston..... .926
Ron Tugnutt, Ottawa..... .925
Arturs Irbe, Carolina..... .92299
Nikolai Khabibulin, Phoenix..... .92267

Lowest save percentage (25 games played minimum)

Bill Ranford, T.B.-Det...... .885
Jamie McLennan, St. Louis..... .8906
Corey Schwab, Tampa Bay..... .8907
Peter Skudra, Pittsburgh..... .8917
Grant Fuhr, St. Louis..... .8924

STATISTICS OF PLAYERS WITH TWO OR MORE TEAMS

SCORING

	Games	G	A	Pts.	PIM	+/-	PPG	SHG	Shots	Shooting Pct.
Mikael Andersson, Tampa Bay	40	2	3	5	4	-8	0	0	40	5.0
Mikael Andersson, Philadelphia	7	0	1	1	0	1	0	0	11	0.0
Totals	47	2	4	6	4	-7	0	0	51	3.9
Blair Atcheynum, Nashville	53	8	6	14	16	-10	2	0	70	11.4
Blair Atcheynum, St. Louis	12	2	2	4	2	2	0	0	23	8.7
Totals	65	10	8	18	18	-8	2	0	93	10.8
Dave Babych, Philadelphia	33	2	4	6	20	0	2	0	44	4.5
Dave Babych, Los Angeles	8	0	2	2	2	-2	0	0	5	0.0
Totals	41	2	6	8	22	-2	2	0	49	4.1
Matthew Barnaby, Buffalo	44	4	14	18	143	-2	0	0	52	7.7
Matthew Barnaby, Pittsburgh	18	2	2	4	34	-10	1	0	27	7.4
Totals	62	6	16	22	177	-12	1	0	79	7.6
Stu Barnes, Pittsburgh	64	20	12	32	20	-12	13	0	155	12.9
Stu Barnes, Buffalo	17	0	4	4	10	1	0	0	25	0.0
Totals	81	20	16	36	30	-11	13	0	180	11.1
Wade Belak, Colorado	22	0	0	0	71	-2	0	0	5	0.0
Wade Belak, Calgary	9	0	1	1	23	3	0	0	2	0.0
Totals	31	0	1	1	94	1	0	0	7	0.0
Ken Belanger, N.Y. Islanders	9	1	1	2	30	1	0	0	3	33.3
Ken Belanger, Boston	45	1	4	5	152	-2	0	0	16	6.3
Totals	54	2	5	7	182	-1	0	0	19	10.5
Bryan Berard, N.Y. Islanders	31	4	11	15	26	-6	2	0	72	5.6
Bryan Berard, Toronto	38	5	14	19	22	7	2	0	63	7.9
Totals	69	9	25	34	48	1	4	0	135	6.7
Craig Berube, Washington	66	5	4	9	166	-7	0	0	45	11.1
Craig Berube, Philadelphia	11	0	0	0	28	-3	0	0	7	0.0
Totals	77	5	4	9	194	-10	0	0	52	9.6
Radim Bicanek, Ottawa	7	0	0	0	4	-1	0	0	6	0.0
Radim Bicanek, Chicago	7	0	0	0	6	-3	0	0	7	0.0

	Games	G	A	Pts.	PIM	+/–	PPG	SHG	Shots	Shooting Pct.
Totals	14	0	0	0	10	-4	0	0	13	0.0
Brad Brown, Montreal	5	0	0	0	21	0	0	0	0	0.0
Brad Brown, Chicago	61	1	7	8	184	-4	0	0	26	3.8
Totals	66	1	7	8	205	-4	0	0	26	3.8
Adam Burt, Carolina	51	0	3	3	46	3	0	0	37	0.0
Adam Burt, Philadelphia	17	0	1	1	14	1	0	0	24	0.0
Totals	68	0	4	4	60	4	0	0	61	0.0
Viacheslav Butsayev, Florida	1	0	0	0	2	-1	0	0	0	0.0
Viacheslav Butsayev, Ottawa	2	0	1	1	2	0	0	0	5	0.0
Totals	3	0	1	1	4	-1	0	0	5	0.0
Chris Chelios, Chicago	65	8	26	34	89	-4	2	1	172	4.7
Chris Chelios, Detroit	10	1	1	2	4	5	1	0	15	6.7
Totals	75	9	27	36	93	1	3	1	187	4.8
Tom Chorske, N.Y. Islanders	2	0	1	1	2	1	0	0	9	0.0
Tom Chorske, Washington	17	0	2	2	4	-4	0	0	22	0.0
Tom Chorske, Calgary	7	0	0	0	2	-5	0	0	13	0.0
Totals	26	0	3	3	8	-8	0	0	44	0.0
Enrico Ciccone, Tampa Bay	16	1	1	2	24	-1	0	0	9	11.1
Enrico Ciccone, Washington	43	2	0	2	103	-6	0	0	43	4.7
Totals	59	3	1	4	127	-7	0	0	52	5.8
Wendel Clark, Tampa Bay	65	28	14	42	35	-25	11	0	171	16.4
Wendel Clark, Detroit	12	4	2	6	2	1	0	0	44	9.1
Totals	77	32	16	48	37	-24	11	0	215	14.9
Paul Coffey, Chicago	10	0	4	4	0	-6	0	0	8	0.0
Paul Coffey, Carolina	44	2	8	10	28	-1	1	0	79	2.5
Totals	54	2	12	14	28	-7	1	0	87	2.3
Brandon Convery, Vancouver	12	2	7	9	8	5	0	0	12	16.7
Brandon Convery, Los Angeles	3	0	0	0	4	-1	0	0	2	0.0
Totals	15	2	7	9	12	4	0	0	14	14.3
Rene Corbet, Colorado	53	8	14	22	58	3	2	0	82	9.8
Rene Corbet, Calgary	20	5	4	9	10	-2	1	0	45	11.1
Totals	73	13	18	31	68	1	3	0	127	10.2
Ted Crowley, Colorado	7	0	1	1	2	-1	0	0	10	0.0
Ted Crowley, N.Y. Islanders	6	1	1	2	0	0	1	0	10	10.0
Totals	13	1	2	3	2	-1	1	0	20	5.0
Alexandre Daigle, Philadelphia	31	3	2	5	2	-1	1	0	26	11.5
Alexandre Daigle, Tampa Bay	32	6	6	12	2	-12	3	0	56	10.7
Totals	63	9	8	17	4	-13	4	0	82	11.0
J.J. Daigneault, Nashville	35	2	2	4	38	-4	1	0	38	5.3
J.J. Daigneault, Phoenix	35	0	7	7	32	-8	0	0	27	0.0
Totals	70	2	9	11	70	-12	1	0	65	3.1
Vincent Damphousse, Montreal	65	12	24	36	46	-7	3	2	147	8.2
Vincent Damphousse, San Jose	12	7	6	13	4	3	3	0	43	16.3
Totals	77	19	30	49	50	-4	6	2	190	10.0
Jason Dawe, N.Y. Islanders	22	2	3	5	8	0	0	0	29	6.9
Jason Dawe, Montreal	37	4	5	9	14	0	1	0	52	7.7
Totals	59	6	8	14	22	0	1	0	81	7.4
Greg De Vries, Nashville	6	0	0	0	4	-4	0	0	1	0.0
Greg De Vries, Colorado	67	1	3	4	60	-3	0	0	56	1.8
Totals	73	1	3	4	64	-7	0	0	57	1.8
Chris Dingman, Calgary	2	0	0	0	17	-2	0	0	1	0.0
Chris Dingman, Colorado	1	0	0	0	7	0	0	0	0	0.0
Totals	3	0	0	0	24	-2	0	0	1	0.0
Ted Donato, Boston	14	1	3	4	4	0	0	0	22	4.5
Ted Donato, N.Y. Islanders	55	7	11	18	27	-10	2	0	68	10.3
Ted Donato, Ottawa	13	3	2	5	10	2	1	0	16	18.8
Totals	82	11	16	27	41	-8	3	0	106	10.4
Steve Dubinsky, Chicago	1	0	0	0	0	0	0	0	1	0.0
Steve Dubinsky, Calgary	61	4	10	14	14	-7	0	2	69	5.8
Totals	62	4	10	14	14	-7	0	2	70	5.7
Steve Duchesne, Los Angeles	60	4	19	23	22	-6	1	0	99	4.0
Steve Duchesne, Philadelphia	11	2	5	7	2	0	1	0	19	10.5
Totals	71	6	24	30	24	-6	2	0	118	5.1
Karl Dykhuis, Tampa Bay	33	2	1	3	18	-21	0	0	27	7.4
Karl Dykhuis, Philadelphia	45	2	4	6	32	-2	1	0	61	3.3
Totals	78	4	5	9	50	-23	1	0	88	4.5
Nelson Emerson, Carolina	35	8	13	21	36	1	3	0	84	9.5
Nelson Emerson, Chicago	27	4	10	14	13	8	0	0	94	4.3
Nelson Emerson, Ottawa	3	1	1	2	2	-1	0	0	10	10.0
Totals	65	13	24	37	51	8	3	0	188	6.9
Anders Eriksson, Detroit	61	2	10	12	34	5	0	0	67	3.0

	Games	G	A	Pts.	PIM	+/–	PPG	SHG	Shots	Shooting Pct.
Anders Eriksson, Chicago	11	0	8	8	0	6	0	0	12	0.0
Totals	72	2	18	20	34	11	0	0	79	2.5
Jeff Finley, N.Y. Rangers	2	0	0	0	0	-1	0	0	0	0.0
Jeff Finley, St. Louis	30	1	2	3	20	12	0	0	16	6.3
Totals	32	1	2	3	20	11	0	0	16	6.3
Theoren Fleury, Calgary	60	30	39	69	68	18	7	3	250	12.0
Theoren Fleury, Colorado	15	10	14	24	18	8	1	0	51	19.6
Totals	75	40	53	93	86	26	8	3	301	13.3
Colin Forbes, Philadelphia	66	9	7	16	51	0	0	0	92	9.8
Colin Forbes, Tampa Bay	14	3	1	4	10	-5	0	1	25	12.0
Totals	80	12	8	20	61	-5	0	1	117	10.3
Dave Gagner, Florida	36	4	10	14	39	-7	2	0	50	8.0
Dave Gagner, Vancouver	33	2	12	14	24	-9	0	0	50	4.0
Totals	69	6	22	28	63	-16	2	0	100	6.0
Todd Gill, St. Louis	28	2	3	5	16	-6	1	0	36	5.6
Todd Gill, Detroit	23	2	2	4	11	-4	0	0	25	8.0
Totals	51	4	5	9	27	-10	1	0	61	6.6
Chris Gratton, Philadelphia	26	1	7	8	41	-8	0	0	54	1.9
Chris Gratton, Tampa Bay	52	7	19	26	102	-20	1	0	127	5.5
Totals	78	8	26	34	143	-28	1	0	181	4.4
Sergey Gusev, Dallas	22	1	4	5	6	5	0	0	30	3.3
Sergey Gusev, Tampa Bay	14	0	3	3	10	-8	0	0	16	0.0
Totals	36	1	7	8	16	-3	0	0	46	2.2
Jeff Hackett, Chicago (goalie)	10	0	0	0	6	0	0	0	0	0.0
Jeff Hackett, Montreal (goalie)	53	0	1	1	6	0	0	0	0	0.0
Totals	63	0	1	1	12	0	0	0	0	0.0
Bret Hedican, Vancouver	42	2	11	13	34	7	0	2	52	3.8
Bret Hedican, Florida	25	3	7	10	17	-2	0	0	38	7.9
Totals	67	5	18	23	51	5	0	2	90	5.6
Sami Helenius, Calgary	4	0	0	0	8	-2	0	0	1	0.0
Sami Helenius, Tampa Bay	4	1	0	1	15	-3	0	1	3	33.3
Totals	8	1	0	1	23	-5	0	1	4	25.0
Bryan Helmer, Phoenix	11	0	0	0	23	2	0	0	11	0.0
Bryan Helmer, St. Louis	29	0	4	4	19	3	0	0	38	0.0
Totals	40	0	4	4	42	5	0	0	49	0.0
Darby Hendrickson, Toronto	35	2	3	5	30	-4	0	0	34	5.9
Darby Hendrickson, Vancouver	27	2	2	4	22	-15	1	0	36	5.6
Totals	62	4	5	9	52	-19	1	0	70	5.7
Alex Hicks, San Jose	4	0	1	1	4	-1	0	0	4	0.0
Alex Hicks, Florida	51	0	6	6	58	-4	0	0	47	0.0
Totals	55	0	7	7	62	-5	0	0	51	0.0
Kevin Hodson, Detroit (goalie)	4	0	0	0	0	0	0	0	0	0.0
Kevin Hodson, Tampa Bay (goalie)	5	0	0	0	0	0	0	0	0	0.0
Totals	9	0	0	0	0	0	0	0	0	0.0
Benoit Hogue, Tampa Bay	62	11	14	25	50	-12	2	0	101	10.9
Benoit Hogue, Dallas	12	1	3	4	4	2	0	0	20	5.0
Totals	74	12	17	29	54	-10	2	0	121	9.9
Dale Hunter, Washington	50	0	5	5	102	-7	0	0	18	0.0
Dale Hunter, Colorado	12	2	4	6	17	0	0	0	6	33.3
Totals	62	2	9	11	119	-7	0	0	24	8.3
Jamie Huscroft, Vancouver	26	0	1	1	63	-3	0	0	20	0.0
Jamie Huscroft, Phoenix	11	0	1	1	27	-1	0	0	7	0.0
Totals	37	0	2	2	90	-4	0	0	27	0.0
Craig Janney, Tampa Bay	38	4	18	22	10	-13	2	0	36	11.1
Craig Janney, N.Y. Islanders	18	1	4	5	4	-2	0	0	9	11.1
Totals	56	5	22	27	14	-15	2	0	45	11.1
Jean-Francois Jomphe, Phoenix	1	0	0	0	2	0	0	0	0	0.0
Jean-Francois Jomphe, Montreal	6	0	0	0	0	0	0	0	4	0.0
Totals	7	0	0	0	2	0	0	0	4	0.0
Keith Jones, Colorado	12	2	2	4	20	-6	1	0	11	18.2
Keith Jones, Philadelphia	66	18	31	49	78	29	2	0	124	14.5
Totals	78	20	33	53	98	23	3	0	135	14.8
Ed Jovanovski, Florida	41	3	13	16	82	-4	1	0	68	4.4
Ed Jovanovski, Vancouver	31	2	9	11	44	-5	0	0	41	4.9
Totals	72	5	22	27	126	-9	1	0	109	4.6
Joe Juneau, Washington	63	14	27	41	20	-3	2	1	142	9.9
Joe Juneau, Buffalo	9	1	1	2	2	-1	0	0	8	12.5
Totals	72	15	28	43	22	-4	2	1	150	10.0
Alexander Karpovtsev, N.Y. Rangers	2	1	0	1	0	1	0	0	4	25.0
Alexander Karpovtsev, Toronto	56	2	25	27	52	38	1	0	61	3.3
Totals	58	3	25	28	52	39	1	0	65	4.6

	Games	G	A	Pts.	PIM	+/–	PPG	SHG	Shots	Shooting Pct.
Dan Keczmer, Dallas	22	0	1	1	22	-2	0	0	12	0.0
Dan Keczmer, Nashville	16	0	0	0	12	-3	0	0	12	0.0
Totals	38	0	1	1	34	-5	0	0	24	0.0
Chad Kilger, Chicago	64	14	11	25	30	-1	2	1	68	20.6
Chad Kilger, Edmonton	13	1	1	2	4	-3	0	0	13	7.7
Totals	77	15	12	27	34	-4	2	1	81	18.5
Trent Klatt, Philadelphia	2	0	0	0	0	0	0	0	2	0.0
Trent Klatt, Vancouver	73	4	10	14	12	-3	0	0	58	6.9
Totals	75	4	10	14	12	-3	0	0	60	6.7
Andrei Kovalenko, Edmonton	43	13	14	27	30	-4	2	0	75	17.3
Andrei Kovalenko, Philadelphia	13	0	1	1	2	-5	0	0	8	0.0
Andrei Kovalenko, Carolina	18	6	6	12	0	3	1	0	21	28.6
Totals	74	19	21	40	32	-6	3	0	104	18.3
Alexei Kovalev, N.Y. Rangers	14	3	4	7	12	-6	1	0	35	8.6
Alexei Kovalev, Pittsburgh	63	20	26	46	37	8	5	1	156	12.8
Totals	77	23	30	53	49	2	6	1	191	12.0
Scott Lachance, N.Y. Islanders	59	1	8	9	30	-19	1	0	37	2.7
Scott Lachance, Montreal	17	1	1	2	11	-2	0	0	22	4.5
Totals	76	2	9	11	41	-21	1	0	59	3.4
Eric Lacroix, Colorado	7	0	0	0	2	-2	0	0	4	0.0
Eric Lacroix, Los Angeles	27	0	1	1	12	-5	0	0	17	0.0
Eric Lacroix, N.Y. Rangers	30	2	1	3	4	-5	0	0	17	11.8
Totals	64	2	2	4	18	-12	0	0	38	5.3
Christian Laflamme, Chicago	62	2	11	13	70	0	0	0	53	3.8
Christian Laflamme, Edmonton	11	0	1	1	0	-3	0	0	15	0.0
Totals	73	2	12	14	70	-3	0	0	68	2.9
Daymond Langkow, Tampa Bay	22	4	6	10	15	0	1	0	40	10.0
Daymond Langkow, Philadelphia	56	10	13	23	24	-8	3	1	109	9.2
Totals	78	14	19	33	39	-8	4	1	149	9.4
Stephen Leach, Ottawa	9	0	2	2	6	-1	0	0	4	0.0
Stephen Leach, Phoenix	22	1	1	2	37	-6	0	0	23	4.3
Totals	31	1	3	4	43	-7	0	0	27	3.7
Mats Lindgren, Edmonton	48	5	12	17	22	4	0	1	53	9.4
Mats Lindgren, N.Y. Islanders	12	5	3	8	2	2	3	0	30	16.7
Totals	60	10	15	25	24	6	3	1	83	12.0
Mike Maneluk, Philadelphia	13	2	6	8	8	4	0	0	23	8.7
Mike Maneluk, Chicago	28	4	3	7	8	2	1	0	29	13.8
Mike Maneluk, N.Y. Rangers	4	0	0	0	4	-1	0	0	3	0.0
Totals	45	6	9	15	20	5	1	0	55	10.9
Dave Manson, Montreal	11	0	2	2	48	-3	0	0	11	0.0
Dave Manson, Chicago	64	6	15	21	107	4	2	0	134	4.5
Totals	75	6	17	23	155	1	2	0	145	4.1
Josef Marha, Anaheim	10	0	1	1	0	-4	0	0	13	0.0
Josef Marha, Chicago	22	2	5	7	4	5	1	0	32	6.3
Totals	32	2	6	8	4	1	1	0	45	4.4
Chris McAllister, Vancouver	28	1	1	2	63	-7	0	0	6	16.7
Chris McAllister, Toronto	20	0	2	2	39	4	0	0	12	0.0
Totals	48	1	3	4	102	-3	0	0	18	5.6
Dean McAmmond, Edmonton	65	9	16	25	36	5	1	0	122	7.4
Dean McAmmond, Chicago	12	1	4	5	2	3	0	0	16	6.3
Totals	77	10	20	30	38	8	1	0	138	7.2
Sandy McCarthy, Tampa Bay	67	5	7	12	135	-22	1	0	89	5.6
Sandy McCarthy, Philadelphia	13	0	1	1	25	-2	0	0	18	0.0
Totals	80	5	8	13	160	-24	1	0	107	4.7
Marty McInnis, Calgary	6	1	1	2	6	-1	0	0	7	14.3
Marty McInnis, Anaheim	75	18	34	52	36	-14	11	1	139	12.9
Totals	81	19	35	54	42	-15	11	1	146	13.0
Boris Mironov, Edmonton	63	11	29	40	104	6	5	0	138	8.0
Boris Mironov, Chicago	12	0	9	9	27	7	0	0	35	0.0
Totals	75	11	38	49	131	13	5	0	173	6.4
Ethan Moreau, Chicago	66	9	6	15	84	-5	0	0	80	11.3
Ethan Moreau, Edmonton	14	1	5	6	8	2	0	0	16	6.3
Totals	80	10	11	21	92	-3	0	0	96	10.4
Bryan Muir, New Jersey	1	0	0	0	0	0	0	0	4	0.0
Bryan Muir, Chicago	53	1	4	5	50	1	0	0	78	1.3
Totals	54	1	4	5	50	1	0	0	82	1.2
Chris Murray, Ottawa	38	1	6	7	65	-2	0	0	33	3.0
Chris Murray, Chicago	4	0	0	0	14	0	0	0	4	0.0
Totals	42	1	6	7	79	-2	0	0	37	2.7
Alain Nasreddine, Chicago	7	0	0	0	19	-2	0	0	2	0.0
Alain Nasreddine, Montreal	8	0	0	0	33	1	0	0	1	0.0

	Games	G	A	Pts.	PIM	+/–	PPG	SHG	Shots	Shooting Pct.
Totals	15	0	0	0	52	-1	0	0	3	0.0
Andrei Nazarov, Tampa Bay	26	2	0	2	43	-5	0	0	18	11.1
Andrei Nazarov, Calgary	36	5	9	14	30	1	0	0	53	9.4
Totals	62	7	9	16	73	-4	0	0	71	9.9
Rumun Ndur, Buffalo	8	0	0	0	16	1	0	0	1	0.0
Rumun Ndur, N.Y. Rangers	31	1	3	4	46	-2	0	0	21	4.8
Totals	39	1	3	4	62	-1	0	0	22	4.5
Stan Neckar, Ottawa	3	0	2	2	0	-1	0	0	2	0.0
Stan Neckar, N.Y. Rangers	18	0	0	0	8	-1	0	0	8	0.0
Stan Neckar, Phoenix	11	0	1	1	10	3	0	0	6	0.0
Totals	32	0	3	3	18	1	0	0	16	0.0
Sergei Nemchinov, N.Y. Islanders	67	8	8	16	22	-17	1	0	61	13.1
Sergei Nemchinov, New Jersey	10	4	0	4	6	4	1	0	13	30.8
Totals	77	12	8	20	28	-13	2	0	74	16.2
Jeff Norton, Florida	3	0	0	0	2	0	0	0	2	0.0
Jeff Norton, San Jose	69	4	18	22	42	2	2	0	68	5.9
Totals	72	4	18	22	44	2	2	0	70	5.7
Michael Nylander, Calgary	9	2	3	5	2	1	1	0	7	28.6
Michael Nylander, Tampa Bay	24	2	7	9	6	-10	0	0	26	7.7
Totals	33	4	10	14	8	-9	1	0	33	12.1
Yanic Perreault, Los Angeles	64	10	17	27	30	-3	2	2	113	8.8
Yanic Perreault, Toronto	12	7	8	15	12	10	2	1	28	25.0
Totals	76	17	25	42	42	7	4	3	141	12.1
Derek Plante, Buffalo	41	4	11	15	12	3	0	0	66	6.1
Derek Plante, Dallas	10	2	3	5	4	1	1	0	24	8.3
Totals	51	6	14	20	16	4	1	0	90	6.7
Shjon Podein, Philadelphia	14	1	0	1	0	-2	0	0	26	3.8
Shjon Podein, Colorado	41	2	6	8	24	-3	0	0	49	4.1
Totals	55	3	6	9	24	-5	0	0	75	4.0
Jason Podollan, Toronto	4	0	0	0	0	0	0	0	2	0.0
Jason Podollan, Los Angeles	6	0	0	0	5	-3	0	0	7	0.0
Totals	10	0	0	0	5	-3	0	0	9	0.0
Felix Potvin, Toronto (goalie)	5	0	0	0	0	0	0	0	0	0.0
Felix Potvin, N.Y. Islanders (goalie)	11	0	0	0	0	0	0	0	0	0.0
Totals	16	0	0	0	0	0	0	0	0	0.0
Sean Pronger, Pittsburgh	2	0	0	0	0	0	0	0	3	0.0
Sean Pronger, N.Y. Rangers	14	0	3	3	4	-3	0	0	3	0.0
Sean Pronger, Los Angeles	13	0	1	1	4	2	0	0	8	0.0
Totals	29	0	4	4	8	-1	0	0	14	0.0
Bill Ranford, Tampa Bay (goalie)	32	0	0	0	2	0	0	0	0	0.0
Bill Ranford, Detroit (goalie)	4	0	0	0	0	0	0	0	0	0.0
Totals	36	0	0	0	2	0	0	0	0	0.0
Mark Recchi, Montreal	61	12	35	47	28	-4	3	0	152	7.9
Mark Recchi, Philadelphia	10	4	2	6	6	-3	0	0	19	21.1
Totals	71	16	37	53	34	-7	3	0	171	9.4
Robert Reichel, N.Y. Islanders	70	19	37	56	50	-15	5	1	186	10.2
Robert Reichel, Phoenix	13	7	6	13	4	2	3	0	50	14.0
Totals	83	26	43	69	54	-13	8	1	236	11.0
Mikael Renberg, Tampa Bay	20	4	8	12	4	-2	2	0	42	9.5
Mikael Renberg, Philadelphia	46	11	15	26	14	7	4	0	112	9.8
Totals	66	15	23	38	18	5	6	0	154	9.7
Cliff Ronning, Phoenix	7	2	5	7	2	3	2	0	18	11.1
Cliff Ronning, Nashville	72	18	35	53	40	-6	8	0	239	7.5
Totals	79	20	40	60	42	-3	10	0	257	7.8
Cam Russell, Chicago	7	0	0	0	10	1	0	0	1	0.0
Cam Russell, Colorado	35	1	2	3	84	-5	0	0	14	7.1
Totals	42	1	2	3	94	-4	0	0	15	6.7
Tommy Salo, N.Y. Islanders (goalie)	51	0	0	0	12	0	0	0	0	0.0
Tommy Salo, Edmonton (goalie)	13	0	0	0	0	0	0	0	0	0.0
Totals	64	0	0	0	12	0	0	0	0	0.0
Ulf Samuelsson, N.Y. Rangers	67	4	8	12	93	6	0	0	37	10.8
Ulf Samuelsson, Detroit	4	0	0	0	6	-1	0	0	2	0.0
Totals	71	4	8	12	99	5	0	0	39	10.3
Alexander Selivanov, Tampa Bay	43	6	13	19	18	-8	1	0	120	5.0
Alexander Selivanov, Edmonton	29	8	6	14	24	0	1	0	57	14.0
Totals	72	14	19	33	42	-8	2	0	177	7.9
Jeff Shantz, Chicago	7	1	0	1	4	-1	0	0	5	20.0
Jeff Shantz, Calgary	69	12	17	29	40	15	1	1	77	15.6
Totals	76	13	17	30	44	14	1	1	82	15.9
Brad Shaw, Washington	4	0	0	0	4	0	0	0	5	0.0
Brad Shaw, St. Louis	12	0	0	0	4	0	0	0	10	0.0

	Games	G	A	Pts.	PIM	+/–	PPG	SHG	Shots	Shooting Pct.
Totals	16	0	0	0	8	0	0	0	15	0.0
Mikhail Shtalenkov, Edmonton (goalie)	34	0	0	0	2	0	0	0	0	0.0
Mikhail Shtalenkov, Phoenix (goalie)	4	0	0	0	0	0	0	0	0	0.0
Totals	38	0	0	0	2	0	0	0	0	0.0
Mike Sillinger, Philadelphia	25	0	3	3	8	-9	0	0	23	0.0
Mike Sillinger, Tampa Bay	54	8	2	10	28	-20	0	2	69	11.6
Totals	79	8	5	13	36	-29	0	2	92	8.7
Jason Smith, Toronto	60	2	11	13	40	-9	0	0	53	3.8
Jason Smith, Edmonton	12	1	1	2	11	0	0	0	15	6.7
Totals	72	3	12	15	51	-9	0	0	68	4.4
Petr Svoboda, Philadelphia	25	4	2	6	28	5	1	1	37	10.8
Petr Svoboda, Tampa Bay	34	1	16	17	53	-4	0	0	46	2.2
Totals	59	5	18	23	81	1	1	1	83	6.0
Chris Tamer, Pittsburgh	11	0	0	0	32	-2	0	0	2	0.0
Chris Tamer, N.Y. Rangers	52	1	5	6	92	-12	0	0	46	2.2
Totals	63	1	5	6	124	-14	0	0	48	2.1
Jocelyn Thibault, Montreal (goalie)	10	0	0	0	0	0	0	0	0	0.0
Jocelyn Thibault, Chicago (goalie)	52	0	1	1	2	0	0	0	0	0.0
Totals	62	0	1	1	2	0	0	0	0	0.0
Andrei Trefilov, Chicago (goalie)	1	0	0	0	0	0	0	0	0	0.0
Andrei Trefilov, Calgary (goalie)	4	0	0	0	0	0	0	0	0	0.0
Totals	5	0	0	0	0	0	0	0	0	0.0
Roman Vopat, Los Angeles	3	0	0	0	6	0	0	0	2	0.0
Roman Vopat, Chicago	3	0	0	0	4	-4	0	0	0	0.0
Roman Vopat, Philadelphia	48	0	3	3	80	-3	0	0	25	0.0
Totals	54	0	3	3	90	-7	0	0	27	0.0
Rhett Warrener, Florida	48	0	7	7	64	-1	0	0	33	0.0
Rhett Warrener, Buffalo	13	1	0	1	20	3	0	0	11	9.1
Totals	61	1	7	8	84	2	0	0	44	2.3
Steve Washburn, Florida	4	0	0	0	4	-1	0	0	0	0.0
Steve Washburn, Vancouver	8	0	0	0	2	0	0	0	6	0.0
Totals	12	0	0	0	6	-1	0	0	6	0.0
Eric Weinrich, Chicago	14	1	3	4	12	-13	0	0	24	4.2
Eric Weinrich, Montreal	66	6	12	18	77	-12	4	0	95	6.3
Totals	80	7	15	22	89	-25	4	0	119	5.9
Mike Wilson, Buffalo	30	1	2	3	47	10	0	0	40	2.5
Mike Wilson, Florida	4	0	0	0	0	2	0	0	8	0.0
Totals	34	1	2	3	47	12	0	0	48	2.1
Harry York, N.Y. Rangers	5	0	0	0	4	-1	0	0	5	0.0
Harry York, Pittsburgh	2	0	0	0	0	0	0	0	0	0.0
Harry York, Vancouver	49	7	9	16	20	-2	1	0	55	12.7
Totals	56	7	9	16	24	-3	1	0	60	11.7
Dainius Zubrus, Philadelphia	63	3	5	8	25	-5	0	1	49	6.1
Dainius Zubrus, Montreal	17	3	5	8	4	-3	0	0	31	9.7
Totals	80	6	10	16	29	-8	0	1	80	7.5

GOALTENDING

	Games	Min.	Goals	SO	Avg.	W	L	T	Shots	Sv. Pct.
Jeff Hackett, Chicago	10	524	33	0	3.78	2	6	1	256	.871
Jeff Hackett, Montreal	53	3091	117	5	2.27	24	20	9	1360	.914
Totals	63	3615	150	5	2.49	26	26	10	1616	.907
Kevin Hodson, Detroit	4	175	9	0	3.09	0	2	0	79	.886
Kevin Hodson, Tampa Bay	5	238	11	0	2.77	2	1	1	118	.907
Totals	9	413	20	0	2.91	2	3	1	197	.898
Felix Potvin, Toronto	5	299	19	0	3.81	3	2	0	142	.866
Felix Potvin, N.Y. Islanders	11	606	37	0	3.66	2	7	1	345	.893
Totals	16	905	56	0	3.71	5	9	1	487	.885
Bill Ranford, Tampa Bay	32	1568	102	1	3.90	3	18	3	858	.881
Bill Ranford, Detroit	4	244	8	0	1.97	3	0	1	98	.918
Totals	36	1812	110	1	3.64	6	18	4	956	.885
Tommy Salo, N.Y. Islanders	51	3018	132	5	2.62	17	26	7	1368	.904
Tommy Salo, Edmonton	13	700	27	0	2.31	8	2	2	279	.903
Totals	64	3718	159	5	2.57	25	28	9	1647	.903
Mikhail Shtalenkov, Edmonton	34	1819	81	3	2.67	12	17	3	782	.896
Mikhail Shtalenkov, Phoenix	4	243	9	0	2.22	1	2	1	104	.913
Totals	38	2062	90	3	2.62	13	19	4	886	.898
Jocelyn Thibault, Montreal	10	529	23	1	2.61	3	4	2	250	.908
Jocelyn Thibault, Chicago	52	3014	136	4	2.71	21	26	5	1435	.905
Totals	62	3543	159	5	2.69	24	30	7	1685	.906
Andrei Trefilov, Chicago	1	25	4	0	9.60	0	1	0	20	.800
Andrei Trefilov, Calgary	4	162	11	0	4.07	0	3	0	84	.869
Totals	5	187	15	0	4.81	0	4	0	104	.856

MISCELLANEOUS

HAT TRICKS

(Players scoring three or more goals in a game)

Date	Player, Team	Opp.	Goals
10-10-98	Theoren Fleury, Calgary	S.J.	3
10-12-98	Al MacInnis, St. Louis	NYR	3
10-16-98	John LeClair, Philadelphia	T.B.	3
10-16-98	Brendan Shanahan, Detroit	St.L.	3
10-30-98	Mark Parrish, Florida	Chi.	4
10-31-98	Geoff Sanderson, Buffalo	Tor.	3
11-1-98	Theoren Fleury, Calgary	Chi.	3
11-6-98	Valeri Kamensky, Colorado	Edm.	3
11-7-98	Peter Bondra, Washington	Ott.	3
11-10-98	Kevin Stevens, N.Y. Rangers	T.B.	3
11-10-98	Pierre Turgeon, St. Louis	Chi.	3
11-12-98	Mats Sundin, Toronto	Chi.	3
11-25-98	Dixon Ward, Buffalo	NYR	3
11-25-98	Stu Barnes, Pittsburgh	Was.	3
11-28-98	Martin Straka, Pittsburgh	Mon.	3
11-28-98	Tony Amonte, Chicago	Cal.	3
11-29-98	John LeClair, Philadelphia	Van.	4
12-4-98	Markus Naslund, Vancouver	Dal.	3
12-23-98	Mike Modano, Dallas	Tor.	3
12-23-98	Bobby Holik, New Jersey	St.L.	3
12-23-98	Marco Sturm, San Jose	Edm.	3
12-30-98	Wendel Clark, Tampa Bay	Car.	3
1-1-99	Teemu Selanne, Anaheim	Buf.	3
1-26-99	Pavel Bure, Florida	Phi.	3
2-3-99	Peter Bondra, Washington	T.B.	4
2-4-99	Jason Allison, Boston	NYI	3
2-5-99	Peter Bondra, Washington	Car.	3
2-10-99	Sergei Berezin, Toronto	Car.	3
2-17-99	Alexander Selivanov, Edmonton	Ana.	3
2-19-99	Joe Sakic, Colorado	Nash.	3
2-19-99	Mike Modano, Dallas	Chi.	3
2-21-99	Vyacheslav Kozlov, Detroit	Buf.	3
2-21-99	Dmitri Khristich, Boston	Chi.	3
2-23-99	Mike Modano, Dallas	Nash.	3
2-26-99	Craig Conroy, St. Louis	Cal.	3
2-28-99	Petr Nedved, N.Y. Rangers	Phi.	3
3-3-99	Peter Forsberg, Colorado	Fla.	3
3-3-99	Pavel Bure, Florida	Col.	3
3-4-99	Alexei Yashin, Ottawa	Phi.	3
3-5-99	Brendan Shanahan, Detroit	Pho.	3
3-6-99	Wendel Clark, Tampa Bay	Mon.	3
3-7-99	Keith Tkachuk, Phoenix	Nash.	3
3-8-99	Magnus Arvedson, Ottawa	T.B.	3
3-19-99	Wendel Clark, Tampa Bay	Det.	3
3-20-99	Mike Grier, Edmonton	Van.	3
3-28-99	Tony Amonte, Chicago	St.L.	3
3-28-99	Theoren Fleury, Colorado	L.A.	3
3-30-99	Sami Salo, Ottawa	Pit.	3
4-1-99	Sergei Berezin, Toronto	Edm.	3
4-3-99	Vincent Damphousse, San Jose	Van.	3
4-7-99	Yanic Perreault, Toronto	Ott.	4
4-7-99	Anson Carter, Boston	Fla.	3
4-8-99	Jean-Pierre Dumont, Chicago	NYR	3
4-10-99	Steve Sullivan, Toronto	Fla.	4
4-12-99	Luc Robitaille, Los Angeles	Nash.	3
4-17-99	Zigmund Palffy, N.Y. Islanders	Pit.	3

OVERTIME GOALS

Date	Player, Team	Opponent	Time	Final score
10-16-98	Luc Robitaille, Los Angeles	Boston	2:47	Los Angeles 2, Boston 1
11-8-98	Josef Beranek, Edmonton	Chicago	0:34	Edmonton 3, Chicago 2
11-10-98	Andrew Cassels, Calgary	Los Angeles	1:12	Calgary 5, Los Angeles 4
11-11-98	Steve Rucchin, Anaheim	Carolina	1:04	Anaheim 5, Carolina 4
11-19-98	Jay Pandolfo, New Jersey	Carolina	3:37	New Jersey 3, Carolina 2
11-20-98	Andrei Kovalenko, Edmonton	Anaheim	0:39	Edmonton 3, Anaheim 2
11-20-98	Dallas Drake, Phoenix	San Jose	0:37	Phoenix 2, San Jose 1
11-21-98	Jason Allison, Boston	Washington	4:29	Boston 5, Washington 4
11-21-98	Rick Tocchet, Phoenix	Edmonton	4:08	Phoenix 3, Edmonton 2
11-22-98	Keith Jones, Philadelphia	Florida	0:26	Philadelphia 2, Florida 1
11-28-98	Derek King, Toronto	Ottawa	0:42	Toronto 3, Ottawa 2
12-1-98	Adam Graves, N.Y. Rangers	Florida	2:10	N.Y. Rangers 5, Florida 4
12-5-98	Tomas Kaberle, Toronto	Montreal	0:34	Toronto 4, Montreal 3
12-10-98	Dave Andreychuk, New Jersey	Philadelphia	1:18	New Jersey 5, Philadelphia 4
12-12-98	Benoit Hogue, Tampa Bay	N.Y. Islanders	4:12	Tampa Bay 2, N.Y. Islanders 1
12-15-98	Kevin Hatcher, Pittsburgh	Tampa Bay	3:17	Pittsburgh 3, Tampa Bay 2
12-17-98	Bryan Berard, N.Y. Islanders	Los Angeles	2:00	N.Y. Islanders 5, Los Angeles 4
12-26-98	Jaromir Jagr, Pittsburgh	Ottawa	1:18	Pittsburgh 2, Ottawa 1
12-29-98	Valeri Zelepukin, Philadelphia	Calgary	1:57	Philadelphia 4, Calgary 3
1-1-99	Brett Hull, Dallas	Phoenix	0:37	Dallas 2, Phoenix 1
1-2-99	Marco Sturm, San Jose	N.Y. Islanders	1:47	San Jose 4, N.Y. Islanders 3
1-4-99	Fredrik Modin, Toronto	Tampa Bay	1:54	Toronto 5, Tampa Bay 4
1-5-99	Craig Johnson, Los Angeles	Edmonton	1:07	Los Angeles 4, Edmonton 3
1-6-99	Michael Peca, Buffalo	Anaheim	0:29	Buffalo 3, Anaheim 2
1-10-99	Claude Lemieux, Colorado	Chicago	3:31	Colorado 3, Chicago 2
1-13-99	Adam Graves, N.Y. Rangers	N.Y. Islanders	3:08	N.Y. Rangers 4, N.Y. Islanders 3
1-14-99	Vyacheslav Kozlov, Detroit	Nashville	2:54	Detroit 2, Nashville 1
1-16-99	Kelly Miller, Washington	Carolina	0:09	Washington 3, Carolina 2
1-27-99	Tony Amonte, Chicago	Edmonton	4:52	Chicago 4, Edmonton 3
1-28-99	Gary Roberts, Carolina	N.Y. Rangers	3:18	Carolina 3, N.Y. Rangers 2
1-30-99	Sebastien Bordeleau, Nashville	New Jersey	2:43	Nashville 3, New Jersey 2
1-30-99	Jeff Shantz, Calgary	St. Louis	3:21	Calgary 4, St. Louis 3
2-1-99	Pierre Turgeon, St. Louis	Edmonton	0:35	St. Louis 4, Edmonton 3
12-30-98	Andreas Dackell, Ottawa	Buffalo	2:24	Ottawa 3, Buffalo 2
2-9-99	Alexei Kovalev, Pittsburgh	Montreal	4:31	Pittsburgh 3, Montreal 2
2-11-99	Jaromir Jagr, Pittsburgh	Vancouver	1:21	Pittsburgh 6, Vancouver 5

Date	Player, Team	Opponent	Time	Final score
2-13-99—	Kip Miller, Pittsburgh	Nashville	3:39	Pittsburgh 3, Nashville 2
2-17-99—	Mats Sundin, Toronto	Buffalo	4:04	Toronto 3, Buffalo 2
2-20-99—	Steve Thomas, Toronto	Montreal	3:48	Toronto 3, Montreal 2
2-21-99—	Eric Lacroix, N.Y. Rangers	Edmonton	0:45	N.Y. Rangers 2, Edmonton 1
2-24-99—	Luc Robitaille, Los Angeles	Detroit	1:57	Los Angeles 3, Detroit 2
3-4-99—	Joe Nieuwendyk, Dallas	N.Y. Islanders	4:12	Dallas 3, N.Y. Islanders 2
3-8-99—	Petr Nedved, N.Y. Rangers	Toronto	4:46	N.Y. Rangers 3, Toronto 2
3-9-99—	Sandis Ozolinsh, Colorado	Washington	0:19	Colorado 3, Washington 2
3-10-99—	Kip Miller, Pittsburgh	Carolina	2:49	Pittsburgh 3, Carolina 2
3-13-99—	Valeri Bure, Calgary	Washington	3:31	Calgary 5, Washington 4
3-14-99—	Adam Graves, N.Y. Rangers	N.Y. Islanders	4:05	N.Y. Rangers 3, N.Y. Islanders 2
3-17-99—	Brian Bellows, Washington	Dallas	0:35	Washington 2, Dallas 1
3-19-99—	Miroslav Satan, Buffalo	N.Y. Rangers	1:18	Buffalo 3, N.Y. Rangers 2
3-21-99—	Mike Modano, Dallas	Carolina	0:44	Dallas 3, Carolina 2
3-28-99—	Dixon Ward, Buffalo	Pittsburgh	2:27	Buffalo 4, Pittsburgh 3
3-28-99—	Wendel Clark, Detroit	Philadelphia	2:26	Detroit 3, Philadelphia 2
3-30-99—	Olli Jokinen, Los Angeles	Boston	3:54	Los Angeles 2, Boston 1
4-12-99—	Tom Poti, Edmonton	San Jose	3:55	Edmonton 5, San Jose 4
4-14-99—	Bryan Berard, Toronto	N.Y. Islanders	0:42	Toronto 3, N.Y. Islanders 2
4-14-99—	Marcus Nilson, Florida	Montreal	4:05	Florida 3, Montreal 2
4-15-99—	Ray Ferraro, Los Angeles	Anaheim	2:21	Los Angeles 4, Anaheim 3
4-16-99—	Bobby Holik, New Jersey	Philadelphia	3:27	New Jersey 3, Philadelphia 2
4-17-99—	Hal Gill, Boston	Buffalo	4:46	Boston 2, Buffalo 1
4-18-99—	Jaromir Jagr, Pittsburgh	N.Y. Rangers	1:22	Pittsburgh 2, N.Y. Rangers 1

PENALTY-SHOT INFORMATION

Date	Shooter, Team	Goaltender, Team	Scored	Final score
10-22-98—	Claude Lapointe, N.Y. Islanders	Mike Richter, N.Y. Rangers	No	N.Y. Rangers 3, N.Y. Islanders 2
10-29-98—	Geoff Courtnall, St. Louis	Chris Osgood, Detroit	Yes	St. Louis 3, Detroit 1
11-11-98—	Scott Niedermayer, New Jersey	Jose Theodore, Montreal	Yes	New Jersey 3, Montreal 0
11-18-98—	Adam Oates, Washington	Curtis Joseph, Toronto	Yes	Washington 4, Toronto 1
11-24-98—	Daymond Langkow, Tampa Bay	Robbie Tallas, Boston	No	Boston 4, Tampa Bay 1
12-1-98—	Shaun Van Allen, Ottawa	Eric Fichaud, Nashville	No	Ottawa 3, Nashville 1
12-4-98—	Mariusz Czerkawski, N.Y. Islanders	Rick Tabaracci, Washington	No	Washington 5, N.Y. Islanders 1
12-7-98—	Mike Modano, Dallas	Tyler Moss, Calgary	No	Dallas 3, Calgary 2
12-19-98—	Markus Naslund, Vancouver	Mike Dunham, Nashville	Yes	Nashville 6, Vancouver 4
12-26-98—	Owen Nolan, San Jose	Garth Snow, Vancouver	No	San Jose 2, Vancouver 0
12-30-98—	Jay Pandolfo, New Jersey	Rick Tabaracci, Washington	No	New Jersey 3, Washington 2
1-2-99—	Martin Rucinsky, Montreal	Corey Hirsch, Vancouver	No	Montreal 2, Vancouver 1
1-7-99—	Sami Kapanen, Carolina	Tom Barrasso, Pittsburgh	No	Pittsburgh 4, Carolina 2
1-10-99—	John MacLean, N.Y. Rangers	Bill Ranford, Tampa Bay	Yes	N.Y. Rangers 5, Tampa Bay 2
1-26-99—	Terry Yake, St. Louis	Steve Shields, San Jose	No	St. Louis 3, San Jose 0
1-29-99—	Peter Bondra, Washington	Stephane Fiset, Los Angeles	Yes	Los Angeles 6, Washington 3
2-15-99—	Tomas Sandstrom, Anaheim	Stephane Fiset, Los Angeles	Yes	Anaheim 3, Los Angeles 1
2-20-99—	Paul Kariya, Anaheim	Corey Hirsch, Vancouver	Yes	Anaheim 5, Vancouver 1
2-26-99—	Pavel Bure, Florida	Chris Osgood, Detroit	Yes	Florida 5, Detroit 5
2-26-99—	Todd White, Chicago	Jamie Storr, Los Angeles	No	Los Angeles 2, Chicago 1
3-6-99—	Steve Sullivan, Toronto	Ron Tugnutt, Ottawa	No	Ottawa 3, Toronto 1
3-17-99—	Landon Wilson, Boston	Curtis Joseph, Toronto	No	Boston 4, Toronto 1
3-18-99—	Paul Kariya, Anaheim	Stephane Fiset, Los Angeles	No	Anaheim 4, Los Angeles 2
3-21-99—	Ray Whitney, Florida	Guy Hebert, Anaheim	Yes	Florida 5, Anaheim 2
3-24-99—	Jason Allison, Boston	Ron Tugnutt, Ottawa	Yes	Boston 3, Ottawa 0
3-25-99—	Robert Reichel, Phoenix	Rick Tabaracci, Washington	No	Phoenix 4, Washington 2
4-12-99—	Ted Donato, Ottawa	Kirk McLean, Florida	No	Florida 2, Ottawa 0

TEAM STREAKS

Most consecutive games won

Colorado, Jan. 10-Feb. 7......................12
Pittsburgh, Jan. 28-Feb. 15..................10
Phoenix, Nov. 11-28..............................8
Detroit, Mar. 24-Apr. 7...........................8
Anaheim, Feb. 20-Mar. 7........................7

Most consecutive games undefeated

Dallas, Dec. 6-Jan. 6.............................15
Philadelphia, Dec. 12-Jan. 13...............15
Phoenix, Oct. 25-Nov. 28.....................14
Colorado, Jan. 10-Feb. 7......................12
Ottawa, Dec. 28-Jan. 16.......................11

Most consecutive home games won

Pittsburgh, Jan. 28-Feb. 22....................9
Chicago, Mar. 17-Apr. 17........................9
Toronto, Nov. 11-Dec. 2..........................7
Buffalo, Nov. 14-Dec. 18.........................7
Phoenix, Nov. 14-Dec. 20........................7
Ottawa, Feb. 13-Mar. 8...........................7
Detroit, Mar. 24-Apr. 7............................7

Most consecutive home games undefeated

Phoenix, Oct. 15-Dec. 20.......................11
Pittsburgh, Jan. 28-Mar. 5.....................11
Buffalo, Oct. 30-Dec. 18........................10
New Jersey, Oct. 31-Dec. 16.................10
Colorado, Mar. 18-Apr. 18......................10

Most consecutive road games won

Colorado, Jan. 10-Feb. 7.........................7
Dallas, Jan. 13-Feb. 23...........................7
Phoenix, Oct. 26-Nov. 28........................6
St. Louis, Feb. 1-Mar. 2...........................6
New Jersey, Jan. 20-Feb. 4.....................5
New Jersey, Mar. 3-Mar. 17....................5
Ottawa, Mar. 19-Apr. 3............................5

Most consecutive road games undefeated

Philadelphia, Dec. 8-Jan. 18.................10
Colorado, Jan. 10-Mar. 3........................10
Dallas, Jan. 12-Mar. 4............................10
Dallas, Dec. 6-Jan. 1...............................9
Phoenix, Oct. 25-Nov. 28........................7
New Jersey, Nov. 28-Dec. 30..................7
Buffalo, Nov. 29-Jan. 6............................7
Ottawa, Dec. 30-Jan. 21..........................7
New Jersey, Feb. 22-Mar. 17...................7
Ottawa, Mar. 17-Apr. 5............................7

TEAM OVERTIME GAMES

	OVERALL					HOME					AWAY				
Team	**G**	**W**	**L**	**T**	**Pct.**	**G**	**W**	**L**	**T**	**Pct.**	**G**	**W**	**L**	**T**	**Pct.**
Toronto	14	6	1	7	.679	9	4	0	5	.722	5	2	1	2	.600
Pittsburgh	22	7	1	14	.636	14	4	0	10	.643	8	3	1	4	.625
Los Angeles	12	5	2	5	.625	6	2	1	3	.583	6	3	1	2	.667
Colorado	12	2	0	10	.583	6	0	0	6	.500	6	2	0	4	.667
New Jersey	15	3	1	11	.567	11	2	1	8	.545	4	1	0	3	.625
Calgary	16	3	1	12	.563	9	2	1	6	.556	7	1	0	6	.571
Dallas	16	3	1	12	.563	5	1	0	4	.600	11	2	1	8	.545
N.Y. Rangers	19	5	3	11	.553	10	3	2	5	.550	9	2	1	6	.556
Detroit	10	2	1	7	.550	5	2	1	2	.600	5	0	0	5	.500
Phoenix	15	2	1	12	.533	7	1	1	5	.500	8	1	0	7	.563
Buffalo	23	3	3	17	.500	9	1	2	6	.444	14	2	1	11	.536
Boston	17	2	2	13	.500	12	2	1	9	.542	5	0	1	4	.400
St. Louis	15	1	1	13	.500	6	0	0	6	.500	9	1	1	7	.500
Philadelphia	24	2	3	19	.479	12	0	1	11	.458	12	2	2	8	.500
San Jose	21	1	2	18	.476	11	0	2	9	.409	10	1	0	9	.550
Florida	21	1	2	18	.476	9	1	1	7	.500	12	0	1	11	.458
Ottawa	18	1	2	15	.472	8	0	0	8	.500	10	1	2	7	.450
Chicago	15	1	2	12	.467	6	0	2	4	.333	9	1	0	8	.556
Vancouver	13	0	1	12	.462	6	0	0	6	.500	7	0	1	6	.429
Tampa Bay	12	1	2	9	.458	4	0	0	4	.500	8	1	2	5	.438
Washington	11	2	3	6	.455	5	1	2	2	.400	6	1	1	4	.500
Edmonton	20	3	5	12	.450	9	0	4	5	.278	11	3	1	7	.591
Nashville	10	1	2	7	.450	5	0	1	4	.400	5	1	1	3	.500
Anaheim	17	1	3	13	.441	9	1	2	6	.444	8	0	1	7	.438
Carolina	24	1	5	18	.417	12	1	2	9	.458	12	0	3	9	.375
Montreal	15	0	4	11	.367	6	0	1	5	.417	9	0	3	6	.333
N.Y. Islanders	17	1	6	10	.353	11	0	4	7	.318	6	1	2	3	.417
Totals	222	60	60	162	1.000	222	28	32	162	.491	222	32	28	162	.509

STANLEY CUP PLAYOFFS

RESULTS

CONFERENCE QUARTERFINALS

EASTERN CONFERENCE

	W	L	Pts.	GF	GA
Pittsburgh Penguins	4	3	8	21	18
New Jersey Devils	3	4	6	18	21

(Pittsburgh won Eastern Conference quarterfinals, 4-3)

Thur. April 22—Pittsburgh 1, at New Jersey 3
Sat. April 24—Pittsburgh 4, at New Jersey 1
Sun. April 25—New Jersey 2, at Pittsburgh 4
Tue. April 27—New Jersey 4, at Pittsburgh 2
Fri. April 30—Pittsburgh 3, at New Jersey 4
Sun. May 2—New Jersey 2, at Pittsburgh 3 (a)
Tue. May 4—Pittsburgh 4, at New Jersey 2
(a)—Jaromir Jagr scored at 8:59 (OT) for Pittsburgh.

	W	L	Pts.	GF	GA
Buffalo Sabres	4	0	8	12	6
Ottawa Senators	0	4	0	6	12

(Buffalo won Eastern Conference quarterfinals, 4-0)

Wed. April 21—Buffalo 2, at Ottawa 1
Fri. April 23—Buffalo 3, at Ottawa 2 (b)
Sun. April 25—Ottawa 0, at Buffalo 3
Tue. April 27—Ottawa 3, at Buffalo 4
(b)—Miroslav Satan scored at 10:35 (2OT) for Buffalo.

	W	L	Pts.	GF	GA
Boston Bruins	4	2	8	16	10
Carolina Hurricanes	2	4	4	10	16

(Boston won Eastern Conference quarterfinals, 4-2)

Thur. April 22—Boston 2, at Carolina 0
Sat. April 24—Boston 2, at Carolina 3 (c)
Mon. April 26—Carolina 3, at Boston 2
Wed. April 28—Carolina 1, at Boston 4
Fri. April 30—Boston 4, at Carolina 3 (d)
Sun. May 2—Carolina 0, Boston 2
(c)—Ray Sheppard scored at 17:05 (OT) for Carolina.
(d)—Anson Carter scored at 14:45 (2OT) for Boston.

	W	L	Pts.	GF	GA
Toronto Maple Leafs	4	2	8	9	11
Philadelphia Flyers	2	4	4	11	9

(Toronto won Eastern Conference quarterfinals, 4-2)

Thur. April 22—Philadelphia 3, at Toronto 0
Sat. April 24—Philadelphia 1, at Toronto 2
Mon. April 26—Toronto 2, at Philadelphia 1
Wed. April 28—Toronto 2, at Philadelphia 5
Fri. April 30—Philadelphia 1, at Toronto 2 (e)
Sun. May 2—Toronto 1, at Philadelphia 0
(e)—Yanic Perreault scored at 11:51 (OT) for Toronto.

WESTERN CONFERENCE

	W	L	Pts.	GF	GA
Dallas Stars	4	0	8	11	7
Edmonton Oilers	0	4	0	7	11

(Dallas won Western Conference quarterfinals, 4-0)

Wed. April 21—Edmonton 1, at Dallas 2
Fri. April 23—Edmonton 2, at Dallas 3
Sun. April 25—Dallas 3, at Edmonton 2
Tue. April 27—Dallas 3, at Edmonton 2 (f)
(f)—Joe Nieuwendyk scored at 17:34 (3OT) for Dallas.

	W	L	Pts.	GF	GA
Colorado Avalanche	4	2	8	19	17
San Jose Sharks	2	4	4	17	19

(Colorado won Western Conference quarterfinals, 4-2)

Sat. April 24—Colorado 3, at San Jose 1
Mon. April 26—Colorado 2, at San Jose 1 (g)
Wed. April 28—San Jose 4, at Colorado 2
Fri. April 30—San Jose 7, at Colorado 3
Sat. May 1—San Jose 2, at Colorado 6
Mon. May 3—Colorado 3, at San Jose 2 (h)
(g)—Milan Hejduk scored a 7:53 (OT) for Colorado.
(h)—Milan Hejduk scored at 13:12 (OT) for Colorado.

	W	L	Pts.	GF	GA
Detroit Red Wings	4	0	8	17	6
Mighty Ducks of Anaheim	0	4	0	6	17

(Detroit won Western Conference quarterfinals, 4-0)

Wed. April 21—Anaheim 3, at Detroit 5
Fri. April 23—Anaheim 1, at Detroit 5
Sun. April 25—Detroit 4, at Anaheim 2
Tue. April 27—Detroit 3, at Anaheim 0

	W	L	Pts.	GF	GA
St. Louis Blues	4	3	8	19	16
Phoenix Coyotes	3	4	6	16	19

(St. Louis won Western Conference quarterfinals, 4-3)

Thur. April 22—St. Louis 3, at Phoenix 1
Sat. April 24—St. Louis 3, at Phoenix 4 (i)
Sun. April 25—Phoenix 5, at St. Louis 4
Tue. April 27—Phoenix 2, at St. Louis 1
Fri. April 30—St. Louis 2, at Phoenix 1 (j)
Sun. May 2—Phoenix 3, at St. Louis 5
Tue. May 4—St. Louis 1, at Phoenix 0 (k)
(i)—Shane Doan scored at 8:58 (OT) for Phoenix.
(j)—Scott Young scored at 5:43 (OT) for St. Louis.
(k)—Pierre Turgeon at 17:59 (OT) for St. Louis.

CONFERENCE SEMIFINALS

EASTERN CONFERENCE

	W	L	Pts.	GF	GA
Toronto Maple Leafs	4	2	8	18	14
Pittsburgh Penguins	2	4	4	14	18

(Toronto won Eastern Conference semifinals, 4-2)

Fri. May 7—Pittsburgh 2, at Toronto 0
Sun. May 9—Pittsburgh 2, at Toronto 4
Tue. May 11—Toronto 3, at Pittsburgh 4
Thur. May 13—Toronto 3, at Pittsburgh 2 (l)
Sat. May 15—Pittsburgh 1, at Toronto 4
Mon. May 17—Toronto 4, at Pittsburgh 3 (m)
(l)—Sergei Berezin scored at 2:18 (OT) for Toronto.
(m)—Garry Valk scored at 1:57 (OT) for Toronto.

	W	L	Pts.	GF	GA
Buffalo Sabres	4	2	8	17	14
Boston Bruins	2	4	4	14	17

(Buffalo won Eastern Conference semifinals, 4-2)

Thur. May 6—Buffalo 2, at Boston 4
Sun. May 9—Buffalo 3, at Boston 1
Wed. May 12—Boston 2, at Buffalo 3
Fri. May 14—Boston 0, at Buffalo 3
Sun. May 16—Buffalo 3, at Boston 5
Tue. May 18—Boston 2, at Buffalo 3

WESTERN CONFERENCE

	W	L	Pts.	GF	GA
Dallas Stars	4	2	8	9	5
St. Louis Blues	2	4	4	5	9

(Dallas won Western Conference semifinals, 4-2)

Thur. May 6—St. Louis 0, at Dallas 3
Sat. May 8—St. Louis 4, at Dallas 5 (n)
Mon. May 10—Dallas 2, at St. Louis 3 (o)
Wed. May 12—Dallas 2, at St. Louis 3 (p)
Sat. May 15—St. Louis 1, at Dallas 3
Mon. May 17—Dallas 2, at St. Louis 1 (q)
(n)—Joe Nieuwendyk scored at 8:22 (OT) for Dallas.

(o)—Pavol Demitra scored at 2:43 (OT) for St. Louis.
(p)—Pierre Turgeon scored at 5:52 (OT) for St. Louis.
(q)—Mike Modano scored at 2:21 (OT) for Dallas.

	W	L	Pts.	GF	GA
Colorado Avalanche	4	2	8	23	13
Detroit Red Wings	2	4	4	13	23

(Colorado won Western Conference semifinals, 4-2)

Fri. May 7—Detroit 3, at Colorado 2 (r)
Sun. May 9—Detroit 4, at Colorado 0
Tue. May 11—Colorado 5, at Detroit 3
Thur. May 13—Colorado 6, at Detroit 2
Sun. May 16—Detroit 2, at Colorado 3
Tue. May 18—Colorado 5, at Detroit 2
(r)—Kirk Maltby scored at 4:18 (OT) for Detroit.

CONFERENCE FINALS

EASTERN CONFERENCE

	W	L	Pts.	GF	GA
Buffalo Sabres	4	1	8	21	16
Toronto Maple Leafs	1	4	2	16	21

(Buffalo won Eastern Conference finals, 4-1)

Sun. May 23—Buffalo 5, at Toronto 4
Tues. May 25—Buffalo 3, at Toronto 6
Thur. May 27—Toronto 2, at Buffalo 4
Sat. May 29—Toronto 2, at Buffalo 5
Mon. May 31—Buffalo 4, at Toronto 2

WESTERN CONFERENCE

	W	L	Pts.	GF	GA
Dallas Stars	4	3	8	23	16
Colorado Avalanche	3	4	6	16	23

(Dallas won Western Conference finals, 4-3)

Sat. May 22—Colorado 2, at Dallas 1
Mon. May 24—Colorado 2, at Dallas 4
Wed. May 26—Dallas 3, at Colorado 0
Fri. May 28—Dallas 2, at Colorado 3 (s)
Sun. May 30—Colorado 7, at Dallas 5
Tue. June 1—Dallas 4, at Colorado 1
Fri. June 4—Colorado 1, at Dallas 4
(s)—Chris Drury scored at 19:29 (OT) for Colorado.

STANLEY CUP FINALS

	W	L	Pts.	GF	GA
Dallas Stars	4	2	8	13	9
Buffalo Sabres	2	4	4	9	13

(Dallas won Stanley Cup championship, 4-2)

Tue. June 8—Buffalo 3, at Dallas 2 (t)
Thur. June 10—Buffalo 2, at Dallas 4
Sat. June 12—Dallas 2, at Buffalo 1
Tue. June 15—Dallas 1, at Buffalo 2
Thur. June 17—Buffalo 0, at Dallas 2
Sat. June 19—Dallas 2, at Buffalo 1 (u)
(t)—Jason Woolley scored at 15:30 (OT) for Buffalo.
(u)—Brett Hull scored at 14:51 (3OT) for Dallas.

GAME SUMMARIES, STANLEY CUP FINALS

GAME 1

AT DALLAS, JUNE 8

Buffalo 3, Dallas 2 (OT)

Buffalo	0	0	2	1	—	3
Dallas	1	0	1	0	—	2

FIRST PERIOD—1. Dallas, Hull 6 (Modano, Lehtinen), 10:17 (pp). Penalties—Zubov, Dallas (roughing), 6:36; Satan, Buffalo (boarding), 8:18; Patrick, Buffalo (double high sticking minor), 12:46); Ward, Buffalo (interference), 19:11.

SECOND PERIOD—No scoring. Penalties—Varada, Buffalo (goalie interference), 4:53; Zhitnik, Buffalo (interference), 7:07; Ward, Buffalo (roughing), 9:34; Ludwig, Dallas (hooking), 12:21; Matvichuk, Dallas (interference), 16:33.

THIRD PERIOD—2. Buffalo, Barnes 5 (Juneau, Smehlik), 8:33. 3. Buffalo, Primeau 3 (Zhitnik, Smehlik), 13:37 (pp). 4. Dallas, Lehtinen 8 (Modano, Zubov), 19:11. Penalties—Sydor, Dallas (obstruction-tripping), 12:10; McKee, Buffalo (charging), 14:17.

OVERTIME—5. Buffalo, Woolley 4 (Brown), 15:30. Penalties—Zhitnik, Buffalo (hooking), 6:41; Sanderson, Buffalo (boarding), 9:06.

Shots on goal—Buffalo 5-4-10-5-24; Dallas 11-13-6-7-37. Power-play opportunities—Buffalo 1 of 4; Dallas 1 of 10. Goalies—Buffalo, Hasek 12-2 (37 shots-35 saves); Dallas, Belfour 12-6 (24-21). A—17,001. Referees—Terry Gregson, Bill McCreary. Linesmen—Ray Scapinello, Jay Sharrers.

GAME 2

AT DALLAS, JUNE 10

Dallas 4, Buffalo 2

Buffalo	0	1	1	—	2
Dallas	0	1	3	—	4

FIRST PERIOD—No scoring. Penalties—Penalties—Skrudland, Dallas (charging), 12:25; Zhitnik, Buffalo (boarding), 15:31; Zhitnik, Buffalo (cross-checking), 20:00; Smehlik, Buffalo (roughing), 20:00; Holzinger, Buffalo, (fighting major), 20:00; Modano, Dallas (tripping), 20:00; Hatcher, Dallas (roughing), 20:00; Nieuwendyk, Dallas, (fighting major), 20:00.

SECOND PERIOD—1. Buffalo, Peca 5 (Woolley, Satan), 7:27 (pp). 2. Dallas, Langenbrunner 10 (Matvichuk, Nieuwendyk), 18:26. Penalties—Sydor, Dallas (hooking), 5:41; Woolley, Buffalo (interference), 9:19; Varada, Buffalo (obstruction-tripping), 13:14; Zhitnik, Buffalo (tripping), 20:00.

THIRD PERIOD—3. Dallas, Ludwig 1 (Skrudland), 4:25. 4. Buffalo, Zhitnik 4 (unassisted), 5:36 (pp). 5. Dallas, Hull 7 (Hrkac, Chambers), 17:10. 6. Dallas, Hatcher 1 (Zubov), 19:34 (en). Penalties—Sydor, Dallas (high-sticking), 4:50; Varada, Buffalo (high-sticking), 10:32; Zhitnik, Buffalo (hooking), 11:48; Hatcher, Dallas (high-sticking), 17:31.

Shots on goal—Buffalo 7-10-4-21; Dallas 5-7-19-31. Power-play opportunities—Buffalo 2 of 4; Dallas 0 of 6. Goalies—Buffalo, Hasek 12-3 (30 shots-27 saves); Dallas, Belfour 13-6 (21-19). A—17,001. Referees—Kerry Fraser, Dan Marouelli. Linesmen—Gord Broseker, Kevin Collins.

GAME 3

AT BUFFALO, JUNE 12

Dallas 2, Buffalo 1

Dallas	0	1	1	—	2
Buffalo	0	1	0	—	1

FIRST PERIOD—No scoring. Penalties—Ludwig, Dallas (interference), 7:45; Chambers, Dallas (roughing), 7:45; Rasmussen, Buffalo (roughing), 7:45; Matvichuk, Dallas (roughing), 9:43; Skrudland, Dallas (slashing), 18:13; Hatcher, Dallas (roughing), 18:46.

SECOND PERIOD—1. Buffalo, Barnes 6 (Smehlik, Holzinger), 7:51. 2. Dallas, Nieuwendyk 10 (Reid, Langenbrunner), 15:33. Penalties—Zhitnik, Buffalo (interference), 3:38; Modano, Dallas (obstruction-tripping), 9:54; Modano, Dallas (slashing), 12:21; Holzinger, Buffalo (high sticking), 19:09; Modano, Dallas (interference), 19:23.

THIRD PERIOD—3. Dallas, Nieuwendyk 11 (Langenbrunner, Reid), 9:35. Penalty—Hrkac, Dallas (tripping), 17:38.

Shots on goal—Dallas 8-13-8-29; Buffalo 3-6-3-12. Power-play opportunities—Dallas 0 of 2; Buffalo 0 of 8. Goalies—Dallas, Belfour, 14-6 (12 shots-11 saves); Buffalo, Hasek 12-4 (29-27). A—18,595. Referees—Terry Gregson, Don Koharski. Linesmen—Ray Scapinello, Jay Sharrers.

GAME 4

AT BUFFALO, JUNE 15

Buffalo 2, Dallas 1

Dallas	1	0	0	—	1
Buffalo	1	1	0	—	2

FIRST PERIOD—1. Buffalo, Sanderson 4 (unassisted), 8:09. 2. Dallas, Lehtinen 9 (Modano, Hatcher), 10:14 (pp). Penalties—Matvichuk, Dallas (roughing), 3:48; Primeau, Buffalo (charging), 9:32; Woolley, Buffalo (holding), 19:05.

SECOND PERIOD—3. Buffalo, Ward 7 (unassisted), 7:37. Penalties—Verbeek, Dallas (interference), 0:21; Ludwig, Dallas (interference), 11:07; Skrudland, Dallas (roughing), 14:49; Holzinger, Buffalo (boarding), 16:44; Hatcher, Dallas (roughing), 20:00; Verbeek, Dallas (roughing), 20:00; Hasek, Buffalo, served by Barnes (roughing), 20:00; Zhitnik, Buffalo (roughing), 20:00.

THIRD PERIOD—No scoring. Penalties—Nieuwendyk, Dallas (hooking), 1:06; Langenbrunner, Dallas (slashing), 20:00; Reid, Dallas (roughing), 20:00; Warrener, Buffalo (roughing), 20:00; Ward, Buffalo (double minor-roughing), 20:00.

Shots on goal—Dallas 9-9-13-31; Buffalo 7-9-2-18. Power-play opportunities—Dallas 1 of 3; Buffalo 0 of 5. Goalies—Dallas, Belfour, 14-7 (18 shots-16 saves); Buffalo, Hasek, 13-4 (31-30). A—18,595. Referees—Dan Marouelli, Bill McCreary. Linesmen—Kevin Collins, Gord Broseker.

GAME 5

AT DALLAS, JUNE 17

Dallas 2, Buffalo 0

Buffalo	0	0	0	—	0
Dallas	0	1	1	—	2

FIRST PERIOD—No scoring. Penalty—Ludwig, Dallas (obstruction-tripping), 2:08.

SECOND PERIOD—1. Dallas, Sydor 3 (Modano, Zubov), 2:23 (pp). Penalties—Brown, Buffalo (interference), 1:42; Woolley, Buffalo (obstruction-holding), 3:31; Langenbrunner, Dallas (roughing), 7:44.

THIRD PERIOD—2. Dallas, Verbeek 3 (Matvichuk, Modano), 15:21. Penalties—Sydor, Dallas (roughing), 8:21; Primeau, Buffalo (roughing), 8:21; Warrener, Buffalo (slashing), 16:31; Zhitnik, Buffalo (elbowing), 17:27; Nieuwendyk, Dallas (roughing), 17:27; Skrudland, Dallas (obstruction-tripping), 19:29; Warrener, Buffalo (roughing), 20:00; Hatcher, Dallas (roughing), 20:00.

Shots on goal—Buffalo 9-5-9-23; Dallas 8-7-6-21. Power-play opportunities—Buffalo 0 of 3; Dallas 1 of 3. Goalies—Buffalo, Hasek, 13-5 (21 shots-19 saves); Dallas, Belfour 15-7 (23-23). A—17,001. Referees—Kerry Fraser, Don Koharski. Linesmen—Ray Scapinello, Jay Sharrers.

GAME 6

AT BUFFALO, JUNE 15

Buffalo 2, Dallas 1

Dallas	1	0	0	0	0	1	—	2
Buffalo	0	1	0	0	0	0	—	1

FIRST PERIOD—1. Dallas, Lehtinen 10 (Modano, Ludwig), 8:09. Penalties—None.

SECOND PERIOD—2. Buffalo, Barnes 7 (Primeau, Zhitnik), 18:21. Penalties—Sanderson, Buffalo (interference), 5:19; Ludwig, Dallas (interference), 10:49; Hogue, Dallas (tripping), 14:28; Peca, Buffalo (slashing), 19:27.

THIRD PERIOD—No scoring or penalties.

FIRST OVERTIME—No scoring or penalties.

SECOND OVERTIME—No scoring or penalties.

THIRD OVERTIME—3. Dallas, Hull 8 (Lehtinen, Modano), 14:51. Penalties—None.

Shots on goal—Dallas 5-11-10-4-13-7-50; Buffalo 11-15-6-6-12-4-54. Power-play opportunities—Dallas 0 of 2; Buffalo 0 of 2. Goalies—Dallas, Belfour, 16-7 (54 shots-53 saves); Buffalo, Hasek, 13-6 (50-48). A—18,595. Referees—Terry Gregson, Bill McCreary. Linesmen—Gord Broseker, Kevin Collins.

INDIVIDUAL LEADERS

Goals: Joe Nieuwendyk, Dallas (11)
Assists: Mike Modano, Dallas (18)
Points: Peter Forsberg, Colorado (24)
Penalty minutes: Alexei Zhitnik, Buffalo (52)
Goaltending average: Ed Belfour, Dallas (1.67)
Shutouts: Ed Belfour, Dallas (3)

TOP SCORERS

	Games	G	A	Pts.	PIM
Peter Forsberg, Colorado	19	8	16	24	31
Mike Modano, Dallas	23	5	18	23	16
Joe Nieuwendyk, Dallas	23	11	10	21	19
Joe Sakic, Colorado	19	6	13	19	8
Jamie Langenbrunner, Dallas	23	10	7	17	16
Theoren Fleury, Colorado	18	5	12	17	20
Mats Sundin, Toronto	17	8	8	16	16
Brett Hull, Dallas	22	8	7	15	4
Martin Straka, Pittsburgh	13	6	9	15	6
Jason Woolley, Buffalo	21	4	11	15	10
Alexei Zhitnik, Buffalo	21	4	11	15	52

INDIVIDUAL STATISTICS

MIGHTY DUCKS OF ANAHEIM

(Lost Western Conference quarterfinals to Detroit, 4-0)

SCORING

	Games	G	A	Pts.	PIM
Teemu Selanne	4	2	2	4	2
Paul Kariya	3	1	3	4	0
Steve Rucchin	4	0	3	3	0
Marty McInnis	4	2	0	2	2
Fredrik Olausson	4	0	2	2	4
Jason Marshall	4	1	0	1	10
Travis Green	4	0	1	1	4
Pavel Trnka	4	0	1	1	2
Tom Askey (goalie)	1	0	0	0	0
Johan Davidsson	1	0	0	0	0
Mike Leclerc	1	0	0	0	0
Daniel Trebil	1	0	0	0	2
Stu Grimson	3	0	0	0	30
Ruslan Salei	3	0	0	0	4
Antti Aalto	4	0	0	0	2
Matt Cullen	4	0	0	0	0
Ted Drury	4	0	0	0	0
Kevin Haller	4	0	0	0	2
Guy Hebert (goalie)	4	0	0	0	0
Jim McKenzie	4	0	0	0	4
Jeff Nielsen	4	0	0	0	2
Jamie Pushor	4	0	0	0	6
Tomas Sandstrom	4	0	0	0	4

GOALTENDING

	Gms.	Min.	W	L	T	G	SO	Avg.
Tom Askey	1	30	0	1	0	2	0	4.00
Guy Hebert	4	208	0	3	0	15	0	4.33

BOSTON BRUINS

(Lost Eastern Conference semifinals to Buffalo, 4-2)

SCORING

	Games	G	A	Pts.	PIM
Jason Allison	12	2	9	11	6
Ray Bourque	12	1	9	10	14
Joe Thornton	11	3	6	9	4
Anson Carter	12	4	3	7	0
Steve Heinze	12	4	3	7	0
Dmitri Khristich	12	3	4	7	6
Sergei Samsonov	11	3	1	4	0
Don Sweeney	11	3	0	3	6
Darren Van Impe	11	1	2	3	4
Kyle McLaren	12	0	3	3	10
Tim Taylor	12	0	3	3	8
Rob DiMaio	12	2	0	2	8
Mattias Timander	4	1	1	2	2
Landon Wilson	8	1	1	2	8
P.J. Axelsson	12	1	1	2	4
Ken Belanger	12	1	0	1	16
Cameron Mann	1	0	0	0	0
Eric Nickulas	1	0	0	0	2
Randy Robitaille	1	0	0	0	0
Grant Ledyard	2	0	0	0	2
Ken Baumgartner	3	0	0	0	0
Dave Ellett	8	0	0	0	4
Shawn Bates	12	0	0	0	4
Byron Dafoe (goalie)	12	0	0	0	2
Hal Gill	12	0	0	0	14

GOALTENDING

	Gms.	Min.	W	L	T	G	SO	Avg.
Byron Dafoe	12	768	6	6	0	26	2	2.03

BUFFALO SABRES

(Lost Stanley Cup finals to Dallas, 4-2)

SCORING

	Games	G	A	Pts.	PIM
Jason Woolley	21	4	11	15	10
Alexei Zhitnik	21	4	11	15	52
Curtis Brown	21	7	6	13	10
Michael Peca	21	5	8	13	18
Dixon Ward	21	7	5	12	32
Joe Juneau	20	3	8	11	10
Stu Barnes	21	7	3	10	6
Geoff Sanderson	19	4	6	10	14
Vaclav Varada	21	5	4	9	14
Miroslav Satan	12	3	5	8	2
Brian Holzinger	21	3	5	8	33
Wayne Primeau	19	3	4	7	6
Erik Rasmussen	21	2	4	6	18
Rhett Warrener	20	1	3	4	32
Michal Grosek	13	0	4	4	28
Jay McKee	21	0	3	3	24
Richard Smehlik	21	0	3	3	10
Rob Ray	5	1	0	1	0
Dominik Hasek (goalie)	19	0	1	1	8
James Patrick	20	0	1	1	12
Darryl Shannon	2	0	0	0	0
Randy Cunneyworth	3	0	0	0	0
Dwayne Roloson (goalie)	4	0	0	0	0
Dean Sylvester	4	0	0	0	2
Paul Kruse	10	0	0	0	4

GOALTENDING

	Gms.	Min.	W	L	T	G	SO	Avg.
Dominik Hasek	19	1217	13	6	0	36	2	1.77
Dwayne Roloson	4	139	1	1	0	10	0	4.32

CAROLINA HURRICANES

(Lost Eastern Conference quarterfinals to Boston, 4-2)

SCORING

	Games	G	A	Pts.	PIM
Ray Sheppard	6	5	1	6	2
Steve Chiasson	6	1	2	3	2
Jon Battaglia	6	0	3	3	8
Martin Gelinas	6	0	3	3	2
Keith Primeau	6	0	3	3	6
Robert Kron	5	2	0	2	0
Sami Kapanen	5	1	1	2	0
Gary Roberts	6	1	1	2	8
Andrei Kovalenko	4	0	2	2	2
Ron Francis	3	0	1	1	0
Paul Coffey	5	0	1	1	2
Jeff O'Neill	6	0	1	1	0
Craig MacDonald	1	0	0	0	0
Dave Karpa	2	0	0	0	2
Nolan Pratt	3	0	0	0	2
Steven Halko	4	0	0	0	2
Marek Malik	4	0	0	0	4
Kevin Dineen	6	0	0	0	8
Arturs Irbe (goalie)	6	0	0	0	0
Curtis Leschyshyn	6	0	0	0	6
Kent Manderville	6	0	0	0	2
Paul Ranheim	6	0	0	0	2
Glen Wesley	6	0	0	0	2

GOALTENDING

	Gms.	Min.	W	L	T	G	SO	Avg.
Arturs Irbe	6	408	2	4	0	15	0	2.21

COLORADO AVALANCHE

(Lost Western Conference finals to Dallas, 4-3)

SCORING

	Games	G	A	Pts.	PIM
Peter Forsberg	19	8	16	24	31
Joe Sakic	19	6	13	19	8
Theoren Fleury	18	5	12	17	20
Claude Lemieux	19	3	11	14	26
Adam Deadmarsh	19	8	4	12	20
Milan Hejduk	16	6	6	12	4
Sandis Ozolinsh	19	4	8	12	22
Valeri Kamensky	10	4	5	9	4
Chris Drury	19	6	2	8	4
Aaron Miller	19	1	5	6	10
Adam Foote	19	2	3	5	24
Dale Hunter	19	1	3	4	38
Shjon Podein	19	1	1	2	12
Greg De Vries	19	0	2	2	22
Patrick Roy (goalie)	19	0	2	2	4
Jeff Odgers	15	1	0	1	14
Stephane Yelle	10	0	1	1	6
Warren Rychel	12	0	1	1	14
Jon Klemm	19	0	1	1	10
Sylvain Lefebvre	19	0	1	1	12
Craig Billington (goalie)	1	0	0	0	0
Eric Messier	3	0	0	0	0
Shean Donovan	5	0	0	0	2
Alexei Gusarov	5	0	0	0	2

GOALTENDING

	Gms.	Min.	W	L	T	G	SO	Avg.
Patrick Roy	19	1173	11	8	0	52	1	2.66
Craig Billington	1	9	0	0	0	1	0	6.67

DALLAS STARS

(Winner of 1999 Stanley Cup)

SCORING

	Games	G	A	Pts.	PIM
Mike Modano	23	5	18	23	16
Joe Nieuwendyk	23	11	10	21	19
Jamie Langenbrunner	23	10	7	17	16
Brett Hull	22	8	7	15	4
Jere Lehtinen	23	10	3	13	2
Sergei Zubov	23	1	12	13	4
Darryl Sydor	23	3	9	12	16
Dave Reid	23	2	8	10	14
Mike Keane	23	5	2	7	6
Pat Verbeek	18	3	4	7	14
Derian Hatcher	18	1	6	7	24
Guy Carbonneau	17	2	4	6	6
Richard Matvichuk	22	1	5	6	20
Craig Ludwig	23	1	4	5	20
Grant Marshall	14	0	3	3	20
Tony Hrkac	5	0	2	2	4
Benoit Hogue	14	0	2	2	16
Shawn Chambers	17	0	2	2	18
Brian Skrudland	19	0	2	2	16
Blake Sloan	19	0	2	2	8
Derek Plante	6	1	0	1	4
Brad Lukowich	8	0	1	1	4
Doug Lidster	4	0	0	0	2
Jonathan Sim	4	0	0	0	0
Ed Belfour (goalie)	23	0	0	0	4

GOALTENDING

	Gms.	Min.	W	L	T	G	SO	Avg.
Ed Belfour	23	1544	16	7	0	43	3	1.67

DETROIT RED WINGS

(Lost Western Conference semifinals to Colorado, 4-2)

SCORING

	Games	G	A	Pts.	PIM
Steve Yzerman	10	9	4	13	0
Nicklas Lidstrom	10	2	9	11	4
Brendan Shanahan	10	3	7	10	6
Sergei Fedorov	10	1	8	9	8
Vyacheslav Kozlov	10	6	1	7	4
Tomas Holmstrom	10	4	3	7	4
Wendel Clark	10	2	3	5	10
Doug Brown	10	2	2	4	4
Chris Chelios	10	0	4	4	14
Ulf Samuelsson	9	0	3	3	10
Darren McCarty	10	1	1	2	23
Igor Larionov	7	0	2	2	0
Martin Lapointe	10	0	2	2	20
Larry Murphy	10	0	2	2	8
Kirk Maltby	10	1	0	1	8
Todd Gill	2	0	1	1	0
Aaron Ward	8	0	1	1	8
Mathieu Dandenault	10	0	1	1	0
Kris Draper	10	0	1	1	6
Jamie Macoun	1	0	0	0	0
Norm Maracle (goalie)	2	0	0	0	0
Brent Gilchrist	3	0	0	0	0
Bill Ranford (goalie)	4	0	0	0	0
Chris Osgood (goalie)	6	0	0	0	0

GOALTENDING

	Gms.	Min.	W	L	T	G	SO	Avg.
Chris Osgood	6	358	4	2	0	14	1	2.35
Norm Maracle	2	58	0	0	0	3	0	3.10
Bill Ranford	4	183	2	2	0	10	1	3.28

EDMONTON OILERS

(Lost Western Conference quarterfinals to Dallas, 4-0)

SCORING

	Games	G	A	Pts.	PIM
Ryan Smyth	3	3	0	3	0
Ethan Moreau	4	0	3	3	6
Mike Grier	4	1	1	2	6
Todd Marchant	4	1	1	2	12
Rem Murray	4	1	1	2	2
Doug Weight	4	1	1	2	15
Bill Guerin	3	0	2	2	2
Alexander Selivanov	2	0	1	1	2
Pat Falloon	4	0	1	1	4
Christian Laflamme	4	0	1	1	2
Tom Poti	4	0	1	1	2
Jason Smith	4	0	1	1	4
Sean Brown	1	0	0	0	10
Boyd Devereaux	1	0	0	0	0
Frank Musil	1	0	0	0	2
Vladimir Vorobiev	1	0	0	0	0
Josef Beranek	2	0	0	0	4
Roman Hamrlik	3	0	0	0	2
Marty McSorley	3	0	0	0	2
Kelly Buchberger	4	0	0	0	0
Chad Kilger	4	0	0	0	4
Georges Laraque	4	0	0	0	2
Janne Niinimaa	4	0	0	0	2
Tommy Salo (goalie)	4	0	0	0	0

GOALTENDING

	Gms.	Min.	W	L	T	G	SO	Avg.
Tommy Salo	4	296	0	4	0	11	0	2.23

NEW JERSEY DEVILS

(Lost Eastern Conference quarterfinals to Pittsburgh, 4-3)

SCORING

	Games	G	A	Pts.	PIM
Bobby Holik	7	0	7	7	6
Petr Sykora	7	3	3	6	4
Randy McKay	7	3	2	5	2
Patrik Elias	7	0	5	5	6
Sergei Brylin	5	3	1	4	4
Jason Arnott	7	2	2	4	4
Scott Niedermayer	7	1	3	4	18
Scott Stevens	7	2	1	3	10
Lyle Odelein	7	0	3	3	10
Dave Andreychuk	4	2	0	2	4
Martin Brodeur (goalie)	7	0	2	2	2
Brendan Morrison	7	0	2	2	0
Jay Pandolfo	7	1	0	1	0
Brian Rolston	7	1	0	1	2
Sheldon Souray	2	0	1	1	0
Denis Pederson	3	0	1	1	0
Krzysztof Oliwa	1	0	0	0	2
Sergei Nemchinov	4	0	0	0	0
Vadim Sharifijanov	4	0	0	0	0
Brad Bombardir	5	0	0	0	0
Bob Carpenter	7	0	0	0	2
Ken Daneyko	7	0	0	0	8
Kevin Dean	7	0	0	0	0

GOALTENDING

	Gms.	Min.	W	L	T	G	SO	Avg.
Martin Brodeur	7	425	3	4	0	20	0	2.82

OTTAWA SENATORS

(Lost Eastern Conference quarterfinals to Buffalo, 4-0)

SCORING

	Games	G	A	Pts.	PIM
Nelson Emerson	4	1	3	4	0
Daniel Alfredsson	4	1	2	3	4
Wade Redden	4	1	2	3	2
Shawn McEachern	4	2	0	2	6
Jason York	4	1	1	2	4
Marian Hossa	4	0	2	2	4
Magnus Arvedson	3	0	1	1	2
Andreas Dackell	4	0	1	1	0
Ted Donato	1	0	0	0	0
Bill Berg	2	0	0	0	0
Andreas Johansson	2	0	0	0	0
Lance Pitlick	2	0	0	0	0
Damian Rhodes (goalie)	2	0	0	0	0
Ron Tugnutt (goalie)	2	0	0	0	0
Bruce Gardiner	3	0	0	0	4
Chris Phillips	3	0	0	0	0
Radek Bonk	4	0	0	0	6
Igor Kravchuk	4	0	0	0	0
Janne Laukkanen	4	0	0	0	4
Vaclav Prospal	4	0	0	0	0
Sami Salo	4	0	0	0	0
Shaun Van Allen	4	0	0	0	0
Alexei Yashin	4	0	0	0	10

GOALTENDING

	Gms.	Min.	W	L	T	G	SO	Avg.
Damian Rhodes	2	150	0	2	0	6	0	2.40
Ron Tugnutt	2	118	0	2	0	6	0	3.05

PHILADELPHIA FLYERS

(Lost Eastern Conference quarterfinals to Toronto, 4-2)

SCORING

	Games	G	A	Pts.	PIM
Eric Desjardins	6	2	2	4	4
Rod Brind'Amour	6	1	3	4	0
John LeClair	6	3	0	3	12
Keith Jones	6	2	1	3	14
Marc Bureau	6	0	2	2	2
Steve Duchesne	6	0	2	2	2
Daymond Langkow	6	0	2	2	2
Valeri Zelepukin	4	1	0	1	4
Karl Dykhuis	5	1	0	1	4
Craig Berube	6	1	0	1	4
Mark Greig	2	0	1	1	0
Mikael Andersson	6	0	1	1	2
Sandy McCarthy	6	0	1	1	0
Daniel McGillis	6	0	1	1	12
Mark Recchi	6	0	1	1	2
Mikael Renberg	6	0	1	1	0
Dmitri Tertyshny	1	0	0	0	2
Adam Burt	6	0	0	0	4
Jody Hull	6	0	0	0	4
Chris Therien	6	0	0	0	6
John Vanbiesbrouck (goalie)	6	0	0	0	2

GOALTENDING

	Gms.	Min.	W	L	T	G	SO	Avg.
J. Vanbiesbrouck	6	369	2	4	0	9	1	1.46

PHOENIX COYOTES

(Lost Western Conference quarterfinals to St. Louis, 4-3)

SCORING

	Games	G	A	Pts.	PIM
Dallas Drake	7	4	3	7	4
Shane Doan	7	2	2	4	6
Robert Reichel	7	1	3	4	2
Keith Tkachuk	7	1	3	4	13
Teppo Numminen	7	2	1	3	4
Keith Carney	7	1	2	3	10
Rick Tocchet	7	0	3	3	8
Louie DeBrusk	6	2	0	2	6
Stephen Leach	7	1	1	2	2
Juha Ylonen	2	0	2	2	2
Brian Noonan	5	0	2	2	4
Oleg Tverdovsky	6	0	2	2	6
Greg Adams	3	1	0	1	0
Mike Stapleton	7	1	0	1	0
Jim Cummins	3	0	1	1	0
Stan Neckar	6	0	1	1	4
Bob Corkum	7	0	1	1	4
Jyrki Lumme	7	0	1	1	6
Jeremy Roenick	1	0	0	0	0
Brad Tiley	1	0	0	0	0
Tavis Hansen	2	0	0	0	0
Gerald Diduck	3	0	0	0	2
Mike Sullivan	5	0	0	0	2
J.J. Daigneault	6	0	0	0	8
Nikolai Khabibulin (goalie)	7	0	0	0	2

GOALTENDING

	Gms.	Min.	W	L	T	G	SO	Avg.
Nikolai Khabibulin	7	449	3	4	0	18	0	2.41

PITTSBURGH PENGUINS

(Lost Eastern Conference semifinals to Toronto, 4-2)

SCORING

	Games	G	A	Pts.	PIM
Martin Straka	13	6	9	15	6
Jaromir Jagr	9	5	7	12	16
Alexei Kovalev	10	5	7	12	14
Kip Miller	13	2	7	9	19
German Titov	11	3	5	8	4
Rob Brown	13	2	5	7	8
Jan Hrdina	13	4	1	5	12
Kevin Hatcher	13	2	3	5	4
Jiri Slegr	13	1	3	4	12
Alexei Morozov	10	1	1	2	0
Brad Werenka	13	1	1	2	6
Robert Lang	12	0	2	2	0
Ian Moran	13	0	2	2	8
Greg Andrusak	12	1	0	1	6
Bobby Dollas	13	1	0	1	6
Dan Kesa	13	1	0	1	0
Maxim Galanov	1	0	0	0	0
Victor Ignatjev	1	0	0	0	2
Todd Hlushko	2	0	0	0	0
Brian Bonin	3	0	0	0	0
Martin Sonnenberg	7	0	0	0	0
Matthew Barnaby	13	0	0	0	35
Tom Barrasso (goalie)	13	0	0	0	4
Tyler Wright	13	0	0	0	19

GOALTENDING

	Gms.	Min.	W	L	T	G	SO	Avg.
Tom Barrasso	13	787	6	7	0	35	1	2.67

ST. LOUIS BLUES

(Lost Western Conference semifinals to Dallas, 4-2)

SCORING

	Games	G	A	Pts.	PIM
Pierre Turgeon	13	4	9	13	6
Al MacInnis	13	4	8	12	20
Scott Young	13	4	7	11	10
Pavol Demitra	13	5	4	9	4

	Games	G	A	Pts.	PIM
Geoff Courtnall	13	2	4	6	10
Chris Pronger	13	1	4	5	28
Blair Atcheynum	13	1	3	4	6
Craig Conroy	13	2	1	3	6
Jeff Finley	13	1	2	3	8
Terry Yake	13	1	2	3	14
Ricard Persson	13	0	3	3	17
Jochen Hecht	5	2	0	2	0
Jamie Rivers	9	1	1	2	2
Mike Eastwood	13	1	1	2	6
Michal Handzus	11	0	2	2	8
Pascal Rheaume	5	1	0	1	4
Scott Pellerin	8	1	0	1	4
Jamal Mayers	11	0	1	1	8
Grant Fuhr (goalie)	13	0	1	1	2
Jamie McLennan (goalie)	1	0	0	0	6
Tyson Nash	1	0	0	0	2
Tony Twist	1	0	0	0	0
Brad Shaw	4	0	0	0	0
Lubos Bartecko	5	0	0	0	2
Michel Picard	5	0	0	0	2
Chris McAlpine	13	0	0	0	2

GOALTENDING

	Gms.	Min.	W	L	T	G	SO	Avg.
Jamie McLennan	1	37	0	1	0	0	0	0.00
Grant Fuhr	13	790	6	6	0	31	1	2.35

SAN JOSE SHARKS

(Lost Western Conference quarterfinals to Colorado, 4-2)

SCORING

	Games	G	A	Pts.	PIM
Jeff Norton	6	0	7	7	10
Vincent Damphousse	6	3	2	5	6
Mike Ricci	6	2	3	5	10
Jeff Friesen	6	2	2	4	14
Marco Sturm	6	2	2	4	4
Alexander Korolyuk	6	1	3	4	2
Bill Houlder	6	3	0	3	4
Patrick Marleau	6	2	1	3	4
Joe Murphy	6	0	3	3	4
Tony Granato	6	1	1	2	2
Owen Nolan	6	1	1	2	6
Mike Vernon (goalie)	5	0	1	1	0
Marcus Ragnarsson	6	0	1	1	6
Dave Lowry	1	0	0	0	0
Steve Shields (goalie)	1	0	0	0	0
Stephane Matteau	5	0	0	0	6
Bryan Marchment	6	0	0	0	4
Mike Rathje	6	0	0	0	4
Bob Rouse	6	0	0	0	6
Ronnie Stern	6	0	0	0	6
Ron Sutter	6	0	0	0	4

GOALTENDING

	Gms.	Min.	W	L	T	G	SO	Avg.
Mike Vernon	5	321	2	3	0	13	0	2.43
Steve Shields	1	60	0	1	0	6	0	6.00

TORONTO MAPLE LEAFS

(Lost Eastern Conference finals to Buffalo, 4-1)

SCORING

	Games	G	A	Pts.	PIM
Mats Sundin	17	8	8	16	16
Sergei Berezin	17	6	6	12	4
Steve Thomas	17	6	3	9	12
Lonny Bohonos	9	3	6	9	2
Yanic Perreault	17	3	6	9	6
Bryan Berard	17	1	8	9	8
Garry Valk	17	3	4	7	22
Steve Sullivan	13	3	3	6	14
Dimitri Yushkevich	17	1	5	6	22
Daniil Markov	17	0	6	6	18
Mike Johnson	17	3	2	5	4
Alexander Karpovtsev	14	1	3	4	12
Derek King	16	1	3	4	4
Sylvain Cote	17	2	1	3	10
Tomas Kaberle	14	0	3	3	2
Kris King	17	1	1	2	25
Kevyn Adams	7	0	2	2	14
Tie Domi	14	0	2	2	24
Adam Mair	5	1	0	1	14
Chris McAllister	6	0	1	1	4
Dallas Eakins	1	0	0	0	0
Glenn Healy (goalie)	1	0	0	0	0
Igor Korolev	1	0	0	0	0
Ladislav Kohn	2	0	0	0	5
Fredrik Modin	8	0	0	0	6
Todd Warriner	9	0	0	0	2
Curtis Joseph (goalie)	17	0	0	0	2

GOALTENDING

	Gms.	Min.	W	L	T	G	SO	Avg.
Glenn Healy	1	20	0	0	0	0	0	0.00
Curtis Joseph	17	1011	9	8	0	41	1	2.43

HAT TRICKS

(Players scoring three or more goals in a game)

Date	Player, Team	Opp.	Goals
	None occurred in playoffs.		

OVERTIME GOALS

Date	Player, Team	Opponent	Time	Final score
4-23-99	Miroslav Satan, Buffalo	Ottawa	*10:35	Buffalo 3, Ottawa 2
4-24-99	Ray Sheppard, Carolina	Boston	17:05	Carolina 3, Boston 2
4-24-99	Shane Doan, Phoenix	St. Louis	8:58	Phoenix 4, St. Louis 3
4-26-99	Milan Hejduk, Colorado	San Jose	7:53	Colorado 2, San Jose 1
4-27-99	Joe Nieuwendyk, Dallas	Edmonton	†17:34	Dallas 3, Edmonton 2
4-30-99	Anson Carter, Boston	Carolina	*14:45	Boston 4, Carolina 3
4-30-99	Yanic Perreault, Toronto	Philadelphia	11:51	Toronto 2, Philadelphia 1
4-30-99	Scott Young, St. Louis	Phoenix	5:43	St. Louis 2, Phoenix 1
5-2-99	Jaromir Jagr, Pittsburgh	New Jersey	8:59	Pittsburgh 3, New Jersey 2
5-3-99	Milan Hejduk, Colorado	San Jose	13:12	Colorado 3, San Jose 2
5-4-99	Pierre Turgeon, St. Louis	Phoenix	17:59	St. Louis 1, Phoenix 0
5-7-99	Kirk Maltby, Detroit	Colorado	4:18	Detroit 3, Colorado 2

Date	Player, Team	Opponent	Time	Final score
5-8-99—	Joe Nieuwendyk, Dallas	St. Louis	8:22	Dallas 5, St. Louis 4
5-10-99—	Pavol Demitra, St. Louis	Dallas	2:43	St. Louis 3, Dallas 2
5-12-99—	Pierre Turgeon, St. Louis	Dallas	5:52	St. Louis 3, Dallas 2
5-13-99—	Sergei Berezin, Toronto	Pittsburgh	2:18	Toronto 3, Pittsburgh 2
5-17-99—	Garry Valk, Toronto	Pittsburgh	1:57	Toronto 4, Pittsburgh 3
5-17-99—	Mike Modano, Dallas	St. Louis	2:21	Dallas 2, St. Louis 1
5-28-99—	Chris Drury, Colorado	Dallas	19:29	Colorado 3, Dallas 2
6-8-99—	Jason Woolley, Buffalo	Dallas	15:30	Buffalo 3, Dallas 2
6-19-99—	Brett Hull, Dallas	Buffalo	†14:51	Dallas 2, Buffalo 1

*Goal scored in second overtime.
†Goal scored in third overtime.

PENALTY-SHOT INFORMATION

Date	Shooter	Goaltender	Scored	Final score
4-22-99—	Mats Sundin, Toronto	John Vanbiesbrouck, Philadelphia	No	Philadelphia 3, Toronto 0
5-29-99—	Mats Sundin, Toronto	Dominik Hasek, Buffalo	Yes	Buffalo 5, Toronto 2

ALL-STAR GAME

AT ICE PALACE, TAMPA, JANUARY 24, 1999

ROSTERS

WORLD

Coach: Lindy Ruff, Buffalo Sabres
Assistant coach: Robbie Ftorek, New Jersey Devils

Forwards (Pos.)	**Club**	**Country**
Peter Bondra (RW)	Washington Capitals	Slovakia
Pavol Demitra (LW)	St. Louis Blues	Slovakia
Peter Forsberg (C)*	Colorado Avalanche	Sweden
Bobby Holik (C)	New Jersey Devils	Czech Rep.
Jaromir Jagr (RW)*	Pittsburgh Penguins	Czech Rep.
Dmitri Khristich(RW)	Boston Bruins	Ukraine
Viktor Kozlov (C)	Florida Panthers	Russia
Sergei Krivokrasov (RW)	Nashville Predators	Russia
Markus Naslund (LW)	Vancouver Canucks	Sweden
Teemu Selanne (RW)*	Mighty Ducks of Anaheim	Finland
Martin Straka (C)	Pittsburgh Penguins	Czech Rep.
Marco Sturm (C)	San Jose Sharks	W. Germany
Mats Sundin (C)	Toronto Maple Leafs	Sweden
Alexei Yashin (C)	Ottawa Senators	Russia
Defensemen		
Roman Hamrlik	Edmonton Oilers	Czech Rep.
Nicklas Lidstrom*	Detroit Red Wings	Sweden
Mattias Norstrom	Los Angeles Kings	Sweden
Teppo Numminen*	Phoenix Coyotes	Finland
Mattias Ohlund	Vancouver Canucks	Sweden
Alexei Zhitnik	Buffalo Sabres	Russia
Sergei Zubov	Dallas Stars	Russia
Goaltenders		
Dominik Hasek*	Buffalo Sabres	Czech Rep.
Arturs Irbe	Carolina Hurricanes	Latvia
Nikolai Khabibulin	Phoenix Coyotes	Russia

*In starting lineup.
†Special selection by commissioner.

NORTH AMERICA

Coach: Ken Hitchcock, Dallas Stars
Assistant coach: Jim Schoenfeld, Phoenix Coyotes

Forwards (Pos.)	**Club**	**Country**
Tony Amonte(RW)	Chicago Blackhawks	U.S.A.
Wendel Clark (LW)	Tampa Bay Lightning	Canada
Theoren Fleury (RW)	Calgary Flames	Canada
Wayne Gretzky (C)	New York Rangers	Canada
Paul Kariya (LW)*	Anaheim Mighty Ducks	Canada
John LeClair (LW)	Philadelphia Flyers	U.S.A.
Eric Lindros (C)*	Philadelphia Flyers	Canada
Mike Modano (C)	Dallas Stars	U.S.A.
Keith Primeau (C)	Carolina Hurricanes	Canada
Mark Recchi (RW)	Montreal Canadiens	Canada
Luc Robitaille (C)	Los Angeles Kings	Canada
Jeremy Roenick (C)	Phoenix Coyotes	U.S.A.
Brendan Shanahan (LW)*	Detroit Red Wings	Canada
Keith Tkachuk (LW)	Phoenix Coyotes	U.S.A.
Defensemen		
Ray Bourque*	Boston Bruins	Canada
Al MacInnis*	St. Louis Blues	Canada
Rob Blake	Los Angeles Kings	Canada
Larry Murphy	Detroit Red Wings	Canada
Chris Pronger	St. Louis Blues	Canada
Scott Stevens	New Jersey Devils	Canada
Darryl Sydor	Dallas Stars	Canada
Goaltenders		
Martin Brodeur*	New Jersey Devils	Canada
Ed Belfour	Dallas Stars	Canada
Ron Tugnutt	Ottawa Senators	Canada

*In starting lineup.
†Special selection by commissioner.

GAME SUMMARY

North America 8, World 6

World	1	3	2	—	6
North America	4	3	1	—	8

FIRST PERIOD—1. North America, Modano 1 (Robitaille, Pronger), 4:09. 2. World, Sturm 1 (Forsberg, Sundin), 9:42. 3. North America, Robitaille 1 (Roenick, Clark), 10:06. 4. North America, Kariya 1 (Modano, Amonte), 16:45. 5. North America, Recchi 1 (Gretzky, Fleury), 17:18.

SECOND PERIOD—6. North America, Bourque 1 (Modano), 0:17. 7. North America, Gretzky 1 (Fleury, Pronger), 1:14. 8. World, Selanne 1 (Yashin, Irbe), 2:02. 9. World, Demitra 1 (Zhitnik, Sundin), 8:59. 10. North America, Blake 1 (Gretzky, Recchi), 14:23. 11. World, Ohlund 1 (Naslund, Sundin), 15:09.

THIRD PERIOD—12. World, Sundin 1 (Ohlund, Jagr), 2:57. 13. North America, Sydor 1 (Modano, Amonte), 4:02. 14. World, Zubov 1 (Khristich, Holik), 4:20. Penalty—North America, MacInnis (tripping), 7:22.

Shots on goal—World 9-15-12-36; North America 19-15-15-49. Power-play opportunities—World 0 of 1; North America 0 of 0. Goalies—World, Hasek (19 shots, 15 saves), Irbe L (0:00 second, 15-12), Khabibulin (0:00 third, 15-14); North America, Brodeur (9-8), Tugnutt W (0:00 second, 15-12), Belfour (0:00 third, 12-10). A—19,758. Referee—Paul Devorski. Linesmen—Pierre Champoux, Brian Murphy.

AWARDS

THE SPORTING NEWS

ALL-STAR TEAM

Dominik Hasek, Buffalo .... Goaltender
Al MacInnis, St. Louis .... Defense
Nicklas Lidstrom, Detroit .... Defense
Paul Kariya, Anaheim .... Left wing
Alexei Yashin, Ottawa .... Center
Jaromir Jagr, Pittsburgh .... Right wing

Note: THE SPORTING NEWS All-Star Team is selected by the NHL players.

AWARD WINNERS

Player of the Year: Jaromir Jagr, Pittsburgh
Coach of the Year: Jacques Martin, Ottawa
Rookie of the Year: Chris Drury, Colorado
Executive of the Year: Craig Patrick, Pittsburgh

Note: THE SPORTING NEWS player and rookie awards are selected by the NHL players, the coaches award by the NHL coaches and the executive award by NHL executives.

NATIONAL HOCKEY LEAGUE

ALL-STAR TEAMS

First team	Position	Second team
Dominik Hasek, Buffalo	Goaltender	Byron Dafoe, Boston
Nicklas Lidstrom, Detroit	Defense	Ray Bourque, Boston
Al MacInnis, St. Louis	Defense	Eric Desjardins, Philadelphia
Paul Kariya, Anaheim	Left wing	John LeClair, Philadelphia
Peter Forsberg, Colorado	Center	Alexei Yashin, Ottawa
Jaromir Jagr, Pittsburgh	Right wing	Teemu Selanne, Anaheim

AWARD WINNERS

Art Ross Trophy: Jaromir Jagr, Pittsburgh
Maurice Richard Trophy: Teemu Selanne, Anaheim
Hart Memorial Trophy: Jaromir Jagr, Pittsburgh
James Norris Memorial Trophy: Al MacInnis, St. Louis
Vezina Trophy: Dominik Hasek, Buffalo
Bill Jennings Trophy: Ed Belfour, Dallas
Roman Turek, Dallas
Calder Memorial Trophy: Chris Drury, Colorado
Lady Byng Memorial Trophy: Wayne Gretzky, N.Y. Rangers
Conn Smythe Trophy: Joe Nieuwendyk, Dallas
Bill Masterton Memorial Trophy: John Cullen, Tampa Bay
Frank J. Selke Trophy: Jere Lehtinen, Dallas
Jack Adams Award: Jacques Martin, Ottawa
King Clancy Trophy: Rob Ray, Buffalo

PLAYER DRAFT

ENTRY DRAFT—JUNE 26, 1999

FIRST ROUND

No.—Selecting club	Player	Pos.	Previous team (league)
1—Atlanta (from Tampa Bay)	Patrik Stefan	C	Long Beach (IHL)
2—Vancouver (from Atlanta)	Daniel Sedin	LW	Modo Ornskoldsvik, Sweden
3—Vancouver	Henrik Sedin	C	Modo Ornskoldsvik, Sweden
4—N.Y. Rangers (from Chicago)	Pavel Brendl	RW	Calgary (WHL)
5—N.Y. Islanders (from Los Angeles)	Tim Connolly	C	Erie (OHL)
6—Nashville	Brian Finley	G	Barrie (OHL)
7—Washington	Kris Breech	C	Calgary (WHL)
8—N.Y. Islanders (from Los Angeles)	Taylor Pyatt	LW	Sudbury (OHL)
9—N.Y. Rangers (from Calgary)	Jamie Lundmark	C	Moose Jaw (WHL)
10—N.Y. Islanders (from Montreal)	Branislav Mezei	D	Belleville (OHL)
11—Calgary (from N.Y. Rangers)	Oleg Saprykin	C/LW	Seattle (WHL)
12—Florida	Denis Shvidki	RW	Barrie (OHL)
13—Edmonton	Jani Rita	RW	Jokerit Helsinki, Finland
14—San Jose	Jeff Jillson	D	Michigan (CCHA)
15—Phoenix (from Anaheim)	Scott Kelman	C	Seattle (WHL)
16—Carolina	David Tanabe	D	Wisconsin (WCHA)
17—St. Louis	Barret Jackman	D	Regina (WHL)
18—Pittsburgh	Konstantin Koltsov	LW	Cherepovec, Russia
19—Phoenix	Kirill Safronov	D	SKA St. Petersburg, Russia
20—Buffalo	Barrett Heisten	LW	Maine (H. East)
21—Boston	Nicholas Boynton	D	Ottawa (OHL)
22—Philadelphia	Maxime Ouellet	G	Quebec (QMJHL)
23—Chicago (from Detroit)	Steve McCarthy	D	Kootenay (WHL)
24—Toronto	Luca Cereda	C	Ambri, Switzerland
25—Colorado	Mihail Kuleshov	LW	Cherepovec, Russia
26—Ottawa	Martin Havlat	C/LW	Trinec, Czech Republic
27—New Jersey	Ari Ahonen	G	Jyvaskyla, Finland
28—N.Y. Islanders (from Dallas)	Kristian Kudroc	D	Michalovce, Slovakia

SECOND ROUND

No.—Selecting club	Player	Pos.	Previous team (league)
29—Washington (from Tampa Bay)	Michal Sivec	C	Kladno, Czech Republic
30—Atlanta	Luke Sellars	D	Ottawa (OHL)
31—Washington (from Van. through Col.)	Charlie Stephens	C/RW	Guelph (OHL)
32—Dallas (from N.Y. Islanders)	Michael Ryan	C	Boston College H.S.
33—Nashville	Jonas Andersson	RW	AIK, Sweden
34—Washington	Ross Lupaschuk	D	Prince Albert (WHL)
35—Buffalo (from Los Angeles)	Milan Bartovic	RW	Trencin, Slovakia
36—Edmonton (from Chicago)	Alexei Semenov	D	Sudbury (OHL)
37—Washington	Nolan Yonkman	D	Kelowna (WHL)
38—Calgary	Dan Cavanaugh	C/RW	Boston U. (H. East)
39—Montreal	Alexander Buturlin	LW	CSKA Moskow, Russia
40—Florida (from St.L. through Nash.)	Alexander Auld	G	North Bay (OHL)
41—Edmonton	Tony Salmelainen	LW	IFK Helsinki, Finland
42—New Jersey	Mike Commodore	D	North Dakota (WCHA)
43—Los Angeles	Andrei Shefer	LW	Cherepovec, Russia
44—Anaheim (from Ott. through N.Y.R.)	Jordan Leopold	D	Minnesota (WCHA)
45—Colorado (from Florida)	Martin Grenier	D	Quebec (QMJHL)
46—Chicago (from Edmonton)	Dimitri Levinski	RW	Cherepovec, Russia
47—Tampa Bay (from Det. through S.J.)	Sheldon Keefe	RW	Barrie (OHL)
48—Ottawa (from Anaheim)	Simon Lajeunesse	G	Moncton (QMJHL)
49—Carolina	Brett Lysak	C	Regina (WHL)
50—New Jersey (from St. Louis)	Brett Clouthier	LW	Kingston (OHL)
51—Pittsburgh	Matt Murley	LW	Rensselaer (ECAC)
52—Nashville	Adam Hall	RW	Michigan State (CCHA)
53—Phoenix	Brad Ralph	LW	Oshawa (OHL)
54—Nashville (from Colorado)	Andrew Hutchinson	D	Michigan State (CCHA)
55—Buffalo	Doug Janik	D	Maine (H. East)
56—Boston	Matt Zultek	LW	Ottawa (OHL)
57—Pittsburgh	Jeremy Van Hoof	D	Ottawa (OHL)
58—Montreal (from Philadelphia)	Matt Carkner	D	Peterborough (OHL)
59—N.Y. Rangers (from Detroit)	David Inman	C	Notre Dame (CCHA)
60—Toronto	Peter Reynolds	D	London (OHL)

No.—Selecting club	Player	Pos.	Previous team (league)
61—Nashville (from Colorado)	Ed Hill	D	Barrie (OHL)
62—Ottawa	Teemu Sainomaa	LW	Jokerit Helsinki, Finland
63—Chicago (from New Jersey)	Stepan Mokhov	D	Cherepovec, Russia
64—Buffalo (from Dallas)	Michael Zigomanis	C	Kingston (OHL)
65—Nashville	Jan Lasak	G	Zvolen, Slovakia
66—Dallas (from St. Louis)	Dan Jancevski	D	London (OHL)

THIRD ROUND

No.—Selecting club	Player	Pos.	Previous team (league)
67—Tampa Bay	Evegeny Konstantinov	G	Ak-Bars Kazan, Russia
68—Atlanta	Zdenek Blatny	C/LW	Seattle (WHL)
69—Vancouver	Rene Vydareny	D	Bratislava, Slovakia
70—Florida	Niklas Hagman	LW	IFK Helsinki, Finland
71—Phoenix (from N.Y. Islanders)	Jason Jaspers	C/LW	Sudbury (OHL)
72—Nashville	Brett Angel	D	North Bay (OHL)
73—Buffalo (from Washington)	Tim Preston	LW	Seattle (WHL)
74—Los Angeles	Jason Crain	D	Ohio State (CCHA)
75—Tampa Bay (from Vancouver)	Brett Scheffelmaier	D	Medicine Hat (WHL)
76—Los Angeles (from Chicago)	Frantisek Kaberle	D	Modo Ornskoldsvik, Sweden
77—Calgary	Craig Andersson	G	Guelph (OHL)
78—N.Y. Islanders (from Montreal)	Mattias Weinhandl	RW	Modo Ornskoldsvik, Sweden
79—N.Y. Rangers	Johan Asplund	G	Brynas Gavle, Sweden
80—Florida	Jean-Francois Laniel	G	Shawinigan (QMJHL)
81—Edmonton	Adam Hauser	G	Minnesota (WCHA)
82—San Jose	Mark Concannon	LW	Winchendon H.S.
83—Anaheim	Niklas Havelid	D	Malmo, Sweden
84—Carolina	Brad Fast	D	Prince George (WHL)
85—St. Louis	Peter Smrek	D	Des Moines (USHL)
86—Pittsburgh	Sebastien Caron	G	Rimouski (QMJHL)
87—N.Y. Islanders (from Phoenix)	Brian Collins	C	St. John's H.S.
88—Tampa Bay (from Van. through Buf.)	Jimmie Olvestad	LW	Djurgarden, Sweden
89—Boston	Kyle Wanvig	RW	Kootenay (WHL)
90—N.Y. Rangers (from Cal. through Phi.)	Patrick Aufiero	D	Boston U. (H. East)
91—Edmonton (from Nash. through Det.)	Mike Comrie	C	Michigan (CCHA)
92—Los Angeles (from Toronto)	Cory Campbell	G	Belleville (OHL)
93—Colorado (from Nash. through Col.)	Branko Radivojevic	RW	Belleville (OHL)
94—Ottawa	Chris Kelly	C/LW	London (OHL)
95—New Jersey	Andre Lakos	D	Barrie (OHL)
96—Dallas	Mathias Tjarnqvist	C	Rogle, Sweden

FOURTH ROUND

No.—Selecting club	Player	Pos.	Previous team (league)
97—Montreal (from Chi. through T.B.)	Chris Dyment	D	Boston U. (H. East)
98—Atlanta	David Kaczowka	LW	Seattle (WHL)
99—Atlanta (from Vancouver)	Rob Zepp	G	Plymouth (OHL)
100—New Jersey	Teemu Kesa	D	Ilves Tampere, Finland
101—N.Y. Islanders	Juraj Kolnik	RW	Rimouski (QMJHL)
102—N.Y. Islanders (from Nashville)	Johan Halvardsson	D	HV-71 Jonkoping, Sweden
103—Florida (from Washington)	Morgan McCormick	RW	Kingston (OHL)
104—Los Angeles	Brian McGrattan	RW	Sudbury (OHL)
105—Anaheim (from Chicago)	Alexandr Chagodayev	C	CSKA Moskow, Russia
106—Calgary	Roman Rozakov	D	Togliatti, Russia
107—Montreal	Evan Lindsay	G	Prince Albert (WHL)
108—Toronto (from N.Y. Rangers)	Mirko Murovic	LW	Moncton (QMJHL)
109—Florida	Rod Sarich	D	Calgary (WHL)
110—Toronto (from Edmonton)	Jonathan Zion	D	Ottawa (OHL)
111—San Jose	Willie Levesque	RW	Northeastern (H. East)
112—Colorado (from Anaheim)	Sanny Lindstrom	D	Huddinge, Sweden
113—Carolina	Ryan Murphy	LW	Bowling Green St. (CCHA)
114—St. Louis	Chad Starling	D	Kamloops (WHL)
115—Pittsburgh	Ryan Malone	LW	Omaha (USHL)
116—Phoenix	Ryan Lauzon	C	Hull (QMJHL)
117—Buffalo	Karel Mosovsky	LW	Regina (WHL)
118—Boston	Jaakko Harikkala	D	Lukko, Finland
119—Philadelphia	Jeff Feniak	D	Calgary (WHL)
120—Detroit	Jari Toulsa	C	Frolunda, Sweden
121—Nashville (from Car. through Tor.)	Yevgeny Pavlov	C/RW	Togliatti, Russia
122—Colorado	Kristian Kovac	RW	Kosice, Slovakia
123—Phoenix (from N.Y.I. through Ott.)	Preston Mizzi	C	Peterborough (OHL)

No.—Selecting club	Player	Pos.	Previous team (league)
124—Nashville (from Detroit)	Alexandr Krevsun	RW	Samara, Russia
125—Los Angeles (from N.Y.I. through N.J.)	Daniel Johansson	C	Modo Ornskoldsvik, Sweden
126—Dallas	Jeff Bateman	C	Brampton (OHL)

FIFTH ROUND

No.—Selecting club	Player	Pos.	Previous team (league)
127—Tampa Bay	Kaspars Astashenko	D	Riga HC, Latvia
128—Atlanta	Derek MacKenzie	C	Sudbury (OHL)
129—Vancouver	Ryan Thorpe	LW	Spokane (WHL)
130—N.Y. Islanders	Justin Mapletoft	C	Red Deer (WHL)
131—Nashville	Konstantin Panov	RW	Kamloops (WHL)
132—Washington	Roman Tyrdon	C/LW	Trencin, Slovakia
133—Los Angeles	Jean-Francois Nogues	G	Victoriaville (QMJHL)
134—Chicago	Michael Jacobsen	D	Belleville (OHL)
135—Calgary	Matt Doman	RW	Wisconsin (WCHA)
136—Montreal	Dustin Jamieson	LW	Sarnia (OHL)
137—N.Y. Rangers	Garett Bembridge	RW	Saskatoon (WHL)
138—Buffalo (from Florida)	Ryan Miller	G	Soo (NAHL)
139—Edmonton	Jonathan Fauteux	D	Val d'Or (QMJHL)
140—N.Y. Islanders (from San Jose)	Adam Johnson	D	Greenway H.S., Minn.
141—Anaheim	Maxim Rybin	RW	Spartak Moscow, Russia
142—Colorado (from Carolina)	William Magnuson	D	Lake Superior State (CCHA)
143—St. Louis	Trevor Byrne	D	Deerfield H.S., Mass.
144—Pittsburgh	Tomas Skvaridlo	C/LW	Zvolen, Slovakia
145—Montreal (from S.J. through Pho.)	Marc-Andre Thinel	RW	Victoriaville (QMJHL)
146—Buffalo	Matthew Kinch	D	Calgary (WHL)
147—Boston	Seamus Kotyk	G	Ottawa (OHL)
148—Tampa Bay (from Philadelphia)	Michal Lanicek	G	Slavia Praha, Czech Rep.
149—Detroit (from S.J. through Det.)	Andrei Maximenko	LW	Krylja Sovetov, Russia
150—Montreal	Matt Shasby	D	Des Moines (USHL)
151—Toronto	Vaclav Zavoral	D	Litvinov, Czech Rep.
152—Colorado	Jordan Krestanovich	LW	Calgary (WHL)
153—Calgary	Jesse Cook	D	Denver (WCHA)
154—Ottawa	Andrew Ianiero	LW	Kingston (OHL)
155—San Jose (from New Jersey)	Nicholas Dimitrakos	RW	Maine (H. East)
156—Dallas	Gregor Baumgartner	C	Acadie-Bathurst (QMJHL)
157—Pittsburgh	Vladimir Malenkykh	D	Lada Togliatti, Russia

SIXTH ROUND

No.—Selecting club	Player	Pos.	Previous team (league)
158—Colorado (from Tampa Bay)	Anders Lovdahl	C	HV-71 Jonkoping, Sweden
159—Atlanta	Yuri Dobryshkin	W	Krylja Sovetov, Russia
160—Philadelphia (from Vancouver)	Konstantin Rudenko		Cherepovec, Russia
161—Toronto (from N.Y. Islanders)	Jan Sochor	RW	Slavia Praha, Czech Rep.
162—Nashville	Timo Helbling	D	Davos, Switzerland
163—N.Y. Islanders (from Washington)	Bjorn Melin	RW	HV-71 Jonkoping, Sweden
164—Ottawa (from Chi. through L.A.)	Martin Prusek	G	HC Vitkovice, Czech Rep.
165—Chicago	Michael Leighton	G	Windsor (OHL)
166—Calgary	Cory Pecker	C	Sault Ste. Marie (OHL)
167—Montreal	Sean Dixon	D	Erie (OHL)
168—Phoenix (from Mon. through N.Y.R.)	Erik Leverstrom	D	Grums, Sweden
169—Florida	Brad Woods	D	Brampton (OHL)
170—Calgary	Matt Underhill	G	Cornell (ECAC)
171—Edmonton	Chris Legg	C	London Jr. B (OHA)
172—Vancouver (from San Jose)	Josh Reed	D	Cowichan (BCJHL)
173—Anaheim	Jan Sandstrom	D	AIK, Sweden
174—Carolina	Damian Surma	LW	Plymouth (OHL)
175—Washington (from St. Louis)	Kyle Clark	RW	Harvard (ECAC)
176—Pittsburgh	Doug Meyer	LW	Minnesota (WCHA)
177—N.Y. Rangers (from Phoenix)	Jay Dardis	C	Proctor H.S., Minn.
178—Buffalo	Seneque Hyacinthe	LW	Val d'Or (QMJHL)
179—Boston	Donald Choukalos	G	Regina (WHL)
180—St. Louis (from Philadelphia)	Tore Vikingstad	W	Farjestad, Sweden
181—Detroit	Kent McDonnell	RW	Guelph (OHL)
182—Tampa Bay (from N.Y.I. through Tor.)	Fedor Fedorov	C	Port Huron (UHL)
183—Colorado	Riku Hahl	C	Hameenlinna, Finland
184—Dallas (from Florida through Ottawa)	Justin Cox	RW	Prince George (WHL)
185—New Jersey	Scott Cameron	C	Barrie (OHL)
186—Dallas	Brett Draney	LW	Kamloops (WHL)

SEVENTH ROUND

No.—Selecting club	Player	Pos.	Previous team (league)
187—Tampa Bay	Ivan Rachunek	LW	ZPS-Barum-Zlin, Czech Rep.
188—Atlanta	Stephan Baby	RW	Green Bay (USHL)
189—Vancouver	Kevin Swanson	G	Kelowna (WHL)
190—Calgary (from N.Y. Islanders)	Blair Stayzer	LW	Windsor (OHL)
191—Nashville	Martin Erat	LW	ZPS-Barum-Zlin, Czech Rep.
192—Washington	David Johansson	D	AIK, Sweden
193—Los Angeles	Kevin Baker	RW	Belleville (OHL)
194—Chicago	Mattias Wennerberg	C	Modo Ornskoldsvik, Sweden
195—Chicago (from Calgary)	Yorick Treille	RW	Mass.-Lowell (H. East)
196—Montreal	Vadim Tarasov	G	Novokuznetsk, Russia
197—N.Y. Rangers	Arto Laatikainen	D	Espoo, Finland
198—Florida	Travis Eagles	RW	Prince George (WHL)
199—Edmonton	Christian Chartier	D	Saskatoon (WHL)
200—Philadelphia (from San Jose)	Pavel Kasparik	C	Czech Republic
201—Ottawa (from Anaheim)	Mikko Ruutu	W	IFK Helsinki, Finland
202—Carolina	Jim Baxter	D	Oshawa (OHL)
203—St. Louis	Phil Osaer	G	Ferris State (CCHA)
204—Pittsburgh	Tom Kostopoulos	RW	London (OHL)
205—Nashville (from Phoenix)	Kyle Kettles	G	Neepawa, Manitoba Jr.
206—Buffalo	Bret DeCecco	RW	Seattle (WHL)
207—Boston	Greg Barber	RW	Victoria (BCJHL)
208—Philadelphia	Vaclav Pletka	LW	Trinec, Czech Republic
209—Ottawa	Layne Ulmer	C	Swift Current (WHL)
210—Detroit	Henrik Zetterberg	LW	Timra, Sweden
211—Toronto	Vladimir Kulkov		CSKA Moskow, Russia
212—Colorado	Radim Vrbata	RW	Hull (QMJHL)
213—Ottawa	Alexandre Giroux	C/LW	Hull (QMJHL)
214—New Jersey	Chris Hartsburg	C/RW	Colorado College (WCHA)
215—Dallas	Jeff MacMillan	D	Oshawa (OHL)

EIGHTH ROUND

No.—Selecting club	Player	Pos.	Previous team (league)
216—Tampa Bay	Erkki Rajamaki	W	IFK Helsinki, Finland
217—Atlanta	Garnet Exelby	D	Saskatoon (WHL)
218—Vancouver	Markus Kankaanpera	D	Jyvaskyla, Finland
219—Washington (from N.Y. Islanders)	Maxim Orlov	C	CSKA Moskow, Russia
220—Nashville	Miroslav Durak	D	Bratislava, Slovakia
221—St. Louis (from Washington)	Colin Hemingway	W	Surrey (BCJHL)
222—Los Angeles	George Parros	RW	Chicago (NAHL)
223—Chicago	Andrew Carver	D	Hull (QMJHL)
224—Philadelphia (from Calgary)	David Nystrom	W	Frolunda, Sweden
225—Montreal	Mikko Hyytia	C	Jyvaskyla, Finland
226—N.Y. Rangers	Evgeny Gusakov	LW	Togliatti, Russia
227—Florida	Jonathan Charron	G	Val d'Or (QMJHL)
228—N.Y. Islanders (from Edmonton)	Radek Martinek	W	Ceske-Budejovice, Czech Rep.
229—San Jose	Eric Betournay	C	Acadie-Bathurst (QMJHL)
230—Anaheim	Petr Tenkrat	W	Kladno, Czech Republic
231—Carolina	David Evans	RW	Clarkson (ECAC)
232—St. Louis	Alexander Khavanov	D	Dynamo, Russia
233—Pittsburgh	Darcy Robinson	D	Saskatoon (WHL)
234—Phoenix	Goran Bezina	D	Fribourg Jr.
235—Buffalo	Brad Self	C	Peterborough (OHL)
236—Boston	John Cronin	D	Nobles Prep H.S.
237—Carolina (from Philadelphia)	Antti Jokela	G	Lukko, Finland
238—Detroit	Anton Borodkin	LW	Kamloops (WHL)
239—Toronto	Pierre Hedin	D	Modo Ornskoldsvik, Sweden
240—Colorado	Jeff Finger	D	Green Bay (USHL)
241—San Jose (from Ottawa)	Doug Murray	D	Apple Core (EJHL)
242—New Jersey	Justin Dziama	RW	Nobles Prep H.S.
243—Dallas	Brian Sullivan	D	Thayer Academy

NINTH ROUND

No.—Selecting club	Player	Pos.	Previous team (league)
244—Tampa Bay	Mikko Kuparinen	D	Grand Rapids (IHL)
245—Atlanta	Tommy Santala	C/RW	Jokerit Helsinki, Finland
246—Atlanta (from Vancouver)	Ray DiLauro	D	St. Lawrence (ECAC)
247—Boston (from N.Y. Islanders)	Mikko Eloranta	W	Jokerit Helsinki, Finland

No.—Selecting club	Player	Pos.	Previous team (league)
248—Nashville	Darren Haydar	RW	New Hampshire (H. East)
249—Washington (from Chi. through Was.)	Igor Shadilov	D	Dynamo, Russia
250—Los Angeles	Noah Clarke	LW	Des Moines (USHL)
251—N.Y. Rangers (from Chicago)	Petter Henning	W	Modo Ornskoldsvik, Sweden
252—Calgary	Dimitri Kirilenko	C	CSKA Moskow, Russia
253—Montreal	Jerome Marois	LW	Quebec (QMJHL)
254—N.Y. Rangers	Alexei Bulatov	LW	Yekateringburg, Russia
255—N.Y. Islanders (from Florida)	Brett Henning	C	Notre Dame (CCHA)
256—Edmonton	Tomas Groschl	W	Hungary
257—San Jose	Hannes Hyvonen	D	TPS Turko, Finland
258—Anaheim	Brian Gornick	C	Air Force Academy (Indep.)
259—Carolina	Yauhenni Kurlin	C	
260—St. Louis	Brian McMeekin	D	Cornell (ECAC)
261—Pittsburgh	Andrew McPherson	LW	Rensselaer (ECAC)
262—Phoenix	Alexei Litvinenko		
263—Buffalo	Craig Brunel	RW	Prince Albert (WHL)
264—Boston	Georgijs Pujacs	D	Dynamo Riga, Latvia Jr.
265—Dallas (from Philadelphia)	Jamie Chamberlain	RW	Peterborough (OHL)
266—Detroit	Ken Davis	RW	Portland (WHL)
267—Toronto	Peter Metcalf	D	Maine (H. East)
268—N.Y. Islanders (from Colorado)	Tyler Scott	D	Upper Canada Col. (CCL)
269—Ottawa	Konstantin Gorovikov	F	SKA St. Petersburg, Russia
270—St. Louis (from New Jersey)	James Desmarais	C	Rouyn-Noranda (QMJHL)
271—Vancouver	Darrell Hay	D	Tri-City (WHL)
272—Dallas	Mikhail Donika	D	Torpedo Yaroslavl, Russia

NHL HISTORY

Stanley Cup champions

All-Star Games

Year-by-year standings

Records

Statistical leaders

Award winners

The Sporting News awards

Hall of Fame

Milestones

Team by team

STANLEY CUP CHAMPIONS

LIST OF WINNERS

The Stanley Cup was donated in 1893 to be awarded to signify supremacy in Canadian amateur hockey. Eventually, other teams, including professional clubs and clubs outside of Canada, began vying for the trophy. Since 1926 only NHL clubs have competed for the Stanley Cup.

Season	Club	Coach
1892-93	Montreal Am. Ath. Assn.*	
1893-94	Montreal Am. Ath. Assn.*	
1894-95	Montreal Victorias*	Mike Grant†
1895-96	(Feb. '96) Winnipeg Victorias*	J. Armitage
1895-96	(Dec. '96) Montreal Victorias*	Mike Grant†
1896-97	Montreal Victorias*	Mike Grant†
1897-98	Montreal Victorias*	F. Richardson
1898-99	Montreal Shamrocks*	H.J. Trihey†
1899-1900	Montreal Shamrocks*	H.J. Trihey†
1900-01	Winnipeg Victorias*	D.H. Bain
1901-02	Montreal Am. Ath. Assn.*	C. McKerrow
1902-03	Ottawa Silver Seven*	A.T. Smith
1903-04	Ottawa Silver Seven*	A.T. Smith
1904-05	Ottawa Silver Seven*	A.T. Smith†
1905-06	Montreal Wanderers*	Cecil Blachford†
1906-07	(Jan. '07) Kenora Thistles*	Tommy Phillips†
1906-07	(Mar. '07) Montreal Wanderers*	Cecil Blachford
1907-08	Montreal Wanderers*	Cecil Blachford
1908-09	Ottawa Senators*	Bruce Stuart†
1909-10	Montreal Wanderers*	Pud Glass†
1910-11	Ottawa Senators*	Bruce Stuart†
1911-12	Quebec Bulldogs*	C. Nolan
1912-13	Quebec Bulldogs*	Joe Malone†
1913-14	Toronto Blueshirts*	Scotty Davidson†
1914-15	Vancouver Millionaires*	Frank Patrick
1915-16	Montreal Canadiens*	George Kennedy
1916-17	Seattle Metropolitans*	Pete Muldoon
1917-18	Toronto Arenas	Dick Carroll
1919-20	Ottawa Senators	Pete Green
1920-21	Ottawa Senators	Pete Green
1921-22	Toronto St. Pats	Eddie Powers
1922-23	Ottawa Senators	Pete Green
1923-24	Montreal Canadiens	Leo Dandurand
1924-25	Victoria Cougars*	Lester Patrick
1925-26	Montreal Maroons	Eddie Gerard
1926-27	Ottawa Senators	Dave Gill
1927-28	New York Rangers	Lester Patrick
1928-29	Boston Bruins	Cy Denneny
1929-30	Montreal Canadiens	Cecil Hart
1930-31	Montreal Canadiens	Cecil Hart
1931-32	Toronto Maple Leafs	Dick Irvin
1932-33	New York Rangers	Lester Patrick
1933-34	Chicago Black Hawks	Tommy Gorman
1934-35	Montreal Maroons	Tommy Gorman
1935-36	Detroit Red Wings	Jack Adams
1936-37	Detroit Red Wings	Jack Adams
1937-38	Chicago Black Hawks	Bill Stewart
1938-39	Boston Bruins	Art Ross
1939-40	New York Rangers	Frank Boucher
1940-41	Boston Bruins	Cooney Weiland
1941-42	Toronto Maple Leafs	Hap Day
1942-43	Detroit Red Wings	Jack Adams
1943-44	Montreal Canadiens	Dick Irvin
1944-45	Toronto Maple Leafs	Hap Day
1945-46	Montreal Canadiens	Dick Irvin
1946-47	Toronto Maple Leafs	Hap Day
1947-48	Toronto Maple Leafs	Hap Day
1948-49	Toronto Maple Leafs	Hap Day
1949-50	Detroit Red Wings	Tommy Ivan
1950-51	Toronto Maple Leafs	Joe Primeau
1951-52	Detroit Red Wings	Tommy Ivan
1952-53	Montreal Canadiens	Dick Irvin
1953-54	Detroit Red Wings	Tommy Ivan
1954-55	Detroit Red Wings	Jimmy Skinner
1955-56	Montreal Canadiens	Toe Blake
1956-57	Montreal Canadiens	Toe Blake
1957-58	Montreal Canadiens	Toe Blake
1958-59	Montreal Canadiens	Toe Blake
1959-60	Montreal Canadiens	Toe Blake
1960-61	Chicago Black Hawks	Rudy Pilous
1961-62	Toronto Maple Leafs	Punch Imlach
1962-63	Toronto Maple Leafs	Punch Imlach
1963-64	Toronto Maple Leafs	Punch Imlach
1964-65	Montreal Canadiens	Toe Blake
1965-66	Montreal Canadiens	Toe Blake
1966-67	Toronto Maple Leafs	Punch Imlach
1967-68	Montreal Canadiens	Toe Blake
1968-69	Montreal Canadiens	Claude Ruel
1969-70	Boston Bruins	Harry Sinden
1970-71	Montreal Canadiens	Al MacNeil
1971-72	Boston Bruins	Tom Johnson
1972-73	Montreal Canadiens	Scotty Bowman
1973-74	Philadelphia Flyers	Fred Shero
1974-75	Philadelphia Flyers	Fred Shero
1975-76	Montreal Canadiens	Scotty Bowman
1976-77	Montreal Canadiens	Scotty Bowman
1977-78	Montreal Canadiens	Scotty Bowman
1978-79	Montreal Canadiens	Scotty Bowman
1979-80	New York Islanders	Al Arbour
1980-81	New York Islanders	Al Arbour
1981-82	New York Islanders	Al Arbour
1982-83	New York Islanders	Al Arbour
1983-84	Edmonton Oilers	Glen Sather
1984-85	Edmonton Oilers	Glen Sather
1985-86	Montreal Canadiens	Jean Perron
1986-87	Edmonton Oilers	Glen Sather
1987-88	Edmonton Oilers	Glen Sather
1988-89	Calgary Flames	Terry Crisp
1989-90	Edmonton Oilers	John Muckler
1990-91	Pittsburgh Penguins	Bob Johnson
1991-92	Pittsburgh Penguins	Scotty Bowman
1992-93	Montreal Canadiens	Jacques Demers
1993-94	New York Rangers	Mike Keenan
1994-95	New Jersey Devils	Jacques Lemaire
1995-96	Colorado Avalanche	Marc Crawford
1996-97	Detroit Red Wings	Scotty Bowman
1997-98	Detroit Red Wings	Scotty Bowman
1998-99	Dallas Stars	Ken Hitchcock

NOTE: 1918-19 series between Montreal and Seattle cancelled after five games because of influenza epidemic.

*Stanley Cups won by non-NHL clubs.

†Team captain.

ALL-STAR GAMES

RESULTS

Date	Site	Winning team, score	Losing team, score	Att.
2-14-34†	Maple Leaf Gardens, Toronto	Toronto Maple Leafs, 7	NHL All-Stars, 3	*14,000
11-3-37‡	Montreal Forum	NHL All-Stars, 6	Montreal All-Stars§, 5	8,683
10-29-39§	Montreal Forum	NHL All-Stars, 5	Montreal Canadiens, 2	*6,000
10-13-47	Maple Leaf Gardens, Toronto	NHL All-Stars, 4	Toronto Maple Leafs, 3	14,169
11-3-48	Chicago Stadium	NHL All-Stars, 3	Toronto Maple Leafs, 1	12,794
10-10-49	Maple Leaf Gardens, Toronto	NHL All-Stars, 3	Toronto Maple Leafs, 1	13,541
10-8-50	Olympia Stadium, Detroit	Detroit Red Wings, 7	NHL All-Stars, 1	9,166
10-9-51	Maple Leaf Gardens, Toronto	First Team▲, 2	Second Team▲, 2	11,469
10-5-52	Olympia Stadium, Detroit	First Team▲, 1	Second Team▲, 1	10,680
10-3-53	Montreal Forum	NHL All-Stars, 3	Montreal Canadiens, 1	14,153
10-2-54	Olympia Stadium, Detroit	NHL All-Stars, 2	Detroit Red Wings, 2	10,689
10-2-55	Olympia Stadium, Detroit	Detroit Red Wings, 3	NHL All-Stars, 1	10,111
10-9-56	Montreal Forum	NHL All-Stars, 1	Montreal Canadiens, 1	13,095
10-5-57	Montreal Forum	NHL All-Stars, 5	Montreal Canadiens, 3	13,095
10-4-58	Montreal Forum	Montreal Canadiens, 6	NHL All-Stars, 3	13,989
10-3-59	Montreal Forum	Montreal Canadiens, 6	NHL All-Stars, 1	13,818
10-1-60	Montreal Forum	NHL All-Stars, 2	Montreal Canadiens, 1	13,949
10-7-61	Chicago Stadium	NHL All-Stars, 3	Chicago Blackhawks, 1	14,534
10-6-62	Maple Leaf Gardens, Toronto	Toronto Maple Leafs, 4	NHL All-Stars, 1	14,236
10-5-63	Maple Leaf Gardens, Toronto	NHL All-Stars, 3	Toronto Maple Leafs, 3	14,034
10-10-64	Maple Leaf Gardens, Toronto	NHL All-Stars, 3	Toronto Maple Leafs, 2	14,232
10-20-65	Montreal Forum	NHL All-Stars, 5	Montreal Canadiens, 2	14,284
1-18-67	Montreal Forum	Montreal Canadiens, 3	NHL All-Stars, 0	14,284
1-16-68	Maple Leaf Gardens, Toronto	Toronto Maple Leafs, 4	NHL All-Stars, 3	15,753
1-21-69	Montreal Forum	West Division, 3	East Division, 3	16,260
1-20-70	St. Louis Arena	East Division, 4	West Division, 1	16,587
1-19-71	Boston Garden	West Division, 2	East Division, 1	14,790
1-25-72	Met Sports Center, Bloomington, Minn.	East Division, 3	West Division, 2	15,423
1-30-73	Madison Square Garden, New York	East Division, 5	West Division, 4	16,986
1-29-74	Chicago Stadium	West Division, 6	East Division, 4	16,426
1-21-75	Montreal Forum	Wales Conference, 7	Campbell Conference, 1	16,080
1-20-76	The Spectrum, Philadelphia	Wales Conference, 7	Campbell Conference, 5	16,436
1-25-77	Pacific Coliseum, Vancouver	Wales Conference, 4	Campbell Conference, 3	15,607
1-24-78	Buffalo Memorial Auditorium	Wales Conference, 3	Campbell Conference, 2 (OT)	16,433
	1979 All-Star Game replaced by Challenge Cup series between Team NHL and Soviet Union			
2-5-80	Joe Louis Arena, Detroit	Wales Conference, 6	Campbell Conference, 3	21,002
2-10-81	The Forum, Los Angeles	Campbell Conference, 4	Wales Conference, 1	15,761
2-9-82	Capital Centre, Landover, Md.	Wales Conference, 4	Campbell Conference, 2	18,130
2-8-83	Nassau Coliseum, Long Island, N.Y.	Campbell Conference, 9	Wales Conference, 3	15,230
1-31-84	Meadowlands Arena, East Rutherford, N.J.	Wales Conference, 7	Campbell Conference, 6	18,939
2-12-85	Olympic Saddledome, Calgary	Wales Conference, 6	Campbell Conference, 4	16,683
2-4-86	Hartford Civic Center	Wales Conference, 4	Campbell Conference, 3 (OT)	15,126
	1987 All-Star Game replaced by Rendez-Vous '87 between Team NHL and Soviet Union			
2-9-88	St. Louis Arena	Wales Conference, 6	Campbell Conference, 5 (OT)	17,878
2-7-89	Northlands Coliseum, Edmonton	Campbell Conference, 9	Wales Conference, 5	17,503
1-21-90	Pittsburgh Civic Arena	Wales Conference, 12	Campbell Conference, 7	17,503
1-19-91	Chicago Stadium	Campbell Conference, 11	Wales Conference, 5	18,472
1-18-92	The Spectrum, Philadelphia	Campbell Conference, 10	Wales Conference, 6	17,380
2-6-93	Montreal Forum	Wales Conference, 16	Campbell Conference, 6	17,137
1-22-94	Madison Square Garden, New York	Eastern Conference, 9	Western Conference, 8	18,200
	1995 All-Star Game canceled because of NHL lockout			
1-20-96	FleetCenter, Boston	Eastern Conference 5	Western Conference 4	17,565
1-18-97	San Jose Arena	Eastern Conference 11	Western Conference 7	17,442
1-18-98	General Motors Place, Vancouver	North America 8	World 7	18,422
1-24-99	Ice Palace, Tampa	North America 8	World 6	19,758

*Estimated figure.

†Benefit game for Toronto Maple Leafs left wing Ace Bailey, who suffered a career-ending skull injury earlier in the season.

‡Benefit game for the family of Montreal Canadiens center Howie Morenz, who died of a heart attack earlier in the year.

§Montreal All-Star roster made up of players from Montreal Canadiens and Maroons.

∞Benefit game for the family of Montreal Canadiens defenseman Babe Siebert, who drowned earlier in the year.

▲First Team roster supplemented by players from the four American clubs and Second Team roster supplemented by players from the two Canadian clubs.

MOST VALUABLE PLAYERS

Date	Player, All-Star Game team (regular-season team)
10-6-62	Eddie Shack, Toronto Maple Leafs
10-5-63	Frank Mahovlich, Toronto Maple Leafs
10-10-64	Jean Beliveau, All-Stars (Montreal Canadiens)
10-20-65	Gordie Howe, All-Stars (Detroit Red Wings)
1-18-67	Henri Richard, Montreal Canadiens
1-16-68	Bruce Gamble, Toronto Maple Leafs
1-21-69	Frank Mahovlich, East Div. (Detroit Red Wings)
1-20-70	Bobby Hull, East Div. (Chicago Blackhawks)
1-19-71	Bobby Hull, West Div. (Chicago Blackhawks)
1-25-72	Bobby Orr, East Division (Boston Bruins)
1-30-73	Greg Polis, West Division (Pittsburgh Penguins)
1-29-74	Garry Unger, West Division (St. Louis Blues)
1-21-75	Syl Apps Jr., Wales Conf. (Pittsburgh Penguins)
1-20-76	Peter Mahovlich, Wales Conf. (Montreal Canadiens)
1-25-77	Rick Martin, Wales Conference (Buffalo Sabres)
1-24-78	Billy Smith, Campbell Conf. (New York Islanders)
2-5-80	Reggie Leach, Campbell Conf. (Philadelphia Flyers)
2-10-81	Mike Liut, Campbell Conf. (St. Louis Blues)
2-9-82	Mike Bossy, Wales Conf. (New York Islanders)
2-8-83	Wayne Gretzky, Campbell Conf. (Edmonton Oilers)
1-31-84	Don Maloney, Wales Conf. (New York Rangers)
2-12-85	Mario Lemieux, Wales Conf. (Pittsburgh Penguins)
2-4-86	Grant Fuhr, Campbell Conf. (Edmonton Oilers)
2-9-88	Mario Lemieux, Wales Conf. (Pittsburgh Penguins)
2-7-89	Wayne Gretzky, Campbell Conf. (Los Angeles Kings)
1-21-90	Mario Lemieux, Wales Conf. (Pittsburgh Penguins)
1-19-91	Vincent Damphousse, Camp. Conf. (Tor. Maple Leafs)
1-18-92	Brett Hull, Campbell Conf. (St. Louis Blues)
2-6-93	Mike Gartner, Wales Conf. (New York Rangers)
1-22-94	Mike Richter, Eastern Conf. (New York Rangers)
1-20-96	Ray Bourque, Eastern Conf. (Boston Bruins)
1-18-97	Mark Recchi, Eastern Conf. (Montreal Canadiens)
1-18-98	Teemu Selanne, North America (Ana. Mighty Ducks)
1-24-99	Wayne Gretzky, North America (New York Rangers)

YEAR-BY-YEAR STANDINGS

Note: Prior to 1926-27 season, clubs outside the NHL also competed for the Stanley Cup. Non-NHL clubs are denoted in parentheses. Sometimes playoff rounds were decided by total goals scored, rather than by games won.

1917-18

Team	W	L	T	Pts.	GF	GA
Montreal Canadiens	13	9	0	26	115	84
Toronto Arenas	13	9	0	26	108	109
Ottawa Senators	9	13	0	18	102	114
Montreal Wanderers	1	5	0	2	17	35

PLAYOFFS

Semifinals: Toronto 10 goals, Montreal Canadiens 7 goals (2-game series); Vancouver (PCHL) 3 goals, Seattle (PCHL) 2 goals (2-game series).

Stanley Cup finals: Toronto 3, Vancouver (PCHL) 2.

1918-19

Team	W	L	T	Pts.	GF	GA
Ottawa Senators	12	6	0	24	71	54
Montreal Canadiens	10	8	0	20	88	78
Toronto Arenas	5	13	0	10	65	92

PLAYOFFS

Semifinals: Seattle (PCHL) 7 goals, Vancouver 5 goals (2-game series); Montreal Canadiens 3, Ottawa 1.

Stanley Cup finals: Series between Montreal Canadiens and Seattle (PCHL) abandoned (with each team winning two games and one game tied) due to influenza epidemic.

1919-20

Team	W	L	T	Pts.	GF	GA
Ottawa Senators	19	5	0	38	121	64
Montreal Canadiens	13	11	0	26	129	113
Toronto St. Patricks	12	12	0	24	119	106
Quebec Bulldogs	4	20	0	8	91	177

PLAYOFFS

Semifinals: Seattle (PCHL) 7 goals, Vancouver (PCHL) 3 goals (2-game series).

Stanley Cup finals: Ottawa 3, Seattle (PCHL) 2.

1920-21

Team	W	L	T	Pts.	GF	GA
Toronto St. Patricks	15	9	0	30	105	100
Ottawa Senators	14	10	0	28	97	75
Montreal Canadiens	13	11	0	26	112	99
Hamilton Tigers	6	18	0	12	92	132

PLAYOFFS

Semifinals: Vancouver (PCHL) 2, Seattle (PCHL) 0; Ottawa 2, Toronto 0.

Stanley Cup finals: Ottawa 3, Vancouver (PCHL) 2.

1921-22

Team	W	L	T	Pts.	GF	GA
Ottawa Senators	14	8	2	30	106	84
Toronto St. Patricks	13	10	1	27	98	97
Montreal Canadiens	12	11	1	25	88	94
Hamilton Tigers	7	17	0	14	88	105

PLAYOFFS

Preliminaries: Regina (WCHL) 2 goals, Calgary (WCHL) 1 goal (2-game series); Regina (WCHL) 3, Edmonton (WCHL) 2; Vancouver (PCHL) 2, Seattle (PCHL) 0; Vancouver (PCHL) 5 goals, Regina (WCHL) 2 goals (2-game series); Toronto 5 goals, Ottawa 4 goals (2-game series).

Stanley Cup finals: Toronto 3, Vancouver (PCHL) 2.

1922-23

Team	W	L	T	Pts.	GF	GA
Ottawa Senators	14	9	1	29	77	54
Montreal Canadiens	13	9	2	28	73	61
Toronto St. Patricks	13	10	1	27	82	88
Hamilton Tigers	6	18	0	12	81	110

PLAYOFFS

Quarterfinals: Ottawa 3 goals, Montreal Canadiens 2 goals (2-game series); Vancouver (PCHL) 5 goals, Victoria (PCHL) 3 goals (2-game series). **Semifinals:** Ottawa 3, Vancouver (PCHL) 1; Edmonton (WCHL) 4 goals, Regina (WCHL) 3 goals (2-game series).

Stanley Cup finals: Ottawa 2, Edmonton (WCHL) 0.

1923-24

Team	W	L	T	Pts.	GF	GA
Ottawa Senators	16	8	0	32	74	54
Montreal Canadiens	13	11	0	26	59	48
Toronto St. Patricks	10	14	0	20	59	85
Hamilton Tigers	9	15	0	18	63	68

PLAYOFFS

First round: Vancouver (PCHL) 4 goals, Seattle (PCHL) 3 goals (2-game series); Calgary (WCHL) 4 goals, Regina (WCHL) 2 goals (2-game series). **Second round:** Montreal Canadiens 2, Ottawa 0; Calgary (WCHL) 2, Vancouver (PCHL) 1. **Third round:** Montreal Canadiens 2, Vancouver (PCHL) 0.

Stanley Cup finals: Montreal Canadiens 2, Calgary (WCHL) 0.

1924-25

Team	W	L	T	Pts.	GF	GA
Hamilton Tigers	19	10	1	39	90	60
Toronto St. Patricks	19	11	0	38	90	84
Montreal Canadiens	17	11	2	36	93	56
Ottawa Senators	17	12	1	35	83	66
Montreal Maroons	9	19	2	20	45	65
Boston Bruins	6	24	0	12	49	119

PLAYOFFS

Quarterfinals: Victoria (WCHL) 6 goals, Saskatoon (WCHL) 4 goals (2-game series). **Semifinals:** Montreal Canadiens 2, Toronto 0; Victoria (WCHL) 3 goals, Calgary (WCHL) 1 goal (2-game series).

Stanley Cup finals: Victoria (WCHL) 3, Montreal Canadiens 1.

1925-26

Team	W	L	T	Pts.	GF	GA
Ottawa Senators	24	8	4	52	77	42
Montreal Maroons	20	11	5	45	91	73
Pittsburgh Pirates	19	16	1	39	82	70
Boston Bruins	17	15	4	38	92	85
New York Americans	12	20	4	28	68	89
Toronto St. Patricks	12	21	3	27	92	114
Montreal Canadiens	11	24	1	23	79	108

PLAYOFFS

Quarterfinals: Victoria (WHL) 4 goals, Saskatoon (WHL) 3 goals (2-game series); Montreal Maroons 6 goals, Pittsburgh 4 goals (2-game series). **Semifinals:** Victoria (WHL) 5 goals, Edmonton (WHL) 3 goals (2-game series); Montreal Maroons 2 goals, Ottawa 1 goal (2-game series).

Stanley Cup finals: Montreal Maroons 3, Victoria (WHL) 1.

1926-27

AMERICAN DIVISION

Team	W	L	T	Pts.	GF	GA
New York Rangers	25	13	6	56	95	27
Boston Bruins	21	20	3	45	97	89
Chicago Blackhawks	19	22	3	41	115	116
Pittsburgh Pirates	15	26	3	33	79	108
Detroit Cougars	12	28	4	28	76	105

CANADIAN DIVISION

Team	W	L	T	Pts.	GF	GA
Ottawa Senators	30	10	4	64	89	69
Montreal Canadiens	28	14	2	58	99	67
Montreal Maroons	20	20	4	44	71	68
New York Americans	17	25	2	36	82	91
Toronto St. Patricks	15	24	5	35	79	94

PLAYOFFS

League quarterfinals: Montreal Canadiens 2 goals, Montreal Maroons 1 goal (2-game series); Boston 10 goals, Chicago 5 goals (2-game series). **Semifinals:** Ottawa 5 goals, Montreal Canadiens 1 goal (2-game series); Boston 3 goals, N.Y. Rangers 1 goal (2-game series).

Stanley Cup finals: Ottawa 2, Boston 0.

1927-28

AMERICAN DIVISION

Team	W	L	T	Pts.	GF	GA
Boston Bruins	20	13	11	51	77	70
New York Rangers	19	16	9	47	94	79
Pittsburgh Pirates	19	17	8	46	67	76
Detroit Cougars	19	19	6	44	88	79
Chicago Blackhawks	7	34	3	17	68	134

CANADIAN DIVISION

Team	W	L	T	Pts.	GF	GA
Montreal Canadiens	26	11	7	59	116	48
Montreal Maroons	24	14	6	54	96	77
Ottawa Senators	20	14	10	50	78	57
Toronto Maple Leafs	18	18	8	44	89	88
New York Americans	11	27	6	28	63	128

PLAYOFFS

League quarterfinals: Montreal Maroons 3 goals, Ottawa 1 goal (2-game series); N.Y. Rangers 6 goals, Pittsburgh 4 goals (2-game series). **Semifinals:** Montreal Maroons 3 goals, Montreal Canadiens 2 goals (2-game series); N.Y. Rangers 5 goals, Boston 2 goals (2-game series).

Stanley Cup finals: N.Y. Rangers 3, Montreal Maroons 2.

1928-29

AMERICAN DIVISION

Team	W	L	T	Pts.	GF	GA
Boston Bruins	26	13	5	57	89	52
New York Rangers	21	13	10	52	72	65
Detroit Cougars	19	16	9	47	72	63
Pittsburgh Pirates	9	27	8	26	46	80
Chicago Blackhawks	7	29	8	22	33	85

CANADIAN DIVISION

Team	W	L	T	Pts.	GF	GA
Montreal Canadiens	22	7	15	59	71	43
New York Americans	19	13	12	50	53	53
Toronto Maple Leafs	21	18	5	47	85	69
Ottawa Senators	14	17	13	41	54	67
Montreal Maroons	15	20	9	39	67	65

PLAYOFFS

League quarterfinals: N.Y. Rangers 1 goal, N.Y. Americans 0 goals (2-game series); Toronto 7 goals, Detroit 2 goals (2-game series). **Semifinals:** Boston 3, Montreal Canadiens 0; N.Y. Rangers 2, Toronto 0.

Stanley Cup finals: Boston 2, N.Y. Rangers 0.

1929-30

AMERICAN DIVISION

Team	W	L	T	Pts.	GF	GA
Boston Bruins	38	5	1	77	179	98
Chicago Blackhawks	21	18	5	47	117	111
New York Rangers	17	17	10	44	136	143
Detroit Cougars	14	24	6	34	117	133
Pittsburgh Pirates	5	36	3	13	102	185

CANADIAN DIVISION

Team	W	L	T	Pts.	GF	GA
Montreal Maroons	23	16	5	51	141	114
Montreal Canadiens	21	14	9	51	142	114
Ottawa Senators	21	15	8	50	138	118
Toronto Maple Leafs	17	21	6	40	116	124
New York Americans	14	25	5	33	113	161

PLAYOFFS

League quarterfinals: Montreal Canadiens 3 goals, Chicago 2 goals (2-game series); N.Y. Rangers 6 goals, Ottawa 3 goals (2-game series). **Semifinals:** Boston 3, Montreal Maroons 1; Montreal Canadiens 2, N.Y. Rangers 0.

Stanley Cup finals: Montreal Canadiens 2, Boston 0.

1930-31

AMERICAN DIVISION

Team	W	L	T	Pts.	GF	GA
Boston Bruins	28	10	6	62	143	90
Chicago Blackhawks	24	17	3	51	108	78
New York Rangers	19	16	9	47	106	87
Detroit Falcons	16	21	7	39	102	105
Philadelphia Quakers	4	36	4	12	76	184

CANADIAN DIVISION

Team	W	L	T	Pts.	GF	GA
Montreal Canadiens	26	10	8	60	89	60
Toronto Maple Leafs	22	13	9	53	99	53
Montreal Maroons	20	18	6	46	106	46
New York Americans	18	16	10	46	76	74
Ottawa Senators	10	30	4	24	91	142

PLAYOFFS

League quarterfinals: Chicago 4 goals, Toronto 3 goals (2-game series); N.Y. Rangers 8 goals, Montreal Maroons 1 goal (2-game series). **Semifinals:** Montreal Canadiens 3, Boston 2; Chicago 2, N.Y. Rangers 0.

Stanley Cup finals: Montreal Canadiens 3, Chicago 2.

1931-32

AMERICAN DIVISION

Team	W	L	T	Pts.	GF	GA
New York Rangers	23	17	8	54	134	112
Chicago Blackhawks	18	19	11	47	86	101
Detroit Falcons	18	20	10	46	95	108
Boston Bruins	15	21	12	42	122	117

CANADIAN DIVISION

Team	W	L	T	Pts.	GF	GA
Montreal Canadiens	25	16	7	57	128	111
Toronto Maple Leafs	23	18	7	53	155	127
Montreal Maroons	19	22	7	45	142	139
New York Americans	16	24	8	40	95	142

PLAYOFFS

League quarterfinals: Toronto 6 goals, Chicago 2 goals (2-game series); Montreal Maroons 3 goals, Detroit 1 goal (2-game series). **Semifinals:** N.Y. Rangers 3, Montreal Canadiens 1; Toronto 4 goals, Montreal Maroons 3 (2-game series).
Stanley Cup finals: Toronto 3, N.Y. Rangers 0.

1932-33

AMERICAN DIVISION

Team	W	L	T	Pts.	GF	GA
Boston Bruins	25	15	8	58	124	88
Detroit Red Wings	25	15	8	58	111	93
New York Rangers	23	17	8	54	135	107
Chicago Blackhawks	16	20	12	44	88	101

CANADIAN DIVISION

Team	W	L	T	Pts.	GF	GA
Toronto Maple Leafs	24	18	6	54	119	111
Montreal Maroons	22	20	6	50	135	119
Montreal Canadiens	18	25	5	41	92	115
New York Americans	15	22	11	41	91	118
Ottawa Senators	11	27	10	32	88	131

PLAYOFFS

League quarterfinals: Detroit 5 goals, Montreal Maroons 2 goals (2-game series); N.Y. Rangers 8 goals, Montreal Canadiens 5 goals (2-game series). **Semifinals:** Toronto 3, Boston 2; N.Y. Rangers 6 goals, Detroit 3 goals (2-game series).
Stanley Cup finals: N.Y. Rangers 3, Toronto 1.

1933-34

AMERICAN DIVISION

Team	W	L	T	Pts.	GF	GA
Detroit Red Wings	24	14	10	58	113	98
Chicago Blackhawks	20	17	11	51	88	83
New York Rangers	21	19	8	50	120	113
Boston Bruins	18	25	5	41	111	130

CANADIAN DIVISION

Team	W	L	T	Pts.	GF	GA
Toronto Maple Leafs	26	13	9	61	174	119
Montreal Canadiens	22	20	6	50	99	101
Montreal Maroons	19	18	11	49	117	122
New York Americans	15	23	10	40	104	132
Ottawa Senators	13	29	6	32	115	143

PLAYOFFS

League quarterfinals: Chicago 4 goals, Montreal Canadiens 3 goals (2-game series); Montreal Maroons 2 goals, N.Y. Rangers 1 goal (2-game series). **Semifinals:** Detroit 3, Toronto 2; Chicago 6 goals, Montreal Maroons 2 goals (2-game series).
Stanley Cup finals: Chicago 3, Detroit 1.

1934-35

AMERICAN DIVISION

Team	W	L	T	Pts.	GF	GA
Boston Bruins	26	16	6	58	129	112
Chicago Blackhawks	26	17	5	57	118	88
New York Rangers	22	20	6	50	137	139
Detroit Red Wings	19	22	7	45	127	114

CANADIAN DIVISION

Team	W	L	T	Pts.	GF	GA
Toronto Maple Leafs	30	14	4	64	157	111
Montreal Maroons	24	19	5	53	123	92
Montreal Canadiens	19	23	6	44	110	145
New York Americans	12	27	9	33	100	142
St. Louis Eagles	11	31	6	28	86	144

PLAYOFFS

League quarterfinals: Montreal Maroons 1 goal, Chicago 0 goals (2-game series); N.Y. Rangers 6 goals, Montreal Canadiens 5 goals (2-game series). **Semifinals:** Toronto 3, Boston 1; Montreal Maroons 5 goals, N.Y. Rangers 4 (2-game series).
Stanley Cup finals: Montreal Maroons 3, Toronto 0.

1935-36

AMERICAN DIVISION

Team	W	L	T	Pts.	GF	GA
Detroit Red Wings	24	16	8	56	124	103
Boston Bruins	22	20	6	50	92	83
Chicago Blackhawks	21	19	8	50	93	92
New York Rangers	19	17	12	50	96	50

CANADIAN DIVISION

Team	W	L	T	Pts.	GF	GA
Montreal Maroons	22	16	10	54	114	106
Toronto Maple Leafs	23	19	6	52	126	106
New York Americans	16	25	7	39	109	122
Montreal Canadiens	11	26	11	33	82	123

PLAYOFFS

League quarterfinals: Toronto 8 goals, Boston 6 goals (2-game series); N.Y. Americans 7 goals, Chicago 5 goals (2-game series). **Semifinals:** Detroit 3, Montreal Maroons 0; Toronto 2, N.Y. Americans 1.
Stanley Cup finals: Detroit 3, Toronto 1.

1936-37

AMERICAN DIVISION

Team	W	L	T	Pts.	GF	GA
Detroit Red Wings	25	14	9	59	128	102
Boston Bruins	23	18	7	53	120	110
New York Rangers	19	20	9	47	117	106
Chicago Blackhawks	14	27	7	35	99	131

CANADIAN DIVISION

Team	W	L	T	Pts.	GF	GA
Montreal Canadiens	24	18	6	54	115	111
Montreal Maroons	22	17	9	53	126	110
Toronto Maple Leafs	22	21	5	49	119	115
New York Americans	15	29	4	34	122	161

PLAYOFFS

League quarterfinals: Montreal Maroons 2, Boston 1; N.Y. Rangers 2, Toronto 0. **Semifinals:** Detroit 3, Montreal Canadiens 2; N.Y. Rangers 2, Montreal Maroons 0.
Stanley Cup finals: Detroit 3, N.Y. Rangers 2.

1937-38

AMERICAN DIVISION

Team	W	L	T	Pts.	GF	GA
Boston Bruins	30	11	7	67	142	89
New York Rangers	27	15	6	60	149	96
Chicago Blackhawks	14	25	9	37	97	139
Detroit Red Wings	12	25	11	35	99	133

CANADIAN DIVISION

Team	W	L	T	Pts.	GF	GA
Toronto Maple Leafs	24	15	9	57	151	127
New York Americans	19	18	11	49	110	111
Montreal Canadiens	18	17	13	49	123	128
Montreal Maroons	12	30	6	30	101	149

PLAYOFFS

League quarterfinals: N.Y. Americans 2, N.Y. Rangers 1; Chicago 2, Montreal Canadiens 1. **Semifinals:** Toronto 3, Boston 0; Chicago 2, N.Y. Americans 1.
Stanley Cup finals: Chicago 3, Toronto 1.

1938-39

Team	W	L	T	Pts.	GF	GA
Boston Bruins	36	10	2	74	156	76
New York Rangers	26	16	6	58	149	105
Toronto Maple Leafs	19	20	9	47	114	107
New York Americans	17	21	10	44	119	157
Detroit Red Wings	18	24	6	42	107	128
Montreal Canadiens	15	24	9	39	115	146
Chicago Blackhawks	12	28	8	32	91	132

PLAYOFFS

League quarterfinals: Toronto 2, N.Y. Americans 0; Detroit 2, Montreal 1. **Semifinals:** Boston 4, N.Y. Rangers 3; Toronto 2, Detroit 1.
Stanley Cup finals: Boston 4, Toronto 1.

1939-40

Team	W	L	T	Pts.	GF	GA
Boston Bruins	31	12	5	67	170	98
New York Rangers	27	11	10	64	136	77
Toronto Maple Leafs	25	17	6	56	134	110
Chicago Blackhawks	23	19	6	52	112	120
Detroit Red Wings	16	26	6	38	90	126
New York Americans	15	29	4	34	106	140
Montreal Canadiens	10	33	5	25	90	167

PLAYOFFS

League quarterfinals: Toronto 2, Chicago 0; Detroit 2, N.Y. Americans 1. **Semifinals:** N.Y. Rangers 4, Boston 2; Toronto 2, Detroit 0.
Stanley Cup finals: N.Y. Rangers 4, Toronto 2.

1940-41

Team	W	L	T	Pts.	GF	GA
Boston Bruins	27	8	13	67	168	102
Toronto Maple Leafs	28	14	6	62	145	99
Detroit Red Wings	21	16	11	53	112	102
New York Rangers	21	19	8	50	143	125
Chicago Blackhawks	16	25	7	39	112	139
Montreal Canadiens	16	26	6	38	121	147
New York Americans	8	29	11	27	99	186

PLAYOFFS

League quarterfinals: Detroit 2, N.Y. Rangers 1; Chicago 2, Montreal 1. **Semifinals:** Boston 4, Toronto 3; Detroit 2, Chicago 0.
Stanley Cup finals: Boston 4, Detroit 0.

1941-42

Team	W	L	T	Pts.	GF	GA
New York Rangers	29	17	2	60	177	143
Toronto Maple Leafs	27	18	3	57	158	136
Boston Bruins	25	17	6	56	160	118
Chicago Blackhawks	22	23	3	47	145	155
Detroit Red Wings	19	25	4	42	140	147
Montreal Canadiens	18	27	3	39	134	173
Brooklyn Americans	16	29	3	35	133	175

PLAYOFFS

League quarterfinals: Boston 2, Chicago 1; Detroit 2, Montreal 1. **Semifinals:** Toronto 4, New York 2; Detroit 2, Boston 0.
Stanley Cup finals: Toronto 4, Detroit 3.

1942-43

Team	W	L	T	Pts.	GF	GA
Detroit Red Wings	25	14	11	61	169	124
Boston Bruins	24	17	9	57	195	176
Toronto Maple Leafs	22	19	9	53	198	159
Montreal Canadiens	19	19	12	50	181	191
Chicago Blackhawks	17	18	15	49	179	180
New York Rangers	11	31	8	30	161	253

PLAYOFFS

League semifinals: Detroit 4, Toronto 2; Boston 4, Montreal 1.
Stanley Cup finals: Detroit 4, Boston 0.

1943-44

Team	W	L	T	Pts.	GF	GA
Montreal Canadiens	38	5	7	83	234	109
Detroit Red Wings	26	18	6	58	214	177
Toronto Maple Leafs	23	23	4	50	214	174
Chicago Blackhawks	22	23	5	49	178	187
Boston Bruins	19	26	5	43	223	268
New York Rangers	6	39	5	17	162	310

PLAYOFFS

League semifinals: Montreal 4, Toronto 1; Chicago 4, Detroit 1.
Stanley Cup finals: Montreal 4, Chicago 0.

1944-45

Team	W	L	T	Pts.	GF	GA
Montreal Canadiens	38	8	4	80	228	121
Detroit Red Wings	31	14	5	67	218	161
Toronto Maple Leafs	24	22	4	52	183	161
Boston Bruins	16	30	4	36	179	219
Chicago Blackhawks	13	30	7	33	141	194
New York Rangers	11	29	10	32	154	247

PLAYOFFS

League semifinals: Toronto 4, Montreal 2; Detroit 4, Boston 3.
Stanley Cup finals: Toronto 4, Detroit 3.

1945-46

Team	W	L	T	Pts.	GF	GA
Montreal Canadiens	28	17	5	61	172	134
Boston Bruins	24	18	8	56	167	156
Chicago Blackhawks	23	20	7	53	200	178
Detroit Red Wings	20	20	10	50	146	159
Toronto Maple Leafs	19	24	7	45	174	185
New York Rangers	13	28	9	35	144	191

PLAYOFFS

League semifinals: Montreal 4, Chicago 0; Boston 4, Detroit 1.
Stanley Cup finals: Montreal 4, Boston 1.

1946-47

Team	W	L	T	Pts.	GF	GA
Montreal Canadiens	34	16	10	78	189	138
Toronto Maple Leafs	31	19	10	72	209	172
Boston Bruins	26	23	11	63	190	175
Detroit Red Wings	22	27	11	55	190	193
New York Rangers	22	32	6	50	167	186
Chicago Blackhawks	19	37	4	42	193	274

PLAYOFFS

League semifinals: Montreal 4, Boston 1; Toronto 4, Detroit 1.
Stanley Cup finals: Toronto 4, Montreal 2.

1947-48

Team	W	L	T	Pts.	GF	GA
Toronto Maple Leafs	32	15	13	77	182	143
Detroit Red Wings	30	18	12	72	187	148
Boston Bruins	23	24	13	59	167	168
New York Rangers	21	26	13	55	176	201
Montreal Canadiens	20	29	11	51	147	169
Chicago Blackhawks	20	34	6	46	195	225

PLAYOFFS

League semifinals: Toronto 4, Boston 1; Detroit 4, New York 2.
Stanley Cup finals: Toronto 4, Detroit 0.

1948-49

Team	W	L	T	Pts.	GF	GA
Detroit Red Wings	34	19	7	75	195	145
Boston Bruins	29	23	8	66	178	163
Montreal Canadiens	28	23	9	65	152	126
Toronto Maple Leafs	22	25	13	57	147	161
Chicago Blackhawks	21	31	8	50	173	211
New York Rangers	18	31	11	47	133	172

PLAYOFFS

League semifinals: Detroit 4, Montreal 3; Toronto 4, Boston 1.
Stanley Cup finals: Toronto 4, Detroit 0.

1949-50

Team	W	L	T	Pts.	GF	GA
Detroit Red Wings	37	19	14	88	229	164
Montreal Canadiens	29	22	19	77	172	150
Toronto Maple Leafs	31	27	12	74	176	173
New York Rangers	28	31	11	67	170	189
Boston Bruins	22	32	16	60	198	228
Chicago Blackhawks	22	38	10	54	203	244

PLAYOFFS

League semifinals: Detroit 4, Toronto 3; New York 4, Montreal 1.
Stanley Cup finals: Detroit 4, New York 3.

1950-51

Team	W	L	T	Pts.	GF	GA
Detroit Red Wings	44	13	13	101	236	139
Toronto Maple Leafs	41	16	13	95	212	138
Montreal Canadiens	25	30	15	65	173	184
Boston Bruins	22	30	18	62	178	197
New York Rangers	20	29	21	61	169	201
Chicago Blackhawks	13	47	10	36	171	280

PLAYOFFS

League semifinals: Montreal 4, Detroit 2; Toronto 4, Boston 1.
Stanley Cup finals: Toronto 4, Montreal 1.

1951-52

Team	W	L	T	Pts.	GF	GA
Detroit Red Wings	44	14	12	100	215	133
Montreal Canadiens	34	26	10	78	195	164
Toronto Maple Leafs	29	25	16	74	168	157
Boston Bruins	25	29	16	66	162	176
New York Rangers	23	34	13	59	192	219
Chicago Blackhawks	17	4	9	43	158	241

PLAYOFFS

League semifinals: Detroit 4, Toronto 0; Montreal 4, Boston 3.
Stanley Cup finals: Detroit 4, Montreal 0.

1952-53

Team	W	L	T	Pts.	GF	GA
Detroit Red Wings	36	16	18	90	222	133
Montreal Canadiens	28	23	19	75	155	148
Boston Bruins	28	29	13	69	152	172
Chicago Blackhawks	27	28	15	69	169	175
Toronto Maple Leafs	27	30	13	67	156	167
New York Rangers	17	37	16	50	152	211

PLAYOFFS

League semifinals: Boston 4, Detroit 2; Montreal 4, Chicago 3.
Stanley Cup finals: Montreal 4, Boston 1.

1953-54

Team	W	L	T	Pts.	GF	GA
Detroit Red Wings	37	19	14	88	191	132
Montreal Canadiens	35	24	11	81	195	141
Toronto Maple Leafs	32	24	14	78	152	131
Boston Bruins	32	28	10	74	177	181
New York Rangers	29	31	10	68	161	182
Chicago Blackhawks	12	51	7	31	133	242

PLAYOFFS

League semifinals: Detroit 4, Toronto 1; Montreal 4, Boston 0.
Stanley Cup finals: Detroit 4, Montreal 3.

1954-55

Team	W	L	T	Pts.	GF	GA
Detroit Red Wings	42	17	11	95	204	134
Montreal Canadiens	41	18	11	93	228	157
Toronto Maple Leafs	24	24	22	70	147	135
Boston Bruins	23	26	21	67	169	188
New York Rangers	17	35	18	52	150	210
Chicago Blackhawks	13	40	17	43	161	235

PLAYOFFS

League semifinals: Detroit 4, Toronto 0; Montreal 4, Boston 1.
Stanley Cup finals: Detroit 4, Montreal 3.

1955-56

Team	W	L	T	Pts.	GF	GA
Montreal Canadiens	45	15	10	100	222	131
Detroit Red Wings	30	24	16	76	183	148
New York Rangers	32	28	10	74	204	203
Toronto Maple Leafs	24	33	13	61	153	181
Boston Bruins	23	34	13	59	147	185
Chicago Blackhawks	19	39	12	50	155	216

PLAYOFFS

League semifinals: Montreal 4, New York 1; Detroit 4, Toronto 1.
Stanley Cup finals: Montreal 4, Detroit 1.

1956-57

Team	W	L	T	Pts.	GF	GA
Detroit Red Wings	38	20	12	88	198	157
Montreal Canadiens	35	23	12	82	210	155
Boston Bruins	34	24	12	80	195	174
New York Rangers	26	30	14	66	184	227
Toronto Maple Leafs	21	34	15	57	174	192
Chicago Blackhawks	16	39	15	47	169	225

PLAYOFFS

League semifinals: Boston 4, Detroit 1; Montreal 4, New York 1.
Stanley Cup finals: Montreal 4, Boston 1.

1957-58

Team	W	L	T	Pts.	GF	GA
Montreal Canadiens	43	17	10	96	250	158
New York Rangers	32	25	13	77	195	188
Detroit Red Wings	29	29	12	70	176	207
Boston Bruins	27	28	15	69	199	194
Chicago Blackhawks	24	39	7	55	163	202
Toronto Maple Leafs	21	38	11	53	192	226

PLAYOFFS

League semifinals: Montreal 4, Detroit 0; Boston 4, New York 2.
Stanley Cup finals: Montreal 4, Boston 2.

1958-59

Team	W	L	T	Pts.	GF	GA
Montreal Canadiens	39	18	13	91	258	158
Boston Bruins	32	29	9	73	205	215
Chicago Blackhawks	28	29	13	69	197	208
Toronto Maple Leafs	27	32	11	65	189	201
New York Rangers	26	32	12	64	201	217
Detroit Red Wings	25	37	8	58	167	218

PLAYOFFS

League semifinals: Montreal 4, Chicago 2; Toronto 4, Boston 3.
Stanley Cup finals: Montreal 4, Toronto 1.

1959-60

Team	W	L	T	Pts.	GF	GA
Montreal Canadiens	40	18	12	92	255	178
Toronto Maple Leafs	35	26	9	79	199	195
Chicago Blackhawks	28	29	13	69	191	180
Detroit Red Wings	26	29	15	67	186	197
Boston Bruins	28	34	8	64	220	241
New York Rangers	17	38	15	49	187	247

PLAYOFFS

League semifinals: Montreal 4, Chicago 0; Toronto 4, Detroit 2.
Stanley Cup finals: Montreal 4, Toronto 0.

1960-61

Team	W	L	T	Pts.	GF	GA
Montreal Canadiens	41	19	10	92	254	188
Toronto Maple Leafs	39	19	12	90	234	176
Chicago Blackhawks	29	24	17	75	198	180
Detroit Red Wings	25	29	16	66	195	215
New York Rangers	22	38	10	54	204	248
Boston Bruins	15	42	13	43	176	254

PLAYOFFS

League semifinals: Chicago 4, Montreal 2; Detroit 4, Toronto 1.
Stanley Cup finals: Chicago 4, Detroit 2.

1961-62

Team	W	L	T	Pts.	GF	GA
Montreal Canadiens	42	14	14	98	259	166
Toronto Maple Leafs	37	22	11	85	232	180
Chicago Blackhawks	31	26	13	75	217	186
New York Rangers	26	32	12	64	195	207
Detroit Red Wings	23	33	14	60	184	219
Boston Bruins	15	47	8	38	177	306

PLAYOFFS

League semifinals: Chicago 4, Montreal 2; Toronto 4, New York 2.
Stanley Cup finals: Toronto 4, Chicago 2.

1962-63

Team	W	L	T	Pts.	GF	GA
Toronto Maple Leafs	35	23	12	82	221	180
Chicago Blackhawks	32	21	17	81	194	178
Montreal Canadiens	28	19	23	79	225	183
Detroit Red Wings	32	25	13	77	200	194
New York Rangers	22	36	12	56	211	233
Boston Bruins	14	39	17	45	198	281

PLAYOFFS

League semifinals: Toronto 4, Montreal 1; Detroit 4, Chicago 2.
Stanley Cup finals: Toronto 4, Detroit 1.

1963-64

Team	W	L	T	Pts.	GF	GA
Montreal Canadiens	36	21	13	85	209	167
Chicago Blackhawks	36	22	12	84	218	169
Toronto Maple Leafs	33	25	12	78	192	172
Detroit Red Wings	30	29	11	71	191	204
New York Rangers	22	38	10	54	186	242
Boston Bruins	18	40	12	48	170	212

PLAYOFFS

League semifinals: Toronto 4, Montreal 3; Detroit 4, Chicago 3.
Stanley Cup finals: Toronto 4, Detroit 3.

1964-65

Team	W	L	T	Pts.	GF	GA
Detroit Red Wings	40	23	7	87	224	175
Montreal Canadiens	36	23	11	83	211	185
Chicago Blackhawks	34	28	8	76	224	176
Toronto Maple Leafs	30	26	14	74	204	173
New York Rangers	20	38	12	52	179	246
Boston Bruins	21	43	6	48	166	253

PLAYOFFS

League semifinals: Chicago 4, Detroit 3; Montreal 4, Toronto 2.
Stanley Cup finals: Montreal 4, Chicago 3.

1965-66

Team	W	L	T	Pts.	GF	GA
Montreal Canadiens	41	21	8	90	239	173
Chicago Blackhawks	37	25	8	82	240	187
Toronto Maple Leafs	34	25	11	79	208	187
Detroit Red Wings	31	27	12	74	221	194
Boston Bruins	21	43	6	48	174	275
New York Rangers	18	41	11	47	195	261

PLAYOFFS

League semifinals: Montreal 4, Toronto 0; Detroit 4, Chicago 2.
Stanley Cup finals: Montreal 4, Detroit 2.

1966-67

Team	W	L	T	Pts.	GF	GA
Chicago Blackhawks	41	17	12	94	264	170
Montreal Canadiens	32	25	13	77	202	188
Toronto Maple Leafs	32	27	11	75	204	211
New York Rangers	30	28	12	72	188	189
Detroit Red Wings	27	39	4	58	212	241
Boston Bruins	17	43	10	44	182	253

PLAYOFFS

League semifinals: Toronto 4, Chicago 2; Montreal 4, New York 0.
Stanley Cup finals: Toronto 4, Montreal 2.

1967-68

EAST DIVISION

Team	W	L	T	Pts.	GF	GA
Montreal Canadiens	42	22	10	94	236	167
New York Rangers	39	23	12	90	226	183
Boston Bruins	37	27	10	84	259	216
Chicago Blackhawks	32	26	16	80	212	222
Toronto Maple Leafs	33	31	10	76	209	176
Detroit Red Wings	27	35	12	66	245	257

WEST DIVISION

Team	W	L	T	Pts.	GF	GA
Philadelphia Flyers	31	32	11	73	173	179
Los Angeles Kings	31	33	10	72	200	224

Team	W	L	T	Pts.	GF	GA
St. Louis Blues	27	31	16	70	177	191
Minnesota North Stars	27	32	15	69	191	226
Pittsburgh Penguins	27	34	13	67	195	216
Oakland Seals	15	42	17	42	153	219

PLAYOFFS

Division semifinals: Montreal 4, Boston 0; Chicago 4, New York 2; St. Louis 4, Philadelphia 3; Minnesota 4, Los Angeles 3. **Division finals:** Montreal 4, Chicago 1; St. Louis 4, Minnesota 3.
Stanley Cup finals: Montreal 4, St. Louis 0.

1968-69

EAST DIVISION

Team	W	L	T	Pts.	GF	GA
Montreal Canadiens	46	19	11	103	271	202
Boston Bruins	42	18	16	100	303	221
New York Rangers	41	26	9	91	231	196
Toronto Maple Leafs	35	26	15	85	234	217
Detroit Red Wings	33	31	12	78	239	221
Chicago Blackhawks	34	33	9	77	280	246

WEST DIVISION

Team	W	L	T	Pts.	GF	GA
St. Louis Blues	37	25	14	88	204	157
Oakland Seals	29	36	11	69	219	251
Philadelphia Flyers	20	35	21	61	174	225
Los Angeles Kings	24	42	10	58	185	260
Pittsburgh Penguins	20	45	11	51	189	270
Minnesota North Stars	18	43	15	51	189	252

PLAYOFFS

Division semifinals: Montreal 4, New York 0; Boston 4, Toronto 0; St. Louis 4, Philadelphia 0; Los Angeles 4, Oakland 3. **Division finals:** Montreal 4, Boston 2; St. Louis 4, Los Angeles 0.
Stanley Cup finals: Montreal 4, St. Louis 0.

1969-70

EAST DIVISION

Team	W	L	T	Pts.	GF	GA
Chicago Blackhawks	45	22	9	99	250	170
Boston Bruins	40	17	19	99	277	216
Detroit Red Wings	40	21	15	95	246	199
New York Rangers	38	22	16	92	246	189
Montreal Canadiens	38	22	16	92	244	201
Toronto Maple Leafs	29	34	13	71	222	242

WEST DIVISION

Team	W	L	T	Pts.	GF	GA
St. Louis Blues	37	27	12	86	224	179
Pittsburgh Penguins	26	38	12	64	182	238
Minnesota North Stars	19	35	22	60	224	257
Oakland Seals	22	40	14	58	169	243
Philadelphia Flyers	17	35	24	58	197	225
Los Angeles Kings	14	52	10	38	168	290

PLAYOFFS

Division semifinals: Chicago 4, Detroit 0; Boston 4, N.Y. Rangers 2; St. Louis 4, Minnesota 2; Pittsburgh 4, Oakland 0. **Division finals:** Boston 4, Chicago 0; St. Louis 4, Pittsburgh 2.
Stanley Cup finals: Boston 4, St. Louis 0.

1970-71

EAST DIVISION

Team	W	L	T	Pts.	GF	GA
Boston Bruins	57	14	7	121	399	207
New York Rangers	49	18	11	109	259	177
Montreal Canadiens	42	23	13	97	291	216
Toronto Maple Leafs	37	33	8	82	248	211
Buffalo Sabres	24	39	15	63	217	291
Vancouver Canucks	24	46	8	56	229	296
Detroit Red Wings	22	45	11	55	209	308

WEST DIVISION

Team	W	L	T	Pts.	GF	GA
Chicago Blackhawks	49	20	9	107	277	184
St. Louis Blues	34	25	19	87	223	208
Philadelphia Flyers	28	33	17	73	207	225
Minnesota North Stars	28	34	16	72	191	223
Los Angeles Kings	25	40	13	63	239	303
Pittsburgh Penguins	21	37	20	62	221	240
California Golden Seals	20	53	5	45	199	320

PLAYOFFS

Division semifinals: Montreal 4, Boston 3; N.Y Rangers 4, Toronto 2; Chicago 4, Philadelphia 0; Minnesota 4, St. Louis 2. **Division finals:** Montreal 4, Minnesota 2; Chicago 4, N.Y. Rangers 3.
Stanley Cup finals: Montreal 4, Chicago 3.

1971-72

EAST DIVISION

Team	W	L	T	Pts.	GF	GA
Boston Bruins	54	13	11	119	330	204
New York Rangers	48	17	13	109	317	192
Montreal Canadiens	46	16	16	108	307	205
Toronto Maple Leafs	33	31	14	80	209	208
Detroit Red Wings	33	35	10	76	261	262
Buffalo Sabres	16	43	19	51	203	289
Vancouver Canucks	20	50	8	48	203	297

WEST DIVISION

Team	W	L	T	Pts.	GF	GA
Chicago Blackhawks	46	17	15	107	256	166
Minnesota North Stars	37	29	12	86	212	191
St. Louis Blues	28	39	11	67	208	247
Philadelphia Flyers	26	38	14	66	220	258
Pittsburgh Penguins	26	38	14	66	200	236
California Golden Seals	21	39	18	60	216	288
Los Angeles Kings	20	49	9	49	206	305

PLAYOFFS

Division semifinals: Boston 4, Toronto 1; N.Y. Rangers 4, Montreal 2; Chicago 4, Pittsburgh 0; St. Louis 4, Minnesota 3. **Division finals:** N.Y. Rangers 4, Chicago 0; Boston 4, St. Louis 0.
Stanley Cup finals: Boston 4, N.Y. Rangers 2.

1972-73

EAST DIVISION

Team	W	L	T	Pts.	GF	GA
Montreal Canadiens	52	10	16	120	329	184
Boston Bruins	51	22	5	107	330	235
New York Rangers	47	23	8	102	297	208
Buffalo Sabres	37	27	14	88	257	219
Detroit Red Wings	37	29	12	86	265	243
Toronto Maple Leafs	27	41	10	64	247	279
Vancouver Canucks	22	47	9	53	233	339
New York Islanders	12	60	6	30	170	347

WEST DIVISION

Team	W	L	T	Pts.	GF	GA
Chicago Blackhawks	42	27	9	93	284	225
Philadelphia Flyers	37	30	11	85	296	256
Minnesota North Stars	37	30	11	85	254	230
St. Louis Blues	32	34	12	76	233	251
Pittsburgh Penguins	32	37	9	73	257	265

Team	W	L	T	Pts.	GF	GA
Los Angeles Kings	31	36	11	73	232	245
Atlanta Flames	25	38	15	65	191	239
California Golden Seals	16	46	16	48	213	323

PLAYOFFS

Division semifinals: Montreal 4, Buffalo 2; N.Y. Rangers 4, Boston 1; Chicago 4, St. Louis 1; Philadelphia 4, Minnesota 2. **Division finals:** Montreal 4, Philadelphia 1; Chicago 4, N.Y. Rangers 1.

Stanley Cup finals: Montreal 4, Chicago 2.

1973-74

EAST DIVISION

Team	W	L	T	Pts.	GF	GA
Boston Bruins	52	17	9	113	349	221
Montreal Canadiens	45	42	9	99	293	240
New York Rangers	40	24	14	94	300	251
Toronto Maple Leafs	35	27	16	86	274	230
Buffalo Sabres	32	34	12	76	242	250
Detroit Red Wings	29	39	10	68	255	319
Vancouver Canucks	24	43	11	59	224	296
New York Islanders	19	41	18	56	182	247

WEST DIVISION

Team	W	L	T	Pts.	GF	GA
Philadelphia Flyers	50	16	12	112	273	164
Chicago Blackhawks	41	14	23	105	272	164
Los Angeles Kings	33	33	12	78	233	231
Atlanta Flames	30	34	14	74	214	238
Pittsburgh Penguins	28	41	9	65	242	273
St. Louis Blues	26	40	12	64	206	248
Minnesota North Stars	23	38	17	63	235	275
California Golden Seals	13	55	10	36	195	342

PLAYOFFS

Division semifinals: Boston 4, Toronto 0; N.Y. Rangers 4, Montreal 2; Philadelphia 4, Atlanta 0; Chicago 4, Los Angeles 1. **Division finals:** Boston 4, Chicago 2; Philadelphia 4, N.Y. Rangers 3.

Stanley Cup finals: Philadelphia 4, Boston 2.

1974-75

PRINCE OF WALES CONFERENCE

ADAMS DIVISION

Team	W	L	T	Pts.	GF	GA
Buffalo Sabres	49	16	15	113	354	240
Boston Bruins	40	26	14	94	345	245
Toronto Maple Leafs	31	33	16	78	280	309
California Golden Seals	19	48	13	51	212	316

NORRIS DIVISION

Team	W	L	T	Pts.	GF	GA
Montreal Canadiens	47	14	19	113	374	225
Los Angeles Kings	42	17	21	105	269	185
Pittsburgh Penguins	37	28	15	89	326	289
Detroit Red Wings	23	45	12	58	259	335
Washington Capitals	8	67	5	21	181	446

CLARENCE CAMPBELL CONFERENCE

PATRICK DIVISION

Team	W	L	T	Pts.	GF	GA
Philadelphia Flyers	51	18	11	113	293	181
New York Rangers	37	29	14	88	319	276
New York Islanders	33	25	22	88	264	221
Atlanta Flames	34	31	15	83	243	233

SMYTHE DIVISION

Team	W	L	T	Pts.	GF	GA
Vancouver Canucks	38	32	10	86	271	254
St. Louis Blues	35	31	14	84	269	267
Chicago Blackhawks	37	35	8	82	268	241
Minnesota North Stars	23	50	7	53	221	341
Kansas City Scouts	15	54	11	41	184	328

PLAYOFFS

Preliminaries: Toronto 2, Los Angeles 1; Chicago 2, Boston 1; Pittsburgh 2, St. Louis 0; N.Y. Islanders 2, N.Y. Rangers 1. **Quarterfinals:** Philadelphia 4, Toronto 0; Buffalo 4, Chicago 1; Montreal 4, Vancouver 1; N.Y. Islanders 4, Pittsburgh 3. **Semifinals:** Philadelphia 4, N.Y. Islanders 3; Buffalo 4, Montreal 2.

Stanley Cup finals: Philadelphia 4, Buffalo 2.

1975-76

PRINCE OF WALES CONFERENCE

ADAMS DIVISION

Team	W	L	T	Pts.	GF	GA
Boston Bruins	48	15	17	113	313	237
Buffalo Sabres	46	21	13	105	339	240
Toronto Maple Leafs	34	31	15	83	294	276
California Golden Seals	27	42	11	65	250	278

NORRIS DIVISION

Team	W	L	T	Pts.	GF	GA
Montreal Canadiens	58	11	11	127	337	174
Los Angeles Kings	38	33	9	85	263	265
Pittsburgh Penguins	35	33	12	82	339	303
Detroit Red Wings	26	44	10	62	226	300
Washington Capitals	11	59	10	32	224	394

CLARENCE CAMPBELL CONFERENCE

PATRICK DIVISION

Team	W	L	T	Pts.	GF	GA
Philadelphia Flyers	51	13	16	118	348	209
New York Islanders	42	21	17	101	297	190
Atlanta Flames	35	33	12	82	262	237
New York Rangers	29	42	9	67	262	333

SMYTHE DIVISION

Team	W	L	T	Pts.	GF	GA
Chicago Blackhawks	32	30	18	82	254	261
Vancouver Canucks	33	32	15	81	271	272
St. Louis Blues	29	37	14	72	249	290
Minnesota North Stars	20	53	7	47	195	303
Kansas City Scouts	12	56	12	36	190	351

PLAYOFFS

Preliminaries: Buffalo 2, St. Louis 1; N.Y. Islanders 2, Vancouver 0; Los Angeles 2, Atlanta 0; Toronto 2, Pittsburgh 1. **Quarterfinals:** Montreal 4, Chicago 0; Philadelphia 4, Toronto 3; Boston 4, Los Angeles 3; N.Y. Islanders 4, Buffalo 2. **Semifinals:** Montreal 4, N.Y. Islanders 1; Philadelphia 4, Boston 1.

Stanley Cup finals: Montreal 4, Philadelphia 0.

1976-77

PRINCE OF WALES CONFERENCE

ADAMS DIVISION

Team	W	L	T	Pts.	GF	GA
Boston Bruins	49	23	8	106	312	240
Buffalo Sabres	48	24	8	104	301	220
Toronto Maple Leafs	33	32	15	81	301	285
Cleveland Barons	25	42	13	63	240	292

NORRIS DIVISION

Team	W	L	T	Pts.	GF	GA
Montreal Canadiens	60	8	12	132	387	171
Los Angeles Kings	34	31	15	83	271	241
Pittsburgh Penguins	34	33	13	81	240	252
Washington Capitals	24	42	14	62	221	307
Detroit Red Wings	16	55	9	41	183	309

CLARENCE CAMPBELL CONFERENCE

PATRICK DIVISION

Team	W	L	T	Pts.	GF	GA
Philadelphia Flyers	48	16	16	112	323	213
New York Islanders	47	21	12	106	288	193
Atlanta Flames	34	34	12	80	264	265
New York Rangers	29	37	14	72	272	310

SMYTHE DIVISION

Team	W	L	T	Pts.	GF	GA
St. Louis Blues	32	39	9	73	239	276
Minnesota North Stars	23	39	18	64	240	310
Chicago Blackhawks	26	43	11	63	240	298
Vancouver Canucks	25	42	13	63	235	294
Colorado Rockies	20	46	14	54	226	307

PLAYOFFS

Preliminaries: N.Y. Islanders 2, Chicago 0; Buffalo 2, Minnesota 0; Los Angeles 2, Atlanta 1; Toronto 2, Pittsburgh 1. **Quarterfinals:** Montreal 4, St. Louis 0; Philadelphia 4, Toronto 2; Boston 4, Los Angeles 2; N.Y. Islanders 4, Buffalo 0. **Semifinals:** Montreal 4, N.Y. Islanders 2; Boston 4, Philadelphia 0.

Stanley Cup finals: Montreal 4, Boston 0.

1977-78

PRINCE OF WALES CONFERENCE

ADAMS DIVISION

Team	W	L	T	Pts.	GF	GA
Boston Bruins	51	18	11	113	333	218
Buffalo Sabres	44	19	17	105	288	215
Toronto Maple Leafs	41	29	10	92	271	237
Cleveland Barons	22	45	13	57	230	325

NORRIS DIVISION

Team	W	L	T	Pts.	GF	GA
Montreal Canadiens	59	10	11	129	359	183
Detroit Red Wings	32	34	14	78	252	266
Los Angeles Kings	31	34	15	77	243	245
Pittsburgh Penguins	25	37	18	68	254	321
Washington Capitals	17	49	14	48	195	321

CLARENCE CAMPBELL CONFERENCE

PATRICK DIVISION

Team	W	L	T	Pts.	GF	GA
New York Islanders	48	17	15	111	334	210
Philadelphia Flyers	45	20	15	105	296	200
Atlanta Flames	34	27	19	87	274	252
New York Rangers	30	37	13	73	279	280

SMYTHE DIVISION

Team	W	L	T	Pts.	GF	GA
Chicago Blackhawks	32	29	19	83	230	220
Colorado Rockies	19	40	21	59	257	305
Vancouver Canucks	20	43	17	57	239	320
St. Louis Blues	20	47	13	53	195	304
Minnesota North Stars	18	53	9	45	218	325

PLAYOFFS

Preliminaries: Philadelphia 2, Colorado 0; Buffalo 2, N.Y. Rangers 1; Toronto 2, Los Angeles 0; Detroit 2, Atlanta 0. **Quarterfinals:** Montreal 4, Detroit 1; Boston 4, Chicago 0; Toronto 4, N.Y. Islanders 3; Philadelphia 4, Buffalo 1. **Semifinals:** Montreal 4, Toronto 0; Boston 4, Philadelphia 1.

Stanley Cup finals: Montreal 4, Boston 2.

1978-79

PRINCE OF WALES CONFERENCE

ADAMS DIVISION

Team	W	L	T	Pts.	GF	GA
Boston Bruins	43	23	14	100	316	270
Buffalo Sabres	36	28	16	88	280	263
Toronto Maple Leafs	34	33	13	81	267	252
Minnesota North Stars	28	40	12	68	257	289

NORRIS DIVISION

Team	W	L	T	Pts.	GF	GA
Montreal Canadiens	52	17	11	115	337	204
Pittsburgh Penguins	36	31	13	85	281	279
Los Angeles Kings	34	34	12	80	292	286
Washington Capitals	24	41	15	63	273	338
Detroit Red Wings	23	41	16	62	252	295

CLARENCE CAMPBELL CONFERENCE

PATRICK DIVISION

Team	W	L	T	Pts.	GF	GA
New York Islanders	51	15	14	116	358	214
Philadelphia Flyers	40	25	15	95	281	248
New York Rangers	40	29	11	91	316	292
Atlanta Flames	41	31	8	90	327	280

SMYTHE DIVISION

Team	W	L	T	Pts.	GF	GA
Chicago Blackhawks	29	36	15	73	244	277
Vancouver Canucks	25	42	13	63	217	291
St. Louis Blues	18	50	12	48	249	348
Colorado Rockies	15	53	12	42	210	331

PLAYOFFS

Preliminaries: Philadelphia 2, Vancouver 1; N.Y. Rangers 2, Los Angeles 0; Toronto 2, Atlanta 0; Pittsburgh 2, Buffalo 1. **Quarterfinals:** N.Y. Islanders 4, Chicago 0; Montreal 4, Toronto 0; Boston 4, Pittsburgh 0; N.Y. Rangers 4, Philadelphia 1. **Semifinals:** N.Y. Rangers 4, N.Y. Islanders 2; Montreal 4, Boston 3.

Stanley Cup finals: Montreal 4, N.Y. Rangers 1.

1979-80

PRINCE OF WALES CONFERENCE

ADAMS DIVISION

Team	W	L	T	Pts.	GF	GA
Buffalo Sabres	47	17	16	110	318	201
Boston Bruins	46	21	13	105	310	234
Minnesota North Stars	36	28	16	88	311	253
Toronto Maple Leafs	35	40	5	75	304	327
Quebec Nordiques	25	44	11	61	248	313

NORRIS DIVISION

Team	W	L	T	Pts.	GF	GA
Montreal Canadiens	47	20	13	107	328	240
Los Angeles Kings	30	36	14	74	290	313
Pittsburgh Penguins	30	37	13	73	251	303
Hartford Whalers	27	34	19	73	303	312
Detroit Red Wings	26	43	11	63	268	306

CLARENCE CAMPBELL CONFERENCE

PATRICK DIVISION

Team	W	L	T	Pts.	GF	GA
Philadelphia Flyers	48	12	20	116	327	254
New York Islanders	39	28	13	91	281	247

Team	W	L	T	Pts.	GF	GA
New York Rangers	38	32	10	86	308	284
Atlanta Flames	35	32	13	83	282	269
Washington Capitals	27	40	13	67	261	293

SMYTHE DIVISION

Team	W	L	T	Pts.	GF	GA
Chicago Blackhawks	34	27	19	87	241	250
St. Louis Blues	34	34	12	80	266	278
Vancouver Canucks	27	37	16	70	256	281
Edmonton Oilers	28	39	13	69	301	322
Winnipeg Jets	20	49	11	51	214	314
Colorado Rockies	19	48	13	51	234	308

PLAYOFFS

Preliminaries: Philadelphia 3, Edmonton 0; Buffalo 3, Vancouver 1; Montreal 3, Hartford 0; Boston 3, Pittsburgh 2; N.Y. Islanders 3, Los Angeles 1; Minnesota 3, Toronto 0; Chicago 3, St. Louis 0; N.Y. Rangers 3, Atlanta 1. **Quarterfinals:** Philadelphia 4, N.Y. Rangers 1; Buffalo 4, Chicago 0; Minnesota 4, Montreal 3; N.Y. Islanders 4, Boston 1. **Semifinals:** Philadelphia 4, Minnesota 1; N.Y. Islanders 4, Buffalo 2.

Stanley Cup finals: N.Y. Islanders 4, Philadelphia 2.

1980-81

PRINCE OF WALES CONFERENCE

ADAMS DIVISION

Team	W	L	T	Pts.	GF	GA
Buffalo Sabres	39	20	21	99	327	250
Boston Bruins	37	30	13	87	316	272
Minnesota North Stars	35	28	17	87	291	263
Quebec Nordiques	30	32	18	78	314	318
Toronto Maple Leafs	28	37	15	71	322	367

NORRIS DIVISION

Team	W	L	T	Pts.	GF	GA
Montreal Canadiens	45	22	13	103	332	232
Los Angeles Kings	43	24	13	99	337	290
Pittsburgh Penguins	30	37	13	73	302	345
Hartford Whalers	21	41	18	60	292	372
Detroit Red Wings	19	43	18	56	252	339

CLARENCE CAMPBELL CONFERENCE

PATRICK DIVISION

Team	W	L	T	Pts.	GF	GA
New York Islanders	48	18	14	110	355	260
Philadelphia Flyers	41	24	15	97	313	249
Calgary Flames	39	27	14	92	329	298
New York Rangers	30	36	14	74	312	317
Washington Capitals	26	36	18	70	286	317

SMYTHE DIVISION

Team	W	L	T	Pts.	GF	GA
St. Louis Blues	45	18	17	107	352	281
Chicago Blackhawks	31	33	16	78	304	315
Vancouver Canucks	28	32	20	76	289	301
Edmonton Oilers	29	35	16	74	328	327
Colorado Rockies	22	45	13	57	258	344
Winnipeg Jets	9	57	14	32	246	400

PLAYOFFS

Preliminaries: N.Y. Islanders 3, Toronto 0; St. Louis 3, Pittsburgh 2; Edmonton 3, Montreal 0; N.Y. Rangers 3, Los Angeles 1; Buffalo 3, Vancouver 0; Philadelphia 3, Quebec 2; Calgary 3, Chicago 0; Minnesota 3, Boston 0. **Quarterfinals:** N.Y. Islanders 4, Edmonton 2; N.Y. Rangers 4, St. Louis 2; Minnesota 4, Buffalo 1; Calgary 4, Philadelphia 3. **Semifinals:** N.Y. Islanders 4, N.Y. Rangers 0; Minnesota 4, Calgary 2.

Stanley Cup finals: N.Y. Islanders 4, Minnesota 1.

1981-82

PRINCE OF WALES CONFERENCE

ADAMS DIVISION

Team	W	L	T	Pts.	GF	GA
Montreal Canadiens	46	17	17	109	360	223
Boston Bruins	43	27	10	96	323	285
Buffalo Sabres	39	26	15	93	307	273
Quebec Nordiques	33	31	16	82	356	345
Hartford Whalers	21	41	18	60	264	351

PATRICK DIVISION

Team	W	L	T	Pts.	GF	GA
New York Islanders	54	16	10	118	385	250
New York Rangers	39	27	14	92	316	306
Philadelphia Flyers	38	31	11	87	325	313
Pittsburgh Penguins	31	36	13	75	310	337
Washington Capitals	26	41	13	65	319	338

CLARENCE CAMPBELL CONFERENCE

NORRIS DIVISION

Team	W	L	T	Pts.	GF	GA
Minnesota North Stars	37	23	20	94	346	288
Winnipeg Jets	33	33	14	80	319	332
St. Louis Blues	32	40	8	72	315	349
Chicago Blackhawks	30	38	12	72	332	363
Toronto Maple Leafs	20	44	16	56	298	380
Detroit Red Wings	21	47	12	54	270	351

SMYTHE DIVISION

Team	W	L	T	Pts.	GF	GA
Edmonton Oilers	48	17	15	111	417	295
Vancouver Canucks	30	33	17	77	290	286
Calgary Flames	29	34	17	75	334	345
Los Angeles Kings	24	41	15	63	314	369
Colorado Rockies	18	49	13	49	241	362

PLAYOFFS

Wales Conference division semifinals: Quebec 3, Montreal 2; Boston 3, Buffalo 1; N.Y. Islanders 3, Pittsburgh 2; N.Y. Rangers 3, Philadelphia 1. **Division finals:** Quebec 4, Boston 3; N.Y. Islanders 4, N.Y. Rangers 2. **Conference finals:** N.Y. Islanders 4, Quebec 0.

Campbell Conference division semifinals: Chicago 3, Minnesota 1; St. Louis 3, Winnipeg 1; Los Angeles 3, Edmonton 2; Vancouver 3, Calgary 0. **Division finals:** Chicago 4, St. Louis 2; Vancouver 4, Los Angeles 1. **Conference finals:** Vancouver 4, Chicago 1.

Stanley Cup finals: N.Y. Islanders 4, Vancouver 0.

1982-83

PRINCE OF WALES CONFERENCE

ADAMS DIVISION

Team	W	L	T	Pts.	GF	GA
Boston Bruins	50	20	10	110	327	228
Montreal Canadiens	42	24	14	98	350	286
Buffalo Sabres	38	29	13	89	318	285
Quebec Nordiques	34	34	12	80	343	336
Hartford Whalers	19	54	7	45	261	403

PATRICK DIVISION

Team	W	L	T	Pts.	GF	GA
Philadelphia Flyers	49	23	8	106	326	240
New York Islanders	42	26	12	96	302	226
Washington Capitals	39	25	16	94	306	283
New York Rangers	35	35	10	80	306	287
New Jersey Devils	17	49	14	48	230	338
Pittsburgh Penguins	18	53	9	45	257	394

CLARENCE CAMPBELL CONFERENCE

NORRIS DIVISION

Team	W	L	T	Pts.	GF	GA
Chicago Blackhawks	47	23	10	104	338	268
Minnesota North Stars	40	24	16	96	321	290
Toronto Maple Leafs	28	40	12	68	293	330
St. Louis Blues	25	40	15	65	285	316
Detroit Red Wings	21	44	15	57	263	344

SMYTHE DIVISION

Team	W	L	T	Pts.	GF	GA
Edmonton Oilers	47	21	12	106	424	315
Calgary Flames	32	34	14	78	321	317
Vancouver Canucks	30	35	15	75	303	309
Winnipeg Jets	33	39	8	74	311	333
Los Angeles Kings	27	41	12	66	308	365

PLAYOFFS

Wales Conference division semifinals: Boston 3, Quebec 1; Buffalo 3, Montreal 0; N.Y. Rangers 3, Philadelphia 0; N.Y. Islanders 3, Washington 1. **Division finals:** Boston 4, Buffalo 3; N.Y. Islanders 4, N.Y. Rangers 2. **Conference finals:** N.Y. Islanders 4, Boston 2.

Campbell Conference division semifinals: Chicago 3, St. Louis 1; Minnesota 3, Toronto 1; Edmonton 3, Winnipeg 0; Calgary 3, Vancouver 1. **Division finals:** Chicago 4, Minnesota 1; Edmonton 4, Calgary 1. **Conference finals:** Edmonton 4, Chicago 0.

Stanley Cup finals: N.Y. Islanders 4, Edmonton 0.

1983-84

PRINCE OF WALES CONFERENCE

ADAMS DIVISION

Team	W	L	T	Pts.	GF	GA
Boston Bruins	49	25	6	104	336	261
Buffalo Sabres	48	25	7	103	315	257
Quebec Nordiques	42	28	10	94	360	278
Montreal Canadiens	35	40	5	75	286	295
Hartford Whalers	28	42	10	66	288	320

PATRICK DIVISION

Team	W	L	T	Pts.	GF	GA
New York Islanders	50	26	4	104	357	269
Washington Capitals	48	27	5	101	308	226
Philadelphia Flyers	44	26	10	98	350	290
New York Rangers	42	29	9	93	314	304
New Jersey Devils	17	56	7	41	231	350
Pittsburgh Penguins	16	58	6	38	254	390

CLARENCE CAMPBELL CONFERENCE

NORRIS DIVISION

Team	W	L	T	Pts.	GF	GA
Minnesota North Stars	39	31	10	88	345	344
St. Louis Blues	32	41	7	71	293	316
Detroit Red Wings	31	42	7	69	298	323
Chicago Blackhawks	30	42	8	68	277	311
Toronto Maple Leafs	26	45	9	61	303	387

SMYTHE DIVISION

Team	W	L	T	Pts.	GF	GA
Edmonton Oilers	57	18	5	119	446	314
Calgary Flames	34	32	14	82	311	314
Vancouver Canucks	32	39	9	73	306	328
Winnipeg Jets	31	38	11	73	340	374
Los Angeles Kings	23	44	13	59	309	376

PLAYOFFS

Wales Conference division semifinals: Montreal 3, Boston 0; Quebec 3, Buffalo 0; N.Y. Islanders 3, N.Y. Rangers 2; Washington 3, Philadelphia 0. **Division finals:** Montreal 4, Quebec 2; N.Y. Islanders 4, Washington 1. **Conference finals:** N.Y. Islanders 4, Montreal 2.

Campbell Conference division semifinals: Minnesota 3, Chicago 2; St. Louis 3, Detroit 1; Edmonton 3, Winnipeg 0; Calgary 3, Vancouver 1. **Division finals:** Minnesota 4, St. Louis 3; Edmonton 4, Calgary 3. **Conference finals:** Edmonton 4, Minnesota 0.

Stanley Cup finals: Edmonton 4, N.Y. Islanders 1.

1984-85

PRINCE OF WALES CONFERENCE

ADAMS DIVISION

Team	W	L	T	Pts.	GF	GA
Montreal Canadiens	41	27	12	94	309	262
Quebec Nordiques	41	30	9	91	323	275
Buffalo Sabres	38	28	14	90	290	237
Boston Bruins	36	34	10	82	303	287
Hartford Whalers	30	41	9	69	268	318

PATRICK DIVISION

Team	W	L	T	Pts.	GF	GA
Philadelphia Flyers	53	20	7	113	348	241
Washington Capitals	46	25	9	101	322	240
New York Islanders	40	34	6	86	345	312
New York Rangers	26	44	10	62	295	345
New Jersey Devils	22	48	10	54	264	346
Pittsburgh Penguins	24	51	5	53	276	385

CLARENCE CAMPBELL CONFERENCE

NORRIS DIVISION

Team	W	L	T	Pts.	GF	GA
St. Louis Blues	37	31	12	86	299	288
Chicago Blackhawks	38	35	7	83	309	299
Detroit Red Wings	27	41	12	66	313	357
Minnesota North Stars	25	43	12	62	268	321
Toronto Maple Leafs	20	52	8	48	253	358

SMYTHE DIVISION

Team	W	L	T	Pts.	GF	GA
Edmonton Oilers	49	20	11	109	401	298
Winnipeg Jets	43	27	10	96	358	332
Calgary Flames	41	27	12	94	363	302
Los Angeles Kings	34	32	14	82	339	326
Vancouver Canucks	25	46	9	59	284	401

PLAYOFFS

Wales Conference division semifinals: Montreal 3, Boston 2; Quebec 3, Buffalo 2; Philadelphia 3, N.Y. Rangers 0; N.Y. Islanders 3, Washington 2. **Division finals:** Quebec 4, Montreal 3; Philadelphia 4, N.Y. Islanders 1. **Conference finals:** Philadelphia 4, Quebec 2.

Campbell Conference division semifinals: Minnesota 3, St. Louis 0; Chicago 3, Detroit 0; Edmonton 3, Los Angelse 0; Winnipeg 3, Calgary 1. **Division finals:** Chicago 4, Minnesota 2; Edmonton 4, Winnipeg 0. **Conference finals:** Edmonton 4, Chicago 2.

Stanley Cup finals: Edmonton 4, Philadelphia 1.

1985-86

PRINCE OF WALES CONFERENCE

ADAMS DIVISION

Team	W	L	T	Pts.	GF	GA
Quebec Nordiques	43	31	6	92	330	289
Montreal Canadiens	40	33	7	87	330	280
Boston Bruins	37	31	12	86	311	288
Hartford Whalers	40	36	4	84	332	302
Buffalo Sabres	37	37	6	80	296	291

PATRICK DIVISION

Team	W	L	T	Pts.	GF	GA
Philadelphia Flyers	53	23	4	110	335	241
Washington Capitals	50	23	7	107	315	272
New York Islanders	39	29	12	90	327	284
New York Rangers	36	38	6	78	280	276
Pittsburgh Penguins	34	38	8	76	313	305
New Jersey Devils	28	49	3	59	300	374

CLARENCE CAMPBELL CONFERENCE

NORRIS DIVISION

Team	W	L	T	Pts.	GF	GA
Chicago Blackhawks	39	33	8	86	351	349
Minnesota North Stars	38	33	9	85	327	305
St. Louis Blues	37	34	9	83	302	291
Toronto Maple Leafs	25	48	7	57	311	386
Detroit Red Wings	17	57	6	40	266	415

SMYTHE DIVISION

Team	W	L	T	Pts.	GF	GA
Edmonton Oilers	56	17	7	119	426	310
Calgary Flames	40	31	9	89	354	315
Winnipeg Jets	26	47	7	59	295	372
Vancouver Canucks	23	44	13	59	282	333
Los Angeles Kings	23	49	8	54	284	389

PLAYOFFS

Wales Conference division semifinals: Hartford 3, Quebec 0; Montreal 3, Boston 0; N.Y. Rangers 3, Philadelphia 2; Washington 3, N.Y. Rangers 0. **Division finals:** Montreal 4, Hartford 3; N.Y. Rangers 4, Washington 2. **Conference finals:** Montreal 4, N.Y. Rangers 1.

Campbell Conference division semifinals: Toronto 3, Chicago 0; St. Louis 3, Minnesota 2; Edmonton 3, Vancouver 0; Calgary 3, Winnipeg 0. **Division finals:** St. Louis 4, Toronto 3; Calgary 4, Edmonton 3. **Conference finals:** Calgary 4, St. Louis 3.

Stanley Cup finals: Montreal 4, Calgary 1.

1986-87

PRINCE OF WALES CONFERENCE

ADAMS DIVISION

Team	W	L	T	Pts.	GF	GA
Hartford Whalers	43	30	7	93	287	270
Montreal Canadiens	41	29	10	92	277	241
Boston Bruins	39	34	7	85	301	276
Quebec Nordiques	31	39	10	72	267	276
Buffalo Sabres	28	44	8	64	280	308

PATRICK DIVISION

Team	W	L	T	Pts.	GF	GA
Philadelphia Flyers	46	26	8	100	310	245
Washington Capitals	38	32	10	86	285	278
New York Islanders	35	33	12	82	279	281
New York Rangers	34	38	8	76	307	323
Pittsburgh Penguins	30	38	12	72	297	290
New Jersey Devils	29	45	6	64	293	368

CLARENCE CAMPBELL CONFERENCE

NORRIS DIVISION

Team	W	L	T	Pts.	GF	GA
St. Louis Blues	32	33	15	79	281	293
Detroit Red Wings	34	36	10	78	260	274
Chicago Blackhawks	29	37	14	72	290	310
Toronto Maple Leafs	32	42	6	70	286	319
Minnesota North Stars	30	40	10	70	296	314

SMYTHE DIVISION

Team	W	L	T	Pts.	GF	GA
Edmonton Oilers	50	24	6	106	372	284
Calgary Flames	46	31	3	95	318	289
Winnipeg Jets	40	32	8	88	279	271
Los Angeles Kings	31	41	8	70	318	341
Vancouver Canucks	29	43	8	66	282	314

PLAYOFFS

Wales Conference division semifinals: Quebec 4, Hartford 2; Montreal 4, Boston 0; Philadelphia 4, N.Y. Rangers 2; N.Y. Islanders 4, Washington 3. **Division finals:** Montreal 4, Quebec 3; Philadelphia 4, N.Y. Islanders 3. **Conference finals:** Philadelphia 4, N.Y. Islanders 3.

Campbell Conference division semifinals: Toronto 4, St. Louis 2; Detroit 4, Chicago 0; Edmonton 4, Los Angeles 1; Winnipeg 4, Calgary 2. **Division finals:** Detroit 4, Toronto 3; Edmonton 4, Winnipeg 0. **Conference finals:** Edmonton 4, Detroit 1.

Stanley Cup finals: Edmonton 4, Philadelphia 3.

1987-88

PRINCE OF WALES CONFERENCE

ADAMS DIVISION

Team	W	L	T	Pts.	GF	GA
Montreal Canadiens	45	22	13	103	298	238
Boston Bruins	44	30	6	94	300	251
Buffalo Sabres	37	32	11	85	283	305
Hartford Whalers	35	38	7	77	249	267
Quebec Nordiques	32	43	5	69	271	306

PATRICK DIVISION

Team	W	L	T	Pts.	GF	GA
New York Islanders	39	31	10	88	308	267
Philadelphia Flyers	38	33	9	85	292	282
Washington Capitals	38	33	9	85	281	249
New Jersey Devils	38	36	6	82	295	296
New York Rangers	36	34	10	82	300	283
Pittsburgh Penguins	36	35	9	81	319	316

CLARENCE CAMPBELL CONFERENCE

NORRIS DIVISION

Team	W	L	T	Pts.	GF	GA
Detroit Red Wings	41	28	11	93	322	269
St. Louis Blues	34	38	8	76	278	294
Chicago Blackhawks	30	41	9	69	284	326
Toronto Maple Leafs	21	49	10	52	273	345
Minnesota North Stars	19	48	13	51	242	349

SMYTHE DIVISION

Team	W	L	T	Pts.	GF	GA
Calgary Flames	48	23	9	105	397	305
Edmonton Oilers	44	25	11	99	363	288
Winnipeg Jets	33	36	11	77	292	310
Los Angeles Kings	30	42	8	68	318	359
Vancouver Canucks	25	46	9	59	272	320

PLAYOFFS

Wales Conference division semifinals: Montreal 4, Hartford 2; Boston 4, Buffalo 2; New Jersey 4, N.Y. Islanders 2; Washington 4, Philadelphia 3. **Division finals:** Boston 4, Montreal 1; New Jersey 4, Washington 3. **Conference finals:** Boston 4, New Jersey 3.

Campbell Conference division semifinals: Detroit 4, Toronto 2; St. Louis 4, Chicago 1; Calgary 4, Los Angeles 1; Edmonton 4, Winnipeg 1. **Division finals:** Detroit 4, St. Louis 1; Edmonton 4, Calgary 0. **Conference finals:** Edmonton 4, Detroit 1.

Stanley Cup finals: Edmonton 4, Boston 0.

1988-89

PRINCE OF WALES CONFERENCE

ADAMS DIVISION

Team	W	L	T	Pts.	GF	GA
Montreal Canadiens	53	18	9	115	315	218
Boston Bruins	37	29	14	88	289	256
Buffalo Sabres	38	35	7	83	291	299
Hartford Whalers	37	38	5	79	299	290
Quebec Nordiques	27	46	7	61	269	342

PATRICK DIVISION

Team	W	L	T	Pts.	GF	GA
Washington Capitals	41	29	10	92	305	259
Pittsburgh Penguins	40	33	7	87	347	349
New York Rangers	37	35	8	82	310	307
Philadelphia Flyers	36	36	8	80	307	285
New Jersey Devils	27	41	12	66	281	325
New York Islanders	28	47	5	61	265	325

CLARENCE CAMPBELL CONFERENCE

NORRIS DIVISION

Team	W	L	T	Pts.	GF	GA
Detroit Red Wings	34	34	12	80	313	316
St. Louis Blues	33	35	12	78	275	285
Minnesota North Stars	27	37	16	70	258	278
Chicago Blackhawks	27	41	12	66	297	335
Toronto Maple Leafs	28	46	6	62	259	342

SMYTHE DIVISION

Team	W	L	T	Pts.	GF	GA
Calgary Flames	54	17	9	117	354	226
Los Angeles Kings	42	31	7	91	376	335
Edmonton Oilers	38	34	8	84	325	306
Vancouver Canucks	33	39	8	74	251	253
Winnipeg Jets	26	42	12	64	300	355

PLAYOFFS

Wales Conference division semifinals: Montreal 4, Hartford 0; Boston 4, Buffalo 1; Philadelphia 4, Washington 2; Pittsburgh 4, N.Y. Rangers 0. **Division finals:** Montreal 4, Boston 1; Philadelphia 4, Pittsburgh 3. **Conference finals:** Montreal 4, Philadelphia 2.

Campbell Conference division semifinals: Chicago 4, Detroit 2; St. Louis 4, Minnesota 1; Calgary 4, Vancouver 3; Los Angeles 4, Edmonton 3. **Division finals:** Chicago 4, St. Louis 1; Calgary 4, Los Angeles 0. **Conference finals:** Calgary 4, Chicago 1.

Stanley Cup finals: Calgary 4, Montreal 2.

1989-90

PRINCE OF WALES CONFERENCE

ADAMS DIVISION

Team	W	L	T	Pts.	GF	GA
Boston Bruins	46	25	9	101	289	232
Buffalo Sabres	45	27	8	98	286	248
Montreal Canadiens	41	28	11	93	288	234
Hartford Whalers	38	33	9	85	275	268
Quebec Nordiques	12	61	7	31	240	407

PATRICK DIVISION

Team	W	L	T	Pts.	GF	GA
New York Rangers	36	31	13	85	279	267
New Jersey Devils	37	34	9	83	295	288
Washington Capitals	36	38	6	78	284	275
New York Islanders	31	38	11	73	281	288
Pittsburgh Penguins	32	40	8	72	318	359
Philadelphia Flyers	30	39	11	71	290	297

CLARENCE CAMPBELL CONFERENCE

NORRIS DIVISION

Team	W	L	T	Pts.	GF	GA
Chicago Blackhawks	41	33	6	88	316	294
St. Louis Blues	37	34	9	83	295	279
Toronto Maple Leafs	38	38	4	80	337	358
Minnesota North Stars	36	40	4	76	284	291
Detroit Red Wings	28	38	14	70	288	323

SMYTHE DIVISION

Team	W	L	T	Pts.	GF	GA
Calgary Flames	42	23	15	99	348	265
Edmonton Oilers	38	28	14	90	315	283
Winnipeg Jets	37	32	11	85	298	290
Los Angeles Kings	34	39	7	75	338	337
Vancouver Canucks	25	41	14	64	245	306

PLAYOFFS

Wales Conference division semifinals: Boston 4, Hartford 3; Montreal 4, Buffalo 3; N.Y. Rangers 4, N.Y. Islanders 1; Washington 4, New Jersey 2. **Division finals:** Boston 4, Montreal 1; Washington 4, N.Y. Rangers 1. **Conference finals:** Boston 4, Washington 0.

Campbell Conference division semifinals: Chicago 4, Minnesota 3; St. Louis 4, Toronto 1; Los Angeles 4, Calgary 2; Edmonton 4, Winnipeg 3. **Division finals:** Chicago 4, St. Louis 3; Edmonton 4, Los Angeles 0. **Conference finals:** Edmonton 4, Chicago 2.

Stanley Cup finals: Edmonton 4, Boston 1.

1990-91

PRINCE OF WALES CONFERENCE

ADAMS DIVISION

Team	W	L	T	Pts.	GF	GA
Boston Bruins	44	24	12	100	299	264
Montreal Canadiens	39	30	11	89	273	249
Buffalo Sabres	31	30	19	81	292	278
Hartford Whalers	31	38	11	73	238	276
Quebec Nordiques	16	50	14	46	236	354

PATRICK DIVISION

Team	W	L	T	Pts.	GF	GA
Pittsburgh Penguins	41	33	6	88	342	305
New York Rangers	36	31	13	85	297	265
Washington Capitals	37	36	7	81	258	258
New Jersey Devils	32	33	15	79	272	264
Philadelphia Flyers	33	37	10	76	252	267
New York Islanders	25	45	10	60	223	290

CLARENCE CAMPBELL CONFERENCE

NORRIS DIVISION

Team	W	L	T	Pts.	GF	GA
Chicago Blackhawks	49	23	8	106	284	211
St. Louis Blues	47	22	11	105	310	250
Detroit Red Wings	34	38	8	76	273	298
Minnesota North Stars	27	39	14	68	256	266
Toronto Maple Leafs	23	46	11	57	241	318

SMYTHE DIVISION

Team	W	L	T	Pts.	GF	GA
Los Angeles Kings	46	24	10	102	340	254
Calgary Flames	46	26	8	100	344	263
Edmonton Oilers	37	37	6	80	272	272
Vancouver Canucks	28	43	9	65	243	315
Winnipeg Jets	26	43	11	63	260	288

PLAYOFFS

Wales Conference division semifinals: Boston 4, Hartford 2; Montreal 4, Buffalo 2; Pittsburgh 4, New Jersey 3; Washington

4, N.Y. Rangers 2. **Division finals:** Boston 4, Montreal 3; Pittsburgh 4, Washington 1. **Conference finals:** Pittsburgh 4, Boston 2.

Campbell Conference division semifinals: Minnesota 4, Chicago 2; St. Louis 4, Detroit 3; Los Angeles 4, Vancouver 2; Edmonton 4, Calgary 3. **Division finals:** Minnesota 4, St. Louis 2; Edmonton 4, Los Angeles 2. **Conference finals:** Minnesota 4, Edmonton 1.

Stanley Cup finals: Pittsburgh 4, Minnesota 2.

1991-92

PRINCE OF WALES CONFERENCE

ADAMS DIVISION

Team	W	L	T	Pts.	GF	GA
Montreal Canadiens	41	28	11	93	267	207
Boston Bruins	36	32	12	84	270	275
Buffalo Sabres	31	37	12	74	289	299
Hartford Whalers	26	41	13	65	247	283
Quebec Nordiques	20	48	12	52	255	318

PATRICK DIVISION

Team	W	L	T	Pts.	GF	GA
New York Rangers	50	25	5	105	321	246
Washington Capitals	45	27	8	98	330	275
Pittsburgh Penguins	39	32	9	87	343	308
New Jersey Devils	38	31	11	87	289	259
New York Islanders	34	35	11	79	291	299
Philadelphia Flyers	32	37	11	75	252	273

CLARENCE CAMPBELL CONFERENCE

NORRIS DIVISION

Team	W	L	T	Pts.	GF	GA
Detroit Red Wings	43	25	12	98	320	256
Chicago Blackhawks	36	29	15	87	257	236
St. Louis Blues	36	33	11	83	279	266
Minnesota North Stars	32	42	6	70	246	278
Toronto Maple Leafs	30	43	7	67	234	294

SMYTHE DIVISION

Team	W	L	T	Pts.	GF	GA
Vancouver Canucks	42	26	12	96	285	250
Los Angeles Kings	35	31	14	84	287	296
Edmonton Oilers	36	34	10	82	295	297
Winnipeg Jets	33	32	15	81	251	244
Calgary Flames	31	37	12	74	296	305
San Jose Sharks	17	58	5	39	219	359

PLAYOFFS

Wales Conference division semifinals: Montreal 4, Hartford 3; Boston 4, Buffalo 3; N.Y. Rangers 4, New Jersey 3; Pittsburgh 4, Washington 3. **Division finals:** Boston 4, Montreal 0; Pittsburgh 4, N.Y. Rangers 2. **Conference finals:** Pittsburgh 4, Boston 0.

Campbell Conference division semifinals: Detroit 4, Minnesota 3; Chicago 4, St. Louis 2; Vancouver 4, Winnipeg 3; Edmonton 4, Los Angeles 2. **Division finals:** Chicago 4, Detroit 0; Edmonton 4, Vancouver 2. **Conference finals:** Chicago 4, Edmonton 0.

Stanley Cup finals: Pittsburgh 4, Chicago 0.

1992-93

PRINCE OF WALES CONFERENCE

ADAMS DIVISION

Team	W	L	T	Pts.	GF	GA
Boston Bruins	51	26	7	109	332	268
Quebec Nordiques	47	27	10	104	351	300
Montreal Canadiens	48	30	6	102	326	280
Buffalo Sabres	38	36	10	86	335	297
Hartford Whalers	26	52	6	58	284	369
Ottawa Senators	10	70	4	24	202	395

PATRICK DIVISION

Team	W	L	T	Pts.	GF	GA
Pittsburgh Penguins	56	21	7	119	367	268
Washington Capitals	43	34	7	93	325	286
New York Islanders	40	37	7	87	308	299
New Jersey Devils	40	37	7	87	335	297
Philadelphia Flyers	36	37	11	83	319	319
New York Rangers	34	39	11	79	304	308

CLARENCE CAMPBELL CONFERENCE

NORRIS DIVISION

Team	W	L	T	Pts.	GF	GA
Chicago Blackhawks	47	25	12	106	279	230
Detroit Red Wings	47	28	9	103	369	280
Toronto Maple Leafs	44	29	11	99	288	241
St. Louis Blues	37	36	11	85	282	278
Minnesota North Stars	36	38	10	82	272	293
Tampa Bay Lightning	23	54	7	53	245	332

SMYTHE DIVISION

Team	W	L	T	Pts.	GF	GA
Vancouver Canucks	46	29	9	101	346	278
Calgary Flames	43	30	11	97	322	282
Los Angeles Kings	39	35	10	88	338	340
Winnipeg Jets	40	37	7	87	322	320
Edmonton Oilers	26	50	8	60	242	337
San Jose Sharks	11	71	2	24	218	414

PLAYOFFS

Wales Conference division semifinals: Buffalo 4, Boston 0; Montreal 4, Quebec 2; Pittsburgh 4, New Jersey 1; N.Y. Islanders 4, Washington 2. **Division finals:** Montreal 4, Buffalo 0; N.Y. Islanders 4, Pittsburgh 3. **Conference finals:** Montreal 4, N.Y. Islanders 1.

Campbell Conference division semifinals: St. Louis 4, Chicago 0; Toronto 4, Detroit 3; Vancouver 4, Winnipeg 2; Los Angeles 4, Calgary 2. **Division finals:** Toronto 4, St. Louis 3; Los Angeles 4, Vancouver 2. **Conference finals:** Los Angeles 4, Toronto 3.

Stanley Cup finals: Montreal 4, Los Angeles 1.

1993-94

EASTERN CONFERENCE

ATLANTIC DIVISION

Team	W	L	T	Pts.	GF	GA
New York Rangers	52	24	8	112	299	231
New Jersey Devils	47	25	12	106	306	220
Washington Capitals	39	35	10	88	277	263
New York Islanders	36	36	12	84	282	264
Florida Panthers	33	34	17	83	233	233
Philadelphia Flyers	35	39	10	80	294	314
Tampa Bay Lightning	30	43	11	71	224	251

NORTHEAST DIVISION

Team	W	L	T	Pts.	GF	GA
Pittsburgh Penguins	44	27	13	101	299	285
Boston Bruins	42	29	13	97	289	252
Montreal Canadiens	41	29	14	96	283	248
Buffalo Sabres	43	32	9	95	282	218
Quebec Nordiques	34	42	8	76	277	292
Hartford Whalers	27	48	9	63	227	288
Ottawa Senators	14	61	9	37	201	397

WESTERN CONFERENCE

CENTRAL DIVISION

Team	W	L	T	Pts.	GF	GA
Detroit Red Wings	46	30	8	100	356	275
Toronto Maple Leafs	43	29	12	98	280	243
Dallas Stars	42	29	13	97	286	265
St. Louis Blues	40	33	11	91	270	283
Chicago Blackhawks	39	36	9	87	254	240
Winnipeg Jets	24	51	9	57	245	344

PACIFIC DIVISION

Team	W	L	T	Pts.	GF	GA
Calgary Flames	42	29	13	97	302	256
Vancouver Canucks	41	40	3	85	279	276
San Jose Sharks	33	35	16	82	252	265
Mighty Ducks of Anaheim	33	46	5	71	229	251
Los Angeles Kings	27	45	12	66	294	322
Edmonton Oilers	25	45	14	64	261	305

PLAYOFFS

Eastern Conference quarterfinals: N.Y. Rangers 4, N.Y. Islanders 0; Washington 4, Pittsburgh 2; New Jersey 4, Buffalo 3; Boston 4, Montreal 3. **Semifinals:** N.Y. Rangers 4, Washington 1; New Jersey 4, Boston 2. **Finals:** N.Y. Rangers 4, New Jersey 3.

Western Conference quarterfinals: San Jose 4, Detroit 3; Vancouver 4, Calgary 3; Toronto 4, Chicago 2; Dallas 4, St. Louis 0. **Semifinals:** Toronto 4, San Jose 3; Vancouver 4, Dallas 1. **Finals:** Vancouver 4, Toronto 1.

Stanley Cup finals: N.Y. Rangers 4, Vancouver 3.

1994-95

EASTERN CONFERENCE

ATLANTIC DIVISION

Team	W	L	T	Pts.	GF	GA
Philadelphia Flyers	28	16	4	60	150	132
New Jersey Devils	22	18	8	52	136	121
Washington Capitals	22	18	8	52	136	120
New York Rangers	22	23	3	47	139	134
Florida Panthers	20	22	6	46	115	127
Tampa Bay Lightning	17	28	3	37	120	144
New York Islanders	15	28	5	35	126	158

NORTHEAST DIVISION

Team	W	L	T	Pts.	GF	GA
Quebec Nordiques	30	13	5	65	185	134
Pittsburgh Penguins	29	16	3	61	181	158
Boston Bruins	27	18	3	57	150	127
Buffalo Sabres	22	19	7	51	130	119
Hartford Whalers	19	24	5	43	127	141
Montreal Canadiens	18	23	7	43	125	148
Ottawa Senators	9	34	5	23	117	174

WESTERN CONFERENCE

CENTRAL DIVISION

Team	W	L	T	Pts.	GF	GA
Detroit Red Wings	33	11	4	70	180	117
St. Louis Blues	28	15	5	61	178	135
Chicago Blackhawks	24	19	5	53	156	115
Toronto Maple Leafs	21	19	8	50	135	146
Dallas Stars	17	23	8	42	136	135
Winnipeg Jets	16	25	7	39	157	177

PACIFIC DIVISION

Team	W	L	T	Pts.	GF	GA
Calgary Flames	24	17	7	55	163	135
Vancouver Canucks	18	18	12	48	153	148
San Jose Sharks	19	25	4	42	129	161
Los Angeles Kings	16	23	9	41	142	174
Edmonton Oilers	17	27	4	38	136	183
Mighty Ducks of Anaheim	16	27	5	37	125	164

PLAYOFFS

Eastern Conference quarterfinals: N.Y. Rangers 4, Quebec 2; Pittsburgh 4, Washington 3; Philadelphia 4, Buffalo 1; New Jersey 4, Boston 1. **Semifinals:** New Jersey 4, Pittsburgh 1; Philadelphia 4, N.Y. Rangers 0. **Finals:** New Jersey 4, Philadelphia 2.

Western Conference quarterfinals: Detroit 4, Dallas 1; Vancouver 4, St. Louis 3; Chicago 4, Toronto 3; San Jose 4, Calgary 3. **Semifinals:** Detroit 4, San Jose 0; Chicago 4, Vancouver 0. **Finals:** Detroit 4, Chicago 1.

Stanley Cup finals: New Jersey 4, Detroit 0.

1995-96

EASTERN CONFERENCE

ATLANTIC DIVISION

Team	W	L	T	Pts.	GF	GA
Philadelphia Flyers	45	24	13	103	282	208
New York Rangers	41	27	14	96	272	237
Florida Panthers	41	31	10	92	254	234
Washington Capitals	39	32	11	89	234	204
Tampa Bay Lightning	38	32	12	88	238	248
New Jersey Devils	37	33	12	86	215	202
New York Islanders	22	50	10	54	229	315

NORTHEAST DIVISION

Team	W	L	T	Pts.	GF	GA
Pittsburgh Penguins	49	29	4	102	362	284
Boston Bruins	40	31	11	91	282	269
Montreal Canadiens	40	32	10	90	265	248
Hartford Whalers	34	39	9	77	237	259
Buffalo Sabres	33	42	7	73	247	262
Ottawa Senators	18	59	5	41	191	291

WESTERN CONFERENCE

CENTRAL DIVISION

Team	W	L	T	Pts.	GF	GA
Detroit Red Wings	62	13	7	131	325	181
Chicago Blackhawks	40	28	14	94	273	220
Toronto Maple Leafs	34	36	12	80	247	252
St. Louis Blues	32	34	16	80	219	248
Winnipeg Jets	36	40	6	78	275	291
Dallas Stars	26	42	14	66	227	280

PACIFIC DIVISION

Team	W	L	T	Pts.	GF	GA
Colorado Avalanche	47	25	10	104	326	240
Calgary Flames	34	37	11	79	241	240
Vancouver Canucks	32	35	15	79	278	278
Mighty Ducks of Anaheim	35	39	8	78	234	247
Edmonton Oilers	30	44	8	68	240	304
Los Angeles Kings	24	40	18	66	256	302
San Jose Sharks	20	55	7	47	252	357

PLAYOFFS

Eastern Conference quarterfinals: Philadelphia 4, Tampa Bay 2; Pittsburgh 4, Washington 2; N.Y. Rangers 4, Montreal 2; Florida 4, Boston 1. **Semifinals:** Florida 4, Philadelphia 2; Pittsburgh 4, N.Y. Rangers 1. **Finals:** Florida 4, Pittsburgh 3.

Western Conference quarterfinals: Detroit 4, Winnipeg 2; Colorado 4, Vancouver 2; Chicago 4, Calgary 0; St. Louis 4, Toronto 2. **Semifinals:** Detroit 4, St. Louis 3; Colorado 4, Chicago 2. **Finals:** Colorado 4, Detroit 2.

Stanley Cup finals: Colorado 4, Florida 0.

1996-97

EASTERN CONFERENCE

ATLANTIC DIVISION

Team	W	L	T	Pts.	GF	GA
New Jersey Devils	45	23	14	104	231	182
Philadelphia Flyers	45	24	13	103	274	217
Florida Panthers	35	28	19	89	221	201
New York Rangers	38	34	10	86	258	231
Washington Capitals	33	40	9	75	214	231
Tampa Bay Lightning	32	40	10	74	217	247
New York Islanders	29	41	12	70	240	250

NORTHEAST DIVISION

Team	W	L	T	Pts.	GF	GA
Buffalo Sabres	40	30	12	92	237	208
Pittsburgh Penguins	38	36	8	84	285	280
Ottawa Senators	31	36	15	77	226	234
Montreal Canadiens	31	36	15	77	249	276
Hartford Whalers	32	39	11	75	226	256
Boston Bruins	26	47	9	61	234	300

WESTERN CONFERENCE

CENTRAL DIVISION

Team	W	L	T	Pts.	GF	GA
Dallas Stars	48	26	8	104	252	198
Detroit Red Wings	38	26	18	94	253	197
Phoenix Coyotes	38	37	7	83	240	243
St. Louis Blues	36	35	11	83	236	239
Chicago Blackhawks	34	35	13	81	223	210
Toronto Maple Leafs	30	44	8	68	230	273

PACIFIC DIVISION

Team	W	L	T	Pts.	GF	GA
Colorado Avalanche	49	24	9	107	277	205
Mighty Ducks of Anaheim	36	33	13	85	245	233
Edmonton Oilers	36	37	9	81	252	247
Vancouver Canucks	35	40	7	77	257	273
Calgary Flames	32	41	9	73	214	239
Los Angeles Kings	28	43	11	67	214	268
San Jose Sharks	27	47	8	62	211	278

PLAYOFFS

Eastern Conference quarterfinals: New Jersey 4, Montreal 1; Buffalo 4, Ottawa 3; Philadelphia 4, Pittsburgh 1; N.Y. Rangers 4, Florida 1. **Semifinals:** N.Y. Rangers 4, New Jersey 1; Philadelphia 4, Buffalo 1. **Finals:** Philadelphia 4, N.Y. Rangers 1.

Western Conference quarterfinals: Colorado 4, Chicago 2; Edmonton 4, Dallas 3; Detroit 4, St. Louis 2; Anaheim 4, Phoenix 3. **Semifinals:** Colorado 4, Edmonton 1; Detroit 4, Anaheim 0. **Finals:** Detroit 4, Colorado 2.

Stanley Cup finals: Detroit 4, Philadelphia 0.

1997-98

EASTERN CONFERENCE

ATLANTIC DIVISION

Team	W	L	T	Pts.	GF	GA
New Jersey Devils	48	23	11	107	225	166
Philadelphia Flyers	42	29	11	95	242	193
Washington Capitals	40	30	12	92	219	202
New York Islanders	30	41	11	71	212	225
New York Rangers	25	39	18	68	197	231
Florida Panthers	24	43	15	63	203	256
Tampa Bay Lightning	17	55	10	44	151	269

NORTHEAST DIVISION

Team	W	L	T	Pts.	GF	GA
Pittsburgh Penguins	40	24	18	98	228	188
Boston Bruins	39	30	13	91	221	194
Buffalo Sabres	36	29	17	89	211	187
Montreal Canadiens	37	32	13	87	235	208
Ottawa Senators	34	33	15	83	193	200
Carolina Hurricanes	33	41	8	74	200	219

WESTERN CONFERENCE

CENTRAL DIVISION

Team	W	L	T	Pts.	GF	GA
Dallas Stars	49	22	11	109	242	167
Detroit Red Wings	44	23	15	103	250	196
St. Louis Blues	45	29	8	98	256	204
Phoenix Coyotes	35	35	12	82	224	227
Chicago Blackhawks	30	39	13	73	192	199
Toronto Maple Leafs	30	43	9	69	194	237

PACIFIC DIVISION

Team	W	L	T	Pts.	GF	GA
Colorado Avalanche	39	26	17	95	231	205
Los Angeles Kings	38	33	11	87	227	225
Edmonton Oilers	35	37	10	80	215	224
San Jose Sharks	34	38	10	78	210	216
Calgary Flames	26	41	15	67	217	252
Mighty Ducks of Anaheim	26	43	13	65	205	261
Vancouver Canucks	25	43	14	64	224	273

PLAYOFFS

Eastern Conference quarterfinals: Ottawa 4, New Jersey 2; Washington 4, Boston 2; Buffalo 4, Philadelphia 1; Montreal 4, Pittsburgh 2. **Semifinals:** Washington 4, Ottawa 1; Buffalo 4, Montreal 0. **Finals:** Washington 4, Buffalo 2.

Western Conference quarterfinals: Edmonton 4, Colorado 3; Dallas 4, San Jose 2; Detroit 4, Phoenix 2; St. Louis 4, Los Angeles 0. **Semifinals:** Dallas 4, Edmonton 1; Detroit 4, St. Louis 2. **Finals:** Detroit 4, Dallas 2.

Stanley Cup finals: Detroit 4, Washington 0.

RECORDS

REGULAR SEASON

INDIVIDUAL—CAREER

Most seasons

NHL: 26—Gordie Howe, Detroit Red Wings and Hartford Whalers, 1946-47 through 1970-71 and 1979-80.
CHL: 9—Richie Hansen, Fort Worth Texans, Salt Lake Golden Eagles, Wichita Wind, 1975-76 through 1983-84.
AHL: 20—Fred Glover, Indianapolis Caps, St. Louis Flyers, Cleveland Barons.
Willie Marshall, Pittsburgh Hornets, Rochester Americans, Hershey Bears, Providence Reds, Baltimore Clippers.
IHL: 18—Glenn Ramsay, Cincinnati Mohawks, Fort Wayne Komets, Troy Bruins, Toledo Blades, St. Paul Saints, Omaha Knights, Des Moines Oak Leafs, Toledo Hornets, Port Huron Flags, 1956-57 through 1973-74.

Most games played

NHL: 1,767—Gordie Howe, Detroit Red Wings and Hartford Whalers (26 seasons).
AHL: 1,205—Willie Marshall, Pittsburgh Hornets, Rochester Americans, Hershey Bears, Providence Reds, Baltimore Clippers (20 seasons).
IHL: 1,053—Glenn Ramsay, Cincinnati Mohawks, Fort Wayne Komets, Troy Bruins, Toledo Blades, St. Paul Saints, Omaha Knights, Des Moines Oak Leafs, Toledo Hornets, Port Huron Flags (18 seasons).
CHL: 575—Richie Hansen, Fort Worth Texans, Salt Lake Golden Eagles, Wichita Wind (9 seasons).
WHA: 551—Andre Lacroix, Philadelphia Blazers, New York Golden Blades, Jersey Knights, San Diego Mariners, Houston Aeros and New England Whalers (7 seasons).

Most goals

NHL: 894—Wayne Gretzky, Edmonton Oilers, Los Angeles Kings, St. Louis Blues, New York Rangers (20 seasons).
IHL: 547—Dave Michayluk, Kalamazoo Wings, Muskegon Lumberjacks, Cleveland Lumberjacks (13 seasons).
AHL: 523—Willie Marshall, Pittsburgh Hornets, Rochester Americans, Hershey Bears, Providence Reds, Baltimore Clippers (20 seasons).
WHA: 316—Marc Tardif, Quebec Nordiques (6 seasons).
CHL: 204—Richie Hansen, Fort Worth Texans, Salt Lake Golden Eagles, Wichita Wind (9 seasons).

Most assists

NHL: 1,963—Wayne Gretzky, Edmonton Oilers, Los Angeles Kings, St. Louis Blues, New York Rangers (20 seasons).
AHL: 852—Willie Marshall, Pittsburgh Hornets, Hershey Bears, Rochester Americans, Providence Reds, Baltimore Clippers (20 seasons).
IHL: 826—Len Thornson, Huntington Hornets, Indianapolis Chiefs, Fort Wayne Komets (13 seasons).
WHA: 547—Andre Lacroix, Philadelphia Blazers, Jersey Knights, San Diego Mariners, Houston Aeros, New England Whalers (7 seasons).
CHL: 374—Richie Hansen, Fort Worth Texans, Salt Lake Golden Eagles, Wichita Wind (9 seasons).

Most points

NHL: 2,857—Wayne Gretzky, Edmonton Oilers, Los Angeles Kings, St. Louis Blues, New York Rangers (20 seasons).
AHL: 1,375—Willie Marshall, Pittsburgh Hornets, Hershey Bears, Rochester Americans, Providence Reds, Baltimore Clippers (20 seasons).
IHL: 1,252—Len Thornson, Huntington Hornets, Indianapolis Chiefs, Fort Wayne Komets (13 seasons).
WHA: 798—Andre Lacroix, Philadelphia Blazers, Jersey Knights, San Diego Mariners, Houston Aeros, New England Whalers (7 seasons).
CHL: 578—Richie Hansen, Fort Worth Texans, Salt Lake Golden Eagles, Wichita Wind (9 seasons).

Most penalty minutes

NHL: 3,966—Dave "Tiger" Williams, Toronto Maple Leafs, Vancouver Canucks, Detroit Red Wings, Los Angeles Kings, Hartford Whalers (13 seasons).
AHL: 2,402—Fred Glover, Indianapolis Caps, St. Louis Flyers, Cleveland Barons (20 seasons).
IHL: 2,175—Gord Malinoski, Dayton Gems, Saginaw Gears (9 seasons).
WHA: 962—Paul Baxter, Cleveland Crusaders, Quebec Nordiques (5 seasons).
CHL: 899—Brad Gassoff, Tulsa Oilers, Dallas Black Hawks (5 seasons).

Most shutouts

NHL: 103—Terry Sawchuk, Detroit Red Wings, Boston Bruins, Los Angeles Kings, New York Rangers, Toronto Maple Leafs (20 seasons).
AHL: 45—Johnny Bower, Cleveland Barons, Providence Reds (11 seasons).
IHL: 45—Glenn Ramsay, Cincinnati Mohawks, Fort Wayne Komets, Troy Bruins, Toledo Blades, St. Paul Saints, Omaha Knights, Des Moines Oak Leafs, Toledo Hornets, Port Huron Flags (18 seasons).
WHA: 16—Ernie Wakely, Winnipeg Jets, San Diego Mariners, Houston Aeros (6 seasons).
CHL: 12—Michel Dumas, Dallas Black Hawks (4 seasons).
Mike Veisor, Dallas Black Hawks (5 seasons).

INDIVIDUAL—SEASON

Most goals

NHL: 92—Wayne Gretzky, Edmonton Oilers, 1981-82 season.
WHA: 77—Bobby Hull, Winnipeg Jets, 1974-75 season.
CHL: 77—Alain Caron, St. Louis Braves, 1963-64 season.
IHL: 75—Dan Lecours, Milwaukee Admirals, 1982-83 season.
AHL: 70—Stephan Lebeau, Sherbrooke Canadiens, 1988-89 season.

Most goals by a defenseman

NHL: 48—Paul Coffey, Edmonton Oilers, 1985-86 season.
IHL: 34—Roly McLenahan, Cincinnati Mohawks, 1955-56 season.

CHL: 29—Dan Poulin, Nashville South Stars, 1981-82 season.
AHL: 28—Greg Tebbutt, Baltimore Skipjacks, 1982-83 season.
WHA: 24—Kevin Morrison, Jersey Knights, 1973-74 season.

Most assists

NHL: 163—Wayne Gretzky, Edmonton Oilers, 1985-86 season.
IHL: 109—John Cullen, Flint Spirits, 1987-88 season.
WHA: 106—Andre Lacroix, San Diego Mariners, 1974-75 season.
AHL: 89—George "Red" Sullivan, Hershey Bears, 1953-54 season.
CHL: 81—Richie Hansen, Salt Lake Golden Eagles, 1981-82 season.

Most assists by a defenseman

NHL: 102—Bobby Orr, Boston Bruins, 1970-71 season.
IHL: 86—Gerry Glaude, Muskegon Zephyrs, 1962-63 season.
WHA: 77—J. C. Tremblay, Quebec Nordiques, 1975-76 season.
AHL: 62—Craig Levie, Nova Scotia Voyageurs, 1980-81 season.
Shawn Evans, Nova Scotia Oilers, 1987-88 season.
CHL: 61—Barclay Plager, Omaha Knights, 1963-64 season.

Most points

NHL: 215—Wayne Gretzky, Edmonton Oilers, 1985-86 season.
IHL: 157—John Cullen, Flint Spirits, 1987-88 season.
WHA: 154—Marc Tardif, Quebec Nordiques, 1977-78 season.
AHL: 138—Don Biggs, Binghamton Rangers, 1992-93 season.
CHL: 125—Alain Caron, St. Louis Braves, 1963-64 season.

Most points by a defenseman

NHL: 139—Bobby Orr, Boston Bruins, 1970-71 season.
IHL: 101—Gerry Glaude, Muskegon Zephyrs, 1962-63 season.
WHA: 89—J. C. Tremblay, Quebec Nordiques, 1972-73 and 1975-76 seasons.
CHL: 85—Dan Poulin, Nashville South Stars, 1981-82 season.
AHL: 84—Greg Tebbutt, Baltimore Skipjacks, 1982-83 season.

Most penalty minutes

IHL: 648—Kevin Evans, Kalamazoo, 1986-87 season.
NHL: 472—Dave Schultz, Philadelphia Flyers, 1974-75 season.
AHL: 446—Robert Ray, Rochester Americans, 1988-89 season.
CHL: 411—Randy Holt, Dallas Black Hawks, 1974-75 season.
WHA: 365—Curt Brackenbury, Minnesota Fighting Saints and Quebec Nordiques, 1975-76 season.

Most shutouts

NHL: 22—George Hainsworth, Montreal Canadiens, 1928-29 season.
NHL: 15—(modern era) Tony Esposito, Chicago Black Hawks, 1969-70 season.
IHL: 10—Charlie Hodge, Cincinnati Mohawks, 1953-54 season.
Joe Daley, Winnipeg Jets, 1975-76 season.
CHL: 9—Marcel Pelletier, St. Paul Rangers, 1963-64 season.
AHL: 9—Gordie Bell, Buffalo Bisons, 1942-43 season.
WHA: 5—Gerry Cheevers, Cleveland Crusaders, 1972-73 season.

Lowest goals against average

NHL: 0.98—George Hainsworth, Montreal Canadiens, 1928-29 season.
AHL: 1.79—Frank Brimsek, Providence Reds, 1937-38 season.
IHL: 1.88—Glenn Ramsay, Cincinnati Mohawks, 1956-57 season.
CHL: 2.16—Russ Gillow, Oklahoma City Blazers, 1967-68 season.
WHA: 2.57—Don McLeod, Houston Aeros, 1973-74 season.

INDIVIDUAL—GAME

Most goals

NHL: 7—Joe Malone, Quebec Bulldogs vs. Toronto St. Pats, January 31, 1920.
NHL: 6—(modern era) Syd Howe, Detroit Red Wings vs. N.Y. Rangers, Feb. 3, 1944.
Gordon "Red" Berenson, St. Louis Blues vs. Philadelphia, Nov. 7, 1968.
Darryl Sittler, Toronto Maple Leafs vs. Boston, Feb. 7, 1976.
CHL: 6—Jim Mayer, Dallas Black Hawks, February 23, 1979.
AHL: 6—Bob Heron, Pittsburgh Hornets, 1941-42.
Harry Pidhirny, Springfield Indians, 1953-54.
Camille Henry, Providence Reds, 1955-56.
Patrick Lebeau, Fredericton Canadiens, Feb. 1, 1991.
IHL: 6—Pierre Brillant, Indianapolis Chiefs, Feb. 18, 1959.
Bryan McLay, Muskegon Zephyrs, Mar. 8, 1961.
Elliott Chorley, St. Paul Saints, Jan. 17, 1962.
Joe Kastelic, Muskegon Zephyrs, Mar. 1, 1962.
Tom St. James, Flint Generals, Mar. 15, 1985.
WHA: 5—Ron Ward, New York Raiders vs. Ottawa, January 4, 1973.
Ron Climie, Edmonton Oilers vs. N.Y. Golden Blades, November 6, 1973.
Andre Hinse, Houston Aeros vs. Edmonton, Jan. 16, 1975.
Vaclav Nedomansky, Toronto Toros vs. Denver Spurs, Nov. 13, 1975.
Wayne Connelly, Minnesota Fighting Saints vs. Cincinnati Stingers, Nov. 27, 1975.
Ron Ward, Cleveland Crusaders vs. Toronto Toros, Nov. 30, 1975.
Real Cloutier, Quebec Nordiques fs. Phoenix Roadrunners, Oct. 26, 1976.

Most assists

AHL: 9—Art Stratton, Buffalo Bisons vs. Pittsburgh, Mar. 17, 1963.
IHL: 9—Jean-Paul Denis, St. Paul Saints, Jan. 17, 1962.
NHL: 7—Billy Taylor, Detroit Red Wings vs. Chicago, Mar. 16, 1947.
Wayne Gretzky, Edmonton Oilers vs. Washington, Feb. 15, 1980.
WHA: 7—Jim Harrison, Alberta Oilers vs. New York, January 30, 1973.
Jim Harrison, Cleveland Crusaders vs. Toronto, Nov. 30, 1975.
CHL: 6—Art Stratton, St. Louis Braves, 1966-67.
Ron Ward, Tulsa Oilers, 1967-68.
Bill Hogaboam, Omaha Knights, January 15, 1972.
Jim Wiley, Tulsa Oilers, 1974-75.

Most points

IHL: 11—Elliott Chorley, St. Paul Saints, Jan. 17, 1962.
Jean-Paul Denis, St. Paul Saints, Jan. 17, 1962.
NHL: 10—Darryl Sittler, Toronto Maple Leafs vs. Boston, Feb. 7, 1976.
WHA: 10—Jim Harrison, Alberta Oilers vs. New York, January 30, 1973.
AHL: 9—Art Stratton, Buffalo Bisons vs Pittsburgh, Mar. 17, 1963.
CHL: 8—Steve Vickers, Omaha Knights vs. Kansas City, Jan. 15, 1972.

Most penalty minutes

NHL: 67—Randy Holt, Los Angeles Kings vs. Philadelphia, March 11, 1979.
IHL: 63—Willie Trognitz, Dayton Gems, Oct. 29, 1977.
AHL: 54—Wally Weir, Rochester Americans vs. New Brunswick, Jan. 16, 1981.
CHL: 49—Gary Rissling, Birmingham Bulls vs. Salt Lake, Dec. 5, 1980.
WHA: 46—Dave Hanson, Birmingham Bulls vs. Indianapolis, Feb. 5, 1978.

STANLEY CUP PLAYOFFS

INDIVIDUAL—CAREER

Most years in playoffs: 20—Gordie Howe, Detroit, Hartford.
Larry Robinson, Montreal, Los Angeles.
Most consecutive years in playoffs: 20—Larry Robinson, Montreal, Los Angeles.
Most games: 236—Mark Messier, Edmonton, New York Rangers.
Most games by goaltender: 179—Patrick Roy, Montreal, Colorado.
Most goals: 122—Wayne Gretzky, Edmonton, Los Angeles, St. Louis, New York Rangers.
Most assists: 260—Wayne Gretzky, Edmonton, Los Angeles, St. Louis, New York Rangers.
Most points: 382—Wayne Gretzky, Edmonton, Los Angeles, St. Louis, New York Rangers.
Most penalty minutes: 729—Dale Hunter, Quebec, Washington, Colorado.
Most shutouts: 14—Jacques Plante, Montreal, St. Louis.

INDIVIDUAL—SEASON

Most goals: 19—Reggie Leach, Philadelphia (1975-76).
Jari Kurri, Edmonton (1984-85).
Most goals by a defenseman: 12—Paul Coffey, Edmonton (1984-85).
Most assists: 31—Wayne Gretzky, Edmonton (1987-88).
Most assists by a defenseman: 25—Paul Coffey, Edmonton (1984-85).
Most points: 47—Wayne Gretzky, Edmonton (1984-85).
Most points by a defenseman: 37—Paul Coffey, Edmonton (1984-85).
Most penalty minutes: 141—Chris Nilan, Montreal (1985-86).
Most shutouts: 4—Clint Benedict, Montreal Maroons (1927-28); Dave Kerr, N.Y. Rangers (1936-37); Frank McCool, Toronto (1944-45); Terry Sawchuk, Detroit (1951-52); Bernie Parent, Philadelphia (1974-75); Ken Dryden, Montreal (1976-77).
Most consecutive shutouts: 3—Frank McCool, Toronto (1944-45).

INDIVIDUAL—GAME

Most goals: 5—Maurice Richard, Montreal vs. Toronto, March 23, 1944.
Darryl Sittler, Toronto vs. Philadelphia, April 22, 1976.
Reggie Leach, Philadelphia vs. Boston, May 6, 1976.
Mario Lemieux, Pittsburgh vs. Philadelphia, April 25, 1989.
Most assists: 6—Mikko Leinonen, N.Y. Rangers vs. Philadelphia, April 8, 1982.
Wayne Gretzky, Edmonton vs. Los Angeles, April 9, 1987.
Most points: 8—Patrik Sundstrom, New Jersey vs. Washington, April 22, 1988.
Mario Lemieux, Pittsburgh vs. Philadelphia, April 25, 1989.

CLUB

Most Stanley Cup championships: 24—Montreal Canadiens.
Most consecutive Stanley Cup championships: 5—Montreal Canadiens.
Most final series apperances: 32—Montreal Canadiens.
Most years in playoffs: 72—Montreal Canadiens.
Most consecutive playoff appearances: 29—Boston Bruins.
Most consecutive playoff game victories: 12—Edmonton Oilers.
Most goals, one team, one game: 13—Edmonton vs. Los Angeles, April 9, 1987.
Most goals, one team, one period: 7—Montreal Canadiens vs. Toronto, March 30, 1944, 3rd period.

STATISTICAL LEADERS

YEAR BY YEAR

1917-18

Goals

Joe Malone, Mon. Canadiens....44
Cy Denneny, Ottawa....36
Reg Noble, Toronto....28
Newsy Lalonde, Mon. Canadiens....23
Corbett Denneny, Toronto....20

Lowest goals-against average (Min. 15 games)

Georges Vezina, Mon. Canadiens....3.82
Hap Holmes, Toronto....4.75
Clint Benedict, Ottawa....5.18

Shutouts

Clint Benedict, Ottawa....1
Georges Vezina, Mon. Canadiens....1

1918-19

Goals

Odie Cleghorn, Montreal....24
Newsy Lalonde, Montreal....21
Cy Denneny, Ottawa....18
Frank Nighbor, Ottawa....17
Didier Pitre, Montreal....15

Lowest goals-against average (Min. 15 games)

Clint Benedict, Ottawa....2.94
Georges Vezina, Montreal....4.33
Bert Lindsay, Toronto....5.19

Shutouts

Clint Benedict, Ottawa....2
Georges Vezina, Montreal....1

1919-20

Goals

Joe Malone, Quebec....39
Newsy Lalonde, Montreal....36
Frank Nighbor, Ottawa....26
Corbett Denneny, Toronto....23
Reg Noble, Toronto....24

Lowest goals-against average (Min. 15 games)

Clint Benedict, Ottawa....2.67
Georges Vezina, Montreal....4.71
Frank Brophy, Quebec....7.05

Shutouts

Clint Benedict, Ottawa....5

1920-21

Goals

Cecil Dye, Tor.-Ham....35
Cy Denneny, Ottawa....34
Newsy Lalonde, Montreal....32
Joe Malone, Hamilton....28
Three players tied with....19

Lowest goals-against average (Min. 15 games)

Clint Benedict, Ottawa....3.13
Jake Forbes, Toronto....3.90
Georges Vezina, Montreal....4.13
Howard Lockhart, Hamilton....5.50

Shutouts

Clint Benedict, Ottawa....2
Howard Lockhart, Hamilton....1
Georges Vezina, Montreal....1

1921-22

Goals

Harry Broadbent, Ottawa....30
Cecil Dye, Toronto....30
Cy Denneny, Ottawa....28
Joe Malone, Hamilton....23
Odie Cleghorn, Montreal....21

Lowest goals-against average (Min. 15 games)

Clint Benedict, Ottawa....3.50
Georges Vezina, Montreal....3.92
John Roach, Toronto....4.14
Howard Lockhart, Hamilton....4.29

Shutouts

Clint Benedict, Ottawa....2

1922-23

Goals

Cecil Dye, Toronto....26
Billy Boucher, Montreal....25
Cy Denneny, Ottawa....23
Odie Cleghorn, Montreal....18
Jack Adams, Toronto....18

Lowest goals-against average (Min. 15 games)

Clint Benedict, Ottawa....2.25
Georges Vezina, Montreal....2.54
John Roach, Toronto....3.67
Jake Forbes, Hamilton....4.58

Shutouts

Clint Benedict, Ottawa....4
Georges Vezina, Montreal....2
John Roach, Toronto....1

1923-24

Goals

Cy Denneny, Ottawa....22
Billy Burch, Hamilton....16
Billy Boucher, Montreal....16
Cecil Dye, Toronto....16
Aurel Joliat, Montreal....15

Lowest goals-against average (Min. 15 games)

Georges Vezina, Montreal....2.00
Clint Benedict, Ottawa....2.05
Jake Forbes, Hamilton....2.83
John Roach, Toronto....3.48

Shutouts

Clint Benedict, Ottawa....3
Georges Vezina, Montreal....3
Jake Forbes, Hamilton....1
John Roach, Toronto....1

1924-25

Goals

Cecil Dye, Toronto....38
Howie Morenz, Mon. Canadiens....30
Aurel Joliat, Mon. Canadiens....29
Cy Denneny, Ottawa....28
Jack Adams, Toronto....21
Billy Burch, Hamilton....21

Points

Cecil Dye, Toronto....44
Cy Denneny, Ottawa....42
Aurel Joliat, Mon. Canadiens....40
Howie Morenz, Mon. Canadiens....34
Billy Boucher, Mon. Canadiens....31

Lowest goals-against average (Min. 15 games)

Georges Vezina, Mon. Canadiens....1.87
Jake Forbes, Hamilton....2.00
Clint Benedict, Mon. Maroons....2.17
Alex Connell, Ottawa....2.20
John Roach, Toronto....2.80

Shutouts

Alex Connell, Ottawa....7
Jake Forbes, Hamilton....6
Georges Vezina, Mon. Canadiens....5
Clint Benedict, Mon. Maroons....2
Charles Stewart, Boston....2

1925-26

Goals

Nels Stewart, Mon. Maroons....34
Carson Cooper, Boston....28
Jimmy Herberts, Boston....26
Cy Denneny, Ottawa....24
Howie Morenz, Mon. Canadiens....23

Points

Nels Stewart, Mon. Maroons....42
Cy Denneny, Ottawa....36
Carson Cooper, Boston....31
Jimmy Heberts, Boston....31
Three players tied with....26

Lowest goals-against average (Min. 15 games)

Alex Connell, Ottawa....1.17
Roy Worters, Pittsburgh....1.94
Clint Benedict, Mon. Maroons....2.03
Charles Stewart, Boston....2.29
Jake Forbes, New York....2.39

Shutouts

Alex Connell, Ottawa....15
Roy Worters, Pittsburgh....7
Clint Benedict, Mon. Maroons....6
Charles Stewart, Boston....6
Jake Forbes, New York....2
John Roach, Toronto....2

1926-27

Goals

Bill Cook, N.Y. Rangers....33
Cecil Dye, Chicago....25

Howie Morenz, Mon. Canadiens..........25
Billy Burch, N.Y. Americans..................19
Three players tied with..........................18

Assists

Dick Irvine, Chicago 18
Frank Boucher, N.Y. Rangers................15
Irvine Bailey, Toronto 13
Frank Fredrickson, Bos.-Det. 13
Frank Clancy, Ottawa.............................10

Points

Bill Cook, N.Y. Rangers 37
Dick Irvin, Chicago...............................36
Howie Morenz, Mon. Canadiens...........32
Frank Fredrickson, Det.-Bos. 31
Babe Dye, Chicago 30

Penalty minutes

Nels Stewart, Mon. Maroons..............133
Eddie Shore, Boston...........................130
Reginald Smith, Ottawa.......................125
Albert Siebert, Mon. Maroons 116
George Boucher, Ottawa.....................115

Lowest goals-against average (Min. 25 games)

Clint Benedict, Mon. Maroons...........1.51
George Hainsworth, Mon. Canadiens..1.52
Lorne Chabot, N.Y. Rangers 1.56
Alex Connell, Ottawa 1.57
Hal Winkler, NYR-Bos. 1.81

Shutouts

George Hainsworth, Mon. Canadiens...14
Clint Benedict, Mon. Maroons.............13
Alex Connell, Ottawa 12
Lorne Chabot, N.Y. Rangers 10
Jake Forbes, N.Y. Americans..................8

1927-28

Goals

Howie Morenz, Mon. Canadiens...........33
Aurel Joliat, Mon. Canadiens................28
Nels Stewart, Mon. Maroons................27
Frank Boucher, N.Y. Rangers................23
George Hay, Detroit..............................22

Assists

Howie Morenz, Mon. Canadiens...........18
Fred Cook, N.Y. Rangers 14
George Hay, Detroit..............................13
Frank Boucher, N.Y. Rangers................12
Aurel Joliat, Mon. Canadiens................11
Sylvio Mantha, Mon. Canadiens...........11

Points

Howie Morenz, Mon. Canadiens...........51
Aurel Joliat, Mon. Canadiens................39
Frank Boucher, N.Y. Rangers................35
George Hay, Detroit..............................35
Nels Stewart, Mon. Maroons................34

Penalty minutes

Eddie Shore, Boston...........................165
Ivan Johnson, N.Y. Rangers...............146
Clarence Boucher, N.Y. Americans 129
Albert Siebert, Mon. Maroons 109
Aurel Joliat, Mon. Canadiens..............105

Lowest goals-against average (Min. 25 games)

George Hainsworth, Mon. Canadiens...1.09
Alex Connell, Ottawa 1.29
Hal Winkler, Boston............................1.59
Roy Worters, Pittsburgh 1.73
Clint Benedict, Mon. Maroons...........1.75

Shutouts

Alex Connell, Ottawa 15
Hal Winkler, Boston..............................15
George Hainsworth, Mon. Canadiens...13
Lorne Chabot, N.Y. Rangers 11
Harry Holmes, Detroit 11

1928-29

Goals

Irvine Bailey, Toronto 22
Nels Stewart, Mon. Maroons................21
Carson Cooper, Detroit.........................18
Howie Morenz, Mon. Canadiens...........17
Harry Oliver, Boston 17

Assists

Frank Boucher, N.Y. Rangers................16
Andy Blair, Toronto...............................15
Gerald Lowrey, Pit.-Tor. 12
Irvine Bailey, Toronto 10
Howie Morenz, Mon. Canadiens...........10

Points

Irvine Bailey, Toronto 32
Nels Stewart, Mon. Maroons................29
Carson Cooper, Detroit.........................27
Howie Morenz, Mon. Canadiens...........27
Andy Blair, Toronto...............................27

Penalty minutes

Mervyn Dutton, Mon. Maroons..........139
Lionel Conacher, N.Y. Americans........132
Reginald Smith, Mon. Maroons 120
Eddie Shore, Boston..............................96
Alex Smith, Ottawa...............................96

Lowest goals-against average (Min. 25 games)

George Hainsworth, Mon. Canadiens..0.98
Tiny Thompson, Boston 1.18
Roy Worters, N.Y. Americans............1.21
Clarence Dolson, Detroit 1.43
John Roach, N.Y. Rangers 1.48

Shutouts

George Hainsworth, Mon. Canadiens.....22
John Roach, N.Y. Rangers 13
Roy Worters, N.Y. Americans...............13
Lorne Chabot, Toronto 12
Tiny Thompson, Boston 12

1929-30

Goals

Ralph Weiland, Boston..........................43
Aubrey Clapper, Boston........................41
Howie Morenz, Mon. Canadiens...........40
Nels Stewart, Mon. Maroons................39
Hec Kilrea, Ottawa................................36

Assists

Frank Boucher, N.Y. Rangers................36
Norman Gainor, Boston........................31
Bill Cook, N.Y. Rangers 30
Ralph Weiland, Boston..........................30
Frank Clancy, Ottawa............................23

Points

Ralph Weiland, Boston..........................73
Frank Boucher, N.Y. Rangers................62
Aubrey Clapper, Boston........................61
Bill Cook, N.Y. Rangers 59
Hec Kilrea, Ottawa................................58

Penalty minutes

Joe Lamb, Ottawa 119
Sylvio Mantha, Mon. Canadiens.........108
Eddie Shore, Boston...........................105
Mervyn Dutton, Mon. Maroons 98
Harvey Rockburn, Detroit......................97

Lowest goals-against average (Min. 25 games)

Tiny Thompson, Boston 2.23
Charles Gardiner, Chicago 2.52
James Walsh, Mon. Maroons............2.55
George Hainsworth, Mon. Canadiens..2.57
Alex Connell, Ottawa 2.68

Shutouts

Lorne Chabot, Toronto 6
George Hainsworth, Mon. Canadiens.....4
Alex Connell, Ottawa 3
Charles Gardiner, Chicago 3
Tiny Thompson, Boston 3

1930-31

Goals

Charlie Conacher, Toronto 31
Bill Cook, N.Y. Rangers 30
Howie Morenz, Mon. Canadiens...........28
Ebbie Goodfellow, Detroit.....................25
Nels Stewart, Mon. Maroons................25
Ralph Weiland, Boston..........................25

Assists

Joe Primeau, Toronto............................32
Frank Boucher, N.Y. Rangers................27
Ebbie Goodfellow, Detroit.....................23
Howie Morenz, Mon. Canadiens...........23
Aurel Joliat, Mon. Canadiens................22

Points

Howie Morenz, Mon. Canadiens...........51
Ebbie Goodfellow, Detroit.....................48
Charlie Conacher, Toronto 43
Bill Cook, N.Y. Rangers 42
Ace Bailey, Toronto...............................42

Penalty minutes

Harvey Rockburn, Detroit....................118
Eddie Shore, Boston...........................105
Darcy Coulson, Philadelphia...............103
Allan Shields, Philadelphia 98
Marty Burke, Mon. Canadiens..............91
Joe Lamb, Ottawa 91

Lowest goals-against average (Min. 25 games)

Roy Worters, N.Y. Americans............1.68
Charles Gardiner, Chicago 1.77
John Roach, N.Y. Rangers 1.98
George Hainsworth, Mon. Canadiens...2.02
Tiny Thompson, Boston 2.05

Shutouts

Charles Gardiner, Chicago 12
George Hainsworth, Mon. Canadiens.....8
Roy Worters, N.Y. Americans.................8
John Roach, N.Y. Rangers 7
Lorne Chabot, Toronto 6
Clarence Dolson, Detroit 6

1931-32

Goals

Charles Conacher, Toronto 34
Bill Cook, N.Y. Rangers 34
Harvey Jackson, Toronto.......................28
Dave Trottier, Mon. Maroons................26
Howie Morenz, Mon. Canadiens...........24

Assists

Joe Primeau, Toronto............................37
Reginald Smith, Mon. Maroons 33

Harvey Jackson, Toronto......................25
Howie Morenz, Mon. Canadiens...........25
Aurel Joliat, Mon. Canadiens................24

Points

Harvey Jackson, Toronto......................53
Joe Primeau, Toronto..........................50
Howie Morenz, Mon. Canadiens...........49
Charlie Conacher, Toronto...................48
Bill Cook, N.Y. Rangers.......................48

Penalty minutes

Georges Mantha, N.Y. Americans.......107
Nick Wasnie, N.Y. Rangers.................106
Reginald Horner, Toronto.....................97
Dave Trottier, Mon. Maroons................94
Alex Levinsky, N.Y. Rangers.................88

Lowest goals-against average (Min. 25 games)

Charles Gardiner, Chicago.................2.10
Alex Connell, Detroit..........................2.25
George Hainsworth, Mon. Canadiens..2.32
John Roach, N.Y. Rangers.................2.34
Tiny Thompson, Boston......................2.42

Shutouts

John Roach, N.Y. Rangers.....................9
Tiny Thompson, Boston.........................9
Alex Connell, Detroit.............................6
George Hainsworth, Mon. Canadiens.....6
Roy Worters, N.Y. Americans.................5

1932-33

Goals

Bill Cook, N.Y. Rangers........................28
Harvey Jackson, Toronto......................27
Martin Barry, Boston............................24
Fred Cook, N.Y. Rangers......................22
Lawrence Northcott, Mon. Maroons 22

Assists

Frank Boucher, N.Y. Rangers................28
Eddie Shore, Boston.............................27
Paul Haynes, Mon. Maroons.................25
Norman Himes, N.Y. Americans...........25
Johnny Gagnon, Mon. Canadiens 23

Points

Bill Cook, N.Y. Rangers........................50
Harvey Jackson, Toronto......................44
Lawrence Northcott, Mon. Maroons 43
Reg Smith, Mon. Maroons....................41
Paul Haynes, Mon. Maroons.................41

Penalty minutes

Reginald Horner, Toronto...................144
Ivan Johnson, N.Y. Rangers...............127
Allan Shields, Ottawa.........................119
Eddie Shore, Boston...........................102
Vern Ayres, N.Y. Americans..................97

Lowest goals-against average (Min. 25 games)

Tiny Thompson, Boston......................1.83
John Roach, Detroit...........................1.93
Charles Gardiner, Chicago.................2.10
Dave Kerr, Mon. Maroons..................2.20
Andy Aitkenhead, N.Y. Rangers.........2.23

Shutouts

Tiny Thompson, Boston.......................11
John Roach, Detroit.............................10
George Hainsworth, Mon. Canadiens.....8
Bill Beveridge, Ottawa...........................5
Lorne Chabot, Toronto...........................5
Charles Gardiner, Chicago......................5
Roy Worters, N.Y. Americans.................5

1933-34

Goals

Charlie Conacher, Toronto...................32
Marty Barry, Boston.............................27
Aurel Joliat, Mon. Canadiens................22
Nels Stewart, Boston............................22
Johnny Sorrell, Detroit.........................21

Assists

Joe Primeau, Toronto..........................32
Frank Boucher, N.Y. Rangers...............30
Cecil Dillon, N.Y. Rangers...................26
Elwyn Romnes, Chicago......................21
Charlie Conacher, Toronto..................20

Points

Charlie Conacher, Toronto..................52
Joe Primeau, Toronto..........................46
Frank Boucher, N.Y. Rangers...............44
Marty Barry, Boston.............................39
Cecil Dillon, N.Y. Rangers...................39

Penalty minutes

Reginald Horner, Toronto..................146
Lionel Conacher, Chicago....................87
Ivan Johnson, N.Y. Rangers.................86
Nels Stewart, Boston...........................68
Earl Seibert, N.Y. Rangers...................66

Lowest goals-against average (Min. 25 games)

Charles Gardiner, Chicago.................1.73
Wilfred Cude, Det.-Mon. C. 1.57
Roy Worters, N.Y. Americans............2.14
Lorne Chabot, Mon. Canadiens.........2.15
Andy Aitkenhead, N.Y. Rangers.........2.35

Shutouts

Charles Gardiner, Chicago..................10
Lorne Chabot, Mtl Canadiens.................8
Andy Aitkenhead, N.Y. Rangers.............7
Dave Kerr, Mon. Maroons.......................6
Wilfred Cude, Det.-Mon. C. 5
Tiny Thompson, Boston.........................5

1934-35

Goals

Charlie Conacher, Toronto...................36
Cecil Dillon, N.Y. Rangers....................25
Syd Howe, St.L.-Det............................22
Harvey Jackson, Toronto......................22
Three players tied with........................21

Assists

Art Chapman, N.Y. Americans.............34
Frank Boucher, N.Y. Rangers...............32
Larry Aurie, Detroit.............................29
Herb Lewis, Detroit.............................27
Howie Morenz, Chicago.......................26
Eddie Shore, Boston............................26

Points

Charlie Conacher, Toronto...................57
Syd Howe, St. Louis-Detroit.................47
Larry Aurie, Detroit.............................46
Frank Boucher, N.Y. Rangers...............45
Harvey Jackson, Toronto......................44

Penalty minutes

Reginald Horner, Toronto..................125
Irvine Frew, St. Louis..........................89
Earl Seibert, N.Y. Rangers...................86
Albert Siebert, Boston..........................80
Ralph Bowman, St.L.-Det.....................72

Lowest goals-against average (Min. 25 games)

Lorne Chabot, Chicago......................1.83
Alex Connell, Mon. Maroons.............1.92
Norman Smith, Detroit.......................2.08
George Hainsworth, Toronto.............2.28
Tiny Thompson, Boston......................2.33

Shutouts

Alex Connell, Mon. Maroons..................9
Lorne Chabot, Chicago...........................8
George Hainsworth, Toronto..................8
Tiny Thompson, Boston..........................8
Dave Kerr, N.Y. Rangers........................4
John Roach, Det.-Tor. 4

1935-36

Goals

Charlie Conacher, Toronto....................23
Bill Thoms, Toronto..............................23
Marty Barry, Detroit.............................21
David Schriner, N.Y. Americans...........19
Reginald Smith, Mon. Maroons 19

Assists

Art Chapman, N.Y. Americans..............28
David Schriner, N.Y. Americans............26
Elwyn Romnes, Chicago.......................25
Herb Lewis, Detroit..............................23
Paul Thompson, Chicago.....................23

Points

David Schriner, N.Y. Americans............45
Marty Barry, Detroit.............................40
Paul Thompson, Chicago.....................40
Five players tied with...........................38

Penalty minutes

Reginald Horner, Toronto...................167
Allan Shields, Mon. Maroons................81
Reginald Smith, Mon. Maroons 75
Charlie Conacher, Toronto...................74
Three players tied with.........................69

Lowest goals-against average (Min. 25 games)

Tiny Thompson, Boston.....................1.73
Mike Karakas, Chicago.......................1.92
Dave Kerr, N.Y. Rangers....................2.02
Norman Smith, Detroit.......................2.14
Bill Beveridge, Mon. Maroons............2.22

Shutouts

Tiny Thompson, Boston.......................10
Mike Karakas, Chicago...........................9
George Hainsworth, Toronto..................8
Dave Kerr, N.Y. Rangers........................8
Wilfred Cude, Mon. Canadiens...............6
Norman Smith, Detroit...........................6

1936-37

Goals

Larry Aurie, Detroit..............................23
Nels Stewart, Bos.-NYA........................23
Mehlville Keeling, N.Y. Rangers............22
Harvey Jackson, Toronto......................21
David Schriner, N.Y. Americans............21

Assists

Syl Apps, Toronto................................29
Marty Barry, Detroit.............................27
Bob Gracie, Mon. Maroons..................25
David Schriner, N.Y. Americans............25
Art Chapman, N.Y. Americans..............23

Points

David Schriner, N.Y. Americans............46
Syl Apps, Toronto................................45
Marty Barry, Detroit............................44
Larry Aurie, Detroit 43
Harvey Jackson, Toronto.....................40

Penalty minutes

Reginald Horner, Toronto 124
Allan Shields, NYA-Bos. 94
Lionel Conacher, Mon. Maroons 64
Jack Portland, Boston 58
Joe Jerwa, Bos.-NYA............................57

Lowest goals-against average (Min. 25 games)

Norman Smith, Detroit......................2.13
Dave Kerr, N.Y. Rangers 2.21
Wilfred Cude, Mon. Canadiens..........2.24
Tiny Thompson, Boston 2.29
Turk Broda, Toronto 2.32

Shutouts

Norman Smith, Detroit...........................6
Tiny Thompson, Boston 6
Wilfred Cude, Mon. Canadiens...............5
Mike Karakas, Chicago 5
Dave Kerr, N.Y. Rangers 4

1937-38

Goals

Gord Drillon, Toronto 26
Georges Mantha, Mon. Canadiens 23
Paul Thompson, Chicago 22
Syl Apps, Toronto.................................21
Cecil Dillon, N.Y. Rangers.....................21
David Schriner, N.Y. Americans............21

Assists

Syl Apps, Toronto.................................29
Art Chapman, N.Y. Americans 27
Gord Drillon, Toronto 26
Phil Watson, N.Y. Rangers 25
Bill Thoms, Toronto..............................24

Points

Gord Drillon, Toronto 52
Syl Apps, Toronto.................................50
Paul Thompson, Chicago 44
Georges Mantha, Mon. Canadiens 42
Cecil Dillon, N.Y. Rangers.....................39
Bill Cowley, Boston...............................39

Penalty minutes

Reginald Horner, Toronto 82
Art Coulter, N.Y. Rangers......................80
Ott Heller, N.Y. Rangers........................68
Stew Evans, Mon. Maroons 59
Four players tied with...........................56

Lowest goals-against average (Min. 25 games)

Tiny Thompson, Boston 1.85
Dave Kerr, N.Y. Rangers 2.00
Earl Robertson, N.Y. Americans 2.31
Turk Broda, Toronto 2.64
Wilfred, Cude, Mon. Canadiens.........2.68

Shutouts

Dave Kerr, N.Y. Rangers 8
Tiny Thompson, Boston 7
Turk Broda, Toronto 6
Earl Robertson, N.Y. Americans 6
Wilfred Cude, Mon. Canadiens...............3
Norman Smith, Detroit 3

1938-39

Goals

Roy Conacher, Boston..........................26
Toe Blake, Montreal..............................24
Alex Shibicky, N.Y. Rangers 24
Clint Smith, N.Y. Rangers......................21
Brian Hextall, N.Y. Rangers 20

Assists

Bill Cowley, Boston...............................34
Paul Haynes, Montreal 33
David Schriner, N.Y. Americans............31
Marty Barry, Detroit..............................28
Tom Anderson, N.Y. Americans............27

Points

Toe Blake, Montreal..............................47
David Schriner, N.Y. Americans............44
Bill Cowley, Boston...............................42
Clint Smith, N.Y. Rangers......................41
Marty Barry, Detroit..............................41

Penalty minutes

Reginald Horner, Toronto 85
Murray Patrick, N.Y. Rangers 64
Art Coulter, N.Y. Rangers......................58
Stew Evans, Montreal...........................58
Earl Seibert, Chicago 57

Lowest goals-against average (Min. 25 games)

Frank Brimsek, Boston 1.59
Dave Kerr, N.Y. Rangers 2.18
Turk Broda, Toronto 2.23
Tiny Thompson, Bos.-Det. 2.49
Mike Karakas, Chicago 2.75

Shutouts

Frank Brimsek, Boston 10
Turk Broda, Toronto 8
Dave Kerr, N.Y. Rangers 6
Mike Karakas, Chicago 5
Tiny Thompson, Bos.-Det. 4

1939-40

Goals

Brian Hextall, N.Y. Rangers 24
Woody Dumart, Boston.........................22
Milt Schmidt, Boston 22
Herb Cain, Boston 21
Gord Drillon, Toronto 21

Assists

Milt Schmidt, Boston 30
Phil Watson, N.Y. Rangers 28
Bill Cowley, Boston...............................27
Bob Bauer, Boston 26
Syd Howe, Detroit 23

Points

Milt Schmidt, Boston 52
Woody Dumart, Boston.........................43
Bob Bauer, Boston 43
Gord Drillon, Toronto 40
Bill Cowley, Boston...............................40

Penalty minutes

Reginald Horner, Toronto 87
Art Coulter, N.Y. Rangers......................68
Erwin Chamberlain, Toronto.................63
Jack Church, Toronto 62
Walter Pratt, N.Y. Rangers....................61

Lowest goals-against average (Min. 25 games)

Dave Kerr, N.Y. Rangers 1.60
Paul Goodman, Chicago 2.00
Frank Brimsek, Boston 2.04
Turk Broda, Toronto 2.30
Tiny Thompson, Detroit 2.61

Shutouts

Dave Kerr, N.Y. Rangers 8
Frank Brimsek, Boston 6
Earl Robertson, N.Y. Americans 6
Turk Broda, Toronto 4
Paul Goodman, Chicago 4

1940-41

Goals

Brian Hextall, N.Y. Rangers 26
Roy Conacher, Boston..........................24
David Schriner, Toronto........................24
Gord Drillon, Toronto 23
Three players tied with.........................20

Assists

Bill Cowley, Boston...............................45
Neil Colville, N.Y. Rangers.....................28
Bill Taylor, Toronto 26
Milton Schmidt, Boston 25
Phil Watson, N.Y. Rangers 25

Points

Bill Cowley, Boston...............................62
Brian Hextall, N.Y. Rangers 44
Gord Drillon, Toronto 44
Syl Apps, Toronto.................................44
Lynn Patrick, N.Y. Rangers....................44
Syd Howe, Detroit 44

Penalty minutes

Jimmy Orlando, Detroit.........................99
Clifford Goupille, Montreal 81
Erwin Chamberlain, Montreal...............75
Joe Cooper, Chicago 66
Des Smith, Boston 61

Lowest goals-against average (Min. 25 games)

Turk Broda, Toronto 2.06
Frank Brimsek, Boston 2.12
John Mowers, Detroit.........................2.12
Dave Kerr, N.Y. Rangers 2.60
Bert Gardiner, Montreal 2.84

Shutouts

Frank Brimsek, Boston 6
Turk Broda, Toronto 5
John Mowers, Detroit.............................4
Bert Gardiner, Montreal 2
Paul Goodman, Chicago.........................2
Dave Kerr, N.Y. Rangers 2

1941-42

Goals

Lynn Patrick, New York 32
Roy Conacher, Boston..........................24
Robert Hamill, Bos.-Chi........................24
Brian Hextall, New York.........................24
Gord Drillon, Toronto 23
Don Grosso, Detroit 23

Assists

Phil Watson, New York..........................37
Brian Hextall, New York.........................32
Syd Abel, Detroit 31
Don Grosso, Detroit 30
Bill Thoms, Chicago 30

Points

Brian Hextall, New York.........................56
Lynn Patrick, New York 54
Don Grosso, Detroit 53

Phil Watson, New York....52
Syd Abel, Detroit....49

Penalty minutes

Pat Egan, Brooklyn....104
Jack Stewart, Detroit....93
Ken Reardon, Montreal....83
Jimmy Orlando, Detroit....81
Bingo Kampman, Toronto....67

Lowest goals-against average (Min. 25 games)

Frank Brimsek, Boston....2.44
Turk Broda, Toronto....2.83
Jim Henry, New York....2.98
John Mowers, Detroit....3.06
Sam LoPresti, Chicago....3.23

Shutouts

Turk Broda, Toronto....6
John Mowers, Detroit....5
Frank Brimsek, Boston....3
Sam LoPresti, Chicago....3
Three players tied with....1

1942-43

Goals

Doug Bentley, Chicago....33
Joseph Benoit, Montreal....30
Gord Drillon, Montreal....28
Lorne Carr, Toronto....27
Bill Cowley, Boston....27
Brian Hextall, New York....27

Assists

Bill Cowley, Boston....45
Max Bentley, Chicago....44
Herbert O'Connor, Montreal....43
Billy Taylor, Toronto....42
Doug Bentley, Chicago....40
Elmer Lach, Montreal....40

Points

Doug Bentley, Chicago....73
Bill Cowley, Boston....72
Max Bentley, Chicago....70
Lynn Patrick, New York....61
Lorne Carr, Toronto....60
Billy Taylor, Toronto....60

Penalty minutes

James Orlando, Detroit....89
Reginald Hamilton, Toronto....68
Jack Stewart, Detroit....68
Erwin Chamberlain, Boston....67
Victor Myles, New York....57

Lowest goals-against average (Min. 25 games)

John Mowers, Detroit....2.48
Turk Broda, Toronto....3.18
Frank Brimsek, Boston....3.52
Bert Gardiner, Chicago....3.60
Paul Bibeault, Montreal....3.82

Shutouts

John Mowers, Detroit....6
Bill Beveridge, New York....1
Paul Bibeault, Montreal....1
Frank Brimsek, Boston....1
Turk Broda, Toronto....1
Bert Gardiner, Chicago....1

1943-44

Goals

Doug Bentley, Chicago....38
Herb Cain, Boston....36
Lorne Carr, Toronto....36
Carl Liscombe, Detroit....36
Moderre Bruneteau, Detroit....35

Assists

Clint Smith, Chicago....49
Elmer Lach, Montreal....48
Herb Cain, Boston....46
Herbert O'Connor, Montreal....42
Bill Cowley, Boston....41
Art Jackson, Boston....41

Points

Herb Cain, Boston....82
Doug Bentley, Chicago....77
Lorne Carr, Toronto....74
Carl Liscombe, Detroit....73
Elmer Lach, Montreal....72
Clint Smith, Chicago....72

Penalty minutes

Mike McMahon, Montreal....78
Harold Jackson, Detroit....76
Pat Egan Det.-Bos.....75
Bob Dill, New York....66
Erwin Chamberlain, Montreal....65

Lowest goals-against average (Min. 25 games)

Bill Durnan, Montreal....2.18
Paul Bibeault, Toronto....3.00
Connie Dion, Detroit....3.08
Mike Karakas, Chicago....3.04
Bert Gardiner, Boston....5.17

Shutouts

Paul Bibeault, Toronto....5
Mike Karakas, Chicago....3
Bill Durnan, Montreal....2
Connie Dion, Detroit....1
Jim Franks, Bos.-Det.....1
Bert Gardiner, Boston....1

1944-45

Goals

Maurice Richard, Montreal....50
Herb Cain, Boston....32
Toe Blake, Montreal....29
Ted Kennedy, Toronto....29
Bill Mosienko, Chicago....28

Assists

Elmer Lach, Montreal....54
Bill Cowley, Boston....40
Toe Blake, Montreal....38
Gus Bodnar, Toronto....36
Syd Howe, Detroit....36

Points

Elmer Lach, Montreal....80
Maurice Richard, Montreal....73
Toe Blake, Montreal....67
Bill Cowley, Boston....65
Five players tied with....54

Penalty minutes

Bob Dill, New York....59
Joe Cooper, Chicago....50
Hal Jackson, Detroit....45
Pete Horeck, Chicago....44
Ted Lindsay, Detroit....43

Lowest goals-against average (Min. 25 games)

Bill Durnan, Montreal....2.42
Harry Lumley, Detroit....3.22
Frank McCool, Toronto....3.22
Mike Karakas, Chicago....3.90
Paul Bibeault, Boston....4.46

Shutouts

Mike Karakas, Chicago....4
Frank McCool, Toronto....4
Bill Durnan, Montreal....1
Harry Lumley, Detroit....1
Ken McAuley, New York....1

1945-46

Goals

Gaye Stewart, Toronto....37
Max Bentley, Chicago....31
Toe Blake, Montreal....29
Maurice Richard, Montreal....27
Clint Smith, Chicago....26

Assists

Elmer Lach, Montreal....34
Max Bentley, Chicago....30
Bill Mosienko, Chicago....30
Albert DeMarco, New York....27
Alex Kaleta, Chicago....27

Points

Max Bentley, Chicago....61
Gaye Stewart, Toronto....52
Toe Blake, Montreal....50
Clint Smith, Chicago....50
Maurice Richard, Montreal....48
Bill Mosienko, Chicago....48

Penalty minutes

Jack Stewart, Detroit....73
Armand Guidolin, Boston....62
John Mariucci, Chicago....58
Emile Bouchard, Montreal....52
Maurice Richard, Montreal....50

Lowest goals-against average (Min. 25 games)

Bill Durnan, Montreal....2.60
Paul Bibeault, Bos.-Mon.....2.88
Harry Lumley, Detroit....3.18
Frank Brimsek, Boston....3.26
Mike Karakas, Chicago....3.46

Shutouts

Bill Durnan, Montreal....4
Paul Bibeault, Bos.-Mon.....2
Frank Brimsek, Boston....2
Harry Lumley, Detroit....2
Three players tied with....1

1946-47

Goals

Maurice Richard, Montreal....45
Bobby Bauer, Boston....30
Roy Conacher, Detroit....30
Max Bentley, Chicago....29
Ted Kennedy, Toronto....28

Assists

Billy Taylor, Detroit....46
Max Bentley, Chicago....43
Milt Schmidt, Boston....35
Doug Bentley, Chicago....34
Ted Kennedy, Toronto....32

Points

Max Bentley, Chicago....72
Maurice Richard, Montreal....71
Billy Taylor, Detroit....63
Milt Schmidt, Boston....62
Ted Kennedy, Toronto....60

Penalty minutes

Gus Mortson, Toronto....133
Johnny Mariucci, Chicago....110
Murph Chamberlain, Montreal....97
Jimmy Thomson, Toronto....97
Bill Ezinicki, Toronto....93

Lowest goals-against average (Min. 25 games)

Bill Durnan, Montreal....2.30
Turk Broda, Toronto....2.86
Frank Brimsek, Boston....2.91
Charlie Rayner, New York....3.05
Harry Lumley, Detroit....3.05

Shutouts

Charlie Rayner, New York....5
Turk Broda, Toronto....4
Bill Durnan, Montreal....4
Frank Brimsek, Boston....3
Harry Lumley, Detroit....3

1947-48

Goals

Ted Lindsay, Detroit....33
Elmer Lach, Montreal....30
Maurice Richard, Montreal....28
Gaye Stewart, Tor.-Chi....27
Syl Apps, Toronto....26
Max Bentley, Chi.-Tor....26

Assists

Doug Bentley, Chicago....37
Buddy O'Connor, New York....36
Edgar Laprade, New York....34
Elmer Lach, Montreal....31
Sid Abel, Detroit....30

Points

Elmer Lach, Montreal....61
Buddy O'Connor, New York....60
Doug Bentley, Chicago....57
Gaye Stewart, Tor.-Chi....56
Max Bentley, Chi.-Tor....54
Bud Poile, Tor.-Chi....54

Penalty minutes

Bill Barilko, Toronto....147
Ken Reardon, Montreal....129
Gus Mortson, Toronto....118
Bill Ezinicki, Toronto....97
Ted Lindsay, Detroit....95

Lowest goals-against average (Min. 25 games)

Turk Broda, Toronto....2.38
Harry Lumley, Detroit....2.45
Bill Durnan, Montreal....2.74
Frank Brimsek, Boston....2.82
Jim Henry, New York....3.19

Shutouts

Harry Lumley, Detroit....7
Turk Broda, Toronto....5
Bill Durnan, Montreal....5
Frank Brimsek, Boston....3
Jim Henry, New York....2

1948-49

Goals

Sid Abel, Detroit....28
Doug Bentley, Chicago....28
Jim Conacher, Det.-Chi....26
Roy Conacher, Chicago....26
Ted Lindsay, Detroit....26
Harry Watson, Toronto....26

Assists

Doug Bentley, Chicago....43
Roy Conacher, Chicago....42
Paul Ronty, Boston....29
Ted Lindsay, Detroit....28
Sid Abel, Detroit....26
Gus Bodnar, Chicago....26

Points

Roy Conacher, Chicago....68
Doug Bentley, Chicago....66
Sid Abel, Detroit....54
Ted Lindsay, Detroit....54
Jim Conacher, Det.-Chi....49
Paul Ronty, Boston....49

Penalty minutes

Bill Ezinicki, Toronto....145
Bep Guidolin, Det.-Chi....116
Erwin Chamberlain, Montreal....111
Maurice Richard, Montreal....110
Ken Reardon, Montreal....103

Lowest goals-against average (Min. 25 games)

Bill Durnan, Montreal....2.10
Harry Lumley, Detroit....2.42
Turk Broda, Toronto....2.68
Frank Brimsek, Boston....2.72
Claude Rayner, New York....2.90

Shutouts

Bill Durnan, Montreal....10
Claude Rayner, New York....7
Harry Lumley, Detroit....6
Turk Broda, Toronto....5
Frank Brimsek, Boston....1
Gordon Henry, Boston....1

1949-50

Goals

Maurice Richard, Montreal....43
Gordie Howe, Detroit....35
Sid Abel, Detroit....34
Gordie Howe, Detroit....35
Metro Prystai, Chicago....29
John Peirson, Boston....27

Assists

Ted Lindsay, Detroit....55
Paul Ronty, Boston....36
Sid Abel, Detroit....35
Bep Guidolin, Chicago....34
Doug Bentley, Chicago....33
Gordie Howe, Detroit....33
Elmer Lach, Montreal....33

Points

Ted Lindsay, Detroit....78
Sid Abel, Detroit....69
Gordie Howe, Detroit....68
Maurice Richard, Montreal....65
Paul Ronty, Boston....59

Penalty minutes

Bill Ezinicki, Toronto....144
Gus Kyle, New York....143
Ted Lindsay, Detroit....141
Bill Gadsby, Chicago....138
Gus Mortson, Toronto....125

Lowest goals-against average (Min. 25 games)

Bill Durnan, Montreal....2.20
Harry Lumley, Detroit....2.35
Turk Broda, Toronto....2.45
Chuck Rayner, New York....2.62
Jack Gelineau, Boston....3.28

Shutouts

Tuck Broda, Toronto....9
Bill Durnan, Montreal....8
Harry Lumley, Detroit....7
Chuck Rayner, New York....6
Frank Brimsek, Chicago....5

1950-51

Goals

Gordie Howe, Detroit....43
Maurice Richard, Montreal....42
Tod Sloan, Toronto....31
Sid Smith, Toronto....30
Roy Conacher, Chicago....26

Assists

Gordie Howe, Detroit....43
Ted Kennedy Toronto....43
Max Bentley, Toronto....41
Milton Schmidt, Boston....39
Sid Abel, Detroit....38

Points

Gordie Howe, Detroit....86
Maurice Richard, Montreal....66
Max Bentley, Toronto....62
Sid Abel, Detroit....61
Milt Schmidt, Boston....61
Ted Kennedy, Toronto....61

Penalty minutes

Gus Mortson, Toronto....142
Tom Johnson, Montreal....128
Bill Ezinicki, Boston....119
Tony Leswick, New York....112
Ted Lindsay, Detroit....110

Lowest goals-against average (Min. 25 games)

Al Rollins, Toronto....1.75
Terry Sawchuk, Detroit....1.98
Turk Broda, Toronto....2.19
Gerry McNeil, Montreal....2.63
Jack Gelineau, Boston....2.81

Shutouts

Terry Sawchuk, Detroit....11
Turk Broda, Toronto....6
Gerry McNeil, Montreal....6
Al Rollins, Toronto....5
Jack Gelineau, Boston....4

1951-52

Goals

Gordie Howe, Detroit....47
Bill Mosienko, Chicago....31
Bernie Geoffrion, Montreal....30
Ted Lindsay, Detroit....30
Maurice Richard, Montreal....27
Sid Smith, Toronto....27

Assists

Elmer Lach, Montreal....50
Don Raleigh, New York....42
Gordie Howe, Detroit....39
Ted Lindsay, Detroit....39
Sid Abel, Detroit....36

Points

Gordie Howe, Detroit....86
Ted Lindsay, Detroit....69
Elmer Lach, Montreal....65
Don Raleigh, New York....61
Sid Smith, Toronto....57

Penalty minutes

Gus Kyle, Boston ... 127
Ted Lindsay, Detroit ... 123
Fern Flaman, Toronto ... 110
Gus Mortson, Toronto ... 106
Al Dewsbury, Chicago ... 99

Lowest goals-against average (Min. 25 games)

Terry Sawchuk, Detroit ... 1.90
Al Rollins, Toronto ... 2.20
Gerry McNeil, Montreal ... 2.34
Jim Henry, Boston ... 2.51
Claude Rayner, New York ... 3.00

Shutouts

Terry Sawchuk, Detroit ... 12
Jim Henry, Boston ... 7
Gerry McNeil, Montreal ... 5
Al Rollins, Toronto ... 5
Harry Lumley, Chicago ... 2
Claude Rayner, New York ... 2

1952-53

Goals

Gordie Howe, Detroit ... 49
Ted Lindsay, Detroit ... 32
Wally Hergesheimer, New York ... 30
Maurice Richard, Montreal ... 28
Fleming Mackell, Boston ... 27

Assists

Gordie Howe, Detroit ... 46
Alex Delvecchio, Detroit ... 43
Ted Lindsay, Detroit ... 39
Paul Ronty, New York ... 38
Metro Prystai, Detroit ... 34

Points

Gordie Howe, Detroit ... 95
Ted Lindsay, Detroit ... 71
Maurice Richard, Montreal ... 61
Wally Hergesheimer, New York ... 59
Alex Delvecchio, Detroit ... 59

Penalty minutes

Maurice Richard, Montreal ... 112
Ted Lindsay, Detroit ... 111
Fern Flaman, Toronto ... 110
George Gee, Chicago ... 99
Leo Boivin, Toronto ... 97
Al Dewsbury, Chicago ... 97

Lowest goals-against average (Min. 25 games)

Terry Sawchuk, Detroit ... 1.90
Gerry McNeil, Montreal ... 2.12
Harry Lumley, Toronto ... 2.38
Jim Henry, Boston ... 2.46
Al Rollins, Chicago ... 2.50

Shutouts

Harry Lumley, Toronto ... 10
Gerry McNeil, Montreal ... 10
Terry Sawchuk, Detroit ... 9
Jim Henry, Boston ... 7
Al Rollins, Chicago ... 6

1953-54

Goals

Maurice Richard, Montreal ... 37
Gordie Howe, Detroit ... 33
Bernie Geoffrion, Montreal ... 29
Wally Hergesheimer, New York ... 27
Ted Lindsay, Detroit ... 26

Assists

Gordie Howe, Detroit ... 48
Bert Olmstead, Montreal ... 37
Ted Lindsay, Detroit ... 36
Four players tied with ... 33

Points

Gordie Howe, Detroit ... 81
Maurice Richard, Montreal ... 67
Ted Lindsay, Detroit ... 62
Bernie Geoffrion, Montreal ... 54
Bert Olmstead, Montreal ... 52

Penalty minutes

Gus Mortson, Chicago ... 132
Maurice Richard, Montreal ... 112
Douglas Harvey, Montreal ... 110
Ted Lindsay, Detroit ... 110
Gordie Howe, Detroit ... 109
Ivan Irwin, New York ... 109

Lowest goals-against average (Min. 25 games)

Harry Lumley, Toronto ... 1.85
Terry Sawchuk, Detroit ... 1.92
Gerry McNeil, Montreal ... 2.15
Jim Henry, Boston ... 2.58
John Bower, New York ... 2.60

Shutouts

Harry Lumley, Toronto ... 13
Terry Sawchuk, Detroit ... 12
Jim Henry, Boston ... 8
Gerry McNeil, Montreal ... 6
John Bower, New York ... 5
Jacques Plante, Montreal ... 5

1954-55

Goals

Bernie Geoffrion, Montreal ... 38
Maurice Richard, Montreal ... 38
Jean Beliveau, Montreal ... 37
Sid Smith, Toronto ... 33
Gordie Howe, Detrot ... 29
Danny Lewicki, New York ... 29

Assists

Bert Olmstead, Montreal ... 48
Doug Harvey, Montreal ... 43
Ted Kennedy, Toronto ... 42
George Sullivan, Chicago ... 42
Earl Reibel, Detroit ... 41

Points

Bernie Geoffrion, Montreal ... 75
Maurice Richard, Montreal ... 74
Jean Beliveau, Montreal ... 73
Earl Reibel, Detroit ... 66
Gordie Howe, Detroit ... 62

Penalty minutes

Fern Flaman, Boston ... 150
Tony Leswick, Detroit ... 137
Bucky Hollingworth, Chicago ... 135
Gus Mortson, Chicago ... 133
Jean Beliveau, Montreal ... 125

Lowest goals-against average (Min. 25 games)

Terry Sawchuk, Detroit ... 1.94
Harry Lumley, Toronto ... 1.94
Jacques Plante, Montreal ... 2.11
John Henderson, Boston ... 2.40
Jim Henry, Boston ... 3.00

Shutouts

Terry Sawchuk, Detroit ... 12
Harry Lumley, Toronto ... 8
John Henderson, Boston ... 5
Jacques Plante, Montreal ... 5
Gump Worsley, New York ... 4

1955-56

Goals

Jean Beliveau, Montreal ... 47
Gordie Howe, Detroit ... 38
Maurice Richard, Montreal ... 38
Tod Sloan, Toronto ... 37
Bernie Goeffrion, Montreal ... 29

Assists

Bert Olmstead, Montreal ... 56
Andy Bathgate, New York ... 47
Bill Gadsby, New York ... 42
Jean Beliveau, Montreal ... 41
Gordie Howe, Detroit ... 41

Points

Jean Beliveau, Montreal ... 88
Gordie Howe, Detroit ... 79
Maurice Richard, Montreal ... 71
Bert Olmstead, Montreal ... 70
Tod Sloan, Toronto ... 66
Andy Bathgate, New York ... 66

Penalty minutes

Lou Fontinato, New York ... 202
Ted Lindsay, Detroit ... 161
Jean Beliveau, Montreal ... 143
Bob Armstrong, Boston ... 122
Vic Stasiuk, Boston ... 118

Lowest goals-against average (Min. 25 games)

Jacques Plante, Montreal ... 1.86
Glenn Hall, Detroit ... 2.11
Terry Sawchuk, Boston ... 2.66
Harry Lumley, Toronto ... 2.69
Gump Worsley, New York ... 2.90

Shutouts

Glenn Hall, Detroit ... 12
Terry Sawchuk, Boston ... 9
Jacques Plante, Montreal ... 7
Gump Worsley, New York ... 4
Harry Lumley, Toronto ... 3
Al Rollins, Chicago ... 3

1956-57

Goals

Gordie Howe, Detroit ... 44
Jean Beliveau, Montreal ... 33
Maurice Richard, Montreal ... 33
Ed Litzenberger, Chicago ... 32
Real Chevrefils, Boston ... 31

Assists

Ted Lindsay, Detroit ... 55
Jean Beliveau, Montreal ... 51
Andy Bathgate, New York ... 50
Gordie Howe, Detroit ... 45
Doug Harvey, Montreal ... 44

Points

Gordie Howe, Detroit ... 89
Ted Lindsay, Detroit ... 85
Jean Beliveau, Montreal ... 84
Andy Bathgate, New York ... 77
Ed Litzenberger, Chicago ... 64

Penalty minutes

Gus Mortson, Chicago ... 147
Lou Fontinato, New York ... 139

Leo LaBine, Boston 128
Pierre Pilote, Chicago.........................117
Jack Evans, New York.........................110

Lowest goals-against average (Min. 25 games)

Jacques Plante, Montreal..................2.02
Glenn Hall, Detroit.............................2.24
Terry Sawchuk, Boston.......................2.38
Don Simmons, Boston........................2.42
Ed Chadwich, Toronto........................2.74

Shutouts

Jacques Plante, Montreal........................9
Ed Chadwick, Toronto.............................5
Glenn Hall, Detroit..................................4
Don Simmons, Boston..............................4
Al Rollins, Chicago..................................3
Gump Worsley, New York........................3

1957-58

Goals

Dickie Moore, Montreal..........................36
Gordie Howe, Detroit..............................33
Camille Henry, New York........................32
Fleming Mackell, Boston.........................32
Andy Bathgate, New York........................30
Bronco Horvath, Boston..........................30

Assists

Henri Richard, Montreal..........................52
Andy Bathgate, New York........................48
Dickie Moore, Montreal...........................48
Gordie Howe, Detroit..............................44
Fleming Mackell, Boston.........................40

Points

Dickie Moore, Montreal...........................84
Henri Richard, Montreal..........................80
Andy Bathgate, New York........................78
Gordie Howe, Detroit...............................77
Bronco Horvath, Boston..........................66

Penalty minutes

Lou Fontinato, New York.......................152
Forbes Kennedy, Detroit........................135
Doug Harvey, Montreal..........................131
Ted Lindsay, Chicago.............................110
Jack Evans, New York............................108

Lowest goals-against average (Min. 25 games)

Jacques Plante, Montreal...................2.09
Gump Worsley, New York....................2.32
Don Simmons, Boston.........................2.45
Harry Lumley, Boston.........................2.84
Glenn Hall, Chicago............................2.88

Shutouts

Jacques Plante, Montreal.........................9
Glenn Hall, Chicago.................................7
Don Simmons, Boston..............................5
Gump Worsley, New York........................4
Ed Chadwick, Toronto..............................4

1958-59

Goals

Jean Beliveau, Montreal..........................45
Dickie Moore, Montreal...........................41
Andy Bathgate, N.Y Rangers..................40
Ed Litzenberger, Chicago........................33
Andy Hebenton, New York.......................33

Assists

Dickie Moore, Montreal...........................55
Andy Bathgate, New York........................48
Jean Beliveau, Montreal..........................46
Bill Gadsby, New York.............................46
Gordie Howe, Detroit...............................46

Points

Dickie Moore, Montreal...........................96
Jean Beliveau, Montreal..........................91
Andy Bathgate, New York........................88
Gordie Howe, Detroit...............................78
Ed Litzenberger, Chicago........................77

Penalty minutes

Ted Lindsay, Chicago.............................184
Lou Fontinato, New York.......................149
Carl Brewer, Toronto.............................125
Jim Bartlett, New York...........................118
Pete Goegan, Detroit.............................109
Eddie Shack, New York..........................109

Lowest goals-against average (Min. 25 games)

Jacques Plante, Montreal...................2.15
Johnny Bower, Toronto......................2.74
Glenn Hall, Chicago............................2.97
Eddie Chadwick, Toronto....................3.00
Gump Worsley, New York....................3.06

Shutouts

Jacques Plante, Montreal.........................9
Terry Sawchuk, Detroit.............................5
Johnny Bower, Toronto............................3
Eddie Chadwick, Toronto.........................3
Don Simmons, Boston..............................3

1959-60

Goals

Bobby Hull, Chicago................................39
Bronco Horvath, Boston..........................39
Jean Beliveau, Montreal..........................34
Dean Prentice, New York........................32
Bernie Geoffrion, Montreal......................30
Henri Richard, Montreal..........................30

Assists

Don McKenney, Boston...........................49
Andy Bathgate, New York........................48
Gordie Howe, Detroit...............................45
Henri Richard, Montreal..........................43
Bobby Hull, Chicago................................42

Points

Bobby Hull, Chicago................................81
Bronco Horvath, Boston..........................80
Jean Beliveau, Montreal..........................74
Andy Bathgate, New York........................74
Henri Richard, Montreal..........................73
Gordie Howe, Detroit...............................73

Penalty minutes

Carl Brewer, Toronto.............................150
Lou Fontinato, New York.......................137
Vic Stasiuk, Boston...............................121
Stan Mikita, Chicago..............................119
Fern Flamen, Boston..............................112

Lowest goals-against average (Min. 25 games)

Jacques Plante, Montreal...................2.54
Glenn Hall, Chicago............................2.57
Terry Sawchuk, Detroit.......................2.69
Johnny Bower, Toronto......................2.73
Don Simmons, Boston.........................3.36

Shutouts

Glenn Hall, Chicago.................................6
Johnny Bower, Toronto............................5
Terry Sawchuk, Detroit.............................5
Jacques Plante, Montreal.........................3
Harry Lumley, Boston..............................2
Don Simmons, Boston..............................2

1960-61

Goals

Bernie Geoffrion, Montreal......................50
Frank Mahovlich, Toronto........................48
Dickie Moore, Montreal...........................35
Jean Beliveau, Montreal..........................32
Bobby Hull, Chicago................................31

Assists

Jean Beliveau, Montreal..........................58
Red Kelly, Toronto..................................50
Gordie Howe, Detroit...............................49
Andy Bathgate, New York........................48
Bill Hay, Chicago....................................48

Points

Bernie Geoffrion, Montreal......................95
Jean Beliveau, Montreal..........................90
Frank Mahovlich, Toronto........................84
Andy Bathgate, New York........................77
Gordie Howe, Detroit...............................72

Penalty minutes

Pierre Pilote, Chicago............................165
Reg Fleming, Chicago............................145
Jean Guy Talbot, Montreal.....................143
Frank Mahovlich, Toronto.......................131
Eric Nesterenko, Chicago.......................125

Lowest goals-against average (Min. 25 games)

Johnny Bower, Toronto......................2.50
Charlie Hodge, Montreal.....................2.53
Jacques Plante, Montreal...................2.80
Hank Bassen, Detroit.........................2.97
Terry Sawchuk, Detroit.......................3.17

Shutouts

Glenn Hall, Chicago.................................6
Charlie Hodge, Montreal..........................4
Johnny Bower, Toronto............................2
Jacques Plante, Montreal.........................2
Terry Sawchuk, Detroit.............................2

1961-62

Goals

Bobby Hull, Chicago................................50
Gordie Howe, Detroit...............................33
Frank Mahovlich, Toronto........................33
Claude Provost, Montreal........................33
Gilles Tremblay, Montreal........................32

Assists

Andy Bathgate, New York........................56
Bill Hay, Chicago....................................52
Stan Mikita, Chicago...............................52
Gordie Howe, Detroit...............................44
Alex Delvecchio, Detroit..........................43

Points

Bobby Hull, Chicago................................84
Andy Bathgate, New York........................84
Gordie Howe, Detroit...............................77
Stan Mikita, Chicago...............................77
Frank Mahovlich, Toronto........................71

Penalty minutes

Lou Fontinato, Montreal.........................167
Ted Green, Boston..................................116
Bob Pulford, Toronto................................98
Stan Mikita, Chicago................................97
Eric Nesterenko, Chicago.........................97
Pierre Pilote, Chicago..............................97

Lowest goals-against average (Min. 25 games)

Jacques Plante, Montreal 2.37
John Bower, Toronto 2.58
Glenn Hall, Chicago 2.66
Henry Bassen, Detroit 2.81
Gump Worsley, New York 2.90

Shutouts

Glenn Hall, Chicago 9
Terry Sawchuk, Detroit 5
Jacques Plante, Montreal 4
Henry Bassen, Detroit 3
Three players tied with 2

1962-63

Goals

Gordie Howe, Detroit 38
Camille Henry, New York 37
Frank Mahovlich, Toronto 36
Andy Bathgate, New York 35
Parker MacDonald, Detroit 33

Assists

Henri Richard, Montreal 50
Jean Beliveau, Montreal 49
Gordie Howe, Detroit 48
Andy Bathgate, New York 46
Stan Mikita, Chicago 45

Points

Gordie Howe, Detroit 86
Andy Bathgate, New York 81
Stan Mikita, Chicago 76
Frank Mahovlich, Toronto 73
Henri Richard, Montreal 73

Penalty minutes

Howie Young, Detroit 273
Carl Brewer, Tornoto 168
Lou Fontinato, Montreal 141
Ted Green, Boston 117
Bill Gladsby, Detroit 116

Lowest goals-against average (Min. 25 games)

Jacques Plante, Montreal 2.46
Terry Sawchuk, Detroit 2.48
Don Simmons, Toronto 2.50
Glenn Hall, Chicago 2.51
Johnny Bower, Toronto 2.62

Shutouts

Glenn Hall, Chicago 5
Jacques Plante, Montreal 5
Terry Sawchuk, Detroit 3
Gump Worsley, New York 2
Four players tied with 1

1963-64

Goals

Bobby Hull, Chicago 43
Stan Mikita, Chicago 39
Ken Wharram, Chicago 39
Camille Henry, New York 29
Jean Beliveau, Montreal 28

Assists

Andy Bathgate, N.Y.-Tor. 58
Jean Beliveau, Montreal 50
Stan Mikita, Chicago 50
Gordie Howe, Detroit 47
Pierre Pilote, Chicago 46

Points

Stan Mikita, Chicago 89
Bobby Hull, Chicago 87
Jean Beliveau, Montreal 78
Andy Bathgate, N.Y.-Tor. 77
Gordie Howe, Detroit 73

Penalty minutes

Vic Hadfield, New York 151
Terry Harper, Montreal 149
Stan Mikita, Chicago 146
Ted Green, Boston 145
Reg Fleming, Chicago 140

Lowest goals-against average (Min. 25 games)

Johnny Bower, Toronto 2.12
Charlie Hodge, Montreal 2.26
Glenn Hall, Chicago 2.30
Terry Sawchuk, Detroit 2.70
Eddie Johnston, Boston 3.01

Shutouts

Charlie Hodge, Montreal 8
Glenn Hall, Chicago 7
Ed Johnston, Boston 6
Johnny Bower, Toronto 5
Terry Sawchuk, Detroit 5

1964-65

Goals

Norm Ullman, Detroit 42
Bobby Hull, Chicago 39
Gordie Howe, Detroit 29
Stan Mikita, Chicago 28
Claude Provost, Montreal 27

Assists

Stan Mikita, Chicago 59
Gordie Howe, Detroit 47
Pierre Pilote, Chicago 45
Alex Delvecchio, Detroit 42
Norm Ullman, Detroit 41

Points

Stan Mikita, Chicago 87
Norm Ullman, Detroit 83
Gordie Howe, Detroit 76
Bobby Hull, Chicago 71
Alex Delvecchio, Detroit 67

Penalty minutes

Carl Brewer, Toronto 177
Ted Lindsay, Detroit 173
Pierre Pilote, Chicago 162
Bob Baun, Toronto 160
John Ferguson, Montreal 156
Ted Green, Boston 156

Lowest goals-against average (Min. 25 games)

Johnny Bower, Toronto 2.38
Roger Crozier, Detroit 2.42
Glenn Hall, Chicago 2.43
Denis DeJordy, Chicago 2.52
Terry Sawchuk, Toronto 2.56

Shutouts

Roger Crozier, Detroit 6
Glenn Hall, Chicago 4
Johnny Bower, Toronto 3
Denis DeJordy, Chicago 3
Charlie Hodge, Montreal 3
Ed Johnston, Boston 3

1965-66

Goals

Bobby Hull, Chicago 54
Frank Mahovlich, Toronto 32
Alex Delvecchio, Detroit 31
Norm Ullman, Detroit 31
Stan Mikita, Chicago 30
Bobby Rousseau, Montreal 30

Assists

Jean Beliveau, Montreal 48
Stan Mikita, Chicago 48
Bobby Rousseau, Montreal 48
Gordie Howe, Detroit 46
Bobby Hull, Chicago 43

Points

Bobby Hull, Chicago 97
Stan Mikita, Chicago 78
Bobby Rousseau, Montreal 78
Jean Beliveau, Montreal 77
Gordie Howe, Detroit 75

Penalty minutes

Reg Fleming, Bos.-N.Y. 166
John Ferguson, Montreal 153
Bryan Watson, Detroit 133
Ted Green, Boston 113
Vic Hadfield, New York 112

Lowest goals-against average (Min. 25 games)

Johnny Bower, Toronto 2.25
Gump Worsley, Montreal 2.36
Charlie Hodge, Montreal 2.58
Glenn Hall, Chicago 2.63
Roger Crozier, Detroit 2.78

Shutouts

Roger Crozier, Detroit 7
Bruce Gamble, Toronto 4
Glenn Hall, Chicago 4
Johnny Bower, Toronto 3
Cesare Maniago, New York 2
Gump Worsley, Montreal 2

1966-67

Goals

Bobby Hull, Chicago 52
Stan Mikita, Chicago 35
Ken Wharram, Chicago 31
Rod Gilbert, New York 28
Bruce MacGregor, Detroit 28

Assists

Stan Mikita, Chicago 62
Phil Goyette, New York 49
Pierre Pilote, Chicago 46
Bobby Rousseau, Montreal 44
Norm Ullman, Detroit 44

Points

Stan Mikita, Chicago 97
Bobby Hull, Chicago 80
Norm Ullman, Detroit 70
Ken Wharram, Chicago 65
Gordie Howe, Detroit 65

Penalty minutes

John Ferguson, Montreal 177
Reg Fleming, New York 146
Gary Bergman, Detroit 129
Gilles Marotte, Boston 112
Ed Van Impe, Chicago 111

Lowest goals-against average (Min. 25 games)

Glenn Hall, Chicago 2.38
Denis DeJordy, Chicago 2.46
Charlie Hodge, Montreal 2.60
Ed Giacomin, New York 2.61
Johnny Bower, Toronto 2.64

Shutouts

Ed Giacomin, New York 9
Roger Crozier, Detroit 4

Denis DeJordy, Chicago 4
Charlie Hodge, Montreal........................3
Three players tied with 2

1967-68

Goals

Bobby Hull, Chicago..........................44
Stan Mikita, Chicago 40
Gordie Howe, Detroit..........................39
Phil Esposito, Boston..........................35
Wayne Connelly, Minnesota 35

Assists

Phil Esposito, Boston..........................49
Alex Delvecchio, Detroit......................48
Rod Gilbert, New York.........................48
Stan Mikita, Chicago 47
Jean Ratelle, New York.........................46

Points

Stan Mikita, Chicago 87
Phil Esposito, Boston..........................84
Gordie Howe, Detroit..........................82
Jean Ratelle, New York.........................78
Rod Gilbert, New York.........................77

Penalty minutes

Gary Dornhoefer, Philadelphia............134
Ted Green, Boston.............................133
Reg Fleming, New York......................132
Forbes Kennedy, Philadelphia.............130
Kent Douglas, Oak.-Det. 126

Lowest goals-against average (Min. 25 games)

Gump Worsley, Montreal 1.98
Johnny Bower, Toronto 2.25
Boug Favell, Philadelphia 2.27
Bruce Gamble, Toronto 2.31
Ed Giacomin, New York....................2.44

Shutouts

Ed Giacomin, New York.........................8
Les Binkley, Pittburgh 6
Cesare Maniago, Minnesota 6
Lorn Worsley, Montreal..........................6
Bruce Gamble, Toronto 5
Glen Hall, St. Louis 5

1968-69

Goals

Bobby Hull, Chicago............................58
Phil Esposito, Boston..........................49
Frank Mahovlich, Detroit......................49
Ken Hodge, Boston 45
Gordie Howe, Detroit..........................44

Assists

Phil Esposito, Boston..........................77
Stan Mikita, Chicago 67
Gordie Howe, Detroit..........................59
Alex Delvecchio, Detroit......................58
Four players tied with..........................49

Points

Phil Esposito, Boston........................126
Bobby Hull, Chicago..........................107
Gordie Howe, Detroit........................103
Stan Mikita, Chicago 97
Ken Hodge, Boston 90

Penalty minutes

Forbes Kennedy, Phi.-Tor. 219
Jim Dorey, Toronto............................200
John Ferguson, Montreal 185
Carol Vadnais, Oakland 151
Don Awrey, Bosotn............................149

Lowest goals-against average (Min. 25 games)

Jacques Plante, St. Louis.................1.96
Glenn Hall, St. Louis 2.17
Gump Worsley, Montreal 2.26
Ron Edwards, Detroit........................2.54
Ed Giacomin, New York....................2.55

Shutouts

Ed Giacomin, New York.........................7
Jaques Plante, St. Louis.........................5
Gump Worsley, Montreal 5
Roy Edwards, Detroit 4
Gary Smith, Oakland 4
Gerry Desjardins, Los Angeles..............4

1969-70

Goals

Phil Esposito, Boston..........................43
Garry Unger, Detroit............................42
Stan Mikita, Chicago 39
Bobby Hull, Chicago............................38
Frank Mahovlich, Detroit......................38

Assists

Bobby Orr, Boston..............................87
Phil Esposito, Boston..........................56
Tommy Williams, Minnesota...............52
Walt Tkaczuk, New York......................50
Phil Goyette, St. Louis.........................49

Points

Bobby Orr, Boston............................120
Phil Esposito, Boston..........................99
Stan Mikita, Chicago 86
Phil Goyette, St. Louis.........................78
Walt Tkaczuk, New York......................77

Penalty minutes

Keith Magnuson, Chicago 213
Carol Vadnais, California 212
Bryan Watson, Pittsburgh 189
Barry Gibbs, Minnesota.....................182
Earl Heiskala, Philadelphia 171

Lowest goals-against average (Min. 25 games)

Ernie Wakely, St. Louis.....................2.11
Tony Esposito, Chicago 2.17
Jacques Plante St. Louis..................2.19
Ed Giacomin, New York....................2.36
Roy Edwards, Detroit 2.59

Shutouts

Tony Esposito, Chicago 15
Ed Giacomin, New York.........................6
Bruce Gambel, Toronto 5
Jacques Plante, St. Louis.......................5
Gerry Cheevers, Boston 4
Rogie Vachon, Montreal........................4
Ernie Wakely, St. Louis..........................4

Wins by goaltenders

Tony Esposito, Chicago 38
Ed Giacomin, New York.......................35
Rogie Vachon, Montreal.......................31
Gerry Cheevers, Boston 24
Roy Edwards, Detroit 24

1970-71

Goals

Phil Esposito, Boston..........................76
John Bucyk, Boston 51
Bobby Hull, Chicago............................44
Ken Hodge, Boston 43
Dennis Hull, Chicago 40

Assists

Bobby Orr, Boston............................102
Phil Esposito, Boston..........................76
John Bucyk, Boston 65
Ken Hodge, Boston 62
Wayne Cashman, Boston 58

Points

Phil Esposito, Boston........................152
Bobby Orr, Boston............................139
John Bucyk, Boston 116
Ken Hodge, Boston 105
Bobby Hull, Chicago............................96

Penalty minutes

Keith Magnuson, Chicago 291
Dennis Hextall, California 217
Jim Dorey, Toronto............................198
Pete Mahovlich, Montreal..................181
Tracy Pratt, Buffalo............................179

Lowest goals-against average (Min. 25 games)

Jacques Plante, Toronto...................1.88
Ed Giacomin, New York....................2.15
Tony Esposito, Chicago 2.27
Gilles Villemure, New York 2.29
Glenn Hall, St. Louis 2.41

Shutouts

Ed Giacomin, New York.........................8
Tony Esposito, Chicago 6
Cesare Maniago, Minnesota 5
Jacques Plante, Toronto 4
Ed Johnston, Boston 4
Gilles Villemure, New York 4

Wins by goaltenders

Tony Esposito, Chicago 35
Ed Johnston, Boston 30
Gerry Cheevers, Boston 27
Ed Giacomin, New York.......................27
Jacques Plante, Toronto......................24

1971-72

Goals

Phil Esposito, Boston..........................66
Vic Hadfield, New York.........................50
Bobby Hull, Chicago............................50
Yvan Cournoyer, Montreal...................47
Jean Ratelle, New York.........................46

Assists

Bobby Orr, Boston..............................80
Phil Esposito, Boston..........................67
Jean Ratelle, New York.........................63
Vic Hadfield, New York.........................56
Fred Stanfield, Boston 56

Points

Phil Esposito, Boston........................133
Bobby Orr, Boston............................117
Jean Ratelle, New York.......................109
Vic Hadfield, New York.......................106
Rod Gilbert, New York.........................97

Penalty minutes

Bryan Watson, Pittsburgh 212
Keith Magnuson, Chicago 199
Gary Dornhoefer, Philadelphia............183
Barclay Plager, St. Louis 176
Rick Floey, Philadelphia.....................168

Lowest goals-against average (Min. 25 games)

Tony Esposito, Chicago 1.76
Gilles Villemure, New York 2.08

Lorne Worsley, Minnesota................2.12
Ken Dryden, Montreal.......................2.34
Gary Smith, Chicago.........................2.41

Shutouts

Tony Esposito, Chicago..........................9
Ken Dryden, Montreal............................8
Gary Smith, Chicago..............................5
Doug Favell, Philadelphia........................5
Al Smith, Detroit......................................4
Gilles Meloche, California.......................4

Wins by goaltenders

Tony Esposito, Chicago........................31
Gerry Cheevers, Boston.......................27
Ed Johnston, Boston............................27
Ed Giacomin, New York.........................24
Gilles Villemure, New York...................24

1972-73

Goals

Phil Esposito, Boston...........................55
Mickey Redmond, Detroit......................52
Rick McLeish, Philadelphia...................50
Jacques Lemaire, Montreal...................44
Three players tied with.........................41

Assists

Phil Esposito, Boston...........................75
Bobby Orr, Boston................................72
Bobby Clarke, Philadelphia...................67
Pit Martin, Chicago...............................61
Gilbert Perreault, Buffalo......................60

Points

Phil Esposito, Boston.........................130
Bobby Clarke, Philadelphia.................104
Bobby Orr, Boston..............................101
Rick MacLeish, Philadelphia...............100
Jacques Lemaire, Montreal...................95

Penalty minutes

Dave Shultz, Philadelphia...................259
Bob Kelly, Philadelphia.......................238
Steve Durbano, St. Louis...................231
Andre Dupont, St.L.-Phi......................215
Don Saleski, Philadelphia...................205

Lowest goals-against average (Min. 25 games)

Ken Dryden, Montreal........................2.26
Gilles Villemure, N.Y. Rangers...........2.29
Tony Esposito, Chicago.....................2.51
Roy Edwards, Detroit........................2.63
Dave Dryden, Buffalo........................2.68

Shutouts

Ken Dryden, Montreal............................6
Roy Edwards, Detroit.............................6
Tony Esposito, Chicago..........................4
Cesare Maniago, Minnesota....................4
Rogie Vachon, Los Angeles....................4

Wins by goaltenders

Ken Dryden, Montreal..........................33
Tony Esposito, Chicago........................32
Roy Edwards, Detroit............................27
Ed Giacomin, N.Y. Rangers..................26
Ed Johnston, Boston............................24

1973-74

Goals

Phil Esposito, Boston...........................61
Ken Hodge, Boston..............................50
Richard Martin, Buffalo.........................52
Mickey Redmond, Detroit......................51
Bill Goldsworthy, Minnesota..................48

Assists

Bobby Orr, Boston................................90
Phil Esposito, Boston...........................77
Dennis Hextall, Minnesota....................62
Syl Apps, Pittsburgh.............................61
Andre Boudrias, Vancouver..................59
Wayne Cashman, Boston.....................59

Points

Phil Esposito, Boston.........................145
Bobby Orr, Boston..............................122
Ken Hodge, Boston.............................105
Wayne Cashman, Boston......................89
Bobby Clarke, Philadelphia...................87

Penalty minutes

Dave Schultz, Philadelphia.................348
Steve Durbano, St.L.-Pit.....................284
Bryan Watson, Pit.-St.L.-Det...............255
Andre Dupont, Philadelphia.................216
Gary Howatt, N.Y. Islanders................204

Lowest goals-against average (Min. 25 games)

Bernie Parent, Philadelphia...............1.89
Tony Esposito, Chicago.....................2.04
Doug Favell, Toronto.........................2.71
Wayne Thomas, Montreal..................2.76
Dan Bouchard, Atlanta.......................2.77

Shutouts

Bernie Parent, Philadelphia.................12
Tony Esposito, Chicago........................10
Gilles Gilbert, Boston.............................6
Dan Bouchard, Atlanta...........................5
Ed Giacomin, N.Y. Rangers....................5
Rogie Vachon, Los Angeles....................5

Wins by goaltenders

Bernie Parent, Philadelphia.................47
Tony Esposito, Chicago........................34
Gilles Gilbert, Boston............................34
Ed Giacomin, N.Y. Rangers..................30
Rogie Vachon, Los Angeles..................28

1974-75

Goals

Phil Esposito, Boston...........................61
Guy Lafleur, Montreal...........................53
Rick Martin, Buffalo..............................52
Danny Grant, Detroit.............................50
Marcel Dionne, Detroit..........................47

Assists

Bobby Clarke, Philadelphia...................89
Bobby Orr, Boston................................89
Pete Mahovlich, Montreal.....................82
Marcel Dionne, Detroit..........................74
Phil Esposito, Boston...........................66
Guy Lafleur, Montreal...........................66

Points

Bobby Orr, Boston..............................135
Phil Esposito, Boston.........................127
Marcel Dionne, Detroit........................121
Guy Lafleur, Montreal.........................119
Pete Mahovlich, Montreal....................117

Penalty minutes

Dave Schultz, Philadelphia.................472
Andre Dupont, Philadelphia.................276
Phil Russell, Chicago..........................260
Bryan Watson, Detroit.........................238
Bob Gassoff, St. Louis........................222

Lowest goals-against average (Min. 25 games)

Bernie Parent, Philadelphia...............2.03
Rogie Vachon, Los Angeles...............2.24
Gary Edwards, Los Angeles...............2.34
Chico Resch, N.Y. Islanaders............2.47
Ken Dryden, Montreal........................2.69

Shutouts

Bernie Parent, Philadelphia.................12
Tony Esposito, Chicago..........................6
Gary Smith, Vancouver...........................6
Rogie Vachon, Los Angeles....................6
Phil Myre, Atlanta...................................5

Wins by goaltenders

Bernie Parent, Philadelphia.................44
Tony Esposito, Chicago........................34
Gary Smith, Vancouver.........................32
Ken Dryden, Montreal..........................30
Rogie Vachon, Los Angeles..................27

1975-76

Goals

Reggie Leach, Philadelphia..................61
Guy Lafleur, Montreal...........................56
Pierre Larouche, Pittsburgh..................53
Jean Pronovost, Pittsburgh...................52
Bill Barber, Philadelphia........................50
Danny Gare, Buffalo.............................50

Assists

Bobby Clarke, Philadelphia...................89
Pete Mahovlich, Montreal.....................71
Guy Lafleur, Montreal...........................69
Gilbert Perreault, Buffalo......................69
Jean Ratelle, NYR-Bos.........................69

Points

Guy Lafleur, Montreal.........................125
Bobby Clarke, Philadelphia.................119
Gilbert Perreault, Buffalo....................113
Bill Barber, Philadelphia......................112
Pierre Larouche, Pittsburgh.................111

Penalty minutes

Steve Durbano, Pit.-K.C......................370
Bryan Watson, Detroit.........................322
Dave Schultz, Philadelphia.................307
Bob Gassoff, St. Louis........................306
Dave Williams, Toronto.......................306

Lowest goals-against average (Min. 25 games)

Ken Dryden, Montreal........................2.03
Chico Resch, N.Y. Islanders..............2.07
Dan Bouchard, Atlanta.......................2.54
Wayne Stephenson, Philadelphia......2.58
Billy Smith, N.Y. Islanders.................2.61

Shutouts

Ken Dryden, Montreal............................8
Chico Resch, N.Y. Islanders...................7
Rogie Vachon, Los Angeles....................5
Tony Esposito, Chicago..........................4
Jim Rutherford, Detroit..........................4

Wins by goaltenders

Ken Dryden, Montreal..........................42
Wayne Stephenson, Philadelphia.........40
Gilles Gilbert, Boston............................33
Tony Esposito, Chicago........................30
Gerry Desjardins, Buffalo.....................29

1976-77

Goals

Steve Shutt, Montreal...........................60
Guy Lafleur, Montreal...........................56

Marcel Dionne, Los Angeles.....53
Rick MacLeish, Philadelphia.....49
Wilf Paiement, Colorado.....41

Assists

Guy Lafleur, Montreal.....80
Marcel Dionne, Los Angeles.....69
Larry Robinson, Montreal.....66
Borje Salming, Toronto.....66
Tim Young, Minnesota.....66

Points

Guy Lafleur, Montreal.....136
Marcel Dionne, Los Angeles.....122
Steve Shutt, Montreal.....105
Rick MacLeish, Philadelphia.....97
Gilbert Perreault, Buffalo.....95
Tim Young, Minnesota.....95

Penalty minutes

Dave Williams, Toronto.....338
Dennis Polonich, Detroit.....274
Bob Gassoff, St. Louis.....254
Phil Russell, Chicago.....233
Dave Schultz, Los Angeles.....232

Lowest goals-against average (Min. 25 games)

Michel Larocque, Montreal.....2.09
Ken Dryden, Montreal.....2.14
Chico Resch, N.Y. Islanders.....2.28
Billy Smith, N.Y. Islanders.....2.50
Don Edwards, Buffalo.....2.51

Shutouts

Ken Dryden, Montreal.....10
Rogie Vachon, Los Angeles.....8
Bernie Parent, Philadelphia.....5
Dunc Wilson, Pittsburgh.....5
Michel Larocque, Montreal.....4
Mike Palmateer, Toronto.....4

Wins by goaltenders

Ken Dryden, Montreal.....41
Bernie Parent, Philadelphia.....35
Rogie Vachon, Los Angeles.....33
Gerry Desjardins, Buffalo.....31
Gerry Cheevers, Boston.....30

1977-78

Goals

Guy Lafleur, Montreal.....60
Mike Bossy, N.Y. Islanders.....53
Steve Shutt, Montreal.....49
Lanny McDonald, Toronto.....47
Bryan Trottier, N.Y. Islanders.....46

Assists

Bryan Trottier, N.Y. Islanders.....77
Guy Lafleur, Montreal.....72
Darryl Sittler, Toronto.....72
Bobby Clarke, Philadelphia.....68
Denis Potvin, N.Y. Islanders.....64

Points

Guy Lafleur, Montreal.....132
Bryan Trottier, N.Y. Islanders.....123
Darryl Sittler, Toronto.....117
Jacques Lemaire, Montreal.....97
Denis Potvin, N.Y. Islanders.....94

Penalty minutes

Dave Schultz, L.A.-Pit.....405
Dave Williams, Toronto.....351
Dennis Polonich, Detroit.....254
Randy Holt, Chi.-Cle......249
Andre Dupont, Philadelphia.....225

Lowest goals-against average (Min. 25 games)

Ken Dryden, Montreal.....2.05
Bernie Parent, Philadelphia.....2.22
Gilles Gilbert, Boston.....2.53
Chico Resch, N.Y. Islanders.....2.55
Tony Esposito, Chicago.....2.63

Shutouts

Bernie Parent, Philadelphia.....7
Ken Dryden, Montreal.....5
Don Edwards, Buffalo.....5
Tony Esposito, Chicago.....5
Mike Palmateer, Toronto.....5

Wins by goaltenders

Don Edwards, Buffalo.....38
Ken Dryden, Montreal.....37
Mike Palmateer, Toronto.....34
Bernie Parent, Philadelphia.....29
Rogie Vachon, Los Angeles.....29

1978-79

Goals

Mike Bossy, N.Y. Islanders.....69
Marcel Dionne, Los Angeles.....59
Guy Lafleur, Montreal.....52
Guy Chouinard, Atlanta.....50
Bryan Trottier, N.Y. Islanders.....47

Assists

Bryan Trottier, N.Y. Islanders.....87
Guy Lafleur, Montreal.....77
Marcel Dionne, Los Angeles.....71
Bob MacMillan, Atlanta.....71
Denis Potvin, N.Y. Islanders.....70

Points

Bryan Trottier, N.Y. Islanders.....134
Marcel Dionne, Los Angeles.....130
Guy Lafleur, Montreal.....129
Mike Bossy, N.Y. Islanders.....126
Bob MacMillan, Atlanta.....108

Penalty minutes

Dave Williams, Toronto.....298
Randy Holt, Van.-L.A......282
Dave Schultz, Pit.-Buf......243
Dave Hutchison, Toronto.....235
Willi Plett, Atlanta.....213

Lowest goals-against average (Min. 25 games)

Ken Dryden, Montreal.....2.30
Chico Resch, N.Y. Islanders.....2.50
Bernie Parent, Philadelphia.....2.70
Michel Larocque, Montreal.....2.84
Billy Smith, N.Y. Islanders.....2.87

Shutouts

Ken Dryden, Montreal.....5
Tony Esposito, Chicago.....4
Mario Lessard, Los Angeles.....4
Mike Palmateer, Toronto.....4
Bernie Parent, Philadelphia.....4

Wins by goaltenders

Dan Bouchard, Atlanta.....32
Ken Dryden, Montreal.....30
Don Edwards, Buffalo.....26
Mike Palmateer, Toronto.....26
Chico Resch, N.Y. Islanders.....26

1979-80

Goals

Charlie Simmer, Los Angeles.....56
Blaine Stoughton, Hartford.....56
Danny Gare, Buffalo.....56
Marcel Dionne, Los Angeles.....53
Mike Bossy, N.Y. Islanders.....51
Wayne Gretzky, Edmonton.....51

Assists

Wayne Gretzky, Edmonton.....86
Marcel Dionne, Los Angeles.....84
Guy Lafleur, Montreal.....75
Gil Perreault, Buffalo.....66
Bryan Trottier, N.Y. Islanders.....62

Points

Marcel Dionne, Los Angeles.....137
Wayne Gretzky, Edmonton.....137
Guy Lafleur, Montreal.....125
Gil Perreault, Buffalo.....106
Mike Rogers, Hartford.....105

Penalty minutes

Jimmy Mann, Winnipeg.....287
Paul Holmgren, Philadelphia.....267
Terry O'Reilly, Boston.....265
Terry Ruskowski, Chicago.....252
Paul Mulvey, Washington.....240

Lowest goals-against average (Min. 25 games)

Bob Sauve, Buffalo.....2.36
Denis Herron, Montreal.....2.51
Don Edwards, Buffalo.....2.57
Gilles Gilbert, Boston.....2.73
Pete Peeters, Philadelphia.....2.73

Shutouts

Tony Esposito, Chicago.....6
Gerry Cheevers, Boston.....4
Bob Sauve, Buffalo.....4
Rogie Vachon, Detroit.....4
Michel Larocque, Montreal.....3
Chico Resch, N.Y. Islanders.....3

Wins by goaltenders

Mike Liut, St. Louis.....32
Tony Esposito, Chicago.....31
Pete Peeters, Philadelphia.....29
Gilles Meloche, Minnesota.....27
Denis Herron, Montreal.....25

1980-81

Goals

Mike Bossy, N.Y. Islanders.....68
Marcel Dionne, Los Angeles.....58
Charlie Simmer, Los Angeles.....56
Wayne Gretzky, Edmonton.....55
Rick Kehoe, Pittsburgh.....55

Assists

Wayne Gretzky, Edmonton.....109
Kent Nilsson, Calgary.....82
Marcel Dionne, Los Angeles.....77
Bernie Federko, St. Louis.....73
Bryan Trottier, N.Y. Islanders.....72

Points

Wayne Gretzky, Edmonton.....164
Marcel Dionne, Los Angeles.....135
Kent Nilsson, Calgary.....131
Mike Bossy, N.Y. Islanders.....119
Dave Taylor, Los Angeles.....112

Penalty minutes

Dave Williams, Vancouver.....333
Paul Holmgren, Philadelphia.....306
Chris Nilan, Montreal.....262
Jim Korn, Detroit.....246
Willi Plett, Calgary.....237
Behn Wilson, Philadelphia.....237

Lowest goals-against average (Min. 25 games)

Richard Sevigny, Montreal 2.40
Rick St. Croix, Philadelphia 2.49
Don Edwards, Buffalo 2.96
Pete Peeters, Philadelphia 2.96
Michel Larocque, Montreal 3.03

Shutouts

Don Edwards, Buffalo 3
Chico Resch, N.Y. Islanders 3
11 goalies tied with 2

Wins by goaltenders

Mario Lessard, Los Angeles 35
Mike Liut, St. Louis 33
Tony Esposito, Chicago 29
Greg Millen, Pittsburgh 25
Rogie Vachon, Boston 25

1981-82

Goals

Wayne Gretzky, Edmonton 92
Mike Bossy, N.Y. Islanders 64
Dennis Maruk, Washington 60
Dino Ciccarelli, Minnesota 55
Rick Vaive, Toronto 54

Assists

Wayne Gretzky, Edmonton 120
Peter Stastny, Quebec 93
Denis Savard, Chicago 87
Mike Bossy, N.Y. Islanders 83
Bryan Trottier, N.Y. Islanders 79

Points

Wayne Gretzky, Edmonton 212
Mike Bossy, N.Y. Islanders 147
Peter Stastny, Quebec 139
Dennis Maruk, Washington 136
Bryan Trottier, N.Y. Islanders 129

Penalty minutes

Paul Baxter, Pittsburgh 407
Dave Williams, Toronto 341
Glen Cochrane, Philadelphia 329
Pat Price, Pittsburgh 322
Al Secord, Chicago 303

Lowest goals-against average (Min. 25 games)

Denis Herron, Montreal 2.64
Rick Wamsley, Montreal 2.75
Bill Smith, N.Y.Islanders 2.97
Roland Melanson, N.Y. Islanders 3.23
Grant Fuhr, Edmonton 3.31

Shutouts

Denis Herron, Montreal 3
Richard Brodeur, Vancouver 2
Mario Lessard, Los Angeles 2
Mike Liut, St. Louis 2
Pat Riggin, Calgary 2
Doug Soetaert, Winnipeg 2
Rick Wamsley, Montreal 2

Wins by goaltenders

Billy Smith, N.Y. Islanders 32
Grant Fuhr, Edmonton 28
Mike Liut, St. Louis 28
Dan Bouchard, Quebec 27
Don Edwards, Buffalo 26
Gilles Meloche, Minnesota 26

1982-83

Goals

Wayne Gretzky, Edmonton 71
Lanny McDonald, Calgary 66
Mike Bossy, N.Y. Islanders 60
Michel Goulet, Quebec 57
Marcel Dionne, Los Angeles 56

Assists

Wayne Gretzky, Edmonton 125
Denis Savard, Chicago 85
Peter Stastny, Quebec 77
Paul Coffey, Edmonton 67
Bobby Clarke, Philadelphia 62

Points

Wayne Gretzky, Edmonton 196
Peter Stastny, Quebec 124
Denis Savard, Chicago 120
Mike Bossy, N.Y. Islanders 118
Marcel Dionne, Los Angeles 107
Barry Pederson, Boston 107

Penalty minutes

Randy Holt, Washington 275
Dave Williams, Vancouver 265
Brian Sutter, St. Louis 254
Paul Baxter, Pittsburgh 238
Jim Korn, Toronto 238

Lowest goals-against average (Min. 25 games)

Pete Peeters, Boston 2.36
Roland Melanson, N.Y. Islanders 2.66
Billy Smith, N.Y. Islanders 2.87
Pelle Lindbergh, Philadelphia 2.98
Murray Bannerman, Chicago 3.10

Shutouts

Pete Peeters, Boston 8
Murray Bannerman, Chicago 4
Bob Froese, Philadelphia 4
Pelle Lindbergh, Philadelphia 3
Corrado Micalef, Detroit 2
Ed Mio, N.Y. Rangers 2

Wins by goaltenders

Pete Peeters, Boston 40
Andy Moog, Edmonton 33
Rick Wamsley, Montreal 27
Bob Sauve, Buffalo 25
Murray Bannerman, Chicago 24
Roland Melanson, N.Y. Islanders 24

1983-84

Goals

Wayne Gretzky, Edmonton 87
Michel Goulet, Quebec 56
Glenn Anderson, Edmonton 54
Tim Kerr, Philadelphia 54
Jari Kurri, Edmonton 52
Rick Vaive, Toronto 52

Assists

Wayne Gretzky, Edmonton 118
Paul Coffey, Edmonton 86
Barry Pederson, Boston 77
Peter Stastny, Quebec 73
Bryan Trottier, N.Y. Islanders 71

Points

Wayne Gretzky, Edmonton 205
Paul Coffey, Edmonton 126
Michel Goulet, Quebec 121
Peter Stastny, Quebec 119
Mike Bossy, N.Y. Islanders 118

Penalty minutes

Chris Nilan, Montreal 338
Willie Plett, Minnesota 316
Gary Rissling, Pittsburgh 297
Dave Williams, Vancouver 294
Jim Korn, Toronto 257

Lowest goals-against average (Min. 25 games)

Pat Riggin, Washington 2.66
Tom Barrasso, Buffalo 2.84
Al Jensen, Washington 2.91
Doug Keans, Boston 2.84
Bob Froese, Philadelphia 3.14

Shutouts

Pat Riggin, Washington 4
Al Jensen, Washington 4
Mike Liut, St. Louis 3
Nine goalies tied with 2

Wins by goaltenders

Grant Fuhr, Edmonton 30
Peter Peeters, Boston 29
Dan Bouchard, Quebec 29
Bob Froese, Philadelphia 28
Glen Hanlon, N.Y. Rangers 28

1984-85

Goals

Wayne Gretzky, Edmonton 73
Jari Kurri, Edmonton 71
Mike Bossy, N.Y. Islanders 58
Michel Goulet, Quebec 55
John Ogrodnick, Detroit 55

Assists

Wayne Gretzky, Edmonton 135
Paul Coffey, Edmonton 84
Marcel Dionne, Los Angeles 80
Dale Hawerchuk, Winnipeg 77
Bernie Federko, St. Louis 73

Points

Wayne Gretzky, Edmonton 208
Jari Kurri, Edmonton 135
Dale Hawerchuk, Winnipeg 130
Marcel Dionne, Los Angeles 126
Paul Coffey, Edmonton 121

Penalty minutes

Chris Nilan, Montreal 358
Torrie Robertson, Hartford 337
John Blum, Boston 263
Tim Hunter, Calgary 259
Bob McGill, Toronto 250

Lowest goals-against average (Min. 25 games)

Tom Barrasso, Buffalo 2.66
Pat Riggin, Washington 2.98
Pelle Lindbergh, Philadelphia 3.02
Steve Penney, Montreal 3.08
Bob Sauve, Buffalo 3.22
Warren Skorodenski, Chicago 3.22

Shutouts

Tom Barrasso, Buffalo 5
Kelly Hrudey, N.Y. Islanders 2
Bob Janecyk, Los Angeles 2
Pelle Lindbergh, Philadelphia 2
Pat Riggin, Washington 2
Warren Skorodenski, Chicago 2
Steve Weeks, Hartford 2

Wins by goaltenders

Pelle Lindbergh, Philadelphia 40
Brian Hayward, Winnipeg 33
Reggie Lemelin, Calgary 30
Pat Riggin, Washington 28
Murray Bannerman, Chicago 27

1985-86

Goals

Jari Kurri, Edmonton 68
Mike Bossy, N.Y. Islanders 61
Tim Kerr, Philadelphia 58
Glenn Anderson, Edmonton 54
Michel Goulet, Quebec 53

Assists

Wayne Gretzky, Edmonton 163
Mario Lemieux, Pittsburgh 93
Paul Coffey, Edmonton 90
Peter Stastny, Quebec 81
Neal Broten, Minnesota 76

Points

Wayne Gretzky, Edmonton 215
Mario Lemieux, Pittsburgh 141
Paul Coffey, Edmonton 138
Jari Kurri, Edmonton 131
Mike Bossy, N.Y. Islanders 123

Penalty minutes

Joey Kocur, Detroit 377
Torrie Robertson, Hartford 358
Dave Williams, Los Angeles 320
Tim Hunter, Calgary 291
Dave Brown, Philadelphia 277

Lowest goals-against average (Min. 25 games)

Bob Froese, Philadelphia 2.55
Al Jensen, Washington 3.18
Kelly Hrudey, N.Y. Islanders 3.21
Clint Malarchuk, Quebec 3.21
John Vanbiesbrouck, N.Y. Rangers ...3.32

Shutouts

Bob Froese, Philadelphia 5
Clint Malarchuk, Quebec 4
Doug Soetaert, Montreal 3
John Vanbiesbrouck, N.Y. Rangers 3

Wins by goaltenders

Bob Froese, Philadelphia 31
John Vanbiesbrouck, N.Y. Rangers 31
Tom Barrasso, Buffalo 29
Rejean Lemelin, Calgary 29
Grant Fuhr, Edmonton 29

1986-87

Goals

Wayne Gretzky, Edmonton 62
Tim Kerr, Philadelphia 58
Mario Lemieux, Pittsburgh 54
Jari Kurri, Edmonton 54
Dino Ciccarelli, Minnesota 52

Assists

Wayne Gretzky, Edmonton 121
Ray Bourque, Boston 72
Mark Messier, Edmonton 70
Kevin Dineen, Hartford 69
Bryan Trottier, N.Y. Islanders 64

Points

Wayne Gretzky, Edmonton 183
Jari Kurri, Edmonton 108
Mario Lemieux, Pittsburgh 107
Mark Messier, Edmonton 107
Doug Gilmour, St. Louis 105

Penalty minutes

Dave Williams, Los Angeles 358
Tim Hunter, Calgary 357
Brian Curran, N.Y. Islanders 356
Basil McRae, Det.-Que. 342
Rick Tocchet, Philadelphia 286

Lowest goals-against average (Min. 25 games)

Brian Hayward, Montreal 2.81
Patrick Roy, Montreal 2.93
Ron Hextall, Philadelphia 3.00
Daniel Berthiaume, Winnipeg 3.17
Mario Gosselin, Quebec 3.18
Glen Hanlon, Detroit 3.18

Shutouts

Mike Liut, Hartford 4
Bill Ranford, Boston 3
Rejean Lemelin, Calgary 2
Allan Bester, Toronto 2
Tom Barrasso, Buffalo 2

Wins by goaltenders

Ron Hextall, Philadelphia 37
Mike Liut, Hartford 31
Mike Vernon, Calgary 30
Andy Moog, Edmonton 28
Alain Chevrier, New Jersey 24

1987-88

Goals

Mario Lemieux, Pittsburgh 70
Craig Simpson, Pit.-Edm. 56
Jimmy Carson, Los Angeles 55
Luc Robitaille, Los Angeles 53
Joe Nieuwendyk, Calgary 51

Assists

Wayne Gretzky, Edmonton 109
Mario Lemieux, Pittsburgh 98
Denis Savard, Chicago 87
Dale Hawerchuk, Winnipeg 77
Mark Messier, Edmonton 74

Points

Mario Lemieux, Pittsburgh 168
Wayne Gretzky, Edmonton 149
Denis Savard, Chicago 131
Dale Hawerchuk, Winnipeg 121
Luc Robitaille, Los Angeles 111
Peter Stastny, Quebec 111
Mark Messier, Edmonton 111

Penalty minutes

Bob Probert, Detroit 398
Basil McRae, Minnesota 378
Tim Hunter, Calgary 337
Richard Zemlak, Minnesota 307
Jay Miller, Boston 304

Lowest goals-against average (Min. 25 games)

Pete Peeters, Washington 2.78
Brian Hayward, Montreal 2.86
Patrick Roy, Montreal 2.90
Rejean Lemelin, Boston 2.93
Greg Stefan, Detroit 3.11

Shutouts

Grant Fuhr, Edmonton 4
Glen Hanlon, Detroit 4
Clint Malarchuk, Washington 4
Kelly Hrudey, N.Y. Islanders 3
Rejean Lemelin, Boston 3
Patrick Roy, Montreal 3

Wins by goaltenders

Grant Fuhr, Edmonton 40
Mike Vernon, Calgary 39
Ron Hextall, Philadelphia 30
John Vanbiesbrouck, N.Y. Rangers 27
Tom Barrasso, Buffalo 25
Mike Liut, Hartford 25

1988-89

Goals

Mario Lemieux, Pittsburgh 85
Bernie Nicholls, Los Angeles 70
Steve Yzerman, Detroit 65
Wayne Gretzky, Los Angeles 54
Joe Nieuwendyk, Calgary 51
Joe Mullen, Calgary 51

Assists

Mario Lemieux, Pittsburgh 114
Wayne Gretzky, Los Angeles 114
Steve Yzerman, Detroit 90
Paul Coffey, Pittsburgh 83
Bernie Nicholls, Los Angeles 80

Points

Mario Lemieux, Pittsburgh 199
Wayne Gretzky, Los Angeles 168
Steve Yzerman, Detroit 155
Bernie Nicholls, Los Angeles 150
Rob Brown, Pittsburgh 115

Penalty minutes

Tim Hunter, Calgary 375
Basil McRae, Minnesota 365
Dave Manson, Chicago 352
Marty McSorley, Los Angeles 350
Mike Hartman, Buffalo 316

Lowest goals-against average (Min. 25 games)

Patrick Roy, Montreal 2.47
Mike Vernon, Calgary 2.65
Pete Peeters, Washington 2.85
Brian Hayward, Montreal 2.90
Rick Wamsley, Calgary 2.96

Shutouts

Greg Millen, St. Louis 6
Pete Peeters, Washington 4
Kirk McLean, Vancouver 4
Peter Sidorkiewicz, Hartford 4
Patrick Roy, Montreal 4

Wins by goaltenders

Mike Vernon, Calgary 37
Patrick Roy, Montreal 33
Ron Hextall, Philadelphia 30
John Vanbiesbrouck, N.Y. Rangers 28
Kelly Hrudey, NYI-L.A. 28

1989-90

Goals

Brett Hull, St. Louis 72
Steve Yzerman, Detroit 62
Cam Neely, Boston 55
Brian Bellows, Minnesota 55
Pat LaFontaine, N.Y. Islanders 54

Assists

Wayne Gretzky, Los Angeles 102
Mark Messier, Edmonton 84
Adam Oates, St. Louis 79
Mario Lemieux, Pittsburgh 78
Paul Coffey, Pittsburgh 74

Points

Wayne Gretzky, Los Angeles 142
Mark Messier, Edmonton 129
Steve Yzerman, Detroit 127
Mario Lemieux, Pittsburgh 123
Brett Hull, St. Louis 113

Penalty minutes

Basil McRae, Minnesota....................351
Alan May, Washington 339
Marty McSorley, Los Angeles............322
Troy Mallette, N.Y. Rangers...............305
Wayne Van Dorp, Chicago.................303

Lowest goals-against average (Min. 25 games)

Mike Liut, Har.-Was........................2.527
Patrick Roy, Montreal......................2.534
Rejean Lemelin, Boston 2.805
Andy Moog, Boston 2.886
Daren Puppa, Buffalo 2.888

Shutouts

Mike Liut, Har.-Was..............................4
Andy Moog, Boston 3
Mike Fitzpatrick, N.Y. Islanders 3
Patrick Roy, Montreal.............................3
Jon Casey, Minnesota 3

Wins by goaltenders

Patrick Roy, Montreal..........................31
Daren Puppa, Buffalo 31
Jon Casey, Minnesota 31
Andy Moog, Boston 24
Bill Ranford, Edmonton.........................24

1990-91

Goals

Brett Hull, St. Louis...............................86
Cam Neely, Boston 51
Theo Fleury, Calgary.............................51
Steve Yzerman, Detroit..........................51
Mike Gartner, N.Y. Rangers 49

Assists

Wayne Gretzky, Los Angeles 122
Adam Oates, St. Louis...........................90
Al MacInnis, Calgary 75
Ray Bourque, Boston 73
Mark Recchi, Pittsburgh.........................73

Points

Wayne Gretzky, Los Angeles 163
Brett Hull, St. Louis.............................131
Adam Oates, St. Louis.........................115
Mark Recchi, Pittsburgh.......................113
John Cullen, Pit.-Har. 110

Penalty minutes

Rob Ray, Buffalo 350
Mike Peluso, Chicago...........................320
Bob Probert, Detroit.............................315
Craig Berube, Philadelphia 293
Gino Odjick, Vancouver........................296

Lowest goals-against average (Min. 25 games)

Ed Belfour, Chicago 2.47
Don Beaupre, Washington 2.64
Patrick Roy, Montreal..........................2.71
Andy Moog, Boston 2.87
Pete Peters, Philadelphia.....................2.88

Shutouts

Don Beaupre, Washington 5
Andy Moog, Boston 4
Bob Essesna, Winnipeg..........................4
Ed Belfour, Chicago 4
John Vanbiesbrouck, N.Y. Rangers 3
Jon Casey, Minnesota 3
Kelly Hrudey, Los Angeles......................3
Vincent Riendeau, St. Louis 3

Wins by goaltenders

Ed Belfour, Chicago 43
Mike Vernon, Calgary 31
Tim Cheveldae, Detroit 30
Vincent Riendeau, St. Louis 29
Tom Barrasso, Pittsburgh 27
Bill Ranford, Edmonton.........................27

1991-92

Goals

Brett Hull, St. Louis...............................70
Kevin Stephens, Pittsburgh..................54
Gary Roberts, Calgary 53
Jeremy Roenick, Chicago......................53
Pat LaFontaine, Buffalo 46

Assists

Wayne Gretzky, Los Angeles 90
Mario Lemieux, Pittsburgh....................87
Brian Leech, N.Y. Rangers....................80
Adam Oates, St.L.-Bos. 79
Dale Hawerchuck, Buffalo 75

Points

Mario Lemieux, Pittsburgh..................131
Kevin Stephens, Pittsburgh.................123
Wayne Gretzky, Los Angeles 121
Brett Hull, St. Louis.............................109
Luc Robitaille, Los Angeles..................107
Mark Messier, N.Y. Rangers 107

Penalty minutes

Mike Peluso, Chicago..........................408
Rob Ray, Buffalo 354
Gino Odjick, Vancouver.......................348
Ronnie Stern, Calgary 338
Link Gaetz, San Jose 326

Lowest goals-against average (Min. 25 games)

Patrick Roy, Montreal.........................2.36
Ed Belfour, Chicago 2.70
Kirk McLean, Vancouver 2.74
John Vanbiesbrouck, N.Y Rangers....2.85
Bob Essensa, Winnipeg......................2.88

Shutouts

Ed Belfour, Chicago 5
Bob Essesna, Winnipeg..........................5
Kirk McLean, Vancouver 5
Patrick Roy, Montreal.............................5
Ron Hextall, Philadelphia 3
Mike Richter, N.Y Rangers 3
Kay Whitmore, Hartford 3

Wins by goaltenders

Tim Cheveldae, Detroit 38
Kirk McLean, Vancouver 38
Patrick Roy, Montreal...........................36
Don Beaupre, Washington 29
Andy Moog, Boston 28

1992-93

Goals

Alexander Mogilny, Buffalo...................76
Teemu Selanne, Winnipeg 76
Mario Lemieux, Pittsburgh....................69
Luc Robitaille, Los Angeles...................63
Pavel Bure, Vancouver 60

Assists

Adam Oates, Boston.............................97
Doug Gilmour, Toronto.........................95
Pat LaFontaine, Buffalo 95
Mario Lemieux, Pittsburgh....................91
Craig Janney, St. Louis 82

Points

Mario Lemieux, Pittburgh...................160
Pat LaFontaine, Buffalo 148
Adam Oates, Boston...........................142
Steve Yzerman, Detroit.......................137
Teemu Selanne, Winnipeg 137

Penalty minutes

Marty McSorley, Los Angeles.............399
Gino Odjick, Vancouver......................370
Tie Domi, NYR-Win. 344
Nick Kypreos, Hartford.......................325
Mike Peluso, Ottawa...........................318

Lowest goals-against average (Min. 25 games)

Felix Potvin, Toronto 2.50
Ed Belfour, Chicago 2.59
Tom Barrasso, Pittsburgh 3.01
Curtis Joseph, St. Louis......................3.02
Kay Whitmore, Vancouver..................3.10

Shutouts

Ed Belfour, Chicago 7
Tommy Soderstrom, Philadelphia 5
Tom Barrasso, Pittsburgh 4
Tim Cheveldae, Detroit 4
John Vanbiesbrouck, N.Y. Rangers 4

Wins by goaltenders

Tom Barrasso, Pittsburgh 43
Ed Belfour, Chicago 41
Andy Moog, Boston 37
Tim Cheveldae, Detroit 34
Bob Essensa, Winnipeg........................33

1993-94

Goals

Pavel Bure, Vancouver 60
Brett Hull, St. Louis..............................57
Sergei Federov, Detroit.........................56
Dave Andreychuk, Toronto 53
Adam Graves, N.Y. Rangers 52
Brendan Shannahan, St. Louis 52
Ray Sheppard, Detroit..........................52

Assists

Wayne Gretzky, Los Angeles 92
Doug Gilmour, Toronto.........................84
Adam Oates, Boston.............................80
Sergei Zubov, N.Y. Rangers..................77
Ray Bourque, Boston 71

Points

Wayne Gretzky, Los Angeles 130
Segei Fedorov, Detroit........................120
Adam Oates, Boston...........................112
Doug Gilmour, Toronto.......................111
Pavel Bure, Vancouver 107
Mike Recchi, Philadelphia 107
Jeremy Roenick, Chicago...................107

Penalty minutes

Tie Domi, Winnipeg............................347
Shane Churla, Dallas 333
Warren Rychel, Los Angeles 322
Craig Berube, Washington 305
Kelly Chase, St. Louis 278

Lowest goals-against average (Min. 27 games)

Dominik Hasek, Buffalo.......................1.95
Martin Brodeur, New Jersey...............2.40
Patrick Roy, Montreal.........................2.50
John Vanbiesbrouck, Florida..............2.53
Mike Richter, N.Y. Rangers.................2.57

Shutouts

Ed Belfour, Chicago....7
Dominik Hasek, Buffalo....7
Patrick Roy, Montreal....7
Ron Hextall, N.Y. Islanders....5
Mike Richter, N.Y. Rangers....5

Wins by goaltenders

Mike Richter, N.Y. Rangers....42
Ed Belfour, Chicago....37
Curtis Joseph, St. Louis....36
Patrick Roy, Montreal....35
Felix Potvin, Toronto....34

1994-95

Goals

Peter Bondra, Washington....34
Jaromir Jagr, Pittsburgh....32
Owen Nolan, Quebec....30
Ray Sheppard, Detroit....30
Alexei Zhamnov, Winnipeg....30

Assists

Ron Francis, Pittsburgh....48
Paul Coffey, Detroit....44
Joe Sakic, Quebec....43
Eric Lindros, Philadelphia....41
Adam Oates, Boston....41

Points

Jaromir Jagr, Pittsburgh....70
Eric Lindros, Philadelphia....70
Alexei Zhamnov, Winnipeg....65
Joe Sakic, Quebec....62
Ron Francis, Pittsburgh....59

Penalty minutes

Enrico Ciccone, Tampa Bay....225
Shane Churla, Dallas....186
Bryan Marchment, Edmonton....184
Craig Berube, Washington....173
Rob Ray, Buffalo....173

Lowest goals-against average (Min. 13 games)

Dominik Hasek, Buffalo....2.111
Rick Tabaracci, Was.-Cal.....2.114
Jim Carey, Washington....2.13
Chris Osgood, Detroit....2.26
Ed Belfour, Chicago....2.28

Shutouts

Ed Belfour, Chicago....5
Dominik Hasek, Buffalo....5
Jim Carey, Washington....4
Arturs Irbe, San Jose....4
Blaine Lacher, Boston....4
John Vanbiesbrouck, Florida....4

Wins by goaltenders

Ken Wregget, Pittsburgh....25
Ed Belfour, Chicago....22
Trevor Kidd, Calgary....22
Curtis Joseph, St. Louis....20
Martin Broduer, New Jersey....19
Dominik Hasek, Buffalo....19
Blaine Lacher, Boston....19
Mike Vernon, Detroit....19

1995-96

Goals

Mario Lemieux, Pittsburgh....69
Jaromir Jagr, Pittsburgh....62
Alexander Mogilny, Vancouver....55
Peter Bondra, Washington....52
John LeClair, Philadelphia....51
Joe Sakic, Colorado....51

Assists

Ron Francis, Pittsburgh....92
Mario Lemieux, Pittsburgh....92
Jaromir Jagr, Pittsburgh....87
Peter Forsberg, Colorado....86
Wayne Gretzky, L.A.-St.L.....79
Doug Weight, Edmonton....79

Points

Mario Lemieux, Pittsburgh....161
Jaromir Jagr, Pittsburgh....149
Joe Sakic, Colorado....120
Ron Francis, Pittsburgh....119
Peter Forsberg, Colorado....116

Penalty minutes

Matthew Barnaby, Buffalo....335
Enrico Ciccone, T.B.-Chi.....306
Tie Domi, Toronto....297
Brad May, Buffalo....295
Rob Ray, Buffalo....287

Lowest goals-against average (Min. 25 games)

Ron Hextall, Philadelphia....2.176
Chris Osgood, Detroit....2.178
Jim Carey, Washington....2.256
Mike Vernon, Detroit....2.264
Martin Brodeur, New Jersey....2.34

Shutouts

Jim Carey, Washington....9
Martin Brodeur, New Jersey....6
Chris Osgood, Detroit....5
Daren Puppa, Tampa Bay....5
Sean Burke, Hartford....4
Jeff Hackett, Chicago....4
Guy Hebert, Anaheim....4
Ron Hextall, Philadelphia....4

Wins by goaltenders

Chris Osgood, Detroit....39
Jim Carey, Washington....35
Martin Brodeur, New Jersey....34
Bill Ranford, Edm.-Bos.....34
Patrick Roy, Mon.-Col.....34

1996-97

Goals

Keith Tkachuk, Phoenix....52
Teemu Selanne, Anaheim....51
John LeClair, Philadelphia....50
Mario Lemieux, Pittsburgh....50
Zigmund Pfaffy, N.Y. Islanders....48

Assists

Wayne Gretzky, N.Y. Rangers....72
Mario Lemieux, Pittsburgh....72
Ron Francis, Pittsburgh....63
Steve Yzerman, Detroit....63
Doug Weight, Edmonton....61

Points

Mario Lemieux, Pittsburgh....122
Teemu Selanne, Anaheim....109
Paul Kariya, Anaheim....99
Wayne Gretzky, N.Y. Rangers....97
John LeClair, Philadelphia....97

Penalty minutes

Gino Odjick, Vancouver....371
Bob Probert, Chicago....326
Paul Laus, Florida....313
Rob Ray, Buffalo....286
Tie Domi, Toronto....275

Lowest goals-against average (Min. 25 games)

Martin Brodeur, New Jersey....1.88
Andy Moog, Dallas....2.15
Jeff Hackett, Chicago....2.16
Dominik Hasek, Buffalo....2.27
John Vanbiesbrouck, Florida....2.29

Shutouts

Martin Brodeur, New Jersey....10
Nikolai Khabibulin, Phoenix....7
Patrick Roy, Colorado....7
Curtis Joseph, Edmonton....6
Chris Osgood, Detroit....6

Wins by goaltenders

Patrick Roy, Colorado....38
Martin Brodeur, New Jersey....37
Dominik Hasek, Buffalo....37
Grant Fuhr, St. Louis....33
Mike Richter, N.Y. Rangers....33

1997-98

Goals

Peter Bondra, Washington....52
Teemu Selanne, Anaheim....52
Pavel Bure, Vancouver....51
John LeClair, Philadelphia....51
Zigmund Palffy, N.Y. Islanders....45

Assists

Wayne Gretzky, N.Y. Rangers....67
Jaromir Jagr, Pittsburgh....67
Peter Forsberg, Colorado....66
Ron Francis, Pittsburgh....62
Adam Oates, Washington....58
Jozef Stumpel, Los Angeles....58

Points

Jaromir Jagr, Pittsburgh....102
Peter Forsberg, Colorado....91
Pavel Bure, Vancouver....90
Wayne Gretzky, N.Y. Rangers....90
John LeClair, Philadelphia....87
Zigmund Palffy, N.Y. Islanders....87
Ron Francis, Pittsburgh....87

Penalty minutes

Donald Brashear, Vancouver....372
Tie Domi, Toronto....365
Krzysztof Oliwa, New Jersey....295
Paul Laus, Florida....293
Richard Pilon, N.Y. Islanders....291

Lowest goals-against average (Min. 25 games)

Ed Belfour, Dallas....1.88
Martin Brodeur, New Jersey....1.89
Tom Barrasso, Pittsburgh....2.07
Dominik Hasek, Buffalo....2.09
Ron Hextall, Philadelphia....2.165
Trevor Kidd, Carolina....2.168
Jamie McLennan, St. Louis....2.171

Shutouts

Dominik Hasek, Buffalo....13
Martin Brodeur, New Jersey....10
Ed Belfour, Dallas....9
Jeff Hackett, Chicago....8
Curtis Joseph, Edmonton....8

Wins by goaltenders

Martin Brodeur, New Jersey....41
Ed Belfour, Dallas....37
Dominik Hasek, Buffalo....33
Olaf Kolzig, Washington....33
Chris Osgood, Detroit....33

AWARD WINNERS

LEAGUE AWARDS

ART ROSS TROPHY

(Leading scorer)

Season	Player, Team	Pts.
1917-18	Joe Malone, Montreal	44
1918-19	Newsy Lalonde, Montreal	32
1919-20	Joe Malone, Quebec Bulldogs	45
1920-21	Newsy Lalonde, Montreal	41
1921-22	Punch Broadbelt, Ottawa	46
1922-23	Babe Dye, Toronto	37
1923-24	Cy Denneny, Ottawa	23
1924-25	Babe Dye, Toronto	44
1925-26	Nels Stewart, Montreal Maroons	42
1926-27	Bill Cook, N.Y. Rangers	37
1927-28	Howie Morenz, Montreal	51
1928-29	Ace Bailey, Toronto	32
1929-30	Cooney Weiland, Boston	73
1930-31	Howie Morenz, Montreal	51
1931-32	Harvey Jackson, Toronto	53
1932-33	Bill Cook, N.Y. Rangers	50
1933-34	Charlie Conacher, Toronto	52
1934-35	Charlie Conacher, Toronto	57
1935-36	Dave Schriner, N.Y. Americans	45
1936-37	Dave Schriner, N.Y. Americans	46
1937-38	Gordie Drillion, Toronto	52
1938-39	Toe Blake, Montreal	47
1939-40	Milt Schmidt, Boston	52
1940-41	Bill Cowley, Boston	62
1941-42	Bryan Hextall, N.Y. Rangers	56
1942-43	Doug Bentley, Chicago	73
1943-44	Herbie Cain, Boston	82
1944-45	Elmer Lach, Montreal	80
1945-46	Max Bentley, Chicago	61
1946-47	Max Bentley, Chicago	72
1947-48	Elmer Lach, Montreal	61
1948-49	Roy Conacher, Chicago	68
1949-50	Ted Lindsay, Detroit	78
1950-51	Gordie Howe, Detroit	86
1951-52	Gordie Howe, Detroit	86
1952-53	Gordie Howe, Detroit	95
1953-54	Gordie Howe, Detroit	81
1954-55	Bernie Geoffrion, Montreal	75
1955-56	Jean Beliveau, Montreal	88
1956-57	Gordie Howe, Detroit	89
1957-58	Dickie Moore, Montreal	84
1958-59	Dickie Moore, Montreal	96
1959-60	Bobby Hull, Chicago	81
1960-61	Bernie Geoffrion, Montreal	95
1961-62	Bobby Hull, Chicago	84
1962-63	Gordie Howe, Detroit	86
1963-64	Stan Mikita, Chicago	89
1964-65	Stan Mikita, Chicago	87
1965-66	Bobby Hull, Chicago	97
1966-67	Stan Mikita, Chicago	97
1967-68	Stan Mikita, Chicago	87
1968-69	Phil Esposito, Boston	126
1969-70	Bobby Orr, Boston	120
1970-71	Phil Esposito, Boston	152
1971-72	Phil Esposito, Boston	133
1972-73	Phil Esposito, Boston	130
1973-74	Phil Esposito, Boston	145
1974-75	Bobby Orr, Boston	135
1975-76	Guy Lafleur, Montreal	125
1976-77	Guy Lafleur, Montreal	136
1977-78	Guy Lafleur, Montreal	132
1978-79	Bryan Trottier, N.Y. Islanders	134
1979-80	Marcel Dionne, Los Angeles	137
1980-81	Wayne Gretzky, Edmonton	164
1981-82	Wayne Gretzky, Edmonton	212
1982-83	Wayne Gretzky, Edmonton	196
1983-84	Wayne Gretzky, Edmonton	205
1984-85	Wayne Gretzky, Edmonton	208
1985-86	Wayne Gretzky, Edmonton	215
1986-87	Wayne Gretzky, Edmonton	183
1987-88	Mario Lemieux, Pittsburgh	168
1988-89	Mario Lemieux, Pittsburgh	199
1989-90	Wayne Gretzky, Los Angeles	142
1990-91	Wayne Gretzky, Los Angeles	163
1991-92	Mario Lemieux, Pittsburgh	131
1992-93	Mario Lemieux, Pittsburgh	160
1993-94	Wayne Gretzky, Los Angeles	130
1994-95	Jaromir Jagr, Pittsburgh	70
1995-96	Mario Lemieux, Pittsburgh	161
1996-97	Mario Lemieux, Pittsburgh	122
1997-98	Jaromir Jagr, Pittsburgh	102
1998-99	Jaromir Jagr, Pittsburgh	127

The award was originally known as the Leading Scorer Trophy. The present trophy, first given in 1947, was presented to the NHL by Art Ross, former manager-coach of the Boston Bruins. In event of a tie, the player with the most goals receives the award.

MAURICE RICHARD TROPHY

(Leading goal scorer)

Season	Player, Team	Goals
1998-99	Teemu Selanne, Anaheim	47

HART MEMORIAL TROPHY

(Most Valuable Player)

Season	Player, Team
1923-24	Frank Nighbor, Ottawa
1924-25	Billy Burch, Hamilton
1925-26	Nels Stewart, Montreal Maroons
1926-27	Herb Gardiner, Montreal
1927-28	Howie Morenz, Montreal
1928-29	Roy Worters, N.Y. Americans
1929-30	Nels Stewart, Montreal Maroons
1930-31	Howie Morenz, Montreal
1931-32	Howie Morenz, Montreal
1932-33	Eddie Shore, Boston
1933-34	Aurel Joliat, Montreal
1934-35	Eddie Shore, Boston
1935-36	Eddie Shore, Boston
1936-37	Babe Siebert, Montreal
1937-38	Eddie Shore, Boston
1938-39	Toe Blake, Montreal
1939-40	Ebbie Goodfellow, Detroit
1940-41	Bill Cowley, Boston
1941-42	Tom Anderson, N.Y. Americans
1942-43	Bill Cowley, Boston
1943-44	Babe Pratt, Toronto
1944-45	Elmer Lach, Montreal
1945-46	Max Bentley, Chicago
1946-47	Maurice Richard, Montreal
1947-48	Buddy O'Connor, N.Y. Rangers
1948-49	Sid Abel, Detroit
1949-50	Chuck Rayner, N.Y. Rangers
1950-51	Milt Schmidt, Boston
1951-52	Gordie Howe, Detroit
1952-53	Gordie Howe, Detroit
1953-54	Al Rollins, Chicago

Season Player, Team
1954-55—Ted Kennedy, Toronto
1955-56—Jean Beliveau, Montreal
1956-57—Gordie Howe, Detroit
1957-58—Gordie Howe, Detroit
1958-59—Andy Bathgate, N.Y. Rangers
1959-60—Gordie Howe, Detroit
1960-61—Bernie Geoffrion, Montreal
1961-62—Jacques Plante, Montreal
1962-63—Gordie Howe, Detroit
1963-64—Jean Beliveau, Montreal
1964-65—Bobby Hull, Chicago
1965-66—Bobby Hull, Chicago
1966-67—Stan Mikita, Chicago
1967-68—Stan Mikita, Chicago
1968-69—Phil Esposito, Boston
1969-70—Bobby Orr, Boston
1970-71—Bobby Orr, Boston
1971-72—Bobby Orr, Boston
1972-73—Bobby Clarke, Philadelphia
1973-74—Phil Esposito, Boston
1974-75—Bobby Clarke, Philadelphia
1975-76—Bobby Clarke, Philadelphia
1976-77—Guy Lafleur, Montreal
1977-78—Guy Lafleur, Montreal
1978-79—Bryan Trottier, N.Y. Islanders
1979-80—Wayne Gretzky, Edmonton
1980-81—Wayne Gretzky, Edmonton
1981-82—Wayne Gretzky, Edmonton
1982-83—Wayne Gretzky, Edmonton
1983-84—Wayne Gretzky, Edmonton
1984-85—Wayne Gretzky, Edmonton
1985-86—Wayne Gretzky, Edmonton
1986-87—Wayne Gretzky, Edmonton
1987-88—Mario Lemieux, Pittsburgh
1988-89—Wayne Gretzky, Los Angeles
1989-90—Mark Messier, Edmonton
1990-91—Brett Hull, St. Louis
1991-92—Mark Messier, N.Y. Rangers
1992-93—Mario Lemieux, Pittsburgh
1993-94—Sergei Fedorov, Detroit
1994-95—Eric Lindros, Philadelphia
1995-96—Mario Lemieux, Pittsburgh
1996-97—Dominik Hasek, Buffalo
1997-98—Dominik Hasek, Buffalo
1998-99—Jaromir Jagr, Pittsburgh

JAMES NORRIS MEMORIAL TROPHY

(Outstanding defenseman)

Season Player, Team
1953-54—Red Kelly, Detroit
1954-55—Doug Harvey, Montreal
1955-56—Doug Harvey, Montreal
1956-57—Doug Harvey, Montreal
1957-58—Doug Harvey, Montreal
1958-59—Tom Johnson, Montreal
1959-60—Doug Harvey, Montreal
1960-61—Doug Harvey, Montreal
1961-62—Doug Harvey, N.Y. Rangers
1962-63—Pierre Pilote, Chicago
1963-64—Pierre Pilote, Chicago
1964-65—Pierre Pilote, Chicago
1965-66—Jacques Laperriere, Montreal
1966-67—Harry Howell, N.Y. Rangers
1967-68—Bobby Orr, Boston
1968-69—Bobby Orr, Boston
1969-70—Bobby Orr, Boston
1970-71—Bobby Orr, Boston
1971-72—Bobby Orr, Boston
1972-73—Bobby Orr, Boston
1973-74—Bobby Orr, Boston
1974-75—Bobby Orr, Boston

Season Player, Team
1975-76—Denis Potvin, N.Y. Islanders
1976-77—Larry Robinson, Montreal
1977-78—Denis Potvin, N.Y. Islanders
1978-79—Denis Potvin, N.Y. Islanders
1979-80—Larry Robinson, Montreal
1980-81—Randy Carlyle, Pittsburgh
1981-82—Doug Wilson, Chicago
1982-83—Rod Langway, Washington
1983-84—Rod Langway, Washington
1984-85—Paul Coffey, Edmonton
1985-86—Paul Coffey, Edmonton
1986-87—Ray Bourque, Boston
1987-88—Ray Bourque, Boston
1988-89—Chris Chelios, Montreal
1989-90—Ray Bourque, Boston
1990-91—Ray Bourque, Boston
1991-92—Brian Leetch, N.Y. Rangers
1992-93—Chris Chelios, Chicago
1993-94—Ray Bourque, Boston
1994-95—Paul Coffey, Detroit
1995-96—Chris Chelios, Chicago
1996-97—Brian Leetch, N.Y. Rangers
1997-98—Rob Blake, Los Angeles
1998-99—Al MacInnis, St. Louis

VEZINA TROPHY

(Outstanding goaltender)

Season	Player, Team	GAA
1926-27	George Hainsworth, Montreal	1.52
1927-28	George Hainsworth, Montreal	1.09
1928-29	George Hainsworth, Montreal	0.98
1929-30	Tiny Thompson, Boston	2.23
1930-31	Roy Worters, N.Y. Americans	1.68
1931-32	Charlie Gardiner, Chicago	2.10
1932-33	Tiny Thompson, Boston	1.83
1933-34	Charlie Gardiner, Chicago	1.73
1934-35	Lorne Chabot, Chicago	1.83
1935-36	Tiny Thompson, Boston	1.71
1936-37	Normie Smith, Detroit	2.13
1937-38	Tiny Thompson, Boston	1.85
1938-39	Frank Brimsek, Boston	1.60
1939-40	Dave Kerr, N.Y. Rangers	1.60
1940-41	Turk Broda, Toronto	2.60
1941-42	Frank Brimsek, Boston	2.38
1942-43	Johnny Mowers, Detroit	2.48
1943-44	Bill Durnan, Montreal	2.18
1944-45	Bill Durnan, Montreal	2.42
1945-46	Bill Durnan, Montreal	2.60
1946-47	Bill Durnan, Montreal	2.30
1947-48	Turk Broda, Toronto	2.38
1948-49	Bill Durnan, Montreal	2.10
1949-50	Bill Durnan, Montreal	2.20
1950-51	Al Rollins, Toronto	1.75
1951-52	Terry Sawchuk, Detroit	1.98
1952-53	Terry Sawchuk, Detroit	1.94
1953-54	Harry Lumley, Toronto	1.85
1954-55	Terry Sawchuk, Detroit	1.94
1955-56	Jacques Plante, Montreal	1.86
1956-57	Jacques Plante, Montreal	2.02
1957-58	Jacques Plante, Montreal	2.09
1958-59	Jacques Plante, Montreal	2.15
1959-60	Jacques Plante, Montreal	2.54
1960-61	Johnny Bower, Toronto	2.50
1961-62	Jacques Plante, Montreal	2.37
1962-63	Glenn Hall, Chicago	2.51
1963-64	Charlie Hodge, Montreal	2.26
1964-65	Terry Sawchuk, Toronto	2.56
	Johnny Bower, Toronto	2.38
1965-66	Lorne Worsley, Montreal	2.36
	Charlie Hodge, Montreal	2.58

Season	Player, Team	GAA
1966-67	—Glenn Hall, Chicago	2.38
	Denis DeJordy, Chicago	2.46
1967-68	—Lorne Worsley, Montreal	1.98
	Rogatien Vachon, Montreal	2.48
1968-69	—Glenn Hall, St. Louis	2.17
	Jacques Plante, St. Louis	1.96
1969-70	—Tony Esposito, Chicago	2.17
1970-71	—Ed Giacomin, N.Y. Rangers	2.15
	Gilles Villemure, N.Y. Rangers	2.29
1971-72	—Tony Esposito, Chicago	1.76
	Gary Smith, Chicago	2.41
1972-73	—Ken Dryden, Montreal	2.26
1973-74	—Bernie Parent, Philadelphia	1.89
	Tony Esposito, Chicago	2.04
1974-75	—Bernie Parent, Philadelphia	2.03
1975-76	—Ken Dryden, Montreal	2.03
1976-77	—Ken Dryden, Montreal	2.14
	Michel Larocque, Montreal	2.09
1977-78	—Ken Dryden, Montreal	2.05
	Michel Larocque, Montreal	2.67
1978-79	—Ken Dryden, Montreal	2.30
	Michel Larocque, Montreal	2.84
1979-80	—Bob Sauve, Buffalo	2.36
	Don Edwards, Buffalo	2.57
1980-81	—Richard Sevigny, Montreal	2.40
	Michel Larocque, Montreal	3.03
	Denis Herron, Montreal	3.50
1981-82	—Billy Smith, N.Y. Islanders	2.97
1982-83	—Pete Peeters, Boston	2.36
1983-84	—Tom Barrasso, Buffalo	2.84
1984-85	—Pelle Lindbergh, Philadelphia	3.02
1985-86	—John Vanbiesbrouck, N.Y. Rangers	3.32
1986-87	—Ron Hextall, Philadelphia	3.00
1987-88	—Grant Fuhr, Edmonton	3.43
1988-89	—Patrick Roy, Montreal	2.47
1989-90	—Patrick Roy, Montreal	2.53
1990-91	—Ed Belfour, Chicago	2.47
1991-92	—Patrick Roy, Montreal	2.36
1992-93	—Ed Belfour, Chicago	2.59
1993-94	—Dominik Hasek, Buffalo	1.95
1994-95	—Dominik Hasek, Buffalo	2.11
1995-96	—Jim Carey, Washington	2.26
1996-97	—Dominik Hasek, Buffalo	2.27
1997-98	—Dominik Hasek, Buffalo	2.09
1998-99	—Dominik Hasek, Buffalo	1.87

The award was formerly presented to the goaltender(s) having played a minimum of 25 games for the team with the fewest goals scored against. Beginning with the 1981-82 season, it was awarded to the outstanding goaltender.

BILL JENNINGS TROPHY

(Leading goaltender)

Season	Player, Team	GAA
1981-82	—Denis Herron, Montreal	2.64
	Rick Wamsley, Montreal	2.75
1982-83	—Roland Melanson, N.Y. Islanders	2.66
	Billy Smith, N.Y. Islanders	2.87
1983-84	—Pat Riggin, Washington	2.66
	Al Jensen, Washington	2.91
1984-85	—Tom Barrasso, Buffalo	2.66
	Bob Sauve, Buffalo	3.22
1985-86	—Bob Froese, Philadelphia	2.55
	Darren Jensen, Philadelphia	3.68
1986-87	—Brian Hayward, Montreal	2.81
	Patrick Roy, Montreal	2.93
1987-88	—Brian Hayward, Montreal	2.86
	Patrick Roy, Montreal	2.90
1988-89	—Patrick Roy, Montreal	2.47
	Brian Hayward, Montreal	2.90
1989-90	—Rejean Lemelin, Boston	2.81
	Andy Moog, Boston	2.89
1990-91	—Ed Belfour, Chicago	2.47
1991-92	—Patrick Roy, Montreal	2.36
1992-93	—Ed Belfour, Chicago	2.59
1993-94	—Dominik Hasek, Buffalo	1.95
	Grant Fuhr, Buffalo	3.68
1994-95	—Ed Belfour, Chicago	2.28
1995-96	—Chris Osgood, Detroit	2.17
	Mike Vernon, Detroit	2.26
1996-97	—Martin Brodeur, New Jersey	1.88
	Mike Dunham, New Jersey	2.55
1997-98	—Martin Brodeur, New Jersey	1.89
1998-99	—Ed Belfour, Dallas	1.99
	Roman Turek, Dallas	2.08

The award is presented to the goaltender(s) having played a minimum of 25 games for the team with the fewest goals scored against.

CALDER MEMORIAL TROPHY

(Rookie of the year)

Season	Player, Team
1932-33	—Carl Voss, Detroit
1933-34	—Russ Blinco, Montreal Maroons
1934-35	—Dave Schriner, N.Y. Americans
1935-36	—Mike Karakas, Chicago
1936-37	—Syl Apps, Toronto
1937-38	—Cully Dahlstrom, Chicago
1938-39	—Frank Brimsek, Boston
1939-40	—Kilby Macdonald, N.Y. Rangers
1940-41	—John Quilty, Montreal
1941-42	—Grant Warwick, N.Y. Rangers
1942-43	—Gaye Stewart, Toronto
1943-44	—Gus Bodnar, Toronto
1944-45	—Frank McCool, Toronto
1945-46	—Edgar Laprade, N.Y. Rangers
1946-47	—Howie Meeker, Toronto
1947-48	—Jim McFadden, Detroit
1948-49	—Pentti Lund, N.Y. Rangers
1949-50	—Jack Gelineau, Boston
1950-51	—Terry Sawchuk, Detroit
1951-52	—Bernie Geoffrion, Montreal
1952-53	—Lorne Worsley, N.Y. Rangers
1953-54	—Camille Henry, N.Y. Rangers
1954-55	—Ed Litzenberger, Chicago
1955-56	—Glenn Hall, Detroit
1956-57	—Larry Regan, Boston
1957-58	—Frank Mahovlich, Toronto
1958-59	—Ralph Backstrom, Montreal
1959-60	—Bill Hay, Chicago
1960-61	—Dave Keon, Toronto
1961-62	—Bobby Rousseau, Montreal
1962-63	—Kent Douglas, Toronto
1963-64	—Jacques Laperriere, Montreal
1964-65	—Roger Crozier, Detroit
1965-66	—Brit Selby, Toronto
1966-67	—Bobby Orr, Boston
1967-68	—Derek Sanderson, Boston
1968-69	—Danny Grant, Minnesota
1969-70	—Tony Esposito, Chicago
1970-71	—Gilbert Perreault, Buffalo
1971-72	—Ken Dryden, Montreal
1972-73	—Steve Vickers, N.Y. Rangers
1973-74	—Denis Potvin, N.Y. Islanders
1974-75	—Eric Vail, Atlanta
1975-76	—Bryan Trottier, N.Y. Islanders
1976-77	—Willi Plett, Atlanta
1977-78	—Mike Bossy, N.Y. Islanders
1978-79	—Bobby Smith, Minnesota
1979-80	—Ray Bourque, Boston
1980-81	—Peter Stastny, Quebec
1981-82	—Dale Hawerchuk, Winnipeg
1982-83	—Steve Larmer, Chicago
1983-84	—Tom Barrasso, Buffalo

Season Player, Team
1984-85—Mario Lemieux, Pittsburgh
1985-86—Gary Suter, Calgary
1986-87—Luc Robitaille, Los Angeles
1987-88—Joe Nieuwendyk, Calgary
1988-89—Brian Leetch, N.Y. Rangers
1989-90—Sergei Makarov, Calgary
1990-91—Ed Belfour, Chicago
1991-92—Pavel Bure, Vancouver
1992-93—Teemu Selanne, Winnipeg
1993-94—Martin Brodeur, New Jersey
1994-95—Peter Forsberg, Quebec
1995-96—Daniel Alfredsson, Ottawa
1996-97—Bryan Berard, N.Y. Islanders
1997-98—Sergei Samsonov, Boston
1998-99—Chris Drury, Colorado

The award was originally known as the Leading Rookie Award. It was renamed the Calder Trophy in 1936-37 and became the Calder Memorial Trophy in 1942-43, following the death of NHL President Frank Calder.

LADY BYNG MEMORIAL TROPHY

(Most gentlemanly player)

Season Player, Team
1924-25—Frank Nighbor, Ottawa
1925-26—Frank Nighbor, Ottawa
1926-27—Billy Burch, N.Y. Americans
1927-28—Frank Boucher, N.Y. Rangers
1928-29—Frank Boucher, N.Y. Rangers
1929-30—Frank Boucher, N.Y. Rangers
1930-31—Frank Boucher, N.Y. Rangers
1931-32—Joe Primeau, Toronto
1932-33—Frank Boucher, N.Y. Rangers
1933-34—Frank Boucher, N.Y. Rangers
1934-35—Frank Boucher, N.Y. Rangers
1935-36—Doc Romnes, Chicago
1936-37—Marty Barry, Detroit
1937-38—Gordie Drillon, Toronto
1938-39—Clint Smith, N.Y. Rangers
1939-40—Bobby Bauer, Boston
1940-41—Bobby Bauer, Boston
1941-42—Syl Apps, Toronto
1942-43—Max Bentley, Chicago
1943-44—Clint Smith, Chicago
1944-45—Bill Mosienko, Chicago
1945-46—Toe Blake, Montreal
1946-47—Bobby Bauer, Boston
1947-48—Buddy O'Connor, N.Y. Rangers
1948-49—Bill Quackenbush, Detroit
1949-50—Edgar Laprade, N.Y. Rangers
1950-51—Red Kelly, Detroit
1951-52—Sid Smith, Toronto
1952-53—Red Kelly, Detroit
1953-54—Red Kelly, Detroit
1954-55—Sid Smith, Toronto
1955-56—Earl Reibel, Detroit
1956-57—Andy Hebenton, N.Y. Rangers
1957-58—Camille Henry, N.Y. Rangers
1958-59—Alex Delvecchio, Detroit
1959-60—Don McKenney, Boston
1960-61—Red Kelly, Toronto
1961-62—Dave Keon, Toronto
1962-63—Dave Keon, Toronto
1963-64—Ken Wharram, Chicago
1964-65—Bobby Hull, Chicago
1965-66—Alex Delvecchio, Detroit
1966-67—Stan Mikita, Chicago
1967-68—Stan Mikita, Chicago
1968-69—Alex Delvecchio, Detroit
1969-70—Phil Goyette, St. Louis
1970-71—John Bucyk, Boston
1971-72—Jean Ratelle, N.Y. Rangers

Season Player, Team
1972-73—Gilbert Perreault, Buffalo
1973-74—John Bucyk, Boston
1974-75—Marcel Dionne, Detroit
1975-76—Jean Ratelle, N.Y. R.-Boston
1976-77—Marcel Dionne, Los Angeles
1977-78—Butch Goring, Los Angeles
1978-79—Bob MacMillan, Atlanta
1979-80—Wayne Gretzky, Edmonton
1980-81—Rick Kehoe, Pittsburgh
1981-82—Rick Middleton, Boston
1982-83—Mike Bossy, N.Y. Islanders
1983-84—Mike Bossy, N.Y. Islanders
1984-85—Jari Kurri, Edmonton
1985-86—Mike Bossy, N.Y. Islanders
1986-87—Joe Mullen, Calgary
1987-88—Mats Naslund, Montreal
1988-89—Joe Mullen, Calgary
1989-90—Brett Hull, St. Louis
1990-91—Wayne Gretzky, Los Angeles
1991-92—Wayne Gretzky, Los Angeles
1992-93—Pierre Turgeon, N.Y. Islanders
1993-94—Wayne Gretzky, Los Angeles
1994-95—Ron Francis, Pittsburgh
1995-96—Paul Kariya, Anaheim
1996-97—Paul Kariya, Anaheim
1997-98—Ron Francis, Pittsburgh
1998-99—Wayne Gretzky, N.Y. Rangers

The award was originally known as the Lady Byng Trophy. After winning the award seven times, Frank Boucher received permanent possession and a new trophy was donated to the NHL in 1936. After Lady Byng's death in 1949, the NHL changed the name to Lady Byng Memorial Trophy.

CONN SMYTHE TROPHY

(Playoff MVP)

Season Player, Team
1964-65—Jean Beliveau, Montreal
1965-66—Roger Crozier, Detroit
1966-67—Dave Keon, Toronto
1967-68—Glenn Hall, St. Louis
1968-69—Serge Savard, Montreal
1969-70—Bobby Orr, Boston
1970-71—Ken Dryden, Montreal
1971-72—Bobby Orr, Boston
1972-73—Yvan Cournoyer, Montreal
1973-74—Bernie Parent, Philadelphia
1974-75—Bernie Parent, Philadelphia
1975-76—Reggie Leach, Philadelphia
1976-77—Guy Lafleur, Montreal
1977-78—Larry Robinson, Montreal
1978-79—Bob Gainey, Montreal
1979-80—Bryan Trottier, N.Y. Islanders
1980-81—Butch Goring, N.Y. Islanders
1981-82—Mike Bossy, N.Y. Islanders
1982-83—Billy Smith, N.Y. Islanders
1983-84—Mark Messier, Edmonton
1984-85—Wayne Gretzky, Edmonton
1985-86—Patrick Roy, Montreal
1986-87—Ron Hextall, Philadelphia
1987-88—Wayne Gretzky, Edmonton
1988-89—Al MacInnis, Calgary
1989-90—Bill Ranford, Edmonton
1990-91—Mario Lemieux, Pittsburgh
1991-92—Mario Lemieux, Pittsburgh
1992-93—Patrick Roy, Montreal
1993-94—Brian Leetch, N.Y. Rangers
1994-95—Claude Lemieux, New Jersey
1995-96—Joe Sakic, Colorado
1996-97—Mike Vernon, Detroit
1997-98—Steve Yzerman, Detroit
1998-99—Joe Nieuwendyk, Dallas

BILL MASTERTON MEMORIAL TROPHY

(Sportsmanship—dedication to hockey)

Season Player, Team
1967-68—Claude Provost, Montreal
1968-69—Ted Hampson, Oakland
1969-70—Pit Martin, Chicago
1970-71—Jean Ratelle, N.Y. Rangers
1971-72—Bobby Clarke, Philadelphia
1972-73—Lowell MacDonald, Pittsburgh
1973-74—Henri Richard, Montreal
1974-75—Don Luce, Buffalo
1975-76—Rod Gilbert, N.Y. Rangers
1976-77—Ed Westfall, N.Y. Islanders
1977-78—Butch Goring, Los Angeles
1978-79—Serge Savard, Montreal
1979-80—Al MacAdam, Minnesota
1980-81—Blake Dunlop, St. Louis
1981-82—Glenn Resch, Colorado
1982-83—Lanny McDonald, Calgary
1983-84—Brad Park, Detroit
1984-85—Anders Hedberg, N.Y. Rangers
1985-86—Charlie Simmer, Boston
1986-87—Doug Jarvis, Hartford
1987-88—Bob Bourne, Los Angeles
1988-89—Tim Kerr, Philadelphia
1989-90—Gord Kluzak, Boston
1990-91—Dave Taylor, Los Angeles
1991-92—Mark Fitzpatrick, N.Y. Islanders
1992-93—Mario Lemieux, Pittsburgh
1993-94—Cam Neely, Boston
1994-95—Pat LaFontaine, Buffalo
1995-96—Gary Roberts, Calgary
1996-97—Tony Granato, San Jose
1997-98—Jamie McLennan, St. Louis
1998-99—John Cullen, Tampa Bay

Presented by the Professional Hockey Writers' Association to the player who best exemplifies the qualities of perseverance, sportsmanship and dedication to hockey.

FRANK J. SELKE TROPHY

(Best defensive forward)

Season Player, Team
1977-78—Bob Gainey, Montreal
1978-79—Bob Gainey, Montreal
1979-80—Bob Gainey, Montreal
1980-81—Bob Gainey, Montreal
1981-82—Steve Kasper, Boston
1982-83—Bobby Clarke, Philadelphia
1983-84—Doug Jarvis, Washington
1984-85—Craig Ramsay, Buffalo
1985-86—Troy Murray, Chicago
1986-87—Dave Poulin, Philadelphia
1987-88—Guy Carbonneau, Montreal
1988-89—Guy Carbonneau, Montreal
1989-90—Rick Meagher, St. Louis
1990-91—Dirk Graham, Chicago
1991-92—Guy Carbonneau, Montreal
1992-93—Doug Gilmour, Toronto
1993-94—Sergei Fedorov, Detroit
1994-95—Ron Francis, Pittsburgh
1995-96—Sergei Fedorov, Detroit
1996-97—Michael Peca, Buffalo
1997-98—Jere Lehtinen, Dallas
1998-99—Jere Lehtinen, Dallas

JACK ADAMS TROPHY

(Coach of the year)

Season Coach, Team
1973-74—Fred Shero, Philadelphia
1974-75—Bob Pulford, Los Angeles

Season Coach, Team
1975-76—Don Cherry, Boston
1976-77—Scotty Bowman, Montreal
1977-78—Bobby Kromm, Detroit
1978-79—Al Arbour, N.Y. Islanders
1979-80—Pat Quinn, Philadelphia
1980-81—Red Berenson, St. Louis
1981-82—Tom Watt, Winnipeg
1982-83—Orval Tessier, Chicago
1983-84—Bryan Murray, Washington
1984-85—Mike Keenan, Philadelphia
1985-86—Glen Sather, Edmonton
1986-87—Jacques Demers, Detroit
1987-88—Jacques Demers, Detroit
1988-89—Pat Burns, Montreal
1989-90—Bob Murdoch, Winnipeg
1990-91—Brian Sutter, St. Louis
1991-92—Pat Quinn, Vancouver
1992-93—Pat Burns, Toronto
1993-94—Jacques Lemaire, New Jersey
1994-95—Marc Crawford, Quebec
1995-96—Scotty Bowman, Detroit
1996-97—Ted Nolan, Buffalo
1997-98—Pat Burns, Boston
1998-99—Jacques Martin, Ottawa

KING CLANCY TROPHY

(Humanitarian contributions)

Season Player, Team
1987-88—Lanny McDonald, Calgary
1988-89—Bryan Trottier, N.Y. Islanders
1989-90—Kevin Lowe, Edmonton
1990-91—Dave Taylor, Los Angeles
1991-92—Ray Bourque, Boston
1992-93—Dave Poulin, Boston
1993-94—Adam Graves, N.Y. Rangers
1994-95—Joe Nieuwendyk, Calgary
1995-96—Kris King, Winnipeg
1996-97—Trevor Linden, Vancouver
1997-98—Kelly Chase, St. Louis
1998-99—Rob Ray, Buffalo

ALL-STAR TEAMS

(As selected by members of the Professional Hockey Writers' Association at the end of each season)

1930-31

First team		Second team
Aurel Joliet, Mon. C.	LW	Bun Cook, N.Y.R.
Howie Morenz, Mon. C.	C	Frank Boucher, N.Y.R.
Bill Cook, N.Y.R.	RW	Dit Clapper, Bos.
Eddie Shore, Bos.	D	Sylvio Mantha, Mon.
King Clancy, Tor.	D	Ching Johnson, N.Y.R.
Charlie Gardiner, Chi.	G	Tiny Thompson, Bos.

1931-32

First team		Second team
Harvey Jackson, Tor.	LW	Aurel Joliat, Mon. C.
Howie Morenz, Mon. C.	C	Hooley Smith, Mon. M.
Bill Cook, N.Y.R.	RW	Charlie Conacher, Tor.
Eddie Shore, Bos.	D	Sylvio Mantha, Mon. C.
Ching Johnson, N.Y.R.	D	King Clancy, Tor.
Charlie Gardiner, Chi.	G	Roy Worters, N.Y.A.

1932-33

First team		Second team
Baldy Northcott, Mon. M.	LW	Harvey Jackson, Tor.
Frank Boucher, N.Y.R.	C	Howie Morenz, Mon.
Bill Cook, N.Y.R.	RW	Charlie Conacher, Tor.
Eddie Shore, Bos.	D	King Clancy, Tor.
Ching Johnson, N.Y.R.	D	Lionel Conacher, Mon. M.
John Ross Roach, Det.	G	Charlie Gardiner, Chi.

1933-34

First team		Second team
Harvey Jackson, Tor.	LW	Aurel Joliat, Mon. C.
Frank Boucher, N.Y.R.	C	Joe Primeau, Tor.
Charlie Conacher, Tor.	RW	Bill Cook, N.Y.R.
King Clancy, Tor.	D	Eddie Shore, Bos.
Lionel Conacher, Chi.	D	Ching Johnson, N.Y.R.
Charlie Gardiner, Chi.	G	Roy Worters, N.Y.A.

1934-35

First team		Second team
Harvey Jackson, Tor.	LW	Aurel Joliat, Mon. C.
Frank Boucher, N.Y.R.	C	Cooney Welland, Det.
Charlie Conacher, Tor.	RW	Dit Clapper, Bos.
Eddie Shore, Bos.	D	Cy Wentworth, Mon. M.
Earl Seibert, N.Y.R.	D	Art Coulter, Chi.
Lorne Chabot, Chi.	G	Tiny Thompson, Bos.

1935-36

First team		Second team
Dave Schriner, N.Y.A.	LW	Paul Thompson, Chi.
Hooley Smith, Mon. M.	C	Bill Thoms, Tor.
Charlie Conacher, Tor.	RW	Cecil Dillon, N.Y.R.
Eddie Shore, Bos.	D	Earl Seibert, Chi.
Babe Siebert, Bos.	D	Ebbie Goodfellow, Det.
Tiny Thompson, Bos.	G	Wilf Cude, Mon. C.

1936-37

First team		Second team
Harvey Jackson, Tor.	LW	Dave Schriner, N.Y.A.
Marty Barry, Det.	C	Art Chapman, N.Y.A.
Larry Aurie, Det.	RW	Cecil Dillon, N.Y.R.
Babe Siebert, Mon. C.	D	Earl Seibert, Chi.
Ebbie Goodfellow, Det.	D	Lionel Conacher, Mon. M.
Norm Smith, Det.	G	Wilf Cude, Mon. C.

1937-38

First team		Second team
Paul Thompson, Chi.	LW	Toe Blake, Mon. C.
Bill Cowley, Bos.	C	Syl Apps, Tor.
Cecil Dillon, N.Y.R.	RW	Cecil Dillon, N.Y.R.
Gord Drillon, Tor.	(tied)	Gord Drillon, Tor.
Eddie Shore, Bos.	D	Art Coulter, N.Y.R.
Babe Siebert, Mon. C.	D	Earl Seibert, Chi.
Tiny Thompson, Bos.	G	Dave Kerr, N.Y.R.

1938-39

First team		Second team
Toe Blake, Mon.	LW	Johnny Gottselig, Chi.
Syl Apps, Tor.	C	Neil Colville, N.Y.R.
Gord Drillon, Tor.	RW	Bobby Bauer, Bos.
Eddie Shore, Bos.	D	Earl Seibert, Chi.
Dit Clapper, Bos.	D	Art Coulter, N.Y.R.
Frank Brimsek, Bos.	G	Earl Robertson, N.Y.A.

1939-40

First team		Second team
Toe Blake, Mon.	LW	Woody Dumart, Bos.
Milt Schmidt, Bos.	C	Neil Colville, N.Y.R.
Bryan Hextall, N.Y.R.	RW	Bobby Bauer, Bos.
Dit Clapper, Bos.	D	Art Coulter, N.Y.R.
Ebbie Goodfellow, Det.	D	Earl Seibert, Chi.
Dave Kerr, N.Y.R.	G	Frank Brimsek, Bos.

1940-41

First team		Second team
Dave Schriner, Tor.	LW	Woody Dumart, Bos.
Bill Cowley, Bos.	C	Syl Apps, Tor.
Bryan Hextall, N.Y.R.	RW	Bobby Bauer, Bos.
Dit Clapper, Bos.	D	Earl Seibert, Chi.
Wally Stanowski, Tor.	D	Ott Heller, N.Y.R.
Turk Broda, Tor.	G	Frank Brimsek, Bos.

1941-42

First team		Second team
Lynn Patrick, N.Y.R.	LW	Sid Abel, Det.
Syl Apps, Tor.	C	Phil Watson, N.Y.R.
Bryan Hextall, N.Y.R.	RW	Gord Drillon, Tor.
Earl Seibert, Chi.	D	Pat Egan, Bkl.
Tommy Anderson, Bkl.	D	Bucko McDonald, Tor.
Frank Brimsek, Bos.	G	Turk Broda, Tor.

1942-43

First team		Second team
Doug Bentley, Chi.	LW	Lynn Patrick, N.Y.R.
Bill Cowley, Bos.	C	Syl Apps, Tor.
Lorne Carr, Tor.	RW	Bryan Hextall, N.Y.R.
Earl Seibert, Chi.	D	Jack Crawford, Bos.
Jack Stewart, Det.	D	Bill Hollett, Bos.
Johnny Mowers, Det.	G	Frank Brimsek, Bos.

1943-44

First team		Second team
Doug Bentley, Chi.	LW	Herb Cain, Bos.
Bill Cowley, Bos.	C	Elmer Lach, Mon.
Lorne Carr, Tor.	RW	Maurice Richard, Mon.
Earl Seibert, Chi.	D	Emile Bouchard, Mon.
Babe Pratt, Tor.	D	Dit Clapper, Bos.
Bill Durnan, Mon.	G	Paul Bibeault, Tor.

1944-45

First team		Second team
Toe Blake, Mon.	LW	Syd Howe, Det.
Elmer Lach, Mon.	C	Bill Cowley, Bos.
Maurice Richard, Mon.	RW	Bill Mosienko, Chi.
Emile Bouchard, Mon.	D	Glen Harmon, Mon.
Bill Hollett, Det.	D	Babe Pratt, Tor.
Bill Durnan, Mon.	G	Mike Karakas, Chi.

1945-46

First team		Second team
Gaye Stewart, Tor.	LW	Toe Blake, Mon.
Max Bentley, Chi.	C	Elmer Lach, Mon.
Maurice Richard, Mon.	RW	Bill Mosienko, Chi.
Jack Crawford, Bos.	D	Kenny Reardon, Mon.
Emile Bouchard, Mon.	D	Jack Stewart, Det.
Bill Durnan, Mon.	G	Frank Brimsek, Bos.

1946-47

First team		Second team
Doug Bentley, Chi.	LW	Woody Dumart, Bos.
Milt Schmidt, Bos.	C	Max Bentley, Chi.
Maurice Richard, Mon.	RW	Bobby Bauer, Bos.
Kenny Reardon, Mon.	D	Jack Stewart, Det.
Emile Bouchard, Mon.	D	Bill Quackenbush, Det.
Bill Durnan, Mon.	G	Frank Brimsek, Bos.

1947-48

First team		Second team
Ted Lindsay, Det.	LW	Gaye Stewart, Chi.
Elmer Lach, Mon.	C	Buddy O'Connor, N.Y.R.
Maurice Richard, Mon.	RW	Bud Poile, Chi.
Bill Quackenbush, Det.	D	Kenny Reardon, Mon.
Jack Stewart, Det.	D	Neil Colville, N.Y.R.
Turk Broda, Tor.	G	Frank Brimsek, Bos.

1948-49

First team		Second team
Roy Conacher, Chi.	LW	Ted Lindsay, Det.
Sid Abel, Det.	C	Doug Bentley, Chi.
Maurice Richard, Mon.	RW	Gordie Howe, Det.
Bill Quackenbush, Det.	D	Glen Harmon, Mon.
Jack Stewart, Det.	D	Kenny Reardon, Mon.
Bill Durnan, Mon.	G	Chuck Rayner, N.Y.R.

1949-50

First team		Second team
Ted Lindsay, Det.	LW	Tony Leswick, N.Y.R.
Sid Abel, Det.	C	Ted Kennedy, Tor.
Maurice Richard, Mon.	RW	Gordie Howe, Det.
Gus Mortson, Tor.	D	Leo Reise, Det.
Kenny Reardon, Mon.	D	Red Kelly, Det.
Bill Durnan, Mon.	G	Chuck Rayner, N.Y.R.

1950-51

First team		Second team
Ted Lindsay, Det.	LW	Sid Smith, Tor.
Milt Schmidt, Bos.	C	Sid Abel, Det.
	(tied)	Ted Kennedy, Tor.
Gordie Howe, Det.	RW	Maurice Richard, Mon.
Red Kelly, Det.	D	Jim Thomson, Tor.
Bill Quackenbush, Bos.	D	Leo Reise, Det.
Terry Sawchuk, Det.	G	Chuck Rayner, N.Y.R.

1951-52

First team		Second team
Ted Lindsay, Det.	LW	Sid Smith, Tor.
Elmer Lach, Mon.	C	Milt Schmidt, Bos.
Gordie Howe, Det.	RW	Maurice Richard, Mon.
Red Kelly, Det.	D	Hy Buller, N.Y.R.
Doug Harvey, Mon.	D	Jim Thomson, Tor.
Terry Sawchuk, Det.	G	Jim Henry, Bos.

1952-53

First team		Second team
Ted Lindsay, Det.	LW	Bert Olmstead, Mon.
Fleming Mackell, Bos.	C	Alex Delvecchio, Det.
Gordie Howe, Det.	RW	Maurice Richard, Mon.
Red Kelly, Det.	D	Bill Quackenbush, Bos.
Doug Harvey, Mon.	D	Bill Gadsby, Chi.
Terry Sawchuk, Det.	G	Gerry McNeil, Mon.

1953-54

First team		Second team
Ted Lindsay, Det.	LW	Ed Sandford, Bos.
Ken Mosdell, Mon.	C	Ted Kennedy, Tor.
Gordie Howe, Det.	RW	Maurice Richard, Mon.
Red Kelly, Det.	D	Bill Gadsby, Chi.
Doug Harvey, Mon.	D	Tim Horton, Tor.
Harry Lumley, Tor.	G	Terry Sawchuk, Det.

1954-55

First team		Second team
Sid Smith, Tor.	LW	Danny Lewicki, N.Y.R.
Jean Beliveau, Mon.	C	Ken Mosdell, Mon.
Maurice Richard, Mon.	RW	Bernie Geoffrion, Mon.
Doug Harvey, Mon.	D	Bob Goldham, Det.
Red Kelly, Det.	D	Fern Flaman, Bos.
Harry Lumley, Tor.	G	Terry Sawchuk, Det.

1955-56

First team		Second team
Ted Lindsay, Det.	LW	Bert Olmstead, Mon.
Jean Beliveau, Mon.	C	Tod Sloan, Tor.
Maurice Richard, Mon.	RW	Gordie Howe, Det.
Doug Harvey, Mon.	D	Red Kelly, Det.
Bill Gadsby, N.Y.R.	D	Tom Johnson, Mon.
Jacques Plante, Mon.	G	Glenn Hall, Det.

1956-57

First team		Second team
Ted Lindsay, Det.	LW	Real Chevrefils, Bos.
Jean Beliveau, Mon.	C	Eddie Litzenberger, Chi.
Gordie Howe, Det.	RW	Maurice Richard, Mon.
Doug Harvey, Mon.	D	Fern Flaman, Bos.
Red Kelly, Det.	D	Bill Gadsby, N.Y.R.
Glenn Hall, Det.	G	Jacques Plante, Mon.

1957-58

First team		Second team
Dickie Moore, Mon.	LW	Camille Henry, N.Y.R.
Henri Richard, Mon.	C	Jean Beliveau, Mon.
Gordie Howe, Det.	RW	Andy Bathgate, N.Y.R.
Doug Harvey, Mon.	D	Fern Flaman, Bos.
Bill Gadsby, N.Y.R.	D	Marcel Pronovost, Det.
Glenn Hall, Chi.	G	Jacques Plante, Mon.

1958-59

First team		Second team
Dickie Moore, Mon.	LW	Alex Delvecchio, Det.
Jean Beliveau, Mon.	C	Henri Richard, Mon.
Andy Bathgate, N.Y.R.	RW	Gordie Howe, Det.
Tom Johnson, Mon.	D	Marcel Pronovost, Det.
Bill Gadsby, N.Y.R.	D	Doug Harvey, Mon.
Jacques Plante, Mon.	G	Terry Sawchuk, Det.

1959-60

First team		Second team
Bobby Hull, Chi.	LW	Dean Prentice, N.Y.R.
Jean Beliveau, Mon.	C	Bronco Horvath, Bos.
Gordie Howe, Det.	RW	Bernie Geoffrion, Mon.
Doug Harvey, Mon.	D	Allan Stanley, Tor.
Marcel Pronovost, Det.	D	Pierre Pilote, Chi.
Glenn Hall, Chi.	G	Jacques Plante, Mon.

1960-61

First team		Second team
Frank Mahovlich, Mon.	LW	Dickie Moore, Mon.
Jean Beliveau, Mon.	C	Henri Richard, Mon.
Bernie Geoffrion, Mon.	RW	Gordie Howe, Det.
Doug Harvey, Mon.	D	Allan Stanley, Tor.
Marcel Pronovost, Det.	D	Pierre Pilote, Chi.
Johnny Bower, Tor.	G	Glenn Hall, Chi.

1961-62

First team		Second team
Bobby Hull, Chi.	LW	Frank Mahovlich, Tor.
Stan Mikita, Chi.	C	Dave Keon, Tor.
Andy Bathgate, N.Y.R.	RW	Gordie Howe, Det.
Doug Harvey, N.Y.R.	D	Carl Brewer, Tor.
Jean-Guy Talbot, Mon.	D	Pierre Pilote, Chi.
Jacques Plante, Mon.	G	Glenn Hall, Chi.

1962-63

First team		Second team
Frank Mahovlich, Tor.	LW	Bobby Hull, Chi.
Stan Mikita, Chi.	C	Henri Richard, Mon.
Gordie Howe, Det.	RW	Andy Bathgate, N.Y.R.
Pierre Pilote, Chi.	D	Tim Horton, Tor.
Carl Brewer, Tor.	D	Elmer Vasko, Chi.
Glenn Hall, Chi.	G	Terry Sawchuk, Det.

1963-64

First team		Second team
Bobby Hull, Chi.	LW	Frank Mahovlich, Tor.
Stan Mikita, Chi.	C	Jean Beliveau, Mon.
Ken Wharram, Chi.	RW	Gordie Howe, Det.
Pierre Pilote, Chi.	D	Elmer Vasko, Chi.
Tim Horton, Tor.	D	Jacques Laperriere, Mon.
Glenn Hall, Chi.	G	Charlie Hodge, Mon.

1964-65

First team		Second team
Bobby Hull, Chi.	LW	Frank Mahovlich, Tor.
Norm Ullman, Det.	C	Stan Mikita, Chi.
Claude Provost, Mon.	RW	Gordie Howe, Det.
Pierre Pilote, Chi.	D	Bill Gadsby, Det.
Jacques Laperriere, Mon.	D	Carl Brewer, Tor.
Roger Crozier, Det.	G	Charlie Hodge, Mon.

1965-66

First team		Second team
Bobby Hull, Chi.	LW	Frank Mahovlich, Tor.
Stan Mikita, Chi.	C	Jean Beliveau, Mon.
Gordie Howe, Det.	RW	Bobby Rousseau, Mon.
Jacques Laperriere, Mon.	D	Allan Stanley, Tor.
Pierre Pilote, Chi.	D	Pat Stapleton, Chi.
Glenn Hall, Chi.	G	Gump Worsley, Mon.

1966-67

First team		Second team
Bobby Hull, Chi.	LW	Don Marshall, N.Y.R.
Stan Mikita, Chi.	C	Norm Ullman, Det.
Ken Wharram, Chi.	RW	Gordie Howe, Det.
Pierre Pilote, Chi.	D	Tim Horton, Tor.
Harry Howell, N.Y.R.	D	Bobby Orr, Bos.
Ed Giacomin, N.Y.R.	G	Glenn Hall, Chi.

1967-68

First team		Second team
Bobby Hull, Chi.	LW	Johnny Bucyk, Bos.
Stan Mikita, Chi.	C	Phil Esposito, Bos.
Gordie Howe, Det.	RW	Rod Gilbert, N.Y.R.
Bobby Orr, Bos.	D	J.C. Tremblay, Mon.
Tim Horton, Tor.	D	Jim Neilson, N.Y.R.
Gump Worsley, Mon.	G	Ed Giacomin, N.Y.R.

1968-69

First team		Second team
Bobby Hull, Chi.	LW	Frank Mahovlich, Det.
Phil Esposito, Bos.	C	Jean Beliveau, Mon.
Gordie Howe, Det.	RW	Yvan Cournoyer, Mon.
Bobby Orr, Bos.	D	Ted Green, Bos.
Tim Horton, Tor.	D	Ted Harris, Mon.
Glenn Hall, St.L.	G	Ed Giacomin, N.Y.R.

1969-70

First team		Second team
Bobby Hull, Chi.	LW	Frank Mahovlich, Det.
Phil Esposito, Bos.	C	Stan Mikita, Chi.
Gordie Howe, Det.	RW	John McKenzie, Bos.
Bobby Orr, Bos.	D	Carl Brewer, Det.
Brad Park, N.Y.R.	D	Jacques Laperriere, Mon.
Tony Esposito, Chi.	G	Ed Giacomin, N.Y.R.

1970-71

First team		Second team
Johnny Bucyk, Bos.	LW	Bobby Hull, Chi.
Phil Esposito, Bos.	C	Dave Keon, Tor.
Ken Hodge, Bos.	RW	Yvan Cournoyer, Mon.
Bobby Orr, Bos.	D	Brad Park, N.Y.R.
J.C. Tremblay, Mon.	D	Pat Stapleton, Chi.
Ed Giacomin, N.Y.R.	G	Jacques Plante, Tor.

1971-72

First team		Second team
Bobby Hull, Chi.	LW	Vic Hadfield, N.Y.R.
Phil Esposito, Bos.	C	Jean Ratelle, N.Y.R.
Rod Gilbert, N.Y.R.	RW	Yvan Cournoyer, Mon.
Bobby Orr, Bos.	D	Bill White, Chi.
Brad Park, N.Y.R.	D	Pat Stapleton, Chi.
Tony Esposito, Chi.	G	Ken Dryden, Mon.

1972-73

First team		Second team
Frank Mahovlich, Mon.	LW	Dennis Hull, Chi.
Phil Esposito, Bos.	C	Bobby Clarke, Phi.
Mickey Redmond, Det.	RW	Yvan Cournoyer, Mon.
Bobby Orr, Bos.	D	Brad Park, N.Y.R.
Guy Lapointe, Mon.	D	Bill White, Chi.
Ken Dryden, Mon.	G	Tony Esposito, Chi.

1973-74

First team		Second team
Richard Martin, Buf.	LW	Wayne Cashman, Bos.
Phil Esposito, Bos.	C	Bobby Clarke, Phi.
Ken Hodge, Bos.	RW	Mickey Redmond, Det.
Bobby Orr, Bos.	D	Bill White, Chi.
Brad Park, N.Y.R.	D	Barry Ashbee, Phi.
Bernie Parent, Phi.	G	Tony Esposito, Chi.

1974-75

First team		Second team
Richard Martin, Buf.	LW	Steve Vickers, N.Y.R.
Bobby Clarke, Phi.	C	Phil Esposito, Bos.
Guy Lafleur, Mon.	RW	Rene Robert, Buf.
Bobby Orr, Bos.	D	Guy Lapointe, Mon.
Denis Potvin, N.Y.I.	D	Borje Salming, Tor.
Bernie Parent, Phi.	G	Rogie Vachon, L.A.

1975-76

First team		Second team
Bill Barber, Phi.	LW	Richard Martin, Buf.
Bobby Clarke, Phi.	C	Gilbert Perreault, Buf.
Guy Lafleur, Mon.	RW	Reggie Leach, Phi.
Denis Potvin, N.Y.I.	D	Borje Salming, Tor.
Brad Park, Bos.	D	Guy Lapointe, Mon.
Ken Dryden, Mon.	G	Glenn Resch, N.Y.I.

1976-77

First team		Second team
Steve Shutt, Mon.	LW	Richard Martin, Buf.
Marcel Dionne, L.A.	C	Gilbert Perreault, Buf.
Guy Lafleur, Mon.	RW	Lanny McDonald, Tor.
Larry Robinson, Mon.	D	Denis Potvin, N.Y.I.
Borje Salming, Tor.	D	Guy Lapointe, Mon.
Ken Dryden, Mon.	G	Rogie Vachon, L.A.

1977-78

First team		Second team
Clark Gillies, N.Y.I.	LW	Steve Shutt, Mon.
Bryan Trottier, N.Y.I.	C	Darryl Sittler, Tor.
Guy Lafleur, Mon.	RW	Mike Bossy, N.Y.I.
Denis Potvin, N.Y.I.	D	Larry Robinson, Mon.
Brad Park, Bos.	D	Borje Salming, Tor.
Ken Dryden, Mon.	G	Don Edwards, Buf.

1978-79

First team		Second team
Clark Gillies, N.Y.I.	LW	Bill Barber, Phi.
Bryan Trottier, N.Y.I.	C	Marcel Dionne, L.A.
Guy Lafleur, Mon.	RW	Mike Bossy, N.Y.I.
Denis Potvin, N.Y.I.	D	Borje Salming, Tor.
Larry Robinson, Mon.	D	Serge Savard, Mon.
Ken Dryden, Mon.	G	Glenn Resch, N.Y.I.

1979-80

First team		Second team
Charlie Simmer, L.A.	LW	Steve Shutt, Mon.
Marcel Dionne, L.A.	C	Wayne Gretzky, Edm.
Guy Lafleur, Mon.	RW	Danny Gare, Buf.
Larry Robinson, Mon.	D	Borje Salming, Tor.
Ray Bourque, Bos.	D	Jim Schoenfeld, Buf.
Tony Esposito, Chi.	G	Don Edwards, Buf.

1980-81

First team		Second team
Charlie Simmer, L.A.	LW	Bill Barber, Phi.
Wayne Gretzky, Edm.	C	Marcel Dionne, L.A.
Mike Bossy, N.Y.I.	RW	Dave Taylor, L.A.
Denis Potvin, N.Y.I.	D	Larry Robinson, Mon.
Randy Carlyle, Pit.	D	Ray Bourque, Bos.
Mike Liut, St.L.	G	Mario Lessard, L.A.

1981-82

First team		Second team
Mark Messier, Edm.	LW	John Tonelli, N.Y.I.
Wayne Gretzky, Edm.	C	Bryan Trottier, N.Y.I.
Mike Bossy, N.Y.I.	RW	Rick Middleton, Bos.
Doug Wilson, Chi.	D	Paul Coffey, Edm.
Ray Bourque, Bos.	D	Brian Engblom, Mon.
Bill Smith, N.Y.I.	G	Grant Fuhr, Edm.

1982-83

First team		Second team
Mark Messier, Edm.	LW	Michel Goulet, Que.
Wayne Gretzky, Edm.	C	Denis Savard, Chi.
Mike Bossy, N.Y.I.	RW	Lanny McDonald, Cal.
Mark Howe, Phi.	D	Ray Bourque, Bos.
Rod Langway, Was.	D	Paul Coffey, Edm.
Pete Peeters, Bos.	G	Roland Melanson, N.Y.I.

1983-84

First team		Second team
Michel Goulet, Que.	LW	Mark Messier, Edm.
Wayne Gretzky, Edm.	C	Bryan Trottier, N.Y.I.
Mike Bossy, N.Y.I.	RW	Jari Kurri, Edm.
Rod Langway, Was.	D	Paul Coffey, Edm.
Ray Bourque, Bos.	D	Denis Potvin, N.Y.I.
Tom Barrasso, Buf.	G	Pat Riggin, Was.

1984-85

First team		Second team
John Ogrodnick, Det.	LW	John Tonelli, N.Y.I.
Wayne Gretzky, Edm.	C	Dale Hawerchuk, Win.
Jari Kurri, Edm.	RW	Mike Bossy, N.Y.I.
Paul Coffey, Edm.	D	Rod Langway, Was.
Ray Bourque, Bos.	D	Doug Wilson, Chi.
Pelle Lindbergh, Phi.	G	Tom Barrasso, Buf.

1985-86

First team		Second team
Michel Goulet, Que.	LW	Mats Naslund, Mon.
Wayne Gretzky, Edm.	C	Mario Lemieux, Pit.
Mike Bossy, N.Y.I.	RW	Jari Kurri, Edm.
Paul Coffey, Edm.	D	Larry Robinson, Mon.
Mark Howe, Phi.	D	Ray Bourque, Bos.
John Vanbiesbrouck, N.Y.R.	G	Bob Froese, Phi.

1986-87

First team		Second team
Michel Goulet, Que.	LW	Luc Robitaille, L.A.
Wayne Gretzky, Edm.	C	Mario Lemieux, Pit.
Jari Kurri, Edm.	RW	Tim Kerr, Phi.
Ray Bourque, Bos.	D	Larry Murphy, Was.
Mark Howe, Phi.	D	Al MacInnis, Cal.
Ron Hextall, Phi.	G	Mike Liut, Har.

1987-88

First team		Second team
Luc Robitaille, L.A.	LW	Michel Goulet, Que.
Mario Lemieux, Pit.	C	Wayne Gretzky, Edm.
Hakan Loob, Cal.	RW	Cam Neely, Bos.
Ray Bourque, Bos.	D	Gary Suter, Cal.
Scott Stevens, Was.	D	Brad McCrimmon, Cal.
Grant Fuhr, Edm.	G	Patrick Roy, Mon.

1988-89

First team		Second team
Luc Robitaille, L.A.	LW	Gerard Gallant, Det.
Mario Lemieux, Pit.	C	Wayne Gretzky, L.A.
Joe Mullen, Cal.	RW	Jari Kurri, Edm.
Chris Chelios, Mon.	D	Al MacInnis, Cal.
Paul Coffey, Pit.	D	Ray Bourque, Bos.
Patrick Roy, Mon.	G	Mike Vernon, Cal.

1989-90

First team		Second team
Luc Robitaille, L.A.	LW	Brian Bellows, Min.
Mark Messier, Edm.	C	Wayne Gretzky, L.A.
Brett Hull, St.L.	RW	Cam Neely, Bos.
Ray Bourque, Bos.	D	Paul Coffey, Pit.
Al MacInnis, Cal.	D	Doug Wilson, Chi.
Patrick Roy, Mon.	G	Daren Puppa, Buf.

1990-91

First team		Second team
Luc Robitaille, L.A.	LW	Kevin Stevens, Pit.
Wayne Gretzky, L.A.	C	Adam Oates, St.L.
Brett Hull, St.L.	RW	Cam Neely, Bos.
Ray Bourque, Bos.	D	Chris Chelios, Chi.
Al MacInnis, Cal.	D	Brian Leetch, N.Y.R.
Ed Belfour, Chi.	G	Patrick Roy, Mon.

1991-92

First team		Second team
Kevin Stevens, Pit.	LW	Luc Robitaille, L.A.
Mark Messier, N.Y.R.	C	Mario Lemieux, Pit.
Brett Hull, St.L.	RW	Mark Recchi, Pit., Phi.
Brian Leetch, N.Y.R.	D	Phil Housley, Win.
Ray Bourque, Bos.	D	Scott Stevens, N.J.
Patrick Roy, Mon.	G	Kirk McLean, Van.

1992-93

First team		Second team
Luc Robitaille, L.A.	LW	Kevin Stevens, Pit.
Mario Lemieux, Pit.	C	Pat LaFontaine, Buf.
Teemu Selanne, Win.	RW	Alexander Mogilny, Buf.
Chris Chelios, Chi.	D	Larry Murphy, Pit.
Ray Bourque, Bos.	D	Al Iafrate, Was.
Ed Belfour, Chi.	G	Tom Barrasso, Pit.

1993-94

First team		Second team
Brendan Shanahan, St.L.	LW	Adam Graves, N.Y.R.
Sergei Fedorov, Det.	C	Wayne Gretzky, L.A.
Pavel Bure, Van.	RW	Cam Neely, Bos.
Ray Bourque, Bos.	D	Al MacInnis, Cal.
Scott Stevens, N.J.	D	Brian Leetch, N.Y.R.
Dominik Hasek, Buf.	G	John Vanbiesbrouck, Fla.

1994-95

First team		Second team
John LeClair, Mon., Phi.	LW	Keith Tkachuk, Win.
Eric Lindros, Phi.	C	Alexei Zhamnov, Win.
Jaromir Jagr, Pit.	RW	Theoren Fleury, Cal.
Paul Coffey, Det.	D	Ray Bourque, Bos.
Chris Chelios, Chi.	D	Larry Murphy, Pit.
Dominik Hasek, Buf.	G	Ed Belfour, Chi.

1995-96

First team		Second team
Paul Kariya, Ana.	LW	John LeClair, Phi.
Mario Lemieux, Pit.	C	Eric Lindros, Phi.
Jaromir Jagr, Pit.	RW	Alexander Mogilny, Van.
Chris Chelios, Chi.	D	Vladimir Konstantinov, Det.
Ray Bourque, Bos.	D	Brian Leetch, N.Y.R.
Jim Carey, Was.	G	Chris Osgood, Det.

1996-97

First team		Second team
Paul Kariya, Ana.	LW	John LeClair, Phi.
Mario Lemieux, Pit.	C	Wayne Gretzky, N.Y.R.
Teemu Selanne, Ana.	RW	Jaromir Jagr, Pit.
Brian Leetch, N.Y.R.	D	Chris Chelios, Chi.
Sandis Ozolinsh, Col.	D	Scott Stevens, N.J.
Dominik Hasek, Buf.	G	Martin Brodeur, N.J.

1997-98

First team		Second team
John LeClair, Phi.	LW	Keith Tkachuk, Phoenix
Peter Forsberg, Col.	C	Wayne Gretzky, N.Y.R.
Jaromir Jagr, Pit.	RW	Teemu Selanne, Ana.
Nicklas Lidstrom, Det.	D	Chris Pronger, St.L.
Rob Blake, L.A.	D	Scott Niedermayer, N.J.
Dominik Hasek, Buf.	G	Martin Brodeur, N.J.

THE SPORTING NEWS AWARDS

PLAYER OF THE YEAR

1967-68—E. Div.: Stan Mikita, Chicago
W. Div.: Red Berenson, St. Louis
1968-69—E. Div.: Phil Esposito, Boston
W. Div.: Red Berenson, St. Louis
1969-70—E. Div.: Bobby Orr, Boston
W. Div.: Red Berenson, St. Louis
1970-71—E. Div.: Phil Esposito, Boston
W. Div.: Bobby Hull, Chicago
1971-72—E. Div.: Jean Ratelle, N.Y. Rangers
W. Div.: Bobby Hull, Chicago
1972-73—E. Div.: Phil Esposito, Boston
W. Div.: Bobby Clarke, Philadelphia
1973-74—E. Div.: Phil Esposito, Boston
W. Div.: Bernie Parent, Philadelphia
1974-75—Camp. Conf.: Bobby Clarke, Philadelphia
Wales Conf.: Guy Lafleur, Montreal
1975-76—Bobby Clarke, Philadelphia
1976-77—Guy Lafleur, Montreal
1977-78—Guy Lafleur, Montreal
1978-79—Bryan Trottier, N.Y. Islanders
1979-80—Marcel Dionne, Los Angeles
1980-81—Wayne Gretzky, Edmonton
1981-82—Wayne Gretzky, Edmonton
1982-83—Wayne Gretzky, Edmonton
1983-84—Wayne Gretzky, Edmonton
1984-85—Wayne Gretzky, Edmonton
1985-86—Wayne Gretzky, Edmonton
1986-87—Wayne Gretzky, Edmonton
1987-88—Mario Lemieux, Pittsburgh
1988-89—Mario Lemieux, Pittsburgh
1989-90—Mark Messier, Edmonton
1990-91—Brett Hull, St. Louis
1991-92—Mark Messier, N.Y. Rangers
1992-93—Mario Lemieux, Pittsburgh
1993-94—Sergei Fedorov, Detroit
1994-95—Eric Lindros, Philadelphia
1995-96—Mario Lemieux, Pittsburgh
1996-97—Dominik Hasek, Buffalo
1997-98—Dominik Hasek, Buffalo
1998-99—Jaromir Jagr, Pittsburgh

ROOKIE OF THE YEAR

1967-68—E. Div.: Derek Sanderson, Boston
W. Div.: Bill Flett, Los Angeles
1968-69—E. Div.: Brad Park, N.Y. Rangers
W. Div.: Norm Ferguson, Oakland
1969-70—E. Div.: Tony Esposito, Chicago
W. Div.: Bobby Clarke, Philadelphia
1970-71—E. Div.: Gil Perreault, Buffalo
W. Div.: Jude Drouin, Minnesota
1971-72—E. Div.: Richard Martin, Buffalo
W. Div.: Gilles Meloche, California
1972-73—E. Div.: Steve Vickers, N.Y. Rangers
W. Div.: Bill Barber, Philadelphia
1973-74—E. Div.: Denis Potvin, N.Y. Islanders
W. Div.: Tom Lysiak, Atlanta
1974-75—Camp. Conf.: Eric Vail, Atlanta
Wales Conf.: Pierre Larouche, Pittsburgh
1975-76—Bryan Trottier, N.Y. Islanders
1976-77—Willi Plett, Atlanta
1977-78—Mike Bossy, N.Y. Islanders
1978-79—Bobby Smith, Minnesota
1979-80—Ray Bourque, Boston
1980-81—Peter Stastny, Quebec
1981-82—Dale Hawerchuk, Winnipeg
1982-83—Steve Larmer, Chicago
1983-84—Steve Yzerman, Detroit
1984-85—Mario Lemieux, Pittsburgh
1985-86—Wendel Clark, Toronto
1986-87—Ron Hextall, Philadelphia
1987-88—Joe Nieuwendyk, Calgary
1988-89—Brian Leetch, N.Y. Rangers
1989-90—Jeremy Roenick, Chicago
1990-91—Ed Belfour, Chicago
1991-92—Tony Amonte, N.Y. Rangers
1992-93—Teemu Selanne, Winnipeg
1993-94—Jason Arnott, Edmonton
1994-95—Peter Forsberg, Quebec
1995-96—Eric Daze, Chicago
1996-97—Bryan Berard, N.Y. Islanders
1997-98—Sergei Samsonov, Boston
1998-99—Chris Drury, Colorado

NHL COACH OF THE YEAR

1944-45—Dick Irvin, Montreal
1945-46—Johnny Gottselig, Chicago
1979-80—Pat Quinn, Philadelphia
1980-81—Red Berenson, St. Louis
1981-82—Herb Brooks, N.Y. Rangers
1982-83—Gerry Cheevers, Boston
1983-84—Bryan Murray, Washington
1984-85—Mike Keenan, Philadelphia
1985-86—Jacques Demers, St. Louis
1986-87—Jacques Demers, Detroit
1987-88—Terry Crisp, Calgary
1988-89—Pat Burns, Montreal
1989-90—Mike Milbury, Boston
1990-91—Tom Webster, Los Angeles
1991-92—Pat Quinn, Vancouver
1992-93—Pat Burns, Toronto
1993-94—Jacques Lemaire, New Jersey
1994-95—Marc Crawford, Quebec
1995-96—Scotty Bowman, Detroit
1996-97—Ken Hitchcock, Dallas
1997-98—Pat Burns, Boston
1998-99—Jacques Martin, Ottawa

NOTE: The Coach of the Year Award was not given from 1946-47 through 1978-79 seasons.

NHL EXECUTIVE OF THE YEAR

1972-73—Sam Pollock, Montreal
1973-74—Keith Allen, Philadelphia
1974-75—Bill Torrey, N.Y. Islanders
1975-76—Sam Pollock, Montreal
1976-77—Harry Sinden, Boston
1977-78—Ted Lindsay, Detroit
1978-79—Bill Torrey, N.Y. Islanders

1979-80—Scotty Bowman, Buffalo
1980-81—Emile Francis, St. Louis
1981-82—John Ferguson, Winnipeg
1982-83—David Poile, Washington
1983-84—David Poile, Washington
1984-85—John Ferguson, Winnipeg
1985-86—Emile Francis, Hartford
1986-87—John Ferguson, Winnipeg
1987-88—Cliff Fletcher, Calgary
1988-89—Bruce McNall, Los Angeles
1989-90—Harry Sinden, Boston
1990-91—Craig Patrick, Pittsburgh
1991-92—Neil Smith, N.Y. Rangers
1992-93—Cliff Fletcher, Toronto
1993-94—Bobby Clarke, Florida
1994-95—Bobby Clarke, Philadelphia
1995-96—Bryan Murray, Florida
1996-97—John Muckler, Buffalo
1997-98—Craig Patrick, Pittsburgh
1998-99—Craig Patrick, Pittsburgh

THE SPORTING NEWS ALL-STAR TEAMS

(As selected by six hockey writers in 1944-45 and 1945-46 and by a vote of league players since 1967-68; no teams selected from 1946-47 through 1966-67)

1944-45

First team		Second team
Maurice Richard, Mon.	W	Bill Mosienko, Chi.
Toe Blake, Mon.	W	Sweeney Schriner, Tor.
Elmer Lach, Mon.	C	Bill Cowley, Bos.
Emile Bouchard, Mon.	D	Earl Seibert, Det.
Bill Hollett, Det.	D	Babe Pratt, Tor.
Bill Durnan, Mon.	G	Frank McCool, Tor.

1945-46

First team		Second team
Gaye Stewart, Tor.	LW	Doug Bentley, Chi.
Max Bentley, Chi.	C	Elmer Lach, Mon.
Bill Mosienko, Chi.	RW	Maurice Richard, Mon.
Emile Bouchard, Mon.	D	Jack Crawford, Bos.
Jack Stewart, Det.	D	Babe Pratt, Tor.
Bill Durnan, Mon.	G	Harry Lumley, Det.

1967-68

EAST DIVISION		WEST DIVISION
First team		**First team**
Bobby Hull, Chi.	LW	Ab McDonald, Pit.
Stan Mikita, Chi.	C	Red Berenson, St.L.
Gordie Howe, Det.	RW	Wayne Connelly, Min.
Bobby Orr, Bos.	D	Bill White, L.A.
Tim Horton, Tor.	D	Mike McMahon, Min.
Ed Giacomin, N.Y.R.	G	Glenn Hall, St.L.
Second team		**Second team**
Johnny Bucyk, Bos.	LW	Bill Sutherland, Phi.
Phil Esposito, Bos.	C	Ray Cullen, Min.
Rod Gilbert, N.Y.R.	RW	Bill Flett, L.A.
J.C. Tremblay, Mon.	D	Ar Arbour, St.L.
Gary Bergman, Det.	D	Ed Van Impe, Phi.
Gump Worsley, Mon.	G	Doug Favell, Phi.

1968-69

EAST DIVISION		WEST DIVISION
First team		**First team**
Bobby Hull, Chi.	LW	Danny Grant, Min.
Phil Esposito, Bos.	C	Red Berenson, St.L.
Gordie Howe, Det.	RW	Norm Ferguson, Oak.
Bobby Orr, Bos.	D	Bill White, L.A.
Tim Horton, Tor.	D	Ar Arbour, St.L.
Ed Giacomin, N.Y.R.	G	Glenn Hall, St.L.
Second team		**Second team**
Frank Mahovlich, Det.	LW	Ab McDonald, St.L.
Stan Mikita, Chi.	C	Ted Hampson, Oak.
Yvan Cournoyer, Mon.	RW	Claude LaRose, Min.
J.C. Tremblay, Mon.	D	Carol Vadnais, Oak.
Jim Neilson, N.Y.R.	D	Ed Van Impe, Phi.
Bruce Gamble, Tor.	G	Bernie Parent, Phi.

1969-70

EAST DIVISION		WEST DIVISION
Bobby Hull, Chi.	LW	Dean Prentice, Pit.
Stan Mikita, Chi.	C	Red Berenson, St.L.
Ron Ellis, Tor.	RW	Bill Goldsworthy, Min.
Bobby Orr, Bos.	D	Al Arbour, St.L.
Brad Park, N.Y.R.	D	Bob Woytowich, Pit.
Tony Esposito, Chi.	G	Bernie Parent, Phi.

1970-71

EAST DIVISION		WEST DIVISION
Johnny Bucyk, Bos.	LW	Bobby Hull, Chi.
Phil Esposito, Bos.	C	Stan Mikita, Chi.
Ken Hodge, Bos.	RW	Bill Goldsworthy, Min.
Bobby Orr, Bos.	D	Pat Stapleton, Chi.
J.C. Tremblay, Mon.	D	Bill White, Chi.
Ed Giacomin, N.Y.R.	G	Tony Esposito, Chi.

1971-72

EAST DIVISION		WEST DIVISION
Vic Hadfield, N.Y.R.	LW	Bobby Hull, Chi.
Phil Esposito, Bos.	C	Bobby Clarke, Phi.
Rod Gilbert, N.Y.R.	RW	Bill Goldsworthy, Min.
Bobby Orr, Bos.	D	Pat Stapleton, Chi.
Brad Park, N.Y.R.	D	Bill White, Chi.
Ken Dryden, Mon.	G	Tony Esposito, Chi.

1972-73

EAST DIVISION		WEST DIVISION
Frank Mahovlich, Mon.	LW	Dennis Hull, Chi.
Phil Esposito, Bos.	C	Bobby Clarke, Phi.
Mickey Redmond, Det.	RW	Bill Flett, Phi.
Bobby Orr, Bos.	D	Bill White, Chi.
Guy Lapointe, Mon.	D	Barry Gibbs, Min.
Ken Dryden, Mon.	G	Tony Esposito, Chi.

1973-74

EAST DIVISION		WEST DIVISION
First team		**First team**
Richard Martin, Buf.	LW	Lowell MacDonald, Pit.
Phil Esposito, Bos.	C	Bobby Clarke, Phi.
Ken Hodge, Bos.	RW	Bill Goldsworthy, Min.
Bobby Orr, Bos.	D	Bill White, Chi.
Brad Park, N.Y.R.	D	Barry Ashbee, Phi.
Gilles Gilbert, Bos.	G	Bernie Parent, Phi.
Second team		**Second team**
Frank Mahovlich, Mon.	LW	Dennis Hull, Chi.
Darryl Sittler, Tor.	C	Stan Mikita, Chi.
Mickey Redmond, Det.	RW	Jean Pronovost, Pit.
Guy Lapointe, Mon.	D	Don Awrey, St.L.
Borje Salming, Tor.	D	Dave Burrows, Pit.
Ed Giacomin, N.Y.R.	D	Tony Esposito, Chi.

1974-75

CAMPBELL CONFERENCE		WALES CONFERENCE
First team		**First team**
Steve Vickers, N.Y.R.	LW	Richard Martin, Buf.
Bobby Clarke, Phi.	C	Phil Esposito, Bos.
Rod Gilbert, N.Y.R.	RW	Guy Lafleur, Mon.
Denis Potvin, N.Y.I.	D	Bobby Orr, Bos.
Brad Park, N.Y.R.	D	Guy Lapointe, Mon.
Bernie Parent, Phi.	G	Rogie Vachon, L.A.

Second team		Second team
Eric Vail, Atl.	LW	Danny Grant, Det.
Stan Mikita, Chi.	C	Gilbert Perreault, Buf.
Reggie Leach, Phi.	RW	Rene Robert, Buf.
Jim Watson, Phi.	D	Borje Salming, Tor.
Phil Russell, Chi.	D	Terry Harper, L.A.
Gary Smith, Van.	D	Ken Dryden, Mon.

1975-76

First team		Second team
Bill Barber, Phi.	LW	Richard Martin, Buf.
Bobby Clarke, Phi.	C	Pete Mahovlich, Mon.
Guy Lafleur, Mon.	RW	Reggie Leach, Phi.
Denis Potvin, N.Y.I.	D	Guy Lapointe, Mon.
Brad Park, Bos.	D	Borje Salming, Tor.
Ken Dryden, Mon.	G	Glenn Resch, N.Y.I.

1976-77

First team		Second team
Steve Shutt, Mon.	LW	Clark Gillies, N.Y.I.
Marcel Dionne, L.A.	C	Gilbert Perreault, Buf.
Guy Lafleur, Mon.	RW	Lanny McDonald, Tor.
Larry Robinson, Mon.	D	Guy Lapointe, Mon.
Borje Salming, Tor.	D	Serge Savard, Mon.
	(tied)	Denis Potvin, N.Y.I.
Rogie Vachon, L.A.	G	Ken Dryden, Mon.

1977-78

First team		Second team
Clark Gillies, N.Y.I.	LW	Steve Shutt, Mon.
Bryan Trottier, N.Y.I.	C	Darryl Sittler, Tor.
Guy Lafleur, Mon.	RW	Terry O'Reilly, Bos.
Borje Salming, Tor.	D	Denis Potvin, N.Y.I.
Larry Robinson, Mon.	D	Serge Savard, Mon.
Ken Dryden, Mon.	G	Don Edwards, Buf.

1978-79

First team		Second team
Clark Gillies, N.Y.I.	LW	Bob Gainey, Mon.
Bryan Trottier, N.Y.I.	C	Marcel Dionne, L.A.
Guy Lafleur, Mon.	RW	Mike Bossy, N.Y.I.
Denis Potvin, N.Y.I.	D	Borje Salming, Tor.
Larry Robinson, Mon.	D	Serge Savard, Mon.
Ken Dryden, Mon.	G	Glenn Resch, N.Y.I.

1979-80

First team		Second team
Charlie Simmer, L.A.	LW	Steve Shutt, Mon.
Marcel Dionne, L.A.	C	Wayne Gretzky, Edm.
Guy Lafleur, Mon.	RW	Danny Gare, Buf.
Larry Robinson, Mon.	D	Barry Beck, Col., N.Y.R.
Borje Salming, Tor.	D	Mark Howe, Har.
Tony Esposito, Chi.	G	Don Edwards, Buf.

1980-81

First team		Second team
Charlie Simmer, L.A.	LW	Bill Barber, Phi.
Wayne Gretzky, Edm.	C	Marcel Dionne, L.A.
Mike Bossy, N.Y.I.	RW	Dave Taylor, L.A.
Randy Carlyle, Pit.	D	Larry Robinson, Mon.
Denis Potvin, N.Y.I.	D	Ray Bourque, Bos.
Mike Liut, St.L.	G	Don Beaupre, Min.

1981-82

First team		Second team
Mark Messier, Edm.	LW	John Tonelli, N.Y.I.
Wayne Gretzky, Edm.	C	Bryan Trottier, N.Y.I.
Mike Bossy, N.Y.I.	RW	Rick Middleton, Bos.
Doug Wilson, Chi.	D	Paul Coffey, Edm.
Ray Bourque, Bos.	D	Larry Robinson, Mon.
Bill Smith, N.Y.I.	G	Grant Fuhr, Edm.

1982-83

First team		Second team
Mark Messier, Edm.	LW	Michel Goulet, Que.
Wayne Gretzky, Edm.	C	Denis Savard, Chi.
Lanny McDonald, Cal.	RW	Mike Bossy, N.Y.I.
Mark Howe, Phi.	D	Ray Bourque, Bos.
Rod Langway, Was.	D	Paul Coffey, Edm.
Pete Peeters, Bos.	G	Andy Moog, Edm.

1983-84

First team		Second team
Michel Goulet, Que.	LW	John Ogrodnick, Det.
Wayne Gretzky, Edm.	C	Bryan Trottier, N.Y.I.
Rick Middleton, Bos.	RW	Mike Bossy, N.Y.I.
Ray Bourque, Bos.	D	Paul Coffey, Edm.
Rod Langway, Was.	D	Denis Potvin, N.Y.I.
Pat Riggin, Was.	G	Tom Barrasso, Buf.

1984-85

First team		Second team
Michel Goulet, Que.	LW	John Ogrodnick, Det.
Wayne Gretzky, Edm.	C	Dale Hawerchuk, Win.
Jari Kurri, Edm.	RW	Mike Bossy, N.Y.I.
Ray Bourque, Bos.	D	Rod Langway, Was.
Paul Coffey, Edm.	D	Doug Wilson, Chi.
Pelle Lindbergh, Phi.	G	Tom Barrasso, Buf.

1985-86

First team		Second team
Michel Goulet, Que.	LW	Mats Naslund, Mon.
Wayne Gretzky, Edm.	C	Mario Lemieux, Pit.
Mike Bossy, N.Y.I.	RW	Jari Kurri, Edm.
Paul Coffey, Edm.	D	Ray Bourque, Bos.
Mark Howe, Phi.	D	Larry Robinson, Mon.
John Vanbiesbrouck, N.Y.R.	G	Grant Fuhr, Edm.

1986-87

First team		Second team
Michel Goulet, Que.	LW	Luc Robitaille, L.A.
Wayne Gretzky, Edm.	C	Mark Messier, Edm.
Tim Kerr, Phi.	RW	Kevin Dineen, Har.
Ray Bourque, Bos.	D	Larry Murphy, Was.
Mark Howe, Phi.	D	Paul Coffey, Edm.
Mike Liut, Har.	G	Ron Hextall, Phi.

1987-88

First team		Second team
Luc Robitaille, L.A.	LW	Michel Goulet, Que.
Mario Lemieux, Pit.	C	Wayne Gretzky, Edm.
Cam Neely, Bos.	RW	Hakan Loob, Cal.
Ray Bourque, Bos.	D	Scott Stevens, Was.
Gary Suter, Cal.	D	Brad McCrimmon, Cal.
Grant Fuhr, Edm.	G	Tom Barrasso, Buf.

1988-89

First team		Second team
Luc Robitaille, L.A.	LW	Mats Naslund, Mon.
Mario Lemieux, Pit.	C	Wayne Gretzky, L.A.
Joe Mullen, Cal.	RW	Jari Kurri, Edm.
Paul Coffey, Pit.	D	Ray Bourque, Bos.
Chris Chelios, Mon.	D	Gary Suter, Cal.
Patrick Roy, Mon.	G	Mike Vernon, Cal.

1989-90

First team		Second team
Luc Robitaille, L.A.	LW	Brian Bellows, Min.
Mark Messier, Edm.	C	Pat LaFontaine, N.Y.I.
Brett Hull, St.L.	RW	Cam Neely, Bos.
Ray Bourque, Bos.	D	Doug Wilson, Chi.
Al MacInnis, Cal.	D	Paul Coffey, Pit.
Patrick Roy, Mon.	G	Daren Puppa, Buf.

1990-91

First team		Second team
Luc Robitaille, L.A.	LW	Kevin Stevens, Pit.
Wayne Gretzky, L.A.	C	Adam Oates, St.L.
Brett Hull, St.L.	RW	Cam Neely, Bos.
Ray Bourque, Bos.	D	Brian Leetch, N.Y.R.
Al MacInnis, Cal.	D	Chris Chelios, Chi.
Ed Belfour, Chi.	G	Patrick Roy, Mon.

1991-92

First team		Second team
Kevin Stevens, Pit.	LW	Luc Robitaille, L.A.
Mark Messier, N.Y.R.	C	Wayne Gretzky, L.A.
Brett Hull, St.L.	RW	Joe Mullen, Pit.
Brian Leetch, N.Y.R.	D	Phil Housley, Win.
Ray Bourque, Bos.	D	Chris Chelios, Chi.
Patrick Roy, Mon.	G	Kirk McLean, Van.

1992-93

First team		Second team
Luc Robitaille, L.A.	LW	Kevin Stevens, Pit.
Mario Lemieux, Pit.	C	Doug Gilmour, Tor.
Teemu Selanne, Win.	RW	Alexander Mogilny, Buf.
Chris Chelios, Chi.	D	Larry Murphy, Pit.
Ray Bourque, Bos.	D	Al Iafrate, Was.
Tom Barrasso, Pit.	G	Ed Belfour, Chi.

1993-94

First team		Second team
Adam Graves, N.Y.R.	LW	Dave Andreychuk, Tor.
Sergei Fedorov, Det.	C	Wayne Gretzky, L.A.
Cam Neely, Bos.	RW	Pavel Bure, Van.
Ray Bourque, Bos.	D	Brian Leetch, N.Y.R.
Scott Stevens, N.J.	D	Al MacInnis, Cal.
John Vanbiesbrouck, Fla.	G	Dominik Hasek, Buf.

1994-95

LW	John LeClair, Mon.-Phi.
C	Eric Lindros, Philadelphia
RW	Jaromir Jagr, Pittsburgh
D	Paul Coffey, Detroit
D	Ray Bourque, Boston
G	Dominik Hasek, Buffalo

1995-96

LW	Keith Tkachuk, Winnipeg
C	Mario Lemieux, Pittsburgh
RW	Jaromir Jagr, Pittsburgh
D	Chris Chelios, Chicago
D	Ray Bourque, Boston
G	Chris Osgood, Detroit

1996-97

LW	John LeClair, Philadelphia
C	Mario Lemieux, Pittsburgh
RW	Teemu Selanne, Anaheim
D	Chris Chelios, Chicago
D	Brian Leetch, N.Y. Rangers
G	Dominik Hasek, Buffalo

1997-98

LW	John LeClair, Philadelphia
C	Peter Forsberg, Colorado
RW	Teemu Selanne, Anaheim
D	Rob Blake, Los Angeles
D	Nicklas Lidstrom, Detroit
G	Dominik Hasek, Buffalo

HALL OF FAME

ROSTER OF MEMBERS

NOTE: Leagues other than the NHL with which Hall of Fame members are associated are denoted in parentheses. Abbreviations: **AAHA:** Alberta Amateur Hockey Association. **AHA:** Amateur Hockey Association of Canada. **CAHL:** Canadian Amateur Hockey League. **EAA:** Eaton Athletic Association. **ECAHA:** Eastern Canada Amateur Hockey Association. **ECHA:** Eastern Canada Hockey Association. **FAHL:** Federal Amateur Hockey League. **IHL:** International Professional Hockey League. **MHL:** Manitoba Hockey League. **MNSHL:** Manitoba and Northwestern Senior Hockey League. **MPHL:** Maritime Pro Hockey League. **MSHL:** Manitoba Senior Hockey League. **NHA:** National Hockey Association. **NOHA:** Northern Ontario Hockey Association. **OHA:** Ontario Hockey Association. **OPHL:** Ontario Professional Hockey League. **PCHA:** Pacific Coast Hockey Association. **WCHL:** Western Canada Hockey League. **WHA:** World Hockey Association. **WHL:** Western Hockey League. **WinHL:** Winnipeg Hockey League. **WOHA:** Western Ontario Hockey Association.

PLAYERS

Player	Elec. year/ how elected*	Pos.†	First season	Last season	Stanley Cup wins‡	Teams as player
Abel, Sid	1969/P	C	1938-39	1953-54	3	Detroit Red Wings, Chicago Blackhawks
Adams, Jack	1959/P	C	1917-18	1926-27	2	Toronto Arenas, Vancouver Millionaires (PCHA), Toronto St. Pats, Ottawa Senators
Apps, Syl	1961/P	C	1936-37	1947-48	3	Toronto Maple Leafs
Armstrong, George	1975/P	RW	1949-50	1970-71	4	Toronto Maple Leafs
Bailey, Ace	1975/P	RW	1926-27	1933-34	1	Toronto Maple Leafs
Bain, Dan	1945/P	C	1895-96	1901-02	3	Winnipeg Victorias (MHL)
Baker, Hobey	1945/P	Ro.	1910	1915	0	Princeton University, St. Nicholas
Barber, Bill	1990/P	LW	1972-73	1983-84	2	Philadelphia Flyers
Barry, Marty	1965/P	C	1927-28	1939-40	2	New York Americans, Boston Bruins, Detroit Red Wings, Montreal Canadiens
Bathgate, Andy	1978/P	RW	1952-53	1974-75	1	New York Rangers, Toronto Maple Leafs, Detroit Red Wings, Pittsburgh Penguins, Vancouver Blazers (WHA)
Bauer, Bobby	1996/V	LW	1935-36	1951-52	2	Boston Bruins
Beliveau, Jean	1972/P	C	1950-51	1970-71	10	Montreal Canadiens
Benedict, Clint	1965/P	G	1917-18	1929-30	4	Ottawa Senators, Montreal Maroons
Bentley, Doug	1964/P	LW	1939-40	1953-54	0	Chicago Blackhawks, New York Rangers
Bentley, Max	1966/P	C	1940-41	1953-54	3	Toronto Maple Leafs, New York Rangers
Blake, Toe	1966/P	LW	1932-33	1947-48	3	Montreal Maroons, Montreal Canadiens
Boivin, Leo	1986/P	D	1951-52	1969-70	0	Toronto Maple Leafs, Boston Bruins, Detroit Red Wings, Pittsburgh Penguins, Minnesota North Stars
Boon, Dickie	1952/P	D	1897	1905	2	Montreal Monarchs, Montreal AAA (CAHL), Montreal Wanderers (FAHL)
Bossy, Mike	1991/P	RW	1977-78	1986-87	4	New York Islanders
Bouchard, Butch	1966/P	D	1941-42	1955-56	4	Montreal Canadiens
Boucher, Frank	1958/P	C	1921-22	1943-44	2	Ottawa Senators, Vancouver Maroons, New York Rangers
Boucher, George	1960/P	F/D	1915-16	1931-32	4	Ottawa Senators, Montreal Maroons, Chicago Blackhawks
Bower, Johnny	1976/P	G	1953-54	1969-70	0	New York Rangers, Toronto Maple Leafs
Bowie, Russell	1945/P	C	1898-99	1907-08	1	Montreal Victorias
Brimsek, Frank	1966/P	G	1938-39	1951-52	0	Boston Bruins, Chicago Blackhawks
Broadbent, Punch	1962/P	RW	1912-13	1928-29	4	Ottawa Senators, Montreal Maroons, New York Americans
Broda, Turk	1967/P	G	1936-37	1928-29	0	Toronto Maple Leafs
Bucyk, John	1981/P	LW	1955-56	1977-78	2	Detroit Red Wings, Boston Bruins
Burch, Billy	1974/P	C	1922-23	1932-33	0	Hamilton Tigers, New York Americans, Chicago Blackhawks
Cameron, Harry	1962/P	D	1912-13	1925-26	3	Toronto Blueshirts, Toronto Arenas, Montreal Wanderers, Ottawa Senators, Toronto St. Pats, Montreal Canadiens, Saskatoon (WCHL)
Cheevers, Gary	1985/P	G	1961-62	1979-80	2	Toronto Maple Leafs, Boston Bruins, Cleveland Crusaders (WHA)
Clancy, King	1958/P	D	1921-22	1936-37	3	Ottawa Senators, Toronto Maple Leafs
Clapper, Dit	1947/P	RW	1927-28	1946-47	3	Boston Bruins
Clarke, Bobby	1987/P	C	1969-70	1983-84	2	Philadelphia Flyers
Cleghorn, Sprague	1958/P	D	1909-10	1927-28	3	New York Crescents, Renfrew Creamery Kings (NHA), Montreal Wanderers, Ottawa Senators, Toronto St. Pats, Toronto St. Pats, Montreal Canadiens, Boston Bruins
Colville, Neil	1967/P	C/D	1935-36	1948-49	1	New York Rangers
Conacher, Charlie	1961/P	RW	1929-30	1940-41	1	Toronto Maple Leafs, Detroit Red Wings, New York Americans
Conacher, Lionel	1994/V	D	1925-26	1936-37	2	Pittsburgh Pirates, New York Americans, Montreal Maroons, Chicago Blackhawks
Conacher, Roy	1998/V	LW	1938-39	1951-52	2	Boston Bruins, Detroit Red Wings, Chicago Blackhawks
Connell, Alex	1958/P	G	1924-25	1936-37	2	Ottawa Senators, Detroit Red Wings, New York Americans, Montreal Maroons

Player	Elec. year/ how elected*	Pos.†	First season	Last season	Stanley Cup wins‡	Teams as player
Cook, Bill	1952/P	RW	1921-22	1936-37	2	Saskatoon, New York Rangers
Cook, Bun	1995/V	LW	1926-27	1936-37	2	New York Rangers, Boston Bruins
Coulter, Art	1974/P	D	1931-32	1941-42	2	Chicago Blackhawks, New York Rangers
Cournoyer, Yvan	1982/P	RW	1963-64	1978-79	10	Montreal Canadiens
Cowley, Bill	1968/P	C	1934-35	1946-47	2	St. Louis Eagles, Boston Bruins
Crawford, Rusty	1962/P	LW	1912-13	1925-26	1	Quebec Bulldogs, Ottawa Senators, Toronto Arenas, Saskatoon (WCHL), Calgary (WCHL), Vancouver (WHL)
Darragh, Jack	1962/P	RW	1910-11	1923-24	4	Ottawa Senators
Davidson, Scotty	1950/P	RW	1912-13	1913-14	0	Toronto (NHA)
Day, Hap	1961/P	LW	1924-25	1937-38	1	Toronto St. Pats, Toronto Maple Leafs, New York Americans
Delvecchio, Alex	1977/P	C	1950-51	1973-74	3	Detroit Red Wings
Denneny, Cy	1959/P	LW	1914-15	1928-29	5	Toronto Shamrocks (NHA), Toronto Arenas (NHA), Ottawa Senators, Boston Bruins
Dionne, Marcel	1992/P	C	1971-72	1988-89	0	Detroit Red Wings, Los Angeles Kings, New York Rangers
Drillon, Gord	1975/P	LW	1936-37	1942-43	1	Toronto Maple Leafs, Montreal Canadiens
Drinkwater, Graham	1950/P	F/D	1892-93	1898-99	5	Montreal Victorias
Dryden, Ken	1983/P	G	1970-71	1978-79	6	Montreal Canadiens
Dumart, Woody	1992/V	LW	1935-36	1953-54	2	Boston Bruins
Dunderdale, Tommy	1974/P	C	1906-07	1923-24	0	Winnipeg Maple Leafs (MHL), Montreal Shamrocks (NHA), Quebec Bulldogs (NHA), Victoria (PCHA), Portland (PCHA), Saskatoon (WCHL), Edmonton (WCHL)
Durnan, Bill	1964/P	G	1943-44	1949-50	2	Montreal Canadiens
Dutton, Red	1958/P	D	1921-22	1935-36	0	Calgary Tigers (WCHL), Montreal Maroons, New York Americans
Dye, Babe	1970/P	RW	1919-20	1930-31	1	Toronto St. Pats, Hamilton Tigers, Chicago Blackhawks, New York Americans, Toronto Maple Leafs
Esposito, Phil	1984/P	C	1963-64	1980-81	2	Chicago Blackhawks, Boston Bruins, New York Rangers
Esposito, Tony	1988/P	G	1968-69	1983-84	1	Montreal Canadiens, Chicago Blackhawks
Farrell, Arthur	1965/P	F	1896-97	1900-01	2	Montreal Shamrocks (AHA/CAHL)
Flaman, Fern	1990/V	D	1944-45	1960-61	1	Boston Bruins, Toronto Maple Leafs
Foyston, Frank	1958/P	C	1912-13	1927-28	3	Toronto Blueshirts (NHA), Seattle Metropolitans (PCHA), Victoria Cougars (WCHL/WHL), Detroit Cougars
Fredrickson, Frank	1958/P	C	1920-21	1930-31	1	Victoria Aristocrats (PCHA), Victoria Cougars (PCHA/WCHL/WHL), Detroit Cougars, Boston Bruins, Pittsburgh Pirates, Detroit Falcons
Gadsby, Bill	1970/P	D	1946-47	1965-66	0	Chicago Blackhawks, New York Rangers, Detroit Red Wings
Gainey, Bob	1992/P	LW	1973-74	1988-89	5	Montreal Canadiens
Gardiner, Chuck	1945/P	G	1927-28	1933-34	1	Chicago Blackhawks
Gardiner, Herb	1958/P	D	1921-22	1928-29	0	Calgary Tigers (WCHL), Montreal Canadiens, Chicago Blackhawks
Gardner, Jimmy	1962/P	LW	1900-01	1914-15	3	Montreal Hockey Club (CAHL), Montreal Wanderers (FAHL/ECHA/NHA), Calumet (IHL), Pittsburgh (IHL), Montreal Shamrocks (ECAHA),New Westminster Royals (PCHA), Montreal Canadiens (NHA)
Geoffrion, Boom Boom	1972/P	RW	1950-51	1967-68	6	Montreal Canadiens, New York Rangers
Gerard, Eddie	1945/P	F/D	1913-14	1922-23	4	Ottawa Senators (NHA/NHL), Toronto St. Pats
Giacomin, Eddie	1987/P	G	1965-66	1977-78	0	New York Rangers, Detroit Red Wings
Gilbert, Rod	1982/P	RW	1960-61	1977-78	0	New York Rangers
Gilmour, Billy	1962/P	RW	1902-03	1915-16	5	Ottawa Silver Seven (CAHL/FAHL/ECAHA), Montreal Victorias (ECAHA), Ottawa Senators (ECHA/NHA)
Goheen, Moose	1952/P	D	1914	1918	0	St. Paul Athletic Club, 1920 U.S. Olympic Team
Goodfellow, Ebbie	1963/P	C	1929-30	1942-43	3	Detroit Cougars, Detroit Falcons, Detroit Red Wings
Goulet, Michel	1998/P	LW	1978-79	1993-94	0	Birmingham Bulls (WHA), Quebec Nordiques, Chicago Blackhawks
Grant, Mike	1950/P	D	1893-94	1901-02	5	Montreal Victorias (AHA/CAHL), Montreal Shamrocks (CAHL)
Green, Shorty	1962/P	RW	1923-24	1926-27	0	Hamilton Tigers, New York Americans
Gretzky, Wayne	1999/P	C	1978-79	1998-99	4	Indianapolis Racers (WHA), Edmonton (WHA/NHL), Los Angeles Kings, St. Louis Blues, New York Rangers
Griffis, Si	1950/P	Ro./D	1902-03	1918-19	2	Rat Portage Thistles (MNSHL), Kenora Thistles (MSHL), Vancouver Millionaires (PCHA)
Hainsworth, George	1961/P	G	1923-24	1936-37	2	Saskatoon Crescents (WCHL/WHL), Montreal Canadiens
Hall, Glenn	1975/P	G	1952-53	1970-71	1	Detriot Red Wings, Chicago Blackhawks, St. Louis Blues
Hall, Joe	1961/P	F/D	1903-04	1918-19	2	Winnipeg (MSHL), Quebec Bulldogs (ECAHA/NHA), Brandon (MHL), Montreal (ECAHA), Montreal Shamrocks (ECAHA/NHA), Montreal Wanderers (ECHA), Montreal Canadiens

Player	Elec. year/ how elected*	Pos.†	First season	Last season	Stanley Cup wins‡	Teams as player
Harvey, Doug	1973/P	D	1947-48	1968-69	6	Montreal Canadiens, New York Rangers, Detroit Red Wings, St. Louis Blues
Hay, George	1958/P	LW	1921-22	1933-34	0	Regina Capitals (WCHL), Portland Rosebuds (WHL), Chicago Blackhawks, Detroit Cougars, Detroit Falcons, Detroit Red Wings
Hern, Riley	1962/P	G	1906-07	1910-11	3	Montreal Wanderers (ECAHA/ECHA/NHA)
Hextall, Bryan	1969/P	RW	1936-37	1947-48	1	New York Rangers
Holmes, Hap	1972/P	G	1912-13	1927-28	0	Toronto Blueshirts (NHA), Seattle Metropolitans (PCHA), Toronto Arenas, Victoria Cougars, Detroit Cougars
Hooper, Tom	1962/P	F	1904-05	1907-08	2	Rat Portage Thistles (MNSHL), Kenora Thistles (SHL), Montreal Wanderers (ECAHA), Montreal (ECAHA)
Horner, Red	1965/P	D	1928-29	1939-40	1	Toronto Maple Leafs
Horton, Tim	1977/P	D	1949-50	1973-74	4	Toronto Maple Leafs, New York Rangers, Pittsburgh Penguins, Buffalo Sabres
Howe, Gordie	1972/P	RW	1946-47	1979-80	4	Detroit Red Wings, Houston Aeros (WHA), New England Whalers (WHA), Hartford Whalers
Howe, Syd	1965/P	F/D	1929-30	1945-46	3	Ottawa Senators, Philadelphia Quakers, Toronto Maple Leafs, St. Louis Eagles, Detroit Red Wings
Howell, Harry	1979/P	D	1952-53	1975-76	0	New York Rangers, Oakland Seals, California Golden Seals, New York Golden Blades/Jersey Knights (WHA), San Diego Mariners (WHA), Calgary Cowboys (WHA)
Hull, Bobby	1983/P	LW	1957-58	1979-80	1	Chicago Blackhawks, Winnipeg Jets (WHA/NHL), Hartford Whalers
Hutton, Bouse	1962/P	G	1898-99	1903-04	1	Ottawa Silver Seven (CAHL)
Hyland, Harry	1962/P	RW	1908-09	1917-18	1	Montreal Shamrocks (ECHA), Montreal Wanderers (NHA), New Westminster Royals (PCHA), Ottawa Senators
Irvin, Dick	1958/P	C	1916-17	1928-29	0	Portland Rosebuds (PCHA), Regina Capitals (WCHL), Chicago Blackhawks
Jackson, Busher	1971/P	LW	1929-30	1943-44	1	Toronto Maple Leafs, New York Americans, Boston Bruins
Johnson, Ching	1958/P	D	1926-27	1937-38	2	New York Rangers, New York Americans
Johnson, Moose	1952/P	LW/D	1903-04	1921-22	4	Montreal AAA (CAHL), Montreal Wanderers (ECAHA/ECHA/NHA), New Westminster Royals (PCHA), Portland Rosebuds (PCHA), Victoria Aristocrats (PCHA)
Johnson, Tom	1970/P	D	1947-48	1964-65	6	Montreal Canadiens, Boston Bruins
Joliat, Aurel	1947/P	LW	1922-23	1937-38	3	Montreal Canadiens
Keats, Duke	1958/P	C	1915-16	1928-29	0	Toronto Arenas (NHA), Edmonton Eskimos (WCHL/WHL), Detroit Cougars, Chicago Blackhawks
Kelly, Red	1969/P	C	1947-48	1966-67	8	Detroit Red Wings, Toronto Maple Leafs
Kennedy, Ted	1966/P	C	1942-43	1956-57	5	Toronto Maple Leafs
Keon, Dave	1986/P	C	1960-61	1981-82	4	Toronto Maple Leafs, Minnesota Fighting Saints (WHA) Indianapolis Racers (WHA), New England Whalers (WHA), Hartford Whalers
Lach, Elmer	1966/P	C	1940-41	1953-54	3	Montreal Canadiens
Lafleur, Guy	1988/P	RW	1971-72	1990-91	5	Montreal Canadiens, New York Rangers, Quebec Nordiques
Lalonde, Newsy	1950/P	C/Ro.	1904-05	1926-27	1	Cornwall (FAHL), Portage La Prairie (MHL), Toronto (OPHL), Montreal Canadiens (NHA/NHL), Renfrew Creamery Kings (NHA), Vancouver Millionaires (PCHA), Saskatoon Sheiks (WCHL), Saskatoon Crescents (WCHL/WHL), New York Americans
Laperriere, Jacques	1987/P	D	1962-63	1973-74	6	Montreal Canadiens
Lapointe, Guy	1993/P	D	1968-69	1983-84	6	Montreal Canadiens, St. Louis Blues, Boston Bruins
Laprade, Edgar	1993/V	C	1945-46	1954-55	0	New York Rangers
Laviolette, Jack	1962/P	D/LW	1903-04	1917-18	1	Montreal Nationals (FAHL), Montreal Shamrocks (ECAHA/ECHA), Montreal Canadiens (NHA/NHL)
Lehman, Hughie	1958/P	G	1908-09	1927-28	1	Berlin Dutchmen (OPHL), Galt (OPHL), New Westminster Royals (PCHA), Vancouver Millionaires, Vancouver Maroons, Chicago Blackhawks
Lemaire, Jacques	1984/P	C	1967-68	1978-79	8	Montreal Canadiens
Lemieux, Mario	1997/P	C	1984-85	1996-97	2	Pittsburgh Penguins
LeSueur, Percy	1961/P	G	1905-06	1915-16	3	Smith Falls (FAHL), Ottawa Senators (ECAHA/ECHA/NHA), Toronto Shamrocks (NHA), Toronto Blueshirts (NHA)
Lewis, Herbie	1989/V	LW	1928-29	1938-39	2	Detroit Cougars, Detroit Falcons, Detroit Red Wings
Lindsay, Ted	1966/P	LW	1944-45	1964-65	4	Detroit Red Wings, Chicago Blackhawks
Lumley, Harry	1980/P	G	1943-44	1959-60	1	Detroit Red Wings, New York Rangers, Chicago Blackhawks, Toronto Maple Leafs, Boston Bruins

Player	Elec. year/ how elected*	Pos.†	First season	Last season	Stanley Cup wins‡	Teams as player
MacKay, Mickey	1952/P	C/Ro.	1914-15	1929-30	1	Vancouver Millionaires (PCHA), Vancouver Maroons (PCHA/WCHL/WHL), Chicago Blackhawks, Pittsburgh Pirates, Boston Bruins
Mahovlich, Frank	1981/P	LW	1956-57	1977-78	6	Toronto Maple Leafs, Detroit Red Wings, Montreal Canadiens, Toronto Toros (WHA), Birmingham Bulls (WHA)
Malone, Joe	1950/P	C/LW	1908-09	1923-24	3	Quebec (ECHA), Waterloo (OPHL), Quebec Bulldogs (NHA/NHL), Montreal Canadiens, Hamilton Tigers
Mantha, Sylvio	1960/P	D	1923-24	1936-37	3	Montreal Canadiens, Boston Bruins
Marshall, Jack	1965/P	C/D	1900-01	1916-17	6	Winnipeg Victorias, Montreal AAA (CAHL), Montreal Wanderers (FAHL/ECAHA/NHA), Montreal Montagnards (FAHL), Montreal Shamrocks (ECAHA/ECHA), Toronto Blueshirts (NHA)
Maxwell, Fred	1962/P	Ro.	1914	1925	0	Winnipeg Monarchs (MSHL), Winnipeg Falcons (MSHL)
McDonald, Lanny	1992/P	RW	1973-74	1988-89	1	Toronto Maple Leafs, Colorado Rockies, Calgary Flames
McGee, Frank	1945/P	C/Ro.	1902-03	1905-06	4	Ottawa Silver Seven
McGimsie, Billy	1962/P	F	1902-03	1906-07	1	Rat Portage Thistles (MNSHL/MSHL), Kenora Thistles (MSHL)
McNamara, George	1958/P	D	1907-08	1916-17	1	Montreal Shamrocks (ECAHA/ECHA), Waterloo (OPHL), Toronto Tecumsehs (NHA), Toronto Ontarios (NHA), Toronto Blueshirts (NHA), Toronto Shamrocks (NHA), 228th Battalion (NHA)
Mikita, Stan	1983/P	C	1958-59	1979-80	1	Chicago Blackhawks
Moore, Dickie	1974/P	RW	1951-52	1967-68	6	Montreal Canadiens, Toronto Maple Leafs, St. Louis Blues
Moran, Paddy	1958/P	G	1901-02	1916-17	2	Quebec Bulldogs (CAHL/ECAHA/ECHA/NHA), Haileybury (NHA)
Morenz, Howie	1945/P	C	1923-24	1936-37	3	Montreal Canadiens, Chicago Blackhawks, New York Rangers
Mosienko, Bill	1965/P	RW	1941-42	1954-55	0	Chicago Blackhawks
Nighbor, Frank	1947/P	LW/C	1912-13	1929-30	5	Toronto Blueshirts (NHA), Vancouver Millionaires, (PCHA), Ottawa Senators, Toronto Maple Leafs
Noble, Reg	1962/P	LW/C/D	1916-17	1932-33	3	Toronto Blueshirts (NHA), Montreal Canadiens (NHA), Toronto Arenas, Toronto St. Pats, Montreal Maroons, Detroit Cougars, Detroit Falcons, Detroit Red Wings
O'Connor, Buddy	1988/V	C	1941-42	1950-51	2	Montreal Canadiens, New York Rangers
Oliver, Harry	1967/P	F	1921-22	1936-37	1	Calgary Tigers (WCHL/WHL), Boston Bruins, New York Americans
Olmstead, Bert	1985/P	LW	1948-49	1961-62	5	Chicago Blackhawks, Montreal Canadiens, Toronto Maple Leafs
Orr, Bobby	1979/P	D	1966-67	1978-79	2	Boston Bruins, Chicago Blackhawks
Parent, Bernie	1984/P	G	1965-66	1978-79	2	Boston Bruins, Philadelphia Flyers, Toronto Maple Leafs, Philadelphia Blazers (WHA)
Park, Brad	1988/P	D	1968-69	1984-85	0	New York Rangers, Boston Bruins, Detroit Red Wings
Patrick, Lester	1947/P	D/Ro./G	1903-04	1926-27	3	Brandon, Westmount (CAHL), Montreal Wanderers (ECAHA), Edmonton Eskimos (AAHA), Renfrew Millionaires (NHA), Victoria Aristocrats (PCHA), Spokane Canaries (PCHA), Seattle Metropolitans (PCHA), Seattle Metropolitans(PCHA), Victoria Cougars (WHA), New York Rangers
Patrick, Lynn	1980/P	LW	1934-35	1945-46	1	New York Rangers
Perreault, Gilbert	1990/P	C	1970-71	1986-87	0	Buffalo Sabres
Phillips, Tommy	1945/P	LW	1902-03	1911-12	1	Montreal AAA (CAHL), Toronto Marlboros (OHA), Rat Portage Thistles, Kenora Thistles (MHL), Ottawa Ottawa Senators (ECAHA), Edmonton Eskimos (AAHA), Vancouver Millionaires (PCHA)
Pilote, Pierre	1975/P	D	1955-56	1968-69	1	Chicago Blackhawks, Toronto Maple Leafs
Pitre, Didier	1962/P	D/Ro.	1903-04	1922-23	0	Montreal Nationals (FAHL/CAHL), Montreal Shamrocks (ECAHA), Edmonton Eskimos (AAHA), Montreal Canadiens (NHA/NHL), Vancouver Millionaires (PCHA)
Plante, Jacques	1978/P	G	1952-53	1974-75	6	Montreal Canadiens, New York Rangers, St. Louis Blues, Toronto Maple Leafs, Boston Bruins, Edmonton Oilers
Potvin, Denis	1991/P	D	1973-74	1987-88	4	New York Islanders
Pratt, Babe	1966/P	D	1935-36	1946-47	2	New York Rangers, Toronto Maple Leafs, Boston Bruins
Primeau, Joe	1963/P	C	1927-28	1935-36	1	Toronto Maple Leafs
Pronovost, Marcel	1978/P	D	1950-51	1966-67	5	Detroit Red Wings, Toronto Maple Leafs
Pulford, Bob	1991/P	LW	1956-57	1971-72	4	Toronto Maple Leafs, Los Angeles Kings
Pulford, Harvey	1945/P	D	1893-94	1907-08	4	Ottawa Silver Seven/Senators (AHA/CAHL/FAHL/ECAHA)
Quackenbush, Bill	1976/P	D	1942-43	1955-56	0	Detroit Red Wings, Boston Bruins
Rankin, Frank	1961/P	Ro.	1906	1914	0	Stratford (OHA), Eatons (EAA), Toronto St. Michaels (OHA)

Player	Elec. year/ how elected*	Pos.†	First season	Last season	Stanley Cup wins‡	Teams as player
Ratelle, Jean	1985/P	C	1960-61	1980-81	0	New York Rangers, Boston Bruins
Rayner, Chuck	1973/P	G	1940-41	1952-53	0	New York Americans, New York Rangers
Reardon, Ken	1966/P	D	1940-41	1949-50	1	Montreal Canadiens
Richard, Henri	1979/P	C	1955-56	1974-75	11	Montreal Canadiens
Richard, Rocket	1961/P	RW	1942-43	1959-60	8	Montreal Canadiens
Richardson, George	1950/P		1906	1912	0	14th Regiment, Queen's University
Roberts, Gordon	1971/P	LW	1909-10	1919-20	0	Ottawa Senators (NHA), Montreal Wanderers (NHA), Vancouver Millionaires (PCHA), Seattle Metropolitans (PCHA)
Robinson, Larry	1995/P	D	1972-73	1991-92	6	Montreal Canadiens, Los Angeles Kings
Ross, Art	1945/P	D	1904-05	1917-18	2	Westmount (CAHL), Brandon (MHL), Kenora Thistles (MHL), Montreal Wanderers (ECAHA/ECHA/NHA/NHL), Haileybury (NHA), Ottawa Senators (NHA)
Russell, Blair	1965/P	RW/C	1899-00	1907-08	0	Montreal Victorias (CAHL/ECAHA)
Russell, Ernie	1965/P	Ro./C	1904-05	1913-14	4	Montreal Winged Wheelers (CAHL), Montreal Wanderers (ECAHA/NHA)
Ruttan, Jack	1962/P		1905	1913	0	Armstrong's Point, Rustler, St. John's College, Manitoba Varsity (WSHL), Winnipeg (WinHL)
Salming, Borje	1996/P	D	1973-74	1989-90	0	Toronto Maple Leafs, Detroit Red Wings
Savard, Serge	1986/P	D	1966-67	1982-83	7	Montreal Canadiens, Winnipeg Jets
Sawchuk, Terry	1971/P	G	1949-50	1969-70	4	Detroit Red Wings, Boston Bruins, Toronto Maple Leafs, Los Angeles Kings, New York Rangers
Scanlan, Fred	1965/P	F	1897-98	1902-03	3	Montreal Shamrocks (AHA/CAHL), Winnipeg Victorias (MSHL)
Schmidt, Milt	1961/P	C	1936-37	1954-55	2	Boston Bruins
Schriner, Sweeney	1962/P	LW	1934-35	1945-46	2	New York Americans, Toronto Maple Leafs
Seibert, Earl	1963/P	D	1931-32	1945-46	2	New York Rangers, Chicago Blackhawks, Detroit Red Wings
Seibert, Oliver	1961/P	D	1900	1906	0	Berlin Rangers (WOHA), Houghton (IHL), Guelph (OPHL), London (OPHL)
Shore, Eddie	1947/P	D	1924-25	1939-40	2	Regina Capitals (WCHL), Edmonton Eskimos (WHL), Boston Bruins, New York Americans
Shutt, Steve	1993/P	LW	1972-73	1984-85	5	Montreal Canadiens, Los Angeles Kings
Siebert, Babe	1964/P	LW/D	1925-26	1938-39	2	Montreal Maroons, New York Rangers, Boston Bruins, Montreal Canadiens
Simpson, Joe	1962/P	D	1921-22	1930-31	0	Edmonton Eskimos (WCHL), New York Americans
Sittler, Darryl	1989/P	C	1970-71	1984-85	0	Toronto Maple Leafs, Philadelphia Flyers, Detroit Red Wings
Smith, Alf	1962/P	RW	1894-95	1907-08	4	Ottawa Silver Seven/Senators (AHA/CAHL/FAHL/ECAHA), Kenora Thistles (MHL)
Smith, Billy	1993/P	G	1971-72	1988-89	4	Los Angeles Kings, New York Islanders
Smith, Clint	1991/V	C	1936-37	1946-47	1	New York Rangers, Chicago Blackhawks
Smith, Hooley	1972/P	RW	1924-25	1940-41	2	1924 Canadian Olympic Team, Ottawa Senators, Montreal Maroons, Boston Bruins, New York Americans
Smith, Tommy	1973/P	LW/C	1905-06	1919-20	1	Ottawa Vics (FAHL), Ottawa Senators (ECAHA), Brantford (OPHL), Moncton (MPHL), Quebec Bulldogs (NHA/NHL), Toronto Ontarios (NHA), Montreal Canadiens (NHA)
Stanley, Allan	1981/P	D	1948-49	1968-69	4	New York Rangers, Chicago Blackhawks, Boston Bruins, Toronto Maple Leafs, Philadelphia Flyers
Stanley, Barney	1962/P	RW/D	1914-15	1925-26	1	Vancouver Millionaires (PCHA), Calgary Tigers (WCHL), Regina Capitals (WCHL), Edmonton Eskimos (WCHL/WHL)
Stastny, Peter	1998/P	C	1980-81	1994-95	0	Quebec Nordiques, New Jersey Devils, St. Louis Blues
Stewart, Black Jack	1964/P	D	1938-39	1951-52	2	Detroit Red Wings, Chicago Blackhawks
Stewart, Nels	1962/P	C	1925-26	1939-40	1	Montreal Maroons, Boston Bruins, New York Americans, Boston Bruins
Stuart, Bruce	1961/P	F	1989-99	1910-11	3	Ottawa Senators (CAHL/ECHA/NHA), Quebec Bulldogs (CAHL), Pittsburgh (IHL), Houghton (IHL), Portage Lake (IHL), Montreal Wanderers (ECAHA)
Stuart, Hod	1945/P	D	1898-99	1906-07	1	Ottawa Senators, Quebec Bulldogs, Calumet (IHL), Pittsburgh (IHL), Montreal Wanderers
Taylor, Cyclone	1947/P	D/Ro./C	1907-08	1922-23	2	Ottawa Senators (ECAHA/ECHA), Renfrew Creamery Kings (NHA), Vancouver Maroons (PCHA)
Thompson, Tiny	1959/P	G	1928-29	1939-40	1	Boston Bruins, Detroit Red Wings
Tretiak, Vladislav	1989/P	G	1969	1984	0	Central Red Army
Trihey, Harry	1950/P	C	1896-97	1900-01	2	Montreal Shamrocks (AHA/CAHL)
Trottier, Bryan	1997/P	C	1975-76	1993-94	6	New York Islanders, Pittsburgh Penguins
Ullman, Norm	1982/P	C	1955-56	1976-77	0	Detroit Red Wings, Toronto Maple Leafs, Edmonton Oilers (WHA)

Player	Elec. year/ how elected*	Pos.†	First season	Last season	Stanley Cup wins‡	Teams as player
Vezina, Georges	1945/P	G	1910-11	1925-26	2	Montreal Canadiens (NHA/NHL)
Walker, Jack	1960/P	LW/Ro.	1910-11	1927-28	3	Port Arthur, Toronto Blueshirts (NHA), Seattle Metropolitans (PCHA), Victoria Cougars (WCHL/WHL), Detroit Cougars
Walsh, Marty	1962/P	C	1905-06	1911-12	2	Queens University (OHA), Ottawa Senators (ECAHA/ECHA/NHA)
Watson, Harry E.	1962/P	C	1915	1931	0	St. Andrews (OHA), Aura Lee Juniors (OHA), Toronto Dentals (OHA), Toronto Granites (OHA), 1924 Canadian Olympic Team, Toronto National Sea Fleas (OHA)
Watson, Harry P.	1994/V	LW	1941-42	1956-57	5	Brooklyn Americans, Detroit Red Wings, Toronto Maple Leafs, Chicago Blackhawks
Weiland, Cooney	1971/P	C	1928-29	1938-39	0	Boston Bruins, Ottawa Senators, Detroit Red Wings
Westwick, Harry	1962/P	Ro.	1894-95	1907-08	4	Ottawa Senators/Silver Seven (AHA/CAHL/FAHL/ECAHA/), Kenora Thistles
Whitcroft, Frederick	1962/P	Ro.	1906-07	1909-10	0	Kenora Thistles (MSHL), Edmonton Eskimos (AAHA), Renfrew Millionaires (NHA)
Wilson, Gord	1962/P	D	1918	1933	0	Port Arthur War Veterans (OHA), Iroquois Falls (NOHA), Port Arthur Bearcats (OHA)
Worsley, Gump	1980/P	G	1952-53	1973-74	4	New York Rangers, Montreal Canadiens, Minnesota North Stars
Worters, Roy	1969/P	G	1925-26	1936-37	0	Pittsburgh Pirates, New York Americans, Montreal Canadiens

*Denotes whether enshrinee was elected by regular election (P) or veterans committee (V).
†Primary positions played during career: C—center; D—defense; G—goaltender; LW—left wing; Ro.—rover; RW—right wing.
‡Stanley Cup wins column refers to wins as a player in the players section and as a coach in the coaches section.

BUILDERS

Builder	Election year	Stanley Cup wins‡	Designation for induction
Adams, Charles F.	1960		Founder, Boston Bruins (1924)
Adams, Weston W.	1972		President and chairman, Boston Bruins(1936-69)
Aheam, Frank	1962		Owner, Ottawa Senators (1924-34)
Ahearne, Bunny	1977		President, International Hockey Federation (1957-75)
Allan, Sir Montagu	1945		Donator of Allan Cup, awarded anually to senior amateur champion of Canada (1908)
Allen, Keith	1992	0	Coach, Philadelphia Flyers (1967-68 and 1968-69); general manager and executive, Philadelphia Flyers (1966-present)
Arbour, Al	1996	4	Coach, St. Louis Blues, New York Islanders, 1970-71, 1971-72 to 1972-73, 1973-74 through 1985-86 and 1988-89 to 1993-94; vice president of hockey operations and consultant, New York Islanders (1994 to present)
Ballard, Harold	1977		Owner and chief executive, Toronto Maple Leafs (1961-90)
Bauer, Father David	1989		Developer and coach of first Canadian National Hockey Team
Bickell, J.P.	1978		First president and chairman of the board, Toronto Maple Leafs (1927-51)
Bowman, Scotty	1991	8	Coach, St. Louis Blues, Montreal Canadiens, Buffalo Sabres, Pittsburgh Penguins, Detroit Red Wings (1967-68 through 1979-80, 1981-82 through 1986-87 and 1991-92 through present); general manager, St. Louis Blues, Buffalo Sabres (1969-70, 1970-71 and 1979-80 through 1986-87)
Brown, George V.	1961		U.S. hockey pioneer; organizer, Boston Athletic Association hockey team (1910); general manager, Boston Arena and Boston Garden (1934-37)
Brown, Walter A.	1962		Co-owner and president, Boston Bruins (1951-64); general manager, Boston Gardens
Buckland, Frank	1975		Amateur hockey coach and manager; president and treasurer, Ontario Hockey Association
Butterfield, Jack	1980		President, American Hockey League
Calder, Frank	1947		First president, National Hockey League (1917-43)
Campbell, Angus	1964		First president, Northern Ontario Hockey Association (1919); executive, Ontario Hockey Association
Campbell, Clarence	1966		Referee (1929-40); president, National Hockey League (1946-77)
Cattarinich, Joseph	1977		General manager, Montreal Canadiens (1909-10); co-owner, Montreal Canadiens (1921-35)
Dandurand, Leo	1963	1	Co-owner, Montreal Canadiens (1921-35); coach, Montreal Canadiens (1920-21 through 1924-25 and 1934-35); general manager, Montreal Canadiens (1920-21 through 1934-35)
Dilio, Frank	1964		Secretary and president, Junior Amateur Hockey Association; registrar and secretary, Quebec Amateur Hockey League (1943-62)
Dudley, George	1958		President, Canadian Amateur Hockey Association (1940-42); treasurer, Ontario Hockey Association; president, International Ice Hockey Federation
Dunn, Jimmy	1968		President, Manitoba Amateur Hockey Association (1945-51); president, Canadian Amateur Hockey Association

Builder	Election year	Stanley Cup wins‡	Designation for induction
Francis, Emile	1982	0	General manager, New York Rangers,St. Louis Blues, Hartford Whalers (1964-65 through 1988-89); coach, New York Rangers, St. Louis Blues (1965-66 through 1974-75, 1976-77, 1981-82 and 1982-83); president, Hartford Whalers (1983-1993)
Gibson, Jack	1976		Organizer, International League (1903-07), world's first professional hockey league
Gorman, Tommy	1963	2	Co-founder, National Hockey League (1917); coach, Ottawa Senators, New York Americans, Chicago Blackhawks, Montreal Maroons (1917-1938); general manager, Montreal Canadiens (1941-42 through 1945-46)
Griffiths, Frank	1993		Chairman, Vancouver Canucks (1974 through 1994)
Hanley, Bill	1986		Secretary-manager, Ontario Hockey Association
Hay, Charles	1974		Coordinator, 1972 series between Canada and Soviet Union; president, Hockey Canada
Hendy, Jim	1968		President, United States Hockey League; general manager, Cleveland Barons (AHL); publisher, Hockey Guide (1933-51)
Hewitt, Foster	1965		Hockey broadcaster
Hewitt, William	1947		Sports editor, Toronto Star; secretary, Ontario Hockey Association (1903-61); registrar and treasurer, Canadian Amateur Hockey Association
Hume, Fred	1962		Co-developer, Western Hockey League, New Westminster Royals
Imlach, Punch	1984	4	Coach, Toronto Maple Leafs, Buffalo Sabres (1958-59 through 1968-69, 1970-71, 1971-72 and 1979-80); general manager, Toronto Maple Leafs, Buffalo Sabres (1958-59 through 1968-69, 1970-71 through 1977-78 and 1979-80 through 1981-82)
Ivan, Tommy	1974	3	Coach, Detroit Red Wings, Chicago Blackhawks (1947-48 through 1953-54, 1956-57 and 1957-58); general manager, Chicago Blackhawks (1954-55 through 1976-77)
Jennings, Bill	1975		President, New York Rangers
Johnson, Bob	1992	1	Coach, Calgary Flames, Pittsburgh Penguins (1982-83 through 1986-87, 1990-91 and 1991-92)
Juckes, Gordon	1979		President, Saskatchewan Amateur Hockey Association; director, Canadian Amateur Hockey Association (1960-78)
Kilpatrick,General J.R.	1960		President, New York Rangers, Madison Square Garden; director, NHL Players' Pension Society; NHL Governor
Knox III, Seymour	1993		Chairman and president, Buffalo Sabres (1970-71 through 1995-96)
Leader, Al	1969		President, Western Hockey League (1944-69)
LeBel, Bob	1970		Founder and president, Interprovincial Senior League (1944-47); president, Quebec Amateur Hockey League, Canadian Amateur Hockey Association, International Ice Hockey Federation (1955-63)
Lockhart, Tommy	1965		Organizer and president, Eastern Amateur Hockey League, Amateur Hockey Association of the United States; business manager, New York Rangers
Loicq, Paul	1961		President and referee, International Ice Hockey Federation (1922-47)
Mariucci, John	1985		Minnesota hockey pioneer; coach, 1956 U.S. Olympic Team
Mathers, Frank	1992		Coach, president and general manager, Hershey Bears (AHL)
McLaughlin, Major Frederic	1963		Owner and first president, Chicago Blackhawks; general manager, Chicago Blackhawks (1926-27 through 1941-42)
Milford, Jake	1984		Coach, New York Rangers organization; general manager, Los Angeles Kings, Vancouver Canucks (1973-74 through 1981-82)
Molson, Senator Hartland De Montarville	1973		President and chairman, Montreal Canadiens (1957-68)
Morrison, Scotty	1999		Referee-in-chief; chairman, Hall of Fame
Murray, Monsignor Athol	1998		Founded hockey programs in Saskatchewan; founded Notre Dame College in Wilcox
Nelson, Francis	1947		Sports editor, Toronto Globe; vice president, Ontario Hockey Association (1903-05); Governor, Amateur Athletic Union of Canada
Norris, Bruce	1969		Owner, Detroit Red Wings, Olympic Stadium (1955-82)
Norris, James Sr.	1958		Co-owner, Detroit Red Wings (1933-43)
Norris, James Dougan	1962		Co-owner, Detroit Red Wings (1933-43), Chicago Blackhawks (1946-66)
Northey, William	1947		President, Montreal Amateur Athletic Association; managing director, Montreal Forum; first trustee, Allan Cup (1908)
O'Brien, J. Ambrose	1962		Organizer, National Hockey Association (1909); co-founder, Montreal Canadiens
O'Neil, Brian	1994		Director of administration, NHL (1966); executive director, NHL (1971); executive vice-president, NHL (1977)
Page, Fred	1993		President, Canadian Amateur Hockey Association (1966-68); chairman of the board, British Columbia Junior Hockey League (1983 through present)
Patrick, Frank	1958		Co-organizer and president, Pacific Coast Hockey Association (1911); owner, manager, player/coach, Vancouver Millionaires (PCHA), managing director, National Hockey League; coach, Boston Bruins (1934-35 and 1935-36); manager, Montreal Canadiens
Pickard, Allan	1958		President, Saskatchewan Amateur Hockey Association, Saskatchewan Senior League, Western Canada Senior League;governor, Saskatchewan Junior League, Western Canada Junior League; president, Canadian Amateur Hockey Association (1947-50)
Pilous, Rudy	1985	1	Coach, Chicago Blackhawks, Winnipeg Jets (1957-58 through 1962-63 and 1974-75); manager, Winnipeg Jets (WHA); scout, Detroit Red Wings, Los Angeles Kings
Poile, Bud	1990		General manager, Philadelphia Flyers, Vancouver Canucks (1967-68 through 1972-73); vice president, World Hockey Association; commissioner, Central Hockey League, International Hockey League

Builder	Election year	Stanley Cup wins‡	Designation for induction
Pollock, Sam	1978		Director of personnel, Montreal Canadiens (1950-64); general manager, Montreal Canadiens (1964-65 through 1977-78)
Raymond, Sen. Donat	1958		President, Canadian Arena Company (Montreal Maroons, Montreal Canadiens) (1924-25 through 1955); chairman, Canadian Arena Company (1955-63)
Robertson, John Ross	1947		President, Ontario Hockey Association (1901-05)
Robinson, Claude	1947		First secretary, Canadian Amateur Hockey Association (1914); manager, 1932 Canadian Olympic Team
Ross, Philip	1976		Trustee, Stanley Cup (1893-1949)
Sabetzki, Gunther	1995		President, International Ice Hockey Federation (1975-1994)
Sather, Glen	1997	4	Coach, Edmonton Oilers (1976-89 and 1993-94); general manager, Edmonton Oilers (1979 to present)
Selke, Frank	1960		Assistant general manager, Toronto Maple Leafs; general manager, Montreal Canadiens (1946-47 through 1963-64)
Sinden, Harry	1983	1	Coach, Boston Bruins (1966-67 through 1969-70, 1979-80 and 1984-85); coach, 1972 Team Canada; general manager, Boston Bruins (1972-73 through present)
Smith, Frank	1962		Co-founder and secretary, Beaches Hockey League (later Metropolitan Toronto Hockey League (1911-62)
Smythe, Conn	1958	0	President, Toronto Maple Leafs, Maple Leaf Gardens, general manager, Toronto Maple Leafs (1927-28 through 1956-57); coach, Toronto Maple Leafs (1926-27 through 1930-31)
Snider, Ed	1988		Owner, Philadelphia Flyers (1967-68 through present)
Stanley of Preston, Lord	1945		Donator, Stanley Cup (1893)
Sutherland, Capt. James	1947		President, Ontario Hockey Association (1915-17); president, Canadian Amateur Hockey Association (1919-21)
Tarasov, Anatoli	1974		Coach, Soviet National Team
Torrey, Bill	1995		Executive vice president, California Seals; general manager, New York Islanders; president, Florida Panthers (1967-present)
Turner, Lloyd	1958		Co-organizer, Western Canadian Hockey League (1918); organizer, Calgary Tigers
Tutt, Thayer	1978		President, International Ice Hockey Federation (1966-69), Amateur Hockey Association of the United States
Voss, Carl	1974		President, U.S. Hockey League; first NHL referee-in-chief
Waghorne, Fred	1961		Pioneer and hockey official, Toronto Hockey League
Wirtz, Arthur	1971		Co-owner, Detroit Red Wings, Olympia Stadium, Chicago Stadium, St. Louis Arena, Madison Square Garden, Chicago Blackhawks
Wirtz, Bill	1976		President, Chicago Blackhawks (1966 through present); chairman, NHL Board of Governors
Ziegler, John	1987		President, National Hockey League (1977-92)

‡Stanley Cup wins column refers to wins as a player in the players section and as a coach in the builders section.

REFEREES/LINESMEN

Referee/linesman	Election year	First season	Last season	Position
Armstrong, Neil	1991	1957	1977	Linesman and referee
Ashley, John	1981	1959	1972	Referee
Chadwick, Bill	1964	1940	1955	Linesman and referee
D'Amico, John	1993	1964-65	1987-88	Linesman
Elliott, Chaucer	1961	1903	1913	Referee (OHA)
Hayes, George	1988	1946-47	1964-65	Linesman
Hewitson, Bobby	1963	1924	1934	Referee
Ion, Mickey	1961	1913	1943	Referee (PCHL/NHL)
Pavelich, Marty	1987	1956-57	1978-79	Linesman
Rodden, Mike	1962			Referee
Smeaton, Cooper	1961			Referee (NHA/NHL); referee-in-chief (NHL) (1931-37); trustee, Stanley Cup (1946-78)
Storey, Red	1967	1951	1959	Referee
Udvari, Frank	1973	1951-52	1965-66	Referee; supervisor of NHL officials
Van Hellemond, Andy	1999	1972-73	1995-96	Referee

MILESTONES

(Players and coaches active in the NHL in the 1998-99 season are in boldface)

CAREER

FORWARDS/DEFENSEMEN

20 SEASONS

Rk.	Player	No.
1.	Gordie Howe	26
2.	Alex Delvecchio	24
	Tim Horton	24
4.	John Bucyk	23
5.	Stan Mikita	22
	Doug Mohns	22
	Dean Prentice	22
8.	George Armstrong	21
	Harry Howell	21
	Eric Nesterenko	21
	Marcel Pronovost	21
	Jean Ratelle	21
	Allan Stanley	21
	Ron Stewart	21
15.	Jean Beliveau	20
	Ray Bourque	**20**
	Bill Gadsby	20
	Wayne Gretzky	**20**
	Red Kelly	20
	Mark Messier	**20**
	Henri Richard	20
	Larry Robinson	20
	Norm Ullman	20

Total number of players: (23)

1,200 GAMES

Rk.	Player	No.
1.	Gordie Howe	1,767
2.	Alex Delvecchio	1,549
3.	John Bucyk	1,540
4.	**Wayne Gretzky**	**1,487**
5.	**Larry Murphy**	**1,477**
6.	**Ray Bourque**	**1,453**
7.	Tim Horton	1,446
8.	Mike Gartner	1,432
9.	**Mark Messier**	**1,413**
10.	Harry Howell	1,411
11.	Norm Ullman	1,410
12.	**Dale Hunter**	**1,407**
13.	Stan Mikita	1,394
14.	Doug Mohns	1,390
15.	Larry Robinson	1,384
16.	Dean Prentice	1,378
17.	Ron Stewart	1,353
18.	Marcel Dionne	1,348
19.	**Ron Francis**	**1,329**
20.	**Paul Coffey**	**1,322**
21.	Red Kelly	1,316
22.	Dave Keon	1,296
23.	Phil Esposito	1,282
24.	Jean Ratelle	1,281
25.	Bryan Trottier	1,279
26.	**Scott Stevens**	**1,275**
27.	**Craig Ludwig**	**1,256**
	Henri Richard	1,256
29.	Kevin Lowe	1,254
30.	Jari Kurri	1,251
31.	**Guy Carbonneau**	**1,249**
32.	Bill Gadsby	1,248
33.	Allan Stanley	1,244
34.	**Dino Ciccarelli**	**1,232**
35.	Eddie Westfall	1,227
36.	**Pat Verbeek**	**1,225**
37.	Brad McCrimmon	1,222
38.	Eric Nesterenko	1,219
39.	**Dave Andreychuk**	**1,210**
	Phil Housley	**1,210**
41.	Marcel Pronovost	1,206

Total number of players: (41)

500 GOALS

Rk.	Player	No.
1.	**Wayne Gretzky**	**894**
2.	Gordie Howe	801
3.	Marcel Dionne	731
4.	Phil Esposito	717
5.	Mike Gartner	708
6.	Mario Lemieux	613
7.	Bobby Hull	610
	Mark Messier	**610**
9.	**Dino Ciccarelli**	**608**
10.	Jari Kurri	601
11.	**Steve Yzerman**	**592**
12.	**Brett Hull**	**586**
13.	Mike Bossy	573
14.	Guy Lafleur	560
15.	John Bucyk	556
16.	Michel Goulet	548
17.	Maurice Richard	544
18.	Stan Mikita	541
19.	Frank Mahovlich	533
20.	**Dave Andreychuk**	**532**
21.	Bryan Trottier	524
22.	Dale Hawerchuk	518
23.	**Luc Robitaille**	**517**
24.	Gilbert Perreault	512
25.	Jean Beliveau	507
26.	Joe Mullen	502
27.	Lanny McDonald	500

Total number of players: (27)

700 ASSISTS

Rk.	Player	No.
1.	**Wayne Gretzky**	**1,963**
2.	**Paul Coffey**	**1,102**
3.	**Ray Bourque**	**1,083**
4.	**Mark Messier**	**1,050**
5.	Gordie Howe	1,049
6.	Marcel Dionne	1,040
7.	**Ron Francis**	**1,037**
8.	Stan Mikita	926
9.	Bryan Trottier	901
10.	Dale Hawerchuk	891
	Steve Yzerman	**891**
12.	Mario Lemieux	881
13.	**Larry Murphy**	**880**
14.	Phil Esposito	873
15.	Denis Savard	865
16.	Bobby Clarke	852
17.	**Adam Oates**	**838**
18.	**Doug Gilmour**	**835**
19.	Alex Delvecchio	825
20.	Gilbert Perreault	814
21.	John Bucyk	813
22.	Jari Kurri	797
23.	Guy Lafleur	793
24.	Peter Stastny	789
25.	Jean Ratelle	776
26.	**Al MacInnis**	**775**
27.	**Phil Housley**	**773**
28.	Bernie Federko	761
29.	Larry Robinson	750
30.	Denis Potvin	742
31.	Norm Ullman	739
32.	**Bernie Nicholls**	**734**
33.	Jean Beliveau	712

Total number of players: (33)

1,000 POINTS

Rk.	Player	No.
1.	**Wayne Gretzky**	**2,857**
2.	Gordie Howe	1,850
3.	Marcel Dionne	1,771
4.	**Mark Messier**	**1,660**
5.	Phil Esposito	1,590
6.	Mario Lemieux	1,494
7.	**Paul Coffey**	**1,487**
8.	**Ron Francis**	**1,486**
9.	**Steve Yzerman**	**1,483**
10.	**Ray Bourque**	**1,468**
11.	Stan Mikita	1,467
12.	Bryan Trottier	1,425
13.	Dale Hawerchuk	1,409
14.	Jari Kurri	1,398
15.	John Bucyk	1,369
16.	Guy Lafleur	1,353
17.	Denis Savard	1,338
18.	Mike Gartner	1,335
19.	Gilbert Perreault	1,326
20.	Alex Delvecchio	1,281
21.	Jean Ratelle	1,267
22.	Peter Stastny	1,239
23.	**Doug Gilmour**	**1,232**
24.	Norm Ullman	1,229
25.	Jean Beliveau	1,219
26.	Bobby Clarke	1,210
27.	**Bernie Nicholls**	**1,209**
28.	**Dino Ciccarelli**	**1,200**
29.	Bobby Hull	1,170
30.	**Larry Murphy**	**1,155**
31.	Michel Goulet	1,152
32.	**Dave Andreychuk**	**1,140**
33.	Bernie Federko	1,130
34.	Mike Bossy	1,126
	Adam Oates	**1,126**
36.	Darryl Sittler	1,121
37.	Frank Mahovlich	1,103
38.	Glenn Anderson	1,099
39.	**Luc Robitaille**	**1,076**
40.	**Phil Housley**	**1,075**
41.	Dave Taylor	1,069
42.	**Al MacInnis**	**1,065**
43.	Joe Mullen	1,063
44.	Denis Potvin	1,052
45.	Henri Richard	1,046
46.	**Brett Hull**	**1,045**
47.	Bobby Smith	1,036
48.	**Brian Bellows**	**1,022**
49.	Rod Gilbert	1,021
50.	**Dale Hunter**	**1,020**

Rk.	Player	No.
51.	Pat LaFontaine	1,013
52.	Steve Larmer	1,012
53.	Lanny McDonald	1,006
54.	Brian Propp	1,004

Total number of players: (54)

2,000 PENALTY MINUTES

Rk.	Player	No.
1.	Dave Williams	3,966
2.	**Dale Hunter**	**3,565**
3.	**Marty McSorley**	**3,319**
4.	Tim Hunter	3,146
5.	Chris Nilan	3,043
6.	**Bob Probert**	**2,907**
7.	**Rick Tocchet**	**2,773**
8.	**Pat Verbeek**	**2,665**
9.	**Craig Berube**	**2,651**
10.	**Dave Manson**	**2,604**
11.	Willie Plett	2,572
12.	**Rob Ray**	**2,529**
13.	**Joey Kocur**	**2,519**
14.	**Scott Stevens**	**2,504**
15.	**Tie Domi**	**2,458**
16.	Basil McRae	2,457
17.	**Ulf Samuelsson**	**2,395**
18.	Jay Wells	2,359
19.	Garth Butcher	2,302
20.	Shane Churla	2,301
21.	Dave Schultz	2,294
22.	**Gino Odjick**	**2,291**
23.	**Chris Chelios**	**2,282**
24.	Laurie Boschman	2,265
25.	**Ken Baumgartner**	**2,244**
26.	**Ken Daneyko**	**2,241**
27.	Rob Ramage	2,226
28.	Bryan Watson	2,212
29.	Terry O'Reilly	2,095
30.	Al Secord	2,093
31.	**Steve Smith**	**2,080**
32.	Mick Vukota	2,071
33.	Gord Donnelly	2,069
34.	Mike Foligno	2,049
35.	Phil Russell	2,038
36.	Harold Snepsts	2,009

Total number of players: (36)

GOALTENDERS

15 SEASONS

Rk.	Goaltender	No.
1.	Terry Sawchuk	21
	Gump Worsley	21
3.	**Grant Fuhr**	**18**
	Glenn Hall	18
	Gilles Meloche	18
	Andy Moog	18
	Jacques Plante	18
	Billy Smith	18
9.	Don Beaupre	17
	John Vanbiesbrouck	**17**
11.	**Tom Barrasso**	**16**
	Tony Esposito	16
	Eddie Johnston	16
	Harry Lumley	16
	Rogie Vachon	16
	Mike Vernon	**16**
	Ken Wregget	**16**
18.	Johnny Bower	15
	Kelly Hrudey	15
	Reggie Lemelin	15
	Cesare Maniago	15

Total number of goaltenders: (21)

600 GAMES

Rk.	Goaltender	No.
1.	Terry Sawchuk	971
2.	Glenn Hall	906
3.	Tony Esposito	886
4.	Gump Worsley	862
5.	**Grant Fuhr**	**845**
6.	Jacques Plante	837
7.	Harry Lumley	804
8.	Rogie Vachon	795
9.	Gilles Meloche	788
10.	**John Vanbiesbrouck**	**779**
11.	**Patrick Roy**	**778**
12.	Andy Moog	713
13.	**Tom Barrasso**	**708**
14.	Billy Smith	680
15.	Kelly Hrudey	677
16.	**Mike Vernon**	**673**
17.	Don Beaupre	667
18.	Mike Liut	663
19.	Dan Bouchard	655
20.	**Bill Ranford**	**631**
21.	Turk Broda	629
22.	Ed Giacomin	610
23.	**Ron Hextall**	**608**
	Bernie Parent	608
25.	Greg Millen	604

Total number of goaltenders: (25)

30,000 MINUTES

Rk.	Goaltender	No.
1.	Terry Sawchuk	57,205
2.	Glenn Hall	53,484
3.	Tony Esposito	52,585
4.	Gump Worsley	50,232
5.	Jacques Plante	49,553
6.	Harry Lumley	48,107
7.	**Grant Fuhr**	**47,740**
8.	Rogie Vachon	46,298
9.	**Patrick Roy**	**45,404**
10.	Gilles Meloche	45,401
11.	**John Vanbiesbrouck**	**44,595**
12.	**Tom Barrasso**	**40,472**
13.	Andy Moog	40,151
14.	**Mike Vernon**	**38,587**
15.	Billy Smith	38,431
16.	Turk Broda	38,173
17.	Mike Liut	38,155
18.	Kelly Hrudey	38,084
19.	Dan Bouchard	37,919
20.	Don Beaupre	37,396
21.	Ed Giacomin	35,693
22.	Greg Millen	35,377
23.	**Bill Ranford**	**35,152**
24.	Bernie Parent	35,136
25.	**Ron Hextall**	**34,750**
26.	Eddie Johnston	34,209
27.	Tiny Thompson	34,174
28.	**Kirk McLean**	**32,664**
29.	Cesare Maniago	32,570
30.	Glenn Resch	32,279
31.	Johnny Bower	32,077
32.	**Ed Belfour**	**31,553**
33.	Frank Brimsek	31,210
34.	John Roach	30,423
35.	Roy Worters	30,175
36.	**Curtis Joseph**	**30,156**
37.	**Ken Wregget**	**30,084**

Total number of goaltenders: (37)

2.50 OR UNDER GOALS-AGAINST AVG.

(Goaltenders with 10,000 or more minutes)

Rk.	Goaltender	Min.	GAA
1.	Alex Connell	26,030	1.91
	George Hainsworth	29,415	1.91
3.	Chuck Gardiner	19,687	2.02
4.	Lorne Chabot	25,309	2.04
5.	Tiny Thompson	34,174	2.08
6.	Dave Kerr	26,519	2.17
7.	**Martin Brodeur**	**21,627**	**2.19**
8.	Ken Dryden	23,352	2.24
9.	**Dominik Hasek**	**23,903**	**2.26**
10.	Roy Worters	30,175	2.27
11.	Clint Benedict	22,321	2.32
	Norman Smith	12,297	2.32
13.	Bill Durnan	22,945	2.36
	Gerry McNeil	16,535	2.36
15.	Jacques Plante	49,553	2.38
16.	John Roach	30,423	2.46

Total number of goaltenders: (16)

200 GAMES WON

Rk.	Goaltender	No.
1.	Terry Sawchuk	447
2.	Jacques Plante	434
3.	Tony Esposito	423
4.	Glenn Hall	407
5.	**Patrick Roy**	**412**
6.	**Grant Fuhr**	**398**
7.	Andy Moog	372
8.	Rogie Vachon	355
9.	**Mike Vernon**	**347**
10.	**Tom Barrasso**	**345**
11.	Gump Worsley	335
12.	**John Vanbiesbrouck**	**333**
13.	Harry Lumley	332
14.	Billy Smith	305
15.	Turk Broda	302
16.	**Ron Hextall**	**296**
17.	Mike Liut	293
18.	Ed Giacomin	289
19.	Dan Bouchard	286
20.	Tiny Thompson	284
21.	**Ed Belfour**	**276**
22.	Kelly Hrudey	271
23.	Gilles Meloche	270
	Bernie Parent	270
25.	Don Beaupre	268
26.	Ken Dryden	258
27.	Frank Brimsek	252
28.	Johnny Bower	251
29.	**Curtis Joseph**	**248**
30.	George Hainsworth	247
31.	Pete Peeters	246
32.	Eddie Johnston	236
	Reggie Lemelin	236
	Bill Ranford	**236**
35.	Glenn Resch	231
36.	Gerry Cheevers	230
	Kirk McLean	**230**
	Mike Richter	**230**
39.	John Roach	218
40.	Greg Millen	215
41.	**Ken Wregget**	**211**
42.	Bill Durnan	208
	Don Edwards	208
44.	Lorne Chabot	206
	Roger Crozier	206
46.	Rick Wamsley	204
47.	Dave Kerr	203
48.	**Martin Brodeur**	**201**

Total number of goaltenders: (48)

200 GAMES LOST

Rk.	Goaltender	No.
1.	Gump Worsley	353
2.	Gilles Meloche	351
3.	Terry Sawchuk	337
4.	Glenn Hall	327
5.	Harry Lumley	324
6.	Tony Esposito	307
7.	**John Vanbiesbrouck**	**303**
8.	Rogie Vachon	291
9.	Greg Millen	284
10.	**Grant Fuhr**	**282**
11.	Don Beaupre	277
12.	**Bill Ranford**	**273**
13.	Mike Liut	271
14.	Kelly Hrudey	265
15.	Cesare Maniago	261
16.	Eddie Johnston	256
17.	**Tom Barrasso**	**248**
18.	Jacques Plante	246
19.	**Kirk McLean**	**244**
20.	**Patrick Roy**	**243**
21.	**Ken Wregget**	**238**
22.	Gary Smith	237
23.	Billy Smith	233
	Roy Worters	233
25.	Dan Bouchard	232
26.	Jim Rutherford	227
27.	Turk Broda	224
	Glenn Resch	224
29.	**Mike Vernon**	**223**
30.	**Ron Hextall**	**214**
31.	Andy Moog	209
	Chuck Rayner	209
33.	Ed Giacomin	206
34.	Al Rollins	205
35.	John Roach	204
36.	Denis Herron	203
	Ron Low	203
38.	Glen Hanlon	202

Total number of goaltenders: (38)

75 GAMES TIED

Rk.	Goaltender	No.
1.	Terry Sawchuk	188
2.	Glenn Hall	165
3.	Tony Esposito	151
4.	Gump Worsley	150
5.	Harry Lumley	143
6.	Jacques Plante	137
7.	Gilles Meloche	131
8.	Bernie Parent	121
9.	Rogie Vachon	115
10.	Dan Bouchard	113
11.	**Grant Fuhr**	**112**
12.	Billy Smith	105
	John Vanbiesbrouck	**105**
14.	Turk Broda	101
15.	Ed Giacomin	97
16.	Cesare Maniago	96
17.	**Patrick Roy**	**95**
18.	Johnny Bower	90
19.	Greg Millen	89
20.	Kelly Hrudey	88
	Andy Moog	88
22.	Eddie Johnston	87
23.	Al Rollins	84
24.	**Mike Vernon**	**83**
25.	Glenn Resch	82
26.	Frank Brimsek	80
27.	**Tom Barrasso**	**79**
28.	Don Edwards	77
	Chuck Rayner	77
30.	Denis Herron	76
	Phil Myre	76
32.	Don Beaupre	75
	Ed Belfour	**75**
	Dave Kerr	75
	Tiny Thompson	75

Total number of goaltenders: (35)

25 SHUTOUTS

Rk.	Goaltender	No.
1.	Terry Sawchuk	103
2.	George Hainsworth	94
3.	Glenn Hall	84
4.	Jacques Plante	82
5.	Tiny Thompson	81
	Alex Connell	81
7.	Tony Esposito	76
8.	Lorne Chabot	73
9.	Harry Lumley	71
10.	Roy Worters	66
11.	Turk Broda	62
12.	John Roach	58
13.	Clint Benedict	57
14.	Bernie Parent	55
15.	Ed Giacomin	54
16.	Dave Kerr	51
	Rogie Vachon	51
18.	Ken Dryden	46
	Patrick Roy	**46**
20.	**Ed Belfour**	**45**
21.	Gump Worsley	43
22.	Charlie Gardiner	42
	Dominik Hasek	**42**
24.	Frank Brimsek	40
25.	Johnny Bower	37
26.	**Martin Brodeur**	**36**
27.	**John Vanbiesbrouck**	**35**
28.	**Tom Barrasso**	**34**
	Bill Durnan	34
30.	Eddie Johnston	32
31.	Roger Crozier	30
	Cesare Maniago	30
33.	Jim Henry	28
	Mike Karakas	28
	Gerry McNeil	28
	Andy Moog	28
	Al Rollins	28
38.	Dan Bouchard	27
39.	Gerry Cheevers	26
	Glenn Resch	26
	Gary Smith	26
42.	**Grant Fuhr**	**25**
43.	Mike Liut	25
	Chuck Rayner	25

Total number of goaltenders: (44)

COACHES

500 GAMES

Rk.	Coach	No.
1.	**Scotty Bowman**	**1,900**
2.	Al Arbour	1,606
3.	Dick Irvin	1,437
4.	Billy Reay	1,102
5.	**Jacques Demers**	**1,009**
6.	**Mike Keenan**	**995**
7.	Jack Adams	982
8.	Bryan Murray	975
9.	Sid Abel	963
10.	**Roger Neilson**	**942**
11.	Toe Blake	914
12.	Punch Imlach	879
13.	Bob Berry	860
14.	Glen Sather	842
15.	**Pat Quinn**	**826**
16.	Michel Bergeron	792
17.	Emile Francis	778
18.	Bob Pulford	771
19.	Milt Schmidt	769
20.	**Pat Burns**	**765**
21.	Red Kelly	742
22.	Fred Shero	734
23.	Art Ross	728
24.	**Brian Sutter**	**700**
25.	Terry Crisp	631
26.	**Terry Murray**	**619**
27.	Jack Evans	614
28.	Tommy Ivan	610
29.	Lester Patrick	604
30.	Eddie Johnston	596
31.	**Jim Schoenfeld**	**580**
32.	Hap Day	546
33.	Frank Boucher	525
34.	Johnny Wilson	517
35.	Bob McCammon	511

Total number of coaches: (35)

250 GAMES WON

Rk.	Coach	No.
1.	**Scotty Bowman**	**1,100**
2.	Al Arbour	781
3.	Dick Irvin	690
4.	Billy Reay	542
5.	**Mike Keenan**	**506**
6.	Toe Blake	500
7.	Bryan Murray	484
8.	Glen Sather	464
9.	**Roger Neilson**	**428**
10.	Jack Adams	423
11.	**Jacques Demers**	**409**
12.	**Pat Quinn**	**402**
13.	Punch Imlach	395
14.	Emile Francis	393
15.	Fred Shero	390
16.	**Pat Burns**	**385**
17.	Bob Berry	384
18.	Sid Abel	382
19.	Art Ross	361
20.	Michel Bergeron	338
21.	Bob Pulford	336
22.	**Brian Sutter**	**329**
23.	**Terry Murray**	**311**
24.	Tommy Ivan	302
25.	Terry Crisp	286
26.	Lester Patrick	281
27.	Red Kelly	278
28.	Eddie Johnston	266
29.	Hap Day	259
30.	**Jim Schoenfeld**	**256**
31.	Don Cherry	250
	Milt Schmidt	250

Total number of coaches: (32)

250 GAMES LOST

Rk.	Coach	No.
1.	Al Arbour	577
2.	Dick Irvin	521
3.	**Scotty Bowman**	**515**
4.	**Jacques Demers**	**474**
5.	Sid Abel	426

Rk.	Coach	No.
6.	Jack Adams	397
7.	Milt Schmidt	393
8.	Billy Reay	385
9.	**Mike Keenan**	**372**
10.	Bryan Murray	368
11.	**Roger Neilson**	**361**
12.	Bob Berry	355
13.	Michel Bergeron	350
14.	Punch Imlach	336
15.	Red Kelly	330
16.	**Pat Quinn**	**315**
17.	Bob Pulford	305
18.	Jack Evans	303
19.	**Brian Sutter**	**278**
20.	Art Ross	277
21.	Emile Francis	273
22.	**Pat Burns**	**271**
23.	Glen Sather	268
24.	Terry Crisp	267
25.	Frank Boucher	263
	Tom McVie	263
27.	Toe Blake	255
28.	Tom Watt	252
29.	Eddie Johnston	251
30.	**John Muckler**	**250**

Total number of coaches: (30)

100 GAMES TIED

Rk.	Coach	No.
1.	**Scotty Bowman**	**285**
2.	Al Arbour	248
3.	Dick Irvin	226
4.	Billy Reay	175
5.	Jack Adams	162
6.	Toe Blake	159
7.	Sid Abel	155
8.	**Roger Neilson**	**153**
9.	Punch Imlach	148
10.	Red Kelly	134
11.	**Jacques Demers**	**130**
	Bob Pulford	130
13.	Milt Schmidt	126
14.	Bryan Murray	123
15.	Bob Berry	121
16.	Fred Shero	119
17.	**Mike Keenan**	**117**
18.	Emile Francis	112
	Tommy Ivan	112
20.	Glen Sather	110
21.	**Pat Burns**	**109**
	Pat Quinn	**109**
23.	Lester Patrick	107
24.	Michel Bergeron	104

Total number of coaches: (24)

.525 WINNING PERCENTAGE

(Coaches with 300 or more games)

Rk.	Coach	Games	Pct.
1.	**Scotty Bowman**	**1,900**	**.654**
2.	Claude Ruel	305	.648
3.	Toe Blake	914	.634
4.	Floyd Smith	309	.626
5.	Glen Sather	842	.616
6.	Fred Shero	734	.612
7.	Gerry Cheevers	376	.604
8.	Don Cherry	480	.601
9.	**Marc Crawford**	**331**	**.594**
10.	Tommy Ivan	610	.587
11.	Jacques Lemaire	393	.580
12.	Emile Francis	778	.577
13.	**Pat Burns**	**765**	**.575**
14.	Billy Reay	1,102	.571
15.	**Mike Keenan**	**995**	**.567**
16.	Al Arbour	1,606	.564
	Terry Murray	**698**	**.564**
18.	Dick Irvin	1,437	.559
	Bryan Murray	975	.559
20.	Art Ross	728	.558
21.	Lester Patrick	604	.554
22.	**Pat Quinn**	**826**	**.553**
23.	Hap Day	546	.549
24.	Fred Creighton	421	.548
	Bob Johnson	480	.548
26.	Harry Sinden	330	.545
27.	**Brian Sutter**	**700**	**.536**
28.	Punch Imlach	879	.534
29.	**Darryl Sutter**	**380**	**.532**

Total number of coaches: (29)

STANLEY CUP CHAMPIONSHIPS

(Includes Stanley Cup championships as NHL coach only)

Rk.	Coach	No.
1.	Toe Blake	8
	Scotty Bowman	**8**
3.	Hap Day	5
4.	Al Arbour	4
	Dick Irvin	4
	Punch Imlach	4
	Glen Sather	4
8.	Jack Adams	3
	Pete Green	3
	Tommy Ivan	3
11.	Tommy Gorman	2
	Cecil Hart	2
	Lester Patrick	2
	Fred Shero	2

Total number of coaches: (14)

SEASON

FORWARDS/DEFENSEMEN

60 GOALS

Season	Player, Team	No.
1981-82	**Wayne Gretzky, Edm.**	**92**
1983-84	**Wayne Gretzky, Edm.**	**87**
1990-91	**Brett Hull, St.L.**	**86**
1988-89	Mario Lemieux, Pit.	85
1971-72	Phil Esposito, Bos.	76
1992-93	**Alexander Mogilny, Buf.**	**76**
1992-93	**Teemu Selanne, Win.**	**76**
1984-85	**Wayne Gretzky, Edm.**	**73**
1989-90	**Brett Hull, St.L.**	**72**
1982-83	**Wayne Gretzky, Edm.**	**71**
1984-85	Jari Kurri, Edm.	71
1991-92	**Brett Hull, St.L.**	**70**
1987-88	Mario Lemieux, Pit.	70
1988-89	**Bernie Nicholls, L.A.**	**70**
1978-79	Mike Bossy, NYI	69
1992-93	Mario Lemieux, Pit.	69
1995-96	Mario Lemieux, Pit.	69
1980-81	Mike Bossy, NYI	68
1973-74	Phil Esposito, Bos.	68
1985-86	Jari Kurri, Edm.	68
1972-73	Phil Esposito, Bos.	66
1982-83	Lanny McDonald, Cal.	66
1988-89	**Steve Yzerman, Det.**	**65**
1981-82	Mike Bossy, NYI	64
1992-93	**Luc Robitaille, L.A.**	**63**
1986-87	**Wayne Gretzky, Edm.**	**62**
1995-96	**Jaromir Jagr, Pit.**	**62**
1989-90	**Steve Yzerman, Det.**	**62**
1985-86	Mike Bossy, NYI	61
1974-75	Phil Esposito, Bos.	61
1975-76	Reggie Leach, Phi.	61
1982-83	Mike Bossy, NYI	60
1992-93	**Pavel Bure, Van.**	**60**
1993-94	**Pavel Bure, Van.**	**60**
1977-78	Guy Lafleur, Mon.	60
1981-82	Dennis Maruk, Was.	60
1976-77	Steve Shutt, Mon.	60

Total number of occurrences: (37)

50-GOAL SEASONS

Rk.	Player	No.	Cons.
1.	Mike Bossy	9	9
	Wayne Gretzky	**9**	**8**
3.	Guy Lafleur	6	6
	Marcel Dionne	6	5
	Mario Lemieux	6	3
6.	Phil Esposito	5	5
	Brett Hull	**5**	**5**
	Steve Yzerman	**5**	**4**
	Bobby Hull	5	2
10.	Michel Goulet	4	4
	Tim Kerr	4	4
	Jari Kurri	4	4
13.	**John LeClair**	**3**	**3**
	Rick Vaive	3	3
	Pavel Bure	**3**	**2**
	Cam Neely	3	2
	Teemu Selanne	**3**	**2**
	Luc Robitaille	**3**	**1**
20.	**Dave Andreychuk**	**2**	**2**
	Rick Martin	2	2
	Dennis Maruk	2	2
	Joe Nieuwendyk	**2**	**2**
	Mickey Redmond	2	2
	Jeremy Roenick	**2**	**2**
	Brendan Shanahan	**2**	**2**
	Charlie Simmer	2	2
	Kevin Stevens	**2**	**2**
	Keith Tkachuk	**2**	**2**
	Glenn Anderson	2	1
	Peter Bondra	**2**	**1**
	Dino Ciccarelli	**2**	**1**
	Danny Gare	2	1
	Pat LaFontaine	2	1
	Pierre Larouche	2	1
	Reggie Leach	2	1
	Alexander Mogilny	**2**	**1**
	Stephane Richer	**2**	**1**
	Blaine Stoughton	2	1
40.	Wayne Babych	1	1
	Bill Barber	1	1
	Brian Bellows	**1**	**1**
	John Bucyk	1	1
	Mike Bullard	1	1
	Bob Carpenter	**1**	**1**
	Jimmy Carson	1	1
	Guy Chouinard	1	1
	Sergei Fedorov	**1**	**1**

Rk.	Player	No.	Cons.
	Theoren Fleury	**1**	**1**
	Mike Gartner	1	1
	Bernie Geoffrion	1	1
	Danny Grant	1	1
	Adam Graves	**1**	**1**
	Vic Hadfield	1	1
	Dale Hawerchuk	1	1
	Ken Hodge	1	1
	Jaromir Jagr	**1**	**1**
	Paul Kariya	**1**	**1**
	Rick Kehoe	1	1
	Gary Leeman	1	1
	Hakan Loob	1	1
	Rick MacLeish	1	1
	Lanny McDonald	1	1
	Mark Messier	**1**	**1**
	Rick Middleton	1	1
	Mike Modano	**1**	**1**
	Joe Mullen	1	1
	Bernie Nicholls	**1**	**1**
	John Ogrodnick	1	1
	Jean Pronovost	1	1
	Mark Recchi	**1**	**1**
	Jacques Richard	1	1
	Maurice Richard	1	1
	Gary Roberts	1	1
	Joe Sakic	**1**	**1**
	Al Secord	1	1
	Ray Sheppard	**1**	**1**
	Steve Shutt	1	1
	Craig Simpson	1	1
	Bryan Trottier	1	1
	Pierre Turgeon	**1**	**1**

Total number of players: (81)

40 GOALS BY ROOKIES

Season	Player, Team	No.
1992-93	**Teemu Selanne, Win.**	**76**
1977-78	Mike Bossy, NYI	53
1987-88	**Joe Nieuwendyk, Cal.**	**51**
1981-82	Dale Hawerchuk, Win	45
1986-87	**Luc Robitaille, L.A.**	**45**
1971-72	Rick Martin, Buf.	44
1981-82	Barry Pederson, Bos.	44
1982-83	Steve Larmer, Chi	43
1984-85	Mario Lemieux, Pit	43
1992-93	**Eric Lindros, Phi.**	**41**
1980-81	Darryl Sutter, Chi.	40
1983-84	Sylvain Turgeon, Har.	40
1984-85	Warren Young, Pit	40

Total number of players: (13)

125 POINTS

Season	Player	No.
1985-86	**Wayne Gretzky, Edm.**	**215**
1981-82	**Wayne Gretzky, Edm.**	**212**
1984-85	**Wayne Gretzky, Edm.**	**208**
1983-84	**Wayne Gretzky, Edm.**	**205**
1988-89	Mario Lemieux, Pit	199
1982-83	**Wayne Gretzky, Edm.**	**196**
1986-87	**Wayne Gretzky, Edm.**	**183**
1988-89	**Wayne Gretzky, L.A.**	**168**
1987-88	Mario Lemieux, Pit	168
1980-81	**Wayne Gretzky, Edm.**	**164**
1990-91	**Wayne Gretzky, L.A.**	**163**
1995-96	Mario Lemieux, Pit	161
1992-93	Mario Lemieux, Pit	160
1988-89	**Steve Yzerman, Det.**	**155**
1970-71	Phil Esposito, Bos.	152
1988-89	**Bernie Nicholls, L.A.**	**150**
1987-88	**Wayne Gretzky, Edm.**	**149**
1995-96	**Jaromir Jagr, Pit.**	**149**
1992-93	Pat LaFontaine, Buf.	148
1981-82	Mike Bossy, NYI	147
1973-74	Phil Esposito, Bos.	145
1989-90	**Wayne Gretzky, L.A.**	**142**
1992-93	**Adam Oates, Bos.**	**142**
1985-86	Mario Lemieux, Pit	141
1970-71	Bobby Orr, Bos.	139
1981-82	Peter Stastny, Que.	139
1985-86	**Paul Coffey, Edm**	**138**
1979-80	**Wayne Gretzky, Edm.**	**137**
1979-80	Marcel Dionne, L.A.	137
1992-93	**Steve Yzerman, Det.**	**137**
1976-77	Guy Lafleur, Mon.	136
1981-82	Dennis Maruk, Was.	136
1980-81	Marcel Dionne, L.A.	135
1984-85	Jari Kurri, Edm.	135
1974-75	Bobby Orr, Bos.	135
1978-79	Bryan Trottier, NYI	134
1971-72	Phil Esposito, Bos.	133
1977-78	Guy Lafleur, Mon.	132
1992-93	**Pierre Turgeon, NYI**	**132**
1992-93	**Teemu Selanne, Win.**	**132**
1990-91	**Brett Hull, St.L.**	**131**
1991-92	Mario Lemieux, Pit	131
1985-86	Jari Kurri, Edm.	131
1980-81	Kent Nilsson, Cal.	131
1987-88	Denis Savard, Chi.	131
1972-73	Phil Esposito, Bos.	130
1978-79	Marcel Dionne, L.A.	130
1984-85	Dale Hawerchuk, Win	130
1993-94	**Wayne Gretzky, L.A.**	**130**
1989-90	**Mark Messier, Edm.**	**129**
1978-79	Guy Lafleur, Mon.	129
1981-82	Bryan Trottier, NYI	129
1974-75	Phil Esposito, Bos.	127
1992-93	**Doug Gilmour, Tor.**	**127**
1992-93	**Alexander Mogilny, Buf.**	**127**
1989-90	**Steve Yzerman, Det.**	**127**
1998-99	**Jaromir Jagr, Pit.**	**127**
1968-69	Phil Esposito, Bos.	126
1978-79	Mike Bossy, NYI	126
1983-84	**Paul Coffey, Edm.**	**126**
1984-85	Marcel Dionne, L.A.	126
1975-76	Guy Lafleur, Mon.	125
1979-80	Guy Lafleur, Mon.	125

Total number of occurrences: (63)

100-POINT SEASONS

Rk.	Player	No.	Cons.
1.	**Wayne Gretzky**	**15**	**13**
2.	Mario Lemieux	10	6
3.	Marcel Dionne	8	5
4.	Mike Bossy	7	6
	Peter Stastny	7	6
6.	Guy Lafleur	6	6
	Bobby Orr	6	6
	Steve Yzerman	**6**	**6**
	Dale Hawerchuk	6	5
	Jari Kurri	6	5
	Bryan Trottier	6	5
	Mark Messier	**6**	**2**
13.	Denis Savard	5	2
14.	**Brett Hull**	**4**	**4**
	Paul Coffey	**4**	**3**
	Bernie Federko	4	3
	Michel Goulet	4	2
	Adam Oates	**4**	**2**
	Luc Robitaille	**4**	**2**
	Joe Sakic	**4**	**2**
21.	Mike Rogers	3	3
	Glenn Anderson	3	2
	Bobby Clarke	3	2
	Doug Gilmour	**3**	**2**
	Bernie Nicholls	**3**	**2**
	Mark Recchi	**3**	**2**
	Jaromir Jagr	**3**	**1**
27.	**Pavel Bure**	**2**	**2**
	Jimmy Carson	2	2
	Pete Mahovlich	2	2
	Barry Pederson	2	2
	Jeremy Roenick	**2**	**2**
	Charlie Simmer	2	2
	Kevin Stevens	**2**	**2**
	Dave Taylor	2	2
	Dino Ciccarelli	**2**	**1**
	Sergei Fedorov	**2**	**1**
	Theoren Fleury	**2**	**1**
	Ron Francis	**3**	**1**
	Pat LaFontaine	2	1
	Rick Middleton	2	1
	Alexander Mogilny	**2**	**1**
	Kent Nilsson	2	1
	Gilbert Perreault	2	1
	Jean Ratelle	2	1
	Darryl Sittler	2	1
	Teemu Selanne	**2**	**1**
	Pierre Turgeon	**2**	**1**

Total number of players: (48)

75 POINTS BY ROOKIES

Season	Player, Team	No.
1992-93	**Teemu Selanne, Win.**	**132**
1980-81	Peter Stastny, Que.	109
1981-82	Dale Hawerchuk, Win	103
1992-93	**Joe Juneau, Bos.**	**102**
1984-85	Mario Lemieux, Pit	100
1981-82	Neal Broten, Min.	98
1975-76	Bryan Trottier, NYI	95
1987-88	**Joe Nieuwendyk, Cal.**	**92**
1981-82	Barry Pederson, Bos.	92
1977-78	Mike Bossy, NYI	91
1982-83	Steve Larmer, Chi	90
1981-82	Marian Stastny, Que	89
1983-84	**Steve Yzerman, Det.**	**87**
1989-90	Sergei Makarov, Cal.	86
1980-81	Anton Stastny, Que.	85
1986-87	**Luc Robitaille, L.A.**	**84**
1993-94	**Mikael Renberg, Phi.**	**82**
1986-87	Jimmy Carson, L.A.	79
1990-91	**Sergei Fedorov, Det.**	**79**
1993-94	**Alexei Yashin, Ott.**	**79**
1971-72	Marcel Dionne, L.A.	77
1980-81	**Larry Murphy, L.A.**	**76**
1981-82	Mark Pavelich, NYR	76
1983-84	Dave Poulin, Phi.	76
1992-93	**Eric Lindros, Phi.**	**75**
1980-81	**Jari Kurri, Edm.**	**75**
1989-90	**Mike Modano, Min.**	**75**
1979-80	Brian Propp, Phi.	75
1980-81	Denis Savard, Chi.	75

Total number of players: (29)

350 PENALTY MINUTES

Season	Player, Team	No.
1974-75	Dave Schultz, Phi.	472
1981-82	Paul Baxter, Pit	409
1991-92	**Mike Peluso, Chi.**	**408**
1977-78	Dave Schultz, L.A.-Pit.	405
1992-93	**Marty McSorley, L.A.**	**399**
1987-88	**Bob Probert, Det.**	**398**
1987-88	Basil McRae, Min.	378

Season	Player, Team	No.
1985-86	**Joey Kocur, Det.**	**377**
1988-89	Tim Hunter, Cal.	375
1997-98	**Donald Brashear, Van.**	**372**
1996-97	**Gino Odjick, Van.**	**371**
1975-76	Steve Durbano, Pit.-K.C.	370
1992-93	**Gino Odjick, Van.**	**370**
1988-89	Basil McRae, Min.	365
1997-98	**Tie Domi, Tor.**	**365**
1986-87	Tim Hunter, Cal.	361
1984-85	Chris Nilan, Mon.	358
1985-86	Torrie Robertson, Har.	358
1986-87	Tiger Williams, L.A.	358
1986-87	Brian Curran, NYI	356
1991-92	**Rob Ray, Buf.**	**354**
1988-89	**Dave Manson, Chi.**	**352**
1977-78	Tiger Williams, Tor.	351
1989-90	Basil McRae, Min.	351
1988-89	**Marty McSorley, L.A.**	**350**
1990-91	**Rob Ray, Buf.**	**350**

Total number of occurrences: (26)

GOALTENDERS

10 SHUTOUTS

Season	Goaltender, Team	No.
1928-29	George Hainsworth, Mon. C.	22
1925-26	Alex Connell, Ott.	15
1927-28	Alex Connell, Ott.	15
1927-28	Hal Winkler, Bos.	15
1969-70	Tony Esposito, Chi.	15
1926-27	George Hainsworth, Mon. C.	14
1926-27	Clint Benedict, Mon. M.	13
1926-27	Alex Connell, Ott.	13
1927-28	George Hainsworth, Mon. C.	13
1928-29	John Roach, NYR	13
1928-29	Roy Worters, NYA	13
1953-54	Harry Lumley, Tor.	13
1997-98	**Dominik Hasek, Buf.**	**13**
1928-29	Lorne Chabot, Tor.	12
1928-29	Tiny Thompson, Bos.	12
1930-31	Chuck Gardiner, Chi.	12
1951-52	Terry Sawchuk, Det.	12
1953-54	Terry Sawchuk, Det.	12
1954-55	Terry Sawchuk, Det.	12
1955-56	Glenn Hall, Det.	12
1973-74	Bernie Parent, Phi.	12
1974-75	Bernie Parent, Phi.	12
1927-28	Lorne Chabot, NYR	11
1927-28	Harry Holmes, Det.	11
1928-29	Clint Benedict, Mon. M.	11
1928-29	Joe Miller, Pit.	11
1932-33	Tiny Thompson, Bos.	11
1950-51	Terry Sawchuk, Det.	11
1926-27	Lorne Chabot, NYR	10
1927-28	Roy Worters, Pit.	10
1928-29	Clarence Dolson, Det.	10
1932-33	John Roach, Det.	10
1933-34	Chuck Gardiner, Chi.	10
1935-36	Tiny Thompson, Bos.	10
1938-39	Frank Brimsek, Bos.	10
1948-49	Bill Durnan, Mon.	10
1952-53	Harry Lumley, Tor.	10
1952-53	Gerry McNeil, Mon.	10
1973-74	Tony Esposito, Chi.	10
1976-77	Ken Dryden, Mon.	10
1996-97	**Martin Brodeur, N.J.**	**10**
1997-98	**Martin Brodeur, N.J.**	**10**
1998-99	**Byron Dafoe, Bos.**	**10**

Total number of occurrences: (43)

GAME

FORWARDS/DEFENSEMEN

FIVE GOALS

Date	Player	Team	Opponents	Goals
December 19, 1917	Joe Malone	Montreal	at Ottawa	5
December 19, 1917	Harry Hyland	Montreal Wanderers	vs. Toronto	5
January 12, 1918	Joe Malone	Montreal	vs. Ottawa	5
February 2, 1918	Joe Malone	Montreal	vs. Toronto	5
January 10, 1920	Newsy Lalonde	Montreal	vs Toronto	6
January 31, 1920	Joe Malone	Quebec Bulldogs	vs. Toronto	7
March 6, 1920	Mickey Roach	Toronto St. Pats	vs. Quebec	5
March 10, 1920	Joe Malone	Quebec Bulldogs	vs. Ottawa	6
January 26, 1921	Corb Denneny	Toronto St. Pats	vs. Hamilton	6
February 16, 1921	Newsy Lalonde	Montreal	vs. Hamilton	5
March 7, 1921	Cy Denneny	Ottawa Senators	vs. Hamilton	6
December 16, 1922	Babe Dye	Toronto St. Pats	vs. Montreal	5
December 5, 1924	Redvers Green	Hamilton Tigers	at Toronto	5
December 22, 1924	Babe Dye	Toronto St. Pats	at Boston	5
January 7, 1925	Harry Broadbent	Montreal Maroons	at Hamilton	5
December 14, 1929	Pit Lepine	Montreal	vs. Ottawa	5
March 18, 1930	Howie Morenz	Montreal	vs. New York Americans	5
January 19, 1932	Charlie Conacher	Toronto	vs. New York Americans	5
February 6, 1943	Ray Getliffe	Montreal	vs. Boston	5
December 28, 1944	Maurice Richard	Montreal	vs. Detroit	5
February 3, 1944	Syd Howe	Detroit	vs. New York Rangers	6
January 8, 1947	Howie Meeker	Toronto	vs. Chicago	5
February 19, 1955	Bernie Geoffrion	Montreal	vs. New York Rangers	5
February 1, 1964	Bobby Rousseau	Montreal	vs. Detroit	5
November 7, 1968	Red Berenson	St. Louis	at Philadelphia	6
February 15, 1975	Yvan Cournoyer	Montreal	vs. Chicago	5
October 12, 1976	Don Murdoch	New York Rangers	at Minnesota	5
November 7, 1976	Darryl Sittler	Toronto	vs. Boston	6
February 2, 1977	Ian Turnbull	Toronto	vs. Detroit	5
December 23, 1978	Bryan Trottier	New York Islanders	vs. New York Rangers	5
January 15, 1979	Tim Young	Minnesota	at New York Rangers	5
January 6, 1981	John Tonelli	New York Islanders	vs. Toronto	5
February 18, 1981	**Wayne Gretzky**	**Edmonton**	**vs. St. Louis**	**5**
December 30, 1981	**Wayne Gretzky**	**Edmonton**	**vs. Philadelphia**	**5**
February 3, 1982	Grant Mulvey	Chicago	vs. St. Louis	5
February 13, 1982	Bryan Trottier	New York Islanders	vs. Philadelphia	5
March 2, 1982	Willie Lindstrom	Winnipeg	at Philadelphia	5
February 23, 1983	Mark Pavelich	New York Rangers	vs. Hartford	5
November 19, 1983	Jari Kurri	Edmonton	vs. New Jersey	5
January 8, 1984	Bengt Gustafsson	Washington	at Philadelphia	5

Date	Player	Team	Opponents	Goals
February 3, 1984	Pat Hughes	Edmonton	vs. Calgary	5
December 15, 1984	**Wayne Gretzky**	**Edmonton**	**at St. Louis**	**5**
February 6, 1986	**Dave Andreychuk**	**Buffalo**	**at Boston**	**5**
December 6, 1987	**Wayne Gretzky**	**Edmonton**	**vs. Minnesota**	**5**
December 31, 1988	Mario Lemieux	Pittsburgh	vs. New Jersey	5
January 11, 1989	**Joe Nieuwendyk**	**Calgary**	**vs. Winnipeg**	**5**
March 5, 1992	**Mats Sundin**	**Quebec**	**at Hartford**	**5**
April 9, 1993	Mario Lemieux	Pittsburgh	at New York Rangers	5
February 5, 1994	**Peter Bondra**	**Washington**	**vs. Tampa Bay**	**5**
February 17, 1994	**Mike Ricci**	**Quebec**	**vs. San Jose**	**5**
April 1, 1995	**Alexei Zhamnov**	**Winnipeg**	**at Los Angeles**	**5**
March 26, 1996	Mario Lemieux	Pittsburgh	vs. St. Louis	5
December 26, 1996	**Sergei Fedorov**	**Detroit**	**vs. Washington**	**5**

Total number of occurrences: (53)

TEAM BY TEAM

MIGHTY DUCKS OF ANAHEIM

YEAR-BY-YEAR RECORDS

	REGULAR SEASON					PLAYOFFS			
Season	W	L	T	Pts.	Finish	W	L	Highest round	Coach
1993-94	33	46	5	71	4th/Pacific	—	—		Ron Wilson
1994-95	16	27	5	37	6th/Pacific	—	—		Ron Wilson
1995-96	35	39	8	78	4th/Pacific	—	—		Ron Wilson
1996-97	36	33	13	85	2nd/Pacific	4	7	Conference semifinals	Ron Wilson
1997-98	26	43	13	65	6th/Pacific	—	—		Pierre Page
1998-99	35	34	13	83	3rd/Pacific	0	4	Conference quarterfinals	Craig Hartsburg

FIRST-ROUND ENTRY DRAFT CHOICES

Year Player, Overall, Last amateur team (league)
1993—Paul Kariya, 4, University of Maine
1994—Oleg Tverdovsky, 2, Krylja Sovetov, CIS
1995—Chad Kilger, 4, Kingston (OHL)
1996—Ruslan Salei, 9, Las Vegas (IHL)

Year Player, Overall, Last amateur team (league)
1997—Mikael Holmqvist, 18, Djurgarden Stockholm (Sweden)
1998—Vitali Vishnevsky, 5, Torpedo Yaroslavl (Russia)
1999—No first-round selection

SINGLE-SEASON INDIVIDUAL RECORDS

FORWARDS/DEFENSEMEN

Most goals
52—Teemu Selanne, 1997-98

Most assists
62—Paul Kariya, 1998-99

Most points
109—Teemu Selanne, 1996-97

Most penalty minutes
285—Todd Ewen, 1995-96

Most power play goals
25—Teemu Selanne, 1998-99

Most shorthanded goals
3—Bob Corkum, 1993-94
Paul Kariya, 1995-96
Paul Kariya, 1996-97

Most games with three or more goals
3—Teemu Selanne, 1997-98

Most shots
429—Paul Kariya, 1998-99

GOALTENDERS

Most games
69—Guy Hebert, 1998-99

Most minutes
4,083—Guy Hebert, 1998-99

Most shots against
2,133—Guy Hebert, 1996-97

Most goals allowed
172—Guy Hebert, 1996-97

Lowest goals-against average
2.42—Guy Hebert, 1998-99

Most shutouts
6—Guy Hebert, 1998-99

Most wins
31—Guy Hebert, 1998-99

Most losses
29—Guy Hebert, 1998-99

Most ties
12—Guy Hebert, 1996-97

FRANCHISE LEADERS

Players in boldface played for club in '98-99

FORWARDS/DEFENSEMEN

Games

Joe Sacco ... 333
Steve Rucchin ... 327
Bobby Dollas ... 305
Paul Kariya ... 302
Teemu Selanne ... 254

Goals

Paul Kariya ... 168
Teemu Selanne ... 166
Steve Rucchin ... 84
Joe Sacco ... 62
Garry Valk ... 40

Assists

Paul Kariya ... 210
Teemu Selanne ... 172
Steve Rucchin ... 159
Bobby Dollas ... 68
Fredrik Olausson ... 65

Points

Paul Kariya ... 378
Teemu Selanne ... 338
Steve Rucchin ... 243
Joe Sacco ... 130
Garry Valk ... 92

Penalty minutes

David Karpa ... 788
Todd Ewen ... 647
Jason Marshall ... 513
Stu Grimson ... 467
Warren Rychel ... 416

GOALTENDERS

Games

Guy Hebert ... 332
Mikhail Shtalenkov ... 122
Ron Tugnutt ... 28
Dominic Roussel ... 18
Tom Askey ... 7

Shutouts

Guy Hebert ... 21
Mikhail Shtalenkov ... 3
Dominic Roussel ... 1
Ron Tugnutt ... 1

Goals-against average
(2400 minutes minimum)

Guy Hebert ... 2.76
Mikhail Shtalenkov ... 3.14

Wins

Guy Hebert ... 133
Mikhail Shtalenkov ... 34
Ron Tugnutt ... 10
Dominic Roussel ... 4

ATLANTA FLAMES (DEFUNCT)

YEAR-BY-YEAR RECORDS

	REGULAR SEASON					PLAYOFFS			
Season	W	L	T	Pts.	Finish	W	L	Highest round	Coach
1972-73	25	38	15	65	7th/West	—	—		Bernie Geoffrion
1973-74	30	34	14	74	4th/West	0	4	Division semifinals	Bernie Geoffrion
1974-75	34	31	15	83	4th/Patrick	—	—		Bernie Geoffrion, Fred Creighton
1975-76	35	33	12	82	3rd/Patrick	0	2	Preliminaries	Fred Creighton
1976-77	34	34	12	80	3rd/Patrick	1	2	Preliminaries	Fred Creighton
1977-78	34	27	19	87	3rd/Patrick	0	2	Preliminaries	Fred Creighton
1978-79	41	31	8	90	4th/Patrick	0	2	Preliminaries	Fred Creighton
1979-80	35	32	13	83	4th/Patrick	1	3	Preliminaries	Al MacNeil

Franchise relocated to Calgary following 1979-80 season.

FIRST-ROUND ENTRY DRAFT CHOICES

Year Player, Overall, Last amateur team (league)

1972—Jacques Richard, 2, Quebec (QMJHL)
1973—Tom Lysiak, 2, Medicine Hat (WCHL)
Vic Mercredi, 16, New Westminster (WCHL)
1974—No first-round selection
1975—Richcard Mulhern, 8, Sherbrooke (QMJHL)

Year Player, Overall, Last amateur team (league)

1976—Dave Shand, 8, Peterborough (OHL)
Harold Phillipoff, 10, New Westminster (WCHL)
1977—No first-round selection
1978—Brad Marsh, 11, London (OHL)
1979—Paul Reinhart, 12, Kitchener (OHL)

SINGLE-SEASON INDIVIDUAL RECORDS

FORWARDS/DEFENSEMEN

Most goals
50—Guy Chouinard, 1978-79

Most assists
71—Bob MacMillan, 1978-79

Most points
108—Bob MacMillan, 1978-79

Most penalty minutes
231—Willi Plett, 1979-80

Most power play goals
14—Kent Nilsson, 1979-80

Most shorthanded goals
3—Bill Clement, 1976-77

Most games with three or more goals
3—Eric Vail, 1974-75

Most shots
277—Tom Lysiak, 1976-77

GOALTENDERS

Most games
64—Dan Bouchard, 1978-79

Most minutes
3,624—Dan Bouchard, 1978-79

Most goals allowed
201—Dan Bouchard, 1978-79

Lowest goals-against average
2.54—Dan Bouchard, 1975-76

Most shutouts
5—Dan Bouchard, 1973-74
Phil Myre, 1974-75

Most wins
32—Dan Bouchard, 1978-79

Most losses
23—Phil Myre, 1972-73

Most ties
19—Dan Bouchard, 1977-78

FRANCHISE LEADERS

FORWARDS/DEFENSEMEN

Games

Eric Vail	469
Rey Comeau	468
Tom Lysiak	445
Curt Bennett	405
Randy Manery	377

Goals

Eric Vail	174
Tom Lysiak	155
Curt Bennett	126
Guy Chouinard	126
Ken Houston	91
Willi Plett	91

Assists

Tom Lysiak	276
Eric Vail	209
Guy Chouinard	168
Randy Manery	142
Curt Bennett	140

Points

Tom Lysiak	431
Eric Vail	383
Guy Chouinard	294
Curt Bennett	266
Bob MacMillan	221

Penalty minutes

Willi Plett	740
Ken Houston	332
Tom Lysiak	329
Ed Kea	283
Randy Manery	242

GOALTENDERS

Games

Dan Bouchard	384
Phil Myre	211
Pat Riggin	25
Yves Belanger	22
Reggie Lemelin	21

Shutouts

Dan Bouchard	20
Phil Myre	11
Pat Riggin	2
Yves Belanger	1

Goals-against average (2400 minutes minimum)

Dan Bouchard	3.00
Phil Myre	3.21

Wins

Dan Bouchard	166
Phil Myre	76
Pat Riggin	11
Yves Belanger	8
Reggie Lemelin	8

YEAR-BY-YEAR RECORDS

	REGULAR SEASON					PLAYOFFS			
Season	W	L	T	Pts.	Finish	W	L	Highest round	Coach
1924-25	6	24	0	12	6th	—	—		Art Ross
1925-26	17	15	4	38	4th	—	—		Art Ross
1926-27	21	20	3	45	2nd/American	*2	2	Stanley Cup finals	Art Ross
1927-28	20	13	11	51	1st/American	*0	1	Semifinals	Art Ross
1928-29	26	13	5	57	1st/American	5	0	Stanley Cup champ	Cy Denneny
1929-30	38	5	1	77	1st/American	3	3	Stanley Cup finals	Art Ross
1930-31	28	10	6	62	1st/American	2	3	Semifinals	Art Ross
1931-32	15	21	12	42	4th/American	—	—		Art Ross
1932-33	25	15	8	58	1st/American	2	3	Semifinals	Art Ross
1933-34	18	25	5	41	4th/American	—	—		Art Ross
1934-35	26	16	6	58	1st/American	1	3	Semifinals	Frank Patrick
1935-36	22	20	6	50	2nd/American	1	1	Quarterfinals	Frank Patrick
1936-37	23	18	7	53	2nd/American	1	2	Quarterfinals	Art Ross
1937-38	30	11	7	67	1st/American	0	3	Semifinals	Art Ross
1938-39	36	10	2	74	1st	8	4	Stanley Cup champ	Art Ross
1939-40	31	12	5	67	1st	2	4	Semifinals	Ralph (Cooney) Weiland
1940-41	27	8	13	67	1st	8	3	Stanley Cup champ	Ralph (Cooney) Weiland
1941-42	25	17	6	56	3rd	2	3	Semifinals	Art Ross
1942-43	24	17	9	57	2nd	4	5	Stanley Cup finals	Art Ross
1943-44	19	26	5	43	5th	—	—		Art Ross
1944-45	16	30	4	36	4th	3	4	League semifinals	Art Ross
1945-46	24	18	8	56	2nd	5	5	Stanley Cup finals	Dit Clapper
1946-47	26	23	11	63	3rd	1	4	League semifinals	Dit Clapper
1947-48	23	24	13	59	3rd	1	4	League semifinals	Dit Clapper
1948-49	29	23	8	66	2nd	1	4	League semifinals	Dit Clapper
1949-50	22	32	16	60	5th	—	—		George Boucher
1950-51	22	30	18	62	4th	†1	4	League semifinals	Lynn Patrick
1951-52	25	29	16	66	4th	3	4	League semifinals	Lynn Patrick
1952-53	28	29	13	69	3rd	5	6	League semifinals	Lynn Patrick
1953-54	32	28	10	74	4th	0	4	League semifinals	Lynn Patrick
1954-55	23	26	21	67	4th	1	4	League semifinals	Lynn Patrick, Milt Schmidt
1955-56	23	34	13	59	5th	—	—		Milt Schmidt
1956-57	34	24	12	80	3rd	5	5	Stanley Cup finals	Milt Schmidt
1957-58	27	28	15	69	4th	6	6	Stanley Cup finals	Milt Schmidt
1958-59	32	29	9	73	2nd	3	4	League semifinals	Milt Schmidt
1959-60	28	34	8	64	5th	—	—		Milt Schmidt
1960-61	15	42	13	43	6th	—	—		Milt Schmidt
1961-62	15	47	8	38	6th	—	—		Phil Watson
1962-63	14	39	17	45	6th	—	—		Phil Watson, Milt Schmidt
1963-64	18	40	12	48	6th	—	—		Milt Schmidt
1964-65	21	43	6	48	6th	—	—		Milt Schmidt
1965-66	21	43	6	48	5th	—	—		Milt Schmidt
1966-67	17	43	10	44	6th	—	—		Harry Sinden
1967-68	37	27	10	84	3rd/East	0	4	Division semifinals	Harry Sinden
1968-69	42	18	16	100	2nd/East	6	4	Division finals	Harry Sinden
1969-70	40	17	19	99	2nd/East	12	2	Stanley Cup champ	Harry Sinden
1970-71	57	14	7	121	1st/East	3	4	Division semifinals	Tom Johnson
1971-72	54	13	11	119	1st/East	12	3	Stanley Cup champ	Tom Johnson
1972-73	51	22	5	107	2nd/East	1	4	Division semifinals	Tom Johnson, Bep Guidolin
1973-74	52	17	9	113	1st/East	10	6	Stanley Cup finals	Bep Guidolin
1974-75	40	26	14	94	2nd/Adams	1	2	Preliminaries	Don Cherry
1975-76	48	15	17	113	1st/Adams	5	7	Semifinals	Don Cherry
1976-77	49	23	8	106	1st/Adams	8	6	Stanley Cup finals	Don Cherry
1977-78	51	18	11	113	1st/Adams	10	5	Stanley Cup finals	Don Cherry
1978-79	43	23	14	100	1st/Adams	7	4	Semifinals	Don Cherry
1979-80	46	21	13	105	2nd/Adams	4	6	Quarterfinals	Fred Creighton, Harry Sinden
1980-81	37	30	13	87	2nd/Adams	0	3	Preliminaries	Gerry Cheevers
1981-82	43	27	10	96	2nd/Adams	6	5	Division finals	Gerry Cheevers
1982-83	50	20	10	110	1st/Adams	9	8	Conference finals	Gerry Cheevers
1983-84	49	25	6	104	1st/Adams	0	3	Division semifinals	Gerry Cheevers
1984-85	36	34	10	82	4th/Adams	2	3	Division semifinals	Gerry Cheevers, Harry Sinden
1985-86	37	31	12	86	3rd/Adams	0	3	Division semifinals	Butch Goring
1986-87	39	34	7	85	3rd/Adams	0	4	Division semifinals	Butch Goring, Terry O'Reilly
1987-88	44	30	6	94	2nd/Adams	12	6	Stanley Cup finals	Terry O'Reilly
1988-89	37	29	14	88	2nd/Adams	5	5	Division finals	Terry O'Reilly
1989-90	46	25	9	101	1st/Adams	13	8	Stanley Cup finals	Mike Milbury
1990-91	44	24	12	100	1st/Adams	10	9	Conference finals	Mike Milbury

	REGULAR SEASON					PLAYOFFS			
Season	W	L	T	Pts.	Finish	W	L	Highest round	Coach
1991-92	36	32	12	84	2nd/Adams	8	7	Conference finals	Rick Bowness
1992-93	51	26	7	109	1st/Adams	0	4	Division semifinals	Brian Sutter
1993-94	42	29	13	97	2nd/Northeast	6	7	Conference semifinals	Brian Sutter
1994-95	27	18	3	57	3rd/Northeast	1	4	Conference quarterfinals	Brian Sutter
1995-96	40	31	11	91	2nd/Northeast	1	4	Conference quarterfinals	Steve Kasper
1996-97	26	47	9	61	6th/Northeast	—	—		Steve Kasper
1997-98	39	30	13	91	2nd/Northeast	2	4	Conference quarterfinals	Pat Burns
1998-99	39	30	13	91	3th/Northeast	6	6	Conference semifinals	Pat Burns

*Won-lost record does not indicate tie(s) resulting from two-game, total-goals series that year (two-game, total-goals series were played from 1917-18 through 1935-36).

†Tied after one overtime (curfew law).

FIRST-ROUND ENTRY DRAFT CHOICES

Year Player, Overall, Last amateur team (league)

1969—Don Tannahill, 3, Niagara Falls (OHL)
Frank Spring, 4, Edmonton (WCHL)
Ivan Boldirev, 11, Oshawa (OHL)
1970—Reggie Leach, 3, Flin Flon (WCHL)
Rick MacLeish, 4, Peterborough (OHL)
Ron Plumb, 9, Peterborough (OHL)
Bob Stewart, 13, Oshawa (OHL)
1971—Ron Jones, 6, Edmonton (WCHL)
Terry O'Reilly, 14, Oshawa (OHL)
1972—Mike Bloom, 16, St. Catharines (OHL)
1973—Andre Savard, 6, Quebec (QMJHL)
1974—Don Laraway, 18, Swift Current (WCHL)
1975—Doug Halward, 14, Peterborough (OHL)
1976—Clayton Pachal, 16, New Westminster (WCHL)
1977—Dwight Foster, 16, Kitchener (OHL)
1978—Al Secord, 16, Hamilton (OHL)
1979—Ray Bourque, 8, Verdun (QMJHL)
Brad McCrimmon, 15, Brandon (WHL)
1980—Barry Pederson, 18, Victoria (WHL)
1981—Norm Leveille, 14, Chicoutimi (QMJHL)
1982—Gord Kluzak, 1, Billings (WHL)*

Year Player, Overall, Last amateur team (league)

1983—Nevin Markwart, 21, Regina (WHL)
1984—Dave Pasin, 19, Prince Albert (WHL)
1985—No first-round selection
1986—Craig Janney, 13, Boston College
1987—Glen Wesley, 3, Portland (WHL)
Stephane Quintal, 14, Granby (QMJHL)
1988—Robert Cimetta, 18, Toronto (OHL)
1989—Shayne Stevenson, 17, Kitchener (OHL)
1990—Bryan Smolinski, 21, Michigan State University
1991—Glen Murray, 18, Sudbury (OHL)
1992—Dmitri Kvartalnov, 16, San Diego (IHL)
1993—Kevyn Adams, 25, Miami of Ohio
1994—Evgeni Riabchikov, 21, Molot-Perm (Russia)
1995—Kyle McLaren, 9, Tacoma (WHL)
Sean Brown, 21, Belleville (OHL)
1996—Johnathan Aitken, 8, Medicine Hat (WHL)
1997—Joe Thornton, 1, Sault Ste. Marie (OHL)*
Sergei Samsonov, 8, Detroit (IHL)
1998—No first-round selection
1999—Nicholas Boynton, 21, Ottawa (OHL)
*Designates first player chosen in draft.

SINGLE-SEASON INDIVIDUAL RECORDS

FORWARDS/DEFENSEMEN

Most goals
76—Phil Esposito, 1970-71

Most assists
102—Bobby Orr, 1970-71

Most points
152—Phil Esposito, 1970-71

Most penalty minutes
302—Jay Miller, 1987-88

Most power play goals
28—Phil Esposito, 1971-72

Most shorthanded goals
7—Jerry Toppazzini, 1957-58
Ed Westfall, 1970-71
Derek Sanderson, 1971-72

Most games with three or more goals
7—Phil Esposito, 1970-71

Most shots
550—Phil Esposito, 1970-71

GOALTENDERS

Most games
70—Frank Brimsek, 1949-50
Jack Gelineau, 1950-51
Eddie Johnston, 1964-64

Most minutes
4,200—Frank Brimsek, 1949-50
Jack Gelineau, 1950-51
Eddie Johnston, 1964-64

Most goals allowed
244—Frank Brimsek, 1949-50

Lowest goals-against average
1.18—Tiny Thompson, 1928-29

Most shutouts
15—Hal Winkler, 1927-28

Most wins
40—Pete Peeters, 1982-83

FRANCHISE LEADERS

Players in boldface played for club in '98-99

FORWARDS/DEFENSEMEN

Games

Ray Bourque	**1453**
John Bucyk	1436
Wayne Cashman	1027
Terry O'Reilly	891
Rick Middleton	881

Goals

John Bucyk	545
Phil Esposito	459
Rick Middleton	402
Ray Bourque	**385**
Cam Neely	344

Assists

Ray Bourque	**1083**
John Bucyk	794
Bobby Orr	624
Phil Esposito	553
Wayne Cashman	516

Points

Ray Bourque	**1468**
John Bucyk	1339
Phil Esposito	1012
Rick Middleton	898
Bobby Orr	888

Penalty minutes

Terry O'Reilly 2095
Mike Milbury 1552
Keith Crowder 1261
Wayne Cashman 1041
Ray Bourque 1067

GOALTENDERS

Games

Cecil Thompson 468
Frankie Brimsek 444
Eddie Johnston 443
Gerry Cheevers 416
Gilles Gilbert 277

Shutouts

Cecil Thompson 74
Frankie Brimsek 35
Eddie Johnston 27
Gerry Cheevers 26
Jim Henry 24

Goals-against average (2400 minutes minimum)

Hal Winkler 1.56
Cecil Thompson 1.99
Byron Dafoe 2.11
Charles Stewart 2.46
John Henderson 2.52

Wins

Tiny Thompson 252
Frankie Brimsek 230
Gerry Cheevers 229
Eddie Johnston 182
Gilles Gilbert 155

BUFFALO SABRES

YEAR-BY-YEAR RECORDS

	REGULAR SEASON					PLAYOFFS			
Season	W	L	T	Pts.	Finish	W	L	Highest round	Coach
1970-71	24	39	15	63	5th/East	—	—		Punch Imlach
1971-72	16	43	19	51	6th/East	—	—		Punch Imlach, Joe Crozier
1972-73	37	27	14	88	4th/East	2	4	Division semifinals	Joe Crozier
1973-74	32	34	12	76	5th/East	—	—		Joe Crozier
1974-75	49	16	15	113	1st/Adams	10	7	Stanley Cup finals	Floyd Smith
1975-76	46	21	13	105	2nd/Adams	4	5	Quarterfinals	Floyd Smith
1976-77	48	24	8	104	2nd/Adams	2	4	Quarterfinals	Floyd Smith
1977-78	44	19	17	105	2nd/Adams	3	5	Quarterfinals	Marcel Pronovost
1978-79	36	28	16	88	2nd/Adams	1	2	Preliminaries	Marcel Pronovost, Bill Inglis
1979-80	47	17	16	110	1st/Adams	9	5	Semifinals	Scotty Bowman
1980-81	39	20	21	99	1st/Adams	4	4	Quarterfinals	Roger Neilson
1981-82	39	26	15	93	3rd/Adams	1	3	Division semifinals	Jim Roberts, Scotty Bowman
1982-83	38	29	13	89	3rd/Adams	6	4	Division finals	Scotty Bowman
1983-84	48	25	7	103	2nd/Adams	0	3	Division semifinals	Scotty Bowman
1984-85	38	28	14	90	3rd/Adams	2	3	Divison semifinals	Scotty Bowman
1985-86	37	37	6	80	5th/Adams	—	—		Jim Schoenfeld, Scotty Bowman
1986-87	28	44	8	64	5th/Adams	—	—		Scotty Bowman, Craig Ramsay
1987-88	37	32	11	85	3rd/Adams	2	4	Division semifinals	Ted Sator
1988-89	38	35	7	83	3rd/Adams	1	4	Division semifinals	Ted Sator
1989-90	45	27	8	98	2nd/Adams	2	4	Division semifinals	Rick Dudley
1990-91	31	30	19	81	3rd/Adams	2	4	Division semifinals	Rick Dudley Ted Sator
1991-92	31	37	12	74	3rd/Adams	3	4	Division semifinals	Rick Dudley, John Muckler
1992-93	38	36	10	86	4th/Adams	4	4	Division finals	John Muckler
1993-94	43	32	9	95	4th/Northeast	3	4	Conference quarterfinals	John Muckler
1994-95	22	19	7	51	4th/Northeast	1	4	Conference quarterfinals	John Muckler
1995-96	33	42	7	73	5th/Northeast	—	—		Ted Nolan
1996-97	40	30	12	92	1st/Northeast	5	7	Conference semifinals	Ted Nolan
1997-98	36	29	17	89	3rd/Northeast	10	5	Conference finals	Lindy Ruff
1998-99	37	28	17	91	4rd/Northeast	14	7	Stanley Cup finals	Lindy Ruff

FIRST-ROUND ENTRY DRAFT CHOICES

Year Player, Overall, Last amateur team (league)

1970—Gilbert Perreault, 1, Montreal (OHL)*
1971—Rick Martin, 5, Montreal (OHL)
1972—Jim Schoenfeld, 5, Niagara Falls (OHL)
1973—Morris Titanic, 12, Sudbury (OHL)
1974—Lee Fogolin, 11, Oshawa (OHL)
1975—Robert Sauve, 17, Laval (QMJHL)
1976—No first-round selection
1977—Ric Seiling, 14, St. Catharines (OHL)
1978—Larry Playfair, 13, Portland (WHL)
1979—Mike Ramsey, 11, University of Minnesota
1980—Steve Patrick, 20, Brandon (WHL)
1981—Jiri Dudacek, 17, Kladno (Czechoslovakia)
1982—Phil Housley, 6, South St. Paul H.S. (Minn.)
Paul Cyr, 9, Victoria (WHL)
Dave Andreychuk, 16, Oshawa (OHL)
1983—Tom Barrasso, 5, Acton Boxboro H.S. (Mass.)
Norm Lacombe, 10, Univ. of New Hampshire
Adam Creighton, 11, Ottawa (OHL)

Year Player, Overall, Last amateur team (league)

1984—Bo Andersson, 18, Vastra Frolunda (Sweden)
1985—Carl Johansson, 14, Vastra Frolunda (Sweden)
1986—Shawn Anderson, 5, Team Canada
1987—Pierre Turgeon, 1, Granby (QMJHL)*
1988—Joel Savage, 13, Victoria (WHL)
1989—Kevin Haller, 14, Regina (WHL)
1990—Brad May, 14, Niagara Falls (OHL)
1991—Philippe Boucher, 13, Granby (QMJHL)
1992—David Cooper, 11, Medicine Hat (WHL)
1993—No first-round selection
1994—Wayne Primeau, 17, Owen Sound (OHL)
1995—Jay McKee, 14, Niagara Falls (OHL)
Martin Biron, 16, Beauport (QMJHL)
1996—Erik Rasmussen, 7, University of Minnesota
1997—Mika Noronen, 21, Tappara Tampere (Finland)
1998—Dimitri Kalinin, 18, Traktor Chelyabinsk (Russia)
1999—Barrett Heisten, 20, Maine (H. East)
*Designates first player chosen in draft.

SINGLE-SEASON INDIVIDUAL RECORDS

FORWARDS/DEFENSEMEN

Most goals
76—Alexander Mogilny, 1992-93

Most assists
95—Pat LaFontaine, 1992-93

Most points
148—Pat LaFontaine, 1992-93

Most penalty minutes
354—Rob Ray, 1991-92

Most power play goals
28—Dave Andreychuk, 1991-92

Most shorthanded goals
8—Don Luce, 1994-95

Most games with three or more goals
7—Rick Martin, 1995-96
Alexander Mogilny, 1992-93

Most shots
360—Alexander Mogilny, 1992-93

GOALTENDERS

Most games
72—Don Edwards, 1997-78
Dominik Hasek, 1997-98

Most minutes
4,220—Dominik Hasek, 1997-98

Most shots against
2,190—Roger Crozier, 1971-72

Most goals allowed
214—Roger Crozier, 1971-72
Tom Barrasso, 1985-86

Lowest goals-against average
1.87—Dominik Hasek, 1998-99

Most shutouts
13—Dominik Hasek, 1997-98

Most wins
38—Don Edwards, 1977-78

Most losses
34—Roger Crozier, 1971-72

Most ties
17—Don Edwards, 1977-78

FRANCHISE LEADERS

Players in boldface played for club in '98-99

FORWARDS/DEFENSEMEN

Games

Gilbert Perreault	1191
Craig Ramsay	1070
Mike Ramsey	911
Bill Hajt	854
Don Luce	766

Goals

Gilbert Perreault	512
Rick Martin	382
Dave Andreychuk	348
Danny Gare	267
Craig Ramsay	252

Assists

Gilbert Perreault	814
Dave Andreychuk	423
Craig Ramsay	420
Phil Housley	380
Rene Robert	330

Points

Gilbert Perreault	1326
Dave Andreychuk	771
Rick Martin	695
Craig Ramsay	672
Phil Housley	558

Penalty minutes

Rob Ray	**2529**
Mike Foligno	1450
Larry Playfair	1390
Brad May	**1323**
Matthew Barnaby	**1248**

GOALTENDERS

Games

Dominik Hasek	**389**
Don Edwards	307
Tom Barrasso	266
Bob Sauve	246
Daren Puppa	215

Shutouts

Dominik Hasek	**41**
Don Edwards	14
Tom Barrasso	13
Roger Crozier	10
Bob Sauve	7

Goals-against average (2400 minutes minimum)

Dominik Hasek	**2.24**
Gerry Desjardins	2.81
Don Edwards	2.90
Dave Dryden	3.06
Bob Sauve	3.20

Wins

Dominik Hasek	**182**
Don Edwards	156
Tom Barrasso	124
Bob Sauve	119
Daren Puppa	96

CALGARY FLAMES

YEAR-BY-YEAR RECORDS

	REGULAR SEASON					PLAYOFFS			
Season	**W**	**L**	**T**	**Pts.**	**Finish**	**W**	**L**	**Highest round**	**Coach**
1980-81	39	27	14	92	3rd/Patrick	9	7	Semifinals	Al MacNeil
1981-82	29	34	17	75	3rd/Smythe	0	3	Division semifinals	Al MacNeil
1982-83	32	34	14	78	2nd/Smythe	4	5	Division finals	Bob Johnson
1983-84	34	32	14	82	2nd/Smythe	6	5	Division finals	Bob Johnson
1984-85	41	27	12	94	3rd/Smythe	1	3	Division semifinals	Bob Johnson
1985-86	40	31	9	89	2nd/Smythe	12	10	Stanley Cup finals	Bob Johnson
1986-87	46	31	3	95	2nd/Smythe	2	4	Division semifinals	Bob Johnson
1987-88	48	23	9	105	1st/Smythe	4	5	Division finals	Terry Crisp
1988-89	54	17	9	117	1st/Smythe	16	6	Stanley Cup champ	Terry Crisp
1989-90	42	23	15	99	1st/Smythe	2	4	Division semifinals	Terry Crisp
1990-91	46	26	8	100	2nd/Smythe	3	4	Division semifinals	Doug Risebrough
1991-92	31	37	12	74	5th/Smythe	—	—		Doug Risebrough, Guy Charron
1992-93	43	30	11	97	2nd/Smythe	2	4	Division semifinals	Dave King
1993-94	42	29	13	97	1st/Pacific	3	4	Conference quarterfinals	Dave King
1994-95	24	17	7	55	1st/Pacific	3	4	Conference quarterfinals	Dave King
1995-96	34	37	11	79	T2nd/Pacific	0	4	Conference quarterfinals	Pierre Page
1996-97	32	41	9	73	5th/Pacific	—	—		Pierre Page
1997-98	26	41	15	67	5th/Pacific	—	—		Brian Sutter
1998-99	30	40	12	72	3rd/Pacific	—	—		Brian Sutter

Franchise was formerly in Atlanta from 1972-73 through 1979-80 seasons.

FIRST-ROUND ENTRY DRAFT CHOICES

Year	Player, Overall, Last amateur team (league)
1980	Denis Cyr, 13, Montreal (OHL)
1981	Al MacInnis, 15, Kitchener (OHL)
1982	No first-round selection
1983	Dan Quinn, 13, Belleville (OHL)
1984	Gary Roberts, 12, Ottawa (OHL)
1985	Chris Biotti, 17, Belmont Hill H.S. (Mass.)
1986	George Pelawa, 16, Bemidji H.S. (Minn.)
1987	Bryan Deasley, 19, University of Michigan
1988	Jason Muzzatti, 21, Michigan State University
1989	No first-round selection
1990	Trevor Kidd, 11, Brandon (WHL)
1991	Niklas Sundblad, 19, AIK (Sweden)
1992	Cory Stillman, 6, Windsor (OHL)
1993	Jesper Mattsson, 18, Malmo (Sweden)
1994	Chris Dingman, 19, Brandon (WHL)
1995	Denis Gauthier, 20, Drummondville (QMJHL)
1996	Derek Morris, 13, Regina (WHL)
1997	Daniel Tkaczuk, 6, Barrie (OHL)
1998	Rico Fata, 6, London (OHL)
1999	Oleg Saprykin, 11, Seattle (WHL)

SINGLE-SEASON INDIVIDUAL RECORDS

FORWARDS/DEFENSEMEN

Most goals
66—Lanny McDonald, 1982-83

Most assists
82—Kent Nilsson, 1980-81

Most points
131—Kent Nilsson, 1980-81

Most penalty minutes
375—Tim Hunter, 1988-89

Most power play goals
31—Joe Nieuwendyk, 1987-88

Most shorthanded goals
9—Kent Nilsson, 1984-85

Most games with three or more goals
5—Hakan Loob, 1987-88
Theo Fleury, 1990-91

Most shots
353—Theo Fleury, 1995-96

GOALTENDERS

Most games
64—Mike Vernon, 1987-88
Mike Vernon, 1992-93

Most minutes
3,732—Mike Vernon, 1992-93

Most goals allowed
229—Rejean Lemelin, 1985-86

Lowest goals-against average
2.45—Fred Brathwaite, 1998-99

Most shutouts
4—Trevor Kidd, 1996-97

Most wins
39—Mike Vernon, 1987-88

Most losses
30—Mike Vernon, 1991-92

Most ties
11—Pat Riggin, 1981-82

FRANCHISE LEADERS

Players in boldface played for club in '98-99

FORWARDS/DEFENSEMEN

Games

Al MacInnis	803
Theo Fleury	**791**
Joel Otto	730
Jim Peplinski	711
Gary Suter	617

Goals

Theo Fleury	**334**
Joe Nieuwendyk	314
Gary Roberts	257
Kent Nilsson	229
Lanny McDonald	215

Assists

Al MacInnis	609
Theo Fleury	**466**
Gary Suter	437
Joe Nieuwendyk	302
Paul Reinhart	297

Points

Theo Fleury	**830**
Al MacInnis	822
Joe Nieuwendyk	616
Gary Suter	565
Gary Roberts	505

Penalty minutes

Tim Hunter	2405
Gary Roberts	1736
Joel Otto	1642
Jim Peplinski	1467
Ronnie Stern	1288

GOALTENDERS

Games

Mike Vernon	467
Reggie Lemelin	303
Trevor Kidd	178
Don Edwards	114
Rick Wamsley	111

Shutouts

Trevor Kidd	10
Mike Vernon	9
Reggie Lemelin	6
Rick Tabaracci	4
Rick Wamsley	4

Goals-against average (2400 minutes minimum)

Rick Tabaracci	**2.81**
Trevor Kidd	2.83
Dwayne Roloson	**2.95**
Mike Vernon	3.28
Reggie Lemelin	3.67

Wins

Mike Vernon	248
Reggie Lemelin	136
Trevor Kidd	72
Rick Wamsley	53
Don Edwards	40

CALIFORNIA GOLDEN SEALS (DEFUNCT)

YEAR-BY-YEAR RECORDS

	REGULAR SEASON					PLAYOFFS			
Season	W	L	T	Pts.	Finish	W	L	Highest round	Coach
1967-68*	15	42	17	42	6th/West	—	—		Bert Olmstead, Gordie Fashoway
1968-69*	29	36	11	69	2nd/West	3	4	Division semifinals	Fred Glover
1969-70*	22	40	14	58	4th/West	0	4	Division semifinals	Fred Glover
1970-71	20	53	5	45	7th/West	—	—		Fred Glover
1971-72	21	39	18	60	6th/West	—	—		Fred Glover, Vic Stasiuk
1972-73	16	46	16	48	8th/West	—	—		Garry Young, Fred Glover
1973-74	13	55	10	36	8th/West	—	—		Fred Glover, Marsh Johnston

Season	W	L	T	Pts.	Finish (Regular season)	W	L	Highest round (Playoffs)	Coach
1974-75	19	48	13	51	4th/Adams	—	—		Marsh Johnston
1975-76	27	42	11	65	4th/Adams	—	—		Jack Evans

*Oakland Seals.
Franchise relocated and became Cleveland Barons following 1975-76 season.

FIRST-ROUND ENTRY DRAFT CHOICES

Year Player, Overall, Last amateur team (league)
1969—Tony Featherstone, 7, Peterborough (OHA)
1970—Chris Oddleifson, 10 Winnipeg (WCHL)
1971—No first-round selection
1972—No first-round selection
1973—No first-round selection
1974—Rick Hampton, 3, St. Catharines (OHA)
Ron Chipperfield, 17, Brandon (WCHL)
1975—Ralph Klassen, 3, Saskatoon (WCHL)

INDIVIDUAL SINGLE-SEASON RECORDS

FORWARDS/DEFENSEMEN

Most goals
34—Norm Ferguson, 1968-69

Most assists
49—Ted Hampson, 1968-69

Most points
75—Ted Hampson, 1968-69

Most penalty minutes
217—Dennis Hextall, 1970-71

Most power play goals
12—Bill Hicke, 1967-68

Most shorthanded goals
5—Dennis Maruk, 1975-76

Most games with three or more goals
2—Earl Ingarfield, 1969-70
Reggie Leach, 1973-74
Al MacAdam, 1975-76
Wayne Merrick, 1975-76

Most shots
274—Carol Vadnais, 1968-69

GOALTENDERS

Most games
71—Gary Smith, 1970-71

Most minutes
3,975—Gary Smith, 1970-71

Most goals allowed
256—Gary Smith, 1970-71

Lowest goals-against average
2.86—Charlie Hodge, 1967-68

Most shutouts
4—Gary Smith, 1968-69
Gilles Meloche, 1971-72

Most wins
19—Gary Smith, 1969-70
Gary Smith, 1970-71

Most losses
48—Gary Smith, 1970-71

Most ties
14—Gilles Meloche, 1972-73

FRANCHISE LEADERS

FORWARDS/DEFENSEMEN

Games

Bert Marshall	313
Gary Ehman	297
Joey Johnston	288
Norm Ferguson	279
Gary Croteau	270

Goals

Joey Johnston	84
Bill Hicke	79
Norm Ferguson	73
Gary Ehman	69
Carol Vadnais	63

Assists

Ted Hampson	123
Bill Hicke	101
Joey Johnston	101
Gary Ehman	86
Carol Vadnais	83

Points

Joey Johnston	185
Ted Hampson	184
Bill Hicke	180
Gary Ehman	155
Carol Vadnais	146

Penalty minutes

Carol Vadnais	560
Bob Stewart	499
Bert Marshall	395
Joey Johnston	308
Doug Roberts	280

GOALTENDERS

Games

Gilles Meloche	250
Gary Smith	211
Charlie Hodge	86
Gary Simmons	74
Marv Edwards	35

Shutouts

Gary Smith	9
Gilles Meloche	8
Gary Simmons	4
Charlie Hodge	3
Marv Edwards	1

Goals-against average (2400 minutes minimum)

Charlie Hodge	3.09
Gary Smith	3.33
Gary Simmons	3.49
Gilles Meloche	3.83

Wins

Charlie Hodge	3.09
Gary Smith	3.33
Gary Simmons	3.49
Gilles Meloche	3.83

CAROLINA HURRICANES

YEAR-BY-YEAR RECORDS

Season	W	L	T	Pts.	Finish (Regular season)	W	L	Highest round (Playoffs)	Coach
1997-98	33	41	8	74	6th/Northeast	—	—		Paul Maurice
1998-99	34	30	18	86	1st/Southeast	2	4	Conference quarterfinals	Paul Maurice

Franchise was formerly known as Hartford Whalers and relocated to Carolina following 1996-97 season.

FIRST-ROUND ENTRY DRAFT CHOICES

Year Player, Overall, Last amateur team (league)
1998—Jeff Heerema, 11, Sarnia (OHL)
1999—David Tanabe, 16, Wisconsin (WCHA)

SINGLE-SEASON INDIVIDUAL RECORDS

FORWARDS/DEFENSEMEN

Most goals
26—Keith Primeau, 1998-99

Most assists
37—Sami Kapanen, 1997-98
Keith Primeau, 1997-98

Most points
63—Sami Kapanen, 1997-98
Keith Primeau, 1997-98

Most penalty minutes
204—Stu Grimson, 1997-98

Most power play goals
7—Keith Primeau, 1998-99

Most shorthanded goals
3—Keith Primeau, 1997-98

Most games with three or more goals
2—Sami Kapanen, 1997-98

Most shots
254—Sami Kapanen, 1998-99

GOALTENDERS

Most games
62—Arturs Irbe, 1998-99

Most minutes
3,643—Arturs Irbe, 1998-99

Most shots against
1,753—Arturs Irbe, 1998-99

Most goals allowed
135—Arturs Irbe, 1998-99

Lowest goals-against average
2.17—Trevor Kidd, 1997-98

Most shutouts
6—Arturs Irbe, 1998-99

Most wins
27—Arturs Irbe, 1998-99

Most losses
21—Trevor Kidd, 1997-98

Most ties
12—Arturs Irbe, 1998-99

FRANCHISE LEADERS

Players in boldface played for club in '98-99

FORWARDS/DEFENSEMEN

Games

Sami Kapanen 162
Keith Primeau 159
Kent Manderville 158
Robert Kron 156
Glen Wesley 156

Goals

Keith Primeau 56
Sami Kapanen 50
Jeff O'Neill 35
Gary Roberts 34
Nelson Emerson 29
Ray Sheppard 29

Assists

Sami Kapanen 72
Keith Primeau 69
Gary Roberts 57
Nelson Emerson 37
Robert Kron 36
Glen Wesley 36

Points

Keith Primeau 125
Sami Kapanen 122
Gary Roberts 91
Jeff O'Neill 70
Nelson Emerson 66

Penalty minutes

Gary Roberts 281
Stu Grimson 204
Kevin Dineen 202
Keith Primeau 185
Adam Burt 152

GOALTENDERS

Games

Trevor Kidd 72
Arturs Irbe 62
Sean Burke 25
Kirk McLean 8
Pat Jablonski 5

Shutouts

Arturs Irbe 6
Trevor Kidd 5
Sean Burke 1

Goals-against average (2400 minutes minimum)

Arturs Irbe 2.22
Trevor Kidd 2.34

Wins

Trevor Kidd 28
Arturs Irbe 27
Sean Burke 7
Kirk McLean 4
Pat Jablonski 1

CHICAGO BLACKHAWKS

YEAR-BY-YEAR RECORDS

	REGULAR SEASON					PLAYOFFS			
Season	W	L	T	Pts.	Finish	W	L	Highest round	Coach
1926-27	19	22	3	41	3rd/American	*0	1	Quarterfinals	Pete Muldoon
1927-28	7	34	3	17	5th/American	—	—		Barney Stanley, Hugh Lehman
1928-29	7	29	8	22	5th/American	—	—		Herb Gardiner
1929-30	21	18	5	47	2nd/American	*0	1	Quarterfinals	Tom Schaughnessy, Bill Tobin
1930-31	24	17	3	51	2nd/American	*5	3	Stanley Cup finals	Dick Irvin
1931-32	18	19	11	47	2nd/American	1	1	Quarterfinals	Dick Irvin, Bill Tobin
1932-33	16	20	12	44	4th/American	—	—		Godfrey Matheson, Emil Iverson
1933-34	20	17	11	51	2nd/American	6	2	Stanley Cup champ	Tom Gorman
1934-35	26	17	5	57	2nd/American	*0	1	Quarterfinals	Clem Loughlin
1935-36	21	19	8	50	3rd/American	1	1	Quarterfinals	Clem Loughlin
1936-37	14	27	7	35	4th/American	—	—		Clem Loughlin
1937-38	14	25	9	37	3rd/American	7	3	Stanley Cup champ	Bill Stewart
1938-39	12	28	8	32	7th	—	—		Bill Stewart, Paul Thompson
1939-40	23	19	6	52	4th	0	2	Quarterfinals	Paul Thompson
1940-41	16	25	7	39	5th	2	3	Semifinals	Paul Thompson
1941-42	22	23	3	47	4th	1	2	Quarterfinals	Paul Thompson
1942-43	17	18	15	49	5th	—	—		Paul Thompson
1943-44	22	23	5	49	4th	4	5	Stanley Cup finals	Paul Thompson
1944-45	13	30	7	33	5th	—	—		Paul Thompson, John Gottselig
1945-46	23	20	7	53	3rd	0	4	League semifinals	John Gottselig
1946-47	19	37	4	42	6th	—	—		John Gottselig

	REGULAR SEASON					PLAYOFFS			
Season	W	L	T	Pts.	Finish	W	L	Highest round	Coach
1947-48	20	34	6	46	6th	—	—		John Gottselig, Charlie Conacher
1948-49	21	31	8	50	5th	—	—		Charlie Conacher
1949-50	22	38	10	54	6th	—	—		Charlie Conacher
1950-51	13	47	10	36	6th	—	—		Ebbie Goodfellow
1951-52	17	44	9	43	6th	—	—		Ebbie Goodfellow
1952-53	27	28	15	69	4th	3	4	League semifinals	Sid Abel
1953-54	12	51	7	31	6th	—	—		Sid Abel
1954-55	13	40	17	43	6th	—	—		Frank Eddolls
1955-56	19	39	12	50	6th	—	—		Dick Irvin
1956-57	16	39	15	47	6th	—	—		Tommy Ivan
1957-58	24	39	7	55	5th	—	—		Tommy Ivan, Rudy Pilous
1958-59	28	29	13	69	3rd	2	4	League semifinals	Rudy Pilous
1959-60	28	29	13	69	3rd	0	4	League semifinals	Rudy Pilous
1960-61	29	24	17	75	3rd	8	4	Stanley Cup champ	Rudy Pilous
1961-62	31	26	13	75	3rd	6	6	Stanley Cup finals	Rudy Pilous
1962-63	32	21	17	81	2nd	2	4	League semifinals	Rudy Pilous
1963-64	36	22	12	84	2nd	3	4	League semifinals	Billy Reay
1964-65	34	28	8	76	3rd	7	7	Stanley Cup finals	Billy Reay
1965-66	37	25	8	82	2nd	2	4	League semifinals	Billy Reay
1966-67	41	17	12	94	1st	2	4	League semifinals	Billy Reay
1967-68	32	26	16	80	4th/East	5	6	Division finals	Billy Reay
1968-69	34	33	9	77	6th/East	—	—		Billy Reay
1969-70	45	22	9	99	1st/East	4	4	Division finals	Billy Reay
1970-71	49	20	9	107	1st/West	11	7	Stanley Cup finals	Billy Reay
1971-72	46	17	15	107	1st/West	4	4	Division finals	Billy Reay
1972-73	42	27	9	93	1st/West	10	6	Stanley Cup finals	Billy Reay
1973-74	41	14	23	105	2nd/West	6	5	Division finals	Billy Reay
1974-75	37	35	8	82	3rd/Smythe	3	5	Quarterfinals	Billy Reay
1975-76	32	30	18	82	1st/Smythe	0	4	Quarterfinals	Billy Reay
1976-77	26	43	11	63	3rd/Smythe	0	2	Preliminaries	Billy Reay, Bill White
1977-78	32	29	19	83	1st/Smythe	0	4	Quarterfinals	Bob Pulford
1978-79	29	36	15	73	1st/Smythe	0	4	Quarterfinals	Bob Pulford
1979-80	34	27	19	87	1st/Smythe	3	4	Quarterfinals	Eddie Johnston
1980-81	31	33	16	78	2nd/Smythe	0	3	Preliminaries	Keith Magnuson
1981-82	30	38	12	72	4th/Norris	8	7	Conference finals	Keith Magnuson, Bob Pulford
1982-83	47	23	10	104	1st/Norris	7	6	Conference finals	Orval Tessier
1983-84	30	42	8	68	4th/Norris	2	3	Division semifinals	Orval Tessier
1984-85	38	35	7	83	2nd/Norris	9	6	Conference finals	Orval Tessier, Bob Pulford
1985-86	39	33	8	86	1st/Norris	0	3	Division semifinals	Bob Pulford
1986-87	29	37	14	72	3rd/Norris	0	4	Division semifinals	Bob Pulford
1987-88	30	41	9	69	3rd/Norris	1	4	Division semifinals	Bob Murdoch
1988-89	27	41	12	66	4th/Norris	9	7	Conference finals	Mike Keenan
1989-90	41	33	6	88	1st/Norris	10	10	Conference finals	Mike Keenan
1990-91	49	23	8	106	1st/Norris	2	4	Division semifinals	Mike Keenan
1991-92	36	29	15	87	2nd/Norris	12	6	Stanley Cup finals	Mike Keenan
1992-93	47	25	12	106	1st/Norris	0	4	Division semifinals	Darryl Sutter
1993-94	39	36	9	87	5th/Central	2	4	Conference quarterfinals	Darryl Sutter
1994-95	24	19	5	53	3rd/Central	9	7	Conference finals	Darryl Sutter
1995-96	40	28	14	94	2nd/Central	6	4	Conference semifinals	Craig Hartsburg
1996-97	34	35	13	81	5th/Central	2	4	Conference quarterfinals	Craig Hartsburg
1997-98	30	39	13	73	5th/Central	—	—		Craig Hartsburg
1998-99	29	41	12	70	3rd/Central	—	—		Dirk Graham, Lorne Molleken

*Won-lost record does not indicate tie(s) resulting from two-game, total-goals series that year (two-game, total-goals series were played from 1917-18 through 1935-36).

FIRST-ROUND ENTRY DRAFT CHOICES

Year Player, Overall, Last amateur team (league)
1969—J.P. Bordeleau, 13, Montreal (OHL)
1970—Dan Maloney, 14, London (OHL)
1971—Dan Spring, 12, Edmonton (WCHL)
1972—Phil Russell, 13, Edmonton (WCHL)
1973—Darcy Rota, 13, Edmonton (WCHL)
1974—Grant Mulvey, 16, Calgary (WCHL)
1975—Greg Vaydik, 7, Medicine Hat (WCHL)
1976—Real Cloutier, 9, Quebec (WHA)
1977—Doug Wilson, 6, Ottawa (OHL)
1978—Tim Higgins, 10, Ottawa (OHL)
1979—Keith Brown, 7, Portland (WHL)
1980—Denis Savard, 3, Montreal (QMJHL)
Jerome Dupont, 15, Toronto (OHL)
1981—Tony Tanti, 12, Oshawa (OHL)
1982—Ken Yaremchuk, 7, Portland (WHL)
1983—Bruce Cassidy, 18, Ottawa (OHL)
1984—Ed Olczyk, 3, U.S. Olympic Team

Year Player, Overall, Last amateur team (league)
1985—Dave Manson, 11, Prince Albert (WHL)
1986—Everett Sanipass, 14, Verdun (QMJHL)
1987—Jimmy Waite, 8, Chicoutimi (QMJHL)
1988—Jeremy Roenick, 8, Thayer Academy (Mass.)
1989—Adam Bennett, 6, Sudbury (OHL)
1990—Karl Dykhuis, 16, Hull (QMJHL)
1991—Dean McAmmond, 22, Prince Albert (WHL)
1992—Sergei Krivokrasov, 12, Central Red Army, CIS
1993—Eric Lecompte, 24, Hull (QMJHL)
1994—Ethan Moreau, 14, Niagara Falls (OHL)
1995—Dimitri Nabokov, 19, Krylja Sovetov, CIS
1996—No first-round selection
1997—Daniel Cleary, 13, Belleville (OHL)
Ty Jones, 16, Spokane (WHL)
1998—Mark Bell, 8, Ottawa (OHL)
1999—Steve McCarthy, 23, Kootenay (WHL)

SINGLE-SEASON INDIVIDUAL RECORDS

FORWARDS/DEFENSEMEN

Most goals
58—Bobby Hull, 1968-69

Most assists
87—Denis Savard, 1981-82
Denis Savard, 1987-88

Most points
131—Denis Savard, 1987-88

Most penalty minutes
408—Mike Peluso, 1991-92

Most power play goals
24—Jeremy Roenick, 1993-94

Most shorthanded goals
10—Dirk Graham, 1988-89

Most games with three or more goals
4—Bobby Hull, 1959-60
Bobby Hull, 1965-66

Most shots
414—Bobby Hull, 1968-69

GOALTENDERS

Most games
74—Ed Belfour, 1990-91

Most minutes
4,219—Tony Esposito, 1974-75

Most goals allowed
246—Harry Lumley, 1950-51
Tony Esposito, 1980-81

Lowest goals-against average
1.73—Charles Gardiner, 1933-34

Most shutouts
15—Tony Esposito, 1969-70

Most wins
43—Ed Belfour, 1990-91

Most losses
47—Al Rollins, 1953-54

Most ties
21—Tony Esposito, 1973-74

FRANCHISE LEADERS

Players in boldface played for club in '98-99

FORWARDS/DEFENSEMEN

Games

Stan Mikita	1394
Bobby Hull	1036
Eric Nesterenko	1013
Bob Murray	1008
Doug Wilson	938

Goals

Bobby Hull	604
Stan Mikita	541
Steve Larmer	406
Denis Savard	377
Dennis Hull	298

Assists

Stan Mikita	926
Denis Savard	719
Doug Wilson	554
Bobby Hull	549
Steve Larmer	517

Points

Stan Mikita	1467
Bobby Hull	1153
Denis Savard	1096
Steve Larmer	923
Doug Wilson	779

GOALTENDERS

Games

Tony Esposito	873
Glenn Hall	618
Ed Belfour	415
Mike Karakas	331
Charlie Gardiner	316

Shutouts

Tony Esposito	74
Glenn Hall	51
Chuck Gardiner	42
Ed Belfour	30
Mike Karakas	28

Goals-against average
(2400 minutes minimum)

Lorne Chabot	1.83
Charlie Gardiner	2.02
Paul Goodman	2.17
Jeff Hackett	**2.45**
Dominik Hasek	2.58

Wins

Tony Esposito	418
Glenn Hall	275
Ed Belfour	201
Murray Bannerman	116
Mike Karakas	114

CLEVELAND BARONS (DEFUNCT)

YEAR-BY-YEAR RECORDS

	REGULAR SEASON					PLAYOFFS			
Season	W	L	T	Pts.	Finish	W	L	Highest round	Coach
1976-77	25	42	13	63	4th/Adams	—	—		Jack Evans
1977-78	22	45	13	57	4th/Adams	—	—		Jack Evans

Franchise was formerly known as California Golden Seals and relocated to Cleveland following 1995-96 season. Barons disbanded after 1977-78 season. Owners bought Minnesota franchise and a number of Cleveland players were awarded to North Stars; remaining players were dispersed to other clubs in draft.

FIRST-ROUND ENTRY DRAFT CHOICES

Year Player, Overall, Last amateur team (league)
1976—Bjorn Johansson, 5, Orebro IK (Sweden)

Year Player, Overall, Last amateur team (league)
1977—Mike Crombeen, 5, Kingston (OHA)

SINGLE-SEASON INDIVIDUAL RECORDS

FORWARDS/DEFENSEMEN

Most goals
36—Dennis Maruk, 1977-78

Most assists
50—Dennis Maruk, 1976-77

Most points
78—Dennis Maruk, 1976-77

Most penalty minutes
229—Randy Holt, 1977-78

Most power play goals
7—Mike Fidler, 1976-77
Kris Manery, 1977-78

Most shorthanded goals
2—Dennis Maruk, 1977-78

Most games with three or more goals
1—Bob Murdoch, 1976-77
Dennis Maruk, 1977-78
Chuck Arnason, 1977-78

Most shots
268—Dennis Maruk, 1976-77

GOALTENDERS

Most games
54—Gilles Meloche, 1977-78

Most minutes
3,100—Gilles Meloche, 1977-78

Most goals allowed
195—Gilles Meloche, 1977-78

Lowest goals-against average
3.47—Gilles Meloche, 1976-77

Most shutouts
2—Gary Edwards, 1976-77
Gilles Meloche, 1976-77

Most wins
19—Gilles Meloche, 1976-77

Most losses
27—Gilles Meloche, 1977-78

Most ties
8—Gilles Meloche, 1977-78

FRANCHISE LEADERS

FORWARDS/DEFENSEMEN

Games

Al MacAdam	160
Dennis Maruk	156
Greg Smith	154
Dave Gardner	151
Bob Stewart	145

Goals

Dennis Maruk	64
Mike Fidler	40
Al MacAdam	38
Bob Murdoch	37
Dave Gardner	35

Assists

Dennis Maruk	85
Al MacAdam	73
Dave Gardner	47
Greg Smith	47
Bob Murdoch	45

Points

Dennis Maruk	149
Al MacAdam	111
Mike Fidler	84
Dave Gardner	82
Bob Murdoch	82

Penalty minutes

Randy Holt	229
Len Frig	213
Bob Stewart	192
Greg Smith	157
Mike Christie	128

GOALTENDERS

Games

Gilles Meloche	105
Gary Edwards	47
Gary Simmons	15

Shutouts

Gilles Meloche	3
Gary Edwards	2
Gary Simmons	1

Goals-against average (2400 minutes minimum)

Gary Edwards	4.36
Gilles Meloche	3.62

Wins

Gilles Meloche	35
Gary Edwards	10
Gary Simmons	2

COLORADO AVALANCHE

YEAR-BY-YEAR RECORDS

	REGULAR SEASON					PLAYOFFS			
Season	W	L	T	Pts.	Finish	W	L	Highest round	Coach
1995-96	47	25	10	104	1st/Pacific	16	6	Stanley Cup champ	Marc Crawford
1996-97	49	24	9	107	1st/Pacific	10	7	Conference finals	Marc Crawford
1997-98	39	26	17	95	1st/Pacific	3	4	Conference quarterfinals	Marc Crawford
1998-99	44	28	10	98	1st/Northwest	11	8	Conference finals	Bob Hartley

Franchise was formerly known as Quebec Nordiques and relocated to Colorado following 1994-95 season.

FIRST-ROUND ENTRY DRAFT CHOICES

Year	Player, Overall, Last amateur team (league)
1996	Peter Ratchuk, 25, Shattuck-St. Mary's H.S. (Min.)
1997	Kevin Grimes, 26, Kingston (OHL)
1998	Alex Tanguay, 12, Halifax (QMJHL)
	Martin Skoula, 17, Barrie (OHL)
	Robyn Regehr, 19, Kamloops (WHL)
	Scott Parker, 20, Kelowna (WHL)
1999	Mihail Kuleshov, 25, Cherepovec, Russia

SINGLE-SEASON INDIVIDUAL RECORDS

FORWARDS/DEFENSEMEN

Most goals
51—Joe Sakic, 1995-96

Most assists
86—Peter Forsberg, 1995-96

Most points
120—Joe Sakic, 1995-96

Most penalty minutes
259—Jeff Odgers, 1998-99

Most power play goals
18—Valeri Kamensky, 1995-96

Most shorthanded goals
6—Joe Sakic, 1995-96

Most games with three or more goals
2—Peter Forsberg, 1995-96
Valeri Kamensky, 1995-96
Claude Lemieux, 1995-96

Most shots
315—Claude Lemieux, 1995-96

GOALTENDERS

Most games
65—Patrick Roy, 1997-98

Most minutes
3,835—Patrick Roy, 1997-98

Most shots against
1,861—Patrick Roy, 1996-97

Most goals allowed
153—Patrick Roy, 1997-98

Lowest goals-against average
2.29—Patrick Roy, 1998-99

Most shutouts
7—Patrick Roy, 1996-97

Most wins
38—Patrick Roy, 1996-97

Most losses
19—Patrick Roy, 1997-98
Patrick Roy, 1998-99

Most ties
13—Patrick Roy, 1997-98

FRANCHISE LEADERS

Players in boldface played for club in '98-99

FORWARDS/DEFENSEMEN

Games

Sylvain Lefebvre....303
Stephane Yelle....303
Adam Deadmarsh....295
Adam Foote....292
Valeri Kamensky....289

Goals

Joe Sakic....141
Peter Forsberg....113
Valeri Kamensky....106
Claude Lemieux....103
Adam Deadmarsh....98

Assists

Peter Forsberg....277
Joe Sakic....212
Valeri Kamensky....155
Sandis Ozolinsh....148
Adam Deadmarsh....102

Points

Peter Forsberg....390
Joe Sakic....353
Valeri Kamensky....261
Sandis Ozolinsh....205
Claude Lemieux....203

Penalty minutes

Adam Deadmarsh....502
Jeff Odgers....472
Adam Foote....439
Claude Lemieux....377
Peter Forsberg....322

GOALTENDERS

Games

Patrick Roy....227
Craig Billington....67
Stephane Fiset....37
Marc Denis....5
Jocelyn Thibault....10

Shutouts

Patrick Roy....17
Craig Billington....2
Stephane Fiset....1

Goals-against average (2400 minutes minimum)

Patrick Roy....2.39
Craig Billington....2.61

Wins

Patrick Roy....123
Craig Billington....30
Stephane Fiset....22
Jocelyn Thibault....3
Marc Denis....1

COLORADO ROCKIES (DEFUNCT)

YEAR-BY-YEAR RECORDS

	REGULAR SEASON					PLAYOFFS			
Season	W	L	T	Pts.	Finish	W	L	Highest round	Coach
1976-77	20	46	14	54	5th/Smythe	—	—		John Wilson
1977-78	19	40	21	59	2nd/Smythe	0	2	Preliminaries	Pat Kelly
1978-79	15	53	12	42	4th/Smythe	—	—		Pat Kelly, Bep Guidolin
1979-80	19	48	13	51	6th/Smythe	—	—		Don Cherry
1980-81	22	45	13	57	5th/Smythe	—	—		Billy MacMillan
1981-82	18	49	13	49	5th/Smythe	—	—		Bert Marshall, Marshall Johnston

Franchise was formerly known as Kansas City Scouts and relocated to Colorado following 1975-76 season; franchise relocated and became New Jersey Devils following 1981-82 season.

FIRST-ROUND ENTRY DRAFT CHOICES

Year Player, Overall, Last amateur team (league)
1976—Paul Gardner, 11, Oshawa (OHL)
1977—Barry Beck, 2, New Westminster (WCHL)
1978—Mike Gillis, 5, Kingston (OHL)
1979—Rob Ramage, 1, Birmingham (WHA)*
1980—Paul Gagne, 19, Windsor (OHL)
1981—Joe Cirella, 5, Oshawa (OHL)
*Designates first player chosen in draft.

SINGLE-SEASON INDIVIDUAL RECORDS

FORWARDS/DEFENSEMEN

Most goals
41—Wilf Paiement, 1976-77

Most assists
56—Wilf Paiement, 1977-78

Most points
87—Wilf Paiement, 1977-78

Most penalty minutes
201—Rob Ramage, 1981-82

Most power play goals
14—Paul Gardner, 1978-79

Most shorthanded goals
5—Wilf Paiement, 1976-77

Most games with three or more goals
1—Held by many players

Most shots
298—Lanny McDonald, 1980-81

GOALTENDERS

Most games
61—Chico Resch, 1981-82

Most minutes
3,424—Chico Resch, 1981-82

Most goals allowed
230—Chico Resch, 1981-82

Lowest goals-against average
3.49—Bill McKechnie, 1979-80

Most shutouts
1—Held by many goaltenders

Most wins
16—Chico Resch, 1981-82

Most losses
31—Chico Resch, 1981-82

Most ties
11—Chico Resch, 1981-82
Doug Favell, 1977-78

FRANCHISE LEADERS

FORWARDS/DEFENSEMEN

Games

Mike Kitchen 354
Ron Delorme 314
Wilf Paiement 257
Randy Pierce 240
Gary Croteau 234
Rob Ramage 234

Goals

Wilf Paiement 106
Paul Gardner 83
Ron Delorme 66
Lanny McDonald 66
Gary Croteau 65

Assists

Wilf Paiement 148
Rob Ramage 91
Merlin Malinowski 86
Paul Gardner 77
Lanny McDonald 75

Points

Wilf Paiement 254
Paul Gardner 160
Lanny McDonald 141
Gary Croteau 136
Merlin Malinowski 132
Rob Ramage 132

Penalty minutes

Rob Ramage 529
Wilf Paiement 336
Mike Kitchen 294
Ron Delorme 284
Randy Pierce 206

GOALTENDERS

Games

Michel Plasse 126
Doug Favell 84
Hardy Astrom 79
Chico Resch 69
Bill Oleschuk 54

Shutouts

Doug Favell 1
Bill McKenzie 1
Bill Oleschuk 1

Goals-against average (2400 minutes minimum)

Hardy Astrom 3.77
Doug Favell 3.82
Michel Plasse 3.91
Chico Resch 3.97
Bill Oleschuk 4.00

Wins

Michel Plasse 24
Doug Favell 21
Chico Resch 18
Hardy Astrom 15
Bill McKenzie 12

DALLAS STARS

YEAR-BY-YEAR RECORDS

	REGULAR SEASON					PLAYOFFS			
Season	W	L	T	Pts.	Finish	W	L	Highest round	Coach
1993-94	42	29	13	97	3rd/Central	5	4	Conference semifinals	Bob Gainey
1994-95	17	23	8	42	5th/Central	1	4	Conference quarterfinals	Bob Gainey
1995-96	26	42	14	66	6th/Central	—	—		Bob Gainey, Ken Hitchcock
1996-97	48	26	8	104	1st/Central	3	4	Conference quarterfinals	Ken Hitchcock
1997-98	49	22	11	109	1st/Central	10	7	Conference finals	Ken Hitchcock
1998-99	51	19	12	114	1st/Pacific	16	7	Stanley Cup champ	Ken Hitchcock

Franchise was formerly known as Minnesota North Stars and relocated to Dallas following 1992-93 season.

FIRST-ROUND ENTRY DRAFT CHOICES

Year Player, Overall, Last amateur team (league)

1993—Todd Harvey, 9, Detroit (OHL)
1994—Jason Botterill, 20, Michigan (CCHA)
1995—Jarome Iginla, 11, Kamloops (WHL)
1996—Richard Jackman, 5, Sault Ste. Marie (OHL)

Year Player, Overall, Last amateur team (league)

1997—Brenden Morrow, 25, Portland (WHL)
1998—No first-round selection
1999—No first-round selection

SINGLE-SEASON INDIVIDUAL RECORDS

FORWARDS/DEFENSEMEN

Most goals
50—Mike Modano, 1993-94

Most assists
57—Russ Courtnall, 1993-94

Most points
93—Mike Modano, 1993-94

Most penalty minutes
333—Shane Churla, 1993-94

Most power play goals
18—Mike Modano, 1993-94

Most shorthanded goals
5—Mike Modano, 1996-97
Mike Modano, 1997-98

Most games with three or more goals
3—Mike Modano, 1998-99

Most shots
320—Mike Modano, 1995-96

GOALTENDERS

Most games
61—Ed Belfour, 1997-98
Ed Belfour, 1998-99

Most minutes
3,581—Ed Belfour, 1997-98

Most shots against
1,604—Andy Moog, 1993-94

Most goals allowed
170—Andy Moog, 1993-94

Lowest goals-against average
1.88—Ed Belfour, 1997-98

Most shutouts
9—Ed Belfour, 1997-98

Most wins
37—Ed Belfour, 1997-98

Most losses
20—Andy Moog, 1993-94

Most ties
10—Ed Belfour, 1997-98

FRANCHISE LEADERS

Players in boldface played for club in '98-99

FORWARDS/DEFENSEMEN

Games

Craig Ludwig ... **433**
Derian Hatcher ... **418**
Mike Modano ... **393**
Richard Matvichuk ... **307**
Guy Carbonneau ... **295**

Goals

Mike Modano ... **188**
Joe Nieuwendyk ... **111**
Jere Lehtinen ... **65**
Pat Verbeek ... **65**
Greg Adams ... 60
Dave Gagner ... 60

Assists

Mike Modano ... **238**
Derian Hatcher ... **118**
Sergei Zubov ... **118**
Darryl Sydor ... **115**
Jere Lehtinen ... **100**

Points

Mike Modano ... **426**
Joe Nieuwendyk ... **207**
Jere Lehtinen ... **165**
Derian Hatcher ... **161**
Sergei Zubov ... **151**

Penalty minutes

Derian Hatcher ... **776**
Shane Churla ... 687
Craig Ludwig ... **534**
Todd Harvey ... **449**
Pat Verbeek ... **431**

GOALTENDERS

Games

Andy Moog ... 175
Ed Belfour ... **122**
Darcy Wakaluk ... 88
Roman Turek ... **55**
Arturs Irbe ... 35

Shutouts

Ed Belfour ... **14**
Andy Moog ... 8
Darcy Wakaluk ... 6
Arturs Irbe ... 3
Roman Turek ... **2**

Goals-against average (2400 minutes minimum)

Ed Belfour ... **1.93**
Roman Turek ... **2.14**
Andy Moog ... 2.75
Darcy Wakaluk ... 3.21

Wins

Andy Moog ... 75
Ed Belfour ... **72**
Darcy Wakaluk ... 31
Roman Turek ... **30**
Arturs Irbe ... 17

DETROIT RED WINGS

YEAR-BY-YEAR RECORDS

	REGULAR SEASON					PLAYOFFS			
Season	W	L	T	Pts.	Finish	W	L	Highest round	Coach
1926-27†	12	28	4	28	5th/American	—	—		Art Duncan, Duke Keats
1927-28†	19	19	6	44	4th/American	—	—		Jack Adams
1928-29†	19	16	9	47	3rd/American	0	2	Quarterfinals	Jack Adams
1929-30†	14	24	6	34	4th/American	—	—		Jack Adams
1930-31‡	16	21	7	39	4th/American	—	—		Jack Adams
1931-32‡	18	20	10	46	3rd/American	*0	1	Quarterfinals	Jack Adams
1932-33	25	15	8	58	2nd/American	2	2	Semifinals	Jack Adams
1933-34	24	14	10	58	1st/American	4	5	Stanley Cup finals	Jack Adams
1934-35	19	22	7	45	4th/American	—	—		Jack Adams
1935-36	24	16	8	56	1st/American	6	1	Stanley Cup champ	Jack Adams
1936-37	25	14	9	59	1st/American	6	4	Stanley Cup champ	Jack Adams
1937-38	12	25	11	35	4th/American	—	—		Jack Adams
1938-39	18	24	6	42	5th	3	3	Semifinals	Jack Adams
1939-40	16	26	6	38	5th	2	3	Semifinals	Jack Adams
1940-41	21	16	11	53	3rd	4	5	Stanley Cup finals	Jack Adams
1941-42	19	25	4	42	5th	7	5	Stanley Cup finals	Jack Adams
1942-43	25	14	11	61	1st	8	2	Stanley Cup champ	Jack Adams
1943-44	26	18	6	58	2nd	1	4	League semifinals	Jack Adams
1944-45	31	14	5	67	2nd	7	7	Stanley Cup finals	Jack Adams
1945-46	20	20	10	50	4th	1	4	League semifinals	Jack Adams
1946-47	22	27	11	55	4th	1	4	League semifinals	Jack Adams
1947-48	30	18	12	72	2nd	4	6	Stanley Cup finals	Tommy Ivan
1948-49	34	19	7	75	1st	4	7	Stanley Cup finals	Tommy Ivan
1949-50	37	19	14	88	1st	8	6	Stanley Cup champ	Tommy Ivan
1950-51	44	13	13	101	1st	2	4	League semifinals	Tommy Ivan
1951-52	44	14	12	100	1st	8	0	Stanley Cup champ	Tommy Ivan
1952-53	36	16	18	90	1st	2	4	League semifinals	Tommy Ivan
1953-54	37	19	14	88	1st	8	4	Stanley Cup champ	Tommy Ivan
1954-55	42	17	11	95	1st	8	3	Stanley Cup champ	Jimmy Skinner
1955-56	30	24	16	76	2nd	5	5	Stanley Cup finals	Jimmy Skinner
1956-57	38	20	12	88	1st	1	4	League semifinals	Jimmy Skinner
1957-58	29	29	12	70	3rd	0	4	League semifinals	Jimmy Skinner, Sid Abel
1958-59	25	37	8	58	6th	—	—		Sid Abel
1959-60	26	29	15	67	4th	2	4	League semifinals	Sid Abel
1960-61	25	29	16	66	4th	6	5	Stanley Cup finals	Sid Abel
1961-62	23	33	14	60	5th	—	—		Sid Abel
1962-63	32	25	13	77	4th	5	6	Stanley Cup finals	Sid Abel
1963-64	30	29	11	71	4th	7	7	Stanley Cup finals	Sid Abel
1964-65	40	23	7	87	1st	3	4	League semifinals	Sid Abel
1965-66	31	27	12	74	4th	6	6	Stanley Cup finals	Sid Abel

	REGULAR SEASON					PLAYOFFS			
Season	W	L	T	Pts.	Finish	W	L	Highest round	Coach
1966-67	27	39	4	58	5th	—	—		Sid Abel
1967-68	27	35	12	66	6th/East	—	—		Sid Abel
1968-69	33	31	12	78	5th/East	—	—		Bill Gadsby
1969-70	40	21	15	95	3rd/East	0	4	Division semifinals	Bill Gadsby, Sid Abel
1970-71	22	45	11	55	7th/East	—	—		Ned Harkness, Doug Barkley
1971-72	33	35	10	76	5th/East	—	—		Doug Barkley, Johnny Wilson
1972-73	37	29	12	86	5th/East	—	—		Johnny Wilson
1973-74	29	39	10	68	6th/East	—	—		Ted Garvin, Alex Delvecchio
1974-75	23	45	12	58	4th/Norris	—	—		Alex Delvecchio
1975-76	26	44	10	62	4th/Norris	—	—		Ted Garvin, Alex Delvecchio
1976-77	16	55	9	41	5th/Norris	—	—		Alex Delvecchio, Larry Wilson
1977-78	32	34	14	78	2nd/Norris	3	4	Quarterfinals	Bobby Kromm
1978-79	23	41	16	62	5th/Norris	—	—		Bobby Kromm
1979-80	26	43	11	63	5th/Norris	—	—		Bobby Kromm, Ted Lindsay
1980-81	19	43	18	56	5th/Norris	—	—		Ted Lindsay, Wayne Maxner
1981-82	21	47	12	54	6th/Norris	—	—		Wayne Maxner, Billy Dea
1982-83	21	44	15	57	5th/Norris	—	—		Nick Polano
1983-84	31	42	7	69	3rd/Norris	1	3	Division semifinals	Nick Polano
1984-85	27	41	12	66	3rd/Norris	0	3	Division semifinals	Nick Polano
1985-86	17	57	6	40	5th/Norris	—	—		Harry Neale, Brad Park, Dan Belisle
1986-87	34	36	10	78	2nd/Norris	9	7	Conference finals	Jacques Demers
1987-88	41	28	11	93	1st/Norris	9	7	Conference finals	Jacques Demers
1988-89	34	34	12	80	1st/Norris	2	4	Division semifinals	Jacques Demers
1989-90	28	38	14	70	5th/Norris	—	—		Jacques Demers
1990-91	34	38	8	76	3rd/Norris	3	4	Division semifinals	Bryan Murray
1991-92	43	25	12	98	1st/Norris	4	7	Division finals	Bryan Murray
1992-93	47	28	9	103	2nd/Norris	3	4	Division semifinals	Bryan Murray
1993-94	46	30	8	100	1st/Central	3	4	Division semifinals	Scotty Bowman
1994-95	33	11	4	70	1st/Central	12	6	Stanley Cup finals	Scotty Bowman
1995-96	62	13	7	131	1st/Central	10	9	Conference finals	Scotty Bowman
1996-97	38	26	18	94	2nd/Central	16	4	Stanley Cup champ	Scotty Bowman
1997-98	44	23	15	103	2nd/Central	16	6	Stanley Cup champ	Scotty Bowman
1998-99	43	32	7	93	1st/Central	6	4	Conference semifinals	Scotty Bowman

*Won-lost record does not indicate tie(s) resulting from two-game, total goals series that year (two-game, total-goals series were played from 1917-18 through 1935-36).

†Detroit Cougars.

‡Detroit Falcons.

FIRST-ROUND ENTRY DRAFT CHOICES

Year Player, Overall, Last amateur team (league)

1969—Jim Rutherford, 10, Hamilton (OHL)
1970—Serge Lajeunesse, 12, Montreal (OHL)
1971—Marcel Dionne, 2, St. Catharines (OHL)
1972—No first-round selection
1973—Terry Richardson, 11, New Westminster (WCHL)
1974—Bill Lochead, 9, Oshawa (OHL)
1975—Rick Lapointe, 5, Victoria (WCHL)
1976—Fred Williams, 4, Saskatoon (WCHL)
1977—Dale McCourt, 1, St. Catharines (OHL)*
1978—Willie Huber, 9, Hamilton (OHL)
Brent Peterson, 12, Portland (WCHL)
1979—Mike Foligno, 3, Sudbury (OHL)
1980—Mike Blaisdell, 11, Regina (WHL)
1981—No first-round selection
1982—Murray Craven, 17, Medicine Hat (WHL)
1983—Steve Yzerman, 4, Peterborough (OHL)
1984—Shawn Burr, 7, Kitchener (OHL)

Year Player, Overall, Last amateur team (league)

1985—Brent Fedyk, 8, Regina (WHL)
1986—Joe Murphy, 1, Michigan State University*
1987—Yves Racine, 11, Longueuil (QMJHL)
1988—Kory Kocur, 17, Saskatoon (WHL)
1989—Mike Sillinger, 11, Regina (WHL)
1990—Keith Primeau, 3, Niagara Falls (OHL)
1991—Martin Lapointe, 10, Laval (QMJHL)
1992—Curtis Bowen, 22, Ottawa (OHL)
1993—Anders Eriksson, 22, MoDo (Sweden)
1994—Yan Golvbovsky, 23, Dynamo Moscow, CIS
1995—Maxim Kuznetsov, 26, Dynamo Moscow, CIS
1996—Jesse Wallin, 26, Red Deer (WHL)
1997—No first-round selection
1998—Jiri Fischer, 25, Hull (QMJHL)
1999—No first-round selection
*Designates first player chosen in draft.

SINGLE-SEASON INDIVIDUAL RECORDS

FORWARDS/DEFENSEMEN

Most goals
65—Steve Yzerman, 1988-89

Most assists
90—Steve Yzerman, 1988-89

Most points
155—Steve Yzerman, 1988-89

Most penalty minutes
398—Bob Probert, 1987-88

Most power play goals
21—Mickey Redmond, 1973-74
Dino Ciccarelli, 1992-93

Most shorthanded goals
10—Marcel Dionne, 1974-75

Most games with three or more goals
4—Frank Mahovlich, 1968-69
Steve Yzerman, 1990-91

Most shots
388—Steve Yzerman, 1988-89

GOALTENDERS

Most games
72—Tim Cheveldae, 1991-92

Most minutes
4,236—Tim Cheveldae, 1991-92

Most goals allowed
226—Tim Cheveldae, 1991-92

Lowest goals-against average
1.43—Dolly Dodson, 1928-29

Most shutouts
12—Terry Sawchuk, 1951-52
Terry Sawchuk, 1953-54
Terry Sawchuk, 1954-55
Glenn Hall, 1955-56

Most wins
44—Terry Sawchuk, 1950-51
Terry Sawchuk, 1951-52

FRANCHISE LEADERS

Players in boldface played for club in '98-99

FORWARDS/DEFENSEMEN

Games

Gordie Howe	1687
Alex Delvecchio	1549
Steve Yzerman	**1178**
Marcel Pronovost	983
Norm Ullman	875

Goals

Gordie Howe	786
Steve Yzerman	**592**
Alex Delvecchio	456
Ted Lindsay	335
Norm Ullman	324

Assists

Gordie Howe	1023
Steve Yzerman	**891**
Alex Delvecchio	825
Norm Ullman	434
Ted Lindsay	393

Points

Gordie Howe	1809
Steve Yzerman	**1483**
Alex Delvecchio	1281
Norm Ullman	758
Ted Lindsay	728

GOALTENDERS

Games

Terry Sawchuk	734
Harry Lumley	324
Jim Rutherford	314
Roger Crozier	310
Greg Stefan	299

Shutouts

Terry Sawchuk	85
Harry Lumley	26
Chris Osgood	**23**
Roger Crozier	20
Clarence Dolson	17
Glenn Hall	17
Harry Holmes	17
Norm Smith	17

Goals-against average (2400 minutes minimum)

Clarence Dolson	2.06
Harry Holmes	2.11
Glenn Hall	2.14
Alex Connell	2.25
John Ross Roach	2.26

Wins

Terry Sawchuk	352
Chris Osgood	**166**
Harry Lumley	163
Roger Crozier	130
Tim Cheveldae	128

EDMONTON OILERS

YEAR-BY-YEAR RECORDS

	REGULAR SEASON					PLAYOFFS			
Season	W	L	T	Pts.	Finish	W	L	Highest round	Coach
1972-73*	38	37	3	79	5th	—	—		Ray Kinasewich
1973-74†	38	37	3	79	3rd	1	4	League quarterfinals	Brian Shaw
1974-75†	36	38	4	76	5th	—	—		Brian Shaw, Bill Hunter
1975-76†	27	49	5	59	4th	0	4	League quarterfinals	Clare Drake, Bill Hunter
1976-77†	34	43	4	72	4th	1	4	League quarterfinals	Bep Guidolin, Glen Sather
1977-78†	38	39	3	79	5th	1	4	League quarterfinals	Glen Sather
1978-79†	48	30	2	98	1st	6	7	Avco World Cup finals	Glen Sather
1979-80	28	39	13	69	4th/Smythe	0	3	Preliminaries	Glen Sather
1980-81	29	35	16	74	4th/Smythe	5	4	Quarterfinals	Glen Sather
1981-82	48	17	15	111	1st/Smythe	2	3	Division semifinals	Glen Sather
1982-83	47	21	12	106	1st/Smythe	11	5	Stanley Cup finals	Glen Sather
1983-84	57	18	5	119	1st/Smythe	15	4	Stanley Cup champ	Glen Sather
1984-85	49	20	11	109	1st/Smythe	15	3	Stanley Cup champ	Glen Sather
1985-86	56	17	7	119	1st/Smythe	6	4	Division finals	Glen Sather
1986-87	50	24	6	106	1st/Smythe	16	5	Stanley Cup champ	Glen Sather
1987-88	44	25	11	99	2nd/Smythe	16	2	Stanley Cup champ	Glen Sather
1988-89	38	34	8	84	3rd/Smythe	3	4	Division semifinals	Glen Sather
1989-90	38	28	14	90	2nd/Smythe	16	6	Stanley Cup champ	John Muckler
1990-91	37	37	6	80	3rd/Smythe	9	9	Conference finals	John Muckler
1991-92	36	34	10	82	3rd/Smythe	8	8	Conference finals	Ted Green
1992-93	26	50	8	60	5th/Smythe	—	—		Ted Green
1993-94	25	45	14	64	6th/Pacific	—	—		Ted Green, Glen Sather
1994-95	17	27	4	38	5th/Pacific	—	—		George Burnett, Ron Low
1995-96	30	44	8	68	5th/Pacific	—	—		Ron Low
1996-97	36	37	9	81	3rd/Pacific	5	7	Conference semifinals	Ron Low
1997-98	35	37	10	80	3rd/Pacific	5	7	Conference semifinals	Ron Low
1998-99	33	37	12	78	2nd/Northwest	0	4	Conference quarterfinals	Ron Low

*Alberta Oilers, members of World Hockey Association.
†Members of World Hockey Association.

FIRST-ROUND ENTRY DRAFT CHOICES

Year	Player, Overall, Last amateur team (league)
1979	Kevin Lowe, 21, Quebec (QMJHL)
1980	Paul Coffey, 6, Kitchener (OHL)
1981	Grant Fuhr, 8, Victoria (WHL)
1982	Jim Playfair, 20, Portland (WHL)
1983	Jeff Beukeboom, 19, Sault Ste. Marie (OHL)
1984	Selmar Odelein, 21, Regina (WHL)
1985	Scott Metcalfe, 20, Kingston (OHL)
1986	Kim Issel, 21, Prince Albert (WHL)
1987	Peter Soberlak, 21, Swift Current (WHL)
1988	Francois Leroux, 19, St. Jean (QMJHL)
1989	Jason Soules, 15, Niagara Falls (OHL)
1990	Scott Allison, 17, Prince Albert (WHL)
1991	Tyler Wright, 12, Swift Current (WHL)
	Martin Rucinsky, 20, Litvinov (Czech.)
1992	Joe Hulbig, 13, St. Sebastian H.S. (Mass.)
1993	Jason Arnott, 7, Oshawa (OHL)
	Nick Stajduhar, 16, London (OHL)
1994	Jason Bonsignore, 4, Niagara Falls (OHL)
	Ryan Smyth, 6, Moose Jaw (WHL)
1995	Steve Kelly, 6, Prince Albert (WHL)
1996	Boyd Devereaux, 6, Kitchener (OHL)
	Matthieu Descoteaux, 19, Shawinigan (QMJHL)
1997	Michel Riessen, 14, HC Biel (Switzerland)
1998	Michael Henrich, 13, Barrie (OHL)
1999	Jani Rita, 13, Jokerit Helsinki, Finland

NOTE: Edmonton chose Dave Dryden, Bengt Gustafsson and Ed Mio as priority selections before the 1979 expansion draft.

SINGLE-SEASON INDIVIDUAL RECORDS

FORWARDS/DEFENSEMEN

Most goals
92—Wayne Gretzky, 1981-82

Most assists
163—Wayne Gretzky, 1985-86

Most points
215—Wayne Gretzky, 1985-86

Most penalty minutes
286—Steve Smith, 1987-88

Most power play goals
20—Wayne Gretzky, 1983-84
Ryan Smyth, 1996-97

Most shorthanded goals
12—Wayne Gretzky, 1983-84

Most games with three or more goals
10—Wayne Gretzky, 1981-82
Wayne Gretzky, 1983-84

Most shots
369—Wayne Gretzky, 1981-82

GOALTENDERS

Most games
75—Grant Fuhr, 1987-88

Most minutes
4,304—Grant Fuhr, 1987-88

Most goals allowed
246—Grant Fuhr, 1987-88

Lowest goals-against average
2.63—Curtis Joseph, 1997-98

Most shutouts
8—Curtis Joseph, 1997-98

Most wins
40—Grant Fuhr, 1987-88

Most losses
38—Bill Ranford, 1992-93

Most ties
14—Grant Fuhr, 1981-82

FRANCHISE LEADERS

Players in boldface played for club in '98-99

FORWARDS/DEFENSEMEN

Games

Kevin Lowe	1037
Mark Messier	851
Glenn Anderson	828
Kelly Buchberger	**795**
Jari Kurri	754

Goals

Wayne Gretzky	583
Jari Kurri	474
Glenn Anderson	413
Mark Messier	392
Paul Coffey	209

Assists

Wayne Gretzky	1086
Mark Messier	642
Jari Kurri	569
Glenn Anderson	483
Paul Coffey	460

Points

Wayne Gretzky	1669
Jari Kurri	1043
Mark Messier	1034
Glenn Anderson	896
Paul Coffey	669

Penalty minutes

Kelly Buchberger	**1647**
Kevin McClelland	1298
Kevin Lowe	1236
Mark Messier	1122
Steve Smith	1080

GOALTENDERS

Games

Bill Ranford	433
Grant Fuhr	423
Andy Moog	235
Curtis Joseph	177
Eddie Mio	77

Shutouts

Curtis Joseph	14
Grant Fuhr	9
Bill Ranford	8
Andy Moog	4
Mikhail Shtalenkov	**3**

Goals-against average (2400 minutes minimum)

Bob Essensa	**2.73**
Curtis Joseph	2.90
Bill Ranford	3.51
Andy Moog	3.61
Grant Fuhr	3.69

Wins

Grant Fuhr	226
Bill Ranford	163
Andy Moog	143
Curtis Joseph	76
Ron Low	30

FLORIDA PANTHERS

YEAR-BY-YEAR RECORDS

	REGULAR SEASON					PLAYOFFS			
Season	W	L	T	Pts.	Finish	W	L	Highest round	Coach
1993-94	33	34	17	83	5th/Atlantic	—	—		Roger Neilson
1994-95	20	22	6	46	5th/Atlantic	—	—		Roger Neilson
1995-96	41	31	10	92	3rd/Atlantic	12	10	Stanley Cup finals	Doug MacLean

Season	W	L	T	Pts.	Finish	W	L	Highest round	Coach
	REGULAR SEASON					PLAYOFFS			
1996-97	35	28	19	89	3rd/Atlantic	1	4	Conference quarterfinals	Doug MacLean
1997-98	24	43	15	63	6th/Atlantic	—	—		Doug MacLean, Bryan Murray
1998-99	30	34	18	78	2nd/Southeast	—	—		Terry Murray

FIRST-ROUND ENTRY DRAFT CHOICES

Year Player, Overall, Last amateur team (league)
1993—Rob Niedermayer, 5, Medicine Hat (WHL)
1994—Ed Jovanovski, 1, Windsor (OHL)*
1995—Radek Dvorak, 10, Budejovice, Czech Republic
1996—Marcus Nilson, 20, Djurgarden-Stockholm, Sweden
1997—Mike Brown, 20, Red Deer (WHL)
1998—No first-round selection
1999—Denis Shvidki, 12, Barrie (OHL)
*Designates first player chosen in draft.

SINGLE-SEASON INDIVIDUAL RECORDS

FORWARDS/DEFENSEMEN

Most goals
32—Scott Mellanby, 1995-96
Ray Whitney, 1997-98

Most assists
49—Robert Svehla, 1995-96

Most points
70—Scott Mellanby, 1995-96

Most penalty minutes
313—Paul Laus, 1996-97

Most power play goals
19—Scott Mellanby, 1995-96

Most shorthanded goals
6—Tom Fitzgerald, 1995-96

Most games with three or more goals
3—Ray Sheppard, 1996-97

Most shots
226—Ray Sheppard, 1996-97

GOALTENDERS

Most games
60—John Vanbiesbrouck, 1996-97

Most minutes
3,451—John Vanbiesbrouck, 1997-98

Most shots against
1,912—John Vanbiesbrouck, 1993-94

Most goals allowed
165—John Vanbiesbrouck, 1997-98

Lowest goals-against average
2.29—John Vanbiesbrouck, 1996-97

Most shutouts
4—John Vanbiesbrouck, 1994-95
John Vanbiesbrouck, 1997-98

Most wins
27—John Vanbiesbrouck, 1996-97

Most losses
29—John Vanbiesbrouck, 1997-98

Most ties
11—Sean Burke, 1998-99

FRANCHISE LEADERS

Players in boldface played for club in '98-99

FORWARDS/DEFENSEMEN

Games
Bill Lindsay ... **368**
Scott Mellanby ... **368**
Gord Murphy ... **359**
Tom Fitzgerald ... **353**
Paul Laus ... **308**

Goals
Scott Mellanby ... **117**
Jody Hull ... **56**
Rob Niedermayer ... **61**
Tom Fitzgerald ... **54**
Bill Lindsay ... **51**
Ray Sheppard ... **51**

Assists
Scott Mellanby ... **133**
Robert Svehla ... **116**
Gord Murphy ... **93**
Rob Niedermayer ... **89**
Bill Lindsay ... **76**

Points
Scott Mellanby ... **250**
Rob Niedermayer ... **150**
Robert Svehla ... **147**
Gord Murphy ... **135**
Bill Lindsay ... **127**

Penalty minutes
Paul Laus ... **1089**
Scott Mellanby ... **696**
Ed Jovanovski ... **467**
Brian Skrudland ... 401
Bill Lindsay ... **400**

GOALTENDERS

Games
John Vanbiesbrouck ... 268
Mark Fitzpatrick ... 119
Sean Burke ... **59**
Kirk McLean ... **37**
Kevin Weekes ... 11

Shutouts
John Vanbiesbrouck ... 13
Mark Fitzpatrick ... 4
Sean Burke ... **3**
Kirk McLean ... **2**

Goals-against average (2400 minutes minimum)
John Vanbiesbrouck ... 2.58
Sean Burke ... **2.66**
Mark Fitzpatrick ... 2.71

Wins
John Vanbiesbrouck ... 106
Mark Fitzpatrick ... 43
Sean Burke ... **21**
Kirk McLean ... **13**

HAMILTON TIGERS (DEFUNCT)

YEAR-BY-YEAR RECORDS

Season	W	L	T	Pts.	Finish	W	L	Highest round	Coach
	REGULAR SEASON					PLAYOFFS			
1920-21	6	18	0	12	4th	—	—		Percy Thompson
1921-22	7	17	0	14	4th	—	—		Percy Thompson
1922-23	6	18	0	12	4th	—	—		Art Ross
1923-24	9	15	0	18	4th	—	—		Percy Lesueur
1924-25	19	10	1	39	1st	*—	—		Jimmy Gardner

*Refused to participate in playoffs—held out for more compensation.

Franchise was formerly known as Quebec Bulldogs and relocated to Hamilton following 1919-20 season; franchise relocated and became New York Americans following 1924-1925 season.

HARTFORD WHALERS (DEFUNCT)

YEAR-BY-YEAR RECORDS

	REGULAR SEASON					PLAYOFFS			
Season	W	L	T	Pts.	Finish	W	L	Highest round	Coach
1972-73*	46	30	2	94	1st	12	3	Avco World Cup champ	Jack Kelley
1973-74*	43	31	4	90	1st	3	4	League quarterfinals	Ron Ryan
1974-75*	43	30	5	91	1st	2	4	League quarterfinals	Ron Ryan, Jack Kelley
1975-76*	33	40	7	73	3rd	6	4	League semifinals	Jack Kelley, Don Blackburn, Harry Neale
1976-77*	35	40	6	76	4th	1	4	League quarterfinals	Harry Neale
1977-78*	44	31	5	93	2nd	8	6	Avco World Cup finals	Harry Neale
1978-79*	37	34	9	83	4th	5	5	League semifinals	Bill Dineen, Don Blackburn
1979-80	27	34	19	73	4th/Norris	0	3	Preliminaries	Don Blackburn
1980-81	21	41	18	60	4th/Norris	—	—		Don Blackburn, Larry Pleau
1981-82	21	41	18	60	5th/Adams	—	—		Larry Pleau
1982-83	19	54	7	45	5th/Adams	—	—		Larry Kish, Larry Pleau, John Cunniff
1983-84	28	42	10	66	5th/Adams	—	—		Jack Evans
1984-85	30	41	9	69	5th/Adams	—	—		Jack Evans
1985-86	40	36	4	84	4th/Adams	6	4	Division finals	Jack Evans
1986-87	43	30	7	93	1st/Adams	2	4	Division semifinals	Jack Evans
1987-88	35	38	7	77	4th/Adams	2	4	Division semifinals	Jack Evans, Larry Pleau
1988-89	37	38	5	79	4th/Adams	0	4	Division semifinals	Larry Pleau
1989-90	38	33	9	85	4th/Adams	3	4	Division semifinals	Rick Ley
1990-91	31	38	11	73	4th/Adams	2	4	Division semifinals	Rick Ley
1991-92	26	41	13	65	4th/Adams	3	4	Division semifinals	Jim Roberts
1992-93	26	52	6	58	5th/Adams	—	—		Paul Holmgren
1993-94	27	48	9	63	6th/Northeast	—	—		Paul Holmgren, Pierre McGuire
1994-95	19	24	5	43	5th/Northeast	—	—		Paul Holmgren
1995-96	34	39	9	77	4th/Northeast	—	—		Paul Holmgren, Paul Maurice
1996-97	32	39	11	75	5th/Northeast	—	—		Paul Maurice

*New England Whalers, members of World Hockey Association.

Franchise relocated and became Carolina Hurricanes following 1996-97 season.

FIRST-ROUND ENTRY DRAFT CHOICES

Year Player, Overall, Last amateur team (league)

1979—Ray Allison, 18, Brandon (WHL)
1980—Fred Arthur, 8, Cornwall (QMJHL)
1981—Ron Francis, 4, Sault Ste. Marie (OHL)
1982—Paul Lawless, 14, Windsor (OHL)
1983—Sylvain Turgeon, 2, Hull (QMJHL)
David A. Jensen, 20, Lawrence Academy (Mass.)
1984—Sylvain Cote, 11, Quebec (QMJHL)
1985—Dana Murzyn, 5, Calgary (WHL)
1986—Scott Young, 11, Boston University
1987—Jody Hull, 18, Peterborough (OHL)
1988—Chris Govedaris, 11, Toronto (OHL)

Year Player, Overall, Last amateur team (league)

1989—Robert Holik, 10, Jihlava (Czechoslovakia)
1990—Mark Greig, 15, Lethbridge (WHL)
1991—Patrick Poulin, 9, St. Hyacinthe (QMJHL)
1992—Robert Petrovicky, 9, Dukla Trencin (Czech.)
1993—Chris Pronger, 2, Peterborough (OHL)
1994—Jeff O'Neill, 5, Guelph (OHL)
1995—Jean-Sebastien Giguere, 13, Halifax (QMJHL)
1996—No first-round selection
1997—Nikos Tselios, 22, Belleville (OHL)

NOTE: Hartford chose Jordy Douglas, John Garrett and Mark Howe as priority selections before the 1979 expansion draft.

SINGLE-SEASON INDIVIDUAL RECORDS

FORWARDS/DEFENSEMEN

Most goals
56—Blaine Stoughton, 1979-80

Most assists
69—Ron Francis, 1989-90

Most points
105—Mike Rogers, 1979-80
Mike Rogers, 1980-81

Most penalty minutes
358—Torrie Robertson, 1985-86

Most power play goals
21—Geoff Sanderson, 1992-93

Most shorthanded goals
4—Mike Rogers, 1980-81
Kevin Dineen, 1984-85

Most games with three or more goals
3—Mike Rogers, 1980-81
Blaine Stoughton, 1981-82

GOALTENDERS

Most games
66—Sean Burke, 1995-96

Most minutes
3,669—Sean Burke, 1995-96

Most goals allowed
282—Greg Millen, 1982-83

Lowest goals-against average
2.64—Mike Liut, 1989-90

Most shutouts
4—Mike Liut, 1986-87
Peter Sidorkiewicz, 1988-89
Sean Burke, 1995-96
Sean Burke, 1996-97

Most wins
31—Mike Liut, 1986-87

Most losses
38—Greg Millen, 1982-83

Most ties
12—John Garrett, 1980-81
Greg Millen, 1982-83

FRANCHISE LEADERS

FORWARDS/DEFENSEMEN

Games

Ron Francis	714
Kevin Dineen	587
Adam Burt	499
Dave Tippett	483
Ulf Samuelsson	463

Goals

Ron Francis	264
Kevin Dineen	235
Blaine Stoughton	219
Pat Verbeek	192
Geoff Sanderson	189

Assists

Ron Francis	557
Kevin Dineen	268
Andrew Cassels	253
Pat Verbeek	211
Dave Babych	196

Points

Ron Francis	821
Kevin Dineen	503
Pat Verbeek	403
Blaine Stoughton	377
Geoff Sanderson	352

Penalty minutes

Torrie Robertson	1368
Kevin Dineen	1239
Pat Verbeek	1144
Ulf Samuelsson	1108
Adam Burt	723

GOALTENDERS

Games

Sean Burke	256
Mike Liut	252
Greg Millen	219
Peter Sidorkiewicz	178
John Garrett	122

Shutouts

Mike Liut	13
Sean Burke	10
Peter Sidorkiewicz	8
Greg Millen	4
Steve Weeks	4

Goals-against average
(2400 minutes minimum)

Sean Burke	3.12
Jason Muzzatti	3.23
Peter Sidorkiewicz	3.33
Mike Liut	3.36
Kay Whitmore	3.61

Wins

Mike Liut	115
Sean Burke	101
Peter Sidorkiewicz	71
Greg Millen	62
Steve Weeks	42

KANSAS CITY SCOUTS (DEFUNCT)

YEAR-BY-YEAR RECORDS

	REGULAR SEASON					PLAYOFFS			
Season	W	L	T	Pts.	Finish	W	L	Highest round	Coach
1974-75	15	54	11	41	5th/Smythe	—	—		Bep Guidolin
1975-76	12	56	12	36	5th/Smythe	—	—		Bep Guidolin, Sid Abel, Eddie Bush

Franchise relocated and became Colorado Rockies following 1975-76 season; franchise later relocated and became New Jersey Devils after 1981-82 season.

FIRST-ROUND ENTRY DRAFT CHOICES

Year Player, Overall, Last amateur team (league)
1974—Wilf Paiement, 2, St. Catharines (OHL)

Year Player, Overall, Last amateur team (league)
1975—Barry Dean, 2, Medicine Hat (WCHL)

SINGLE-SEASON INDIVIDUAL RECORDS

FORWARDS/DEFENSEMEN

Most goals
27—Guy Charron, 1975-76

Most assists
44—Guy Charron, 1975-76

Most points
71—Guy Charron, 1975-76

Most penalty minutes
209—Steve Durbano, 1975-76

Most power play goals
11—Simon Nolet, 1974-75

Most shorthanded goals
2—Ed Gilbert, 1974-75
Simon Nolet, 1974-75

Most games with three or more goals
1—Wilf Paiement, 1975-76

Most shots
226—Guy Charron, 1975-76

GOALTENDERS

Most games
64—Denis Herron, 1975-76

Most minutes
3,620—Denis Herron, 1975-76

Most goals allowed
243—Denis Herron, 1975-76

Lowest goals-against average
4.03—Denis Herron, 1975-76

Most shutouts
Never accomplished

Most wins
11—Denis Herron, 1975-76

Most losses
39—Denis Herron, 1975-76

Most ties
11—Denis Herron, 1975-76

FRANCHISE LEADERS

FORWARDS/DEFENSEMEN

Games

Gary Croteau	156
Randy Rota	151
Robin Burns	149
Dave Hudson	144
Wilf Paiement	135

Goals

Wilf Paiement	47
Guy Charron	40
Simon Nolet	36
Robin Burns	31
Gary Croteau	27
Randy Rota	27

Assists

Guy Charron	73
Dave Hudson	52
Simon Nolet	47
Wilf Paiement	35
Gary Bergman	33
Robin Burns	33

Points

Guy Charron.......113
Simon Nolet.......83
Wilf Paiement.......82
Dave Hudson.......72
Robin Burns.......64

Penalty minutes

Wilf Paiement.......222
Steve Durbano.......209
Jean-Guy Lagace.......130
Larry Johnston.......122
Robin Burns.......107

GOALTENDERS

Games

Denis Herron.......86
Peter McDuffe.......36
Michel Plasse.......24
Bill McKenzie.......22
Bill Oleschuk.......1

Shutouts

Never occurred

Goals-against average (2400 minutes minimum)

Denis Herron.......3.96

Wins

Denis Herron.......15
Peter McDuffe.......7
Michel Plasse.......4
Bill McKenzie.......1

LOS ANGELES KINGS

YEAR-BY-YEAR RECORDS

	REGULAR SEASON					PLAYOFFS			
Season	W	L	T	Pts.	Finish	W	L	Highest round	Coach
1967-68	31	33	10	72	2nd/West	3	4	Division semifinals	Red Kelly
1968-69	24	42	10	58	4th/West	4	7	Division finals	Red Kelly
1969-70	14	52	10	38	6th/West	—	—		Hal Laycoe, Johnny Wilson
1970-71	25	40	13	63	5th/West	—	—		Larry Regan
1971-72	20	49	9	49	7th/West	—	—		Larry Regan, Fred Glover
1972-73	31	36	11	73	6th/West	—	—		Bob Pulford
1973-74	33	33	12	78	3rd/West	1	4	Division semifinals	Bob Pulford
1974-75	42	17	21	105	2nd/Norris	1	2	Preliminaries	Bob Pulford
1975-76	38	33	9	85	2nd/Norris	5	4	Quarterfinals	Bob Pulford
1976-77	34	31	15	83	2nd/Norris	4	5	Quarterfinals	Bob Pulford
1977-78	31	34	15	77	3rd/Norris	0	2	Preliminaries	Ron Stewart
1978-79	34	34	12	80	3rd/Norris	0	2	Preliminaries	Bob Berry
1979-80	30	36	14	74	2nd/Norris	1	3	Preliminaries	Bob Berry
1980-81	43	24	13	99	2nd/Norris	1	3	Preliminaries	Bob Berry
1981-82	24	41	15	63	4th/Smythe	4	6	Division finals	Parker MacDonald, Don Perry,
1982-83	27	41	12	66	5th/Smythe	—	—		Don Perry
1983-84	23	44	13	59	5th/Smythe	—	—		Don Perry, Rogie Vachon, Roger Neilson
1984-85	34	32	14	82	4th/Smythe	0	3	Division semifinals	Pat Quinn
1985-86	23	49	8	54	5th/Smythe	—	—		Pat Quinn
1986-87	31	41	8	70	4th/Smythe	1	4	Division semifinals	Pat Quinn, Mike Murphy
1987-88	30	42	8	68	4th/Smythe	1	4	Division semifinals	Mike Murphy, Rogie Vachon, Robbie Ftorek
1988-89	42	31	7	91	2nd/Smythe	4	7	Division finals	Robbie Ftorek
1989-90	34	39	7	75	4th/Smythe	4	6	Division finals	Tom Webster
1990-91	46	24	10	102	1st/Smythe	6	6	Division finals	Tom Webster
1991-92	35	31	14	84	2nd/Smythe	2	4	Division semifinals	Tom Webster
1992-93	39	35	10	88	3rd/Smythe	13	11	Stanley Cup finals	Barry Melrose
1993-94	27	45	12	66	5th/Pacific	—	—		Barry Melrose
1994-95	16	23	9	41	4th/Pacific	—	—		Barry Melrose, Rogie Vachon
1995-96	24	40	18	66	6th/Pacific	—	—		Larry Robinson
1996-97	28	43	11	67	6th/Pacific	—	—		Larry Robinson
1997-98	38	33	11	87	2nd/Pacific	0	4	Conference quarterfinals	Larry Robinson
1998-99	32	45	5	69	5th/Pacific	—	—		Larry Robinson

FIRST-ROUND ENTRY DRAFT CHOICES

Year Player, Overall, Last amateur team (league)

1969—No first-round selection
1970—No first-round selection
1971—No first-round selection
1972—No first-round selection
1973—No first-round selection
1974—No first-round selection
1975—Tim Young, 16, Ottawa (OHL)
1976—No first-round selection
1977—No first-round selection
1978—No first-round selection
1979—Jay Wells, 16, Kingston (OHL)
1980—Larry Murphy, 4, Peterborough (OHL)
Jim Fox, 10, Ottawa (OHL)
1981—Doug Smith, 2, Ottawa (OHL)

Year Player, Overall, Last amateur team (league)

1982—No first-round selection
1983—No first-round selection
1984—Craig Redmond, 6, Canadian Olympic Team
1985—Craig Duncanson, 9, Sudbury (OHL)
Dan Gratton, 10, Oshawa (OHL)
1986—Jimmy Carson, 2, Verdun (QMJHL)
1987—Wayne McBean, 4, Medicine Hat (WHL)
1988—Martin Gelinas, 7, Hull (QMJHL)
1989—No first-round selection
1990—Darryl Sydor, 7, Kamloops (WHL)
1991—No first-round selection
1992—No first-round selection
1993—No first-round selection
1994—Jamie Storr, 7, Owen Sound (OHL)

Year	Player, Overall, Last amateur team (league)
1995	Aki-Petteri Berg, 3, TPS Jrs., Finland
1996	No first-round selection
1997	Olli Jokinen, 3, IFK Helsinki (Finland) Matt Zultek, 15, Ottawa (OHL)
1998	Mathieu Biron, 21, Shawinigan (QMJHL)
1999	No first-round selection

SINGLE-SEASON INDIVIDUAL RECORDS

FORWARDS/DEFENSEMEN

Most goals
70—Bernie Nicholls, 1988-89

Most assists
122—Wayne Gretzky, 1990-91

Most points
168—Wayne Gretzky, 1988-89

Most penalty minutes
399—Marty McSorley, 1992-93

Most power play goals
26—Luc Robitaille, 1991-92

Most shorthanded goals
8—Bernie Nicholls, 1988-89

Most games with three or more goals
5—Jimmy Carson, 1987-88

Most shots
385—Bernie Nicholls, 1988-89

GOALTENDERS

Most games
70—Rogie Vachon, 1977-78

Most minutes
4,107—Rogie Vachon, 1977-78

Most shots against
2,219—Kelly Hrudey, 1993-94

Most goals allowed
228—Kelly Hrudey, 1993-94

Lowest goals-against average
2.24—Rogie Vachon, 1974-75

Most shutouts
8—Rogie Vachon, 1977-78

Most wins
35—Mario Lessard, 1980-81

Most losses
31—Kelly Hrudey, 1993-94

Most ties
13—Rogie Vachon, 1974-75
Rogie Vachon, 1977-78
Kelly Hrudey, 1991-92

FRANCHISE LEADERS

Players in boldface played for club in '98-99

FORWARDS/DEFENSEMEN

Games

Dave Taylor	1111
Marcel Dionne	921
Luc Robitaille	**779**
Butch Goring	736
Mike Murphy	673

Goals

Marcel Dionne	550
Luc Robitaille	**447**
Dave Taylor	431
Bernie Nicholls	327
Butch Goring	275

Assists

Marcel Dionne	757
Wayne Gretzky	672
Dave Taylor	638
Luc Robitaille	**470**
Bernie Nicholls	431

Points

Marcel Dionne	1307
Dave Taylor	1069
Wayne Gretzky	918
Luc Robitaille	**917**
Bernie Nicholls	758

Penalty minutes

Marty McSorley	1846
Dave Taylor	1589
Jay Wells	1446
Rob Blake	**870**
Mark Hardy	858

GOALTENDERS

Games

Rogie Vachon	389
Kelly Hrudey	360
Mario Lessard	240
Gary Edwards	155
Stephane Fiset	**146**

Shutouts

Rogie Vachon	32
Kelly Hrudey	10
Stephane Fiset	**9**
Mario Lessard	9
Gerry Desjardins	7
Gary Edwards	7

Goals-against average (2400 minutes minimum)

Jamie Storr	**2.50**
Stephane Fiset	**2.82**
Rogie Vachon	2.86
Wayne Rutledge	3.34
Gary Edwards	3.39

Wins

Rogie Vachon	171
Kelly Hrudey	145
Mario Lessard	92
Stephane Fiset	**57**
Gary Edwards	54

MINNESOTA NORTH STARS (DEFUNCT)

YEAR-BY-YEAR RECORDS

	REGULAR SEASON					PLAYOFFS			
Season	W	L	T	Pts.	Finish	W	L	Highest round	Coach
1967-68	27	32	15	69	4th/West	7	7	Division finals	Wren Blair
1968-69	18	43	15	51	6th/West	—	—		Wren Blair, John Muckler
1969-70	19	35	22	60	3rd/West	2	4	Division semifinals	Wren Blair, Charlie Burns
1970-71	28	34	16	72	4th/West	6	6	Division finals	Jack Gordon
1971-72	37	29	12	86	2nd/West	3	4	Division semifinals	Jack Gordon
1972-73	37	30	11	85	3rd/West	2	4	Division semifinals	Jack Gordon
1973-74	23	38	17	63	7th/West	—	—		Jack Gordon, Parker MacDonald
1974-75	23	50	7	53	4th/Smythe	—	—		Jack Gordon, Charlie Burns
1975-76	20	53	7	47	4th/Smythe	—	—		Ted Harris
1976-77	23	39	18	64	2nd/Smythe	0	2	Preliminaries	Ted Harris
1977-78	18	53	9	45	5th/Smythe	—	—		Ted Harris, Andre Beaulieu, Lou Nanne
1978-79	28	40	12	68	4th/Adams	—	—		Harry Howell, Glen Sonmor
1979-80	36	28	16	88	3rd/Adams	8	7	Semifinals	Glen Sonmor

Season	W	L	T	Pts.	Finish	W	L	Highest round	Coach
	REGULAR SEASON					PLAYOFFS			
1980-81	35	28	17	87	3rd/Adams	12	7	Stanley Cup finals	Glen Sonmor
1981-82	37	23	20	94	1st/Norris	1	3	Division semifinals	Glen Sonmor, Murray Oliver
1982-83	40	24	16	96	2nd/Norris	4	5	Division finals	Glen Sonmor, Murray Oliver
1983-84	39	31	10	88	1st/Norris	7	9	Conference finals	Bill Maloney
1984-85	25	43	12	62	4th/Norris	5	4	Division finals	Bill Maloney, Glen Sonmor
1985-86	38	33	9	85	2nd/Norris	2	3	Division semifinals	Lorne Henning
1986-87	30	40	10	70	5th/Norris	—	—		Lorne Henning, Glen Sonmor
1987-88	19	48	13	51	5th/Norris	—	—		Herb Brooks
1988-89	27	37	16	70	3rd/Norris	1	4	Division semifinals	Pierre Page
1989-90	36	40	4	76	4th/Norris	3	4	Division semifinals	Pierre Page
1990-91	27	39	14	68	4th/Norris	14	9	Stanley Cup finals	Bob Gainey
1991-92	32	42	6	70	4th/Norris	3	4	Division semifinals	Bob Gainey
1992-93	36	38	10	82	5th/Norris	—	—		Bob Gainey

Franchise relocated and became Dallas Stars following 1992-93 season.

FIRST-ROUND ENTRY DRAFT CHOICES

Year Player, Overall, Last amateur team (league)

1969—Dick Redmond, 5, St. Catharines (OHL)
Dennis O'Brien, 14, St. Catharines (OHL)
1970—No first-round selection
1971—No first-round selection
1972—Jerry Byers, 12, Kitchener (OHL)
1973—No first-round selection
1974—Doug Hicks, 6, Flin Flon (WCHL)
1975—Brian Maxwell, 4, Medicine Hat (WCHL)
1976—Glen Sharpley, 3, Hull (QMJHL)
1977—Brad Maxwell, 7, New Westminster (WCHL)
1978—Bobby Smith, 1, Ottawa (OHL)*
1979—Craig Hartsburg, 6, Birmingham (WHA)
Tom McCarthy, 10, Oshawa (OHL)
1980—Brad Palmer, 16, Victoria (WHL)

Year Player, Overall, Last amateur team (league)

1981—Ron Meighan, 13, Niagara Falls (OHL)
1982—Brian Bellows, 2, Kitchener (OHL)
1983—Brian Lawton, 1, Mount St. Charles H.S. (R.I.)*
1984—David Quinn, 13, Kent H.S. (Ct.)
1985—No first-round selection
1986—Warren Babe, 12, Lethbridge (WHL)
1987—Dave Archibald, 6, Portland (WHL)
1988—Mike Modano, 1, Prince Albert (WHL)*
1989—Doug Zmolek, 7, John Marshall H.S. (Minn.)
1990—Derian Hatcher, 8, North Bay (OHL)
1991—Richard Matvichuk, 8, Saskatoon (WHL)
1992—No first-round selection
*Designates first player chosen in draft.

SINGLE-SEASON INDIVIDUAL RECORDS

FORWARDS/DEFENSEMEN

Most goals
55—Dino Ciccarelli, 1981-82
Brian Bellows, 1989-90

Most assists
76—Neal Broten, 1985-86

Most points
114—Bobby Smith, 1981-82

Most penalty minutes
382—Basil McRae, 1987-88

Most power play goals
22—Dino Ciccarelli, 1986-87

Most shorthanded goals
6—Bill Collins, 1969-70

Most games with three or more goals
3—Bill Goldsworthy, 1973-74
Dino Ciccarelli, 1981-82
Dino Ciccarelli, 1983-84
Tom McCarthy, 1984-85
Scott Bjugstad, 1985-86
Dino Ciccarelli, 1985-86

Most shots
321—Bill Goldsworthy, 1973-74

GOALTENDERS

Most games
64—Cesare Maniago, 1968-69

Most minutes
3,599—Cesare Maniago, 1968-69

Most goals allowed
216—Pete LoPresti, 1977-78

Lowest goals-against average
2.12—Gump Worsley, 1971-72

Most shutouts
6—Cesare Maniago, 1967-68

Most wins
31—Jon Casey, 1989-90

Most losses
35—Pete LoPresti, 1977-78

Most ties
16—Cesare Maniago, 1969-70

FRANCHISE LEADERS

FORWARDS/DEFENSEMEN

Games
Neal Broten 876
Curt Giles 760
Brian Bellows 753
Fred Barrett 730
Bill Goldsworthy 670

Goals
Brian Bellows 342
Dino Ciccarelli 332
Bill Goldsworthy 267
Neal Broten 249
Steve Payne 228

Assists
Neal Broten 547
Brian Bellows 380
Bobby Smith 369
Dino Ciccarelli 319
Tim Young 316

Points
Neal Broten 796
Brian Bellows 722
Dino Ciccarelli 651
Bobby Smith 554
Bill Goldsworthy 506

Penalty minutes
Basil McRae 1567
Shane Churla 1194
Willi Plett 1137
Brad Maxwell 1031
Mark Tinordi 872

GOALTENDERS

Games

Cesare Maniago	420
Gilles Meloche	328
Jon Casey	325
Don Beaupre	316
Pete LoPresti	173

Shutouts

Cesare Maniago	29
Jon Casey	12
Gilles Meloche	9
Pete LoPresti	5
Don Beaupre	4
Brian Hayward	4

Goals-against average (2400 minutes minimum)

Gump Worsley	2.62
Cesare Maniago	3.17
Jon Casey	3.28
Gilles Gilbert	3.39
Gary Edwards	3.44
Darcy Wakaluk	3.44

Wins

Cesare Maniago	143
Gilles Meloche	141
Jon Casey	128
Don Beaupre	126
Pete LoPresti	43

MONTREAL CANADIENS

YEAR-BY-YEAR RECORDS

	REGULAR SEASON					PLAYOFFS			
Season	W	L	T	Pts.	Finish	W	L	Highest round	Coach
1917-18	13	9	0	26	1st/3rd	1	1	Semifinals	George Kennedy
1918-19	10	8	0	20	1st/2nd	†*6	3	Stanley Cup finals	George Kennedy
1919-20	13	11	0	26	2nd/3rd	—	—		George Kennedy
1920-21	13	11	0	26	3rd/2nd	—	—		George Kennedy
1921-22	12	11	1	25	3rd	—	—		Leo Dandurand
1922-23	13	9	2	28	2nd	1	1	Quarterfinals	Leo Dandurand
1923-24	13	11	0	26	2nd	6	0	Stanley Cup champ	Leo Dandurand
1924-25	17	11	2	36	3rd	3	3	Stanley Cup finals	Leo Dandurand
1925-26	11	24	1	23	7th	—	—		Cecil Hart
1926-27	28	14	2	58	2nd/Canadian	*1	1	Semifinals	Cecil Hart
1927-28	26	11	7	59	1st/Canadian	*0	1	Semifinals	Cecil Hart
1928-29	22	7	15	59	1st/Canadian	0	3	Semifinals	Cecil Hart
1929-30	21	14	9	51	2nd/Canadian	*5	0	Stanley Cup champ	Cecil Hart
1930-31	26	10	8	60	1st/Canadian	6	4	Stanley Cup champ	Cecil Hart
1931-32	25	16	7	57	1st/Canadian	1	3	Semifinals	Cecil Hart
1932-33	18	25	5	41	3rd/Canadian	*0	1	Quarterfinals	Newsy Lalonde
1933-34	22	20	6	50	2nd/Canadian	*0	1	Quarterfinals	Newsy Lalonde
1934-35	19	23	6	44	3rd/Canadian	*0	1	Quarterfinals	Newsy Lalonde, Leo Dandurand
1935-36	11	26	11	33	4th/Canadian	—	—		Sylvio Mantha
1936-37	24	18	6	54	1st/Canadian	2	3	Semifinals	Cecil Hart
1937-38	18	17	13	49	3rd/Canadian	1	2	Quarterfinals	Cecil Hart
1938-39	15	24	9	39	6th	1	2	Quarterfinals	Cecil Hart, Jules Dugal
1939-40	10	33	5	25	7th	—	—		Pit Lepine
1940-41	16	26	6	38	6th	1	2	Quarterfinals	Dick Irvin
1941-42	18	27	3	39	6th	1	2	Quarterfinals	Dick Irvin
1942-43	19	19	12	50	4th	1	4	League semifinals	Dick Irvin
1943-44	38	5	7	83	1st	8	1	Stanley Cup champ	Dick Irvin
1944-45	38	8	4	80	1st	2	4	League semifinals	Dick Irvin
1945-46	28	17	5	61	1st	8	1	Stanley Cup champ	Dick Irvin
1946-47	34	16	10	78	1st	6	5	Stanley Cup finals	Dick Irvin
1947-48	20	29	11	51	5th	—	—		Dick Irvin
1948-49	28	23	9	65	3rd	3	4	League semifinals	Dick Irvin
1949-50	29	22	19	77	2nd	1	4	League semifinals	Dick Irvin
1950-51	25	30	15	65	3rd	5	6	Stanley Cup finals	Dick Irvin
1951-52	34	26	10	78	2nd	4	7	Stanley Cup finals	Dick Irvin
1952-53	28	23	19	75	2nd	8	4	Stanley Cup champ	Dick Irvin
1953-54	35	24	11	81	2nd	7	4	Stanley Cup finals	Dick Irvin
1954-55	41	18	11	93	2nd	7	5	Stanley Cup finals	Dick Irvin
1955-56	45	15	10	100	1st	8	2	Stanley Cup champ	Toe Blake
1956-57	35	23	12	82	2nd	8	2	Stanley Cup champ	Toe Blake
1957-58	43	17	10	96	1st	8	2	Stanley Cup champ	Toe Blake
1958-59	39	18	13	91	1st	8	3	Stanley Cup champ	Toe Blake
1959-60	40	18	12	92	1st	8	0	Stanley Cup champ	Toe Blake
1960-61	41	19	10	92	1st	2	4	League semifinals	Toe Blake
1961-62	42	14	14	98	1st	2	4	League semifinals	Toe Blake
1962-63	28	19	23	79	3rd	1	4	League semifinals	Toe Blake
1963-64	36	21	13	85	1st	3	4	League semifinals	Toe Blake
1964-65	36	23	11	83	2nd	8	5	Stanley Cup champ	Toe Blake
1965-66	41	21	8	90	1st	8	2	Stanley Cup champ	Toe Blake
1966-67	32	25	13	77	2nd	6	4	Stanley Cup finals	Toe Blake
1967-68	42	22	10	94	1st/East	12	1	Stanley Cup champ	Toe Blake
1968-69	46	19	11	103	1st/East	12	2	Stanley Cup champ	Claude Ruel

	REGULAR SEASON					PLAYOFFS			
Season	W	L	T	Pts.	Finish	W	L	Highest round	Coach
1969-70	38	22	16	92	5th/East	—	—		Claude Ruel
1970-71	42	23	13	97	3rd/East	12	8	Stanley Cup champ	Claude Ruel, Al MacNeil
1971-72	46	16	16	108	3rd/East	2	4	Division semifinals	Scotty Bowman
1972-73	52	10	16	120	1st/East	12	5	Stanley Cup champ	Scotty Bowman
1973-74	45	42	9	99	2nd/East	2	4	Division semifinals	Scotty Bowman
1974-75	47	14	19	113	1st/Norris	6	5	Semifinals	Scotty Bowman
1975-76	58	11	11	127	1st/Norris	12	1	Stanley Cup champ	Scotty Bowman
1976-77	60	8	12	132	1st/Norris	12	2	Stanley Cup champ	Scotty Bowman
1977-78	59	10	11	129	1st/Norris	12	3	Stanley Cup champ	Scotty Bowman
1978-79	52	17	11	115	1st/Norris	12	4	Stanley Cup champ	Scotty Bowman
1979-80	47	20	13	107	1st/Norris	6	4	Quarterfinals	Bernie Geoffrion, Claude Ruel
1980-81	45	22	13	103	1st/Norris	0	3	Preliminaries	Claude Ruel
1981-82	46	17	17	109	1st/Adams	2	3	Division semifinals	Bob Berry
1982-83	42	24	14	98	2nd/Adams	0	3	Division semifinals	Bob Berry
1983-84	35	40	5	75	4th/Adams	9	6	Conference finals	Bob Berry, Jacques Lemaire
1984-85	41	27	12	94	1st/Adams	6	6	Division finals	Jacques Lemaire
1985-86	40	33	7	87	2nd/Adams	15	5	Stanley Cup champ	Jean Perron
1986-87	41	29	10	92	2nd/Adams	10	7	Conference finals	Jean Perron
1987-88	45	22	13	103	1st/Adams	5	6	Division finals	Jean Perron
1988-89	53	18	9	115	1st/Adams	14	7	Stanley Cup finals	Pat Burns
1989-90	41	28	11	93	3rd/Adams	5	6	Division finals	Pat Burns
1990-91	39	30	11	89	2nd/Adams	7	6	Division finals	Pat Burns
1991-92	41	28	11	93	1st/Adams	4	7	Division finals	Pat Burns
1992-93	48	30	6	102	3rd/Adams	16	4	Stanley Cup champ	Jacques Demers
1993-94	41	29	14	96	3rd/Northeast	3	4	Conference quarterfinals	Jacques Demers
1994-95	18	23	7	43	6th/Northeast	—	—		Jacques Demers
1995-96	40	32	10	90	3rd/Northeast	2	4	Conference quarterfinals	Jacques Demers, Mario Tremblay
1996-97	31	36	15	77	T3rd/Northeast	1	4	Conference quarterfinals	Mario Tremblay
1997-98	37	32	13	87	4th/Northeast	4	6	Conference semifinals	Alain Vigneault
1998-99	32	39	11	75	5th/Northeast	—	—		Alain Vigneault

*Won-lost record does not indicate tie(s) resulting from two-game, total-goals series that year (two-game, total-goals series were played from 1917-18 through 1935-36).

†1918-19 series abandoned with no Cup holder due to influenza epidemic.

FIRST-ROUND ENTRY DRAFT CHOICES

Year Player, Overall, Last amateur team (league)

1969—Rejean Houle, 1, Montreal (OHL)*
Marc Tardif, 2, Montreal (OHL)
1970—Ray Martiniuk, 5, Flin Flon (WCHL)
Chuck Lefley, 6, Canadian Nationals
1971—Guy Lafleur, 1, Quebec (QMJHL)*
Chuck Arnason, 7, Flin Flon (WCHL)
Murray Wilson, 11, Ottawa (OHL)
1972—Steve Shutt, 4, Toronto (OHL)
Michel Larocque, 6, Ottawa (OHL)
Dave Gardner, 8, Toronto (OHL)
John Van Boxmeer, 14, Guelph (SOJHL)
1973—Bob Gainey, 8, Peterborough (OHL)
1974—Cam Connor, 5, Flin Flon (WCHL)
Doug Risebrough, 7, Kitchener (OHL)
Rick Chartraw, 10, Kitchener (OHL)
Mario Tremblay, 12, Montreal (OHL)
Gord McTavish, 15, Sudbury (OHL)
1975—Robin Sadler, 9, Edmonton (WCHL)
Pierre Mondou, 15, Montreal (QMJHL)
1976—Peter Lee, 12, Ottawa (OHL)
Rod Schutt, 13, Sudbury (OHL)
Bruce Baker, 18, Ottawa (OHL)
1977—Mark Napier, 10, Birmingham (WHA)
Normand Dupont, 18, Montreal (QMJHL)
1978—Danny Geoffrion, 8, Cornwall (QMJHL)
Dave Hunter, 17, Sudbury (OHL)

Year Player, Overall, Last amateur team (league)

1979—No first-round selection
1980—Doug Wickenheiser, 1, Regina (WHL)*
1981—Mark Hunter, 7, Brantford (OHL)
Gilbert Delorme, 18, Chicoutimi (QMJHL)
Jan Ingman, 19, Farjestads (Sweden)
1982—Alain Heroux, 19, Chicoutimi (QMJHL)
1983—Alfie Turcotte, 17, Portland (WHL)
1984—Petr Svoboda, 5, Czechoslovakia
Shayne Corson, 8, Brantford (OHL)
1985—Jose Charbonneau, 12, Drummondville (QMJHL)
Tom Chorske, 16, Minneapolis SW H.S. (Minn.)
1986—Mark Pederson, 15, Medicine Hat (WHL)
1987—Andrew Cassels, 17, Ottawa (OHL)
1988—Eric Charron, 20, Trois-Rivieres (QMJHL)
1989—Lindsay Vallis, 13, Seattle (WHL)
1990—Turner Stevenson, 12, Seattle (WHL)
1991—Brent Bilodeau, 17, Seattle (WHL)
1992—David Wilkie, 20, Kamloops (WHL)
1993—Saku Koivu, 21, TPS Turku (Finland)
1994—Brad Brown, 18, North Bay (OHL)
1995—Terry Ryan, 8, Tri-City (WHL)
1996—Matt Higgins, 18, Moose Jaw (WHL)
1997—Jason Ward, 11, Erie (OHL)
1998—Eric Chouinard, 16, Quebec (QMJHL)
1999—No first-round selection
*Designates first player chosen in draft.

SINGLE-SEASON INDIVIDUAL RECORDS

FORWARDS/DEFENSEMEN

Most goals
60—Steve Shutt, 1976-77
Guy Lafleur, 1977-78

Most assists
82—Pete Mahovlich, 1974-75

Most points
136—Guy Lafleur, 1976-77

Most penalty minutes
358—Chris Nilan, 1984-85

Most power play goals
20—Yvan Cournoyer, 1966-67

Most shorthanded goals
8—Guy Carbonneau, 1983-84

Most games with three or more goals
7—Joe Malone, 1917-18

GOALTENDERS

Most games
70—Gerry McNeil, 1950-51
Gerry McNeil, 1951-52
Jacques Plante, 1961-62

Most minutes
4,200—Gerry McNeil, 1950-51
Gerry McNeil, 1951-52
Jacques Plante, 1961-62

Lowest goals-against average
0.92—George Hainsworth, 1928-29

Most shutouts
22—George Hainsworth, 1928-29

Most wins
42—Jacques Plante, 1955-56
Jacques Plante, 1961-62
Ken Dryden, 1975-76

FRANCHISE LEADERS

Players in boldface played for club in '98-99

FORWARDS/DEFENSEMEN

Games

Henri Richard	1256
Larry Robinson	1202
Bob Gainey	1160
Jean Beliveau	1125
Claude Provost	1005

Goals

Maurice Richard	544
Guy Lafleur	518
Jean Beliveau	507
Yvan Cournoyer	428
Steve Shutt	408

Assists

Guy Lafleur	728
Jean Beliveau	712
Henri Richard	688
Larry Robinson	686
Jacques Lemaire	469

Points

Guy Lafleur	1246
Jean Beliveau	1219
Henri Richard	1046
Maurice Richard	965
Larry Robinson	883

Penalty minutes

Chris Nilan	2248
Lyle Odelein	1367
Maurice Richard	1285
John Ferguson	1214
Shayne Corson	**1079**

GOALTENDERS

Games

Jacques Plante	556
Patrick Roy	551
Ken Dryden	397
Bill Durnan	383
Georges Vezina	328

Shutouts

George Hainsworth	74
Jacques Plante	58
Ken Dryden	46
Bill Durnan	34
Patrick Roy	29

Wins

Jacques Plante	314
Patrick Roy	289
Ken Dryden	258
Bill Durnan	208
Georges Vezina	174

MONTREAL MAROONS (DEFUNCT)

YEAR-BY-YEAR RECORDS

	REGULAR SEASON					PLAYOFFS			
Season	W	L	T	Pts.	Finish	W	L	Highest round	Coach
1924-25	9	19	2	20	5th	—	—		Eddie Gerard
1925-26	20	11	5	45	2nd	3	1	Stanley Cup champ	Eddie Gerard
1926-27	20	20	4	44	3rd/Canadian	*0	1	Quarterfinals	Eddie Gerard
1927-28	24	14	6	54	2nd/Canadian	*5	3	Stanley Cup finals	Eddie Gerard
1928-29	15	20	9	39	5th/Canadian	—	—		Eddie Gerard
1929-30	23	16	5	51	1st/Canadian	1	3	Semifinals	Dunc Munro
1930-31	20	18	6	46	3rd/Canadian	*0	2	Quarterfinals	Dunc Munro, George Boucher
1931-32	19	22	7	45	3rd/Canadian	*1	1	Semifinals	Sprague Cleghorn
1932-33	22	20	6	50	2nd/Canadian	0	2	Quarterfinals	Eddie Gerard
1933-34	19	18	11	49	3rd/Canadian	*1	2	Semifinals	Eddie Gerard
1934-35	24	19	5	53	2nd/Canadian	*5	0	Stanley Cup champ	Tommy Gorman
1935-36	22	16	10	54	1st/Canadian	0	3	Semifinals	Tommy Gorman
1936-37	22	17	9	53	2nd/Canadian	2	3	Semifinals	Tommy Gorman
1937-38	12	30	6	30	4th/Canadian	—	—		King Clancy, Tommy Gorman

*Won-lost record does not indicate tie(s) resulting from two-game, total goals series that year (two-game, total-goals series were played from 1917-18 through 1935-36).

MONTREAL WANDERERS (DEFUNCT)

YEAR-BY-YEAR RECORDS

	REGULAR SEASON					PLAYOFFS			
Season	W	L	T	Pts.	Finish	W	L	Highest round	Coach
1917-18*	1	5	0	2	4th	—	—		Art Ross

*Franchise disbanded after Montreal Arena burned down. Montreal Canadiens and Toronto each counted one win for defaulted games with Wanderers.

NASHVILLE PREDATORS

YEAR-BY-YEAR RECORDS

	REGULAR SEASON					PLAYOFFS			
Season	W	L	T	Pts.	Finish	W	L	Highest round	Coach
1998-99	28	47	7	63	4th/Central	—	—		Barry Trotz

FIRST-ROUND ENTRY DRAFT CHOICES

Year Player, Overall, Last amateur team (league)
1998—David Legwand, 2, Plymouth (OHL)

Year Player, Overall, Last amateur team (league)
1999—Brian Finley, 6, Barrie (OHL)

SINGLE-SEASON INDIVIDUAL RECORDS

FORWARDS/DEFENSEMEN

Most goals
25—Sergei Krivokrasov, 1998-99

Most assists
35—Cliff Ronning, 1998-99

Most points
53—Cliff Ronning, 1998-99

Most penalty minutes
242—Patrick Cote, 1998-99

Most power play goals
10—Sergei Krivokrasov, 1998-99

Most shorthanded goals
3—Greg Johnson, 1998-99

Most games with three or more goals
Never occurred

Most shots
239—Cliff Ronning, 1998-99

GOALTENDERS

Most games
44—Mike Dunham, 1998-99

Most minutes
2,472—Mike Dunham, 1998-99

Most goals allowed
127—Mike Dunham, 1998-99

Lowest goals-against average
2.95—Tomas Vokoun, 1998-99

Most shutouts
1—Mike Dunham, 1998-99
Tomas Vokoun, 1998-99

Most wins
16—Mike Dunham, 1998-99

Most losses
23—Mike Dunham, 1998-99

Most ties
4—Tomas Vokoun, 1998-99

FRANCHISE LEADERS

Players in boldface played for club in '98-99

FORWARDS/DEFENSEMEN

Games

Tom Fitzgerald 80
Bob Boughner 79
Andrew Brunette 77
Denny Lambert 76
Drake Berehowsky 74

Goals

Sergei Krivokrasov 25
Cliff Ronning 18
Greg Johnson 16
Sebastien Bordeleau 16
Scott Walker 15

Assists

Cliff Ronning 35
Greg Johnson 34
Scott Walker 25
Sebastien Bordeleau 24
Sergei Krivokrasov 23

Points

Cliff Ronning 53
Greg Johnson 50
Sergei Krivokrasov 48
Sebastien Bordeleau 40
Scott Walker 40

Penalty minutes

Patrick Cote 242
Denny Lambert 218
Drake Berehowsky 140
Bob Boughner 137
Scott Walker 103

GOALTENDERS

Games

Mike Dunham 44
Tomas Vokoun 37
Eric Fichaud 9
Chris Mason 3

Shutouts

Mike Dunham 1
Tomas Vokoun 1

Goals-against average

(2400 minutes minimum)

Mike Dunham 3.08

Wins

Mike Dunham 16
Tomas Vokoun 12

NEW JERSEY DEVILS

YEAR-BY-YEAR RECORDS

	REGULAR SEASON					PLAYOFFS			
Season	W	L	T	Pts.	Finish	W	L	Highest round	Coach
1982-83	17	49	14	48	5th/Patrick	—	—		Billy MacMillan
1983-84	17	56	7	41	5th/Patrick	—	—		Billy MacMillan, Tom McVie
1984-85	22	48	10	54	5th/Patrick	—	—		Doug Carpenter
1985-86	28	49	3	59	5th/Patrick	—	—		Doug Carpenter
1986-87	29	45	6	64	6th/Patrick	—	—		Doug Carpenter
1987-88	38	36	6	82	4th/Patrick	11	9	Conference finals	Doug Carpenter, Jim Schoenfeld
1988-89	27	41	12	66	5th/Patrick	—	—		Jim Schoenfeld
1989-90	37	34	9	83	2nd/Patrick	2	4	Division semifinals	Jim Schoenfeld, John Cunniff
1990-91	32	33	15	79	4th/Patrick	3	4	Division semifinals	John Cunniff, Tom McVie
1991-92	38	31	11	87	4th/Patrick	3	4	Division semifinals	Tom McVie
1992-93	40	37	7	87	4th/Patrick	1	4	Division semifinals	Herb Brooks
1993-94	47	25	12	106	2nd/Atlantic	11	9	Conference finals	Jacques Lemaire
1994-95	22	18	8	52	2nd/Atlantic	16	4	Stanley Cup champ	Jacques Lemaire
1995-96	37	33	12	86	6th/Atlantic	—	—		Jacques Lemaire
1996-97	45	23	14	104	1st/Atlantic	5	5	Conference semifinals	Jacques Lemaire
1997-98	48	23	11	107	1st/Atlantic	2	4	Conference quarterfinals	Jacques Lemaire
1998-99	47	24	11	105	1st/Atlantic	3	4	Conference quarterfinals	Robbie Ftorek

Franchise was originally known as Kansas City Scouts and relocated to become Colorado Rockies following 1975-76 season; franchise relocated and became New Jersey Devils following 1981-82 season.

FIRST-ROUND ENTRY DRAFT CHOICES

Year Player, Overall, Last amateur team (league)
1982—Rocky Trottier, 8, Billings (WHL)
Ken Daneyko, 18, Seattle (WHL)
1983—John MacLean, 6, Oshawa (OHL)
1984—Kirk Muller, 2, Guelph (OHL)
1985—Craig Wolanin, 3, Kitchener (OHL)
1986—Neil Brady, 3, Medicine Hat (WHL)
1987—Brendan Shanahan, 2, London (OHL)
1988—Corey Foster, 12, Peterborough (OHL)
1989—Bill Guerin, 5, Springfield (Mass.) Jr.
Jason Miller, 18, Medicine Hat (WHL)
1990—Martin Brodeur, 20, St. Hyacinthe (QMJHL)

Year Player, Overall, Last amateur team (league)
1991—Scott Niedermayer, 3, Kamloops (WHL)
Brian Rolston, 11, Detroit Compuware Jr.
1992—Jason Smith, 18, Regina (WHL)
1993—Denis Pederson, 13, Prince Albert (WHL)
1994—Vadim Sharifjanov, 25, Salavat (Russia)
1995—Petr Sykora, 18, Detroit (IHL)
1996—Lance Ward, 10, Red Deer (WHL)
1997—Jean-Francois Damphousse, 24, Moncton (QMJHL)
1998—Mike Van Ryn, 26, Michigan
Scott Gomez, 27, Tri-City (WHL)
1999—Ari Ahonen, 27, Jyvaskyla, Finland

SINGLE-SEASON INDIVIDUAL RECORDS

FORWARDS/DEFENSEMEN

Most goals
46—Pat Verbeek, 1987-88

Most assists
60—Scott Stevens, 1993-94

Most points
94—Kirk Muller, 1987-88

Most penalty minutes
295—Krzysztof Oliwa, 1997-98

Most power play goals
19—John MacLean, 1990-91

Most shorthanded goals
5—Brian Rolston, 1998-99

Most games with three or more goals
3—Kirk Muller, 1987-88
John MacLean, 1988-89

Most shots
322—John MacLean, 1989-90

GOALTENDERS

Most games
77—Martin Brodeur, 1995-96

Most minutes
4,433—Martin Brodeur, 1995-96

Most goals allowed
242—Chico Resch, 1982-83

Lowest goals-against average
1.88—Martin Brodeur, 1996-97

Most shutouts
10—Martin Brodeur, 1996-97
Martin Brodeur, 1997-98

Most wins
43—Martin Brodeur, 1997-98

Most losses
35—Chico Resch, 1982-83

Most ties
13—Martin Brodeur, 1996-97

FRANCHISE LEADERS

Players in boldface played for club in '98-99

FORWARDS/DEFENSEMEN

Games

Ken Daneyko	**992**
John MacLean	934
Bruce Driver	702
Scott Stevens	**596**
Aaron Broten	581

Goals

John MacLean	347
Kirk Muller	185
Pat Verbeek	170
Aaron Broten	147
Stephane Richer	146

Assists

John MacLean	354
Kirk Muller	335
Bruce Driver	316
Aaron Broten	283
Scott Stevens	**253**

Points

John MacLean	701
Kirk Muller	520
Aaron Broten	430
Bruce Driver	399
Scott Stevens	**321**
Pat Verbeek	321

Penalty minutes

Ken Daneyko	**2241**
John MacLean	1168
Randy McKay	**1223**
Pat Verbeek	943
Joe Cirella	886

GOALTENDERS

Games

Martin Brodeur	**375**
Chris Terreri	268
Chico Resch	198
Sean Burke	162
Alain Chevrier	140

Shutouts

Martin Brodeur	**32**
Chris Terreri	6
Craig Billington	4
Sean Burke	4
Mike Dunham	**3**

Goals-against average (2400 minutes minimum)

Martin Brodeur	**2.16**
Chris Terreri	3.09
Sean Burke	3.66
Bob Sauve	3.87
Craig Billington	3.98

Wins

Martin Brodeur	**162**
Chris Terreri	106
Sean Burke	62
Alain Chevrier	53
Chico Resch	49

NEW YORK AMERICANS (DEFUNCT)

YEAR-BY-YEAR RECORDS

	REGULAR SEASON					PLAYOFFS			
Season	W	L	T	Pts.	Finish	W	L	Highest round	Coach
1925-26	12	20	4	28	5th	—	—		Tommy Gorman
1926-27	17	25	2	36	4th/Canadian	—	—		Newsy Lalonde
1927-28	11	27	6	28	5th/Canadian	—	—		Wilf Green
1928-29	19	13	12	50	2nd/Canadian	*0	1	Semifinals	Tommy Gorman
1929-30	14	25	5	33	5th/Canadian	—	—		Lionel Conacher
1930-31	18	16	10	46	4th/Canadian	—	—		Eddie Gerard
1931-32	16	24	8	40	4th/Canadian	—	—		Eddie Gerard
1932-33	15	22	11	41	4th/Canadian	—	—		Joe Simpson
1933-34	15	23	10	40	4th/Canadian	—	—		Joe Simpson
1934-35	12	27	9	33	4th/Canadian	—	—		Joe Simpson
1935-36	16	25	7	39	3rd/Canadian	2	3	Semifinals	Red Dutton
1936-37	15	29	4	34	4th/Canadian	—	—		Red Dutton
1937-38	19	18	11	49	2nd/Canadian	3	3	Semifinals	Red Dutton
1938-39	17	21	10	44	4th	0	2	Quarterfinals	Red Dutton
1939-40	15	29	4	34	6th	1	2	Quarterfinals	Red Dutton
1940-41	8	29	11	27	7th	—	—		Red Dutton
1941-42†	16	29	3	35	7th	—	—		Red Dutton

Franchise was originally known as Quebec Bulldogs and relocated to become Hamilton Tigers following 1919-20 season; franchise relocated and became New York Americans following 1924-25 season.

*Won-lost record does not indicate tie(s) resulting from two-game, total goals series that year (two-game, total-goals series were played from 1917-18 through 1935-36).

†Brooklyn Americans.

NEW YORK ISLANDERS

YEAR-BY-YEAR RECORDS

	REGULAR SEASON					PLAYOFFS			
Season	W	L	T	Pts.	Finish	W	L	Highest round	Coach
1972-73	12	60	6	30	8th/East	—	—		Phil Goyette, Earl Ingarfield
1973-74	19	41	18	56	8th/East	—	—		Al Arbour
1974-75	33	25	22	88	3rd/Patrick	9	8	Semifinals	Al Arbour
1975-76	42	21	17	101	2nd/Patrick	7	6	Semifinals	Al Arbour
1976-77	47	21	12	106	2nd/Patrick	8	4	Semifinals	Al Arbour
1977-78	48	17	15	111	1st/Patrick	3	4	Quarterfinals	Al Arbour
1978-79	51	15	14	116	1st/Patrick	6	4	Semifinals	Al Arbour
1979-80	39	28	13	91	2nd/Patrick	15	6	Stanley Cup champ	Al Arbour
1980-81	48	18	14	110	1st/Patrick	15	3	Stanley Cup champ	Al Arbour
1981-82	54	16	10	118	1st/Patrick	15	4	Stanley Cup champ	Al Arbour
1982-83	42	26	12	96	2nd/Patrick	15	5	Stanley Cup champ	Al Arbour
1983-84	50	26	4	104	1st/Patrick	12	9	Stanley Cup finals	Al Arbour
1984-85	40	34	6	86	3rd/Patrick	4	6	Division finals	Al Arbour
1985-86	39	29	12	90	3rd/Patrick	0	3	Division semifinals	Al Arbour
1986-87	35	33	12	82	3rd/Patrick	7	7	Division finals	Terry Simpson
1987-88	39	31	10	88	1st/Patrick	2	4	Division semifinals	Terry Simpson
1988-89	28	47	5	61	6th/Patrick	—	—		Terry Simpson, Al Arbour
1989-90	31	38	11	73	4th/Patrick	1	4	Division semifinals	Al Arbour
1990-91	25	45	10	60	6th/Patrick	—	—		Al Arbour
1991-92	34	35	11	79	5th/Patrick	—	—		Al Arbour
1992-93	40	37	7	87	3rd/Patrick	9	9	Conference finals	Al Arbour
1993-94	36	36	12	84	4th/Atlantic	0	4	Conference quarterfinals	Al Arbour, Lorne Henning

Season	W	L	T	Pts.	Finish (Regular Season)	W	L	Highest round (Playoffs)	Coach
1994-95	15	28	5	35	7th/Atlantic	—	—		Lorne Henning
1995-96	22	50	10	54	7th/Atlantic	—	—		Mike Milbury
1996-97	29	41	12	70	7th/Atlantic	—	—		Mike Milbury, Rick Bowness
1997-98	30	41	11	71	4th/Atlantic	—	—		Rick Bowness, Mike Milbury
1998-99	24	48	10	58	5th/Atlantic	—	—		Mike Milbury, Bill Stewart

FIRST-ROUND ENTRY DRAFT CHOICES

Year Player, Overall, Last amateur team (league)
1972—Billy Harris, 1, Toronto (OHL)*
1973—Denis Potvin, 1, Ottawa (OHL)*
1974—Clark Gillies, 4, Regina (WCHL)
1975—Pat Price, 11, Vancouver (WHA)
1976—Alex McKendry, 14, Sudbury (OHL)
1977—Mike Bossy, 15, Laval (QMJHL)
1978—Steve Tambellini, 15, Lethbridge (WCHL)
1979—Duane Sutter, 17, Lethbridge (WHL)
1980—Brent Sutter, 17, Red Deer (AJHL)
1981—Paul Boutilier, 21, Sherbrooke (QMJHL)
1982—Pat Flatley, 21, University of Wisconsin
1983—Pat LaFontaine, 3, Verdun (QMJHL)
Gerald Diduck, 16, Lethbridge (WHL)
1984—Duncan MacPherson, 20, Saskatoon (WHL)
1985—Brad Dalgarno, 6, Hamilton (OHL)
Derek King, 13, Sault Ste. Marie (OHL)
1986—Tom Fitzgerald, 17, Austin Prep (Mass.)
1987—Dean Chynoweth, 13, Medicine Hat (WHL)

Year Player, Overall, Last amateur team (league)
1988—Kevin Cheveldayoff, 16, Brandon (WHL)
1989—Dave Chyzowski, 2, Kamloops (WHL)
1990—Scott Scissons, 6, Saskatoon (WHL)
1991—Scott Lachance, 4, Boston University
1992—Darius Kasparaitis, 5, Dynamo Moscow (CIS)
1993—Todd Bertuzzi, 23, Guelph (OHL)
1994—Brett Lindros, 9, Kingston (OHL)
1995—Wade Redden, 2, Brandon (WHL)
1996—Jean-Pierre Dumont, 3, Val-d'Or (QMJHL)
1997—Roberto Luongo, 4, Val d'Or (QMJHL)
Eric Brewer, 5, Prince George (WHL)
1998—Michael Rupp, 9, Erie (OHL)
1999—Tim Connolly, 5, Erie (OHL)
Taylor Pyatt, 8, Sudbury (OHL)
Branislav Mezei, 10, Belleville (OHL)
Kristian Kudroc, 28, Michalovce, Slovakia

*Designates first player chosen in draft.

SINGLE-SEASON INDIVIDUAL RECORDS

FORWARDS/DEFENSEMEN

Most goals
69—Mike Bossy, 1978-79

Most assists
87—Bryan Trottier, 1978-79

Most points
147—Mike Bossy, 1981-82

Most penalty minutes
356—Brian Curran, 1986-87

Most power play goals
28—Mike Bossy, 1980-81

Most shorthanded goals
7—Bob Bourne, 1980-81

Most games with three or more goals
9—Mike Bossy, 1980-81

GOALTENDERS

Most games
65—Ron Hextall, 1993-94

Most minutes
3,581—Ron Hextall, 1993-94

Most goals allowed
195—Gerry Desjardins, 1972-73

Lowest goals-against average
2.07—Chico Resch, 1975-76

Most shutouts
7—Chico Resch, 1975-76

Most wins
32—Billy Smith, 1981-82

Most losses
35—Gerry Desjardins, 1972-73

Most ties
17—Billy Smith, 1974-75

FRANCHISE LEADERS

Players in boldface played for club in '98-99

FORWARDS/DEFENSEMEN

Games
Bryan Trottier 1123
Denis Potvin 1060
Bob Nystrom 900
Clark Gillies 872
Bob Bourne 814

Goals
Mike Bossy 573
Bryan Trottier 500
Denis Potvin 310
Clark Gillies 304
Pat LaFontaine 287
Brent Sutter 287

Assists
Bryan Trottier 853
Denis Potvin 742
Mike Bossy 553
Clark Gillies 359
John Tonelli 338

Points
Bryan Trottier 1353
Mike Bossy 1126
Denis Potvin 1052
Clark Gillies 663
Brent Sutter 610

Penalty minutes
Mick Vukota 1879
Rich Pilon 1491
Garry Howatt 1466
Denis Potvin 1354
Bob Nystrom 1248

GOALTENDERS

Games
Billy Smith 675
Chico Resch 282
Kelly Hrudey 241
Tommy Salo 187
Glenn Healy 176

Shutouts
Chico Resch 25
Billy Smith 22
Tommy Salo 14
Kelly Hrudey 6
Wade Flaherty 3

Goals-against average (2400 minutes minimum)
Chico Resch 2.56
Tommy Salo 2.77
Ron Hextall 3.08
Eric Fichaud 3.14
Roland Melanson 3.14

Wins
Billy Smith 304
Chico Resch 157
Kelly Hrudey 106
Roland Melanson 77
Glenn Healy 66

NEW YORK RANGERS

YEAR-BY-YEAR RECORDS

	REGULAR SEASON					PLAYOFFS			
Season	W	L	T	Pts.	Finish	W	L	Highest round	Coach
1926-27	25	13	6	56	1st/American	*0	1	Semifinals	Lester Patrick
1927-28	19	16	9	47	2nd/American	*5	3	Stanley Cup champ	Lester Patrick
1928-29	21	13	10	52	2nd/American	*3	2	Stanley Cup finals	Lester Patrick
1929-30	17	17	10	44	3rd/American	*1	2	Semifinals	Lester Patrick
1930-31	19	16	9	47	3rd/American	2	2	Semifinals	Lester Patrick
1931-32	23	17	8	54	1st/American	3	4	Stanley Cup finals	Lester Patrick
1932-33	23	17	8	54	3rd/American	*6	1	Stanley Cup champ	Lester Patrick
1933-34	21	19	8	50	3rd/American	*0	1	Quarterfinals	Lester Patrick
1934-35	22	20	6	50	3rd/American	*1	1	Semifinals	Lester Patrick
1935-36	19	17	12	50	4th/American	—	—		Lester Patrick
1936-37	19	20	9	47	3rd/American	6	3	Stanley Cup finals	Lester Patrick
1937-38	27	15	6	60	2nd/American	1	2	Quarterfinals	Lester Patrick
1938-39	26	16	6	58	2nd	3	4	Semifinals	Lester Patrick
1939-40	27	11	10	64	2nd	8	4	Stanley Cup champ	Frank Boucher
1940-41	21	19	8	50	4th	1	2	Quarterfinals	Frank Boucher
1941-42	29	17	2	60	1st	2	4	Semifinals	Frank Boucher
1942-43	11	31	8	30	6th	—	—		Frank Boucher
1943-44	6	39	5	17	6th	—	—		Frank Boucher
1944-45	11	29	10	32	6th	—	—		Frank Boucher
1945-46	13	28	9	35	6th	—	—		Frank Boucher
1946-47	22	32	6	50	5th	—	—		Frank Boucher
1947-48	21	26	13	55	4th	2	4	League semifinals	Frank Boucher
1948-49	18	31	11	47	6th	—	—		Frank Boucher, Lynn Patrick
1949-50	28	31	11	67	4th	7	5	Stanley Cup finals	Lynn Patrick
1950-51	20	29	21	61	5th	—	—		Neil Colville
1951-52	23	34	13	59	5th	—	—		Neil Colville, Bill Cook
1952-53	17	37	16	50	6th	—	—		Bill Cook
1953-54	29	31	10	68	5th	—	—		Frank Boucher, Muzz Patrick
1954-55	17	35	18	52	5th	—	—		Muzz Patrick
1955-56	32	28	10	74	3rd	1	4	League semifinals	Phil Watson
1956-57	26	30	14	66	4th	1	4	League semifinals	Phil Watson
1957-58	32	25	13	77	2nd	2	4	League semifinals	Phil Watson
1958-59	26	32	12	64	5th	—	—		Phil Watson
1959-60	17	38	15	49	6th	—	—		Phil Watson, Alf Pike
1960-61	22	38	10	54	5th	—	—		Alf Pike
1961-62	26	32	12	64	4th	2	4	League semifinals	Doug Harvey
1962-63	22	36	12	56	5th	—	—		Muzz Patrick, Red Sullivan
1963-64	22	38	10	54	5th	—	—		Red Sullivan
1964-65	20	38	12	52	5th	—	—		Red Sullivan
1965-66	18	41	11	47	6th	—	—		Red Sullivan, Emile Francis
1966-67	30	28	12	72	4th	0	4	League semifinals	Emile Francis
1967-68	39	23	12	90	2nd/East	2	4	Division semifinals	Emile Francis
1968-69	41	26	9	91	3rd/East	0	4	Division semifinals	Bernie Geoffrion, Emile Francis
1969-70	38	22	16	92	4th/East	2	4	Division semifinals	Emile Francis
1970-71	49	18	11	109	2nd/East	7	6	Division finals	Emile Francis
1971-72	48	17	13	109	2nd/East	10	6	Stanley Cup finals	Emile Francis
1972-73	47	23	8	102	3rd/East	5	5	Division finals	Emile Francis
1973-74	40	24	14	94	3rd/East	7	6	Division finals	Larry Popein, Emile Francis
1974-75	37	29	14	88	2nd/Patrick	1	2	Preliminaries	Emile Francis
1975-76	29	42	9	67	4th/Patrick	—	—		Ron Stewart, John Ferguson
1976-77	29	37	14	72	4th/Patrick	—	—		John Ferguson
1977-78	30	37	13	73	4th/Patrick	1	2	Preliminaries	Jean-Guy Talbot
1978-79	40	29	11	91	3rd/Patrick	11	7	Stanley Cup finals	Fred Shero
1979-80	38	32	10	86	3rd/Patrick	4	5	Quarterfinals	Fred Shero
1980-81	30	36	14	74	4th/Patrick	7	7	Semifinals	Fred Shero, Craig Patrick
1981-82	39	27	14	92	2nd/Patrick	5	5	Division finals	Herb Brooks
1982-83	35	35	10	80	4th/Patrick	5	4	Division finals	Herb Brooks
1983-84	42	29	9	93	4th/Patrick	2	3	Division semifinals	Herb Brooks
1984-85	26	44	10	62	4th/Patrick	0	3	Division semifinals	Herb Brooks, Craig Patrick
1985-86	36	38	6	78	4th/Patrick	8	8	Conference finals	Ted Sator
1986-87	34	38	8	76	4th/Patrick	2	4	Division semifinals	Ted Sator, Tom Webster, Phil Esposito
1987-88	36	34	10	82	4th/Patrick	—	—		Michel Bergeron
1988-89	37	35	8	82	3rd/Patrick	0	4	Division semifinals	Michel Bergeron, Phil Esposito
1989-90	36	31	13	85	1st/Patrick	5	5	Division finals	Roger Neilson
1990-91	36	31	13	85	2nd/Patrick	2	4	Division semifinals	Roger Neilson
1991-92	50	25	5	105	1st/Patrick	6	7	Division finals	Roger Neilson

	REGULAR SEASON					PLAYOFFS			
Season	W	L	T	Pts.	Finish	W	L	Highest round	Coach
1992-93	34	39	11	79	6th/Patrick	—	—		Roger Neilson, Ron Smith
1993-94	52	24	8	112	1st/Atlantic	16	7	Stanley Cup champ	Mike Keenan
1994-95	22	23	3	47	4th/Atlantic	4	6	Conference semifinals	Colin Campbell
1995-96	41	27	14	96	2nd/Atlantic	5	6	Conference semifinals	Colin Campbell
1996-97	38	34	10	86	4th/Atlantic	9	6	Conference finals	Colin Campbell
1997-98	25	39	18	68	5th/Atlantic	—	—		Colin Campbell, John Muckler
1998-99	33	38	11	77	4th/Atlantic	—	—		John Muckler

*Won-lost record does not indicate tie(s) resulting from two-game, total goals series that year (two-game, total-goals series were played from 1917-18 through 1935-36).

FIRST-ROUND ENTRY DRAFT CHOICES

Year Player, Overall, Last amateur team (league)

1969—Andre Dupont, 8, Montreal (OHL)
Pierre Jarry, 12, Ottawa (OHL)
1970—Normand Gratton, 11, Montreal (OHL)
1971—Steve Vickers, 10, Toronto (OHL)
Steve Durbano, 13, Toronto (OHL)
1972—Albert Blanchard, 10, Kitchener (OHL)
Bobby MacMillan, 15, St. Catharines (OHL)
1973—Rick Middleton, 14, Oshawa (OHL)
1974—Dave Maloney, 14, Kitchener (OHL)
1975—Wayne Dillon, 12, Toronto (WHA)
1976—Don Murdoch, 6, Medicine Hat (WCHL)
1977—Lucien DeBlois, 8, Sorel (QMJHL)
Ron Duguay, 13, Sudbury (OHL)
1978—No first-round selection
1979—Doug Sulliman, 13, Kitchener (OHL)
1980—Jim Malone, 14, Toronto (OHL)
1981—James Patrick, 9, Prince Albert (AJHL)
1982—Chris Kontos, 15, Toronto (OHL)

Year Player, Overall, Last amateur team (league)

1983—Dave Gagner, 12, Brantford (OHL)
1984—Terry Carkner, 14, Peterborough (OHL)
1985—Ulf Dahlen, 7, Ostersund (Sweden)
1986—Brian Leetch, 9, Avon Old Farms Prep (Ct.)
1987—Jayson More, 10, New Westminster (WCHL)
1988—No first-round selection
1989—Steven Rice, 20, Kitchener (OHL)
1990—Michael Stewart, 13, Michigan State University
1991—Alexei Kovalev, 15, Dynamo Moscow (USSR)
1992—Peter Ferraro, 24, Waterloo (USHL)
1993—Niklas Sundstrom, 8, Ornskoldsvik (Sweden)
1994—Dan Cloutier, 26, Sault Ste. Marie (OHL)
1995—No first-round selection
1996—Jeff Brown, 22, Sarnia (OHL)
1997—Stefan Cherneski, 19, Brandon (WHL)
1998—Manny Malhotra, 7, Guelph (OHL)
1999—Pavel Brendl, 4, Calgary (WHL)
Jamie Lundmark, 9, Moose Jaw (WHL)

SINGLE-SEASON INDIVIDUAL RECORDS

FORWARDS/DEFENSEMEN

Most goals
52—Adam Graves, 1993-94

Most assists
88—Brian Leetch, 1991-92

Most points
109—Jean Ratelle, 1971-72

Most penalty minutes
305—Troy Mallette, 1989-90

Most power play goals
23—Vic Hadfield, 1971-72

Most shorthanded goals
5—Don Maloney, 1980-81
Mike Rogers, 1982-83
Mike Gartner, 1993-94
Mark Messier, 1996-97

Most games with three or more goals
4—Tomas Sandstrom, 1986-87

Most shots
344—Phil Esposito, 1976-77

GOALTENDERS

Most games
72—Mike Richter, 1997-98

Most minutes
4,143—Mike Richter, 1997-98

Lowest goals-against average
1.48—John Ross Roach, 1928-29

Most shutouts
13—John Ross Roach, 1928-29

Most wins
42—Mike Richter, 1993-94

FRANCHISE LEADERS

Players in boldface played for club in '98-99

FORWARDS/DEFENSEMEN

Games

Harry Howell 1160
Rod Gilbert 1065
Ron Greschner 982
Walt Tkaczuk 945
Jean Ratelle 862

Goals

Rod Gilbert 406
Jean Ratelle 336
Andy Bathgate 272
Vic Hadfield 262
Camille Henry 256

Assists

Rod Gilbert 615
Brian Leetch 578
Jean Ratelle 481
Andy Bathgate 457
Walt Tkaczuk 451

Points

Rod Gilbert 1021
Jean Ratelle 817
Brian Leetch 755
Andy Bathgate 729
Walt Tkaczuk 678

Penalty minutes

Ron Greschner 1226
Jeff Beukeboom 1157
Harry Howell 1147
Don Maloney 1113
Vic Hadfield 1036

GOALTENDERS

Games

Gump Worsley 583
Ed Giacomin 539
Mike Richter 492
John Vanbiesbrouck 449
Chuck Rayner 377

Shutouts

Ed Giacomin 49
Dave Kerr 40
John Ross Roach 30

Chuck Rayner..24
Gump Worsley..24

Goals-against average
(2400 minutes minimum)

Lorne Chabot..1.61
Dave Kerr..2.07
John Ross Roach..2.16
Andy Aitkenhead..2.42
Johnny Bower..2.62
Gilles Villemure..2.62

Wins

Ed Giacomin..266
Mike Richter..230
Gump Worsley..204
John Vanbiesbrouck..200
Dave Kerr..157

OTTAWA SENATORS (FIRST CLUB—DEFUNCT)

YEAR-BY-YEAR RECORDS

	REGULAR SEASON					PLAYOFFS			
Season	W	L	T	Pts.	Finish	W	L	Highest round	Coach
1917-18	9	13	0	18	3rd	—	—		Eddie Gerard
1918-19	12	6	0	24	1st	1	4	Semifinals	Alf Smith
1919-20	19	5	0	38	1st	3	2	Stanley Cup champ	Pete Green
1920-21	14	10	0	28	2nd	*4	2	Stanley Cup champ	Pete Green
1921-22	14	8	2	30	1st	*0	1	Semifinals	Pete Green
1922-23	14	9	1	29	1st	6	2	Stanley Cup champ	Pete Green
1923-24	16	8	0	32	1st	0	2	Semifinals	Pete Green
1924-25	17	12	1	35	4th	—	—		Pete Green
1925-26	24	8	4	52	1st	*0	1	Semifinals	Pete Green
1926-27	30	10	4	64	1st/Canadian	*3	0	Stanley Cup champ	Dave Gill
1927-28	20	14	10	50	3rd/Canadian	0	2	Quarterfinals	Dave Gill
1928-29	14	17	13	41	4th/Canadian	—	—		Dave Gill
1929-30	21	15	8	50	3rd/Canadian	*0	1	Semifinals	Newsy Lalonde
1930-31	10	30	4	24	5th/Canadian	—	—		Newsy Lalonde
1931-32	Club suspended operations for one season.								
1932-33	11	27	10	32	5th/Canadian	—	—		Cy Denneny
1933-34	13	29	6	32	5th/Canadian	—	—		George Boucher

*Won-lost record does not indicate tie(s) resulting from two-game, total goals series that year (two-game, total-goals series were played from 1917-18 through 1935-36).

Franchise relocated and became St. Louis Eagles following 1933-34 season.

OTTAWA SENATORS (SECOND CLUB)

YEAR-BY-YEAR RECORDS

	REGULAR SEASON					PLAYOFFS			
Season	W	L	T	Pts.	Finish	W	L	Highest round	Coach
1992-93	10	70	4	24	6th/Adams	—	—		Rick Bowness
1993-94	14	61	9	37	7th/Northeast	—	—		Rick Bowness
1994-95	9	34	5	23	7th/Northeast	—	—		Rick Bowness
1995-96	18	59	5	41	6th/Northeast	—	—		Rick Bowness, Dave Allison, Jacques Martin
1996-97	31	36	15	77	T3rd/Northeast	3	4	Conference quarterfinals	Jacques Martin
1997-98	34	33	15	83	5th/Northeast	5	6	Conference semifinals	Jacques Martin
1998-99	44	23	15	103	1st/Northeast	0	4	Conference quarterfinals	Jacques Martin

FIRST-ROUND ENTRY DRAFT CHOICES

Year Player, Overall, Last amateur team (league)
1992—Alexei Yashin, 2, Dynamo Moscow (CIS)
1993—Alexandre Daigle, 1, Victoriaville (QMJHL)*
1994—Radek Bonk, 3, Las Vegas (IHL)
1995—Bryan Berard, 1, Detroit (OHL)*
1996—Chris Phillips, 1, Prince Albert (WHL)*

Year Player, Overall, Last amateur team (league)
1997—Marian Hossa, 12, Dukla Trencin (Czechoslovakia)
1998—Mathieu Chouinard, 15, Shawinigan (QMJHL)
1999—Martin Havlat, 26, Trinec, Czech Republic
*Designates first player chosen in draft.

SINGLE-SEASON INDIVIDUAL RECORDS

FORWARDS/DEFENSEMEN

Most goals
44—Alexei Yashin, 1998-99

Most assists
50—Alexei Yashin, 1998-99

Most points
94—Alexei Yashin, 1998-99

Most penalty minutes
318—Mike Peluso, 1992-93

Most power play goals
19—Alexei Yashin, 1998-99

Most shorthanded goals
4—Magnus Arvedson, 1998-99

Most games with three or more goals
1—Held by many players

Most shots
337—Alexei Yashin, 1998-99

GOALTENDERS

Most games
64—Peter Sidorkiewicz, 1992-93

Most minutes
3,388—Peter Sidorkiewicz, 1992-93

Most shots against
1,801—Craig Billington, 1993-94

Most goals allowed
254—Craig Billington, 1993-94

Lowest goals-against average
1.79—Ron Tugnutt, 1998-99

Most shutouts
5—Damian Rhodes, 1997-98

Most wins
22—Damian Rhodes, 1998-99
Ron Tugnutt, 1998-99

Most losses
46—Peter Sidorkiewicz, 1992-93

Most ties
14—Damian Rhodes, 1996-97

FRANCHISE LEADERS

Players in boldface played for club in '98-99

FORWARDS/DEFENSEMEN

Games

Alexei Yashin **422**
Radek Bonk **317**
Alexandre Daigle 301
Randy Cunneyworth 276
Daniel Alfredsson **271**

Goals

Alexei Yashin **178**
Daniel Alfredsson **78**
Alexandre Daigle 74
Shawn McEachern **66**
Radek Bonk **47**
Bob Kudelski 47
Sylvain Turgeon 47

Assists

Alexei Yashin **225**
Daniel Alfredsson **132**
Alexandre Daigle 98
Norm Maciver 73
Andreas Dackell **72**

Points

Alexei Yashin **403**
Daniel Alfredsson **210**
Alexandre Daigle 172
Shawn McEachern **135**
Andreas Dackell **114**

Penalty minutes

Dennis Vial 625
Denny Lambert 467
Troy Mallette 372
Randy Cunneyworth 360
Mike Peluso 318

GOALTENDERS

Games

Damian Rhodes **181**
Ron Tugnutt **122**
Craig Billington 72
Don Beaupre 71
Peter Sidorkiewicz 64

Shutouts

Damian Rhodes **11**
Ron Tugnutt **9**
Don Beaupre 2

Goals-against average
(1200 minutes minimum)

Ron Tugnutt **2.24**
Damian Rhodes **2.56**
Don Beaupre 3.53
Darrin Madeley 4.36
Daniel Berthiaume 4.39

Wins

Damian Rhodes **65**
Ron Tugnutt **54**
Don Beaupre 14
Craig Billington 11
Peter Sidorkiewicz 8

PHILADELPHIA FLYERS

YEAR-BY-YEAR RECORDS

	REGULAR SEASON					PLAYOFFS			
Season	**W**	**L**	**T**	**Pts.**	**Finish**	**W**	**L**	**Highest round**	**Coach**
1967-68	31	32	11	73	1st/West	3	4	Division semifinals	Keith Allen
1968-69	20	35	21	61	3rd/West	0	4	Division semifinals	Keith Allen
1969-70	17	35	24	58	5th/West	—	—		Vic Stasiuk
1970-71	28	33	17	73	3rd/West	0	4	Division semifinals	Vic Stasiuk
1971-72	26	38	14	66	5th/West	—	—		Fred Shero
1972-73	37	30	11	85	2nd/West	5	6	Division finals	Fred Shero
1973-74	50	16	12	112	1st/West	12	5	Stanley Cup champ	Fred Shero
1974-75	51	18	11	113	1st/Patrick	12	5	Stanley Cup champ	Fred Shero
1975-76	51	13	16	118	1st/Patrick	8	8	Stanley Cup finals	Fred Shero
1976-77	48	16	16	112	1st/Patrick	4	6	Semifinals	Fred Shero
1977-78	45	20	15	105	2nd/Patrick	7	5	Semifinals	Fred Shero
1978-79	40	25	15	95	2nd/Patrick	3	5	Quarterfinals	Bob McCammon, Pat Quinn
1979-80	48	12	20	116	1st/Patrick	13	6	Stanley Cup finals	Pat Quinn
1980-81	41	24	15	97	2nd/Patrick	6	6	Quarterfinals	Pat Quinn
1981-82	38	31	11	87	3rd/Patrick	1	3	Division semifinals	Pat Quinn, Bob McCammon
1982-83	49	23	8	106	1st/Patrick	0	3	Division semifinals	Bob McCammon
1983-84	44	26	10	98	3rd/Patrick	0	3	Division semifinals	Bob McCammon
1984-85	53	20	7	113	1st/Patrick	12	7	Stanley Cup finals	Mike Keenan
1985-86	53	23	4	110	1st/Patrick	2	3	Division semifinals	Mike Keenan
1986-87	46	26	8	100	1st/Patrick	15	11	Stanley Cup finals	Mike Keenan
1987-88	38	33	9	85	2nd/Patrick	3	4	Division semifinals	Mike Keenan
1988-89	36	36	8	80	4th/Patrick	10	9	Conference finals	Paul Holmgren
1989-90	30	39	11	71	6th/Patrick	—	—		Paul Holmgren
1990-91	33	37	10	76	5th/Patrick	—	—		Paul Holmgren
1991-92	32	37	11	75	6th/Patrick	—	—		Paul Holmgren, Bill Dineen
1992-93	36	37	11	83	5th/Patrick	—	—		Bill Dineen
1993-94	35	39	10	80	6th/Atlantic	—	—		Terry Simpson
1994-95	28	16	4	60	1st/Atlantic	10	5	Conference finals	Terry Murray
1995-96	45	24	13	103	1st/Atlantic	6	6	Conference semifinals	Terry Murray
1996-97	45	24	13	103	2nd/Atlantic	12	7	Stanley Cup finals	Terry Murray
1997-98	42	29	11	95	2nd/Atlantic	1	4	Conference quarterfinals	Wayne Cashman, Roger Neilson
1998-99	37	26	19	93	2nd/Atlantic	2	4	Conference quarterfinals	Roger Neilson

FIRST-ROUND ENTRY DRAFT CHOICES

Year Player, Overall, Last amateur team (league)
1969—Bob Currier, 6, Cornwall (QMJHL)
1970—No first-round selection
1971—Larry Wright, 8, Regina (WCHL)
Pierre Plante, 9, Drummondville (QMJHL)
1972—Bill Barber, 7, Kitchener (OHL)
1973—No first-round selection
1974—No first-round selection
1975—Mel Bridgeman, 1, Victoria (WCHL)*
1976—Mark Suzor, 17, Kingston (OHL)
1977—Kevin McCarthy, 17, Winnipeg (WCHL)
1978—Behn Wilson, 6, Kingston (OHL)
Ken Linseman, 7, Birmingham (WHA)
Dan Lucas, 14, Sault Ste. Marie (OHL)
1979—Brian Propp, 14, Brandon (WHL)
1980—Mike Stothers, 21, Kingston (OHL)
1981—Steve Smith, 16, Sault Ste. Marie (OHL)
1982—Ron Sutter, 4, Lethbridge (WHL)
1983—No first-round selection

Year Player, Overall, Last amateur team (league)
1984—No first-round selection
1985—Glen Seabrooke, 21, Peterborough (OHL)
1986—Kerry Huffman, 20, Guelph (OHL)
1987—Darren Rumble, 20, Kitchener (OHL)
1988—Claude Boivin, 14, Drummondville (QMJHL)
1989—No first-round selection
1990—Mike Ricci, 4, Peterborough (OHL)
1991—Peter Forsberg, 6, Modo (Sweden)
1992—Ryan Sittler, 7, Nichols H.S. (N.Y.)
Jason Bowen, 15, Tri-City (WHL)
1993—No first-round selection
1994—No first-round selection
1995—Brian Boucher, 22, Tri-City (WHL)
1996—Dainius Zubrus, 15, Pembroke, Tier II
1997—No first-round selection
1998—Simon Gagne, 22, Quebec (QMJHL)
1999—Maxime Ouellet, 22, Quebec (QMJHL)
*Designates first player chosen in draft.

SINGLE-SEASON INDIVIDUAL RECORDS

FORWARDS/DEFENSEMEN

Most goals
61—Reggie Leach, 1975-76

Most assists
89—Bobby Clarke, 1974-75
Bobby Clarke, 1975-76

Most points
123—Mark Recchi, 1992-93

Most penalty minutes
472—Dave Schultz, 1974-75

Most power play goals
34—Tim Kerr, 1985-86

Most shorthanded goals
7—Brian Propp, 1984-85
Mark Howe, 1985-86

Most games with three or more goals
5—Tim Kerr, 1984-85

Most shots
380—Bill Barber, 1975-76

GOALTENDERS

Most games
73—Bernie Parent, 1973-74

Most minutes
4,314—Bernie Parent, 1973-74

Most goals allowed
208—Ron Hextall, 1987-88

Lowest goals-against average
1.89—Bernie Parent, 1973-74

Most shutouts
12—Bernie Parent, 1973-74
Bernie Parent, 1974-75

Most wins
47—Bernie Parent, 1973-74

Most losses
29—Bernie Parent, 1969-70

Most ties
20—Bernie Parent, 1969-70

FRANCHISE LEADERS

Players in boldface played for club in '98-99

FORWARDS/DEFENSEMEN

Games

Bobby Clarke	1144
Bill Barber	903
Brian Propp	790
Joe Watson	746
Bob Kelly	741
Rick MacLeish	741

Goals

Bill Barber	420
Brian Propp	369
Tim Kerr	363
Bobby Clarke	358
Rick MacLeish	328

Assists

Bobby Clarke	852
Brian Propp	480
Bill Barber	463
Rick MacLeish	369
Mark Howe	342

Points

Bobby Clarke	1210
Bill Barber	883
Brian Propp	849
Rick MacLeish	697
Tim Kerr	650

Penalty minutes

Rick Tocchet	1683
Paul Holmgren	1600
Andre Dupont	1505
Bobby Clarke	1453
Dave Schultz	1386

GOALTENDERS

Games

Ron Hextall	**489**
Bernie Parent	486
Doug Favell	215
Pete Peeters	179
Wayne Stephenson	165

Shutouts

Bernie Parent	50
Ron Hextall	**18**
Doug Favell	16
Bob Froese	12
Wayne Stephenson	10

Goals-against average (2400 minutes minimum)

Bernie Parent	2.42
Garth Snow	2.59
Bob Froese	2.74
Wayne Stephenson	2.77
Doug Favell	2.78

Wins

Ron Hextall	**240**
Bernie Parent	232
Wayne Stephenson	93
Bob Froese	92
Pelle Lindbergh	87

PHOENIX COYOTES

YEAR-BY-YEAR RECORDS

	REGULAR SEASON					PLAYOFFS			
Season	W	L	T	Pts.	Finish	W	L	Highest round	Coach
1996-97	38	37	7	83	T3rd/Central	3	4	Conference quarterfinals	Don Hay
1997-98	35	35	12	82	4th/Central	2	4	Conference quarterfinals	Jim Schoenfeld
1998-99	39	31	12	90	2nd/Pacific	3	4	Conference quarterfinals	Jim Schoenfeld

Franchise was formerly known as Winnipeg Jets and relocated to Phoenix following 1995-96 season.

FIRST-ROUND ENTRY DRAFT CHOICES

Year Player, Overall, Last amateur team (league)
1997—No first-round selection
1998—Patrick DesRochers, 14, Sarnia (OHL)
1999—Scott Kelman, 15, Seattle (WHL)
Kirill Safronov, 19, SKA St. Petersburg, Russia

SINGLE-SEASON INDIVIDUAL RECORDS

FORWARDS/DEFENSEMEN

Most goals
52—Keith Tkachuk, 1996-97

Most assists
48—Jeremy Roenick, 1998-99

Most points
86—Keith Tkachuk, 1996-97

Most penalty minutes
228—Keith Tkachuk, 1996-97

Most power play goals
13—Mike Gartner, 1996-97

Most shorthanded goals
5—Bob Corkum, 1997-98

Most games with three or more goals
3—Keith Tkachuk, 1996-97
Keith Tkachuk, 1997-98

Most shots
296—Keith Tkachuk, 1996-97

GOALTENDERS

Most games
72—Nikolai Khabibulin, 1996-97

Most minutes
4,091—Nikolai Khabibulin, 1996-97

Most shots against
2,094—Nikolai Khabibulin, 1996-97

Most goals allowed
193—Nikolai Khabibulin, 1996-97

Lowest goals-against average
2.74—Nikolai Khabibulin, 1996-97

Most shutouts
8—Nikolai Khabibulin, 1998-99

Most wins
32—Nikolai Khabibulin, 1998-99

Most losses
33—Nikolai Khabibulin, 1996-97

Most ties
10—Nikolai Khabibulin, 1997-98

FRANCHISE LEADERS

Players in boldface played for club in '98-99

FORWARDS/DEFENSEMEN

Games

Teppo Numminen.......................246
Bob Corkum.............................233
Jeremy Roenick........................229
Keith Tkachuk..........................218
Oleg Tverdovsky........................210

Goals

Keith Tkachuk..........................128
Jeremy Roenick..........................77
Rick Tocchet.............................52
Mike Gartner.....................................44
Dallas Drake.............................37

Assists

Jeremy Roenick........................120
Teppo Numminen........................95
Keith Tkachuk............................92
Craig Janney.....................................81
Cliff Ronning.............................81

Points

Keith Tkachuk..........................220
Jeremy Roenick........................197
Teppo Numminen.......................118
Cliff Ronning...........................113
Dallas Drake............................107

Penalty minutes

Keith Tkachuk..........................526
Jeremy Roenick........................348
Jim McKenzie....................................346
Jim Cummins............................237
Gerald Diduck...........................213

GOALTENDERS

Games

Nikolai Khabibulin....................205
Jim Waite..................................33
Darcy Wakaluk....................................16
Scott Langkow.............................4
Mikhail Shtalenkov........................4

Shutouts

Nikolai Khabibulin......................19
Jim Waite....................................2
Darcy Wakaluk.......................................1

Goals-against average (2400 minutes minimum)

Nikolai Khabibulin....................2.58

Wins

Nikolai Khabibulin......................92
Jim Waite...................................11
Darcy Wakaluk.......................................8
Mikhail Shtalenkov........................1

PITTSBURGH PENGUINS

YEAR-BY-YEAR RECORDS

	REGULAR SEASON					PLAYOFFS			
Season	W	L	T	Pts.	Finish	W	L	Highest round	Coach
1967-68	27	34	13	67	5th/West	—	—		Red Sullivan
1968-69	20	45	11	51	5th/West	—	—		Red Sullivan
1969-70	26	38	12	64	2nd/West	6	4	Division finals	Red Kelly

	REGULAR SEASON					PLAYOFFS			
Season	W	L	T	Pts.	Finish	W	L	Highest round	Coach
1970-71	21	37	20	62	6th/West	—	—		Red Kelly
1971-72	26	38	14	66	4th/West	0	4	Division semifinals	Red Kelly
1972-73	32	37	9	73	5th/West	—	—		Red Kelly, Ken Schinkel
1973-74	28	41	9	65	5th/West	—	—		Ken Schinkel, Marc Boileau
1974-75	37	28	15	89	3rd/Norris	5	4	Quarterfinals	Marc Boileau
1975-76	35	33	12	82	3rd/Norris	1	2	Preliminaries	Marc Boileau, Ken Schinkel
1976-77	34	33	13	81	3rd/Norris	1	2	Preliminaries	Ken Schinkel
1977-78	25	37	18	68	4th/Norris	—	—		Johnny Wilson
1978-79	36	31	13	85	2nd/Norris	2	5	Quarterfinals	Johnny Wilson
1979-80	30	37	13	73	3rd/Norris	2	3	Preliminaries	Johnny Wilson
1980-81	30	37	13	73	3rd/Norris	2	3	Preliminaries	Eddie Johnston
1981-82	31	36	13	75	4th/Patrick	2	3	Division semifinals	Eddie Johnston
1982-83	18	53	9	45	6th/Patrick	—	—		Eddie Johnston
1983-84	16	58	6	38	6th/Patrick	—	—		Lou Angotti
1984-85	24	51	5	53	5th/Patrick	—	—		Bob Berry
1985-86	34	38	8	76	5th/Patrick	—	—		Bob Berry
1986-87	30	38	12	72	5th/Patrick	—	—		Bob Berry
1987-88	36	35	9	81	6th/Patrick	—	—		Pierre Creamer
1988-89	40	33	7	87	2nd/Patrick	7	4	Division finals	Gene Ubriaco
1989-90	32	40	8	72	5th/Patrick	—	—		Gene Ubriaco, Craig Patrick
1990-91	41	33	6	88	1st/Patrick	16	8	Stanley Cup champ	Bob Johnson
1991-92	39	32	9	87	3rd/Patrick	16	5	Stanley Cup champ	Scotty Bowman
1992-93	56	21	7	119	1st/Patrick	7	5	Division finals	Scotty Bowman
1993-94	44	27	13	101	1st/Northeast	2	4	Conference quarterfinals	Eddie Johnston
1994-95	29	16	3	61	2nd/Northeast	5	7	Conference semifinals	Eddie Johnston
1995-96	49	29	4	102	1st/Northeast	11	7	Conference finals	Eddie Johnston
1996-97	38	36	8	84	2nd/Northeast	1	4	Conference quarterfinals	Eddie Johnston, Craig Patrick
1997-98	40	24	18	98	1st/Northeast	2	4	Conference quarterfinals	Kevin Constantine
1998-99	38	30	14	90	3rd/Atlantic	6	7	Conference semifinals	Kevin Constantine

FIRST-ROUND ENTRY DRAFT CHOICES

Year Player, Overall, Last amateur team (league)
1969—No first-round selection
1970—Greg Polis, 7, Estevan (WCHL)
1971—No first-round selection
1972—No first-round selection
1973—Blaine Stoughton, 7, Flin Flon (WCHL)
1974—Pierre Larouche, 8, Sorel (QMJHL)
1975—Gord Laxton, 13, New Westminster (WCHL)
1976—Blair Chapman, 2, Saskatoon (WCHL)
1977—No first-round selection
1978—No first-round selection
1979—No first-round selection
1980—MIke Bullard, 9, Brantford (OHL)
1981—No first-round selection
1982—Rich Sutter, 10, Lethbridge (WHL)
1983—Bob Errey, 15, Peterborough (OHL)
1984—Mario Lemieux, 1, Laval (QMJHL)*
Doug Bodger, 9, Kamloops (WHL)
Roger Belanger, 16, Kingston (OHL)

Year Player, Overall, Last amateur team (league)
1985—Craig Simpson, 2, Michigan State University
1986—Zarley Zalapski, 4, Team Canada
1987—Chris Joseph, 5, Seattle (WHL)
1988—Darrin Shannon, 4, Windsor (OHL)
1989—Jamie Heward, 16, Regina (WHL)
1990—Jaromir Jagr, 5, Poldi Kladno (Czech.)
1991—Markus Naslund, 16, MoDo (Sweden)
1992—Martin Straka, 19, Skoda Plzen (Czech.)
1993—Stefan Bergqvist, 26, Leksand (Sweden)
1994—Chris Wells, 24, Seattle (WHL)
1995—Alexei Morozov, 24, Krylja Sovetov, CIS
1996—Craig Hillier, 23, Ottawa (OHL)
1997—Robert Dome, 17, Las Vegas (IHL)
1998—Milan Kraft, 23, Plzen (Czech.)
1999—Konstantin Koltsov, 18, Cherepovec, Russia
*Designates first player chosen in draft.

SINGLE-SEASON INDIVIDUAL RECORDS

FORWARDS/DEFENSEMEN

Most goals
85—Mario Lemieux, 1988-89

Most assists
114—Mario Lemieux, 1988-89

Most points
199—Mario Lemieux, 1988-89

Most penalty minutes
409—Paul Baxter, 1981-82

Most power play goals
31—Mario Lemieux, 1988-89
Mario Lemieux, 1995-96

Most shorthanded goals
13—Mario Lemieux, 1988-89

Most games with three or more goals
9—Mario Lemieux, 1988-89

Most shots
403—Jaromir Jagr, 1995-96

GOALTENDERS

Most games
63—Greg Millen, 1980-81
Tom Barrasso, 1992-93
Tom Barrasso, 1997-98

Most minutes
3,721—Greg Millen, 1980-81

Most goals allowed
258—Greg Millen, 1980-81

Lowest goals-against average
2.07—Tom Barrasso, 1997-98

Most shutouts
7—Tom Barrasso, 1997-98

Most wins
43—Tom Barrasso, 1992-93

Most losses
31—Les Binkley, 1968-69

Most ties
15—Denis Herron, 1977-78

FRANCHISE LEADERS

Players in boldface played for club in '98-99

FORWARDS/DEFENSEMEN

Games

Jean Pronovost.....753
Mario Lemieux.....745
Rick Kehoe.....722
Jaromir Jagr.....662
Ron Stackhouse.....621

Goals

Mario Lemieux.....613
Jaromir Jagr.....345
Jean Pronovost.....316
Rick Kehoe.....312
Kevin Stevens.....251

Assists

Mario Lemieux.....867
Jaromir Jagr.....517
Ron Francis.....449
Syl Apps.....349
Paul Coffey.....332

Points

Mario Lemieux.....1494
Jaromir Jagr.....862
Rick Kehoe.....636
Ron Francis.....613
Jean Pronovost.....603

Penalty minutes

Troy Loney.....980
Kevin Stevens.....968
Rod Buskas.....959
Bryan Watson.....871
Paul Baxter.....851

GOALTENDERS

Games

Tom Barrasso.....440
Denis Herron.....290
Ken Wregget.....212
Les Binkley.....196
Michel Dion.....151

Shutouts

Tom Barrasso.....21
Les Binkley.....11
Denis Herron.....6
Ken Wregget.....6
Dunc Wilson.....5

Goals-against average (2400 minutes minimum)

Peter Skudra.....2.50
Al Smith.....3.07
Les Binkley.....3.12
Jim Rutherford.....3.14
Tom Barrasso.....3.27

Wins

Tom Barrasso.....221
Ken Wregget.....104
Denis Herron.....88
Les Binkley.....58
Greg Millen.....57

PITTSBURGH PIRATES (DEFUNCT)

YEAR-BY-YEAR RECORDS

	REGULAR SEASON					PLAYOFFS			
Season	**W**	**L**	**T**	**Pts.**	**Finish**	**W**	**L**	**Highest round**	**Coach**
1925-26	19	16	1	39	3rd	—	—		Odie Cleghorn
1926-27	15	26	3	33	4th/American	—	—		Odie Cleghorn
1927-28	19	17	8	46	3rd/American	1	1	Quarterfinals	Odie Cleghorn
1928-29	9	27	8	26	4th/American	—	—		Odie Cleghorn
1929-30	5	36	3	13	5th/American	—	—		Frank Frederickson
1930-31*	4	36	4	12	5th/American	—	—		Cooper Smeaton

*Philadelphia Quakers.

QUEBEC BULLDOGS (DEFUNCT)

YEAR-BY-YEAR RECORDS

	REGULAR SEASON					PLAYOFFS			
Season	**W**	**L**	**T**	**Pts.**	**Finish**	**W**	**L**	**Highest round**	**Coach**
1919-20	4	20	0	8	4th	—	—		Mike Quinn

Franchise relocated and became Hamilton Tigers following 1919-20 season; franchise later relocated and became New York Americans after 1924-25 season.

QUEBEC NORDIQUES (DEFUNCT)

YEAR-BY-YEAR RECORDS

	REGULAR SEASON					PLAYOFFS			
Season	**W**	**L**	**T**	**Pts.**	**Finish**	**W**	**L**	**Highest round**	**Coach**
1972-73*	33	40	5	71	5th	—	—		Maurice Richard, Maurice Filion
1973-74*	38	36	4	80	5th	—	—		Jacques Plante
1974-75*	46	32	0	92	1st	8	7	Avco World Cup finals	Jean-Guy Gendron
1975-76*	50	27	4	104	2nd	1	4	League quarterfinals	Jean-Guy Gendron
1976-77*	47	31	3	97	1st	12	5	Avco World Cup champ	Marc Boileau
1977-78*	40	37	3	83	4th	5	6	League semifinals	Marc Boileau
1978-79*	41	34	5	87	2nd	0	4	League semifinals	Jacques Demers
1979-80	25	44	11	61	5th/Adams	—	—		Jacques Demers
1980-81	30	32	18	78	4th/Adams	2	3	Preliminaries	Maurice Filion, Michel Bergeron
1981-82	33	31	16	82	4th/Adams	7	9	Conference finals	Michel Bergeron
1982-83	34	34	12	80	4th/Adams	1	3	Division semifinals	Michel Bergeron
1983-84	42	28	10	94	3rd/Adams	5	4	Division finals	Michel Bergeron
1984-85	41	30	9	91	2nd/Adams	9	9	Conference finals	Michel Bergeron
1985-86	43	31	6	92	1st/Adams	0	3	Division semifinals	Michel Bergeron
1986-87	31	39	10	72	4th/Adams	7	6	Division finals	Michel Bergeron
1987-88	32	43	5	69	5th/Adams	—	—		Andre Savard, Ron Lapointe

	REGULAR SEASON					PLAYOFFS			
Season	W	L	T	Pts.	Finish	W	L	Highest round	Coach
1988-89	27	46	7	61	5th/Adams	—	—		Ron Lapointe, Jean Perron
1989-90	12	61	7	31	5th/Adams	—	—		Michel Bergeron
1990-91	16	50	14	46	5th/Adams	—	—		Dave Chambers
1991-92	20	48	12	52	5th/Adams	—	—		Dave Chambers, Pierre Page
1992-93	47	27	10	104	2nd/Adams	2	4	Division semifinals	Pierre Page
1993-94	34	42	8	76	5th/Northeast	—	—		Pierre Page
1994-95	30	13	5	65	1st/Northeast	2	4	Conference quarterfinals	Marc Crawford

*Members of World Hockey Association.
Franchise relocated and became Colorado Avalanche following 1994-95 season.

FIRST-ROUND ENTRY DRAFT CHOICES

Year Player, Overall, Last amateur team (league)
1979—Michel Goulet, 20, Birmingham (WHA)
1980—No first-round selection
1981—Randy Moller, 11, Lethbridge (WHL)
1982—David Shaw, 13, Kitchener (OHL)
1983—No first-round selection
1984—Trevor Steinburg, 15, Guelph (OHL)
1985—Dave Latta, 15, Kitchener (OHL)
1986—Ken McRae, 18, Sudbury (OHL)
1987—Bryan Fogarty, 9, Kingston (OHL)
Joe Sakic, 15, Swift Current (WHL)
1988—Curtis Leschyshyn, 3, Saskatoon (WHL)
Daniel Dore, 5, Drummondville (QMJHL)

Year Player, Overall, Last amateur team (league)
1989—Mats Sundin, 1, Nacka (Sweden)*
1990—Owen Nolan, 1, Cornwall (OHL)*
1991—Eric Lindros, 1, Oshawa (OHL)*
1992—Todd Warriner, 4, Windsor (OHL)
1993—Jocelyn Thibault, 10, Sherbrooke (QMJHL)
Adam Deadmarsh, 14, Portland (WHL)
1994—Wade Belak, 12, Saskatoon (WHL)
Jeffrey Kealty, 22, Catholic Memorial H.S.
1995—Marc Denis, 25, Chicoutimi (QMJHL)
*Designates first player chosen in draft.
NOTE: Quebec chose Paul Baxter, Richard Brodeur and Garry Larivierre as priority selections before the 1979 expansion draft.

SINGLE-SEASON INDIVIDUAL RECORDS

FORWARDS/DEFENSEMEN

Most goals
57—Michel Goulet, 1982-83

Most assists
93—Peter Stastny, 1981-82

Most points
139—Peter Stastny, 1981-82

Most penalty minutes
301—Gord Donnelly, 1987-88

Most power play goals
29—Michel Goulet, 1987-88

Most shorthanded goals
6—Michel Goulet, 1981-82
Scott Young, 1992-93

Most games with three or more goals
4—Miroslav Frycer, 1981-82
Peter Stastny, 1982-83

GOALTENDERS

Most games
60—Dan Bouchard, 1981-82

Most minutes
3,572—Dan Bouchard, 1981-82

Most goals allowed
230—Dan Bouchard, 1981-82

Lowest goals-against average
2.78—Stephane Fiset, 1994-95

Most shutouts
4—Clint Malarchuk, 1985-86

Most wins
29—Dan Bouchard, 1983-84
Ron Hextall, 1992-93

Most losses
29—Ron Tugnutt, 1990-91

Most ties
11—Dan Bouchard, 1981-82

FRANCHISE LEADERS

FORWARDS/DEFENSEMEN

Games
Michel Goulet 813
Peter Stastny 737
Alain Cote 696
Anton Stastny 650
Steven Finn 606

Goals
Michel Goulet 456
Peter Stastny 380
Anton Stastny 252
Joe Sakic 235
Dale Hunter 140

Assists
Peter Stastny 668
Michel Goulet 489
Joe Sakic 391
Anton Stastny 384
Dale Hunter 318

Points
Peter Stastny 1048
Michel Goulet 945
Anton Stastny 636
Joe Sakic 626
Dale Hunter 458

Penalty minutes
Dale Hunter 1545
Steven Finn 1511
Paul Gillis 1351
Randy Moller 1002
Mario Marois 778

GOALTENDERS

Games
Dan Bouchard 225
Mario Gosselin 192
Ron Tugnutt 153
Stephane Fiset 152
Clint Malarchuk 140

Shutouts
Mario Gosselin 6
Dan Bouchard 5
Stephane Fiset 5
Clint Malarchuk 5
Michel Dion 2

Goals-against average (2400 minutes minimum)
Jocelyn Thibault 2.95
Ron Hextall 3.45
Dan Bouchard 3.59
Clint Malarchuk 3.63
Maril Gosselin 3.67

Wins
Dan Bouchard 107
Mario Gosselin 79
Stephane Fiset 62
Clint Malarchuk 62
Ron Tugnutt 35

ST. LOUIS BLUES

YEAR-BY-YEAR RECORDS

	REGULAR SEASON					PLAYOFFS			
Season	W	L	T	Pts.	Finish	W	L	Highest round	Coach
1967-68	27	31	16	70	3rd/West	8	10	Stanley Cup finals	Lynn Patrick, Scotty Bowman
1968-69	37	25	14	88	1st/West	8	4	Stanley Cup finals	Scotty Bowman
1969-70	37	27	12	86	1st/West	8	8	Stanley Cup finals	Scotty Bowman
1970-71	34	25	19	87	2nd/West	2	4	Division semifinals	Al Arbour, Scotty Bowman
1971-72	28	39	11	67	3rd/West	4	7	Division finals	Sid Abel, Bill McCreary, Al Arbour
1972-73	32	34	12	76	4th/West	1	4	Division semifinals	Al Arbour, Jean-Guy Talbot
1973-74	26	40	12	64	6th/West	—	—		Jean-Guy Talbot, Lou Angotti
1974-75	35	31	14	84	2nd/Smythe	0	2	Preliminaries	Lou Angotti, Lynn Patrick, Garry Young
1975-76	29	37	14	72	3rd/Smythe	1	2	Preliminaries	Garry Young, Lynn Patrick, Leo Boivin
1976-77	32	39	9	73	1st/Smythe	0	4	Quarterfinals	Emile Francis
1977-78	20	47	13	53	4th/Smythe	—	—		Leo Boivin, Barclay Plager
1978-79	18	50	12	48	3rd/Smythe	—	—		Barclay Plager
1979-80	34	34	12	80	2nd/Smythe	0	3	Preliminaries	Barclay Plager, Red Berenson
1980-81	45	18	17	107	1st/Smythe	5	6	Quarterfinals	Red Berenson
1981-82	32	40	8	72	3rd/Norris	5	5	Division finals	Red Berenson, Emile Francis
1982-83	25	40	15	65	4th/Norris	1	3	Division semifinals	Emile Francis, Barclay Plager
1983-84	32	41	7	71	2nd/Norris	6	5	Division finals	Jacques Demers
1984-85	37	31	12	86	1st/Norris	0	3	Division semifinals	Jacques Demers
1985-86	37	34	9	83	3rd/Norris	10	9	Conference finals	Jacques Demers
1986-87	32	33	15	79	1st/Norris	2	4	Division semifinals	Jacques Martin
1987-88	34	38	8	76	2nd/Norris	5	5	Division finals	Jacques Martin
1988-89	33	35	12	78	2nd/Norris	5	5	Division finals	Brian Sutter
1989-90	37	34	9	83	2nd/Norris	7	5	Division finals	Brian Sutter
1990-91	47	22	11	105	2nd/Norris	6	7	Division finals	Brian Sutter
1991-92	36	33	11	83	3rd/Norris	2	4	Division semifinals	Brian Sutter
1992-93	37	36	11	85	4th/Norris	7	4	Division finals	Bob Plager, Bob Berry
1993-94	40	33	11	91	4th/Central	0	4	Conference quarterfinals	Bob Berry
1994-95	28	15	5	61	2nd/Central	3	4	Conference quarterfinals	Mike Keenan
1995-96	32	34	16	80	T3rd/Central	7	6	Conference semifinals	Mike Keenan
1996-97	36	35	11	83	T3rd/Central	2	4	Conference quarterfinals	Mike Keenan, Jimmy Roberts, Joel Quenneville
1997-98	45	29	8	98	3rd/Central	6	4	Conference semifinals	Joel Quenneville
1998-99	37	32	13	87	2nd/Central	6	7	Conference semifinals	Joel Quenneville

FIRST-ROUND ENTRY DRAFT CHOICES

Year Player, Overall, Last amateur team (league)
1969—No first-round selection
1970—No first-round selection
1971—Gene Carr, 4, Flin Flon (WCHL)
1972—Wayne Merrick, 9, Ottawa (OHL)
1973—John Davidson, 5, Calgary (WCHL)
1974—No first-round selection
1975—No first-round selection
1976—Bernie Federko, 7, Saskatoon (WCHL)
1977—Scott Campbell, 9, London (OHL)
1978—Wayne Babych, 3, Portland (WCHL)
1979—Perry Turnbull, 2, Portland (WHL)
1980—Rik Wilson, 12, Kingston (OHL)
1981—Marty Ruff, 20, Lethbridge (WHL)
1982—No first-round selection
1983—No first-round selection
1984—No first-round selection

Year Player, Overall, Last amateur team (league)
1985—No first-round selection
1986—Jocelyn Lemieux, 10, Laval (QMJHL)
1987—Keith Osborne, 12, North Bay (OHL)
1988—Rod Brind'Amour, 9, Notre Dame Academy (Sask.)
1989—Jason Marshall, 9, Vernon (B.C.) Tier II
1990—No first-round selection
1991—No first-round selection
1992—No first-round selection
1993—No first-round selection
1994—No first-round selection
1995—No first-round selection
1996—Marty Reasoner, 14, Boston College
1997—No first-round selection
1998—Christian Backman, 24, Frolunda HC Goteborg (Sweden)
1999—Barret Jackman, 17, Regina (WHL)

SINGLE-SEASON INDIVIDUAL RECORDS

FORWARDS/DEFENSEMEN

Most goals
86—Brett Hull, 1990-91

Most assists
90—Adam Oates, 1990-91

Most points
131—Brett Hull, 1990-91

Most penalty minutes
306—Bob Gassoff, 1975-76

Most power play goals
29—Brett Hull, 1990-91
Brett Hull, 1992-93

Most shorthanded goals
8—Chuck Lefley, 1975-76
Larry Patey, 1980-81

Most games with three or more goals
8—Brett Hull, 1991-92

Most shots
408—Brett Hull, 1991-92

GOALTENDERS

Most games
79—Grant Fuhr, 1995-96

Most minutes
4,365—Grant Fuhr, 1995-96

Most shots against
2,382—Curtis Joseph, 1993-94

Most goals allowed
250—Mike Liut, 1991-92

Lowest goals-against average
1.96—Jacques Plante, 1968-69

Most shutouts
8—Glenn Hall, 1968-69

Most wins
36—Curtis Joseph, 1993-94

Most losses
29—Mike Liut, 1983-84

Most ties
16—Grant Fuhr, 1995-96

FRANCHISE LEADERS

Players in boldface played for club in '98-99

FORWARDS/DEFENSEMEN

Games

Bernie Federko 927
Brian Sutter 779
Brett Hull 744
Garry Unger 662
Bob Plager 615

Goals

Brett Hull 527
Bernie Federko 352
Brian Sutter 303
Garry Unger 292
Red Berenson 172

Assists

Bernie Federko 721
Brett Hull 409
Brian Sutter 334
Garry Unger 283
Red Berenson 240

Points

Bernie Federko 1073
Brett Hull 936
Brian Sutter 636
Garry Unger 575
Red Berenson 412

Penalty minutes

Brian Sutter 1786
Kelly Chase 1379
Barclay Plager 1115
Rob Ramage 998
Bob Gassoff 866

GOALTENDERS

Games

Mike Liut 347
Curtis Joseph 280
Grant Fuhr 249
Greg Millen 209
Rick Wamsley 154

Shutouts

Glenn Hall 16
Grant Fuhr 11
Mike Liut 10
Jacques Plante 10
Greg Millen 9

Goals-against average (2400 minutes minimum)

Jacques Plante 2.07
Glenn Hall 2.43
Grant Fuhr 2.68
Ernie Wakely 2.77
Jacques Caron 3.02

Wins

Mike Liut 151
Curtis Joseph 137
Grant Fuhr 108
Greg Millen 85
Rick Wamsley 75

ST. LOUIS EAGLES (DEFUNCT)

YEAR-BY-YEAR RECORDS

	REGULAR SEASON					PLAYOFFS			
Season	**W**	**L**	**T**	**Pts.**	**Finish**	**W**	**L**	**Highest round**	**Coach**
1934-35	11	31	6	28	5th/Canadian	—	—		Eddie Gerard, George Boucher

Franchise was formerly known as Ottawa Senators and relocated to St. Louis following 1933-34 season.

SAN JOSE SHARKS

YEAR-BY-YEAR RECORDS

	REGULAR SEASON					PLAYOFFS			
Season	**W**	**L**	**T**	**Pts.**	**Finish**	**W**	**L**	**Highest round**	**Coach**
1991-92	17	58	5	39	6th/Smythe	—	—		George Kingston
1992-93	11	71	2	24	6th/Smythe	—	—		George Kingston
1993-94	33	35	16	82	3rd/Pacific	7	7	Conference semifinals	Kevin Constantine
1994-95	19	25	4	42	3rd/Pacific	4	7	Conference semifinals	Kevin Constantine
1995-96	20	55	7	47	7th/Pacific	—	—		Kevin Constantine, Jim Wiley
1996-97	27	47	8	62	7th/Pacific	—	—		Al Sims
1997-98	34	38	10	78	4th/Pacific	2	4	Conference quarterfinals	Darryl Sutter
1998-89	31	33	18	80	4th/Pacific	2	4	Conference quarterfinals	Darryl Sutter

FIRST-ROUND ENTRY DRAFT CHOICES

Year Player, Overall, Last amateur team (league)
1991—Pat Falloon, 2, Spokane (WHL)
1992—Mike Rathje, 3, Medicine Hat (WHL)
Andrei Nazarov, 10, Dynamo Moscow, CIS
1993—Viktor Kozlov, 6, Moscow, CIS
1994—Jeff Friesen, 11, Regina (WHL)
1995—Teemu Riihijarvi, 12, Espoo Jrs., Finland

Year Player, Overall, Last amateur team (league)
1996—Andrei Zyuzin, 2, Salavat Yulayev UFA, CIS
Marco Sturm, 21, Landshut, Germany
1997—Patrick Marleau, 2, Seattle (WHL)
Scott Hannan, 23, Kelowna (WHL)
1998—Brad Stuart, 3, Regina (WHL)
1999—Jeff Jillson, 14, Michigan (CCHA)

SINGLE-SEASON INDIVIDUAL RECORDS

FORWARDS/DEFENSEMEN

Most goals
31—Owen Nolan, 1996-97
Jeff Friesen, 1997-98

Most assists
52—Kelly Kisio, 1992-93

Most points
78—Kelly Kisio, 1992-93

Most penalty minutes
326—Link Gaetz, 1991-92

Most power play goals
14—Johan Garpenlov, 1992-93

Most shorthanded goals
6—Jamie Baker, 1995-96

Most games with three or more goals
2—Rob Gaudreau, 1992-93
Igor Larionov, 1993-94
Tony Granato, 1996-97

Most shots
231—Tony Granato, 1996-97

GOALTENDERS

Most games
74—Arturs Irbe, 1993-94

Most minutes
4,412—Arturs Irbe, 1993-94

Most shots against
2,064—Arturs Irbe, 1993-94

Most goals allowed
209—Arturs Irbe, 1993-94

Lowest goals-against average
2.46—Mike Vernon, 1997-98

Most shutouts
5—Mike Vernon, 1997-98

Most wins
30—Arturs Irbe, 1993-94
Mike Vernon, 1997-98

Most losses
30—Jeff Hackett, 1992-93

Most ties
16—Arturs Irbe, 1993-94

FRANCHISE LEADERS

Players in boldface played for club in '98-99

FORWARDS/DEFENSEMEN

Games

Jeff Friesen	**366**
Jeff Odgers	334
Mike Rathje	**310**
Owen Nolan	**297**
Marcus Ragnarsson	**293**

Goals

Jeff Friesen	**111**
Owen Nolan	**93**
Pat Falloon	76
Jeff Odgers	48
Ray Whitney	48

Assists

Jeff Friesen	**142**
Owen Nolan	**117**
Pat Falloon	86
Johan Garpenlov	86
Kelly Kisio	78
Marcus Ragnarsson	**78**

Points

Jeff Friesen	**253**
Owen Nolan	**210**
Pat Falloon	162
Johan Garpenlov	132
Ray Whitney	121

Penalty minutes

Jeff Odgers	1001
Owen Nolan	**565**
Jay More	545
Andrei Nazarov	490
Dody Wood	471

GOALTENDERS

Games

Arturs Irbe	183
Mike Vernon	**111**
Jeff Hackett	78
Kelly Hrudey	76
Chris Terreri	68

Shutouts

Mike Vernon	**9**
Arturs Irbe	8
Steve Shields	**4**
Ed Belfour	1
Wade Flaherty	1
Kelly Hrudey	1

Goals-against average (2400 minutes minimum)

Mike Vernon	**2.37**
Kelly Hrudey	3.04
Chris Terreri	3.39
Arturs Irbe	3.47
Wade Flaherty	4.29

Wins

Arturs Irbe	57
Mike Vernon	**46**
Kelly Hrudey	20
Chris Terreri	19
Steve Shields	**15**

TAMPA BAY LIGHTNING

YEAR-BY-YEAR RECORDS

	REGULAR SEASON					PLAYOFFS			
Season	W	L	T	Pts.	Finish	W	L	Highest round	Coach
1992-93	23	54	7	53	6th/Norris	—	—		Terry Crisp
1993-94	30	43	11	71	7th/Atlantic	—	—		Terry Crisp
1994-95	17	28	3	37	6th/Atlantic	—	—		Terry Crisp
1995-96	38	32	12	88	5th/Atlantic	2	4	Conference quarterfinals	Terry Crisp
1996-97	32	40	10	74	6th/Atlantic	—	—		Terry Crisp
1997-98	17	55	10	44	7th/Atlantic	—	—		Terry Crisp, Rick Paterson, Jacques Demers
1998-99	19	54	9	47	4th/Southeast	—	—		Jacques Demers

FIRST-ROUND ENTRY DRAFT CHOICES

Year Player, Overall, Last amateur team (league)
1992—Roman Hamrlik, 1, Zlin (Czech.)*
1993—Chris Gratton, 3, Kingston (OHL)
1994—Jason Weimer, 8, Portland (WHL)
1995—Daymond Langkow, 5, Tri-City (WHL)
1996—Mario Larocque, 16, Hull (QMJHL)
1997—Paul Mara, 7, Sudbury (OHL)
1998—Vincent Lecavalier, 1, Rimouski (QMJHL)*
1999—No first-round selection
*Designates first player chosen in draft.

SINGLE-SEASON INDIVIDUAL RECORDS

FORWARDS/DEFENSEMEN

Most goals
42—Brian Bradley, 1992-93

Most assists
56—Brian Bradley, 1995-96

Most points
86—Brian Bradley, 1992-93

Most penalty minutes
258—Enrico Ciccone, 1995-96

Most power play goals
16—Brian Bradley, 1992-93

Most shorthanded goals
4—Rob Zamuner, 1994-95
Rob Zamuner, 1995-96

Most games with three or more goals
3—Wendel Clark, 1998-99

Most shots
281—Roman Hamrlik, 1995-96

GOALTENDERS

Most games
63—Daren Puppa, 1993-94

Most minutes
3,653—Daren Puppa, 1993-94

Most shots against
1,637—Daren Puppa, 1993-94

Most goals allowed
165—Daren Puppa, 1993-94

Lowest goals-against average
2.46—Daren Puppa, 1995-96

Most shutouts
5—Daren Puppa, 1995-96

Most wins
29—Daren Puppa, 1995-96

Most losses
33—Daren Puppa, 1993-94

Most ties
9—Daren Puppa, 1995-96

FRANCHISE LEADERS

Players in boldface played for club in '98-99

FORWARDS/DEFENSEMEN

Games

Rob Zamuner **475**
Mikael Andersson **435**
Roman Hamrlik 377
Cory Cross **336**
Brian Bradley 328

Goals

Brian Bradley 111
Rob Zamuner **84**
Alexander Selivanov **78**
Chris Gratton 67
Petr Klima 63

Assists

Brian Bradley 189
Roman Hamrlik 133
Rob Zamuner **116**
Chris Gratton 102
John Tucker 82

Points

Brian Bradley 300
Rob Zamuner **200**
Roman Hamrlik 185
Chris Gratton 169
Alexander Selivanov **155**

Penalty minutes

Enrico Ciccone **604**
Chris Gratton 518
Roman Hamrlik 472
Rudy Poeschek 418
Jason Wiemer 391

GOALTENDERS

Games

Daren Puppa **201**
Corey Schwab **87**
Pat Jablonski 58
Rick Tabaracci 55
J.C. Bergeron 53

Shutouts

Daren Puppa **12**
Rick Tabaracci 4
Corey Schwab **3**
J.C. Bergeron 1
Mark Fitzpatrick 1
Pat Jablonski 1
Bill Ranford **1**
Wendell Young 1

Goals-against average (2400 minutes minimum)

Daren Puppa **2.64**
Rick Tabaracci 2.75
Corey Schwab **3.25**
J.C. Bergeron 3.65
Pat Jablonski 3.95

Wins

Daren Puppa **76**
Corey Schwab **21**
Rick Tabaracci 20
J.C. Bergeron 14
Pat Jablonski 13

TORONTO MAPLE LEAFS

YEAR-BY-YEAR RECORDS

	REGULAR SEASON					PLAYOFFS			
Season	W	L	T	Pts.	Finish	W	L	Highest round	Coach
1917-18‡	13	9	0	26	2nd	4	3	Stanley Cup champ	Dick Carroll
1918-19‡	5	13	0	10	3rd	—	—		Dick Carroll
1919-20§	12	12	0	24	3rd	—	—		Frank Heffernan, Harry Sproule
1920-21§	15	9	0	30	1st	0	2	Semifinals	Dick Carroll
1921-22§	13	10	1	27	2nd	*4	2	Stanley Cup champ	Eddie Powers
1922-23§	13	10	1	27	3rd	—	—		Charlie Querrie, Jack Adams
1923-24§	10	14	0	20	3rd	—	—		Eddie Powers
1924-25§	19	11	0	38	2nd	0	2	Semifinals	Eddie Powers
1925-26§	12	21	3	27	6th	—	—		Eddie Powers
1926-27§	15	24	5	35	5th/Canadian	—	—		Conn Smythe
1927-28	18	18	8	44	4th/Canadian	—	—		Alex Roveril, Conn Smythe
1928-29	21	18	5	47	3rd/Canadian	2	2	Semifinals	Alex Roveril, Conn Smythe
1929-30	17	21	6	40	4th/Canadian	—	—		Alex Roveril, Conn Smythe
1930-31	22	13	9	53	2nd/Canadian	*0	1	Quarterfinals	Conn Smythe, Art Duncan
1931-32	23	18	7	53	2nd/Canadian	5	2	Stanley Cup champ	Art Duncan, Dick Irvin
1932-33	24	18	6	54	1st/Canadian	4	5	Stanley Cup finals	Dick Irvin
1933-34	26	13	9	61	1st/Canadian	2	3	Semifinals	Dick Irvin
1934-35	30	14	4	64	1st/Canadian	3	4	Stanley Cup finals	Dick Irvin

Season	W	L	T	Pts.	Finish	W	L	Highest round	Coach
					REGULAR SEASON			PLAYOFFS	
1935-36	23	19	6	52	2nd/Canadian	4	5	Stanley Cup finals	Dick Irvin
1936-37	22	21	5	49	3rd/Canadian	0	2	Quarterfinals	Dick Irvin
1937-38	24	15	9	57	1st/Canadian			Stanley Cup finals	Dick Irvin
1938-39	19	20	9	47	3rd	5	5	Stanley Cup finals	Dick Irvin
1939-40	25	17	6	56	3rd	6	4	Stanley Cup finals	Dick Irvin
1940-41	28	14	6	62	2nd	3	4	Semifinals	Hap Day
1941-42	27	18	3	57	2nd	8	5	Stanley Cup champ	Hap Day
1942-43	22	19	9	53	3rd	2	4	League semifinals	Hap Day
1943-44	23	23	4	50	3rd	1	4	League semifinals	Hap Day
1944-45	24	22	4	52	3rd	8	5	Stanley Cup champ	Hap Day
1945-46	19	24	7	45	5th	—	—		Hap Day
1946-47	31	19	10	72	2nd	8	3	Stanley Cup champ	Hap Day
1947-48	32	15	13	77	1st	8	1	Stanley Cup champ	Hap Day
1948-49	22	25	13	57	4th	8	1	Stanley Cup champ	Hap Day
1949-50	31	27	12	74	3rd	3	4	League semifinals	Hap Day
1950-51	41	16	13	95	2nd	†8	2	Stanley Cup champ	Joe Primeau
1951-52	29	25	16	74	3rd	0	4	League semifinals	Joe Primeau
1952-53	27	30	13	67	5th	—	—		Joe Primeau
1953-54	32	24	14	78	3rd	1	4	League semifinals	King Clancy
1954-55	24	24	22	70	3rd	0	4	League semifinals	King Clancy
1955-56	24	33	13	61	4th	1	4	League semifinals	King Clancy
1956-57	21	34	15	57	5th	—	—		Howie Meeker
1957-58	21	38	11	53	6th	—	—		Billy Reay
1958-59	27	32	11	65	4th	5	7	Stanley Cup finals	Billy Reay, Punch Imlach
1959-60	35	26	9	79	2nd	4	6	Stanley Cup finals	Punch Imlach
1960-61	39	19	12	90	2nd	1	4	League semifinals	Punch Imlach
1961-62	37	22	11	85	2nd	8	4	Stanley Cup champ	Punch Imlach
1962-63	35	23	12	82	1st	8	2	Stanley Cup champ	Punch Imlach
1963-64	33	25	12	78	3rd	8	6	Stanley Cup champ	Punch Imlach
1964-65	30	26	14	74	4th	2	4	League semifinals	Punch Imlach
1965-66	34	25	11	79	3rd	0	4	League semifinals	Punch Imlach
1966-67	32	27	11	75	3rd	8	4	Stanley Cup champ	Punch Imlach
1967-68	33	31	10	76	5th/East	—	—		Punch Imlach
1968-69	35	26	15	85	4th/East	0	4	Division semifinals	Punch Imlach
1969-70	29	34	13	71	6th/East	—	—		John McLellan
1970-71	37	33	8	82	4th/East	2	4	Division semifinals	John McLellan
1971-72	33	31	14	80	4th/East	1	4	Division semifinals	John McLellan
1972-73	27	41	10	64	6th/East	—	—		John McLellan
1973-74	35	27	16	86	4th/East	0	4	Division semifinals	Red Kelly
1974-75	31	33	16	78	3rd/Adams	2	5	Quarterfinals	Red Kelly
1975-76	34	31	15	83	3rd/Adams	5	5	Quarterfinals	Red Kelly
1976-77	33	32	15	81	3rd/Adams	4	5	Quarterfinals	Red Kelly
1977-78	41	29	10	92	3rd/Adams	4	2	Quarterfinals	Roger Neilson
1978-79	34	33	13	81	3rd/Adams	4	7	Quarterfinals	Roger Neilson
1979-80	35	40	5	75	4th/Adams	0	3	Preliminaries	Floyd Smith
1980-81	28	37	15	71	5th/Adams	0	3	Preliminaries	Punch Imlach, Joe Crozier
1981-82	20	44	16	56	5th/Norris	—	—		Mike Nykoluk
1982-83	28	40	12	68	3rd/Norris	1	3	Division semifinals	Mike Nykoluk
1983-84	26	45	9	61	5th/Norris	—	—		Mike Nykoluk
1984-85	20	52	8	48	5th/Norris	—	—		Dan Maloney
1985-86	25	48	7	57	4th/Norris	6	4	Division finals	Dan Maloney
1986-87	32	42	6	70	4th/Norris	7	6	Division finals	John Brophy
1987-88	21	49	10	52	4th/Norris	2	4	Division semifinals	John Brophy
1988-89	28	46	6	62	5th/Norris	—	—		John Brophy, George Armstrong
1989-90	38	38	4	80	3rd/Norris	1	4	Division semifinals	Doug Carpenter
1990-91	23	46	11	57	5th/Norris	—	—		Doug Carpenter, Tom Watt
1991-92	30	43	7	67	5th/Norris	—	—		Tom Watt
1992-93	44	29	11	99	3rd/Norris	11	10	Conference finals	Pat Burns
1993-94	43	29	12	98	2nd/Central	9	9	Conference finals	Pat Burns
1994-95	21	19	8	50	4th/Central	3	4	Conference quarterfinals	Pat Burns
1995-96	34	36	12	80	T3rd/Central	2	4	Conference quarterfinals	Pat Burns, Nick Beverley
1996-97	30	44	8	68	6th/Central	—	—		Mike Murphy
1997-98	30	43	9	69	6th/Central	—	—		Mike Murphy
1998-99	45	30	7	97	2nd/Northeast	9	8	Conference finals	Pat Quinn

*Won-lost record does not indicate tie(s) resulting from two-game, total-goals series that year (two-game, total-goals series were played from 1917-18 through 1935-36).

†Tied after one overtime (curfew law).

‡Toronto Arenas.

§Toronto St. Patricks (until April 14, 1927).

FIRST-ROUND ENTRY DRAFT CHOICES

Year Player, Overall, Last amateur team (league)
1969—Ernie Moser, 9, Esteven (WCHL)
1970—Darryl Sittler, 8, London (OHL)
1971—No first-round selection
1972—George Ferguson, 11, Toronto (OHL)
1973—Lanny McDonald, 4, Medicine Hat (WCHL)
Bob Neely, 10, Peterborough (OHL)
Ian Turnbull, 15, Ottawa (OHL)
1974—Jack Valiquette, 13, Sault Ste. Marie (OHL)
1975—Don Ashby, 6, Calgary (WCHL)
1976—No first-round selection
1977—John Anderson, 11, Toronto (OHA)
Trevor Johansen, 12, Toronto (OHA)
1978—No first-round selection
1979—Laurie Boschman, 9, Brandon (WHL)
1980—No first-round selection
1981—Jim Benning, 6, Portland (WHL)
1982—Gary Nylund, 3, Portland (WHL)
1983—Russ Courtnall, 7, Victoria (WHL)
1984—Al Iafrate, 4, U.S. Olympics/Belleville (OHL)
1985—*Wendel Clark, 1, Saskatoon (WHL)

Year Player, Overall, Last amateur team (league)
1986—Vincent Damphousse, 6, Laval (QMJHL)
1987—Luke Richardson, 7, Peterborough (OHL)
1988—Scott Pearson, 6, Kingston (OHL)
1989—Scott Thornton, 3, Belleville (OHL)
Rob Pearson, 12, Belleville (OHL)
Steve Bancroft, 21, Belleville (OHL)
1990—Drake Berehowsky, 10, Kingston (OHL)
1991—No first-round selection
1992—Brandon Convery, 8, Sudbury (OHL)
Grant Marshall, 23, Ottawa (OHL)
1993—Kenny Jonsson, 12, Rogle (Sweden)
Landon Wilson, 19, Dubuque (USHL)
1994—Eric Fichaud, 16, Chicoutimi (QMJHL)
1995—Jeff Ware, 15, Oshawa (OHL)
1996—No first-round selection
1997—No first-round selection
1998—Nikolai Antropov, 10, Torpedo, Russia
1999—Luca Cereda, 24, Ambri, Switzerland
*Designates first player chosen in draft.

SINGLE-SEASON INDIVIDUAL RECORDS

FORWARDS/DEFENSEMEN

Most goals
54—Rick Vaive, 1981-82

Most assists
95—Doug Gilmour, 1992-93

Most points
127—Doug Gilmour, 1992-93

Most penalty minutes
351—Tiger Williams, 1977-78

Most shorthanded goals
8—Dave Keon, 1970-71
Dave Reid, 1990-91

Most games with three or more goals
5—Darryl Sittler, 1980-81

GOALTENDERS

Most games
74—Felix Potvin, 1996-97

Most minutes
4,271—Felix Potvin, 1996-97

Lowest goals-against average
1.56—Lorne Chabot, 1928-29

Most shutouts
13—Harry Lumley, 1953-54

Most wins
35—Curtis Joseph, 1998-99

Most losses
38—Ed Chadwick, 1957-58

Most ties
22—Harry Lumley, 1954-55

FRANCHISE LEADERS

Players in boldface played for club in '98-99

FORWARDS/DEFENSEMEN

Games

George Armstrong	1187
Tim Horton	1185
Borje Salming	1099
Dave Keon	1062
Ron Ellis	1034

Goals

Darryl Sittler	389
Dave Keon	365
Ron Ellis	332
Rick Vaive	299
Frank Mahovlich	296
George Armstrong	296

Assists

Borje Salming	620
Darryl Sittler	527
Dave Keon	493
George Armstrong	417
Tim Horton	349

Points

Darryl Sittler	916
Dave Keon	858
Borje Salming	768
George Armstrong	713
Ron Ellis	640

Penalty minutes

Dave Williams	1670
Wendel Clark	**1514**
Tim Horton	1389
Borje Salming	1292
Red Horner	1264

GOALTENDERS

Games

Turk Broda	629
Johnny Bower	472
Felix Potvin	**369**
Mike Palmateer	296
Harry Lumley	267

Shutouts

Turk Broda	62
Harry Lumley	34
Lorne Chabot	33
Johnny Bower	32
George Hainsworth	19

Goals-against average (2400 minutes minimum)

John Ross Roach	2.00
Al Rollins	2.05
Lorne Chabot	2.20
Harry Lumley	2.21
George Hainsworth	2.26

Wins

Turk Broda	302
Johnny Bower	220
Felix Potvin	**160**
Mike Palmateer	129
Lorne Chabot	108

VANCOUVER CANUCKS

YEAR-BY-YEAR RECORDS

	REGULAR SEASON					PLAYOFFS			
Season	W	L	T	Pts.	Finish	W	L	Highest round	Coach
1970-71	24	46	8	56	6th/East	—	—		Hal Laycoe
1971-72	20	50	8	48	7th/East	—	—		Hal Laycoe
1972-73	22	47	9	53	7th/East	—	—		Vic Stasiuk
1973-74	24	43	11	59	7th/East	—	—		Bill McCreary, Phil Maloney
1974-75	38	32	10	86	1st/Smythe	1	4	Quarterfinals	Phil Maloney
1975-76	33	32	15	81	2nd/Smythe	0	2	Preliminaries	Phil Maloney
1976-77	25	42	13	63	4th/Smythe	—	—		Phil Maloney, Orland Kurtenbach
1977-78	20	43	17	57	3rd/Smythe	—	—		Orland Kurtenbach
1978-79	25	42	13	63	2nd/Smythe	1	2	Preliminaries	Harry Neale
1979-80	27	37	16	70	3rd/Smythe	1	3	Preliminaries	Harry Neale
1980-81	28	32	20	76	3rd/Smythe	0	3	Preliminaries	Harry Neale
1981-82	30	33	17	77	2nd/Smythe	11	6	Stanley Cup finals	Harry Neale, Roger Neilson
1982-83	30	35	15	75	3rd/Smythe	1	3	Division semifinals	Roger Neilson
1983-84	32	39	9	73	3rd/Smythe	1	3	Division semifinals	Roger Neilson, Harry Neale
1984-85	25	46	9	59	5th/Smythe	—	—		Bill Laforge, Harry Neale
1985-86	23	44	13	59	4th/Smythe	0	3	Division semifinals	Tom Watt
1986-87	29	43	8	66	5th/Smythe	—	—		Tom Watt
1987-88	25	46	9	59	5th/Smythe	—	—		Bob McCammon
1988-89	33	39	8	74	4th/Smythe	3	4	Division semifinals	Bob McCammon
1989-90	25	41	14	64	5th/Smythe	—	—		Bob McCammon
1990-91	28	43	9	65	4th/Smythe	2	4	Division semifinals	Bob McCammon, Pat Quinn
1991-92	42	26	12	96	1st/Smythe	6	7	Division finals	Pat Quinn
1992-93	46	29	9	101	1st/Smythe	6	6	Division finals	Pat Quinn
1993-94	41	40	3	85	2nd/Pacific	15	9	Stanley Cup finals	Pat Quinn
1994-95	18	18	12	48	2nd/Pacific	4	7	Conference semifinals	Rick Ley
1995-96	32	35	15	79	T2nd/Pacific	2	4	Conference quarterfinals	Rick Ley, Pat Quinn
1996-97	35	40	7	77	4th/Pacific	—	—		Tom Renney
1997-98	25	43	14	64	7th/Pacific	—	—		Tom Renney, Mike Keenan
1998-99	23	47	12	58	4th/Northwest	—	—		Mike Keenan, Marc Crawford

FIRST-ROUND ENTRY DRAFT CHOICES

Year Player, Overall, Last amateur team (league)
1970—Dale Tallon, 2, Toronto (OHL)
1971—Jocelyn Guevremont, 3, Montreal (OHL)
1972—Don Lever, 3, Niagara Falls (OHL)
1973—Dennis Ververgaert, 3, London (OHL)
Bob Dailey, 9, Toronto (OHL)
1974—No first-round selection
1975—Rick Blight, 10, Brandon (WCHL)
1976—No first-round selection
1977—Jere Gillis, 4, Sherbrooke (QMJHL)
1978—Bill Derlago, 4, Brandon (WCHL)
1979—Rick Vaive, 5, Birmingham (WHA)
1980—Rick Lanz, 7, Oshawa (OHL)
1981—Garth Butcher, 10, Regina (WHL)
1982—Michel Petit, 11, Sherbrooke (QMJHL)
1983—Cam Neely, 9, Portland (WHL)
1984—J.J. Daigneault, 10, Can. Ol./Longueuil (QMJHL)
1985—Jim Sandlak, 4, London (OHL)

Year Player, Overall, Last amateur team (league)
1986—Dan Woodley, 7, Portland (WHL)
1987—No first-round selection
1988—Trevor Linden, 2, Medicine Hat (WHL)
1989—Jason Herter, 8, University of North Dakota
1990—Petr Nedved, 2, Seattle (WHL)
Shawn Antoski, 18, North Bay (OHL)
1991—Alex Stojanov, 7, Hamilton (OHL)
1992—Libor Polasek, 21, TJ Vikovice (Czech.)
1993—Mike Wilson, 20, Sudbury (OHL)
1994—Mattias Ohlund, 13, Pitea Div. I (Sweden)
1995—No first-round selection
1996—Josh Holden, 12, Regina (WHL)
1997—Brad Ference, 10, Spokane (WHL)
1998—Bryan Allen, 4, Oshawa (OHL)
1999—Daniel Sedin, 2, Modo Ornskoldsvik, Sweden
Henrik Sedin, 3, Modo Ornskoldsvik, Sweden

SINGLE-SEASON INDIVIDUAL RECORDS

FORWARDS/DEFENSEMEN

Most goals
60—Pavel Bure, 1992-93
Pavel Bure, 1993-94

Most assists
62—Andre Boudrias, 1974-75

Most points
110—Pavel Bure, 1992-93

Most penalty minutes
372—Donald Brashear, 1997-98

Most power play goals
25—Pavel Bure, 1993-94

Most shorthanded goals
7—Pavel Bure, 1992-93

Most games with three or more goals
4—Petri Skriko, 1986-87

Most shots
407—Pavel Bure, 1992-93

GOALTENDERS

Most games
72—Gary Smith, 1974-75

Most minutes
3,852—Kirk McLean, 1991-92

Most goals allowed
240—Richard Brodeur, 1985-86

Lowest goals-against average
2.73—Arturs Irbe, 1997-98

Most shutouts
6—Gary Smith, 1974-75
Garth Snow, 1998-99

Most wins
38—Kirk McLean, 1991-92

Most losses
33—Gary Smith, 1973-74

Most ties
16—Richard Brodeur, 1980-81

FRANCHISE LEADERS

Players in boldface played for club in '98-99

FORWARDS/DEFENSEMEN

Games

Stan Smyl....896
Harold Snepsts....781
Trevor Linden....702
Dennis Kearns....677
Doug Lidster....666

Goals

Stan Smyl....262
Pavel Bure....254
Tony Tanti....250
Trevor Linden....247
Thomas Gradin....197

Assists

Stan Smyl....411
Thomas Gradin....353
Trevor Linden....322
Dennis Kearns....290
Andre Boudrias....267

Points

Stan Smyl....673
Trevor Linden....569
Thomas Gradin....550
Pavel Bure....478
Tony Tanti....470

Penalty minutes

Gino Odjick....2127
Garth Butcher....1668
Stan Smyl....1556
Harold Snepsts....1446
Tiger Williams....1314

GOALTENDERS

Games

Kirk McLean....516
Richard Brodeur....377
Gary Smith....208
Dunc Wilson....148
Glen Hanlon....137

Shutouts

Kirk McLean....20
Gary Smith....11
Richard Brodeur....6
Garth Snow....6
Glen Hanlon....5

Goals-against average (2400 minutes minimum)

Garth Snow....2.95
Corey Hirsch....3.12
Kirk McLean....3.28
Gary Smith....3.33
Kay Whitmore....3.41

Wins

Kirk McLean....211
Richard Brodeur....126
Gary Smith....72
Glen Hanlon....43
Kay Whitmore....36

WASHINGTON CAPITALS

YEAR-BY-YEAR RECORDS

	REGULAR SEASON					PLAYOFFS			
Season	W	L	T	Pts.	Finish	W	L	Highest round	Coach
1974-75	8	67	5	21	5th/Norris	—	—		Jim Anderson, Red Sullivan, Milt Schmidt
1975-76	11	59	10	32	5th/Norris	—	—		Milt Schmidt, Tom McVie
1976-77	24	42	14	62	4th/Norris	—	—		Tom McVie
1977-78	17	49	14	48	5th/Norris	—	—		Tom McVie
1978-79	24	41	15	63	4th/Norris	—	—		Dan Belisle
1979-80	27	40	13	67	5th/Patrick	—	—		Dan Belisle, Gary Green
1980-81	26	36	18	70	5th/Patrick	—	—		Gary Green
1981-82	26	41	13	65	5th/Patrick	—	—		Gary Green, Roger Crozier, Bryan Murray
1982-83	39	25	16	94	3rd/Patrick	1	3	Division semifinals	Bryan Murray
1983-84	48	27	5	101	2nd/Patrick	4	4	Division finals	Bryan Murray
1984-85	46	25	9	101	2nd/Patrick	2	3	Division semifinals	Bryan Murray
1985-86	50	23	7	107	2nd/Patrick	5	4	Division finals	Bryan Murray
1986-87	38	32	10	86	2nd/Patrick	3	4	Division semifinals	Bryan Murray
1987-88	38	33	9	85	2nd/Patrick	7	7	Division finals	Bryan Murray
1988-89	41	29	10	92	1st/Patrick	2	4	Division semifinals	Bryan Murray
1989-90	36	38	6	78	3rd/Patrick	8	7	Conference finals	Bryan Murray, Terry Murray
1990-91	37	36	7	81	3rd/Patrick	5	6	Division finals	Terry Murray
1991-92	45	27	8	98	2nd/Patrick	3	4	Division semifinals	Terry Murray
1992-93	43	34	7	93	2nd/Patrick	2	4	Division semifinals	Terry Murray
1993-94	39	35	10	88	3rd/Atlantic	5	6	Conference semifinals	Terry Murray, Jim Schoenfeld
1994-95	22	18	8	52	3rd/Atlantic	4	3	Conference quarterfinals	Jim Schoenfeld
1995-96	39	32	11	89	4th/Atlantic	2	4	Conference quarterfinals	Jim Schoenfeld
1996-97	33	40	9	75	5th/Atlantic	—	—		Jim Schoenfeld
1997-98	40	30	12	92	3rd/Atlantic	12	9	Stanley Cup finals	Ron Wilson
1998-99	31	45	6	68	3rd/Southeast	—	—		Ron Wilson

FIRST-ROUND ENTRY DRAFT CHOICES

Year Player, Overall, Last amateur team (league)

1974—Greg Joly, 1, Regina (WCHL)*
1975—Alex Forsyth, 18, Kingston (OHA)
1976—Rick Green, 1, London (OHL)*
Greg Carroll, 15, Medicine Hat (WCHL)
1977—Robert Picard, 3, Montreal (QMJHL)
1978—Ryan Walter, 2, Seattle (WCHL)
Tim Coulis, 18, Hamilton (OHL)
1979—Mike Gartner, 4, Cincinnati (WHA)
1980—Darren Veitch, 5, Regina (WHL)

Year Player, Overall, Last amateur team (league)

1981—Bobby Carpenter, 3, St. John's H.S. (Mass.)
1982—Scott Stevens, 5, Kitchener (OHL)
1983—No first-round selection
1984—Kevin Hatcher, 17, North Bay (OHL)
1985—Yvon Corriveau, 19, Toronto (OHL)
1986—Jeff Greenlaw, 19, Team Canada
1987—No first-round selection
1988—Reggie Savage, 15, Victoriaville (QMJHL)
1989—Olaf Kolzig, 19, Tri-City (WHL)

1990—John Slaney, 9, Cornwall (OHL)
1991—Pat Peake, 14, Detroit (OHL)
Trevor Halverson, 21, North Bay (OHL)
1992—Sergei Gonchar, 14, Dynamo Moscow, CIS
1993—Brendan Witt, 11, Seattle (WHL)
Jason Allison, 17, London (OHL)
1994—Nolan Baumgartner, 10, Kamloops (WHL)
Alexander Kharlamov, 15, CSKA Moscow, CIS
1995—Brad Church, 17, Prince Albert (WHL)
Miikka Elomo, 23, Kiekko-67, Finland
1996—Alexander Volchkov, 4, Barrie (OHL)
1997—Nick Boynton, 9, Ottawa (OHL)
Jaroslav Svejkovsky, 17, Tri-City (WHL)
1998—No first-round selection
1999—Kris Breech, 7, Calgary (WHL)
*Designates first player chosen in draft.

SINGLE-SEASON INDIVIDUAL RECORDS

FORWARDS/DEFENSEMEN

Most goals
60—Dennis Maruk, 1981-82

Most assists
76—Dennis Maruk, 1981-82

Most points
136—Dennis Maruk, 1981-82

Most penalty minutes
339—Alan May, 1989-90

Most power play goals
20—Dennis Maruk, 1981-82

Most shorthanded goals
6—Mike Gartner, 1986-87
Peter Bondra, 1994-95

Most games with three or more goals
4—Dennis Maruk, 1980-81
Dennis Maruk, 1981-82
Peter Bondra, 1995-96

Most shots
330—Mike Gartner, 1984-85

GOALTENDERS

Most games
71—Jim Carey, 1995-96

Most minutes
4,069—Jim Carey, 1995-96

Most shots against
1,631—Jim Carey, 1995-96

Most goals allowed
235—Ron Low, 1974-75

Lowest goals-against average
2.13—Jim Carey, 1994-95

Most shutouts
9—Jim Carey, 1995-96

Most wins
35—Jim Carey, 1995-96

Most losses
36—Ron Low, 1974-75

Most ties
10—Wayne Stephenson, 1979-80

FRANCHISE LEADERS

Players in boldface played for club in '98-99

FORWARDS/DEFENSEMEN

Games

Kelly Miller	**940**
Dale Hunter	**872**
Michal Pivonka	**825**
Mike Gartner	758
Calle Johansson	**732**

Goals

Mike Gartner	397
Peter Bondra	**316**
Mike Ridley	218
Bengt Gustafsson	196
Dave Christian	193

Assists

Michal Pivonka	**418**
Mike Gartner	392
Dale Hunter	**375**
Bengt Gustafsson	359
Scott Stevens	331

Points

Mike Gartner	789
Michal Pivonka	**599**
Dale Hunter	**556**
Bengt Gustafsson	555
Mike Ridley	547

Penalty minutes

Dale Hunter	**2003**
Scott Stevens	1630
Craig Berube	**1202**
Alan May	1189
Kevin Hatcher	998

GOALTENDERS

Games

Don Beaupre	269
Olaf Kolzig	**199**
Al Jensen	173
Ron Low	145
Pat Riggin	143

Goals-against average (2400 minutes minimum)

Jim Carey	2.37
Olaf Kolzig	**2.58**
Rick Tabaracci	**2.71**
Pat Riggin	3.02
Don Beaupre	3.05

Wins

Don Beaupre	128
Al Jensen	94
Olaf Kolzig	**73**
Jim Carey	70
Pete Peeters	70

Shutouts

Jim Carey	14
Don Beaupre	12
Olaf Kolzig	**11**
Al Jensen	8
Pete Peeters	7

WINNIPEG JETS (DEFUNCT)

YEAR-BY-YEAR RECORDS

	REGULAR SEASON					PLAYOFFS			
Season	W	L	T	Pts.	Finish	W	L	Highest round	Coach
1972-73*	43	31	4	90	1st	9	5	Avco World Cup finals	Nick Mickoski, Bobby Hull
1973-74*	34	39	5	73	4th	0	4	League quarterfinals	Nick Mickoski, Bobby Hull
1974-75*	38	35	5	81	3rd	—	—		Rudy Pilous
1975-76*	52	27	2	106	1st	12	1	Avco World Cup champ	Bobby Kromm
1976-77*	46	32	2	94	2nd	11	9	Avco World Cup finals	Bobby Kromm
1977-78*	50	28	2	102	1st	8	1	Avco World Cup champ	Larry Hillman
1978-79*	39	35	6	84	3rd	8	2	Avco World Cup champ	Larry Hillman, Tom McVie
1979-80	20	49	11	51	5th/Smythe	—	—		Tom McVie
1980-81	9	57	14	32	6th/Smythe	—	—		Tom McVie, Bill Sutherland, Mike Smith

	REGULAR SEASON					PLAYOFFS			
Season	W	L	T	Pts.	Finish	W	L	Highest round	Coach
1981-82	33	33	14	80	2nd/Norris	1	3	Division semifinals	Tom Watt
1982-83	33	39	8	74	4th/Smythe	0	3	Division semifinals	Tom Watt
1983-84	31	38	11	73	3rd/Smythe	0	3	Division semifinals	Tom Watt, Barry Long
1984-85	43	27	10	96	2nd/Smythe	3	5	Division finals	Barry Long
1985-86	26	47	7	59	3rd/Smythe	0	3	Division semifinals	Barry Long, John Ferguson
1986-87	40	32	8	88	3rd/Smythe	4	6	Division finals	Dan Maloney
1987-88	33	36	11	77	3rd/Smythe	1	4	Division semifinals	Dan Maloney
1988-89	26	42	12	64	5th/Smythe	—	—		Dan Maloney, Rick Bowness
1989-90	37	32	11	85	3rd/Smythe	3	4	Division semifinals	Bob Murdoch
1990-91	26	43	11	63	5th/Smythe	—	—		Bob Murdoch
1991-92	33	32	15	81	4th/Smythe	3	4	Division semifinals	John Paddock
1992-93	40	37	7	87	4th/Smythe	2	4	Division semifinals	John Paddock
1993-94	24	51	9	57	6th/Central	—	—		John Paddock
1994-95	16	25	7	39	6th/Central	—	—		John Paddock, Terry Simpson
1995-96	36	40	6	78	5th/Central	—	—		Terry Simpson

*Members of World Hockey Association.
Franchise relocated and became Phoenix Coyotes following 1995-96 season.

FIRST-ROUND ENTRY DRAFT CHOICES

Year Player, Overall, Last amateur team (league)
1979—Jimmy Mann, 19, Sherbrooke (QMJHL)
1980—David Babych, 2, Portland (WHL)
1981—Dale Hawerchuk, 1, Cornwall (QMJHL)*
1982—Jim Kyte, 12, Cornwall (OHL)
1983—Andrew McBain, 8, North Bay (OHL)
Bobby Dollas, 14, Laval (QMJHL)
1984—No first-round selection
1985—Ryan Stewart, 18, Kamloops (WHL)
1986—Pat Elynuik, 8, Prince Albert (WHL)
1987—Bryan Marchment, 16, Belleville (OHL)
1988—Teemu Selanne, 10, Jokerit (Finland)
1989—Stu Barnes, 4, Tri-City (WHL)

Year Player, Overall, Last amateur team (league)
1990—Keith Tkachuk, 19, Malden Cath. H.S. (Mass.)
1991—Aaron Ward, 5, University of Michigan
1992—Sergei Bautin, 17, Dynamo Moscow (CIS)
1993—Mats Lindgren, 15, Skelleftea (Sweden)
1994—No first-round selection
1995—Shane Doan, 7, Kamloops (WHL)
1996—Dan Focht, 11, Tri-City (WHL)
Daniel Briere, 24, Drummondville (QMJHL)

*Designates first player chosen in draft.
NOTE: Winnipeg chose Scott Campbell, Morris Lukowich and Markus Mattsson as priority selections before the 1979 expansion draft.

SINGLE-SEASON INDIVIDUAL RECORDS

FORWARDS/DEFENSEMEN

Most goals
76—Teemu Selanne, 1992-93

Most assists
79—Phil Housley, 1992-93

Most points
132—Teemu Selanne, 1992-93

Most penalty minutes
347—Tie Domi, 1993-94

Most power play goals
24—Teemu Selanne, 1992-93

Most shorthanded goals
7—Dave McLlwain, 1989-90

Most games with three or more goals
5—Teemu Selanne, 1992-93

Most shots
387—Teemu Selanne, 1992-93

GOALTENDERS

Most games
67—Bob Essensa, 1992-93

Most minutes
3,855—Bob Essensa, 1992-93

Most goals allowed
227—Bob Essensa, 1992-93

Lowest goals-against average
2.88—Bob Essensa, 1991-92

Most shutouts
5—Bob Essensa, 1991-92

Most wins
33—Brian Hayward, 1984-85
Bob Essensa, 1992-93

Most losses
30—Bob Essensa, 1993-94

Most ties
8—Doug Soetaert, 1981-82

FRANCHISE LEADERS

FORWARDS/DEFENSEMEN

Games
Thomas Steen 950
Dale Hawerchuk 713
Doug Smail 691
Randy Carlyle 564
Teppo Numminen 547

Goals
Dale Hawerchuk 379
Thomas Steen 264
Paul MacLean 248
Doug Smail 189
Morris Lukowich 168

Assists
Thomas Steen 553
Dale Hawerchuk 550
Paul MacLean 270
Fredrik Olausson 249
Dave Babych 248

Points
Dale Hawerchuk 929
Thomas Steen 817
Paul MacLean 518
Doug Smail 397
Laurie Boschman 379

Penalty minutes
Laurie Boschman 1338
Keith Tkachuk 792
Jim Kyte 772
Tim Watters 760
Thomas Steen 753

GOALTENDERS

Games
Bob Essensa 281
Brian Hayward 165
Doug Soetaert 130
Daniel Berthiaume 120
Pokey Reddick 117

Shutouts

Bob Essensa	14
Daniel Berthiaume	4
Markus Mattsson	3
Stephane Beauregard	2
Dan Bouchard	2
Doug Soetaert	2
Ed Staniowski	2

Goals-against average (2400 minutes minimum)

Nikolai Khabibulin	3.22
Bob Essensa	3.38
Stephane Beauregard	3.48
Daniel Berthiaume	3.63
Pokey Reddick	3.73

Wins

Bob Essensa	116
Brian Hayward	63
Daniel Berthiaume	50
Doug Soetaert	50
Pokey Reddick	41

MINOR LEAGUES

American Hockey League

International Hockey League

East Coast Hockey League

Central Hockey League

United Hockey League

AMERICAN HOCKEY LEAGUE

LEAGUE OFFICE

Chairman of the board
Jack A. Butterfield
President/CEO and treasurer
David A. Andrews
General counsel
Joe Rodio
Director, finance and administration
Drew Griffin
Director of hockey operations
Jim Mill
Executive assistant, hockey operations
Edward Culver
Manager, corporate sales and licensing
Michael Churchill
Dir. of corporate sales & bus. dev.
Ross Yanco
Coordinator of marketing services
Chris Nikolis
Manager of communications
Bret Stothart
Manager of media relations
Jamie Leaver
Address
1 Monarch Place
Springfield, MA 01144
Phone
413-781-2030
Fax
413-733-4767

TEAMS

ALBANY RIVER RATS

Chief executive officer
Garen Szableski
Head coach
John Cunniff
Home ice
Pepsi Arena
Address
51 South Pearl St.
Albany, NY 12207
Seating capacity
13,311
Phone
518-487-2244
FAX
518-487-2248

CINCINNATI MIGHTY DUCKS

General manager
David McNab
Head coach
Moe Mantha
Home ice
Cincinnati Gardens
Address
2250 Seymour Ave.
Cincinnati, OH 45212
Seating capacity
10,326
Phone
513-351-3999
FAX
513-351-5898

HAMILTON BULLDOGS

General manager
Scott Howson
Head coach
Walt Kyle
Home ice
Copps Coliseum
Address
85 York Blvd.
Hamilton, Ont. L8R 3L4
Seating capacity
8,919
Phone
905-529-8500
FAX
905-529-1188

HARTFORD WOLF PACK

Vice president
Don Maloney
Head coach
John Paddock
Home ice
Hartford Civic Center
Address
196 Trumbull Street, Third Floor
Hartford, CT 06103
Seating capacity
15,635
Phone
860-246-7825
FAX
860-240-7618

HERSHEY BEARS

General manager
Doug Yingst
Head coach
Mike Foligno
Home ice
Hersheypark Arena
Address
P.O. Box 866
Hershey, PA 17033
Seating capacity
7,256
Phone
717-534-3380
FAX
717-534-3383

KENTUCKY THOROUGHBLADES

General manager
Wayne Thomas
Head coach
Roy Sommer
Home ice
Rupp Arena
Address
410 West Vine St.
Lexington, KY 40507
Seating capacity
21,300
Phone
606-259-1996
FAX
606-252-3684

LOUISVILLE PANTHERS

President
Tamer Afr
Head coach
Joe Paterson
Home ice
Freedom Hall
Address
P.O. Box 9227
Louisville, KY 40209
Seating capacity
17,200
Phone
502-992-7825
FAX
502-992-7834

LOWELL LOCK MONSTERS

General manager
Tom Rowe
Head coach
Bruce Boudreau
Home ice
Tsongas Arena
Address
300 Arcand Dr.
Lowell, MA 01852
Seating capacity
6,500
Phone
978-458-7825
FAX
978-453-8452

PHILADELPHIA PHANTOMS

Chief operating officer
Frank Miceli
Head coach
Bill Barber
Home ice
First Union Spectrum
Address
3601 S. Broad Street
Philadelphia, PA 19148
Seating capacity
17,380
Phone
215-465-4522
FAX
215-952-5245

PORTLAND PIRATES

President
Jeff Eisenberg
Head coach
Glen Hanlon
Home ice
Cumberland County Civic Center
Address
85 Free St.
Portland, ME 04101
Seating capacity
6,746
Phone
207-828-4665
FAX
207-773-3278

PROVIDENCE BRUINS

Chief executive officer
Ed Anderson
Head coach
Peter Laviolette
Home ice
Providence Civic Center
Address
1 LaSalle Square
Providence, RI 02903
Seating capacity
11,911
Phone
401-273-5000
FAX
401-273-5004

QUEBEC CITADELLES

General manager
Raymond Bolduc
Head coach
Michel Therrien
Home ice
Colisee de Quebec
Address
250 Hamel Blvd.
Quebec City, Que. G1L 5A7
Seating capacity
15,399
Phone
418-525-5333
FAX
418-525-2242

ROCHESTER AMERICANS

General manager
Jody Gage
Head coach
Brian McCutcheon
Home ice
Rochester War Memorial
Address
One War Memorial Square
Rochester, NY 14614
Seating capacity
11,200
Phone
716-454-5335
FAX
716-454-3954

SAINT JOHN FLAMES

General manager
Nick Polano
Head coach
Rick Vaive
Home ice
Harbour Station
Address
P.O. Box 4040, Station B
Saint John, NB E2M 5E6
Seating capacity
6,153
Phone
506-635-2637
FAX
506-633-4625

ST. JOHN'S MAPLE LEAFS

Director of operations
Glenn Stanford
Head coach
Al MacAdam
Home ice
St. John's Memorial Stadium
Address
49 Elizabeth Ave., Suite 302
St. John's, Newfoundland A1A 1W9
Seating capacity
3,765
Phone
709-726-1010
FAX
709-726-1511

SPRINGFIELD FALCONS

President
Bruce Landon
Head coach
Dave Farrish
Home ice
Springfield Civic Center
Address
P.O. Box 3190
Springfield, MA 01101
Seating capacity
7,452
Phone
413-739-3344
FAX
413-739-3389

SYRACUSE CRUNCH

General manager
Vance Lederman
Head coach
Stan Smyl
Home ice
Onondaga County War Memorial
Address
800 South State St.
Syracuse, NY 13202
Seating capacity
6,230
Phone
315-473-4444
FAX
315-473-4449

WILKES-BARRE/SCRANTON PENGUINS

President
Jeff Barrett
Head coach
Glenn Patrick
Home ice
Northeastern Pennsylvania Civic & Convention Center
Address
60 Public Square, Suite 150
Wilkes-Barre, PA 18701
Seating capacity
8,500
Phone
570-208-7367
FAX
570-208-5432

WORCESTER ICECATS

Vice president
John Ferguson Jr.
Head coach
Greg Gilbert
Home ice
Worcester's Centrum Centre
Address
303 Main St.
Worcester, MA 01608
Seating capacity
12,316
Phone
508-798-5400
FAX
508-799-5267

1998-99 REGULAR SEASON

FINAL STANDINGS

EASTERN CONFERENCE

ATLANTIC DIVISION

Team	G	W	L	T	Pts.	GF	GA
Lowell	80	33	32	13	81	219	237
St. John's	80	34	35	7	79	246	270
Fredericton	80	33	36	6	77	246	246
Saint John	80	31	40	8	71	238	296
Portland	80	23	48	7	55	214	273

NEW ENGLAND DIVISION

Team	G	W	L	T	Pts.	GF	GA
Providence	80	56	16	4	120	321	223
Hartford	80	38	31	5	87	256	256
Springfield	80	35	35	9	80	245	232
Worcester	80	34	36	8	78	237	260
New Haven	80	33	35	7	78	240	250

WESTERN CONFERENCE

EMPIRE DIVISION

Team	G	W	L	T	Pts.	GF	GA
Rochester	80	52	21	6	111	287	176
Albany	80	46	26	6	100	275	230
Hamilton	80	40	29	7	91	229	206
Adirondack	80	21	48	8	53	184	280
Syracuse	80	18	50	9	48	220	327

MID-ATLANTIC DIVISION

Team	G	W	L	T	Pts.	GF	GA
Philadelphia	80	47	22	9	105	272	221
Kentucky	80	44	26	7	98	272	214
Hershey	80	37	32	10	85	242	224
Cincinnati	80	35	39	4	76	227	249

The following teams also had overtime losses (worth one point each): Hartford 6; Fredericton, New Haven 5 each; Hamilton, Providence, St. John's 4 each; Adirondack, Kentucky, Syracuse 3 each; Albany, Cincinnati, Lowell, Philadelphia, Portland, Worcester 2 each; Hershey, Rochester, Saint John, Springfield 1 each.

INDIVIDUAL LEADERS

Goals: Jeff Williams, Albany (46)
Assists: Randy Robitaille, Providence (74)
Points: Domenic Pittis, Rochester (104)
Penalty minutes: Aaron Downey, Providence (401)
Goaltending average: Martin Biron, Rochester (2.07)
Shutouts: Martin Biron, Rochester (6)

TOP SCORERS

	Games	G	A	Pts.
Domenic Pittis, Rochester	76	38	66	104
Randy Robitaille, Providence	74	28	74	102
John Madden, Albany	75	38	60	98
Peter White, Philadelphia	77	31	59	90
Jim Montgomery, Philadelphia	78	29	58	87
Steve Brule, Albany	78	32	52	84
Richard Park, Philadelphia	75	41	42	83
Lonny Bohonos, St. John's	70	34	48	82
Shane Willis, New Haven	73	31	50	81
Craig Fisher, Rochester	70	29	52	81
Derek Armstrong, Hartford	59	29	51	80
Mike Harder, Rochester	79	31	48	79
Christian Matte, Hershey	60	31	47	78
Chris Ferraro, Hamilton	72	35	41	76
Steve Guolla, Kentucky	53	29	47	76
Herbert Vasiljevs, Kentucky	76	28	48	76
Vladimir Vorobiev, Hamilton	73	27	47	74
Jeff Williams, Albany	74	46	27	73
Bob Wren, Cincinnati	73	27	43	70
Serge Aubin, Hershey	64	30	39	69
Craig Reichert, Cincinnati	72	28	41	69
Ladislav Kohn, St. John's	61	27	42	69
Andre Savage, Providence	63	27	42	69
Mark Greig, Philadelphia	67	23	46	69

INDIVIDUAL STATISTICS

ADIRONDACK RED WINGS

SCORING

	Games	G	A	Pts.	PIM
Marc Rodgers	80	19	38	57	66
Philippe Audet	70	20	20	40	77
Dave Paradise	74	17	23	40	62
Jon Coleman	72	12	26	38	32
Brian Bonin	54	19	16	35	31
Darryl Laplante	71	17	15	32	96
B.J. Young	58	13	17	30	150
Shane Hnidy	68	9	20	29	121
Doug Houda	73	7	21	28	122
Ryan Tobler	64	9	18	27	157
Alexandre Jacques	68	9	13	22	25
Xavier Majic	33	2	15	17	12
Barry Potomski	75	9	7	16	220
Jesse Wallin	76	4	12	16	34
Martin Laitre	63	5	7	12	345
Sean Gillam	68	1	10	11	75
Jeff Lazaro	16	2	8	10	10
Petr Klima	15	2	6	8	8
Kirby Law	11	2	3	5	40
Ivan Ciernik	21	1	4	5	4
Yan Golubovsky	43	2	2	4	32
Barry Dreger	65	2	2	4	259
Maxim Kuznetsov	60	0	4	4	30
Kelly Harper	4	1	1	2	0
Jason Elliott (goalie)	51	0	2	2	4
Stacy Roest	2	0	1	1	0
Colin Beardsmore	17	0	1	1	2
Toivo Suursoo	2	0	0	0	0
Colin Chaulk	4	0	0	0	4
Dave Arsenault (goalie)	5	0	0	0	0
Kevin Hodson (goalie)	6	0	0	0	0
Norm Maracle (goalie)	6	0	0	0	0
Aren Miller (goalie)	25	0	0	0	15

GOALTENDING

	Gms.	Min.	W	L	T	G	SO	Avg.
Norm Maracle	6	359	3	3	0	18	0	3.01
Jason Elliott	51	2710	14	27	5	146	2	3.23
Kevin Hodson	6	349	1	3	2	19	0	3.27
Aren Miller	25	1155	3	14	1	68	1	3.53
Dave Arsenault	5	250	0	4	0	20	0	4.80

ALBANY RIVER RATS

SCORING

	Games	G	A	Pts.	PIM
John Madden	75	38	60	98	44
Steve Brule	78	32	52	84	35
Jeff Williams	74	46	27	73	39
Eric Bertrand	78	34	31	65	160
Alexander Semak	70	20	42	62	62
Jiri Bicek	79	15	45	60	102
Ken Sutton	75	13	42	55	118
Sergei Vyshedkevich	79	11	38	49	28
Pierre Dagenais	69	17	13	30	37
Richard Rochefort	70	16	10	26	26
Josh DeWolf	75	1	17	18	111
Rob Pattison	40	9	6	15	17
Colin White	77	2	12	14	265
Geordie Kinnear	55	1	13	14	162
Sascha Goc	55	1	12	13	24
Matt Ruchty	29	6	6	12	134
David Cunniff	48	2	9	11	118
Wes Mason	27	4	4	8	36
Scott Daniels	13	1	5	6	97
Henrik Rehnberg	55	1	4	5	49
William Mitchell	6	1	3	4	29
Vadim Sharifijanov	2	1	1	2	0
Sasha Lakovic	10	1	1	2	93
George Awada	10	1	1	2	8
Rob Skrlac	61	1	1	2	203

	Games	G	A	Pts.	PIM
Vlastimil Kroupa	2	0	1	1	4
Frederic Henry (goalie)	35	0	1	1	0
Jean-Francois Damphousse (g).	1	0	0	0	0
Bobby House	1	0	0	0	0
Judd Lambert (goalie)	2	0	0	0	0
Bryan Duce	2	0	0	0	2
Chris Thompson	9	0	0	0	14
Bryan Muir	10	0	0	0	29
Richard Shulmistra (goalie)	12	0	0	0	2
Mike Buzak (goalie)	48	0	0	0	2

GOALTENDING

	Gms.	Min.	W	L	T	G	SO	Avg.
Judd Lambert	2	102	1	0	0	3	0	1.76
Mike Buzak	48	2382	22	13	3	102	0	2.57
Frederic Henry	35	1690	17	10	3	84	1	2.98
J.-F. Damphousse	1	59	0	1	0	3	0	3.06
Richard Shulmistra	12	596	6	4	0	34	0	3.42

CINCINNATI MIGHTY DUCKS

SCORING

	Games	G	A	Pts.	PIM
Bob Wren	73	27	43	70	102
Craig Reichert	72	28	41	69	56
Mike Leclerc	65	25	28	53	153
Frank Banham	66	22	27	49	20
Igor Nikulin	74	18	26	44	26
Rastisl Pavlikovsky	36	12	23	35	59
Scott Ferguson	78	4	31	35	144
Joel Kwiatkowski	80	12	21	33	48
Eric Lecompte	67	11	22	33	183
Mike Crowley	44	5	23	28	42
Peter LeBoutillier	63	12	12	24	189
Dan Trebil	52	6	15	21	31
Marc Chouinard	69	7	8	15	20
Tony Tuzzolino	50	4	10	14	55
Ivan Ciernik	32	10	3	13	10
Anders Bjork	36	5	8	13	22
Jeremy Stevenson	22	4	4	8	83
Chris Albert	17	4	3	7	109
Johan Davidsson	9	1	6	7	2
Terran Sandwith	40	0	6	6	77
Byron Briske	55	0	6	6	130
Lee Jinman	9	2	2	4	20
Mike Pomichter	25	2	2	4	14
Matt Cullen	3	1	2	3	8
Brett McLean	7	0	3	3	6
Lloyd Shaw	50	2	0	2	170
Dany Bousquet	8	0	2	2	4
Rick Goldmann	32	0	2	2	18
Tom Askey (goalie)	53	0	2	2	15
Beau Bilek	2	1	0	1	2
Josef Marha	3	1	0	1	4
Jeff Winter	55	1	0	1	42
Matt Loen	21	0	1	1	0
Tony Mohagen	1	0	0	0	5
Calvin Elfring	4	0	0	0	0
Eric Hallman	5	0	0	0	0
Ryan Brindley	8	0	0	0	16
Jamie Ram (goalie)	35	0	0	0	4

GOALTENDING

	Gms.	Min.	W	L	T	G	SO	Avg.
Tom Askey	53	2893	21	22	3	131	3	2.72
Jamie Ram	35	1916	14	19	1	109	2	3.41

FREDERICTON CANADIENS

SCORING

	Games	G	A	Pts.	PIM
Martin Gendron	65	33	34	67	26
Eric Houde	69	27	37	64	32
Francis Bouillon	79	19	36	55	174
Marc Beaucage	79	25	26	51	64
Terry Ryan	55	16	27	43	189
Scott King	70	14	29	43	42
Stephane Robidas	79	8	33	41	59
Alexei Lojkin	71	20	20	40	16
Jonathan Delisle	78	7	29	36	118
Aaron Asham	60	16	18	34	118
Jean-Francois Houle	62	7	22	29	101
Boyd Olson	61	10	16	26	60
Miloslav Guren	63	5	16	21	24
Sylvain Blouin	67	6	10	16	333
Jimmy Drolet	57	3	10	13	61
Andrei Bashkirov	13	7	5	12	4
Alain Nasreddine	38	0	10	10	108
Dave Morrisette	39	4	4	8	152
Marc Hussey	51	3	5	8	105
Sergei Zholtok	7	3	4	7	0
Matt Higgins	11	3	4	7	6
Samy Nasserdine	49	3	4	7	77
Darcy Harris	31	3	3	6	97
Aris Brimanis	8	2	4	6	6
J.F. Jomphe	3	1	3	4	6
Gennady Razin	48	0	3	3	16
Brett Clark	3	1	0	1	0
Jose Theodore (goalie)	27	0	1	1	6
Mathieu Garon (goalie)	40	0	1	1	8
Martin Villeneuve (goalie)	2	0	0	0	0
Chris Aldous	3	0	0	0	2
Lee Jinman	4	0	0	0	2
Konstantin Sidulov	5	0	0	0	6
Gordie Dwyer	14	0	0	0	46
Philippe DeRouville (goalie)	19	0	0	0	2

GOALTENDING

	Gms.	Min.	W	L	T	G	SO	Avg.
Jose Theodore	27	1609	12	13	2	77	2	2.87
Philippe DeRouville	19	921	6	6	2	46	0	3.00
Mathieu Garon	40	2222	14	22	2	114	3	3.08
Martin Villeneuve	2	75	1	0	0	4	0	3.22

HAMILTON BULLDOGS

SCORING

	Games	G	A	Pts.	PIM
Chris Ferraro	72	35	41	76	104
Fredrik Lindquist	57	18	36	54	20
Jeff Daw	66	18	29	47	10
Joe Hulbig	76	22	24	46	68
Jim Dowd	51	15	29	44	82
Todd Reirden	58	9	25	34	84
Dan LaCouture	72	17	14	31	73
Steve Potvin	71	9	21	30	79
Kevin J. Brown	32	9	14	23	47
Michel Riesen	60	6	17	23	6
Daniel Lacroix	46	13	9	22	260
Terry Marchant	47	12	8	20	10
Craig Millar	43	3	17	20	38
Sergei Yerkovich	69	7	11	18	103
Mathieu Descoteaux	74	6	12	18	49
David Matsos	55	8	6	14	32
Georges Laraque	25	6	8	14	93
Boyd Devereaux	7	4	6	10	2
Vladimir Vorobiev	8	3	6	9	2
Adam Copeland	30	3	6	9	6
Brad Norton	58	1	8	9	134
Kevin Bolibruck	64	1	6	7	42
Jason Bowen	58	3	3	6	178
Steve Passmore (goalie)	54	0	4	4	16
Chris Hajt	64	0	4	4	36
Brad Church	9	0	2	2	4
Stephane Soulliere	2	1	0	1	0
Paul Comrie	7	0	1	1	0

	Games	G	A	Pts.	PIM
Daniel Cleary	9	0	1	1	7
Alex Stojanov	12	0	1	1	35
Tim Thomas (goalie)	15	0	1	1	2
Darryl LaFrance	1	0	0	0	0
Ted Laviolette	1	0	0	0	0
Chris Wickenheiser (goalie)	2	0	0	0	4
Eric Heffler (goalie)	2	0	0	0	0
Joe Seroski	2	0	0	0	0
Sergei Radchenko	3	0	0	0	7
Kevin Pozzo	3	0	0	0	4
Chad Hinz	3	0	0	0	2
Mike Minard (goalie)	11	0	0	0	4

GOALTENDING

	Gms.	Min.	W	L	T	G	SO	Avg.
Steve Passmore	54	3148	24	21	7	117	4	2.23
Chris Wickenheiser	2	80	1	0	0	3	0	2.25
Eric Heffler	2	119	1	1	0	5	0	2.52
Mike Minard	11	645	8	3	0	30	1	2.79
Tim Thomas	15	837	6	8	0	45	0	3.23

HARTFORD WOLF PACK

SCORING

	Games	G	A	Pts.	PIM
Derek Armstrong	59	29	51	80	73
Vladimir Vorobiev	65	24	41	65	22
Chris Dube	58	21	30	51	20
Ken Gernander	70	23	26	49	32
Bob Errey	69	18	27	45	59
Brad Smyth	36	25	19	44	48
Daniel Goneau	72	20	19	39	56
Scott Fraser	36	13	24	37	20
Johan Witehall	62	14	15	29	56
Todd Hall	72	14	15	29	12
Rich Brennan	47	4	24	28	42
Alexei Vasiliev	75	8	19	27	24
P.J. Stock	55	4	14	18	250
Brent Thompson	76	3	15	18	265
Chris Winnes	33	7	6	13	25
Marc Savard	9	3	10	13	16
Jeff Finley	42	2	10	12	28
Bill Berg	16	4	7	11	23
Boyd Kane	56	3	5	8	23
Chris Kenady	22	2	6	8	52
Kevin J. Brown	9	3	2	5	14
Jan Mertzig	35	3	2	5	14
Jason Doig	8	1	4	5	40
Geoff Smith	9	1	4	5	10
Chris O'Sullivan	10	1	4	5	0
Adam Smith	29	1	4	5	54
Ryan Risidore	49	1	4	5	81
Michael York	3	2	2	4	0
Dale Purinton	45	1	3	4	306
Stefan Cherneski	11	1	2	3	41
Ed Campbell	18	0	3	3	24
Jean-Francois Labbe (goalie)	59	0	3	3	25
Jeff Brown	9	0	2	2	21
Eric Cairns	11	0	2	2	49
Lee Sorochan	16	0	2	2	33
Rumun Ndur	6	0	1	1	4
Kay Whitmore (goalie)	18	0	1	1	0
Benjamin Carpentier	21	0	1	1	31
Francois Fortier	1	0	0	0	0
Mike Sylvia	3	0	0	0	0
Brian Swanson	4	0	0	0	4
David Oliver	4	0	0	0	29
Jeff Heil (goalie)	11	0	0	0	0

GOALTENDING

	Gms.	Min.	W	L	T	G	SO	Avg.
Kay Whitmore	18	1080	8	8	2	47	0	2.61
J.-Francois Labbe	59	3392	28	26	3	182	2	3.22
Jeff Heil	11	367	2	3	0	22	0	3.60

HERSHEY BEARS

SCORING

	Games	G	A	Pts.	PIM
Christian Matte	60	31	47	78	48
Serge Aubin	64	30	39	69	58
Rob Shearer	77	24	42	66	43
Mitch Lamoureux	70	19	34	53	58
Chris Armstrong	65	12	32	44	30
Ville Nieminen	67	24	19	43	127
Mike Gaul	43	9	31	40	22
Paul Brousseau	39	11	21	32	15
Brian Willsie	72	19	10	29	28
Yuri Babenko	74	11	15	26	47
Evgeny Lazarev	53	6	15	21	18
Dan Hinote	65	4	16	20	95
Shannon Finn	42	4	15	19	57
Dan Smith	54	5	7	12	72
Brian White	71	4	8	12	41
Bruce Richardson	44	4	7	11	132
Jeff Buchanan	38	4	6	10	102
Nick Bootland	62	3	6	9	122
Rick Berry	62	2	6	8	153
Scott Parker	32	4	3	7	143
Brad Larsen	18	3	4	7	11
Ted Crowley	18	1	5	6	27
Brent Gretzky	6	2	2	4	2
Eric Messier	6	1	3	4	4
Chris Dingman	17	1	3	4	102
Alex Tanguay	5	1	2	3	2
Calvin Elfring	7	1	1	2	0
Rick Goldmann	21	1	1	2	23
Lindsay Vallis	4	1	0	1	0
Emmanuel LaBranche	5	0	1	1	28
Wade Belak	17	0	1	1	49
Troy Crowder	25	0	1	1	44
David Aebischer (goalie)	38	0	1	1	0
Marc Denis (goalie)	52	0	1	1	17
Jeremy Thompson	1	0	0	0	2
Alexander Ryazantsev	2	0	0	0	0
Scott Ricci	4	0	0	0	2
Ryan Brown	4	0	0	0	9
Greg Callahan	5	0	0	0	29
Travis Tucker	5	0	0	0	0
Ben Storey	5	0	0	0	0
Sami Helenius	8	0	0	0	29

GOALTENDING

	Gms.	Min.	W	L	T	G	SO	Avg.
David Aebischer	38	1932	17	10	5	79	2	2.45
Marc Denis	52	2908	20	23	5	137	4	2.83

KENTUCKY THOROUGHBLADES

SCORING

	Games	G	A	Pts.	PIM
Steve Guolla	53	29	47	76	33
Herbert Vasiljevs	76	28	48	76	66
Jarrod Skalde	54	17	40	57	75
Jarrett Deuling	60	22	31	53	68
Mike Craig	52	27	17	44	72
Matt Bradley	79	23	20	43	57
Dan Boyle	53	8	34	42	87
Mark Smith	78	18	21	39	101
Eric Veilleux	68	8	25	33	114
Steve Lingren	74	11	19	30	60
Andy MacIntyre	61	9	16	25	68
Shawn Burr	26	10	14	24	29
Alexander Korolyuk	23	9	13	22	16
Peter Allen	72	3	17	20	48
Alexandre Boikov	55	5	13	18	116
David Duerden	36	8	9	17	9
Andy Sutton	21	5	10	15	53
Harold Hersh	63	7	7	14	30
Andrei Zyuzin	23	2	12	14	42

	Games	G	A	Pts.	PIM
Steffon Walby	11	8	4	12	6
Filip Kuba	45	2	8	10	33
Curtis Doell	53	2	8	10	166
Joe Blaznek	15	1	7	8	4
Eric Boulton	34	3	3	6	154
Greg Pankewicz	10	2	3	5	7
Shawn Heins	18	2	2	4	108
Mathieu Raby	26	1	1	2	132
Christian Gosselin	31	1	1	2	107
Jan Slavik	3	0	2	2	2
Sean Gauthier (goalie)	40	0	2	2	6
Garrett Burnett	31	1	0	1	186
Xavier Majic	1	0	1	1	0
Mike Kucsulain	4	0	1	1	14
Jon Rohloff	12	0	1	1	8
John Nabokov (goalie)	43	0	1	1	12
Terry Friesen (goalie)	1	0	0	0	0
David Lambeth	1	0	0	0	0
Forrest Gore	1	0	0	0	7
Beau Bilek	1	0	0	0	0
Craig Paterson	2	0	0	0	7
Scott Hannan	2	0	0	0	2
Eric Hallman	3	0	0	0	12
Mark Pivetz	3	0	0	0	0
Darren Wetherill	4	0	0	0	4
Brantt Myhres	4	0	0	0	16

GOALTENDING

	Gms.	Min.	W	L	T	G	SO	Avg.
Sean Gauthier	40	2376	18	15	6	99	1	2.50
John Nabokov	43	2429	26	14	1	106	5	2.62
Terry Friesen	1	26	0	0	0	2	0	4.66

LOWELL LOCK MONSTERS

SCORING

	Games	G	A	Pts.	PIM
Craig Charron	71	22	39	61	41
Sean Haggerty	77	19	27	46	40
Dane Jackson	80	16	27	43	103
Dmitri Nabokov	73	17	25	42	46
Vladimir Orszagh	68	18	23	41	57
Warren Luhning	56	20	20	40	67
Mike Kennedy	62	14	26	40	52
Ray Giroux	59	13	19	32	92
John Namestnikov	42	12	14	26	42
Ted Crowley	41	3	22	25	51
Buddy Wallace	70	11	11	22	57
Nic Beaudoin	49	9	9	18	18
Ryan Huska	60	5	13	18	70
Mark Lawrence	21	10	6	16	28
Mike Mader	52	5	9	14	91
Vladimi Chebaturkin	69	2	12	14	85
Dean Malkoc	61	2	8	10	193
Mike Gaul	18	3	5	8	14
Evgeny Korolev	54	2	6	8	48
Bret Meyers	11	5	2	7	2
Steve Webb	23	2	4	6	80
Vaclav Nedomansky	11	4	1	5	4
Zdeno Chara	23	2	2	4	47
Mike Hough	11	0	3	3	21
Ray Schultz	54	0	3	3	184
Mike Peron	5	1	1	2	2
Jon Sarg	3	0	2	2	2
Duane Harmer	14	0	2	2	16
Jason Stewart	31	0	2	2	7
Marcel Cousineau (goalie)	53	0	2	2	41
Chris Lipsett	2	1	0	1	0
Jim Birmingham	5	1	0	1	0
Wade Flaherty (goalie)	5	0	1	1	0
Kelly Harper	7	0	1	1	0
Nicholas Windsor	8	0	1	1	0
Steve Valiquette (goalie)	1	0	0	0	0
Pavel Smirnov	1	0	0	0	2
Ritchie Bronilla	2	0	0	0	0
Blair Manning	2	0	0	0	2
Jeff Romfo	3	0	0	0	2
Jeff Libby	5	0	0	0	2
Travis Smith	7	0	0	0	0
Eric Cairns	24	0	0	0	91
Mark McArthur (goalie)	26	0	0	0	14

GOALTENDING

	Gms.	Min.	W	L	T	G	SO	Avg.
Marcel Cousineau	53	3034	26	17	7	139	3	2.75
Steve Valiquette	1	59	0	1	0	3	0	3.05
Mark McArthur	26	1457	6	13	5	75	3	3.09
Wade Flaherty	5	305	1	3	1	16	0	3.15

BEAST OF NEW HAVEN

SCORING

	Games	G	A	Pts.	PIM
Shane Willis	73	31	50	81	49
Scott Levins	80	32	26	58	189
Byron Ritchie	66	24	33	57	139
Craig MacDonald	62	17	31	48	77
Craig Ferguson	61	18	27	45	76
Dwayne Hay	46	18	17	35	22
Chris Allen	58	8	27	35	43
Marcus Nilson	69	8	25	33	10
Ryan Johnson	37	8	19	27	18
Peter Ratchuk	53	7	20	27	44
Tommy Westlund	50	8	18	26	31
Tom Buckley	73	8	16	24	48
Pat Mikesch	34	5	15	20	46
Joey Tetarenko	65	4	10	14	154
Jaroslav Spacek	14	4	8	12	15
Chad Cabana	66	6	5	11	251
Ashlin Halfnight	71	2	9	11	45
Ian MacNeil	47	6	4	10	62
Marek Malik	21	2	8	10	28
Steve Halko	42	2	7	9	58
John Jakopin	60	2	7	9	154
Mike Rucinski	23	2	6	8	27
Steve Washburn	10	4	3	7	6
Lance Ward	43	2	5	7	51
Greg Koehler	26	4	0	4	29
Chris Wells	9	3	1	4	28
Peter Worrell	10	3	1	4	65
Andrew Long	16	0	3	3	8
Mark Parrish	2	1	0	1	0
Greg Kuznik	27	1	0	1	33
Jeff Ware	20	0	1	1	26
Mike Fountain (goalie)	51	0	1	1	0
Hugh Hamilton	1	0	0	0	0
Randy Petruk (goalie)	1	0	0	0	0
Sergei Fedotov	3	0	0	0	2
Kevin McDonald	8	0	0	0	14
Todd MacDonald (goalie)	31	0	0	0	0

GOALTENDING

	Gms.	Min.	W	L	T	G	SO	Avg.
Randy Petruk	1	65	0	0	1	3	0	2.77
Mike Fountain	51	2989	23	24	3	150	2	3.01
Todd MacDonald	31	1775	10	16	3	91	0	3.08

PHILADELPHIA PHANTOMS

SCORING

	Games	G	A	Pts.	PIM
Peter White	77	31	59	90	20
Jim Montgomery	78	29	58	87	89
Richard Park	75	41	42	83	33
Mark Greig	67	23	46	69	102
Paul Healey	72	26	20	46	39
Brian Wesenberg	71	23	20	43	169

	Games	G	A	Pts.	PIM
Chris Joseph	51	9	29	38	26
Shawn McCosh	38	12	25	37	43
Mark Eaton	74	9	27	36	38
Francis Belanger	58	13	13	26	242
Jason Zent	64	13	13	26	82
Andy Delmore	70	5	18	23	51
Dave MacIsaac	47	6	15	21	98
Sergei Klimentiev	43	5	12	17	99
Jeff Lank	51	5	10	15	36
Dennis Bonvie	37	4	10	14	158
Ryan Bast	69	0	11	11	160
Martin Cerven	46	6	4	10	20
Steve McLaren	52	4	3	7	216
Mikhial Chernov	56	4	3	7	98
Chris Albert	22	1	3	4	88
Sean O'Brien	18	1	2	3	60
Jesse Boulerice	24	1	2	3	82
Frank Bialowas	24	0	3	3	42
John Pelletier (goalie)	47	0	3	3	0
Dan Kordic	9	1	1	2	43
Martin Boisvenue	5	0	1	1	2
Andre Payette	12	0	1	1	34
John Stevens	25	0	1	1	19
Brian Boucher (goalie)	36	0	1	1	2
Trevor Koenig (goalie)	1	0	0	0	0
Bujar Amidovski (goalie)	2	0	0	0	0

GOALTENDING

	Gms.	Min.	W	L	T	G	SO	Avg.
Bujar Amidovski	2	120	2	0	0	5	0	2.50
Brian Boucher	36	2061	20	8	5	89	2	2.59
John Pelletier	47	2636	25	16	4	122	2	2.78
Trevor Koenig	1	29	0	0	0	2	0	4.14

PORTLAND PIRATES

SCORING

	Games	G	A	Pts.	PIM
Benoit Gratton	64	18	42	60	135
Trevor Halverson	57	24	25	49	153
Jean-Pierre Dumont	50	32	14	46	39
Kent Hulst	72	16	23	39	52
Matt Herr	46	15	14	29	29
Daniel Cleary	30	9	17	26	74
Patrick Boileau	52	6	18	24	52
Steve Poapst	54	3	21	24	36
Casey Hankinson	72	10	13	23	106
Rick Kowalsky	47	6	15	21	85
Nolan Baumgartner	38	5	14	19	62
Trent Whitfield	50	10	8	18	20
Craig Mills	48	7	11	18	59
Mike Peluso	26	7	6	13	6
Rick Mrozik	70	4	8	12	63
Stewart Malgunas	33	2	10	12	49
Alexandre Volchkov	27	3	8	11	24
Steve Tardif	33	2	9	11	48
Jeff Toms	20	3	7	10	8
Barrie Moore	23	3	7	10	4
Tim Murray	28	1	9	10	14
Mark Major	66	5	4	9	250
Josef Marha	8	0	8	8	2
Todd Rohloff	58	1	6	7	59
Mike Omicioli	9	3	3	6	2
Dwight Parrish	54	2	4	6	138
Ryan Vandenbussche	37	4	1	5	119
Jakub Ficenec	5	3	2	5	4
Brad Church	10	1	3	4	18
Jeff Halpern	6	2	1	3	4
Jason Goulet	8	2	1	3	0
Ryan Gillis	8	0	3	3	4
Curtis Sheptak	13	0	3	3	32
Bryan Muir	2	1	1	2	2
Geoff Peters	4	1	1	2	9
Anthony Cappelletti	5	1	1	2	4
Alain St. Hilaire	9	1	1	2	0
Dean Stork	10	0	2	2	13
Martin Brochu (goalie)	20	0	2	2	2
Dennis Bonvie	3	1	0	1	16
Christian LaFlamme	2	0	1	1	2
Remi Royer	2	0	1	1	2
Luke Curtin	4	0	1	1	4
Alain Nasreddine	7	0	1	1	36
Carlin Nordstrom	10	0	1	1	36
Joaquin Gage (goalie)	26	0	1	1	4
Brian LaFleur	1	0	0	0	2
Harlin Hayes (goalie)	1	0	0	0	0
Travis Tucker	2	0	0	0	0
Garry Gulash	2	0	0	0	11
Jeff Salajko (goalie)	2	0	0	0	0
Sebasti Charpentier (goalie)	3	0	0	0	0
Frederic Deschenes (goalie)	3	0	0	0	0
Gerad Adams	3	0	0	0	4
Colin Pepperall	4	0	0	0	6
Jason Hamilton	4	0	0	0	0
Darren Maloney	4	0	0	0	6
Darren Wetherill	5	0	0	0	2
Olaf Kjenstad	5	0	0	0	4
Frank Bialowas	6	0	0	0	10
Jeff Paul	6	0	0	0	4
Denis Chervyakov	13	0	0	0	15
Mike Rosati (goalie)	32	0	0	0	6

GOALTENDING

	Gms.	Min.	W	L	T	G	SO	Avg.
Harlin Hayes	1	20	0	0	0	0	0	0.00
Joaquin Gage	26	1429	8	11	3	69	2	2.90
Martin Brochu	20	1164	6	10	3	57	2	2.94
S. Charpentier	3	180	0	3	0	10	0	3.34
Mike Rosati	32	1783	9	23	0	111	1	3.74
Frederic Deschenes	3	165	0	2	1	14	0	5.09
Jeff Salajko	2	80	0	1	0	7	0	5.25

PROVIDENCE BRUINS

SCORING

	Games	G	A	Pts.	PIM
Randy Robitaille	74	28	74	102	34
Andre Savage	63	27	42	69	54
Brandon Smith	72	16	46	62	32
Eric Nickulas	75	31	27	58	83
Antti Laaksonen	66	25	33	58	52
Terry Virtue	76	8	48	56	117
Landon Wilson	48	31	22	53	89
Shawn Bates	37	25	21	46	39
Cameron Mann	43	21	25	46	65
Steve Bancroft	62	7	34	41	78
Marquis Mathieu	64	15	15	30	166
Joel Prpic	75	14	16	30	163
Peter Ferraro	16	15	10	25	14
Jeremy Brown	47	12	12	24	20
Mattias Timander	43	2	22	24	24
Aaron Downey	75	10	12	22	401
Chris Taylor	21	6	11	17	6
Jay Henderson	55	7	9	16	172
Dennis Vaske	43	2	13	15	56
Johnathan Aitken	65	2	9	11	92
Elias Abrahamsson	75	2	9	11	184
Jason McBain	9	1	7	8	10
Roger Maxwell	29	2	3	5	153
Joe Harney	13	1	4	5	14
Matt Ruchty	17	1	3	4	54
Duane Harmer	9	0	4	4	4
Joel Trottier	7	3	0	3	17
Peter Nordstrom	13	2	1	3	2
Bob Beers	10	1	2	3	4
Mark Cornforth	15	1	1	2	16

	Games	G	A	Pts.	PIM
Jim Bermingham	2	1	0	1	4
Steven King	3	1	0	1	0
Dan Ceman	3	1	0	1	0
Yevgeny Shaldybin	1	0	0	0	0
Paxton Schafer (goalie)	1	0	0	0	0
Dana Mulvihill	2	0	0	0	2
David Brumby (goalie)	2	0	0	0	0
Tim Sweeney	2	0	0	0	0
Joaquin Gage (goalie)	3	0	0	0	0
Shane Belter	5	0	0	0	0
Bill Armstrong	6	0	0	0	32
Jim Carey (goalie)	30	0	0	0	4
John Grahame (goalie)	48	0	0	0	31

GOALTENDING

	Gms.	Min.	W	L	T	G	SO	Avg.
Jim Carey	30	1750	17	8	3	68	3	2.33
John Grahame	48	2771	37	9	1	134	3	2.90
Paxton Schafer	1	61	1	0	0	3	0	2.94
David Brumby	2	119	1	1	0	6	0	3.02
Joaquin Gage	3	130	0	2	0	9	0	4.16

ROCHESTER AMERICANS

SCORING

	Games	G	A	Pts.	PIM
Domenic Pittis	76	38	66	104	110
Craig Fisher	70	29	52	81	28
Mike Harder	79	31	48	79	39
Dean Sylvester	76	35	30	65	46
Mike Hurlbut	72	15	39	54	46
Matt Davidson	80	26	15	41	42
Dean Melanson	79	7	27	34	192
Denis Hamel	74	16	17	33	121
Scott Nichol	53	13	20	33	120
Darren VanOene	73	11	20	31	143
Jason Holland	74	4	25	29	36
Cory Sarich	77	3	26	29	82
Steffon Walby	48	15	13	28	52
Randy Cunneyworth	52	10	18	28	55
Erik Rasmussen	37	12	14	26	47
Greg Walters	56	6	8	14	200
Francois Methot	58	5	8	13	8
Alexei Tezikov	31	3	7	10	41
Jean-L. Grand-Pierre	56	5	4	9	90
Shane Kenny	23	2	1	3	25
Jason Mansoff	26	0	3	3	14
Martin Biron (goalie)	52	0	3	3	22
Marc Dupuis	11	0	2	2	2
Peter Vandermeer	2	1	0	1	16
Dimitri Kalinin	3	0	1	1	14
Alexandre Boikov	13	0	1	1	15
Chris Hynnes	1	0	0	0	0
Dwayne Roloson (goalie)	2	0	0	0	0
Mark Dutiaume	3	0	0	0	0
Derek Wood	3	0	0	0	0
Carlin Nordstrom	11	0	0	0	29
Tom Draper (goalie)	26	0	0	0	2

GOALTENDING

	Gms.	Min.	W	L	T	G	SO	Avg.
Dwayne Roloson	2	120	2	0	0	4	0	2.00
Martin Biron	52	3129	36	13	3	108	6	2.07
Tom Draper	26	1568	14	9	3	60	0	2.30

SAINT JOHN FLAMES

SCORING

	Games	G	A	Pts.	PIM
Martin St. Louis	53	28	34	62	30
Sergei Varlamov	76	24	33	57	66
Travis Brigley	74	15	35	50	48
Hnat Domenichelli	51	25	21	46	26
David Cooper	65	18	24	42	121
Eric M. Landry	56	19	22	41	158
Chris Clark	73	13	27	40	123
Eric Healey	64	14	24	38	77
Chris O'Sullivan	41	7	29	36	24
Ronald Petrovicky	78	12	21	33	114
Greg Pankewicz	30	10	14	24	84
Eric Charron	50	10	12	22	148
Steve Begin	73	11	9	20	156
Jeff Cowan	71	7	12	19	117
Mickey Elick	62	2	11	13	50
Chris Dingman	50	5	7	12	140
Allan Egeland	14	5	5	10	49
Derrick Walser	40	3	7	10	24
Darrel Scoville	61	1	7	8	66
Steve Bancroft	8	1	4	5	22
Rocky Thompson	27	2	2	4	108
Lee Sorochan	3	1	3	4	4
Arttu Kayhko	14	1	3	4	14
Dave Roche	7	0	3	3	6
Denis Gauthier	16	0	3	3	31
Sean Berens	11	2	0	2	6
Dan Price	7	1	1	2	2
Fredrik Oduya	12	0	2	2	48
Wade Belak	12	0	2	2	43
Gaetan Royer	15	1	0	1	36
Mike Vellinga	15	0	1	1	6
Igor Karpenko (goalie)	23	0	1	1	2
J.-Sebastien Giguere (goalie)	39	0	1	1	10
Matt O'Dette	42	0	1	1	82
Trevor Doyle	2	0	0	0	5
Steve Duke	2	0	0	0	0
John Tripp	2	0	0	0	10
Ryan Bast	2	0	0	0	5
Erik Andersson	5	0	0	0	4
Jamie Allison	5	0	0	0	23
Joel Irving	5	0	0	0	2
Bujar Amidovski (goalie)	6	0	0	0	0
Kam White	6	0	0	0	17
Jody Shelley	8	0	0	0	46
Tyler Moss (goalie)	9	0	0	0	0
Matt Eisler (goalie)	15	0	0	0	2

GOALTENDING

	Gms.	Min.	W	L	T	G	SO	Avg.
Tyler Moss	9	475	2	5	1	25	0	3.16
Igor Karpenko	23	1207	5	10	3	69	0	3.43
J.-S. Giguere	39	2145	18	16	3	123	3	3.44
Matt Eisler	15	760	4	8	1	53	0	4.18
Bujar Amidovski	6	243	2	2	0	19	0	4.69

ST. JOHN'S MAPLE LEAFS

SCORING

	Games	G	A	Pts.	PIM
Lonny Bohonos	70	34	48	82	40
Ladislav Kohn	61	27	42	69	90
Jason Podollan	68	42	26	68	65
Kevyn Adams	80	15	35	50	85
Mark Deyell	44	20	27	47	39
D.J. Smith	79	7	28	35	216
Yuri Khmylev	48	12	21	33	19
Aaron Brand	80	7	26	33	88
Nathan Dempsey	67	2	29	31	70
Brad Chartrand	64	16	14	30	48
Dennis Maxwell	41	9	16	25	212
Ryan Pepperall	79	16	8	24	70
Todd Gillingham	61	4	16	20	128
Shawn Thornton	78	8	11	19	354
Jason Sessa	56	9	4	13	25
David Nemirovsky	22	3	9	12	18
Justin Hocking	44	4	6	10	99
Dallas Eakins	20	3	7	10	16
Dimitri Yakushin	71	2	6	8	65

	Games	G	A	Pts.	PIM
Konstantin Kalmikov	52	3	4	7	4
Greg Smyth	40	0	7	7	159
Jeff Ware	55	1	4	5	130
Jeff Reese (goalie)	27	0	3	3	4
Dave Gilmore	3	1	1	2	0
Marek Posymk	41	1	0	1	36
Doug Bonner (goalie)	4	0	0	0	0
Francis Larivee (goalie)	17	0	0	0	12
Marc Robitaille (goalie)	42	0	0	0	8

GOALTENDING

	Gms.	Min.	W	L	T	G	SO	Avg.
Jeff Reese	27	1555	17	7	3	66	1	2.55
Marc Robitaille	42	2269	13	22	1	124	1	3.28
Francis Larivee	17	851	4	7	2	59	0	4.16
Doug Bonner	4	175	0	3	1	13	0	4.47

SPRINGFIELD FALCONS

SCORING

	Games	G	A	Pts.	PIM
Trevor Letowski	67	32	35	67	46
Joe Dziedzic	61	18	27	45	128
Brad Tiley	69	9	35	44	14
Radoslav Suchy	69	4	32	36	10
Tavis Hansen	63	23	11	34	85
Josh Green	41	15	15	30	29
Greg Phillips	63	16	13	29	74
Bobby House	56	11	18	29	27
J.F. Jomphe	29	10	18	28	36
Eric Belanger	33	8	18	26	10
Rob Murray	68	6	19	25	197
Brandon Convery	31	9	14	23	45
Sean McCann	31	8	15	23	31
Sean Gagnon	68	8	14	22	331
Jason Morgan	46	6	16	22	51
Joe Corvo	50	5	15	20	32
Donald Maclean	41	5	14	19	31
Barry Nieckar	67	11	6	17	270
Maxim Spiridonov	23	8	8	16	2
Peter Hogan	71	1	14	15	41
Olli Jokinen	9	3	6	9	6
Steve Leach	13	5	3	8	10
Jason Doig	32	3	5	8	67
Daniel Briere	13	2	6	8	20
Robert Schnabel	77	1	7	8	155
Bruce Coles	9	3	4	7	12
Chris Schmidt	17	3	2	5	19
Sean Tallaire	6	2	1	3	0
John Kosobud	2	2	0	2	4
Jim Brown	7	2	0	2	6
Kevin Hilton	2	1	1	2	0
Brad Isbister	4	1	1	2	12
Dan Bylsma	2	0	2	2	2
Dan Focht	30	0	2	2	58
Tim Harris	1	1	0	1	0
Robert Francz	2	1	0	1	4
Tyler Prosofsky	3	1	0	1	0
Louie DeBrusk	3	1	0	1	0
Karol Bartanus	1	0	1	1	0
Chris Grenville	2	0	1	1	0
Mark Rupnow	3	0	1	1	0
Richard Lintner	8	0	1	1	16
Scott Ricci	9	0	1	1	4
Sean Blanchard	10	0	1	1	4
Robert Esche (goalie)	55	0	1	1	13
Dean Mando	1	0	0	0	0
Jeremy Brown	2	0	0	0	0
Mike Martone	2	0	0	0	2
Mark Cornforth	5	0	0	0	2
Scott Barney	5	0	0	0	2
Jimmy Waite (goalie)	8	0	0	0	4
Sylvain Daigle (goalie)	27	0	0	0	43

GOALTENDING

	Gms.	Min.	W	L	T	G	SO	Avg.
Jimmy Waite	8	483	3	4	1	19	0	2.36
Robert Esche	55	2957	24	20	6	138	1	2.80
Sylvain Daigle	27	1393	8	12	2	67	1	2.89

SYRACUSE CRUNCH

SCORING

	Games	G	A	Pts.	PIM
Boris Protsenko	65	24	24	48	84
Larry Courville	71	13	28	41	155
Valentin Morozov	63	17	23	40	10
Robb Gordon	68	16	22	38	98
Robert Dome	48	18	17	35	70
Mark Wotton	72	4	31	35	74
Matt Cooke	37	15	18	33	119
Brent Sopel	53	10	21	31	59
Ryan Savoia	54	9	22	31	40
Josh Holden	38	14	15	29	48
Peter Schaefer	41	10	19	29	66
Zenith Komarniski	58	9	19	28	89
Martin Sonnenberg	37	16	9	25	31
Michal Rozsival	49	3	22	25	72
Pavel Skrbek	64	6	16	22	38
Alexei Kolkunov	55	5	13	18	20
Sean O'Brien	45	5	11	16	155
Darren Sinclair	68	7	6	13	38
Stewart Bodtker	31	5	5	10	12
Chad Allan	60	2	8	10	98
Steve Washburn	13	1	6	7	6
Dana Murzyn	20	2	4	6	37
Chris Kelleher	45	1	4	5	43
Marcus Gustafsson	3	4	0	4	0
Jonas Soling	29	2	2	4	4
Larry Shapley	50	1	1	2	254
Paul Ferone	28	0	2	2	109
Bert Robertsson	8	1	0	1	21
Tim Keyes (goalie)	11	0	1	1	6
Tom O'Connor	16	0	1	1	8
Clint Cabana	19	0	1	1	86
Mike Valley (goalie)	26	0	1	1	4
Craig Hillier (goalie)	36	0	1	1	6
Patrick Charbonneau (goalie)	1	0	0	0	0
Mark Yannetti	1	0	0	0	0
Andy Powers	1	0	0	0	0
Jamie Bird	1	0	0	0	0
Bobby Stewart	3	0	0	0	0
Chris McAllister	5	0	0	0	24
Kyle Freadrich	5	0	0	0	20
Corey Hirsch (goalie)	5	0	0	0	0
Joaquin Gage (goalie)	12	0	0	0	0

GOALTENDING

	Gms.	Min.	W	L	T	G	SO	Avg.
P. Charbonneau	1	36	1	0	0	0	0	0.00
Corey Hirsch	5	300	2	3	0	14	0	2.80
Joaquin Gage	12	706	2	8	2	46	0	3.91
Craig Hillier	36	1919	9	18	6	126	1	3.94
Mike Valley	26	1281	2	17	1	87	0	4.07
Tim Keyes	11	582	2	7	0	43	0	4.43

WORCESTER ICECATS

SCORING

	Games	G	A	Pts.	PIM
Jochen Hecht	74	21	35	56	48
Shayne Toporowski	75	18	29	47	124
Stephane Roy	64	16	28	44	41
Andrej Podkonicky	61	19	24	43	52
Marty Reasoner	44	17	22	39	24
Lubos Bartecko	49	14	24	38	22
Derek Bekar	51	16	20	36	6
Tyson Nash	55	14	22	36	143

	Games	G	A	Pts.	PIM
Daniel Corso	63	14	14	28	26
Kevin Sawyer	70	8	14	22	299
Rory Fitzpatrick	53	5	16	21	82
Terry Yake	24	8	11	19	26
Tyler Willis	55	8	10	18	227
Bryce Salvador	69	5	13	18	129
Jamal Mayers	20	9	7	16	34
Bryan Helmer	16	7	8	15	18
Jeremiah McCarthy	59	5	10	15	37
Jan Horacek	53	1	13	14	119
Reed Low	77	5	6	11	239
Matt Smith	44	3	8	11	81
Jamie Thompson	25	7	3	10	12
Ricard Persson	19	6	4	10	42
Jaroslav Obsut	31	2	8	10	14
Tyler Harlton	58	2	5	7	94
Derek Diener	39	1	5	6	39
Jason Widmer	25	2	3	5	42
Geoff Smith	25	1	3	4	16
Brent Johnson (goalie)	49	0	4	4	10
Quinn Hancock	13	1	2	3	4
Marek Ivan	7	0	2	2	4
J.F. Boutin	2	1	0	1	2
Darren Maloney	6	1	0	1	6
Andrei Petrakov	4	0	1	1	2
Rich Parent (goalie)	20	0	1	1	2
Jim Mullin (goalie)	1	0	0	0	0
Kris Porter	3	0	0	0	2
Libor Zabransky	6	0	0	0	18
Dan Murphy (goalie)	8	0	0	0	2
Scott Roche (goalie)	9	0	0	0	0

GOALTENDING

	Gms.	Min.	W	L	T	G	SO	Avg.
Brent Johnson	49	2925	22	22	4	146	2	2.99
Rich Parent	20	1100	8	8	2	56	1	3.05
Jim Mullin	1	59	0	1	0	3	0	3.06
Scott Roche	9	339	2	3	1	18	0	3.19
Dan Murphy	8	410	2	4	1	26	0	3.81

PLAYERS WITH TWO OR MORE TEAMS

SCORING

	Games	G	A	Pts.	PIM
Chris Albert, Cincinnati	17	4	3	7	109
Chris Albert, Philadelphia	22	1	3	4	88
Totals	39	5	6	11	197
Bujar Amidovski, S. John (g)	6	0	0	0	0
Bujar Amidovski, Phil. (g)	2	0	0	0	0
Totals	8	0	0	0	0
Steve Bancroft, Saint John	8	1	4	5	22
Steve Bancroft, Providence	62	7	34	41	78
Totals	70	8	38	46	100
Ryan Bast, Saint John	2	0	0	0	5
Ryan Bast, Philadelphia	69	0	11	11	160
Totals	71	0	11	11	165
Wade Belak, Hershey	17	0	1	1	49
Wade Belak, Saint John	12	0	2	2	43
Totals	29	0	3	3	92
Frank Bialowas, Philadelphia	24	0	3	3	42
Frank Bialowas, Portland	6	0	0	0	10
Totals	30	0	3	3	52
Beau Bilek, Kentucky	1	0	0	0	0
Beau Bilek, Cincinnati	2	1	0	1	2
Totals	3	1	0	1	2
Alexandre Boikov, Kentucky	55	5	13	18	116
Alexandre Boikov, Rochester	13	0	1	1	15
Totals	68	5	14	19	131
Dennis Bonvie, Portland	3	1	0	1	16
Dennis Bonvie, Philadelphia	37	4	10	14	158
Totals	40	5	10	15	174
Jeremy Brown, Springfield	2	0	0	0	0
Jeremy Brown, Providence	47	12	12	24	20
Totals	49	12	12	24	20
Kevin J. Brown, Hamilton	32	9	14	23	47
Kevin J. Brown, Hartford	9	3	2	5	14
Totals	41	12	16	28	61
Eric Cairns, Hartford	11	0	2	2	49
Eric Cairns, Lowell	24	0	0	0	91
Totals	35	0	2	2	140
Brad Church, Portland	10	1	3	4	18
Brad Church, Hamilton	9	0	2	2	4
Totals	19	1	5	6	22
Ivan Ciernik, Adirondack	21	1	4	5	4
Ivan Ciernik, Cincinnati	32	10	3	13	10
Totals	53	11	7	18	14
Daniel Cleary, Portland	30	9	17	26	74
Daniel Cleary, Hamilton	9	0	1	1	7
Totals	39	9	18	27	81
Mark Cornforth, Providence	15	1	1	2	16
Mark Cornforth, Springfield	5	0	0	0	2
Totals	20	1	1	2	18
Ted Crowley, Hershey	18	1	5	6	27
Ted Crowley, Lowell	41	3	22	25	51
Totals	59	4	27	31	78
Chris Dingman, Saint John	50	5	7	12	140
Chris Dingman, Hershey	17	1	3	4	102
Totals	67	6	10	16	242
Jason Doig, Springfield	32	3	5	8	67
Jason Doig, Hartford	8	1	4	5	40
Totals	40	4	9	13	107
Calvin Elfring, Hershey	7	1	1	2	0
Calvin Elfring, Cincinnati	4	0	0	0	0
Totals	11	1	1	2	0
Joaquin Gage, Portland (g)	26	0	1	1	4
Joaquin Gage, Prov. (g)	3	0	0	0	0
Joaquin Gage, Syracuse (g)	12	0	0	0	0
Totals	41	0	1	1	4
Mike Gaul, Lowell	18	3	5	8	14
Mike Gaul, Hershey	43	9	31	40	22
Totals	61	12	36	48	36
Rick Goldmann, Hershey	21	1	1	2	23
Rick Goldmann, Cincinnati	32	0	2	2	18
Totals	53	1	3	4	41
Eric Hallman, Kentucky	3	0	0	0	12
Eric Hallman, Cincinnati	5	0	0	0	0
Totals	8	0	0	0	12
Duane Harmer, Lowell	14	0	2	2	16
Duane Harmer, Providence	9	0	4	4	4
Totals	23	0	6	6	20
Kelly Harper, Adirondack	4	1	1	2	0
Kelly Harper, Lowell	7	0	1	1	0
Totals	11	1	2	3	0
Bobby House, Albany	1	0	0	0	0
Bobby House, Springfield	56	11	18	29	27
Totals	57	11	18	29	27
Lee Jinman, Cincinnati	9	2	2	4	20
Lee Jinman, Fredericton	4	0	0	0	2
Totals	13	2	2	4	22
J.F. Jomphe, Springfield	29	10	18	28	36
J.F. Jomphe, Fredericton	3	1	3	4	6
Totals	32	11	21	32	42
Xavier Majic, Kentucky	1	0	1	1	0
Xavier Majic, Adirondack	33	2	15	17	12
Totals	34	2	16	18	12
Darren Maloney, Worcester	6	1	0	1	6
Darren Maloney, Portland	4	0	0	0	6
Totals	10	1	0	1	12
Josef Marha, Cincinnati	3	1	0	1	4
Josef Marha, Portland	8	0	8	8	2
Totals	11	1	8	9	6
Bryan Muir, Albany	10	0	0	0	29
Bryan Muir, Portland	2	1	1	2	2

	Games	G	A	Pts.	PIM
Totals	12	1	1	2	31
Alain Nasreddine, Portland	7	0	1	1	36
Alain Nasreddine, Fredericton	38	0	10	10	108
Totals	45	0	11	11	144
Carlin Nordstrom, Portland	10	0	1	1	36
Carlin Nordstrom, Rochester	11	0	0	0	29
Totals	21	0	1	1	65
Sean O'Brien, Syracuse	45	5	11	16	155
Sean O'Brien, Philadelphia	18	1	2	3	60
Totals	63	6	13	19	215
Chris O'Sullivan, Saint John	41	7	29	36	24
Chris O'Sullivan, Hartford	10	1	4	5	0
Totals	51	8	33	41	24
Greg Pankewicz, Saint John	30	10	14	24	84
Greg Pankewicz, Kentucky	10	2	3	5	7
Totals	40	12	17	29	91
Scott Ricci, Springfield	9	0	1	1	4
Scott Ricci, Hershey	4	0	0	0	2
Totals	13	0	1	1	6
Matt Ruchty, Providence	17	1	3	4	54
Matt Ruchty, Albany	29	6	6	12	134
Totals	46	7	9	16	188
Geoff Smith, Hartford	9	1	4	5	10
Geoff Smith, Worcester	25	1	3	4	16
Totals	34	2	7	9	26
Lee Sorochan, Hartford	16	0	2	2	33
Lee Sorochan, Saint John	3	1	3	4	4
Totals	19	1	5	6	37
Travis Tucker, Portland	2	0	0	0	0
Travis Tucker, Hershey	5	0	0	0	0
Totals	7	0	0	0	0
Vladimir Vorobiev, Hartford	65	24	41	65	22
Vladimir Vorobiev, Hamilton	8	3	6	9	2
Totals	73	27	47	74	24
Steffon Walby, Rochester	48	15	13	28	52
Steffon Walby, Kentucky	11	8	4	12	6
Totals	59	23	17	40	58
Jeff Ware, St. John's	55	1	4	5	130
Jeff Ware, New Haven	20	0	1	1	26
Totals	75	1	5	6	156
Steve Washburn, New Haven	10	4	3	7	6
Steve Washburn, Syracuse	13	1	6	7	6
Totals	23	5	9	14	12
Darren Wetherill, Portland	5	0	0	0	2
Darren Wetherill, Kentucky	4	0	0	0	4
Totals	9	0	0	0	6

GOALTENDING

	Gms.	Min.	W	L	T	G	SO	Avg.
B. Amidovski, S.J.	6	243	2	2	0	19	0	4.69
B. Amidovski, Phil.	2	120	2	0	0	5	0	2.50
Totals	8	363	4	2	0	24	0	3.97
J. Gage, Port.	26	1429	8	11	3	69	2	2.90
J. Gage, Prov.	3	130	0	2	0	9	0	4.16
J. Gage, Syr.	12	706	2	8	2	46	0	3.91
Totals	41	2264	10	21	5	124	2	3.29

1999 CALDER CUP PLAYOFFS

RESULTS

CONFERENCE QUARTERFINALS

	W	L	Pts.	GF	GA
Saint John	3	0	6	14	9
Lowell	0	3	0	9	14

(Saint John won series, 3-0)

	W	L	Pts.	GF	GA
Fredericton	3	2	6	17	13
St. John's	2	3	4	13	17

(Fredericton won series, 3-2)

	W	L	Pts.	GF	GA
Providence	3	1	6	16	10
Worcester	1	3	2	10	16

(Providence won series, 3-1)

	W	L	Pts.	GF	GA
Hartford	3	0	6	13	5
Springfield	0	3	0	5	13

(Hartford won series, 3-0)

	W	L	Pts.	GF	GA
Rochester	3	0	6	10	5
Adirondack	0	3	0	5	10

(Rochester won series, 3-0)

	W	L	Pts.	GF	GA
Hamilton	3	2	6	15	14
Albany	2	3	4	14	15

(Hamilton won series, 3-2)

	W	L	Pts.	GF	GA
Philadelphia	3	0	6	14	7
Cincinnati	0	3	0	7	14

(Philadelphia won series, 3-0)

	W	L	Pts.	GF	GA
Kentucky	3	2	6	13	10
Hershey	2	3	4	10	13

(Kentucky won series, 3-2)

CONFERENCE SEMIFINALS

	W	L	Pts.	GF	GA
Fredericton	4	0	8	23	11
Saint John	0	4	0	11	23

(Fredericton won series, 4-0)

	W	L	Pts.	GF	GA
Providence	4	0	8	17	12
Hartford	0	4	0	12	17

(Providence won series, 4-0)

	W	L	Pts.	GF	GA
Rochester	4	2	8	18	11
Hamilton	2	4	4	11	18

(Rochester won series, 4-2)

	W	L	Pts.	GF	GA
Philadelphia	4	3	8	29	21
Kentucky	3	4	6	21	29

(Philadelphia won series, 4-3)

CONFERENCE FINALS

	W	L	Pts.	GF	GA
Providence	4	2	8	24	18
Fredericton	2	4	4	18	24

(Providence won series, 4-2)

	W	L	Pts.	GF	GA
Rochester	4	2	8	19	12
Philadelphia	2	4	4	12	19

(Rochester won series, 4-2)

CALDER CUP FINALS

	W	L	Pts.	GF	GA
Providence	4	1	8	20	9
Rochester	1	4	2	9	20

(Providence won series, 4-1)

INDIVIDUAL LEADERS

Goals: Martin Gendron, Fredericton (12)
Dean Sylvester, Rochester (12)
Assists: Randy Cunneyworth, Rochester (14)
Domenic Pittis, Rochester (14)
Randy Robitaille, Providence (14)
Points: Peter Ferraro, Providence (21)
Domenic Pittis, Rochester (21)
Penalty minutes: Sylvain Blouin, Fredericton (87)
Goaltending average: Martin Biron, Rochester (2.16)
Shutouts: John Nabokov, Kentucky (2)

TOP SCORERS

	Games	G	A	Pts.
Peter Ferraro, Providence	19	9	12	21
Domenic Pittis, Rochester	20	7	14	21
Craig Fisher, Rochester	20	9	11	20
Eric Nickulas, Providence	18	8	12	20
Randy Robitaille, Providence	19	6	14	20
Martin Gendron, Fredericton	15	12	5	17
Dean Sylvester, Rochester	18	12	5	17
Peter White, Philadelphia	16	4	13	17
Randy Cunneyworth, Rochester	20	3	14	17
J.F. Jomphe, Fredericton	15	5	11	16

INDIVIDUAL STATISTICS

ADIRONDACK RED WINGS

(Lost conference quarterfinals to Rochester, 3-0)

SCORING

	Games	G	A	Pts.	PIM
Dave Paradise	3	1	1	2	6
Jesse Wallin	3	0	2	2	2
Philippe Audet	2	1	0	1	4
Sean Gillam	3	1	0	1	6
B.J. Young	3	1	0	1	6
Kirby Law	3	1	0	1	2
Darryl Laplante	3	0	1	1	0
Shane Hnidy	3	0	1	1	0
Doug Houda	3	0	1	1	4
Barry Potomski	1	0	0	0	2
Jason Elliott (goalie)	1	0	0	0	0
Yan Golubovsky	2	0	0	0	4
Xavier Majic	2	0	0	0	0
Brian Bonin	2	0	0	0	0
Aren Miller (goalie)	2	0	0	0	0
Alexandre Jacques	3	0	0	0	0
Maxim Kuznetsov	3	0	0	0	0
Martin Laitre	3	0	0	0	14
Marc Rodgers	3	0	0	0	10
Jon Coleman	3	0	0	0	0
Ryan Tobler	3	0	0	0	2

GOALTENDING

	Gms.	Min.	W	L	T	G	SO	Avg.
Jason Elliott	1	59	0	1	0	2	0	2.04
Aren Miller	2	123	0	2	0	8	0	3.92

ALBANY RIVER RATS

(Lost conference quarterfinals to Hamilton, 3-2)

SCORING

	Games	G	A	Pts.	PIM
Eric Bertrand	5	4	2	6	0
Steve Brule	5	3	1	4	4
John Madden	5	2	2	4	6
Jiri Bicek	5	2	2	4	2
Jeff Williams	5	1	2	3	0
Sergei Vyshedkevich	5	0	3	3	0
Alexander Semak	5	0	2	2	4
Ken Sutton	5	0	2	2	12
Richard Rochefort	5	1	0	1	0
Matt Ruchty	5	1	0	1	16
Geordie Kinnear	5	0	1	1	0
David Cunniff	5	0	1	1	4
Rob Pattison	5	0	1	1	0
Colin White	5	0	1	1	8
George Awada	1	0	0	0	0
Rob Skrlac	1	0	0	0	0
Richard Shulmistra (goalie)	2	0	0	0	0
Henrik Rehnberg	2	0	0	0	0
Sascha Goc	2	0	0	0	0
Pierre Dagenais	4	0	0	0	0
Josh DeWolf	5	0	0	0	2
Mike Buzak (goalie)	5	0	0	0	0

GOALTENDING

	Gms.	Min.	W	L	T	G	SO	Avg.
Mike Buzak	5	272	2	1	0	12	0	2.65
Richard Shulmistra	2	64	0	2	0	3	0	2.82

CINCINNATI MIGHTY DUCKS

(Lost conference quarterfinals to Philadelphia, 3-0)

SCORING

	Games	G	A	Pts.	PIM
Eric Lecompte	3	1	2	3	0
Bob Wren	3	1	2	3	8
Mike Crowley	3	0	3	3	2
Joel Kwiatkowski	3	2	0	2	0
Craig Reichert	3	2	0	2	0
Jeremy Stevenson	3	1	0	1	2
Rastisl Pavlikovsky	2	0	1	1	4
Frank Banham	3	0	1	1	0
Mike Leclerc	3	0	1	1	19
Igor Nikulin	3	0	1	1	4
Anders Bjork	2	0	0	0	0
Ivan Ciernik	2	0	0	0	2
Peter LeBoutillier	3	0	0	0	2
Marc Chouinard	3	0	0	0	4
Scott Ferguson	3	0	0	0	4
Ryan Brindley	3	0	0	0	2
Rick Goldmann	3	0	0	0	2
Byron Briske	3	0	0	0	2
Tom Askey (goalie)	3	0	0	0	0

GOALTENDING

	Gms.	Min.	W	L	T	G	SO	Avg.
Tom Askey	3	178	0	3	0	13	0	4.39

FREDERICTON CANADIENS

(Lost conference finals to Providence, 4-2)

SCORING

	Games	G	A	Pts.	PIM
Martin Gendron	15	12	5	17	2
J.F. Jomphe	15	5	11	16	49
Aaron Asham	13	8	6	14	11
Aris Brimanis	15	3	10	13	18
Miloslav Guren	15	4	7	11	10
Jonathan Delisle	15	3	6	9	39
Eric Houde	14	2	7	9	4
Jean-Francois Houle	12	1	7	8	10
Jason Ward	10	4	2	6	22
Stephane Robidas	15	1	5	6	10
Eric Chouinard	6	3	2	5	0
Scott King	6	2	3	5	2

	Games	G	A	Pts.	PIM
Marc Beaucage	9	2	3	5	12
Terry Ryan	11	1	3	4	10
Boyd Olson	13	1	3	4	16
Francis Bouillon	5	2	1	3	0
Jimmy Drolet	6	1	2	3	0
Alain Nasreddine	15	0	3	3	39
Sylvain Blouin	15	2	0	2	87
Matt Higgins	5	0	2	2	0
Dave Morrisette	12	1	0	1	31
Mike Ribeiro	5	0	1	1	2
Jose Theodore (goalie)	13	0	1	1	2
Darcy Harris	3	0	0	0	0
Gennady Razin	4	0	0	0	2
Mathieu Garon (goalie)	6	0	0	0	0

GOALTENDING

	Gms.	Min.	W	L	T	G	SO	Avg.
Jose Theodore	13	694	8	5	0	35	1	3.03
Mathieu Garon	6	208	1	1	0	12	0	3.47

HAMILTON BULLDOGS

(Lost conference semifinals to Rochester, 4-2)

SCORING

	Games	G	A	Pts.	PIM
Chris Ferraro	11	8	5	13	20
Jim Dowd	11	3	6	9	8
Joe Hulbig	11	4	2	6	18
Craig Millar	11	1	5	6	18
Todd Reirden	11	0	5	5	6
Daniel Lacroix	11	3	1	4	65
Fredrik Lindquist	11	2	2	4	2
Paul Comrie	8	1	3	4	2
Dan LaCouture	9	2	1	3	2
Boyd Devereaux	8	0	3	3	4
Jeff Daw	11	0	3	3	4
Sergei Yerkovich	8	0	2	2	2
Terry Marchant	2	1	0	1	0
David Matsos	8	1	0	1	0
Vladimir Vorobiev	6	0	1	1	2
Steve Potvin	7	0	1	1	6
Kevin Bolibruck	11	0	1	1	4
Jason Bowen	11	0	1	1	16
Brad Norton	11	0	1	1	6
Mike Minard (goalie)	1	0	0	0	0
Daniel Cleary	3	0	0	0	0
Michel Riesen	3	0	0	0	0
Mathieu Descoteaux	4	0	0	0	0
Steve Passmore (goalie)	11	0	0	0	0

GOALTENDING

	Gms.	Min.	W	L	T	G	SO	Avg.
Mike Minard	1	20	0	0	0	0	0	0.00
Steve Passmore	11	680	5	6	0	31	0	2.74

HARTFORD WOLF PACK

(Lost conference semifinals to Providence, 4-0)

SCORING

	Games	G	A	Pts.	PIM
Marc Savard	7	1	12	13	16
Derek Armstrong	7	5	4	9	10
Scott Fraser	6	4	3	7	4
Brad Smyth	7	6	0	6	14
Michael York	6	3	1	4	0
Kevin J. Brown	5	1	3	4	4
Chris O'Sullivan	7	1	3	4	11
Johan Witehall	7	1	2	3	6
Ken Gernander	7	1	2	3	2
Chris Dube	6	0	3	3	4
Ed Campbell	7	0	3	3	14
Bob Errey	7	0	3	3	8
Jason Doig	7	1	1	2	39
Dale Purinton	7	0	2	2	24
Daniel Goneau	2	1	0	1	0
Chris Kenady	2	0	1	1	6
Alexei Vasiliev	6	0	1	1	2
P.J. Stock	6	0	1	1	35
Ryan Risidore	1	0	0	0	0
Chris Winnes	1	0	0	0	0
Todd Hall	1	0	0	0	0
Jean-Francois Labbe (goalie)	7	0	0	0	2
Brent Thompson	7	0	0	0	23

GOALTENDING

	Gms.	Min.	W	L	T	G	SO	Avg.
J.-Francois Labbe	7	447	3	4	0	22	0	2.95

HERSHEY BEARS

(Lost conference quarterfinals to Kentucky, 3-2)

SCORING

	Games	G	A	Pts.	PIM
Dan Hinote	5	3	1	4	6
Christian Matte	5	2	1	3	8
Mitch Lamoureux	4	1	2	3	4
Paul Brousseau	5	1	1	2	0
Mike Gaul	5	1	1	2	6
Chris Dingman	5	0	2	2	6
Alex Tanguay	5	0	2	2	0
Brian Willsie	3	1	0	1	0
Brad Larsen	5	1	0	1	6
Yuri Babenko	2	0	1	1	0
Ville Nieminen	3	0	1	1	0
Serge Aubin	3	0	1	1	2
Brian White	4	0	1	1	2
Chris Armstrong	5	0	1	1	0
Jeff Buchanan	5	0	1	1	4
Dan Smith	5	0	1	1	0
Martin Skoula	1	0	0	0	0
Bruce Richardson	3	0	0	0	15
David Aebischer (goalie)	3	0	0	0	0
Rob Shearer	3	0	0	0	6
Marc Denis (goalie)	3	0	0	0	0
Scott Parker	4	0	0	0	6
Sami Helenius	5	0	0	0	16

GOALTENDING

	Gms.	Min.	W	L	T	G	SO	Avg.
David Aebischer	3	152	1	2	0	6	0	2.37
Marc Denis	3	143	1	1	0	7	0	2.93

KENTUCKY THOROUGHBLADES

(Lost conference semifinals to Philadelphia, 4-3)

SCORING

	Games	G	A	Pts.	PIM
Shawn Burr	12	4	9	13	10
Mike Craig	12	5	4	9	18
Jarrod Skalde	12	4	5	9	16
Jarrett Deuling	12	3	6	9	8
Shawn Heins	12	2	7	9	10
Mark Smith	12	2	7	9	16
Dan Boyle	12	3	5	8	16
Greg Pankewicz	11	4	1	5	10
Steffon Walby	12	3	2	5	14
Matt Bradley	10	1	4	5	4
Steve Lingren	12	0	4	4	0
Herbert Vasiljevs	12	2	1	3	4
Peter Allen	12	1	1	2	8
David Duerden	6	0	2	2	0
Eric Veilleux	6	0	2	2	6
Scott Hannan	12	0	2	2	10
Eric Boulton	10	0	1	1	36
Filip Kuba	10	0	1	1	4
John Nabokov (goalie)	11	0	1	1	2
Andy MacIntyre	1	0	0	0	0
Sean Gauthier (goalie)	4	0	0	0	0
Andy Sutton	5	0	0	0	23

GOALTENDING

	Gms.	Min.	W	L	T	G	SO	Avg.
John Nabokov	11	599	6	5	0	30	2	3.00
Sean Gauthier	4	130	0	1	0	8	0	3.68

LOWELL LOCK MONSTERS

(Lost conference quarterfinals to Saint John, 3-0)

SCORING

	Games	G	A	Pts.	PIM
Vladimir Orszagh	3	2	2	4	2
Craig Charron	3	1	2	3	8
Warren Luhning	3	0	3	3	16
Buddy Wallace	3	1	1	2	2
Ray Giroux	3	1	1	2	0
Mike Watt	2	1	0	1	2
Nic Beaudoin	3	1	0	1	7
Mike Kennedy	3	1	0	1	2
Eric Cairns	3	1	0	1	32
Evgeny Korolev	2	0	1	1	0
Dmitri Nabokov	3	0	1	1	0
Sean Haggerty	3	0	1	1	0
Dane Jackson	3	0	1	1	16
Ray Schultz	1	0	0	0	4
Ryan Huska	2	0	0	0	0
Mike Mader	2	0	0	0	0
Vladimi Chebaturkin	3	0	0	0	0
Marcel Cousineau (goalie)	3	0	0	0	2
Ted Crowley	3	0	0	0	6
Dean Malkoc	3	0	0	0	8

GOALTENDING

	Gms.	Min.	W	L	T	G	SO	Avg.
Marcel Cousineau	3	186	0	3	0	13	0	4.20

PHILADELPHIA PHANTOMS

(Lost conference finals to Rochester, 4-2)

SCORING

	Games	G	A	Pts.	PIM
Peter White	16	4	13	17	12
Richard Park	16	9	6	15	4
Jim Montgomery	16	4	11	15	20
Chris Joseph	16	3	10	13	8
Mark Eaton	16	4	8	12	0
Chris Albert	15	5	5	10	22
Paul Healey	15	4	6	10	11
Brian Wesenberg	16	5	3	8	28
Francis Belanger	16	4	3	7	16
Sean O'Brien	16	3	4	7	24
Dave MacIsaac	16	2	5	7	50
Dennis Bonvie	14	3	3	6	26
Jason Zent	16	2	4	6	22
Mark Greig	7	1	5	6	14
Andy Delmore	15	1	4	5	6
Mikhial Chernov	14	1	0	1	8
Martin Cerven	1	0	1	1	0
Martin Boisvenue	1	0	0	0	0
John Pelletier (goalie)	1	0	0	0	0
Dan Kordic	1	0	0	0	0
Jeff Lank	2	0	0	0	2
Steve McLaren	7	0	0	0	2
Brian Boucher (goalie)	16	0	0	0	4
Ryan Bast	16	0	0	0	30

GOALTENDING

	Gms.	Min.	W	L	T	G	SO	Avg.
John Pelletier	1	27	0	0	0	0	0	0.00
Brian Boucher	16	947	9	7	0	45	0	2.85

PROVIDENCE BRUINS

(Winner of 1999 Calder Cup playoffs)

SCORING

	Games	G	A	Pts.	PIM
Peter Ferraro	19	9	12	21	38
Eric Nickulas	18	8	12	20	33
Randy Robitaille	19	6	14	20	20
Cameron Mann	11	7	7	14	4
Terry Virtue	17	2	12	14	29
Jeremy Brown	19	6	7	13	4
John Spoltore	11	6	6	12	4
Steven King	13	7	4	11	12
Marquis Mathieu	19	4	7	11	30
Joel Prpic	18	4	6	10	48
Brandon Smith	19	1	9	10	12
Antti Laaksonen	19	7	2	9	28
Jason McBain	19	1	8	9	16
Landon Wilson	11	7	1	8	19
Dennis Vaske	19	1	5	6	26
Steve Bancroft	15	0	6	6	28
Aaron Downey	19	1	1	2	46
Andre Savage	5	0	1	1	0
Bob Beers	5	0	1	1	2
Jay Henderson	2	0	0	0	2
Dan Ceman	2	0	0	0	0
Elias Abrahamsson	4	0	0	0	7
Roger Maxwell	7	0	0	0	6
Johnathan Aitken	13	0	0	0	17
John Grahame (goalie)	19	0	0	0	6

GOALTENDING

	Gms.	Min.	W	L	T	G	SO	Avg.
John Grahame	19	1209	15	4	0	48	1	2.38

ROCHESTER AMERICANS

(Lost league finals to Providence, 4-1)

SCORING

	Games	G	A	Pts.	PIM
Domenic Pittis	20	7	14	21	40
Craig Fisher	20	9	11	20	10
Dean Sylvester	18	12	5	17	8
Randy Cunneyworth	20	3	14	17	58
Mike Harder	20	2	9	11	23
Mike Hurlbut	20	4	5	9	12
Denis Hamel	20	3	4	7	10
Jason Holland	20	2	5	7	8
Darren VanOene	12	2	4	6	8
Cory Sarich	20	2	4	6	14
Derek Wood	20	2	4	6	24
Dean Melanson	17	3	2	5	32
Greg Walters	15	1	3	4	14
Alexandre Boikov	17	1	3	4	24
Matt Davidson	18	2	1	3	6
Martin Biron (goalie)	20	0	3	3	10
Peter Vandermeer	16	1	0	1	38
Francois Methot	9	0	1	1	0
Shane Kenny	1	0	0	0	10
Brian Campbell	2	0	0	0	0
Tom Draper (goalie)	2	0	0	0	0
Carlin Nordstrom	6	0	0	0	18
Dimitri Kalinin	7	0	0	0	6
Marc Dupuis	16	0	0	0	4

GOALTENDING

	Gms.	Min.	W	L	T	G	SO	Avg.
Martin Biron	20	1167	12	8	0	42	1	2.16
Tom Draper	2	86	0	0	0	4	0	2.79

SAINT JOHN FLAMES

(Lost conference semifinals to Fredericton, 4-0)

SCORING

	Games	G	A	Pts.	PIM
Hnat Domenichelli	7	4	4	8	2
Martin St. Louis	7	4	4	8	2
Eric M. Landry	7	2	5	7	12
Lee Sorochan	7	3	3	6	29
Chris Clark	7	2	4	6	15
Allan Egeland	7	1	4	5	21
David Cooper	7	1	4	5	10

	Games	G	A	Pts.	PIM
Travis Brigley	7	3	1	4	2
Sergei Varlamov	7	0	4	4	8
Ronald Petrovicky	7	1	2	3	19
Darrel Scoville	7	1	2	3	13
Steve Begin	7	2	0	2	18
Eric Charron	3	1	0	1	22
Arttu Kayhko	4	0	1	1	2
Jeff Cowan	4	0	1	1	10
Wade Belak	6	0	1	1	23
Gaetan Royer	7	0	1	1	8
Dany Sabourin (goalie)	1	0	0	0	0
Igor Karpenko (goalie)	2	0	0	0	0
Matt O'Dette	2	0	0	0	14
Sean Berens	2	0	0	0	0
Fredrik Oduya	6	0	0	0	22
J.-Sebastien Giguere (goalie)	7	0	0	0	0

GOALTENDING

	Gms.	Min.	W	L	T	G	SO	Avg.
J.-S. Giguere	7	304	3	2	0	21	0	4.14
Dany Sabourin	1	57	0	1	0	4	0	4.19
Igor Karpenko	2	63	0	1	0	5	0	4.79

ST. JOHN'S MAPLE LEAFS

(Lost conference quarterfinals to Fredericton, 3-2)

SCORING

	Games	G	A	Pts.	PIM
Lonny Bohonos	5	2	4	6	2
David Nemirovsky	5	4	1	5	0
Yuri Khmylev	5	2	1	3	4
Aaron Brand	5	1	2	3	8
Mark Deyell	3	0	3	3	0
Dennis Maxwell	5	0	3	3	8
Kevyn Adams	5	2	0	2	4
Brad Chartrand	5	0	2	2	2
Adam Mair	3	1	0	1	6
Ryan Pepperall	5	1	0	1	2
Nathan Dempsey	5	0	1	1	2
Dallas Eakins	5	0	1	1	6
D.J. Smith	5	0	1	1	0
Greg Smyth	5	0	1	1	19
Marc Robitaille (goalie)	3	0	0	0	0
Jeff Reese (goalie)	3	0	0	0	0
Dimitri Yakushin	4	0	0	0	0
Todd Gillingham	5	0	0	0	2
Justin Hocking	5	0	0	0	2
Shawn Thornton	5	0	0	0	9

GOALTENDING

	Gms.	Min.	W	L	T	G	SO	Avg.
Marc Robitaille	3	158	1	2	0	8	0	3.04
Jeff Reese	3	142	1	1	0	8	0	3.39

SPRINGFIELD FALCONS

(Lost conference quarterfinals to Hartford, 3-0)

SCORING

	Games	G	A	Pts.	PIM
Joe Dziedzic	3	1	1	2	20
Trevor Letowski	3	1	0	1	2
Robert Schnabel	3	1	0	1	4
Bobby House	3	1	0	1	2
Dan Focht	3	1	0	1	10
Radoslav Suchy	3	0	1	1	0
Eric Belanger	3	0	1	1	2
Daniel Briere	3	0	1	1	2
Tavis Hansen	3	0	1	1	5
Sean McCann	3	0	1	1	4
Robert Francz	1	0	0	0	0
Barry Nieckar	1	0	0	0	2
Chris Schmidt	1	0	0	0	0
Scott Barney	1	0	0	0	2
Robert Esche (goalie)	1	0	0	0	0
Brad Tiley	1	0	0	0	0
Maxim Spiridonov	2	0	0	0	2
Peter Hogan	2	0	0	0	0
Jimmy Waite (goalie)	2	0	0	0	2
Greg Phillips	3	0	0	0	4
Jason Morgan	3	0	0	0	6
Sean Gagnon	3	0	0	0	14
Rob Murray	3	0	0	0	4

GOALTENDING

	Gms.	Min.	W	L	T	G	SO	Avg.
Jimmy Waite	2	118	0	2	0	6	0	3.05
Robert Esche	1	60	0	1	0	4	0	4.02

WORCESTER ICECATS

(Lost conference quarterfinals to Providence, 3-1)

SCORING

	Games	G	A	Pts.	PIM
Tyson Nash	4	4	1	5	27
Ladislav Nagy	3	2	2	4	0
Marty Reasoner	4	2	1	3	6
Jochen Hecht	4	1	1	2	2
Jeremiah McCarthy	4	0	2	2	0
Stephane Roy	4	0	2	2	2
Shayne Toporowski	4	1	0	1	6
Rory Fitzpatrick	4	0	1	1	17
Jaroslav Obsut	4	0	1	1	2
Bryce Salvador	4	0	1	1	2
Brent Johnson (goalie)	4	0	1	1	2
Kevin Sawyer	4	0	1	1	4
Jamie Thompson	1	0	0	0	0
Andrej Podkonicky	4	0	0	0	4
Bryan Helmer	4	0	0	0	12
Derek Bekar	4	0	0	0	0
Jan Horacek	4	0	0	0	6
Geoff Smith	4	0	0	0	4
Reed Low	4	0	0	0	2

GOALTENDING

	Gms.	Min.	W	L	T	G	SO	Avg.
Brent Johnson	4	238	1	3	0	12	0	3.02

1998-99 AWARD WINNERS

ALL-STAR TEAMS

First team	Pos.	Second team
Martin Biron, Rochester	G	Steve Passmore, Hamilton
Ken Sutton, Albany	D	Terry Virtue, Providence
Brandon Smith, Providence	D	Dan Boyle, Kentucky
Landon Wilson, Providence	LW	Jeff Williams, Albany
Randy Robitaille, Providence	C	Steve Guolla, Kentucky
Shane Willis, New Haven	RW	Richard Park, Philadelphia

TROPHY WINNERS

John B. Sollenberger Trophy: Domenic Pittis, Rochester
Les Cunningham Plaque: Randy Robitaille, Providence
Harry (Hap) Holmes Memorial Trophy:
Martin Biron, Rochester
Tom Draper, Rochester
Dudley (Red) Garrett Memorial Trophy: Shane Willis, New Haven
Eddie Shore Award: Ken Sutton, Albany
Fred Hunt Memorial Award: Mitch Lamoureux, Hershey
Louis A.R. Pieri Memorial Award: Peter Laviolette, Providence
Baz Bastien Trophy: Martin Biron, Rochester
Jack Butterfield Trophy: Peter Ferraro, Providence

ALL-TIME AWARD WINNERS

JOHN B. SOLLENBERGER TROPHY

(Leading scorer)

Season Player, Team
1936-37—Jack Markle, Syracuse
1937-38—Jack Markle, Syracuse
1938-39—Don Deacon, Pittsburgh
1939-40—Norm Locking, Syracuse
1940-41—Les Cunningham, Cleveland
1941-42—Pete Kelly, Springfield
1942-43—Wally Kilrea, Hershy
1943-44—Tommy Burlington, Cleveland
1944-45—Bob Gracie, Pittsburgh
Bob Walton, Pittsburgh
1945-46—Les Douglas, Indianapolis
1946-47—Phil Hergesheimer, Philadelphia
1947-48—Carl Liscombe, Providence
1948-49—Sid Smith, Pittsburgh
1949-50—Les Douglas, Cleveland
1950-51—Ab DeMarco, Buffalo
1951-52—Ray Powell, Providence
1952-53—Eddie Olson, Cleveland
1953-54—George Sullivan, Hershey
1954-55—Eddie Olson, Cleveland
1955-56—Zellio Toppazzini, Providence
1956-57—Fred Glover, Cleveland
1957-58—Willie Marshall, Hershey
1958-59—Bill Hicke, Rochester
1959-60—Fred Glover, Cleveland
1960-61—Bill Sweeney, Springfield
1961-62—Bill Sweeney, Springfield
1962-63—Bill Sweeney, Springfield
1963-64—Gerry Ehman, Rochester
1964-65—Art Stratton, Buffalo
1965-66—Dick Gamble, Rochester
1966-67—Gordon Labossiere, Quebec
1967-68—Simon Nolet, Quebec
1968-69—Jeannot Gilbert, Hershey
1969-70—Jude Drouin, Montreal
1970-71—Fred Speck, Baltimore
1971-72—Don Blackburn, Providence
1972-73—Yvon Lambert, Nova Scotia
1973-74—Steve West, New Haven
1974-75—Doug Gibson, Rochester
1975-76—Jean-Guy Gratton, Hershey
1976-77—Andre Peloffy, Springfield
1977-78—Gord Brooks, Philadelphia
Rick Adduono, Rochester
1978-79—Bernie Johnston, Maine
1979-80—Norm Dube, Nova Scotia
1980-81—Mark Lofthouse, Hershey
1981-82—Mike Kasczyki, New Brunswick
1982-83—Ross Yates, Binghamton
1983-84—Claude Larose, Sherbrooke
1984-85—Paul Gardner, Binghamton
1985-86—Paul Gardner, Rochester
1986-87—Tim Tookey, Hershey
1987-88—Bruce Boudreau, Springfield
1988-89—Stephan Lebeau, Sherbrooke
1989-90—Paul Ysebaert, Utica
1990-91—Kevin Todd, Utica
1991-92—Shaun Van Allen, Cape Breton
1992-93—Don Biggs, Binghamton
1993-94—Tim Taylor, Adirondack
1994-95—Peter White, Cape Breton
1995-96—Brad Smyth, Carolina
1996-97—Peter White, Philadelphia
1997-98—Peter White, Philadelphia
1998-99—Domenic Pittis, Rochester

LES CUNNINGHAM PLAQUE

(Most Valuable Player)

Season Player, Team
1947-48—Carl Liscombe, Providence
1948-49—Carl Liscombe, Providence
1949-50—Les Douglas, Cleveland
1950-51—Ab DeMarco, Buffalo
1951-52—Ray Powell, Providence
1952-53—Eddie Olson, Cleveland
1953-54—George "Red" Sullivan, Hershey
1954-55—Ross Lowe, Springfield
1955-56—Johnny Bower, Providence
1956-57—Johnny Bower, Providence
1957-58—Johnny Bower, Cleveland
1958-59—Bill Hicke, Rochester
Rudy Migay, Rochester
1959-60—Fred Glover, Cleveland
1960-61—Phil Maloney, Buffalo
1961-62—Fred Glover, Cleveland
1962-63—Denis DeJordy, Buffalo
1963-64—Fred Glover, Cleveland
1964-65—Art Stratton, Buffalo
1965-66—Dick Gamble, Rochester
1966-67—Mike Nykoluk, Hershey
1967-68—Dave Creighton, Providence
1968-69—Gilles Villemure, Buffalo
1969-70—Gilles Villemure, Buffalo
1970-71—Fred Speck, Baltimore
1971-72—Garry Peters, Boston
1972-73—Billy Inglis, Cincinnati
1973-74—Art Stratton, Rochester
1974-75—Doug Gibson, Rochester
1975-76—Ron Andruff, Nova Scotia
1976-77—Doug Gibson, Rochester
1977-78—Blake Dunlop, Maine
1978-79—Rocky Saganiuk, New Brunswick
1979-80—Norm Dube, Nova Scotia
1980-81—Pelle Lindbergh, Maine
1981-82—Mike Kasczyki, New Brunswick
1982-83—Ross Yates, Binghamton
1983-84—Mal Davis, Rochester
Garry Lariviere, St. Catharines
1984-85—Paul Gardner, Binghamton
1985-86—Paul Gardner, Rochester
1986-87—Tim Tookey, Hershey
1987-88—Jody Gage, Rochester
1988-89—Stephan Lebeau, Sherbrooke
1989-90—Paul Ysebaert, Utica
1990-91—Kevin Todd, Utica
1991-92—John Anderson, Hew Haven
1992-93—Don Biggs, Binghamton
1993-94—Rich Chernomaz, St. John's
1994-95—Steve Larouche, Prince Edward Island
1995-96—Brad Smyth, Carolina
1996-97—Jean-Francois Labbe, Hershey
1997-98—Steve Guolla, Kentucky
1998-99—Randy Robitaille, Providence

HARRY (HAP) HOLMES MEMORIAL TROPHY

(Outstanding goaltender)

Season Player, Team
1936-37—Bert Gardiner, Philadelphia
1937-38—Frank Brimsek, Providence
1938-39—Alfie Moore, Hershey
1939-40—Moe Roberts, Cleveland
1940-41—Chuck Rayner, Springfield
1941-42—Bill Beveridge, Cleveland
1942-43—Gordie Bell, Buffalo
1943-44—Nick Damore, Hershey
1944-45—Yves Nadon, Buffalo
1945-46—Connie Dion, St. Louis-Buffalo
1946-47—Baz Bastien, Pittsburgh
1947-48—Baz Bastien, Pittsburgh
1948-49—Baz Bastien, Pittsburgh
1949-50—Gil Mayer, Pittsburgh
1950-51—Gil Mayer, Pittsburgh
1951-52—Johnny Bower, Cleveland

Season	Player, Team
1952-53	Gil Mayer, Pittsburgh
1953-54	Jacques Plante, Buffalo
1954-55	Gil Mayer, Pittsburgh
1955-56	Gil Mayer, Pittsburgh
1956-57	Johnny Bower, Providence
1957-58	Johnny Bower, Cleveland
1958-59	Bob Perreault, Hershey
1959-60	Ed Chadwick, Rochester
1960-61	Marcel Paille, Springfield
1961-62	Marcel Paille, Springfield
1962-63	Denis DeJordy, Buffalo
1963-64	Roger Crozier, Pittsburgh
1964-65	Gerry Cheevers, Rochester
1965-66	Les Binkley, Cleveland
1966-67	Andre Gill, Hershey
1967-68	Bob Perreault, Rochester
1968-69	Gilles Villemure, Buffalo
1969-70	Gilles Villemure, Buffalo
1970-71	Gary Kurt, Cleveland
1971-72	Dan Bouchard, Boston
	Ross Brooks, Boston
1972-73	Michel Larocque, Nova Scotia
1973-74	Jim Shaw, Nova Scotia
	Dave Elenbaas, Nova Scotia
1974-75	Ed Walsh, Nova Scotia
	Dave Elenbaas, Nova Scotia
1975-76	Dave Elenbaas, Nova Scotia
	Ed Walsh, Nova Scotia
1976-77	Ed Walsh, Nova Scotia
	Dave Elenbaas, Nova Scotia
1977-78	Bob Holland, Nova Scotia
	Maurice Barrette, Nova Scotia
1978-79	Pete Peeters, Maine
	Robbie Moore, Maine
1979-80	Rick St. Croix, Maine
	Robbie Moore, Maine
1980-81	Pelle Lindbergh, Maine
	Robbie Moore, Maine
1981-82	Bob Janecyk, New Brunswick
	Warren Skorodenski, New Brunswick
1982-83	Brian Ford, Fredericton
	Clint Malarchuk, Fredericton
1983-84	Brian Ford, Fredericton
1984-85	Jon Casey, Baltimore
1985-86	Sam St. Laurent, Maine
	Karl Friesen, Maine
1986-87	Vincent Riendeau, Sherbrooke
1987-88	Vincent Riendeau, Sherbrooke
	Jocelyn Perreault, Sherbrooke
1988-89	Randy Exelby, Sherbrooke
	Francois Gravel, Sherbrooke
1989-90	Jean Claude Bergeron, Sherbrooke
	Andre Racicot, Sherbrooke
1990-91	David Littman, Rochester
	Darcy Wakaluk, Rochester
1991-92	David Littman, Rochester
1992-93	Corey Hirsch, Binghamton
	Boris Rousson, Binghamton
1993-94	Byron Dafoe, Portland
	Olaf Kolzig, Portland
1994-95	Mike Dunham, Albany
	Corey Schwab, Albany
1995-96	Scott Langkow, Springfield
	Manny Legace, Springfield
1996-97	Jean-Francois Labbe, Hershey
1997-98	Jean-Sebastien Giguere, Saint John
	Tyler Moss, Saint John
1998-99	Martin Biron, Rochester
	Tom Draper, Rochester

Beginning with the 1983-84 season, the award goes to the top goaltending team with each goaltender having played a minimum of 25 games for the team with the fewest goals against.

DUDLEY (RED) GARRETT MEMORIAL TROPHY

(Top rookie)

Season	Player, Team
1947-48	Bob Solinger, Cleveland
1948-49	Terry Sawchuk, Indianapolis
1949-50	Paul Meger, Buffalo
1950-51	Wally Hergesheimer, Cleveland
1951-52	Earl "Dutch" Reibel, Indianapolis
1952-53	Guyle Fielder, St. Louis
1953-54	Don Marshall, Buffalo
1954-55	Jimmy Anderson, Springfield
1955-56	Bruce Cline, Providence
1956-57	Boris "Bo" Elik, Cleveland
1957-58	Bill Sweeney, Providence
1958-59	Bill Hicke, Rochester
1959-60	Stan Baluik, Providence
1960-61	Ronald "Chico" Maki, Buffalo
1961-62	Les Binkley, Cleveland
1962-63	Doug Robinson, Buffalo
1963-64	Roger Crozier, Pittsburgh
1964-65	Ray Cullen, Buffalo
1965-66	Mike Walton, Rochester
1966-67	Bob Rivard, Quebec
1967-68	Gerry Desjardins, Cleveland
1968-69	Ron Ward, Rochester
1969-70	Jude Drouin, Montreal
1970-71	Fred Speck, Baltimore
1971-72	Terry Caffery, Cleveland
1972-73	Ron Anderson, Boston
1973-74	Rick Middleton, Providence
1974-75	Jerry Holland, Providence
1975-76	Greg Holst, Providence
	Pierre Mondou, Nova Scotia
1976-77	Rod Schutt, Nova Scotia
1977-78	Norm Dupont, Nova Scotia
1978-79	Mike Meeker, Binghamton
1979-80	Darryl Sutter, New Brunswick
1980-81	Pelle Lindbergh, Maine
1981-82	Bob Sullivan, Binghamton
1982-83	Mitch Lamoureux, Baltimore
1983-84	Claude Verret, Rochester
1984-85	Steve Thomas, St. Catharines
1985-86	Ron Hextall, Hershey
1986-87	Brett Hull, Moncton
1987-88	Mike Richard, Binghamton
1988-89	Stephan Lebeau, Sherbrooke
1989-90	Donald Audette, Rochester
1990-91	Patrick Lebeau, Fredericton
1991-92	Felix Potvin, St. John's
1992-93	Corey Hirsch, Binghamton
1993-94	Rene Corbet, Cornwall
1994-95	Jim Carey, Portland
1995-96	Darcy Tucker, Fredericton
1996-97	Jaroslav Svejkovsky, Portland
1997-98	Daniel Briere, Springfield
1998-99	Shane Willis, New Haven

EDDIE SHORE PLAQUE

(Outstanding defenseman)

Season	Player, Team
1958-59	Steve Kraftcheck, Rochester
1959-60	Larry Hillman, Providence
1960-61	Bob McCord, Springfield
1961-62	Kent Douglas, Springfield
1962-63	Marc Reaume, Hershey
1963-64	Ted Harris, Cleveland
1964-65	Al Arbour, Rochester
1965-66	Jim Morrison, Quebec
1966-67	Bob McCord, Pittsburgh
1967-68	Bill Needham, Cleveland
1968-69	Bob Blackburn, Buffalo
1969-70	Noel Price, Springfield
1970-71	Marshall Johnston, Cleveland
1971-72	Noel Price, Nova Scotia

Season Player, Team
1972-73—Ray McKay, Cincinnati
1973-74—Gordon Smith, Springfield
1974-75—Joe Zanussi, Providence
1975-76—Noel Price, Nova Scotia
1976-77—Brian Engblom, Nova Scotia
1977-78—Terry Murray, Maine
1978-79—Terry Murray, Maine
1979-80—Rick Vasko, Adirondack
1980-81—Craig Levie, Nova Scotia
1981-82—Dave Farrish, New Brunswick
1982-83—Greg Tebbutt, Baltimore
1983-84—Garry Lariviere, St. Catharines
1984-85—Richie Dunn, Binghamton
1985-86—Jim Wiemer, New Haven
1986-87—Brad Shaw, Binghamton
1987-88—Dave Fenyves, Hershey
1988-89—Dave Fenyves, Hershey
1989-90—Eric Weinrich, Utica
1990-91—Norm Maciver, Cape Breton
1991-92—Greg Hawgood, Cape Breton
1992-93—Bobby Dollas, Adirondack
1993-94—Chris Snell, St. John's
1994-95—Jeff Serowik, Providence
1995-96—Barry Richter, Binghamton
1996-97—Darren Rumble, Philadelphia
1997-98—Jamie Heward, Philadelphia
1998-99—Ken Sutton, Albany

FRED HUNT MEMORIAL AWARD
(Sportsmanship, determination and dedication)

Season Player, Team
1977-78—Blake Dunlop, Maine
1978-79—Bernie Johnston, Maine
1979-80—Norm Dube, Nova Scotia
1980-81—Tony Cassolato, Hershey
1981-82—Mike Kasczyki, New Brunswick
1982-83—Ross Yates, Binghamton
1983-84—Claude Larose, Sherbrooke
1984-85—Paul Gardner, Binghamton
1985-86—Steve Tsujiura, Maine
1986-87—Glenn Merkosky, Adirondack
1987-88—Bruce Boudreau, Springfield
1988-89—Murray Eaves, Adirondack
1989-90—Murray Eaves, Adirondack
1990-91—Glenn Merkosky, Adirondack
1991-92—John Anderson, New Haven
1992-93—Tim Tookey, Hershey
1993-94—Jim Nesich, Cape Breton
1994-95—Steve Larouche, Prince Edward Island
1995-96—Ken Gernander, Binghamton
1996-97—Steve Passmore, Hamilton
1997-98—Craig Charron, Rochester
1998-99—Mitch Lamoureux, Hershey

LOUIS A.R. PIERI MEMORIAL AWARD
(Top coach)

Season Coach, Team
1967-68—Vic Stasiuk, Quebec
1968-69—Frank Mathers, Hershey
1969-70—Fred Shero, Buffalo
1970-71—Terry Reardon, Baltimore
1971-72—Al MacNeil, Nova Scotia
1972-73—Floyd Smith, Cincinnati
1973-74—Don Cherry, Rochester
1974-75—John Muckler, Providence
1975-76—Chuck Hamilton, Hershey

Season Coach, Team
1976-77—Al MacNeil, Nova Scotia
1977-78—Bob McCammon, Maine
1978-79—Parker MacDonald, New Haven
1979-80—Doug Gibson, Hershey
1980-81—Bob McCammon, Maine
1981-82—Orval Tessier, New Brunswick
1982-83—Jacques Demers, Fredericton
1983-84—Gene Ubriaco, Baltimore
1984-85—Bill Dineen, Adirondack
1985-86—Bill Dineen, Adirondack
1986-87—Larry Pleau, Binghamton
1987-88—John Paddock, Hershey
Mike Milbury, Maine
1988-89—Tom McVie, Utica
1989-90—Jimmy Roberts, Springfield
1990-91—Don Lever, Rochester
1991-92—Doug Carpenter, New Haven
1992-93—Marc Crawford, St. John's
1993-94—Barry Trotz, Portland
1994-95—Robbie Ftorek, Albany
1995-96—Robbie Ftorek, Albany
1996-97—Greg Gilbert, Worcester
1997-98—Bill Stewart, Saint John
1998-99—Peter Laviolette, Providence

BAZ BASTIEN TROPHY
(Coaches pick as top goaltender)

Season Player, Team
1983-84—Brian Ford, Fredericton
1984-85—Jon Casey, Baltimore
1985-86—Sam St. Laurent, Maine
1986-87—Mark Laforest, Adirondack
1987-88—Wendell Young, Hershey
1988-89—Randy Exelby, Sherbrooke
1989-90—Jean Claude Bergeron, Sherbrooke
1990-91—Mark Laforest, Binghamton
1991-92—Felix Potvin, St. John's
1992-93—Corey Hirsch, Binghamton
1993-94—Frederic Chabot, Hershey
1994-95—Jim Carey, Portland
1995-96—Manny Legace, Springfield
1996-97—Jean-Francois Labbe, Hershey
1997-98—Scott Langkow, Springfield
1998-99—Martin Biron, Rochester

JACK BUTTERFIELD TROPHY
(Calder Cup playoff MVP)

Season Player, Team
1983-84—Bud Stefanski, Maine
1984-85—Brian Skrudland, Sherbrooke
1985-86—Tim Tookey, Hershey
1986-87—Dave Fenyves, Rochester
1987-88—Wendell Young, Hershey
1988-89—Sam St. Laurent, Adirondack
1989-90—Jeff Hackett, Springfield
1990-91—Kay Whitmore, Springfield
1991-92—Allan Bester, Adirondack
1992-93—Bill McDougall, Cape Breton
1993-94—Olaf Kolzig, Portland
1994-95—Mike Dunham, Albany
Corey Schwab, Albany
1995-96—Dixon Ward, Rochester
1996-97—Mike McHugh, Hershey
1997-98—Mike Maneluk, Philadelphia
1998-99—Peter Ferraro, Providence

ALL-TIME LEAGUE CHAMPIONS

	REGULAR-SEASON CHAMPION		PLAYOFF CHAMPION	
Season	**Team**	**Coach**	**Team**	**Coach**
1936-37—	Philadelphia (E) Syracuse (W)	Herb Gardiner Eddie Powers	Syracuse	Eddie Powers

Season	REGULAR-SEASON CHAMPION Team	Coach	PLAYOFF CHAMPION Team	Coach
1937-38—	Providence (E)	Bun Cook	Providence	Bun Cook
	Cleveland (W)	Bill Cook		
1938-39—	Philadelphia (E)	Herb Gardiner	Cleveland	Bill Cook
	Hershey (W)	Herb Mitchell		
1939-40—	Providence (E)	Bun Cook	Providence	Bun Cook
	Indianapolis (W)	Herb Lewis		
1940-41—	Providence (E)	Bun Cook	Cleveland	Bill Cook
	Cleveland (W)	Bill Cook		
1941-42—	Springfield (E)	Johnny Mitchell	Indianapolis	Herb Lewis
	Indianapolis (W)	Herb Lewis		
1942-43—	Hershey	Cooney Weiland	Buffalo	Art Chapman
1943-44—	Hershey (E)	Cooney Weiland	Buffalo	Art Chapman
	Cleveland (W)	Bun Cook		
1944-45—	Buffalo (E)	Art Chapman	Cleveland	Bun Cook
	Cleveland (W)	Bun Cook		
1945-46—	Buffalo (E)	Frank Beisler	Buffalo	Frank Beisler
	Indianapolis (W)	Earl Seibert		
1946-47—	Hershey (E)	Don Penniston	Hershey	Don Penniston
	Cleveland (W)	Bun Cook		
1947-48—	Providence (E)	Terry Reardon	Cleveland	Bun Cook
	Cleveland (W)	Bun Cook		
1948-49—	Providence (E)	Terry Reardon	Providence	Terry Reardon
	St. Louis (W)	Ebbie Goodfellow		
1949-50—	Buffalo (E)	Roy Goldsworthy	Indianapolis	Ott Heller
	Cleveland (W)	Bun Cook		
1950-51—	Buffalo (E)	Roy Goldsworthy	Cleveland	Bun Cook
	Cleveland (W)	Bun Cook		
1951-52—	Hershey (E)	John Crawford	Pittsburgh	King Clancy
	Pittsburgh (W)	King Clancy		
1952-53—	Cleveland	Bun Cook	Cleveland	Bun Cook
1953-54—	Buffalo	Frank Eddolls	Cleveland	Bun Cook
1954-55—	Pittsburgh	Howie Meeker	Pittsburgh	Howie Meeker
1955-56—	Providence	John Crawford	Providence	John Crawford
1956-57—	Providence	John Crawford	Cleveland	Jack Gordon
1957-58—	Hershey	Frank Mathers	Hershey	Frank Mathers
1958-59—	Buffalo	Bobby Kirk	Hershey	Frank Mathers
1959-60—	Springfield	Pat Egan	Springfield	Pat Egan
1960-61—	Springfield	Pat Egan	Springfield	Pat Egan
1961-62—	Springfield (E)	Pat Egan	Springfield	Pat Egan
	Cleveland (W)	Jack Gordon		
1962-63—	Providence (E)	Fern Flaman	Buffalo	Billy Reay
	Buffalo (W)	Billy Reay		
1963-64—	Quebec (E)	Floyd Curry	Cleveland	Fred Glover
	Pittsburgh (W)	Vic Stasiuk		
1964-65—	Quebec (E)	Bernie Geoffrion	Rochester	Joe Crozier
	Rochester (W)	Joe Crozier		
1965-66—	Quebec (E)	Bernie Geoffrion	Rochester	Joe Crozier
	Rochester (W)	Joe Crozier		
1966-67—	Hershey (E)	Frank Mathers	Pittsburgh	Baz Bastien
	Pittsburgh (W)	Baz Bastien		
1967-68—	Hershey (E)	Frank Mathers	Rochester	Joe Crozier
	Rochester (W)	Joe Crozier		
1968-69—	Hershey (E)	Frank Mathers	Hershey	Frank Mathers
	Buffalo (W)	Fred Shero		
1969-70—	Montreal (E)	Al MacNeil	Buffalo	Fred Shero
	Buffalo (W)	Fred Shero		
1970-71—	Providence (E)	Larry Wilson	Springfield	John Wilson
	Baltimore (W)	Terry Reardon		
1971-72—	Boston (E)	Bep Guidolin	Nova Scotia	Al MacNeil
	Baltimore (W)	Terry Reardon		
1972-73—	Nova Scotia (E)	Al MacNeil	Cincinnati	Floyd Smith
	Cincinnati (W)	Floyd Smith		
1973-74—	Rochester (N)	Don Cherry	Hershey	Chuck Hamilton
	Baltimore (S)	Terry Reardon		
1974-75—	Providence (N)	John Muckler	Springfield	Ron Stewart
	Virginia (S)	Doug Barkley		
1975-76—	Nova Scotia (N)	Al MacNeil	Nova Scotia	Al MacNeil
	Hershey (S)	Chuck Hamilton		
1976-77—	Nova Scotia	Al MacNeil	Nova Scotia	Al MacNeil
1977-78—	Maine (N)	Bob McCammon	Maine	Bob McCammon
	Rochester (S)	Duane Rupp		

	REGULAR-SEASON CHAMPION		PLAYOFF CHAMPION	
Season	**Team**	**Coach**	**Team**	**Coach**
1978-79—	Maine (N)	Bob McCammon	Maine	Bob McCammon
	New Haven (S)	Parker MacDonald		
1979-80—	New Brunswick (N)	Joe Crozier-Lou Angotti	Hershey	Doug Gibson
	New Haven (S)	Parker MacDonald		
1980-81—	Maine (N)	Bob McCammon	Adirondack	Tom Webster-J.P. LeBlanc
	Hershey (S)	Bryan Murray		
1981-82—	New Brunswick (N)	Orval Tessier	New Brunswick	Orval Tessier
	Binghamton (S)	Larry Kish		
1982-83—	Fredericton (N)	Jacques Demers	Rochester	Mike Keenan
	Rochester (S)	Mike Keenan		
1983-84—	Fredericton (N)	Earl Jessiman	Maine	John Paddock
	Baltimore (S)	Gene Ubriaco		
1984-85—	Maine (N)	Tom McVie-John Paddock	Sherbrooke	Pierre Creamer
	Binghamton (S)	Larry Pleau		
1985-86—	Adirondack (N)	Bill Dineen	Adirondack	Bill Dineen
	Hershey (S)	John Paddock		
1986-87—	Sherbrooke (N)	Pierre Creamer	Rochester	John Van Boxmeer
	Rochester (S)	John Van Boxmeer*		
1987-88—	Maine (N)	Mike Milbury	Hershey	John Paddock
	Hershey (S)	John Paddock		
1988-89—	Sherbrooke (N)	Jean Hamel	Adirondack	Bill Dineen
	Adirondack (S)	Bill Dineen		
1989-90—	Sherbrooke (N)	Jean Hamel	Springfield	Jimmy Roberts
	Rochester (S)	John Van Boxmeer		
1990-91—	Springfield (N)	Jimmy Roberts	Springfield	Jimmy Roberts
	Rochester (S)	Don Lever		
1991-92—	Springfield (N)	Jay Leach	Adirondack	Barry Melrose
	Binghamton (S)	Ron Smith		
	Fredericton (A)	Paulin Bordeleau		
1992-93—	Providence (N)	Mike O'Connell	Cape Breton	George Burnett
	Binghamton (S)	Ron Smith-Colin Campbell		
	St. John's (A)	Marc Crawford		
1993-94—	Adirondack (N)	Newell Brown	Portland	Barry Trotz
	Hershey (S)	Jay Leach		
	St. John's (A)	Marc Crawford		
1994-95—	Albany (N)	Robbie Ftorek	Albany	Robbie Ftorek
	Binghamton (S)	Al Hill		
	Prince Edward Island (A)	Dave Allison		
1995-96—	Albany (N)	Robbie Ftorek	Rochester	John Tortorella
1996-97—	Philadelphia (MA)	Bill Barber	Hershey	Bob Hartley
1997-98—	Philadelphia (MA)	Bill Barber	Philadelphia	Bill Barber
1998-99—	Providence (NE)	Peter Laviolette	Providence	Peter Laviolette

*Rochester awarded division championship based on season-series record.

INTERNATIONAL HOCKEY LEAGUE

LEAGUE OFFICE

President and chief executive officer
Doug Moss
Senior v.p. of business operations
Mike McEvoy
Director of communications
Jim Anderson
Communications manager
Sean Krabach
Vice president of hockey operations
Bob McCammon
Address
1395 East Twelve Mile Road
Madison Heights, MI 48071
Phone
248-546-3230
FAX
248-546-1811

TEAMS

CHICAGO WOLVES

General manager
Kevin Cheveldayoff
Head coach
John Anderson
Home ice
Allstate Arena
Address
2301 Ravine Way
Glenview, IL 60025
Seating capacity
16,882
Phone
847-390-0404
FAX
847-724-1652

CINCINNATI CYCLONES

General manager and head coach
Ron Smith
Home ice
Firststar Center
Address
100 Broadway
Cincinnati, OH 45202
Seating capacity
16,000
Phone
513-421-7825
FAX
513-421-1210

CLEVELAND LUMBERJACKS

General manager
Larry Gordon
Co-coaches
Perry Ganchar
B.J. MacDonald
Phil Russell
Home ice
Gund Arena
Address
One Center Ice
200 Huron Road
Cleveland, OH 44115
Seating capacity
19,941
Phone
216-420-0000
FAX
216-420-2500

DETROIT VIPERS

General manager
John Torchetti
Head coach
Paulin Bordeleau
Home ice
Palace of Auburn Hills
Address
Two Championship Drive
Auburn Hills, MI 48326
Seating capacity
20,804
Phone
248-377-8613
FAX
248-377-2695

GRAND RAPIDS GRIFFINS

General manager
Bob McNamara
Head coach
Guy Charron
Home ice
Van Andel Arena
Address
130 W. Fulton
Grand Rapids, MI 49503
Seating capacity
10,834
Phone
616-774-4585
FAX
616-336-5464

HOUSTON AEROS

General manager/head coach
Ron Low
Home ice
Compaq Center
Address
3100 Wilcrest Drive
Houston, TX 77042
Seating capacity
11,500
Phone
713-974-7825
FAX
713-361-7900

KANSAS CITY BLADES

Vice president and general manager
Doug Soetaert
Head coach
Paul MacLean
Home ice
Kemper Arena
Address
1800 Genesee
Kansas City, MO 64102
Seating capacity
17,857
Phone
816-842-5233
FAX
816-842-5610

LONG BEACH ICE DOGS

General manager and head coach
John Van Boxmeer
Home ice
Long Beach Arena
Address
300 E. Ocean Blvd.
Long Beach, CA 90802
Seating capacity
11,131
Phone
562-423-3647
FAX
562-437-5116

MANITOBA MOOSE

General manager and head coach
Randy Carlyle
Home ice
Winnipeg Arena
Address
1430 Maroons Road
Winnipeg, Manitoba, Canada R3G 0L5
Seating capacity
10,842
Phone
204-987-7825
FAX
204-896-6673

MICHIGAN K-WINGS

General manager
Bill Inglis
Head coach
Bill McDonald
Home ice
Wings Stadium
Address
3620 Van Rick Drive
Kalamazoo, MI 49002
Seating capacity
5,113
Phone
616-349-9772
FAX
616-345-6584

MILWAUKEE ADMIRALS

General manager and executive v.p.
Phil Wittliff
Head coach
Al Sims
Home ice
Bradley Center
Address
1001 North Fourth St.
Milwaukee, WI 53203
Seating capacity
17,845
Phone
414-227-0550
FAX
414-227-0568

ORLANDO SOLAR BEARS

General manager
John Weisbrod
Head coach
To be announced
Home ice
Orlando Arena
Address
8701 Maitland Summit Blvd.
Orlando, FL 32810
Seating capacity
15,820
Phone
407-916-2400
FAX
407-841-6363

UTAH GRIZZLIES

General manager and head coach
Bob Bourne
Home ice
E Center of West Balley City
Address
3200 S. Decker Lake Dr.
West Balley City, UT 84119
Seating capacity
10,500
Phone
801-988-8000
FAX
801-988-7000

1998-99 REGULAR SEASON

FINAL STANDINGS

EASTERN CONFERENCE

NORTHEAST DIVISION

Team	G	W	L	SOL	Pts.	GF	GA
Detroit	82	50	21	11	111	259	195
Orlando	82	45	33	4	94	264	253
Cincinnati	82	44	32	6	94	269	270
Grand Rapids	82	34	40	8	76	256	281

CENTRAL DIVISION

Team	G	W	L	SOL	Pts.	GF	GA
Michigan	82	35	34	13	83	232	253
Fort Wayne	82	33	33	16	82	250	280
Indianapolis	82	33	37	12	78	243	277
Cleveland	82	28	47	7	63	248	310

WESTERN CONFERENCE

MIDWEST DIVISION

Team	G	W	L	SOL	Pts.	GF	GA
Chicago	82	49	21	12	110	285	246
Manitoba	82	47	21	14	108	269	236
Kansas City	82	44	31	7	95	256	270
Milwaukee	82	38	28	16	92	254	265

SOUTHWEST DIVISION

Team	G	W	L	SOL	Pts.	GF	GA
Houston	82	54	15	13	121	307	209
Long Beach	82	48	28	6	102	260	237
Utah	82	39	34	9	87	244	254
Las Vegas	82	35	39	8	78	247	307

INDIVIDUAL LEADERS

Goals: Steve Maltais, Chicago (56)
Assists: Brian Wiseman, Houston (88)
Points: Brian Wiseman, Houston (109)
Penalty minutes: Mel Angelstad, Michigan (421)
Goaltending average: Kevin Weekes, Detroit (2.07)
Shutouts: Kevin Weekes, Detroit (4)

TOP SCORERS

	Games	G	A	Pts.
Brian Wiseman, Houston	77	21	88	109
Steve Maltais, Chicago	82	56	44	100
Bill Bowler, Manitoba	82	26	67	93
Gilbert Dionne, Cincinnati	76	35	53	88
Todd Simon, Cincinnati	81	26	61	87
Brett Harkins, Cleveland	74	20	67	87
Jeff Christian, Houston	80	45	41	86
Chris Marinucci, Chicago	82	41	40	81
Glen Metropolit, Grand Rapids	77	28	53	81
Dave Hymovitz, Indianapolis	78	46	30	76
Stan Drulia, Detroit	82	23	52	75
Don Biggs, Utah	83	22	53	75
Greg Hawgood, Houston	76	17	57	74
David Ling, Kansas City	82	30	42	72
Viacheslav Butsayev, Fort Wayne	71	28	44	72
Mark Beaufait, Orlando	71	28	43	71
Brett Hauer, Manitoba	81	15	56	71
Scott Thomas, Manitoba	78	45	25	70
Dave Roberts, Michigan	75	32	38	70
Mark Lamb, Houston	79	21	49	70

INDIVIDUAL STATISTICS

CHICAGO WOLVES

SCORING

	Games	G	A	Pts.	PIM
Steve Maltais	82	56	44	100	164
Chris Marinucci	82	41	40	81	24
Niklas Andersson	65	17	47	64	49
Tom Tilley	73	5	55	60	32
Bob Nardella	82	8	45	53	86
Guy Larose	80	19	22	41	117
Steve Larouche	33	13	25	38	18
Scott Pearson	62	23	13	36	154
Dan Plante	81	21	12	33	119
Kevin Miller	30	11	20	31	8
Brent Gretzky	39	9	19	28	15
Glen Featherstone	62	5	21	26	191
Todd White	25	11	13	24	8
Tim Breslin	72	7	14	21	72
Steve Gosselin	65	2	18	20	107
Glenn Stewart	16	7	6	13	4
Tim Bergland	68	4	9	13	20
Paul Koch	53	0	12	12	85
Jeremy Mylymok	63	4	6	10	194
Chris LiPuma	34	0	10	10	186
Kevin Dahl	34	3	6	9	61

	Games	G	A	Pts.	PIM
James Black	5	6	0	6	0
Dennis Vial	55	1	4	5	213
Ed Olczyk	7	2	2	4	6
Dave Seitz	7	1	2	3	2
Wendell Young (goalie)	35	0	2	2	32
Pat Jablonski (goalie)	36	0	2	2	12
Mike Melas	3	0	1	1	0
Andrei Petronin	7	0	1	1	2
Neal Martin	8	0	1	1	2
Glenn Healy (goalie)	10	0	1	1	2
David Craievich	1	0	0	0	0
Francis Larivee (goalie)	1	0	0	0	0
Patrick Rochon	1	0	0	0	2
Cory Banika	1	0	0	0	6
Mark Pivetz	1	0	0	0	0
Stas Tkatch	1	0	0	0	0
Dallas Eakins	2	0	0	0	0
Scott LaGrand (goalie)	2	0	0	0	0
Paul Willett	3	0	0	0	0
Sami Helenius	4	0	0	0	11
Craig Mills	5	0	0	0	14

GOALTENDING

	Gms.	Min.	W	L	T	G	SO	Avg.
Scott LaGrand	2	78	1	0	0	3	0	2.31
Wendell Young	35	2047	20	10	4	84	3	2.46
Pat Jablonski	36	2119	22	7	7	106	1	3.00
Glenn Healy	10	597	6	3	1	33	0	3.32
Francis Larivee	1	60	0	1	0	5	0	5.00

CINCINNATI CYCLONES

SCORING

	Games	G	A	Pts.	PIM
Gilbert Dionne	76	35	53	88	123
Todd Simon	81	26	61	87	72
Jeff Shevalier	76	29	34	63	57
Todd Hawkins	82	20	32	52	171
Scott Morrow	80	29	22	51	116
Jeff Wells	82	9	29	38	41
Kirk Nielsen	82	12	22	34	58
Burt Henderson	80	9	24	33	84
Ed Patterson	73	8	25	33	227
Chris Joseph	27	11	19	30	38
Fred Knipscheer	43	14	15	29	44
Don Biggs	23	3	17	20	33
Doug MacDonald	33	7	11	18	22
Eric Dandenault	63	4	13	17	180
Rastisl Pavlikovsky	31	4	12	16	28
Tom Nemeth	36	9	6	15	16
Kaspars Ashtashenko	74	3	11	14	166
Pat MacLeod	18	5	5	10	4
Phil Crowe	39	2	6	8	62
Olaf Kjenstad	22	2	5	7	43
Brian Secord	32	1	6	7	26
Geoff Smith	31	3	3	6	20
Denis Chervyakov	32	3	3	6	62
Jan Bulis	10	2	2	4	14
Ryan Gillis	15	2	2	4	14
Alexandre Volchkov	25	1	3	4	8
Jamie Ling	2	1	2	3	0
Brandon Sugden	6	0	2	2	51
Jani Hurme (goalie)	26	0	2	2	4
Norm Dezainde	2	1	0	1	0
Aaron Kriss	4	1	0	1	6
Chris Bergeron	1	0	1	1	2
Kiley Hill	1	0	1	1	0
Earl Cronan	4	0	1	1	0
Brian Regan (goalie)	4	0	1	1	0
Rick Goldmann	5	0	1	1	7
Dave Van Drunen	1	0	0	0	0
Kelly Harper	1	0	0	0	0
Justin Krall	1	0	0	0	0
Mike Sylvia	1	0	0	0	0
Bobby Brown	2	0	0	0	0
Jim Carey (goalie)	2	0	0	0	0
Chris Wismer	4	0	0	0	6
Alexei Tezikov	5	0	0	0	2
Geoff Sarjeant (goalie)	14	0	0	0	2
Frederic Cassivi (goalie)	44	0	0	0	2

GOALTENDING

	Gms.	Min.	W	L	T	G	SO	Avg.
Jim Carey	2	120	1	0	1	2	0	1.00
Brian Regan	4	197	2	1	0	9	0	2.73
Frederic Cassivi	44	2418	21	17	2	123	1	3.05
Jani Hurme	26	1428	14	9	2	81	0	3.40
Geoff Sarjeant	14	733	6	5	1	42	1	3.44

CLEVELAND LUMBERJACKS

SCORING

	Games	G	A	Pts.	PIM
Brett Harkins	74	20	67	87	84
Jock Callander	81	28	26	54	121
Xavier Delisle	77	15	29	44	36
Dave Baseggio	55	12	30	42	72
Jason Ruff	44	13	27	40	57
Chris Longo	69	13	23	36	109
Jason Bonsignore	48	14	19	33	68
Corey Spring	48	18	10	28	98
Jesse Belanger	22	9	13	22	10
Eduard Pershin	68	9	12	21	71
Eric Lavigne	66	11	7	18	259
Lane Lambert	36	8	10	18	61
Paul Ysebaert	27	6	11	17	14
Karel Betik	74	5	11	16	97
Jim Paek	65	4	11	15	34
Joe Cardarelli	50	7	7	14	8
Brent Peterson	18	6	7	13	31
Steve Kelly	18	6	7	13	36
Rob Pearson	20	3	10	13	27
Ryan Mougenel	45	5	7	12	46
Mario Larocque	59	5	7	12	202
Jeff Rucinski	63	4	5	9	72
John Cullen	6	2	7	9	0
Samuel St. Pierre	13	2	5	7	4
Tony Tuzzolino	15	2	4	6	22
Mike McBain	28	2	4	6	15
Steve Wilson	18	1	5	6	21
Andrei Skopintsev	19	3	2	5	8
Jason Robinson	29	2	3	5	26
Pavel Kubina	6	2	2	4	16
Derek Wilkinson (goalie)	34	0	3	3	6
Andrew Williamson	3	2	0	2	0
Daymond Langkow	4	1	1	2	18
David Wilkie	2	0	2	2	0
Alexander Selivanov	2	0	1	1	4
Jarret Whidden	3	0	1	1	2
Corey Schwab (goalie)	8	0	1	1	4
Mike Tamburro (goalie)	17	0	1	1	6
Tim Fingerhut	1	0	0	0	0
Brian Regan (goalie)	1	0	0	0	0
Beau Bilek	3	0	0	0	2
Dean Shmyr	3	0	0	0	8
Martin Bradette (goalie)	4	0	0	0	0
Ryan Brown	4	0	0	0	5
Enrico Ciccone	6	0	0	0	23
Zac Bierk (goalie)	27	0	0	0	4

GOALTENDING

	Gms.	Min.	W	L	T	G	SO	Avg.
Brian Regan	1	60	0	1	0	3	0	3.02
Zac Bierk	27	1556	11	12	4	79	0	3.05
Derek Wilkinson	34	1760	10	15	2	108	1	3.68
Corey Schwab	8	477	1	6	1	31	0	3.90
Mike Tamburro	17	835	5	11	0	58	0	4.17
Martin Bradette	4	206	1	2	0	17	0	4.95

DETROIT VIPERS

SCORING

	Games	G	A	Pts.	PIM
Stan Drulia	82	23	52	75	64
Peter Ciavaglia	59	27	31	58	33
Steve Walker	80	25	32	57	72
Brian Felsner	72	20	35	55	49
Mike Prokopec	75	25	28	53	125
Brad Shaw	61	10	35	45	44
Keith Aldridge	66	15	28	43	130
Bobby Reynolds	67	21	20	41	60
John Gruden	59	10	28	38	52
John Emmons	75	13	22	35	172
Ian Herbers	82	8	16	24	142
Yves Sarault	36	11	12	23	52
Darren Banks	58	6	12	18	296
Mike Maurice	29	5	9	14	18
Peter Ambroziak	33	5	8	13	30
Stefan Ustorf	14	3	7	10	11
Andy Bezeau	44	2	7	9	308
Tim Murray	39	1	8	9	17
Dan Kesa	8	3	5	8	12
Steve Martins	4	1	6	7	16
Luch Nasato	26	2	4	6	111
Mike Gaffney	38	2	4	6	33
Kory Karlander	22	4	1	5	8
Craig Wolanin	16	0	5	5	21
Mike Bondy	14	3	1	4	2
Alex Stojanov	27	1	3	4	91
Bobby Jay	44	1	3	4	51
Brian Mueller	12	1	2	3	4
Jeff Whittle	8	0	3	3	2
Sami Salo	5	0	2	2	0
Stewart Malgunas	9	0	2	2	10
Andrei Trefilov (goalie)	27	0	2	2	16
Jim Logan	1	0	1	1	0
Chris Luongo	11	0	1	1	4
Kevin Weekes (goalie)	33	0	1	1	2
Tony Martino (goalie)	1	0	0	0	0
Emmanuel LaBranche	2	0	0	0	2
Chad Dameworth	2	0	0	0	0
Bret Meyers	2	0	0	0	2
Phil Crowe	2	0	0	0	9
Eric Naud	2	0	0	0	21
Carlin Nordstrom	3	0	0	0	6
Aaron Kriss	3	0	0	0	16
Chris Wismer	4	0	0	0	21
Mathieu Raby	5	0	0	0	11
Trevor Koenig (goalie)	6	0	0	0	0
Mark Vilneff	7	0	0	0	2
Geoff Sarjeant (goalie)	8	0	0	0	6
Jani Hurme (goalie)	12	0	0	0	0

GOALTENDING

	Gms.	Min.	W	L	T	G	SO	Avg.
Tony Martino	1	60	1	0	0	1	0	1.00
Andrei Trefilov	27	1613	17	8	2	53	3	1.97
Kevin Weekes	33	1857	19	5	7	64	4	2.07
Trevor Koenig	6	300	5	0	0	11	1	2.20
Jani Hurme	12	643	7	3	1	26	1	2.43
Geoff Sarjeant	8	421	1	5	1	26	0	3.70

FORT WAYNE KOMETS

SCORING

	Games	G	A	Pts.	PIM
Viacheslav Butsayev	71	28	44	72	123
Brad Purdie	80	27	41	68	45
Eric Boguniecki	72	32	34	66	100
Oleg Shargorodsky	79	18	30	48	100
Ian Boyce	75	20	24	44	80
Tero Lehtera	69	15	24	39	8
Andrei Bashkirov	34	11	25	36	10
David Nemirovsky	44	22	13	35	24
Robin Bawa	74	11	17	28	194
Sean Selmser	80	9	17	26	200
Mike Martin	75	6	20	26	89
Dion Darling	71	4	18	22	267
Andre Roy	65	15	6	21	395
Guy Dupuis	58	3	15	18	52
Ed Campbell	46	1	16	17	137
Tracy Egeland	26	10	5	15	24
Shawn Penn	78	3	11	14	308
Lee Sorochan	45	0	10	10	204
Derek Wood	25	0	8	8	36
Andrei Petrakov	11	2	4	6	0
Chad Dameworth	36	0	6	6	33
Nikolai Tsulygin	17	1	4	5	8
Jed Fiebelkorn	10	0	5	5	6
Adam Smith	27	3	1	4	44
Johnny Brdarovic	2	0	3	3	0
Chris Newans	11	0	3	3	7
Bob Woods	1	2	0	2	0
Hugo Belanger	6	0	2	2	0
Lance Ward	13	0	2	2	28
Pokey Reddick (goalie)	33	0	1	1	19
Bruce Racine (goalie)	53	0	1	1	24
Bryan McKinney	1	0	0	0	0
Andrei Sryubko	1	0	0	0	0
Dave Doucette	1	0	0	0	0
Paul Willett	1	0	0	0	2
Mike Legg	2	0	0	0	0
Jan Kobezda	4	0	0	0	4

GOALTENDING

	Gms.	Min.	W	L	T	G	SO	Avg.
Bruce Racine	53	3024	21	18	11	154	1	3.06
Pokey Reddick	33	1874	12	15	5	102	1	3.27

GRAND RAPIDS GRIFFINS

SCORING

	Games	G	A	Pts.	PIM
Glen Metropolit	77	28	53	81	92
Robert Petrovicky	49	26	32	58	87
Todd Hlushko	82	24	27	51	78
Andrei Vasilyev	59	21	27	48	24
Joe Frederick	45	23	18	41	98
Aris Brimanis	66	16	21	37	70
Travis Richards	82	9	23	32	84
Maxim Spiridonov	41	11	17	28	12
Kory Karlander	44	9	19	28	58
Darren Rumble	53	6	22	28	44
Danton Cole	72	14	11	25	50
Radim Bicanek	46	8	17	25	48
Jared Bednar	74	3	18	21	220
Donald Maclean	28	6	13	19	8
Gaetan Royer	52	12	6	18	177
Anders Bjork	35	8	6	14	17
Brent Peterson	17	7	6	13	14
Mickey Elick	17	3	6	9	8
Bruce Coles	15	1	7	8	10
Tom Ashe	76	1	7	8	84
Vashi Nedomansky	12	3	4	7	6
Marc Hussey	13	0	7	7	14
Darrin Shannon	10	1	5	6	12
Gord Kruppke	42	0	5	5	93
Michel Picard	6	2	2	4	2
Bruce Ramsay	47	1	3	4	165
Alexei Lojkin	10	1	2	3	4
Ashley Buckberger	11	1	2	3	0
Chris Szysky	6	1	1	2	10
Francois Leroux	13	1	1	2	22
Jed Fiebelkorn	5	0	2	2	5
Yan Kaminsky	7	0	2	2	0
Mikko Kuparinen	19	0	2	2	35

	Games	G	A	Pts.	PIM
Neil Little (goalie)	50	0	2	2	6
Matt Ruchty	13	1	0	1	59
Kerry Huffman	4	0	1	1	6
Tom Nolan	6	0	1	1	2
Jason Weaver	10	0	1	1	28
Ian Gordon (goalie)	41	0	1	1	0
Francois Sasseville	3	0	0	0	2
Dan Kordic	3	0	0	0	0
Brian LaFleur	4	0	0	0	2
Warren Norris	4	0	0	0	0
Sean Tallaire	4	0	0	0	0
Luke Curtin	4	0	0	0	2
Adam Smith	5	0	0	0	12
Mark DeSantis	7	0	0	0	9
Travis Tucker	10	0	0	0	31

GOALTENDING

	Gms.	Min.	W	L	T	G	SO	Avg.
Neil Little	50	2740	18	21	5	144	3	3.15
Ian Gordon	41	2149	16	19	3	123	2	3.43

HOUSTON AEROS

SCORING

	Games	G	A	Pts.	PIM
Brian Wiseman	77	21	88	109	106
Jeff Christian	80	45	41	86	252
Greg Hawgood	76	17	57	74	90
Mark Lamb	79	21	49	70	72
Cam Stewart	61	36	26	62	75
Jeff Tory	79	19	36	55	46
Rob Valicevic	57	16	33	49	62
Mark Freer	79	17	28	45	66
Zac Boyer	61	16	23	39	40
David Oliver	37	18	17	35	30
Norm MacIver	49	6	25	31	48
Paul Dyck	76	4	18	22	62
Sean Pronger	16	11	7	18	32
Blake Sloan	62	8	10	18	76
Mike Yeo	57	6	12	18	65
Brian Sullivan	53	9	7	16	32
Trent Cull	72	2	14	16	232
Bill Huard	38	9	5	14	201
Brent Hughes	29	4	2	6	87
Robert Dome	20	2	4	6	24
Sven Butenschon	57	1	4	5	81
Jim Shepherd	5	2	2	4	0
Lane Lambert	9	2	1	3	4
Jim Paek	11	0	3	3	2
Gord Kruppke	19	0	2	2	58
Brian Pellerin	6	1	0	1	16
Eric Boulton	7	1	0	1	41
Greg Andrusak	3	0	1	1	2
Chad Alban (goalie)	5	0	1	1	0
Chris Valicevic	1	0	0	0	0
Chris Johnston	1	0	0	0	0
Craig Johnson	1	0	0	0	0
Kelly Smart	1	0	0	0	0
Jason Ruff	1	0	0	0	0
Phil Valk	1	0	0	0	2
Darren Maloney	2	0	0	0	4
Danny Lorenz (goalie)	7	0	0	0	0
Tom Nolan	8	0	0	0	2
Travis Van Tighem	13	0	0	0	9
Frederic Chabot (goalie)	21	0	0	0	6
Manny Fernandez (goalie)	50	0	0	0	4

GOALTENDING

	Gms.	Min.	W	L	T	G	SO	Avg.
Danny Lorenz	7	418	3	2	2	13	0	1.86
Frederic Chabot	21	1259	16	4	1	49	3	2.34
Manny Fernandez	50	2949	34	6	9	116	2	2.36
Chad Alban	5	284	1	3	1	14	0	2.95

INDIANAPOLIS ICE

SCORING

	Games	G	A	Pts.	PIM
Dave Hymovitz	78	46	30	76	42
Brian Noonan	65	19	44	63	128
Bob Lachance	70	17	46	63	59
Sylvain Cloutier	73	21	33	54	128
Chris Herperger	79	19	29	48	81
Mike Hall	73	12	25	37	10
Mike Vukonich	70	9	17	26	20
Nathan Perrott	72	14	11	25	307
Bryan Fogarty	36	7	15	22	28
Patrick Boileau	29	8	13	21	27
Marc Dupuis	55	4	17	21	56
Cail MacLean	35	13	7	20	20
Barrie Moore	43	9	10	19	18
Remi Royer	54	4	15	19	164
Marty Wilford	80	3	13	16	116
Dale DeGray	27	3	11	14	18
Ryan Vandenbussche	34	3	10	13	130
Erik Andersson	48	5	7	12	24
Matt Cooney	29	2	9	11	52
Jeff Paul	55	0	7	7	120
Justin Hocking	34	2	4	6	111
Craig Mills	12	2	3	5	14
Vince Williams	33	2	3	5	30
Colin Pepperall	9	2	2	4	12
Andrei Kozyrev	61	1	2	3	81
Justin Cardwell	4	2	0	2	0
Todd Rohloff	12	2	0	2	8
Jason Glover	1	0	2	2	0
Kirk Daubenspeck (goalie)	12	0	2	2	4
Jamie Allison	3	1	0	1	10
Frank Bialowas	16	1	0	1	27
Jamie Ling	1	0	1	1	0
Andrei Trefilov (goalie)	18	0	1	1	0
Geoff Sarjeant (goalie)	23	0	1	1	16
Marc Lamothe (goalie)	32	0	1	1	23
Rob Woodward	1	0	0	0	0
Dan Hodge	1	0	0	0	2
Richard Keyes	2	0	0	0	0
Jeff Salajko (goalie)	2	0	0	0	0
Bret Meyers	4	0	0	0	4
Marko Makinen	5	0	0	0	0
Steve Tardif	6	0	0	0	40

GOALTENDING

	Gms.	Min.	W	L	T	G	SO	Avg.
Andrei Trefilov	18	986	9	6	2	39	0	2.37
Geoff Sarjeant	23	1354	13	7	2	57	2	2.53
Jeff Salajko	2	80	0	0	1	5	0	3.75
Marc Lamothe	32	1823	9	16	6	115	1	3.78
Kirk Daubenspeck	12	650	2	8	1	43	0	3.97

KANSAS CITY BLADES

SCORING

	Games	G	A	Pts.	PIM
David Ling	82	30	42	72	112
Jason Cirone	82	42	26	68	151
Eric Perrin	82	24	37	61	71
Jean-Guy Trudel	76	24	25	49	66
Pat Ferschweiler	80	7	38	45	66
Dan Ratushny	70	9	32	41	38
Dave Chyzowski	67	24	15	39	147
Dale Craigwell	61	11	28	39	14
Vlastimil Kroupa	77	6	32	38	52
Brendan Yarema	69	11	21	32	163
Dody Wood	60	11	16	27	286
David Vallieres	61	9	12	21	63
Ryan Mulhern	59	7	11	18	82
Jon Rohloff	41	5	13	18	42
Steven Low	64	3	14	17	100

	Games	G	A	Pts.	PIM
Lonnie Loach	22	9	5	14	6
Nick Naumenko	21	3	8	11	4
Dan Harrison	10	1	8	9	4
Grant Richison	65	0	8	8	58
Brian Bonin	19	2	5	7	10
Rocky Welsing	45	3	2	5	79
Brent Bilodeau	35	0	4	4	66
Andrew Ference	5	1	2	3	4
Trevor Sherban	35	1	1	2	40
Eric Rud	11	0	1	1	6
Patrick Lalime (goalie)	66	0	1	1	6
Marty Melnychuk	1	0	0	0	7
Brian Sullivan	2	0	0	0	0
Walker McDonald	3	0	0	0	7
Brian Leitza (goalie)	3	0	0	0	0
Ryan Hoople (goalie)	3	0	0	0	0
Jason Kelly	3	0	0	0	0
Greg Smith (goalie)	3	0	0	0	0
Tuomas Gronman	4	0	0	0	0
Jean-Sebastien Aubin (goalie)	13	0	0	0	0

GOALTENDING

	Gms.	Min.	W	L	T	G	SO	Avg.
Greg Smith	3	98	0	0	1	3	0	1.83
Patrick Lalime	66	3789	39	20	4	190	2	3.01
J.-Sebastien Aubin	13	751	5	7	1	41	0	3.27
Ryan Hoople	3	131	0	2	1	10	0	4.57
Brian Leitza	3	131	0	2	0	10	0	4.58

LAS VEGAS THUNDER

SCORING

	Games	G	A	Pts.	PIM
Russ Romaniuk	82	43	20	63	91
Jason McBain	65	9	37	46	54
Scott Hollis	53	20	25	45	67
Sean Berens	61	24	18	42	62
Patrice Lefebvre	42	11	26	37	40
Lee Jinman	52	11	23	34	36
Stefan Ustorf	40	11	17	28	40
Taj Melson	72	8	20	28	48
Shawn Wansborough	62	7	20	27	144
Nick Naumenko	34	5	16	21	37
Brad Miller	73	5	16	21	264
Jean-Francois Jomphe	32	6	14	20	63
Randy Burridge	25	7	12	19	8
Petr Nedved	13	8	10	18	32
Kevin Kaminski	39	7	10	17	217
Ryan Mulhern	23	9	6	15	8
Chris Taylor	14	3	12	15	2
David Shaw	24	3	10	13	22
Andrei Vasilyev	15	3	6	9	6
Louie DeBrusk	26	3	6	9	160
Ashley Buckberger	24	3	5	8	6
Dean Ewen	66	3	5	8	251
Andrei Sryubko	51	0	8	8	164
Trevor Roenick	32	3	4	7	43
Peter Zurba	24	2	3	5	89
Sami Helenius	42	2	3	5	193
Mike Wilson	6	3	1	4	6
Bryan Helmer	8	1	3	4	28
Yevgeny Shaldybin	13	1	3	4	6
Phil Crowe	14	1	3	4	18
Drew Bannister	16	2	1	3	73
Keith McCambridge	18	1	2	3	56
Alex Alexeev	10	0	3	3	4
Pavel Evstigneev	10	2	0	2	0
Daniel Briere	1	1	1	2	0
Kevin St. Jacques	2	1	1	2	2
Vadim Sharapov	2	0	2	2	0
Luch Nasato	13	0	2	2	52
Petr Franek (goalie)	37	0	2	2	4
Brad Mehalko	8	1	0	1	7
Dampy Brar	8	1	0	1	0
Lorne Toews	13	1	0	1	15
Michel Petit	6	0	1	1	10
Mike Gaffney	10	0	1	1	8
Konstantin Simchuk (goalie)	30	0	1	1	23
Edgars Zaltkovskis	1	0	0	0	0
Scott Drevitch	1	0	0	0	0
Hakan Jansson	1	0	0	0	2
Jeff Mercer	1	0	0	0	4
Kevin Smyth	1	0	0	0	0
Paul Taylor (goalie)	1	0	0	0	0
Ray Clarke	1	0	0	0	0
Sam Fields	1	0	0	0	10
Marc Giannetti	2	0	0	0	0
Brad Isbister	2	0	0	0	9
Brett Larson	2	0	0	0	0
Igor Bondarev	3	0	0	0	0
Brad Guzda (goalie)	3	0	0	0	0
Alexei Podalinski	4	0	0	0	0
Chad Wagner	4	0	0	0	29
Tim Lovell	9	0	0	0	8
Bob Quinnell	10	0	0	0	2
Nikolai Syrtsov	12	0	0	0	4
Scott Langkow (goalie)	27	0	0	0	18

GOALTENDING

	Gms.	Min.	W	L	T	G	SO	Avg.
Konstantin Simchuk	30	1471	10	10	3	75	0	3.06
Petr Franek	37	1879	17	13	2	107	0	3.42
Scott Langkow	27	1402	7	14	2	97	1	4.15
Brad Guzda	3	138	1	2	0	10	0	4.34
Paul Taylor	1	9	0	0	1	1	0	7.02

LONG BEACH ICE DOGS

SCORING

	Games	G	A	Pts.	PIM
Patrik Augusta	68	24	35	59	125
Dan Lambert	50	17	36	53	91
Sean Tallaire	56	24	19	43	68
Doug Ast	50	16	22	38	54
Patrik Stefan	33	11	24	35	26
Jaroslav Modry	64	6	29	35	44
Claude Jutras	74	13	19	32	408
Pavel Rosa	31	17	13	30	28
Darryl Williams	65	13	15	28	122
Eric Manlow	51	9	19	28	30
Andy Roach	41	5	21	26	34
Mark Ferner	59	2	24	26	78
Nathan LaFayette	41	9	13	22	24
Lonnie Loach	30	12	9	21	18
Jan Nemecek	66	5	16	21	42
John Byce	37	8	11	19	8
Dan Bylsma	58	10	8	18	53
Patrice Lefebvre	14	1	12	13	8
Mike Matteucci	79	3	9	12	253
Dmitri Leonov	34	6	4	10	59
Louie DeBrusk	24	5	5	10	134
Jason Morgan	13	4	6	10	18
Brandon Convery	14	3	7	10	8
Jason Podollan	8	5	3	8	2
Jocelyn Lemieux	17	4	4	8	16
Frederick Jobin	35	4	4	8	88
Scott Hollis	13	2	5	7	21
Keith McCambridge	52	2	5	7	200
Chris Kenady	19	1	6	7	47
Shawn Wansborough	8	1	5	6	16
Sacha Molin	19	2	2	4	10
Pierre Sevigny	6	1	3	4	7
B.J. MacPherson	4	1	2	3	2
Mike Jickling	9	1	1	2	4
Rene Chapdelaine	29	1	1	2	28
Neil Martin	3	0	2	2	6

	Games	G	A	Pts.	PIM
Petr Marek	6	0	2	2	2
Ryan Bach (goalie)	27	0	1	1	8
Manny Legace (goalie)	33	0	1	1	6
Geoff Sarjeant (goalie)	1	0	0	0	0
Eric Belanger	1	0	0	0	0
Petr Jaros (goalie)	1	0	0	0	0
Steve Vezina (goalie)	2	0	0	0	0
Eric Brule	2	0	0	0	0
Steven Low	2	0	0	0	2
Trevor Converse	3	0	0	0	7
Dave MacIntyre	3	0	0	0	0
Andy Powers	3	0	0	0	0
Brett Larson	4	0	0	0	2
Jason Shmyr	8	0	0	0	35
Trevor Koenig (goalie)	11	0	0	0	0
Sergei Naumov (goalie)	15	0	0	0	2

GOALTENDING

	Gms.	Min.	W	L	T	G	SO	Avg.
Manny Legace	33	1796	22	8	1	67	2	2.24
Trevor Koenig	11	635	5	5	0	29	0	2.74
Ryan Bach	27	1491	10	9	5	74	1	2.98
Geoff Sarjeant	1	60	1	0	0	1	0	3.41
Steve Vezina	2	52	0	1	0	3	0	3.48
Sergei Naumov	15	808	10	4	0	47	0	3.49
Petr Jaros	1	60	0	1	0	5	0	5.00

MANITOBA MOOSE

SCORING

	Games	G	A	Pts.	PIM
Bill Bowler	82	26	67	93	59
Brett Hauer	81	15	56	71	66
Scott Thomas	78	45	25	70	32
Ralph Intranuovo	71	29	31	60	70
Patrice Tardif	63	21	35	56	88
Jason MacDonald	82	25	27	52	283
Scott Arniel	70	16	35	51	82
Kent Fearns	66	14	27	41	66
Rhett Gordon	76	14	23	37	61
Jimmy Roy	78	10	16	26	185
Curt Bowen	45	10	12	22	54
Jeff Parrott	82	2	18	20	82
Cory Cyrenne	46	4	14	18	18
Brian Chapman	76	3	15	18	127
Michael Stewart	77	5	10	15	136
Sheldon Kennedy	24	7	7	14	14
Mike Ruark	53	5	6	11	179
Justin Kurtz	38	4	6	10	40
Neil Brady	13	1	5	6	8
Bruce Coles	11	1	3	4	6
Chris Winnes	11	2	0	2	0
Jason Shmyr	57	1	1	2	227
Christian Bronsard (goalie)	33	0	2	2	6
Richard Shulmistra (goalie)	44	0	2	2	0
Jonathan DuBois	2	1	0	1	0
Mike Rosati (goalie)	8	0	1	1	0
Derek Landmesser	1	0	0	0	0
Xavier Majic	1	0	0	0	0
Jaroslav Obsut	2	0	0	0	0
Bobby Brown	2	0	0	0	0
Don Parsons	2	0	0	0	0
Robb Stauber (goalie)	5	0	0	0	0
Kelly Perrault	17	0	0	0	23

GOALTENDING

	Gms.	Min.	W	L	T	G	SO	Avg.
Mike Rosati	8	479	5	1	2	16	1	2.00
Christian Bronsard	33	1746	15	8	4	71	1	2.44
Richard Shulmistra	44	2469	25	11	7	117	2	2.84
Robb Stauber	5	213	2	1	1	17	0	4.78

MICHIGAN K-WINGS

SCORING

	Games	G	A	Pts.	PIM
Dave Roberts	75	32	38	70	77
Aaron Gavey	67	24	33	57	128
Jon Sim	68	24	27	51	91
Kelly Fairchild	74	17	33	50	88
Greg Leeb	77	16	27	43	18
Marty Flichel	70	15	28	43	57
Jason Botterill	56	13	25	38	106
Jamie Wright	64	16	15	31	92
Richard Jackman	71	13	17	30	106
Brad Lukowich	67	8	21	29	95
Petr Buzek	74	5	14	19	68
Doug Doull	55	4	11	15	227
Matt Martin	76	3	12	15	114
Shawn McCosh	12	4	9	13	18
Paul Traynor	39	3	9	12	12
Ryan Christie	48	4	5	9	74
Jeff Mitchell	50	4	4	8	122
Mel Angelstad	78	3	5	8	421
Alan Letang	12	3	3	6	0
Chris Albert	23	3	3	6	44
Sergey Gusev	12	0	6	6	14
Ryan Gillis	21	2	3	5	13
Evgueni Tsybouk	42	1	3	4	69
Paul Vincent	2	2	1	3	0
Jim Logan	20	2	1	3	54
Eric Brule	9	0	3	3	2
Milt Mastad	16	1	1	2	63
Mike Bales (goalie)	32	0	2	2	16
Frederic Bouchard	3	0	1	1	17
Dan Keczmer	5	0	1	1	2
Brad Berry	5	0	1	1	10
Marty Turco (goalie)	54	0	1	1	21
Jason Disher	1	0	0	0	0
Vadim Podrezov	2	0	0	0	2
Brent Severyn	3	0	0	0	0
Lee Jinman	3	0	0	0	0
Trevor Doyle	4	0	0	0	2
Akil Adams	8	0	0	0	6

GOALTENDING

	Gms.	Min.	W	L	T	G	SO	Avg.
Marty Turco	54	3127	24	17	10	136	1	2.61
Mike Bales	32	1773	11	17	3	96	1	3.25

MILWAUKEE ADMIRALS

SCORING

	Games	G	A	Pts.	PIM
Jason Cipolla	79	21	46	67	122
Craig Darby	81	32	22	54	33
Doug Friedman	69	26	25	51	251
Jeff Nelson	70	20	31	51	66
Karlis Skrastins	75	8	36	44	47
Jeff Daniels	62	12	31	43	19
Matt Henderson	77	19	19	38	117
Mark Mowers	51	14	22	36	24
Petr Sykora	73	14	15	29	50
David Gosselin	74	17	11	28	78
Marian Cisar	51	11	17	28	31
Brad Smyth	34	11	16	27	21
Richard Lintner	66	9	16	25	75
Jeff Kealty	70	8	14	22	134
Shannon Finn	35	6	11	17	22
Sergei Klimentiev	35	4	11	15	59
Kimmo Timonen	29	2	13	15	22
Vitali Yachmenev	16	7	6	13	0
Jeff Staples	69	2	10	12	155
Bobby Russell	31	3	3	6	8
Marc Moro	80	0	5	5	264

	Games	G	A	Pts.	PIM
Eric Fenton	5	1	2	3	24
Chris Armstrong	5	0	3	3	4
Paul Brousseau	5	1	1	2	2
Dan Riva	8	0	2	2	4
Darryl Gilmour (goalie)	5	0	1	1	0
Brian Downey	5	0	1	1	0
John Slaney	7	0	1	1	0
Mike Minard (goalie)	10	0	1	1	0
Kaj Linna	11	0	1	1	25
Alex Stojanov	13	0	1	1	58
Kay Whitmore (goalie)	23	0	1	1	25
Chris Mason (goalie)	34	0	1	1	6
Jason Disher	2	0	0	0	0
Ryan Aikia	2	0	0	0	0
Jeff Blum	2	0	0	0	5
Eric Fichaud (goalie)	8	0	0	0	0
Tomas Vokoun (goalie)	9	0	0	0	0
Matt Eldred	15	0	0	0	31

GOALTENDING

	Gms.	Min.	W	L	T	G	SO	Avg.
Tomas Vokoun	9	539	3	2	4	22	1	2.45
Chris Mason	34	1901	15	12	6	92	1	2.90
Kay Whitmore	23	1304	10	6	4	64	0	2.95
Mike Minard	10	531	3	5	0	27	0	3.05
Eric Fichaud	8	480	5	2	1	25	0	3.13
Darryl Gilmour	5	155	2	1	1	11	0	4.25

ORLANDO SOLAR BEARS

SCORING

	Games	G	A	Pts.	PIM
Mark Beaufait	71	28	43	71	38
Grigori Panteleyev	77	25	37	62	51
Todd Krygier	65	19	40	59	82
Curtis Murphy	80	22	35	57	60
Hubie McDonough	74	20	33	53	52
Dave Mackey	78	21	20	41	192
Shawn Carter	79	13	26	39	103
Todd Richards	67	11	26	37	61
Pierre Sevigny	43	11	21	32	44
Kirby Law	67	18	13	31	136
Allan Egeland	62	7	23	30	182
Patrick Neaton	75	5	22	27	98
Rob Bonneau	45	7	13	20	34
Terry Hollinger	21	9	9	18	18
Fredrik Oduya	64	2	14	16	259
Rob Kenny	20	9	5	14	10
Mike Nicholishen	45	1	13	14	61
Sean McCann	42	4	9	13	28
Clayton Norris	66	6	5	11	327
Eric Healey	13	5	4	9	13
Rob Pearson	11	6	2	8	41
Jason Blake	5	3	5	8	6
Ken Sabourin	72	3	4	7	248
Arttu Kayhko	23	0	5	5	18
Brent Cullaton	6	1	2	3	7
Scott Hollis	3	1	1	2	6
Denis Chervyakov	12	0	2	2	39
David Littman (goalie)	55	0	1	1	21
Karl Infanger	1	0	0	0	0
Mike Vellinga	1	0	0	0	4
Jeff Collard	1	0	0	0	4
Max Gingras (goalie)	1	0	0	0	0
J.F. Boutin	2	0	0	0	4
Shawn Wansborough	3	0	0	0	6
Martin Masa	3	0	0	0	2
Barry Dreger	8	0	0	0	57
Tyler Moss (goalie)	9	0	0	0	0
Frederic Deschenes (goalie)	12	0	0	0	0
Scott Bailey (goalie)	17	0	0	0	0

GOALTENDING

	Gms.	Min.	W	L	T	G	SO	Avg.
Tyler Moss	9	515	6	2	1	21	1	2.44
Scott Bailey	17	749	5	7	0	36	0	2.88
David Littman	55	2981	32	17	1	144	2	2.90
Frederic Deschenes	12	638	2	7	2	38	1	3.58
Max Gingras	1	18	0	0	0	3	0	9.78

UTAH GRIZZLIES

SCORING

	Games	G	A	Pts.	PIM
John Purves	80	24	39	63	24
Brad Lauer	78	31	30	61	68
Don Biggs	60	19	36	55	73
Dave Archibald	76	23	25	48	32
Micah Aivazoff	79	25	22	47	67
Jeff Sharples	78	8	29	37	93
John Byce	35	11	20	31	18
Yan Kaminsky	56	11	17	28	12
Gord Dineen	77	5	22	27	78
Brent Hughes	51	13	11	24	80
Terry Hollinger	58	4	19	23	40
Rob Bonneau	20	6	13	19	8
Rob Zettler	77	2	16	18	136
Andy Roach	44	7	10	17	18
Mick Vukota	48	8	7	15	226
Curtis Sheptak	60	7	8	15	99
Chris Kenady	35	7	6	13	68
Fred Knipscheer	21	4	9	13	20
Mike Hough	26	5	7	12	8
Rod Miller	72	2	8	10	95
Nick Naumenko	20	4	3	7	20
Darren Rumble	10	1	4	5	10
Rene Chapdelaine	19	2	2	4	16
Stanislav Gron	4	0	3	3	0
Anson Carter	6	1	1	2	0
Colin Chaulk	6	1	1	2	2
Andrei Lupandin	8	1	1	2	0
Scott Niedermayer	5	0	2	2	0
Bryan Randall	9	0	2	2	8
Trevor Roenick	21	0	2	2	17
Mike Taylor	1	0	1	1	4
Mike Larkin	2	0	1	1	0
Jan Mertzig	5	0	1	1	6
Mike Nicholishen	11	0	1	1	14
Mark McArthur (goalie)	1	0	0	0	0
Brett Larson	1	0	0	0	0
Johnny Brdarovic	2	0	0	0	0
Mark Vilneff	3	0	0	0	0
Ryan Bach (goalie)	4	0	0	0	0
Philippe DeRouville (goalie)	5	0	0	0	0
Martin Brochu (goalie)	5	0	0	0	0
Frederick Beaubien (goalie)	7	0	0	0	2
Scott LaGrand (goalie)	8	0	0	0	2
Petr Franek (goalie)	8	0	0	0	0
Jimmy Waite (goalie)	11	0	0	0	0
Steve Vezina (goalie)	20	0	0	0	0
Scott Langkow (goalie)	21	0	0	0	0
Rhett Trombley	36	0	0	0	86

GOALTENDING

	Gms.	Min.	W	L	T	G	SO	Avg.
Scott LaGrand	8	474	4	3	1	20	1	2.53
Martin Brochu	5	298	1	3	1	13	0	2.62
Ryan Bach	4	197	2	1	0	9	0	2.74
Steve Vezina	20	1066	12	4	1	49	0	2.76
Scott Langkow	21	1227	10	9	2	59	1	2.89
Jimmy Waite	11	622	6	3	2	30	0	2.89
Frederick Beaubien	7	371	3	2	1	18	0	2.91
Petr Franek	8	446	1	6	1	26	0	3.50
Mark McArthur	1	60	0	1	0	5	0	5.00
Philippe DeRouville	5	142	0	2	0	12	0	5.07

PLAYERS WITH TWO OR MORE TEAMS

SCORING

	Games	G	A	Pts.	PIM
Ryan Bach, Utah (goalie)	4	0	0	0	0
Ryan Bach, Long Beach (g)	27	0	1	1	8
Totals	31	0	1	1	8
Don Biggs, Cincinnati	23	3	17	20	33
Don Biggs, Utah	60	19	36	55	73
Totals	83	22	53	75	106
Rob Bonneau, Orlando	45	7	13	20	34
Rob Bonneau, Utah	20	6	13	19	8
Totals	65	13	26	39	42
Johnny Brdarovic, Utah	2	0	0	0	0
Johnny Brdarovic, F.W.	2	0	3	3	0
Totals	4	0	3	3	0
Bobby Brown, Manitoba	2	0	0	0	0
Bobby Brown, Cincinnati	2	0	0	0	0
Totals	4	0	0	0	0
Eric Brule, Michigan	9	0	3	3	2
Eric Brule, Long Beach	2	0	0	0	0
Totals	11	0	3	3	2
Ashley Buckberger, G.R.	11	1	2	3	0
Ashley Buckberger, L.V.	24	3	5	8	6
Totals	35	4	7	11	6
John Byce, Long Beach	37	8	11	19	8
John Byce, Utah	35	11	20	31	18
Totals	72	19	31	50	26
Rene Chapdelaine, Utah	19	2	2	4	16
Rene Chapdelaine, L.B.	29	1	1	2	28
Totals	48	3	3	6	44
Denis Chervyakov, Cincinnati	32	3	3	6	62
Denis Chervyakov, Orlando	12	0	2	2	39
Totals	44	3	5	8	101
Bruce Coles, Grand Rapids	15	1	7	8	10
Bruce Coles, Manitoba	11	1	3	4	6
Totals	26	2	10	12	16
Phil Crowe, Detroit	2	0	0	0	9
Phil Crowe, Cincinnati	39	2	6	8	62
Phil Crowe, Las Vegas	14	1	3	4	18
Totals	55	3	9	12	89
Chad Dameworth, Detroit	2	0	0	0	0
Chad Dameworth, F.W.	36	0	6	6	33
Totals	38	0	6	6	33
Louie DeBrusk, Las Vegas	26	3	6	9	160
Louie DeBrusk, Long Beach	24	5	5	10	134
Totals	50	8	11	19	294
Jason Disher, Michigan	1	0	0	0	0
Jason Disher, Milwaukee	2	0	0	0	0
Totals	3	0	0	0	0
Jed Fiebelkorn, Grand Rapids	5	0	2	2	5
Jed Fiebelkorn, Fort Wayne	10	0	5	5	6
Totals	15	0	7	7	11
Petr Franek, Utah (goalie)	8	0	0	0	0
Petr Franek, Las Vegas (g)	37	0	2	2	4
Totals	45	0	2	2	4
Mike Gaffney, Detroit	38	2	4	6	33
Mike Gaffney, Las Vegas	10	0	1	1	8
Totals	48	2	5	7	41
Ryan Gillis, Michigan	21	2	3	5	13
Ryan Gillis, Cincinnati	15	2	2	4	14
Totals	36	4	5	9	27
Sami Helenius, Chicago	4	0	0	0	11
Sami Helenius, Las Vegas	42	2	3	5	193
Totals	46	2	3	5	204
Terry Hollinger, Utah	58	4	19	23	40
Terry Hollinger, Orlando	21	9	9	18	18
Totals	79	13	28	41	58
Scott Hollis, Orlando	3	1	1	2	6
Scott Hollis, Long Beach	13	2	5	7	21
Scott Hollis, Las Vegas	53	20	25	45	67
Totals	69	23	31	54	94
Brent Hughes, Houston	29	4	2	6	87
Brent Hughes, Utah	51	13	11	24	80
Totals	80	17	13	30	167
Jani Hurme, Detroit (goalie)	12	0	0	0	0
Jani Hurme, Cincinnati (g)	26	0	2	2	4
Totals	38	0	2	2	4
Lee Jinman, Michigan	3	0	0	0	0
Lee Jinman, Las Vegas	52	11	23	34	36
Totals	55	11	23	34	36
Yan Kaminsky, Utah	56	11	17	28	12
Yan Kaminsky, Grand Rapids	7	0	2	2	0
Totals	63	11	19	30	12
Kory Karlander, Detroit	22	4	1	5	8
Kory Karlander, G.R.	44	9	19	28	58
Totals	66	13	20	33	66
Chris Kenady, Utah	35	7	6	13	68
Chris Kenady, Long Beach	19	1	6	7	47
Totals	54	8	12	20	115
Fred Knipscheer, Utah	21	4	9	13	20
Fred Knipscheer, Cincinnati	43	14	15	29	44
Totals	64	18	24	42	64
Trevor Koenig, L.B. (goalie)	11	0	0	0	0
Trevor Koenig, Detroit (g)	6	0	0	0	0
Totals	17	0	0	0	0
Aaron Kriss, Detroit	3	0	0	0	16
Aaron Kriss, Cincinnati	4	1	0	1	6
Totals	7	1	0	1	22
Gord Kruppke, Houston	19	0	2	2	58
Gord Kruppke, Grand Rapids	42	0	5	5	93
Totals	61	0	7	7	151
Scott LaGrand, Utah (goalie)	8	0	0	0	2
Scott LaGrand, Chicago (g)	2	0	0	0	0
Totals	10	0	0	0	2
Lane Lambert, Cleveland	36	8	10	18	61
Lane Lambert, Houston	9	2	1	3	4
Totals	45	10	11	21	65
Scott Langkow, L.V. (goalie)	27	0	0	0	18
Scott Langkow, Utah (goalie)	21	0	0	0	0
Totals	48	0	0	0	18
Brett Larson, Long Beach	4	0	0	0	2
Brett Larson, Utah	1	0	0	0	0
Brett Larson, Las Vegas	2	0	0	0	0
Totals	7	0	0	0	2
Patrice Lefebvre, Las Vegas	42	11	26	37	40
Patrice Lefebvre, Long Beach	14	1	12	13	8
Totals	56	12	38	50	48
Jamie Ling, Cincinnati	2	1	2	3	0
Jamie Ling, Indianapolis	1	0	1	1	0
Totals	3	1	3	4	0
Lonnie Loach, Long Beach	30	12	9	21	18
Lonnie Loach, Kansas City	22	9	5	14	6
Totals	52	21	14	35	24
Jim Logan, Detroit	1	0	1	1	0
Jim Logan, Michigan	20	2	1	3	54
Totals	21	2	2	4	54
Steven Low, Long Beach	2	0	0	0	2
Steven Low, Kansas City	64	3	14	17	100
Totals	66	3	14	17	102
Keith McCambridge, L.V.	18	1	2	3	56
Keith McCambridge, L.B.	52	2	5	7	200
Totals	70	3	7	10	256
Bret Meyers, Detroit	2	0	0	0	2
Bret Meyers, Indianapolis	4	0	0	0	4
Totals	6	0	0	0	6
Craig Mills, Chicago	5	0	0	0	14
Craig Mills, Indianapolis	12	2	3	5	14
Totals	17	2	3	5	28
Ryan Mulhern, Kansas City	59	7	11	18	82
Ryan Mulhern, Las Vegas	23	9	6	15	8
Totals	82	16	17	33	90
Luch Nasato, Detroit	26	2	4	6	111
Luch Nasato, Las Vegas	13	0	2	2	52

	Games	G	A	Pts.	PIM
Totals	39	2	6	8	163
Nick Naumenko, Utah	20	4	3	7	20
Nick Naumenko, Las Vegas	34	5	16	21	37
Nick Naumenko, Kansas City	21	3	8	11	4
Totals	75	12	27	39	61
Mike Nicholishen, Orlando	45	1	13	14	61
Mike Nicholishen, Utah	11	0	1	1	14
Totals	56	1	14	15	75
Tom Nolan, Grand Rapids	6	0	1	1	2
Tom Nolan, Houston	8	0	0	0	2
Totals	14	0	1	1	4
Jim Paek, Cleveland	65	4	11	15	34
Jim Paek, Houston	11	0	3	3	2
Totals	76	4	14	18	36
Rob Pearson, Cleveland	20	3	10	13	27
Rob Pearson, Orlando	11	6	2	8	41
Totals	31	9	12	21	68
Brent Peterson, Cleveland	18	6	7	13	31
Brent Peterson, G.R.	17	7	6	13	14
Totals	35	13	13	26	45
Brian Regan, Cleveland (g)	1	0	0	0	0
Brian Regan, Cincinnati (g)	4	0	1	1	0
Totals	5	0	1	1	0
Andy Roach, Long Beach	41	5	21	26	34
Andy Roach, Utah	44	7	10	17	18
Totals	85	12	31	43	52
Trevor Roenick, Las Vegas	32	3	4	7	43
Trevor Roenick, Utah	21	0	2	2	17
Totals	53	3	6	9	60
Jason Ruff, Cleveland	44	13	27	40	57
Jason Ruff, Houston	1	0	0	0	0
Totals	45	13	27	40	57
Darren Rumble, G.R.	53	6	22	28	44
Darren Rumble, Utah	10	1	4	5	10
Totals	63	7	26	33	54
Geoff Sarjeant, Cincinnati (g)	14	0	0	0	2
Geoff Sarjeant, Detroit (g)	8	0	0	0	6
Geoff Sarjeant, L.B. (goalie)	1	0	0	0	0
Geoff Sarjeant, Ind. (goalie)	23	0	1	1	16
Totals	46	0	1	1	24
Pierre Sevigny, Long Beach	6	1	3	4	7
Pierre Sevigny, Orlando	43	11	21	32	44
Totals	49	12	24	36	51
Jason Shmyr, Long Beach	8	0	0	0	35
Jason Shmyr, Manitoba	57	1	1	2	227
Totals	65	1	1	2	262
Adam Smith, Grand Rapids	5	0	0	0	12
Adam Smith, Fort Wayne	27	3	1	4	44
Totals	32	3	1	4	56
Andrei Sryubko, Fort Wayne	1	0	0	0	0
Andrei Sryubko, Las Vegas	51	0	8	8	164
Totals	52	0	8	8	164
Alex Stojanov, Milwaukee	13	0	1	1	58
Alex Stojanov, Detroit	27	1	3	4	91
Totals	40	1	4	5	149
Brian Sullivan, Houston	53	9	7	16	32
Brian Sullivan, Kansas City	2	0	0	0	0
Totals	55	9	7	16	32
Sean Tallaire, Grand Rapids	4	0	0	0	0
Sean Tallaire, Long Beach	56	24	19	43	68
Totals	60	24	19	43	68
Andrei Trefilov, Ind. (goalie)	18	0	1	1	0
Andrei Trefilov, Detroit (g)	27	0	2	2	16
Totals	45	0	3	3	16
Stefan Ustorf, Las Vegas	40	11	17	28	40
Stefan Ustorf, Detroit	14	3	7	10	11
Totals	54	14	24	38	51
Andrei Vasilyev, Las Vegas	15	3	6	9	6
Andrei Vasilyev, G.R.	59	21	27	48	24
Totals	74	24	33	57	30
Steve Vezina, L.B. (goalie)	2	0	0	0	0
Steve Vezina, Utah (goalie)	20	0	0	0	0
Totals	22	0	0	0	0
Mark Vilneff, Utah	3	0	0	0	0
Mark Vilneff, Detroit	7	0	0	0	2
Totals	10	0	0	0	2
Shawn Wansborough, Orl.	3	0	0	0	6
Shawn Wansborough, L.B.	8	1	5	6	16
Shawn Wansborough, L.V.	62	7	20	27	144
Totals	73	8	25	33	166
Paul Willett, Chicago	3	0	0	0	0
Paul Willett, Fort Wayne	1	0	0	0	2
Totals	4	0	0	0	2
Chris Wismer, Detroit	4	0	0	0	21
Chris Wismer, Cincinnati	4	0	0	0	6
Totals	8	0	0	0	27

GOALTENDING

	Gms.	Min.	W	L	T	G	SO	Avg.
Ryan Bach, Utah	4	197	2	1	0	9	0	2.74
Ryan Bach, L.B.	27	1491	10	9	5	74	1	2.98
Totals	31	1689	12	10	5	83	1	2.95
Petr Franek, Utah	8	446	1	6	1	26	0	3.50
Petr Franek, L.V.	37	1879	17	13	2	107	0	3.42
Totals	45	2325	18	19	3	133	0	3.43
Jani Hurme, Det.	12	643	7	3	1	26	1	2.43
Jani Hurme, Cin.	26	1428	14	9	2	81	0	3.40
Totals	38	2070	21	12	3	107	1	3.10
Trevor Koenig, L.B.	11	635	5	5	0	29	0	2.74
Trevor Koenig, Det.	6	300	5	0	0	11	1	2.20
Totals	17	935	10	5	0	40	1	2.57
Scott LaGrand, Ut.	8	474	4	3	1	20	1	2.53
Scott LaGrand, Chi.	2	78	1	0	0	3	0	2.31
Totals	10	552	5	3	1	23	1	2.50
S. Langkow, L.V.	27	1402	7	14	2	97	1	4.15
S. Langkow, Utah	21	1227	10	9	2	59	1	2.89
Totals	48	2628	17	23	4	156	2	3.56
Brian Regan, Cle.	1	60	0	1	0	3	0	3.02
Brian Regan, Cin.	4	197	2	1	0	9	0	2.73
Totals	5	257	2	2	0	12	0	2.80
Geoff Sarjeant, Cin.	14	733	6	5	1	42	1	3.44
Geoff Sarjeant, Det.	8	421	1	5	1	26	0	3.70
Geoff Sarjeant, L.B.	1	60	1	0	0	1	0	3.41
Geoff Sarjeant, Ind.	23	1354	13	7	2	57	2	2.53
Totals	46	2569	21	17	4	126	3	2.94
Andrei Trefilov, Ind.	18	986	9	6	2	39	0	2.37
Andrei Trefilov, Det.	27	1613	17	8	2	53	3	1.97
Totals	45	2600	26	14	4	92	3	2.12
Steve Vezina, L.B.	2	52	0	1	0	3	0	3.48
Steve Vezina, Utah	20	1066	12	4	1	49	0	2.76
Totals	22	1117	12	5	1	52	0	2.79

1999 TURNER CUP PLAYOFFS

RESULTS

PRELIMINARY ROUND

	W	L	Pts.	GF	GA
Indianapolis	2	1	4	7	7
Cincinnati	1	2	2	7	7

(Indianapolis won series, 2-1)

	W	L	Pts.	GF	GA
Michigan	2	0	4	9	3
Fort Wayne	0	2	0	3	9

(Michigan won series, 2-0)

	W	L	Pts.	GF	GA
Manitoba	2	0	4	8	6
Milwaukee	0	2	0	6	8

(Manitoba won series, 2-0)

	W	L	Pts.	GF	GA
Long Beach	2	1	4	6	5
Kansas City	1	2	2	5	6

(Long Beach won series, 2-1)

CONFERENCE SEMIFINALS

	W	L	Pts.	GF	GA
Detroit	3	1	6	13	7
Indianapolis	1	3	2	7	13

(Detroit won series, 3-1)

	W	L	Pts.	GF	GA
Orlando	3	0	6	11	5
Michigan	0	3	0	5	11

(Orlando won series, 3-0)

	W	L	Pts.	GF	GA
Houston	3	2	6	13	14
Long Beach	2	3	4	14	13

(Houston won series, 3-2)

	W	L	Pts.	GF	GA
Chicago	3	0	6	12	9
Manitoba	0	3	0	9	12

(Chicago won series, 3-0)

CONFERENCE FINALS

	W	L	Pts.	GF	GA
Orlando	4	3	8	20	23
Detroit	3	4	6	23	20

(Orlando won series, 4-3)

	W	L	Pts.	GF	GA
Houston	4	3	8	23	15
Chicago	3	4	6	15	23

(Houston won series, 4-3)

TURNER CUP FINALS

	W	L	Pts.	GF	GA
Houston	4	3	8	30	23
Orlando	3	4	6	23	30

(Houston won series, 4-3)

INDIVIDUAL LEADERS

Goals: Mark Freer, Houston (11)
Assists: Brian Wiseman, Houston (13)
Points: Mark Freer, Houston (22)
Penalty minutes: Scott Pearson, Chicago (50)
Goaltending average: Manny Legace, Long Beach (1.60)
Shutouts: Marc Lamothe, Detroit (2)

TOP SCORERS

	Games	G	A	Pts.
Mark Freer, Houston	19	11	11	22
Todd Krygier, Orlando	17	9	10	19
Rob Valicevic, Houston	19	7	10	17
David Oliver, Houston	19	10	6	16
Grigori Panteleyev, Orlando	17	8	8	16
Jeff Christian, Houston	18	4	12	16
Brian Wiseman, Houston	19	3	13	16
Cam Stewart, Houston	19	10	5	15
Rob Pearson, Orlando	17	8	6	14
Hubie McDonough, Orlando	17	2	12	14
Mark Beaufait, Orlando	15	2	12	14

INDIVIDUAL STATISTICS

CHICAGO WOLVES

(Lost conference finals to Houston, 4-3)

SCORING

	Games	G	A	Pts.	PIM
Steve Maltais	10	4	6	10	2
Kevin Miller	10	2	7	9	22
Chris Marinucci	10	3	5	8	10
Dan Plante	10	1	5	6	10
Scott Pearson	8	4	1	5	50
Jean-Pierre Dumont	10	4	1	5	6
Kevin Dahl	10	2	3	5	8
Todd White	10	1	4	5	8
Niklas Andersson	10	2	2	4	10
Guy Larose	10	1	3	4	14
Glen Featherstone	10	0	3	3	26
Jean-Yves Leroux	10	1	1	2	18
Jeremy Mylymok	10	1	1	2	23
Tom Tilley	10	1	1	2	2
Bob Nardella	10	0	2	2	6
Brent Gretzky	3	0	1	1	0
Wendell Young (goalie)	7	0	1	1	4
Steve Gosselin	2	0	0	0	4
Pat Jablonski (goalie)	3	0	0	0	0
Paul Koch	3	0	0	0	2
Tim Breslin	4	0	0	0	4

GOALTENDING

	Gms.	Min.	W	L	T	G	SO	Avg.
Wendell Young	7	421	4	3	0	19	1	2.70
Pat Jablonski	3	185	2	1	0	11	0	3.57

CINCINNATI CYCLONES

(Lost preliminary round to Indianapolis, 2-1)

SCORING

	Games	G	A	Pts.	PIM
Fred Knipscheer	3	2	1	3	4
Todd Hawkins	3	2	1	3	8
Jeff Shevalier	3	1	1	2	0
Todd Simon	3	1	1	2	12
Kaspars Ashtashenko	3	0	2	2	6
Gilbert Dionne	3	0	2	2	6
Scott Morrow	3	0	2	2	2
Pat MacLeod	3	0	2	2	4
Ed Patterson	3	1	0	1	4
Jeff Wells	3	0	1	1	0
Brian Regan (goalie)	1	0	0	0	0
Frederic Cassivi (goalie)	3	0	0	0	0
Eric Dandenault	3	0	0	0	2
Chris Bergeron	3	0	0	0	0
Burt Henderson	3	0	0	0	4
Alexei Tezikov	3	0	0	0	10
Kirk Nielsen	3	0	0	0	4
Tom Nemeth	3	0	0	0	4

GOALTENDING

	Gms.	Min.	W	L	T	G	SO	Avg.
Brian Regan	1	43	0	0	0	1	0	1.41
Frederic Cassivi	3	139	1	1	1	6	0	2.59

DETROIT VIPERS

(Lost conference finals to Detroit, 4-3)

SCORING

	Games	G	A	Pts.	PIM
Stefan Ustorf	11	4	7	11	2
Brian Felsner	11	4	6	10	12
Yves Sarault	11	7	2	9	40
Stan Drulia	11	5	4	9	10
John Emmons	11	4	5	9	22
Mike Prokopec	10	3	6	9	26
Keith Aldridge	11	2	7	9	49
Peter Ciavaglia	11	1	8	9	10
Bobby Reynolds	10	2	4	6	6
Steve Walker	11	1	4	5	4
Ian Herbers	11	1	3	4	18
Chris Luongo	11	0	4	4	16
Andy Bezeau	8	2	1	3	31
Brian Mueller	1	0	1	1	0
Andrei Trefilov (goalie)	10	0	1	1	20
John Gruden	10	0	1	1	6
Stewart Malgunas	11	0	1	1	21
Marc Lamothe (goalie)	1	0	0	0	0
Peter Ambroziak	2	0	0	0	0
Darren Banks	3	0	0	0	35
Craig Wolanin	11	0	0	0	12

GOALTENDING

	Gms.	Min.	W	L	T	G	SO	Avg.
Andrei Trefilov	10	647	6	3	1	22	0	2.04
Marc Lamothe	1	80	0	0	1	5	0	3.73

FORT WAYNE KOMETS

(Lost preliminary round to Michigan, 2-0)

SCORING

	Games	G	A	Pts.	PIM
Brad Purdie	2	0	2	2	0
Viacheslav Butsayev	2	1	0	1	4
Guy Dupuis	2	1	0	1	0
Adam Smith	2	1	0	1	0
Konstanti Shafranov	2	0	1	1	0
Eric Boguniecki	2	0	1	1	2
Tracy Egeland	2	0	1	1	0
Tero Lehtera	2	0	1	1	0
Pokey Reddick (goalie)	1	0	0	0	0
Bruce Racine (goalie)	1	0	0	0	0
Oleg Shargorodsky	2	0	0	0	0
Chad Dameworth	2	0	0	0	0
Dion Darling	2	0	0	0	4
Sean Selmser	2	0	0	0	2
Mike Martin	2	0	0	0	4
Shawn Penn	2	0	0	0	2
Ian Boyce	2	0	0	0	0
Andre Roy	2	0	0	0	11

GOALTENDING

	Gms.	Min.	W	L	T	G	SO	Avg.
Pokey Reddick	1	60	0	1	0	4	0	4.00
Bruce Racine	1	60	0	1	0	5	0	5.00

HOUSTON AEROS

(Winner of 1999 Turner Cup playoffs)

SCORING

	Games	G	A	Pts.	PIM
David Oliver	19 1	0	6	16	22
Cam Stewart	19 1	0	5	15	26
Mark Freer	19 1	1	11	22	12
Rob Valicevic	19	7	10	17	8
Jeff Christian	18	4	12	16	32
Brian Wiseman	19	3	13	16	26
Greg Hawgood	19	4	8	12	24
Mark Lamb	19	1	10	11	12
Jason Ruff	19	5	5	10	12
Jeff Tory	18	2	6	8	8
Jim Paek	19	2	4	6	10
Lane Lambert	19	4	1	5	26
Paul Dyck	19	2	3	5	18
Greg Andrusak	6	1	4	5	16
Norm MacIver	10	0	5	5	14
Mike Yeo	9	0	4	4	11
Trent Cull	19	0	2	2	34
Danny Lorenz (goalie)	1	0	0	0	0
Zac Boyer	1	0	0	0	0
Brian Goudie	4	0	0	0	6
Bill Huard	10	0	0	0	8
Manny Fernandez (goalie)	19	0	0	0	4

GOALTENDING

	Gms.	Min.	W	L	T	G	SO	Avg.
Manny Fernandez	19	1126	11	6	2	49	1	2.61
Danny Lorenz	1	38	0	0	0	2	0	3.19

INDIANAPOLIS ICE

(Lost conference semifinals to Detroit, 3-1)

SCORING

	Games	G	A	Pts.	PIM
Bob Lachance	7	1	5	6	16
Sylvain Cloutier	7	3	2	5	12
Dave Hymovitz	5	2	3	5	2
Nathan Perrott	7	3	1	4	45
Cail MacLean	7	2	2	4	0
Chris Herperger	7	0	4	4	4
Todd Rohloff	5	1	1	2	6
Mike Hall	7	1	1	2	0
Justin Cardwell	7	0	2	2	6
Jeff Paul	7	0	2	2	12
Craig Mills	6	1	0	1	5
Geoff Sarjeant (goalie)	3	0	1	1	0
Patrick Boileau	4	0	1	1	2
Marty Wilford	7	0	1	1	16
Frank Bialowas	2	0	0	0	6
Erik Andersson	4	0	0	0	12
Mike Vukonich	4	0	0	0	0
Andrei Kozyrev	5	0	0	0	2
Marc Lamothe (goalie)	6	0	0	0	2
Vince Williams	7	0	0	0	10
Remi Royer	7	0	0	0	44

GOALTENDING

	Gms.	Min.	W	L	T	G	SO	Avg.
Marc Lamothe	6	338	3	2	1	10	2	1.78
Geoff Sarjeant	3	115	0	1	0	10	0	5.21

KANSAS CITY BLADES

(Lost preliminary round to Long Beach, 2-1)

SCORING

	Games	G	A	Pts.	PIM
Nick Naumenko	3	1	2	3	4
Dale Craigwell	3	0	2	2	2
Jean-Guy Trudel	3	1	0	1	0
Jason Cirone	3	1	0	1	8
Lonnie Loach	3	1	0	1	0
David Ling	3	1	0	1	20
Pat Ferschweiler	3	0	1	1	2
Vlastimil Kroupa	3	0	1	1	0
Dody Wood	3	0	1	1	25
David Vallieres	3	0	0	0	2
Andrew Ference	3	0	0	0	9
Patrick Lalime (goalie)	3	0	0	0	0
Grant Richison	3	0	0	0	4
Brendan Yarema	3	0	0	0	12
Dan Ratushny	3	0	0	0	4
Eric Perrin	3	0	0	0	0
Jon Rohloff	3	0	0	0	18

GOALTENDING

	Gms.	Min.	W	L	T	G	SO	Avg.
Patrick Lalime	3	179	1	2	0	6	1	2.01

LONG BEACH ICE DOGS

(Lost conference semifinals to Houston, 3-2)

SCORING

	Games	G	A	Pts.	PIM
Patrik Augusta	8	4	6	10	4
Jaroslav Modry	8	4	2	6	4
Doug Ast	8	4	2	6	6
Dan Lambert	8	0	6	6	12
Sean Tallaire	8	4	1	5	8
Mark Ferner	8	1	3	4	14
Jason Podollan	6	1	2	3	4
Pavel Rosa	6	1	2	3	0
Patrice Lefebvre	8	0	3	3	2
Rene Chapdelaine	8	0	2	2	18
Jocelyn Lemieux	8	0	2	2	15
Nathan LaFayette	7	1	0	1	8
Mike Matteucci	8	0	1	1	12
Claude Jutras	1	0	0	0	2
Ryan Bach (goalie)	3	0	0	0	0
Dan Bylsma	4	0	0	0	8
Manny Legace (goalie)	6	0	0	0	0
Keith McCambridge	8	0	0	0	20
Dmitri Leonov	8	0	0	0	9
Eric Manlow	8	0	0	0	8

GOALTENDING

	Gms.	Min.	W	L	T	G	SO	Avg.
Manny Legace	6	338	4	2	0	9	0	1.60
Ryan Bach	3	152	0	1	1	7	0	2.77

MANITOBA MOOSE

(Lost conference semifinals to Chicago, 3-0)

SCORING

	Games	G	A	Pts.	PIM
Bill Bowler	5	6	5	11	6
Scott Thomas	5	3	4	7	4
Kent Fearns	5	1	5	6	8
Brett Hauer	5	0	5	5	4
Jason MacDonald	5	2	2	4	13
Ralph Intranuovo	5	2	1	3	4
Patrice Tardif	5	1	2	3	0
Scott Arniel	5	1	2	3	0
Cory Cyrenne	5	1	0	1	2
Bruce Coles	2	0	1	1	0
Michael Stewart	5	0	1	1	11
Jimmy Roy	5	0	1	1	6
Christian Bronsard (goalie)	1	0	0	0	0
Jason Shmyr	3	0	0	0	0
Brian Chapman	5	0	0	0	12
Rhett Gordon	5	0	0	0	0
Justin Kurtz	5	0	0	0	4
Jeff Parrott	5	0	0	0	6
Mike Rosati (goalie)	5	0	0	0	6

GOALTENDING

	Gms.	Min.	W	L	T	G	SO	Avg.
Christian Bronsard	1	19	0	0	0	0	0	0.00
Mike Rosati	5	314	2	2	1	18	0	3.44

MICHIGAN K-WINGS

(Lost conference semifinals to Orlando, 3-0)

SCORING

	Games	G	A	Pts.	PIM
Aaron Gavey	5	2	3	5	4
Jon Sim	5	3	1	4	18
Kelly Fairchild	5	2	2	4	16
Richard Jackman	5	0	4	4	6
Jason Botterill	5	2	1	3	4
Dave Roberts	4	1	2	3	2
Shawn McCosh	5	1	2	3	6
Greg Leeb	5	0	3	3	4
Ryan Christie	3	1	1	2	2
Doug Doull	3	1	1	2	4
Alan Letang	5	0	2	2	0
Mel Angelstad	5	1	0	1	16
Marty Flichel	1	0	0	0	0
Evgueni Tsybouk	2	0	0	0	2
Jeff Mitchell	2	0	0	0	0
Jamie Wright	2	0	0	0	2
Milt Mastad	3	0	0	0	24
Paul Traynor	5	0	0	0	2
Matt Martin	5	0	0	0	10
Marty Turco (goalie)	5	0	0	0	0
Petr Buzek	5	0	0	0	10

GOALTENDING

	Gms.	Min.	W	L	T	G	SO	Avg.
Marty Turco	5	300	2	2	1	14	0	2.80

MILWAUKEE ADMIRALS

(Lost preliminary round to Manitoba, 2-0)

SCORING

	Games	G	A	Pts.	PIM
Craig Darby	2	3	0	3	0
Doug Friedman	2	1	2	3	8
Jeff Daniels	2	1	1	2	0
Petr Sykora	2	1	1	2	0
David Gosselin	2	0	2	2	2
Jason Cipolla	2	0	2	2	6
Dan Riva	1	0	1	1	0
Karlis Skrastins	2	0	1	1	2
Jeff Kealty	2	0	1	1	4
Mark Mowers	1	0	0	0	0
Sergei Klimentiev	2	0	0	0	6
Matt Henderson	2	0	0	0	0
Marian Cisar	2	0	0	0	12
Shannon Finn	2	0	0	0	6
Jeff Staples	2	0	0	0	2
Tomas Vokoun (goalie)	2	0	0	0	2
Jeff Nelson	2	0	0	0	0
Marc Moro	2	0	0	0	4

GOALTENDING

	Gms.	Min.	W	L	T	G	SO	Avg.
Tomas Vokoun	2	149	0	1	1	8	0	3.22

ORLANDO SOLAR BEARS

(Lost league finals to Houston, 4-3)

SCORING

	Games	G	A	Pts.	PIM
Todd Krygier	17	9	10	19	16
Grigori Panteleyev	17	8	8	16	4
Rob Pearson	17	8	6	14	24
Mark Beaufait	15	2	12	14	14
Hubie McDonough	17	2	12	14	14
Todd Richards	16	3	7	10	14
Pierre Sevigny	15	4	5	9	32
Curtis Murphy	17	4	5	9	16
Terry Hollinger	17	3	5	8	14
Jason Blake	13	3	4	7	20
Shawn Carter	17	1	4	5	10
Patrick Neaton	17	2	2	4	14
Barry Dreger	13	1	3	4	38
Dave Mackey	17	3	0	3	38
Eric Healey	8	1	0	1	12
Rob Kenny	9	0	1	1	16
David Littman (goalie)	2	0	0	0	2
Clayton Norris	7	0	0	0	25
Denis Chervyakov	9	0	0	0	16
Ken Sabourin	14	0	0	0	49
Tyler Moss (goalie)	17	0	0	0	6

GOALTENDING

	Gms.	Min.	W	L	T	G	SO	Avg.
Tyler Moss	17	1017	10	5	2	53	0	3.13
David Littman	2	46	0	0	0	4	0	5.19

1998-99 AWARD WINNERS

ALL-STAR TEAMS

First team	Pos.	Second team
Patrick Lalime, Kansas City	G	Andrei Trefilov, Detroit
Brett Hauer, Manitoba	D	Dan Lambert, Long Beach
Greg Hawgood, Houston	D	Tom Tilley, Chicago
Steve Maltais, Chicago	LW	Dave Hymovitz, Indianapolis
Brian Wiseman, Houston	C	Bill Bowler, Manitoba
Scott Thomas, Manitoba	RW	Chris Marinucci, Chicago

TROPHY WINNERS

James Gatschene Memorial Trophy: Brian Wiseman, Houston
Leo P. Lamoureux Memorial Trophy: Brian Wiseman, Houston
James Norris Memorial Trophy: Andrei Trefilov, Detroit
Steve Weekes, Detroit
Governors Trophy: Greg Hawgood, Houston
Garry F. Longman Memorial Trophy: Marty Turco, Michigan
Ken McKenzie Trophy: Mark Mowers, Milwaukee
Commissioner's Trophy: Dave Tippett, Houston
N.R. (Bud) Poile Trophy: Mark Freer, Houston

ALL-TIME AWARD WINNERS

JAMES GATSCHENE MEMORIAL TROPHY

(Most Valuable Player)

Season Player, Team
1946-47—Herb Jones, Detroit Auto Club
1947-48—Lyle Dowell, Det. Bright's Goodyears
1948-49—Bob McFadden, Det. Jerry Lynch
1949-50—Dick Kowcinak, Sarnia
1950-51—John McGrath, Toledo
1951-52—Ernie Dick, Chatham
1952-53—Donnie Marshall, Cincinnati
1953-54—No award given
1954-55—Phil Goyette, Cincinnati
1955-56—George Hayes, Grand Rapids
1956-57—Pierre Brillant, Indianapolis
1957-58—Pierre Brillant, Indianapolis
1958-59—Len Thornson, Fort Wayne
1959-60—Billy Reichart, Minneapolis
1960-61—Len Thornson, Fort Wayne
1961-62—Len Thornson, Fort Wayne
1962-63—Len Thornson, Fort Wayne
Eddie Lang, Fort Wayne
1963-64—Len Thornson, Fort Wayne
1964-65—Chick Chalmers, Toledo
1965-66—Gary Schall, Muskegon
1966-67—Len Thornson, Fort Wayne
1967-68—Len Thornson, Fort Wayne
Don Westbrooke, Dayton
1968-69—Don Westbrooke, Dayton
1969-70—Cliff Pennington, Des Moines
1970-71—Lyle Carter, Muskegon
1971-72—Len Fontaine, Port Huron
1972-73—Gary Ford, Muskegon
1973-74—Pete Mara, Des Moines
1974-75—Gary Ford, Muskegon
1975-76—Len Fontaine, Port Huron
1976-77—Tom Mellor, Toledo
1977-78—Dan Bonar, Fort Wayne
1978-79—Terry McDougall, Fort Wayne
1979-80—Al Dumba, Fort Wayne
1980-81—Marcel Comeau, Saginaw
1981-82—Brent Jarrett, Kalamazoo
1982-83—Claude Noel, Toledo
1983-84—Darren Jensen, Fort Wayne
1984-85—Scott Gruhl, Muskegon
1985-86—Darrell May, Peoria
1986-87—Jeff Pyle, Saginaw
Jock Callander, Muskegon
1987-88—John Cullen, Flint
1988-89—Dave Michayluk, Muskegon
1989-90—Michel Mongeau, Peoria
1990-91—David Bruce, Peoria
1991-92—Dmitri Kvartalnov, San Diego
1992-93—Tony Hrkac, Indianapolis
1993-94—Rob Brown, Kalamazoo
1994-95—Tommy Salo, Denver
1995-96—Stephane Beauregard, San Francisco

Season Player, Team
1996-97—Frederic Chabot, Houston
1997-98—Patrice Lefebvre, Las Vegas
1998-99—Brian Wiseman, Houston

LEO P. LAMOUREUX MEMORIAL TROPHY

(Leading scorer)

Season Player, Team
1946-47—Harry Marchand, Windsor
1947-48—Dick Kowcinak, Det. Auto Club
1948-49—Leo Richard, Toledo
1949-50—Dick Kowcinak, Sarnia
1950-51—Herve Parent, Grand Rapids
1951-52—George Parker, Grand Rapids
1952-53—Alex Irving, Milwaukee
1953-54—Don Hall, Johnstown
1954-55—Phil Goyette, Cincinnati
1955-56—Max Mekilok, Cincinnati
1956-57—Pierre Brillant, Indianapolis
1957-58—Warren Hynes, Cincinnati
1958-59—George Ranieri, Louisville
1959-60—Chick Chalmers, Louisville
1960-61—Ken Yackel, Minneapolis
1961-62—Len Thornson, Fort Wayne
1962-63—Moe Bartoli, Minneapolis
1963-64—Len Thornson, Fort Wayne
1964-65—Lloyd Maxfield, Port Huron
1965-66—Bob Rivard, Fort Wayne
1966-67—Len Thornson, Fort Wayne
1967-68—Gary Ford, Muskegon
1968-69—Don Westbrooke, Dayton
1969-70—Don Westbrooke, Dayton
1970-71—Darrel Knibbs, Muskegon
1971-72—Gary Ford, Muskegon
1972-73—Gary Ford, Muskegon
1973-74—Pete Mara, Des Moines
1974-75—Rick Bragnalo, Dayton
1975-76—Len Fontaine, Port Huron
1976-77—Jim Koleff, Flint
1977-78—Jim Johnston, Flint
1978-79—Terry McDougall, Fort Wayne
1979-80—Al Dumba, Fort Wayne
1980-81—Marcel Comeau, Saginaw
1981-82—Brent Jarrett, Kalamazoo
1982-83—Dale Yakiwchuk, Milwaukee
1983-84—Wally Schreiber, Fort Wayne
1984-85—Scott MacLeod, Salt Lake
1985-86—Scott MacLeod, Salt Lake
1986-87—Jock Callander, Muskegon
Jeff Pyle, Saginaw
1987-88—John Cullen, Flint
1988-89—Dave Michayluk, Muskegon
1989-90—Michel Mongeau, Peoria
1990-91—Lonnie Loach, Fort Wayne
1991-92—Dmitri Kvartalnov, San Diego
1992-93—Tony Hrkac, Indianapolis
1993-94—Rob Brown, Kalamazoo

Season	Player, Team
1994-95	Stephane Morin, Minnesota
1995-96	Rob Brown, Chicago
1996-97	Rob Brown, Chicago
1997-98	Patrice Lefebvre, Las Vegas
1998-99	Brian Wiseman, Houston

The award was originally known as the George H. Wilkinson Trophy from 1946-47 through 1959-60.

JAMES NORRIS MEMORIAL TROPHY

(Outstanding goaltenders)

Season Player, Team
1955-56—Bill Tibbs,Troy
1956-57—Glenn Ramsey, Cincinnati
1957-58—Glenn Ramsey, Cincinnati
1958-59—Don Rigazio, Louisville
1959-60—Rene Zanier, Fort Wayne
1960-61—Ray Mikulan, Minneapolis
1961-62—Glenn Ramsey, Omaha
1962-63—Glenn Ramsey, Omaha
1963-64—Glenn Ramsey, Toledo
1964-65—Chuck Adamson, Fort Wayne
1965-66—Bob Sneddon, Port Huron
1966-67—Glenn Ramsey, Toledo
1967-68—Tim Tabor, Muskegon
Bob Perani, Muskegon
1968-69—Pat Rupp, Dayton
John Adams, Dayton
1969-70—Gaye Cooley, Des Moines
Bob Perreault, Des Moines
1970-71—Lyle Carter, Muskegon
1971-72—Glenn Resch, Muskegon
1972-73—Robbie Irons, Fort Wayne
Don Atchison, Fort Wayne
1973-74—Bill Hughes, Muskegon
1974-75—Bob Volpe, Flint
Merlin Jenner, Flint
1975-76—Don Cutts, Muskegon
1976-77—Terry Richardson, Kalamazoo
1977-78—Lorne Molleken, Saginaw
Pierre Chagnon, Saginaw
1978-79—Gord Laxton, Grand Rapids
1979-80—Larry Lozinski, Kalamazoo
1980-81—Claude Legris, Kalamazoo
Georges Gagnon, Kalamazoo
1981-82—Lorne Molleken, Toledo
Dave Tardich, Toledo
1982-83—Lorne Molleken, Toledo
1983-84—Darren Jensen, Fort Wayne
1984-85—Rick Heinz, Peoria
1985-86—Rick St. Croix, Fort Wayne
Pokey Reddick, Fort Wayne
1986-87—Alain Raymond, Fort Wayne
Michel Dufour, Fort Wayne
1987-88—Steve Guenette, Muskegon
1988-89—Rick Knickle, Fort Wayne
1989-90—Jimmy Waite, Indianapolis
1990-91—Guy Hebert, Peoria
Pat Jablonski, Peoria
1991-92—Arturs Irbe, Kansas City
Wade Flaherty, Kansas City
1992-93—Rick Knickle, San Diego
Clint Malarchuk, San Diego
1993-94—J.C. Bergeron, Atlanta
Mike Greenlay, Atlanta
1994-95—Tommy Salo, Denver
1995-96—Mark McArthur, Utah
Tommy Salo, Utah
1996-97—Rich Parent, Detroit
Jeff Reese, Detroit
1997-98—Mike Buzak, Long Beach
Kay Whitmore, Long Beach
1998-99—Andrei Trefilov, Detroit
Steve Weekes, Detroit

GOVERNORS TROPHY

(Outstanding defenseman)

Season Player, Team
1964-65—Lionel Repka, Fort Wayne
1965-66—Bob Lemieux, Muskegon
1966-67—Larry Mavety, Port Huron
1967-68—Carl Brewer, Muskegon
1968-69—Al Breaule, Dayton
Moe Benoit, Dayton
1969-70—John Gravel, Toledo
1970-71—Bob LaPage, Des Moines
1971-72—Rick Pagnutti, Fort Wayne
1972-73—Bob McCammon, Port Huron
1973-74—Dave Simpson, Dayton
1974-75—Murry Flegel, Muskegon
1975-76—Murry Flegel, Muskegon
1976-77—Tom Mellor, Toledo
1977-78—Michel LaChance, Milwaukee
1978-79—Guido Tenesi, Grand Rapids
1979-80—John Gibson, Saginaw
1980-81—Larry Goodenough, Saginaw
1981-82—Don Waddell, Saginaw
1982-83—Jim Burton, Fort Wayne
Kevin Willison, Milwaukee
1983-84—Kevin Willison, Milwaukee
1984-85—Lee Norwood, Peoria
1985-86—Jim Burton, Fort Wayne
1986-87—Jim Burton, Fort Wayne
1987-88—Phil Bourque, Muskegon
1988-89—Randy Boyd, Milwaukee
1989-90—Brian Glynn, Salt Lake
1990-91—Brian McKee, Fort Wayne
1991-92—Jean-Marc Richard, Fort Wayne
1992-93—Bill Houlder, San Diego
1993-94—Darren Veitch, Peoria
1994-95—Todd Richards, Las Vegas
1995-96—Greg Hawgood, Las Vegas
1996-97—Brad Werenka, Indianapolis
1997-98—Dan Lambert, Long Beach
1998-99—Greg Hawgood, Houston

GARRY F. LONGMAN MEMORIAL TROPHY

(Outstanding rookie)

Season Player, Team
1961-62—Dave Richardson, Fort Wayne
1962-63—John Gravel, Omaha
1963-64—Don Westbrooke, Toledo
1964-65—Bob Thomas, Toledo
1965-66—Frank Golembrowsky, Port Huron
1966-67—Kerry Bond, Columbus
1967-68—Gary Ford, Muskegon
1968-69—Doug Volmar, Columbus
1969-70—Wayne Zuk, Toledo
1970-71—Corky Agar, Flint
Herb Howdle, Dayton
1971-72—Glenn Resch, Muskegon
1972-73—Danny Gloor, Des Moines
1973-74—Frank DeMarco, Des Moines
1974-75—Rick Bragnalo, Dayton
1975-76—Sid Veysey, Fort Wayne
1976-77—Ron Zanussi, Fort Wayne
Garth MacGuigan, Muskegon
1977-78—Dan Bonar, Fort Wayne
1978-79—Wes Jarvis, Port Huron
1979-80—Doug Robb, Milwaukee
1980-81—Scott Vanderburgh, Kalamazoo
1981-82—Scott Howson, Toledo
1982-83—Tony Fiore, Flint
1983-84—Darren Jensen, Fort Wayne
1984-85—Gilles Thibaudeau, Flint
1965-66—Guy Benoit, Muskegon
1986-87—Michel Mongeau, Saginaw

Season	Player, Team
1987-88	Ed Belfour, Saginaw; John Cullen, Flint
1988-89	Paul Ranheim, Salt Lake
1989-90	Rob Murphy, Milwaukee
1990-91	Nelson Emerson, Peoria
1991-92	Dmitri Kvartalnov, Kansas City
1992-93	Mikhail Shtalenkov, Milwaukee
1993-94	Radek Bonk, Las Vegas
1994-95	Tommy Salo, Denver
1995-96	Konstantin Shafranov, Fort Wayne
1996-97	Sergei Samsonov, Detroit
1997-98	Todd White, Indianapolis
1998-99	Marty Turco, Michigan

KEN MC KENZIE TROPHY

(Outstanding American-born rookie)

Season	Player, Team
1977-78	Mike Eruzione, Toledo
1978-79	Jon Fontas, Saginaw
1979-80	Bob Janecyk, Fort Wayne
1980-81	Mike Labianca, Toledo; Steve Janaszak, Fort Wayne
1981-82	Steve Salvucci, Saginaw
1982-83	Paul Fenton, Peoria
1983-84	Mike Krensing, Muskegon
1984-85	Bill Schafhauser, Kalamazoo
1985-86	Brian Noonan, Saginaw
1986-87	Ray LeBlanc, Flint
1987-88	Dan Woodley, Flint
1988-89	Paul Ranheim, Salt Lake
1989-90	Tim Sweeney, Salt Lake
1990-91	C.J. Young, Salt Lake
1991-92	Kevin Wortman, Salt Lake
1992-93	Mark Beaufait, Kansas City
1993-94	Chris Rogles, Indianapolis
1994-95	Chris Marinucci, Denver
1995-96	Brett Lievers, Utah
1996-97	Brian Felsner, Orlando
1997-98	Eric Nickulas, Orlando
1998-99	Mark Mowers, Milwaukee

COMMISSIONER'S TROPHY

(Coach of the year)

Season	Coach, Team
1984-85	Rick Ley, Muskegon; Pat Kelly, Peoria
1985-86	Rob Laird, Fort Wayne
1986-87	Wayne Thomas, Salt Lake
1987-88	Rick Dudley, Flint
1988-89	B. J. MacDonald, Muskegon; Phil Russell, Muskegon
1989-90	Darryl Sutter, Indianapolis
1990-91	Bob Plager, Peoria
1991-92	Kevin Constantine, Kansas City
1992-93	Al Sims, Fort Wayne
1993-94	Bruce Boudreau, Fort Wayne
1994-95	Butch Goring, Denver
1995-96	Butch Goring, Utah
1996-97	John Van Boxmeer, Long Beach
1997-98	John Torchetti, Fort Wayne
1998-99	Dave Tippett, Houston

N.R. (BUD) POILE TROPHY

(Playoff MVP)

Season	Player, Team
1984-85	Denis Cyr, Peoria
1985-86	Jock Callander, Muskegon
1986-87	Rick Heinz, Salt Lake
1987-88	Peter Lappin, Salt Lake
1988-89	Dave Michayluk, Muskegon
1989-90	Mike McNeill, Indianapolis
1990-91	Michel Mongeau, Peoria
1991-92	Ron Handy, Kansas City
1992-93	Pokey Reddick, Fort Wayne
1993-94	Stan Drulia, Atlanta
1994-95	Kip Miller, Denver
1995-96	Tommy Salo, Utah
1996-97	Peter Ciavaglia, Detroit
1997-98	Alexander Semak, Chicago
1998-99	Mark Freer, Houston

The award was originally known as the Turner Cup Playoff MVP from 1984-85 through 1988-89.

ALL-TIME LEAGUE CHAMPIONS

	REGULAR-SEASON CHAMPION		PLAYOFF CHAMPION	
Season	Team	Coach	Team	Coach
1945-46	No trophy awarded		Detroit Auto Club	Jack Ward
1946-47	Windsor Staffords	Jack Ward	Windsor Spitfires	Ebbie Goodfellow
1947-48	Windsor Hettche Spitfires	Dent-Goodfellow	Toledo Mercurys	Andy Mulligan
1948-49	Toledo Mercurys	Andy Mulligan	Windsor Hettche Spitfires	Jimmy Skinner
1949-50	Sarnia Sailors	Dick Kowcinak	Catham Maroons	Bob Stoddart
1950-51	Grand Rapids Rockets	Lou Trudell	Toledo Mercurys	Alex Wood
1951-52	Grand Rapids Rockets	Lou Trudell	Toledo Mercurys	Alex Wood
1952-53	Cincinnati Mohawks	Buddy O'Conner	Cincinnati Mohawks	Buddy O'Conner
1953-54	Cincinnati Mohawks	Roly McLenahan	Cincinnati Mohawks	Roly McLenahan
1954-55	Cincinnati Mohawks	Roly McLenahan	Cincinnati Mohawks	Roly McLenahan
1955-56	Cincinnati Mohawks	Roly McLenahan	Cincinnati Mohawks	Roly McLenahan
1956-57	Cincinnati Mohawks	Roly McLenahan	Cincinnati Mohawks	Roly McLenahan
1957-58	Cincinnati Mohawks	Bill Gould	Indiana. Chiefs	Leo Lamoureux
1958-59	Louisville Rebels	Leo Gasparini	Louisville Rebels	Leo Gasparini
1959-60	Fort Wayne Komets	Ken Ullyot	St. Paul Saints	Fred Shero
1960-61	Minneapolis Millers	Ken Yachel	St. Paul Saints	Fred Shero
1961-62	Muskegon Zephrys	Moose Lallo	Muskegon Zephrys	Moose Lallo
1962-63	Fort Wayne Komets	Ken Ullyot	Fort Wayne Komets	Ken Ullyot
1963-64	Toledo Blades	Moe Benoit	Toledo Blades	Moe Benoit
1964-65	Port Huron Flags	Lloyd Maxfield	Fort Wayne Komets	Eddie Long
1965-66	Muskegon Mohawks	Moose Lallo	Port Huron Flags	Lloyd Maxfield
1966-67	Dayton Gems	Warren Back	Toledo Blades	Terry Slater
1967-68	Muskegon Mohawks	Moose Lallo	Muskegon Mohawks	Moose Lallo
1968-69	Dayton Gems	Larry Wilson	Dayton Gems	Larry Wilson
1969-70	Muskegon Mohawks	Moose Lallo	Dayton Gems	Larry Wilson
1970-71	Muskegon Mohawks	Moose Lallo	Port Huron Flags	Ted Garvin

	REGULAR-SEASON CHAMPION		PLAYOFF CHAMPION	
Season	Team	Coach	Team	Coach
1971-72—	Muskegon Mohawks	Moose Lallo	Port Huron Flags	Ted Garvin
1972-73—	Fort Wayne Komets	Marc Boileau	Fort Wayne Komets	Marc Boileau
1973-74—	Des Moines Capitals	Dan Belisle	Des Moines Capitals	Dan Belisle
1974-75—	Muskegon Mohawks	Moose Lallo	Toledo Goaldiggers	Ted Garvin
1975-76—	Dayton Gems	Ivan Prediger	Dayton Gems	Ivan Prediger
1976-77—	Saginaw Gears	Don Perry	Saginaw Gears	Don Perry
1977-78—	Fort Wayne Komets	Gregg Pilling	Toledo Goaldiggers	Ted Garvin
1978-79—	Grand Rapids Owls	Moe Bartoli	Kalamazoo Wings	Bill Purcell
1979-80—	Kalamazoo Wings	Doug McKay	Kalamazoo Wings	Doug McKay
1980-81—	Kalamazoo Wings	Doug McKay	Saginaw Gears	Don Perry
1981-82—	Toledo Goaldiggers	Bill Inglis	Toledo Goaldiggers	Bill Inglis
1982-83—	Toledo Goaldiggers	Bill Inglis	Toledo Goaldiggers	Bill Inglis
1983-84—	Fort Wayne Komets	Ron Ullyot	Flint Generals	Dennis Desrosiers
1984-85—	Peoria Rivermen	Pat Kelly	Peoria Rivermen	Pat Kelly
1985-86—	Fort Wayne Komets	Rob Laird	Muskegon Lumberjacks	Rick Ley
1986-87—	Fort Wayne Komets	Rob Laird	Salt Lake Golden Eagles	Wayne Thomas
1987-88—	Muskegon Lumberjacks	Rick Ley	Salt Lake Golden Eagles	Paul Baxter
1988-89—	Muskegon Lumberjacks	B.J. MacDonald	Muskegon Lumberjacks	B.J. MacDonald
1989-90—	Muskegon Lumberjacks	B.J. MacDonald	Indianapolis Ice	Darryl Sutter
1990-91—	Peoria Rivermen	Bob Plager	Peoria Rivermen	Bob Plager
1991-92—	Kansas City Blades	Kevin Constantine	Kansas City Blades	Kevin Constantine
1992-93—	San Diego Gulls	Rick Dudley	Fort Wayne Komets	Al Sims
1993-94—	Las Vegas Thunder	Butch Goring	Atlanta Knights	Gene Ubriaco
1994-95—	Denver Grizzlies	Butch Goring	Denver Grizzlies	Butch Goring
1995-96—	Las Vegas Thunder	Chris McSorley	Utah Grizzlies	Butch Goring
1996-97—	Detroit Vipers	Steve Ludzik	Detroit Vipers	Steve Ludzik
1997-98—	Long Beach Ice Dogs	John Van Boxmeer	Chicago Wolves	John Anderson
1998-99—	Houston Aeros	Dave Tippett	Houston Aeros	Dave Tippett

The IHL regular-season champion is awarded the Fred A. Huber Trophy and the playoff champion is awarded the Joseph Turner Memorial Cup.

The regular-season championship award was originally called the J.P. McGuire Trophy from 1946-47 through 1953-54.

EAST COAST HOCKEY LEAGUE

LEAGUE OFFICE

President/chief executive officer
Richard W. Adams
Sr. v.p. of hockey operations
Andy Van Hellemond
Commissioner emeritus
Patrick J. Kelly
Sr. v.p. of business operations
Scott Sabatino
V.p of marketing and sales
Jason Siegel
Vice president of hockey administration
Doug Price
Director of communications
Jason Rothwell
Director of finance
Anthony King
Director of special projects
Melissa Adams
Assistant director of sales/marketing
Kelly Jutras
Address
103 Main Street
Princeton, NJ 08540
Phone
609-452-0770
FAX
609-452-7147

TEAMS

ARKANSAS RIVERBLADES

President and chief executive officer
Dave Berryman
Head coach
Geoff Ward
Home ice
Alltel Arena
Address
425 W. Broadway, Suite B
North Little Rock, AR 72114
Seating capacity
16,377
Phone
501-975-2327
FAX
501-907-2327

AUGUSTA LYNX

General manager
Paul Gamsby
Head coach
Dan Wiebe
Home ice
Richmond County Civic Center
Address
712 Telfair St.
Augusta, GA 30901
Seating capacity
6,604
Phone
706-724-4423
FAX
706-724-2423

BATON ROUGE KINGFISH

General manager
Ron Hansis
Head coach
Bob McGill
Home ice
Centroplex
Address
P.O. Box 2142
Baton Rouge, LA 70821
Seating capacity
8,600
Phone
504-336-4625
FAX
504-336-4011

BIRMINGHAM BULLS

President
Charles Felix
Head coach
Dennis Desrosiers
Home ice
Jefferson County Civic Center
Address
P.O. Box 1506
Birmingham, AL 35201
Seating capacity
16,850
Phone
205-458-8833
FAX
205-458-8489

CHARLOTTE CHECKERS

General manager
Steve Camp
Head coach
Shawn Wheeler
Home ice
Independence Arena
Address
2700 E. Independence Blvd.
Charlotte, NC 28205
Seating capacity
9,570
Phone
704-342-4423
FAX
704-377-4595

DAYTON BOMBERS

General manager
John Gagnon
Head coach
Greg Ireland
Home ice
Nutter Center
Address
3640 Colonel Glenn Highway, Suite 417
Dayton, OH 45435
Seating capacity
9,950
Phone
937-775-4747
FAX
937-775-4749

FLORIDA EVERBLADES

President
Craig Brush
Head coach
Bob Ferguson
Home ice
Everblades Arena
Address
11000 Everblades Parkway
Estero, FL 33928
Seating capacity
7,209
Phone
941-948-7825
FAX
941-948-2248

GREENSBORO HOCKEY CLUB

General manager
To be announced
Head coach
Jeff Brubaker
Home ice
Greensboro Coliseum
Address
P.O. Box 3387
Greensboro, NC 27402
Seating capacity
20,800
Phone
336-218-5428
FAX
336-218-5498

GREENVILLE GRRROWL

President
Carl Scheer
Head coach
John Marks
Home ice
BI-LO Center
Address
P.O. Box 10348
Greenville, SC 29603
Seating capacity
14,108
Phone
864-467-4777
FAX
864-241-3872

HAMPTON ROADS ADMIRALS

General manager
Al MacIsaac
Head coach
John Brophy
Home ice
Norfolk Scope
Address
P.O. Box 56230
Virginia Beach, VA 23456

Seating capacity
8,994
Phone
757-430-8873
FAX
757-430-8803

HUNTINGTON BLIZZARD

General manager
Morris Jeffreys
Head coach
Ray Edwards
Home ice
Huntington Civic Center
Address
763 Third Avenue
Huntington, WV 25701
Seating capacity
5,780
Phone
304-697-7825
FAX
304-697-7832

JACKSON HOCKEY CLUB

General manager
Brad Ewing
Head coach
Derek Clancey
Home ice
Mississippi Coliseum
Address
Jackson, MS
Seating capacity
6,200
Phone
To be announced
FAX
To be announced

JACKSONVILLE LIZARD KINGS

Vice president of sales
Brendan Cunningham
Head coach
Alain Lemieux
Home ice
Jacksonville Coliseum
Address
1000 W. Bay St.
Jacksonville, FL 32204
Seating capacity
8,000
Phone
904-358-7825
FAX
904-358-9999

JOHNSTOWN CHIEFS

General manager
Toby O'Brien
Head coach
Scott Allen
Home ice
Cambria County War Memorial
Address
326 Napoleon Street
Johnstown, PA 15901
Seating capacity
4,050
Phone
814-539-1799
FAX
814-536-1316

LOUISIANA ICEGATORS

General manager
Jady Regard
Head coach
To be announced
Home ice
Cajundome
Address
444 Cajundome Blvd.
Lafayette, LA 70506
Seating capacity
11,700
Phone
318-234-4423
FAX
318-232-1254

MISSISSIPPI SEA WOLVES

General manager
Brian Kelley
Head coach
To be announced
Home ice
Mississippi Coast Coliseum
Address
2350 Beach Blvd.
Biloxi, MS 39531
Seating capacity
9,150
Phone
228-388-6151
FAX
228-338-5848

MOBILE MYSTICKS

General manager
Steve Chapman
Head coach
Jeff Pyle
Home ice
Mobile Civic Center
Address
P.O. Box 263
Mobile, AL 36601-0263
Seating capacity
8,033
Phone
334-208-7825
FAX
334-434-7931

NEW ORLEANS BRASS

General manager
Dan Belisle
Head coach
Ted Sator
Home ice
New Orleans Arena
Address
1201 St. Peter St., Suite 200
New Orleans, LA 70116
Seating capacity
17,000
Phone
504-522-7825
FAX
504-523-7295

PEE DEE PRIDE

Senior vice president
Jack Capuano
Head coach
Frank Anzalone
Home ice
Florence City-County Civic Center
Address
One Civic Center Plaza
3300 West Radio Drive
Florence, SC 29501
Seating capacity
7,426
Phone
843-669-7825
FAX
843-669-7149

PENSACOLA ICE PILOTS

Director of hockey operations
Joe Bucchino
Head coach
Al Pederson
Home ice
Pensacola Civic Center
Address
201 East Gregory St.-Rear
Pensacola, FL 32501-4956
Seating capacity
8,150
Phone
850-432-7825
FAX
850-432-1929

PEORIA RIVERMEN

President
John Butler
Head coach
Don Granato
Home ice
Peoria Civic Center
Address
201 SW Jefferson
Peoria, IL 61602
Seating capacity
9,470
Phone
309-676-1040
FAX
309-676-2488

RICHMOND RENEGADES

President/hockey operations
Craig Laughlin
Head coach
Mark Kaufman
Home ice
Richmond Coliseum
Address
601 East Leigh St.
Richmond, VA 23219
Seating capacity
11,088
Phone
804-643-7865
FAX
804-649-0651

ROANOKE EXPRESS

General manager
Tony Benizio
Head coach
Scott Gordon
Home ice
Roanoke Civic Center
Address
4504 Starkey Road S.W., Suite 208
Roanoke, VA 24014
Seating capacity
8,706

Phone
540-989-4625
FAX
540-989-8681

SOUTH CAROLINA STRINGRAYS

President
Gary Grondines
Head coach
Rick Adduono
Home ice
North Charleston Coliseum
Address
3107 Firestone Road
N. Charleston, SC 29418
Seating capacity
10,529
Phone
803-744-2248
FAX
803-744-2898

TALLAHASSEE TIGER SHARKS

General manager
Larry Kish
Head coach
To be announced
Home ice
Leon County Civic Center
Address
505 W. Pensacola St., Suite B
Tallahassee, FL 32301
Seating capacity
11,048
Phone
850-224-4625
FAX
850-224-6300

TOLEDO STORM

General manager
Pat Pylypuik
Head coach
To be announced
Home ice
Toledo Sports Arena
Address
One Main Street
Toledo, OH 43605
Seating capacity
5,160
Phone
419-691-0200
FAX
419-698-8998

TRENTON TITANS

President and general manager
Brian McKenna
Head coach
Bruce Cassidy
Home ice
Sovereign Bank Arena
Address
P.O. Box 4570
Trenton, NJ 08611
Seating capacity
7,850
Phone
609-599-9500
FAX
609-599-3600

WHEELING NAILERS

General manager
Fred Traynor
Head coach
Murray Eaves
Home ice
Wheeling Civic Center
Address
1144 Market Street, Suite 202
Wheeling, WV 26003
Seating capacity
5,406
Phone
304-234-4625
FAX
304-233-4846

1998-99 REGULAR SEASON

FINAL STANDINGS

NORTHERN CONFERENCE

NORTHEAST DIVISION

Team	G	W	L	T	Pts.	GF	GA
Roanoke	70	38	22	10	86	224	201
Hampton Roads	70	38	24	8	84	215	213
Richmond	70	40	27	3	83	239	196
Chesapeake	70	34	25	11	79	229	206
Johnstown	70	27	34	9	63	218	265

NORTHWEST DIVISION

Team	G	W	L	T	Pts.	GF	GA
Columbus	70	39	24	7	85	257	242
Peoria	70	39	25	6	84	243	230
Toledo	70	39	26	5	83	256	246
Dayton	70	34	27	9	77	239	241
Huntington	70	31	33	6	68	221	253
Wheeling	70	27	37	6	60	206	249

SOUTHERN CONFERENCE

SOUTHEAST DIVISION

Team	G	W	L	T	Pts.	GF	GA
Pee Dee	70	51	15	4	106	289	191
Florida	70	45	20	5	95	253	180
South Carolina	70	40	20	10	90	235	216
Augusta	70	38	27	5	81	235	233
Jacksonville	70	35	33	2	72	235	255
Charlotte	70	29	30	11	69	221	262
Miami	70	28	32	10	66	208	266
Greenville	70	26	33	11	63	208	241

SOUTHWEST DIVISION

Team	G	W	L	T	Pts.	GF	GA
Louisiana	70	46	18	6	98	297	205
Mississippi	70	41	22	7	89	251	215
Birmingham	70	37	29	4	78	251	267
New Orleans	70	30	27	13	73	244	261
Mobile	70	31	31	8	70	231	259
Baton Rouge	70	30	30	10	70	222	228
Tallahassee	70	27	34	9	63	212	250
Pensacola	70	25	41	4	54	199	267

INDIVIDUAL LEADERS

Goals: Rob DeCiantis, New Orleans (47)
Assists: Jamey Hicks, Birmingham (75)
Points: John Spoltore, Louisiana (109)
Penalty minutes: L.P. Charbonneau, Greenville (366)
Goaltending average: Maxime Gingras, Richmond (2.26)
Shutouts: Maxime Gingras, Richmond (7)

TOP SCORERS

	Games	G	A	Pts.
John Spoltore, Louisiana	69	36	73	109
Jamie Ling, Dayton	70	39	56	95
Chris Valicevic, Louisiana	70	20	72	92
Jamey Hicks, Birmingham	65	16	75	91
Dany Bousquet, Pee Dee	62	36	54	90
Rob DeCiantis, New Orleans	70	47	41	88
Allan Sirois, Pee Dee	70	35	49	84
John Varga, Louisiana	65	39	44	83
J.F. Aube, Charlotte	70	32	50	82
Matt Oates, Columbus	70	24	57	81
Bryan Richardson, Baton Rouge	69	32	47	79
Derek Clancey, Chesapeake	70	21	58	79
Jim Bermingham, Huntington	64	16	63	79
Darryl LaFrance, New Orleans	55	39	39	78

	Games	G	A	Pts.
Dan Ceman, Hampton Roads	70	38	39	77
Pierre Gendron, Pensacola	68	34	42	76
Darryl Noren, Charlotte	70	26	50	76
Jason Elders, Mobile	68	29	46	75
Hugo Belanger, Birmingham	70	34	40	74
Louis Dumont, Louisiana	55	30	44	74
Denny Felsner, Chesapeake	50	29	45	74

INDIVIDUAL STATISTICS

AUGUSTA LYNX

SCORING

	Games	G	A	Pts.	PIM
Darren Colbourne	70	30	37	67	54
Bob Berg	69	28	39	67	104
Lars Pettersen	70	20	46	66	56
Jonas Soling	50	27	20	47	71
Bryan Duce	68	17	27	44	33
Jaroslav Obsut	41	11	25	36	42
Stu Bodtker	47	17	15	32	58
Chris Thompson	57	16	14	30	221
Sam Ftorek	62	11	18	29	128
Wes Mason	30	13	14	27	75
Jessie Rezansoff	67	8	17	25	283
Rob Pattison	30	11	13	24	63
Garry Gruber	42	5	11	16	45
John Whitwell	70	3	13	16	92
Mark DeSantis	25	1	13	14	46
Henry Kuster	20	5	5	10	4
Chad Wilson	46	3	7	10	35
Alexandre LaPorte	34	0	9	9	56
Dan Kopec	65	2	6	8	313
Ken Ruddick	15	2	4	6	26
Richard Irwin	41	3	2	5	65
Bryan Forslund	8	1	2	3	20
Peter Constantine	5	0	2	2	2
Mark Blesenthal	8	0	2	2	6
Bobby House	5	1	0	1	15
Jason Carriere	5	0	1	1	16
Luke Murphy	6	0	1	1	0
Judd Lambert (goalie)	51	0	1	1	6
Igor Yankovitch	1	0	0	0	2
Andy Borggaard	1	0	0	0	0
Rick Nichol (goalie)	1	0	0	0	0
Phil Milbourne	2	0	0	0	0
Bob Bell (goalie)	2	0	0	0	0
Frederic Tremblay	3	0	0	0	0
Joaquin Gage (goalie)	5	0	0	0	0
Clint Cabana	6	0	0	0	37
Tim Keyes (goalie)	8	0	0	0	0
Mike Valley (goalie)	9	0	0	0	0

GOALTENDING

	Gms.	Min.	W	L	T	G	SO	Avg.
Rick Nichol	1	11	0	0	0	0	0	0.00
Judd Lambert	51	2949	24	20	5	150	1	3.05
Mike Valley	9	494	5	3	0	26	1	3.16
Joaquin Gage	5	300	5	0	0	16	0	3.20
Tim Keyes	8	411	4	3	0	25	0	3.65
Bob Bell	2	24	0	1	0	3	0	7.53

BATON ROUGE KINGFISH

SCORING

	Games	G	A	Pts.	PIM
Bryan Richardson	69	32	47	79	56
B.J. Johnston	68	28	34	62	68
Dan Shermerhorn	61	25	34	59	63
Luke Curtin	56	28	29	57	32
Cam Brown	68	17	23	40	213
Scott Humeniuk	53	9	27	36	88
Paul Croteau	68	8	23	31	14
Bruce Coles	23	8	16	24	43
Trevor Jobe	22	11	12	23	26
Chris Aldous	55	3	20	23	22
Eric Normandin	29	8	12	20	14
Eric Montreuil	70	5	15	20	103
Bob Westerby	59	5	10	15	211
Martin Laroche	25	9	4	13	2
Brett Abrahamson	70	5	8	13	35
Derrick Smith	6	3	7	10	9
Mike Josephson	29	3	7	10	29
Lee Hamilton	41	2	6	8	110
Bryan Fogarty	5	4	3	7	24
Daniel Bienvenue	37	3	3	6	19
Michel Massie	20	2	4	6	9
Joe Eagan	46	0	5	5	79
Denis Chervyakov	4	1	3	4	16
Jason Byrnes	27	1	2	3	42
Jordan Willis (goalie)	47	0	3	3	25
Jon Rempel	12	1	1	2	39
Andy Borggaard	5	1	0	1	24
Kaleb Toth	7	0	1	1	2
Christian Soucy (goalie)	25	0	1	1	2
Geordie Hyland	2	0	0	0	6
Casey Wolak	3	0	0	0	17
Eric Brown	4	0	0	0	2
Mike Hurley	6	0	0	0	6
Kevin Holliday	7	0	0	0	54
Allan Hitchen (goalie)	7	0	0	0	10
Jeff Boettger	16	0	0	0	8

GOALTENDING

	Gms.	Min.	W	L	T	G	SO	Avg.
Christian Soucy	25	1386	9	9	4	69	2	2.99
Allan Hitchen	7	277	2	1	1	14	0	3.03
Jordan Willis	47	2521	19	20	5	131	4	3.12

BIRMINGHAM BULLS

SCORING

	Games	G	A	Pts.	PIM
Jamey Hicks	65	16	75	91	60
Hugo Belanger	70	34	40	74	20
Craig Lutes	68	23	25	48	64
Stefan Rivard	70	21	26	47	149
Rob DeCiantis	39	24	19	43	24
Patrick Nadeau	38	22	20	42	13
Kelly Perrault	50	7	32	39	59
Chad Power	30	22	10	32	8
Joe Seroski	29	12	18	30	8
Tyler Prosofsky	27	15	14	29	115
Mike Barrie	23	13	15	28	85
Justin Martin	70	10	16	26	93
Jeff Scharf	41	5	21	26	29
Tyler Johnston	66	5	21	26	67
Adam Lewis	54	5	9	14	80
Kory Mullin	48	1	13	14	59
Emmanuel LaBranche	56	6	3	9	216
Dennis Pinfold	43	4	5	9	323
Kevin Popp	59	3	4	7	300
Jay McGee	61	1	4	5	49
Scott Bailey (goalie)	27	0	3	3	32
Rick Smith	4	1	1	2	0
Yves Bertrand	4	1	0	1	0
Niklas Henrikkson	4	0	1	1	2
Frederic Deschenes (goalie)	39	0	1	1	0
Joe Spencer	1	0	0	0	0
Chad Cavanaugh	2	0	0	0	0
Daniel Passero	2	0	0	0	0
Eric Andersen	2	0	0	0	0
Jason Polera	2	0	0	0	0

	Games	G	A	Pts.	PIM
Martin Bradette (goalie)	3	0	0	0	0
Randy Best	4	0	0	0	0
Chad Wilchynski	5	0	0	0	2
Greg Dreveny (goalie)	8	0	0	0	2
Wally Wuttunee	11	0	0	0	2
Everett Caldwell	12	0	0	0	6
Ken Tasker	18	0	0	0	131

GOALTENDING

	Gms.	Min.	W	L	T	G	SO	Avg.
Frederic Deschenes	39	2224	20	16	2	128	2	3.45
Scott Bailey	27	1557	16	8	2	90	1	3.47
Greg Dreveny	8	312	0	4	0	30	0	5.78
Martin Bradette	3	100	1	1	0	11	0	6.59

CHARLOTTE CHECKERS

SCORING

	Games	G	A	Pts.	PIM
J.F. Aube	70	32	50	82	32
Darryl Noren	70	26	50	76	89
David Brosseau	70	33	28	61	66
Martin Sychra	64	20	25	45	41
Mike Sylvia	56	9	26	35	56
Jon Sturgis	53	18	16	34	14
Shannon Basaraba	58	10	21	31	34
Louis Bernard	55	7	17	24	62
Kurt Seher	68	7	17	24	65
Mike Rucinski	16	6	10	16	4
Dean Zayonce	62	2	14	16	118
Brooke Chateau	66	8	7	15	107
John Gurskis	32	6	6	12	12
Ryan Sittler	33	3	9	12	112
Boyd Kane	12	5	6	11	14
Doug Battaglia	23	5	5	10	6
Benjamin Carpentier	23	4	6	10	68
Bobby Sheehan	24	2	7	9	26
Tom Brown	48	1	8	9	57
Jon Pratt	19	4	4	8	14
Trevor Sim	9	3	5	8	12
Pat Brownlee	22	1	6	7	28
Pete Brearley	8	3	3	6	7
Reggie Brezeault	24	3	3	6	63
Jeff Brown	12	1	2	3	20
Garry Gruber	21	1	2	3	17
Rob Smillie	9	0	2	2	0
Jason Norrie	11	1	0	1	30
Nikolai Pronin	10	0	1	1	2
Taras Lendzyk (goalie)	36	0	1	1	8
Andy Borggaard	2	0	0	0	0
Erik Olsen	2	0	0	0	6
Tim Keyes (goalie)	2	0	0	0	2
Gerry Daley	3	0	0	0	2
Allan Hitchen (goalie)	4	0	0	0	0
Andrew Pearsall	6	0	0	0	4
David Brumby (goalie)	6	0	0	0	6
Rocky Welsing	7	0	0	0	8
Dave Risk	7	0	0	0	2
Kevin Kreutzer (goalie)	9	0	0	0	10
Jeff Heil (goalie)	22	0	0	0	24

GOALTENDING

	Gms.	Min.	W	L	T	G	SO	Avg.
Allan Hitchen	4	81	0	1	1	4	0	0.00
Taras Lendzyk	36	2005	14	14	6	111	0	3.32
David Brumby	6	300	3	1	0	18	0	3.61
Kevin Kreutzer	9	481	4	3	1	29	0	3.62
Jeff Heil	22	1236	7	11	3	77	0	3.74
Tim Keyes	2	86	1	0	0	6	0	4.17

CHESAPEAKE ICEBREAKERS

SCORING

	Games	G	A	Pts.	PIM
Derek Clancey	70	21	58	79	48
Denny Felsner	50	29	45	74	32
Marc Tropper	63	26	24	50	83
Arturs Kupaks	48	16	32	48	61
Brad Holzinger	60	12	31	43	47
Kaleb Toth	57	26	15	41	37
Earl Cronan	50	19	16	35	95
Brian Callahan	70	20	14	34	132
J.P. O'Connor	70	11	20	31	86
Jamie O'Leary	70	9	19	28	68
Steve Wilson	47	5	18	23	128
L.P. Charbonneau	46	9	7	16	271
Bob Thornton	27	7	7	14	19
Ryan Brown	37	5	9	14	102
Cory Murphy	62	2	12	14	87
Joe Cardarelli	17	2	6	8	8
Eric Linkowski	55	1	6	7	22
Jason Robinson	37	1	5	6	57
Jeff Boettger	56	1	5	6	59
Ryan Mougenel	8	2	3	5	19
Jeff Rucinski	17	1	3	4	27
Tony McCauley	18	1	3	4	10
Gaston Gingras	5	0	4	4	6
Kam White	13	1	1	2	59
Phil Milbourne	17	0	2	2	26
John Cirjak	5	1	0	1	0
Nate DeMars	6	1	0	1	9
Eduard Pershin	2	0	1	1	2
Erasmo Saltarelli (goalie)	27	0	1	1	4
Troy Christensen	1	0	0	0	0
Scott Parmentier	1	0	0	0	2
Martin Bradette (goalie)	1	0	0	0	0
Taner Gorcia	2	0	0	0	0
Marco Emond (goalie)	2	0	0	0	0
Marcin Cwikla	5	0	0	0	7
Erik Kaminski	5	0	0	0	0
Kirk Daubenspeck (goalie)	13	0	0	0	20
Mike Tamburro (goalie)	35	0	0	0	26

GOALTENDING

	Gms.	Min.	W	L	T	G	SO	Avg.
Kirk Daubenspeck	13	774	7	2	4	31	2	2.40
Mike Tamburro	35	1935	19	11	2	79	2	2.45
Marco Emond	2	43	0	1	0	2	0	2.82
Erasmo Saltarelli	27	1421	8	11	5	74	1	3.12
Martin Bradette	1	13	0	0	0	2	0	9.33

COLUMBUS CHILL

SCORING

	Games	G	A	Pts.	PIM
Matt Oates	70	24	57	81	81
Richard Keyes	65	38	32	70	91
Bret Meyers	53	33	30	63	104
Tim Fingerhut	62	24	29	53	148
Mike Legg	49	19	33	52	24
Beau Bilek	68	9	37	46	94
Steve Moffat	63	17	21	38	39
Jason Christie	35	9	28	37	70
Matt Golden	61	10	19	29	98
Jay Pecora	50	12	15	27	45
Rob Woodward	50	11	16	27	48
Martin Laroche	37	8	18	26	10
Matt Cooney	25	5	16	21	72
Andrew Fagan	63	7	7	14	257
Mark Pivetz	59	4	10	14	57
Vince Williams	43	5	8	13	57
Matt Lahey	25	7	5	12	73
Matt Peterson	70	3	9	12	44
John Gurskis	23	5	2	7	6
Todd Norman	13	2	2	4	0
Rob Schriner	5	2	1	3	0
Rob White	8	1	2	3	21
Ryan Root	8	0	2	2	4
Lee Hamilton	22	0	2	2	82
Dan Cousineau	3	1	0	1	2
Bryan Fuss	10	1	0	1	21

	Games	G	A	Pts.	PIM
Andrei Kozyrev	3	0	1	1	11
Marc Dupuis	4	0	1	1	2
Dan MacKinnon	1	0	0	0	4
Erik Raygor	2	0	0	0	10
Marcel Kuris (goalie)	3	0	0	0	0
Dennis Burke	5	0	0	0	0
Tyler MacMillan	11	0	0	0	0
Andrew Chlebus	16	0	0	0	0
Harlin Hayes (goalie)	18	0	0	0	2
Jeff Salajko (goalie)	54	0	0	0	25

GOALTENDING

	Gms.	Min.	W	L	T	G	SO	Avg.
Jeff Salajko	54	3077	30	16	6	162	2	3.16
Harlin Hayes	18	934	7	7	1	53	1	3.40
Marcel Kuris	3	179	2	1	0	13	0	4.35

DAYTON BOMBERS

SCORING

	Games	G	A	Pts.	PIM
Jamie Ling	70	39	56	95	32
Bobby Brown	66	30	30	60	125
Colin Miller	68	20	36	56	126
Brian Ridolfi	70	17	35	52	73
Justin Krall	68	16	24	40	56
Dan Hendrickson	70	14	26	40	96
Tom Nemeth	43	13	23	36	28
Norm Dezainde	30	14	17	31	123
Brian Secord	37	11	20	31	66
Kiley Hill	59	20	10	30	227
Aaron Kriss	62	7	22	29	106
Travis Dillabough	54	7	18	25	91
Frederic Bouchard	50	3	18	21	75
Ryan Furness	55	7	10	17	106
Jim Logan	23	7	9	16	27
Chris Wismer	40	2	8	10	107
Dave Van Drunen	9	2	4	6	12
Calvin Crowe	14	2	3	5	70
Josh Harrold	7	1	4	5	8
Ryan Brindley	4	1	2	3	16
Colin Schmidt	10	1	2	3	7
Mike Sylvia	9	0	3	3	4
Bob Thornton	13	2	0	2	10
Chuck Mindell	4	1	1	2	2
Troy Christensen	16	0	2	2	11
Brian Regan (goalie)	32	0	2	2	2
Shayne Tomlinson	34	0	2	2	30
Olaf Kjenstad	2	1	0	1	32
Steve Sabo	18	1	0	1	12
Kaspars Astashenko	2	0	1	1	4
Bryan Kennedy	5	0	1	1	2
Roland Grelle	6	0	1	1	6
Mike Minard (goalie)	15	0	1	1	2
Brandon Sugden	44	0	1	1	233
Michael MacPherson	1	0	0	0	0
Tyler MacMillan	1	0	0	0	0
Scott Thompson	1	0	0	0	0
Andy Prokspec	1	0	0	0	0
Dave Smith	1	0	0	0	0
Rob Payne (goalie)	1	0	0	0	0
Chris Fawcett	2	0	0	0	0
Chris Farion (goalie)	2	0	0	0	0
Matt Barnes (goalie)	2	0	0	0	2
Nick Robinson	3	0	0	0	0
Rick Nichol (goalie)	3	0	0	0	0
Sam Fields	4	0	0	0	7
Sergei Radchenko	7	0	0	0	24
Kevin Kreutzer (goalie)	7	0	0	0	10
Trevor Koenig (goalie)	15	0	0	0	4

GOALTENDING

	Gms.	Min.	W	L	T	G	SO	Avg.
Matt Barnes	2	63	0	0	0	2	0	1.90
Brian Regan	32	1831	14	12	5	92	3	3.01
Trevor Koenig	15	888	9	5	0	45	0	3.04
Mike Minard	15	788	8	5	2	42	1	3.20
Kevin Kreutzer	7	394	3	3	1	23	0	3.50
Rick Nichol	3	164	0	1	1	13	0	4.46
Chris Farion	2	28	0	1	0	4	0	8.70
Rob Payne	1	27	0	0	0	4	0	8.74

FLORIDA EVERBLADES

SCORING

	Games	G	A	Pts.	PIM
Tim Ferguson	67	33	36	69	53
Pat Mikesch	45	23	37	60	67
Matt Demarski	65	31	28	59	36
Mike Jickling	47	13	32	45	35
Andrew Taylor	70	12	33	45	77
Kevin McDonald	41	17	24	41	153
Dane Litke	67	10	25	35	21
Hugh Hamilton	65	8	25	33	57
Eric Rud	50	11	18	29	36
Greg Koehler	29	13	14	27	62
Steve Tardif	25	13	12	25	75
Nick Checco	61	11	14	25	31
Sergei Fedotov	47	9	15	24	28
Eric Manlow	18	8	15	23	11
Eric Boulton	26	9	13	22	143
Matt Brush	63	6	14	20	14
Jason Prokopetz	59	6	9	15	191
Greg Kuznik	50	6	8	14	110
Eric Ricard	47	1	12	13	100
Brett Bruininks	42	3	5	8	26
Mike Rucinski	16	2	5	7	13
Mark McMahon	13	1	4	5	59
Jon Sturgis	11	2	2	4	4
Mike Kucsulain	6	1	2	3	12
Dan Reimann	59	0	3	3	53
Cal McGowan	5	2	0	2	14
Andrew Luciuk	11	2	0	2	4
Mark Polak	5	0	2	2	8
Marc Magliarditi (goalie)	47	0	2	2	8
Askhat Rakhmatulin	6	0	1	1	2
Randy Petruk (goalie)	25	0	0	0	2

GOALTENDING

	Gms.	Min.	W	L	T	G	SO	Avg.
Marc Magliarditi	47	2746	32	10	3	104	5	2.27
Randy Petruk	25	1441	13	10	2	66	1	2.75

GREENVILLE GRRROWL

SCORING

	Games	G	A	Pts.	PIM
Dana Mulvihill	69	31	27	58	94
Sean Venedam	70	29	24	53	42
Rick Judson	70	16	32	48	22
Bill McCauley	61	11	29	40	74
Davis Payne	43	19	20	39	96
Colin Pepperall	55	15	20	35	128
Matt Alvey	65	15	16	31	26
Joel Trottier	53	15	15	30	49
Charlie Moxham	66	12	14	26	33
Mike Kolenda	56	4	19	23	81
Shane Belter	54	5	17	22	59
Ryan Stewart	39	8	13	21	43
Charles Paquette	57	3	8	11	211
Dan Back	38	1	8	9	38
Marko Makinen	20	3	5	8	14
Jason Hamilton	45	2	6	8	206
L.P. Charbonneau	19	4	3	7	95
Andy Johnson	42	2	5	7	30
Paul Bailley	29	0	7	7	22
Darcy Anderson	14	3	2	5	0
Jon Pratt	7	2	3	5	8
Randy Best	23	2	3	5	27
Kam White	34	1	4	5	127

	Games	G	A	Pts.	PIM
Jeff Scharf	6	1	3	4	2
Dennis Burke	4	2	0	2	0
Jim Alauria	16	1	1	2	17
John Blessman	19	1	0	1	19
Nick Vitucci (goalie)	32	0	0	0	2
Paxton Schafer (goalie)	40	0	0	0	16

GOALTENDING

	Gms.	Min.	W	L	T	G	SO	Avg.
Paxton Schafer	40	2326	17	16	7	115	2	2.97
Nick Vitucci	32	1855	9	17	4	103	0	3.33

HAMPTON ROADS ADMIRALS

SCORING

	Games	G	A	Pts.	PIM
Dan Ceman	70	38	39	77	66
Dominic Maltais	70	22	37	59	217
Marty Clapton	70	18	36	54	79
Rod Taylor	70	23	27	50	97
Joel Poirier	67	11	32	43	93
Chad Ackerman	69	10	26	36	49
Chris Phelps	50	3	24	27	34
Trent Whitfield	19	13	12	25	12
Bobby Russell	44	15	8	23	25
Boris Zelenko	29	11	10	21	20
Brad Church	24	10	9	19	129
Alexander Kharlamov	32	4	14	18	25
Jason Deleurme	26	9	6	15	74
Dean Campanale	34	9	5	14	12
Trevor Johnson	65	3	9	12	135
Trever Fraser	65	4	7	11	122
Louis Bedard	32	3	6	9	208
Francois Bourdeau	23	1	8	9	34
Milt Mastad	44	2	6	8	142
Ryan Gillis	13	2	4	6	27
Henry Higdon	23	2	3	5	32
Derek Ernest	60	1	4	5	234
Jami Yoder	17	0	3	3	29
Andy Doktorchik	10	1	1	2	4
Dustin McArthur	9	0	2	2	13
Rob Boleski	9	0	1	1	18
Dennis McEwen	13	0	1	1	8
Joe Corvo	5	0	0	0	15
Charlie Retter	10	0	0	0	7
Jeff Corbett	30	0	0	0	145
Steve Valiquette (goalie)	31	0	0	0	2
Jason Saal (goalie)	44	0	0	0	12

GOALTENDING

	Gms.	Min.	W	L	T	G	SO	Avg.
Jason Saal	44	2478	20	17	5	114	4	2.76
Steve Valiquette	31	1713	18	7	3	84	1	2.94

HUNTINGTON BLIZZARD

SCORING

	Games	G	A	Pts.	PIM
Jim Bermingham	64	16	63	79	85
Kelly Harper	57	23	42	65	43
Tracy Egeland	47	38	18	56	113
Karson Kaebel	63	21	32	53	60
Jan Slavik	68	12	37	49	75
Jamie Sokolsky	65	12	30	42	79
Jason Bermingham	69	22	19	41	62
Butch Kaebel	70	14	26	40	42
Brodie Coffin	63	16	18	34	151
Ritchie Bronilla	62	6	26	32	30
Derek Smith	70	8	15	23	95
Kevin Paden	48	8	12	20	50
Pete Brearley	39	10	8	18	11
Rob Stanfield	54	3	9	12	108
Bill Baaki	57	5	4	9	54
Mike Perna	49	1	7	8	200
D.J. Harding	70	0	7	7	39
Joe Craigen	13	4	1	5	2

	Games	G	A	Pts.	PIM
Mike Schultz	11	2	0	2	4
Rob Boleski	9	0	2	2	45
Jim Mullin (goalie)	30	0	2	2	8
Steve Barnes	4	0	1	1	4
Kevin Kreutzer (goalie)	13	0	1	1	2
Owen Lessard	1	0	0	0	0
Jon Pirrong	1	0	0	0	0
Lloyd Shaw	2	0	0	0	4
Mark Petercak	3	0	0	0	2
Jake Deadmarsh	5	0	0	0	8
Blaine Russell (goalie)	12	0	0	0	2
Francis Larivee (goalie)	16	0	0	0	18
Chad Lang (goalie)	16	0	0	0	2

GOALTENDING

	Gms.	Min.	W	L	T	G	SO	Avg.
Francis Larivee	16	767	5	7	1	35	1	2.74
Blaine Russell	12	516	6	1	0	25	1	2.90
Jim Mullin	30	1446	13	9	3	86	0	3.57
Kevin Kreutzer	13	651	3	7	0	42	0	3.76
Chad Lang	16	798	4	9	2	54	0	4.06

JACKSONVILLE LIZARD KINGS

SCORING

	Games	G	A	Pts.	PIM
Bryan Forslund	65	23	46	69	46
Brad Federenko	69	27	39	66	34
Cail MacLean	40	29	28	57	14
Derek Eberle	70	19	34	53	82
Eric Long	68	13	35	48	78
Xavier Majic	33	16	28	44	30
Matt Cressman	69	16	23	39	55
Bill McKay	65	12	18	30	119
Colin Chaulk	24	8	22	30	49
Patrick Gingras	61	9	20	29	132
Mike Pomichter	33	10	18	28	31
Lukas Smital	23	12	9	21	19
Dean Campanale	25	9	8	17	16
Brett Punchard	20	6	9	15	38
Matt Eldred	38	5	6	11	108
Jami Yoder	47	2	9	11	30
Ryan Cirillo	38	5	5	10	49
Joel Theriault	43	4	5	9	164
Duncan Dalmao	68	1	7	8	78
Erik Olsen	60	2	5	7	106
Ray LeBlanc (goalie)	53	0	6	6	4
Andy Borggaard	8	3	1	4	2
Chad Wilson	5	3	0	3	6
Billy Pierce	5	0	3	3	12
Chad Nelson	12	2	0	2	57
C.J. Carlson	18	1	1	2	4
Brad Holzinger	5	0	2	2	4
Jason Desloover	4	0	1	1	2
Kirk Daubenspeck (goalie)	8	0	1	1	4
Jan Labraaten	1	0	0	0	0
Dennis Pybip	1	0	0	0	0
Jason Gaggi (goalie)	1	0	0	0	0
Ron Duguay	1	0	0	0	0
Eric Kelly	1	0	0	0	2
Daniel Bienvenue	2	0	0	0	2
Sean Freeman	2	0	0	0	12
Troy Maguire (goalie)	2	0	0	0	0
Tim Winkleman	3	0	0	0	7
Jay Pylypuik	3	0	0	0	0
Simon Alary	3	0	0	0	0
Josh Evans (goalie)	3	0	0	0	0
Scott Page	3	0	0	0	4
Sergei Petrov	4	0	0	0	0
Jack Greig	4	0	0	0	5
Jean-Phillipe Soucy	6	0	0	0	5
Justin McPolin	7	0	0	0	55
Rick MacDonald	8	0	0	0	6
Joe Eagan	14	0	0	0	24
Rob Murdoch (goalie)	16	0	0	0	14

GOALTENDING

	Gms.	Min.	W	L	T	G	SO	Avg.
Kirk Daubenspeck	8	424	5	3	0	18	0	2.55
Ray LeBlanc	53	2982	29	19	1	163	1	3.28
Josh Evans	3	53	0	1	0	4	0	4.50
Troy Maguire	2	119	0	1	1	9	0	4.52
Rob Murdoch	16	591	2	7	0	49	0	4.97
Jason Gaggi	1	20	0	1	0	4	0	12.00

JOHNSTOWN CHIEFS

SCORING

	Games	G	A	Pts.	PIM
Martin Masa	64	27	30	57	83
Joel Irving	65	26	20	46	112
Casey Kesselring	46	18	25	43	21
Jakub Ficenec	59	18	23	41	54
E.J. Bradley	66	13	22	35	36
Lukas Smital	34	12	21	33	38
Ian Smith	60	4	28	32	72
Jody Shelley	52	12	17	29	325
Brad Englehart	50	15	13	28	63
Kent Simpson	55	6	21	27	56
Steve Duke	54	4	23	27	58
Aaron Cain	68	14	12	26	100
Shawn Frappier	58	4	21	25	48
Eric Normandin	31	9	11	20	30
Derrick Walser	24	8	12	20	29
Jon Sorg	38	4	13	17	99
Mike Vellinga	45	1	14	15	22
Carl Fleury	22	7	7	14	31
Dmitri Tarabrin	31	7	6	13	6
Jeremy Thompson	54	3	6	9	224
Bryan McKinney	29	1	7	8	28
Etienne Drapeau	14	2	4	6	4
Matt Eldred	22	1	4	5	68
John Tripp	7	2	0	2	12
Igor Karpenko (goalie)	7	0	2	2	0
Roby Gropp (goalie)	7	0	2	2	2
Matt Eisler (goalie)	43	0	2	2	10
Mikhail Strelkov	8	0	1	1	67
David Ficenec	21	0	1	1	2
Eric Hamlet	1	0	0	0	2
Mike Beale (goalie)	1	0	0	0	0
Kevin Hill	1	0	0	0	0
Pavel Nestak (goalie)	19	0	0	0	10

GOALTENDING

	Gms.	Min.	W	L	T	G	SO	Avg.
Mike Beale	1	8	0	0	0	0	0	0.00
Igor Karpenko	7	369	4	3	0	20	0	3.25
Matt Eisler	43	2457	14	20	7	145	2	3.54
Pavel Nestak	19	1061	7	9	2	65	2	3.68
Roby Gropp	7	303	2	2	0	21	0	4.15

LOUISIANA ICEGATORS

SCORING

	Games	G	A	Pts.	PIM
John Spoltore	69	36	73	109	96
Chris Valicevic	70	20	72	92	63
John Varga	65	39	44	83	77
Louis Dumont	55	30	44	74	66
Mike Murray	66	31	40	71	97
Don Parsons	44	34	29	63	44
Jay Murphy	47	29	29	58	189
Gary Roach	65	9	37	46	45
Rob Weingartner	59	20	22	42	203
Blair Manning	65	9	19	28	57
Nick Stajduhar	30	5	18	23	26
Matthew Pagnutti	64	2	19	21	76
Cory Cyrenne	21	6	9	15	6
Mark DeSantis	27	4	10	14	85
Eric Cloutier	33	6	6	12	284
Ken Ruddick	25	2	5	7	23
Ryan Shanahan	27	3	3	6	91
Justin Kurtz	6	1	4	5	6
Jason McQuat	26	3	1	4	112
Stan Melanson	49	2	2	4	191
Rob McQuat	14	1	2	3	36
Roger Maxwell	36	1	2	3	285
Chad Nelson	15	2	0	2	73
Mark Edmundson	13	1	1	2	2
Doug Bonner (goalie)	45	0	2	2	8
Peter Zurba	14	1	0	1	103
John DePourcq	3	0	1	1	4
Bujar Amidovski (goalie)	27	0	1	1	0
Robert Gorman (goalie)	1	0	0	0	0
Lance Franz (goalie)	1	0	0	0	0
Eric Andersen	2	0	0	0	14
Brendan Concannon	4	0	0	0	6
Kyle Freadrich	5	0	0	0	17

GOALTENDING

	Gms.	Min.	W	L	T	G	SO	Avg.
Lance Franz	1	60	1	0	0	1	0	1.00
Bujar Amidovski	27	1525	17	5	3	59	3	2.32
Doug Bonner	45	2593	28	13	3	131	1	3.03
Robert Gorman	1	9	0	0	0	4	0	25.99

MIAMI MATADORS

SCORING

	Games	G	A	Pts.	PIM
Michael Flynn	70	20	50	70	30
Greg Clancy	59	28	25	53	40
Jack Kowal	65	14	32	46	44
Rob Kenny	58	22	20	42	62
Jed Fiebelkorn	46	18	17	35	103
Terry Lindgren	66	6	25	31	114
Sheldon Gorski	36	15	11	26	46
Chris Rowland	70	14	12	26	264
Darren Meek	59	4	22	26	78
David Bell	68	7	15	22	213
Dan Lupo	32	6	14	20	23
Jeff Kostuch	37	8	10	18	32
David Duerden	13	10	7	17	0
Thom Cullen	64	4	12	16	60
Andrew Long	25	7	8	15	16
Paul Doherty	27	5	8	13	34
Wes Swinson	17	1	11	12	37
Pasi Nielikainen	39	5	6	11	40
Eon Macfarlane	21	4	6	10	8
John Badduke	53	3	5	8	255
Mike Sancimino	11	4	3	7	12
Konstantin Sidulov	45	1	4	5	60
Jan Jas	6	0	3	3	0
Matt Redmond	10	1	1	2	0
John Finstrom	8	0	2	2	6
Brent Belecki (goalie)	54	0	2	2	2
Lance Ward	6	1	0	1	12
Jason Carriere	3	0	0	0	5
Kevin Powell	4	0	0	0	2
Aaron MacDonald (goalie)	29	0	0	0	0

GOALTENDING

	Gms.	Min.	W	L	T	G	SO	Avg.
Brent Belecki	54	2938	21	24	5	173	0	3.53
Aaron MacDonald	29	1243	7	8	5	74	0	3.57

MISSISSIPPI SEA WOLVES

SCORING

	Games	G	A	Pts.	PIM
Bob Woods	70	24	38	62	41
Mikhail Kravets	59	17	42	59	136
Kelly Hurd	54	20	33	53	40
Mark Rupnow	67	13	39	52	36
Kevin Hilton	48	16	29	45	22
Cody Bowtell	49	18	24	42	25
Karol Bartanus	50	19	21	40	50

	Games	G	A	Pts.	PIM
John Kosobud	66	18	21	39	38
Patrick Rochon	70	3	35	38	113
Vaclav Nedomansky	23	24	10	34	116
D.J. Mando	68	13	17	30	156
Brad Essex	59	15	14	29	190
Quinn Fair	69	11	18	29	38
Sean Blanchard	58	5	24	29	30
Troy Mann	50	12	15	27	34
Mike Martone	44	5	11	16	59
Arttu Kayhko	38	5	8	13	51
Andrew Dale	21	6	2	8	15
Pavol Pekarik	48	4	1	5	54
Karl Infanger	11	1	3	4	4
Travis Scott (goalie)	44	0	4	4	36
Travis Tucker	3	0	2	2	20
Bob Brandon	4	0	2	2	0
Chris Schmidt	6	1	0	1	2
Shawn Frappier	10	1	0	1	21
Mattias Cederlund	2	0	1	1	2
Jay Hebert	3	0	1	1	0
Chuck Thuss (goalie)	37	0	1	1	10
Dan Focht	2	0	0	0	6

GOALTENDING

	Gms.	Min.	W	L	T	G	SO	Avg.
Travis Scott	44	2337	22	12	5	112	1	2.88
Chuck Thuss	37	1850	19	10	2	93	3	3.02

MOBILE MYSTICKS

SCORING

	Games	G	A	Pts.	PIM
Jason Elders	68	29	46	75	24
Jim Shepherd	68	21	41	62	161
Russ Monteith	69	25	32	57	26
Hugues Gervais	66	31	20	51	167
David Craievich	60	10	38	48	90
Lee Giffin	54	16	21	37	44
Stacey Rayan	44	10	26	36	16
Brandon Carper	69	7	29	36	57
Tom Nolan	42	18	17	35	44
Andrew Will	70	9	23	32	34
Russ Guzior	20	16	12	28	46
Dalen Hrooshkin	56	6	16	22	6
Yanick Jean	68	2	18	20	126
Charlie Retter	47	8	11	19	26
Alain Savage	19	3	12	15	27
Kevin Kerr	12	6	8	14	57
Greg Callahan	38	5	9	14	138
Mike Olaski	52	2	6	8	25
Craig Binns	53	0	8	8	94
Mitch Vig	20	1	6	7	14
Francois Page	14	3	1	4	48
Chad Alban (goalie)	34	0	3	3	2
Joel Theriault	19	2	0	2	95
Chad Wilchynski	4	1	0	1	2
Frederic Tremblay	10	0	1	1	4
Thierry Ryckman	1	0	0	0	0
Chris Farion (goalie)	1	0	0	0	0
Mike Dennis	1	0	0	0	0
Nico Pyka	1	0	0	0	0
Todd Chinnick	2	0	0	0	5
John McCabe	7	0	0	0	5
Ryan Schmidt	8	0	0	0	8
Steve Debus (goalie)	39	0	0	0	2

GOALTENDING

	Gms.	Min.	W	L	T	G	SO	Avg.
Chad Alban	34	1960	16	14	3	111	1	3.40
Steve Debus	39	2215	15	17	5	132	0	3.58
Chris Farion	1	13	0	0	0	1	0	4.63

NEW ORLEANS BRASS

SCORING

	Games	G	A	Pts.	PIM
Darryl LaFrance	55	39	39	78	41
Jeff Lazaro	52	26	44	70	81
Mark Turner	63	14	38	52	47
Rob DeCiantis	31	23	22	45	32
Stephane Soulliere	59	20	22	42	94
Kimbi Daniels	29	11	28	39	61
Martin Woods	67	9	27	36	170
Kevin Pozzo	53	1	25	26	79
Russ Guzior	37	10	14	24	22
Chad Power	39	13	10	23	43
Steve Cheredaryk	58	8	15	23	135
Martin Hohenberger	57	10	9	19	38
Dean Moore	67	10	9	19	248
Joe Seroski	36	9	10	19	8
Adam Copeland	23	9	9	18	15
Olivier Morin	54	9	8	17	61
Ted Laviolette	50	5	7	12	78
Brad Symes	67	3	6	9	76
Jason Downey	51	1	8	9	213
Chris Fox	23	3	5	8	22
Brad Church	5	3	4	7	4
Mike Morrone	21	1	5	6	37
Dalen Hrooshkin	9	4	1	5	2
Martin Villeneuve (goalie)	43	0	5	5	18
Gordie Dwyer	36	1	3	4	163
Chris Slater	9	0	2	2	10
Chris Wickenheiser (goalie)	35	0	2	2	42
Todd Norman	5	1	0	1	0
Martin Chouinard	9	1	0	1	4
Jesse Boulerice	12	0	1	1	38
John Hultberg (goalie)	1	0	0	0	0
Kyle Peterson	1	0	0	0	0
Kam White	1	0	0	0	6
Bill McKay	3	0	0	0	5

GOALTENDING

	Gms.	Min.	W	L	T	G	SO	Avg.
Martin Villeneuve	43	2334	17	14	8	133	0	3.42
Chris Wickenheiser	35	1848	13	13	5	111	0	3.60
John Hultberg	1	11	0	0	0	1	0	5.40

PEE DEE PRIDE

SCORING

	Games	G	A	Pts.	PIM
Dany Bousquet	62	36	54	90	63
Allan Sirois	70	35	49	84	105
Jim Brown	60	23	42	65	44
Ryan Petz	70	28	34	62	71
Kurt Mallett	70	27	31	58	23
Brendan Flynn	67	14	44	58	30
Peter Geronazzo	57	27	25	52	93
Chris Lipsett	45	24	21	45	34
Rod Aldoff	70	12	32	44	55
Rick Bennett	66	21	18	39	103
Darcy Dallas	70	15	24	39	123
Brian Goudie	55	5	28	33	189
Jan Vodrazka	64	8	12	20	262
Bryan Tapper	70	5	15	20	58
Tom Field	39	4	9	13	30
Mark Cadotte	18	1	8	9	29
Trevor Demmans	14	1	7	8	8
Cory Peterson	49	1	7	8	50
Calvin Elfring	10	1	2	3	14
Mike Payne	14	1	2	3	65
Mark Richards (goalie)	40	0	3	3	4
Gregg Gripentrog	16	0	1	1	10
Ryan Pisiak	22	0	1	1	174
Sandy Allan (goalie)	35	0	1	1	12
Jessie Grenier	1	0	0	0	7
Eric Kelly	2	0	0	0	0

GOALTENDING

	Gms.	Min.	W	L	T	G	SO	Avg.
Sandy Allan	35	1958	21	11	2	81	1	2.48
Mark Richards	40	2234	29	4	3	105	3	2.82

PENSACOLA ICE PILOTS

SCORING

	Games	G	A	Pts.	PIM
Chad Quenneville	70	24	38	62	22
Mike Sullivan	56	27	34	61	22
Shane Calder	70	17	39	56	213
Pierre Gendron	47	23	27	50	51
Don Chase	67	21	24	45	55
Keli Corpse	43	8	29	37	14
Sheldon Gorski	32	16	17	33	24
Nick Stajduhar	33	7	18	25	66
Mark Polak	62	7	15	22	54
Brandon Gray	44	6	11	17	28
Todd Norman	45	7	7	14	12
Bob Wilkie	16	2	11	13	18
Joe Harney	21	2	10	12	45
Brendan Concannon	21	4	7	11	4
Kelly Hultgren	28	4	7	11	12
Dave Ivaska	61	3	7	10	80
Etienne Beaudry	37	4	4	8	34
Eon Macfarlane	36	3	4	7	26
Kirk Dewaele	47	3	3	6	63
Rob Phillips	22	2	4	6	2
Chris Sbrocca	3	1	4	5	6
Steve Naughton	23	1	4	5	8
Chris Libett	28	1	4	5	36
Taj Schaffnit	30	1	3	4	35
Andrew Rodgers	41	2	1	3	105
Keith O'Connell	22	1	2	3	60
Tim Lozinik	29	0	3	3	20
Jay Hebert	10	1	0	1	4
Calvin Crowe	12	1	0	1	39
Jason Clarke	2	0	1	1	27
John Rumeo	6	0	1	1	0
Tom Noble (goalie)	25	0	1	1	4
Dave Kennedy (goalie)	1	0	0	0	0
Sam Dietelbaum (goalie)	2	0	0	0	0
Steve LaFleur	3	0	0	0	7
Mikhail Strelkov	4	0	0	0	35
Craig Brown (goalie)	16	0	0	0	6
Darrin Madeley (goalie)	32	0	0	0	14

GOALTENDING

	Gms.	Min.	W	L	T	G	SO	Avg.
Dave Kennedy	1	20	0	0	0	1	0	3.00
Darrin Madeley	32	1792	12	16	3	92	3	3.08
Sam Dietelbaum	2	73	0	0	0	4	0	3.28
Craig Brown	16	910	5	10	0	57	0	3.76
Tom Noble	25	1380	8	15	1	98	1	4.26

PEORIA RIVERMEN

SCORING

	Games	G	A	Pts.	PIM
Joe Rybar	70	32	41	73	30
J.F. Boutin	61	28	34	62	114
Doug Evans	57	14	46	60	112
Marek Ivan	61	27	25	52	206
Jeff Trembecky	68	21	26	47	40
Daniel Hodge	68	12	35	47	58
Jamie Thompson	43	21	22	43	37
Darren Maloney	61	9	30	39	120
Blaine Fitzpatrick	50	14	13	27	159
Alexandre Couture	58	7	20	27	78
Joe Craigen	50	10	14	24	20
Chris Coveny	58	4	19	23	138
Quinn Hancock	28	8	13	21	6
Mike Schultz	39	8	6	14	11
Steve MacKinnan	34	7	6	13	21
Kory Karlander	8	6	3	9	6
Jay Kenney	39	0	9	9	8
Dan Carney	35	5	3	8	26
Ken Boone	61	3	4	7	318
Kevin Paden	17	4	2	6	6
Darcy Smith	42	1	3	4	175
Jeremiah McCarthy	6	1	2	3	6
Matt Smith	6	0	3	3	6
Niklas Henrikkson	8	0	3	3	8
Michal Dvorak	4	0	2	2	0
Tyler Harlton	6	0	2	2	40
Anthony Aquino	10	1	0	1	19
Brian Regan (goalie)	10	0	1	1	0
Rick MacDonald	15	0	1	1	8
Chad Lang (goalie)	20	0	1	1	0
Dan Murphy (goalie)	29	0	1	1	10
Mike Pietrangelo	31	0	1	1	17
Brian Hamilton (goalie)	1	0	0	0	0
Marc Terris	1	0	0	0	0
Mike Beale (goalie)	1	0	0	0	0
Mark Petercak	2	0	0	0	2
Scott Roche (goalie)	7	0	0	0	4
Jim Mullin (goalie)	7	0	0	0	12

GOALTENDING

	Gms.	Min.	W	L	T	G	SO	Avg.
Scott Roche	7	418	3	3	1	19	0	2.72
Chad Lang	20	1116	12	6	1	51	2	2.74
Brian Regan	10	500	4	2	2	23	1	2.76
Dan Murphy	29	1672	16	10	2	92	0	3.30
Jim Mullin	7	399	4	3	0	26	0	3.91
Brian Hamilton	1	53	0	1	0	4	0	4.50
Mike Beale	1	30	0	0	0	4	0	7.95

RICHMOND RENEGADES

SCORING

	Games	G	A	Pts.	PIM
Ryan Kraft	63	28	36	64	35
Andrew Shier	70	27	37	64	76
Joe Blaznek	59	38	23	61	37
Joe Bianchi	53	26	26	52	68
Peter Roed	60	26	24	50	68
Forrest Gore	69	24	24	48	173
Joe Vandermeer	70	1	35	36	80
David Lambeth	68	6	22	28	76
Sal Manganaro	26	10	14	24	33
Valentin Passarelli	42	10	14	24	34
Kevin Knopp	63	6	17	23	70
Steve Dumonski	64	7	12	19	199
Trevor Senn	42	7	11	18	271
Craig Paterson	59	9	7	16	135
Darren Wetherill	68	1	14	15	146
Pat Brownlee	22	2	10	12	22
Brandon Gray	18	3	5	8	6
Dan Fournel	26	2	5	7	87
Keith O'Connell	35	0	6	6	72
Chris Libett	37	0	6	6	23
Maxime Gingras (goalie)	50	0	6	6	19
Andy MacIntyre	4	3	2	5	2
John Lovell	12	2	1	3	12
Bryan McKinney	7	1	1	2	7
Terry Friesen (goalie)	24	0	2	2	6
Todd Cary	3	0	1	1	0
Dan Vandermeer	6	0	1	1	7
Troy Maguire (goalie)	1	0	0	0	0
Avi Karuhakar (goalie)	2	0	0	0	0
Joel Irwin	2	0	0	0	0
Jean Paul Tessier	9	0	0	0	4
Dan Back	11	0	0	0	10

GOALTENDING

	Gms.	Min.	W	L	T	G	SO	Avg.
Troy Maguire	1	40	1	0	0	1	0	1.50
Maxime Gingras	50	2808	30	13	3	106	7	2.26
Terry Friesen	24	1278	9	13	0	76	1	3.57
Avi Karuhakar	2	60	0	1	0	5	0	5.00

ROANOKE EXPRESS

SCORING

	Games	G	A	Pts.	PIM
Kris Cantu	59	27	26	53	104
Tim Christian	70	22	30	52	29

	Games	G	A	Pts.	PIM
Dru Burgess	64	21	23	44	20
Mike Peron	50	15	24	39	118
Nicholas Windsor	59	14	22	36	48
Ben Schust	67	10	22	32	34
J.F. Tremblay	54	17	14	31	153
Scott Campbell	46	11	15	26	24
Calvin Elfring	40	8	16	24	41
J.C. Ruid	39	6	18	24	38
Duane Harmer	41	6	18	24	56
Dan O'Connell	37	9	14	23	85
Mark Cadotte	44	10	10	20	77
Jason Stewart	31	7	13	20	39
Jason Dailey	63	5	15	20	41
Travis Smith	59	7	11	18	83
Chris Lipsett	21	7	6	13	19
Nic Beaudoin	22	6	7	13	38
Doug Searle	68	1	10	11	70
Steve Sabo	47	2	5	7	75
Jeremy Schaefer	39	4	2	6	182
Mike Mader	14	3	2	5	38
Mike Oliveira	3	2	1	3	0
Chad Spurr	3	2	0	2	2
Pete Brearley	8	2	0	2	6
Chris Wismer	20	0	2	2	33
Evgeny Korolev	2	0	1	1	0
Craig Perrett	3	0	1	1	0
Andrew Tortorella	5	0	1	1	4
Dave Gagnon (goalie)	34	0	1	1	6
Daniel Berthiaume (goalie)	35	0	1	1	0
Rob Murdoch (goalie)	1	0	0	0	0
Rick Boyd	4	0	0	0	8
Drew Felder	6	0	0	0	12

GOALTENDING

	Gms.	Min.	W	L	T	G	SO	Avg.
Rob Murdoch	1	59	0	1	0	1	0	1.02
Dave Gagnon	34	2033	20	9	5	87	2	2.57
Daniel Berthiaume	35	2105	18	12	5	97	2	2.77

SOUTH CAROLINA STINGRAYS

SCORING

	Games	G	A	Pts.	PIM
Jeff Romfo	69	25	44	69	124
Dave Seitz	53	30	37	67	69
Brett Marietti	65	16	40	56	142
Brad Dexter	70	19	36	55	46
Chris Hynnes	70	19	29	48	77
Jay Moser	64	18	27	45	135
Rob Concannon	69	21	16	37	258
Damian Prescott	70	19	13	32	107
Greg Schmidt	62	13	18	31	99
Marc Tardif	36	9	15	24	149
Matt Garzone	50	4	19	23	33
Chris Felix	70	5	15	20	70
Jeff McLean	28	8	11	19	17
Brendan Concannon	22	7	12	19	6
Jeff Edwards	67	6	9	15	75
Chris Wheaton	70	7	4	11	112
Paul Traynor	27	0	9	9	31
Mike MacKay	23	3	2	5	2
Dustin McArthur	19	2	2	4	48
Chris Jacobson	19	0	4	4	59
Cory Cadden (goalie)	45	0	4	4	26
Jody Lehman (goalie)	33	0	3	3	12
Steve Zoryk	9	2	0	2	0
Jason Hughes	9	1	1	2	10
Jason Carriere	11	1	1	2	22
Cam Danyluk	3	0	2	2	8
Martin Lapointe	3	0	1	1	0
Petro Kantzavelos	1	0	0	0	0
Chris Snell	1	0	0	0	0
Andy Davis (goalie)	1	0	0	0	10
Rick Findlay	4	0	0	0	0
Matthew Garver	5	0	0	0	0
Jason Hehr	5	0	0	0	0
Jessie Grenier	6	0	0	0	52
Jason Mucciarone	8	0	0	0	4

GOALTENDING

	Gms.	Min.	W	L	T	G	SO	Avg.
Jody Lehman	33	1743	18	7	4	79	1	2.72
Cory Cadden	45	2449	22	13	6	126	3	3.09

TALLAHASSEE TIGER SHARKS

SCORING

	Games	G	A	Pts.	PIM
Brent Cullaton	59	23	38	61	72
Brett Punchard	49	20	29	49	40
Pavel Smirnov	64	26	21	47	125
Reg Cardinal	50	13	21	34	34
Brian Farrell	53	20	13	33	71
David Dartsch	61	12	21	33	169
Tim Chase	65	10	22	32	46
Jeff McLean	21	16	15	31	12
Scott Chartier	41	12	18	30	107
Pierre Gendron	21	11	15	26	41
Wes Swinson	26	3	18	21	67
Jan Kobezda	60	6	14	20	56
Jason Clarke	48	12	5	17	287
Alexei Krovopuskov	23	6	9	15	73
Mike Sancimino	45	6	9	15	51
Louis Bedard	32	2	9	11	117
Alexandre LaPorte	30	3	6	9	42
T.J. Tanberg	42	2	7	9	22
Mitch Vig	45	2	7	9	87
Greg Callahan	21	1	5	6	42
Taj Schaffnit	23	1	4	5	37
Andy Silverman	26	1	4	5	14
Colin Chaulk	7	0	5	5	14
Dan Shermerhorn	10	2	2	4	8
Janis Tomans	14	1	3	4	12
Drew Palmer	41	0	4	4	86
Kirk Dewaele	21	0	3	3	36
Garry Gruber	9	1	1	2	2
Scott LaGrand (goalie)	39	0	2	2	2
Greg Taylor (goalie)	35	0	1	1	30
Andy Borggaard	2	0	0	0	4
Niklas Henrikkson	5	0	0	0	4
Rick Nichol (goalie)	5	0	0	0	0
Erasmo Saltarelli (goalie)	6	0	0	0	0

GOALTENDING

	Gms.	Min.	W	L	T	G	SO	Avg.
Scott LaGrand	39	2159	15	18	4	121	0	3.36
Greg Taylor	35	1664	11	14	4	94	1	3.39
Erasmo Saltarelli	6	216	1	1	1	13	1	3.61
Rick Nichol	5	144	0	1	0	10	0	4.17

TOLEDO STORM

SCORING

	Games	G	A	Pts.	PIM
Anthony Terzo	70	32	36	68	37
David Lessard	66	30	31	61	130
Colin Beardsmore	52	22	35	57	33
Andrew Williamson	55	34	20	54	65
Jeremy Rebek	70	10	39	49	90
Jason Gladney	70	5	43	48	109
Aaron Boh	65	11	28	39	226
Harlan Pratt	61	4	35	39	32
Scott Burt	58	18	19	37	111
Rob Merrill	68	13	22	35	89
Rob Thorpe	40	20	13	33	63
Shawn Maltby	64	15	15	30	94
Jason Norrie	55	9	18	27	164
Darcy George	58	8	15	23	51
Andrei Shurupov	30	7	12	19	50
Mark Deazeley	36	9	7	16	96

	Games	G	A	Pts.	PIM
Louis Bernard	11	0	9	9	4
Chris Gignac	3	3	3	6	2
Jeff Scharf	12	1	5	6	12
Bryan McKinney	24	1	4	5	25
Darren Wright	32	1	3	4	93
Scott Hillman	3	1	2	3	0
Ken Tasker	29	1	2	3	188
Jason Cannon	8	1	1	2	27
Matt Mullin (goalie)	45	0	2	2	2
Nicolas Perreault	3	0	1	1	0
Jay Pylypuik	4	0	1	1	0
Mike Schultz	7	0	1	1	0
Dave Arsenault (goalie)	21	0	1	1	6
Bruce MacDonald	1	0	0	0	0
Mike Beale (goalie)	1	0	0	0	0
Link Gaetz	1	0	0	0	2
Brad Perry	2	0	0	0	2
Stewart Nowosad	3	0	0	0	0
Kevin Diachina	3	0	0	0	4
Nikolai Pronin	3	0	0	0	19
Mark Petercak	3	0	0	0	6
Mike Loach	3	0	0	0	12
Scott Tolstropp (goalie)	4	0	0	0	0
Mike Pietrangelo	6	0	0	0	2
Gerald Moriarity	7	0	0	0	39
Aren Miller (goalie)	7	0	0	0	0

GOALTENDING

	Gms.	Min.	W	L	T	G	SO	Avg.
Mike Beale	1	15	0	0	0	1	0	2.53
Matt Mullin	45	2480	27	13	3	121	0	2.93
Dave Arsenault	21	1171	10	8	1	72	0	3.69
Scott Tolstropp	4	141	1	1	0	9	0	3.83
Aren Miller	7	374	1	4	1	33	0	5.30

WHEELING NAILERS

SCORING

	Games	G	A	Pts.	PIM
Darren Schwartz	68	27	29	56	148
Jeff Loder	67	24	27	51	82
Rob Giffin	67	20	27	47	85
Dmitri Tarabrin	41	12	22	34	30
Mike Latendresse	63	15	17	32	34
Keli Corpse	30	7	23	30	18
Karl Infanger	54	7	20	27	67
Tobias Holm	60	9	17	26	108
Tom O'Connor	54	5	20	25	58
Jon Pratt	25	11	11	22	49
Trevor Demmans	42	5	15	20	83
Stefan Brannare	60	7	12	19	149
Jeremy Brown	22	9	9	18	24
Matt Van Horlick	66	8	10	18	260
Dimitri Sergeev	31	8	9	17	12
Chris Jacobson	46	4	12	16	176
Matt Garzone	20	4	10	14	14
Karol Bartanus	13	6	5	11	8
Ladislav Hampeis	51	0	11	11	130
Doug Battaglia	39	4	4	8	26
Jon Sorg	27	1	6	7	42
Ryan Furness	16	3	3	6	43
Joe Harney	15	2	4	6	24
Pavol Pekarik	16	2	3	5	8
Sergei Radchenko	28	2	3	5	98
Wally Wuttunee	25	0	3	3	44
Mike Pietrangelo	4	2	0	2	0
Leon Delorme	32	1	1	2	208
Mike Nicholson	4	0	2	2	0
Luciano Caravaggio (goalie)	43	0	2	2	10
Tom Brown	18	1	0	1	29
Jay Pylypuik	6	0	1	1	15
Grant Van Laar (goalie)	1	0	0	0	0
Allan Hitchen (goalie)	4	0	0	0	14
David Brumby (goalie)	31	0	0	0	56

GOALTENDING

	Gms.	Min.	W	L	T	G	SO	Avg.
David Brumby	31	1741	11	14	4	89	0	3.07
Luciano Caravaggio	43	2289	16	22	2	139	3	3.64
Allan Hitchen	4	148	0	1	0	11	0	4.45
Grant Van Laar	1	7	0	0	0	1	0	8.74

PLAYERS WITH TWO OR MORE TEAMS

SCORING

	Games	G	A	Pts.	PIM
Eric Andersen, Louisiana	2	0	0	0	14
Eric Andersen, Birmingham	2	0	0	0	0
Totals	4	0	0	0	14
Dan Back, Richmond	11	0	0	0	10
Dan Back, Grand Rapids	38	1	8	9	38
Totals	49	1	8	9	48
Karol Bartanus, Mississippi	50	19	21	40	50
Karol Bartanus, Wheeling	13	6	5	11	8
Totals	63	25	26	51	58
Doug Battaglia, Charlotte	23	5	5	10	6
Doug Battaglia, Wheeling	39	4	4	8	26
Totals	62	9	9	18	32
Mike Beale, Johnstown (g)	1	0	0	0	0
Mike Beale, Toledo (goalie)	1	0	0	0	0
Mike Beale, Peoria (goalie)	1	0	0	0	0
Totals	3	0	0	0	0
Louis Bedard, Tallahassee	32	2	9	11	117
Louis Bedard, Hartford	32	3	6	9	208
Totals	64	5	15	20	325
Louis Bernard, Toledo	11	0	9	9	4
Louis Bernard, Charlotte	55	7	17	24	62
Totals	66	7	26	33	66
Randy Best, Grand Rapids	23	2	3	5	27
Randy Best, Birmingham	4	0	0	0	0
Totals	27	2	3	5	27
Daniel Bienvenue, Jack.	2	0	0	0	2
Daniel Bienvenue, B.R.	37	3	3	6	19
Totals	39	3	3	6	21
Jeff Boettger, Chesapeake	56	1	5	6	59
Jeff Boettger, Baton Rouge	16	0	0	0	8
Totals	72	1	5	6	67
Rob Boleski, Hartford	9	0	1	1	18
Rob Boleski, Huntington	9	0	2	2	45
Totals	18	0	3	3	63
Andy Borggaard, Tallahassee	2	0	0	0	4
Andy Borggaard, Augusta	1	0	0	0	0
Andy Borggaard, Char.	2	0	0	0	0
Andy Borggaard, B.R.	5	1	0	1	24
Andy Borggaard, Jack.	8	3	1	4	2
Martin Bradette, Ches. (g)	1	0	0	0	0
Martin Bradette, Birm. (g)	3	0	0	0	0
Totals	4	0	0	0	0
Pete Brearley, Roanoke	8	2	0	2	6
Pete Brearley, Charlotte	8	3	3	6	7
Pete Brearley, Huntington	39	10	8	18	11
Totals	55	15	11	26	24
Tom Brown, Charlotte	48	1	8	9	57
Tom Brown, Wheeling	18	1	0	1	29
Totals	66	2	8	10	86
Pat Brownlee, Charlotte	22	1	6	7	28
Pat Brownlee, Richmond	22	2	10	12	22
Totals	44	3	16	19	50
David Brumby, Wheeling (g)	31	0	0	0	56
David Brumby, Charlotte (g)	6	0	0	0	6
Totals	37	0	0	0	62
Dennis Burke, Grand Rapids	4	2	0	2	0
Dennis Burke, Columbus	5	0	0	0	0
Totals	9	2	0	2	0
Mark Cadotte, Pee Dee	18	1	8	9	29
Mark Cadotte, Roanoke	44	10	10	20	77
Totals	62	11	18	29	106
Greg Callahan, Mobile	38	5	9	14	138
Greg Callahan, Tallahassee	21	1	5	6	42

	Games	G	A	Pts.	PIM
Totals	59	6	14	20	180
Dean Campanale, Jack.	25	9	8	17	16
Dean Campanale, Hartford	34	9	5	14	12
Totals	59	18	13	31	28
Jason Carriere, S.C.	11	1	1	2	22
Jason Carriere, Augusta	5	0	1	1	16
Jason Carriere, Miami	3	0	0	0	5
Totals	19	1	2	3	43
L.P. Charbonneau, Ches.	46	9	7	16	271
L.P. Charbonneau, G.R.	19	4	3	7	95
Totals	65	13	10	23	366
Colin Chaulk, Tallahassee	7	0	5	5	14
Colin Chaulk, Jacksonville	24	8	22	30	49
Totals	31	8	27	35	63
Troy Christensen, Ches.	1	0	0	0	0
Troy Christensen, Dayton	16	0	2	2	11
Totals	17	0	2	2	11
Brad Church, Hartford	24	10	9	19	129
Brad Church, New Orleans	5	3	4	7	4
Totals	29	13	13	26	133
Jason Clarke, Tallahassee	48	12	5	17	287
Jason Clarke, Pensacola	2	0	1	1	27
Totals	50	12	6	18	314
Brendan Concannon, Pen.	21	4	7	11	4
Brendan Concannon, Lou.	4	0	0	0	6
Brendan Concannon, S.C.	22	7	12	19	6
Totals	47	11	19	30	16
Keli Corpse, Pensacola	43	8	29	37	14
Keli Corpse, Wheeling	30	7	23	30	18
Totals	73	15	52	67	32
Joe Craigen, Peoria	50	10	14	24	20
Joe Craigen, Huntington	13	4	1	5	2
Totals	63	14	15	29	22
Calvin Crowe, Dayton	14	2	3	5	70
Calvin Crowe, Pensacola	12	1	0	1	39
Totals	26	3	3	6	109
Kirk Daubenspeck, Jack. (g)	8	0	1	1	4
Kirk Daubenspeck, Ches. (g)	13	0	0	0	20
Totals	21	0	1	1	24
Rob DeCiantis, Birmingham	39	24	19	43	24
Rob DeCiantis, New Orleans	31	23	22	45	32
Totals	70	47	41	88	56
Mark DeSantis, Louisiana	27	4	10	14	85
Mark DeSantis, Augusta	25	1	13	14	46
Totals	52	5	23	28	131
Trevor Demmans, Wheeling	42	5	15	20	83
Trevor Demmans, Pee Dee	14	1	7	8	8
Totals	56	6	22	28	91
Kirk Dewaele, Tallahassee	21	0	3	3	36
Kirk Dewaele, Pensacola	47	3	3	6	63
Totals	68	3	6	9	99
Joe Eagan, Jacksonville	14	0	0	0	24
Joe Eagan, Baton Rouge	46	0	5	5	79
Totals	60	0	5	5	103
Matt Eldred, Jacksonville	38	5	6	11	108
Matt Eldred, Johnstown	22	1	4	5	68
Totals	60	6	10	16	176
Calvin Elfring, Pee Dee	10	1	2	3	14
Calvin Elfring, Roanoke	40	8	16	24	41
Totals	50	9	18	27	55
Chris Farion, Dayton (goalie)	2	0	0	0	0
Chris Farion, Mobile (goalie)	1	0	0	0	0
Totals	3	0	0	0	0
Bryan Forslund, Augusta	8	1	2	3	20
Bryan Forslund, Jacksonville	65	23	46	69	46
Totals	73	24	48	72	66
Shawn Frappier, Mississippi	10	1	0	1	21
Shawn Frappier, Johnstown	58	4	21	25	48
Totals	68	5	21	26	69
Ryan Furness, Dayton	55	7	10	17	106
Ryan Furness, Wheeling	16	3	3	6	43
Totals	71	10	13	23	149
Matt Garzone, Wheeling	20	4	10	14	14
Matt Garzone, S.C.	50	4	19	23	33

	Games	G	A	Pts.	PIM
Totals	70	8	29	37	47
Pierre Gendron, Tallahassee	21	11	15	26	41
Pierre Gendron, Pensacola	47	23	27	50	51
Totals	68	34	42	76	92
Sheldon Gorski, Miami	36	15	11	26	46
Sheldon Gorski, Pensacola	32	16	17	33	24
Totals	68	31	28	59	70
Brandon Gray, Richmond	18	3	5	8	6
Brandon Gray, Pensacola	44	6	11	17	28
Totals	62	9	16	25	34
Jessie Grenier, S.C.	6	0	0	0	52
Jessie Grenier, Pee Dee	1	0	0	0	7
Totals	7	0	0	0	59
Garry Gruber, Augusta	42	5	11	16	45
Garry Gruber, Tallahassee	9	1	1	2	2
Garry Gruber, Charlotte	21	1	2	3	17
Totals	72	7	14	21	64
John Gurskis, Columbus	23	5	2	7	6
John Gurskis, Charlotte	32	6	6	12	12
Totals	55	11	8	19	18
Russ Guzior, New Orleans	37	10	14	24	22
Russ Guzior, Mobile	20	16	12	28	46
Totals	57	26	26	52	68
Lee Hamilton, Columbus	22	0	2	2	82
Lee Hamilton, Baton Rouge	41	2	6	8	110
Totals	63	2	8	10	192
Joe Harney, Wheeling	15	2	4	6	24
Joe Harney, Pensacola	21	2	10	12	45
Totals	36	4	14	18	69
Jay Hebert, Mississippi	3	0	1	1	0
Jay Hebert, Pensacola	10	1	0	1	4
Totals	13	1	1	2	4
Niklas Henrikkson, Tall.	5	0	0	0	4
Niklas Henrikkson, Birm.	4	0	1	1	2
Niklas Henrikkson, Peoria	8	0	3	3	8
Totals	17	0	4	4	14
Allan Hitchen, B.R. (g)	7	0	0	0	10
Allan Hitchen, Charlotte (g)	4	0	0	0	0
Allan Hitchen, Wheeling (g)	4	0	0	0	14
Totals	15	0	0	0	24
Brad Holzinger, Jacksonville	5	0	2	2	4
Brad Holzinger, Chesapeake	60	12	31	43	47
Totals	65	12	33	45	51
Dalen Hrooshkin, N.O.	9	4	1	5	2
Dalen Hrooshkin, Mobile	56	6	16	22	6
Totals	65	10	17	27	8
Karl Infanger, Wheeling	54	7	20	27	67
Karl Infanger, Mississippi	11	1	3	4	4
Totals	65	8	23	31	71
Chris Jacobson, S.C.	19	0	4	4	59
Chris Jacobson, Wheeling	46	4	12	16	176
Totals	65	4	16	20	235
Eric Kelly, Pee Dee	2	0	0	0	0
Eric Kelly, Jacksonville	1	0	0	0	2
Totals	3	0	0	0	2
Tim Keyes, Augusta (goalie)	8	0	0	0	0
Tim Keyes, Charlotte (goalie)	2	0	0	0	2
Totals	10	0	0	0	2
Kevin Kreutzer, Charlotte (g)	9	0	0	0	10
Kevin Kreutzer, Hunt. (g)	13	0	1	1	2
Kevin Kreutzer, Dayton (g)	7	0	0	0	10
Totals	29	0	1	1	22
Marc Lamothe, Ind. (goalie)	6	0	0	0	2
Marc Lamothe, Detroit (g)	1	0	0	0	0
Totals	7	0	0	0	2
Chad Lang, Huntington (g)	16	0	0	0	2
Chad Lang, Peoria (goalie)	20	0	1	1	0
Totals	36	0	1	1	2
Alexandre LaPorte, Augusta	34	0	9	9	56
Alexandre LaPorte, Tall.	30	3	6	9	42
Totals	64	3	15	18	98
Martin Laroche, Baton Rouge	25	9	4	13	2
Martin Laroche, Columbus	37	8	18	26	10
Totals	62	17	22	39	12

	Games	G	A	Pts.	PIM
Chris Libett, Richmond	37	0	6	6	23
Chris Libett, Pensacola	28	1	4	5	36
Totals	65	1	10	11	59
Chris Lipsett, Roanoke	21	7	6	13	19
Chris Lipsett, Pee Dee	45	24	21	45	34
Totals	66	31	27	58	53
Rick MacDonald, Peoria	15	0	1	1	8
Rick MacDonald, Jack.	8	0	0	0	6
Totals	23	0	1	1	14
Tyler MacMillan, Dayton	1	0	0	0	0
Tyler MacMillan, Columbus	11	0	0	0	0
Totals	12	0	0	0	0
Eon Macfarlane, Pensacola.....	36	3	4	7	26
Eon Macfarlane, Miami	21	4	6	10	8
Totals	57	7	10	17	34
Troy Maguire, Jack. (g)..........	2	0	0	0	0
Troy Maguire, Richmond (g) ..	1	0	0	0	0
Totals	3	0	0	0	0
Dustin McArthur, S.C.	19	2	2	4	48
Dustin McArthur, Hartford	9	0	2	2	13
Totals	28	2	4	6	61
Bill McKay, New Orleans	3	0	0	0	5
Bill McKay, Jacksonville..........	65	12	18	30	119
Totals	68	12	18	30	124
Bryan McKinney, Richmond ...	7	1	1	2	7
Bryan McKinney, Toledo	24	1	4	5	25
Bryan McKinney, Johnstown ..	29	1	7	8	28
Totals	60	3	12	15	60
Jeff McLean, South Carolina...	28	8	11	19	17
Jeff McLean, Tallahassee	21	16	15	31	12
Totals	49	24	26	50	29
Phil Milbourne, Chesapeake ...	17	0	2	2	26
Phil Milbourne, Augusta	2	0	0	0	0
Totals	19	0	2	2	26
Jim Mullin, Peoria (goalie)	7	0	0	0	12
Jim Mullin, Huntington (g)	30	0	2	2	8
Totals	37	0	2	2	20
Rob Murdoch, Roanoke (g)....	1	0	0	0	0
Rob Murdoch, Jack. (g)..........	16	0	0	0	14
Totals	17	0	0	0	14
Chad Nelson, Louisiana	15	2	0	2	73
Chad Nelson, Jacksonville	12	2	0	2	57
Totals	27	4	0	4	130
Rick Nichol, Augusta (goalie) .	1	0	0	0	0
Rick Nichol, Dayton (goalie) ...	3	0	0	0	0
Rick Nichol, Tallahassee (g)....	5	0	0	0	0
Totals	9	0	0	0	0
Todd Norman, New Orleans....	5	1	0	1	0
Todd Norman, Columbus........	13	2	2	4	0
Todd Norman, Pensacola........	45	7	7	14	12
Totals	63	10	9	19	12
Eric Normandin, Johnstown ...	31	9	11	20	30
Eric Normandin, B.R.	29	8	12	20	14
Totals	60	17	23	40	44
Jason Norrie, Charlotte...........	11	1	0	1	30
Jason Norrie, Toledo..............	55	9	18	27	164
Totals	66	10	18	28	194
Keith O'Connell, Pensacola.....	22	1	2	3	60
Keith O'Connell, Richmond.....	35	0	6	6	72
Totals	57	1	8	9	132
Erik Olsen, Charlotte	2	0	0	0	6
Erik Olsen, Jacksonville	60	2	5	7	106
Totals	62	2	5	7	112
Kevin Paden, Huntington	48	8	12	20	50
Kevin Paden, Peoria...............	17	4	2	6	6
Totals	65	12	14	26	56
Pavol Pekarik, Mississippi	48	4	1	5	54
Pavol Pekarik, Wheeling	16	2	3	5	8
Totals	64	6	4	10	62
Mark Petercak, Toledo	3	0	0	0	6
Mark Petercak, Huntington	3	0	0	0	2
Mark Petercak, Peoria............	2	0	0	0	2
Totals	8	0	0	0	10

	Games	G	A	Pts.	PIM
Mike Pietrangelo, Wheeling	4	2	0	2	0
Mike Pietrangelo, Peoria........	31	0	1	1	17
Mike Pietrangelo, Toledo	6	0	0	0	2
Totals	41	2	1	3	19
Mark Polak, Florida................	5	0	2	2	8
Mark Polak, Pensacola	62	7	15	22	54
Totals	67	7	17	24	62
Chad Power, New Orleans	39	13	10	23	43
Chad Power, Birmingham	30	22	10	32	8
Totals	69	35	20	55	51
Jon Pratt, Wheeling	25	11	11	22	49
Jon Pratt, Charlotte................	19	4	4	8	14
Jon Pratt, Grand Rapids	7	2	3	5	8
Totals	51	17	18	35	71
Nikolai Pronin, Charlotte.........	10	0	1	1	2
Nikolai Pronin, Toledo............	3	0	0	0	19
Totals	13	0	1	1	21
Brett Punchard, Jacksonville ..	20	6	9	15	38
Brett Punchard, Tallahassee....	49	20	29	49	40
Totals	69	26	38	64	78
Jay Pylypuik, Toledo	4	0	1	1	0
Jay Pylypuik, Wheeling...........	6	0	1	1	15
Jay Pylypuik, Jacksonville	3	0	0	0	0
Totals	13	0	2	2	15
Sergei Radchenko, Wheeling..	28	2	3	5	98
Sergei Radchenko, Dayton	7	0	0	0	24
Totals	35	2	3	5	122
Brian Regan, Peoria (goalie)...	10	0	1	1	0
Brian Regan, Dayton (goalie)..	32	0	2	2	2
Totals	42	0	3	3	2
Charlie Retter, Hartford	10	0	0	0	7
Charlie Retter, Mobile	47	8	11	19	26
Totals	57	8	11	19	33
Mike Rucinski, Florida	16	2	5	7	13
Mike Rucinski, Charlotte.........	16	6	10	16	4
Totals	32	8	15	23	17
Ken Ruddick, Louisiana	25	2	5	7	23
Ken Ruddick, Augusta	15	2	4	6	26
Totals	40	4	9	13	49
Steve Sabo, Dayton	18	1	0	1	12
Steve Sabo, Roanoke.............	47	2	5	7	75
Totals	65	3	5	8	87
Erasmo Saltarelli, Ches. (g)	27	0	1	1	4
Erasmo Saltarelli, Tall. (g).......	6	0	0	0	0
Totals	33	0	1	1	4
Mike Sancimino, Miami	11	4	3	7	12
Mike Sancimino, Tallahassee ..	45	6	9	15	51
Totals	56	10	12	22	63
Taj Schaffnit, Tallahassee	23	1	4	5	37
Taj Schaffnit, Pensacola..........	30	1	3	4	35
Totals	53	2	7	9	72
Jeff Scharf, Grand Rapids	6	1	3	4	2
Jeff Scharf, Toledo.................	12	1	5	6	12
Jeff Scharf, Birmingham.........	41	5	21	26	29
Totals	59	7	29	36	43
Mike Schultz, Toledo..............	7	0	1	1	0
Mike Schultz, Huntington	11	2	0	2	4
Mike Schultz, Peoria	39	8	6	14	11
Totals	57	10	7	17	15
Joe Seroski, New Orleans.......	36	9	10	19	8
Joe Seroski, Birmingham	29	12	18	30	8
Totals	65	21	28	49	16
Dan Shermerhorn, Tall.	10	2	2	4	8
Dan Shermerhorn, B.R.	61	25	34	59	63
Totals	71	27	36	63	71
Lukas Smital, Johnstown	34	12	21	33	38
Lukas Smital, Jacksonville......	23	12	9	21	19
Totals	57	24	30	54	57
Jon Sorg, Johnstown	38	4	13	17	99
Jon Sorg, Wheeling	27	1	6	7	42
Totals	65	5	19	24	141
Nick Stajduhar, Pensacola	33	7	18	25	66
Nick Stajduhar, Louisiana	30	5	18	23	26

	Games	G	A	Pts.	PIM
Totals	63	12	36	48	92
Mikhail Strelkov, Johnstown	8	0	1	1	67
Mikhail Strelkov, Pensacola	4	0	0	0	35
Totals	12	0	1	1	102
Jon Sturgis, Florida	11	2	2	4	4
Jon Sturgis, Charlotte	53	18	16	34	14
Totals	64	20	18	38	18
Wes Swinson, Miami	17	1	11	12	37
Wes Swinson, Tallahassee	26	3	18	21	67
Totals	43	4	29	33	104
Mike Sylvia, Dayton	9	0	3	3	4
Mike Sylvia, Charlotte	56	9	26	35	56
Totals	65	9	29	38	60
Dmitri Tarabrin, Wheeling	41	12	22	34	30
Dmitri Tarabrin, Johnstown	31	7	6	13	6
Totals	72	19	28	47	36
Ken Tasker, Birmingham	18	0	0	0	131
Ken Tasker, Toledo	29	1	2	3	188
Totals	47	1	2	3	319
Joel Theriault, Mobile	19	2	0	2	95
Joel Theriault, Jacksonville	43	4	5	9	164
Totals	62	6	5	11	259
Bob Thornton, Dayton	13	2	0	2	10
Bob Thornton, Chesapeake	27	7	7	14	19
Totals	40	9	7	16	29
Kaleb Toth, Baton Rouge	7	0	1	1	2
Kaleb Toth, Chesapeake	57	26	15	41	37
Totals	64	26	16	42	39
Frederic Tremblay, Augusta	3	0	0	0	0
Frederic Tremblay, Mobile	10	0	1	1	4
Totals	13	0	1	1	4
Mitch Vig, Tallahassee	45	2	7	9	87
Mitch Vig, Mobile	20	1	6	7	14
Totals	65	3	13	16	101
Kam White, New Orleans	1	0	0	0	6
Kam White, Grand Rapids	34	1	4	5	127
Kam White, Chesapeake	13	1	1	2	59
Totals	48	2	5	7	192
Chad Wilchynski, Birm.	5	0	0	0	2
Chad Wilchynski, Mobile	4	1	0	1	2
Totals	9	1	0	1	4
Chad Wilson, Jacksonville	5	3	0	3	6
Chad Wilson, Augusta	46	3	7	10	35
Totals	51	6	7	13	41
Chris Wismer, Roanoke	20	0	2	2	33
Chris Wismer, Dayton	40	2	8	10	107
Totals	60	2	10	12	140
Wally Wuttunee, Wheeling	25	0	3	3	44
Wally Wuttunee, Birmingham	11	0	0	0	2
Totals	36	0	3	3	46
Jami Yoder, Hartford	17	0	3	3	29
Jami Yoder, Jacksonville	47	2	9	11	30
Totals	64	2	12	14	59

GOALTENDING

	Gms.	Min.	W	L	T	G	SO	Avg.
Mike Beale, John.	1	8	0	0	0	0	0	0.00
Mike Beale, Toledo	1	15	0	0	0	1	0	2.53
Mike Beale, Peoria	1	30	0	0	0	4	0	7.95
Totals	3	54	0	0	0	5	0	5.57
M. Bradette, Ches.	1	13	0	0	0	2	0	9.33
M. Bradette, Birm.	3	100	1	1	0	11	0	6.59
Totals	4	113	1	1	0	13	0	6.90
D. Brumby, Whe.	31	1741	11	14	4	89	0	3.07
D. Brumby, Char.	6	300	3	1	0	18	0	3.61
Totals	37	2041	14	15	4	107	0	3.15
K. Daubenspeck, J.	8	424	5	3	0	18	0	2.55
K. Daubenspeck, Che.	13	774	7	2	4	31	2	2.40
Totals	21	1198	12	5	4	49	2	2.45
Chris Farion, Day.	2	28	0	1	0	4	0	8.70
Chris Farion, Mob.	1	13	0	0	0	1	0	4.63
Totals	3	41	0	1	0	5	0	7.40
Allan Hitchen, B.R.	7	277	2	1	1	14	0	3.03
Allan Hitchen, Char.	4	81	0	1	1	4	0	0.00
Allan Hitchen, Whe.	4	148	0	1	0	11	0	4.45
Totals	15	506	2	3	2	29	0	3.44
Tim Keyes, Aug.	8	411	4	3	0	25	0	3.65
Tim Keyes, Char.	2	86	1	0	0	6	0	4.17
Totals	10	498	5	3	0	31	0	3.74
K. Kreutzer, Char.	9	481	4	3	1	29	0	3.62
K. Kreutzer, Hunt.	13	651	3	7	0	42	0	3.76
K. Kreutzer, Day.	7	394	3	3	1	23	0	3.50
Totals	29	1526	10	13	2	94	0	3.70
Chad Lang, Hunt.	16	798	4	9	2	54	0	4.06
Chad Lang, Peoria	20	1116	12	6	1	51	2	2.74
Totals	36	1914	16	15	3	105	2	3.29
Troy Maguire, Jack.	2	119	0	1	1	9	0	4.52
Troy Maguire, Rich.	1	40	1	0	0	1	0	1.50
Totals	3	159	1	1	1	10	0	3.76
Jim Mullin, Peoria	7	399	4	3	0	26	0	3.91
Jim Mullin, Hunt.	30	1446	13	9	3	86	0	3.57
Totals	37	1845	17	12	3	112	0	3.64
R. Murdoch, Roan.	1	59	0	1	0	1	0	1.02
R. Murdoch, Jack.	16	591	2	7	0	49	0	4.97
Totals	17	650	2	8	0	50	0	4.62
Rick Nichol, Aug.	1	11	0	0	0	0	0	0.00
Rick Nichol, Day.	3	164	0	1	1	13	0	4.46
Rick Nichol, Tall.	5	144	0	1	0	10	0	4.17
Totals	9	319	0	2	1	23	0	4.33
Brian Regan, Peo.	10	500	4	2	2	23	1	2.76
Brian Regan, Day.	32	1831	14	12	5	92	3	3.01
Totals	42	2331	18	14	7	115	4	2.96
E. Saltarelli, Ches.	27	1421	8	11	5	74	1	3.12
E. Saltarelli, Tall.	6	216	1	1	1	13	1	3.61
Totals	33	1637	9	12	6	87	2	3.19

1999 KELLY CUP PLAYOFFS

RESULTS

WILD-CARD ROUND

	W	L	Pts.	GF	GA
Baton Rouge	2	0	4	6	2
Augusta	0	2	0	2	6

(Baton Rouge won series, 2-0)

	W	L	Pts.	GF	GA
Birmingham	2	0	4	9	5
Mobile	0	2	0	5	9

(Birmingham won series, 2-0)

	W	L	Pts.	GF	GA
New Orleans	2	0	4	10	6
Jacksonville	0	2	0	6	10

(New Orleans won series, 2-0)

CONFERENCE QUARTERFINALS

	W	L	Pts.	GF	GA
Roanoke	3	1	6	12	10
Dayton	1	3	2	10	12

(Roanoke won series, 3-1)

	W	L	Pts.	GF	GA
Chesapeake	3	1	6	13	10
Columbus	1	3	2	10	13

(Chesapeake won series, 3-1)

	W	L	Pts.	GF	GA
Toledo	3	1	6	17	13
Peoria	1	3	2	13	17

(Toledo won series, 3-1)

	W	L	Pts.	GF	GA
Richmond	3	1	6	19	11
Hampton Roads	1	3	2	11	19

(Richmond won series, 3-1)

	W	L	Pts.	GF	GA
Pee Dee	3	1	6	17	7
Baton Rouge	1	3	2	7	17

(Pee Dee won series, 3-1)

	W	L	Pts.	GF	GA
New Orleans	3	2	6	13	10
Louisiana	2	3	4	10	13

(New Orleans won series, 3-2)

	W	L	Pts.	GF	GA
Florida	3	0	6	16	5
Birmingham	0	3	0	5	16

(Florida won series, 3-0)

	W	L	Pts.	GF	GA
Mississippi	3	0	6	11	6
South Carolina	0	3	0	6	11

(Mississippi won series, 3-0)

CONFERENCE SEMIFINALS

	W	L	Pts.	GF	GA
Roanoke	3	1	6	5	4
Chesapeake	1	3	2	4	5

(Roanoke won series, 3-1)

	W	L	Pts.	GF	GA
Richmond	3	0	6	13	7
Toledo	0	3	0	7	13

(Richmond won series, 3-0)

	W	L	Pts.	GF	GA
Pee Dee	3	1	6	15	14
New Orleans	1	3	2	14	15

(Pee Dee won series, 3-1)

	W	L	Pts.	GF	GA
Mississippi	3	0	6	14	7
Florida	0	3	0	7	14

(Mississippi won series, 3-0)

CONFERENCE FINALS

	W	L	Pts.	GF	GA
Richmond	4	0	8	13	4
Roanoke	0	4	0	4	13

(Richmond won series, 4-0)

	W	L	Pts.	GF	GA
Mississippi	4	1	8	17	12
Pee Dee	1	4	2	12	17

(Mississippi won series, 4-1)

LEAGUE FINALS

	W	L	Pts.	GF	GA
Mississippi	4	3	8	21	17
Richmond	3	4	6	17	21

(Mississippi won series, 4-3)

INDIVIDUAL LEADERS

Goals: Chris Lipsett, Pee Dee (13)
Assists: Andrew Shier, Richmond (14)
Points: Rob DeCiantis, New Orleans (22)
Penalty minutes: Trevor Senn, Richmond (89)
Goaltending average: Kirk Daubenspeck, Chesapeake (1.70)
Shutouts: Maxime Gingras, Richmond (5)

TOP SCORERS

	Games	G	A	Pts.
Rob DeCiantis, New Orleans	11	11	11	22
Ryan Kraft, Richmond	18	10	10	20
Kelly Hurd, Mississippi	18	9	11	20
Dany Bousquet, Pee Dee	13	7	12	19
Chris Lipsett, Pee Dee	13	13	4	17
Vaclav Nedomansky, Mississippi	18	8	9	17
Darryl LaFrance, New Orleans	11	6	11	17
Allan Sirois, Pee Dee	13	4	13	17
Jeff Lazaro, New Orleans	11	9	7	16
Peter Roed, Richmond	18	6	10	16
Andrew Shier, Richmond	18	2	14	16

INDIVIDUAL STATISTICS

AUGUSTA LYNX

(Lost wild-card round to Baton Rouge, 2-0)

SCORING

	Games	G	A	Pts.	PIM
Darren Colbourne	2	1	0	1	0
Wes Mason	2	1	0	1	6
Jessie Rezansoff	2	0	1	1	2
Bob Berg	2	0	1	1	0
Peter Constantine	2	0	0	0	0
Mark Blesenthal	2	0	0	0	0
Lars Pettersen	2	0	0	0	2
Chris Thompson	2	0	0	0	4
Mark DeSantis	2	0	0	0	2
John Whitwell	2	0	0	0	2
Clint Cabana	2	0	0	0	2
Judd Lambert (goalie)	2	0	0	0	0
Luke Murphy	2	0	0	0	2
Ken Ruddick	2	0	0	0	4
Bryan Duce	2	0	0	0	0
Sam Ftorek	2	0	0	0	4
Dan Kopec	2	0	0	0	8

GOALTENDING

	Gms.	Min.	W	L	T	G	SO	Avg.
Judd Lambert	2	119	0	2	0	5	0	2.52

BATON ROUGE KINGFISH

(Lost conference quarterfinals to Pee Dee, 3-1)

SCORING

	Games	G	A	Pts.	PIM
Cam Brown	6	6	1	7	42
Luke Curtin	6	3	4	7	4
Bryan Richardson	6	2	4	6	4
Bryan Fogarty	4	1	3	4	8
Brett Abrahamson	6	0	2	2	0
Dan Shermerhorn	6	0	2	2	4
B.J. Johnston	6	0	2	2	4
Paul Croteau	6	1	0	1	4
Eric Montreuil	6	0	1	1	2
Eric Normandin	6	0	1	1	8
Lee Hamilton	6	0	1	1	14
Jeff Boettger	6	0	0	0	0
Derrick Smith	6	0	0	0	0
Jordan Willis (goalie)	6	0	0	0	0
Bob Westerby	6	0	0	0	28
Casey Wolak	6	0	0	0	18
Joe Eagan	6	0	0	0	6

GOALTENDING

	Gms.	Min.	W	L	T	G	SO	Avg.
Jordan Willis	6	374	3	3	0	18	1	2.89

BIRMINGHAM BULLS

(Lost conference quarterfinals to Florida, 3-0)

SCORING

	Games	G	A	Pts.	PIM
Jamey Hicks	5	4	4	8	4
Patrick Nadeau	5	0	4	4	2
Kory Mullin	5	0	4	4	2
Stefan Rivard	5	2	1	3	10
Chad Power	5	2	1	3	4
Craig Lutes	5	1	2	3	10
Hugo Belanger	5	2	0	2	2
Emmanuel LaBranche	5	1	1	2	8
Daniel Passard	4	0	2	2	6
Dennis Pinfold	1	1	0	1	2
Chad Cavanaugh	5	1	0	1	0
Tyler Johnston	5	0	1	1	6
Justin Martin	5	0	1	1	8
Jeff Scharf	5	0	1	1	2
Joe Seroski	5	0	1	1	0
Rick Smith	5	0	1	1	0
Scott Bailey (goalie)	5	0	0	0	2
Adam Lewis	5	0	0	0	4

GOALTENDING

	Gms.	Min.	W	L	T	G	SO	Avg.
Scott Bailey	5	299	2	3	0	21	0	4.21

CHESAPEAKE ICEBREAKERS

(Lost conference semifinals to Roanoke, 3-1)

SCORING

	Games	G	A	Pts.	PIM
Derek Clancey	8	1	8	9	12
Denny Felsner	8	4	1	5	2
Arturs Kupaks	8	2	2	4	15
Earl Cronan	8	2	1	3	15
Kaleb Toth	8	2	1	3	4
Brad Holzinger	8	1	2	3	6
Ryan Brown	8	1	2	3	18
J.P. O'Connor	8	2	0	2	2
Marc Tropper	6	1	1	2	4
Jamie O'Leary	8	0	2	2	4
Steve Wilson	8	0	2	2	10
Ryan Mougenel	2	1	0	1	0
Jeff Rucinski	2	0	1	1	0
Brian Callahan	8	0	1	1	12
Bob Thornton	8	0	1	1	12
Cory Murphy	8	0	1	1	8
Mike Tamburro (goalie)	1	0	0	0	2
Tony McCauley	5	0	0	0	4
Kirk Daubenspeck (goalie)	7	0	0	0	2
Kam White	8	0	0	0	24

GOALTENDING

	Gms.	Min.	W	L	T	G	SO	Avg.
Kirk Daubenspeck	7	424	3	4	0	12	1	1.70
Mike Tamburro	1	60	1	0	0	2	0	2.00

COLUMBUS CHILL

(Lost conference quarterfinals to Chesapeake, 3-1)

SCORING

	Games	G	A	Pts.	PIM
Tim Fingerhut	4	1	3	4	4
Martin Laroche	4	0	4	4	4
Steve Moffat	3	3	0	3	6
Richard Keyes	4	2	1	3	0
Bret Meyers	4	2	1	3	2
Jason Christie	4	1	1	2	4
Jay Pecora	4	0	2	2	4
Mark Pivetz	4	1	0	1	2
Dan Cousineau	2	0	1	1	0
Matt Cooney	3	0	1	1	11
Matt Oates	4	0	1	1	8
Rob White	4	0	1	1	7
Harlin Hayes (goalie)	2	0	0	0	0
Jeff Salajko (goalie)	3	0	0	0	0
Matt Peterson	4	0	0	0	6
Andrew Fagan	4	0	0	0	16
Rob Woodward	4	0	0	0	0
Matt Golden	4	0	0	0	6
Beau Bilek	4	0	0	0	8

GOALTENDING

	Gms.	Min.	W	L	T	G	SO	Avg.
Harlin Hayes	2	107	0	0	1	2	0	1.12
Jeff Salajko	3	139	1	2	0	10	0	4.32

DAYTON BOMBERS

(Lost conference quarterfinals to Roanoke, 3-1)

SCORING

	Games	G	A	Pts.	PIM
Jamie Ling	4	1	4	5	4
Norm Dezainde	4	2	2	4	18
Bobby Brown	4	2	1	3	2
Justin Krall	4	1	2	3	2
Travis Dillabough	4	0	2	2	8
Sergei Radchenko	2	1	0	1	0
Chuck Mindell	2	1	0	1	0
Dan Hendrickson	4	1	0	1	6
Brian Ridolfi	4	1	0	1	4
Colin Miller	4	0	1	1	16
Brian Secord	4	0	1	1	24
Kiley Hill	4	0	1	1	12
Brandon Sugden	1	0	0	0	17
Aaron Kriss	1	0	0	0	4
Brian Regan (goalie)	1	0	0	0	0
Nick Robinson	3	0	0	0	4
Dave Van Drunen	4	0	0	0	12
Trevor Koenig (goalie)	4	0	0	0	0
Josh Harrold	4	0	0	0	2
Chris Wismer	4	0	0	0	16

GOALTENDING

	Gms.	Min.	W	L	T	G	SO	Avg.
Trevor Koenig	4	203	1	2	0	6	1	1.78
Brian Regan	1	36	0	1	0	4	0	6.68

FLORIDA EVERBLADES

(Lost conference semifinals to Mississippi, 3-0)

SCORING

	Games	G	A	Pts.	PIM
Steve Tardif	6	4	3	7	18
Pat Mikesch	4	1	5	6	4
Kevin McDonald	6	3	2	5	10
Eric Rud	6	3	2	5	2
Greg Koehler	6	2	3	5	12
Mike Jickling	6	1	4	5	2
Eric Ricard	6	0	5	5	12
Nick Checco	6	2	2	4	2
Andrew Taylor	6	1	3	4	0
Hugh Hamilton	6	0	4	4	6
Matt Demarski	3	2	1	3	2
Tim Ferguson	6	2	1	3	2
Matt Brush	6	0	2	2	2
Sergei Fedotov	3	1	0	1	2
Greg Kuznik	5	1	0	1	0
Marc Magliarditi (goalie)	5	0	1	1	0
Dane Litke	5	0	1	1	0
Randy Petruk (goalie)	1	0	0	0	0
Jason Prokopetz	5	0	0	0	2
Dan Reimann	5	0	0	0	0

GOALTENDING

	Gms.	Min.	W	L	T	G	SO	Avg.
Marc Magliarditi	5	332	3	1	1	14	1	2.53
Randy Petruk	1	60	0	1	0	5	0	5.00

HAMPTON ROADS ADMIRALS

(Lost conference quarterfinals to Richmond, 3-1)

SCORING

	Games	G	A	Pts.	PIM
Dominic Maltais	4	4	1	5	15
Dan Ceman	4	1	4	5	2
Joel Poirier	4	1	3	4	2
Chris Phelps	4	0	4	4	10
Chad Ackerman	4	1	2	3	0
Trent Whitfield	4	2	0	2	14
Andy Doktorchik	4	1	0	1	6
Marty Clapton	4	1	0	1	15
Trever Fraser	2	0	1	1	6
Francois Bourdeau	4	0	1	1	2
Dean Campanale	4	0	1	1	0
Ryan Gillis	4	0	1	1	8
Joe Corvo	4	0	1	1	0
Derek Ernest	1	0	0	0	2
Steve Valiquette (goalie)	2	0	0	0	0
Henry Higdon	2	0	0	0	0
Trevor Johnson	3	0	0	0	16
Louis Bedard	4	0	0	0	24
Jason Saal (goalie)	4	0	0	0	0
Rod Taylor	4	0	0	0	30

GOALTENDING

	Gms.	Min.	W	L	T	G	SO	Avg.
Jason Saal	4	179	1	2	0	12	0	4.02
Steve Valiquette	2	60	0	1	0	7	0	7.00

JACKSONVILLE LIZARD KINGS

(Lost wild-card round to New Orleans, 2-0)

SCORING

	Games	G	A	Pts.	PIM
Colin Chaulk	2	2	1	3	6
Mike Pomichter	2	1	2	3	0
Bill McKay	2	1	2	3	2
Bryan Forslund	2	0	2	2	8
Derek Eberle	2	0	2	2	0
Brad Federenko	2	1	0	1	2
Eric Long	2	1	0	1	2
Ray LeBlanc (goalie)	2	0	1	1	0
Jean-Phillipe Soucy	2	0	0	0	0
Patrick Gingras	2	0	0	0	10
Joel Theriault	2	0	0	0	19
Matt Cressman	2	0	0	0	2
Duncan Dalmao	2	0	0	0	0
Lukas Smital	2	0	0	0	0
Erik Olsen	2	0	0	0	0
Scott Page	2	0	0	0	0
Jami Yoder	2	0	0	0	0

GOALTENDING

	Gms.	Min.	W	L	T	G	SO	Avg.
Ray LeBlanc	2	118	0	2	0	8	0	4.06

LOUISIANA ICEGATORS

(Lost conference quarterfinals to New Orleans, 3-2)

SCORING

	Games	G	A	Pts.	PIM
John Spoltore	5	2	3	5	0
Mike Murray	5	2	3	5	6
Chris Valicevic	5	1	3	4	4
John Varga	5	1	2	3	10
Nick Stajduhar	5	1	1	2	10
Louis Dumont	5	1	1	2	10
Jay Murphy	5	1	1	2	23
Gary Roach	5	0	2	2	6
Rob Weingartner	2	1	0	1	19
Don Parsons	4	0	1	1	4
Blair Manning	5	0	1	1	6
Kyle Freadrich	4	0	0	0	2
Matthew Pagnutti	5	0	0	0	4
Stan Melanson	5	0	0	0	4
Ryan Shanahan	5	0	0	0	8
Jason McQuat	5	0	0	0	13
Doug Bonner (goalie)	5	0	0	0	0

GOALTENDING

	Gms.	Min.	W	L	T	G	SO	Avg.
Doug Bonner	5	299	2	3	0	13	0	2.61

MISSISSIPPI SEA WOLVES

(Winner of 1999 Kelly Cup playoffs)

SCORING

	Games	G	A	Pts.	PIM
Kelly Hurd	18	9	11	20	4
Vaclav Nedomansky	18	8	9	17	40
Kevin Hilton	18	7	8	15	14
Mark Rupnow	18	6	9	15	10
Mikhail Kravets	18	5	8	13	10
Chris Schmidt	18	5	8	13	10
Quinn Fair	18	3	10	13	22
John Kosobud	18	3	6	9	25
Patrick Rochon	17	2	7	9	28
Andrew Dale	12	5	3	8	10
Bob Woods	18	2	6	8	12
Karl Infanger	18	1	7	8	14
Sean Blanchard	17	0	8	8	4
Cody Bowtell	18	3	4	7	4
Brad Essex	14	2	4	6	25
Mike Martone	18	0	3	3	40
D.J. Mando	8	1	1	2	25
Troy Mann	4	1	0	1	2
Travis Scott (goalie)	18	0	1	1	2

GOALTENDING

	Gms.	Min.	W	L	T	G	SO	Avg.
Travis Scott	18	1252	14	3	1	42	3	2.01

MOBILE MYSTICS

(Lost wild-card round to Birmingham, 2-0)

SCORING

	Games	G	A	Pts.	PIM
Jim Shepherd	2	1	2	3	6
Russ Guzior	2	2	0	2	0
Dalen Hrooshkin	2	1	1	2	0
Charlie Retter	2	1	0	1	2
Russ Monteith	2	0	1	1	0
Jason Elders	2	0	1	1	0
Yanick Jean	2	0	1	1	4
Andrew Will	2	0	1	1	0
Lee Giffin	2	0	1	1	24
Chad Wilchynski	2	0	0	0	2
Brandon Carper	2	0	0	0	4
Hugues Gervais	2	0	0	0	19
Craig Binns	2	0	0	0	2
Mike Olaski	2	0	0	0	2
Chad Alban (goalie)	2	0	0	0	0
Tom Nolan	2	0	0	0	10
Mitch Vig	2	0	0	0	14

GOALTENDING

	Gms.	Min.	W	L	T	G	SO	Avg.
Chad Alban	2	119	0	2	0	9	0	4.53

NEW ORLEANS BRASS

(Lost conference semifinals to Pee Dee, 3-1)

SCORING

	Games	G	A	Pts.	PIM
Rob DeCiantis	11	11	11	22	8
Darryl LaFrance	11	6	11	17	12
Jeff Lazaro	11	9	7	16	14
Steve Cheredaryk	11	3	4	7	26
Mark Turner	11	2	5	7	22

	Games	G	A	Pts.	PIM
Martin Woods	11	1	6	7	12
Adam Copeland	11	3	1	4	6
Kevin Pozzo	10	1	3	4	23
Stephane Soulliere	10	0	3	3	8
Brad Church	11	1	1	2	22
Jason Downey	11	0	2	2	37
Martin Villeneuve (goalie)	8	0	1	1	2
Dean Moore	10	0	1	1	25
Chris Slater	11	0	1	1	16
Martin Hohenberger	3	0	0	0	2
Chris Wickenheiser (goalie)	3	0	0	0	2
Olivier Morin	9	0	0	0	2
Gordie Dwyer	11	0	0	0	27
Brad Symes	11	0	0	0	21

GOALTENDING

	Gms.	Min.	W	L	T	G	SO	Avg.
Martin Villeneuve	8	479	5	3	0	18	2	2.25
Chris Wickenheiser	3	180	1	2	0	12	0	4.01

PEE DEE PRIDE

(Lost conference finals to Mississippi, 4-1)

SCORING

	Games	G	A	Pts.	PIM
Dany Bousquet	13	7	12	19	20
Chris Lipsett	13	13	4	17	20
Allan Sirois	13	4	13	17	14
Ryan Petz	13	7	6	13	14
Peter Geronazzo	13	2	5	7	20
Trevor Demmans	13	1	6	7	12
Brendan Flynn	10	1	4	5	18
Rod Aldoff	13	1	4	5	10
Brian Goudie	13	0	5	5	66
Rick Bennett	11	3	1	4	33
Tom Field	13	3	1	4	0
Kurt Mallett	13	1	3	4	12
Jim Brown	8	1	2	3	4
Darcy Dallas	13	0	3	3	42
Mike Payne	8	0	1	1	7
Sandy Allan (goalie)	11	0	1	1	0
Mark Richards (goalie)	5	0	0	0	0
Bryan Tapper	13	0	0	0	10
Jan Vodrazka	13	0	0	0	56

GOALTENDING

	Gms.	Min.	W	L	T	G	SO	Avg.
Mark Richards	5	226	0	1	1	9	0	2.38
Sandy Allan	11	627	7	2	2	28	0	2.68

PEORIA RIVERMEN

(Lost conference quarterfinals to Toledo, 3-1)

SCORING

	Games	G	A	Pts.	PIM
Joe Rybar	4	1	4	5	0
Doug Evans	4	0	5	5	10
Jamie Thompson	2	3	0	3	2
Darren Maloney	4	2	1	3	21
Marek Ivan	4	2	1	3	20
J.F. Boutin	4	1	2	3	4
Jeff Trembecky	4	1	1	2	4
Matt Smith	4	1	1	2	6
Blaine Fitzpatrick	3	0	2	2	17
Alex Couture	4	0	2	2	4
Daniel Hodge	4	1	0	1	2
Ken Boone	4	1	0	1	13
Michal Dvorak	3	0	1	1	2
Chris Coveny	4	0	1	1	4
Kevin Paden	4	0	1	1	8
Dan Carney	4	0	1	1	6
Chad Lang (goalie)	1	0	0	0	2
Jay Kenney	3	0	0	0	0
Dan Murphy (goalie)	3	0	0	0	0

GOALTENDING

	Gms.	Min.	W	L	T	G	SO	Avg.
Dan Murphy	3	180	1	2	0	11	0	3.67
Chad Lang	1	60	0	1	0	5	0	5.03

RICHMOND RENEGADES

(Lost finals to Mississippi, 4-3)

SCORING

	Games	G	A	Pts.	PIM
Ryan Kraft	18	10	10	20	4
Peter Roed	18	6	10	16	14
Andrew Shier	18	2	14	16	22
Joe Blaznek	18	10	5	15	8
Joe Bianchi	18	7	5	12	22
Kevin Knopp	15	2	10	12	39
Joe Vandermeer	18	4	7	11	8
Valentin Passarelli	18	5	4	9	4
Steve Dumonski	17	7	1	8	38
Trevor Senn	18	4	4	8	89
Sal Manganaro	18	3	5	8	37
David Lambeth	18	0	7	7	18
Forrest Gore	10	0	4	4	6
Dan Vandermeer	16	0	4	4	8
Craig Paterson	17	1	2	3	19
Darren Wetherill	18	1	1	2	26
Jean Paul Tessier	14	0	1	1	15
Terry Friesen (goalie)	1	0	0	0	0
Maxime Gingras (goalie)	18	0	0	0	2

GOALTENDING

	Gms.	Min.	W	L	T	G	SO	Avg.
Terry Friesen	1	20	1	0	0	0	0	0.00
Maxime Gingras	18	1117	12	4	1	43	5	2.31

ROANOKE EXPRESS

(Lost conference finals to Richmond, 4-0)

SCORING

	Games	G	A	Pts.	PIM
Calvin Elfring	11	3	5	8	10
Duane Harmer	12	2	5	7	0
Mike Peron	11	4	2	6	26
Tim Christian	12	4	2	6	6
Chad Spurr	12	4	2	6	12
Mike Oliveira	12	0	4	4	4
Dru Burgess	12	1	2	3	4
Ben Schust	12	2	0	2	8
Nicholas Windsor	12	1	1	2	8
J.F. Tremblay	6	0	2	2	12
Dan O'Connell	11	0	2	2	22
Kris Cantu	6	0	1	1	6
Scott Campbell	12	0	1	1	8
Drew Felder	3	0	0	0	5
Dave Gagnon (goalie)	3	0	0	0	2
Daniel Berthiaume (goalie)	10	0	0	0	8
Steve Sabo	11	0	0	0	16
Jason Stewart	12	0	0	0	2
Travis Smith	12	0	0	0	44
Doug Searle	12	0	0	0	8

GOALTENDING

	Gms.	Min.	W	L	T	G	SO	Avg.
Daniel Berthiaume	10	608	6	3	1	19	1	1.87
Dave Gagnon	3	139	0	2	0	6	0	2.59

SOUTH CAROLINA STINGRAYS

(Lost conference quarterfinals to Mississippi, 3-0)

SCORING

	Games	G	A	Pts.	PIM
Brett Marietti	3	2	1	3	6
Brendan Concannon	3	1	1	2	0
Rob Concannon	3	1	1	2	20
Brad Dexter	3	1	1	2	2
Chris Hynnes	3	0	2	2	2

	Games	G	A	Pts.	PIM
Chris Felix	3	0	2	2	8
Jeff Romfo	3	1	0	1	0
Damian Prescott	3	0	1	1	2
Dave Seitz	3	0	1	1	4
Jay Moser	3	0	1	1	0
Chris Wheaton	1	0	0	0	17
Jeff Edwards	1	0	0	0	2
Jason Hughes	2	0	0	0	17
Matt Garzone	3	0	0	0	2
Greg Schmidt	3	0	0	0	0
Cam Danyluk	3	0	0	0	4
Jody Lehman (goalie)	3	0	0	0	2
Marc Tardif	3	0	0	0	18

GOALTENDING

	Gms.	Min.	W	L	T	G	SO	Avg.
Jody Lehman	3	230	0	2	1	11	0	2.87

TOLEDO STORM

(Lost conference semifinals to Richmond, 3-0)

SCORING

	Games	G	A	Pts.	PIM
Aaron Boh	7	3	6	9	28
Shawn Maltby	7	2	6	8	6
Scott Hillman	7	0	7	7	6
Colin Beardsmore	7	4	2	6	2
Scott Burt	7	1	5	6	6
Andrew Williamson	7	2	3	5	10
David Lessard	7	1	3	4	6
Jeremy Rebek	7	1	3	4	6
Rob Thorpe	7	3	0	3	12
Chris Gignac	4	1	2	3	2
Mark Deazeley	7	2	0	2	5
Anthony Terzo	4	1	1	2	4
Jason Cannon	7	1	1	2	12
Jason Norrie	7	1	1	2	15
Rob Merrill	4	1	0	1	2
Darcy George	6	0	1	1	4
Harlan Pratt	3	0	0	0	0
Kevin Diachina	5	0	0	0	11
Matt Mullin (goalie)	7	0	0	0	4

GOALTENDING

	Gms.	Min.	W	L	T	G	SO	Avg.
Matt Mullin	7	419	3	4	0	26	0	3.73

1998-99 AWARD WINNERS

ALL-STAR TEAMS

First team	Pos.	Second team
Maxime Gingras, Richmond	G	Marc Magliarditi, Florida
Chris Valicevic, Louisiana	D	Bob Woods, Mississippi
Arturs Kupaks, Chesapeake	D	Brad Dexter, South Carolina
Allan Sirois, Pee Dee	LW	Jason Elders, Mobile
John Spoltore, Louisiana	C	Jamey Hicks, Birmingham
Denny Felsner, Chesapeake	RW	Rob DeCiantis, New Orleans

TROPHY WINNERS

Most Valuable Player: Chris Valicevic, Louisiana
Scoring leader: John Spoltore, Louisiana
Outstanding defenseman: Chris Valicevic, Louisiana
Outstanding goaltender: Maxime Gingras, Richmond
Rookie of the Year: Maxime Gingras, Richmond
Playoff MVP: Travis Scott, Mississippi
Coach of the Year: Bob Ferguson, Florida

ALL-TIME AWARD WINNERS

MOST VALUABLE PLAYER

Season Player, Team
1988-89—Daryl Harpe, Erie
1989-90—Bill McDougall, Erie
1990-91—Stan Drulia, Knoxville
1991-92—Phil Berger, Greensboro
1992-93—Trevor Jobe, Nashville
1993-94—Joe Flanagan, Birmingham
1994-95—Vadim Slivchenko, Wheeling
1995-96—Hugo Belanger, Nashville
1996-97—Mike Ross, South Carolina
1997-98—Jamey Hicks, Birmingham
1998-99—Chris Valicevic, Louisiana

TOP SCORER

Season Player, Team
1988-89—Daryl Harpe, Erie
1989-90—Bill McDougall, Erie
1990-91—Stan Drulia, Knoxville
1991-92—Phil Berger, Greensboro
1992-93—Trevor Jobe, Nashville
1993-94—Phil Berger, Greensboro
1994-95—Scott Burfoot, Erie
1995-96—Hugo Belanger, Nashville
1996-97—Ed Courtenay, South Carolina
Mike Ross, South Carolina
1997-98—Jamey Hicks, Birmingham
1998-99—John Spoltore, Louisiana

ROOKIE OF THE YEAR

Season Player, Team
1988-89—Tom Sasso, Johnstown
1989-90—Bill McDougall, Erie
1990-91—Dan Gauthier, Knoxville
1991-92—Darren Colbourne, Dayton
1992-93—Joe Flanagan, Birmingham
1993-94—Dan Gravelle, Greensboro
1994-95—Kevin McKinnon, Erie
1995-96—Keli Corpse, Wheeling
1996-97—Dany Bousquet, Birmingham
1997-98—Sean Venedam, Toledo
1998-99—Maxime Gingras, Richmond

TOP GOALTENDER

Season Player, Team
1988-89—Scott Gordon, Johnstown
1989-90—Alain Raymond, Hampton Roads
1990-91—Dean Anderson, Knoxville
1991-92—Frederic Chabot, Winston-Salem
1992-93—Nick Vitucci, Hampton Roads
1993-94—Cory Cadden, Knoxville
1994-95—Chris Gordon, Huntington
1995-96—Alain Morissette, Louisville
1996-97—Marc Delorme, Louisiana
1997-98—Nick Vitucci, Toledo
1998-99—Maxime Gingras, Richmond

PLAYOFF MVP

Season Player, Team
1988-89—Nick Vitucci, Carolina
1989-90—Wade Flaherty, Greensboro
1990-91—Dave Gagnon, Hampton Rds.
Flanagan, Hampton Roads
1991-92—Mark Bernard, Hampton Roads
1992-93—Rick Judson, Toledo

Season	Player, Team
1993-94	Dave Gagnon, Toledo
1994-95	Blaine Moore, Richmond
1995-96	Nick Vitucci, Charlotte
1996-97	Jason Fitzsimmons, South Carolina
1997-98	Sebastian Charpentier, Hampton Roads
1998-99	Travis Scott, Mississippi

COACH OF THE YEAR

Season	Coach, Team
1988-89	Ron Hansis, Erie
1989-90	Dave Allison, Virginia
1990-91	Don Jackson, Knoxville
1991-92	Doug Sauter, Winston-Salem
1992-93	Kurt Kleinendorst, Raleigh
1993-94	Barry Smith, Knoxville
1994-95	Jim Playfair, Dayton
1995-96	Roy Sommer, Richmond
1996-97	Brian McCutcheon, Columbus
1997-98	Chris Nilan, Chesapeake
1998-99	Bob Ferguson, Florida

TOP DEFENSEMAN

Season	Player, Team
1988-89	Kelly Szautner, Erie
1989-90	Bill Whitfield, Virginia
1990-91	Brett McDonald, Nashville
1991-92	Scott White, Greensboro
1992-93	Derek Booth, Toledo
1993-94	Tom Nemeth, Dayton
1994-95	Brandon Smith, Dayton
1995-96	Chris Valicevic, Louisiana
1996-97	Chris Valicevic, Louisiana
1997-98	Chris Valicevic, Louisiana
1998-99	Chris Valicevic, Louisiana

ALL-TIME LEAGUE CHAMPIONS

	REGULAR-SEASON CHAMPION		PLAYOFF CHAMPION	
Season	Team	Coach	Team	Coach
1988-89	Erie Panthers	Ron Hansis	Carolina Thunderbirds	Brendon Watson
1989-90	Winston-Salem Thunderbirds	C. McSorley, J. Fraser	Greensboro Monarchs	Jeff Brubaker
1990-91	Knoxville Cherokees	Don Jackson	Hampton Roads Admirals	John Brophy
1991-92	Toledo Storm	Chris McSorley	Hampton Roads Admirals	John Brophy
1992-93	Wheeling Thunderbirds	Doug Sauter	Toledo Storm	Chris McSorley
1993-94	Knoxville Cherokees	Barry Smith	Toledo Storm	Chris McSorley
1994-95	Wheeling Thunderbirds	Doug Sauter	Richmond Renegades	Roy Sommer
1995-96	Richmond Renegades	Roy Sommer	Charlotte Checkers	John Marks
1996-97	South Carolina Stingrays	Rick Vaive	South Carolina Stingrays	Rick Vaive
1997-98	Louisiana Icegators	Doug Shedden	Hampton Roads Admirals	John Brophy
1998-99	Pee Dee Pride	Jack Capuano	Mississippi Sea Wolves	Bruce Boudreau

The ECHL regular season champion is awarded the Brabham Cup. The playoff champion was awarded the Riley Cup through the 1995-96 season. Playoff champions are now awarded the Patrick J. Kelly Cup.

CENTRAL HOCKEY LEAGUE

LEAGUE OFFICE

Commissioner
N. Thomas Berry Jr.
Special assignments
Michael A. Meyers
Director of finance
Charlene Smoll
Director of marketing
Brad Johnson
Director of communications
Lisa M. Peppin
Administrative assistant
Amy Pickett
Address
222 E. Ohio Street, Suite 320
Indianapolis, IN 46204
Phone
317-931-4245
FAX
317-916-0563

TEAMS

COLUMBUS COTTONMOUTHS

General manager
Phil Roberto
Head coach
Bruce Garber
Home ice
Columbus Civic Center
Address
P.O. Box 1886
Columbus, GA 31902-1886
Seating capacity
7,509
Phone
706-571-0086
FAX
706-571-0080

FAYETTEVILLE FORCE

General manager
Kevin MacNaught
Head coach
David Lohrei
Home ice
Crown Coliseum
Address
1960 Coliseum Drive
Fayetteville, NC 28306
Seating Capacity
10,000
Phone
910-438-9000
FAX
910-438-9004

HUNTSVILLE CHANNEL CATS

President
Matt Ingram
Head coach
Pat Bingham
Home ice
Von Braun Center
Address
700 Monroe Street
Huntsville, AL 35801
Seating capacity
6,552
Phone
256-551-2383
FAX
256-551-2382

INDIANAPOLIS ICE

General manager
Brad Beery
Coach
To be announced
Home ice
Pepsi Coliseum/Market Square Arena
Address
1202 East 38th Street
Indianapolis, IN 46205
Seating capacity
8,200/15,993
Phone
317-925-4423
FAX
317-931-4511

MACON WHOOPEE

President
Keith Burdette
General manager and head coach
Graeme Townshend
Home ice
Macon Centreplex
Address
200 Coliseum St.
Macon, GA 31217
Seating capacity
7,300
Phone
912-741-1000
FAX
912-741-0089

MEMPHIS RIVERKINGS

General manager
Jim Riggs
Head coach
Kevin Evans
Home ice
Mid-South Coliseum
Address
315 S. Hollywood, Bldg. F
Memphis, TN 38104
Seating capacity
9,551
Phone
901-278-9009
FAX
901-323-3262

OKLAHOMA CITY BLAZERS

General manager
Brad Lund
Head coach
Doug Sauter
Home ice
Myriad Convention Center
Address
119 N. Robinson, Suite 230
Oklahoma City, OK 73102
Seating capacity
13,479
Phone
405-235-7825
FAX
405-272-9875

SAN ANTONIO IGUANAS

General manager
David Oldham
Head coach
Chris Stewart
Home ice
Freeman Coliseum
Address
5757 Hwy. 90 W.
San Antonio, TX 78227
Seating Capacity
9,500
Phone
210-227-4449
FAX
210-670-0001

TOPEKA SCARECROWS

General manager
Chris Presson
Head coach
Paul Kelly
Home ice
Landon Arena
Address
1800 Exduster Blvd.
Topeka, KS 66612-1442
Seating Capacity
8,000
Phone
785-232-7697
FAX
785-232-7423

TULSA OILERS

General manager
Jeff Lund
Head coach
Shaun Clouston
Home ice
Tulsa Convention Center
Address
6413 S. Mingo, Suite 200
Tulsa, OK 74133
Seating Capacity
7,111
Phone
918-252-7825
FAX
918-249-0310

WICHITA THUNDER

General manager
Bill Shuck
Head coach
Bryan Wells
Home ice
Kansas Coliseum

Address
505 W. Maple, Suite 100
Wichita, KS 67213
Seating Capacity
9,685

Phone
316-264-4625
FAX
316-264-3037

1998-99 REGULAR SEASON

FINAL STANDINGS

EASTERN DIVISION

Team	G	W	L	SOL	Pts.	GF	GA
Huntsville	70	47	19	4	98	310	251
Columbus	70	41	21	8	90	276	210
Macon	70	36	25	9	81	241	233
Memphis	70	36	27	7	79	313	307
Fayetteville	70	35	27	8	78	267	285

WESTERN DIVISION

Team	G	W	L	SOL	Pts.	GF	GA
Oklahoma City	70	49	19	2	100	322	203
San Antonio	70	37	26	7	81	286	283
Wichita	70	34	26	10	78	257	262
Topeka	70	28	38	4	60	189	251
Fort Worth	70	22	43	5	49	245	322
Tulsa	70	20	41	9	49	261	360

INDIVIDUAL LEADERS

Goals: Joe Burton, Oklahoma City (73)
Assists: Hardy Sauter, Oklahoma City (80)
Points: Derek Grant, Memphis (123)
Penalty minutes: Curtis Voth, Tulsa (426)
Goaltending average: Jean-Ian Filiatrault, Oklahoma City (2.54)
Shutouts: Jean-Ian Filiatrault, Oklahoma City (6)

TOP SCORERS

	Games	G	A	Pts.
Derek Grant, Memphis	65	45	78	123
Denis Lamoureux, Memphis	69	67	54	121
Johnny Brdarovic, San Antonio	68	56	59	115
Joe Burton, Oklahoma City	69	73	37	110
Chris George, Huntsville	70	59	48	107
Igor Bondarev, Huntsville	64	26	78	104
Paul Jackson, San Antonio	62	41	62	103
Jocelyn Langlois, Macon	70	38	65	103
Chad Remackel, Fayetteville	70	36	67	103
Jeff Antonovich, Tulsa	70	40	60	100
Hardy Sauter, Oklahoma City	70	20	80	100
Jonathan DuBois, Huntsville	58	28	71	99
Brian Shantz, San Antonio	69	26	63	89
Travis Clayton, Wichita	69	25	57	82
Corey MacIntyre, Oklahoma City	56	22	60	82
Mark Karpen, Wichita	69	35	46	81
Brett Seguin, Topeka	70	24	56	80
Leonard Bonanno, Memphis	67	26	53	79
Mike Martens, Columbus	64	37	41	78
Craig Conley, Fort Worth	70	25	52	77
Roddy MacCormick, Fayetteville	70	23	54	77

INDIVIDUAL STATISTICS

COLUMBUS COTTONMOUTHS

SCORING

	Games	G	A	Pts.	PIM
Mike Martens	64	37	41	78	44
Mick Kempffer	69	19	57	76	135
Rob Sinclair	70	40	35	75	8
Thomas Stewart	45	22	30	52	48
Derek Crimin	64	23	28	51	52
Grady Manson	69	19	31	50	99
Dave Neilson	50	22	26	48	122
Dan Brown	52	5	39	44	93
Marcel Richard	43	19	24	43	35
Jerome Bechard	70	21	20	41	298
Kevin Plager	45	10	16	26	137
Roman Marakhovski	51	2	16	18	45
Claude Fillion	30	2	15	17	75
Oleg Tsirkounov	20	4	8	12	15
Brad Prefontaine	65	0	10	10	177
Brian Idalski	62	2	6	8	116
Olaf Kjenstad	3	5	1	6	2
Corwin Saurdiff (goalie)	34	0	6	6	4
Travis Riggin	14	5	0	5	8
J.A. Schneider	36	2	3	5	31
Tom Wilson	51	1	4	5	243
Jeff Mikesch	6	1	3	4	4
Mike Bajurny	10	1	2	3	29
Doug Mann	17	1	2	3	87
Francis Ouellette (goalie)	40	0	3	3	2
Rich Metro	2	2	0	2	2
Buddy Smith	2	1	1	2	4
Derek Marchand	8	0	1	1	8
Stewart Nowosad	1	0	0	0	2
Mike Sinerate	1	0	0	0	0
Craig Willard	1	0	0	0	2
Josh Dobbyn	2	0	0	0	5
Mike Rusk	2	0	0	0	0

GOALTENDING

	Games	Min.	W	L	SOL	G	SO	Avg.
Francis Ouellette	40	2262	24	10	3	104	0	2.76
Corwin Saurdiff	34	1939	18	11	4	94	1	2.91

FAYETTEVILLE FORCE

SCORING

	Games	G	A	Pts.	PIM
Chad Remackel	70	36	67	103	68
Roddy MacCormick	70	23	54	77	95
Steve Sangermano	47	35	41	76	174
Justin Tomberlin	70	29	37	66	42
Alexsand Chunchukov	45	24	36	60	36
Jason Wright	70	8	40	48	68
Steven Toll	59	19	26	45	21
Chris Ford	67	17	26	43	108
Lon Hovland	70	9	22	31	113
Janis Tomans	37	12	16	28	48
Tim Hill	47	9	15	24	102
Brett Colborne	23	10	11	21	21
Rod Butler	40	4	12	16	76
Ryan Guzior	40	2	12	14	42
Darren McLean	55	7	6	13	212

	Games	G	A	Pts.	PIM
Erik Raygor	31	7	5	12	67
Colin Muldoon	70	2	10	12	53
Jasen Rintala	25	5	6	11	26
Chris Brassard	11	1	7	8	11
Brad Barton	19	1	5	6	24
Ronalds Ozolinsh	31	1	4	5	22
Gairin Smith	3	3	1	4	25
Casey Hungle	10	1	3	4	12
Lance Robson	10	0	2	2	0
Mark Bernard (goalie)	15	0	1	1	6
Dan Dennis (goalie)	16	0	1	1	0
Ken Shepard (goalie)	16	0	1	1	17
Maurice Hall	1	0	0	0	2
Chris Duncan	2	0	0	0	6
Askhat Rakhmatulin	4	0	0	0	4
Geoff Derouin (goalie)	5	0	0	0	0
Chris Bernard (goalie)	13	0	0	0	0
Colum Cavilla (goalie)	13	0	0	0	2

GOALTENDING

	Games	Min.	W	L	SOL	G	SO	Avg.
Ken Shepard	16	894	11	3	1	43	0	2.88
Geoff Derouin	5	213	0	3	1	11	0	3.10
Dan Dennis	16	920	8	5	2	53	0	3.46
Colum Cavilla	13	727	4	6	2	50	1	4.12
Chris Bernard	13	620	6	5	0	43	0	4.16
Mark Bernard	15	821	6	5	2	74	0	5.41

FORT WORTH FIRE

SCORING

	Games	G	A	Pts.	PIM
Craig Conley	70	25	52	77	92
Alex Kholomeyev	45	22	33	55	73
Gatis Tseplis	52	16	37	53	26
J.D. Eaton	67	15	32	47	251
Dan Menard	58	19	23	42	104
Andre Quesnel	51	18	24	42	37
Cosmo Clarke	61	21	19	40	24
Craig Mittleholt	42	9	19	28	8
Mike Dick	28	13	13	26	14
Jason Carriere	38	12	11	23	80
Ben White	39	3	14	17	110
Kelly Leroux	69	3	14	17	107
Dave Lylyk	21	7	6	13	10
Bobby Clouston	16	3	10	13	73
David Grant	39	7	5	12	32
Roland Monilaws	37	5	6	11	30
Mike McCormick	22	4	7	11	26
Ray DeSouza	39	3	7	10	76
Anders Sorensen	17	3	6	9	4
Greg Cherne	21	6	2	8	12
Sam Katsuras	9	3	5	8	2
Chris O'Rourke	47	2	6	8	189
Warren Sachs	12	3	4	7	0
Troy MacCormick	10	2	5	7	4
Sheldon Flaman	7	2	3	5	10
Scott Usmail	7	2	3	5	6
Keith Kinvig	12	3	1	4	21
Jayme Adduono	7	1	3	4	8
Ryan Connolly	9	2	1	3	39
Marty Wells	10	1	2	3	19
Rick Findlay	15	1	2	3	19
Kurt Walston	3	1	1	2	4
Charlie Lawson	3	0	2	2	2
Gary Golczewski	6	1	0	1	20
Francois Albert	2	0	1	1	0
Jason Ricci	7	0	1	1	0
Ryan Schmidt	7	0	1	1	24
Nathan Grobins (goalie)	60	0	1	1	56
David Bouskill	1	0	0	0	2
Dave MacLean	1	0	0	0	0
Darryl Sinclair	1	0	0	0	0
Aaron Starnyski	1	0	0	0	0
Steve Wachter (goalie)	1	0	0	0	0
Brent Swarbrick	2	0	0	0	0
Jordan Hines	3	0	0	0	0
John Herrick (goalie)	6	0	0	0	0
Jason Desjardins (goalie)	8	0	0	0	0
Steve Noble	9	0	0	0	6

GOALTENDING

	Games	Min.	W	L	SOL	G	SO	Avg.
Kelly Leroux	1	17	0	0	0	0	0	0.00
Steve Wachter	1	58	0	1	0	4	0	4.15
Nathan Grobins	60	3504	18	37	4	256	1	4.38
Jason Desjardins	8	363	3	2	1	32	0	5.29
John Herrick	6	246	1	3	0	22	0	5.37

HUNTSVILLE CHANNEL CATS

SCORING

	Games	G	A	Pts.	PIM
Chris George	70	59	48	107	28
Igor Bondarev	64	26	78	104	86
Jonathan DuBois	58	28	71	99	140
Tyler Quiring	61	17	42	59	78
John Gibson	70	10	35	45	120
Mike Gamble	55	22	22	44	117
Phil Daigle	70	19	23	42	264
Mike DeGurse	44	23	18	41	212
Ryan Wood	64	14	27	41	61
Ken Richardson	53	17	21	38	240
Greg Lakovic	59	17	18	35	180
Josh Erdman	67	8	18	26	107
Wade Gibson	57	10	14	24	142
Marc Vachon	55	2	22	24	84
Todd Dougherty	61	4	12	16	96
Alex Kholomeyev	11	6	6	12	20
Clint Collins	25	6	5	11	212
Scott Lindsay	14	6	1	7	36
Aigars Mironovics	15	3	4	7	19
Chris Morgan	15	1	2	3	32
David Defrancesco	5	1	1	2	5
Derek Puppa (goalie)	55	0	2	2	2
Jon Sikkema (goalie)	12	0	1	1	0
Cedric Billequet	2	0	0	0	0
Matt Stone	2	0	0	0	4
Ryan Esselmont	5	0	0	0	0
Troy Seibel (goalie)	7	0	0	0	0

GOALTENDING

	Games	Min.	W	L	SOL	G	SO	Avg.
Cedric Billequet	2	120	2	0	0	4	0	2.00
Derek Puppa	55	3104	39	11	2	162	1	3.13
Jon Sikkema	12	589	2	6	1	44	0	4.48
Troy Seibel	7	379	4	2	1	32	0	5.06

MACON WHOOPEE

SCORING

	Games	G	A	Pts.	PIM
Jocelyn Langlois	70	38	65	103	34
Steve Suk	63	18	44	62	40
Mark Green	30	21	24	45	6
Todd MacIsaac	60	18	23	41	41
Joe Suk	68	15	26	41	63
Jason Renard	41	15	20	35	376
Corey Isen	52	15	19	34	121
Mike Anastasio	52	16	12	28	45
Carl Menard	43	11	16	27	32
Raymond Delarosbil	69	8	18	26	69
Rob Phillips	34	8	14	22	21
Dave Wilejto	70	8	14	22	117
Chris Brassard	24	6	13	19	64
Jason Price	49	6	13	19	64
Martin Belanger	55	2	17	19	22
Bruno Villeneuve	31	11	6	17	4
Patrice Charbonneau	66	3	14	17	78
Paul Berrington	22	4	12	16	13
Dan Carney	17	2	5	7	14
Per Schlyter	15	2	4	6	12

	Games	G	A	Pts.	PIM
Ryan Schmidt	27	0	6	6	60
Richie Walcott	16	3	0	3	54
Ben Gagnon	13	1	1	2	24
Raitis Ivanans	16	1	1	2	20
Tomas Meixner	8	0	2	2	0
Chris Haskett	3	1	0	1	2
Eoin McInerney (goalie)	2	0	1	1	0
Marc Vachon	7	0	1	1	12
Eric Patry (goalie)	28	0	1	1	24
Pierre Gagnon (goalie)	50	0	1	1	8
Marty Wells	2	0	0	0	2

GOALTENDING

	Games	Min.	W	L	SOL	G	SO	Avg.
Eoin McInerney	2	120	0	1	1	6	0	3.00
Eric Patry	28	1342	11	9	3	70	1	3.13
Pierre Gagnon	50	2735	24	17	4	150	0	3.29

MEMPHIS RIVERKINGS

SCORING

	Games	G	A	Pts.	PIM
Derek Grant	65	45	78	123	45
Denis Lamoureux	69	67	54	121	20
Leonard Bonanno	67	26	53	79	220
Scot Bell	66	15	54	69	83
Randy Stevens	62	30	34	64	90
Kyle Peterson	61	18	30	48	48
Jason Sangiuliano	69	17	28	45	71
Vladimir Rubes	56	24	20	44	34
Nico Pyka	66	9	35	44	149
Ryan Esselmont	48	7	30	37	42
Stas Tkatch	30	12	19	31	24
Kurt Johnston	57	17	12	29	140
Derrek Harper	54	0	14	14	198
Ray DeSouza	12	2	9	11	28
Carl Greenhous	69	3	7	10	159
Bryan Cossette	40	2	8	10	50
Thierry Ryckman	12	5	4	9	31
Dave Lylyk	15	5	3	8	24
Trent Gleason	17	0	5	5	12
Jay Pylypuik	16	2	2	4	20
Sam Fields	21	1	3	4	95
Yanic Sylvester	5	0	3	3	0
Martin Kolesar	8	0	3	3	18
Bob Cancelli	7	1	1	2	8
Rob Friesen (goalie)	48	0	2	2	14
Wesley Neild	4	0	1	1	2
Maurice Hall	5	0	1	1	0
Greg Cherne	7	0	1	1	0
Jason Mucciarone	1	0	0	0	0
Pavel Navrat	1	0	0	0	0
Dana Carnegie (goalie)	2	0	0	0	0
Maxim Priyatel (goalie)	2	0	0	0	0
Paul Shantz	2	0	0	0	4
Benoit Thibert (goalie)	2	0	0	0	0
Frank Marciello	3	0	0	0	0
Anthony Segala	3	0	0	0	0
Darren Thomas (goalie)	3	0	0	0	0
Brian Renfrew (goalie)	20	0	0	0	4

GOALTENDING

	Games	Min.	W	L	SOL	G	SO	Avg.
Brian Renfrew	20	1140	12	3	3	64	0	3.37
Darren Thomas	3	93	1	1	0	6	1	3.89
Rob Friesen	48	2692	23	18	4	191	0	4.26
Maxim Priyatel	2	80	0	1	0	9	0	6.75
Dana Carnegie	2	99	0	2	0	12	0	7.29
Benoit Thibert	2	91	0	2	0	14	0	9.21

OKLAHOMA CITY BLAZERS

SCORING

	Games	G	A	Pts.	PIM
Joe Burton	69	73	37	110	41
Hardy Sauter	70	20	80	100	56
Corey MacIntyre	56	22	60	82	86
Steve Moore	53	30	41	71	136
Brad Preston	70	18	36	54	56
Tom Gomes	70	18	31	49	112
Jim Jensen	66	23	25	48	147
Simon Olivier	51	14	34	48	153
Mike Pozzo	60	21	25	46	26
Peter Arvanitis	58	13	20	33	280
Dominic Fafard	67	3	26	29	86
Jasen Rintala	45	13	14	27	78
Chris Johnston	15	9	10	19	20
Rod Butler	25	7	9	16	40
Sean McKegney	28	6	8	14	46
Sheldon Flaman	56	2	12	14	91
Dan Fournel	30	8	4	12	176
Chris Duncan	26	1	11	12	40
Qamil Elezi	41	4	7	11	188
Craig Johnson	9	3	7	10	63
Cam Severson	5	6	3	9	4
Troy MacCormick	16	2	6	8	20
Daniel Larin	7	0	4	4	34
Mike Tobin	10	1	2	3	53
Craig Willard	14	1	2	3	48
Dave Lylyk	8	0	2	2	8
Travis Riggin	8	0	1	1	30
Mike Williams (goalie)	23	0	1	1	6
Charlie Lawson	1	0	0	0	0
Brian Elder (goalie)	6	0	0	0	17
Jean-Ian Filiatrault (goalie)	43	0	0	0	23

GOALTENDING

	Games	Min.	W	L	SOL	G	SO	Avg.
Jean-Ian Filiatrault	43	2532	30	12	1	107	6	2.54
Brian Elder	6	317	5	0	0	16	0	3.03
Mike Williams	23	1335	14	7	1	72	1	3.24
Hardy Sauter	1	4	0	0	0	1	0	15.86

SAN ANTONIO IGUANAS

SCORING

	Games	G	A	Pts.	PIM
Johnny Brdarovic	68	56	59	115	38
Paul Jackson	62	41	62	103	239
Brian Shantz	69	26	63	89	48
Dave Doucette	58	11	59	70	110
Ricky Jacob	66	27	30	57	47
Kevin Lune	42	14	27	41	84
Jason McIntyre	62	6	28	34	223
Blair Rota	70	16	16	32	82
Cheyne Lazar	62	17	14	31	21
Pat Caron	33	17	10	27	95
Scott Green	21	8	16	24	8
Mike Tobin	51	5	16	21	186
Gatis Tseplis	18	5	14	19	18
Trevor Matschke	69	5	13	18	58
Fred Goltz	22	7	8	15	31
Mike Legg	10	5	7	12	11
Roy Gray	34	0	10	10	37
Warren Sachs	14	3	5	8	14
Marc LaForge	58	0	8	8	302
Steve Wagg	26	4	3	7	10
Mike Loach	13	2	5	7	34
Don McGrath	24	2	4	6	225
Jay Pylypuik	17	1	4	5	4
Rhett Trombley	4	0	5	5	44
Nicholas Ouimet	15	3	1	4	29
Ken Shepard (goalie)	31	0	2	2	38
Levi Clegg	1	0	1	1	0
Jason DesJardins (goalie)	1	0	0	0	0
Tony Deynzer	1	0	0	0	0
Dave Dow	1	0	0	0	0
Trevor Converse	3	0	0	0	28
Andy Meth	3	0	0	0	2
Philippe DeRouville (goalie)	5	0	0	0	0
Scott Usmail	5	0	0	0	0
Paul Taylor (goalie)	19	0	0	0	24
John Hultberg (goalie)	22	0	0	0	4

GOALTENDING

	Games	Min.	W	L	SOL	G	SO	Avg.
Ken Shepard	31	1778	16	11	2	108	1	3.64
Paul Taylor	19	1019	9	5	2	66	0	3.89
Philippe DeRouville	5	201	3	2	0	13	0	3.89
John Hultberg	22	1112	9	7	3	79	0	4.26
Dave Dow	1	20	0	0	0	2	0	6.00
Jason DesJardins	1	36	0	1	0	6	0	10.00

TOPEKA SCARECROWS

SCORING

	Games	G	A	Pts.	PIM
Brett Seguin	70	24	56	80	48
Joe Coombs	47	19	19	38	49
Oleg Tsirkounov	44	19	17	36	61
Troy Frederick	64	19	17	36	87
Ryan Phillips	49	9	19	28	40
Mike Rusk	62	4	23	27	87
Jordon Shields	44	14	11	25	16
Stephane Desjardins	60	5	20	25	123
Sergei Olympiev	43	10	9	19	45
Thomas Stewart	26	12	6	18	50
Jan Melichar	43	2	14	16	28
Travis Riggin	32	9	6	15	17
Trevor Hanas	29	3	11	14	60
Shawn Randall	47	5	7	12	136
Chris Belanger	10	3	6	9	27
Kyle Haviland	63	5	3	8	147
Joey Beaudry	38	3	4	7	115
Paul Godfrey	10	2	5	7	6
Dave Gregory	23	2	4	6	39
Chris Bowen	47	3	2	5	96
Kevin Lune	21	2	3	5	75
Scott Dickson	30	2	3	5	48
Alex Motley	19	1	2	3	25
Chad Antonishyn	47	0	3	3	89
Marco Emond (goalie)	5	0	2	2	0
Michal Podolka (goalie)	22	0	2	2	4
Zybnek Neckar	13	1	0	1	8
Rod Branch (goalie)	37	0	1	1	10
Chris King (goalie)	1	0	0	0	0
Travis Sinden (goalie)	1	0	0	0	0
Mike Migen	2	0	0	0	0
Virgil Rutili	2	0	0	0	0
Steve Adams	3	0	0	0	10
Ken Eddy	3	0	0	0	0
Roy Gray	3	0	0	0	4
Brad Klyn	3	0	0	0	4
Marcus Nilson	3	0	0	0	2
Bob Pardy	8	0	0	0	6
Andy Adams (goalie)	9	0	0	0	2

GOALTENDING

	Games	Min.	W	L	SOL	G	SO	Avg.
Rod Branch	37	2181	20	16	0	101	3	2.78
Michal Podolka	22	1183	7	10	3	76	0	3.85
Andy Adams	9	524	1	8	0	38	0	4.35
Chris King	1	40	0	1	0	3	0	4.50
Marco Emond	5	219	0	2	1	17	0	4.66
Travis Sinden	1	40	0	1	0	5	0	7.50

TULSA OILERS

SCORING

	Games	G	A	Pts.	PIM
Jeff Antonovich	70	40	60	100	66
Chris Smith	66	18	56	74	136
Troy Caley	65	41	29	70	68
Luc Beausoleil	48	29	39	68	30
Francois Leroux	62	23	40	63	64
Mike Berger	69	25	35	60	93
Doug Lawrence	23	6	39	45	159
Clint Black	70	8	33	41	127
Carlos Assayag	63	21	18	39	99
Doug Pirnak	68	11	13	24	254
Troy MacCormick	39	6	15	21	56
Daniel Villeneuve	56	3	16	19	266
Curtis Voth	56	7	4	11	426
Brent Hoiness	16	4	5	9	5
Raitis Ivanans	32	2	7	9	39
Duane Ward	15	2	4	6	2
Mike Loach	9	2	3	5	28
Nolan Weir	12	2	3	5	15
Troy Yarosh	26	1	3	4	53
Ryan Mair	8	1	2	3	6
Ben White	12	1	2	3	18
J.A. Schneider	16	1	2	3	20
Scott Usmail	19	1	2	3	25
Jan Klimes	5	1	1	2	0
Virgil Rutili	8	1	1	2	6
Randy Hankinson	16	1	1	2	6
Jason Desjardins (goalie)	6	0	2	2	10
Paul Van De Perre	2	1	0	1	8
John Rockbrune	18	1	0	1	56
Jean-Franc Bouchard	2	0	1	1	0
Adam Patterson	7	0	1	1	38
Rod Branch (goalie)	11	0	1	1	2
Steph Lefebvre	2	0	0	0	0
Craig Lochhead	2	0	0	0	4
Nicholas Ouimet	2	0	0	0	0
Mark Petercak	3	0	0	0	6
Brian Rasmussen	3	0	0	0	5
Ryan Connolly	5	0	0	0	8
Pascal Gasse (goalie)	19	0	0	0	8
Martin Legault (goalie)	43	0	0	0	4

GOALTENDING

	Games	Min.	W	L	SOL	G	SO	Avg.
Luc Beausoleil	1	14	0	0	0	1	0	4.35
Rod Branch	11	636	2	5	2	48	0	4.53
Martin Legault	43	2369	9	25	6	180	1	4.56
Pascal Gasse	19	864	8	8	1	67	0	4.65
Jason Desjardins	5	296	1	3	0	46	0	9.33

WICHITA THUNDER

SCORING

	Games	G	A	Pts.	PIM
Travis Clayton	69	25	57	82	95
Mark Karpen	69	35	46	81	44
John Kachur	65	32	25	57	60
Todd Howarth	48	23	20	43	86
Jim McGeough	27	18	22	40	24
Jason Duda	34	13	24	37	20
Rhett Dudley	53	8	26	34	149
Chris Dashney	61	5	28	33	94
Sean O'Reilly	67	8	23	31	253
Trevor Folk	64	7	21	28	186
Kevin Powell	34	11	16	27	29
Thomas Migdal	61	15	10	25	51
Aaron Novak	55	9	16	25	86
Nolan Weir	51	10	12	22	101
Walker McDonald	32	8	9	17	86
Mark Macera	52	3	13	16	203
Dan Brown	8	1	7	8	40
Travis Tipler	10	4	3	7	14
Mike Donaghue	25	1	6	7	10
Ron Aubrey	6	3	1	4	33
Jason Modopoulos	30	1	3	4	224
Mike Olaski	3	3	0	3	2
Ryan Phillips	4	2	1	3	0
Jason Neath	11	2	1	3	86
Vern Beardy	25	1	2	3	13
Cory Dosdall	1	2	0	2	0
Trevor Sherban	4	0	2	2	0
Lance Leslie (goalie)	43	0	2	2	14
Geoff Derouin (goalie)	6	0	1	1	2
Jason Fortier	6	0	1	1	21
Pascal Gasse (goalie)	8	0	1	1	0
Brad Bourhis	1	0	0	0	0
Brian Langlot (goalie)	1	0	0	0	0

	Games	G	A	Pts.	PIM
Brad Link (goalie)	1	0	0	0	0
Karl Johnson	3	0	0	0	2
Scott Dickson	6	0	0	0	28
Greg Harvey	6	0	0	0	6
Troy Yarosh	9	0	0	0	23
Greg Smith (goalie)	17	0	0	0	29

GOALTENDING

	Games	Min.	W	L	SOL	G	SO	Avg.
Brad Link	1	31	0	0	0	1	0	1.97
Greg Smith	17	932	9	4	2	53	3	3.41
Lance Leslie	43	2484	21	16	6	143	1	3.45
Pascal Gasse	8	324	2	2	2	20	0	3.70
Geoff Derouin	6	339	2	3	0	26	0	4.60
Brian Langlot	1	55	0	1	0	5	0	5.48

PLAYERS WITH TWO OR MORE TEAMS

SCORING

	Games	G	A	Pts.	PIM
Rod Branch, Tulsa (goalie)	11	0	1	1	2
Rod Branch, Topeka (goalie)	37	0	1	1	10
Totals	48	0	2	2	12
Chris Brassard, Fayetteville	11	1	7	8	11
Chris Brassard, Macon	24	6	13	19	64
Totals	35	7	20	27	75
Dan Brown, Columbus	52	5	39	44	93
Dan Brown, Wichita	8	1	7	8	40
Totals	60	6	46	52	133
Rod Butler, Fayetteville	40	4	12	16	76
Rod Butler, Oklahoma City	25	7	9	16	40
Totals	65	11	21	32	116
Greg Cherne, Fort Worth	21	6	2	8	12
Greg Cherne, Memphis	7	0	1	1	0
Totals	28	6	3	9	12
Ryan Connolly, Tulsa	5	0	0	0	8
Ryan Connolly, Fort Worth	9	2	1	3	39
Totals	14	2	1	3	47
Geoff Derouin, Wichita (g)	6	0	1	1	2
Geoff Derouin, Fayetteville (g)	5	0	0	0	0
Totals	11	0	1	1	2
Jason Desjardins, F.W. (goalie)	8	0	0	0	0
Jason DesJardins, S.A. (g)	1	0	0	0	0
Jason Desjardins, Tulsa (g)	6	0	2	2	10
Totals	14	0	2	2	10
Scott Dickson, Wichita	6	0	0	0	28
Scott Dickson, Topeka	30	2	3	5	48
Totals	36	2	3	5	76
Chris Duncan, Fayetteville	2	0	0	0	6
Chris Duncan, Oklahoma City	26	1	11	12	40
Totals	28	1	11	12	46
Ryan Esselmont, Huntsville	5	0	0	0	0
Ryan Esselmont, Memphis	48	7	30	37	42
Totals	53	7	30	37	42
Sheldon Flaman, Okla. City	56	2	12	14	91
Sheldon Flaman, Fort Worth	7	2	3	5	10
Totals	63	4	15	19	101
Pascal Gasse, Tulsa (goalie)	19	0	0	0	8
Pascal Gasse, Wichita (goalie)	8	0	1	1	0
Totals	27	0	1	1	8
Roy Gray, San Antonio	34	0	10	10	37
Roy Gray, Topeka	3	0	0	0	4
Totals	37	0	10	10	41
Maurice Hall, Fayetteville	1	0	0	0	2
Maurice Hall, Memphis	5	0	1	1	0
Totals	6	0	1	1	2
Raitis Ivanans, Macon	16	1	1	2	20
Raitis Ivanans, Tulsa	32	2	7	9	39
Totals	48	3	8	11	59
Alex Kholomeyev, Fort Worth	45	22	33	55	73
Alex Kholomeyev, Huntsville	11	6	6	12	20
Totals	56	28	39	67	93
Charlie Lawson, Oklahoma City	1	0	0	0	0
Charlie Lawson, Fort Worth	3	0	2	2	2
Totals	4	0	2	2	2
Mike Loach, San Antonio	13	2	5	7	34
Mike Loach, Tulsa	9	2	3	5	28
Totals	22	4	8	12	62
Kevin Lune, Topeka	21	2	3	5	75
Kevin Lune, San Antonio	42	14	27	41	84
Totals	63	16	30	46	159
Dave Lylyk, Memphis	15	5	3	8	24
Dave Lylyk, Oklahoma City	8	0	2	2	8
Dave Lylyk, Fort Worth	21	7	6	13	10
Totals	44	12	11	23	42
Troy MacCormick, Tulsa	39	6	15	21	56
Troy MacCormick, Okla. City	16	2	6	8	20
Troy MacCormick, Fort Worth	10	2	5	7	4
Totals	65	10	26	36	80
Ryan Phillips, Wichita	4	2	1	3	0
Ryan Phillips, Topeka	49	9	19	28	40
Totals	53	11	20	31	40
Jay Pylypuik, San Antonio	17	1	4	5	4
Jay Pylypuik, Memphis	16	2	2	4	20
Totals	33	3	6	9	24
Travis Riggin, Oklahoma City	8	0	1	1	30
Travis Riggin, Columbus	14	5	0	5	8
Travis Riggin, Topeka	32	9	6	15	17
Totals	54	14	7	21	55
Jasen Rintala, Oklahoma City	45	13	14	27	78
Jasen Rintala, Fayetteville	25	5	6	11	26
Totals	70	18	20	38	104
Mike Rusk, Columbus	2	0	0	0	0
Mike Rusk, Topeka	62	4	23	27	87
Totals	64	4	23	27	87
Virgil Rutili, Topeka	2	0	0	0	0
Virgil Rutili, Tulsa	8	1	1	2	6
Totals	10	1	1	2	6
Warren Sachs, San Antonio	14	3	5	8	14
Warren Sachs, Fort Worth	12	3	4	7	0
Totals	26	6	9	15	14
Ryan Schmidt, Macon	27	0	6	6	60
Ryan Schmidt, Fort Worth	7	0	1	1	24
Totals	34	0	7	7	84
J.A. Schneider, Columbus	36	2	3	5	31
J.A. Schneider, Tulsa	16	1	2	3	20
Totals	52	3	5	8	51
Ken Shepard, San Antonio (g)	31	0	2	2	38
Ken Shepard, Fayetteville (g)	16	0	1	1	17
Totals	47	0	3	3	55
Thomas Stewart, Topeka	26	12	6	18	50
Thomas Stewart, Columbus	45	22	30	52	48
Totals	71	34	36	70	98
Mike Tobin, San Antonio	51	5	16	21	186
Mike Tobin, Oklahoma City	10	1	2	3	53
Totals	61	6	18	24	239
Gatis Tseplis, Fort Worth	52	16	37	53	26
Gatis Tseplis, San Antonio	18	5	14	19	18
Totals	70	21	51	72	44
Oleg Tsirkounov, Columbus	20	4	8	12	15
Oleg Tsirkounov, Topeka	44	19	17	36	61
Totals	64	23	25	48	76
Scott Usmail, Tulsa	19	1	2	3	25
Scott Usmail, San Antonio	5	0	0	0	0
Scott Usmail, Fort Worth	7	2	3	5	6
Totals	31	3	5	8	31
Marc Vachon, Huntsville	55	2	22	24	84
Marc Vachon, Macon	7	0	1	1	12
Totals	62	2	23	25	96
Nolan Weir, Wichita	51	412	12	22	101
Nolan Weir, Tulsa	12	359	3	5	15
Totals	63	12	15	27	116
Marty Wells, Macon	2	0	0	0	2
Marty Wells, Fort Worth	10	1	2	3	19
Totals	12	1	2	3	21
Ben White, Fort Worth	39	3	14	17	110
Ben White, Tulsa	12	1	2	3	18
Totals	51	4	16	20	128

	Games	G	A	Pts.	PIM
Craig Willard, Columbus	1	0	0	0	2
Craig Willard, Oklahoma City	14	1	2	3	48
Totals	15	1	2	3	50
Troy Yarosh, Tulsa	26	1	3	4	53
Troy Yarosh, Wichita	9	0	0	0	23
Totals	35	1	3	4	76

GOALTENDING

	Gms.	Min.	W	L	SOL	G	SO	Avg.
Rod Branch, Tul.	11	636	2	5	2	48	0	4.53
Rod Branch, Top.	37	2181	20	16	0	101	3	2.78
Totals	48	2816	22	21	2	149	3	3.17
Geoff Derouin, Wich.	6	339	2	3	0	26	0	4.60
Geoff Derouin, Fay.	5	213	0	3	1	11	0	3.10
Totals	11	552	2	6	1	37	0	4.02
J. Desjardins, F.W.	8	363	3	2	1	32	0	5.29
J. Desjardins, Tul.	5	296	1	3	0	46	0	9.33
Totals	13	659	4	5	1	78	0	7.10
Pascal Gasse, Tul.	19	864	8	8	1	67	0	4.65
Pascal Gasse, Wich.	8	324	2	2	2	20	0	3.70
Totals	27	1189	10	10	3	87	0	4.39

1999 PLAYOFFS

RESULTS

QUARTERFINALS

	W	L	Pts.	GF	GA
Huntsville	3	0	6	14	7
Macon	0	3	0	7	14

(Huntsville won series, 3-0)

	W	L	Pts.	GF	GA
Columbus	3	1	6	19	14
Memphis	1	3	2	14	19

(Columbus won series, 3-1)

	W	L	Pts.	GF	GA
Oklahoma City	3	0	6	14	2
Topeka	0	3	0	2	14

(Oklahoma City won series, 3-0)

	W	L	Pts.	GF	GA
San Antonio	3	1	6	21	12
Wichita	1	3	2	12	21

(San Antonio won series, 3-1)

SEMIFINALS

	W	L	Pts.	GF	GA
Huntsville	4	2	8	25	16
Columbus	2	4	4	16	25

(Huntsville won series, 4-2)

	W	L	Pts.	GF	GA
Oklahoma City	4	0	8	20	12
San Antonio	0	4	0	12	20

(Oklahoma City won series, 4-0)

FINALS

	W	L	Pts.	GF	GA
Huntsville	4	2	8	19	11
Oklahoma City	2	4	4	11	19

(Huntsville won series, 4-2)

INDIVIDUAL LEADERS

Goals: Scott Green, San Antonio (8)
Mike DeGurse, Huntsville (8)
Assists: Jonathan DuBois, Huntsville (16)
Points: Jonathan DuBois, Huntsville (19)
Penalty minutes: Craig Johnson (73)
Goaltending average: Derek Puppa, Huntsville (2.12)
Shutouts: Jean-Ian Filiatrault, Oklahoma City (1)
Derek Puppa, Huntsville (1)

TOP SCORERS

	Games	G	A	Pts.
Jonathan DuBois, Huntsville	15	3	16	19
Igor Bondarev, Huntsville	15	5	11	16
Mick Kempffer, Columbus	10	3	13	16
Mike Martens, Columbus	10	6	9	15
Ken Richardson, Huntsville	15	6	9	15
Hardy Sauter, Oklahoma City	13	5	9	14
Joe Burton, Oklahoma City	11	6	7	13
Jim Jensen, Oklahoma City	13	5	8	13
Scott Green, San Antonio	8	8	4	12
Chris George, Huntsville	15	6	6	12
Johnny Brdarovic, San Antonio	8	4	8	12
Brian Shantz, San Antonio	8	3	9	12

INDIVIDUAL STATISTICS

COLUMBUS COTTONMOUTHS

(Lost semifinals to Huntsville, 4-2)

SCORING

	Games	G	A	Pts.	PIM
Mick Kempffer	10	3	13	16	30
Mike Martens	10	6	9	15	25
Marcel Richard	10	4	6	10	26
Buddy Smith	9	2	6	8	0
Dave Neilson	10	5	1	6	13
Claude Fillion	8	1	5	6	38
Olaf Kjenstad	9	4	1	5	23
Thomas Stewart	8	2	2	4	12
Rich Metro	4	2	1	3	0
Grady Manson	8	2	1	3	6
Jerome Bechard	10	2	1	3	43
Brian Idalski	6	0	3	3	10
Rob Sinclair	9	0	3	3	5
Derek Crimin	9	2	0	2	12
Roman Marakhovski	10	0	2	2	10
Corwin Saurdiff (goalie)	2	0	1	1	0
Brad Prefontaine	8	0	1	1	6
Francis Ouellette (goalie)	10	0	1	1	2
Greg Taylor (goalie)	1	0	0	0	0
Kevin Plager	3	0	0	0	0
Tom Wilson	10	0	0	0	20

GOALTENDING

	Games	Min.	W	L	T	G	SO	Avg.
Greg Taylor	1	20	0	0	0	0	0	0.00
Francis Ouellette	10	503	4	4	0	28	0	3.34
Corwin Saurdiff	2	105	1	1	0	9	0	5.14

HUNTSVILLE CHANNEL CATS

(Winner of 1999 playoffs)

SCORING

	Games	G	A	Pts.	PIM
Jonathan DuBois	15	3	16	19	19
Igor Bondarev	15	5	11	16	12
Ken Richardson	15	6	9	15	44
Chris George	15	6	6	12	6

	Games	G	A	Pts.	PIM
Scott Lindsay	15	5	6	11	16
Alex Kholomeyev	15	6	4	10	30
Tyler Quiring	12	5	5	10	15
Mike DeGurse	14	8	0	8	32
John Gibson	15	2	5	7	33
Aigars Mironovics	15	1	6	7	8
Wade Gibson	15	1	6	7	32
Greg Lakovic	12	2	4	6	48
Phil Daigle	15	2	4	6	31
Joe Murphy	13	1	5	6	20
Ryan Wood	15	4	1	5	6
Josh Erdman	7	1	1	2	4
Derek Puppa (goalie)	15	0	1	1	0
Todd Dougherty	2	0	0	0	0

GOALTENDING

	Games	Min.	W	L	T	G	SO	Avg.
Derek Puppa	15	961	11	4	0	34	1	2.12

MACON WHOOPEE

(Lost quarterfinals to Huntsville, 3-0)

SCORING

	Games	G	A	Pts.	PIM
Corey Isen	3	2	0	2	8
Carl Menard	3	2	0	2	0
Todd MacIsaac	3	2	0	2	0
Steve Suk	3	0	2	2	0
Jocelyn Langlois	3	0	2	2	0
Per Schlyter	3	0	2	2	0
Jason Renard	3	1	0	1	21
Chris Brassard	3	0	1	1	11
Mark Green	3	0	1	1	4
Joe Suk	3	0	1	1	4
Patrice Charbonneau	1	0	0	0	0
Rob Phillips	2	0	0	0	0
Marc Vachon	3	0	0	0	4
Jason Price	3	0	0	0	2
Dave Wilejto	3	0	0	0	2
Raymond Delarosbil	3	0	0	0	0
Pierre Gagnon (goalie)	3	0	0	0	0

GOALTENDING

	Games	Min.	W	L	T	G	SO	Avg.
Pierre Gagnon	3	205	0	3	0	12	0	3.51

MEMPHIS RIVERKINGS

(Lost quarterfinals to Columbus, 3-1)

SCORING

	Games	G	A	Pts.	PIM
Scot Bell	4	3	4	7	12
Denis Lamoureux	4	3	2	5	10
Leonard Bonanno	4	2	3	5	28
Randy Stevens	4	2	2	4	0
Derek Grant	4	0	4	4	8
Stas Tkatch	2	1	2	3	4
Carl Greenhous	4	1	1	2	0
Kyle Peterson	4	0	2	2	8
Nico Pyka	4	1	0	1	16
Kurt Johnston	4	1	0	1	28
Vladimir Rubes	4	0	1	1	2
Ray DeSouza	4	0	1	1	10
Jay Pylypuik	1	0	0	0	0
Derrek Harper	1	0	0	0	28
Ryan Esselmont	3	0	0	0	2
Jason Sangiuliano	4	0	0	0	2
Brian Renfrew (goalie)	4	0	0	0	0

GOALTENDING

	Games	Min.	W	L	T	G	SO	Avg.
Brian Renfrew	4	243	1	3	0	18	0	4.45

OKLAHOMA CITY BLAZERS

(Lost finals to Huntsville, 4-2)

SCORING

	Games	G	A	Pts.	PIM
Hardy Sauter	13	5	9	14	37
Joe Burton	11	6	7	13	2
Jim Jensen	13	5	8	13	24
Chris Johnston	13	6	5	11	49
Steve Moore	10	3	6	9	31
Corey MacIntyre	11	3	5	8	18
Tom Gomes	13	2	6	8	34
Mike Tobin	13	0	6	6	34
Daniel Larin	12	3	2	5	4
Cam Severson	10	4	0	4	26
Peter Arvanitis	10	1	3	4	26
Craig Johnson	10	2	1	3	73
Rod Butler	12	2	1	3	33
Dan Fournel	9	2	0	2	28
Mike Pozzo	5	1	0	1	0
Brad Preston	10	0	1	1	4
Jean-la Filiatrault (goalie)	12	0	1	1	4
Brian Elder (goalie)	1	0	0	0	0
Drew Schoneck	7	0	0	0	7
Dominic Fafard	13	0	0	0	10

GOALTENDING

	Games	Min.	W	L	T	G	SO	Avg.
Brian Elder	1	60	0	1	0	2	0	2.01
Jean-Ian Filiatrault	12	733	9	3	0	30	1	2.45

SAN ANTONIO IGUANAS

(Lost semifinals to Oklahoma City, 4-0)

SCORING

	Games	G	A	Pts.	PIM
Scott Green	8	8	4	12	16
Johnny Brdarovic	8	4	8	12	6
Brian Shantz	8	3	9	12	16
Paul Jackson	8	1	10	11	67
Gatis Tseplis	8	4	5	9	4
Ricky Jacob	8	5	1	6	10
Cheyne Lazar	8	2	3	5	10
Blair Rota	7	3	1	4	12
Scott Wray	8	1	3	4	2
Trevor Matschke	8	0	4	4	2
Jason MacIntyre	8	1	2	3	48
Kevin Lune	8	0	3	3	23
Nicholas Ouimet	8	1	1	2	6
Marc LaForge	7	0	0	0	43
Don McGrath	8	0	0	0	43
Paul Taylor (goalie)	8	0	0	0	14

GOALTENDING

	Games	Min.	W	L	T	G	SO	Avg.
Paul Taylor	8	488	3	5	0	30	0	3.69

TOPEKA SCARECROWS

(Lost quarterfinals to Oklahoma City, 3-0)

SCORING

	Games	G	A	Pts.	PIM
Oleg Tsirkounov	3	1	0	1	9
Troy Frederick	3	1	0	1	0
Brett Seguin	3	0	1	1	8
Sergei Olympiev	3	0	1	1	7
Mike Tilson	1	0	0	0	0
Jordon Shields	2	0	0	0	2
Kyle Haviland	3	0	0	0	30
Zybnek Neckar	3	0	0	0	2
Joey Beaudry	3	0	0	0	14
Shawn Randall	3	0	0	0	17
Joe Coombs	3	0	0	0	6
Mike Rusk	3	0	0	0	8
Jan Melichar	3	0	0	0	2
Chris Bowen	3	0	0	0	0
Stephane Desjardins	3	0	0	0	4
Rod Branch (goalie)	3	0	0	0	0

GOALTENDING

	Games	Min.	W	L	T	G	SO	Avg.
Rod Branch	3	179	0	3	0	14	0	4.70

WICHITA THUNDER

(Lost quarterfinals to San Antonio, 3-1)

SCORING

	Games	G	A	Pts.	PIM
Mark Karpen	4	3	1	4	2
Jim McGeough	4	1	3	4	6

	Games	G	A	Pts.	PIM
Chris Dashney	4	1	2	3	0
Dan Brown	4	0	3	3	2
Rhett Dudley	4	0	3	3	6
Kevin Powell	4	2	0	2	4
John Kachur	4	1	1	2	10
Sean O'Reilly	4	0	2	2	18
Travis Tipler	4	1	0	1	7
Jason Duda	4	1	0	1	2
Walker McDonald	4	1	0	1	2
Travis Clayton	4	1	0	1	8
Thomas Migdal	4	0	1	1	2
Mike Donaghue	4	0	1	1	2
Trevor Folk	1	0	0	0	2
Aaron Novak	1	0	0	0	2
Pascal Gasse (goalie)	2	0	0	0	2
Mark Macera	2	0	0	0	0
Greg Smith (goalie)	3	0	0	0	0

GOALTENDING

	Games	Min.	W	L	T	G	SO	Avg.
Greg Smith	3	165	1	2	0	13	0	4.71
Pascal Gasse	2	82	0	1	0	7	0	5.11

1998-99 AWARD WINNERS

ALL-STAR TEAMS

The Central Hockey League did not name an All-Star team for the 1998-99 season.

TROPHY WINNERS

Most Valuable Player: Derek Puppa, Huntsville
Ken McKenzie Trophy: Derek Grant, Memphis
Goaltender of the Year: Jean-Ian Filiatrault, Oklahoma City
Defenseman of the Year: Igor Bondarev, Huntsville
Rookie of the Year: Johnny Brdarovic, San Antonio
President's Trophy: Derek Puppa, Huntsville
Commissioner's Trophy: Chris Stewart, Huntsville

ALL-TIME AWARD WINNERS

MOST VALUABLE PLAYER

Season Player, Team
1992-93—Sylvain Fleury, Oklahoma City
1993-94—Robert Desjardins, Wichita
1994-95—Paul Jackson, San Antonio
1995-96—Brian Shantz, San Antonio
1996-97—Trevor Jobe, Columbus-Wichita
1997-98—Joe Burton, Oklahoma City
1998-99—Derek Puppa, Huntsville

KEN MCKENZIE TROPHY

(Leading Scorer)

Season Player, Team
1992-93—Sylvain Fleury, Oklahoma City
1993-94—Paul Jackson, Wichita
1994-95—Brian Shantz, San Antonio
1995-96—Brian Shantz, San Antonio
1996-97—Trevor Jobe, Columbus-Wichita
1997-98—Luc Beausoleil, Tulsa
1998-99—Derek Grant, Memphis

GOALTENDER OF THE YEAR

Season Player, Team
1992-93—Tony Martino, Tulsa
1993-94—Alan Perry, Oklahoma City
1994-95—Alan Perry, Oklahoma City
1995-96—Jean-ian Filiatrault, Oklahoma City
1996-97—Jean-ian Filiatrault, Oklahoma City
1997-98—Brian Elder, Oklahoma City
1998-99—Jean-Ian Filiatrault, Oklahoma City

DEFENSEMAN OF THE YEAR

Season Player, Team
1992-93—Dave Doucette, Dallas
1993-94—Guy Girouard, Oklahoma City
1994-95—Eric Ricard, Fort Worth

Season Player, Team
1995-96—Dan Brown, Memphis
1996-97—Hardy Sauter, Oklahoma City
1997-98—Hardy Sauter, Oklahoma City
1998-99—Igor Bondarev, Huntsville

ROOKIE OF THE YEAR

Season Player, Team
1992-93—Robert Desjardins, Wichita
1993-94—Chad Seibel, Memphis
1994-95—Michel St. Jacques, Oklahoma City
1995-96—Derek Grant, Memphis
1996-97—Cory Dosdall, Wichita
1997-98—David Beauregard, Wichita
1998-99—Johnny Brdarovic, San Antonio

PRESIDENT'S TROPHY

(Playoff MVP)

Season Player, Team
1992-93—Tony Fiore, Tulsa
1993-94—Ron Handy, Wichita
1994-95—Ron Handy, Wichita
1995-96—Jean-ian Filiatrault, Oklahoma City
1996-97—Steve Plouffe, Fort Worth
1997-98—Mike Martens, Columbus
1998-99—Derek Puppa, Huntsville

COMMISSIONER'S TROPHY

(Coach of the year)

Season Coach, Team
1992-93—Garry Unger, Tulsa
1993-94—Doug Shedden, Wichita
1994-95—John Torchetti, San Antonio
1995-96—Doug Sauter, Oklahoma City
1996-97—Bill McDonald, Fort Worth
1997-98—David Lohrei, Nashville
1998-99—Chris Stewart, Huntsville

ALL-TIME LEAGUE CHAMPIONS

	REGULAR-SEASON CHAMPION		PLAYOFF CHAMPION	
Season	Team	Coach	Team	Coach
1992-93—	Oklahoma City Blazers	Michael McEwen	Tulsa Oilers	Garry Unger
1993-94—	Wichita Thunder	Doug Shedden	Wichita Thunder	Doug Shedden
1994-95—	Wichita Thunder	Doug Shedden	Wichita Thunder	Doug Shedden
1995-96—	Oklahoma City Blazers	Doug Sauter	Oklahoma City Blazers	Doug Sauter
1996-97—	Oklahoma City Blazers	Doug Sauter	Fort Worth Fire	Bill McDonald
1997-98—	Columbus Cottonmouths	Bruce Garber	Columbus Cottonmouths	Bruce Garber
1998-99—	Oklahoma City Blazers	Doug Sauter	Huntsville Channel Cats	Chris Stewart

The Central League regular season champion is awarded the Adams Cup. The playoff champion is awarded the William "Bill" Levins Cup.

UNITED HOCKEY LEAGUE

(NOTE: The United Hockey League operated under the name Colonial Hockey League through the 1996-97 season.)

LEAGUE OFFICE

Chief operating officer/commissioner
Richard Brosal
Director of business operations
Ron Caron
Director of hockey administration
Lori Kessel
Director of media relations
Will Wolper
Director of player discipline
Mike Hoberg
Director of officiating
Dave Madsen
Address
1301 Edgewater Point, Suite 301
Lake St. Louis, MO 63367
Phone
314-625-6011
FAX
314-625-2009

TEAMS

ADIRONDACK ICEHAWKS

President
Art Shaver
Head coach
Robbie Nichols
Home ice
Glens Falls Civic Center
Address
1 Civic Center Plaza
Glens Falls, NY 12801
Seating capacity
4,806
Phone
518-926-7825
FAX
518-761-9112

ASHEVILLE SMOKE

President and general manager
Dan Wilhelm
Head coach
Keith Gretzky
Home ice
Asheville Civic Center
Address
87 Haywood Street
Asheville, NC 28801
Seating capacity
6,434
Phone
828-252-7825
FAX
828-252-8756

B.C. ICEMEN

General manager
Patrick Snyder
Head coach
Brad Jones
Home ice
Broome County Veterans Memorial
Address
One Stuart Street
Binghamton, NY 13901
Seating capacity
4,680
Phone
607-772-9300
FAX
607-772-0707

FLINT GENERALS

General manager
To be announced
Head coach
To be announced
Home ice
IMA Sports Arena
Address
3501 Lapeer Road
Flint, MI 48503
Seating capacity
4,021
Phone
810-742-9422
FAX
810-742-5892

FORT WAYNE KOMETS

General manager
David Franke
Head coach
To be announced
Home ice
Allen County War Memorial
Address
1010 Memorial Way, Suite 100
Fort Wayne, IN 46805
Seating capacity
8,003
Phone
219-483-0011
FAX
219-483-3899

KNOXVILLE SPEED

President
Andy Wilhelm
Head coach
Terry Ruskowski
Home ice
Knoxville Civic Coliseum
Address
500 East Church Street
Knoxville, TN 37915
Seating capacity
5,000
Phone
423-521-9991
FAX
423-524-2639

MADISON PRO HOCKEY

General manager
Leo Hunstiger
Head coach
Kent Hawley
Home ice
Dane County Coliseum
Address
1881 Expo Mall East
Madison, WI 53713
Seating capacity
8,500
Phone
608-250-2611
FAX
608-250-2614

MISSOURI RIVER OTTERS

General manager
Matt McSparin
Head coach
Mark Reeds
Home ice
SSM Healthcare Arena
Address
324 Main Street
St. Charles, MO 63301
Seating capacity
10,000
Phone
314-946-0003
FAX
314-946-3844

MOHAWK VALLEY PROWLERS

General manager and head coach
Dave Schultz
Home ice
Utica Memorial Auditorium
Address
400 West Oriskany Street
Utica, NY 13502
Seating capacity
3,992
Phone
315-733-0100
FAX
315-733-8154

MUSKEGON FURY

General manager
Tony Lisman
Head coach
Rich Kromm
Home ice
L.C. Walker Arena
Address
470 West Western Avenue
Muskegon, MI 49440
Seating capacity
5,100
Phone
616-726-3879
FAX
616-728-0428

PORT HURON BORDER CATS

General manager and head coach
Greg Puhalski
Home ice
McMorran Arena
Address
215 Huron Avenue
Port Huron, MI 48060
Seating capacity
3,300
Phone
810-982-2287
FAX
810-982-9838

QUAD CITY MALLARDS

General manager
Mark Mead
Head coach
Matt Shaw
Home ice
The MARK of the Quad Cities
Address
1509 Third Avenue A
Moline, IL 61265
Seating capacity
9,237
Phone
309-764-7825
FAX
309-764-7858

ROCKFORD ICEHOGS

General manager
Kevin Cummings
Head coach
To be announced
Home ice
Rockford Metro Centre
Address
P.O. Box 5984
Rockford, IL 61125-0984
Seating capacity
7,600
Phone
807-623-7121
FAX
807-622-3306

SAGINAW GEARS

General manager
Brian Dobbin
Head coach
Robert Dirk
Home ice
Wendler Arena
Address
3030 Johnson Street, Suite 105
Saginaw, MI 48607
Seating capacity
4,727
Phone
517-753-4801
FAX
517-753-4907

1998-99 REGULAR SEASON

FINAL STANDINGS

CENTRAL DIVISION

Team	G	W	L	SOL	Pts.	GF	GA
Muskegon	74	50	18	6	106	304	208
Port Huron	74	41	26	7	89	261	239
Flint	74	37	32	5	79	318	299
Saginaw	74	20	46	8	48	212	332

EASTERN DIVISION

Team	G	W	L	SOL	Pts.	GF	GA
Binghamton	74	39	30	5	83	280	238
Asheville	74	36	35	3	75	292	331
Winston-Salem	74	31	40	3	65	245	311
Mohawk Valley	74	27	39	8	62	214	300

WESTERN DIVISION

Team	G	W	L	SOL	Pts.	GF	GA
Quad City	74	50	19	5	105	364	253
Thunder Bay	74	47	20	7	101	325	247
Madison	74	29	40	5	63	237	294

INDIVIDUAL LEADERS

Goals: Wayne Strachan, Thunder Bay (57)
Assists: Jason Firth, Thunder Bay (91)
Points: Jason Firth, Thunder Bay (141)
Penalty minutes: Pete Vandermeer, Binghamton (390)
Goaltending average: Joe Dimaline, Muskegon (2.36)
Shutouts: Joe Dimaline, Muskegon (4)
Jon Hillebrandt, Port Huron (4)

TOP SCORERS

	Games	G	A	Pts.
Jason Firth, Thunder Bay	73	50	91	141
Wayne Strachan, Thunder Bay	72	57	71	128
Ross Wilson, Flint	74	43	66	109
Brian Sakic, Flint	71	36	72	108
Paul Polillo, Port Huron	73	28	79	107
Sergei Kharin, Muskegon	70	37	63	100
Lindsay Vallis, Asheville	66	27	73	100
Glenn Stewart, Quad City	56	50	49	99
Jason Glover, Flint	66	48	48	96
Brant Blackned, Thunder Bay	70	41	55	96
Shawn Ulrich, Asheville	67	39	57	96
Dion Delmonte, Madison	72	40	53	93
Mike Melas, Quad City	67	40	52	92
Paul Willett, Muskegon	62	24	68	92
Alexei Deev, Winston-Salem	74	35	49	84
Jeff Azar, Winston-Salem	71	38	45	83
Robin Bouchard, Muskegon	70	48	34	82
Greg Pajor, Binghamton	74	40	42	82
David Beauregard, Flint	69	52	29	81
Scott Burfoot, Quad City	58	18	61	79

INDIVIDUAL STATISTICS

ASHEVILLE SMOKE

SCORING

	Games	G	A	Pts.	PIM
Lindsay Vallis	66	27	73	100	46
Shawn Ulrich	67	39	57	96	71
Brent Gretzky	32	28	42	70	29
Rob Milliken	61	15	38	53	119
Jim McGroarty	61	13	34	47	36
Fredrik Svensson	68	19	19	38	69
Wade Welte	67	18	20	38	258
Frank DeFrenza	36	19	16	35	30
Andrew Luciuk	38	16	16	32	31
Jon Pirrong	70	13	16	29	97
Chris Newans	21	6	19	25	81
Jason Dexter	26	12	11	23	12
Jeff Jubenville	34	12	9	21	26
Dan Davies	63	11	7	18	95
Lubos Krajcovic	54	6	11	17	24
Askhat Rakhmatulin	31	6	10	16	23
Dale Greenwood	9	6	6	12	15
Bob Brandon	15	4	8	12	25

	Games	G	A	Pts.	PIM
Kris Schultz	70	5	5	10	281
Jeff Foster	33	2	8	10	22
Joakim Wassberger	9	1	5	6	2
Chris Torkoff	24	1	4	5	59
Jeff Smith	21	2	2	4	46
Myles Zomok	62	2	2	4	53
Gairin Smith	4	1	2	3	9
William Laird	11	2	0	2	24
Andy Johnson	1	1	1	2	0
Eric Kelly	8	1	1	2	27
Marc Salsman	14	0	2	2	41
Per Schlyter	9	0	2	2	6
Joey Centrella	2	0	1	1	6
Robert Ferm	1	0	1	1	0
Danny Laviolette (goalie)	45	0	1	1	22
Jason Lehman	9	0	1	1	4
Kurt Roberts	3	0	1	1	0
Lee Schill (goalie)	34	0	1	1	8
Josh Tymchak	11	0	1	1	35
Chris Simms	1	0	0	0	0
Mark Howell	2	0	0	0	0
Chris King (goalie)	2	0	0	0	0
Dave MacLean	2	0	0	0	0
Troy Christensen	4	0	0	0	4
Darren Guidinger	5	0	0	0	2
Grant Gessell	9	0	0	0	9
Ron Paleczny	9	0	0	0	8

GOALTENDING

	Gms.	Min.	W	L	T	G	SO	Avg.
Danny Laviolette	44	2434	23	17	2	170	0	4.19
Lee Schill	34	1919	13	16	1	140	0	4.38
Chris King	2	68	0	2	0	8	0	7.02

B.C. ICEMEN

SCORING

	Games	G	A	Pts.	PIM
Greg Pajor	74	40	42	82	52
Patrice Robitaille	71	18	57	75	38
Chris Grenville	74	37	34	71	105
Derek Knorr	63	31	33	64	142
Mark Dutiaume	67	27	35	62	43
Yevgeny Shaldybin	61	14	38	52	38
Jamie Bird	71	6	45	51	45
Justin Plamondon	72	16	32	48	40
Pete Vandermeer	62	15	21	36	390
Peter Cermak	67	16	15	31	20
Justin Kearns	65	16	13	29	57
Scott Ricci	57	6	20	26	70
Derek Wood	18	12	10	22	29
Jarno Mensonen	49	3	8	11	8
Mike O'Grady	21	5	5	10	47
Igor Yefimov	25	5	3	8	21
Doug Johnson	69	1	6	7	114
Ales Dvorak	58	1	5	6	34
Eric Kelly	28	2	2	4	36
Ben White	12	1	2	3	11
Shane Kenny	7	1	1	2	4
Jack Greig	15	0	2	2	51
Olie Sundstrom (goalie)	19	0	2	2	21
Chris Kavanagh	34	1	0	1	34
Dieter Kochan (goalie)	40	1	0	1	4
Dimitry Deryabin	12	0	1	1	10
Jim Dinneen (goalie)	2	0	0	0	0
Scott Souffel	2	0	0	0	0
Dallas Mann	3	0	0	0	7
Shane Dow	12	0	0	0	6
Jon Hillebrandt (goalie)	17	0	0	0	6

GOALTENDING

	Gms.	Min.	W	L	T	G	SO	Avg.
Dieter Kochan	40	2322	18	16	5	115	2	2.97
Olie Sundstrom	19	1133	13	6	0	56	0	2.97
Jon Hillebrandt	17	902	8	7	0	53	1	3.53
Jim Dinneen	2	63	0	1	0	5	0	4.75

FLINT GENERALS

SCORING

	Games	G	A	Pts.	PIM
Ross Wilson	74	43	66	109	36
Brian Sakic	71	36	72	108	10
Jason Glover	66	48	48	96	91
Stephan Brochu	58	12	55	67	39
Nick Forbes	61	20	26	46	173
Peter Ambroziak	40	19	27	46	90
Kahlil Thomas	35	19	20	39	26
Chad Grills	42	10	26	36	105
Lorne Knauft	54	9	25	34	143
Luch Nasato	21	7	27	34	97
Mikhail Nemirovsky	40	17	16	33	28
Corey Ignas	54	12	17	29	38
Mike Bondy	46	6	22	28	68
David Beauregard	18	18	8	26	10
Don MacPherson	35	10	13	23	57
Jan Klimes	19	9	9	18	16
Brett MacDonald	23	2	9	11	16
Craig O'Brien	19	5	2	7	27
Bobby Reynolds	4	4	2	6	0
Randy Hankinson	36	0	6	6	35
Rob Laurie (goalie)	66	0	6	6	22
Tom Moulton	30	0	6	6	31
Jeff Whittle	5	1	4	5	54
Rob Fitzgerald	14	2	2	4	6
Trevor Bremner	29	0	4	4	80
Mark Collicutt	33	0	4	4	141
Jason Payne	44	2	1	3	149
Jason Desloover	24	1	2	3	19
Jeff Smith	15	1	2	3	4
Mark Vilneff	13	1	2	3	25
Chris Newans	7	0	3	3	22
Steve Beadle	6	1	1	2	0
Geordie Hyland	26	1	1	2	44
Jean-Yves Dube (goalie)	12	0	1	1	0
Paul Godfrey	3	0	1	1	0
Jeremy Sladovnik	6	0	1	1	34
Duane Ward	6	0	1	1	15
Igor Yankovitch	7	0	1	1	40
Andrej Blasko	5	0	0	0	2
Chuck Carvey	2	0	0	0	0
Troy Glover	3	0	0	0	2
Andrei Grechushkin	5	0	0	0	5
Daryl Lavoie	1	0	0	0	5
Ryan Miles (goalie)	1	0	0	0	0
Darcy Pengelly	2	0	0	0	4
Mark Robinson	3	0	0	0	9
Geoff Sarjeant (goalie)	3	0	0	0	2
Jamie Weatherston	3	0	0	0	0
Libor Scindl	4	0	0	0	2
Nick Ross	5	0	0	0	0
Pat Parthenais	6	0	0	0	4
Dan McIntyre (goalie)	7	0	0	0	0
Wes Neild	7	0	0	0	2

GOALTENDING

	Gms.	Min.	W	L	T	G	SO	Avg.
Ryan Miles	1	29	0	0	0	1	0	2.04
Dan McIntyre	7	213	2	1	0	13	0	3.67
Geoff Sarjeant	3	179	0	2	1	11	0	3.69
Rob Laurie	66	3750	35	27	4	239	1	3.82
Jean-Yves Dube	12	260	0	2	0	25	0	5.77

MADISON MONSTERS

SCORING

	Games	G	A	Pts.	PIM
Dion Delmonte	72	40	53	93	86
Brian Downey	63	23	49	72	41
Jim Duhart	72	40	28	68	218
Matt Loen	47	26	35	61	30
Ryan Aikia	64	5	43	48	141
Andy Faulkner	74	23	24	47	30

	Games	G	A	Pts.	PIM
Jamie Dabanovich	74	10	37	47	48
Jason Dexter	37	13	24	37	4
Mike Maurice	20	13	13	26	6
Luke Strand	74	4	17	21	130
Jason Disher	51	6	9	15	158
Derek Beuselink	74	3	9	12	129
Kelly Stephens	67	6	4	10	92
Jarno Mensonen	18	3	6	9	4
Chris Newans	18	2	7	9	27
Jeff Foster	25	3	5	8	24
Daniel Ruoho	25	3	5	8	30
Ben Gorwich	13	1	5	6	2
Chris Torkoff	9	2	3	5	18
Brian Hill	15	0	5	5	10
Dan Myre	9	0	4	4	2
Brian Wilson	2	3	0	3	0
Cory Holland	48	1	1	2	143
Trevor Bremner	18	0	2	2	48
Joel Gardner	4	0	2	2	0
Ben Verhaagh	39	0	2	2	19
Sean Freeman	11	1	0	1	8
Doug Altschul	4	0	1	1	9
David Fletcher (goalie)	36	0	1	1	11
Myles Zomok	3	0	1	1	5
Chris Clancy	1	0	0	0	0
Kevin Fricke	1	0	0	0	0
Dan Gardner	1	0	0	0	0
Dave Gregory	1	0	0	0	0
Troy Walczak	2	0	0	0	0
Kurt Semandel	3	0	0	0	0
Shane Googins	4	0	0	0	0
Chris Olsen	4	0	0	0	0
Jeff Smith	4	0	0	0	4
Erik Zachrisson	4	0	0	0	0
Brad Michalski	9	0	0	0	11
Darryl Gilmour (goalie)	43	0	0	0	4

GOALTENDING

	Gms.	Min.	W	L	T	G	SO	Avg.
David Fletcher	36	2001	13	16	3	118	2	3.54
Darryl Gilmour	43	2424	16	24	2	164	1	4.06

MOHAWK VALLEY PROWLERS

SCORING

	Games	G	A	Pts.	PIM
Joel Gardner	44	15	35	50	16
Mark Yannetti	66	7	39	46	15
Tim Harris	71	18	27	45	60
David Evans	72	19	25	44	72
Mark Bultje	39	17	25	42	47
Andre Payette	51	9	21	30	241
Dominic Chiasson	23	15	8	23	6
Sandy MacKenzie	49	15	8	23	46
Robert Ferraris	74	3	19	22	139
Jason Taylor	36	5	15	20	24
Chris Palmer	13	11	7	18	18
Daniel Larin	21	10	7	17	6
Mark Kotary	37	10	6	16	21
Jason Dexter	12	7	7	14	2
Libor Svindl	43	3	10	13	31
Martin Cerven	16	4	8	12	20
Serge Roberge	61	7	4	11	268
Ryan Mair	26	6	3	9	33
Jeremy Baker	22	5	4	9	10
Paul Constantin	18	4	5	9	0
Daniel Leckelt	73	0	9	9	141
Greg Bailey	44	0	8	8	123
Brian Rasmussen	17	0	8	8	35
Mike Hiebert	33	2	5	7	114
Dmitri Emilyantsev	9	3	2	5	2
Shawn Evans	11	0	5	5	20
Eric Hallman	15	2	2	4	25
Marty Wells	5	2	1	3	2
Sean Freeman	11	1	2	3	4
Philip Tremblay	4	1	2	3	0
Eric Kelly	8	0	3	3	8
Dan Wildfong	4	0	3	3	2
Ken Blum	11	2	0	2	6
Kris Kavanaugh	12	0	2	2	21
Radim Haupt	6	1	0	1	15
Derek Prue	2	1	0	1	0
Thierry Ryckman	12	1	0	1	22
Josh Tymchak	12	1	0	1	36
Kevin Westlake	2	1	0	1	0
Mark Petercak	2	0	1	1	2
Peter Romeo	4	0	1	1	2
Doug Reynolds	12	0	1	1	2
Ryan Caley (goalie)	19	0	1	1	7
Patrick Charbonneau (goalie)	54	0	1	1	41
Dan Colacito	1	0	0	0	0
Steve Adams	2	0	0	0	29
Jayme Adduono	2	0	0	0	2
John Cherubini	2	0	0	0	0
Dennis Dunphy	2	0	0	0	2
John Herrick (goalie)	2	0	0	0	0
Chris King (goalie)	2	0	0	0	0
Geoff Kufta	2	0	0	0	0
Kurt Roberts	2	0	0	0	0
Sergei Stakhovich	2	0	0	0	2
Ryan Connolly	3	0	0	0	7
John Finstrom	3	0	0	0	2
Tony Frenette	3	0	0	0	0
Jason Mucciarone	3	0	0	0	4
Bartek Wrobel	3	0	0	0	4
Chad Ford (goalie)	4	0	0	0	8
Chris Bernard (goalie)	6	0	0	0	0
Craig Perrett	6	0	0	0	5
Scott Usmail	9	0	0	0	17

GOALTENDING

	Gms.	Min.	W	L	T	G	SO	Avg.
Ryan Caley	19	1046	7	8	3	63	0	3.32
P. Charbonneau	54	2881	19	26	5	173	2	3.60
Chad Ford	4	168	1	2	0	12	0	4.29
John Herrick	2	65	0	1	0	5	0	4.60
Chris King	2	31	0	0	0	3	0	5.81
Chris Bernard	6	232	0	2	0	27	0	6.99

MUSKEGON FURY

SCORING

	Games	G	A	Pts.	PIM
Sergei Kharin	70	37	63	100	77
Paul Willett	62	24	68	92	37
Robin Bouchard	70	48	34	82	148
Andrei Petrunin	63	37	37	74	63
John Vary	62	14	47	61	75
Vadim Podrezov	69	8	53	61	78
David Beauregard	51	34	21	55	30
Denis Afinogenov	30	15	13	28	12
Cory Banika	50	11	17	28	184
Frankie Nault	73	11	16	27	62
Joakim Wassberger	50	8	18	26	18
Igor Malykhin	29	5	17	22	29
Chad Grills	23	12	8	20	68
Scott Feasby	60	3	16	19	117
Jan Klimes	39	8	10	18	8
Rob Melanson	69	0	13	13	251
Mark Vilneff	37	0	11	11	45
Chris Maillett	67	5	5	10	174
Joel Gardner	7	0	10	10	0
Mike Feasby	49	0	8	8	80
Andrei Petrakov	5	4	3	7	0
Lubos Krajcovic	16	2	3	5	10
Don McSween	7	1	4	5	4
Jason Pain	18	3	1	4	6
Duke Bouskill	40	2	2	4	28

	Games	G	A	Pts.	PIM
Kevin Boyd	7	1	3	4	17
Grant Richison	2	1	0	1	2
Bob Brandon	7	0	1	1	17
Denis Khlopotnov (goalie)	38	0	1	1	0
Nick Foley	1	0	0	0	0
Dale Gignac	1	0	0	0	0
Mike Masini	4	0	0	0	0
Dmitri Emilyantsev	5	0	0	0	2
Joe Dimaline (goalie)	44	0	0	0	2

GOALTENDING

	Gms.	Min.	W	L	T	G	SO	Avg.
Joe Dimaline	44	2412	29	9	4	95	4	2.36
Denis Khlopotnov	37	1950	21	8	2	98	1	3.02
Nick Foley	1	60	0	1	0	4	0	4.00

PORT HURON BORDER CATS

SCORING

	Games	G	A	Pts.	PIM
Paul Polillo	73	28	79	107	14
Chris Bergeron	53	26	43	69	18
Bob McKillop	58	34	30	64	10
Kevin Brown	45	23	20	43	36
Adam Robbins	70	16	25	41	85
Wayne Muir	47	16	22	38	83
Kraig Nienhuis	29	15	22	37	12
Bernie John	70	7	29	36	12
Bruce Watson	66	12	15	27	136
Kevin Boyd	49	10	15	25	67
Nikolai Syrtsov	58	7	18	25	69
Jeff Blum	71	6	18	24	79
Brian Dobbin	21	10	13	23	16
Lee Cole	68	4	18	22	246
Mike O'Grady	46	8	7	15	86
Chad Dameworth	32	6	7	13	31
Mark Kotary	17	5	7	12	12
Paul Rosebush	7	4	4	8	0
Curtis Sayler	66	4	4	8	201
Fedor Fedorov	42	2	5	7	20
Brian Mueller	7	0	7	7	10
Jeff Winter	13	0	6	6	2
Rob Fitzgerald	13	3	2	5	6
Andrei Srubko	22	2	2	4	78
Jim Logan	8	1	2	3	9
Steve Martell	13	2	0	2	6
Bruce Rendall	3	1	1	2	5
Olie Sundstrom (goalie)	33	0	2	2	14
Mike Hiebert	5	0	1	1	23
Denis LeBlanc	2	0	1	1	0
Thomas Makinen	4	0	1	1	0
Eoin McInerney (goalie)	12	0	1	1	4
Jon Hillebrandt (goalie)	17	0	1	1	2
Darrin Fisher	1	0	0	0	0
Mike Dark	2	0	0	0	0
Ryan Caley (goalie)	4	0	0	0	2
Dave Chudomel	4	0	0	0	7
Jason Ricci	6	0	0	0	0
Konstantin Simchuk (goalie)	8	0	0	0	4
Matt Carmichael (goalie)	11	0	0	0	0
Wally Wuttunee	19	0	0	0	8

GOALTENDING

	Gms.	Min.	W	L	T	G	SO	Avg.
Ryan Caley	4	240	3	1	0	8	0	2.00
Konstantin Simchuk	8	405	5	1	1	15	0	2.22
Jon Hillebrandt	17	967	10	5	1	37	3	2.30
Olie Sundstrom	33	1712	17	10	3	85	2	2.98
Eoin McInerney	12	572	4	4	1	41	0	4.30
Matt Carmichael	11	536	2	5	1	41	1	4.59

QUAD CITY MALLARDS

SCORING

	Games	G	A	Pts.	PIM
Glenn Stewart	56	50	49	99	38
Mike Melas	67	40	52	92	111
Scott Burfoot	58	18	61	79	40
Brian LaFleur	61	28	41	69	20
Kevin Kerr	49	32	36	68	108
Mark McFarlane	72	31	25	56	274
Rusty Fitzgerald	53	29	25	54	40
Hugo Proulx	50	19	33	52	60
Carl LeBlanc	66	6	46	52	173
Rick Emmett	55	12	34	46	72
Garry Gulash	56	10	35	45	342
Steve Gibson	33	14	29	43	44
Brendan Brooks	61	18	17	35	67
Bill Weir	63	10	19	29	68
Stephane Madore	57	1	19	20	206
Matt Carey	41	5	9	14	27
Kelly Hultgren	23	5	9	14	14
Howie Rosenblatt	29	6	7	13	119
Mike Gaffney	19	5	7	12	10
Robert Frid	38	1	11	12	201
Bruce Richardson	16	4	7	11	75
Travis Tucker	27	2	8	10	71
Scott Thompson	49	1	8	9	120
Jay Hebert	16	4	3	7	13
Mario Kazda	8	2	0	2	8
Erik Zachrisson	9	2	0	2	6
Martin Hlinka	2	1	1	2	0
Ken Eddy	13	0	2	2	10
Martin Fillion (goalie)	38	0	2	2	42
Dave Bolduc	8	1	0	1	13
Mark Best	1	0	0	0	0
Dustin Kersey	1	0	0	0	0
Sean Flynn	3	0	0	0	0
Carlin Nordstrom	3	0	0	0	4
Chris Torkoff	4	0	0	0	28
Rob Boleski	6	0	0	0	23
Sebastian Charpentier (goalie)	6	0	0	0	0
Sergei Zvyagin (goalie)	20	0	0	0	4
Chad Ford (goalie)	25	0	0	0	37

GOALTENDING

	Gms.	Min.	W	L	T	G	SO	Avg.
Sebasti Charpentier	6	4	0	0	0	0	0	0.00
Sergei Zvyagin	20	1084	11	5	1	57	2	3.15
Martin Fillion	38	2028	21	8	3	114	1	3.37
Chad Ford	25	1316	18	6	1	75	1	3.42

SAGINAW LUMBER KINGS

SCORING

	Games	G	A	Pts.	PIM
Keith Osborne	73	20	49	69	72
Francois Sasseville	70	23	30	53	49
Justin Morrison	59	24	27	51	109
Mark Giannetti	56	22	25	47	24
Dominic Chiasson	49	15	26	41	8
John Evangelista	67	17	21	38	32
Brian Mueller	51	12	20	32	38
Patrick Charbonneau	72	10	17	27	92
John Nelson	34	7	18	25	93
David VanDrunen	63	5	17	22	126
Kevin Tucker	35	7	14	21	0
Jamie Hayden	74	3	14	17	33
Mike Senior	64	11	5	16	30
Peter Romeo	30	3	9	12	41
Mike Pomichter	10	8	2	10	0
Randy Best	28	2	7	9	12
Chris Palmer	6	5	2	7	4
Mike Hiebert	16	2	5	7	64
Doug Reynolds	7	2	5	7	2
Jason Ricci	14	0	7	7	10
Phil Husak	30	2	4	6	25
Marty Wells	11	1	3	4	4
Darryl Sinclair	6	3	0	3	4
John Finstrom	20	1	2	3	21
Joel Gardner	3	0	3	3	2

	Games	G	A	Pts.	PIM
Anthony Segala	28	0	3	3	16
Jack Greig	26	1	1	2	146
Kevin Westlake	4	1	1	2	0
D.J. Conte	35	0	2	2	103
Chad Holloway	8	0	2	2	4
Matt Hoffman	2	0	1	1	7
Joe Smaza	7	0	1	1	2
Dave Gregory	9	0	1	1	8
Rick MacDonald	9	0	1	1	4
Trevor Bremner	10	0	1	1	32
Brian Scott	12	0	1	1	5
Marc Delorme (goalie)	33	0	1	1	14
Kevin Butt (goalie)	1	0	0	0	0
Shawn Grenier (goalie)	1	0	0	0	0
Kevin Hill	1	0	0	0	0
Jean-Yves Dube (goalie)	2	0	0	0	0
Steve Adams	3	0	0	0	14
Mike Alunno	3	0	0	0	0
Jessie Grenier	3	0	0	0	41
Craig Griese	3	0	0	0	0
Todd Chinnick	4	0	0	0	0
Brian Steiner	9	0	1	1	12
Brian Kreft (goalie)	13	0	0	0	2
Avi Karunakar (goalie)	28	0	0	0	8

GOALTENDING

	Gms.	Min.	W	L	T	G	SO	Avg.
Shawn Grenier	1	60	1	0	0	3	0	3.00
Marc Delorme	33	1946	10	19	4	126	1	3.88
Brian Kreft	13	739	2	8	1	55	0	4.47
Avi Karunakar	28	1516	7	17	3	116	1	4.59
Kevin Butt	1	60	0	1	0	5	0	5.00
Jean-Yves Dube	2	109	0	1	0	15	0	8.29

THUNDER BAY THUNDER CATS

SCORING

	Games	G	A	Pts.	PIM
Jason Firth	73	50	91	141	32
Wayne Strachan	72	57	71	128	91
Brant Blackned	70	41	55	96	60
Norm Paquet	74	22	41	63	32
Neal Purdon	58	32	22	54	28
Michael Henderson	57	24	30	54	287
David Mayes	72	10	36	46	68
Derek Landmesser	72	7	36	43	180
Barry McKinlay	34	15	27	42	24
Dan Myre	59	11	19	30	36
Darren Szczygiel	53	8	22	30	63
Allan Roulette	63	11	16	27	53
Nikolai Pronin	41	6	13	19	49
Jason Lehman	59	5	12	17	43
Sean McEachran	66	10	3	13	186
Shawn Smith	46	1	12	13	66
Kevin Holliday	41	2	5	7	352
Jason Payne	17	5	1	6	83
Jeff Smith	17	3	3	6	34
Jason Garatti	10	2	2	4	2
J.F. Rivard (goalie)	55	0	3	3	17
Harkie Singh	6	0	2	2	32
Dave Stewart	6	0	2	2	12
Mark Cupolo	7	0	2	2	2
Jason Disher	7	0	2	2	21
Dan Brenzavich (goalie)	23	0	2	2	2
Grant Gessell	17	0	1	1	15
Brian Walker	2	0	0	0	20
Chad MacLeod (goalie)	3	0	0	0	0
Greg Fullerton	4	0	0	0	10
J.C. Larocque	4	0	0	0	0

GOALTENDING

	Gms.	Min.	W	L	T	G	SO	Avg.
Dan Brenzavich	23	1160	12	5	1	58	1	3.00
J.F. Rivard	55	3159	34	14	6	163	2	3.10
Chad MacLeod	3	111	1	1	0	14	0	7.55

WINSTON-SALEM ICEHAWKS

SCORING

	Games	G	A	Pts.	PIM
Alexei Deev	74	35	49	84	14
Jeff Azar	71	38	45	83	45
Sergei Petrov	66	30	39	69	121
Dmitri Rodine	73	11	44	55	57
Shawn Yakimishyn	65	24	26	50	172
Trent Schachle	74	14	35	49	145
Chris Palmer	23	10	23	33	19
Dean Roach	64	7	19	26	93
Kevin Tucker	35	11	11	22	24
Doug Reynolds	44	7	13	20	12
Mark Bultje	18	6	11	17	14
Chad Holloway	61	1	14	15	47
Bruno Villeneuve	24	7	6	13	2
Bob Brandon	39	7	5	12	72
Chris Torkoff	27	6	6	12	61
Justin Morrison	11	3	9	12	27
Mark Giannetti	10	3	7	10	12
Jason Desloover	41	2	8	10	59
Larry Empey	74	0	8	8	120
Trevor Rapchalk	32	4	3	7	58
Josh Tymchak	46	4	3	7	135
John Nelson	12	2	3	5	67
Jason Currie	14	1	3	4	23
Simon Alary	37	2	1	3	96
Pat Barton	24	1	1	2	42
Tom Moulton	28	1	1	2	51
Ryan Caley (goalie)	14	0	2	2	19
Brian Kreft (goalie)	23	0	2	2	35
Derrick Robson	4	1	0	1	0
Mike Bajurny	6	0	1	1	7
Martin Bradette (goalie)	17	0	1	1	21
Tim Winkleman	8	0	1	1	48
Brian Clark	1	0	0	0	0
Cam Colborne	1	0	0	0	2
Joe Curran	1	0	0	0	0
Clint Lomenda	2	0	0	0	0
Justin Lund	2	0	0	0	0
Ian MacDonald	2	0	0	0	5
Andy Ristau	2	0	0	0	0
Jason White (goalie)	3	0	0	0	2
Darren Srochenski	5	0	0	0	13
Dan Tice	5	0	0	0	45
Robert Cardinal	6	0	0	0	0
Phil Husak	6	0	0	0	2
John Taggert	8	0	0	0	0
Marc Delorme (goalie)	27	0	0	0	8

GOALTENDING

	Gms.	Min.	W	L	T	G	SO	Avg.
Ryan Caley	14	688	4	5	1	41	0	3.58
Marc Delorme	27	1465	12	13	1	98	1	4.01
Brian Kreft	23	1240	9	12	0	84	1	4.07
Martin Bradette	17	864	5	8	1	65	0	4.52
Jason White	3	164	1	2	0	15	0	5.48
John Nelson	1	7	0	0	0	1	0	8.57

PLAYERS WITH TWO OR MORE TEAMS

SCORING

	Games	G	A	Pts.	PIM
Steve Adams, Mohawk Valley	2	0	0	0	29
Steve Adams, Saginaw	3	0	0	0	14
Totals	5	0	0	0	43
David Beauregard, Muskegon	51	34	21	55	30
David Beauregard, Flint	18	18	8	26	10
Totals	69	52	29	81	40
Kevin Boyd, Port Huron	49	10	15	25	67
Kevin Boyd, Muskegon	7	1	3	4	17
Totals	56	11	18	29	84
Bob Brandon, Muskegon	7	0	1	1	17
Bob Brandon, Asheville	15	4	8	12	25

	Games	G	A	Pts.	PIM
Bob Brandon, Winston-Salem	39	7	5	12	72
Totals	61	11	14	25	114
Trevor Bremner, Saginaw	10	0	1	1	32
Trevor Bremner, Madison	18	0	2	2	48
Trevor Bremner, Flint	29	0	4	4	80
Totals	57	0	7	7	160
Mark Bultje, Mohawk Valley	39	17	25	42	47
Mark Bultje, Winston-Salem	18	6	11	17	14
Totals	57	23	36	59	61
Ryan Caley, Port Huron (g)	4	0	0	0	2
Ryan Caley, Mohawk Valley (g)	19	0	1	1	7
Ryan Caley, Winston-Salem (g)	14	0	2	2	19
Totals	37	0	3	3	28
Dominic Chiasson, Saginaw	49	15	26	41	8
Dominic Chiasson, M. Valley	23	15	8	23	6
Totals	72	30	34	64	14
Marc Delorme, Saginaw (g)	33	0	1	1	14
Marc Delorme, W.-Salem (g)	27	0	0	0	8
Totals	60	0	1	1	22
Jason Desloover, W.-Salem	41	2	8	10	59
Jason Desloover, Flint	24	1	2	3	19
Totals	65	3	10	13	78
Jason Dexter, Madison	37	13	24	37	4
Jason Dexter, Asheville	26	12	11	23	12
Jason Dexter, Mohawk Valley	12	7	7	14	2
Totals	75	32	42	74	18
Jason Disher, Madison	51	6	9	15	158
Jason Disher, Thunder Bay	7	0	2	2	21
Totals	58	6	11	17	179
Jean-Yves Dube, Flint (g)	12	0	1	1	0
Jean-Yves Dube, Saginaw (g)	2	0	0	0	0
Totals	14	0	1	1	0
Dmitri Emilyantsev, Muskegon	5	0	0	0	2
Dmitri Emilyantsev, M. Valley	9	3	2	5	2
Totals	14	3	2	5	4
John Finstrom, Mohawk Valley	3	0	0	0	2
John Finstrom, Saginaw	20	1	2	3	21
Totals	23	1	2	3	23
Rob Fitzgerald, Flint	14	2	2	4	6
Rob Fitzgerald, Port Huron	13	3	2	5	6
Totals	27	5	4	9	12
Chad Ford, Quad City (g)	25	0	0	0	37
Chad Ford, Mohawk Valley (g)	4	0	0	0	8
Totals	29	0	0	0	45
Jeff Foster, Madison	25	3	5	8	24
Jeff Foster, Asheville	33	2	8	10	22
Totals	58	5	13	18	46
Sean Freeman, Madison	11	1	0	1	8
Sean Freeman, Mohawk Valley	11	1	2	3	4
Totals	22	2	2	4	12
Joel Gardner, Saginaw	3	0	3	3	2
Joel Gardner, Muskegon	7	0	10	10	0
Joel Gardner, Madison	4	0	2	2	0
Joel Gardner, Mohawk Valley	44	15	35	50	16
Totals	58	15	50	65	18
Grant Gessell, Thunder Bay	17	0	1	1	15
Grant Gessell, Asheville	9	0	0	0	9
Totals	26	0	1	1	24
Mark Giannetti, Saginaw	56	22	25	47	24
Mark Giannetti, W.-Salem	10	3	7	10	12
Totals	66	25	32	57	36
Dave Gregory, Madison	1	0	0	0	0
Dave Gregory, Saginaw	9	0	1	1	8
Totals	10	0	1	1	8
Jack Greig, Saginaw	26	1	1	2	146
Jack Greig, B.C.	15	0	2	2	51
Totals	41	1	3	4	197
Chad Grills, Flint	42	10	26	36	105
Chad Grills, Muskegon	23	12	8	20	68
Totals	65	22	34	56	173
Mike Hiebert, Port Huron	5	0	1	1	23
Mike Hiebert, Mohawk Valley	33	2	5	7	114
Mike Hiebert, Saginaw	16	2	5	7	64

	Games	G	A	Pts.	PIM
Totals	54	4	11	15	201
Jon Hillebrandt, B.C. (g)	17	0	0	0	6
Jon Hillebrandt, Port Huron (g)	17	0	1	1	2
Totals	34	0	1	1	8
Chad Holloway, W.-Salem	61	1	14	15	47
Chad Holloway, Saginaw	8	0	2	2	4
Totals	69	1	16	17	51
Phil Husak, Winston-Salem	6	0	0	0	2
Phil Husak, Saginaw	30	2	4	6	25
Totals	36	2	4	6	27
Eric Kelly, B.C.	28	2	2	4	36
Eric Kelly, Mohawk Valley	8	0	3	3	8
Eric Kelly, Asheville	8	1	1	2	27
Totals	44	3	6	9	71
Chris King, Mohawk Valley (g)	2	0	0	0	0
Chris King, Asheville (g)	2	0	0	0	0
Totals	4	0	0	0	0
Jan Klimes, Muskegon	39	8	10	18	8
Jan Klimes, Flint	19	9	9	18	16
Totals	58	17	19	36	24
Mark Kotary, Mohawk Valley	37	10	6	16	21
Mark Kotary, Port Huron	17	5	7	12	12
Totals	54	15	13	28	33
Lubos Krajcovic, Muskegon	16	2	3	5	10
Lubos Krajcovic, Asheville	54	6	11	17	24
Totals	70	8	14	22	34
Brian Kreft, Winston-Salem (g)	23	0	2	2	35
Brian Kreft, Saginaw (g)	13	0	0	0	2
Totals	36	0	2	2	37
Jason Lehman, Thunder Bay	59	5	12	17	43
Jason Lehman, Asheville	9	0	1	1	4
Totals	68	5	13	18	47
Jarno Mensonen, B.C.	49	3	8	11	8
Jarno Mensonen, Madison	18	3	6	9	4
Totals	67	6	14	20	12
Justin Morrison, Saginaw	59	24	27	51	109
Justin Morrison, W.-Salem	11	3	9	12	27
Totals	70	27	36	63	136
Tom Moulton, Flint	30	0	6	6	31
Tom Moulton, Winston-Salem	28	1	1	2	51
Totals	58	1	7	8	82
Brian Mueller, Saginaw	51	12	20	32	38
Brian Mueller, Port Huron	7	0	7	7	10
Totals	58	12	27	39	48
Dan Myre, Thunder Bay	59	11	19	30	36
Dan Myre, Madison	9	0	4	4	2
Totals	68	11	23	34	38
John Nelson, Winston-Salem	12	2	3	5	67
John Nelson, Saginaw	34	7	18	25	93
Totals	46	9	21	30	160
Chris Newans, Asheville	21	6	19	25	81
Chris Newans, Madison	18	2	7	9	27
Chris Newans, Flint	7	0	3	3	22
Totals	46	8	29	37	130
Mike O'Grady, Port Huron	46	8	7	15	86
Mike O'Grady, B.C.	21	5	5	10	47
Totals	67	13	12	25	133
Chris Palmer, Winston-Salem	23	10	23	33	19
Chris Palmer, Saginaw	6	5	2	7	4
Chris Palmer, Mohawk Valley	13	11	7	18	18
Totals	42	26	32	58	41
Jason Payne, Thunder Bay	17	5	1	6	83
Jason Payne, Flint	44	2	1	3	149
Totals	61	7	2	9	232
Doug Reynolds, W.-Salem	44	7	13	20	12
Doug Reynolds, M. Valley	12	0	1	1	2
Doug Reynolds, Saginaw	7	2	5	7	2
Totals	63	9	19	28	16
Jason Ricci, Port Huron	6	0	0	0	0
Jason Ricci, Saginaw	14	0	7	7	10
Totals	20	0	7	7	10
Kurt Roberts, Asheville	3	0	1	1	0
Kurt Roberts, Mohawk Valley	2	0	0	0	0

	Games	G	A	Pts.	PIM
Totals	5	0	1	1	0
Peter Romeo, Saginaw	30	3	9	12	41
Peter Romeo, Mohawk Valley	4	0	1	1	2
Totals	34	3	10	13	43
Jeff Smith, Thunder Bay	17	3	3	6	34
Jeff Smith, Asheville	21	2	2	4	46
Jeff Smith, Madison	4	0	0	0	4
Jeff Smith, Flint	15	1	2	3	4
Totals	57	6	7	13	88
Olie Sundstrom, P. Huron (g)	33	0	2	2	14
Olie Sundstrom, B.C. (g)	19	0	2	2	21
Totals	52	0	4	4	35
Chris Torkoff, Quad City	4	0	0	0	28
Chris Torkoff, Winston-Salem	27	6	6	12	61
Chris Torkoff, Asheville	24	1	4	5	59
Chris Torkoff, Madison	9	2	3	5	18
Totals	64	9	13	22	166
Kevin Tucker, Winston-Salem	35	11	11	22	24
Kevin Tucker, Saginaw	35	7	14	21	0
Totals	70	18	25	43	24
Josh Tymchak, Winston-Salem	46	4	3	7	135
Josh Tymchak, Mohawk Valley	12	1	0	1	36
Josh Tymchak, Asheville	11	0	1	1	35
Totals	69	5	4	9	206
Mark Vilneff, Muskegon	37	0	11	11	45
Mark Vilneff, Flint	13	1	2	3	25
Totals	50	1	13	14	70
Joakim Wassberger, Asheville	9	1	5	6	2
Joakim Wassberger, Musk.	50	8	18	26	18
Totals	59	9	23	32	20
Marty Wells, Mohawk Valley	5	2	1	3	2
Marty Wells, Saginaw	11	1	3	4	4
Totals	16	3	4	7	6
Kevin Westlake, M. Valley	2	1	0	1	0
Kevin Westlake, Saginaw	4	1	1	2	0
Totals	6	2	1	3	0
Erik Zachrisson, Quad City	9	2	0	2	6
Erik Zachrisson, Madison	4	0	0	0	0
Totals	13	2	0	2	6
Myles Zomok, Madison	3	0	1	1	5
Myles Zomok, Asheville	62	2	2	4	53
Totals	65	2	3	5	58

GOALTENDING

	Gms.	Min.	W	L	T	G	SO	Avg.
Ryan Caley, P.H.	4	240	3	1	0	8	0	2.00
Ryan Caley, M.V.	19	1046	7	8	3	63	0	3.32
Ryan Caley, W.-S.	14	688	4	5	1	41	0	3.58
Totals	37	1973	14	14	4	112	0	3.41
M. Delorme, Sag.	33	1946	10	19	4	126	1	3.88
M. Delorme, W.-S.	27	1465	12	13	1	98	1	4.01
Totals	60	3411	22	32	5	224	2	3.94
J.-Yves Dube, Flint	12	260	0	2	0	25	0	5.77
J.-Yves Dube, Sag.	2	109	0	1	0	15	0	8.29
Totals	14	369	0	3	0	40	0	6.51
Chad Ford, Q.C.	25	1316	18	6	1	75	1	3.42
Chad Ford, M.V.	4	168	1	2	0	12	0	4.29
Totals	29	1484	19	8	1	87	1	3.52
J. Hillebrandt, B.C.	17	902	8	7	0	53	1	3.53
J. Hillebrandt, P.H.	17	967	10	5	1	37	3	2.30
Totals	34	1868	18	12	1	90	4	2.89
Chris King, M.V.	2	31	0	0	0	3	0	5.81
Chris King, Ash.	2	68	0	2	0	8	0	7.02
Totals	4	99	0	2	0	11	0	6.71
Brian Kreft, W.-S.	23	1240	9	12	0	84	1	4.07
Brian Kreft, Sag.	13	739	2	8	1	55	0	4.47
Totals	36	1978	11	20	1	139	1	4.22
O. Sundstrom, P.H.	33	1712	17	10	3	85	2	2.98
O. Sundstrom, B.C.	19	1133	13	6	0	56	0	2.97
Totals	52	2845	30	16	3	141	2	2.97

1999 COLONIAL CUP PLAYOFFS

RESULTS

QUARTERFINALS

	W	L	Pts.	GF	GA
Muskegon	4	1	8	25	14
Winston-Salem	1	4	2	14	25

(Muskegon won series, 4-1)

	W	L	Pts.	GF	GA
Quad City	4	0	8	19	7
Asheville	0	4	0	7	19

(Quad City won series, 4-0)

	W	L	Pts.	GF	GA
Flint	4	1	8	19	13
Binghamton	1	4	2	13	19

(Flint won series, 4-1)

	W	L	Pts.	GF	GA
Thunder Bay	4	3	8	16	12
Port Huron	3	4	6	12	16

(Thunder Bay won series, 4-3)

SEMIFINALS

	W	L	Pts.	GF	GA
Quad City	4	2	8	18	17
Thunder Bay	2	4	4	17	18

(Quad City won series, 4-2)

	W	L	Pts.	GF	GA
Muskegon	4	3	8	27	20
Flint	3	4	6	20	27

(Muskegon won series, 4-3)

FINALS

	W	L	Pts.	GF	GA
Muskegon	4	2	8	16	18
Quad City	2	4	4	18	16

(Muskegon won series, 4-2

INDIVIDUAL LEADERS

Goals: Robin Bouchard, Muskegon (13)
Assists: Sergei Kharin, Muskegon (17)
Points: Paul Willett, Muskegon (26)
Penalty minutes: Michael Henderson, Thunder Bay (65)
Goaltending average: J.F. Rivard, Thunder Bay (2.12)
Shutouts: Joe Dimaline, Muskegon (2)
Sergei Zvyagin, Quad City (2)

TOP SCORERS

	Games	G	A	Pts.
Paul Willett, Muskegon	18	11	15	26
Sergei Kharin, Muskegon	18	7	17	24
Robin Bouchard, Muskegon	18	13	9	22
Jason Firth, Thunder Bay	13	6	13	19
Brian Sakic, Flint	12	4	15	19
John Vary, Muskegon	17	6	12	18
Glenn Stewart, Quad City	16	10	7	17
Chad Grills, Muskegon	18	5	11	16
Hugo Proulx, Quad City	16	3	13	16
Scott Burfoot, Quad City	16	4	11	15

INDIVIDUAL STATISTICS

ASHEVILLE SMOKE

(Lost quarterfinals to Quad City, 4-0)

SCORING

	Games	G	A	Pts.	PIM
Lindsay Vallis	4	3	0	3	0
Fredrik Svensson	4	2	0	2	0
Andrew Luciuk	4	1	1	2	6
Lubos Krajcovic	2	0	2	2	0
Rob Milliken	3	0	2	2	4
Jeff Jubenville	4	0	2	2	0
Wade Welte	4	0	2	2	13
Askhat Rakhmatulin	4	1	0	1	0
Jon Pirrong	3	0	1	1	2
Jason Lehman	4	0	1	1	2
Kris Schultz	4	0	1	1	9
Josh Tymchak	4	0	1	1	0
Dan Davies	2	0	0	0	4
Danny Laviolette (goalie)	2	0	0	0	0
Lee Schill (goalie)	2	0	0	0	0
Eric Kelly	3	0	0	0	2
Shawn Ulrich	3	0	0	0	0
Jeff Foster	4	0	0	0	6
Kris Knoblauch	4	0	0	0	5
Jim McGroarty	4	0	0	0	2

GOALTENDING

	Gms.	Min.	W	L	T	G	SO	Avg.
Lee Schill	2	119	0	2	0	8	0	4.04
Danny Laviolette	2	119	0	2	0	9	0	4.54

B.C. ICEMEN

(Lost quarterfinals to Flint, 4-1)

SCORING

	Games	G	A	Pts.	PIM
Chris Grenville	5	2	3	5	4
Derek Knorr	5	2	2	4	8
Pete Vandermeer	5	2	2	4	0
Greg Pajor	5	1	3	4	22
Patrice Robitaille	5	2	1	3	0
Mike O'Grady	4	1	2	3	8
Derek Wood	5	0	3	3	2
Peter Cermak	5	1	1	2	15
Jamie Bird	5	0	2	2	2
Scott Ricci	5	0	2	2	2
Mark Dutiaume	1	1	0	1	0
Doug Johnson	5	1	0	1	4
Justin Kearns	5	0	1	1	6
Ben White	5	0	1	1	2
Olie Sundstrom (goalie)	2	0	0	0	0
Jack Greig	4	0	0	0	0
Dieter Kochan (goalie)	4	0	0	0	2
Ales Dvorak	5	0	0	0	2
Justin Plamondon	5	0	0	0	0

GOALTENDING

	Gms.	Min.	W	L	T	G	SO	Avg.
Dieter Kochan	4	208	1	2	0	9	0	2.60
Olie Sundstrom	2	95	0	2	0	8	0	5.06

FLINT GENERALS

(Lost semifinals to Muskegon, 4-3)

SCORING

	Games	G	A	Pts.	PIM
Brian Sakic	12	4	15	19	2
Ross Wilson	12	11	2	13	14
Jason Glover	11	1	8	9	38
David Beauregard	12	5	3	8	12
Corey Ignas	12	3	3	6	8
Luch Nasato	5	0	6	6	16
Kahlil Thomas	12	5	0	5	6
Nick Forbes	10	2	3	5	4
Don MacPherson	12	2	3	5	11
Chris Newans	4	1	4	5	12
Stephan Brochu	8	1	3	4	8
Brett MacDonald	12	1	3	4	12
Greg Labenski	12	0	4	4	2
Jan Klimes	11	2	1	3	0
Lorne Knauft	10	1	2	3	50
Peter Ambroziak	5	0	2	2	12
Jason Desloover	9	0	2	2	2
Mark Vilneff	11	0	2	2	12
Pat Parthenais	3	0	0	0	0
Dan McIntyre (goalie)	6	0	0	0	0
Jason Payne	7	0	0	0	9
Rob Laurie (goalie)	9	0	0	0	0

GOALTENDING

	Gms.	Min.	W	L	T	G	SO	Avg.
Dan McIntyre	6	325	3	2	0	15	1	2.77
Rob Laurie	9	397	4	3	0	25	0	3.77

MUSKEGON FURY

(Winner of 1999 United Hockey League playoffs)

SCORING

	Games	G	A	Pts.	PIM
Paul Willett	18	11	15	26	22
Sergei Kharin	18	7	17	24	10
Robin Bouchard	18	13	9	22	34
John Vary	17	6	12	18	16
Chad Grills	18	5	11	16	48
Denis Afinogenov	17	7	6	13	10
Vadim Podrezov	18	3	9	12	14
Andrei Petrunin	13	3	8	11	8
Cory Banika	15	3	5	8	58
Joakim Wassberger	13	3	4	7	0
Scott Feasby	17	3	4	7	38
Frankie Nault	18	0	7	7	24
Igor Malykhin	11	0	5	5	4
Don McSween	8	2	2	4	10
Chris Neil	18	1	3	4	61
Kevin Boyd	9	1	0	1	29
Rob Melanson	18	0	1	1	46
Duke Bouskill	2	0	0	0	0
Mike Feasby	2	0	0	0	4
Denis Khlopotnov (goalie)	4	0	0	0	0
Joe Dimaline (goalie)	16	0	0	0	8
Chris Maillett	18	0	0	0	8

GOALTENDING

	Gms.	Min.	W	L	T	G	SO	Avg.
Joe Dimaline	16	921	11	5	0	42	2	2.74
Denis Khlopotnov	4	166	1	1	0	9	0	3.26

PORT HURON BORDER CATS

(Lost quarterfinals to Thunder Bay, 4-3)

SCORING

	Games	G	A	Pts.	PIM
Kraig Nienhuis	7	3	4	7	4
Paul Polillo	7	1	4	5	2
Chris Bergeron	7	3	1	4	4
Bob McKillop	7	1	2	3	2
Mike Bondy	7	2	0	2	6
Jim Logan	7	2	0	2	8
Paul Rosebush	5	0	2	2	0
Jeff Blum	7	0	1	1	16
Lee Cole	7	0	1	1	12
Kevin Brown	1	0	0	0	0
Chad Dameworth	1	0	0	0	0
Andrei Srubko	2	0	0	0	4
Adam Robbins	4	0	0	0	12
Mark Kotary	5	0	0	0	0
Curtis Sayler	5	0	0	0	5
Brian Dobbin	7	0	0	0	0

	Games	G	A	Pts.	PIM
Jon Hillebrandt (goalie)	7	0	0	0	0
Bernie John	7	0	0	0	0
Nikolai Syrtsov	7	0	0	0	8
Bruce Watson	7	0	0	0	31

GOALTENDING

	Gms.	Min.	W	L	T	G	SO	Avg.
Jon Hillebrandt	7	438	3	4	0	16	1	2.19

QUAD CITY MALLARDS

(Lost finals to Muskegon, 4-2)

SCORING

	Games	G	A	Pts.	PIM
Glenn Stewart	16	10	7	17	8
Hugo Proulx	16	3	13	16	16
Scott Burfoot	16	4	11	15	18
Steve Gibson	14	8	6	14	12
Mike Gaffney	10	2	10	12	12
Kevin Kerr	16	5	6	11	29
Howie Rosenblatt	10	3	7	10	14
Rusty Fitzgerald	12	4	4	8	9
Garry Gulash	16	3	4	7	53
Rick Emmett	13	2	5	7	16
Mark McFarlane	13	2	5	7	43
Kelly Hultgren	15	3	3	6	4
Brendan Brooks	15	3	1	4	8
Brian LaFleur	14	1	3	4	4
Mike Melas	5	1	1	2	2
Stephane Madore	14	1	0	1	43
Travis Tucker	10	0	1	1	44
Bill Weir	10	0	1	1	2
Carl LeBlanc	12	0	1	1	20
Martin Hlinka	1	0	0	0	0
Martin Fillion (goalie)	3	0	0	0	6
Michael Hanson	8	0	0	0	21
Sergei Zvyagin (goalie)	14	0	0	0	2

GOALTENDING

	Gms.	Min.	W	L	T	G	SO	Avg.
Sergei Zvyagin	14	847	9	5	0	32	2	2.27
Martin Fillion	3	164	1	1	0	7	0	2.57

THUNDER BAY THUNDER CATS

(Lost semifinals to Quad City, 4-2)

SCORING

	Games	G	A	Pts.	PIM
Jason Firth	13	6	13	19	0
Brant Blackned	13	5	8	13	12
Wayne Strachan	13	6	6	12	14
Barry McKinlay	13	5	4	9	8
Michael Henderson	12	1	6	7	65
Derek Landmesser	13	3	3	6	26
Neal Purdon	10	3	1	4	4
Jason Disher	13	0	4	4	14
Nikolai Pronin	13	3	0	3	2
Norm Paquet	12	0	3	3	12
David Mayes	13	0	3	3	12
Allan Roulette	13	1	1	2	4
Darren Szczygiel	6	0	2	2	4
Dave Stewart	12	0	1	1	37
Greg Fullerton	4	0	0	0	2
Sean McEachran	8	0	0	0	7
Shawn Smith	10	0	0	0	10
Kevin Holliday	12	0	0	0	42
J.F. Rivard (goalie)	13	0	0	0	0

GOALTENDING

	Gms.	Min.	W	L	T	G	SO	Avg.
J.F. Rivard	13	849	6	7	0	30	1	2.12

WINSTON-SALEM ICEHAWKS

(Lost quarterfinals to Muskegon, 4-1)

SCORING

	Games	G	A	Pts.	PIM
Dmitri Rodine	5	1	4	5	4
Alexei Deev	5	2	2	4	2
Sergei Petrov	5	2	2	4	14
Justin Morrison	5	1	3	4	29
Dean Roach	5	3	0	3	2
Mark Giannetti	5	2	1	3	27
Jeff Azar	5	1	2	3	21
Mark Bultje	5	2	0	2	6
Bob Brandon	5	0	2	2	2
Trent Schachle	5	0	2	2	0
Pat Barton	3	0	1	1	2
Bruno Villeneuve	3	0	1	1	0
Trevor Rapchalk	5	0	1	1	6
Ryan Caley (goalie)	1	0	0	0	2
Marc Delorme (goalie)	4	0	0	0	2
John Taggert	4	0	0	0	0
Larry Empey	5	0	0	0	4
Tom Moulton	5	0	0	0	10

GOALTENDING

	Gms.	Min.	W	L	T	G	SO	Avg.
Marc Delorme	4	247	1	3	0	20	0	4.86
Ryan Caley	1	60	0	1	0	5	0	5.00

1998-99 AWARD WINNERS

ALL-STAR TEAMS

First team	Pos.	Second team
Joe Dimaline, Muskegon	G	J.F. Rivard, Thunder Bay
Stephan Brochu, Flint	D	John Vary, Muskegon
Brian LaFleur, Quad City	D	Vadim Podrezov, Muskegon
Jason Firth, Thunder Bay	C	Brian Sakic, Flint
Glenn Stewart, Quad City	LW	Sergei Kharin, Muskegon
Wayne Strachan, T. Bay	RW	Ross Wilson, Flint

TROPHY WINNERS

Most Valuable Player: Jason Firth, Thunder Bay
Scoring leader: Jason Firth, Thunder Bay
Outstanding defenseman: Stephan Brochu, Flint
Outstanding defensive forward: Paul Willett, Muskegon
Outstanding goaltender: Joe Dimaline, Muskegon
Rookie of the Year: Mike Melas, Quad City
Most sportsmanlike player: Brian Sakic, Flint
Playoff MVP: Sergei Kharin, Muskegon
Coach of the Year: Rich Kromm, Muskegon

ALL-TIME AWARD WINNERS

MOST VALUABLE PLAYER

Season Player, Team
1991-92—Terry McCutcheon, Brantford
1992-93—Jason Firth, Thunder Bay
1993-94—Kevin Kerr, Flint
1994-95—Mark Green, Utica
Paul Polillo, Brantford
1995-96—Paul Polillo, Brantford
1996-97—Paul Polillo, Brantford
1997-98—Jason Firth, Thunder Bay
1998-99—Jason Firth, Thunder Bay

SCORING LEADER

Season Player, Team
1991-92—Tom Sasso, Flint
1992-93—Len Soccio, St. Thomas
1993-94—Paul Polillo, Brantford
1994-95—Paul Polillo, Brantford
1995-96—Paul Polillo, Brantford
1996-97—Paul Polillo, Brantford
1997-98—Paul Polillo, Brantford
1998-99—Jason Firth, Thunder Bay

ROOKIE OF THE YEAR

Season Player, Team
1991-92—Kevin Butt, St. Thomas
1992-93—Jason Firth, Thunder Bay
1993-94—Jean-Francois Labbe, Thunder Bay
1994-95—Lance Leslie, Thunder Bay
1995-96—Matt Loen, Madison
1996-97—Forbes MacPherson, Thunder Bay
1997-98—Jason Weaver, Muskegon
1998-99—Mike Melas, Quad City

DEFENSEMAN OF THE YEAR

Season Player, Team
1991-92—Tom Searle, Brantford
1992-93—Tom Searle, Brantford
1993-94—Barry McKinlay, Thunder Bay
1994-95—Barry McKinlay, Thunder Bay
1995-96—Chris Hynnes, Thunder Bay
1996-97—Barry McKinlay, Thunder Bay
1997-98—John Vary, Muskegon
1998-99—Stephan Brochu, Flint

BEST DEFENSIVE FORWARD

Season Player, Team
1991-92—Tim Bean, St. Thomas
1992-93—Todd Howarth, Thunder Bay
1993-94—Jamie Hicks, Brantford
1994-95—Terry Menard, Thunder Bay
1995-96—Brian Downey, Madison
1996-97—Brian Downey, Madison
1997-98—Brad Jones, B.C.
1998-99—Paul Willett, Muskegon

BEST GOALTENDER

Season Player, Team
1991-92—Jamie Stewart, Detroit
1992-93—Jamie Stewart, Detroit
1993-94—J.F. Labbe, Thunder Bay
1994-95—Maxim Machialovsky, Detroit
1995-96—Rich Parent, Muskegon
1996-97—Sergei Zvyagin, Quad City
1997-98—Darryl Gilmour, Madison
1998-99—Joe Dimaline, Muskegon

MOST SPORTSMANLIKE PLAYER

Season Player, Team
1991-92—Tom Sasso, Flint
1992-93—Paul Polillo, Brantford
1993-94—Paul Polillo, Brantford
1994-95—Paul Polillo, Brantford
1995-96—Scott Burfoot, Flint
1996-97—Kent Hawley, Madison
1997-98—Brian Sakic, Flint
1998-99—Brian Sakic, Flint

PLAYOFF MVP

Season Player, Team
1991-92—Gary Callaghan, Thunder Bay
1992-93—Roland Melanson, Brantford
1993-94—Jean-Francois Labbe, Thunder Bay
1994-95—Lance Leslie, Thunder Bay
1995-96—Scott Burfoot, Flint
1996-97—Sergei Zvyagin, Quad City
1997-98—Jim Brown, Quad City
1998-99—Sergei Kharin, Muskegon

COACH OF THE YEAR

Season Coach, Team
1991-92—Peter Horachek, St. Thomas
1992-93—Bill McDonald, Thunder Bay
1993-94—Tom Barrett, Chatham
1994-95—Steve Ludzik, Muskegon
1995-96—Mark Johnson, Madison
1996-97—Robbie Nichols, Flint
1997-98—Robert Dirk, Winston-Salem
1998-99—Rich Kromm, Muskegon

ALL-TIME LEAGUE CHAMPIONS

	REGULAR-SEASON CHAMPION		PLAYOFF CHAMPION	
Season	**Team**	**Coach**	**Team**	**Coach**
1991-92—	Michigan Falcons	Terry Christensen	Thunder Bay Thunder Hawks	Bill MacDonald
1992-93—	Brantford Smoke	Ken Mann & Ken Gratton	Brantford Smoke	Ken Gratton
1993-94—	Thunder Bay Senators	Bill MacDonald	Thunder Bay Senators	Bill MacDonald
1994-95—	Thunder Bay Senators	Bill MacDonald	Thunder Bay Senators	Bill MacDonald
1995-96—	Flint Generals	Robbie Nichols	Flint Generals	Robbie Nichols
1996-97—	Flint Generals	Robbie Nichols	Quad City Mallards	John Anderson
1997-98—	Quad City Mallards	Paul Gillis	Quad City Mallards	Paul Gillis
1998-99—	Muskegon Fury	Rich Kromm	Muskegon Fury	Rich Kromm

MAJOR JUNIOR LEAGUES

Canadian Hockey League

Ontario Hockey League

Quebec Major Junior Hockey League

Western Hockey League

CANADIAN HOCKEY LEAGUE

GENERAL INFORMATION

The Canadian Hockey League is an alliance of the three Major Junior leagues—Ontario Hockey League, Quebec Major Junior Hockey League and Western Hockey League. After the regular season, the three leagues compete in a round-robin tournament to decide the Memorial Cup championship. Originally awarded to the national Junior champion, the Memorial Cup later signified Junior A supremacy (after Junior hockey in Canada was divided into ``A'' and ``B'' classes). Beginning in 1971, when Junior A hockey was split into Major Junior and Tier II Junior A, the Memorial Cup was awarded to the Major Junior champion.

LEAGUE OFFICE

Member leagues
Ontario Hockey League
Quebec Major Junior Hockey League
Western Hockey League
President
David E. Branch
Vice presidents
Gilles Courteau
Dev Dley
Directors
Bruce Hamilton
Charles Henry
Jim Rooney
Secretary treasurer
John Horman
Director of marketing
Colin Campbell
Director of information
Dave Lord
Director of officiating
Richard Doerksen
Address
2235 Sheppard Ave. East, Suite 1710
Willowdale, Ont. M2J 5B8
Phone
416-497-1907
FAX
416-490-9998

1999 MEMORIAL CUP

FINAL STANDINGS

Team (League)	W	L	Pts.	GF	GA
Ottawa (OHL)	4	1	8	24	17
Calgary (WHL)	2	2	4	17	14
Belleville (OHL)	2	2	4	13	14
Acadie-Bathurst (QMJHL)	0	3	0	3	12

RESULTS

SATURDAY, MAY 15

Ottawa 5, Acadie-Bathurst 1

SUNDAY, MAY 16

Calgary 5, Belleville 2

MONDAY, MAY 17

Ottawa 4, Calgary 3

TUESDAY, MAY 18

Belleville 4, Acadie-Bathurst 1

WEDNESDAY, MAY 19

Calgary 3, Acadie-Bathurst 1

THURSDAY, MAY 20

Belleville 5, Ottawa 4 (2 OT)

SATURDAY, MAY 22

Ottawa 4, Belleville 2

SUNDAY, MAY 23

Ottawa 7, Calgary 6 (OT)

TOP TOURNAMENT SCORERS

	Games	G	A	Pts.
Justin Davis, Ottawa	5	3	*6	*9
Mark Bell, Ottawa	5	2	*6	8
Pavel Brendl, Calgary	4	*4	3	7
Joe Talbot, Ottawa	5	3	4	7
Nick Boynton, Ottawa	5	1	*6	7
Brad Moran, Calgary	4	3	3	6
Matt Kinch, Calgary	4	0	6	6
Matt Zultek, Ottawa	5	3	2	5
Glenn Crawford, Belleville	4	3	1	4
Ian Jacobs, Ottawa	5	3	1	4
Kris Beech, Calgary	4	2	2	4
Dan Tessier, Ottawa	5	2	2	4
Brent Dodginghorse, Calgary	4	1	3	4
Brian Campbell, Ottawa	5	1	3	4
Miguel Delisle, Ottawa	5	1	3	4

*Indicates tournament leader.

1998-99 AWARD WINNERS

ALL-STAR TEAMS

First team	Pos.	Second team
Cody Rudkowsky, Seattle	G	Brian Finley, Barrie
Brian Campbell, Ottawa	D	Jiri Fischer, Hull
Brad Stuart, Calgary	D	Matt Kinch, Calgary
Jerome Tremblay, R.-N.	LW	Ryan Ready, Belleville
Mike Ribeiro, Rouyn-Noranda	C	Daniel Tkaczuk, Barrie
Pavel Brendl, Calgary	RW	James Desmarais, R.-N.

TROPHY WINNERS

Player of the year: Brian Campbell, Ottawa
Plus/minus award: Simon Tremblay, Quebec
Rookie of the year: Pavel Brendl, Calgary
Defenseman of the year: Brad Stuart, Calgary
Goaltender of the year: Cody Rudkowsky, Seattle
Scholastic player of the year: Rob Zepp, Plymouth
Coach of the year: Guy Chouinard, Quebec
Executive of the year: Jeff Hunt, Ottawa
Most sportsmanlike player of the year: Matt Kinch, Calgary
Top draft prospect award: Pavel Brendl, Calgary
Humanitarian award: Philippe Sauve, Rimouski

ALL-TIME MEMORIAL CUP WINNERS

Season Team
1918-19—Univ. of Toronto Schools
1919-20—Toronto Canoe Club
1920-21—Winnipeg Falcons
1921-22—Fort William War Veterans
1922-23—Univ. of Manitoba-Winnipeg
1923-24—Owen Sound Greys
1924-25—Regina Pats
1925-26—Calgary Canadians
1926-27—Owen Sound Greys
1927-28—Regina Monarchs
1928-29—Toronto Marlboros
1929-30—Regina Pats
1930-31—Winnipeg Elmwoods
1931-32—Sudbury Wolves
1932-33—Newmarket
1933-34—Toronto St. Michael's
1934-35—Winnipeg Monarchs
1935-36—West Toronto Redmen
1936-37—Winnipeg Monarchs
1937-38—St. Boniface Seals
1938-39—Oshawa Generals
1939-40—Oshawa Generals
1940-41—Winnipeg Rangers
1941-42—Portage la Prairie
1942-43—Winnipeg Rangers
1943-44—Oshawa Generals
1944-45—Toronto St. Michael's

Season Team
1945-46—Winnipeg Monarchs
1946-47—Toronto St. Michael's
1947-48—Port Arthur W. End Bruins
1948-49—Montreal Royals
1949-50—Montreal Jr. Canadiens
1950-51—Barrie Flyers
1951-52—Guelph Biltmores
1952-53—Barrie Flyers
1953-54—St. Catharines Tee Pees
1954-55—Toronto Marlboros
1955-56—Toronto Marlboros
1956-57—Flin Flon Bombers
1957-58—Ottawa-Hull Jr. Canadiens
1958-59—Winnipeg Braves
1959-60—St. Catharines Tee Pees
1960-61—Tor. St. Michael's Majors
1961-62—Hamilton Red Wings
1962-63—Edmonton Oil Kings
1963-64—Toronto Marlboros
1964-65—Niagara Falls Flyers
1965-66—Edmonton Oil Kings
1966-67—Toronto Marlboros
1967-68—Niagara Falls Flyers
1968-69—Montreal Jr. Canadiens
1969-70—Montreal Jr. Canadiens
1970-71—Quebec Remparts
1971-72—Cornwall Royals

Season Team
1972-73—Toronto Marlboros
1973-74—Regina Pats
1974-75—Toronto Marlboros
1975-76—Hamilton Fincups
1976-77—New Westminster Bruins
1977-78—New Westminster Bruins
1978-79—Peterborough Petes
1979-80—Cornwall Royals
1980-81—Cornwall Royals
1981-82—Kitchener Rangers
1982-83—Portland Winter Hawks
1983-84—Ottawa 67's
1984-85—Prince Albert Raiders
1985-86—Guelph Platers
1986-87—Medicine Hat Tigers
1987-88—Medicine Hat Tigers
1988-89—Swift Current Broncos
1989-90—Oshawa Generals
1990-91—Spokane Chiefs
1991-92—Kamloops Blazers
1992-93—Sault Ste. Marie Greyhounds
1993-94—Kamloops Blazers
1994-95—Kamloops Blazers
1995-96—Granby Predateurs
1996-97—Hull Olympics
1997-98—Portland Winter Hawks
1998-99—Ottawa 67's

ALL-TIME AWARD WINNERS

PLAYER OF THE YEAR AWARD

Season Player, Team
1974-75—Ed Staniowski, Regina
1975-76—Peter Lee, Ottawa
1976-77—Dale McCourt, Ste. Catharines
1977-78—Bobby Smith, Ottawa
1978-79—Pierre LaCroix, Trois-Rivieres
1979-80—Doug Wickenheiser, Regina
1980-81—Dale Hawerchuk, Cornwall
1981-82—Dave Simpson, London
1982-83—Pat LaFontaine, Verdun
1983-84—Mario Lemieux, Laval
1984-85—Dan Hodgson, Prince Albert
1985-86—Luc Robitaille, Hull
1986-87—Rob Brown, Kamloops
1987-88—Joe Sakic, Swift Current
1988-89—Bryan Fogarty, Niagara Falls
1989-90—Mike Ricci, Peterborough
1990-91—Eric Lindros, Oshawa
1991-92—Charles Poulin, St. Hyacinthe
1992-93—Pat Peake, Detroit
1993-94—Jason Allison, London
1994-95—David Ling, Kingston
1995-96—Christian Dube, Sherbrooke
1996-97—Alyn McCauley, Ottawa
1997-98—Sergei Varlamov, Swift Current
1998-99—Brian Campbell, Ottawa

PLUS/MINUS AWARD

Season Player, Team
1986-87—Rob Brown, Kamloops
1987-88—Marc Saumier, Hull
1988-89—Bryan Fogarty, Niagara Falls
1989-90—Len Barrie, Kamloops
1990-91—Eric Lindros, Oshawa
1991-92—Dean McAmmond, Prince Albert
1992-93—Chris Pronger, Peterborough

Season Player, Team
1993-94—Mark Wotton, Saskatoon
1994-95—Darren Ritchie, Brandon
1995-96—Daniel Goneau, Granby
1996-97—Nick Boynton, Ottawa
1997-98—Andrew Ference, Portland
1998-99—Simon Tremblay, Quebec

ROOKIE OF THE YEAR AWARD

Season Player, Team
1987-88—Martin Gelinas, Hull
1988-89—Yanic Perreault, Trois-Rivieres
1989-90—Petr Nedved, Seattle
1990-91—Philippe Boucher, Granby
1991-92—Alexandre Daigle, Victoriaville
1992-93—Jeff Freisen, Regina
1993-94—Vitali Yachmenev, North Bay
1994-95—Bryan Berard, Detroit
1995-96—Joe Thornton, Sault Ste. Marie
1996-97—Vincent Lecavalier, Rimouski
1997-98—David Legwand, Plymouth
1998-99—Pavel Brendl, Calgary

DEFENSEMAN OF THE YEAR AWARD

Season Player, Team
1987-88—Greg Hawgood, Kamloops
1988-89—Bryan Fogarty, Niagara Falls
1989-90—John Slaney, Cornwall
1990-91—Patrice Brisebois, Drummondville
1991-92—Drake Berehowsky, North Bay
1992-93—Chris Pronger, Peterborough
1993-94—Steve Gosselin, Chicoutimi
1994-95—Nolan Baumgartner, Kamloops
1995-96—Bryan Berard, Detroit
1996-97—Sean Blanchard, Ottawa
1997-98—Derrick Walser, Rimouski
1998-99—Brad Stuart, Calgary

GOALTENDER OF THE YEAR AWARD

Season Player, Team
1987-88—Stephane Beauregard, St. Jean
1988-89—Stephane Fiset, Victoriaville
1989-90—Trevor Kidd, Brandon
1990-91—Felix Potvin, Chicoutimi
1991-92—Corey Hirsch, Kamloops
1992-93—Jocelyn Thibault, Sherbrooke
1993-94—Norm Maracle, Saskatoon
1994-95—Martin Biron, Beauport
1995-96—Frederic Deschenes, Granby
1996-97—Marc Denis, Chicoutimi
1997-98—Mathieu Garon, Victoriaville
1998-99—Cody Rudkowsky, Seattle

SCHOLASTIC PLAYER OF THE YEAR AWARD

Season Player, Team
1987-88—Darrin Shannon, Windsor
1988-89—Jeff Nelson, Prince Albert
1989-90—Jeff Nelson, Prince Albert
1990-91—Scott Niedermayer, Kamloops
1991-92—Nathan LaFayette, Cornwall
1992-93—David Trofimenkoff, Lethbridge
1993-94—Patrick Boileau, Laval
1994-95—Perry Johnson, Regina
1995-96—Boyd Devereaux, Kitchener
1996-97—Stefan Cherneski, Brandon
1997-98—Kyle Rossiter, Spokane
1998-99—Rob Zepp, Plymouth

COACH OF THE YEAR AWARD

Season Coach, Team
1987-88—Alain Vigneault, Hull
1988-89—Joe McDonnell, Kitchener
1989-90—Ken Hitchcock, Kamloops
1990-91—Joe Canale, Chicoutimi
1991-92—Bryan Maxwell, Spokane
1992-93—Marcel Comeau, Tacoma
1993-94—Bert Templeton, North Bay
1994-95—Craig Hartsburg, Guelph
1995-96—Bob Lowes, Brandon
1996-97—Brian Kilrea, Ottawa
1997-98—Dean Clark, Calgary
1998-99—Guy Chouinard, Quebec

EXECUTIVE OF THE YEAR AWARD

Season Executive, Team or League
1988-89—John Horman, QMJHL
1989-90—Russ Farwell, Seattle
1990-91—Sherwood Bassin, Sault Ste. Marie
1991-92—Bert Templeton, North Bay
1992-93—Jim Rutherford, Detroit
1993-94—Bob Brown, Kamloops
1994-95—Kelly McCrimmon, Brandon
1995-96—Tim Speltz, Spokane
1996-97—Harold MacKay, Halifax
1997-98—Paul McIntosh, London
1998-99—Jeff Hunt, Ottawa

MOST SPORTSMANLIKE PLAYER OF THE YEAR AWARD

Season Player, Team
1989-90—Andrew McKim, Hull
1990-91—Pat Falloon, Spokane
1991-92—Martin Gendron, St. Hyacinthe
1992-93—Rick Girard, Swift Current
1993-94—Yanick Dube, Laval
1994-95—Eric Daze, Beauport
1995-96—Hnat Domenichelli, Kamloops
1996-97—Kelly Smart, Brandon
1997-98—Cory Cyrenne, Brandon
1998-99—Matt Kinch, Calgary

TOP DRAFT PROSPECT AWARD

Season Player, Team
1990-91—Eric Lindros, Oshawa
1991-92—Todd Warriner, Windsor
1992-93—Alexandre Daigle, Victoriaville
1993-94—Jeff O'Neill, Guelph
1994-95—Bryan Berard, Detroit
1995-96—Chris Phillips, Prince Albert
1996-97—Joe Thornton, Sault Ste. Marie
1997-98—Vincent Lecavalier, Rimouski
1998-99—Pavel Brendl, Calgary

HUMANITARIAN AWARD

Season Player, Team
1992-93—Keli Corpse, Kingston
1993-94—Stephane Roy, Val d'Or
1994-95—David-Alexandre Beauregard, St. Hyacinthe
1995-96—Craig Mills, Belleville
1996-97—Jesse Wallin, Red Deer
1997-98—Jason Metcalfe, London
1998-99—Philippe Sauve, Rimouski

ONTARIO HOCKEY LEAGUE

LEAGUE OFFICE

Commissioner
David E. Branch
Chairman of the board
Jim Rooney
Director of administration
Herb Morell
Dir. of hockey op./referee in chief
Ted Baker
Director of information & special events
Aaron Bell
Director of central scouting
Bill Neeham
Address
305 Milner Avenue
Suite 208
Scarborough, Ontario M1B 3V4
Phone
416-299-8700
FAX
416-299-8787

1998-99 REGULAR SEASON

FINAL STANDINGS

EAST DIVISION

Team	G	W	L	T	Pts.	GF	GA
Ottawa	68	48	13	7	103	305	164
Belleville	68	39	22	7	85	334	246
Oshawa	68	39	24	5	83	280	217
Peterborough	68	40	26	2	82	266	213
Kingston	68	22	42	4	48	240	320

CENTRAL DIVISION

Team	G	W	L	T	Pts.	GF	GA
Barrie	68	49	13	6	104	343	192
Sudbury	68	25	35	8	58	261	288
North Bay	68	22	40	6	50	215	248
Toronto	68	20	42	6	46	214	316
Mississauga	68	4	61	3	11	145	426

MIDWEST DIVISION

Team	G	W	L	T	Pts.	GF	GA
Guelph	68	44	22	2	90	300	218
Owen Sound	68	39	24	5	83	312	293
Erie	68	31	33	4	66	271	297
Kitchener	68	23	39	6	52	205	257
Brampton	68	8	57	3	19	198	362

WEST DIVISION

Team	G	W	L	T	Pts.	GF	GA
Plymouth	68	51	13	4	106	313	162
Sarnia	68	37	25	6	80	279	216
London	68	34	30	4	72	260	217
Sault Ste. Marie	68	31	29	8	70	244	242
Windsor	68	23	39	6	52	203	294

INDIVIDUAL LEADERS

Goals: Harold Druken, Plymouth (58)
Assists: Peter Sarno, Sarnia (93)
Points: Peter Sarno, Sarnia (130)
Penalty minutes: Ryan Barnes, Barrie (399)
Goaltending average: Robert Holsinger, Plymouth (2.08)
Shutouts: Robert Holsinger, Plymouth (5)
Seamus Kotyk, Ottawa (5)

TOP SCORERS

	Games	G	A	Pts.
Peter Sarno, Sarnia	68	37	93	130
Norm Milley, Sudbury	68	52	68	120
Sheldon Keefe, Barrie	66	51	65	116
Adam Colagiacomo, Plymouth	67	40	68	108
Mike Fisher, Sudbury	68	41	65	106
Daniel Tkaczuk, Barrie	58	43	62	105
Harold Druken, Plymouth	60	58	45	103
Kevin Colley, Oshawa	63	39	62	101
Justin Papineau, Belleville	68	52	47	99
Ivan Novoseltsev, Sarnia	68	57	39	96
Brent Gauvreau, Oshawa	68	33	62	95
Jay Legault, London	65	43	51	94
Denis Shvidki, Barrie	61	35	59	94
Dan Snyder, Owen Sound	64	27	67	94
Ryan Ready, Belleville	63	33	59	92
Mike Oliveira, Kingston	68	37	52	89
Peter Campbell, Owen Sound	67	45	43	88
Brett Gibson, North Bay	67	42	46	88
Tom Kostopoulos, London	66	27	60	87
Derek MacKenzie, Sudbury	68	22	65	87
Brian Campbell, Ottawa	62	12	75	87

INDIVIDUAL STATISTICS

BARRIE COLTS

SCORING

	Games	G	A	Pts.	PIM
Daniel Tkaczuk	58	43	62	105	58
Denis Shvidki	61	35	59	94	8
Michael Henrich	62	38	33	71	42
Martin Skoula	67	13	46	59	46
Nick Smith	68	19	34	53	18
Joel Dezainde	36	15	33	48	52
Mike Christian	60	20	26	46	160
Sheldon Keefe	28	14	28	42	60
Scott Cameron	66	10	32	42	14
Chris Feil	67	10	31	41	158
Mike Jefferson	26	15	20	35	62
Keith Delaney	38	12	21	33	10
Jeff Tetzlaff	59	12	20	32	32
Adam DeLeeuw	39	15	16	31	146
Ryan Barnes	24	16	14	30	161
Darryl Bootland	38	18	11	29	89
Tim Verbeek	66	15	14	29	96
Andre Lakos	62	4	23	27	40
Ed Hill	53	7	17	24	42
Jerry Connell	45	3	14	17	43
Shawn Cation	27	3	8	11	49
Fraser Clair	25	4	3	7	14
Ryan O'Keefe	57	2	5	7	52

	Games	G	A	Pts.	PIM
Kevin Parfrey	16	0	4	4	0
Brad Pierce	34	0	4	4	36
Mike Brito	4	0	1	1	2
Danny Gould (goalie)	2	0	1	1	0
Ben Vanderklok (goalie)	19	0	1	1	16
Chad Moreau	1	0	0	0	0
Lyle Rolling	1	0	0	0	0
Casey Burnette	3	0	0	0	0
Sebastian Harts	3	0	0	0	5
Mihajlo Martinovich	3	0	0	0	2
Greg Patton	5	0	0	0	0
Rick Hwodeky	15	0	0	0	9
Brian Finley (goalie)	52	0	0	0	2

GOALTENDING

	Gms.	Min.	W	L	T	G	SO	Avg.
Brian Finley	52	3063	36	10	4	136	3	2.66
Ben Vanderklok	19	1004	13	2	2	45	3	2.69
Danny Gould	2	47	0	1	0	8	0	10.21

BELLEVILLE BULLS

SCORING

	Games	G	A	Pts.	PIM
Justin Papineau	68	52	47	99	28
Ryan Ready	63	33	59	92	73
Jonathan Cheechoo	63	35	47	82	74
Kevin Baker	68	44	37	81	66
Chris Stanley	51	29	40	69	32
Randy Rowe	65	24	38	62	21
Branko Radivojevic	68	20	38	58	61
Mark Chaplin	66	21	33	54	13
Glenn Crawford	42	14	25	39	20
Jason Lawmaster	61	6	32	38	227
Derek Campbell	49	14	21	35	40
Michael Jacobsen	68	5	27	32	33
Kelly Paddon	67	5	26	31	44
Branislav Mezei	60	5	18	23	90
Nathan Robinson	50	11	8	19	23
Kris Newbury	51	6	8	14	89
Mike Renzi	51	4	10	14	65
Nick Policelli	65	1	12	13	216
Rick Bertran	17	0	10	10	35
Adam Collins	17	2	5	7	2
Tyler Longo	15	2	3	5	4
Doug MacIver	36	0	3	3	56
Sam Katsuras	6	0	2	2	4
Justin Grady	15	1	0	1	24
Joe Groleau	13	0	1	1	6
Chad Mehlenbacher (goalie)	18	0	1	1	2
Dustin Dagenais	20	0	1	1	20
Cory Campbell (goalie)	46	0	1	1	8
Brent Mulder	6	0	0	0	0
Shawn Gallant (goalie)	9	0	0	0	10

GOALTENDING

	Gms.	Min.	W	L	T	G	SO	Avg.
Cory Campbell	46	2679	28	13	4	156	1	3.49
Chad Mehlenbacher	18	893	8	4	2	53	0	3.56
Shawn Gallant	9	545	3	5	1	34	0	3.74

BRAMPTON BATTALION

SCORING

	Games	G	A	Pts.	PIM
Jason Spezza	67	22	49	71	18
Raffi Torres	62	35	27	62	32
Jeff Bateman	68	23	35	58	27
Lukas Havel	64	19	31	50	29
Brian Barker	66	21	25	46	71
Scott Thompson	62	19	18	37	33
Jason Maleyko	68	7	25	32	155
Kurt MacSweyn	60	16	13	29	23
Aaron VanLeusen	58	7	8	15	15
Jay Harrison	63	1	14	15	108
Matt Reynolds	62	6	8	14	29
Shane Fryia	39	6	4	10	42
Matt Lecce	64	4	4	8	42
Pat Parthenais	46	0	8	8	55
Richard Kearns	58	2	5	7	27
Cam McLaughlin	46	1	6	7	21
Jim Bradley	37	5	1	6	33
Brad Woods	58	1	5	6	42
Matthew Hodges	53	1	4	5	92
Jason Doyle	4	2	1	3	7
Tony Gutilla	19	0	3	3	44
Tyler Hanchuck	57	0	3	3	87
Blair McLaughlin	20	0	2	2	6
Scott Della Vedova (goalie)	34	0	1	1	4
Steve Van de Oetelaar	1	0	0	0	0
Bryan Blair	2	0	0	0	0
David Chant (goalie)	46	0	0	0	6

GOALTENDING

	Gms.	Min.	W	L	T	G	SO	Avg.
David Chant	46	2462	7	31	2	191	0	4.65
Scott Della Vedova	34	1638	1	26	1	167	0	6.12

ERIE OTTERS

SCORING

	Games	G	A	Pts.	PIM
Tim Connolly	46	34	34	68	50
Tyler Rennette	61	30	37	67	40
Shane Nash	66	28	39	67	37
Brad Boyes	59	24	36	60	30
Jason Baird	65	25	31	56	186
Michael Rupp	63	22	25	47	102
Jeff Zehr	28	20	23	43	78
Steve Montador	61	9	33	42	114
Nikita Alexeev	61	17	18	35	14
Arvid Rekis	60	5	29	34	66
Paul Harvey	61	16	17	33	132
Brad Yeo	42	9	16	25	81
Warren Hefford	31	4	11	15	22
Ryan Lee	67	5	9	14	143
Sean Dixon	55	2	12	14	57
Andrew Proskurnicki	15	6	5	11	39
Darren McMillan	62	1	9	10	37
Jourdan Lagace	52	4	5	9	27
Wade Clubb	56	2	7	9	87
Derek Watson	12	3	3	6	47
Steve Nobili	45	1	2	3	22
Derek McDonald	11	1	1	2	20
Julius Halfkenny	29	1	1	2	8
Jim McGillivray	44	1	1	2	69
Ryan Fraser	45	1	1	2	75
Corey Batten (goalie)	36	0	2	2	4
Adam Munroe	1	0	0	0	0
Patrick Dovigi (goalie)	12	0	0	0	0
Ryan Scott	15	0	0	0	4
J.F. Perras (goalie)	32	0	0	0	8

GOALTENDING

	Gms.	Min.	W	L	T	G	SO	Avg.
J.F. Perras	32	1522	12	10	3	104	0	4.10
Corey Batten	36	1930	13	18	1	138	1	4.29
Patrick Dovigi	12	655	6	5	0	50	1	4.58

GUELPH STORM

SCORING

	Games	G	A	Pts.	PIM
Joe Gerbe	68	30	48	78	31
Kevin Mitchell	68	26	52	78	107
Eric Beaudoin	66	28	43	71	79
Kent McDonell	60	31	38	69	110
Lindsay Plunkett	65	29	34	63	90

	Games	G	A	Pts.	PIM
Ryan Davis	61	25	28	53	77
Charlie Stephens	61	24	28	52	72
Darryl Knight	56	15	30	45	28
Darryl McArthur	68	7	34	41	100
Bob Crummer	68	15	25	40	213
Kevin Dallman	68	8	30	38	52
Bohuslav Subr	64	22	12	34	62
Nathan Herrington	62	11	17	28	24
Lucas Nehrling	60	5	14	19	131
Brent Kelly	30	8	8	16	8
Matt Rock	68	3	7	10	35
Dusty Jamieson	12	2	7	9	0
Ian Forbes	60	1	8	9	182
Yevgeny Krivomaz	16	1	6	7	16
Francois Jolette	39	4	2	6	35
Brian McGrattan	6	1	3	4	15
Mike DePetrillo	14	2	1	3	38
Joey Bartley	3	0	2	2	4
Garrett McAiney	36	0	2	2	8
Greg Jacina	6	1	0	1	0
Aaron Bailie	8	1	0	1	6
John Dickie	2	0	1	1	5
Mike D'Alessandro (goalie)	13	0	0	0	0
Jean-Sebastien Larocque	13	0	0	0	0
Craig Andersson (goalie)	21	0	0	0	6
Chris Madden (goalie)	50	0	0	0	12

GOALTENDING

	Gms.	Min.	W	L	T	G	SO	Avg.
Craig Andersson	21	1006	12	5	1	52	1	3.10
Chris Madden	50	2567	28	13	0	133	2	3.11
Mike D'Alessandro	13	518	4	4	1	29	0	3.36

KINGSTON FRONTENACS

SCORING

	Games	G	A	Pts.	PIM
Mike Oliveira	68	37	52	89	26
Michael Zigomanis	67	29	56	85	36
Matt Elich	67	44	30	74	32
Jonathan Schill	68	32	27	59	93
Andrew Ianiero	68	21	26	47	81
Sean Avery	33	14	25	39	88
Aaron Fransen	25	11	15	26	98
Kevin Grimes	56	5	20	25	184
Brett Clouthier	64	8	14	22	227
Sean Griffin	59	1	19	20	151
Brett Ormond	56	4	15	19	26
Eric Braff	68	0	19	19	46
Darryl Thomson	55	9	9	18	32
D.J. Maracle	28	6	8	14	114
Morgan McCormick	34	6	5	11	43
Ian Turner	62	3	8	11	23
Matt Price	19	2	9	11	43
Stephen Lafleur	35	1	10	11	47
Jamie Young	62	2	8	10	6
Jan Sulc	13	4	4	8	6
Patrick DesRochers (goalie)	44	0	4	4	4
Nathan Tennant	63	0	4	4	61
Rob Mailloux	7	0	2	2	6
Ryan Rivard	49	1	0	1	16
Lucas Nehrling	2	0	1	1	13
Curtis Cruickshank (goalie)	16	0	1	1	9
Gerald MacNeil	18	0	1	1	0
Ryan Chapman	2	0	0	0	0
Shayne Kanyo	2	0	0	0	0
Mark Boisvert	3	0	0	0	0
Danny Gould (goalie)	3	0	0	0	0
Walker MacDonald	15	0	0	0	9
Chad Lynch (goalie)	18	0	0	0	2
Colin Scotland	31	0	0	0	27

GOALTENDING

	Gms.	Min.	W	L	T	G	SO	Avg.
Patrick DesRochers	44	2389	14	22	3	177	1	4.45
Curtis Cruickshank	16	835	5	9	0	63	1	4.53
Chad Lynch	18	821	3	11	1	71	0	5.19
Danny Gould	3	60	0	0	0	7	0	7.00

KITCHENER RANGERS

SCORING

	Games	G	A	Pts.	PIM
Darren Mortier	66	19	28	47	41
Michal Dvorak	50	23	23	46	40
Ryan Held	65	18	25	43	45
Brandon Merli	61	23	16	39	35
Allan Rourke	66	11	28	39	79
Serge Payer	40	18	19	37	22
Ryan Milanovic	61	15	18	33	114
Nick Robinson	66	11	22	33	80
Vratislav Cech	66	6	21	27	73
Casey Wolak	41	10	14	24	117
Wes Jarvis	52	5	18	23	80
Josh Seabrook	66	8	12	20	106
Rick Smith	30	9	9	18	37
Sal Lettieri	66	2	16	18	53
Travis Lisabeth	65	9	7	16	57
Mike Wehrstedt	58	6	8	14	10
Richard Kazda	61	5	7	12	77
Joe DiBiase	36	2	4	6	38
Mike Vaillaincourt	49	2	2	4	13
Dallas Ashford	18	1	2	3	45
Rick Bertran	38	1	2	3	78
Barry Graham	48	1	2	3	93
Alain Veilleux	16	0	2	2	6
Reg Bourcier (goalie)	45	0	2	2	4
Tony Demola	1	0	0	0	0
Andrew Yardy	4	0	0	0	0
Bobby Naylor	9	0	0	0	9
Alain Veilleux	9	0	2	2	4
Mark Aggio (goalie)	10	0	0	0	0
Mike Gorman (goalie)	28	0	0	0	10
Mike Laceby	12	0	0	0	6
Jeff MacLean	9	0	0	0	4

GOALTENDING

	Gms.	Min.	W	L	T	G	SO	Avg.
Reg Bourcier	45	2240	14	21	4	126	0	3.38
Mike Gorman	28	1515	7	16	2	96	1	3.80
Mark Aggio	10	364	2	2	0	26	0	4.29

LONDON KNIGHTS

SCORING

	Games	G	A	Pts.	PIM
Jay Legault	65	43	51	94	99
Tom Kostopoulos	66	27	60	87	114
Chris Kelly	68	36	41	77	60
Richard Pitirri	65	35	41	76	56
Joel Scherban	68	22	32	54	14
Jason Doyle	54	20	31	51	61
Krys Barch	66	18	20	38	66
Rico Fata	23	15	18	33	41
Alex Henry	68	5	23	28	105
Peter Reynolds	59	2	25	27	55
John Erskine	57	8	12	20	208
Mike Mazzuca	67	4	13	17	130
Adam Saffer	51	11	5	16	40
Tomas Gron	66	3	12	15	4
Dan Jancevski	68	2	12	14	115
Jason Metcalfe	46	2	9	11	145
Tyler Durham	59	1	5	6	30
Mike DePetrillo	14	3	2	5	30
Jason Lange	14	2	1	3	2
Bobby Turner	60	1	2	3	119

	Games	G	A	Pts.	PIM
Gene Chiarello (goalie)	62	0	3	3	16
Matt Belanger	40	0	1	1	47
Taylor Cummings (goalie)	4	0	0	0	2
Jeff Kaufman	7	0	0	0	2
Bill Ruggiero (goalie)	8	0	0	0	0
Dan Sullivan	18	0	0	0	10
Steven Rawski	29	0	0	0	2

GOALTENDING

	Gms.	Min.	W	L	T	G	SO	Avg.
Gene Chiarello	62	3633	32	25	3	182	2	3.01
Taylor Cummings	4	177	0	2	1	10	0	3.39
Bill Ruggiero	8	305	2	3	0	19	0	3.74

MISSISSAUGA ICEDOGS

SCORING

	Games	G	A	Pts.	PIM
Scott Page	66	20	30	50	251
Lou Dickenson	62	19	27	46	12
Chad Wiseman	64	11	25	36	29
Adam Nittel	34	15	16	31	235
Sebastien Savage	57	10	15	25	55
Brent Theobald	65	10	14	24	25
Joel Dezainde	24	4	20	24	35
Chris Thaler	66	12	10	22	34
Nick Jones	29	10	6	16	116
Blake Orr	61	3	13	16	28
Fraser Clair	34	2	9	11	30
Andrew Davis	65	4	6	10	50
Nathan Kalverda	63	3	7	10	115
Danny Armstrong	56	2	7	9	121
Darrell Cowen	61	3	5	8	40
Drew Felder	36	1	7	8	68
Mark Jerant	48	6	1	7	68
Brad Simms	23	3	3	6	24
John Zubyck	48	1	4	5	44
Sebastian Harts	30	2	2	4	31
Matt Coughlin	61	1	3	4	152
Phil Vandenbeukal	31	1	2	3	28
Ivan Curic	36	1	1	2	12
Nick Foley (goalie)	37	0	2	2	0
Michael Ancuta	35	1	0	1	64
Josh Evans (goalie)	41	0	1	1	10
Spencer Fowler	50	0	1	1	138
Casey Wolak	1	0	0	0	0
Mike Nixon	2	0	0	0	0

GOALTENDING

	Gms.	Min.	W	L	T	G	SO	Avg.
Nick Foley	37	1890	3	26	1	186	0	5.90
Josh Evans	41	2212	1	35	2	235	0	6.37

NORTH BAY CENTENNIALS

SCORING

	Games	G	A	Pts.	PIM
Brett Gibson	67	42	46	88	98
Chris Neil	66	26	46	72	215
Greg Labenski	68	16	40	56	73
Lorne Misita	65	18	24	42	54
Scott Wray	61	23	18	41	61
Mike Cirillo	57	10	27	37	144
Samu Isosalo	59	13	12	25	19
Ryan Armstrong	68	6	15	21	23
Oak Hewer	40	11	9	20	34
Rob Davison	59	2	17	19	150
John Dean	67	9	9	18	47
Steve Chabbert	64	1	16	17	83
Rodney Richard	64	8	8	16	12
Brett Angel	55	5	9	14	139
Omar Ennaffati	61	4	10	14	99
Jamie Piercey	41	6	6	12	24
Gabriel Spilar	38	4	4	8	4

	Games	G	A	Pts.	PIM
Chris Eade	46	1	6	7	32
Mark Jerant	8	2	3	5	10
Josh Legge	59	1	4	5	75
Warren Holmes	14	1	3	4	25
Scott McKenzie	22	1	1	2	0
Alex Auld (goalie)	37	0	1	1	2
Shawn Degagne (goalie)	42	0	1	1	0
Michael Barber (goalie)	1	0	0	0	0
Luc Messier	1	0	0	0	0
Nick Vukovic	10	0	0	0	2

GOALTENDING

	Gms.	Min.	W	L	T	G	SO	Avg.
Michael Barber	1	36	0	0	0	2	0	3.33
Alex Auld	37	1894	9	20	1	106	1	3.36
Shawn Degagne	42	2182	13	20	5	133	0	3.66

OSHAWA GENERALS

SCORING

	Games	G	A	Pts.	PIM
Kevin Colley	63	39	62	101	68
Brent Gauvreau	68	33	62	95	57
Brad Ralph	67	31	44	75	93
Jim Baxter	66	22	52	74	20
Derrell Upton	62	23	25	48	22
Brian Passmore	63	18	25	43	53
Vladimir Repnev	59	14	24	38	28
John Kozoriz	60	22	13	35	25
Ilja Demidov	62	4	23	27	72
Andrew Peters	54	14	10	24	137
Richard Scott	54	12	12	24	193
Brandon Coalter	55	12	11	23	95
Bryan Allen	37	7	15	22	77
Jeff MacMillan	65	3	18	21	109
Trevor Gillies	66	6	9	15	270
Drew Bucktooth	54	4	11	15	82
Jonah Leroux	56	5	9	14	27
Ian Courville	28	3	8	11	15
Richard Spence	55	3	8	11	134
Brandon Cullen	40	2	3	5	70
Matt Rusenstrom	49	1	3	4	36
Tyrone Garner (goalie)	44	0	4	4	18
T.J. Reynolds	17	0	1	1	27
Steve Mongrain (goalie)	1	0	0	0	0
Matt Neely	3	0	0	0	5
David Riddell (goalie)	11	0	0	0	2
Derek Dolson (goalie)	18	0	0	0	0

GOALTENDING

	Gms.	Min.	W	L	T	G	SO	Avg.
Steve Mongrain	1	60	1	0	0	1	0	1.00
Derek Dolson	18	950	11	3	1	39	1	2.46
Tyrone Garner	44	2496	24	15	3	124	4	2.98
David Riddell	11	592	3	6	1	47	0	4.76

OTTAWA 67'S

SCORING

	Games	G	A	Pts.	PIM
Brian Campbell	62	12	75	87	27
Dan Tessier	68	36	48	84	64
Matt Zultek	56	33	33	66	71
Justin Davis	61	22	37	59	13
Nick Boynton	51	11	48	59	83
Dan Tudin	61	24	33	57	40
Ben Gustavson	63	27	29	56	98
Mark Bell	44	29	26	55	69
Joe Talbot	68	22	30	52	43
Jonathan Zion	60	8	33	41	10
Henric Alfredsson	65	22	18	40	16
Lance Galbraith	64	17	23	40	210
Miguel Delisle	57	16	17	33	34
Ian Jacobs	63	7	17	24	46

	Games	G	A	Pts.	PIM
Luke Sellars	56	4	19	23	87
Zenon Konopka	56	7	8	15	62
Jeremy Van Hoof	54	0	13	13	46
Chris Cava	27	2	10	12	68
Kyle McAllister	23	1	9	10	27
Dallas Ashford	37	1	4	5	18
Jonathan Boone	28	2	2	4	20
Scott O'Connor	31	1	3	4	9
Jeff MacLean	26	1	2	3	23
Ryan Crowther	1	0	1	1	2
Lavente Szuper (goalie)	32	0	1	1	0
Alain Veilleux	7	0	0	0	2
Seamus Kotyk (goalie)	41	0	0	0	14

GOALTENDING

	Gms.	Min.	W	L	T	G	SO	Avg.
Lavente Szuper	32	1800	22	6	3	70	4	2.33
Seamus Kotyk	41	2314	26	7	4	92	5	2.39

OWEN SOUND PLATERS

SCORING

	Games	G	A	Pts.	PIM
Dan Snyder	64	27	67	94	110
Peter Campbell	67	45	43	88	37
Wes Goldie	61	46	37	83	63
Adam Mair	43	23	41	64	109
Mike Dombkiewicz	66	13	50	63	83
Chad Woollard	50	28	29	57	79
Jan Sulc	53	20	29	49	59
Sean Avery	28	22	23	45	70
Aaron Fransen	32	9	27	36	86
Joel Ward	58	19	16	35	23
Adam Campbell	60	10	22	32	153
Juri Golicic	38	15	12	27	0
Randy Davidson	53	11	16	27	13
Nick Vukovic	55	4	17	21	31
Chris Minard	43	6	9	15	18
Chris Hopiavuori	68	1	13	14	41
Dave Stephenson	61	2	9	11	172
Stephen Lafleur	30	1	10	11	45
Brent Sullivan	65	2	7	9	78
Kyle Flaxey	34	1	8	9	17
Mike Barrett	66	2	6	8	17
Mike Lankshear	26	2	5	7	44
Bryan Kazarian	41	1	5	6	27
Curtis Sanford (goalie)	56	0	5	5	4
D.J. Maracle	12	2	2	4	48
Warren Holmes	13	2	2	4	20
Jeff Alcombrack	1	0	1	1	0
Richard Boyd (goalie)	1	0	1	1	0
Ryan Rivard	5	0	1	1	2
Jeff Kaufman	11	0	1	1	2
Luc Bergeron (goalie)	3	0	0	0	0
Stephane Savage	4	0	0	0	2
Corey Roberts (goalie)	20	0	0	0	0

GOALTENDING

	Gms.	Min.	W	L	T	G	SO	Avg.
Curtis Sanford	56	2998	30	16	5	191	2	3.82
Luc Bergeron	3	176	2	1	0	12	0	4.09
Richard Boyd	1	40	0	0	0	3	0	4.50
Corey Roberts	20	896	7	7	0	83	0	5.56

PETERBOROUGH PETES

SCORING

	Games	G	A	Pts.	PIM
Jason Williams	68	26	48	74	42
Pat Kavanagh	68	26	43	69	118
Scott Barney	44	41	26	67	80
Preston Mizzi	67	29	29	58	74
Robert Francz	65	25	32	57	171
Adam Dewan	62	20	29	49	126

	Games	G	A	Pts.	PIM
John Brioux	66	14	28	42	26
Jamie Chamberlain	68	15	24	39	26
Brad Self	48	17	12	29	8
Derek McNamara	62	5	24	29	37
Sergei Kuznetzov	65	8	17	25	39
Jack Hardill	66	11	13	24	143
B.J. Ketcheson	62	1	20	21	86
Matt Carkner	60	2	16	18	173
Mark Phibbs	39	7	10	17	49
Brandon Verner	40	6	10	16	22
Kris MacPhee	50	7	8	15	2
Kurtis Foster	54	2	13	15	59
Dustin Wood	62	1	8	9	14
Jeff McKercher	57	1	7	8	22
Jesse MacLeish	9	1	1	2	0
Darcy Morris	29	1	1	2	48
Mike Pickard (goalie)	32	0	2	2	4
Brad Gibbs	4	0	1	1	9
Brett Ormond	9	0	1	1	4
Joey MacDonald (goalie)	47	0	1	1	6

GOALTENDING

	Gms.	Min.	W	L	T	G	SO	Avg.
Joey MacDonald	47	2483	22	15	2	123	3	2.97
Mike Pickard	32	1605	18	11	0	84	1	3.14

PLYMOUTH WHALERS

SCORING

	Games	G	A	Pts.	PIM
Adam Colagiacomo	67	40	68	108	89
Harold Druken	60	58	45	103	34
David Legwand	55	31	49	80	65
Eric Gooldy	67	23	38	61	167
Nikos Tselios	60	21	39	60	60
Paul Mara	52	13	41	54	95
Randy Fitzgerald	64	15	34	49	144
Shaun Fisher	67	9	31	40	43
Damian Surma	65	17	15	32	62
Jason Ward	23	14	13	27	28
Julian Smith	59	13	13	26	12
Rick Smith	30	13	12	25	44
Tomek Valtonen	43	8	16	24	53
Jamie Lalonde	52	14	6	20	162
Troy Smith	54	6	13	19	40
Kevin Holdridge	64	2	17	19	118
Kristopher Vernarsky	45	3	14	17	30
Jared Newman	66	2	15	17	57
Mark McMahon	34	2	12	14	91
Justin Williams	47	4	8	12	28
James Ramsay	47	2	2	4	169
Max Linnik	21	0	3	3	19
Kristopher Purdy	18	0	2	2	8
Robert Holsinger (goalie)	40	0	2	2	4
Kyle Chapman	23	2	0	2	29
Andre Robichaud	17	1	0	1	4
Dwayne Bateman (goalie)	4	0	0	0	0
Rob Zepp (goalie)	31	0	0	0	2

GOALTENDING

	Gms.	Min.	W	L	T	G	SO	Avg.
Robert Holsinger	40	2252	28	10	0	78	5	2.08
Dwayne Bateman	4	200	4	0	0	7	0	2.10
Rob Zepp	31	1662	19	3	4	76	3	2.74

SARNIA STING

SCORING

	Games	G	A	Pts.	PIM
Peter Sarno	68	37	93	130	49
Ivan Novoseltsev	68	57	39	96	45
Peter Cava	62	33	48	81	63
Jeff Heerema	62	31	39	70	113
Greg Willers	68	16	38	54	32

	Games	G	A	Pts.	PIM
Ryan VanBuskirk	66	15	33	48	85
Robb Palahnuk	68	16	27	43	114
Dusty Jamieson	54	14	21	35	10
Matt Price	36	6	17	23	59
Kevin Malcolm	64	12	10	22	184
Chris Berti	68	10	12	22	114
Dan Watson	68	2	18	20	27
Andrew Proskurnicki	36	4	14	18	136
David Cornacchia	43	4	12	16	106
Jeff Zehr	14	4	10	14	43
Ryan Hare	52	6	4	10	14
Travis Albers	50	0	10	10	38
Corey Brekelmans	68	4	3	7	69
Darryl Knight	9	1	5	6	2
Tyler Coleman	30	4	1	5	4
Abe Herbst	11	0	4	4	15
Julius Halfkenny	29	0	3	3	15
Casey Wolak	15	1	1	2	31
Doug MacIver	21	1	1	2	31
Kevin Mota	12	0	2	2	17
Derek McKinley	35	0	2	2	26
Greg Hewitt (goalie)	39	0	2	2	8
Tony Gutilla	25	1	0	1	15
Mike Hooker	11	0	1	1	0
Curtis Cruickshank (goalie)	28	0	1	1	21
Paul Guthrie (goalie)	6	0	0	0	0
Luke Blackbird	8	0	0	0	16
Patrick DesRochers (goalie)	8	0	0	0	0

GOALTENDING

	Gms.	Min.	W	L	T	G	SO	Avg.
Curtis Cruickshank	28	1557	18	5	1	66	2	2.54
Greg Hewitt	39	1960	16	12	5	104	2	3.18
Patrick DesRochers	8	425	3	5	0	26	0	3.67
Paul Guthrie	6	168	0	3	0	12	0	4.29

SAULT STE. MARIE GREYHOUNDS

SCORING

	Games	G	A	Pts.	PIM
Chad Cavanagh	68	40	39	79	77
Chad Spurr	65	27	45	72	73
Daniel Passero	61	11	51	62	46
Ryan Jardine	68	27	34	61	56
Cory Pecker	68	25	34	59	24
Josef Vasicek	66	21	35	56	30
Martin Galik	61	23	27	50	24
Josh Bennett	63	14	12	26	102
Tim Zafiris	62	15	10	25	155
John Osborne	50	13	11	24	95
Bill Browne	68	2	12	14	171
Robert Mulick	66	1	12	13	83
Shawn Snider	41	5	7	12	39
Adam Nittel	21	3	8	11	101
Ryan Healy	45	3	7	10	53
Jouni Kuokkanen	20	3	5	8	2
Nick Jones	29	3	3	6	156
Cleon Smith	42	3	3	6	15
Jake Gibson	52	0	6	6	99
Paul Ballantyne	53	0	6	6	33
Mike Nelson	36	1	4	5	15
Darren Strilchuk	58	2	2	4	50
Oak Hewer	10	1	3	4	16
Derek Fox	32	1	2	3	45
Jeremy Elliott (goalie)	1	0	0	0	0
Marc Mazzuca	1	0	0	0	0
Robert Zago (goalie)	3	0	0	0	0
Jeff McKercher	8	0	0	0	0
Jason Flick (goalie)	31	0	0	0	2
Jake McCracken (goalie)	41	0	0	0	0

GOALTENDING

	Gms.	Min.	W	L	T	G	SO	Avg.
Jason Flick	31	1706	16	11	3	82	2	2.88
Jake McCracken	41	2290	15	16	4	140	0	3.67
Jeremy Elliott	1	25	0	0	1	2	0	4.80
Robert Zago	3	115	0	2	0	14	0	7.30

SUDBURY WOLVES

SCORING

	Games	G	A	Pts.	PIM
Norm Milley	68	52	68	120	47
Mike Fisher	68	41	65	106	55
Derek MacKenzie	68	22	65	87	74
Taylor Pyatt	68	37	38	75	95
Jason Jaspers	68	28	33	61	81
Brad Morgan	58	7	31	38	77
Alexei Salashenko	63	15	9	24	20
Glenn Crawford	22	7	16	23	12
Serge Dube	60	5	17	22	26
Kip Brennan	38	9	12	21	160
Matt Barnhardt	46	8	10	18	14
Brian McGrattan	53	7	10	17	153
Marc Long	54	5	9	14	16
Ryan McKie	68	1	12	13	77
Abe Herbst	19	2	8	10	16
Kyle Dafoe	66	3	6	9	239
Mike Laceby	28	1	8	9	8
Kevin Mota	51	1	8	9	35
Warren Hefford	28	3	4	7	38
Corey Sabourin	62	1	4	5	34
Tom Kotsopoulos	26	0	4	4	16
Troy Turyk	12	2	1	3	24
Alexei Semenov	28	0	3	3	28
Ryan Barnes	8	2	0	2	23
Kevin Beaumont	34	1	1	2	13
Colin Scotland	6	0	2	2	0
Andrew Raycroft (goalie)	45	0	2	2	2
David Cornacchia	7	1	0	1	15
Nevin Patterson	5	0	1	1	0
Mike Gorman (goalie)	16	0	1	1	10
B.J. VanMierlo (goalie)	1	0	0	0	0
Chris Kerr	3	0	0	0	2
Ryan Philips	3	0	0	0	2
Luc Messier	4	0	0	0	0
Matthew Hodges	10	0	0	0	17
Mark Aggio (goalie)	13	0	0	0	2

GOALTENDING

	Gms.	Min.	W	L	T	G	SO	Avg.
Mike Gorman	16	913	6	7	2	55	2	3.61
Andrew Raycroft	45	2528	17	22	5	173	1	4.11
Mark Aggio	13	654	2	6	1	49	0	4.50
B.J. VanMierlo	1	28	0	0	0	4	0	8.57

TORONTO ST. MICHAEL'S MAJORS

SCORING

	Games	G	A	Pts.	PIM
Sheldon Keefe	38	37	37	74	80
Kenny Corupe	68	22	33	55	24
Mike Jefferson	27	18	22	40	116
Jason Cannon	61	8	26	34	52
George Nistas	57	9	24	33	14
Mark Popovic	60	6	26	32	46
Shawn Cation	36	9	21	30	129
Keith Delaney	28	9	17	26	12
Ryan Barnes	31	11	14	25	215
Jason Pinizzotto	64	10	14	24	28
Brock Boucher	35	6	18	24	17
Ryan Walsh	66	10	10	20	36
Darryl Bootland	28	12	6	18	80
Matt Ellis	47	10	8	18	6
Adam DeLeeuw	29	10	5	15	55

	Games	G	A	Pts.	PIM
Kyle McAllister	30	5	10	15	24
Brian Simpson	60	6	6	12	105
Brent Mulder	57	4	4	8	97
Michael Gough	64	4	2	6	42
Charlie Stephens	7	2	4	6	8
Mark Hynes	64	1	5	6	66
Brad Pierce	28	2	3	5	40
Kevin Parfrey	17	0	4	4	0
Chris Cava	30	0	4	4	153
Chris Boucher	55	1	1	2	49
Ryan Rasmussen	39	0	2	2	30
Scott MacKenzie	6	1	0	1	0
Philippe Lakos	38	1	0	1	41
Gerald Moriarity	53	0	1	1	199
Kevin Parfrey	1	0	0	0	0
Jamie Ritskos	1	0	0	0	0
Troy Turyk	1	0	0	0	2
Cody Leibel	3	0	0	0	0
Ryan Robichaud	4	0	0	0	2
Jeff Thomson (goalie)	6	0	0	0	0
Corey Batten (goalie)	13	0	0	0	6
Dwayne Bateman (goalie)	24	0	0	0	2
Patrick Dovigi (goalie)	39	0	0	0	8

GOALTENDING

	Gms.	Min.	W	L	T	G	SO	Avg.
Corey Batten	13	757	3	7	3	48	0	3.80
Patrick Dovigi	39	2004	13	21	1	143	0	4.28
Dwayne Bateman	24	1179	4	12	2	100	0	5.09
Jeff Thomson	6	179	0	2	0	20	0	6.70

WINDSOR SPITFIRES

SCORING

	Games	G	A	Pts.	PIM
Jeff Martin	65	30	38	68	38
Michael Hanson	58	28	30	58	216
Jason Polera	65	33	22	55	64
Pavel Shtefan	67	14	27	41	24
Patrick Finnegan	63	8	33	41	44
Luc Rioux	68	14	25	39	26
Robin Boucher	55	10	29	39	33
Blair Stayzer	62	12	19	31	140
Jason Ward	12	8	11	19	25
Ryan Courtney	60	7	10	17	13
Andy Burnham	51	7	7	14	165
Curtis Watson	50	5	9	14	67
Craig Mahon	57	3	11	14	81
Kyle Chapman	28	6	3	9	49
Brent L'Heureux	52	1	6	7	24
Joey Sewell	63	3	3	6	143
Mark Ridout	44	1	5	6	95
Dan Growden	62	1	5	6	20
Jeff Kapitanchuk	27	3	2	5	25
John Cilladi	47	2	2	4	83
Tim Sinasac	61	2	2	4	203
Brad Simms	12	1	2	3	8
Max Linnik	19	1	2	3	14
Nick Young	35	0	3	3	8
Mike Leighton (goalie)	28	0	2	2	2
Jason Goldenberg	2	1	0	1	2
Darren Forbes	5	1	0	1	4
Boris Ivanov	5	1	0	1	0
Ron Vogel (goalie)	50	0	1	1	4
Terry Banjavic	1	0	0	0	0
J. Asadorian	3	0	0	0	2
Ryan Leblanc	3	0	0	0	2
Bryan Blair	4	0	0	0	2
Jeff Kugel	6	0	0	0	13

GOALTENDING

	Gms.	Min.	W	L	T	G	SO	Avg.
Ron Vogel	50	2745	19	22	4	177	0	3.87
Mike Leighton	28	1389	4	17	2	112	0	4.84

PLAYERS WITH TWO OR MORE TEAMS

SCORING

	Games	G	A	Pts.	PIM
Mark Aggio, Sudbury (goalie)	13	0	0	0	2
Mark Aggio, Kitchener (goalie)	10	0	0	0	0
Totals	23	0	0	0	2
Dallas Ashford, Kitchener	18	1	2	3	45
Dallas Ashford, Ottawa	37	1	4	5	18
Totals	55	2	6	8	63
Sean Avery, Owen Sound	28	22	23	45	70
Sean Avery, Kingston	33	14	25	39	88
Totals	61	36	48	84	158
Ryan Barnes, Sudbury	8	2	0	2	23
Ryan Barnes, Toronto	31	11	14	25	215
Ryan Barnes, Barrie	24	16	14	30	161
Totals	63	29	28	57	399
Dwayne Bateman, Ply. (goalie)	4	0	0	0	0
Dwayne Bateman, Toronto (g)	24	0	0	0	2
Totals	28	0	0	0	2
Corey Batten, Toronto (goalie)	13	0	0	0	6
Corey Batten, Erie (goalie)	36	0	2	2	4
Totals	49	0	2	2	10
Rick Bertran, Kitchener	38	1	2	3	78
Rick Bertran, Belleville	17	0	10	10	35
Totals	55	1	12	13	113
Bryan Blair, Windsor	4	0	0	0	2
Bryan Blair, Brampton	2	0	0	0	0
Totals	6	0	0	0	2
Darryl Bootland, Barrie	38	18	11	29	89
Darryl Bootland, Toronto	28	12	6	18	80
Totals	66	30	17	47	169
Shawn Cation, Toronto	36	9	21	30	129
Shawn Cation, Barrie	27	3	8	11	49
Totals	63	12	29	41	178
Chris Cava, Toronto	30	0	4	4	153
Chris Cava, Ottawa	27	2	10	12	68
Totals	57	2	14	16	221
Kyle Chapman, Plymouth	23	2	0	2	29
Kyle Chapman, Windsor	28	6	3	9	49
Totals	51	8	3	11	78
Fraser Clair, Barrie	25	4	3	7	14
Fraser Clair, Mississauga	34	2	9	11	30
Totals	59	6	12	18	44
David Cornacchia, Sudbury	7	1	0	1	15
David Cornacchia, Sarnia	43	4	12	16	106
Totals	50	5	12	17	121
Glenn Crawford, Sudbury	22	7	16	23	12
Glenn Crawford, Belleville	42	14	25	39	20
Totals	64	21	41	62	32
Curtis Cruickshank, Kings. (g)	16	0	1	1	9
Curtis Cruickshank, Sarnia (g)	28	0	1	1	21
Totals	44	0	2	2	30
Keith Delaney, Barrie	38	12	21	33	10
Keith Delaney, Toronto	28	9	17	26	12
Totals	66	21	38	59	22
Adam DeLeeuw, Barrie	39	15	16	31	146
Adam DeLeeuw, Toronto	29	10	5	15	55
Totals	68	25	21	46	201
Mike DePetrillo, London	14	3	2	5	30
Mike DePetrillo, Guelph	14	2	1	3	38
Totals	28	5	3	8	68
Patrick DesRochers, Sarnia (g)	8	0	0	0	0

	Games	G	A	Pts.	PIM
Patrick DesRochers, Kings. (g)	44	0	4	4	4
Totals	52	0	4	4	4
Joel Dezainde, Mississauga	24	4	20	24	35
Joel Dezainde, Barrie	36	15	33	48	52
Totals	60	19	53	72	87
Patrick Dovigi, Erie (goalie)	12	0	0	0	0
Patrick Dovigi, Toronto (goalie)	39	0	0	0	8
Totals	51	0	0	0	8
Jason Doyle, Brampton	4	2	1	3	7
Jason Doyle, London	54	20	31	51	61
Totals	58	22	32	54	68
Aaron Fransen, Kingston	25	11	15	26	98
Aaron Fransen, Owen Sound	32	9	27	36	86
Totals	57	20	42	62	184
Mike Gorman, Kitchener (g)	28	0	0	0	10
Mike Gorman, Sudbury (g)	16	0	1	1	10
Totals	44	0	1	1	20
Danny Gould, Kingston (goalie)	3	0	0	0	0
Danny Gould, Barrie (goalie)	2	0	1	1	0
Totals	5	0	1	1	0
Tony Gutilla, Brampton	19	0	3	3	44
Tony Gutilla, Sarnia	25	1	0	1	15
Totals	44	1	3	4	59
Julius Halfkenny, Sarnia	29	0	3	3	15
Julius Halfkenny, Erie	29	1	1	2	8
Totals	58	1	4	5	23
Sebastian Harts, Barrie	3	0	0	0	5
Sebastian Harts, Mississauga	30	2	2	4	31
Totals	33	2	2	4	36
Warren Hefford, Erie	31	4	11	15	22
Warren Hefford, Sudbury	28	3	4	7	38
Totals	59	7	15	22	60
Abe Herbst, Sarnia	11	0	4	4	15
Abe Herbst, Sudbury	19	2	8	10	16
Totals	30	2	12	14	31
Oak Hewer, Sault Ste. Marie	10	1	3	4	16
Oak Hewer, North Bay	40	11	9	20	34
Totals	50	12	12	24	50
Matthew Hodges, Sudbury	10	0	0	0	17
Matthew Hodges, Brampton	53	1	4	5	92
Totals	63	1	4	5	109
Warren Holmes, Owen Sound	13	2	2	4	20
Warren Holmes, North Bay	14	1	3	4	25
Totals	27	3	5	8	45
Dusty Jamieson, Guelph	12	2	7	9	0
Dusty Jamieson, Sarnia	54	14	21	35	10
Totals	66	16	28	44	10
Mike Jefferson, Toronto	27	18	22	40	116
Mike Jefferson, Barrie	26	15	20	35	62
Totals	53	33	42	75	178
Mark Jerant, North Bay	8	2	3	5	10
Mark Jerant, Mississauga	48	6	1	7	68
Totals	56	8	4	12	78
Nick Jones, Sault Ste. Marie	29	3	3	6	156
Nick Jones, Mississauga	29	10	6	16	116
Totals	58	13	9	22	272
Jeff Kaufman, Owen Sound	11	0	1	1	2
Jeff Kaufman, London	7	0	0	0	2
Totals	18	0	1	1	4
Sheldon Keefe, Toronto	38	37	37	74	80
Sheldon Keefe, Barrie	28	14	28	42	60
Totals	66	51	65	116	140
Darryl Knight, Sarnia	9	1	5	6	2
Darryl Knight, Guelph	56	15	30	45	28
Totals	65	16	35	51	30
Mike Laceby, Kitchener	12	0	0	0	6
Mike Laceby, Sudbury	28	1	8	9	8
Totals	40	1	8	9	14
Stephen Lafleur, Owen Sound	30	1	10	11	45
Stephen Lafleur, Kingston	35	1	10	11	47
Totals	65	2	20	22	92
Max Linnik, Plymouth	21	0	3	3	19

	Games	G	A	Pts.	PIM
Max Linnik, Windsor	19	1	2	3	14
Totals	40	1	5	6	33
Doug MacIver, Belleville	36	0	3	3	56
Doug MacIver, Sarnia	21	1	1	2	31
Totals	57	1	4	5	87
Jeff MacLean, Kitchener	9	0	0	0	4
Jeff MacLean, Ottawa	26	1	2	3	23
Totals	35	1	2	3	27
D.J. Maracle, Kingston	28	6	8	14	114
D.J. Maracle, Owen Sound	12	2	2	4	48
Totals	40	8	10	18	162
Kyle McAllister, Ottawa	23	1	9	10	27
Kyle McAllister, Toronto	30	5	10	15	24
Totals	53	6	19	25	51
Brian McGrattan, Guelph	6	1	3	4	15
Brian McGrattan, Sudbury	53	7	10	17	153
Totals	59	8	13	21	168
Jeff McKercher, S. Ste. Marie	8	0	0	0	0
Jeff McKercher, Peterborough	57	1	7	8	22
Totals	65	1	7	8	22
Luc Messier, North Bay	1	0	0	0	0
Luc Messier, Sudbury	4	0	0	0	0
Totals	5	0	0	0	0
Kevin Mota, Sarnia	12	0	2	2	17
Kevin Mota, Sudbury	51	1	8	9	35
Totals	63	1	10	11	52
Brent Mulder, Belleville	6	0	0	0	0
Brent Mulder, Toronto	57	4	4	8	97
Totals	63	4	4	8	97
Lucas Nehrling, Kingston	2	0	1	1	13
Lucas Nehrling, Guelph	60	5	14	19	131
Totals	62	5	15	20	144
Adam Nittel, Mississauga	34	15	16	31	235
Adam Nittel, Sault Ste. Marie	21	3	8	11	101
Totals	55	18	24	42	336
Brett Ormond, Peterborough	9	0	1	1	4
Brett Ormond, Kingston	56	4	15	19	26
Totals	65	4	16	20	30
Kevin Parfrey, Barrie	16	0	4	4	0
Kevin Parfrey, Toronto	1	0	0	0	0
Totals	17	0	4	4	0
Brad Pierce, Barrie	34	0	4	4	36
Brad Pierce, Toronto	28	2	3	5	40
Totals	62	2	7	9	76
Matt Price, Kingston	19	2	9	11	43
Matt Price, Sarnia	36	6	17	23	59
Totals	55	8	26	34	102
Andrew Proskurnicki, Sarnia	36	4	14	18	136
Andrew Proskurnicki, Erie	15	6	5	11	39
Totals	51	10	19	29	175
Ryan Rivard, Owen Sound	5	0	1	1	2
Ryan Rivard, Kingston	49	1	0	1	16
Totals	54	1	1	2	18
Colin Scotland, Sudbury	6	0	2	2	0
Colin Scotland, Kingston	31	0	0	0	27
Totals	37	0	2	2	27
Brad Simms, Mississauga	23	3	3	6	24
Brad Simms, Windsor	12	1	2	3	8
Totals	35	4	5	9	32
Rick Smith, Plymouth	30	13	12	25	44
Rick Smith, Kitchener	30	9	9	18	37
Totals	60	22	21	43	81
Charlie Stephens, Toronto	7	2	4	6	8
Charlie Stephens, Guelph	61	24	28	52	72
Totals	68	26	32	58	80
Jan Sulc, Kingston	13	4	4	8	6
Jan Sulc, Owen Sound	53	20	29	49	59
Totals	66	24	33	57	65
Troy Turyk, Toronto	1	0	0	0	2
Troy Turyk, Sudbury	12	2	1	3	24
Totals	13	2	1	3	26
Alain Veilleux, Ottawa	7	0	0	0	2

	Games	G	A	Pts.	PIM
Alain Veilleux, Kitchener	9	0	2	2	4
Totals	16	0	2	2	6
Nick Vukovic, North Bay	10	0	0	0	2
Nick Vukovic, Owen Sound	55	4	17	21	31
Totals	65	4	17	21	33
Jason Ward, Windsor	12	8	11	19	25
Jason Ward, Plymouth	23	14	13	27	28
Totals	35	22	24	46	53
Casey Wolak, Mississauga	1	0	0	0	0
Casey Wolak, Sarnia	15	1	1	2	31
Casey Wolak, Kitchener	41	10	14	24	117
Totals	57	11	15	26	148
Jeff Zehr, Erie	28	20	23	43	78
Jeff Zehr, Sarnia	14	4	10	14	43
Totals	42	24	33	57	121

GOALTENDING

	Games	Min.	W	L	T	G	SO	Avg.
Mark Aggio, Sud.	13	654	2	6	1	49	0	4.50
Mark Aggio, Kit.	10	364	2	2	0	26	0	4.29
Totals	23	1018	4	8	1	75	0	4.42
D. Bateman, Ply.	4	200	4	0	0	7	0	2.10
D. Bateman, Tor.	24	1179	4	12	2	100	0	5.09
Totals	28	1379	8	12	2	107	0	4.66
Corey Batten, Tor.	13	757	3	7	3	48	0	3.80
Corey Batten, Erie	36	1930	13	18	1	138	1	4.29
Totals	49	2687	16	25	4	186	1	4.15
C. Cruickshank, Kin.	16	835	5	9	0	63	1	4.53
C. Cruickshank, Sar.	28	1557	18	5	1	66	2	2.54
Totals	44	2392	23	14	1	129	3	3.24
P. DesRochers, Sar.	8	425	3	5	0	26	0	3.67
P. DesRochers, Kin.	44	2389	14	22	3	177	1	4.45
Totals	52	2814	17	27	3	203	1	4.33
Patrick Dovigi, Erie	12	655	6	5	0	50	1	4.58
Patrick Dovigi, Tor.	39	2004	13	21	1	143	0	4.28
Totals	51	2659	19	26	1	193	1	4.36
Mike Gorman, Kit.	28	1515	7	16	2	96	1	3.80
M. Gorman, Sud.	16	913	6	7	2	55	2	3.61
Totals	44	2428	13	23	4	151	3	3.73
D. Gould, Kings.	3	60	0	0	0	7	0	7.00
Danny Gould, Bar.	2	47	0	1	0	8	0	10.21
Totals	5	107	0	1	0	15	0	8.41

1999 J. ROSS ROBERTSON CUP PLAYOFFS

RESULTS

SUDDEN DEATH PLAYOFF GAME

	W	L	Pts.	GF	GA
Windsor	1	0	2	2	1
Kitchener	0	1	0	1	2

(Windsor won game for final playoff spot)

PRELIMINARY ROUND

	W	L	Pts.	GF	GA
Barrie	4	1	8	23	15
Kingston	1	4	2	15	23

(Barrie won series, 4-1)

	W	L	Pts.	GF	GA
Ottawa	4	0	8	14	3
North Bay	0	4	0	3	14

(Ottawa won series, 4-0)

	W	L	Pts.	GF	GA
Belleville	4	0	8	31	12
Sudbury	0	4	0	12	31

(London won series, 4-3)

	W	L	Pts.	GF	GA
Oshawa	4	1	8	24	13
Peterborough	1	4	2	13	24

(Oshawa won series, 4-1)

	W	L	Pts.	GF	GA
Plymouth	4	0	8	27	6
Windsor	0	4	0	6	27

(Plymouth won series, 4-0)

	W	L	Pts.	GF	GA
Guelph	4	1	8	15	14
Erie	1	4	2	14	15

(Guelph won series, 4-1)

	W	L	Pts.	GF	GA
Owen Sound	4	1	8	24	19
Sault Ste. Marie	1	4	2	19	24

(Owen Sound won series, 4-1)

	W	L	Pts.	GF	GA
London	4	2	8	22	19
Sarnia	2	4	4	19	22

(London won series, 4-2)

QUARTERFINALS

	W	L	Pts.	GF	GA
Oshawa	4	3	8	23	30
Barrie	3	4	6	30	23

(Oshawa won series, 4-3)

	W	L	Pts.	GF	GA
Belleville	4	1	8	21	15
Ottawa	1	4	2	15	21

(Belleville won series, 4-1)

	W	L	Pts.	GF	GA
London	4	3	8	35	26
Plymouth	3	4	6	26	35

(London won series, 4-3)

	W	L	Pts.	GF	GA
Owen Sound	4	2	8	29	24
Guelph	2	4	4	24	29

(Owen Sound won series, 4-2)

SEMIFINALS

	W	L	Pts.	GF	GA
Belleville	4	1	8	30	15
Oshawa	1	4	2	15	30

(Belleville won series, 4-1)

	W	L	Pts.	GF	GA
London	4	1	8	16	10
Owen Sound	1	4	2	10	16

(London won series, 4-1)

J. ROSS ROBERTSON CUP FINALS

	W	L	Pts.	GF	GA
Belleville	4	3	8	36	25
London	3	4	6	25	36

(Belleville won series, 4-3)

INDIVIDUAL LEADERS

Goals: Justin Papineau, Belleville (21)
Assists: Justin Papineau, Belleville (30)
Points: Justin Papineau, Belleville (51)
Penalty minutes: Aaron Fransen, Owen Sound (50)
Goaltending average: Seamus Kotyk, Ottawa (2.31)
Shutouts: Gene Chiarello, London (1)
Robert Holsinger, Plymouth (1)
Chris Madden, Guelph (1)
Lavente Szuper, Ottawa (1)

TOP SCORERS

	Games	G	A	Pts.
Justin Papineau, Belleville	21	21	30	51
Ryan Ready, Belleville	21	10	28	38
Tom Kostopoulos, London	25	19	16	35
Richard Pitirri, London	25	12	22	34
Jonathan Cheechoo, Belleville	21	15	15	30
Krys Barch, London	25	9	17	26
Chris Kelly, London	25	9	17	26
Jay Legault, London	25	8	18	26
Mike Dombkiewicz, Owen Sound	16	3	22	25
Glenn Crawford, Belleville	21	13	11	24
Brent Gauvreau, Oshawa	17	10	14	24
Kevin Colley, Oshawa	16	8	16	24
Branko Radivojevic, Belleville	21	7	17	24

INDIVIDUAL STATISTICS

BARRIE COLTS

(Lost quarterfinals to Oshawa, 4-3)

SCORING

	Games	G	A	Pts.	PIM
Denis Shvidki	12	7	9	16	2
Daniel Tkaczuk	12	7	8	15	10
Martin Skoula	12	3	10	13	13
Mike Jefferson	9	6	5	11	38
Mike Christian	12	5	6	11	24
Nick Smith	12	3	8	11	8
Joel Dezainde	12	2	9	11	27
Sheldon Keefe	10	5	5	10	31
Jeff Tetzlaff	12	1	7	8	13
Tim Verbeek	12	4	3	7	14
Chris Feil	12	1	6	7	25
Andre Lakos	12	3	3	6	8
Ryan Barnes	12	2	4	6	40
Shawn Cation	11	1	4	5	15
Scott Cameron	12	2	2	4	2
Brian Finley (goalie)	5	0	2	2	2
Michael Henrich	12	0	2	2	4
Ed Hill	12	0	2	2	8
Jerry Connell	11	1	0	1	10
Danny Gould	0	0	0	0	0
Ryan O'Keefe	6	0	0	0	0
Ben Vanderklok (goalie)	7	0	0	0	2

GOALTENDING

	Gms.	Min.	W	L	T	G	SO	Avg.
Brian Finley	5	323	4	1	0	15	0	2.79
Ben Vanderklok	7	428	3	4	0	23	0	3.22

BELLEVILLE BULLS

(Winner of 1999 J. Ross Robertson Cup)

SCORING

	Games	G	A	Pts.	PIM
Justin Papineau	21	21	30	51	20
Ryan Ready	21	10	28	38	22
Jonathan Cheechoo	21	15	15	30	27
Glenn Crawford	21	13	11	24	22
Branko Radivojevic	21	7	17	24	18
Kelly Paddon	21	3	17	20	28
Derek Campbell	21	6	12	18	32
Jason Lawmaster	21	5	13	18	34
Kevin Baker	12	12	5	17	12
Randy Rowe	21	9	8	17	0
Mike Renzi	21	5	8	13	17
Kris Newbury	21	4	6	10	23
Nathan Robinson	21	4	4	8	14
Mark Chaplin	20	2	6	8	2
Nick Policelli	12	0	5	5	8
Adam Collins	20	0	5	5	10
Branislav Mezei	18	0	4	4	29
Michael Jacobsen	21	0	4	4	10
Chris Stanley	8	1	0	1	0
Chad Mehlenbacher (goalie)	1	0	0	0	0
Tyler Longo	2	0	0	0	2
Rick Bertran	13	0	0	0	21
Cory Campbell (goalie)	21	0	0	0	4

GOALTENDING

	Gms.	Min.	W	L	T	G	SO	Avg.
Cory Campbell	21	1296	16	5	0	65	0	3.01
C. Mehlenbacher	1	11	0	0	0	2	0	10.91

ERIE OTTERS

(Lost preliminary round to Guelph, 4-1)

SCORING

	Games	G	A	Pts.	PIM
Tyler Rennette	5	6	1	7	8
Andrew Proskurnicki	5	2	2	4	16
Darren McMillan	5	0	4	4	4
Brad Boyes	5	1	2	3	10
Nikita Alexeev	5	1	1	2	4
Julius Halfkenny	5	1	1	2	2
Arvid Rekis	5	1	1	2	0
Jason Baird	5	0	2	2	19
Steve Montador	5	0	2	2	9
Michael Rupp	5	0	2	2	25
Paul Harvey	5	1	0	1	15
Brad Yeo	5	1	0	1	14
Steve Nobili	2	0	1	1	0
Ryan Lee	5	0	1	1	12
Tyler Rennette	0	0	0	0	0
Corey Batten (goalie)	2	0	0	0	0
Jim McGillivray	3	0	0	0	2
Wade Clubb	5	0	0	0	19
Ryan Fraser	5	0	0	0	9
Jourdan Lagace	5	0	0	0	7
Shane Nash	5	0	0	0	4
J.F. Perras (goalie)	5	0	0	0	2

GOALTENDING

	Gms.	Min.	W	L	T	G	SO	Avg.
J.F. Perras	5	245	1	3	0	11	0	2.69
Corey Batten	2	59	0	1	0	4	0	4.07

GUELPH STORM

(Lost quarterfinals to Owen Sound, 4-2)

SCORING

	Games	G	A	Pts.	PIM
Kevin Mitchell	11	3	10	13	29
Bob Crummer	11	5	5	10	30
Lindsay Plunkett	11	4	5	9	14
Ryan Davis	11	1	8	9	13
Eric Beaudoin	11	5	3	8	12
Charlie Stephens	11	3	5	8	19
Joe Gerbe	11	5	2	7	15
Kent McDonell	11	4	3	7	36
Darryl Knight	11	2	3	5	2
Kevin Dallman	11	1	4	5	2
Bohuslav Subr	11	1	4	5	15
Brent Kelly	11	3	1	4	6
Darryl McArthur	11	1	3	4	20
Ian Forbes	5	0	1	1	8
Yevgeny Krivomaz	11	0	1	1	17
Lucas Nehrling	11	0	1	1	35
Craig Andersson (goalie)	3	0	0	0	2
Francois Jolette	5	0	0	0	4
John Dickie	7	0	0	0	16
Nathan Herrington	7	0	0	0	0
Matt Rock	9	0	0	0	2
Chris Madden (goalie)	10	0	0	0	2

GOALTENDING

	Gms.	Min.	W	L	T	G	SO	Avg.
Chris Madden	10	550	6	3	0	32	1	3.49
Craig Andersson	3	114	0	2	0	9	0	4.74

KINGSTON FRONTENACS

(Lost preliminary round to Barrie, 4-1)

SCORING

	Games	G	A	Pts.	PIM
Andrew Ianiero	5	5	3	8	15
Matt Elich	5	3	5	8	0
Michael Zigomanis	5	1	7	8	2
Kevin Grimes	5	2	3	5	12
Sean Avery	5	1	3	4	13
Mike Oliveira	5	0	4	4	2
Jonathan Schill	5	2	1	3	6
Brett Clouthier	5	1	1	2	4
Stephen Lafleur	5	0	1	1	12
Chad Lynch	0	0	0	0	0
Eric Braff	5	0	0	0	2
Patrick DesRochers (goalie)	5	0	0	0	4
Sean Griffin	5	0	0	0	10
Morgan McCormick	5	0	0	0	13
Brett Ormond	5	0	0	0	4
Ryan Rivard	5	0	0	0	5
Nathan Tennant	5	0	0	0	0
Darryl Thomson	5	0	0	0	2
Ian Turner	5	0	0	0	2
Jamie Young	5	0	0	0	0

GOALTENDING

	Gms.	Min.	W	L	T	G	SO	Avg.
Patrick DesRochers	5	323	1	4	0	21	0	3.90

KITCHENER RANGERS

(Lost sudden death game for final playoff position to Windsor)

SCORING

	Games	G	A	Pts.	PIM
Ryan Milanovic	1	1	0	1	0
Vratislav Cech	1	0	1	1	4
Mark Aggio	0	0	0	0	0
Reg Bourcier (goalie)	1	0	0	0	0
Michal Dvorak	1	0	0	0	0
Barry Graham	1	0	0	0	0
Ryan Held	1	0	0	0	0
Wes Jarvis	1	0	0	0	2
Richard Kazda	1	0	0	0	0
Sal Lettieri	1	0	0	0	5
Travis Lisabeth	1	0	0	0	0
Brandon Merli	1	0	0	0	2
Darren Mortier	1	0	0	0	0
Nick Robinson	1	0	0	0	0
Allan Rourke	1	0	0	0	2
Josh Seabrook	1	0	0	0	0
Rick Smith	1	0	0	0	4
Mike Vaillaincourt	1	0	0	0	0
Mike Wehrstedt	1	0	0	0	0
Casey Wolak	1	0	0	0	4

GOALTENDING

	Gms.	Min.	W	L	T	G	SO	Avg.
Reg Bourcier	1	81	0	1	0	2	0	1.48

LONDON KNIGHTS

(Lost finals to Belleville, 4-3)

SCORING

	Games	G	A	Pts.	PIM
Tom Kostopoulos	25	19	16	35	32
Richard Pitirri	25	12	22	34	24
Krys Barch	25	9	17	26	15
Chris Kelly	25	9	17	26	22
Jay Legault	25	8	18	26	40
Rico Fata	25	10	12	22	42
Jason Doyle	25	7	12	19	20
Joel Scherban	25	5	11	16	4
John Erskine	25	5	10	15	38
Alex Henry	25	3	10	13	22
Dan Jancevski	25	1	7	8	24
Mike Mazzuca	25	4	1	5	12
Peter Reynolds	23	2	3	5	24
Jason Metcalfe	25	1	2	3	45
Adam Saffer	25	2	0	2	2
Tyler Durham	23	1	0	1	0
Bobby Turner	25	0	1	1	0
Taylor Cummings	0	0	0	0	0
Bill Ruggiero	0	0	0	0	0
Tomas Gron	2	0	0	0	0
Jeff Kaufman	2	0	0	0	0
Gene Chiarello (goalie)	25	0	0	0	8
Steven Rawski	25	0	0	0	0

GOALTENDING

	Gms.	Min.	W	L	T	G	SO	Avg.
Gene Chiarello	25	1550	15	10	0	88	1	3.41

NORTH BAY CENTENNIALS

(Lost preliminary round to Ottawa, 4-0)

SCORING

	Games	G	A	Pts.	PIM
Brett Gibson	4	1	1	2	10
Greg Labenski	4	0	2	2	2
Lorne Misita	4	1	0	1	4
Chris Neil	4	1	0	1	15
Rob Davison	4	0	1	1	12
Oak Hewer	4	0	1	1	0
Scott McKenzie	1	0	0	0	0
Shawn Degagne (goalie)	2	0	0	0	0
Alex Auld (goalie)	3	0	0	0	0
Rodney Richard	3	0	0	0	2
Brett Angel	4	0	0	0	7
Ryan Armstrong	4	0	0	0	2
Steve Chabbert	4	0	0	0	0
John Dean	4	0	0	0	6
Chris Eade	4	0	0	0	0
Omar Ennaffati	4	0	0	0	10
Samu Isosalo	4	0	0	0	4
Josh Legge	4	0	0	0	0

	Games	G	A	Pts.	PIM
Jamie Piercey	4	0	0	0	0
Gabriel Spilar	4	0	0	0	2
Scott Wray	4	0	0	0	6

GOALTENDING

	Gms.	Min.	W	L	T	G	SO	Avg.
Shawn Degagne	2	69	0	1	0	3	0	2.61
Alex Auld	3	170	0	3	0	10	0	3.53

OSHAWA GENERALS

(Lost semifinals to Belleville, 4-1)

SCORING

	Games	G	A	Pts.	PIM
Brent Gauvreau	17	10	14	24	17
Kevin Colley	16	8	16	24	38
Brad Ralph	16	8	7	15	12
Brian Passmore	17	6	9	15	33
Derrell Upton	17	6	6	12	4
Jim Baxter	14	4	8	12	6
Jeff MacMillan	17	3	7	10	28
Andrew Peters	17	2	7	9	36
Brandon Coalter	17	4	4	8	29
Ilja Demidov	17	2	6	8	30
John Kozoriz	17	5	2	7	10
Richard Scott	10	1	3	4	27
Vladimir Repnev	14	0	3	3	0
Bryan Allen	17	0	3	3	30
Brandon Cullen	17	2	0	2	18
Drew Bucktooth	16	1	1	2	16
Trevor Gillies	13	0	2	2	28
Tyrone Garner (goalie)	17	0	2	2	2
Richard Spence	15	0	1	1	21
Derek Dolson (goalie)	1	0	0	0	0
T.J. Reynolds	1	0	0	0	5
Mike Rusenstrom	10	0	0	0	0
Jonah Leroux	11	0	0	0	2

GOALTENDING

	Gms.	Min.	W	L	T	G	SO	Avg.
Tyrone Garner	17	1021	9	8	0	70	0	4.11
Derek Dolson	1	6	0	0	0	2	0	20.00

OTTAWA 67'S

(Lost quarterfinals to Belleville, 4-1)

SCORING

	Games	G	A	Pts.	PIM
Brian Campbell	9	2	10	12	6
Mark Bell	9	6	5	11	8
Justin Davis	9	2	8	10	4
Nick Boynton	9	1	9	10	18
Matt Zultek	9	6	2	8	4
Ben Gustavson	9	2	3	5	16
Jonathan Zion	9	2	3	5	8
Dan Tudin	9	3	1	4	6
Joe Talbot	9	2	2	4	4
Ian Jacobs	9	1	2	3	7
Lance Galbraith	9	0	3	3	16
Dan Tessier	8	0	2	2	10
Jeremy Van Hoof	5	1	0	1	2
Miguel Delisle	9	1	0	1	4
Seamus Kotyk (goalie)	5	0	1	1	0
Chris Cava	9	0	1	1	10
Lavente Szuper (goalie)	4	0	0	0	0
Dallas Ashford	6	0	0	0	2
Zenon Konopka	7	0	0	0	2
Henric Alfredsson	9	0	0	0	0
Jeff MacLean	9	0	0	0	4

GOALTENDING

	Gms.	Min.	W	L	T	G	SO	Avg.
Seamus Kotyk	5	338	3	2	0	13	0	2.31
Lavente Szuper	4	241	2	2	0	11	1	2.74

OWEN SOUND PLATERS

(Lost semifinals to London, 4-1)

SCORING

	Games	G	A	Pts.	PIM
Mike Dombkiewicz	16	3	22	25	22
Adam Mair	16	10	10	20	47
Aaron Fransen	16	4	14	18	50
Peter Campbell	16	8	9	17	22
Mike Lankshear	16	3	13	16	23
Wes Goldie	13	11	3	14	10
Dan Snyder	16	8	5	13	30
Jan Sulc	16	4	8	12	18
Chad Woollard	15	2	9	11	22
Joel Ward	16	2	4	6	0
Dave Stephenson	12	2	3	5	13
Adam Campbell	16	2	2	4	33
Randy Davidson	16	1	3	4	2
Juri Golicic	16	0	2	2	0
Brent Sullivan	16	0	2	2	0
D.J. Maracle	11	1	0	1	32
Nick Vukovic	16	1	0	1	12
Bryan Kazarian	3	0	1	1	0
Curtis Sanford (goalie)	16	0	1	1	0
Corey Roberts	0	0	0	0	0
Mike Barrett	13	0	0	0	2
Chris Hopiavuori	13	0	0	0	4

GOALTENDING

	Gms.	Min.	W	L	T	G	SO	Avg.
Curtis Sanford	16	960	9	7	0	58	0	3.63

PETERBOROUGH PETES

(Lost preliminary round to Oshawa, 4-1)

SCORING

	Games	G	A	Pts.	PIM
Scott Barney	5	4	1	5	4
Preston Mizzi	5	2	3	5	15
Pat Kavanagh	5	0	5	5	10
John Brioux	5	2	1	3	2
Sergei Kuznetzov	5	2	1	3	2
Jason Williams	5	1	2	3	2
Derek McNamara	5	1	1	2	4
Adam Dewan	5	0	2	2	12
Robert Francz	5	0	2	2	12
Brad Self	5	1	0	1	4
Jamie Chamberlain	4	0	1	1	4
B.J. Ketcheson	5	0	1	1	4
Mark Phibbs	5	0	1	1	0
David Currie	0	0	0	0	0
Darcy Morris	1	0	0	0	2
Joey MacDonald (goalie)	3	0	0	0	0
Mike Pickard (goalie)	3	0	0	0	0
Matt Carkner	5	0	0	0	20
Kurtis Foster	5	0	0	0	6
Jack Hardill	5	0	0	0	2
Jeff McKercher	5	0	0	0	4
Dustin Wood	5	0	0	0	0

GOALTENDING

	Gms.	Min.	W	L	T	G	SO	Avg.
Mike Pickard	3	154	1	2	0	11	0	4.29
Joey MacDonald	3	145	0	2	0	13	0	5.38

PLYMOUTH WHALERS

(Lost quarterfinals to London, 4-3)

SCORING

	Games	G	A	Pts.	PIM
Harold Druken	11	9	12	21	14
Adam Colagiacomo	10	6	9	15	14
Jason Ward	11	6	8	14	12
Nikos Tselios	11	4	10	14	8
Paul Mara	11	5	7	12	28

	Games	G	A	Pts.	PIM
David Legwand	11	3	8	11	8
Randy Fitzgerald	11	3	7	10	16
Damian Surma	11	3	6	9	15
Julian Smith	11	2	5	7	4
Jamie Lalonde	8	1	5	6	10
Shaun Fisher	10	1	5	6	0
Eric Gooldy	9	3	1	4	10
Troy Smith	11	3	0	3	2
Justin Williams	7	1	2	3	0
Jared Newman	11	1	2	3	9
James Ramsay	4	1	0	1	5
Tomek Valtonen	7	1	0	1	0
Kevin Holdridge	11	0	1	1	15
Mark McMahon	11	0	1	1	25
Rob Zepp (goalie)	3	0	0	0	0
Robert Holsinger (goalie)	10	0	0	0	4
Kristopher Vernarsky	11	0	0	0	2

GOALTENDING

	Gms.	Min.	W	L	T	G	SO	Avg.
Robert Holsinger	10	567	6	4	0	31	1	3.28
Rob Zepp	3	100	1	0	0	10	0	6.00

SARNIA STING

(Lost preliminary round to London, 4-2)

SCORING

	Games	G	A	Pts.	PIM
Peter Sarno	6	1	7	8	2
Jeff Zehr	6	3	4	7	27
Jeff Heerema	6	5	1	6	0
Ivan Novoseltsev	5	2	4	6	6
Peter Cava	5	1	5	6	8
Ryan VanBuskirk	6	1	2	3	4
Ryan Hare	6	0	3	3	0
Kevin Malcolm	6	2	0	2	0
Robb Palahnuk	6	1	1	2	6
Greg Willers	6	1	1	2	6
David Cornacchia	5	1	0	1	19
Dusty Jamieson	6	1	0	1	2
Chris Berti	6	0	1	1	0
Corey Brekelmans	6	0	1	1	4
Tony Gutilla	2	0	0	0	0
Matt Price	2	0	0	0	4
Derek McKinley	3	0	0	0	0
Curtis Cruickshank (goalie)	4	0	0	0	4
Doug MacIver	4	0	0	0	0
Travis Albers	5	0	0	0	2
Tyler Coleman	5	0	0	0	0
Greg Hewitt (goalie)	5	0	0	0	0
Dan Watson	6	0	0	0	4

GOALTENDING

	Gms.	Min.	W	L	T	G	SO	Avg.
Greg Hewitt	5	322	1	4	0	15	0	2.80
Curtis Cruickshank	4	71	1	0	0	6	0	5.07

SAULT STE. MARIE GREYHOUNDS

(Lost preliminary round to Owen Sound, 4-1)

SCORING

	Games	G	A	Pts.	PIM
Chad Cavanagh	5	5	4	9	4
Chad Spurr	5	4	3	7	4
Tim Zafiris	4	2	3	5	9
Daniel Passero	5	1	4	5	8
Josef Vasicek	5	3	0	3	10
Adam Nittel	5	1	2	3	30
Cory Pecker	5	1	2	3	2
Martin Galik	5	0	3	3	2
Shawn Snider	5	1	1	2	0
Bill Browne	5	0	2	2	6
Paul Ballantyne	5	1	0	1	4
Darren Strilchuk	4	0	1	1	8
Jake Gibson	5	0	1	1	6
Ryan Jardine	5	0	1	1	6
Robert Mulick	5	0	1	1	10
Cleon Smith	5	0	1	1	6
Jeremy Elliott (goalie)	1	0	0	0	0
Jake McCracken (goalie)	1	0	0	0	0
Ryan Healy	3	0	0	0	4
Jason Flick (goalie)	4	0	0	0	0
Derek Fox	4	0	0	0	4
Josh Bennett	5	0	0	0	9

GOALTENDING

	Gms.	Min.	W	L	T	G	SO	Avg.
Jason Flick	4	240	1	3	0	13	0	3.25
Jake McCracken	1	45	0	0	0	7	0	9.33
Jeremy Elliott	1	14	0	1	0	3	0	12.86

SUDBURY WOLVES

(Lost preliminary round to Belleville, 4-0)

SCORING

	Games	G	A	Pts.	PIM
Derek MacKenzie	4	2	4	6	2
Brad Morgan	4	3	2	5	4
Norm Milley	4	2	3	5	4
Taylor Pyatt	4	0	4	4	6
Mike Fisher	4	2	1	3	4
Jason Jaspers	4	2	1	3	13
Matt Barnhardt	4	0	3	3	0
Ryan McKie	4	0	2	2	8
Tom Kotsopoulos	3	1	0	1	2
Mike Laceby	4	0	1	1	2
B.J. VanMierlo	0	0	0	0	0
Troy Turyk	1	0	0	0	0
Corey Sabourin	2	0	0	0	0
Alexei Semenov	2	0	0	0	4
Mike Gorman (goalie)	3	0	0	0	0
Andrew Raycroft (goalie)	3	0	0	0	0
Kyle Dafoe	4	0	0	0	4
Serge Dube	4	0	0	0	6
Warren Hefford	4	0	0	0	6
Marc Long	4	0	0	0	2
Brian McGrattan	4	0	0	0	8
Kevin Mota	4	0	0	0	6
Alexei Salashenko	4	0	0	0	2

GOALTENDING

	Gms.	Min.	W	L	T	G	SO	Avg.
Mike Gorman	3	144	0	2	0	18	0	7.50
Andrew Raycroft	3	96	0	2	0	13	0	8.13

WINDSOR SPITFIRES

(Lost preliminary round to Plymouth, 4-0)

SCORING

	Games	G	A	Pts.	PIM
Michael Hanson	5	4	2	6	27
Jason Polera	5	0	4	4	0
Jeff Martin	5	2	0	2	2
Blair Stayzer	5	2	0	2	14
Ron Vogel (goalie)	4	0	2	2	2
Luc Rioux	5	0	2	2	4
Max Linnik	3	0	1	1	0
Patrick Finnegan	5	0	1	1	4
Dan Growden	5	0	1	1	6
Joey Sewell	5	0	1	1	2
Mark Ridout	1	0	0	0	0
Mike Leighton (goalie)	3	0	0	0	0
Robin Boucher	5	0	0	0	2
Kyle Chapman	5	0	0	0	4
John Cilladi	5	0	0	0	0
Ryan Courtney	5	0	0	0	7

	Games	G	A	Pts.	PIM
Brent L'Heureux	5	0	0	0	0
Craig Mahon	5	0	0	0	14
Pavel Shtefan	5	0	0	0	2
Tim Sinasac	5	0	0	0	11
Curtis Watson	5	0	0	0	11

GOALTENDING

	Gms.	Min.	W	L	T	G	SO	Avg.
Ron Vogel	4	240	1	3	0	18	0	4.50
Mike Leighton	3	80	0	1	0	10	0	7.50

1998-99 AWARD WINNERS

ALL-STAR TEAMS

First team	Pos.	Second team
Brian Finley, Barrie	G	Tyrone Garner, Oshawa
Brian Campbell, Ottawa	D	Kevin Mitchell, Guelph
Bryan Allen, Oshawa	D	Martin Skoula, Barrie
Ryan Ready, Belleville	LW	Denis Shvidki, Barrie
Daniel Tkaczuk, Barrie	C	Harold Druken, Plymouth
Ivan Novoseltsev, Sarnia	RW	Norm Milley, Sudbury

TROPHY WINNERS

Red Tilson Trophy: Brian Campbell, Ottawa
Eddie Powers Memorial Trophy: Peter Sarno, Sarnia
Dave Pinkney Trophy: Robert Holsinger, Plymouth
Rob Zepp, Plymouth
Max Kaminsky Trophy: Brian Campbell, Ottawa
William Hanley Trophy: Brian Campbell, Ottawa
Emms Family Award: Sheldon Keefe, Barrie
Matt Leyden Trophy: Peter DeBoer, Plymouth
Jim Mahon Memorial Trophy: Norm Milley, Sudbury
F.W. Dinty Moore Trophy: Lavente Szuper, Ottawa
Leo Lalonde Memorial Trophy: Ryan Ready, Belleville
Hamilton Spectator Trophy: Plymouth Whalers
J. Ross Robertson Cup: Belleville Bulls

ALL-TIME AWARD WINNERS

RED TILSON TROPHY

(Outstanding player)

Season Player, Team
1944-45—Doug McMurdy, St. Catharines
1945-46—Tod Sloan, St. Michael's
1946-47—Ed Sanford, St. Michael's
1947-48—George Armstrong, Stratford
1948-49—Gil Mayer, Barrie
1949-50—George Armstrong, Marlboros
1950-51—Glenn Hall, Windsor
1951-52—Bill Harrington, Kitchener
1952-53—Bob Attersley, Oshawa
1953-54—Brian Cullen, St. Catharines
1954-55—Hank Ciesla, St. Catharines
1955-56—Ron Howell, Guelph
1956-57—Frank Mahovlich, St. Michael's
1957-58—Murray Oliver, Hamilton
1958-59—Stan Mikita, St. Catharines
1959-60—Wayne Connelly, Peterborough
1960-61—Rod Gilbert, Guelph
1961-62—Pit Martin, Hamilton
1962-63—Wayne Maxner, Niagara Falls
1963-64—Yvan Cournoyer, Montreal
1964-65—Andre Lacroix, Peterborough
1965-66—Andre Lacroix, Peterborough
1966-67—Mickey Redmond, Peterborough
1967-68—Walt Tkaczuk, Kitchener
1968-69—Rejean Houle, Montreal
1969-70—Gilbert Perreault, Montreal
1970-71—Dave Gardner, Marlboros
1971-72—Don Lever, Niagara Falls
1972-73—Rick Middleton, Oshawa
1973-74—Jack Valiquette, Sault Ste. Marie
1974-75—Dennis Maruk, London
1975-76—Peter Lee, Ottawa
1976-77—Dale McCourt, St. Catharines
1977-78—Bobby Smith, Ottawa
1978-79—Mike Foligno, Sudbury
1979-80—Jim Fox, Ottawa
1980-81—Ernie Godden, Windsor
1981-82—Dave Simpson, London
1982-83—Doug Gilmour, Cornwall
1983-84—John Tucker, Kitchener
1984-85—Wayne Groulx, Sault Ste. Marie

Season Player, Team
1985-86—Ray Sheppard, Cornwall
1986-87—Scott McCrory, Oshawa
1987-88—Andrew Cassels, Ottawa
1988-89—Bryan Fogarty, Niagara Falls
1989-90—Mike Ricci, Peterborough
1990-91—Eric Lindros, Oshawa
1991-92—Todd Simon, Niagara Falls
1992-93—Pat Peake, Detroit
1993-94—Jason Allison, London
1994-95—David Ling, Kingston
1995-96—Alyn McCauley, Ottawa
1996-97—Alyn McCauley, Ottawa
1997-98—David Legwand, Plymouth
1998-99—Brian Campbell, Ottawa

EDDIE POWERS MEMORIAL TROPHY

(Scoring champion)

Season Player, Team
1933-34—J. Groboski, Oshawa
1934-35—J. Good, Toronto Lions
1935-36—John O'Flaherty, West Toronto
1936-37—Billy Taylor, Oshawa
1937-38—Hank Goldup, Tor. Marlboros
1938-39—Billy Taylor, Oshawa
1939-40—Jud McAtee, Oshawa
1940-41—Gaye Stewart, Tor. Marlboros
1941-42—Bob Wiest, Brantford
1942-43—Norman ``Red'' Tilson, Oshawa
1943-44—Ken Smith, Oshawa
1944-45—Leo Gravelle, St. Michael's
1945-46—Tod Sloan, St. Michael's
1946-47—Fleming Mackell, St. Michael's
1947-48—George Armstrong, Stratford
1948-49—Bert Giesebrecht, Windsor
1949-50—Earl Reibel, Windsor
1950-51—Lou Jankowski, Oshawa
1951-52—Ken Laufman, Guelph
1952-53—Jim McBurney, Galt
1953-54—Brian Cullen, St. Catharines
1954-55—Hank Ciesla, St. Catharines
1955-56—Stan Baliuk, Kitchener
1956-57—Bill Sweeney, Guelph
1957-58—John McKenzie, St. Catharines

Season	Player, Team
1958-59	Stan Mikita, St. Catharines
1959-60	Chico Maki, St. Catharines
1960-61	Rod Gilbert, Guelph
1961-62	Andre Boudrias, Montreal
1962-63	Wayne Maxner, Niagara Falls
1963-64	Andre Boudrias, Montreal
1964-65	Ken Hodge, St. Catharines
1965-66	Andre Lacroix, Peterborough
1966-67	Derek Sanderson, Niagara Falls
1967-68	Tom Webster, Niagara Falls
1968-69	Rejean Houle, Montreal
1969-70	Marcel Dionne, St. Catharines
1970-71	Marcel Dionne, St. Catharines
1971-72	Bill Harris, Toronto
1972-73	Blake Dunlop, Ottawa
1973-74	Jack Valiquette, Sault Ste. Marie Rick Adduono, St. Catharines
1974-75	Bruce Boudreau, Toronto
1975-76	Mike Kaszycki, Sault Ste. Marie
1976-77	Dwight Foster, Kitchener
1977-78	Bobby Smith, Ottawa
1978-79	Mike Foligno, Sudbury
1979-80	Jim Fox, Ottawa
1980-81	John Goodwin, Sault Ste. Marie
1981-82	Dave Simpson, London
1982-83	Doug Gilmour, Cornwall
1983-84	Tim Salmon, Kingston
1984-85	Dave MacLean, Belleville
1985-86	Ray Sheppard, Cornwall
1986-87	Scott McCrory, Oshawa
1987-88	Andrew Cassels, Ottawa
1988-89	Bryan Fogarty, Niagara Falls
1989-90	Keith Primeau, Niagara Falls
1990-91	Eric Lindros, Oshawa
1991-92	Todd Simon, Niagara Falls
1992-93	Andrew Brunette, Owen Sound
1993-94	Jason Allison, London
1994-95	Marc Savard, Oshawa
1995-96	Aaron Brand, Sarnia
1996-97	Marc Savard, Oshawa
1997-98	Peter Sarno, Windsor
1998-99	Peter Sarno, Sarnia

DAVE PINKNEY TROPHY

(Top team goaltending)

Season	Player, Team
1948-49	Gil Mayer, Barrie
1949-50	Don Lockhart, Marlboros
1950-51	Don Lockhart, Marlboros Lorne Howes, Barrie
1951-52	Don Head, Marlboros
1952-53	John Henderson, Marlboros
1953-54	Dennis Riggin, Hamilton
1954-55	John Albani, Marlboros
1955-56	Jim Crockett, Marlboros
1956-57	Len Broderick, Marlboros
1957-58	Len Broderick, Marlboros
1958-59	Jacques Caron, Peterborough
1959-60	Gerry Cheevers, St. Michael's
1960-61	Bud Blom, Hamilton
1961-62	George Holmes, Montreal
1962-63	Chuck Goddard, Peterborough
1963-64	Bernie Parent, Niagara Falls
1964-65	Bernie Parent, Niagara Falls
1965-66	Ted Quimet, Montreal
1966-67	Peter MacDuffe, St. Catharines
1967-68	Bruce Mullet, Montreal
1968-69	Wayne Wood, Montreal
1969-70	John Garrett, Peterborough
1970-71	John Garrett, Peterborough
1971-72	Michel Larocque, Ottawa
1972-73	Mike Palmateer, Toronto
1973-74	Don Edwards, Kitchener
1974-75	Greg Millen, Peterborough
1975-76	Jim Bedard, Sudbury
1976-77	Pat Riggin, London
1977-78	Al Jensen, Hamilton
1978-79	Nick Ricci, Niagara Falls
1979-80	Rick LaFerriere, Peterborough
1980-81	Jim Ralph, Ottawa
1981-82	Marc D'Amour, Sault Ste. Marie
1982-83	Peter Sidorkiewicz, Oshawa Jeff Hogg, Oshawa
1983-84	Darren Pang, Ottawa Greg Coram, Ottawa
1984-85	Scott Mosey, Sault Ste. Marie Marty Abrams, Sault Ste. Marie
1985-86	Kay Whitmore, Peterborough Ron Tugnutt, Peterborough
1986-87	Sean Evoy, Oshawa Jeff Hackett, Oshawa
1987-88	Todd Bojcun, Peterborough John Tanner, Peterborough
1988-89	Todd Bojcun, Peterborough John Tanner, Peterborough
1989-90	Jeff Wilson, Peterborough Sean Gauthier, Kingston
1990-91	Kevin Hodson, Sault Ste. Marie Mike Lenarduzzi, Sault Ste. Marie
1991-92	Kevin Hodson, Sault Ste. Marie
1992-93	Chad Lang, Peterborough Ryan Douglas, Peterborough
1993-94	Sandy Allan, North Bay Scott Roche, North Bay
1994-95	Andy Adams, Guelph Mark McArthur, Guelph
1995-96	Dan Cloutier, Guelph Brett Thompson, Guelph
1996-97	Craig Hillier, Ottawa Tim Keyes, Ottawa
1997-98	Craig Hillier, Ottawa Seamus Kotyk, Ottawa
1998-99	Robert Holsinger, Plymouth Rob Zepp, Plymouth

MAX KAMINSKY TROPHY

(Outstanding defenseman)

Season	Player, Team
1969-70	Ron Plumb, Peterborough
1970-71	Jocelyn Guevremont, Montreal
1971-72	Denis Potvin, Ottawa
1972-73	Denis Potvin, Ottawa
1973-74	Jim Turkiewicz, Peterborough
1974-75	Mike O'Connell, Kingston
1975-76	Rick Green, London
1976-77	Craig Hartsburg, S. Ste. Marie
1977-78	Brad Marsh, London Rob Ramage, London
1978-79	Greg Theberge, Peterborough
1979-80	Larry Murphy, Peterborough
1980-81	Steve Smith, Sault Ste. Marie
1981-82	Ron Meighan, Niagara Falls
1982-83	Allan MacInnis, Kitchener
1983-84	Brad Shaw, Ottawa
1984-85	Bob Halkidis, London
1985-86	Terry Carkner, Peterborough Jeff Brown, Sudbury
1986-87	Kerry Huffman, Guelph
1987-88	Darryl Shannon, Windsor
1988-89	Bryan Fogarty, Niagara Falls
1989-90	John Slaney, Cornwall
1990-91	Chris Snell, Ottawa
1991-92	Drake Berehowsky, North Bay
1992-93	Chris Pronger, Peterborough

Season Player, Team
1993-94—Jamie Rivers, Sudbury
1994-95—Bryan Berard, Detroit
1995-96—Bryan Berard, Detroit
1996-97—Sean Blanchard, Ottawa
1997-98—Chris Allen, Kingston
1998-99—Brian Campbell, Ottawa

WILLIAM HANLEY TROPHY

(Most gentlemanly)

Season Player, Team
1960-61—Bruce Draper, St. Michael's
1961-62—Lowell MacDonald, Hamilton
1962-63—Paul Henderson, Hamilton
1963-64—Fred Stanfield, St. Catharines
1964-65—Jimmy Peters, Hamilton
1965-66—Andre Lacroix, Peterborough
1966-67—Mickey Redmond, Peterborough
1967-68—Tom Webster, Niagara Falls
1968-69—Rejean Houle, Montreal
1969-74—No award presented
1974-75—Doug Jarvis, Peterborough
1975-76—Dale McCourt, Hamilton
1976-77—Dale McCourt, St. Catharines
1977-78—Wayne Gretzky, S.S. Marie
1978-79—Sean Simpson, Ottawa
1979-80—Sean Simpson, Ottawa
1980-81—John Goodwin, Sault Ste. Marie
1981-82—Dave Simpson, London
1982-83—Kirk Muller, Guelph
1983-84—Kevin Conway, Kingston
1984-85—Scott Tottle, Peterborough
1985-86—Jason Lafreniere, Belleville
1986-87—Scott McCrory, Oshawa
Keith Gretzky, Hamilton
1987-88—Andrew Cassels, Ottawa
1988-89—Kevin Miehm, Oshawa
1989-90—Mike Ricci, Peterborough
1990-91—Dale Craigwell, Oshawa
1991-92—John Spoltore, North Bay
1992-93—Pat Peake, Detroit
1993-94—Jason Allison, London
1994-95—Vitali Yachmenev, North Bay
1995-96—Jeff Williams, Guelph
1996-97—Alyn McCauley, Ottawa
1997-98—Matt Bradley, Kingston
1998-99—Brian Campbell, Ottawa

EMMS FAMILY AWARD

(Rookie of the year)

Season Player, Team
1972-73—Dennis Maruk, London
1973-74—Jack Valiquette, Sault Ste. Marie
1974-75—Danny Shearer, Hamilton
1975-76—John Travella, Sault Ste. Marie
1976-77—Yvan Joly, Ottawa
1977-78—Wayne Gretzky, S.S. Marie
1978-79—John Goodwin, Sault Ste. Marie
1979-80—Bruce Dowie, Toronto
1980-81—Tony Tanti, Oshawa
1981-82—Pat Verbeek, Sudbury
1982-83—Bruce Cassidy, Ottawa
1983-84—Shawn Burr, Kitchener
1984-85—Derek King, Sault Ste. Marie
1985-86—Lonnie Loach, Guelph
1986-87—Andrew Cassels, Ottawa
1987-88—Rick Corriveau, London
1988-89—Owen Nolan, Cornwall
1989-90—Chris Longo, Peterborough
1990-91—Cory Stillman, Windsor
1991-92—Chris Gratton, Kingston
1992-93—Jeff O'Neill, Guelph

Season Player, Team
1993-94—Vitali Yachmenev, North Bay
1994-95—Bryan Berard, Detroit
1995-96—Joe Thornton, Sault Ste. Marie
1996-97—Peter Sarno, Windsor
1997-98—David Legwand, Plymouth
1998-99—Sheldon Keefe, Barrie

MATT LEYDEN TROPHY

(Coach of the year)

Season Coach, Team
1971-72—Gus Bodnar, Oshawa
1972-73—George Armstrong, Toronto
1973-74—Jack Bownass, Kingston
1974-75—Bert Templeton, Hamilton
1975-76—Jerry Toppazzini, Sudbury
1976-77—Bill Long, London
1977-78—Bill White, Oshawa
1978-79—Gary Green, Peterborough
1979-80—Dave Chambers, Toronto
1980-81—Brian Kilrea, Ottawa
1981-82—Brian Kilrea, Ottawa
1982-83—Terry Crisp, Sault Ste. Marie
1983-84—Tom Barrett, Kitchener
1984-85—Terry Crisp, Sault Ste. Marie
1985-86—Jacques Martin, Guelph
1986-87—Paul Theriault, Oshawa
1987-88—Dick Todd, Peterborough
1988-89—Joe McDonnell, Kitchener
1989-90—Larry Mavety, Kingston
1990-91—George Burnett, Niagara Falls
1991-92—George Burnett, Niagara Falls
1992-93—Gary Agnew, London
1993-94—Bert Templeton, North Bay
1994-95—Craig Hartsburg, Guelph
1995-96—Brian Kilrea, Ottawa
1996-97—Brian Kilrea, Ottawa
1997-98—Gary Agnew, London
1998-99—Peter DeBoer, Plymouth

JIM MAHON MEMORIAL TROPHY

(Top scoring right wing)

Season Player, Team
1971-72—Bill Harris, Toronto
1972-73—Dennis Ververgaert, London
1973-74—Dave Gorman, St. Catharines
1974-75—Mark Napier, Toronto
1975-76—Peter Lee, Ottawa
1976-77—John Anderson, Toronto
1977-78—Dino Ciccarelli, London
1978-79—Mike Foligno, Sudbury
1979-80—Jim Fox, Ottawa
1980-81—Tony Tanti, Oshawa
1981-82—Tony Tanti, Oshawa
1982-83—Ian MacInnis, Cornwall
1983-84—Wayne Presley, Kitchener
1984-85—Dave MacLean, Belleville
1985-86—Ray Sheppard, Cornwall
1986-87—Ron Goodall, Kitchener
1987-88—Sean Williams, Oshawa
1988-89—Stan Drulia, Niagara Falls
1989-90—Owen Nolan, Cornwall
1990-91—Rob Pearson, Oshawa
1991-92—Darren McCarty, Belleville
1992-93—Kevin J. Brown, Detroit
1993-94—Kevin J. Brown, Detroit
1994-95—David Ling, Kingston
1995-96—Cameron Mann, Peterborough
1996-97—Joe Seroski, Sault Ste. Marie
1997-98—Maxim Spiridonov, London
1998-99—Norm Milley, Sudbury

F.W. DINTY MOORE TROPHY

(Lowest average by a rookie goalie)

Season Player, Team

1975-76—Mark Locken, Hamilton
1976-77—Barry Heard, London
1977-78—Ken Ellacott, Peterborough
1978-79—Nick Ricci, Niagara Falls
1979-80—Mike Vezina, Ottawa
1980-81—John Vanbiesbrouck, Sault Ste. Marie
1981-82—Shawn Kilroy, Peterborough
1982-83—Dan Burrows, Belleville
1983-84—Jerry Iuliano, Sault Ste. Marie
1984-85—Ron Tugnutt, Peterborough
1985-86—Paul Henriques, Belleville
1986-87—Jeff Hackett, Oshawa
1987-88—Todd Bojcun, Peterborough
1988-89—Jeff Wilson, Kingston
1989-90—Sean Basilio, London
1990-91—Kevin Hodson, Sault Ste. Marie
1991-92—Sandy Allan, North Bay
1992-93—Ken Shepard, Oshawa
1993-94—Scott Roche, North Bay
1994-95—David MacDonald, Sudbury
1995-96—Brett Thompson, Guelph

Season Player, Team

1996-97—Shawn Degane, Kitchener
1997-98—Seamus Kotyk, Ottawa
1998-99—Lavente Szuper, Ottawa

LEO LALONDE MEMORIAL TROPHY

(Overage player of the year)

Season Player, Team

1983-84—Don McLaren, Ottawa
1984-85—Dunc MacIntyre, Belleville
1985-86—Steve Guenette, Guelph
1986-87—Mike Richard, Toronto
1987-88—Len Soccio, North Bay
1988-89—Stan Drulia, Niagara Falls
1989-90—Iain Fraser, Oshawa
1990-91—Joey St. Aubin, Kitchener
1991-92—John Spoltore, North Bay
1992-93—Scott Hollis, Oshawa
1993-94—B.J. MacPherson, North Bay
1994-95—Bill Bowler, Windsor
1995-96—Aaron Brand, Sarnia
1996-97—Zac Bierk, Peterborough
1997-98—Bujar Amidovski, Toronto
1998-99—Ryan Ready, Belleville

ALL-TIME LEAGUE CHAMPIONS

Season	REGULAR-SEASON CHAMPION Team	PLAYOFF CHAMPION Team
1933-34—	No trophy awarded	St. Michael's College
1934-35—	No trophy awarded	Kitchener
1935-36—	No trophy awarded	West Toronto Redmen
1936-37—	No trophy awarded	St. Michael's College
1937-38—	No trophy awarded	Oshawa Generals
1938-39—	No trophy awarded	Oshawa Generals
1939-40—	No trophy awarded	Oshawa Generals
1940-41—	No trophy awarded	Oshawa Generals
1941-42—	No trophy awarded	Oshawa Generals
1942-43—	No trophy awarded	Oshawa Generals
1943-44—	No trophy awarded	Oshawa Generals
1944-45—	No trophy awarded	St. Michael's College
1945-46—	No trophy awarded	St. Michael's College
1946-47—	No trophy awarded	St. Michael's College
1947-48—	No trophy awarded	Barrie Flyers
1948-49—	No trophy awarded	Barrie Flyers
1949-50—	No trophy awarded	Guelph Biltmores
1950-51—	No trophy awarded	Barrie Flyers
1951-52—	No trophy awarded	Guelph Biltmores
1952-53—	No trophy awarded	Barrie Flyers
1953-54—	No trophy awarded	St. Catharines Tee Pees
1954-55—	No trophy awarded	Toronto Marlboros
1955-56—	No trophy awarded	Toronto Marlboros
1956-57—	No trophy awarded	Guelph Biltmores
1957-58—	St. Catharines Tee Pees	Toronto Marlboros
1958-59—	St. Catharines Tee Pees	Peterborough TPTs
1959-60—	Toronto Marlboros	St. Catharines Tee Pees
1960-61—	Guelph Royals	St. Michael's College
1961-62—	Montreal Jr. Canadiens	Hamilton Red Wings
1962-63—	Niagara Falls Flyers	Niagara Falls Flyers
1963-64—	Toronto Marlboros	Toronto Marlboros
1964-65—	Niagara Falls Flyers	Niagara Falls Flyers
1965-66—	Peterborough Petes	Oshawa Generals
1966-67—	Kitchener Rangers	Toronto Marlboros
1967-68—	Kitchener Rangers	Niagara Falls Flyers
1968-69—	Montreal Jr. Canadiens	Montreal Jr. Canadiens
1969-70—	Montreal Jr. Canadiens	Montreal Jr. Canadiens
1970-71—	Peterborough Petes	St. Catharines Black Hawks
1971-72—	Toronto Marlboros	Peterborough Petes
1972-73—	Toronto Marlboros	Toronto Marlboros
1973-74—	Kitchener Rangers	St. Catharines Black Hawks
1974-75—	Toronto Marlboros	Toronto Marlboros

REGULAR-SEASON CHAMPION		PLAYOFF CHAMPION
Season	**Team**	**Team**
1975-76—	Sudbury Wolves	Hamilton Steelhawks
1976-77—	St. Catharines Fincups	Ottawa 67's
1977-78—	Ottawa 67's	Peterborough Petes
1978-79—	Peterborough Petes	Peterborough Petes
1979-80—	Peterborough Petes	Peterborough Petes
1980-81—	Sault St. Marie Greyhounds	Kitchener Rangers
1981-82—	Ottawa 67's	Kitchener Rangers
1982-83—	Sault Ste. Marie Greyhounds	Oshawa Generals
1983-84—	Kitchener Rangers	Ottawa 67's
1984-85—	Sault Ste. Marie Greyhounds	Sault Ste. Marie Greyhounds
1985-86—	Peterborough Petes	Guelph Platers
1986-87—	Oshawa Generals	Oshawa Generals
1987-88—	Windsor Compuware Spitfires	Windsor Compuware Spitfires
1988-89—	Kitchener Rangers	Peterborough Petes
1989-90—	Oshawa Generals	Oshawa Generals
1990-91—	Oshawa Generals	Sault Ste. Marie Greyhounds
1991-92—	Peterborough Petes	Sault Ste. Marie Greyhounds
1992-93—	Peterborough Petes	Peterborough Petes
1993-94—	North Bay Centennials	North Bay Centennials
1994-95—	Guelph Storm	Detroit Jr. Red Wings
1995-96—	Guelph Storm	Peterborough Petes
1996-97—	Ottawa 67's	Oshawa Generals
1997-98—	Guelph Storm	Guelph Storm
1998-99—	Plymouth Whalers	Belleville Bulls

The OHL regular-season champion is awarded the Hamilton Spectator Trophy and the playoff champion is awarded the J. Ross Robertson Cup.

QUEBEC MAJOR JUNIOR HOCKEY LEAGUE

LEAGUE OFFICE

President
Gilles Courteau
Chairman of the board
Conrad Chapdelaine
Vice president
Maurice Filion
Statistician
Denis Demers
Director of public relations
Manon Gagnon-Leroux

Referee in chief
Doug Hayward
Director of hockey operations
Marcel Patenaude
Marketing director
Paul Girard
Address
255 Roland-Therien Blvd.
Suite 101
Longueuil, Quebec J4H 4A6

Phone
450-442-3590
FAX
450-442-3593

1998-99 REGULAR SEASON

FINAL STANDINGS

ROBERT LE BEL DIVISION

Team	G	W	L	T	Pts.	GF	GA
Shawinigan	70	44	22	4	92	275	212
Rouyn-Noranda	70	36	23	11	83	314	261
Victoriaville	70	34	30	6	74	275	253
Sherbrooke	70	31	34	5	67	268	272
Val-d'Or	70	30	35	5	65	312	319
Hull	70	23	38	9	55	276	298
Drummondville	70	18	48	4	40	233	349

FRANK DILIO DIVISION

Team	G	W	L	T	Pts.	GF	GA
Quebec	70	51	13	6	108	316	207
Halifax	70	46	20	4	96	298	206
Acadie-Bathurst	70	42	25	3	87	315	255
Moncton	70	38	27	5	81	257	235
Rimouski	70	30	32	8	68	270	263
Cape Breton	70	22	44	4	48	226	272
Baie-Comeau	70	18	44	8	44	208	297
Chicoutimi	70	20	48	2	42	200	344

INDIVIDUAL LEADERS

Goals: Ladislav Nagy, Halifax (71)
Assists: Mike Ribeiro, Rouyn-Noranda (100)
Points: Mike Ribeiro, Rouyn-Noranda (167)
Penalty minutes: Martin Grenier, Quebec (479)
Goaltending average: Maxime Ouellet, Quebec (2.698)
Shutouts: Mathieu Chouinard, Shawinigan (5)

TOP SCORERS

	Games	G	A	Pts.
Mike Ribeiro, Rouyn-Noranda	69	67	100	167
James Desmarais, Rouyn-Noranda	66	62	73	135
Jerome Tremblay, Rouyn-Noranda	69	38	94	132
Brad Richards, Rimouski	59	39	92	131
Ladislav Nagy, Halifax	63	71	55	126
Simon Gagne, Quebec	61	50	70	120
Benoit Dusablon, Val-d'Or	67	42	74	116
Patrick Grandmaitre, Victoriaville	70	37	78	115
Mathieu Benoit, Acadie-Bathurst	68	62	47	109
Eric Choinard, Quebec	62	50	59	109
Ryan Walsh, Shawinigan	59	45	59	104
Marc-Andre Thinel, Victoriaville	66	45	58	103
Jean-Philippe Pare, Shawinigan	69	36	67	103
David Thibeault, Victoriaville	63	43	59	102
Martin Fillion, Acadie-Bathurst	66	49	50	99
Alexandre Tremblay, Shawinigan	70	47	48	95
Christian Daigle, Val-d'Or	54	33	58	91
Gregor Baumgartner, A.-Bathurst	68	33	58	91
Sebastien Roger, Moncton	64	38	50	88
Michael Ryder, Hull	69	44	43	87
Paul Spadafora, Hull	70	29	58	87

INDIVIDUAL STATISTICS

BAIE-COMEAU DRAKKAR

SCORING

	Games	G	A	Pts.	PIM
Oleg Timchenko	44	34	25	59	44
Sylvain Deschatelets	69	23	32	55	108
Christopher Page	69	15	38	53	14
Marco Charpentier	52	16	23	39	34
Eric Tremblay	70	6	29	35	272
Yanick Lehoux	63	10	20	30	31
Jonathan Gautier	49	9	21	30	72
Edo Terglav	48	13	16	29	35
Marc-Andre Bergeron	46	8	14	22	57
Marc-Etienne Hubert	28	12	9	21	50
Bruno St. Jacques	49	8	13	21	85
Domenico Scali	22	7	12	19	24
Ken Arsenault	24	5	14	19	20
Jean-Nicolas Bordeleau	51	4	15	19	49
Steve Castonguay	41	6	12	18	10
Mario Favreau	39	4	12	16	18
Olivier Maltais	61	7	8	15	28
Jerome Bergeron	23	5	10	15	14
Dominic Periard	62	3	9	12	170
Duilio Grande	58	3	8	11	49
Eric VanAcker	65	1	6	7	192
Benoit Beausoleil	41	2	4	6	216
Nicolas Besner	22	2	3	5	27
Marc-Andre Guerard	21	1	4	5	7
Joey Fetta	10	1	2	3	102

	Games	G	A	Pts.	PIM
Serge Crochetiere	27	1	1	2	123
Nicolas Chabot (goalie)	33	0	2	2	0
Guillaume Gilbert	37	1	0	1	69
Martin Blanchet	3	0	1	1	0
Philippe Germain	3	0	1	1	0
Christopher Greene	18	0	1	1	12
Mathieu Chicoine	18	0	1	1	13
Eric Desjardins (goalie)	39	0	1	1	27
Alexandre Lapointe	1	0	0	0	0
Martin Leclerc	1	0	0	0	0
Guy Turmel	2	0	0	0	5
Sebastien Lortie	3	0	0	0	0
Shawn Lauzon (goalie)	3	0	0	0	0
Billy Harvey	4	0	0	0	23
Andre Bouchard	9	0	0	0	0
Steve Vallee (goalie)	34	0	0	0	0
Nicolas Joyal (goalie)	36	0	0	0	27

GOALTENDING

	Games	Min.	W	L	T	G	SO	Avg.
Eric Desjardins	31	1761	9	16	3	98	0	3.34
Nicolas Joyal	8	354	3	4	0	23	0	3.90
Nicolas Chabot	30	1666	6	16	5	121	0	4.36
Shawn Lauzon	2	119	0	2	0	11	0	5.57
Steve Vallee	10	375	0	6	0	42	0	6.72

ACADIE-BATHURST TITANS

SCORING

	Games	G	A	Pts.	PIM
Martin Fillion	66	49	50	99	59
Gregor Baumgartner	68	33	58	91	14
Philippe Plante	70	16	64	80	42
Alain O'Driscoll	68	35	42	77	74
Jonathan Girard	50	9	58	67	60
Mathieu Benoit	32	23	33	56	6
Eric Betournay	70	16	29	45	57
Denis Boily	31	16	23	39	65
Alain Charbonneau	36	23	15	38	67
Ramzi Abid	24	14	22	36	102
Marc Bouchard	33	15	20	35	20
Jules-Edy Laraque	52	16	17	33	52
Seneque Hyacinthe	31	13	17	30	70
Martin Lavergne	64	5	20	25	81
Francois Beauchemin	31	4	17	21	53
Jean-Philippe Soucy	36	1	17	18	108
Danny Groulx	36	2	15	17	51
Jonathan Francoeur	34	5	6	11	11
Hugo Levesque	62	2	7	9	44
Roberto Luongo (goalie)	52	0	8	8	2
Bryan Dube	34	4	3	7	159
Ryan Flinn	44	3	4	7	195
Philippe Gervais	25	2	5	7	13
Shawn Scanzano	23	1	5	6	23
Martin Autotte	37	3	2	5	87
Jean-Sebastien Trudelle	30	0	5	5	145
Samuel Lavoie	26	1	3	4	47
Denis Boudreau	38	2	1	3	4
Alexandre Morel	25	1	1	2	10
Jerome Dumont	31	1	0	1	17
Philippe Ozga (goalie)	58	0	1	1	2
Kevin Carrier	1	0	0	0	0
Jean-Philippe Cote	3	0	0	0	2
Adam Carter	10	0	0	0	17
Frederic Cloutier (goalie)	24	0	0	0	2
Benoit Beausoleil	26	0	0	0	82

GOALTENDING

	Games	Min.	W	L	T	G	SO	Avg.
Philippe Ozga	26	1457	16	6	2	80	1	3.30
Roberto Luongo	22	1341	14	7	1	74	0	3.31
Jonathan Charron	19	1065	10	9	0	64	0	3.61
Frederic Cloutier	8	382	2	3	0	30	0	4.71

CAPE BRETON SCREAMING EAGLES

SCORING

	Games	G	A	Pts.	PIM
Philippe Tremblay	64	30	55	85	101
Ryan Walsh	42	35	44	79	58
Yannick Carpentier	67	30	35	65	58
Jonathan Gagnon	68	27	37	64	39
Artem Rybin	70	19	30	49	63
Josh Dill	67	7	25	32	144
Randy Copley	25	8	22	30	60
Chris Lyness	42	12	17	29	35
Robbie Sutherland	58	11	14	25	97
Sebastien Gagnon	58	5	18	23	237
Tomas Kloucek	59	4	17	21	162
Travis Zachary	33	10	5	15	127
Jean Mallette	59	2	13	15	76
Patrick Yetman	26	5	9	14	21
Olivier Proulx	59	5	9	14	53
Robbie Bennett	63	1	10	11	55
Guillaume Lefebvre	24	2	7	9	13
Sandro Sbrocca	65	1	8	9	256
Pierre-Luc Laprise	52	3	4	7	31
Kevin Bergin	18	2	4	6	22
Matt House	29	4	1	5	23
Trevor Ettinger	61	0	5	5	376
Alexandre Page	19	2	2	4	52
Hunter Lahache	29	1	2	3	55
Steve Castonguay	7	0	2	2	2
Alain Turcotte	17	0	2	2	52
David St. Germain (goalie)	73	0	2	2	2
Chris Tellum	3	0	0	0	0
Jamie Mattie	12	0	0	0	4
Nicolas Chatham (goalie)	12	0	0	0	0
Marc-Andre Leclerc (goalie)	31	0	0	0	17
Donald Johnstone	36	0	0	0	24

GOALTENDING

	Games	Min.	W	L	T	G	SO	Avg.
Danny Lavoie	28	1586	11	13	3	84	2	3.18
Jonathan Wilhelmy	11	518	1	6	0	30	0	3.47
David St. Germain	35	1959	10	23	1	127	1	3.89
Marc-Andre Leclerc	9	202	0	2	0	14	0	4.16
Nicolas Chatham	3	37	0	0	0	7	0	11.31

CHICOUTIMI SAGUENEENS

SCORING

	Games	G	A	Pts.	PIM
Mathieu Benoit	36	39	14	53	28
Francois Fortin	70	12	36	48	48
Gregory Dupre	62	10	37	47	67
Gilbert Lefrancois	69	18	21	39	58
Marc Bouchard	37	12	27	39	30
Vincent Dionne	40	16	22	38	61
Roustam Bakhriddinov	68	7	27	34	95
Jonathan Francoeur	31	15	13	28	20
Ramzi Abid	21	11	15	26	97
Sacha Fillion	58	6	19	25	137
Guillaume Karrer	45	5	17	22	57
David Girard	27	9	10	19	34
Alex Turcotte	69	4	11	15	61
Michel Nault	62	5	8	13	48
Yves Bellerose	53	4	9	13	144
Jean-Sebastien Trudelle	36	1	12	13	110
Simon Tremblay	26	7	5	12	85
Pierre-Antoine Paquet	58	5	7	12	30
Marc Villeneuve	62	4	6	10	30
Karl St. Pierre	62	1	8	9	67
Sylvain Watt	64	2	6	8	12
Joey D'Amico	13	3	3	6	22
Jean-Philippe Soucy	5	0	4	4	9
Sebastien Lucier	23	0	4	4	9
Jerome Dumont	28	2	1	3	28
Vincent Blanchette	48	0	3	3	37

	Games	G	A	Pts.	PIM
Rémi Bergeron (goalie)	68	0	2	2	22
Eryc Collin	6	1	0	1	21
Simon Duplessis	7	1	0	1	0
Alexandre Piche	4	0	1	1	4
Alexandre Morel	3	0	0	0	0
Jean-Francois Belanger	3	0	0	0	0
Jean-Francois Talbot	4	0	0	0	2
Patrick Provencal (goalie)	5	0	0	0	0
Jean-Francois Rousseau	7	0	0	0	2
Patrick Mbaraga	19	0	0	0	13
Yann Collin (goalie)	67	0	0	0	29

GOALTENDING

	Games	Min.	W	L	T	G	SO	Avg.
Remi Bergeron	55	2719	14	33	1	202	0	4.46
Yann Collin	35	1463	6	14	1	127	0	5.21
Patrick Provencal	4	48	0	1	0	6	0	7.61

DRUMMONDVILLE VOLTIGEURS

SCORING

	Games	G	A	Pts.	PIM
Samuel St. Pierre	68	47	28	75	65
Zoltan Batovsky	62	29	42	71	126
Jonathan Roy	65	24	37	61	44
Miroslav Zalesak	45	24	27	51	18
Francis Lessard	53	12	36	48	295
Eric Laplante	42	14	25	39	258
Jean-Philippe Morin	69	2	31	33	158
Domenico Scali	42	11	13	24	20
David Girard	46	10	12	22	19
Daniel Hudgin	64	7	14	21	34
Yannick Noiseux	68	10	10	20	64
Eric Perricone	20	6	11	17	10
Alexandre Couture	34	5	12	17	32
Philippe Paris	70	7	9	16	32
Eric Drouin	34	5	11	16	29
Jean-Philippe Soucy	24	2	13	15	53
Jean-Philippe Glaude	64	2	13	15	110
Philippe Gelinas	54	5	6	11	67
Luc Roy	32	1	9	10	218
Marc-Etienne Hubert	22	1	8	9	43
Simon Lagace-Daigle	44	3	5	8	17
Jonathan St. Louis	32	3	4	7	131
Patrice Auger	43	0	5	5	29
Jeff Leblanc	25	1	3	4	109
Marc-Andre Jacob	29	2	0	2	49
Eric Jean	23	0	2	2	7
Mathieu Loiselle	41	0	2	2	54
Jean-Michel Martin	22	0	1	1	0
Jonathan Pelletier (goalie)	69	0	1	1	10
Danny Dallaire (goalie)	70	0	1	1	2
Pascal Poirier (goalie)	1	0	0	0	0
Sebastien Briere	1	0	0	0	0
Francis Larivee	3	0	0	0	4
Jean-Francois Poulin	4	0	0	0	7

GOALTENDING

	Games	Min.	W	L	T	G	SO	Avg.
Jonathan Pelletier	54	2803	13	30	3	212	0	4.54
Danny Dallaire	32	1455	5	18	1	131	0	5.40

HALIFAX MOOSEHEADS

SCORING

	Games	G	A	Pts.	PIM
Ladislav Nagy	63	71	55	126	148
Jason Troini	70	23	40	63	78
Alex Tanguay	31	27	34	61	30
Brandon Reid	70	32	25	57	33
Samuel Seguin	70	16	33	49	45
Alexandre Mathieu	69	21	27	48	90
Carlyle Lewis	65	20	27	47	425
Frederic Belanger	54	6	41	47	115
Jasmin Gelinas	59	7	36	43	80
Mauro DiPaolo	53	11	29	40	238
Marc-Andre Binette	70	13	26	39	20
Ali MacEachern	70	9	28	37	87
Jeffrey Sullivan	69	7	30	37	320
Brandon Benedict	64	18	12	30	12
Billy Manley	36	11	12	23	20
Mathieu Paul	43	1	10	11	22
Alex Johnstone	60	1	8	9	248
P.J. Lynch	23	3	4	7	42
Alexei Volkov (goalie)	56	0	2	2	21
Pascal Leclaire (goalie)	62	0	2	2	2
Jimmy Bilodeau	22	1	0	1	0
Dustin Dagenais	4	0	1	1	23
Eric Perricone	7	0	1	1	2
Nathan States	8	0	1	1	4
Michael Riendeau	11	0	1	1	4
Brett Bower	16	0	1	1	24
Vincent Laroche (goalie)	21	0	1	1	5
David McCutcheon	28	0	1	1	67
Tyler Reid	49	0	1	1	42
David Ouellet (goalie)	1	0	0	0	0
Dwight Wolfe	1	0	0	0	9
Francois Pichette	1	0	0	0	0
Ryan Power	2	0	0	0	2
A.J. Rivers	3	0	0	0	4
Eric Frechette	4	0	0	0	17
Mike Bray	28	0	0	0	4
Jeff Towriss	32	0	0	0	13

GOALTENDING

	Games	Min.	W	L	T	G	SO	Avg.
Vincent Laroche	4	118	2	0	0	4	0	2.04
Alexei Volkov	39	2332	25	9	3	105	2	2.70
Pascal Leclaire	33	1828	19	11	1	96	2	3.15

HULL OLYMPIQUES

SCORING

	Games	G	A	Pts.	PIM
Michael Ryder	69	44	43	87	65
Paul Spadafora	70	29	58	87	153
Marty Johnston	56	35	47	82	74
Jiri Fischer	65	22	56	78	141
Ryan Lauzon	57	21	47	68	36
Radim Vrbata	54	22	38	60	16
Alexandre Giroux	67	15	22	37	124
Bruno Lemire	67	17	17	34	57
Dustin Russell	70	11	19	30	41
Yannick Lachance	58	12	9	21	121
Adam Rivet	59	3	17	20	67
Brock Boucher	23	9	10	19	26
Andrew Carver	65	2	15	17	104
Daniel Clermont	60	4	10	14	49
Roberto Bissonnette	44	7	6	13	183
Mario Joly	61	3	8	11	375
Vince Malts	12	5	5	10	36
Adam Collins	21	4	5	9	8
Casey Burnette	48	2	7	9	131
Philippe Lacasse	18	2	5	7	4
Michael Lanthier	47	1	5	6	197
Jonathan Andrews	45	2	3	5	112
Michaël Parent	41	2	1	3	49
Jonathan Pilotte	19	1	2	3	25
Brian Jollimore	22	0	2	2	11
David McCutcheon	20	1	0	1	77
Erich Paroshy	3	0	1	1	4
Frederic Malette (goalie)	66	0	1	1	2
Francis Nault	1	0	0	0	0
Maxime Plouffe (goalie)	3	0	0	0	0
Jean-Francois Monfils (goalie)	5	0	0	0	0
Yannick Bourgeois (goalie)	17	0	0	0	0
Philippe Bergeron (goalie)	49	0	0	0	37

GOALTENDING

	Games	Min.	W	L	T	G	SO	Avg.
Maxime Plouffe	1	1	0	0	0	0	0	0.00
Frederic Malette	51	2676	14	23	5	174	0	3.90
Philippe Bergeron	30	1568	8	14	4	112	0	4.29
Yannick Bourgeois	3	62	1	1	0	7	0	6.84

MONCTON WILDCATS

SCORING

	Games	G	A	Pts.	PIM
Sebastien Roger	64	38	50	88	91
Eric Demers	70	35	38	73	36
Simon Laliberte	70	31	39	70	64
David Comeau	70	18	46	64	163
Alexandre Vigneault	69	7	48	55	38
Mirko Murovic	69	21	33	54	60
Morgan Warren	48	20	16	36	68
Jonathan Desroches	70	5	29	34	54
Alexei Tezikov	25	9	21	30	52
Shane Reagh	48	14	13	27	41
Dimitri Kalinin	39	7	18	25	44
Clark Udle	24	6	15	21	140
Simon Tremblay	40	8	12	20	40
Olivier Dubuc	61	5	15	20	31
Vincent Dionne	23	7	11	18	28
Daniel MacLeod	69	4	12	16	188
Jonathan Gauthier	39	5	8	13	41
Louis-Philippe Lessard	67	1	10	11	36
Dimitri Afanasenkov	15	5	5	10	12
Jacques Lariviere	66	5	5	10	306
Dominic Noel	51	3	7	10	12
David Walker	41	0	8	8	226
Patrice Theriault	56	2	5	7	34
Yannick Theriault	8	1	3	4	2
Jeff Washbrook	4	0	1	1	4
J.-F. Damphousse (goalie)	61	0	1	1	2
Simon Lajeunesse (goalie)	70	0	1	1	2
Branwell Beck	1	0	0	0	2
Jean-Francois Gouin	1	0	0	0	20
Howard Beaton	2	0	0	0	0
Joel Boudreau (goalie)	2	0	0	0	0
Martin Leon	2	0	0	0	0
Tyson Maloney	5	0	0	0	4
Ryan Dodge	6	0	0	0	19
Danny Bowie (goalie)	7	0	0	0	0
Andrew MacDonald	32	0	0	0	49

GOALTENDING

	Games	Min.	W	L	T	G	SO	Avg.
Simon Lajeunesse	36	1993	18	9	3	98	1	2.95
J.-F. Damphousse	40	2163	19	17	2	121	1	3.36
Danny Bowie	2	129	1	1	0	11	0	5.14

QUEBEC REMPARTS

SCORING

	Games	G	A	Pts.	PIM
Simon Gagne	61	50	70	120	42
Eric Chouinard	62	50	59	109	56
David Bernier	50	34	50	84	69
Martin Moise	67	36	38	74	34
Dmitri Tolkunov	69	11	57	68	110
Wesley Scanzano	70	23	31	54	64
Andre Martineau	70	18	33	51	22
Simon Tremblay	70	13	27	40	86
Maxim Balmochnykh	21	9	22	31	38
Daniel Archambault	70	4	24	28	382
Antoine Vermette	57	9	17	26	32
Martin Grenier	60	7	18	25	479
Jerome Marois	52	8	15	23	48
Eric Laplante	23	4	17	21	58
Raymond Dalton	35	8	9	17	17
Nicholas Bilotto	35	1	16	17	72
Joey Fetta	28	2	10	12	80
Juraj Kolnik	12	6	5	11	6
Marco Charpentier	12	4	7	11	4
Sebastien Lucier	42	5	4	9	8
Travis Zachary	17	4	4	8	37
Sylvain Plamondon	24	3	5	8	112
Jeff Leblanc	21	2	6	8	109
Cameron Lowe	25	0	7	7	8
Tommy Bolduc	54	2	4	6	108
Pierre Loiselle	20	2	2	4	65
Alexandre Morel	20	1	2	3	16
Stuart MacRae	7	0	2	2	0
Jonathan Wilhelmy (goalie)	55	0	1	1	0
Martin Pare (goalie)	1	0	0	0	0
Nicolas Pelletier	4	0	0	0	0
Sebastien Crete (goalie)	4	0	0	0	0
Jean-Philippe Cote	8	0	0	0	2
Danick Jomphe	9	0	0	0	2
Hunter Lahache	27	0	0	0	33
Martin Bilodeau (goalie)	39	0	0	0	4
Eric Jean	43	0	0	0	28
Maxime Ouellet (goalie)	68	0	0	0	4

GOALTENDING

	Games	Min.	W	L	T	G	SO	Avg.
Maxime Ouellet	59	3447	40	12	6	155	3	2.70
Martin Bilodeau	10	427	5	1	0	24	0	3.38
Jonathan Wilhelmy	8	426	6	0	0	25	0	3.52

RIMOUSKI OCEANIC

SCORING

	Games	G	A	Pts.	PIM
Brad Richards	59	39	92	131	55
Juraj Kolnik	50	36	37	73	34
Julien Desrosiers	64	31	37	68	40
Jonathan Beaulieu	58	24	34	58	182
Thatcher Bell	64	16	38	54	67
Francois Page	35	22	21	43	194
Joe Rullier	54	7	32	39	202
Philippe Grondin	58	19	17	36	118
Adam Borzecki	61	6	30	36	134
Jan-Philippe Cadieux	47	13	15	28	8
Casey Leggett	69	11	16	27	101
David St. Onge	56	9	18	27	69
Michel Ouellet	28	7	13	20	10
Eric Drouin	29	4	12	16	65
Benoit Martin	68	7	7	14	41
David Bilodeau	53	4	9	13	26
David Boilard	66	3	10	13	113
Jonathan St. Louis	30	4	6	10	133
Denis Desmarais	66	4	3	7	105
Nicolas Poirier	54	3	4	7	107
Kris Barnett	32	1	4	5	25
Antoine Bergeron	20	0	4	4	28
Guillaume Couture	43	0	4	4	178
Jean-Philippe Briere	1	0	2	2	2
Jean-Francois Babin	50	0	2	2	136
Sebastien Caron (goalie)	61	0	2	2	4
Mathieu Pigeon	3	0	1	1	0
Pierre Levesque	8	0	1	1	0
Alex Castonguay	12	0	1	1	31
Philippe Sauve (goalie)	62	0	1	1	13
Frederic Faucher	1	0	0	0	0
Mike Ouellet	1	0	0	0	0
Vincent Tougas	1	0	0	0	0
Francis Pelletier	2	0	0	0	0
Alexandre Belzile	3	0	0	0	4
Billy Poirier	3	0	0	0	0
Eric Salvail (goalie)	3	0	0	0	0
Bruno Levesque (goalie)	9	0	0	0	0

GOALTENDING

	Games	Min.	W	L	T	G	SO	Avg.
Sebastien Caron	30	1570	13	10	3	85	0	3.25
Philippe Sauve	44	2401	16	19	4	155	0	3.87
Eric Desjardins	5	292	1	3	1	20	0	4.11
Bruno Levesque	1	20	0	0	0	2	0	6.00

ROUYN-NORANDA HUSKIES

SCORING

	Games	G	A	Pts.	PIM
Mike Ribeiro	69	67	100	167	137
James Desmarais	66	62	73	135	127
Jerome Tremblay	69	38	94	132	36
Steeve Vandal	64	35	35	70	183
Kevin Cloutier	69	15	27	42	40
Samuel Gagnon	64	18	22	40	297
Jimmy Verdule	42	5	33	38	172
Jason Lehoux	64	13	20	33	288
Randy Copley	38	7	25	32	87
Oleg Timchenko	24	15	10	25	20
Didier Pietropaulo	37	3	19	22	190
Jerome Bergeron	39	11	8	19	64
Jonathan Gauthier	22	2	13	15	25
Patrick Gilbert	62	2	12	14	60
Jean-Luc Legault	43	5	7	12	19
Kyrill Alexeyev	52	2	10	12	125
Steve Waters	56	2	9	11	16
Jason Tessier	57	1	9	10	59
Chris Lyness	25	3	6	9	49
Mathieu Rancourt	38	1	6	7	99
Jonathan Blais	34	2	4	6	19
Joey D'Amico	38	2	4	6	65
Alexandre Audet	57	1	4	5	126
Guillaume Marcoux	18	1	3	4	22
Roberto Baldris	8	0	4	4	23
Danny Lavoie (goalie)	67	0	4	4	10
Alain Turcotte	28	1	2	3	32
Benoit Vezina	12	0	3	3	23
Danny Couette	1	0	1	1	0
Luc Vaillancourt (goalie)	27	0	1	1	0
Sebastien Centomo (goalie)	70	0	1	1	6
Jean-Jacques Gauthier	1	0	0	0	0
Patrick Couture (goalie)	1	0	0	0	0
Shawn Scanzano	5	0	0	0	7
Eric Naudi	8	0	0	0	2
Philip Page (goalie)	9	0	0	0	0
Peter Kassa	10	0	0	0	14
Vincent Labelle	14	0	0	0	0
Kenny Moore	21	0	0	0	21

GOALTENDING

	Games	Min.	W	L	T	G	SO	Avg.
Danny Lavoie	28	1556	14	7	4	87	0	3.36
Luc Vaillancourt	18	1000	8	6	2	58	1	3.48
Sebastien Centomo	32	1658	14	9	4	104	1	3.76
Philip Page	2	70	0	0	1	5	0	4.27
Patrick Couture	1	40	0	1	0	4	0	5.97

SHAWINIGAN CATARACTES

SCORING

	Games	G	A	Pts.	PIM
Jean-Philippe Pare	69	36	67	103	72
Alexandre Tremblay	70	47	48	95	96
Dominic Forget	66	34	47	81	24
Pascal Dupuis	57	30	42	72	118
Michel Periard	64	14	40	54	90
Michel Tremblay	63	17	29	46	81
Yann Joseph	65	17	28	45	70
Mathieu Biron	69	13	32	45	116
Philippe Deblois	58	11	25	36	71
Jimmy Grondin	52	10	24	34	199
Ryan Walsh	17	10	15	25	43
Benoit Cote	70	6	10	16	102
Frederic Levac	36	3	13	16	77
Jean-Francois Pilon	58	6	9	15	22
Francis Emery	65	7	7	14	210
Simon Poirier	43	0	14	14	102
Marc-Andre Bergeron	24	6	7	13	66
Juraj Slovak	44	2	8	10	50
Jonathan Lessard	53	1	5	6	75
Philippe Ouellette	35	2	3	5	98
Guillaume Lefebvre	40	3	1	4	49
Dominic Desbiens	25	0	4	4	47
Francis Deslauriers	35	1	1	2	18
Jean-Francois David	7	0	1	1	0
Samuel Duplain	46	0	1	1	169
Mathieu Chouinard (goalie)	63	0	1	1	35
Andre Landry	1	0	0	0	0
Daniel Bergeron	2	0	0	0	2
Dustin Traylen (goalie)	2	0	0	0	0
Jason Pominville	2	0	0	0	0
Jean-Francois Dufort	3	0	0	0	0
Sylvain Castilloux	4	0	0	0	10
Steve Mongrain (goalie)	8	0	0	0	0
Martin Brière (goalie)	12	0	0	0	0
Justin Grenier	13	0	0	0	0
Jean-Francois Laniel (goalie)	55	0	0	0	0

GOALTENDING

	Games	Min.	W	L	T	G	SO	Avg.
Steve Mongrain	2	94	2	0	0	4	0	2.57
Mathieu Chouinard	56	3288	36	16	4	150	5	2.74
Jean-Francois Laniel	18	876	6	6	0	56	0	3.84

SHERBROOKE FAUCONS

SCORING

	Games	G	A	Pts.	PIM
Francois Fortier	48	36	40	76	8
Eric Pinoul	68	17	56	73	134
Maxim Potapov	58	20	43	63	34
Dimitri Afanasenkov	51	23	30	53	22
Yannick Landry	67	23	28	51	14
Sylvain Dufresne	70	21	30	51	75
Jean-Francois Lortie	59	17	33	50	29
Jean-Francois Fortin	64	17	33	50	78
Eric Lavigne	67	11	26	37	80
Patrick Vincent	57	17	14	31	246
Eric Perricone	28	12	18	30	30
Alexandre Couture	35	9	18	27	52
Pierre-Luc Courchesne	60	6	19	25	88
Jean Morin	70	3	20	23	114
Clark Udle	26	8	12	20	73
Jean-Philippe Paradis	52	9	10	19	39
Bryan Lachance	53	4	13	17	130
Jason Spence	67	3	10	13	248
Martin Beauchesne	46	1	8	9	76
Philippe Parent	53	1	7	8	57
Philippe Denicourt	24	4	2	6	6
Sylvain Plamondon	33	3	3	6	92
David Cloutier	46	2	2	4	39
Marc-Andre Jacob	19	0	2	2	28
Dany Sabourin (goalie)	70	0	2	2	2
Frederik Brindamour (goalie)	70	0	2	2	8
Michel Beausoleil	6	1	0	1	10
Jonathan Moreau	1	0	0	0	0
Sebastien Favreau	2	0	0	0	0
Sebastien Nadeau	7	0	0	0	0
Francis Pare	10	0	0	0	4

GOALTENDING

	Games	Min.	W	L	T	G	SO	Avg.
Frederik Brindamour	54	2785	23	21	3	163	0	3.51
Dany Sabourin	30	1477	8	13	2	102	1	4.14

VAL D'OR FOREURS

SCORING

	Games	G	A	Pts.	PIM
Benoit Dusablon	67	42	74	116	63
Christian Daigle	54	33	58	91	64
Didier Tremblay	63	23	51	74	56
Simon Gamache	70	19	43	62	54
Guillaume Lamoureux	67	29	32	61	39
Lucio Demartinis	68	20	31	51	100
Jonathan Fauteux	59	15	33	48	139
Alain Charbonneau	35	24	18	42	28
Eric Dubois	64	17	16	33	46

	Games	G	A	Pts.	PIM
Anthony Quessy	62	18	13	31	152
Danny Groulx	36	3	26	29	55
Denis Boily	22	9	19	28	33
Seneque Hyacinthe	32	11	16	27	36
Mathieu Lendick	68	10	13	23	67
Sebastien Laprise	63	12	10	22	20
Alexandre Page	33	2	12	14	40
Francois Hardy	39	3	10	13	118
Jerome Petit	25	5	7	12	26
Steve Morency	51	5	7	12	23
Luc Girard	69	1	11	12	49
Nick Greenough	49	3	8	11	169
Lee Cousineau	9	3	6	9	16
Philippe Ouellette	22	2	6	8	60
Dwight Wolfe	52	2	5	7	57
Daniel Cloutier	10	1	3	4	2
Charles-Philippe Barbe	5	0	2	2	5
Eric Fortier	8	0	2	2	4
Sergei Moziakin	4	0	1	1	2
Daniel Savoie	2	0	0	0	0
Igor Yemeleev	2	0	0	0	0
Bobby Paquette	3	0	0	0	0
Hugo Lehoux	15	0	0	0	16
Carl Gauthier	31	0	0	0	30
Dave Verville (goalie)	46	0	0	0	2
Jonathan Charron (goalie)	63	0	0	0	6

GOALTENDING

	Games	Min.	W	L	T	G	SO	Avg.
Roberto Luongo	21	1177	6	10	2	77	1	3.93
Jonathan Charron	26	1364	12	8	2	97	0	4.27
David St. Germain	16	833	7	7	1	68	0	4.90
Dave Verville	21	895	5	10	0	76	0	5.09

VICTORIAVILLE TIGRES

SCORING

	Games	G	A	Pts.	PIM
Patrick Grandmaitre	70	37	78	115	139
Marc-Andre Thinel	66	45	58	103	16
David Thibeault	63	43	59	102	72
Carl Mallette	62	27	46	73	51
Alexander Ryazantsev	64	17	40	57	57
Eric Cote	55	16	36	52	8
Sebastien Thinel	60	15	24	39	18
Tomas Baluch	39	15	21	36	29
Christian Robichaud	53	10	13	23	116
Hugo Marchand	62	8	14	22	163
Edin Burazerovic	50	6	13	19	249
Stephane Veilleux	65	6	13	19	35
Frederic Girard	69	4	14	18	150
Matthew Lombardi	47	6	10	16	8
Marc-Andre Gaudet	68	3	13	16	109
Antoine Bergeron	30	3	6	9	73
Jordan Trew	56	3	6	9	241
David Bouchard	51	4	4	8	6
Etienne Drapeau	4	1	3	4	7
Richard Paul	48	1	3	4	171
Andre Corbeil	36	1	2	3	269
Patrick Chouinard	63	0	3	3	113
Michael McIntyre	33	1	1	2	75
Martin Gascon	1	1	0	1	0
Jean-Francois Touchette	3	1	0	1	0
David Landry	12	1	0	1	21
Pierre-Luc Therrien (goalie)	64	0	1	1	33
Martin Meilleur	2	0	0	0	0
Luc Levesque	4	0	0	0	33
Louis-Pier Asselin	5	0	0	0	0
Eric Joly (goalie)	6	0	0	0	0
Jean-Francois Aumont	13	0	0	0	35
Jean-Francois Nogues (goalie)	70	0	0	0	17

GOALTENDING

	Games	Min.	W	L	T	G	SO	Avg.
Pierre-Luc Therrien	48	2628	22	19	2	133	2	3.04
Eric Joly	3	115	1	1	0	7	0	3.67
Jean-Francois Nogues	32	1556	11	10	4	108	0	4.17

PLAYERS WITH TWO OR MORE TEAMS

SCORING

	Games	G	A	Pts.	PIM
Ramzi Abid, Chicoutimi	21	11	15	26	97
Ramzi Abid, Acadie-Bathurst	24	14	22	36	102
Totals	45	25	37	62	199
Dimitri Afanasenkov, Moncton	15	5	5	10	12
Dimitri Afanasenkov, Sher.	51	23	30	53	22
Totals	66	28	35	63	34
Benoit Beausoleil, Baie-Com.	41	2	4	6	216
Benoit Beausoleil, A.-Bathurst	26	0	0	0	82
Totals	67	2	4	6	298
Mathieu Benoit, Chicoutimi	36	39	14	53	28
Mathieu Benoit, A.-Bathurst	32	23	33	56	6
Totals	68	62	47	109	34
Antoine Bergeron, Rimouski	20	0	4	4	28
Antoine Bergeron, Victoriaville	30	3	6	9	73
Totals	50	3	10	13	101
Jerome Bergeron, Rouyn-Nor.	39	11	8	19	64
Jerome Bergeron, Baie-Com.	23	5	10	15	14
Totals	62	16	18	34	78
Marc-Andre Bergeron, B.-C.	46	8	14	22	57
Marc-Andre Bergeron, Shaw.	24	6	7	13	66
Totals	70	14	21	35	123
Denis Boily, Acadie-Bathurst	31	16	23	39	65
Denis Boily, Val-d'Or	22	9	19	28	33
Totals	53	25	42	67	98
Marc Bouchard, Chicoutimi	37	12	27	39	30
Marc Bouchard, A.-Bathurst	33	15	20	35	20
Totals	70	27	47	74	50
Steve Castonguay, Cape Breton.	7	0	2	2	2
Steve Castonguay, Baie-Com.	41	6	12	18	10
Totals	48	6	14	20	12
Alain Charbonneau, Val-d'Or	35	24	18	42	28
Alain Charbonneau, A.-Bathurst	36	23	15	38	67
Totals	71	47	33	80	95
Marco Charpentier, Quebec	12	4	7	11	4
Marco Charpentier, Baie-Com.	52	16	23	39	34
Totals	64	20	30	50	38
Randy Copley, Cape Breton	25	8	22	30	60
Randy Copley, Rouyn-Noranda	38	7	25	32	87
Totals	63	15	47	62	147
Alexandre Couture, Sher.	35	9	18	27	52
Alexandre Couture, Drum.	34	5	12	17	32
Totals	69	14	30	44	84
Joey D'Amico, Rouyn-Noranda	38	2	4	6	65
Joey D'Amico, Chicoutimi	13	3	3	6	22
Totals	51	5	7	12	87
Vincent Dionne, Chicoutimi	40	16	22	38	61
Vincent Dionne, Moncton	23	7	11	18	28
Totals	63	23	33	56	89
Eric Drouin, Rimouski	29	4	12	16	65
Eric Drouin, Drummondville	34	5	11	16	29
Totals	63	9	23	32	94
Jerome Dumont, Chicoutimi	28	2	1	3	28
Jerome Dumont, A.-Bathurst	31	1	0	1	17
Totals	59	3	1	4	45
Joey Fetta, Baie-Comeau	10	1	2	3	102
Joey Fetta, Quebec	28	2	10	12	80
Totals	38	3	12	15	182
Jon. Francoeur, A.-Bathurst	34	5	6	11	11
Jonathan Francoeur, Chi.	31	15	13	28	20

	Games	G	A	Pts.	PIM
Totals	65	20	19	39	31
Jonathan Gauthier, Moncton	39	5	8	13	41
Jonathan Gauthier, Rouyn-Nor.	22	2	13	15	25
Totals	61	7	21	28	66
David Girard, Drummondville	46	10	12	22	19
David Girard, Chicoutimi	27	9	10	19	34
Totals	73	19	22	41	53
Danny Groulx, Val-d'Or	36	3	26	29	55
Danny Groulx, Acadie-Bathurst	36	2	15	17	51
Totals	72	5	41	46	106
Marc-Etienne Hubert, Drum.	22	1	8	9	43
Marc-Etienne Hubert, Baie-C.	28	12	9	21	50
Totals	50	13	17	30	93
Seneque Hyacinthe, A.-Bathurst	31	13	17	30	70
Seneque Hyacinthe, Val-d'Or	32	11	16	27	36
Totals	63	24	33	57	106
Marc-Andre Jacob, Drum.	29	2	0	2	49
Marc-Andre Jacob, Sher.	19	0	2	2	28
Totals	48	2	2	4	77
Eric Jean, Quebec	43	0	0	0	28
Eric Jean, Drummondville	23	0	2	2	7
Totals	66	0	2	2	35
Juraj Kolnik, Quebec	12	6	5	11	6
Juraj Kolnik, Rimouski	50	36	37	73	34
Totals	62	42	42	84	40
Hunter Lahache, Quebec	27	0	0	0	33
Hunter Lahache, Cape Breton	29	1	2	3	55
Totals	56	1	2	3	88
Eric Laplante, Drummondville	42	14	25	39	258
Eric Laplante, Quebec	23	4	17	21	58
Totals	65	18	42	60	316
Jeff Leblanc, Drummondville	25	1	3	4	109
Jeff Leblanc, Quebec	21	2	6	8	109
Totals	46	3	9	12	218
Guillaume Lefebvre, Shaw.	40	3	1	4	49
Guillaume Lefebvre, C. Breton	24	2	7	9	13
Totals	64	5	8	13	62
Sebastien Lucier, Quebec	42	5	4	9	8
Sebastien Lucier, Chicoutimi	23	0	4	4	9
Totals	65	5	8	13	17
Chris Lyness, Rouyn-Noranda	25	3	6	9	49
Chris Lyness, Cape Breton	42	12	17	29	35
Totals	67	15	23	38	84
David McCutcheon, Hull	20	1	0	1	77
David McCutcheon, Halifax	28	0	1	1	67
Totals	48	1	1	2	144
Alexandre Morel, A.-Bathurst	25	1	1	2	10
Alexandre Morel, Chicoutimi	3	0	0	0	0
Alexandre Morel, Quebec	20	1	2	3	16
Totals	48	2	3	5	26
Philippe Ouellette, Shawinigan	35	2	3	5	98
Philippe Ouellette, Val-d'Or	22	2	6	8	60
Totals	57	4	9	13	158
Alexandre Page, Cape Breton	19	2	2	4	52
Alexandre Page, Val-d'Or	33	2	12	14	40
Totals	52	4	14	18	92
Eric Perricone, Drummondville	20	6	11	17	10
Eric Perricone, Halifax	7	0	1	1	2
Eric Perricone, Sherbrooke	28	12	18	30	30
Totals	55	18	30	48	42
Sylvain Plamondon, Sher.	33	3	3	6	92
Sylvain Plamondon, Quebec	24	3	5	8	112
Totals	57	6	8	14	204
Jonathan St. Louis, Rimouski	30	4	6	10	133
Jonathan St. Louis, Drum.	32	3	4	7	131
Totals	62	7	10	17	264
Domenico Scali, Baie-Comeau	22	7	12	19	24
Domenico Scali, Drum.	42	11	13	24	20
Totals	64	18	25	43	44
Shawn Scanzano, A.-Bathurst	23	1	5	6	23
Shawn Scanzano, Rouyn-Nor.	5	0	0	0	7
Totals	28	1	5	6	30
J.-Philippe Soucy, A.-Bathurst	36	1	17	18	108
Jean-Philippe Soucy, Chi.	5	0	4	4	9
Jean-Philippe Soucy, Drum.	24	2	13	15	53
Totals	65	3	34	37	170
Oleg Timchenko, Baie-Comeau	44	34	25	59	44
Oleg Timchenko, Rouyn-Nor.	24	15	10	25	20
Totals	68	49	35	84	64
Simon Tremblay, Moncton	40	8	12	20	40
Simon Tremblay, Chicoutimi	26	7	5	12	85
Totals	66	15	17	32	125
Jean-Sebastien Trudelle, Chi.	36	1	12	13	110
Jean-Sebastien Trudelle, A.-B.	30	0	5	5	145
Totals	66	1	17	18	255
Alain Turcotte, Cape Breton	17	0	2	2	52
Alain Turcotte, Rouyn-Noranda	28	1	2	3	32
Totals	45	1	4	5	84
Clark Udle, Sherbrooke	26	8	12	20	73
Clark Udle, Moncton	24	6	15	21	140
Totals	50	14	27	41	213
Ryan Walsh, Cape Breton	42	35	44	79	58
Ryan Walsh, Shawinigan	17	10	15	25	43
Totals	59	45	59	104	101
Dwight Wolfe, Halifax	1	0	0	0	9
Dwight Wolfe, Val-d'Or	52	2	5	7	57
Totals	53	2	5	7	66
Travis Zachary, Cape Breton	33	10	5	15	127
Travis Zachary, Quebec	17	4	4	8	37
Totals	50	14	9	23	164

GOALTENDING

	Games	Min.	W	L	T	G	SO	Avg.
Jon. Charron, A.-Bath.	19	1065	10	9	0	64	0	3.61
Jon. Charron, Val.	26	1364	12	8	2	97	0	4.27
Totals	45	2429	22	17	2	161	0	3.98
Eric Desjardins, Rim.	5	292	1	3	1	20	0	4.11
Eric Desjardins, B.-C.	31	1761	9	16	3	98	0	3.34
Totals	36	2053	10	19	4	118	0	3.45
Danny Lavoie, C.B.	28	1586	11	13	3	84	2	3.18
Danny Lavoie, R.-N.	28	1556	14	7	4	87	0	3.36
Totals	56	3142	25	20	7	171	2	3.27
Roberto Luongo, Val.	21	1177	6	10	2	77	1	3.93
Roberto Luongo, A.-B.	22	1341	14	7	1	74	0	3.31
Totals	43	2518	20	17	3	151	1	3.60
D. St. Germain, Val.	16	833	7	7	1	68	0	4.90
D. St. Germain, C.B.	35	1959	10	23	1	127	1	3.89
Totals	51	2792	17	30	2	195	1	4.19
Jon. Wilhelmy, C.B.	11	518	1	6	0	30	0	3.47
Jon. Wilhelmy, Que.	8	426	6	0	0	25	0	3.52
Totals	19	944	7	6	0	55	0	3.50

1999 PRESIDENT CUP PLAYOFFS

RESULTS

DIVISION QUARTERFINALS

	W	L	Pts.	GF	GA
Acadie-Bathurst	4	1	8	20	14
Cape Breton	1	4	2	14	20

(Acadie-Bathurst won series, 4-1)

	W	L	Pts.	GF	GA
Rimouski	4	0	8	16	7
Moncton	0	4	0	7	16

(Rimouski won series, 4-0)

	W	L	Pts.	GF	GA
Sherbrooke	4	2	8	30	19
Val-d'Or	2	4	4	19	30

(Sherbrooke won series, 4-2)

	W	L	Pts.	GF	GA
Hull	4	2	8	15	17
Victoriaville	2	4	4	17	15

(Hull won series, 4-2)

DIVISION SEMIFINALS

	W	L	Pts.	GF	GA
Acadie-Bathurst	4	1	8	24	14
Halifax	1	4	2	14	24

(Acadie-Bathurst won series, 4-1)

	W	L	Pts.	GF	GA
Quebec	4	3	8	23	18
Rimouski	3	4	6	18	23

(Quebec won series, 4-3)

	W	L	Pts.	GF	GA
Hull	4	2	8	27	23
Shawinigan	2	4	4	23	27

(Hull won series, 4-2)

	W	L	Pts.	GF	GA
Rouyn-Noranda	4	3	8	24	25
Sherbrooke	3	4	6	25	24

(Rouyn-Noranda won series, 4-3)

DIVISION FINALS

	W	L	Pts.	GF	GA
Acadie-Bathurst	4	2	8	24	17
Quebec	2	4	4	17	24

(Acadie-Bathurst won series, 4-2)

	W	L	Pts.	GF	GA
Hull	4	0	8	22	10
Rouyn-Noranda	0	4	0	10	22

(Hull won series, 4-0)

LEAGUE FINALS

	W	L	Pts.	GF	GA
Acadie-Bathurst	4	3	8	23	21
Hull	3	4	6	21	23

(Acadie-Bathurst won series, 4-3)

INDIVIDUAL LEADERS

Goals: Mathieu Benoit, Acadie-Bathurst (20)
Michael Ryder, Hull (20)
Assists: Mathieu Benoit, Acadie-Bathurst (21)
Points: Mathieu Benoit, Acadie-Bathurst (41)
Penalty minutes: Mario Joly, Hull (86)
Goaltending average: Pierre-Luc Therrien, Victoriaville (1.89)
Shutouts: Maxime Ouellet, Quebec (1)
Philippe Sauve, Rimouski (1)

TOP SCORERS

	Games	G	A	Pts.
Mathieu Benoit, Acadie-Bathurst	23	20	21	41
Michael Ryder, Hull	23	20	16	36
Ramzi Abid, Acadie-Bathurst	23	14	20	34
Jonathan Girard, Acadie-Bathurst	23	13	18	31
Marty Johnston, Hull	23	10	16	26
Paul Spadafora, Hull	22	9	17	26
Marc Bouchard, Acadie-Bathurst	21	5	19	24
Jiri Fischer, Hull	23	6	17	23
Ryan Lauzon, Hull	23	3	20	23
Brad Richards, Rimouski	11	9	12	21
Brock Boucher, Hull	23	9	12	21

INDIVIDUAL STATISTICS

ACADIE-BATHURST TITANS

(Winner of 1999 President Cup playoffs)

SCORING

	Games	G	A	Pts.	PIM
Mathieu Benoit	23	20	21	41	16
Ramzi Abid	23	14	20	34	84
Jonathan Girard	23	13	18	31	22
Marc Bouchard	21	5	19	24	27
Philippe Plante	23	7	13	20	28
Francois Beauchemin	23	2	16	18	55
Gregor Baumgartner	23	8	8	16	8
Martin Fillion	23	8	8	16	30
Alain O'Driscoll	23	3	6	9	18
Jules-Edy Laraque	23	2	7	9	14
Eric Betournay	23	2	6	8	18
Jean-Sebastien Trudelle	23	0	6	6	43
Alain Charbonneau	21	3	1	4	34
Martin Lavergne	23	2	2	4	42
Ryan Flinn	23	2	0	2	37
Danny Groulx	18	0	2	2	6
Roberto Luongo (goalie)	23	0	2	2	0
Jerome Dumont	4	0	0	0	0
Benoit Beausoleil	12	0	0	0	42
Bryan Dube	16	0	0	0	17
Hugo Levesque	23	0	0	0	6
Philippe Ozga (goalie)	23	0	0	0	0

GOALTENDING

	Games	Min.	W	L	T	G	SO	Avg.
Philippe Ozga	1	34	0	1	0	1	0	1.75
Roberto Luongo	23	1400	16	6	0	64	0	2.74

CAPE BRETON SCREAMING EAGLES

(Lost division quarterfinals to Bathurst, 4-1)

SCORING

	Games	G	A	Pts.	PIM
Artem Rybin	5	3	4	7	4
Jonathan Gagnon	5	2	4	6	2
Philippe Tremblay	3	2	2	4	4
Yannick Carpentier	5	2	2	4	2
Josh Dill	5	3	0	3	2
Sandro Sbrocca	5	1	2	3	41
Robbie Sutherland	5	0	3	3	0
Sebastien Gagnon	5	0	2	2	12
Jean Mallette	5	0	2	2	12
Pierre-Luc Laprise	5	1	0	1	0
Kevin Bergin	3	0	1	1	0
Trevor Ettinger	5	0	1	1	23
Guillaume Lefebvre	5	0	1	1	0
Chris Lyness	5	0	1	1	4
Olivier Proulx	5	0	1	1	0
David St. Germain (goalie)	5	0	1	1	0
Tomas Kloucek	2	0	0	0	4
Hunter Lahache	2	0	0	0	0
Robbie Bennett	5	0	0	0	6
Donald Johnstone	5	0	0	0	0
Matt House	5	0	0	0	2
Marc-Andre Leclerc	5	0	0	0	0

GOALTENDING

	Games	Min.	W	L	T	G	SO	Avg.
David St. Germain	5	299	1	4	0	19	0	3.82

HALIFAX MOOSEHEADS

(Lost division semifinals to Bathurst, 4-1)

SCORING

	Games	G	A	Pts.	PIM
Ladislav Nagy	5	3	3	6	18
Brandon Reid	5	2	2	4	0
Frederic Belanger	5	1	3	4	10
Jasmin Gelinas	5	1	2	3	2
Alex Tanguay	5	1	2	3	2
Mauro DiPaolo	5	1	1	2	15
Carlyle Lewis	5	1	1	2	18
Ali MacEachern	5	1	1	2	0
Jeffrey Sullivan	5	1	1	2	14
P.J. Lynch	5	1	0	1	4
Billy Manley	5	1	0	1	0
Alex Johnstone	5	0	1	1	4
Alexandre Mathieu	5	0	1	1	4
Samuel Seguin	5	0	1	1	4
Jason Troini	5	0	1	1	12
Alexei Volkov (goalie)	5	0	1	1	0
David McCutcheon	1	0	0	0	0
Mathieu Paul	4	0	0	0	2
Brandon Benedict	5	0	0	0	0
Marc-Andre Binette	5	0	0	0	0
Pascal Leclaire (goalie)	5	0	0	0	0

GOALTENDING

	Games	Min.	W	L	T	G	SO	Avg.
Alexei Volkov	5	282	1	4	0	21	0	4.47
Pascal Leclaire	1	17	0	0	0	2	0	7.32

HULL OLYMPIQUES

(Lost league finals to Bathurst, 4-3)

SCORING

	Games	G	A	Pts.	PIM
Michael Ryder	23	20	16	36	39
Marty Johnston	23	10	16	26	14
Paul Spadafora	22	9	17	26	73
Jiri Fischer	23	6	17	23	44
Ryan Lauzon	23	3	20	23	10
Brock Boucher	23	9	12	21	18
Radim Vrbata	23	6	13	19	6
Bruno Lemire	23	3	6	9	16
Adam Rivet	23	2	7	9	22
Roberto Bissonnette	23	4	4	8	33
Dustin Russell	23	4	4	8	25
Erich Paroshy	21	3	3	6	43
Yannick Lachance	21	2	3	5	34
Alexandre Giroux	22	2	2	4	8
Mario Joly	23	2	2	4	86
Daniel Clermont	23	0	2	2	10
Andrew Carver	23	0	1	1	22
Philippe Bergeron (goalie)	23	0	1	1	0
Michaël Parent	1	0	0	0	0
Michael Lanthier	7	0	0	0	6
Casey Burnette	21	0	0	0	25
Frederic Malette (goalie)	23	0	0	0	2

GOALTENDING

	Games	Min.	W	L	T	G	SO	Avg.
Frederic Malette	3	152	2	0	0	3	0	1.18
Philippe Bergeron	22	1372	13	8	0	69	0	3.02

MONCTON WILDCATS

(Lost division quarterfinals to Rimouski, 4-0)

SCORING

	Games	G	A	Pts.	PIM
Sebastien Roger	4	1	3	4	6
Simon Laliberte	4	2	1	3	6
David Comeau	4	1	1	2	10
Dimitri Kalinin	4	1	1	2	0
Alexandre Vigneault	4	0	2	2	2
Jonathan Desroches	4	1	0	1	0
Dominic Noel	4	1	0	1	0
Olivier Dubuc	4	0	1	1	4
Jacques Lariviere	4	0	1	1	12
Mirko Murovic	4	0	1	1	2
Morgan Warren	1	0	0	0	2
Branwell Beck	3	0	0	0	0
Eric Demers	4	0	0	0	2
Vincent Dionne	4	0	0	0	4
Louis-Philippe Lessard	4	0	0	0	0
Daniel MacLeod	4	0	0	0	18
Patrice Theriault	4	0	0	0	0
Clark Udle	4	0	0	0	2
David Walker	4	0	0	0	14
Jean-Francois Damphousse (g)	4	0	0	0	0
Simon Lajeunesse (goalie)	4	0	0	0	0

GOALTENDING

	Games	Min.	W	L	T	G	SO	Avg.
Simon Lajeunesse	1	43	0	0	0	2	0	2.83
J.-F. Damphousse	4	200	0	4	0	12	0	3.60

QUEBEC REMPARTS

(Lost division finals to Bathurst, 4-2)

SCORING

	Games	G	A	Pts.	PIM
Eric Chouinard	13	8	10	18	8
Simon Gagne	13	9	8	17	4
David Bernier	13	6	10	16	12
Eric Laplante	13	8	7	15	45
Martin Moise	13	2	10	12	2
Dmitri Tolkunov	13	2	7	9	22
Andre Martineau	12	1	4	5	0
Simon Tremblay	13	1	4	5	25
Nicholas Bilotto	13	1	3	4	18
Jerome Marois	12	0	4	4	13
Martin Grenier	13	0	4	4	29
Daniel Archambault	13	0	3	3	16
Wesley Scanzano	12	1	1	2	4
Raymond Dalton	12	1	0	1	6
Travis Zachary	13	0	1	1	14
Tommy Bolduc	1	0	0	0	0
Pierre Loiselle	1	0	0	0	0
Alexandre Morel	2	0	0	0	0
Jeff Leblanc	13	0	0	0	22
Sylvain Plamondon	13	0	0	0	18
Antoine Vermette	13	0	0	0	2
Maxime Ouellet (goalie)	13	0	0	0	2
Jonathan Wilhelmy (goalie)	13	0	0	0	0

GOALTENDING

	Games	Min.	W	L	T	G	SO	Avg.
Jonathan Wilhelmy	1	0	0	0	0	0	0	0.00
Maxime Ouellet	13	803	6	7	0	41	1	3.06

RIMOUSKI OCEANIC

(Lost division semifinals to Quebec, 4-3)

SCORING

	Games	G	A	Pts.	PIM
Brad Richards	11	9	12	21	6
Juraj Kolnik	11	9	6	15	6
Francois Page	11	3	6	9	33
Jonathan Beaulieu	11	3	4	7	4
Julien Desrosiers	11	3	4	7	8
Adam Borzecki	11	0	6	6	12
Joe Rullier	11	2	3	5	26
Philippe Grondin	7	1	4	5	16
Thatcher Bell	11	3	1	4	0
David St. Onge	11	0	4	4	10
Jan-Philippe Cadieux	8	1	1	2	0
David Bilodeau	11	0	2	2	14
Kris Barnett	5	0	1	1	2
Benoit Martin	11	0	1	1	4
Michel Ouellet	11	0	1	1	6
Guillaume Couture	5	0	0	0	0
Nicolas Poirier	5	0	0	0	4

	Games	G	A	Pts.	PIM
David Boilard	6	0	0	0	4
Jean-Francois Babin	8	0	0	0	4
Denis Desmarais	11	0	0	0	15
Casey Leggett	11	0	0	0	20
Sebastien Caron (goalie)	11	0	0	0	0
Philippe Sauve (goalie)	11	0	0	0	4

GOALTENDING

	Games	Min.	W	L	T	G	SO	Avg.
Sebastien Caron	2	68	1	0	0	0	0	0.00
Philippe Sauve	11	595	6	4	0	30	1	3.03

ROUYN-NORANDA HUSKIES

(Lost division finals to Hull, 4-0)

SCORING

	Games	G	A	Pts.	PIM
Mike Ribeiro	11	5	11	16	12
James Desmarais	11	6	7	13	14
Jerome Tremblay	11	3	8	11	10
Randy Copley	11	3	5	8	14
Oleg Timchenko	11	3	5	8	17
Jonathan Gauthier	11	2	4	6	14
Kevin Cloutier	11	2	3	5	14
Alain Turcotte	11	2	3	5	19
Didier Pietropaulo	11	2	2	4	20
Samuel Gagnon	11	2	1	3	50
Benoit Vezina	5	1	2	3	4
Jason Lehoux	6	1	2	3	49
Jason Tessier	11	0	3	3	29
Kyrill Alexeyev	11	1	1	2	23
Mathieu Rancourt	11	0	2	2	16
Steve Waters	10	1	0	1	0
Jean-Luc Legault	8	0	1	1	6
Patrick Gilbert	10	0	1	1	6
Jonathan Blais	5	0	0	0	2
Alexandre Audet	11	0	0	0	32
Sebastien Centomo (goalie)	11	0	0	0	2
Danny Lavoie (goalie)	11	0	0	0	0

GOALTENDING

	Games	Min.	W	L	T	G	SO	Avg.
Danny Lavoie	11	645	4	6	0	42	0	3.91
Sebastien Centomo	2	28	0	1	0	5	0	10.87

SHAWINIGAN CATARACTES

(Lost division semifinals to Hull, 4-2)

SCORING

	Games	G	A	Pts.	PIM
Dominic Forget	6	2	7	9	4
Pascal Dupuis	6	1	8	9	18
Jean-Philippe Pare	6	3	5	8	6
Alexandre Tremblay	6	1	6	7	8
Francis Emery	6	4	2	6	30
Philippe Deblois	6	3	2	5	4
Marc-Andre Bergeron	5	2	2	4	24
Juraj Slovak	6	1	3	4	6
Michel Periard	6	1	2	3	4
Benoit Cote	6	0	3	3	19
Michel Tremblay	6	2	0	2	17
Jimmy Grondin	6	1	1	2	40
Mathieu Biron	6	0	2	2	6
Ryan Walsh	4	1	0	1	2
Simon Poirier	6	1	0	1	27
Jean-Francois David	1	0	0	0	2
Jean-Francois Pilon	2	0	0	0	0
Samuel Duplain	6	0	0	0	0
Yann Joseph	6	0	0	0	6
Jonathan Lessard	6	0	0	0	10
Mathieu Chouinard (goalie)	6	0	0	0	0
Jean-Francois Laniel	6	0	0	0	0

GOALTENDING

	Games	Min.	W	L	T	G	SO	Avg.
Mathieu Chouinard	6	392	2	4	0	27	0	4.14

SHERBROOKE FAUCONS

(Lost division semifinals to Rouyn-Noranda, 4-3)

SCORING

	Games	G	A	Pts.	PIM
Eric Perricone	13	7	13	20	23
Eric Pinoul	13	4	16	20	11
Jean-Francois Fortin	12	5	13	18	20
Dimitri Afanasenkov	13	10	6	16	6
Francois Fortier	13	6	9	15	4
Jean-Francois Lortie	13	2	11	13	6
Sylvain Dufresne	13	8	3	11	6
Yannick Landry	13	6	5	11	4
Patrick Vincent	13	1	6	7	26
Eric Lavigne	13	0	7	7	2
Jason Spence	13	2	2	4	15
Maxim Potapov	11	1	3	4	4
Jean Morin	13	2	1	3	10
Martin Beauchesne	13	0	2	2	27
Marc-Andre Jacob	7	1	0	1	4
Jean-Philippe Paradis	13	0	1	1	0
Philippe Parent	13	0	1	1	29
Frederik Brindamour (goalie)	13	0	1	1	2
David Cloutier	4	0	0	0	2
Bryan Lachance	5	0	0	0	5
Pierre-Luc Courchesne	13	0	0	0	18
Dany Sabourin (goalie)	13	0	0	0	0

GOALTENDING

	Games	Min.	W	L	T	G	SO	Avg.
Dany Sabourin	1	49	0	1	0	2	0	2.44
Frederik Brindamour	13	740	7	5	0	40	0	3.24

VAL-D'OR FOREURS

(Lost division quarterfinals to Sherbrooke, 4-2)

SCORING

	Games	G	A	Pts.	PIM
Christian Daigle	6	4	5	9	0
Benoit Dusablon	6	2	6	8	4
Denis Boily	6	1	5	6	18
Anthony Quessy	6	3	2	5	10
Didier Tremblay	6	1	4	5	4
Eric Dubois	6	1	3	4	2
Francois Hardy	3	2	1	3	6
Guillaume Lamoureux	6	2	1	3	4
Jonathan Fauteux	6	1	2	3	8
Simon Gamache	6	1	2	3	4
Seneque Hyacinthe	4	0	2	2	2
Jerome Petit	6	1	0	1	2
Lucio Demartinis	6	0	1	1	2
Mathieu Lendick	6	0	1	1	6
Alexandre Page	6	0	1	1	10
Carl Gauthier	1	0	0	0	0
Steve Morency	4	0	0	0	0
Luc Girard	6	0	0	0	0
Sebastien Laprise	6	0	0	0	0
Philippe Ouellette	6	0	0	0	10
Jonathan Charron (goalie)	6	0	0	0	0
Dave Verville (goalie)	6	0	0	0	0

GOALTENDING

	Games	Min.	W	L	T	G	SO	Avg.
Dave Verville	6	339	2	3	0	27	0	4.78
Jonathan Charron	1	21	0	1	0	3	0	8.82

VICTORIAVILLE TIGRES

(Lost division quarterfinals to Hull, 4-2)

SCORING

	Games	G	A	Pts.	PIM
Sebastien Thinel	6	2	8	10	4
Marc-Andre Thinel	6	5	3	8	4
Patrick Grandmaitre	6	2	6	8	6
David Thibeault	6	5	2	7	8
Stephane Veilleux	6	1	3	4	2
Eric Cote	6	0	4	4	2

	Games	G	A	Pts.	PIM
Carl Mallette	6	1	2	3	2
Alexander Ryazantsev	6	0	3	3	10
Christian Robichaud	6	1	0	1	4
Hugo Marchand	6	0	1	1	10
David Bouchard	1	0	0	0	0
Antoine Bergeron	2	0	0	0	0
Edin Burazerovic	5	0	0	0	2
Matthew Lombardi	5	0	0	0	0
Richard Paul	5	0	0	0	10
Tomas Baluch	6	0	0	0	0
Patrick Chouinard	6	0	0	0	4
Marc-Andre Gaudet	6	0	0	0	6
Frederic Girard	6	0	0	0	4
Jordan Trew	6	0	0	0	12
Jean-Francois Nogues	6	0	0	0	0
Pierre-Luc Therrien (goalie)	6	0	0	0	0

GOALTENDING

	Games	Min.	W	L	T	G	SO	Avg.
Pierre-Luc Therrien	6	444	2	4	0	14	0	1.89

1998-99 AWARD WINNERS

ALL-STAR TEAMS

First team	Pos.	Second team
Mathieu Chouinard, Shaw.	G	Maxime Ouellet, Quebec
Jonathan Girard, A.-Bath.	D	Dmitri Tolkunov, Quebec
Jiri Fischer, Hull	D	Simon Tremblay, Quebec
Jerome Tremblay, R.-N.	LW	David Thibeault, Victoriaville
Mike Ribeiro, R.-Noranda	C	Simon Gagne, Quebec
James Desmarais, R.-N.	RW	Mathieu Benoit, A.-Bathurst

TROPHY WINNERS

Frank Selke Trophy: Eric Chouinard, Quebec
Michel Bergeron Trophy: Ladislav Nagy, Halifax
Raymond Lagace Trophy: Alexei Volkov, Halifax
Jean Beliveau Trophy: Mike Ribeiro, Rouyn-Noranda
Michel Briere Trophy: Mathieu Chouinard, Shawinigan
Marcel Robert Trophy: Christian Robichaud, Victoriaville
Mike Bossy Trophy: Maxime Ouellet, Quebec
Emile "Butch" Bouchard Trophy: Jiri Fischer, Hull
Jacques Plante Trophy: Maxime Ouellet, Quebec
Guy Lafleur Trophy: Mathieu Benoit, Acadie-Bathurst
Robert LeBel Trophy: Halifax Mooseheads
John Rougeau Trophy: Quebec Remparts
President Cup: Acadie-Bathurst Titans

ALL-TIME AWARD WINNERS

FRANK SELKE TROPHY

(Most gentlemanly player)

Season Player, Team
1970-71—Norm Dube, Sherbrooke
1971-72—Gerry Teeple, Cornwall
1972-73—Claude Larose, Drummondville
1973-74—Gary MacGregor, Cornwall
1974-75—Jean-Luc Phaneuf, Montreal
1975-76—Norm Dupont, Montreal
1976-77—Mike Bossy, Laval
1977-78—Kevin Reeves, Montreal
1978-79—Ray Bourque, Verdun
Jean-Francois Sauve, Trois-Rivieres
1979-80—Jean-Francois Sauve, Trois-Rivieres
1980-81—Claude Verret, Trois-Rivieres
1981-82—Claude Verret, Trois-Rivieres
1982-83—Pat LaFontaine, Verdun
1983-84—Jerome Carrier, Verdun
1984-85—Patrick Emond, Chicoutimi
1985-86—Jimmy Carson, Verdun
1986-87—Luc Beausoleil, Laval
1987-88—Stephan Lebeau, Shawinigan
1988-89—Steve Cadieux, Shawinigan
1989-90—Andrew McKim, Hull
1990-91—Yanic Perreault, Trois-Rivieres
1991-92—Martin Gendron, St. Hyacinthe
1992-93—Martin Gendron, St. Hyacinthe
1993-94—Yanick Dube, Laval
1994-95—Eric Daze, Beauport
1995-96—Christian Dube, Sherbrooke
1996-97—Daniel Briere, Drummondville
1997-98—Simon Laliberte, Moncton
1998-99—Eric Chouinard, Quebec

MICHEL BERGERON TROPHY

(Top rookie forward)

Season Player, Team
1969-70—Serge Martel, Verdun
1970-71—Bob Murphy, Cornwall
1971-72—Bob Murray, Cornwall
1972-73—Pierre Larouche, Sorel
1973-74—Mike Bossy, Laval
1974-75—Dennis Pomerleau, Hull
1975-76—Jean-Marc Bonamie, Shawinigan
1976-77—Rick Vaive, Sherbrooke
1977-78—Norm Rochefort, Trois-Rivieres
Denis Savard, Montreal
1978-79—Alan Grenier, Laval
1979-80—Dale Hawerchuk, Cornwall
1980-81—Claude Verret, Trois-Rivieres
1981-82—Sylvain Turgeon, Hull
1982-83—Pat LaFontaine, Verdun
1983-84—Stephane Richer, Granby
1984-85—Jimmy Carson, Verdun
1985-86—Pierre Turgeon, Granby
1986-87—Rob Murphy, Laval
1987-88—Martin Gelinas, Hull
1988-89—Yanic Perreault, Trois-Rivieres
1989-90—Martin Lapointe, Laval
1990-91—Rene Corbet, Drummondville
1991-92—Alexandre Daigle, Victoriaville
1992-93—Steve Brule, St. Jean
1993-94—Christian Dube, Sherbrooke
1994-95—Daniel Briere, Drummondville
1995-96—Pavel Rosa, Hull
1996-97—Vincent Lecavalier, Rimouski
1997-98—Mike Ribeiro, Rouyn-Noranda
1998-99—Ladislav Nagy, Halifax

Prior to 1980-81 season, award was given to QMJHL rookie of the year.

RAYMOND LAGACE TROPHY

(Top rookie defenseman or goaltender)

Season Player, Team
1980-81—Billy Campbell, Montreal
1981-82—Michel Petit, Sherbrooke
1982-83—Bobby Dollas, Laval
1983-84—James Gasseau, Drummondville
1984-85—Robert Desjardins, Shawinigan
1985-86—Stephane Guerard, Shawinigan

Season Player, Team
1986-87—Jimmy Waite, Chicoutimi
1987-88—Stephane Beauregard, St. Jean
1988-89—Karl Dykhuis, Hull
1989-90—Francois Groleau, Shawinigan
1990-91—Philippe Boucher, Granby
1991-92—Philippe DeRouville, Longueuil
1992-93—Stephane Routhier, Drummondville
1993-94—Jimmy Drolet, St. Hyacinthe
1994-95—Martin Biron, Beauport
1995-96—Mathieu Garon, Victoriaville
1996-97—Christian Bronsard, Hull
1997-98—Alexei Tezikov, Moncton
1998-99—Alexei Volkov, Halifax

JEAN BELIVEAU TROPHY
(Scoring leader)

Season Player, Team
1969-70—Luc Simard, Trois-Rivieres
1970-71—Guy Lafleur, Quebec
1971-72—Jacques Richard, Quebec
1972-73—Andre Savard, Quebec
1973-74—Pierre Larouche, Sorel
1974-75—Norm Dupont, Montreal
1975-76—Richard Dalpe, Trois-Rivieres
Sylvain Locas, Chicoutimi
1976-77—Jean Savard, Quebec
1977-78—Ron Carter, Sherbooke
1978-79—Jean-Francois Sauve, Trois-Rivieres
1979-80—Jean-Francois Sauve, Trois-Rivieres
1980-81—Dale Hawerchuk, Cornwall
1981-82—Claude Verret, Trois-Rivieres
1982-83—Pat LaFontaine, Verdun
1983-84—Mario Lemieux, Laval
1984-85—Guy Rouleau, Longueuil
1985-86—Guy Rouleau, Hull
1986-87—Marc Fortier, Chicoutimi
1987-88—Patrice Lefebvre, Shawinigan
1988-89—Stephane Morin, Chicoutimi
1989-90—Patrick Lebeau, Victoriaville
1990-91—Yanic Perreault, Trois-Rivieres
1991-92—Patrick Poulin, St. Hyacinthe
1992-93—Rene Corbet, Drummondville
1993-94—Yanick Dube, Laval
1994-95—Patrick Carignan, Shawinigan
1995-96—Daniel Briere, Drummondville
1996-97—Pavel Rosa, Hull
1997-98—Ramzi Abid, Chicoutimi
1998-99—Mike Ribeiro, Rouyn-Noranda

MICHEL BRIERE TROPHY
(Most Valuable Player)

Season Player, Team
1972-73—Andre Savard, Quebec
1973-74—Gary MacGregor, Cornwall
1974-75—Mario Viens, Cornwall
1975-76—Peter Marsh, Sherbrooke
1976-77—Lucien DeBlois, Sorel
1977-78—Kevin Reeves, Montreal
1978-79—Pierre Lacroix, Trois-Rivieres
1979-80—Denis Savard, Montreal
1980-81—Dale Hawerchuk, Cornwall
1981-82—John Chabot, Sherbrooke
1982-83—Pat LaFontaine, Verdun
1983-84—Mario Lemieux, Laval
1984-85—Daniel Berthiaune, Chicoutimi
1985-86—Guy Rouleau, Hull
1986-87—Robert Desjardins, Longueuil
1987-88—Marc Saumier, Hull
1988-89—Stephane Morin, Chicoutimi
1989-90—Andrew McKim, Hull
1990-91—Yanic Perreault, Trois-Rivieres
1991-92—Charles Poulin, St. Hyacinthe
1992-93—Jocelyn Thibault, Sherbrooke
1993-94—Emmanuel Fernandez, Laval

Season Player, Team
1994-95—Frederic Chartier, Laval
1995-96—Christian Dube, Sherbrooke
1996-97—Daniel Corso, Victoriaville
1997-98—Ramzi Abid, Chicoutimi
1998-99—Mathieu Chouinard, Shawinigan

MARCEL ROBERT TROPHY
(Top scholastic/athletic performer)

Season Player, Team
1981-82—Jacques Sylvestre, Granby
1982-83—Claude Gosselin, Quebec
1983-84—Gilbert Paiement, Chicoutimi
1984-85—Claude Gosselin, Longueuil
1985-86—Bernard Morin, Laval
1986-87—Patrice Tremblay, Chicoutimi
1987-88—Stephane Beauregard, St. Jean
1988-89—Daniel Lacroix, Granby
1989-90—Yanic Perreault, Trois-Rivieres
1990-91—Benoit Larose, Laval
1991-92—Simon Toupin, Beauport
1992-93—Jocelyn Thibault, Sherbrooke
1993-94—Patrick Boileau, Laval
1994-95—Daniel Briere, Drummondville
1995-96—Marc Denis, Chicoutimi
1996-97—Luc Vaillancourt, Beauport
1997-98—Michel Tremblay, Shawinigan
1998-99—Christian Robichaud, Victoriaville

MIKE BOSSY TROPHY
(Top pro prospect)

Season Player, Team
1980-81—Dale Hawerchuk, Cornwall
1981-82—Michel Petit, Sherbrooke
1982-83—Pat LaFontaine, Verdun
Sylvain Turgeon, Hull
1983-84—Mario Lemieux, Laval
1984-85—Jose Charbonneau, Drummondville
1985-86—Jimmy Carson, Verdun
1986-87—Pierre Turgeon, Granby
1987-88—Daniel Dore, Drummondville
1988-89—Patrice Brisebois, Laval
1989-90—Karl Dykhuis, Hull
1990-91—Philippe Boucher, Granby
1991-92—Paul Brousseau, Hull
1992-93—Alexandre Daigle, Victoriaville
1993-94—Eric Fichaud, Chicoutimi
1994-95—Martin Biron, Beauport
1995-96—Jean-Pierre Dumont, Val d'Or
1996-97—Roberto Luongo, Val d'Or
1997-98—Vincent Lecavalier, Rimouski
1998-99—Maxime Ouellet, Quebec

Originally known as Association of Journalism of Hockey Trophy from 1980-81 through 1982-83.

EMILE "BUTCH" BOUCHARD TROPHY
(Top defenseman)

Season Player, Team
1975-76—Jean Gagnon, Quebec
1976-77—Robert Picard, Montreal
1977-78—Mark Hardy, Montreal
1978-79—Ray Bourque, Verdun
1979-80—Gaston Therrien, Quebec
1980-81—Fred Boimistruck, Cornwall
1981-82—Paul Andre Boutilier, Sherbrooke
1982-83—J.J. Daigneault, Longueuil
1983-84—Billy Campbell, Verdun
1984-85—Yves Beaudoin, Shawinigan
1985-86—Sylvain Cote, Hull
1986-87—Jean Marc Richard, Chicoutimi
1987-88—Eric Desjardins, Granby
1988-89—Yves Racine, Victoriaville
1989-90—Claude Barthe, Victoriaville
1990-91—Patrice Brisebois, Drummondville
1991-92—Francois Groleau, Shawinigan

Season Player, Team
1992-93—Benoit Larose, Laval
1993-94—Steve Gosselin, Chicoutimi
1994-95—Stephane Julien, Sherbrooke
1995-96—Denis Gauthier, Drummondville
1996-97—Stephane Robidas, Shawinigan
1997-98—Derrick Walser, Rimouski
1998-99—Jiri Fischer, Hull

JACQUES PLANTE TROPHY
(Top goaltender)

Season Player, Team
1969-70—Michael Deguise, Sorel
1970-71—Reynald Fortier, Quebec
1971-72—Richard Brodeur, Cornwall
1972-73—Pierre Perusee, Quebec
1973-74—Claude Legris, Sorel
1974-75—Nick Sanza, Sherbrooke
1975-76—Tim Bernhardt, Cornwall
1976-77—Tim Bernhardt, Cornwall
1977-78—Tim Bernhardt, Cornwall
1978-79—Jacques Cloutier, Trois-Rivieres
1979-80—Corrado Micalef, Sherbrooke
1980-81—Michel Dufour,Sorel
1981-82—Jeff Barratt, Montreal
1982-83—Tony Haladuick, Laval
1983-84—Tony Haladuick, Laval
1984-85—Daniel Berthiaume, Chicoutimi
1985-86—Robert Desjardins, Hull
1986-87—Robert Desjardins, Longueuil
1987-88—Stephane Beauregard, St. Jean
1988-89—Stephane Fiset, Victoriaville
1989-90—Pierre Gagnon, Victoriaville
1990-91—Felix Potvin, Chicoutimi
1991-92—Jean-Francois Labbe, Trois-Rivieres
1992-93—Jocelyn Thibault, Sherbrooke
1993-94—Philippe DeRouville, Verdun
1994-95—Martin Biron, Beauport
1995-96—Frederic Deschenes, Granby
1996-97—Marc Denis, Chicoutimi
1997-98—Mathieu Garon, Victoriaville
1998-99—Maxime Ouellet, Quebec

GUY LAFLEUR TROPHY
(Playoff MVP)

Season Player, Team
1977-78—Richard David, Trois-Rivieres
1978-79—Jean-Francois Sauve, Trois-Rivieres
1979-80—Dale Hawerchuk, Cornwall
1980-81—Alain Lemieux, Trois-Rivieres
1981-82—Michel Morissette, Sherbrooke
1982-83—Pat LaFontaine, Verdun
1983-84—Mario Lemieux, Laval
1984-85—Claude Lemieux, Verdun
1985-86—Sylvain Cote, Hull
Luc Robitaille, Hull
1986-87—Marc Saumier, Longueuil
1987-88—Marc Saumier, Hull
1988-89—Donald Audette, Laval
1989-90—Denis Chalifoux, Laval
1990-91—Felix Potvin, Chicoutimi
1991-92—Robert Guillet, Longueuil
1992-93—Emmanuel Fernandez, Laval
1993-94—Eric Fichaud, Chicoutimi
1994-95—Jose Theodore, Hull
1995-96—Jason Doig, Granby
1996-97—Christian Bronsard, Hull
1997-98—Jean-Pierre Dumont, Val d'Or
1998-99—Mathieu Benoit, Acadie-Bathurst

ROBERT LEBEL TROPHY
(Best team defensive average)

Season Team
1977-78—Trois-Rivieres Draveurs
1978-79—Trois-Rivieres Draveurs
1979-80—Sherbrooke Beavers
1980-81—Sorel Black Hawks
1981-82—Montreal Juniors
1982-83—Shawinigan Cataracts
1983-84—Shawinigan Cataracts
1984-85—Shawinigan Cataracts
1985-86—Hull Olympiques
1986-78—Longueuil Chevaliers
1987-88—St. Jean Castors
1988-89—Hull Olympiques
1989-90—Victoriaville Tigres
1990-91—Chicoutimi Sagueneens
1991-92—Trois-Rivieres Draveurs
1992-93—Sherbrooke Faucons
1993-94—College Francais de Verdun
1994-95—Beauport Harfangs
1995-96—Granby Predateurs
1996-97—Hull Olympics
1997-98—Quebec Remparts
1998-99—Halifax Mooseheads

ALL-TIME LEAGUE CHAMPIONS

	REGULAR-SEASON CHAMPION	PLAYOFF CHAMPION
Season	**Team**	**Team**
1969-70—	Quebec Remparts	Quebec Remparts
1970-71—	Quebec Remparts	Quebec Remparts
1971-72—	Cornwall Royals	Cornwall Royals
1972-73—	Quebec Remparts	Quebec Remparts
1973-74—	Sorel Black Hawks	Quebec Remparts
1974-75—	Sherbrooke Beavers	Sherbrooke Beavers
1975-76—	Sherbrooke Beavers	Quebec Remparts
1976-77—	Quebec Remparts	Sherbrooke Beavers
1977-78—	Trois-Rivieres Draveurs	Trois-Rivieres Draveurs
1978-79—	Trois-Rivieres Draveurs	Trois-Rivieres Draveurs
1979-80—	Sherbrooke Beavers	Cornwall Royals
1980-81—	Cornwall Royals	Cornwall Royals
1981-82—	Sherbrooke Beavers	Sherbrooke Beavers
1982-83—	Laval Voisins	Verdun Juniors
1983-84—	Laval Voisins	Laval Voisins
1984-85—	Shawinigan Cataracts	Verdun Junior Canadiens
1985-86—	Hull Olympiques	Hull Olympiques
1986-87—	Granby Bisons	Longueuil Chevaliers
1987-88—	Hull Olympiques	Hull Olympiques
1988-89—	Trois-Rivieres Draveurs	Laval Titans
1989-90—	Victoriaville Tigres	Laval Titans

REGULAR-SEASON CHAMPION		PLAYOFF CHAMPION
Season	**Team**	**Team**
1990-91—	Chicoutimi Sagueneens	Chicoutimi Saguenees
1991-92—	Longueuil College Francais	Longueuil College Francais
1992-93—	Sherbrooke Faucons	Laval Titans
1993-94—	Laval Titans	Chicoutimi Sagueneens
1994-95—	Laval Titans	Hull Olympiques
1995-96—	Granby Predateurs	Granby Predateurs
1996-97—	Hull Olympics	Hull Olympics
1997-98—	Quebec Remparts	Val d'Or Foreurs
1998-99—	Quebec Remparts	Acadie-Bathurst Titans

The QMJHL regular-season champion is awarded the John Rougeau Trophy and the playoff champion is awarded the Presidents Cup. The John Rougeau Trophy was originally called the Governors Trophy from 1969-70 through 1982-83.

WESTERN HOCKEY LEAGUE

LEAGUE OFFICE

Note: League was known as Canadian Major Junior Hockey League in 1966-67 and Western Canadian Hockey League from 1967-68 through 1977-78.

Commissioner
Dev Dley
Vice president
Richard Doerksen
Executive assistant
Norman Dueck
Director of information
Lloyd Hamshaw

Education consultant
Jim Donlevy
Address
Suite 521, 10333 Southport Road SW
Calgary, Alberta T2W 3X6

Phone
403-253-8113
FAX
403-258-1455

1998-99 REGULAR SEASON

FINAL STANDINGS

EAST DIVISION

Team	G	W	L	T	Pts.	GF	GA
Prince Albert	72	45	22	5	95	288	213
Brandon	72	39	29	4	82	293	267
Moose Jaw	72	39	31	2	80	292	262
Swift Current	72	34	32	6	74	232	211
Regina	72	24	43	5	53	238	312
Saskatoon	72	16	49	7	39	184	291

CENTRAL DIVISION

Team	G	W	L	T	Pts.	GF	GA
Calgary	72	51	13	8	110	319	187
Red Deer	72	34	33	5	73	274	250
Lethbridge	72	31	32	9	71	224	215
Kootenay	72	30	35	7	67	245	276
Medicine Hat	72	15	56	1	31	185	323

WEST DIVISION

Team	G	W	L	T	Pts.	GF	GA
Kamloops	72	48	11	13	109	298	195
Tri-City	72	43	23	6	92	311	219
Seattle	72	37	24	11	85	279	236
Prince George	72	34	32	6	74	255	264
Portland	72	23	36	13	59	215	278
Kelowna	72	25	42	5	55	224	282
Spokane	72	19	44	9	47	193	268

INDIVIDUAL LEADERS

Goals: Pavel Brendl, Calgary (73)
Assists: Scott Gomez, Tri-City (78)
Points: Pavel Brendl, Calgary (134)
Penalty minutes: Mike Brown, Kamloops (285)
Goaltending average: Kenric Exner, Kamloops (2.31)
Shutouts: Cody Rudkowsky, Seattle (7)

TOP SCORERS

	Games	G	A	Pts.
Pavel Brendl, Calgary	68	73	61	134
Brad Moran, Calgary	71	60	58	118
Dylan Gyori, Tri-City	69	53	65	118
Chad Hinz, Moose Jaw	71	42	75	117
Scott Gomez, Tri-City	58	30	78	108
Shawn McNeil, Red Deer	72	44	59	103
Brett McLean, Kelowna-Brandon	65	47	54	101
Bret DeCecco, Seattle	72	57	43	100
Ryan Robson, Brandon	72	33	61	94
Oleg Saprykin, Seattle	66	47	46	93
Jamie Lundmark, Moose Jaw	70	40	51	91
Kyle Calder, Kamloops	61	42	46	88
Brett Lysak, Regina	61	39	49	88
Milan Kraft, Prince Albert	68	40	46	86
Jaroslav Kristek, Tri-City	70	38	48	86
Brenden Morrow, Portland	61	41	44	85
Dustin Paul, Moose Jaw	71	31	52	83
Matt Kinch, Calgary	68	14	69	83
Ken McKay, Tri-City	64	37	45	82
Mike Green, Kootenay	71	35	45	80
Marc Brown, Prince Albert	72	35	45	80

INDIVIDUAL STATISTICS

BRANDON WHEAT KINGS

SCORING

	Games	G	A	Pts.	PIM
Ryan Robson	72	33	61	94	35
Burke Henry	68	18	58	76	151
Andrei Lupandin	69	25	50	75	171
Brad Twordik	57	29	45	74	67
Aaron Goldade	64	27	33	60	56
Brett Girard	63	23	34	57	33
Dan Tetrault	57	10	36	46	91
Alex Argyriou	57	19	21	40	11
Mike Wirll	44	16	21	37	12
Brett McLean	21	15	16	31	20
Jason Chimera	21	14	12	26	32
Ryan Craig	54	11	12	23	46
Ryan Johnston	27	7	14	21	73
Jan Fadrny	45	4	17	21	36
Randy Ponte	54	4	14	18	235
Andrew Kaminsky	50	9	7	16	71
Wade Skolney	39	3	10	13	60

	Games	G	A	Pts.	PIM
Scott McCallum	52	3	7	10	111
Richard Mueller	39	7	2	9	14
Cory Unser	56	3	6	9	59
Petr Kudrna	39	4	3	7	31
Brett Thurston	46	2	3	5	27
Les Borsheim	27	0	5	5	94
J.D. Kehler	26	3	1	4	6
Kevin Harris	9	2	2	4	9
Justin Yeoman	32	1	1	2	27
Brooks Paisley	24	1	0	1	26
Jamie Hodson (goalie)	43	0	1	1	2
Brett Dickie	1	0	0	0	2
Mike Gerstenbuhler	2	0	0	0	0
Mitchell Virostek	2	0	0	0	0
Travis Young	5	0	0	0	0
Jomar Cruz (goalie)	38	0	0	0	7

GOALTENDING

	Games	Min.	W	L	T	G	SO	Avg.
Jamie Hodson	43	2295	23	12	3	123	4	3.22
Jomar Cruz	38	2057	16	17	1	139	1	4.05

CALGARY HITMEN

SCORING

	Games	G	A	Pts.	PIM
Pavel Brendl	68	73	61	134	40
Brad Moran	71	60	58	118	96
Matt Kinch	68	14	69	83	16
Kris Beech	68	26	41	67	103
Kenton Smith	69	19	35	54	138
Chris Nielsen	70	22	24	46	45
Brent Dodginghorse	50	13	31	44	153
Jerred Smithson	63	14	22	36	108
Peter Bergman	60	16	19	35	91
Brad Stuart	30	11	22	33	26
Lyle Steenbergen	70	15	16	31	80
Sean McAslan	71	7	16	23	110
Jordan Krestanovich	62	6	13	19	10
Rod Sarich	65	3	15	18	22
Curtis Rich	68	3	15	18	215
Ryan Shannon	67	3	13	16	252
Ryan Geremia	35	4	9	13	42
Ryan Andres	61	6	6	12	192
Michael Bubnick	49	3	2	5	8
Jeff Feniak	39	1	4	5	81
Eric Clark	44	0	3	3	9
Wade Davis	38	0	2	2	21
Brent Williams (goalie)	9	0	1	1	0
Donald Choukalos, (goalie)	10	0	1	1	4
Alexandre Fomitchev (goalie)	57	0	1	1	4
Chad Wolkowski	3	0	0	0	0
Shaun Norrie	4	0	0	0	0

GOALTENDING

	Games	Min.	W	L	T	G	SO	Avg.
Donald Choukalos	10	571	8	1	0	20	1	2.10
Alex Fomitchev	57	3317	39	10	7	142	4	2.57
Brent Williams	9	462	4	2	1	21	0	2.73

KAMLOOPS BLAZERS

SCORING

	Games	G	A	Pts.	PIM
Steve Shrum	72	28	40	68	63
Ajay Baines	72	33	32	65	145
Steve Gainey	68	30	34	64	155
Konstantin Panov	62	33	30	63	62
Donnie Kinney	65	24	35	59	47
Mike Brown	69	28	16	44	285
Kyle Calder	27	19	18	37	30
Anton Borodkin	71	8	29	37	98
Micki DuPont	59	8	27	35	110
Chris St. Croix	64	8	27	35	123
Robyn Regehr	54	12	20	32	130
Jonathan Hobson	61	11	19	30	38
Jared Aulin	55	7	19	26	23
Alan Manness	40	8	17	25	34
Paul Deniset	57	5	18	23	46
Kyle Kos	28	6	14	20	42
Kevin Mackle	35	5	15	20	78
Ty Jones	20	3	16	19	84
Brett Draney	58	7	10	17	48
Chad Starling	65	4	13	17	101
Wade Burt	4	2	5	7	2
Gable Gross	37	2	5	7	50
Jordon Flodell	27	3	3	6	88
Ryan Thorpe	22	2	1	3	68
Kenric Exner (goalie)	51	0	3	3	10
Adam Dombrowski	22	1	1	2	43
Aaron Glonet	53	1	1	2	70
Kyle Ladobruk	1	0	0	0	0
Brett Bartell	2	0	0	0	0
Chris Thompson (goalie)	3	0	0	0	4
Shawn Thompson	4	0	0	0	0
Blaine Depper	5	0	0	0	2
David Haun (goalie)	10	0	0	0	2
David Klatt (goalie)	13	0	0	0	0

GOALTENDING

	Games	Min.	W	L	T	G	SO	Avg.
Kenric Exner	51	2966	34	6	8	114	5	2.31
David Klatt	13	706	5	3	3	36	0	3.06
David Haun	10	574	8	0	2	31	0	3.24
Chris Thompson	3	141	1	2	0	12	0	5.11

KELOWNA ROCKETS

SCORING

	Games	G	A	Pts.	PIM
Brett McLean	44	32	38	70	46
J.J. Hunter	66	18	32	50	61
Scott Hannan	47	15	30	45	92
Rory McDade	47	11	33	44	83
Vernon Fiddler	68	22	21	43	82
Kevin Korol	68	19	21	40	55
Ryan Wade	43	13	25	38	82
Lubomir Pistek	55	13	16	29	38
Kiel McLeod	55	12	15	27	48
Quintin Laing	70	11	10	21	107
Gavin McLeod	49	5	15	20	140
Gerad Adams	15	6	10	16	28
Carsen Germyn	59	6	10	16	61
Bruce Harrison	68	6	9	15	170
Rob Sandrock	37	4	11	15	62
Trevor Hitchings	38	1	13	14	16
Ryan Cuthbert	54	6	5	11	63
Jan Dusanek	27	4	6	10	30
Mitch Fritz	52	9	0	9	156
Ryan Johnston	20	4	5	9	40
Nolan Yonkman	61	1	6	7	129
Clint Keichinger	41	1	4	5	122
Joe Suderman	49	0	5	5	82
Brad Rohrig	9	2	2	4	14
David Selthun	49	2	2	4	49
Seth Leonard	3	1	2	3	4
B. J. Fehr	53	0	3	3	50
Lindsey Materi (goalie)	27	0	2	2	2
Chris Noble (goalie)	1	0	0	0	0
Ryan Johnson	2	0	0	0	4
Richie Regehr	2	0	0	0	0
Kyle Stanton (goalie)	2	0	0	0	0
Corey Koskl	3	0	0	0	0
Travis Moen	4	0	0	0	0
Aaron Sproule (goalie)	6	0	0	0	0
Jordan Watt (goalie)	6	0	0	0	0
Kris Mallette	9	0	0	0	40
Justin Jack	22	0	0	0	43
Kevin Swanson (goalie)	50	0	0	0	0

GOALTENDING

	Games	Min.	W	L	T	G	SO	Avg.
Kevin Swanson	50	2507	18	23	3	144	2	3.45
Jordan Watt	6	323	1	2	1	20	0	3.72
Aaron Sproule	6	278	2	4	0	19	0	4.10
Lindsey Materi	27	1150	4	12	1	80	0	4.17
Chris Noble	1	60	0	1	0	7	0	7.00
Kyle Stanton	2	29	0	0	0	4	0	8.28

KOOTENAY ICE

SCORING

	Games	G	A	Pts.	PIM
Mike Green	71	35	45	80	37
Jaroslav Svoboda	54	26	33	59	46
Steve McCarthy	57	19	33	52	79
Stanislav Gron	49	28	18	46	18
Trevor Wasyluk	43	17	26	43	76
Scott Roles	64	7	34	41	75
Wade Burt	58	14	21	35	59
Jarret Stoll	57	13	21	34	38
Kyle Wanvig	71	12	20	32	119
Brad Tutschek	68	16	13	29	123
Jason Jaffray	57	14	12	26	50
Tyler Beechey	57	14	9	23	24
Jesse Ferguson	61	3	18	21	77
Colin Sinclair	62	6	11	17	54
Trevor Johnson	56	1	14	15	51
Kris Knoblauch	21	7	3	10	36
Mark Thompson	36	2	7	9	76
Dion Lassu	72	1	6	7	216
Nick Marach	57	3	3	6	81
Andy Penny	10	2	4	6	5
Dean Arsene	68	1	4	5	111
Graham Belak	45	3	1	4	201
Jeremy Yablonski	27	1	1	2	77
Tyler Dyck	4	0	2	2	2
Brian Ballman	18	0	2	2	36
Rod Leroux	30	0	2	2	51
Clayton Pool (goalie)	57	0	2	2	8
B.J. Boxma (goalie)	16	0	1	1	0
Brian Dafoe (goalie)	10	0	0	0	0

GOALTENDING

	Games	Min.	W	L	T	G	SO	Avg.
B.J. Boxma	16	666	4	3	1	37	0	3.33
Clayton Pool	57	3174	26	24	6	184	1	3.48
Brian Dafoe	10	516	0	8	0	54	0	6.28

LETHBRIDGE HURRICANES

SCORING

	Games	G	A	Pts.	PIM
Jason Hegberg	71	27	48	75	94
Curtis Huppe	48	33	23	56	34
Luc Theoret	46	13	39	52	92
Sean Robertson	65	19	24	43	125
Kris Knoblauch	52	20	22	42	102
Derek Holland	51	8	29	37	128
Brandon Janes	55	6	31	37	38
Brian Ballman	52	11	13	24	95
Dave Taylor	39	6	18	24	34
Scott Borders	69	11	12	23	98
Dennis Kozyrev	59	10	13	23	25
Nathan Barrett	22	12	9	21	19
Chad Kletzel	55	9	10	19	76
Thomas Scantlebury	67	4	14	18	109
Bart Rushmer	71	4	12	16	154
Shaun Sutter	35	8	4	12	43
Derrick Ruck	63	4	7	11	36
Trevor Wasyluk	17	3	8	11	30
Ryan Jorde	21	2	5	7	22
Eric Godard	66	2	5	7	213
Igor Valeev	8	2	3	5	13
Derek Atkinson	39	1	4	5	29
Andrew Guindon	33	1	3	4	52
Brent Hope	24	2	1	3	15
Phil Cole	45	2	1	3	64
Todd Hornung	13	1	1	2	26
Blair Simpson	24	0	2	2	21
Brady Block (goalie)	55	0	2	2	21
Andy Penny	10	1	0	1	0
Mike Varhaug	15	0	1	1	60
Jason McLean (goalie)	19	0	1	1	8
Dustin Kazak	23	0	1	1	9
Darren Lynch	1	0	0	0	2
Mike Trussler (goalie)	4	0	0	0	0
Kyle Chant	2	0	0	0	6

GOALTENDING

	Games	Min.	W	L	T	G	SO	Avg.
Jason McLean	19	1077	11	4	2	49	1	2.73
Brady Block	55	3098	19	26	7	150	1	2.91
Mark Trussler	4	179	1	2	0	13	0	4.36

MEDICINE HAT TIGERS

SCORING

	Games	G	A	Pts.	PIM
Aaron Millar	72	28	39	67	36
Burkeley Buchko	66	26	21	47	55
Martin Cibak	66	21	26	47	72
Paul Elliott	71	11	36	47	80
Jason Chimera	37	18	22	40	84
Denny Johnston	65	9	24	33	22
Ben Thomson	67	10	14	24	22
Jason Boyd	67	9	12	21	56
Shaun Sutter	23	9	5	14	38
Kris Graf	35	6	8	14	37
Kevin Young	58	1	13	14	19
Brett Scheffelmaier	70	3	10	13	252
Brad Voth	40	4	6	10	102
Konrad Brand	63	4	6	10	140
Derek Rupprecht	65	4	6	10	40
Vladimir Sicak	35	1	9	10	71
Steve Wilejto	33	2	6	8	18
Blair Simpson	43	1	7	8	70
Cody Lyseng	47	4	2	6	94
Brady Austin	60	1	5	6	197
Frazer Donahue	23	4	1	5	19
Kevin Labbe	33	4	0	4	6
Justin Yeoman	22	3	1	4	12
Jay Bouwmeester	8	2	1	3	2
Tyson Kentel	51	0	2	2	109
Scott Stewart	4	0	1	1	0
Shaun Aebig	8	0	1	1	4
Josh Morrow	10	0	1	1	2
Scott Buhler (goalie)	44	0	1	1	2
Rob Sandrock	1	0	0	0	0
Ryan Trotter	1	0	0	0	5
Shaune Draper	2	0	0	0	2
Ryan Kinasewich	3	0	0	0	2
Jordan Roach	8	0	0	0	15
Travis Willie	8	0	0	0	11
Shaun Hill	25	0	0	0	86
Cam Ondrik (goalie)	39	0	0	0	11

GOALTENDING

	Games	Min.	W	L	T	G	SO	Avg.
Scott Buhler	44	2401	11	28	1	166	1	4.15
Cam Ondrik	39	1922	4	28	0	149	0	4.65

MOOSE JAW WARRIORS

SCORING

	Games	G	A	Pts.	PIM
Chad Hinz	71	42	75	117	40
Jamie Lundmark	70	40	51	91	121
Dustin Paul	71	31	52	83	75
Scott Schoneck	72	20	56	76	44
Brent Hobday	72	40	26	66	135

	Games	G	A	Pts.	PIM
Jason Weitzel	70	19	35	54	60
Garnet Jacobson	68	16	24	40	176
Shawn Limpright	69	12	19	31	101
Alex Andreyev	60	11	11	22	80
Cory Hintz	60	10	12	22	42
Shawn Skolney	48	11	10	21	107
Brian Sutherby	66	9	12	21	47
Dreu Volk	55	3	17	20	93
Chris Twerdun	55	4	15	19	67
Dayle Wilcox	51	5	12	17	21
Steven Crampton	52	7	5	12	31
Kris Mallette	49	1	10	11	187
Dustin Bru	44	3	5	8	17
Craig Strain	50	2	6	8	88
Justin Hansen	10	4	3	7	11
Rastislav Stana (goalie)	36	0	5	5	4
Bobby Chad Mitchell	36	0	4	4	38
Kevin Lapp	17	2	1	3	74
Jordon Flodell	25	0	1	1	65
Tim Barlow (goalie)	33	0	1	1	2
Regan Rome	42	0	1	1	31
Jared Smith	1	0	0	0	0
Deryk Engelland	2	0	0	0	0
Nathan Paetsch	2	0	0	0	0
Jay Ewasiuk (goalie)	5	0	0	0	2

GOALTENDING

	Games	Min.	W	L	T	G	SO	Avg.
Tim Barlow	33	1905	17	13	1	108	2	3.40
Rastislav Stana	36	2131	21	14	1	123	2	3.46
Jay Ewasiuk	5	297	1	4	0	25	0	5.05

PORTLAND WINTER HAWKS

SCORING

	Games	G	A	Pts.	PIM
Brenden Morrow	61	41	44	85	248
Marty Standish	72	26	40	66	192
Todd Robinson	36	22	35	57	46
Kevin Haupt	67	11	40	51	32
Dean Beuker	70	19	24	43	58
Blake Robson	61	14	18	32	54
Andrew Ference	40	11	21	32	104
Todd Hornung	45	15	15	30	86
Ken Davis	72	13	14	27	76
Marcel Hossa	70	7	14	21	66
Jan Koznar	67	9	11	20	56
Ryan Kehrig	66	2	11	13	12
Ryan Thrussell	70	1	11	12	78
Scott Botterill	52	6	5	11	16
Christian Bolding	50	1	10	11	53
Matt Walker	64	1	10	11	151
Derek MacLean	52	3	7	10	41
Shon Jones-Parry	44	4	5	9	145
Gerry King	32	2	6	8	71
Steve Fetter	54	2	5	7	20
Michael Kiesman	26	3	3	6	65
Jason LaBarbera (goalie)	51	0	5	5	14
Harlan Pratt	10	1	3	4	10
James DeMone	64	1	2	3	81
Tyler Cronk	2	0	0	0	0
Duane Perillat (goalie)	2	0	0	0	0
Kyle Chant	3	0	0	0	0
Luc Theoret	3	0	0	0	10
Mike Gillen	4	0	0	0	0
Tim McEachen	9	0	0	0	7
Shaun Lee (goalie)	27	0	0	0	0

GOALTENDING

	Games	Min.	W	L	T	G	SO	Avg.
Jason LaBarbera	51	299	18	23	9	170	4	3.41
Shaun Lee	27	1327	5	12	4	91	0	4.11
Duane Perillat	2	80	0	1	0	11	0	8.25

PRINCE ALBERT RAIDERS

SCORING

	Games	G	A	Pts.	PIM
Milan Kraft	68	40	46	86	32
Marc Brown	72	35	44	79	47
Cody Jensen	70	34	43	77	62
Derek Paget	72	26	45	71	115
Cory Morgan	66	39	31	70	103
Richard Seeley	61	10	48	58	110
Scott Hartnell	65	10	34	44	104
David Cameron	41	9	30	39	25
Garrett Prosofsky	24	15	16	31	21
Ross Lupaschuk	67	8	19	27	127
Dallas Flaman	71	11	14	25	77
Nick Schultz	58	5	18	23	37
Blaine Stowards	68	8	14	22	39
Clayton Chartrand	67	5	14	19	89
Jeremy Goetzinger	51	2	17	19	42
Craig Brunel	50	10	8	18	173
Kevin Kellett	58	5	12	17	103
Todd Fedoruk	28	6	4	10	75
Justin Kelly	30	3	4	7	13
Derek Brandon	39	1	5	6	90
Riley Cote	37	3	2	5	63
Kerry Nice	59	2	1	3	46
Steve Wilejto	27	0	3	3	17
Grant McCune (goalie)	18	0	2	2	2
Evan Lindsay (goalie)	56	0	2	2	10
Scott Botterill	6	1	0	1	0
Trevor Hitchings	5	0	1	1	6
Aaron Blair	1	0	0	0	0
Travis Willie	1	0	0	0	0
Shaun Hill	2	0	0	0	5
Jason Seery	2	0	0	0	15
Greg Watson	2	0	0	0	5
Jordan Clarke	5	0	0	0	5

GOALTENDING

	Games	Min.	W	L	T	G	SO	Avg.
Evan Lindsay	56	3334	34	16	5	158	1	2.84
Grant McCune	18	1018	11	6	0	50	2	2.95

PRINCE GEORGE COUGARS

SCORING

	Games	G	A	Pts.	PIM
Mike Bayrack	70	37	32	69	71
Jarrett Smith	49	20	37	57	54
Garry Toor	59	14	39	53	28
Tyler Bouck	56	22	25	47	178
Ian Walterson	72	10	34	44	83
Blair Betts	42	20	22	42	39
Jozef Mrena	65	15	26	41	18
Curtis Tipler	55	14	25	39	36
Trent Hunter	50	18	20	38	34
Petr Kubos	70	8	29	37	52
Tyler Brough	65	14	16	30	58
Jordan Walker	37	7	20	27	20
Brent McDonald	34	13	13	26	40
Justin Cox	72	9	13	22	51
Justin Hansen	32	13	7	20	29
Michael Kiesman	41	10	10	20	115
Jeff Zorn	46	5	10	15	50
Travis Eagles	48	1	9	10	66
Jonathan Parker	56	4	5	9	17
Tim Wedderburn	66	0	8	8	20
Shon Jones-Parry	24	0	5	5	114
Dan Hamhuis	56	1	3	4	45
Scott Myers (goalie)	66	0	3	3	6
Mike Leier	5	0	1	1	7
Ryan Driedger (goalie)	11	0	1	1	0
Owen Richey	16	0	1	1	6
Ryan Chieduch	56	0	1	1	64
Billy Thompson (goalie)	1	0	0	0	0
Kevin Seibel	1	0	0	0	0

	Games	G	A	Pts.	PIM
Chris Falloon	1	0	0	0	0
Kevin Swanson (goalie)	4	0	0	0	0
Dustin Ernest	2	0	0	0	0
Adam Loncan	9	0	0	0	2

GOALTENDING

	Games	Min.	W	L	T	G	SO	Avg.
Kevin Swanson	4	180	1	2	0	10	0	3.33
Scott Myers	66	3771	30	28	6	214	0	3.40
Ryan Driedger	11	351	3	1	0	29	0	4.96
Billy Thompson	1	40	0	1	0	6	0	9.00

RED DEER REBELS

SCORING

	Games	G	A	Pts.	PIM
Shawn McNeil	72	44	59	103	87
Brad Leeb	64	32	47	79	84
Frantisek Mrazek	60	34	42	76	79
Kevin Marsh	60	35	26	61	36
Lukas Bednarik	72	25	36	61	16
Justin Mapletoft	72	24	22	46	81
Brent McDonald	38	17	18	35	64
Jim Vandermeer	70	5	23	28	258
Andrew Bergen	61	14	12	26	45
Jordan Walker	33	9	17	26	12
Justin Wallin	72	9	14	23	20
Kyle Kos	37	3	17	20	56
Ryan Bonni	20	3	10	13	41
Chris Ovington	49	1	10	11	73
Drew Kehler	56	1	10	11	163
Devin Francon	40	4	6	10	46
Jarrett Thompson	28	3	7	10	47
Brad Rohrig	33	4	4	8	47
Stephen Peat	31	2	6	8	98
Scott C. McQueen	70	1	7	8	78
Regan Darby	19	1	6	7	90
Adam Dombrowski	24	1	6	7	23
Kent Beagle	36	2	3	5	88
Bobby Duncan	5	0	5	5	2
Jay Batchelor	33	0	4	4	19
Scott D. McQueen	15	0	2	2	25
Dustin Schwartz (goalie)	49	0	2	2	13
Colby Armstrong	1	0	1	1	0
Doug Lynch	3	0	1	1	2
Rhett Nevill	32	0	1	1	14
Andrew Coates	33	0	1	1	6
Jearum Kurtz	1	0	0	0	0
Robert Schnabel	1	0	0	0	2
Chris Cederstrand	2	0	0	0	0
Michael Clague (goalie)	2	0	0	0	0
Joel Stepp	2	0	0	0	0
Shane Bendera (goalie)	3	0	0	0	0
Trevor Nychkalo	3	0	0	0	0
Jay Vidrine	20	0	0	0	2
Jeff Smith	25	0	0	0	9
Jordan Watt (goalie)	27	0	0	0	6

GOALTENDING

	Games	Min.	W	L	T	G	SO	Avg.
Jordan Watt	27	1472	12	9	2	81	2	3.30
Dustin Schwartz	49	2706	21	23	3	149	1	3.30
Michael Clague	2	64	1	0	0	6	0	5.63
Shane Bendera	3	92	0	1	0	7	0	4.57

REGINA PATS

SCORING

	Games	G	A	Pts.	PIM
Brett Lysak	61	39	49	88	84
Radek Duda	65	24	31	55	139
Karel Mosovsky	68	26	25	51	58
Kyle Calder	34	23	28	51	29
Barret Jackman	70	8	36	44	259
David Manuca	68	12	26	38	84
Gerad Adams	42	16	20	36	136
Brad Stuart	29	10	19	29	43
Alan Manness	28	7	18	25	18
Todd Fedoruk	39	12	12	24	107
Kevin Saurette	66	8	16	24	47
Chris Anderson	55	4	19	23	84
Travis Churchman	71	9	11	20	212
Ryan Thomas	60	11	6	17	115
Andrew Kaminsky	19	4	5	9	14
Matt Hubbauer	52	3	6	9	59
Scotty Balan	63	1	8	9	42
Ryan Geremia	27	4	4	8	6
Colin Taylor	54	4	4	8	116
Garth Murray	60	3	5	8	101
Devin Francon	16	3	3	6	21
Jason Steenbergen	47	2	2	4	39
Kyle Freadrich	52	2	2	4	215
Drew Kehler	18	0	4	4	53
Shane Lanigan	6	1	1	2	16
Matko Malbasa	3	1	0	1	0
Ryan Annesley	7	1	0	1	0
Richard Andrew	2	0	1	1	0
Chad Yaremko (goalie)	22	0	1	1	7
Chad Davidson	1	0	0	0	0
Randall Dyck	1	0	0	0	0
Shaun Fleming (goalie)	2	0	0	0	2
Justin Lucyshyn	2	0	0	0	0
Zack Roe	2	0	0	0	0
Grant Jacobsen	3	0	0	0	0
Brett Bartell	4	0	0	0	0
Drew Norman	10	0	0	0	2
Kyle Kautz	12	0	0	0	23
Donald Choukalos (goalie)	24	0	0	0	0
Colin Kobza	27	0	0	0	73
Matt Cockell	33	0	0	0	15
Thomas Johnman	48	0	0	0	38

GOALTENDING

	Games	Min.	W	L	T	G	SO	Avg.
Shaun Fleming	2	79	1	0	0	3	1	2.28
Matt Cockell	33	1890	14	17	1	129	0	4.10
Chad Yaremko	22	1016	3	13	0	72	0	4.25
Donald Choukalos	24	1337	6	12	4	98	0	4.40

SASKATOON BLADES

SCORING

	Games	G	A	Pts.	PIM
Jon Barkman	64	35	35	70	37
Garrett Bernbridge	68	23	27	50	30
Ryan Gaucher	64	14	32	46	92
Mathieu Cusson	43	16	28	44	22
Ryan Bonni	51	6	26	32	211
Bobby Almeida	39	9	16	25	44
Chris Fleury	63	5	17	22	87
David Cameron	24	6	14	20	12
Bevin Guenther	70	6	13	19	77
Tyler Shybunka	52	12	5	17	24
Christian Chartier	62	2	14	16	71
Garrett Prosofsky	25	8	7	15	21
Warren Peters	53	8	6	14	111
Derek Halldorson	44	7	4	11	128
Petja Pietilainen	53	1	10	11	58
Darcy Robinson	48	3	6	9	86
Garnet Exelby	61	5	3	8	91
Justin Kelly	20	3	5	8	6
Darcy Hordichuk	66	3	2	5	246
Ryan Johnston	10	2	2	4	21
Igor Valeev	23	2	2	4	36
Chris Ovington	19	2	1	3	37
Matt Miller	21	2	1	3	36
Ryan Stempfle	31	0	3	3	19
Kyle Hart	44	0	3	3	73
Steven MacIntyre	55	2	0	2	190
Chad Elmy	41	1	1	2	77

	Games	G	A	Pts.	PIM
Tyler MacKay (goalie)	41	0	2	2	27
Owen Richey	3	1	0	1	0
Scott D. McQueen	3	0	1	1	4
Derek Bjornson	10	0	1	1	16
Aaron Baker (goalie)	15	0	1	1	10
Aaron Rome	1	0	0	0	0
Kane Ludwar	2	0	0	0	0
Davin Heintz	2	0	0	0	0
Jeff Coulter	4	0	0	0	0
Brent Henley	15	0	0	0	35
Mike Schlamp	20	0	0	0	5
Jeff Blair (goalie)	28	0	0	0	9

GOALTENDING

	Games	Min.	W	L	T	G	SO	Avg.
Jeff Blair	28	1528	7	17	2	94	0	3.69
Tyler MacKay	41	2117	8	23	3	134	0	3.80
Aaron Baker	15	708	1	9	2	57	0	4.83

SEATTLE THUNDERBIRDS

SCORING

	Games	G	A	Pts.	PIM
Bret DeCecco	72	57	43	100	81
Oleg Saprykin	66	47	46	93	107
Scott Kelman	66	19	54	73	95
Torrey DiRoberto	66	25	42	67	100
Ben Clymer	70	12	44	56	93
Jame Pollock	59	10	32	42	78
Shane Endicott	72	13	26	39	27
Zdenek Blatny	44	18	15	33	25
Mike Siklenka	68	19	13	32	115
Jason Beckett	70	4	26	30	195
Tim Preston	60	12	15	27	98
Nathan Forster	65	5	17	22	153
Justin Ossachuk	56	9	9	18	231
Jeffrey Beatch	66	4	10	14	63
David Ullmann	49	7	6	13	37
Keegan McAvoy	66	2	11	13	87
Craig Olynick	51	1	9	10	89
Paul Hurd	35	5	3	8	67
David Kaczowka	60	3	2	5	247
David Morisset	17	4	0	4	31
Ryan Trsek	38	3	1	4	35
Cody Rudkowsky (goalie)	64	0	4	4	8
Chris Manchakowski	32	0	2	2	24
Darren McLachlan	2	0	1	1	7
Greg Black	2	0	0	0	0
Ray Fraser (goalie)	5	0	0	0	0
Garret Stroshein	11	0	0	0	32
Thomas Vicars (goalie)	16	0	0	0	4

GOALTENDING

	Games	Min.	W	L	T	G	SO	Avg.
Cody Rudkowsky	64	3665	34	17	10	177	7	2.90
Thomas Vicars	16	455	2	4	1	34	0	4.48
Ray Fraser	5	250	1	3	0	21	0	5.04

SPOKANE CHIEFS

SCORING

	Games	G	A	Pts.	PIM
Lynn Loyns	72	20	30	50	43
Dan Vandemeer	69	16	33	49	83
Daniel Bohac	70	26	21	47	58
Brandin Cole	68	15	27	42	114
Cam Severson	46	16	17	33	190
Ty Jones	26	15	12	27	98
Jared Smyth	70	12	15	27	119
Tim Smith	57	5	20	25	21
Brad Ference	31	3	22	25	125
Kyle Rossiter	71	4	17	21	206
Curtis Suter	65	7	13	20	221
Bobby Leavins	52	5	14	19	57
Derek Schutz	56	5	12	17	133
Chris Harper	59	8	8	16	60
Cole Fischer	66	3	11	14	111
Ryan Thorpe	19	10	3	13	21
Tim Krymusa	59	9	3	12	49
Mason Wallin	44	6	5	11	10
Jan Dusanek	27	1	10	11	21
Mark Forth	60	0	8	8	138
Kris Callaway	27	0	4	4	10
Josh Maser	19	2	1	3	89
Shawn Thompson	41	2	1	3	29
David Boychuk	22	0	3	3	41
David Hajek	27	0	3	3	10
Chris Twerdun	8	1	1	2	17
Ben Johnson	7	1	0	1	4
Matthew Keith	7	1	0	1	4
Mike Lencucha (goalie)	43	0	1	1	0
Shaun Fleming (goalie)	1	0	0	0	0
Chris Heid	1	0	0	0	0
Jeff Lucky	1	0	0	0	0
Jeff Peters	3	0	0	0	0
Simon Jones	6	0	0	0	9
David Haun (goalie)	34	0	0	0	0
Jeremy Farr	38	0	0	0	62
Matt Cockell (goalie)	10	0	0	0	0

GOALTENDING

	Games	Min.	W	L	T	G	SO	Avg.
Matt Cockell	10	338	0	2	2	17	0	3.02
David Haun	34	1893	7	21	4	113	1	3.58
Mike Lencucha	43	2099	12	21	3	127	1	3.63
Shaun Fleming	1	24	0	0	0	2	0	5.00

SWIFT CURRENT BRONCOS

SCORING

	Games	G	A	Pts.	PIM
Layne Ulmer	72	40	35	75	34
Kurt Drummond	70	10	51	61	78
Lawrence Nycholat	72	16	44	60	125
Jeremy Reich	67	21	28	49	220
Jeremy Rondeau	67	15	34	49	89
Tyler Murray	71	20	17	37	54
Chad Beagle	53	16	19	35	150
Brett Allan	72	16	18	34	74
Danis Zaripov	62	23	8	31	33
Quinn Sherdahl	62	13	17	30	58
Brent Twordik	67	13	12	25	34
Dan Hulak	68	6	14	20	71
Jay Langager	66	2	12	14	71
Nathan Smith	47	5	8	13	26
Dean Serdachny	72	1	9	10	193
Ben Ondrus	46	4	4	8	58
Scott Henkelman	19	3	5	8	17
Dustan Heintz	40	1	7	8	26
Jakub Cutta	59	3	3	6	63
Brad Rohrig	10	1	2	3	6
Chris Sotiropoulos	26	1	2	3	27
Mike Markell	10	2	0	2	0
Toni Bader	26	0	1	1	39
Josh Maser	44	0	1	1	115
Bryce Wandler (goalie)	51	0	1	1	4
Ryan Finnerty	1	0	0	0	0
James Hiebert	1	0	0	0	0
Matt Sommerfeld	1	0	0	0	0
Clay Thoring	1	0	0	0	0
Colton Orr	2	0	0	0	0
Jay Banach	3	0	0	0	4
Lindsey Materi (goalie)	3	0	0	0	0
Duncan Milroy	3	0	0	0	0
Steve Mongrain (goalie)	4	0	0	0	0
Jeff Froese	5	0	0	0	0
Andrew Milne	8	0	0	0	27
Tyson Motz (goalie)	21	0	0	0	12

GOALTENDING

	Games	Min.	W	L	T	G	SO	Avg.
Bryce Wandler	51	2882	23	20	4	123	3	2.56
Steven Mongrain	4	155	1	1	0	8	0	3.10
Tyson Motz	21	1136	8	10	2	64	1	3.38
Lindsey Materi	3	181	2	1	0	11	0	3.65

TRI-CITY AMERICANS

SCORING

	Games	G	A	Pts.	PIM
Dylan Gyori	69	53	65	118	112
Scott Gomez	58	30	78	108	55
Jaroslav Kristek	70	38	48	86	55
Ken McKay	64	37	45	82	46
Darrell Hay	72	13	49	62	87
Blake Evans	72	18	29	47	131
Josef Melichar	65	8	28	36	125
Jody Lapeyre	61	15	18	33	65
K.C. Timmons	69	13	11	24	113
Curtis Huppe	18	12	10	22	10
Jordan Landry	59	11	11	22	131
Eric Johannson	48	8	14	22	20
Brad Ference	20	6	15	21	116
Nathan Barrett	33	9	9	18	19
Jeff Katcher	60	4	14	18	136
Ryley Layden	51	8	8	16	34
Tim Green	45	7	9	16	27
Mike Lee	56	6	10	16	120
Jarrett Thompson	33	5	9	14	86
Mike Muzechka	70	2	9	11	137
Bobby Almeida	19	1	7	8	17
Regan Darby	38	2	4	6	152
Chris Anderson	10	2	3	5	6
David Boychuk	37	0	4	4	43
Toni Bader	23	0	3	3	47
Scott Henkelman	25	2	0	2	21
Andrew Guindon	14	1	1	2	23
Ryan Jorde	19	0	1	1	7
Blake Ward (goalie)	21	0	1	1	4
Aaron Baker (goalie)	31	0	1	1	4
David Darguzas	1	0	0	0	0
Ryan Thomas	1	0	0	0	2
Andrew DeSousa	2	0	0	0	2
Jay Ewasiuk (goalie)	5	0	0	0	2
Stephen Peat	5	0	0	0	19
Jeff Blair (goalie)	30	0	0	0	2

GOALTENDING

	Games	Min.	W	L	T	G	SO	Avg.
Blake Ward	21	844	5	5	2	34	0	2.42
Jeff Blair	30	1584	19	8	1	78	3	2.95
Aaron Baker	31	1649	17	10	1	88	2	3.20
Jay Ewasiuk	5	261	2	0	2	16	0	3.68

PLAYERS WITH TWO OR MORE TEAMS

SCORING

	Games	G	A	Pts.	PIM
Gerad Adams, Regina	42	16	20	36	136
Gerad Adams, Kelowna	15	6	10	16	28
Totals	57	22	30	52	164
Bobby Almeida, Tri-City	19	1	7	8	17
Bobby Almeida, Saskatoon	39	9	16	25	44
Totals	58	10	23	33	61
Chris Anderson, Tri-City	10	2	3	5	6
Chris Anderson, Regina	55	4	19	23	84
Totals	65	6	22	28	90
Toni Bader, Swift Current	26	0	1	1	39
Toni Bader, Tri-City	23	0	3	3	47
Totals	49	0	4	4	86
Aaron Baker, Tri-City (goalie)	31	0	1	1	4
Aaron Baker, Sask. (goalie)	15	0	1	1	10
Totals	46	0	2	2	14
Brian Ballman, Kootenay	18	0	2	2	36
Brian Ballman, Lethbridge	52	11	13	24	95
Totals	70	11	15	26	131
Nathan Barrett, Tri-City	33	9	9	18	19
Nathan Barrett, Lethbridge	22	12	9	21	19
Totals	55	21	18	39	38
Brett Bartell, Kamloops	2	0	0	0	0
Brett Bartell, Regina	4	0	0	0	0
Totals	6	0	0	0	0
Jeff Blair, Saskatoon (goalie)	28	0	0	0	9
Jeff Blair, Tri-City (goalie)	30	0	0	0	2
Totals	58	0	0	0	11
Ryan Bonni, Saskatoon	51	6	26	32	211
Ryan Bonni, Red Deer	20	3	10	13	41
Totals	71	9	36	45	252
Scott Botterill, Prince Albert	6	1	0	1	0
Scott Botterill, Portland	52	6	5	11	16
Totals	58	7	5	12	16
David Boychuk, Tri-City	37	0	4	4	43
David Boychuk, Spokane	22	0	3	3	41
Totals	59	0	7	7	84
Wade Burt, Kamloops	4	2	5	7	2
Wade Burt, Kootenay	58	14	21	35	59
Totals	62	16	26	42	61
Kyle Calder, Regina	34	23	28	51	29
Kyle Calder, Kamloops	27	19	18	37	30
Totals	61	42	46	88	59
David Cameron, Prince Albert	41	9	30	39	25
David Cameron, Saskatoon	24	6	14	20	12
Totals	65	15	44	59	37
Kyle Chant, Portland	3	0	0	0	0
Kyle Chant, Lethbridge	2	0	0	0	6
Totals	5	0	0	0	6
Jason Chimera, Medicine Hat	37	18	22	40	84
Jason Chimera, Brandon	21	14	12	26	32
Totals	58	32	34	66	116
Donald Choukalos, Calgary (g)	10	0	1	1	4
Donald Choukalos, Regina (g)	24	0	0	0	0
Totals	34	0	1	1	4
Matt Cockell, Regina (goalie)	33	0	0	0	15
Matt Cockell, Spokane (goalie)	10	0	0	0	0
Totals	43	0	0	0	15
Regan Darby, Tri-City	38	2	4	6	152
Regan Darby, Red Deer	19	1	6	7	90
Totals	57	3	10	13	242
Adam Dombrowski, Kamloops	22	1	1	2	43
Adam Dombrowski, Red Deer	24	1	6	7	23
Totals	46	2	7	9	66
Jan Dusanek, Kelowna	27	4	6	10	30
Jan Dusanek, Spokane	27	1	10	11	21
Totals	54	5	16	21	51
Jay Ewasiuk, M.J. (goalie)	5	0	0	0	2
Jay Ewasiuk, Tri-City (goalie)	5	0	0	0	2
Totals	10	0	0	0	4
Todd Fedoruk, Regina	39	12	12	24	107
Todd Fedoruk, Prince Albert	28	6	4	10	75
Totals	67	18	16	34	182
Brad Ference, Spokane	31	3	22	25	125
Brad Ference, Tri-City	20	6	15	21	116
Totals	51	9	37	46	241
Shaun Fleming, Spo. (goalie)	1	0	0	0	0
Shaun Fleming, Reg. (goalie)	2	0	0	0	2
Totals	3	0	0	0	2
Jordon Flodell, Moose Jaw	25	0	1	1	65
Jordon Flodell, Kamloops	27	3	3	6	88
Totals	52	3	4	7	153
Devin Francon, Red Deer	40	4	6	10	46
Devin Francon, Regina	16	3	3	6	21
Totals	56	7	9	16	67

	Games	G	A	Pts.	PIM
Ryan Geremia, Calgary	35	4	9	13	42
Ryan Geremia, Regina	27	4	4	8	6
Totals	62	8	13	21	48
Andrew Guindon, Lethbridge	33	1	3	4	52
Andrew Guindon, Tri-City	14	1	1	2	23
Totals	47	2	4	6	75
Justin Hansen, Moose Jaw	10	4	3	7	11
Justin Hansen, Prince George	32	13	7	20	29
Totals	42	17	10	27	40
David Haun, Spokane (goalie)	34	0	0	0	0
David Haun, Kamloops (goalie)	10	0	0	0	2
Totals	44	0	0	0	2
Scott Henkelman, Tri-City	25	2	0	2	21
Scott Henkelman, S. Current	19	3	5	8	17
Totals	44	5	5	10	38
Shaun Hill, Medicine Hat	25	0	0	0	86
Shaun Hill, Prince Albert	2	0	0	0	5
Totals	27	0	0	0	91
Trevor Hitchings, Prince Albert	5	0	1	1	6
Trevor Hitchings, Kelowna	38	1	13	14	16
Totals	43	1	14	15	22
Todd Hornung, Portland	45	15	15	30	86
Todd Hornung, Lethbridge	13	1	1	2	26
Totals	58	16	16	32	112
Curtis Huppe, Lethbridge	48	33	23	56	34
Curtis Huppe, Tri-City	18	12	10	22	10
Totals	66	45	33	78	44
Ryan Johnston, Saskatoon	10	2	2	4	21
Ryan Johnston, Brandon	27	7	14	21	73
Ryan Johnston, Kelowna	20	4	5	9	40
Totals	57	13	21	34	134
Ty Jones, Spokane	26	15	12	27	98
Ty Jones, Kamloops	20	3	16	19	84
Totals	46	18	28	46	182
Shon Jones-Parry, Portland	44	4	5	9	145
Shon Jones-Parry, P. George	24	0	5	5	114
Totals	68	4	10	14	259
Ryan Jorde, Tri-City	19	0	1	1	7
Ryan Jorde, Lethbridge	21	2	5	7	22
Totals	40	2	6	8	29
Andrew Kaminsky, Brandon	50	9	7	16	71
Andrew Kaminsky, Regina	19	4	5	9	14
Totals	69	13	12	25	85
Drew Kehler, Regina	18	0	4	4	53
Drew Kehler, Red Deer	56	1	10	11	163
Totals	74	1	14	15	216
Justin Kelly, Prince Albert	30	3	4	7	13
Justin Kelly, Saskatoon	20	3	5	8	6
Totals	50	6	9	15	19
Michael Kiesman, P. George	41	10	10	20	115
Michael Kiesman, Portland	26	3	3	6	65
Totals	67	13	13	26	180
Kris Knoblauch, Kootenay	21	7	3	10	36
Kris Knoblauch, Lethbridge	52	20	22	42	102
Totals	73	27	25	52	138
Kyle Kos, Red Deer	37	3	17	20	56
Kyle Kos, Kamloops	28	6	14	20	42
Totals	65	9	31	40	98
Kris Mallette, Kelowna	9	0	0	0	40
Kris Mallette, Moose Jaw	49	1	10	11	187
Totals	58	1	10	11	227
Alan Manness, Kamloops	40	8	17	25	34
Alan Manness, Regina	28	7	18	25	18
Totals	68	15	35	50	52
Josh Maser, Spokane	19	2	1	3	89
Josh Maser, Swift Current	44	0	1	1	115
Totals	63	2	2	4	204
Lindsey Materi, S. Current (g)	3	0	0	0	0
Lindsey Materi, Kelowna (g)	27	0	2	2	2
Totals	30	0	2	2	2
Brent McDonald, Red Deer	38	17	18	35	64
Brent McDonald, P. George	34	13	13	26	40
Totals	72	30	31	61	104

	Games	G	A	Pts.	PIM
Brett McLean, Kelowna	44	32	38	70	46
Brett McLean, Brandon	21	15	16	31	20
Totals	65	47	54	101	66
Scott D. McQueen, Red Deer	15	0	2	2	25
Scott D. McQueen, Saskatoon	3	0	1	1	4
Totals	18	0	3	3	29
Chris Ovington, Red Deer	49	1	10	11	73
Chris Ovington, Saskatoon	19	2	1	3	37
Totals	68	3	11	14	110
Stephen Peat, Red Deer	31	2	6	8	98
Stephen Peat, Tri-City	5	0	0	0	19
Totals	36	2	6	8	117
Andy Penny, Kootenay	10	2	4	6	5
Andy Penny, Lethbridge	10	1	0	1	0
Totals	20	3	4	7	5
Garrett Prosofsky, Saskatoon	25	8	7	15	21
Garrett Prosofsky, P. Albert	24	15	16	31	21
Totals	49	23	23	46	42
Owen Richey, Prince George	16	0	1	1	6
Owen Richey, Saskatoon	3	1	0	1	0
Totals	19	1	1	2	6
Brad Rohrig, Kelowna	9	2	2	4	14
Brad Rohrig, Swift Current	10	1	2	3	6
Brad Rohrig, Red Deer	33	4	4	8	47
Totals	52	7	8	15	67
Rob Sandrock, Medicine Hat	1	0	0	0	0
Rob Sandrock, Kelowna	37	4	11	15	62
Totals	38	4	11	15	62
Blair Simpson, Medicine Hat	43	1	7	8	70
Blair Simpson, Lethbridge	24	0	2	2	21
Totals	67	1	9	10	91
Brad Stuart, Regina	29	10	19	29	43
Brad Stuart, Calgary	30	11	22	33	26
Totals	59	21	41	62	69
Shaun Sutter, Lethbridge	35	8	4	12	43
Shaun Sutter, Medicine Hat	23	9	5	14	38
Totals	58	17	9	26	81
Kevin Swanson, P. George (g)	4	0	0	0	0
Kevin Swanson, Kelowna (g)	50	0	0	0	0
Totals	54	0	0	0	0
Luc Theoret, Lethbridge	46	13	39	52	92
Luc Theoret, Portland	3	0	0	0	10
Totals	49	13	39	52	102
Ryan Thomas, Tri-City	1	0	0	0	2
Ryan Thomas, Regina	60	11	6	17	115
Totals	61	11	6	17	117
Jarrett Thompson, Tri-City	33	5	9	14	86
Jarrett Thompson, Red Deer	28	3	7	10	47
Totals	61	8	16	24	133
Shawn Thompson, Kamloops	4	0	0	0	0
Shawn Thompson, Spokane	41	2	1	3	29
Totals	45	2	1	3	29
Ryan Thorpe, Kamloops	22	2	1	3	68
Ryan Thorpe, Spokane	19	10	3	13	21
Totals	41	12	4	16	89
Chris Twerdun, Spokane	8	1	1	2	17
Chris Twerdun, Moose Jaw	55	4	15	19	67
Totals	63	5	16	21	84
Igor Valeev, Lethbridge	8	2	3	5	13
Igor Valeev, Saskatoon	23	2	2	4	36
Totals	31	4	5	9	49
Jordan Walker, Prince George	37	7	20	27	20
Jordan Walker, Red Deer	33	9	17	26	12
Totals	70	16	37	53	32
Trevor Wasyluk, Lethbridge	17	3	8	11	30
Trevor Wasyluk, Kootenay	43	17	26	43	76
Totals	60	20	34	54	106
Jordan Watt, Kelowna (goalie)	6	0	0	0	0
Jordan Watt, Red Deer (goalie)	27	0	0	0	6
Totals	33	0	0	0	6
Steve Wilejto, Prince Albert	27	0	3	3	17
Steve Wilejto, Medicine Hat	33	2	6	8	18
Totals	60	2	9	11	35

	Games	G	A	Pts.	PIM
Travis Willie, Medicine Hat	8	0	0	0	11
Travis Willie, Prince Albert	1	0	0	0	0
Totals	9	0	0	0	11
Justin Yeoman, Brandon	32	1	1	2	27
Justin Yeoman, Medicine Hat	22	3	1	4	12
Totals	54	4	2	6	39

GOALTENDING

	Games	Min.	W	L	T	G	SO	Avg.
Aaron Baker, T.-C.	31	1649	17	10	1	88	2	3.20
Aaron Baker, Sask.	15	708	1	9	2	57	0	4.83
Totals	46	2357	18	19	3	145	2	3.69
Jeff Blair, Sask.	28	1528	7	17	2	94	0	3.69
Jeff Blair, Tri-City	30	1584	19	8	1	78	3	2.95
Totals	58	3112	26	25	3	172	3	3.32
D. Choukalos, Cal.	10	571	8	1	0	20	1	2.10
D. Choukalos, Reg.	24	1337	6	12	4	98	0	4.40
Totals	34	1908	14	13	4	118	1	3.71
Matt Cockell, Reg.	33	1890	14	17	1	129	0	4.10
Matt Cockell, Spo.	10	338	0	2	2	17	0	3.02
Totals	43	2228	14	19	3	146	0	3.93
Jay Ewasiuk, M.J.	5	297	1	4	0	25	0	5.05
Jay Ewasiuk, T.-C.	5	261	2	0	2	16	0	3.68
Totals	10	558	3	4	2	41	0	4.41
S. Fleming, Spo.	1	24	0	0	0	2	0	5.00
S. Fleming, Reg.	2	79	1	0	0	3	1	2.28
Totals	3	103	1	0	0	5	1	2.91
David Haun, Spo.	34	1893	7	21	4	113	1	3.58
David Haun, Kam.	10	574	8	0	2	31	0	3.24
Totals	44	2467	15	21	6	144	1	3.50
L. Materi, S.C.	3	181	2	1	0	11	0	3.65
L. Materi, Kel.	27	1150	4	12	1	80	0	4.17
Totals	30	1331	6	13	1	91	0	4.10
K. Swanson, P.G.	4	180	1	2	0	10	0	3.33
K. Swanson, Kel.	50	2507	18	23	3	144	2	3.45
Totals	54	2687	19	25	3	154	2	3.44

1999 PLAYOFFS

RESULTS

FIRST ROUND

	W	L	Pts.	GF	GA
Calgary	4	3	8	33	27
Kootenay	3	4	6	27	33

(Calgary won series, 4-3)

	W	L	Pts.	GF	GA
Prince Albert	4	0	8	24	7
Lethbridge	0	4	0	7	24

(Prince Albert won series, 4-0)

	W	L	Pts.	GF	GA
Red Deer	4	1	8	29	15
Brandon	1	4	2	15	29

(Red Deer won series, 4-1)

	W	L	Pts.	GF	GA
Moose Jaw	4	2	8	18	15
Swift Current	2	4	4	15	18

(Moose Jaw won series, 4-2)

	W	L	Pts.	GF	GA
Kamloops	4	2	8	15	11
Kelowna	2	4	4	11	15

(Kamloops won series, 4-2)

	W	L	Pts.	GF	GA
Tri-City	4	0	8	19	9
Portland	0	4	0	9	19

(Tri-City won series, 4-0)

	W	L	Pts.	GF	GA
Seattle	4	3	8	23	17
Prince George	3	4	6	17	23

(Seattle won series, 4-3)

SECOND ROUND

	W	L	Pts.	GF	GA
Calgary	4	0	8	17	9
Red Deer	0	4	0	9	17

(Calgary won series, 4-0)

	W	L	Pts.	GF	GA
Prince Albert	4	1	8	27	10
Moose Jaw	1	4	2	10	27

(Prince Albert won series, 4-1)

	W	L	Pts.	GF	GA
Tri-City	3	1	6	17	6
Seattle	1	3	2	6	17

(Tri-City won series, 3-1)

THIRD ROUND

	W	L	Pts.	GF	GA
Calgary	4	1	8	30	16
Prince Albert	1	4	2	16	30

(Calgary won series, 4-1)

	W	L	Pts.	GF	GA
Kamloops	4	0	8	17	8
Tri-City	0	4	0	8	17

(Kamloops won series, 4-0)

WHL FINALS

	W	L	Pts.	GF	GA
Calgary	4	1	8	19	11
Kamloops	1	4	2	11	19

(Calgary won series, 4-1)

INDIVIDUAL LEADERS

Goals: Pavel Brendl, Calgary (21)
Assists: Pavel Brendl, Calgary (25)
Brad Moran, Calgary (25)
Points: Pavel Brendl, Calgary (46)
Penalty minutes: Brent Dodginghorse, Calgary (72)
Goaltending average: Kenric Exner, Kamloops (2.21)
Shutouts: Jeff Blair, Tri-City (2)
Kenric Exner, Kamloops (2)

TOP SCORERS

	Games	G	A	Pts.
Pavel Brendl, Calgary	20	21	25	46
Brad Moran, Calgary	21	17	25	42
Matt Kinch, Calgary	21	7	23	30
Brent Dodginghorse, Calgary	21	10	15	25
Brad Stuart, Calgary	21	8	15	23
Derek Paget, Prince Albert	12	8	12	20
Cody Jensen, Prince Albert	14	8	12	20
Milan Kraft, Prince Albert	14	7	13	20
Scott Gomez, Tri-City	10	6	13	19
Marc Brown, Prince Albert	14	12	6	18
Dylan Gyori, Tri-City	12	7	11	18

BRANDON WHEAT KINGS

(Lost first round to Red Deer, 4-1)

SCORING

	Games	G	A	Pts.	PIM
Burke Henry	5	1	6	7	9
Brett McLean	5	1	6	7	8
Ryan Robson	5	4	1	5	2
Jason Chimera	5	4	1	5	8
Brad Twordik	5	2	1	3	9
Jan Fadrny	5	1	2	3	4
Andrei Lupandin	5	1	1	2	6
Brett Girard	5	1	0	1	6
Scott McCallum	5	0	1	1	13
Aaron Goldade	5	0	1	1	8
Les Borsheim	5	0	1	1	19
Wade Skolney	5	0	1	1	16
Mike Wirll	5	0	1	1	2
Jomar Cruz (goalie)	1	0	0	0	0
Alex Argyriou	2	0	0	0	0
Richard Mueller	2	0	0	0	0
Brett Thurston	3	0	0	0	0
Dan Tetrault	4	0	0	0	9
Cory Unser	4	0	0	0	2
Ryan Craig	5	0	0	0	4
Jamie Hodson (goalie)	5	0	0	0	0
Randy Ponte	5	0	0	0	14

GOALTENDING

	Games	Min.	W	L	T	G	SO	Avg.
Jomar Cruz	1	23	0	0	0	2	0	5.22
Jamie Hodson	5	275	1	4	0	26	0	5.67

CALGARY HITMEN

(Winner of 1999 WHL playoffs)

SCORING

	Games	G	A	Pts.	PIM
Pavel Brendl	20	21	25	46	18
Brad Moran	21	17	25	42	26
Matt Kinch	21	7	23	30	8
Brent Dodginghorse	21	10	15	25	72
Brad Stuart	21	8	15	23	59
Chris Nielsen	21	11	5	16	28
Kenton Smith	21	1	14	15	34
Jordan Krestanovich	20	3	8	11	4
Jerred Smithson	21	3	7	10	17
Peter Bergman	21	3	5	8	25
Lyle Steenbergen	15	4	3	7	17
Curtis Rich	18	4	1	5	31
Kris Beech	6	1	4	5	8
Sean McAslan	21	2	1	3	18
Eric Clark	20	1	2	3	0
Ryan Andres	21	1	2	3	52
Rod Sarich	21	1	2	3	8
Ryan Shannon	20	1	1	2	35
Jeff Feniak	17	0	1	1	16
Alexandre Fomitchev (goalie)	21	0	1	1	0
Wade Davis	2	0	0	0	0
Brent Williams (goalie)	2	0	0	0	0
Michael Bubnick	4	0	0	0	0
Shaun Norrie	5	0	0	0	0

GOALTENDING

	Games	Min.	W	L	T	G	SO	Avg.
Brent Williams	2	28	0	0	0	1	0	2.14
Alex Fomitchev	21	1299	16	5	0	61	1	2.82

KAMLOOPS BLAZERS

(Lost WHL finals to Calgary, 4-1)

SCORING

	Games	G	A	Pts.	PIM
Kyle Calder	15	6	10	16	6
Ajay Baines	15	7	6	13	20
Donnie Kinney	15	4	7	11	6
Mike Brown	15	3	7	10	68
Micki DuPont	15	2	8	10	22
Steve Gainey	15	5	4	9	38
Konstantin Panov	13	5	3	8	10
Ty Jones	14	5	3	8	22
Steve Shrum	15	1	5	6	4
Robyn Regehr	12	1	4	5	21
Jared Aulin	13	1	3	4	2
Kevin Mackle	15	1	3	4	25
Chris St. Croix	14	0	4	4	16
Brett Draney	15	1	1	2	8
Paul Deniset	13	1	0	1	6
Kenric Exner (goalie)	11	0	1	1	0
Anton Borodkin	12	0	1	1	8
Gable Gross	1	0	0	0	0
David Haun (goalie)	6	0	0	0	0
Jonathan Hobson	9	0	0	0	2
Kyle Kos	9	0	0	0	8
Jordon Flodell	11	0	0	0	8
Chad Starling	14	0	0	0	8

GOALTENDING

	Games	Min.	W	L	T	G	SO	Avg.
Kenric Exner	11	598	7	4	0	22	2	2.21
David Haun	6	356	2	2	0	14	0	2.36

KELOWNA ROCKETS

(Lost first round to Kamloops, 4-2)

SCORING

	Games	G	A	Pts.	PIM
Quintin Laing	6	3	0	3	0
Scott Hannan	6	1	2	3	14
J.J. Hunter	6	1	2	3	2
Ryan Johnston	6	0	3	3	4
Vernon Fiddler	6	2	0	2	8
Gerad Adams	6	1	1	2	6
Ryan Wade	6	1	1	2	10
Kevin Korol	6	1	1	2	6
Rory McDade	6	0	2	2	4
Gavin McLeod	6	1	0	1	6
Bruce Harrison	5	0	1	1	4
Kiel McLeod	6	0	1	1	2
David Selthun	1	0	0	0	0
Mitch Fritz	2	0	0	0	0
Ryan Cuthbert	5	0	0	0	0
Carsen Germyn	5	0	0	0	2
Nolan Yonkman	6	0	0	0	6
Trevor Hitchings	6	0	0	0	2
Kevin Swanson (goalie)	6	0	0	0	0
Joe Suderman	6	0	0	0	8
Lubomir Pistek	6	0	0	0	6

GOALTENDING

	Games	Min.	W	L	T	G	SO	Avg.
Kevin Swanson	6	355	2	4	0	14	0	2.37

KOOTENAY ICE

(Lost first round to Calgary, 4-3)

SCORING

	Games	G	A	Pts.	PIM
Stanislav Gron	7	3	8	11	12
Tyler Beechey	5	4	3	7	2
Scott Roles	7	4	3	7	8
Trevor Wasyluk	7	5	1	6	16
Wade Burt	7	2	4	6	12
Steve McCarthy	6	0	5	5	8
Mike Green	7	2	2	4	4
Jaroslav Svoboda	7	2	2	4	11
Brad Tutschek	6	1	3	4	22
Kyle Wanvig	7	1	3	4	18

	Games	G	A	Pts.	PIM
Jason Jaffray	7	1	2	3	6
Dion Lassu	7	1	1	2	18
Jesse Ferguson	7	1	1	2	16
Clayton Pool (goalie)	7	0	1	1	2
Rod Leroux	1	0	0	0	2
Brian Dafoe (goalie)	1	0	0	0	0
Dean Arsene	4	0	0	0	4
Mark Thompson	4	0	0	0	2
Jarret Stoll	4	0	0	0	2
Trevor Johnson	6	0	0	0	2
Nick Marach	6	0	0	0	2
Graham Belak	7	0	0	0	38
Colin Sinclair	7	0	0	0	2

GOALTENDING

	Games	Min.	W	L	T	G	SO	Avg.
Brian Dafoe	1	4	0	0	0	0	0	0.00
Clayton Pool	7	419	3	4	0	32	0	4.58

LETHBRIDGE HURRICANES

(Lost first round to Prince Albert, 4-0)

SCORING

	Games	G	A	Pts.	PIM
Dave Taylor	4	1	3	4	2
Kris Knoblauch	4	1	3	4	6
Brandon Janes	4	0	2	2	4
Jason Hegberg	4	1	0	1	8
Chad Kletzel	4	1	0	1	4
Bart Rushmer	4	1	0	1	13
Nathan Barrett	4	1	0	1	0
Dennis Kozyrev	3	0	1	1	0
Sean Robertson	4	0	1	1	11
Brian Ballman	4	0	1	1	2
Derrick Ruck	4	0	1	1	2
Jason McLean (goalie)	2	0	0	0	0
Dustin Kazak	2	0	0	0	0
Brent Hope	3	0	0	0	4
Derek Atkinson	4	0	0	0	9
Brady Block (goalie)	4	0	0	0	0
Scott Borders	4	0	0	0	4
Phil Cole	4	0	0	0	0
Ryan Jorde	4	0	0	0	0
Blair Simpson	4	0	0	0	4
Eric Godard	4	0	0	0	14

GOALTENDING

	Games	Min.	W	L	T	G	SO	Avg.
Brady Block	4	163	0	3	0	13	0	4.79
Jason McLean	2	75	0	1	0	12	0	9.60

MOOSE JAW WARRIORS

(Lost second round to Prince Albert, 4-1)

SCORING

	Games	G	A	Pts.	PIM
Chad Hinz	11	4	12	16	12
Jamie Lundmark	11	5	4	9	24
Scott Schoneck	11	4	4	8	10
Dustin Paul	11	2	6	8	26
Garnet Jacobson	11	5	1	6	19
Brent Hobday	11	3	3	6	21
Shawn Skolney	11	2	3	5	21
Jason Weitzel	10	1	4	5	6
Shawn Limpright	10	1	3	4	16
Steven Crampton	9	1	1	2	4
Dustin Bru	9	0	1	1	2
Chris Twerdun	11	0	1	1	4
Brian Sutherby	11	0	1	1	0
Dayle Wilcox	11	0	1	1	2
Nathan Paetsch	1	0	0	0	0
Tim Barlow (goalie)	2	0	0	0	0
Alex Andreyev	5	0	0	0	4
Regan Rome	5	0	0	0	0
Bobby Chad Mitchell	8	0	0	0	17
Kris Mallette	9	0	0	0	39
Rastislav Stana (goalie)	9	0	0	0	0
Dreu Volk	11	0	0	0	4
Craig Strain	11	0	0	0	12

GOALTENDING

	Games	Min.	W	L	T	G	SO	Avg.
Rastislav Stana	9	544	4	5	0	30	0	3.31
Tim Barlow	2	120	1	1	0	11	0	5.50

PORTLAND WINTER HAWKS

(Lost first round to Tri-City, 4-0)

SCORING

	Games	G	A	Pts.	PIM
Todd Robinson	4	3	3	6	8
Andrew Ference	4	1	4	5	10
Brenden Morrow	4	0	4	4	18
Dean Beuker	4	3	0	3	0
Kevin Haupt	4	1	1	2	2
Marty Standish	4	1	1	2	21
Ken Davis	4	0	1	1	11
Matt Walker	4	0	1	1	6
Luke Molotowsky	2	0	0	0	0
Marcel Hossa	2	0	0	0	0
Scott Botterill	4	0	0	0	0
Michael Kiesman	4	0	0	0	2
Jason LaBarbera (goalie)	4	0	0	0	0
Christian Bolding	4	0	0	0	4
James DeMone	4	0	0	0	4
Steve Fetter	4	0	0	0	0
Ryan Kehrig	4	0	0	0	0
Ryan Thrussell	4	0	0	0	6
Blake Robson	4	0	0	0	4
Jan Koznar	4	0	0	0	0

GOALTENDING

	Games	Min.	W	L	T	G	SO	Avg.
Jason LaBarbera	4	252	0	4	0	19	0	4.52

PRINCE ALBERT RAIDERS

(Lost third round to Calgary, 4-1)

SCORING

	Games	G	A	Pts.	PIM
Derek Paget	12	8	12	20	13
Cody Jensen	14	8	12	20	10
Milan Kraft	14	7	13	20	6
Marc Brown	14	12	6	18	6
Garrett Prosofsky	14	7	8	15	20
Ross Lupaschuk	14	4	9	13	16
Cory Morgan	14	6	6	12	19
Richard Seeley	14	1	11	12	14
Kevin Kellett	14	4	6	10	26
Dallas Flaman	14	5	4	9	2
Todd Fedoruk	13	1	6	7	49
Nick Schultz	14	0	7	7	0
Craig Brunel	14	4	2	6	48
Scott Hartnell	14	0	5	5	22
Jeremy Goetzinger	14	0	3	3	4
Blaine Stowards	14	1	1	2	14
Clayton Chartrand	14	0	2	2	9
Grant McCune (goalie)	3	0	0	0	0
Derek Brandon	8	0	0	0	18
Riley Cote	9	0	0	0	9
Evan Lindsay (goalie)	14	0	0	0	4

GOALTENDING

	Games	Min.	W	L	T	G	SO	Avg.
Grant McCune	3	71	0	0	0	3	0	2.54
Evan Lindsay	14	780	9	5	0	43	1	3.31

PRINCE GEORGE COUGARS

(Lost first round to Seattle, 4-3)

SCORING

	Games	G	A	Pts.	PIM
Mike Bayrack	7	7	1	8	17
Trent Hunter	7	2	5	7	2

	Games	G	A	Pts.	PIM
Blair Betts	7	3	2	5	8
Curtis Tipler	7	0	4	4	12
Dan Hamhuis	7	1	2	3	8
Jozef Mrena	7	1	2	3	4
Ian Walterson	7	0	3	3	19
Brent McDonald	7	1	1	2	18
Tyler Bouck	2	0	2	2	10
Jarrett Smith	3	0	2	2	2
Petr Kubos	7	0	2	2	0
Garry Toor	2	1	0	1	2
Justin Cox	7	1	0	1	13
Tyler Brough	5	0	1	1	4
Justin Hansen	4	0	0	0	0
Travis Eagles	5	0	0	0	8
Willy Glover	5	0	0	0	0
Jonathan Parker	5	0	0	0	0
Scott Myers (goalie)	7	0	0	0	2
Shon Jones-Parry	7	0	0	0	50
Ryan Chieduch	7	0	0	0	7
Tim Wedderburn	7	0	0	0	0

GOALTENDING

	Games	Min.	W	L	T	G	SO	Avg.
Scott Myers	7	418	3	4	0	23	0	3.30

RED DEER REBELS

(Lost second round to Calgary, 4-0)

SCORING

	Games	G	A	Pts.	PIM
Shawn McNeil	9	8	7	15	6
Lukas Bednarik	9	6	9	15	0
Brad Leeb	9	5	9	14	10
Kevin Marsh	9	5	7	12	2
Frantisek Mrazek	9	6	4	10	16
Jordan Walker	9	1	5	6	2
Justin Mapletoft	9	2	3	5	12
Drew Kehler	8	0	4	4	18
Ryan Bonni	9	0	4	4	25
Jarrett Thompson	7	2	1	3	21
Andrew Bergen	9	1	2	3	10
Brad Rohrig	9	1	1	2	4
Justin Wallin	9	1	1	2	5
Regan Darby	9	0	1	1	18
Jim Vandermeer	9	0	1	1	24
Jay Batchelor	1	0	0	0	0
Jay Vidrine	5	0	0	0	0
Kent Beagle	6	0	0	0	9
Dustin Schwartz (goalie)	9	0	0	0	0
Scott C. McQueen	9	0	0	0	9
Adam Dombrowski	9	0	0	0	4

GOALTENDING

	Games	Min.	W	L	T	G	SO	Avg.
Dustin Schwartz	9	542	4	4	0	30	0	3.32

SEATTLE THUNDERBIRDS

(Lost second round to Tri-City, 3-1)

SCORING

	Games	G	A	Pts.	PIM
Oleg Saprykin	11	5	11	16	36
Mike Siklenka	11	6	6	12	24
Torrey DiRoberto	11	4	4	8	14
Scott Kelman	11	4	3	7	37
Jame Pollock	11	3	4	7	8
Ben Clymer	11	1	5	6	12
Bret DeCecco	11	1	4	5	21
Zdenek Blatny	11	4	0	4	24
David Morisset	11	1	1	2	22
Nathan Forster	10	0	2	2	26
Jason Beckett	11	0	1	1	40
Jeffrey Beatch	11	0	1	1	10
Shane Endicott	11	0	1	1	0
Tim Preston	11	0	1	1	11
Brennan Evans	1	0	0	0	0
Thomas Vicars (goalie)	1	0	0	0	0
David Ullmann	3	0	0	0	2
Garret Stroshein	4	0	0	0	7
Justin Ossachuk	6	0	0	0	20
David Kaczowka	9	0	0	0	24
Cody Rudkowsky (goalie)	11	0	0	0	2
Paul Hurd	11	0	0	0	13
Craig Olynick	11	0	0	0	14

GOALTENDING

	Games	Min.	W	L	T	G	SO	Avg.
Cody Rudkowsky	11	637	5	6	0	31	1	2.92
Thomas Vicars	1	20	0	0	0	1	0	3.00

SWIFT CURRENT BRONCOS

(Lost first round to Moose Jaw, 4-2)

SCORING

	Games	G	A	Pts.	PIM
Lawrence Nycholat	6	2	2	4	12
Tyler Murray	6	2	1	3	4
Kurt Drummond	6	2	1	3	4
Jeremy Rondeau	6	2	1	3	15
Quinn Sherdahl	6	2	1	3	2
Layne Ulmer	6	2	1	3	4
Jay Langager	6	2	1	3	8
Chad Beagle	6	1	2	3	16
Jeremy Reich	6	0	3	3	26
Brett Allan	6	0	2	2	0
Brent Twordik	6	0	2	2	6
Ben Ondrus	6	0	1	1	8
Dean Serdachny	6	0	1	1	8
Danis Zaripov	6	0	1	1	6
Bryce Wandler (goalie)	6	0	0	0	0
Chris Sotiropoulos	6	0	0	0	0
Scott Henkelman	6	0	0	0	4
Dan Hulak	6	0	0	0	4
Josh Maser	6	0	0	0	2

GOALTENDING

	Games	Min.	W	L	T	G	SO	Avg.
Bryce Wandler	6	364	2	4	0	17	1	2.80

TRI-CITY AMERICANS

(Lost third round to Kamloops, 4-0)

SCORING

	Games	G	A	Pts.	PIM
Scott Gomez	10	6	13	19	31
Dylan Gyori	12	7	11	18	25
Ken McKay	12	8	8	16	8
Darrell Hay	12	2	10	12	22
Brad Ference	12	1	9	10	63
Jaroslav Kristek	12	4	3	7	2
Curtis Huppe	12	4	2	6	12
Blake Evans	12	0	4	4	16
Jody Lapeyre	12	3	0	3	13
Mike Lee	12	1	2	3	19
Jeff Katcher	8	2	0	2	20
Ryley Layden	12	2	0	2	6
Eric Johannson	6	1	1	2	2
Jordan Landry	12	1	1	2	31
K.C. Timmons	12	1	1	2	36
Mike Muzechka	12	0	2	2	33
Josef Melichar	11	1	0	1	15
Tim Green	5	0	1	1	2
Jeff Blair (goalie)	12	0	1	1	0
Blake Ward (goalie)	1	0	0	0	0
Andrew Guindon	7	0	0	0	0
Toni Bader	12	0	0	0	8

GOALTENDING

	Games	Min.	W	L	T	G	SO	Avg.
Jeff Blair	12	721	7	5	0	31	2	2.58
Blake Ward	1	20	0	0	0	1	0	3.00

1998-99 AWARD WINNERS

ALL-STAR TEAMS

EASTERN CONFERENCE

First team	Pos.	Second team
Alexandre Fomitchev, Cal.	G	Evan Lindsay, Prince Albert
Brad Stuart, Calgary	D	Burke Henry, Brandon
Matt Kinch, Calgary	D	Kurt Drummond, S. Current
Pavel Brendl, Calgary	F	Brett Lysak, Regina
Brad Moran, Calgary	F	Jamie Lundmark, Moose Jaw
Chad Hinz, Moose Jaw	F	Brad Leeb, Red Deer

WESTERN CONFERENCE

First team	Pos.	Second team
Cody Rudkowsky, Seattle	G	Kenric Exner, Kamloops
Robyn Regehr, Kamloops	D	Andrew Ference, Portland
Scott Hannan, Kelowna	D	Garry Toor, Prince George
Scott Gomez, Tri-City	F	Bret DeCecco, Seattle
Dylan Gyori, Tri-City	F	Ajay Baines, Kamloops
Brenden Morrow, Portland	F	Oleg Saprykin, Seattle

TROPHY WINNERS

Four Broncos Memorial Trophy: Cody Rudkowsky, Seattle
Bob Clarke Trophy: Pavel Brendl, Calgary
Jim Piggott Memorial Trophy: Pavel Brendl, Calgary
Brad Hornung Trophy: Matt Kinch, Calgary
Bill Hunter Trophy: Brad Stuart, Calgary
Del Wilson Trophy: Cody Rudkowsky, Seattle
Dunc McCallum Memorial Trophy: Don Hay, Tri-City
Scott Munro Memorial Trophy: Calgary Hitmen
President's Cup: Calgary Hitmen
Playoff MVP: Brad Moran, Calgary

ALL-TIME AWARD WINNERS

FOUR BRONCOS MEMORIAL TROPHY

(Player of the year—selected by coaches)

Season Player, Team
1966-67—Gerry Pinder, Saskatoon
1967-68—Jim Harrison, Estevan
1968-69—Bobby Clarke, Flin Flon
1969-70—Reggie Leach, Flin Flon
1970-71—Ed Dyck, Calgary
1971-72—John Davidson, Calgary
1972-73—Dennis Sobchuk, Regina
1973-74—Ron Chipperfield, Brandon
1974-75—Bryan Trottier, Lethbridge
1975-76—Bernie Federko, Saskatoon
1976-77—Barry Beck, New Westminster
1977-78—Ryan Walter, Seattle
1978-79—Perry Turnbull, Portland
1979-80—Doug Wickenheiser, Regina
1980-81—Steve Tsujiura, Medicine Hat
1981-82—Mike Vernon, Calgary
1982-83—Mike Vernon, Calgary
1983-84—Ray Ferraro, Brandon
1984-85—Cliff Ronning, New Westminster
1985-86—Emanuel Viveiros, Prince Albert (East Div.)
Rob Brown, Kamloops (West Div.)
1986-87—Joe Sakic, Swift Current (East Div.)
Rob Brown, Kamloops (West Div.)
1987-88—Joe Sakic, Swift Current
1988-89—Stu Barnes, Tri-City
1989-90—Glen Goodall, Seattle
1990-91—Ray Whitney, Spokane
1991-92—Steve Konowalchuk, Portland
1992-93—Jason Krywulak, Swift Current
1993-94—Sonny Mignacca, Medicine Hat
1994-95—Marty Murray, Brandon
1995-96—Jarome Iginla, Kamloops
1996-97—Peter Schaefer, Brandon
1997-98—Sergei Varlamov, Swift Current
1998-99—Cody Rudkowsky, Seattle

The trophy was awarded to the most valuable player prior to the 1994-95 season.

BOB CLARKE TROPHY

(Top scorer)

Season Player, Team
1966-67—Gerry Pinder, Saskatoon
1967-68—Bobby Clarke, Flin Flon
1968-69—Bobby Clarke, Flin Flon
1969-70—Reggie Leach, Flin Flon
1970-71—Chuck Arnason, Flin Flon
1971-72—Tom Lysiak, Medicine Hat
1972-73—Tom Lysiak, Medicine Hat
1973-74—Ron Chipperfield, Brandon
1974-75—Mel Bridgman, Victoria
1975-76—Bernie Federko, Saskatoon
1976-77—Bill Derlago, Brandon
1977-78—Brian Propp, Brandon
1978-79—Brian Propp, Brandon
1979-80—Doug Wickenheiser, Regina
1980-81—Brian Varga, Regina
1981-82—Jack Callander, Regina
1982-83—Dale Derkatch, Regina
1983-84—Ray Ferraro, Brandon
1984-85—Cliff Ronning, New Westminster
1985-86—Rob Brown, Kamloops
1986-87—Rob Brown, Kamloops
1987-88—Joe Sakic, Swift Current
Theo Fleury, Moose Jaw
1988-89—Dennis Holland, Portland
1989-90—Len Barrie, Kamloops
1990-91—Ray Whitney, Spokane
1991-92—Kevin St. Jacques, Lethbridge
1992-93—Jason Krywulak, Swift Current
1993-94—Lonny Bohonos, Portland
1994-95—Daymond Langkow, Tri-City
1995-96—Mark Deyell, Saskatoon
1996-97—Todd Robinson, Portland
1997-98—Sergei Varlamov, Swift Current
1998-99—Pavel Brendl, Calgary

The award was originally known as the Bob Brownridge Memorial Trophy.

JIM PIGGOTT MEMORIAL TROPHY

(Rookie of the year)

Season Player, Team
1966-67—Ron Garwasiuk, Regina
1967-68—Ron Fairbrother, Saskatoon
1968-69—Ron Williams, Edmonton
1969-70—Gene Carr, Flin Flon
1970-71—Stan Weir, Medicine Hat
1971-72—Dennis Sobchuk, Regina
1972-73—Rick Blight, Brandon
1973-74—Cam Connor, Flin Flon
1974-75—Don Murdoch, Medicine Hat

Season Player, Team

1975-76—Steve Tambellini, Lethbridge
1976-77—Brian Propp, Brandon
1977-78—John Orgrodnick, New Westminster
Keith Brown, Portland
1978-79—Kelly Kisio, Calgary
1979-80—Grant Fuhr, Victoria
1980-81—Dave Michayluk, Regina
1981-82—Dale Derkatch, Regina
1982-83—Dan Hodgson, Prince Albert
1983-84—Cliff Ronning, New Westminster
1984-85—Mark Mackay, Moose Jaw
1985-86—Neil Brady, Medicine Hat (East Div.)
Ron Shudra, Kamloops, (West Div.)
Dave Waldie, Portland (West Div.)
1986-87—Joe Sakic, Swift Current (East Div.)
Dennis Holland, Portland (West Div.)
1987-88—Stu Barnes, New Westminster
1988-89—Wes Walz, Lethbridge
1989-90—Petr Nedved, Seattle
1990-91—Donevan Hextall, Prince Albert
1991-92—Ashley Buckberger, Swift Current
1992-93—Jeff Friesen, Regina
1993-94—Wade Redden, Brandon
1994-95—Todd Robinson, Portland
1995-96—Chris Phillips, Prince Albert
1996-97—Donovan Nunweiler, Moose Jaw
1997-98—Marian Hossa, Portland
1998-99—Pavel Brendl, Calgary

The award was originally known as the Stewart "Butch" Paul Memorial Trophy.

BRAD HORNUNG TROPHY

(Most sportsmanlike player)

Season Player, Team

1966-67—Morris Stefaniw, Estevan
1967-68—Bernie Blanchette, Saskatoon
1968-69—Bob Liddington, Calgary
1969-70—Randy Rota, Calgary
1970-71—Lorne Henning, Estevan
1971-72—Ron Chipperfield, Brandon
1972-73—Ron Chipperfield, Brandon
1973-74—Mike Rogers, Calgary
1974-75—Danny Arndt, Saskatoon
1975-76—Blair Chapman, Saskatoon
1976-77—Steve Tambellini, Lethbridge
1977-78—Steve Tambellini, Lethbridge
1978-79—Errol Rausse, Seattle
1979-80—Steve Tsujiura, Medicine Hat
1980-81—Steve Tsujiura, Medicine Hat
1981-82—Mike Moller, Lethbridge
1982-83—Darren Boyko, Winnipeg
1983-84—Mark Lamb, Medicine Hat
1984-85—Cliff Ronning, New Westminster
1985-86—Randy Smith, Saskatoon (East Division)
Ken Morrison, Kamloops (West Division)
1986-87—Len Nielsen, Regina (East Division)
Dave Archibald, Portland (West Division)
1987-88—Craig Endean, Regina
1988-89—Blair Atcheynum, Moose Jaw
1989-90—Bryan Bosch, Lethbridge
1990-91—Pat Falloon, Spokane
1991-92—Steve Junker, Spokane
1992-93—Rick Girard, Swift Current
1993-94—Lonny Bohonos, Portland
1994-95—Darren Ritchie, Brandon
1995-96—Hnat Domenichelli, Kamloops
1996-97—Kelly Smart, Brandon
1997-98—Cory Cyrenne, Brandon
1998-99—Matt Kinch, Calgary

The award was originally known as the Frank Boucher Memorial Trophy for most gentlemanly player.

BILL HUNTER TROPHY

(Top defenseman)

Season Player, Team

1966-67—Barry Gibbs, Estevan
1967-68—Gerry Hart, Flin Flon
1968-69—Dale Hoganson, Estevan
1969-70—Jim Hargreaves, Winnipeg
1970-71—Ron Jones, Edmonton
1971-72—Jim Watson, Calgary
1972-73—George Pesut, Saskatoon
1973-74—Pat Price, Saskatoon
1974-75—Rick LaPointe, Victoria
1975-76—Kevin McCarthy, Winnipeg
1976-77—Barry Beck, New Westminster
1977-78—Brad McCrimmon, Brandon
1978-79—Keith Brown, Portland
1979-80—David Babych, Portland
1980-81—Jim Benning, Portland
1981-82—Gary Nylund, Portland
1982-83—Gary Leeman, Regina
1983-84—Bob Rouse, Lethbridge
1984-85—Wendel Clark, Saskatoon
1985-86—Emanuel Viveiros, Prince Albert (East Division)
Glen Wesley, Portland (West Division)
1986-87—Wayne McBean, Medicine Hat (East Division)
Glen Wesley, Portland (West Division)
1987-88—Greg Hawgood, Kamloops
1988-89—Dan Lambert, Swift Current
1989-90—Kevin Haller, Regina
1990-91—Darryl Sydor, Kamloops
1991-92—Richard Matvichuk, Saskatoon
1992-93—Jason Smith, Regina
1993-94—Brendan Witt, Seattle
1994-95—Nolan Baumgartner, Kamloops
1995-96—Nolan Baumgartner, Kamloops
1996-97—Chris Phillips, Lethbridge
1997-98—Michal Rozsival, Swift Current
1998-99—Brad Stuart, Calgary

DEL WILSON TROPHY

(Top goaltender)

Season Player, Team

1966-67—Ken Brown, Moose Jaw
1967-68—Chris Worthy, Flin Flon
1968-69—Ray Martyniuk, Flin Flon
1969-70—Ray Martyniuk, Flin Flon
1970-71—Ed Dyck, Calgary
1971-72—John Davidson, Calgary
1972-73—Ed Humphreys, Saskatoon
1973-74—Garth Malarchuk, Calgary
1974-75—Bill Oleschuk, Saskatoon
1975-76—Carey Walker, New Westminster
1976-77—Glen Hanlon, Brandon
1977-78—Bart Hunter, Portland
1978-79—Rick Knickle, Brandon
1979-80—Kevin Eastman, Victoria
1980-81—Grant Fuhr, Victoria
1981-82—Mike Vernon, Calgary
1982-83—Mike Vernon, Calgary
1983-84—Ken Wregget, Lethbridge
1984-85—Troy Gamble, Medicine Hat
1985-86—Mark Fitzpatrick, Medicine Hat
1986-87—Kenton Rein, Prince Albert (East Division)
Dean Cook, Kamloops (West Division)
1987-88—Troy Gamble, Spokane
1988-89—Danny Lorenz, Seattle
1989-90—Trevor Kidd, Brandon
1990-91—Jamie McLennan, Lethbridge
1991-92—Corey Hirsch, Kamloops
1992-93—Trevor Wilson, Brandon
1993-94—Norm Maracle, Saskatoon
1994-95—Paxton Schafer, Medicine Hat
1995-96—David Lemanowicz, Spokane
1996-97—Brian Boucher, Tri-City
1997-98—Brent Belecki, Portland
1998-99—Cody Rudkowsky, Seattle

PLAYER OF THE YEAR

(Selected by fans and media)

Season Player, Team
1974-75—Ed Staniowski, Regina
1975-76—Bernie Federko, Saskatoon
1976-77—Kevin McCarthy, Winnipeg
1977-78—Ryan Walter, Seattle
1978-79—Brian Propp, Brandon
1979-80—Doug Wickenheiser, Regina
1980-81—Barry Pederson, Victoria
1981-82—Mike Vernon, Calgary
1982-83—Dean Evason, Kamloops
1983-84—Ray Ferraro, Brandon
1984-85—Dan Hodgson, Prince Albert
1985-86—Emanuel Viveiros, Prince Albert
1986-87—Rob Brown, Kamloops
1987-88—Joe Sakic, Swift Current
1988-89—Dennis Holland, Portland
1989-90—Wes Walz, Lethbridge
1990-91—Ray Whitney, Spokane
1991-92—Corey Hirsch, Kamloops
1992-93—Jason Krywulak, Swift Current
1993-94—Sonny Mignacca, Medicine Hat

The award merged with the Four Broncos Memorial Trophy after the 1993-94 season.

DUNC MC CALLUM MEMORIAL TROPHY

(Coach of the year)

Season Coach, Team
1968-69—Scotty Munro, Calgary
1969-70—Pat Ginnell, Flin Flon
1970-71—Pat Ginnell, Flin Flon
1971-72—Earl Ingarfield, Regina
1972-73—Pat Ginnell, Flin Flon
1973-74—Stan Dunn, Swift Current
1974-75—Pat Ginnell, Victoria
1975-76—Ernie McLean, New Westminster

Season Coach, Team
1976-77—Dunc McCallum, Brandon
1977-78—Jack Shupe, Victoria
Dave King, Billings
1978-79—Dunc McCallum, Brandon
1979-80—Doug Sauter, Calgary
1980-81—Ken Hodge, Portland
1981-82—Jack Sangster, Seattle
1982-83—Darryl Lubiniecki, Saskatoon
1983-84—Terry Simpson, Prince Albert
1984-85—Doug Sauter, Medicine Hat
1985-86—Terry Simpson, Prince Albert
1986-87—Ken Hitchcock, Kam. (West Division)
Graham James, Swift Current (East Division)
1987-88—Marcel Comeau, Saskatoon
1988-89—Ron Kennedy, Medicine Hat
1989-90—Ken Hitchcock, Kamloops
1990-91—Tom Renney, Kamloops
1991-92—Bryan Maxwell, Spokane
1992-93—Marcel Comeau, Tacoma
1993-94—Lorne Molleken, Saskatoon
1994-95—Don Nachbaur, Seattle
1995-96—Bob Lowes, Brandon
1996-97—Brent Peterson, Portland
1997-98—Dean Clark, Calgary
1998-99—Don Hay, Tri-City

PLAYOFF MVP

Season Player, Team
1991-92—Jarrett Deuling, Kamloops
1992-93—Andy Schneider, Swift Current
1993-94—Steve Passmore, Kamloops
1994-95—Nolan Baumgartner, Kamloops
1995-96—Bob Brown, Brandon
1996-97—Blaine Russell, Lethbridge
1997-98—Brent Belecki, Portland
1998-99—Brad Moran, Calgary

ALL-TIME LEAGUE CHAMPIONS

Season	REGULAR-SEASON CHAMPION Team	PLAYOFF CHAMPION Team
1966-67	Edmonton Oil Kings	Moose Jaw Canucks
1967-68	Flin Flon Bombers	Estevan Bruins
1968-69	Flin Flon Bombers	Flin Flon Bombers
1969-70	Flin Flon Bombers	Flin Flon Bombers
1970-71	Edmonton Oil Kings	Edmonton Oil Kings
1971-72	Calgary Centennials	Edmonton Oil Kings
1972-73	Saskatoon Blades	Medicine Hat Tigers
1973-74	Regina Pats	Regina Pats
1974-75	Victoria Cougars	New Westminster Bruins
1975-76	New Westminster Bruins	New Westminster Bruins
1976-77	New Westminster Bruins	New Westminster Bruins
1977-78	Brandon Wheat Kings	New Westminster Bruins
1978-79	Brandon Wheat Kings	Brandon Wheat Kings
1979-80	Portland Winter Hawks	Regina Pats
1980-81	Victoria Cougars	Victoria Cougars
1981-82	Lethbridge Broncos	Portland Winter Hawks
1982-83	Saskatoon Blades	Lethbridge Broncos
1983-84	Kamloops Junior Oilers	Kamloops Junior Oilers
1984-85	Prince Albert Raiders	Prince Albert Raiders
1985-86	Medicine Hat Tigers	Kamloops Blazers
1986-87	Kamloops Blazers	Medicine Hat Tigers
1987-88	Saskatoon Blades	Medicine Hat Tigers
1988-89	Swift Current Bronocs	Swift Current Broncos
1989-90	Kamloops Blazers	Kamloops Blazers
1990-91	Kamloops Blazers	Spokane Chiefs
1991-92	Kamloops Blazers	Kamloops Blazers
1992-93	Swift Current Broncos	Swift Current Broncos
1993-94	Kamloops Blazers	Kamloops Blazers
1994-95	Kamloops Blazers	Kamloops Blazers
1995-96	Brandon Wheat Kings	Brandon Wheat Kings
1996-97	Lethbridge Hurricanes	Lethbridge Hurricanes
1997-98	Portland Winter Hawks	Portland Winter Hawks
1998-99	Calgary Hitmen	Calgary Hitmen

The WHL regular-season champion is awarded the Scott Munro Memorial Trophy and the playoff champion is awarded the President's Cup.

COLLEGE HOCKEY

NCAA Division I

Central Collegiate Hockey Association

Eastern College Athletic Conference

Hockey East

Western Collegiate Hockey Association

Independents

Canadian Interuniversity Athletic Union

Canadian colleges

NCAA DIVISION I

1998-99 SEASON

NCAA TOURNAMENT

EAST REGIONAL
(Worcester, Mass.)

Maine 4, Ohio State 2
Michigan 5, Denver 3
New Hampshire 2, Michigan 1 (OT)
Maine 7, Clarkson 2

WEST REGIONAL
(Madison, Wis.)

Colorado College 5, St. Lawrence 2
Boston College 2, Northern Michigan 1
Michigan State 4, Colorado College 3
Boston College 3, North Dakota 1

NCAA FINALS
(Anaheim)

Maine 2, Boston College 1 (OT)
New Hampshire 5, Michigan State 3

CHAMPIONSHIP GAME
(Anaheim)

Maine 3, New Hampshire 2 (OT)

ALL-TOURNAMENT TEAM

Player	Pos.	College
Alfie Michaud	G	Maine
David Cullen	D	Maine
Jayme Filipowicz	D	New Hampshire
Niko Dimitrakos	F	Maine
Jason Krog	F	New Hampshire
Mike Souza	F	New Hampshire

ALL-AMERICA TEAMS

EAST

First team	Pos.	Second team
Eric Heffler, St. Lawrence	G	Michel Larocque, Boston U.
David Cullen, Maine	D	Jayme Filipowicz, N. Hamp.
Mike Mottau, Boston College	D	Willie Mitchell, Clarkson
Brian Gionta, Boston College	F	Erik Cole, Clarkson
Steve Kariya, Maine	F	Jeff Hamilton, Yale
Jason Krog, New Hampshire	F	Rejean Stringer, Merrimack

WEST

First team	Pos.	Second team
Joe Blackburn, Michigan St.	G	Jeff Maund, Ohio State
Scott Swanson, Colorado Col.	D	Benoit Cotnoir, Notre Dame
Brad Williamson, N. Dakota	D	Mike Weaver, Michigan State
Jason Blake, North Dakota	F	Hugo Boisvert, Ohio State
Brian Swanson, Colorado Col.	F	Paul Comrie, Denver
Mike York, Michigan State	F	Jay Panzer, North Dakota

HISTORY

TOURNAMENT CHAMPIONS

Year	Champion	Coach	Score	Runner-up	Most outstanding player
1948	Michigan	Vic Heyliger	8-4	Dartmouth	Joe Riley, F, Dartmouth
1949	Boston College	John Kelley	4-3	Dartmouth	Dick Desmond, G, Dartmouth
1950	Colorado College	Cheddy Thompson	13-4	Boston University	Ralph Bevins, G, Boston University
1951	Michigan	Vic Heyliger	7-1	Brown	Ed Whiston, G, Brown
1952	Michigan	Vic Heyliger	4-1	Colorado College	Kenneth Kinsley, G, Colorado College
1953	Michigan	Vic Heyliger	7-3	Minnesota	John Matchefts, F, Michigan
1954	Rensselaer	Ned Harkness	*5-4	Minnesota	Abbie Moore, F, Rensselaer
1955	Michigan	Vic Heyliger	5-3	Colorado College	Philip Hilton, D, Colorado College
1956	Michigan	Vic Heyliger	7-5	Michigan Tech	Lorne Howes, G, Michigan
1957	Colorado College	Thomas Bedecki	13-6	Michigan	Bob McCusker, F, Colorado College
1958	Denver	Murray Armstrong	6-2	North Dakota	Murray Massier, F, Denver
1959	North Dakota	Bob May	*4-3	Michigan State	Reg Morelli, F, North Dakota
1960	Denver	Murray Armstrong	5-3	Michigan Tech	Bob Marquis, F, Boston University Barry Urbanski, G, Boston University Louis Angotti, F, Michigan Tech
1961	Denver	Murray Armstrong	12-2	St. Lawrence	Bill Masterton, F, Denver
1962	Michigan Tech	John MacInnes	7-1	Clarkson	Louis Angotti, F, Michigan Tech
1963	North Dakota	Barney Thorndycraft	6-5	Denver	Al McLean, F, North Dakota
1964	Michigan	Allen Renfrew	6-3	Denver	Bob Gray, G, Michigan
1965	Michigan Tech	John MacInnes	8-2	Boston College	Gary Milroy, F, Michigan Tech
1966	Michigan State	Amo Bessone	6-1	Clarkson	Gaye Cooley, G, Michigan State
1967	Cornell	Ned Harkness	4-1	Boston University	Walt Stanowski, D, Cornell
1968	Denver	Murray Armstrong	4-0	North Dakota	Gerry Powers, G, Denver
1969	Denver	Murray Armstrong	4-3	Cornell	Keith Magnuson, D, Denver
1970	Cornell	Ned Harkness	6-4	Clarkson	Daniel Lodboa, D, Cornell
1971	Boston University	Jack Kelley	4-2	Minnesota	Dan Brady, G, Boston University
1972	Boston University	Jack Kelley	4-0	Cornell	Tim Regan, G, Boston University
1973	Wisconsin	Bob Johnson	4-2	Vacated	Dean Talafous, F, Wisconsin
1974	Minnesota	Herb Brooks	4-2	Michigan Tech	Brad Shelstad, G, Minnesota
1975	Michigan Tech	John MacInnes	6-1	Minnesota	Jim Warden, G, Michigan Tech
1976	Minnesota	Herb Brooks	6-4	Michigan Tech	Tom Vanelli, F, Minnesota

Year	Champion	Coach	Score	Runner-up	Most outstanding player
1977	Wisconsin	Bob Johnson	*6-5	Michigan	Julian Baretta, G, Wisconsin
1978	Boston University	Jack Parker	5-3	Boston College	Jack O'Callahan, D, Boston University
1979	Minnesota	Herb Brooks	4-3	North Dakota	Steve Janaszak, G, Minnesota
1980	North Dakota	John Gasparini	5-2	Northern Michigan	Doug Smail, F, North Dakota
1981	Wisconsin	Bob Johnson	6-3	Minnesota	Marc Behrend, G, Wisconsin
1982	North Dakota	John Gasparini	5-2	Wisconsin	Phil Sykes, F, North Dakota
1983	Wisconsin	Jeff Sauer	6-2	Harvard	Marc Behrend, G, Wisconsin
1984	Bowling Green State	Jerry York	*5-4	Minnesota-Duluth	Gary Kruzich, G, Bowling Green State
1985	Rensselaer	Mike Addesa	2-1	Providence	Chris Terreri, G, Providence
1986	Michigan State	Ron Mason	6-5	Harvard	Mike Donnelly, F, Michigan State
1987	North Dakota	John Gasparini	5-3	Michigan State	Tony Hrkac, F, North Dakota
1988	Lake Superior State	Frank Anzalone	*4-3	St. Lawrence	Bruce Hoffort, G, Lake Superior State
1989	Harvard	Bill Cleary	*4-3	Minnesota	Ted Donato, F, Harvard
1990	Wisconsin	Jeff Sauer	7-3	Colgate	Chris Tancill, F, Wisconsin
1991	Northern Michigan	Rick Comley	*8-7	Boston University	Scott Beattie, F, Northern Michigan
1992	Lake Superior State	Jeff Jackson	5-3	Wisconsin	Paul Constantin, F, Lake Superior State
1993	Maine	Shawn Walsh	5-4	Lake Superior State	Jim Montgomery, F, Maine
1994	Lake Superior State	Jeff Jackson	9-1	Boston University	Sean Tallaire, F, Lake Superior State
1995	Boston University	Jack Parker	6-2	Maine	Chris O'Sullivan, F, Boston University
1996	Michigan	Red Berenson	*3-2	Colorado College	Brendan Morrison, F, Michigan
1997	North Dakota	Dean Blaise	6-4	Boston University	Matt Henderson, F, North Dakota
1998	Michigan	Red Berenson	*3-2	Boston College	Marty Turco, G, Michigan
1999	Maine	Shawn Walsh	*3-2	New Hampshire	Alfie Michaud, G, Maine

*Overtime.

ALL-TIME TOURNAMENT RECORDS

	Visits	W	L	GF	GA	Pct.	Finished 1st	Finished 2nd
Colgate	1	3	1	10	11	.750	0	1
Michigan	22	35	15	260	167	.700	9	2
§Wisconsin	17	29	15	183	138	.659	5	2
North Dakota	16	25	13	154	117	.658	6	3
‡Lake Superior State	10	20	11	143	105	.645	3	1
Maine	8	18	10	115	104	.643	2	1
Denver	14	19	12	144	91	.613	5	2
Michigan Tech	10	13	9	118	85	.591	3	4
Minnesota	22	28	24	259	234	.538	3	6
Boston University	24	32	28	245	244	.533	4	5
†Michigan State	18	23	22	183	173	.511	2	2
Northern Michigan	7	8	8	66	67	.500	1	1
‡Rensselaer Polytechnic Institute	8	8	8	52	55	.500	2	0
Northeastern	3	3	3	30	30	.500	0	0
Merrimack	1	2	2	14	16	.500	0	0
Ohio State	2	2	2	12	12	.500	0	0
Cornell	11	10	12	76	84	.455	2	2
Minnesota-Duluth	4	5	6	43	41	.455	0	1
Colorado College	14	12	15	111	123	.444	2	3
Dartmouth	5	4	5	38	37	.444	0	2
Providence	7	9	12	72	78	.429	0	1
*Bowling Green State	9	8	12	66	88	.400	1	0
§Lowell	3	2	3	19	23	.400	0	0
Clarkson	17	12	20	103	135	.375	0	3
Boston College	20	17	29	160	115	.370	1	3
†Harvard	16	14	24	143	166	.368	1	2
New Hampshire	10	7	14	64	97	.333	0	1
Yale	2	1	2	7	9	.333	0	0
Alaska-Anchorage	3	2	5	22	39	.286	0	0
Brown	4	2	5	31	45	.286	0	1
Vermont	3	1	4	10	21	.200	0	0
St. Lawrence	13	5	22	78	128	.185	0	2
Princeton	1	0	1	1	2	.000	0	0
St. Cloud State	1	0	2	5	10	.000	0	0
Miami of Ohio	2	0	2	3	7	.000	0	0
Western Michigan	3	0	4	8	23	.000	0	0

(Denver also participated in 1973 tournament but its record was voided by the NCAA in 1977 upon discovery of violations by the University. The team had finished second in '73.)

*Bowling Green State and Northeastern played to a 2-2 tie in 1981-82.
†Harvard and Michigan State played to a 3-3 tie in 1982-83.
‡Lake Superior State and RPI played to a 3-3 tie in 1984-85.
§Wisconsin and Lowell played to a 4-4 tie in 1987-88.

HOBEY BAKER AWARD WINNERS

(Top college hockey player in United States)

Year—Player, College
1981—Neal Broten, Minnesota
1982—George McPhee, Bowling Green St.
1983—Mark Fusco, Harvard
1984—Tom Kurvers, Minnesota-Duluth
1985—Bill Watson, Minnesota-Duluth
1986—Scott Fusco, Harvard
1987—Tony Hrkac, North Dakota

Year—Player, College
1988—Robb Stauber, Minnesota
1989—Lane MacDonald, Harvard
1990—Kip Miller, Michigan State
1991—David Emma, Boston College
1992—Scott Pellerin, Maine
1993—Paul Kariya, Maine
1994—Chris Marinucci, Min.-Duluth

Year—Player, College
1995—Brian Holzinger, Bowling Green St.
1996—Brian Bonin, Minnesota
1997—Brendan Morrison, Michigan
1998—Chris Drury, Boston University
1999—Jason Krog, New Hampshire

CENTRAL COLLEGIATE HOCKEY ASSOCIATION

1998-99 SEASON

FINAL STANDINGS

Team	G	W	L	T	Pts.	GF	GA
Michigan St. (29-6-7)	30	20	3	7	47	91	40
Michigan (25-11-6)	30	17	8	5	39	98	72
Ohio State (21-16-4)	30	17	10	3	37	87	66
Notre Dame (19-14-5)	30	15	11	4	34	92	68
N. Michigan (22-15-5)	30	14	11	5	33	94	83
Ferris St. (14-16-6)	30	13	12	5	31	76	69
Bowl. Green (17-18-3)	30	13	14	3	29	102	105
Lake Sup. St. (11-23-4)	30	10	17	3	23	79	93
Mia. of Ohio (11-20-5)	30	9	17	4	22	78	104
W. Michigan (6-20-8)	30	5	17	8	18	69	119
A. Fairbanks (11-22-1)	30	8	21	1	17	77	124

Overall record in parentheses.

PLAYOFF RESULTS

FIRST ROUND

Ohio State 4, Ferris State 2
Ohio State 3, Ferris State 1
(Ohio State won series, 2-0)

Michigan State 3, Lake Superior State 2
Michigan State 4, Lake Superior State 0
(Michigan State won series, 2-0)

Notre Dame 3, Northern Michigan 2
Northern Michigan 7, Notre Dame 1
Northern Michigan 3, Notre Dame 2
(Northern Michigan won series, 2-1)

Michigan 3, Bowling Green State 2
Michigan 9, Bowling Green State 3
(Michigan won series, 2-0)

SEMIFINALS

Michigan 3, Ohio State 2
Northern Michigan 5, Michigan State 3

FINALS

Michigan 5, Northern Michigan 1

ALL-STAR TEAMS

First team	Pos.	Second team
Jeff Maund, Ohio State	G	Joe Blackburn, Mich. State
Mike Weaver, Mich. State	D	Mike Jones, Bowl. Green
Benoit Cotnoir, Notre Dame	D	Andre Signoretti, Ohio State
Hugo Boisvert, Ohio State	F	Dan Price, Bowling Green
Mike York, Mich. State	F	Ben Simon, Notre Dame
Adam Edinger, Bowl. Green	F	J.P. Vigier, N. Michigan

AWARD WINNERS

Player of the year: Mike York, Michigan State
Rookie of the year: Mike Comrie, Michigan
Coach of the year: Ron Mason, Michigan State
Leading scorer: Mike York, Michigan State
Playoff MVP: Mark Kosick, Michigan

INDIVIDUAL LEADERS

Goals: Jason Deskins, Miami of Ohio (26)
Assists: Buddy Smith, Northern Michigan (35)
Points: Mike York, Michigan State (54)
Penalty minutes: Ryan Jestadt, Ohio State (98)
Goaltending average: Joe Blackburn, Michigan State (1.55)

TOP SCORERS

	Games	G	A	Pts.
Mike York, Michigan State	42	22	32	54
Dan Price, Bowling Green State	38	21	32	53
Hugo Boisvert, Ohio State	41	24	27	51
Adam Edinger, Bowling Green State	38	23	25	48
Mike Comrie, Michigan	42	19	25	44
Buddy Smith, Northern Michigan	42	9	35	44
Ben Simon, Notre Dame	37	18	24	42
Brian Urick, Notre Dame	35	16	25	41
Jason Deskins, Miami of Ohio	36	26	14	40
J.P. Vigier, Northern Michigan	42	21	18	39

INDIVIDUAL STATISTICS

ALASKA-FAIRBANKS NANOOKS

SCORING

	Pos.	Class	Games	G	A	Pts.	PIM
Chris Kirwan	F	Sr.	32	14	12	26	40
Jim Lawrence	F	So.	34	8	14	22	16
Jamie Coady	F	Jr.	32	10	9	19	37
Kerry Hafele	F	Jr.	30	8	11	19	22
Sjon Wynia	F	Jr.	34	9	9	18	52
Dwayne Zinger	D	Jr.	33	4	14	18	42
Bobby Andrews	F	Fr.	31	5	11	16	38
Ryan Reinheller	F	So.	32	3	12	15	16
Mike Jaros	D	Sr.	34	4	8	12	30
Kevin McNeill	F	Jr.	34	6	5	11	23
Chad Hamilton	D	So.	31	1	10	11	68
Daniel Carriere	D	Fr.	29	4	6	10	22
Darren Tiemstra	D	So.	34	4	5	9	71
Aaron Grosul	D	Fr.	33	1	8	9	14
Pat Hallett	F	So.	32	7	1	8	30
Nathan Rocheleau	F	Jr.	34	4	4	8	24
Scott McIlroy	F	So.	30	1	3	4	8
Mike Barren	F	So.	23	0	2	2	10
Dennis Gould	F	Fr.	7	1	0	1	0
Ian Perkins	G	Sr.	28	0	1	1	6
Nathan Wheeler	F	So.	3	0	0	0	0
Jacob Flora	F	Fr.	5	0	0	0	0
Jeff McLean	F	Sr.	5	0	0	0	4
Chris Marvel	G	Jr.	10	0	0	0	15
Joe Borro	D	Fr.	23	0	0	0	32

GOALTENDING

	Games	Min.	W	L	T	Goals	SO	Avg.
Ian Perkins	28	1551	9	15	1	95	2	3.67
Chris Marvel	10	493	2	7	0	35	0	4.26

BOWLING GREEN STATE FALCONS

SCORING

	Pos.	Class	Games	G	A	Pts.	PIM
Dan Price	F	Sr.	38	21	32	53	56
Adam Edinger	F	Jr.	38	23	25	48	36
Ryan Murphy	F	So.	34	10	23	33	38
Chris Bonvie	F	So.	34	11	18	29	58
Mike Jones	D	Fr.	38	8	21	29	80
Craig Desjarlais	F	Jr.	38	10	15	25	74
Greg Day	F	Fr.	38	10	11	21	8
Grady Moore	D	Fr.	38	6	10	16	27
Zach Ham	F	Jr.	36	4	8	12	38
Curtis Valentine	F	So.	38	4	8	12	40
Doug Schueller	D	So.	37	7	4	11	54
Marc Barlow	D	Fr.	34	1	8	9	20
Austin de Luis	F	Fr.	34	4	3	7	28
Scott Hewson	F	Fr.	28	1	6	7	45
Dennis Williams	F	So.	33	4	1	5	55
Ryan Wetterberg	F	Fr.	37	1	3	4	14
Mike Savard	G	Sr.	33	0	2	2	16
Louis Mass	D	So.	35	0	2	2	30
Stewart Nowosad	F	So.	19	1	0	1	38
B.J. Adams	D	Jr.	38	0	1	1	93
Jason Piwko	G	Sr.	2	0	0	0	0
Joe Statkus	D	Fr.	5	0	0	0	2
John Hustler	D	Sr.	6	0	0	0	4
Shawn Timm	G	So.	7	0	0	0	0
Brad Newman	F	Jr.	8	0	0	0	0

GOALTENDING

	Games	Min.	W	L	T	Goals	SO	Avg.
Jason Piwko	2	40	0	0	0	1	0	1.51
Mike Savard	33	1916	16	14	2	103	1	3.23
Shawn Timm	7	329	1	4	1	27	0	4.93

FERRIS STATE BULLDOGS

SCORING

	Pos.	Class	Games	G	A	Pts.	PIM
Brian McCullough	F	Jr.	35	14	14	28	28
Joel Irwin	F	Sr.	36	10	13	23	50
Kevin Swider	F	So.	36	12	10	22	14
Jim Dube	D	So.	33	7	13	20	28
Brent Wishart	F	Jr.	36	7	13	20	26
Geoff Bennetts	F	Sr.	36	10	3	13	22
Rob Collins	F	Fr.	36	3	9	12	14
Rob Kozak	F	Jr.	36	3	8	11	28
Kenzie Homer	F	Sr.	28	6	4	10	46
Casey Harris	F	Sr.	35	4	6	10	46
Ed Kowalski	F	Sr.	31	4	5	9	32
Jason Hodel	F	Sr.	33	3	6	9	18
Scott Lewis	D	So.	34	2	5	7	33
J.P. Tessier	D	Sr.	36	0	7	7	56
Todd Steinmetz	F	Sr.	33	2	2	4	50
Jon Rogger	F	So.	17	1	3	4	17
Jason Basile	D	Fr.	32	1	3	4	22
Christian Schroder	D	Fr.	9	0	2	2	10
Chad McIver	D	Fr.	20	0	1	1	42
Ken Sergott	D	Sr.	23	0	1	1	26
Gary Ricciardi	D	Jr.	33	0	1	1	38
Phil Osaer	G	Fr.	9	0	0	0	0
Vince Owen	G	So.	31	0	0	0	2

GOALTENDING

	Games	Min.	W	L	T	Goals	SO	Avg.
Phil Osaer	9	399	2	2	1	10	0	1.51
Vince Owen	31	1786	12	14	5	73	4	2.45

LAKE SUPERIOR STATE LAKERS

SCORING

	Pos.	Class	Games	G	A	Pts.	PIM
Tobin Praznik	F	Sr.	38	13	11	24	50
Trent Walford	F	Jr.	32	10	12	22	14
Mike Vigilante	F	So.	31	4	17	21	18
Ryan Vince	F	So.	36	8	10	18	53
Ben Keup	F	Jr.	34	5	12	17	48
Jeff Cheeseman	F	Jr.	31	11	5	16	52
Fred Slukynsky	F	Jr.	37	8	8	16	68
Jeremy Bachusz	F	Fr.	38	6	7	13	26
Ryan Knox	D	So.	28	3	9	12	26
Blaine McCauley	D	Jr.	37	2	10	12	152
Mike Henderson	F	Fr.	29	6	3	9	8
Mike Kucsulain	F	Sr.	20	4	4	8	75
Tyson Turgeon	D	Fr.	19	0	8	8	6
Bart Redden	F	So.	38	4	3	7	26
Chris Thompson	D	Fr.	32	3	4	7	73
Tyler Palmer	D	Jr.	31	1	5	6	32
Chris McNamara	F	Fr.	14	0	4	4	10
Jamie Garrick	F	Fr.	6	2	0	2	4
Jeff Attard	F	So.	19	1	1	2	12
Matt Frick	D	So.	32	1	1	2	22
Jason Nightingale	F	Fr.	8	1	0	1	2
Cory Bast	F	Fr.	21	0	1	1	16
Will Magnuson	D	Fr.	32	0	1	1	44
Rob Galatiuk	G	So.	10	0	0	0	2
Mike Brusseau	G	Jr.	15	0	0	0	0
Klemen Kelgar	D	So.	18	0	0	0	16
Yevgeniy Dubravin	F	Fr.	20	0	0	0	6

GOALTENDING

	Games	Min.	W	L	T	Goals	SO	Avg.
Jayme Platt	29	1509	8	16	2	78	1	3.10
Mike Brusseau	15	469	3	3	2	26	0	3.33
Rob Galatiuk	10	304	0	4	0	21	0	4.15

MIAMI OF OHIO REDSKINS

SCORING

	Pos.	Class	Games	G	A	Pts.	PIM
Jason Deskins	F	So.	36	26	14	40	70
Mark Shalawylo	F	Jr.	32	13	21	34	14
Pat Leahy	F	So.	34	10	20	30	40
Alex Kim	F	So.	36	11	9	20	36
Josh Mizerek	D	Jr.	36	3	13	16	60
Ryan Brindley	D	Sr.	34	4	11	15	62
Ernie Hartlieb	F	So.	34	6	8	14	26
Josh Harrold	D	Sr.	36	3	10	13	42
Evan Cheverie	F	Fr.	35	4	6	10	28
Gregor Krajnc	F	Jr.	30	5	4	9	12
Jeremy Bautch	F	Jr.	36	2	7	9	42
Ken Marsch	D	Fr.	34	1	6	7	12
Dustin Whitecotton	F	Jr.	12	0	5	5	4
Matt Chandler	F	Fr.	26	2	2	4	4
C.J. Buzzell	F	Sr.	29	2	2	4	32
Pavel Nejezchleb	D	Fr.	36	1	2	3	24
Bart Stevens	D	Fr.	20	0	3	3	18
Michael Glumac	F	Fr.	35	2	0	2	44
Jeremy Vokes	F	Fr.	19	1	1	2	8
Jake Ortmeyer	F	Fr.	25	1	1	2	34
Anthony Donskov	F	So.	30	1	0	1	20
Clarke Walford	F	So.	1	0	0	0	0
Andy Marsch	G	Jr.	14	0	0	0	0
Ian Olsen	G	Jr.	26	0	0	0	2

GOALTENDING

	Games	Min.	W	L	T	Goals	SO	Avg.
Ian Olsen	26	1471	5	14	4	84	0	3.43
Andy Marsch	14	712	6	6	1	43	0	3.62

MICHIGAN WOLVERINES

SCORING

	Pos.	Class	Games	G	A	Pts.	PIM
Mike Comrie	F	Fr.	42	19	25	44	38
Josh Langfeld	F	So.	41	21	14	35	84
Mark Kosick	F	So.	42	12	23	35	14
Bubba Berenzweig	D	Sr.	42	7	24	31	38
Jeff Jillson	D	Fr.	38	5	19	24	71
Dave Huntzicker	D	So.	41	5	19	24	50
Dale Rominski	F	Sr.	41	15	8	23	80
Mike Van Ryn	D	So.	37	10	13	23	52
Bobby Hayes	F	Sr.	41	7	14	21	114
Scott Matzka	F	So.	40	7	12	19	30
Sean Ritchlin	F	Sr.	41	12	5	17	55
Geoff Koch	F	So.	40	4	12	16	101
Sean Peach	D	Jr.	37	3	11	14	42
Greg Crozier	F	Sr.	39	7	6	13	63
Bill Trainor	F	So.	29	1	8	9	8
Justin Clark	F	Sr.	40	4	2	6	6
Andrew Merrick	F	Jr.	34	1	3	4	61
Josh Blackburn	G	Fr.	42	0	3	3	0
Craig Murray	F	Fr.	16	0	1	1	6
Scott Crawford	D	So.	17	0	1	1	16
Greg Daddario	G	Sr.	2	0	0	0	0
Kevin Magnuson	D	Jr.	5	0	0	0	8
Krikor Arman	F	Jr.	8	0	0	0	2
Kevin O'Malley	G	Fr.	8	0	0	0	0
Bob Gassoff	D	So.	21	0	0	0	50
Jay Vancik	D	Fr.	24	0	0	0	26

GOALTENDING

	Games	Min.	W	L	T	Goals	SO	Avg.
Josh Blackburn	42	2398	25	10	6	91	3	2.28
Kevin O'Malley	8	145	0	1	0	6	0	2.48
Greg Daddario	2	11	0	0	0	1	0	5.46

MICHIGAN STATE SPARTANS

SCORING

	Pos.	Class	Games	G	A	Pts.	PIM
Mike York	F	Sr.	42	22	32	54	41
Bryan Adams	F	Sr.	42	21	16	37	56
Shawn Horcoff	F	Jr.	39	12	25	37	70
Rustyn Dolyny	F	So.	41	18	15	33	61
Adam Hall	F	Fr.	36	16	7	23	74
Jeff Kozakowski	D	Sr.	40	5	13	18	24
Brad Hodgins	D	Jr.	42	3	15	18	64
Andrew Hutchinson	D	Fr.	37	3	12	15	26
Damon Whitten	F	So.	42	9	5	14	84
Chris Bogas	D	Sr.	35	1	13	14	86
Joe Goodenow	F	Fr.	36	3	10	13	38
Mark Loeding	F	Sr.	37	4	3	7	18
Mike Weaver	D	Jr.	42	1	6	7	54
Shawn Mather	F	Fr.	37	4	2	6	10
John Nail	F	So.	42	1	5	6	18
Sean Patchell	F	So.	40	3	2	5	82
Andrew Bogle	F	So.	38	2	2	4	18
Curtis Gemmel	F	Sr.	23	0	3	3	6
Joe Blackburn	G	So.	33	0	1	1	4
Jon Insana	D	Fr.	39	0	1	1	59
Mike Ford	F	Sr.	9	0	0	0	4
Mike Gresl	G	Jr.	9	0	0	0	0
Brody Brandstatter	D	So.	17	0	0	0	18

GOALTENDING

	Games	Min.	W	L	T	Goals	SO	Avg.
Mike Gresl	9	539	8	1	0	11	2	1.22
Joe Blackburn	33	2013	21	5	7	52	3	1.55

NORTHERN MICHIGAN WILDCATS

SCORING

	Pos.	Class	Games	G	A	Pts.	PIM
Buddy Smith	F	Sr.	42	9	35	44	40
J.P. Vigier	F	Jr.	42	21	18	39	80
Roger Trudeau	F	Jr.	42	19	14	33	42
Chad Theuer	F	Fr.	40	8	21	29	40
Fred Mattersdorfer	F	So.	42	10	16	26	18
Bryan Phillips	F	Jr.	39	13	10	23	55
Sean Connolly	D	Fr.	34	4	18	22	62
Tyson Holly	F	Jr.	34	14	7	21	61
Brad Frattaroli	F	Sr.	42	9	11	20	42
Jeff White	D	So.	38	6	8	14	24
Rich Metro	F	Sr.	40	4	9	13	42
Doug Schmidt	D	So.	36	7	5	12	77
Ryan Riipi	F	So.	35	4	6	10	44
Kevin Schmidt	D	Jr.	42	3	7	10	34
Lee Ruff	F/D	Jr.	41	1	8	9	22
Sean Owens	D	Fr.	32	4	3	7	51
Mike Sandbeck	F	So.	30	2	5	7	36
Mike Johnson	D	Sr.	18	1	5	6	30
Ian LaRocque	F	So.	8	3	2	5	10
Tyler Barabonoff	D	Jr.	29	1	4	5	42
Bernie Sigrist	F	Fr.	28	0	4	4	10
Colin Young	D	So.	19	1	0	1	30
Duane Hoey	G	Jr.	12	0	1	1	0
Dan Ragusett	G	So.	33	0	1	1	0

GOALTENDING

	Games	Min.	W	L	T	Goals	SO	Avg.
Dan Ragusett	33	1927	16	11	5	80	2	2.49
Duane Hoey	12	613	6	4	0	32	0	3.13

NOTRE DAME FIGHTING IRISH

SCORING

	Pos.	Class	Games	G	A	Pts.	PIM
Ben Simon	F	Jr.	37	18	24	42	65
Brian Urick	F	Sr.	35	16	25	41	45
Aniket Dhadphale	F	Sr.	34	18	11	29	55
Dan Carlson	F	So.	36	7	20	27	51
Benoit Cotnoir	D	Sr.	36	7	18	25	58
David Inman	F	Fr.	38	10	10	20	74
Tyson Fraser	D	Jr.	33	1	16	17	46
Chad Chipchase	F	So.	38	10	5	15	16
Joe Dusbabek	F	Jr.	34	4	10	14	36
Matt Van Arkel	F	So.	35	8	4	12	30
Brett Henning	F	Fr.	38	4	6	10	30
Ryan Dolder	F	So.	35	5	4	9	20
Sean Molina	D	Jr.	36	0	5	5	42
Sam Cornelius	D	Fr.	36	1	3	4	26
Ryan Clark	F	So.	14	1	2	3	26
Craig Hagkull	F	Sr.	18	1	2	3	8
Jay Kopischke	F	So.	29	0	3	3	30
Troy Bagne	F	Jr.	30	1	1	2	8
Andy Jurkowski	D	Jr.	38	1	1	2	31
Nathan Borega	D	Jr.	30	0	2	2	26
John Dwyer	F	Jr.	15	1	0	1	6
Sean Seyferth	D	Jr.	7	0	1	1	4
Scott Giuliani	D	Sr.	2	0	0	0	0
Jeremiah Kimento	G	Fr.	5	0	0	0	0
Forrest Karr	G	Sr.	38	0	0	0	0

GOALTENDING

	Games	Min.	W	L	T	Goals	SO	Avg.
Forrest Karr	38	2160	19	14	5	93	2	2.58
J. Kimento	5	138	0	0	0	6	0	2.61

OHIO STATE BUCKEYES

SCORING

	Pos.	Class	Games	G	A	Pts.	PIM
Hugo Boisvert	F	Jr.	41	24	27	51	54
Chris Richards	F	Sr.	41	9	28	37	48
Eric Meloche	F	Jr.	35	11	16	27	87
Jean-Francois Dufour	F	So.	41	9	15	24	16
Andre Signoretti	D	So.	41	3	21	24	70
Brandon Lafrance	F	Sr.	41	10	7	17	38
Jason Crain	D	Fr.	41	3	14	17	18
Vinnie Grant	F	So.	36	5	11	16	24
Louie Colsant	F	Jr.	39	6	8	14	20
Ryan Jestadt	D	Jr.	41	9	3	12	98
Dan Cousineau	F	Sr.	32	6	4	10	38
Neal Rech	F	Sr.	41	6	3	9	44
Scott Titus	D	Fr.	40	2	7	9	59
Nick Ganga	F	Fr.	35	4	4	8	26
Jaisen Freeman	D	So.	36	3	3	6	22
Brian Morrison	F	Sr.	13	2	3	5	4
Jason Selleke	F	Jr.	38	2	2	4	49
Yan Des Gagne	F	Fr.	14	2	1	3	6
Benji Wolke	F	So.	11	0	3	3	24
Rob Gubala	F	So.	13	2	0	2	4
Ryan Skaleski	D	Jr.	40	2	0	2	95
Mike McCormick	F	Fr.	14	1	1	2	12
Ryan Smith	F	Fr.	8	0	2	2	4
Jeff Maund	G	So.	38	0	1	1	0
Ray Aho	G	Jr.	5	0	0	0	2
Jeff Marshall	D	Fr.	5	0	0	0	2

GOALTENDING

	Games	Min.	W	L	T	Goals	SO	Avg.
Jeff Maund	38	2283	20	14	4	89	3	2.34
Ray Aho	5	201	1	2	0	10	0	2.99

WESTERN MICHIGAN BRONCOS

SCORING

	Pos.	Class	Games	G	A	Pts.	PIM
Chuck Mindel	F	Sr.	34	14	9	23	44
David Gove	F	So.	33	9	14	23	12
Frank Novock	F	Sr.	34	6	16	22	24
Corey Waring	F	Jr.	33	8	7	15	12
Daryl Andrews	D	Jr.	33	3	11	14	42
Jason Redenius	F	Jr.	33	8	5	13	28
Matt Addesa	F	Jr.	31	7	6	13	55
Steve Rymsha	F	So.	31	6	7	13	42
Chad Kline	F	So.	29	4	8	12	45
Ryan Crane	D	Fr.	30	2	7	9	48
Geoff Collard	D	Sr.	34	2	5	7	69
Jeff Lukasak	F	Jr.	29	1	6	7	61
Mark Wilkinson	F	So.	30	1	6	7	56
Austin Miller	D	Fr.	33	0	6	6	26
Anthony Battaglia	F	Fr.	33	0	4	4	14
Bryan Farquhar	F	Fr.	23	2	1	3	14
Matt Barnes	G	Sr.	25	0	3	3	0
Michael Bishai	F	Fr.	26	0	3	3	20
Greg Mitchell	F	Fr.	16	1	1	2	10
Caley Jones	F	Jr.	18	1	0	1	16
Brett Mills	F	So.	3	0	1	1	2
Derek McKinlay	D	Fr.	8	0	1	1	14
Jeff Reynaert	G	Fr.	10	0	1	1	0
Kevin Clauson	D	So.	12	0	1	1	14
Jay McCabe	F	So.	19	0	1	1	10
G.W. King	D	Fr.	2	0	0	0	0
Chris Peck	G	So.	2	0	0	0	0

GOALTENDING

	Games	Min.	W	L	T	Goals	SO	Avg.
Matt Barnes	25	1478	5	12	7	82	0	3.33
Jeff Reynaert	10	522	1	7	1	31	0	3.57
Chris Peck	2	69	0	1	0	9	0	7.78

EASTERN COLLEGE ATHLETIC CONFERENCE

1998-99 SEASON

FINAL STANDINGS

Team	G	W	L	T	Pts.	GF	GA
Clarkson (25-11-1)	22	18	4	0	36	91	48
St. Lawrence (23-13-3)	22	15	4	3	33	80	47
Rensselaer (23-12-2)	22	13	7	2	28	89	62
Princeton (20-12-2)	22	13	8	1	27	69	62
Colgate (19-12-4)	22	12	8	2	26	66	56
Yale (13-14-4)	22	11	7	4	26	65	56
Cornell (12-15-4)	22	9	10	3	21	67	63
Harvard (14-16-2)	22	8	12	2	18	64	87
Vermont (13-18-2)	22	7	13	2	16	53	67
Brown (9-16-6)	22	5	12	5	15	56	72
Dartmouth (10-17-2)	22	6	14	2	14	60	79
Union (3-26-3)	22	1	19	2	4	32	93

Overall record in parentheses.

PLAYOFF RESULTS

PLAY-IN GAME

Princeton 3, Colgate 2

FIRST ROUND

Harvard 2, Rensselaer 1
Rensselaer 4, Harvard 0
Rensselaer 4, Harvard 2
(Rensselaer won series, 2-1)

St. Lawrence 9, Vermont 2
St. Lawrence 4, Vermont 1
(St. Lawrence won series, 2-0)

Clarkson 3, Brown 2 (OT)
Clarkson 3, Brown 1
(Clarkson won series, 2-0)

Colgate 5, Yale 1
Colgate 7, Yale 2
(Colgate won series, 2-0)

Princeton 4, Cornell 4 (OT)
Princeton 6, Cornell 5
(Princeton won series, 1-0-1)

SEMIFINALS

Clarkson 6, Princeton 5
St. Lawrence 5, Rensselaer 3

CONSOLATION GAME

Rensselaer 6, Princeton 4

CHAMPIONSHIP GAME

Clarkson 3, St. Lawrence 2

ALL-STAR TEAMS

First team	Pos.	Second team
Eric Heffler, St. Lawrence	G	Alex Westlund, Yale
Jeff Burgoyne, Cornell	D	Jason Reid, Vermont
Willie Mitchell, Clarkson	D	Steven Shirreffs, Princeton
Erik Cole, Clarkson	F	Jeff Halpern, Princeton
Jeff Hamilton, Yale	F	Andy McDonald, Colgate
Danny Riva, Rensselaer	F	Bob Prier, St. Lawrence

AWARD WINNERS

Player of the year: Eric Heffler, St. Lawrence
Rookies of the year: Brandon Dietrich, St. Lawrence
Coach of the year: Joe Marsh, St. Lawrence
Leading scorer: Danny Riva, Rensselaer
Playoff MVP: Willie Mitchell, Clarkson

INDIVIDUAL LEADERS

Goals: Erik Cole, Clarkson (22)
Jeff Halpern, Princeton (22)
Danny Riva, Rensselaer (22)
Assists: Danny Riva, Rensselaer (35)
Points: Danny Riva, Rensselaer (57)
Penalty minutes: Benoit Morin, Princeton (100)
Goaltending average: Shep Harder, Colgate (2.28)

TOP SCORERS

	Games	G	A	Pts.
Danny Riva, Rensselaer	36	22	35	57
Matt Murley, Rensselaer	36	17	32	49
Jeff Hamilton, Yale	30	20	28	48
Alain St. Hilaire, Rensselaer	33	16	32	48
Andy McDonald, Colgate	35	20	26	46
Bob Prier, St. Lawrence	37	20	26	46
Jeff Halpern, Princeton	33	22	22	44
John Poapst, St. Lawrence	39	16	27	43
Erik Cole, Clarkson	36	22	20	42
Kyle Knopp, Cornell	31	10	32	42

INDIVIDUAL STATISTICS

BROWN BEARS

SCORING

	Pos.	Class	Games	G	A	Pts.	PIM
Michael Bent	F	Jr.	31	14	9	23	0
Adrian Smith	F	Sr.	28	11	11	22	70
Jon Zielinski	F	So.	29	9	13	22	32
Paul Giblin	F	Sr.	30	6	9	15	14
Jade Kersey	F	Sr.	28	5	10	15	8
Josh Barker	D	Fr.	31	2	13	15	38
Gianni Cantini	F	Fr.	27	5	9	14	6
Shawn Brackenridge	F	So.	28	2	12	14	30
Jeff Lawler	F	Jr.	31	10	3	13	18
James Duval	F	Jr.	30	4	9	13	4
Christian Warrington	D	So.	29	1	8	9	22
John Petricig	F	So.	25	6	2	8	19
Matt Kohansky	F	So.	21	3	5	8	2
Tyler Garrow	F	Jr.	31	3	4	7	40
Doug Janjevich	F	So.	13	3	2	5	2
Chris Dirkes	D	Fr.	30	0	5	5	18
Mike Pratt	D	So.	29	1	3	4	48
Darren McPeak	D	Fr.	17	1	2	3	16
Ryan Longfield	D	Jr.	25	1	2	3	18
J.-Francois Labarre	F	Fr.	15	0	2	2	4
Brian O'Neill	D	Jr.	11	0	1	1	6
Ryan MacNevin	D	Jr.	1	0	0	0	2
Jonathan Charbonneau	F	Fr.	1	0	0	0	0

	Pos.	Class	Games	G	A	Pts.	PIM
Graham McNally	G	Fr.	2	0	0	0	0
Brian Eklund	G	Fr.	8	0	0	0	0
Greg Hayes	D	Jr.	13	0	0	0	16
Scott Stirling	G	Jr.	27	0	0	0	10

GOALTENDING

	Games	Min.	W	L	T	Goals	SO	Avg.
Scott Stirling	27	1543	8	13	5	75	2	2.92
Graham McNally	2	42	0	0	1	2	0	2.83
Brian Eklund	8	299	1	3	0	17	0	3.41

CLARKSON GOLDEN KNIGHTS

SCORING

	Pos.	Class	Games	G	A	Pts.	PIM
Erik Cole	F	So.	36	22	20	42	50
Mikko Ollila	F	Sr.	35	9	24	33	14
Ben Maidment	F	Sr.	37	12	17	29	8
Willie Mitchell	D	So.	34	10	19	29	40
Matt Reid	F	Jr.	36	10	13	23	60
Philippe Roy	D	Jr.	36	9	13	22	42
Don Smith	F	So.	37	9	12	21	18
Carl Drakensjo	F	Jr.	37	7	14	21	40
Yan Turgeon	F	Jr.	34	9	11	20	16
Matt Poapst	F	Fr.	37	7	11	18	26
David Evans	F	Fr.	33	6	10	16	6
Kent Huskins	D	So.	37	5	11	16	28
Matt Saper	F	So.	33	6	8	14	26
Kerry Ellis-Toddington	D	Fr.	37	0	12	12	20
Murray Kuntz	F	So.	21	3	5	8	16
Jim Sheehan	F	Jr.	32	3	4	7	22
Aaron Gates	D	Sr.	35	3	4	7	50
Ian Manzano	D	Fr.	37	3	4	7	18
Andrew Leutwiler	F	Fr.	22	0	3	3	6
Nate Strong	D	Sr.	1	0	0	0	10
Christopher Aishford	F	So.	2	0	0	0	4
Gasper Sekelj	D	So.	4	0	0	0	6
Andrew Gibson	G	Fr.	6	0	0	0	0
Chris Line	F	Fr.	14	0	0	0	12
Shawn Grant	G	Fr.	36	0	0	0	6

GOALTENDING

	Games	Min.	W	L	T	Goals	SO	Avg.
Andrew Gibson	6	157	0	1	0	8	0	3.05
Shawn Grant	36	2061	25	10	1	93	2	2.71

COLGATE RED RAIDERS

SCORING

	Pos.	Class	Games	G	A	Pts.	PIM
Andy McDonald	F	Jr.	35	20	26	46	42
Jed Whitchurch	F	Sr.	35	7	20	27	0
Darryl Campbell	F	Jr.	33	15	11	26	39
Cory Murphy	D	So.	34	3	23	26	26
Dan Wildfong	F	Sr.	35	9	16	25	54
Sean Nolan	F	So.	24	11	10	21	10
Michael Marostega	D	Jr.	35	6	14	20	2
Etienne Morin	F	Fr.	35	10	8	18	28
Chad MacDonald	F	So.	34	9	7	16	42
Tim Brokaw	F	Sr.	35	4	8	12	14
Kevin Johns	F	So.	31	3	8	11	22
Bryan Long	D	So.	25	5	5	10	22
Mike O'Malley	F	So.	20	2	6	8	14
Ryan Faubert	D	Sr.	32	2	6	8	14
Bob Vandersluis	F	Fr.	19	0	5	5	6
Mark Holdridge	D	Sr.	27	0	5	5	52
Shep Harder	G	Jr.	24	0	3	3	2
Jeff Potter	D	Jr.	34	0	3	3	18
Brian Owens	F	Sr.	32	2	0	2	38
Pat Varecka	F	So.	23	1	1	2	8
Byron Pool	D	Jr.	11	0	1	1	10
Jason Lefevre	G	Fr.	15	0	1	1	0
Sam Sturgis	F	So.	20	0	1	1	4
Chris Murray	G	Sr.	1	0	0	0	0
Dan Stay	F	So.	8	0	0	0	8
Ben Bryce	D	Fr.	13	0	0	0	22

GOALTENDING

	Games	Min.	W	L	T	Goals	SO	Avg.
Chris Murray	1	3	0	0	0	0	0	0.00
Jason Lefevre	15	745	4	5	3	32	1	2.58
Shep Harder	24	1395	15	7	1	53	1	2.28

CORNELL BIG RED

SCORING

	Pos.	Class	Games	G	A	Pts.	PIM
Kyle Knopp	F	Sr.	31	10	32	42	10
Denis Ladouceur	F	Fr.	31	14	14	28	16
Ryan Moynihan	F	Jr.	31	12	15	27	56
David Kozier	F	Fr.	30	11	13	24	32
Doug Stienstra	F	Jr.	31	12	11	23	30
Jeff Burgoyne	D	Sr.	29	4	18	22	20
Mike Rutter	F	Jr.	26	4	8	12	22
Dan Svoboda	F	So.	30	6	5	11	8
Frank Kovac	F	Jr.	31	5	6	11	60
Krzysztof Wieckowski	F	Fr.	31	3	6	9	20
Larry Pierce	D	So.	28	1	8	9	16
Jeff Oates	F	Sr.	25	5	3	8	38
David Hovey	F	So.	23	4	4	8	12
David Francis	F	Fr.	21	2	5	7	6
Tyler Sutherland	F	So.	18	2	3	5	16
Andrew McNiven	F	So.	17	1	4	5	40
Alex Gregory	D	Fr.	20	0	5	5	20
Danny Powell	D	So.	31	0	5	5	46
Rick Sacchetti	D	Jr.	22	0	4	4	48
Niels Heilmann	F	So.	6	0	1	1	0
David Adler	D	Jr.	19	0	1	1	22
Brian McMeekin	D	Fr.	26	0	1	1	12
Ian Burt	G	So.	12	0	0	0	17
Matt Underhill	G	Fr.	25	0	0	0	0

GOALTENDING

	Games	Min.	W	L	T	Goals	SO	Avg.
Matt Underhill	25	1320	7	10	4	65	1	2.95
Ian Burt	12	551	5	5	0	28	0	3.05

DARTMOUTH BIG GREEN

SCORING

	Pos.	Class	Games	G	A	Pts.	PIM
Mike Maturo	F	Fr.	29	9	16	25	20
Ryan Chaytors	F	Sr.	29	13	10	23	44
Jamie Herrington	F	Fr.	29	8	15	23	26
Christopher Baldwin	F	Fr.	28	6	17	23	20
Curtis Wilgosh	F	Sr.	29	10	12	22	34
Scott Peach	D	Sr.	24	6	12	18	44
Frank Nardella	F	Fr.	29	5	10	15	4
David Risk	D	Sr.	29	2	12	14	6
Michael Byrne	F	So.	28	6	5	11	8
Zach Hafer	F	Sr.	24	5	5	10	29
Dory Tisdale	D	So.	28	4	6	10	12
Chris Taliercio	F	Fr.	26	5	4	9	22
Ryan Poulton	D	Jr.	22	3	5	8	22
Ryan Burkart	D	Sr.	29	1	7	8	30
Dan Casella	F	Fr.	19	3	4	7	18
Craig Lund	F	Fr.	21	2	2	4	4
Shane Ness	D	Sr.	14	1	3	4	12
Matt Giedt	F	Sr.	17	0	4	4	16
Peter Mahler	F	So.	21	0	3	3	16
Gary Hunter	F	Fr.	10	1	1	2	4
Ryan Sinclair	F	Fr.	7	0	1	1	2
Carl Desjardins	D	Fr.	16	0	1	1	10
Eric Almon	G	Jr.	27	0	1	1	0
Dan Lehouillier	F	So.	2	0	0	0	2
Robert Delwo	G	Fr.	5	0	0	0	0
Pascal Lalonde	F	Fr.	12	0	0	0	8

GOALTENDING

	Games	Min.	W	L	T	Goals	SO	Avg.
Eric Almon	27	1543	9	15	2	92	0	3.58
Robert Delwo	5	212	1	2	0	16	0	4.53

HARVARD CRIMSON

SCORING

	Pos.	Class	Games	G	A	Pts.	PIM
Steve Moore	F	So.	30	18	13	31	34
Rob Millar	F	Sr.	32	10	17	27	23
Craig Adams	F	Sr.	31	9	14	23	53
Brett Chodorow	F	Jr.	31	9	10	19	30
Harry Schwefel	F	So.	31	5	13	18	20
Matt Scorsune	D	Sr.	31	8	9	17	34
Scott Turco	F	Jr.	32	5	12	17	10
Trevor Allman	F	Jr.	30	6	10	16	34
Chris Bala	F	So.	28	5	10	15	16
Ben Storey	D	Sr.	23	4	11	15	30
Jeff Stonehouse	F	Fr.	28	6	5	11	20
Peter Capouch	D	Fr.	31	3	3	6	16
Brice Conklin	F	Jr.	26	2	1	3	14
Graham Morrell	D	So.	29	1	2	3	39
Derek Nowak	F	Fr.	30	1	2	3	6
Mark Moore	D	Jr.	31	1	2	3	82
Kyle Clark	F	Fr.	20	0	2	2	30
Jared Cantanucci	F	Fr.	24	1	0	1	6
Matt MacLeod	F	Jr.	6	0	1	1	17
Tim Stay	D	So.	12	0	1	1	8
Leif Ericson	D	Fr.	14	0	1	1	8
Liam McCarthy	D	So.	23	0	1	1	18
Jamin Kerner	F	Jr.	1	0	0	0	0
Clayton Rodgers	F	Sr.	2	0	0	0	0
Oliver Jonas	G	So.	12	0	0	0	0
J.R. Prestifilippo	G	Jr.	24	0	0	0	2

GOALTENDING

	Games	Min.	W	L	T	Goals	SO	Avg.
Oliver Jonas	12	614	4	3	1	33	0	3.22
J.R. Prestifilippo	24	1316	10	13	1	78	0	3.56

PRINCETON TIGERS

SCORING

	Pos.	Class	Games	G	A	Pts.	PIM
Jeff Halpern	F	Sr.	33	22	22	44	32
Scott Bertoli	F	Sr.	34	13	23	36	74
Syl Apps	F	Sr.	34	13	21	34	45
Benoit Morin	F	Jr.	33	12	12	24	100
Steven Shirreffs	D	Sr.	27	2	17	19	39
Chris Corrinet	F	So.	32	10	6	16	38
Michael Acosta	D	Sr.	32	3	13	16	28
Shane Campbell	F	So.	32	4	10	14	28
Ethan Doyle	F	So.	33	7	4	11	24
Brad Meredith	D	Jr.	28	5	6	11	8
J.P. Acosta	F	So.	18	5	5	10	30
Kirk Lamb	F	So.	23	3	6	9	14
Brian Horst	F	Sr.	24	2	7	9	12
Jackson Hegland	D	Sr.	28	3	4	7	18
Darren Yopyk	D	Jr.	33	1	5	6	60
Brad Parsons	F	Fr.	19	3	2	5	2
Jason Given	F	Sr.	14	1	3	4	2
Rob Chisholm	F	Fr.	10	1	2	3	16
David Del Monte	F	Fr.	11	2	0	2	4
Josh Roberts	F	Fr.	23	1	1	2	10
David Schneider	D	Fr.	21	1	0	1	24
Chris Barber	D	Jr.	27	1	0	1	8
Nick Rankin	G	Sr.	13	0	1	1	0
David Bennett	D	Fr.	18	0	1	1	26
Dave Stathos	G	Fr.	22	0	1	1	0
Peter Zavodny	D	So.	24	0	1	1	16
Craig Bradley	G	Jr.	7	0	0	0	0

GOALTENDING

	Games	Min.	W	L	T	Goals	SO	Avg.
Craig Bradley	7	260	1	3	0	19	0	4.39
Nick Rankin	13	652	7	4	0	31	3	2.85
Dave Stathos	22	1139	12	5	2	55	0	2.90

RENSSELAER POLYTECHNIC INSTITUTE ENGINEERS

SCORING

	Pos.	Class	Games	G	A	Pts.	PIM
Danny Riva	F	Sr.	36	22	35	57	35
Matt Murley	F	Fr.	36	17	32	49	32
Alain St. Hilaire	F	Sr.	33	16	32	48	34
Mark Murphy	F	Sr.	37	11	30	41	76
Brad Tapper	F	So.	35	20	20	40	60
Pete Gardiner	F	Jr.	37	17	21	38	76
Doug Shepherd	F	Jr.	37	9	9	18	8
Brian Pothier	D	Jr.	37	5	13	18	36
Jared Reigstad	D	Jr.	37	7	10	17	52
Keith Dupee	F	Jr.	33	7	6	13	6
Steve Caley	F	Jr.	32	4	8	12	24
Andrew McPherson	F	Fr.	29	5	4	9	12
J.-Francois Gosselin	F	Sr.	29	3	6	9	20
Steve Munn	D	Fr.	36	1	7	8	50
Chris Migliore	F	Fr.	21	1	3	4	16
Jim Henkel	F	Fr.	20	0	4	4	14
Glenn Coupal	D	So.	31	0	4	4	28
Jim Vickers	D	Fr.	29	0	3	3	8
George Murray	D	Sr.	36	0	3	3	66
Hamish Cunning	D	Fr.	16	1	1	2	10
Erick James	F	Sr.	29	1	1	2	8
Scott Prekaski	G	Jr.	14	0	0	0	0
Joel Laing	G	Jr.	27	0	0	0	0

GOALTENDING

	Games	Min.	W	L	T	Goals	SO	Avg.
Joel Laing	27	1559	16	9	0	73	5	2.81
Scott Prekaski	14	683	7	3	2	37	1	3.25

ST. LAWRENCE SAINTS

SCORING

	Pos.	Class	Games	G	A	Pts.	PIM
Bob Prier	F	Sr.	37	20	26	46	50
John Poapst	F	Sr.	39	16	27	43	34
Erik Anderson	F	So.	39	10	30	40	18
Brandon Dietrich	F	Fr.	39	20	19	39	22
Justin Harney	D	Jr.	38	5	21	26	48
Al Fyfe	F	So.	37	13	12	25	30
Mike Gellard	F	So.	39	10	11	21	22
Jason Windle	F	Jr.	36	5	11	16	8
Dale Clarke	D	Jr.	39	3	13	16	44
Matt Oikawa	F	Sr.	35	6	8	14	14
Ray DiLauro	D	Fr.	35	4	8	12	12
Matt Desrosiers	D	So.	39	3	9	12	24
Robin Carruthers	F	Fr.	28	6	5	11	8
Victor Natali	F	So.	19	7	2	9	6
Charlie Daniels	F	Fr.	26	3	4	7	12
Josh LeRoy	D	Jr.	37	1	6	7	34
Sean Muir	F	Fr.	30	2	2	4	31
Ryan Ward	F	Jr.	15	1	3	4	14
Kevin Veneruzzo	D	So.	28	0	4	4	20
Kris Margherio	F	Jr.	18	1	1	2	12
Mike Muir	F	Fr.	27	0	2	2	8
Ben Blais	D	Fr.	3	0	1	1	6
Eric Heffler	G	Sr.	37	0	1	1	4
Mike McCabe	F	Jr.	1	0	0	0	0
Andy Marchetti	F	So.	2	0	0	0	2
Sean Coakley	G	So.	2	0	0	0	0
Jeremy Symington	G	So.	3	0	0	0	0
Jake Harney	D	Jr.	16	0	0	0	12

GOALTENDING

	Games	Min.	W	L	T	Goals	SO	Avg.
Eric Heffler	37	2206	22	12	3	88	3	2.39
J. Symington	3	128	1	1	0	7	0	3.27
Sean Coakley	2	27	0	0	0	4	0	8.89

UNION SKATING DUTCHMEN

SCORING

	Pos.	Class	Games	G	A	Pts.	PIM
Mark Szucs	F	Sr.	30	9	5	14	39
Ryan Campbell	F	Jr.	32	5	6	11	48
Dave Smith	F	So.	25	4	6	10	10
Jeff Sproat	D	Jr.	25	2	8	10	8
Drew Taylor	F	Fr.	23	1	9	10	0
Jeff Wilson	F	Fr.	27	8	1	9	30
Joel Bond	D	Sr.	29	3	4	7	8
Jason Ralph	F	So.	25	4	2	6	28
Bryant Westerman	F	So.	27	2	4	6	58
Bryan Yackel	F	So.	32	3	2	5	52
Alex Todd	D	So.	25	2	3	5	44
Mason Anderson	F	So.	18	3	1	4	20
Brent Ozarowski	F	Sr.	30	2	2	4	8
Jeff Hutchins	F	Fr.	19	1	3	4	20
Charles Simard	D	Fr.	14	0	4	4	6
Clark Jones	F	So.	26	0	4	4	18
Doug Christiansen	D	Fr.	18	0	3	3	38
Ryan Boyd	D	Sr.	25	2	0	2	42
Jay Varady	F	So.	30	1	1	2	46
Seamus Galligan	F	Fr.	16	0	2	2	20
Sheldon Pietrzykowski	F	So.	22	0	2	2	2
Paul Kilfoy	D	So.	18	0	1	1	28
Mark Will	D	Sr.	20	0	1	1	12
Frederic Cyr	D	Fr.	20	0	1	1	18
Jeff Movshin	G	So.	1	0	0	0	0
Leeor Shtrom	G	Sr.	16	0	0	0	30
Brandon Snee	G	Fr.	19	0	0	0	0

GOALTENDING

	Games	Min.	W	L	T	Goals	SO	Avg.
Leeor Shtrom	16	917	2	14	0	69	0	4.51
Brandon Snee	19	1011	1	12	3	59	1	3.50
Jeff Movshin	1	3	0	0	0	0	0	0.00

VERMONT CATAMOUNTS

SCORING

	Pos.	Class	Games	G	A	Pts.	PIM
Kevin Karlander	F	Jr.	32	12	10	22	44
Stephane Piche	F	Sr.	31	5	16	21	30
Andreas Moborg	D	So.	33	2	18	20	24
Matt Sanders	F	Jr.	33	13	6	19	34
Jason Reid	D	Sr.	30	7	12	19	54
Philippe Choiniere	F	So.	33	9	9	18	55
B.J. Kilbourne	F	Sr.	31	6	12	18	38
Don Richardson	F	Fr.	32	7	8	15	14
Eric Lundin	F	Sr.	32	7	7	14	22
Martin Wilde	D	So.	33	1	13	14	22
J.-Francois Caudron	F	So.	29	3	10	13	14
Jerry Gernander	F	So.	31	1	6	7	24
Graham Mink	F	Fr.	27	4	2	6	34
Mark Gouett	D	Fr.	33	3	3	6	28
Mike Torney	D	So.	32	2	4	6	42
Ryan Cox	F	Fr.	26	4	1	5	6
Jim Gernander	D	So.	33	0	5	5	20
Joe Flammia	D	Fr.	8	0	2	2	2
Chris Hills	F	Fr.	12	0	1	1	4
Benoit Lampron	F	Jr.	22	0	1	1	0
Shaun Hakala	F	Sr.	1	0	0	0	0
Tim Peters	G	Fr.	3	0	0	0	0
Marty Phillips	G	Sr.	13	0	0	0	0
Isaac Gilbert	F	Sr.	20	0	0	0	20
Andrew Allen	G	So.	24	0	0	0	0

GOALTENDING

	Games	Min.	W	L	T	Goals	SO	Avg.
Marty Phillips	13	640	5	5	0	38	2	3.56
Tim Peters	3	53	0	0	0	7	0	7.88
Andrew Allen	24	1296	8	13	2	56	1	2.59

YALE BULLDOGS

SCORING

	Pos.	Class	Games	G	A	Pts.	PIM
Jeff Hamilton	F	Jr.	30	20	28	48	51
Jeff Brow	F	Jr.	28	16	22	38	22
Jay Quenville	F	Jr.	31	7	15	22	10
Keith McCullough	F	Sr.	31	6	11	17	50
Ben Stafford	F	So.	27	5	8	13	6
Francois Magnant	D	Sr.	31	4	8	12	46
Joe Dart	D	So.	31	2	10	12	10
Cory Shea	F	Jr.	27	5	5	10	46
Keith Fitzpatrick	D	Jr.	30	1	9	10	26
Mark Turco	F	Sr.	31	7	2	9	10
Paul Lawson	F	Jr.	30	5	3	8	26
Mark Sproule	F	Jr.	31	1	5	6	26
Luke Earl	F	Fr.	17	1	4	5	6
Lee Jelenic	F	So.	22	0	4	4	16
Spencer Rodgers	F	Fr.	25	2	1	3	26
James Chyz	D	Jr.	29	1	2	3	40
Adam Sauve	F	So.	15	1	1	2	4
Christian Peterson	F	Sr.	17	1	1	2	6
Jim Morrissey	D	Sr.	22	0	2	2	30
Peter Toomey	F	So.	4	1	0	1	2
Dan Lombard	G	Fr.	2	0	0	0	0
Jason Noe	F	Fr.	3	0	0	0	0
Gabe Polsky	F	Fr.	3	0	0	0	0
David Sproule	D	Fr.	4	0	0	0	2
Trevor Hanger	G	Jr.	6	0	0	0	0
John Gauger	D	So.	17	0	0	0	41
Robert Mutter	D	Fr.	22	0	0	0	8
Alex Westlund	G	Sr.	28	0	0	0	0

GOALTENDING

	Games	Min.	W	L	T	Goals	SO	Avg.
Trevor Hanger	6	191	0	2	0	12	0	3.77
Dan Lombard	2	54	1	0	0	1	0	1.11
Alex Westlund	28	1630	12	12	4	79	0	2.91

HOCKEY EAST

1998-99 SEASON

FINAL STANDINGS

Team	G	W	L	T	Pts.	GF	GA
New Hamp. (31-7-3)....	24	18	3	3	39	100	49
Maine (31-6-4)............	24	17	5	2	36	96	64
Boston Col. (27-12-4)..	24	15	7	2	32	99	73
Providence (20-17-1)...	24	12	11	1	25	90	81
Boston U. (14-20-3)	24	8	13	3	19	72	86
Mass. (12-21-2)..........	24	8	14	2	18	56	86
Lowell (17-19-0)..........	24	9	15	0	18	65	85
Merrimack (11-24-1) ...	24	7	16	1	15	67	94
Northeastern (11-20-3).	24	6	16	2	14	74	101

Overall record in parentheses.

PLAYOFF RESULTS

QUARTERFINALS

Maine 3, Massachusetts 1
Maine 5, Massachusetts 2
(Maine won series, 2-0)

Boston College 5, Lowell 0
Boston College 5, Lowell 4
(Boston College won series, 2-0)

New Hampshire 3, Merrimack 2
New Hampshire 5, Merrimack 4
(New Hampshire won series, 2-0)

Providence 8, Boston University 2
Boston University 8, Providence 2
Providence 5, Boston University 1
(Providence won series, 2-1)

SEMIFINALS

New Hampshire 6, Providence 2
Boston College 3, Maine 2

CHAMPIONSHIP GAME

Boston College 5, New Hampshire 4 (OT)

ALL-STAR TEAM

First team	Pos.	Second team
Michel Larocque, Boston U.	G	Ty Conklin, N. Hampshire
Jayme Filipowicz, N. Hamp.	D	Mike Mottau, Boston College
David Cullen, Maine	D	Anthony Cappelletti, Lowell
Jason Krog, New Hampshire	F	Rejean Stringer, Merrimack
Steve Kariya, Maine	F	Mike Omicioli, Providence
Brian Gionta, Boston College	F	Darren Haydar, N. Hampshire

AWARD WINNERS

Player of the year: Jason Krog, New Hampshire
Rookie of the year: Darren Haydar, New Hampshire
Coach of the year: Richard Umile, New Hampshire
Leading scorer: Jason Krog, New Hampshire
Playoff MVP: Blake Bellefeuille, Boston College

INDIVIDUAL LEADERS

Goals: Jason Krog, New Hampshire (34)
Assists: Jason Krog, New Hampshire (51)
Points: Jason Krog, New Hampshire (85)
Penalty minutes: Brooks Orpik, Boston College (96)
Goaltending average: Ty Conklin, New Hampshire (1.84)

TOP SCORERS

	Games	G	A	Pts.
Jason Krog, New Hampshire............	41	34	51	85
Steve Kariya, Maine..........................	41	27	38	65
Mike Souza, New Hampshire	41	23	42	65
Darren Haydar, New Hampshire........	41	31	30	61
Brian Gionta, Boston College.............	39	27	33	60
Jeff Farkas, Boston College...............	43	32	25	57
Rejean Stringer, Merrimack..............	36	17	39	56
Cory Larose, Maine	38	21	31	52
Jerry Keefe, Providence.....................	35	16	36	52
Fernando Pisani, Providence.............	38	14	37	51

INDIVIDUAL STATISTICS

BOSTON COLLEGE EAGLES

SCORING

	Pos.	Class	Games	G	A	Pts.	PIM
Brian Gionta	F	So.	39	27	33	60	46
Jeff Farkas	F	Jr.	43	32	25	57	56
Blake Bellefeuille	F	Jr.	43	24	25	49	80
Mike Mottau.............	D	Jr.	43	3	39	42	44
Chris Masters...........	F	Sr.	43	16	23	39	50
Bobby Allen..............	D	So.	43	9	23	32	34
Mike Lephart............	F	So.	36	11	16	27	28
Andy Powers............	F	Sr.	43	13	12	25	52
Jeff Giuliano.............	F	Fr.	43	5	15	20	10
Kevin Caulfield	F	Jr.	41	8	8	16	81
Brendan Buckley	D	Sr.	43	1	13	14	75
Tony Hutchins..........	F	Jr.	39	4	9	13	42
Nick Pierandri	F	Sr.	43	3	10	13	12
Matt Mulhern	F	Sr.	43	4	7	11	22
Marty Hughes	D	So.	43	3	8	11	51
Brooks Orpik............	D	Fr.	41	1	10	11	96
Rob Scuderi	D	So.	41	2	8	10	20
Alex Dolinar	F	Fr.	38	3	5	8	8
Cory Bilodeau	F	Jr.	8	1	1	2	0
Mark McLennan.......	F	So.	18	0	1	1	6
Andy McLaughlin.....	G	Sr.	1	0	0	0	0
Mike Correia............	G	Sr.	3	0	0	0	0
Scott Clemmensen...	G	So.	42	0	0	0	4

GOALTENDING

	Games	Min.	W	L	T	Goals	SO	Avg.
A. McLaughlin....	1	30	0	0	0	1	0	2.02
Mike Correia	3	63	1	0	0	3	0	2.85
S. Clemmensen..	42	2507	26	12	4	120	1	2.87

BOSTON UNIVERSITY TERRIERS

SCORING

	Pos.	Class	Games	G	A	Pts.	PIM
Albie O'Connell	F	Sr.	36	9	30	39	66
Chris Heron..............	F	Jr.	36	18	17	35	28
Russ Bartlett	F	So.	35	12	20	32	18
Carl Corazzini	F	So.	37	15	9	24	12
Tommi Degerman	F	Jr.	27	12	9	21	24
Nick Gillis.................	F	So.	33	3	16	19	37
Bobby Hanson	F	Jr.	34	5	13	18	16
Juha Vuori	F	So.	35	4	14	18	40
Mike Pandolfo..........	F	Fr.	34	13	4	17	26
Joe DiPenta..............	D	So.	36	2	15	17	72

	Pos.	Class	Games	G	A	Pts.	PIM
Dan Cavanaugh	F	Fr.	36	6	8	14	60
Jack Baker	F	Fr.	31	6	7	13	40
Scott Perry	F	So.	33	4	8	12	26
Dan Ronan	D	Sr.	37	0	10	10	78
Pat Aufiero	D	Fr.	22	3	4	7	14
Greg Quebec	F	Jr.	33	3	4	7	22
Chris Dyment	D	Fr.	25	1	5	6	18
Colin Sheen	D	So.	33	1	4	5	26
Dave LoPresti	D	Fr.	12	0	1	1	10
Mike DiMella	F	Fr.	26	0	1	1	16
Bob Weston	F	So.	3	0	0	0	2
Jason Tapp	G	Fr.	6	0	0	0	0
Keith Emery	D	So.	29	0	0	0	16
Michel Larocque	G	Sr.	35	0	0	0	30

GOALTENDING

	Games	Min.	W	L	T	Goals	SO	Avg.
M. Larocque	35	2072	14	18	3	117	0	3.39
Jason Tapp	6	161	0	2	0	12	0	4.46

LOWELL RIVER HAWKS

SCORING

	Pos.	Class	Games	G	A	Pts.	PIM
John Campbell	F	Jr.	36	11	25	36	18
Chris Bell	F	Jr.	36	15	18	33	18
Anthony Cappelletti	D	Sr.	36	13	19	32	56
Jeff Boulanger	F	So.	34	14	8	22	48
Brad Rooney	F	So.	34	4	17	21	60
Kevin Bertram	D	Jr.	35	6	13	19	54
Jeremy Kyte	F	So.	30	5	12	17	12
Doug Nolan	F	Sr.	25	8	5	13	41
Mike Mulligan	F	Sr.	36	6	7	13	30
Yorick Trielle	F	Fr.	32	6	5	11	24
Kevin Kotyluk	D	Fr.	36	3	8	11	48
Dan Fontas	F	So.	29	6	4	10	30
Kyle Kidney	F	So.	30	3	7	10	58
Tom Rouleau	F	Fr.	34	4	4	8	28
Craig Brown	F	Jr.	31	4	3	7	26
Chris Gustafson	D	Fr.	33	1	6	7	33
Josh Allison	D	Fr.	34	0	7	7	47
Mark Fontas	D	So.	22	1	4	5	6
Wil Tormey	D	Sr.	25	1	4	5	12
Nicholas Carso	F	So.	18	1	1	2	4
Sean Storozuk	F	Jr.	9	0	2	2	12
Jason Savageau	D	So.	10	0	1	1	2
Brendan Hynes	G	Fr.	1	0	0	0	0
Andrew Korzen	F	Fr.	1	0	0	0	0
R.J. Tolan	F	Fr.	4	0	0	0	2
Jimi St. John	G	Fr.	9	0	0	0	0
Scott Fankhouser	G	Sr.	32	0	0	0	2

GOALTENDING

	Games	Min.	W	L	T	Goals	SO	Avg.
Brendan Hynes	1	4	0	0	0	0	0	0.00
S. Fankhouser	32	1729	9	12	0	80	1	2.78
Jimi St. John	9	424	0	3	0	34	0	4.82

MAINE BLACK BEARS

SCORING

	Pos.	Class	Games	G	A	Pts.	PIM
Steve Kariya	F	Sr.	41	27	38	65	24
Cory Larose	F	Jr.	38	21	31	52	34
David Cullen	D	Sr.	41	11	33	44	24
Dan Kerluke	F	So.	41	23	19	42	18
Marcus Gustafsson	F	Sr.	41	13	15	28	16
Barrett Heisten	F	Fr.	34	12	16	28	72
Ben Guite	F	Jr.	40	12	16	28	30
Niko Dimitrakos	F	Fr.	35	8	19	27	33
Peter Metcalf	D	Fr.	33	6	17	23	34
Brendan Walsh	F	Jr.	30	7	13	20	58
Doug Janik	D	Fr.	35	3	13	16	44
Bobby Stewart	F	Sr.	31	8	5	13	28
Anders Lundback	F	So.	41	1	11	12	20
Matthias Trattnig	F	So.	39	5	5	10	32
Ed Wood	D	Fr.	21	1	9	10	10
Jim Leger	F	Jr.	41	5	2	7	4
Tuomo Jaaskelainen	F	So.	25	1	5	6	14
Robert Ek	D	Jr.	39	0	6	6	44
Jason Vitorino	F	Sr.	35	2	1	3	34
Magnus Lundback	F	So.	13	1	2	3	2
Eric Turgeon	D	So.	12	0	2	2	4
A.J. Begg	F	So.	26	0	2	2	26
Alfie Michaud	G	Jr.	37	0	1	1	0
Adam Tate	D	So.	5	0	0	0	4
Mike Morrison	G	Fr.	11	0	0	0	0

GOALTENDING

	Games	Min.	W	L	T	Goals	SO	Avg.
Mike Morrison	11	347	3	0	1	10	1	1.73
Alfie Michaud	37	2147	28	6	3	83	3	2.32

MASSACHUSETTS MINUTEMEN

SCORING

	Pos.	Class	Games	G	A	Pts.	PIM
Jeff Blanchard	F	Jr.	35	11	16	27	42
Jeff Turner	F	So.	34	9	13	22	22
Dean Stork	D	Jr.	34	9	7	16	44
Nathan Sell	F	Jr.	35	10	4	14	32
Kris Wallis	F	So.	35	5	9	14	22
Ray Geever	F	So.	29	4	10	14	30
Martin Miljko	F	Fr.	28	3	9	12	16
R.J. Gates	F	So.	34	2	9	11	59
Nick Stephens	F	So.	33	7	3	10	47
Jay Shaw	F	So.	34	3	6	9	24
Toni Soderholm	D	Fr.	35	1	8	9	64
Bryan Kennedy	F	Jr.	33	3	5	8	8
Joey Culgin	D	So.	35	3	5	8	42
Bryan Fitzgerald	F	Sr.	29	2	6	8	23
Darcy King	F	Fr.	29	3	4	7	8
Randy Drohan	D	Fr.	32	2	4	6	62
Kevin Poulin	F	Jr.	16	0	5	5	2
Chris Brannen	D	Fr.	35	1	3	4	34
Jedd Crumb	F	Fr.	15	2	1	3	6
Brendan Shaw	D	Sr.	4	0	0	0	0
Dmitri Vasiliev	F	Jr.	6	0	0	0	0
Mike Johnson	G	Fr.	9	0	0	0	0
Kevin Tucker	D	So.	13	0	0	0	6
Justin Shaw	D	Fr.	19	0	0	0	16
Markus Helanen	G	So.	31	0	0	0	10

GOALTENDING

	Games	Min.	W	L	T	Goals	SO	Avg.
Mike Johnson	9	298	2	3	0	13	2	2.62
Markus Helanen	31	1808	10	18	2	100	0	3.32

MERRIMACK WARRIORS

SCORING

	Pos.	Class	Games	G	A	Pts.	PIM
Rejean Stringer	F	Sr.	36	17	39	56	44
Kris Porter	F	Sr.	36	24	21	45	48
Greg Classen	F	Fr.	36	14	11	25	28
John Pyliotis	F	So.	35	4	18	22	24
Sandy Cohen	F	Jr.	34	6	14	20	26
Chris Halecki	F	Jr.	36	6	13	19	20
Drew Halecki	D	Jr.	36	6	12	18	20
Jayson Philbin	F	Jr.	36	2	13	15	32
Vince Clevenger	F	So.	35	6	7	13	20
Ryan Kiley	F	Fr.	30	5	5	10	38
Nick Parillo	F	Fr.	33	3	7	10	10
Tony White	D	Jr.	31	2	8	10	28
Nick Torretti	F	Fr.	29	4	3	7	10
Joey Gray	F	So.	25	3	4	7	25
Andrew Fox	D	Jr.	33	1	6	7	14
Stephen Moon	D	So.	15	3	3	6	25

	Pos.	Class	Games	G	A	Pts.	PIM
Mike Rodrigues	D	Jr.	32	0	4	4	12
Tom Welby	G	So.	30	0	2	2	10
Brad Mills	D	Fr.	23	1	0	1	10
Ron Mongeau	F	So.	16	0	1	1	4
Tim Foster	D	Fr.	29	0	1	1	16
David Brien	D	Fr.	0	0	0	0	0
Joe Savioli	F	So.	0	0	0	0	0
John Kovalsky	F	Jr.	2	0	0	0	0
Roland Sperlich	G	So.	2	0	0	0	0
Jason Wolfe	G	Fr.	2	0	0	0	0
Julien Jorgensen	F	So.	3	0	0	0	2
Fred Nelson	F	So.	6	0	0	0	2
Cris Classen	G	Jr.	9	0	0	0	0
Roland Grelle	D	Sr.	20	0	0	0	35

GOALTENDING

	Games	Min.	W	L	T	Goals	SO	Avg.
Tom Welby	30	1721	9	20	1	102	0	3.56
Cris Classen	9	385	2	4	0	26	0	4.05
Roland Sperlich	2	15	0	0	0	1	0	4.08
Jason Wolfe	2	40	0	0	0	5	0	7.58

NEW HAMPSHIRE WILDCATS

SCORING

	Pos.	Class	Games	G	A	Pts.	PIM
Jason Krog	F	Sr.	41	34	51	85	38
Mike Souza	F	Jr.	41	23	42	65	38
Darren Haydar	F	Fr.	41	31	30	61	34
Jayme Filipowicz	D	Jr.	41	8	30	38	56
Steve O'Brien	D	Sr.	41	4	27	31	20
Jason Shipulski	F	Jr.	41	15	14	29	12
Corey-Joe Ficek	F	So.	40	10	7	17	43
John Sadowski	F	Jr.	41	7	9	16	58
Christian Bragnalo	D	Sr.	41	2	14	16	63
Matt Swain	F	So.	30	9	6	15	10
Chad Onufrechuk	F	Sr.	41	5	10	15	32
Ryan Cordeiro	F	Fr.	39	4	10	14	20
Johnny Rogers	F	So.	36	3	10	13	18
Eric Lind	D	So.	41	3	9	12	20
Dan Enders	D	Jr.	29	3	6	9	22
Tim Walsh	F	Jr.	39	2	7	9	16
Matt Dzieduszycki	F	Fr.	29	2	6	8	34
David Busch	F	Fr.	28	3	1	4	8
Mark White	D	So.	34	1	2	3	16
Sean Austin	D	So.	16	1	1	2	6
Ryan Harris	F	Sr.	6	0	2	2	4
Brendon McEniry	D	Jr.	3	0	1	1	6
Sean Matile	G	Sr.	19	0	1	1	0
Ty Conklin	G	So.	22	0	1	1	2
Michael Filardo	G	So.	3	0	0	0	0

GOALTENDING

	Games	Min.	W	L	T	Goals	SO	Avg.
Ty Conklin	22	1338	18	3	1	41	0	1.84
Sean Matile	19	1143	13	4	2	47	0	2.47
Michael Filardo	3	13	0	0	0	2	0	9.57

NORTHEASTERN HUSKIES

SCORING

	Pos.	Class	Games	G	A	Pts.	PIM
Todd Barclay	F	Jr.	31	19	12	31	20
Roger Holeczy	F	Jr.	34	4	25	29	24
Chris Lynch	F	Fr.	28	10	14	24	36
Graig Mischler	F	So.	33	8	15	23	36
Willie Levesque	F	Fr.	34	12	10	22	38
Mike Jozefowicz	D	So.	31	5	17	22	14
Billy Newson	F	Jr.	26	7	13	20	34
Jim Fahey	D	Fr.	32	5	13	18	34
Ryan Zoller	F	Fr.	30	7	6	13	28
John Peterman	D	So.	30	6	7	13	40
Brian Cummings	F	So.	34	5	8	13	50
Matt Brown	D	So.	29	4	5	9	40
Rich Spiller	D	Fr.	32	2	7	9	44
Bob Haglund	F	So.	27	3	5	8	31
Bobby Davis	F	Jr.	26	3	4	7	6
Sean MacDonald	F	So.	30	2	4	6	8
Leon Hayward	F	Fr.	27	3	1	4	22
Kevin Welch	F	So.	20	1	3	4	20
Matt Keating	F	So.	20	0	3	3	18
Doug Carlson	D	So.	17	1	1	2	4
Brent Thomas	F	Sr.	13	1	0	1	24
Scott Sutton	G	Fr.	6	0	1	1	2
Jason Braun	G	Fr.	30	0	1	1	0
Dan Calore	G	So.	2	0	0	0	0
Joe Mancuso	D	Fr.	24	0	0	0	22

GOALTENDING

	Games	Min.	W	L	T	Goals	SO	Avg.
Jason Braun	30	1728	10	17	3	104	1	3.61
Scott Sutton	6	290	1	2	0	22	0	4.55
Dan Calore	2	40	0	1	0	5	0	7.58

PROVIDENCE FRIARS

SCORING

	Pos.	Class	Games	G	A	Pts.	PIM
Jerry Keefe	F	Jr.	35	16	36	52	34
Fernando Pisani	F	Jr.	38	14	37	51	42
Mike Omicioli	F	Sr.	38	19	31	50	50
Josh MacNevin	D	Jr.	36	6	29	35	52
Troy Lake	F	Sr.	38	19	14	33	48
Doug Sheppard	F	Jr.	38	15	14	29	16
Jason Ialongo	D	Jr.	37	11	18	29	24
Jon Cameron	F	Sr.	36	8	17	25	77
Jon Coe	F	Sr.	37	9	15	24	46
Drew Omicioli	F	Fr.	33	8	9	17	54
Heath Gordon	F	So.	30	7	10	17	16
Mike Farrell	D	So.	29	3	12	15	51
Nick Lent	F	Jr.	36	8	3	11	31
Matt Libby	D	So.	37	4	5	9	45
Leigh Dean	D	Jr.	26	3	6	9	26
Jay Leach	D	So.	33	1	8	9	42
Marc Suderman	F	Fr.	33	2	6	8	10
Cole Gendreau	F	So.	29	3	2	5	23
Rich Miller	D	Jr.	13	1	3	4	12
Adam Lee	F	So.	20	1	2	3	18
Dave Gunderson	D	Jr.	19	0	3	3	12
J.J. Picinic	F	So.	8	1	1	2	0
Josh Faulkner	F	Fr.	4	0	1	1	0
Mark Kane	G	Sr.	16	0	0	0	10
Boyd Ballard	G	So.	28	0	0	0	2

GOALTENDING

	Games	Min.	W	L	T	Goals	SO	Avg.
Mark Kane	16	765	6	5	0	38	0	2.98
Boyd Ballard	28	1516	14	12	1	92	1	3.64

WESTERN COLLEGIATE HOCKEY ASSOCIATION

1998-99 SEASON

FINAL STANDINGS

Team	G	W	L	T	Pts.	GF	GA
N. Dakota (32-6-2)	28	24	2	2	50	142	76
Colorado C. (29-12-1)	28	20	8	0	40	103	68
Denver (26-13-2)	28	15	11	2	32	101	95
Wisconsin (15-19-4)	28	13	12	3	29	76	81
Minnesota (15-19-9)	28	10	12	6	26	90	99
A'ka-Anch. (13-18-5)	28	10	13	5	25	57	71
St. Cloud St. (16-18-5)	28	8	16	4	20	79	95
Mich. Tech (9-28-1)	28	9	19	0	18	67	99
M.-Duluth (7-27-4)	28	4	20	4	12	71	102

Overall record in parentheses.

PLAYOFF RESULTS

FIRST ROUND

Mankato State 3, North Dakota 2 (OT)
North Dakota 3, Mankato State 2
North Dakota 10, Mankato State 0
(North Dakota won series, 2-1)
Minnesota 4, Alaska-Anchorage 0
Minnesota 1, Alaska-Anchorage 0
(Minnesota won series, 2-0)
Colorado College 3, Minnesota-Duluth 1
Colorado College 5, Minnesota-Duluth 4
(Colorado College won series, 2-0)
St. Cloud State 5, Wisconsin 2
St. Cloud State 3, Wisconsin 2
(St. Cloud State won series, 2-0)
Denver 2, Michigan Tech 1
Denver 4, Michigan Tech 2
(Denver won series, 2-0)

PLAY-IN GAME

Minnesota 5, St. Cloud State 3

SEMIFINALS

Denver 3, Colorado College 2 (OT)
North Dakota 6, Minnesota 2

CONSOLATION GAME

Colorado College 7, Minnesota 4

FINALS

Denver 4, North Dakota 3

ALL-STAR TEAMS

First team	Pos.	Second team
Gregg Naumenko, A'ka-Anch.	G	Karl Goehring, North Dakota
Scott Swanson, Colorado C.	D	Dan Peters, Colorado College
Brad Williamson, N. Dakota	D	Trevor Hammer, N. Dakota
Brian Swanson, Colorado Col.	F	Jay Panzer, North Dakota
Jason Blake, North Dakota	F	Darren Clark, Colorado Col.
Paul Comrie, Denver	F	Jeff Panzer, North Dakota

AWARD WINNERS

Player of the year: Jason Blake, North Dakota
Rookie of the year: Gregg Naumenko, Alaska-Anchorage
Coach of the year: Dean Blais, North Dakota
Leading scorer: Jason Blake, North Dakota
Playoff MVP: Stephen Wagner, Denver

INDIVIDUAL LEADERS

Goals: Jason Blake, North Dakota (28)
Assists: Jason Blake, North Dakota (41)
Brian Swanson, Colorado College (41)
Scott Swanson, Colorado College (41)
Points: Jason Blake, North Dakota (69)
Penalty minutes: Mike Commodore, North Dakota (154)
Goaltending average: Gregg Naumenko, Alaska-Anch. (2.31)

TOP SCORERS

	Games	G	A	Pts.
Jason Blake, North Dakota	38	28	41	69
Brian Swanson, Colorado College	42	25	41	66
Jay Panzer, North Dakota	39	21	33	54
Scott Swanson, Colorado College	42	11	41	52
Paul Comrie, Denver	40	18	31	49
Reggie Berg, Minnesota	43	20	28	48
Jeff Panzer, North Dakota	39	21	26	47
Brad Williamson, North Dakota	40	10	37	47
Lee Goren, North Dakota	38	26	19	45
James Patterson, Denver	41	24	21	45

INDIVIDUAL STATISTICS

ALASKA-ANCHORAGE SEAWOLVES

SCORING

	Pos.	Class	Games	G	A	Pts.	PIM
Rob Douglas	F	Jr.	35	12	7	19	28
Steve Cygan	F	Fr.	36	12	6	18	20
Mike Scott	F	Fr.	35	7	11	18	37
Gregg Zaporzan	F	Fr.	29	3	12	15	12
Jeff Carlson	F	Fr.	35	2	12	14	8
Klage Kaebel	F	Jr.	32	7	6	13	0
Clayton Read	F	Sr.	36	6	7	13	20
Chris Pont	F	Sr.	27	7	5	12	8
Matt Williams	D	Jr.	31	4	4	8	10
Eric Lawson	D	Fr.	36	2	5	7	12
Ted Suihkonen	F	So.	35	1	5	6	12
Corey Hessler	D	Fr.	33	3	2	5	20
Matt Mathias	F	Fr.	26	2	3	5	4
Reggie Simon	F	Jr.	34	2	3	5	16
Chris Sikich	F	So.	35	2	3	5	10
Eric Tuott	F	Sr.	10	0	4	4	2
Mark Leitner	D	So.	32	1	2	3	4
Marc Charbonneau	D	Sr.	33	1	2	3	16
Jon Maruk	F	So.	24	0	3	3	2
Steve Ludwig	D	So.	35	0	3	3	10
Curt Malin	F	So.	7	0	1	1	4
Doug Teskey	G	Sr.	8	0	1	1	0
Mark Filipenko	D	Jr.	10	0	1	1	2
Gregg Naumenko	G	Fr.	29	0	1	1	2
Pete Brady	G	So.	1	0	0	0	0
Randy Enders	D	Fr.	2	0	0	0	2

GOALTENDING

	Games	Min.	W	L	T	Goals	SO	Avg.
Gregg Naumenko	29	1692	11	13	5	65	1	2.31
Doug Teskey	8	461	2	5	0	23	1	3.00
Pete Brady	1	34	0	0	0	3	0	5.46

COLORADO COLLEGE TIGERS

SCORING

	Pos.	Class	Games	G	A	Pts.	PIM
Brian Swanson	F	Sr.	42	25	41	66	28
Scott Swanson	D	Sr.	42	11	41	52	16
Darren Clark	F	Sr.	29	17	23	40	38
Jesse Heerema	F	Fr.	42	15	24	39	20
Justin Morrison	F	So.	38	23	15	38	33
Mark Cullen	F	Fr.	42	8	25	33	22
Jon Austin	F	Sr.	32	11	20	31	20
Dan Peters	D	Jr.	36	8	21	29	82
Toby Petersen	F	Jr.	21	12	12	24	2
Cam Kryway	F	Jr.	41	8	12	20	54
Mike Stuart	D	Fr.	40	2	12	14	44
Paul Manning	D	So.	41	3	10	13	75
Aaron Karpan	F	Jr.	37	6	5	11	10
Chris Hartsburg	F	Fr.	34	6	4	10	60
Trent Clark	F	Fr.	41	3	6	9	20
Ian Petersen	F	Jr.	35	4	3	7	12
Berk Nelson	F/D	Jr.	31	1	6	7	61
Paul Johnson	D	Sr.	42	1	5	6	30
Jeff Sanger	G	Fr.	36	0	4	4	2
K.J. Voorhees	F	Jr.	16	3	0	3	12
Shaun Winkler	F	Fr.	21	2	0	2	14
Brent Voorhees	D	So.	13	0	1	1	2
Mike Colgan	D	So.	40	0	1	1	20
Todd Gustin	G	Sr.	1	0	0	0	0
Colin Zulianello	G	So.	9	0	0	0	0

GOALTENDING

	Games	Min.	W	L	T	Goals	SO	Avg.
Todd Gustin	1	20	0	0	0	0	0	0.00
Jeff Sanger	36	2102	23	12	1	89	3	2.54
Colin Zulianello	9	419	6	0	0	20	0	2.87

DENVER PIONEERS

SCORING

	Pos.	Class	Games	G	A	Pts.	PIM
Paul Comrie	F	Sr.	40	18	31	49	84
James Patterson	F	Sr.	41	24	21	45	48
Mark Rycroft	F	So.	41	19	18	37	36
Bjorn Engstrom	F	So.	41	16	18	34	24
Gavin Morgan	F	Sr.	40	13	16	29	85
Joe Ritson	D	Jr.	34	8	13	21	22
Kelly Popadynetz	F	So.	41	9	11	20	36
Matt Pettinger	F	Fr.	38	6	14	20	52
Erik Adams	D	Fr.	37	3	15	18	8
Jon Newman	F	Jr.	37	8	9	17	28
Joe Murphy	F	Sr.	33	3	13	16	25
Todd Kidd	D	Sr.	38	3	12	15	60
Paul Veres	F	Sr.	33	8	6	14	16
Jesse Cook	D	Fr.	33	0	10	10	22
Bryce Wallnutt	F	Jr.	26	6	3	9	34
Chris Paradise	F	Fr.	32	5	4	9	31
Judd Stauss	D	So.	34	2	7	9	22
Ryan Hacker	D	Sr.	35	1	8	9	58
Shawn Kurulak	D	Sr.	36	1	5	6	54
Stephen Wagner	G	Jr.	40	0	5	5	10
David Neale	F	Fr.	19	0	2	2	16
James Armstrong	D	So.	12	1	0	1	6
Ben Henrich	G	Sr.	5	0	1	1	0
Bryan Vines	D	So.	7	0	1	1	2
Joe Casey	F	Jr.	3	0	0	0	0
Paul Cox	F	Fr.	7	0	0	0	0

GOALTENDING

	Games	Min.	W	L	T	Goals	SO	Avg.
Ben Henrich	5	157	2	0	1	7	0	2.67
Stephen Wagner	40	2318	24	13	1	114	4	2.95

MICHIGAN TECH HUSKIES

SCORING

	Pos.	Class	Games	G	A	Pts.	PIM
Matt Ulwelling	F	So.	38	9	17	26	30
Riley Nelson	F	Jr.	36	10	14	24	20
Brad Mueller	F	Jr.	37	11	12	23	25
Devin Hartnell	F	Jr.	37	7	16	23	72
Paul Cabana	F	Fr.	38	12	9	21	50
Adrian Fure	D	So.	33	6	9	15	29
Brad Patterson	F	Fr.	38	4	10	14	12
Tab Lardner	F	So.	38	2	10	12	46
Mat Snesrud	D	So.	37	3	8	11	22
Clint Way	D	So.	38	5	5	10	36
Jarrett Weinberger	F	So.	33	2	6	8	38
Tim Laurila	F	Fr.	36	4	3	7	40
Tom Kaiman	D	Fr.	32	3	4	7	64
Jaron Doetzel	F	Fr.	37	3	4	7	8
Jason McKee	F	So.	27	1	3	4	20
Miles VanTassel	D	Sr.	30	1	3	4	18
Landon Boyko	D	Fr.	31	0	4	4	42
Jim Kotajarvi	F	So.	10	0	3	3	4
Quinton Krueger	D	So.	24	1	1	2	10
Brian Eovaldi	F	Fr.	10	1	0	1	0
A.J. Aitken	F	Jr.	33	1	0	1	48
David Weninger	G	Sr.	32	0	1	1	4
Jason Moilanen	G	So.	2	0	0	0	0
Sean Day	F	So.	5	0	0	0	0
Matt Lewis	D	Fr.	7	0	0	0	6
Todd Weninger	G	So.	10	0	0	0	2

GOALTENDING

	Games	Min.	W	L	T	Goals	SO	Avg.
David Weninger	32	1802	9	21	1	100	0	3.33
Todd Weninger	10	461	0	7	0	37	0	4.82
Jason Moilanen	2	14	0	0	0	3	0	12.46

MINNESOTA GOLDEN GOPHERS

SCORING

	Pos.	Class	Games	G	A	Pts.	PIM
Reggie Berg	F	Sr.	43	20	28	48	64
Wyatt Smith	F	Sr.	43	23	20	43	37
Dave Spehar	F	Jr.	42	13	23	36	32
Erik Westrum	D/F	So.	41	10	26	36	81
Jordon Leopold	D	Fr.	39	7	16	23	20
Aaron Miskovich	F	So.	42	11	11	22	36
Mike Anderson	F	Sr.	43	10	7	17	64
John Pohl	F	Fr.	42	7	10	17	18
Rico Pagel	F	Jr.	32	4	11	15	8
Erik Wendell	F	Fr.	41	7	7	14	46
Nate Miller	F	Jr.	43	6	8	14	70
Dylan Mills	D	So.	39	2	12	14	38
Matt Leimbek	F	So.	28	4	8	12	10
Stuart Senden	F	So.	34	4	5	9	12
Bill Kohn	D	Sr.	43	3	6	9	97
Nick Angell	D	Fr.	37	1	8	9	21
Doug Meyer	F	Fr.	36	4	4	8	18
Mike Lyons	D	Jr.	42	1	4	5	54
Ryan Trebil	D	Jr.	21	1	2	3	40
Brad Timmons	D	Jr.	11	1	2	3	8
Pat O'Leary	F	Fr.	17	0	2	2	8
Cory Miller	F	Jr.	2	0	0	0	6
Willy Marvin	G	Jr.	4	0	0	0	0
Rob LaRue	G	Fr.	5	0	0	0	0
Mark Nenovich	D	Fr.	13	0	0	0	18
Adam Hauser	G	Fr.	40	0	0	0	10

GOALTENDING

	Games	Min.	W	L	T	Goals	SO	Avg.
Rob LaRue	5	63	0	0	0	2	0	1.91
Adam Hauser	40	2350	14	18	8	136	3	3.47
Willy Marvin	4	199	1	1	1	12	0	3.62

MINNESOTA-DULUTH BULLDOGS

SCORING

	Pos.	Class	Games	G	A	Pts.	PIM
Jeff Scissons	F	Jr.	38	18	19	37	42
Ryan Homstol	F	So.	38	12	22	34	30
Colin Anderson	F	Jr.	36	9	14	23	40
Mark Carlson	D	Fr.	36	5	18	23	33
Derek Derow	F	So.	32	13	8	21	23
Jesse Fibiger	D	So.	36	4	16	20	61
Shawn Pogreba	F	Jr.	35	8	7	15	36
Mark Gunderson	F	So.	38	4	9	13	16
Curtis Bois	F	Sr.	35	6	5	11	59
Judd Medak	F	Fr.	37	3	8	11	67
Tom Nelson	F	Fr.	30	2	9	11	27
Ryan Coole	D	So.	36	3	6	9	69
Nate Anderson	F	Fr.	34	2	6	8	16
Richie Anderson	F	Jr.	33	3	4	7	23
Andy Reierson	D	Fr.	34	3	4	7	24
Bert Gilling	D	Sr.	38	1	5	6	30
Eric Ness	F	Fr.	27	2	2	4	2
Kent Sauer	D	Fr.	38	1	3	4	50
Ryan Nosan	F	Jr.	17	1	1	2	10
Nik Patronas	F	Jr.	12	0	1	1	6
Jeremy Zahn	F	Jr.	13	0	1	1	23
Brant Nicklin	G	Jr.	32	0	1	1	4
Ryan Tessier	D	Fr.	1	0	0	0	0
Tony Gasparini	G	Sr.	10	0	0	0	0
Craig Pierce	D	So.	10	0	0	0	12

GOALTENDING

	Games	Min.	W	L	T	Goals	SO	Avg.
Tony Gasparini	10	490	1	4	2	24	1	2.94
Brant Nicklin	32	1807	6	23	2	109	0	3.62

NORTH DAKOTA FIGHTING SIOUX

SCORING

	Pos.	Class	Games	G	A	Pts.	PIM
Jason Blake	F	Sr.	38	28	41	69	49
Jay Panzer	F	Sr.	39	21	33	54	12
Jeff Panzer	F	So.	39	21	26	47	14
Brad Williamson	D	Sr.	40	10	37	47	36
Lee Goren	F	So.	38	26	19	45	20
David Hoogsteen	F	Sr.	31	11	29	40	6
Jeff Ulmer	F	Sr.	38	16	20	36	46
Jesse Bull	F	Sr.	38	8	23	31	16
Adam Calder	F	Sr.	33	13	16	29	71
Brad DeFauw	F	Jr.	34	11	12	23	64
Trevor Hammer	D	So.	39	4	18	22	37
Jason Ulmer	F	Jr.	37	6	15	21	43
Peter Armbrust	F	Jr.	37	6	8	14	42
Mike Commodore	D	So.	39	5	8	13	154
Wes Dorey	F	So.	22	4	8	12	6
Bryan Lundbohm	F	Fr.	32	2	9	11	4
Chad Mazurak	D	Fr.	38	2	7	9	66
Aaron Schneekloth	D	Fr.	35	2	4	6	14
Paul Murphy	D	Fr.	23	1	5	6	23
Tom Philion	F	Sr.	14	1	4	5	6
Tim O'Connell	D	Jr.	22	0	3	3	29
Karl Goehring	G	So.	31	0	3	3	0
Mike Possin	F	Fr.	10	1	0	1	12
Andy Kollar	G	Fr.	13	0	1	1	2
Pat Kenny	F	Fr.	5	0	0	0	0

GOALTENDING

	Games	Min.	W	L	T	Goals	SO	Avg.
Karl Goehring	31	1774	22	5	2	71	3	2.40
Andy Kollar	13	649	10	1	0	31	0	2.87

ST. CLOUD STATE HUSKIES

SCORING

	Pos.	Class	Games	G	A	Pts.	PIM
Matt Noga	F	Jr.	36	9	24	33	39
Tyler Arnason	F	Fr.	38	14	17	31	16
George Awada	F	Sr.	39	14	16	30	38
Brandon Sampair	F	So.	38	15	14	29	10
Jason Goulet	F	Sr.	29	11	16	27	14
Mike Pudlick	D	Fr.	37	13	12	25	74
Geno Parrish	D	Jr.	39	7	10	17	48
Nate DiCasmirro	F	Fr.	34	6	8	14	46
Keith Anderson	F	So.	35	6	6	12	16
Brad Goulet	F	Sr.	39	4	8	12	22
Tom Lund	D	Jr.	39	1	9	10	63
Ryan Forbes	F	So.	31	3	6	9	30
Lee Brooks	F	Fr.	38	4	4	8	8
Brian Gaffaney	D	So.	37	3	5	8	45
Peter Torsson	F	So.	13	3	4	7	40
Kyle McLaughlin	D	Sr.	37	1	5	6	30
Ritchie Larson	D	Jr.	27	2	2	4	6
Mike Rucinski	F	Jr.	11	1	3	4	4
Ryan Frisch	F	Sr.	24	2	1	3	41
Matt Bailey	F	Jr.	21	1	2	3	10
Aaron Dwyer	D	Fr.	20	1	1	2	24
Archie Bifulk	F	Fr.	7	1	0	1	0
Dean Weasler	G	Fr.	31	0	1	1	8
Gert Prohaska	G	Fr.	8	0	0	0	0
Scott Meyer	G	So.	18	0	0	0	0
Bryce Macken	D	Jr.	19	0	0	0	36

GOALTENDING

	Games	Min.	W	L	T	Goals	SO	Avg.
Dean Weasler	30	1716	13	11	4	85	3	2.97
Scott Meyer	9	464	2	5	1	23	0	2.98
Gert Prohaska	3	178	1	2	0	11	0	3.71

WISCONSIN BADGERS

SCORING

	Pos.	Class	Games	G	A	Pts.	PIM
Steve Reinprecht	F	Jr.	38	16	17	33	14
Dustin Kuk	F	Jr.	37	10	22	32	71
Dave Tanabe	D	Fr.	35	10	12	22	44
Jeff Dessner	D	So.	37	7	14	21	46
Matt Hussey	F	Fr.	37	10	5	15	18
Dan Bjornlie	D	Jr.	38	2	12	14	16
Yuri Gusak	F	Sr.	36	5	8	13	14
Chad Stauffacher	F	So.	36	5	7	12	30
Matt Doman	F	Fr.	34	5	5	10	52
Tim Rothering	D/F	Sr.	32	4	6	10	26
David Hukalo	F	Fr.	29	4	5	9	16
Kevin Granato	F	So.	25	2	7	9	18
Matt Murray	F	Fr.	24	6	2	8	38
Luke Gruden	D	Sr.	30	1	6	7	38
Dave Hergert	F	Fr.	16	2	3	6	2
Craig Anderson	D	Sr.	9	2	4	6	6
T.R. Moreau	F	Jr.	19	2	4	6	33
Dave Hergert	F	Fr.	16	2	3	5	2
Kent Davyduke	F	Fr.	33	2	3	5	16
Rob Vega	D	Fr.	30	1	3	4	12
Niki Siren	F	Jr.	28	1	2	3	12
Alex Brooks	D	So.	37	0	3	3	73
Andy Wheeler	F	Fr.	18	1	1	2	2
Graham Melanson	G	So.	38	0	1	1	0
Dan Guenther	F	Jr.	6	0	0	0	0
Rick Spooner	D	So.	9	0	0	0	25
Mike Cerniglia	F	So.	14	0	0	0	2

GOALTENDING

	Games	Min.	W	L	T	Goals	SO	Avg.
G. Melanson	37	2189	15	19	3	102	1	2.80
Jake Soper	3	111	0	0	1	6	0	3.24

INDEPENDENTS

1998-99 SEASON

FINAL STANDINGS

Team	G	W	L	T	Pct.	GF	GA
Niagara	33	18	12	3	.591	108	89
Mankato State	39	18	16	5	.526	149	129
Army	35	16	16	3	.500	133	104
Air Force	36	15	19	2	.444	113	128
Nebraska-Omaha	37	13	24	0	.351	102	137

INDIVIDUAL STATISTICS

AIR FORCE FALCONS

SCORING

	Pos.	Class	Games	G	A	Pts.	PIM
Justin Kieffer	F	Sr.	35	14	24	38	55
Nels Grafstrom	F	Jr.	36	14	12	26	18
Tony Lawrence	F	Fr.	35	13	13	26	92
Scott Bradley	F	So.	35	9	16	25	35
Brendan Connelly	F	Fr.	36	9	13	22	40
Brian Gornick	F	Fr.	34	10	11	21	20
Dan Davies	D	Sr.	32	4	16	20	63
Derek Olson	F	Fr.	34	9	9	18	12
Jace Anders	D	Fr.	34	3	11	14	10
Joe Kramer	D	Sr.	34	3	11	14	54
Brian Rodgers	F	Fr.	32	3	8	11	26
Marcus Peters	F	So.	34	6	4	10	18
Mike McGuire	D	Sr.	34	1	9	10	35
Billy O'Reilly	F	So.	33	5	4	9	30
James Ord	D	So.	23	3	4	7	6
Ryan Smith	D	Fr.	25	2	5	7	49
Kirk Zerkel	F	Jr.	25	1	3	4	76
Matt Zitzlsperger	F	Jr.	19	2	1	3	4
Chad Shenk	D	So.	21	0	3	3	22
Ryan Thompson	F	So.	14	2	0	2	20
Neil Barner	D	Fr.	17	0	2	2	14
Jeff Zurick	D	Fr.	8	0	2	2	2
Mike Keough	D	Jr.	25	0	1	1	30
Jason Mascetta	G	Fr.	1	0	0	0	0
Sean Broderick	G	So.	15	0	0	0	0
Marc Kielkucki	G	So.	33	0	0	0	6

GOALTENDING

	Games	Min.	W	L	T	Goals	SO	Avg.
Jason Mascetta	1	13	0	0	0	0	0	0.00
Marc Kielkucki	33	1709	14	15	2	96	5	3.37
Sean Broderick	15	428	1	4	0	28	0	3.92

ARMY CADETS

SCORING

	Pos.	Class	Games	G	A	Pts.	PIM
Greg Buckmeier	F	Sr.	32	15	20	35	20
Andy Lundbohm	F	Sr.	29	18	16	34	30
Jason Choi	F	Sr.	31	16	10	26	63
Joe Carpenter	F	Fr.	35	3	23	26	10
Nathan Mayfield	F	Fr.	26	7	15	22	28
Tim Fisher	F	Fr.	35	11	8	19	36
T.J. McMeniman	D	Fr.	32	6	13	19	8
Mike Fairman	F	So.	29	7	9	16	10
Paul Gonzalez	F	Fr.	21	4	10	14	8
K.C. Finnegan	F	So.	26	6	6	12	22
Scott Lensky	D	Fr.	25	2	10	12	10
John Williams	D	Jr.	33	3	8	11	22
Mike Dugan	F	Sr.	19	5	4	9	18
Josh Morino	D	Fr.	23	1	8	9	44
Brad Pieper	F	Jr.	8	5	3	8	2
Andy Foss	F	Sr.	27	5	3	8	18
Brody Howatt	F	Sr.	28	4	4	8	46
Chuck Sawicky	F	Sr.	19	1	7	8	8
Joel Jamison	D	Sr.	31	1	7	8	10
Bucky Burleigh	F	Jr.	3	3	3	6	0
Bill Griffith	F	Jr.	25	4	1	5	48
Garrett Brougham	F	Fr.	7	2	2	4	6
Jeff Gallo	F	So.	20	2	1	3	10
Tim Murphy	F	So.	9	1	2	3	0
Pete Edlund	D	So.	12	0	3	3	6
Eric Joyce	D	Fr.	26	0	3	3	56
Mark Rothemich	F	So.	11	1	1	2	2
Tom Kennedy	D	Jr.	1	0	0	0	0
Jason Galui	G	Jr.	2	0	0	0	0
Andy Haskell	D	Fr.	7	0	0	0	2
Scott Hamilton	G	Fr.	16	0	0	0	0
Corey Winer	G	Jr.	21	0	0	0	0

GOALTENDING

	Games	Min.	W	L	T	Goals	SO	Avg.
Jason Galui	2	67	0	0	0	2	0	1.80
Scott Hamilton	16	900	9	5	1	40	1	2.67
Corey Winer	21	1150	7	11	2	61	0	3.18

MANKATO STATE MAVERICKS

SCORING

	Pos.	Class	Games	G	A	Pts.	PIM
Aaron Fox	F	Jr.	38	22	25	47	16
Jesse Rooney	F	So.	39	18	15	33	28
Rob White	F	Sr.	39	17	16	33	32
Tyler Deis	F	Sr.	38	17	15	32	84
Tim Wolfe	F	Jr.	38	18	10	28	56
Ryan Schrick	F	Jr.	35	9	18	27	48
B. Christopherson	D	So.	37	3	21	24	64
Tyler Baines	F	So.	35	7	16	23	12
Todd George	D	Jr.	37	2	21	23	38
T.J. Guidarelli	F	So.	39	4	16	20	30
Peter Holoien	F	So.	38	8	11	19	40
Justin Martin	F	Fr.	37	5	9	14	31
Ryan Severson	F	So.	35	4	9	13	40
Darin Hawn	D	Sr.	37	2	9	11	20
Andy Fermoyle	D	Jr.	37	2	7	9	20
David Graham	D	Fr.	26	0	9	9	10
Jon Bushy	D	So.	21	0	8	8	8
Dwight Hirst	F	Fr.	15	6	0	6	15
B.J. Anderson	F	Fr.	20	4	2	6	16
Andy Hedlund	D	Fr.	34	1	2	3	34
Eric Pateman	G	Fr.	23	0	3	3	0
Jessie Willis	D	Sr.	10	0	3	3	8
Todd Kelzenberg	G	Fr.	14	0	1	1	2
Matt Cunningham	D	Sr.	11	0	1	1	14
Jon Kerr	F	Fr.	6	0	1	1	0
Brian Nelson	G	Jr.	9	0	0	0	0

GOALTENDING

	Games	Min.	W	L	T	Goals	SO	Avg.
Eric Pateman	23	1238	12	6	3	57	2	2.76
Todd Zelzenberg	14	720	4	5	2	43	1	3.58
Brian Nelson	9	430	2	5	0	29	0	4.05

NEBRASKA-OMAHA MAVERICKS

SCORING

	Pos.	Class	Games	G	A	Pts.	PIM
Jason White	F	So.	34	11	16	27	22
Allan Carr	F	So.	25	9	14	23	22
Derek Reynolds	F	Jr.	34	6	16	22	70
Shane Glover	F	Fr.	35	10	9	19	10
James Chalmers	F	So.	30	6	12	18	53
Tom Kowal	D	Jr.	33	6	11	17	44
Jason Cupp	F	So.	27	6	11	17	30
Billy Pugliese	F	So.	33	6	10	16	10
Jeff Hoggan	F	Fr.	37	9	6	15	48
Dave Noel-Bernier	F	So.	27	7	3	10	33
Kyle O'Keefe	F	Fr.	29	5	5	10	28
Daniel Samuelsson	D	Fr.	37	1	9	10	34
Nick Fohr	F	Fr.	29	4	4	8	35
Ryan Bencurik	D	Jr.	28	4	4	8	22
Jeff Edwards	F	Jr.	33	4	2	6	65
Zach Scribner	D	Fr.	31	0	6	6	24
Josh Lampman	D	Jr.	21	2	3	5	36
Joe Yurecko	F	So.	24	2	1	3	20
Darrin Bradley	D	Jr.	12	1	2	3	12
John Rosso	D	So.	16	1	2	3	4
Colin Strom	D	Sr.	18	0	3	3	39
Mike Skogland	F	Jr.	28	1	1	2	12
Sean Cavan	F	Jr.	12	1	0	1	6
Jason Mitchell	G	Sr.	16	0	1	1	0
Kendall Sidoruk	G	Jr.	23	0	1	1	4
Mike Hanson	F	So.	5	0	0	0	2
Rob Facca	F	Jr.	1	0	0	0	0
Christian Graham	D	Sr.	28	0	0	0	22

GOALTENDING

	Games	Min.	W	L	T	Goals	SO	Avg.
Kendall Sidoruk	23	1339	8	14	0	72	1	3.23
Jason Mitchell	16	874	5	10	0	58	0	3.98

NIAGARA PURPLE EAGLES

SCORING

	Pos.	Class	Games	G	A	Pts.	PIM
Mike Isherwood	F	Jr.	33	22	19	41	36
Riku Suuriniemi	F	Fr.	33	10	18	28	52
Mikko Sivonen	F	Jr.	32	15	11	26	54
Peter DeSantis	F	Jr.	32	11	14	25	12
Chris MacKenzie	D	Jr.	33	5	17	22	40
Colin Rows	D	Jr.	29	4	17	21	74
Jas Kasperek	F	Jr.	26	9	10	19	8
P.J. Perry	F	So.	30	5	14	19	58
Kyle Martin	F	Jr.	31	11	7	18	18
Nate Handrahan	D	Jr.	33	5	11	16	18
Timo Makela	D	So.	32	0	12	12	24
Jon Marshall	F	Jr.	33	4	3	7	10
Todd Elliott	F	So.	25	3	4	7	6
Greg Gardner	G	Jr.	30	0	5	5	6
John Heffernan	F	Fr.	12	2	2	4	8
John Maksymiu	F	Jr.	17	2	2	4	4
Thomas Clayton	F	Fr.	15	0	4	4	8
Richard DeCaprio	F	Jr.	10	1	1	2	0
Scott McDonald	F	Jr.	22	0	2	2	16
Darwin Murray	D	So.	31	0	2	2	10
A.J. Melanson	F	Jr.	13	1	0	1	4
Nicholas Carriere	F	So.	5	0	1	1	0
Adam Morris	F	Jr.	22	0	1	1	22
Peter Ricketts	D	Jr.	27	0	1	1	12
Eric DiCarlo	D	Fr.	1	0	1	1	0
Christian Laden	D	So.	11	0	0	0	0
Peter Nastasi	G	So.	6	0	0	0	0
Ilkka Laitinen	F	Fr.	4	0	0	0	0

GOALTENDING

	Games	Min.	W	L	T	Goals	SO	Avg.
Peter Nastasi	6	282	3	2	0	11	0	2.34
Greg Gardner	30	1742	15	10	3	78	4	2.69

CANADIAN INTERUNIVERSITY ATHLETIC UNION

GENERAL INFORMATION

The Canadian Interuniversity Athletic Union is an alliance of three Canadian college leagues—the Atlantic Universities Athletic Association, Canada West University Athletic Association and Ontario Universities Athletic Association. After the regular season, the three leagues compete in an elimination tournament to decide the CIAU national champion. The award and trophy winners are based on regular-season play.

1999 NATIONAL CHAMPIONSHIPS

PLAYOFF STANDINGS

POOL A

Team (League)	W	L	Pts.	GF	GA
Alberta (CWUAA)	3	0	6	15	4
York (OUA)	1	1	2	5	8
Trois-Rivieres (OUA)	0	2	0	6	10

POOL B

Team (League)	W	L	Pts.	GF	GA
Moncton (AUAA)	2	1	4	11	13
Saskatchewan (CWUAA)	1	1	2	8	7
Windsor (OUA)	0	2	0	5	8

RESULTS

ROUND-ROBIN POOL PLAY

THURSDAY, MARCH 25

York 5, Trois-Rivieres 4 (OT)
Moncton 4, Windsor 3

FRIDAY, MARCH 26

Alberta 5, Trois-Rivieres 2
Saskatchewan 4, Windsor 2

SATURDAY, MARCH 27

Alberta 4, York 0
Moncton 5, Saskatchewan 4

FINAL

SUNDAY, MARCH 28

Alberta 6, Moncton 2

1998-99 AWARD WINNERS

ALL-STAR TEAM

Pos.	Player
G	Bobby DaCosta, York
D	Mike Garrow, Alberta
	Scott Hillman, Windsor
F	Russ Hewson, Alberta
	Kevin Pucovsky, Windsor
	Mike Thompson, Alberta

Playoff MVP: Cam Danyluk (Forward), Alberta

TROPHY WINNERS

Player of the year: Luc Belanger, Trois-Rivieres
Rookie of the year: Eric Schneider, Calgary
Most sportsmanlike player: Chris Cignac, Windsor
Scholastic player of the year: Brad Peddle, St. Francis Xavier
Coach of the year: Trevor Steinburg, St. Mary's

TOP SCORERS

	Games	G	A	Pts.
Dave Gilmore, St. Thomas	26	18	44	62
Yanick Evola, St. Francis Xavier	26	23	33	56
Guy Loranger, St. Francis Xavier	26	16	39	55
Russ Hewson, Alberta	26	24	23	47
Brad Peddle, St. Francis Xavier	26	18	29	47
Christian Caron, Trois-Rivieres	23	22	23	45
Mike Thompson, Alberta	28	10	35	45
Mike Harding, Prince Edward Island	26	20	22	42
Eric Schneider, Calgary	28	24	17	41
Paul Andrea, St. Francis Xavier	25	22	19	41
Rob Mailloux, Queen's	22	16	25	41

CANADIAN COLLEGES

ATLANTIC UNIVERSITIES ATHLETIC ASSOCIATION, 1998-99 SEASON

FINAL STANDINGS

KELLY DIVISION

Team (Overall)	G	W	L	T	Pts.	GF	GA
St. F'cis Xavier (21-14-2) .	26	14	10	2	30	129	99
Acadia (24-15-2)	26	14	10	2	30	90	81
St. Mary's (16-17-2)..........	26	13	11	2	28	98	91
Dalhousie (13-18-2)	26	10	14	2	22	93	111

MAC ADAM DIVISION

Team (Overall)	G	W	L	T	Pts.	GF	GA
St. Thomas (18-12-3)........	26	14	9	3	33	130	101
New Brunswick (16-18-1)..	26	13	12	1	28	110	106
Moncton (23-16-3)............	26	12	11	3	28	116	117
P. Edward Island (7-25-1)..	26	6	19	1	16	88	148

PLAYOFF RESULTS

KELLY DIVISION SEMIFINALS

St. F. Xavier 2, Dalhousie 1
St. F. Xavier 6, Dalhousie 1

Acadia 3, St. Mary's 2
St. Mary's 6, Acadia 3
Acadia 1, St. Mary's 0

MAC ADAM DIVISION SEMIFINALS

St. Thomas 2, P.E.I. 1 (2OT)
St. Thomas 6, P.E.I. 5 (OT)

New Brunswick 3, Moncton 2
Moncton 4, New Brunswick 3
Moncton 5, N. B'wick 4 (2OT)

KELLY DIVISION FINALS

St. F. Xavier 5, Acadia 2
Acadia 6, St. F. Xavier 5 (3OT)
Acadia 6, St. F. Xavier 3

MAC ADAM DIVISION FINALS

Moncton 7, St. Thomas 5
Moncton 2, St. Thomas 1

LEAGUE FINALS

Moncton 5, Acadia 2
Acadia 5, Moncton 4 (OT)
Moncton 5, Acadia 3

ALL-STAR TEAMS

KELLY DIVISION Player, team	Pos.	MAC ADAM DIVISION Player, team
Trevor Amundrud, Acadia	G	David Mitchell, P.E.I.
Bob MacIsaac, St. Mary's	D	Serge Bourgeois, Moncton
Brad Peddle, St.F.X.	D	Dan Preston, St. Thomas
Yanick Evola, St.F.X.	F	Mark Edmundson, St. Th's
Chris Pittman, Dalhousie	F	Dave Gilmore, St. Thomas
Josh St. Louis, Acadia	F	Dax MacLean, N. Brunswick

AWARD WINNERS

Most Valuable Player: Dave Gilmore, St. Thomas
Rookie of the year: Jim Midgley, St. Mary's
Most sportsmanlike player: Dan Preston, St. Thomas
Coach of the year: Trevor Stienburg, St. Mary's
Leading scorer: Dave Gilmore, St. Thomas

INDIVIDUAL LEADERS

Goals: Yanick Evola, St. Francis Xavier (23)
Assists: Dave Gilmore, St. Thomas (44)
Points: Dave Gilmore, St. Thomas (62)
Penalty minutes: Jean-Francois Beliveau, Moncton (167)
Goaltending average: Donovan Nunweiler, Acadia (2.76)

TOP SCORERS

	Games	G	A	Pts.
Dave Gilmore, St. Thomas	26	18	44	62
Yanick Evola, St. Francis Xavier.........	26	23	33	56
Guy Loranger, St. Francis Xavier.......	26	16	39	55
Brad Peddle, St. Francis Xavier	26	18	29	47
Mike Harding, Prince Edward Island.	26	20	22	42
Paul Andrea, St. Francis Xavier	25	22	19	41
Mark Edmundson, St. Thomas..........	23	20	18	38
Dax MacLean, New Brunswick..........	26	17	18	35
David Carson, St. Thomas................	26	21	13	34
Jim Midgley, St. Mary's....................	26	14	20	34

CANADA WEST UNIVERSITY ATHLETIC ASSOCIATION, 1998-99 SEASON

FINAL STANDINGS

EAST DIVISION

Team (Overall)	G	W	L	T	Pts.	GF	GA
Sask. (33-12-1)	28	18	9	1	37	146	73
Manitoba (21-20-4)	28	13	11	4	30	109	114
Brandon (16-20-3).............	28	12	13	3	27	87	114
Regina (4-26-4)	28	4	20	4	12	75	122

WEST DIVISION

Team (Overall)	G	W	L	T	Pts.	GF	GA
Alberta (29-14-2)...............	28	20	6	2	42	140	88
Calgary (19-19-6)	28	13	10	5	31	96	105
Lethbridge (18-21-2)	28	13	13	2	28	95	114
Brit. Col. (12-23-3)	28	7	18	3	17	84	102

PLAYOFF RESULTS

EAST DIVISION SEMIFINALS

Manitoba 5, Brandon 2
Manitoba 2, Brandon 1

WEST DIVISION SEMIFINALS

Calgary 7, Lethbridge 6
Lethbridge 6, Calgary 2
Calgary 6, Lethbridge 2

EAST DIVISION FINALS

Saskatchewan 4, Manitoba 2
Saskatchewan 10, Manitoba 4

WEST DIVISION FINALS

Alberta 6, Calgary 3
Alberta 7, Calgary 3

CONFERENCE FINALS

Saskatchewan 5, Alberta 2
Saskatchewan 4, Alberta 1

ALL-STAR TEAMS

First team	Pos.	Second team
Jeff Calvert, Saskatchewan	G	Scott Tollestrup, Lethbridge
Jeff Helperl, Saskatchewan	D	Dion Zukiwsky, Alberta
Shane Zulyniak, Calgary	D	Jason Becker, Saskatchewan
Russ Hewson, Alberta	F	Trevor Ethier, Saskatchewan
Eric Schneider, Calgary	F	Jason Issel, Saskatchewan
Mike Thompson, Alberta	F	Trevor Winkler, Sask.

AWARD WINNERS

Most Valuable Player: Mike Thompson, Alberta
Rookie of the year: Eric Schneider, Calgary
Most sportsmanlike player: Trevor Ethier, Saskatchewan
Coach of the year: Rob Daum, Alberta
Leading scorer: Russ Hewson, Alberta

INDIVIDUAL LEADERS

Goals: Russ Hewson, Alberta (24)
Eric Schneider, Calgary (24)
Assists: Mike Thompson, Alberta (35)
Points: Russ Hewson, Alberta (47)
Penalty minutes: Ryan Vermette, Brandon (169)
Goaltending average: Jeff Calvert, Saskatchewan (2.60)

TOP SCORERS

	Games	G	A	Pts.
Russ Hewson, Alberta	26	24	23	47
Mike Thompson, Alberta	28	10	35	45
Eric Schneider, Calgary	28	24	17	41
Trevor Ethier, Saskatchewan	27	21	18	39
Trevor Winkler, Saskatchewan	28	21	17	38
Marc Gaudet, Manitoba	28	13	24	37
Neil Johnston, Saskatchewan	27	12	23	35
Cam Danyluk, Alberta	26	14	20	34
Jeff Helperl, Saskatchewan	28	5	28	33
Scott Cannam, Saskatchewan	24	13	19	32
Matt Holmes, Calgary	27	8	24	32

ONTARIO UNIVERSITY ATHLETICS, 1998-99 SEASON

FINAL STANDINGS

FAR EAST DIVISION

Team	G	W	L	T	Pts.	GF	GA
Trois-Rivieres (30-7-1)	26	20	5	1	41	125	54
Concordia (22-14-3)	26	16	7	3	35	109	75
Ottawa (18-14-0)	26	17	9	0	34	97	72
McGill (16-14-6)	26	13	9	4	30	100	89

MID EAST DIVISION

Team	G	W	L	T	Pts.	GF	GA
Guelph (16-19-5)	26	11	10	5	27	94	80
Queen's (13-20-7)	26	5	14	7	17	85	113
Toronto (9-23-6)	26	6	16	4	16	66	106
Royal Military (5-30-1)	26	4	21	1	9	69	136

MID WEST DIVISION

Team	G	W	L	T	Pts.	GF	GA
York (16-19-7)	25	8	10	7	23	79	109
Brock (18-20-2)	26	10	14	2	22	90	107
Laurentian (9-20-5)	26	8	13	5	21	92	131
Ryerson (8-25-0)	25	6	19	0	12	74	133

FAR WEST DIVISION

Team	G	W	L	T	Pts.	GF	GA
Windsor (21-14-3)	26	17	6	3	37	115	72
W. Laurier (22-12-5)	26	14	7	5	33	108	72
Waterloo (17-17-7)	26	11	8	7	29	100	83
W. Ontario (18-17-0)	26	14	12	0	28	107	78

PLAYOFF RESULTS

DIVISION SEMIFINALS

Concordia 3, Ottawa 1
Concordia 6, Ottawa 3
Toronto 2, Queen's 1
Queen's 4, Toronto 0
Queen's 3, Toronto 2 (4OT)
Laurentian 8, Brock 2
Brock 7, Laurentian 4
Brock 7, Laurentian 2
Wilfred Laurier 3, Waterloo 2
Waterloo 3, Wilfred Laurier 1
Waterloo 4, Wilfred Laurier 2

DIVISION FINALS

Trois-Rivieres 3, Concordia 1
Trois-Rivieres 5, Concordia 1
Guelph 5, Queen's 0
Queen's 7, Guelph 6
Guelph 4, Queen's 2
Brock 4, York 2
York 6, Brock 5 (OT)
York 4, Brock 2
Windsor 6, Waterloo 3
Windsor 4, Waterloo 3 (2OT)

LEAGUE SEMIFINALS

Trois-Rivieres 3, Guelph 1
York 3, Windsor 2 (OT)

LEAGUE FINALS

Trois-Rivieres 7, York 0

CONSOLATION GAME

Windsor 3, Guelph 1

ALL-STAR TEAMS

EAST DIVISION

First team	Pos.	Second team
Luc Belanger, T.-R.	G	Paulo Della Bella, Ottawa
Daniel Laflamme, T.-R.	D	Mike Van Volsen, Guelph
Luc Bilodeau, T.-R.	D	Wes Booker, Queen's
Christian Caron, T.-R.	F	Hugo Turcotte, T.-R.
Robert Mailloux, Queen's	F	Greg Eisler, Ottawa
Mathieu Darche, McGill	F	Paul Rosebush, Guelph

WEST DIVISION

First team	Pos.	Second team
Frank Ivankovic, W. Laurier	G	Ryan Gelinas, Windsor
Scott Hillman, Windsor	D	Kevin Diachina, Windsor
Paul McInnes, Brock	D	Julian Dal Cin, York
Chris Gignac, Windsor	F	Damon Hardy, W. Ontario
Mike Williams, York	F	Kevin Pucovsky, Windsor
Jeff Petrie, W. Ontario	F	Sasha Cucuz, York

AWARD WINNERS

East Division Most Valuable Player: Luc Belanger, T.-R.
West Division Most Valuable Player: Chris Gignac, Windsor
East Division rookie of the year: Daniel Payette, Trois-Rivieres
West Division rookie of the year: Marcin Snita, Ryerson
East Division most sportsmanlike player: Daniel Laflamme, T.-R.
West Division most sportsmanlike player: Chris Gignac, Windsor
East Division coach of the year: Michel Goulet, Ottawa
West Division coach of the year: Tony Martindale, W. Laurier
Leading scorer: Christian Caron, Trois-Rivieres

INDIVIDUAL LEADERS

Goals: Christian Caron, Trois-Rivieres (22)
Assists: Jean-Francois Brunelle, Trois-Rivieres (29)
Points: Christian Caron, Trois-Rivieres (45)
Penalty minutes: Carl Benoit, Concordia (98)
Goaltending average: Luc Belanger, Trois-Rivieres (2.03)

TOP SCORERS

	Games	G	A	Pts.
Christian Caron, Trois-Rivieres	23	22	23	45
Robert Mailloux, Queen's	22	16	25	41
Hugo Turcotte, Trois-Rivieres	24	20	20	40
Jean-Francois Brunelle, T.-Rivieres	24	11	29	40
Daniel Payette, Trois-Rivieres	23	14	25	39
Chris Gignac, Windsor	22	12	27	39
Alexandre Charette, Concordia	26	11	28	39
Mike Williams, York	21	16	21	37
Sasha Cucuz, York	21	15	21	36
Damon Hardy, Western Ontario	26	15	21	36

INDEX OF TEAMS

NHL, MINOR LEAGUES, MAJOR JUNIOR LEAGUES

COLLEGE TEAMS